# ADVANCED
# ACCOUNTING

# ADVANCED
# ACCOUNTING

## 13TH EDITION

**Floyd A. Beams**
Virginia Polytechnic Institute
and State University

**Joseph H. Anthony**
Michigan State University

**Bruce Bettinghaus**
Grand Valley State University

**Kenneth A. Smith**
Central Washington University

New York, NY

| | |
|---|---|
| **Vice President, Business Publishing:** Donna Battista | **Creative Director:** Blair Brown |
| **Director of Portfolio Management:** Adrienne D'Ambrosio | **Manager, Learning Tools:** Brian Surette |
| **Director, Courseware Portfolio Management:** Ashley Dodge | **Content Developer, Learning Tools:** Sarah Peterson |
| **Senior Sponsoring Editor:** Neeraj Bhalla | **Managing Producer, Digital Studio, Arts and Business:** Diane Lombardo |
| **Vice President, Product Marketing:** Roxanne McCarley | **Digital Studio Producer:** Regina DaSilva |
| **Director of Strategic Marketing:** Brad Parkins | **Digital Studio Producer:** Alana Coles |
| **Strategic Marketing Manager:** Deborah Strickland | **Digital Content Team Lead:** Noel Lotz |
| **Product Marketer:** Tricia Murphy | **Digital Content Project Lead:** Martha Lachance |
| **Field Marketing Manager:** Natalie Wagner | **Full-Service Project Management and Composition:** SPi Global |
| **Field Marketing Assistant:** Kristen Compton | **Interior Design:** SPi Global |
| **Product Marketing Assistant:** Jessica Quazza | **Cover Design:** SPi Global |
| **Vice President, Production and Digital Studio, Arts and Business:** Etain O'Dea | **Cover Art:** Yuttasak Jannarong/Shutterstock |
| **Director of Production, Business:** Jeff Holcomb | **Printer/Binder:** LSC Communications |
| **Managing Producer, Business:** Ashley Santora | **Cover Printer:** LSC Communications |
| **Operations Specialist:** Carol Melville | |

**Library of Congress Cataloging-in-Publication Data**

Names: Beams, Floyd A., author.
Title: Advanced accounting / Floyd A. Beams, Virginia Polytechnic Institute and State University, Joseph H. Anthony, Michigan State University, Bruce Bettinghaus, Grand Valley State University, Kenneth A. Smith, Central Washington University.
Description: 13th Edition. | New York : Pearson Education, [2016] | Revised edition of: Advanced accounting, [2015]
Identifiers: LCCN 2016050010| ISBN 9780134472140 | ISBN 0134472144
Subjects: LCSH: Accounting.
Classification: LCC HF5636 .B43 2016 | DDC 657/.046—dc23 LC record available at https://lccn.loc.gov/2016050010

ISBN-10: 0-13-447214-4
ISBN-13: 978-0-13-447214-0

*To Beth*

JOE ANTHONY

*To Trish*

BRUCE BETTINGHAUS

*To Karen, Madelyn and AJ*

KENNETH A. SMITH

# ABOUT THE
# AUTHORS

**FLOYD A. BEAMS, PH.D.,** authored the first edition of *Advanced Accounting* in 1979 and actively revised his text through the next six revisions and twenty-one years while maintaining an active professional and academic career at Virginia Tech where he rose to the rank of Professor, retiring in 1995.

Beams earned his B.S. and M.A. degrees from the University of Nebraska, and a Ph.D. from the University of Illinois. He published actively in journals, including *The Accounting Review, Journal of Accounting, Auditing and Finance, Journal of Accountancy, The Atlantic Economic Review, Management Accounting,* and others. He was a member of the American Accounting Association and the Institute of Management Accountants and served on committees for both organizations. Beams was honored with the National Association of Accounts' Lybrand Bronze Medal Award for outstanding contribution to accounting literature, the Distinguished Career in Accounting award from the Virginia Society of CPAs, and the Virginia Outstanding Accounting Educator award from the Carman G. Blough student chapter of the Institute of Management Accountants. Professor Beams passed away in 2004; however, we continue to honor his contribution to the field and salute the impact he had on this volume.

**JOSEPH H. ANTHONY, PH.D.,** joined the Michigan State University faculty in 1983 and is an Associate Professor of Accounting at the Eli Broad College of Business. He earned his B.A. in 1971 and his M.S. in 1974, both awarded by Pennsylvania State University, and he earned his Ph.D. from The Ohio State University in 1984. He is a Certified Public Accountant, and is a member of the American Accounting Association, American Institute of Certified Public Accountants, American Finance Association, and Canadian Academic Accounting Association. He has been recognized as a Lilly Foundation Faculty Teaching Fellow and as the MSU Accounting Department's Outstanding Teacher in 1998–1999 and in 2010–2011. He is retiring in May 2016.

Anthony teaches a variety of courses, including undergraduate introductory, intermediate, and advanced financial accounting. He also teaches financial accounting theory and financial statement analysis at the master's level, as well as financial accounting courses in Executive MBA programs, and a doctoral seminar in financial accounting and capital markets research. He co-authored an introductory financial accounting textbook.

Anthony's research interests include financial statement analysis, corporate reporting, and the impact of accounting information in the securities markets. He has published a number of articles in leading accounting and finance journals, including *The Journal of Accounting & Economics, The Journal of Finance, Contemporary Accounting Research, The Journal of Accounting, Auditing, & Finance,* and *Accounting Horizons.*

**BRUCE BETTINGHAUS, PH.D.,** is an Associate Professor of Accounting in the School of Accounting in The Seidman College of Business at Grand Valley State University. His teaching experience includes corporate governance and accounting ethics, as well as accounting theory and financial reporting for both undergraduates and graduate classes. He earned his Ph.D. at Penn State University and his B.B.A. at Grand Valley State University. Bruce has also served on the faculties of the University of Missouri and Michigan State University. He has been recognized for high-quality teaching at both Penn State and Michigan State Universities. His research interests focus on governance and financial reporting for public firms. He has published articles in *The International Journal of Accounting, Management Accounting Quarterly, Strategic Finance,* and *The Journal of Corporate Accounting and Finance.*

**KENNETH A. SMITH, PH.D.,** is an Associate Professor of Accounting and the Department Chair at Central Washington University. He earned his Ph.D. from the University of Missouri, his M.B.A. from Ball State University, and his B.A. in Accounting from Anderson University (IN). He is a Certified Public Accountant. Smith's research interests include government accounting and budgeting, non-profit financial management, non-financial performance reporting, and information systems in government and non-profit organizations. He has published articles in such journals as *Accounting Horizons, Journal of Government Financial Management, Public Performance & Management Review, Nonprofit and Voluntary Sector Quarterly, International Public Management Journal, Government Finance Review,* and *Strategic Finance.*

Smith's professional activities include membership in the American Accounting Association, the Association of Government Accountants, the Government Finance Officers Association, the Institute of Internal Auditors, and the Institute of Management Accountants. He is an elected public official, serving on the School Board for the 10th largest School District in the state of Washington. He formerly served as the Executive Director for the Oregon Public Performance Measurement Association and the not-for-profit Wheels for Humanity.

# BRIEF CONTENTS

# CONTENTS

# PREFACE

## NEW TO THIS EDITION

Important changes in the 13th edition of *Advanced Accounting* include the following:

- The text has been rewritten to align with both the *Financial Accounting Standards Board Accounting Standards Codification* and the *Governmental Accounting Standards Board Codification*. References to original pronouncements have been deleted, except where important in an historical context.

- The text now provides references to official pronouncements parenthetically within the text. Text length is reduced and rendered much more readable for the students. References to the Codification appear parenthetically (e.g., ASC 740-10-15).

- End of chapter materials have been modified to include Professional Research assignments. These assignments require students to access the authoritative literature. Solutions offered to these assignments are up to date as of May 2016. Instructors will want to verify that those have not changed.

- All chapters have been updated to include coverage of the latest international reporting standards and issues, where appropriate. As U.S. and international reporting standards move toward greater harmonization, the international coverage continues to expand in the 13th edition.

- All chapters have been updated to reflect the most recent changes to the *Financial Accounting Standards Board Codification* and *Governmental Accounting Standards Board Codification*.
  - Chapter 16 has been modified to clarify GAAP/non-GAAP issue with partnership accounting in instances where the addition of a new partner may constitute a business combination.

- The governmental and not-for-profit chapters have been updated to include all standards through *GASB No. 81*. These chapters have also been enhanced with illustrations of the financial statements from Golden, Colorado. Coverage now includes the new financial statement elements (deferred inflows and outflows), as well as several new pension standards. Chapter 20 includes an exhibit with t-accounts to help students follow the governmental fund transactions and their financial statement impact.

- Chapter 23 coverage of fiduciary accounting for estates and trusts has been revised and updated to reflect current taxation of these entities as of December 31, 2015. Assignment materials have been modified to enhance student learning.

This 13th edition of *Advanced Accounting* is designed for undergraduate and graduate students majoring in accounting. This edition includes 23 chapters designed for financial accounting courses beyond the intermediate level. Although this text is primarily intended for accounting students, it is also useful for accounting practitioners interested in preparation or analysis of consolidated financial statements, accounting for derivative securities, and governmental and not-for-profit accounting and reporting. This 13th edition has been thoroughly updated to reflect recent business developments, as well as changes in accounting standards and regulatory requirements.

This comprehensive textbook addresses the practical financial reporting problems encountered in consolidated financial statements, goodwill, other intangible assets, and derivative securities. The text also includes coverage of foreign currency transactions and translations, partnerships, corporate liquidations and reorganizations, governmental accounting and reporting, not-for-profit accounting, and estates and trusts.

An important feature of the 13th edition is the continued student orientation, which has been further enhanced with this edition. This 13th edition strives to maintain an interesting and readable text for the students. The focus on the complete equity method is maintained to allow students to focus on accounting concepts rather than bookkeeping techniques in learning the consolidation materials. This edition also maintains the reference text quality of prior editions through the use of appendices to the consolidation chapters. These appendices cover pooling of interests accounting, trial balance workpaper formats, and easy to understand conversions from an incomplete equity method or cost method to the complete equity method. Students can then follow the main text approach to preparing consolidated financial statements using the complete equity method. The presentation of consolidation materials highlights working paper-only entries with shading and presents working papers on single upright pages. All chapters include current excerpts from the popular business press and references to familiar real-world companies, institutions, and events. This book uses examples from annual reports of well-known companies and governmental and not-for-profit institutions to illustrate key concepts and maintain student interest. Assignment materials include adapted items from past CPA examinations and have been updated and expanded to maintain close alignment with coverage of the chapter concepts. Assignments have been updated to include additional research cases and simulation-type problems, as well as the Professional Research assignments mentioned previously. This edition maintains identification of names of parent and subsidiary companies beginning with P and S, allowing immediate identification. It also maintains parenthetical notation in journal entries to clearly indicate the direction and types of accounts affected by the transactions. The 13th edition retains the use of learning objectives throughout all chapters to allow students to better focus study time on the most important concepts.

## ORGANIZATION OF THIS BOOK

Chapters 1 through 11 cover business combinations, the equity, fair value and cost methods of accounting for investments in common stock, and consolidated financial statements. This emphasizes the importance of business combinations and consolidations in advanced accounting courses as well as in financial accounting and reporting practices.

Accounting and reporting standards for acquisitions are introduced in Chapter 1. Chapter 1 also provides necessary background material on the form and economic impact of business combinations. The Appendix to Chapter 1 provides a summary on Pooling of Interests Accounting. Chapter 2 introduces the complete equity method of accounting as a one-line consolidation, and this approach is integrated throughout subsequent chapters on consolidations. This approach permits alternate computations for such key concepts as consolidated net income and consolidated retained earnings, and it helps instructors explain the objectives of consolidation procedures. The alternative computational approaches also assist students by providing a check figure for their logic on these key concepts. The one-line consolidation is maintained as the standard for a parent company in accounting for investments in its subsidiaries. Chapter 3 introduces the preparation of consolidated financial statements. Students learn how to record the fair values of the subsidiary's identifiable net assets and implied goodwill. Chapter 4 continues consolidations coverage, introducing working paper techniques and procedures. The text emphasizes the three-section, vertical financial statement working paper approach throughout, but Appendix A to Chapter 4 also offers a trial balance approach. The standard employed throughout the consolidation chapters is working papers for a parent company that uses the complete equity method of accounting for investments in subsidiaries. Appendix B to Chapter 4 provides a clear approach to convert from either the Incomplete Equity Method or the Cost Method to the complete equity method of accounting.

Chapters 5 through 7 cover intercompany transactions in inventories, plant assets, and bonds.

Chapter 8 discusses changes in the level of subsidiary ownership, and Chapter 9 introduces more complex affiliation structures. Chapter 10 covers several consolidation-related topics: subsidiary preferred stock, consolidated earnings per share, and income taxation for consolidated business entities. Chapter 11 is a theory chapter that discusses alternative consolidation theories, push-down accounting, leveraged buyouts, corporate joint ventures, and key concepts related to accounting and reporting by variable interest entities. Chapters 9 through 11 cover specialized topics and have been written as stand-alone materials. Coverage of these chapters is not necessary for assignment of subsequent text chapters.

Business enterprises become more global in nature with each passing day. Survival of a modern business depends upon access to foreign markets, suppliers, and capital. Some of the unique challenges of international business and financial reporting are covered in Chapters 12 and 13. These chapters cover accounting for derivatives and foreign currency transactions and translations. As in the prior edition, Chapter 12 covers the concepts and common transactions for derivatives and foreign currency, and Chapter 13 covers accounting for derivative and hedging activities. Coverage includes import and export activities and forward or similar contracts used to hedge against potential exchange losses. Chapter 14 focuses on preparation of consolidated financial statements for foreign subsidiaries. This chapter includes translation and remeasurement of foreign-entity financial statements, one-line consolidation of equity method investees, consolidation of foreign subsidiaries for financial reporting purposes, and the combination of foreign branch operations.

Chapter 15 introduces topics of segment reporting under *FASB ASC Topic 280*, as well as interim financial reporting issues. Partnership accounting and reporting are covered in Chapters 16 and 17. Chapter 16 has been updated to include consideration of cases where a partnership change meets the criteria for treatment as a business combination. Chapter 18 discusses accounting and reporting procedures related to corporate liquidations and reorganizations.

Chapters 19 through 20 provide an introduction to governmental accounting, and Chapter 22 introduces accounting for voluntary health and welfare organizations, hospitals, and colleges and universities. These chapters are completely updated through *GASB Statement No. 81*, and provide students with a good grasp of key concepts and procedures related to not-for-profit accounting.

Finally, Chapter 23 provides coverage of fiduciary accounting and reporting for estates and trusts.

## INSTRUCTORS' RESOURCES

The following instructors' resources are available for download at www.pearsonhighered.com:-

- **Solutions Manual:** Prepared by the authors, the solutions manual includes updated answers to questions, and solutions to exercises and problems. Solutions to assignment materials included in the electronic supplements are also included. Solutions are provided in electronic format, making electronic classroom display easier for instructors. All solutions have been accuracy-checked to maintain high-quality work.

- **Instructor's Manual:** The instructor's manual contains comprehensive outlines of all chapters, class illustrations, descriptions for all exercises and problems (including estimated times for completion), and brief outlines of new standards set apart for easy review.

- **Test Bank:** This file includes test questions in true/false, multiple-choice, short-answer, and problem formats. Solutions to all test items are also included.

- **PowerPoint Presentation:** A ready-to-use PowerPoint slideshow designed for classroom presentation is available. Instructors can use it as-is or edit content to fit particular classroom needs.

## STUDENT RESOURCES

To access the student resources, visit www.pearsonhighered.com/beams. It includes problem templates for selected assignments. The templates minimize the time spent on inputting problem data, allowing students to focus their efforts on understanding the concepts and procedures.

## ACKNOWLEDGMENTS

Many people have made valuable contributions to this 13th edition of *Advanced Accounting*, and we are pleased to recognize their contributions. We are indebted to the many users of prior editions for their helpful comments and constructive criticisms. We also acknowledge the help and encouragement that we received from students at Grand Valley State, Michigan State, and Central Washington University, who, often unknowingly, participated in class testing of various sections of the manuscript.

We want to thank our faculty colleagues for the understanding and support that have made 13 editions of *Advanced Accounting* possible.

A special thank you to Carolyn Streuly for her many hours of hard work and continued dedication to the project.

The following accuracy checkers and supplements authors whose contributions we appreciate— David W. Daniel, East Stroudsburg University; Darlene Ely, Carroll Community College, and Regan Garey, Lock Haven University.

We would like to thank the members of the Pearson book team for their hard work and dedication: Donna Battista, Vice President, Product Management; Adrienne D'Ambrosio, Director of Portfolio Management; Ashley Dodge, Director, Courseware Portfolio Management; Director Production– Business, Jeff Holcomb; Managing Producer, Ashley Santora; and Neeraj Bhalla, Senior Sponsoring Editor. We would also like to thank Nicole Suddeth, Editorial Project Manager, Pavithra Kumari, Full Service Project Manager from SPi Global.

Our thanks to the reviewers who helped to shape this 13th edition:

Marie Archambault, Marshall University
Ron R. Barniv, Kent State University
Nat Briscoe, Northwestern State University
Michael Brown, Tabor School of Business
Susan Cain, Southern Oregon University
Kerry Calnan, Elmus College
Eric Carlsen, Kean University
Gregory Cermignano, Widener University
Lawrence Clark, Clemson University
Penny Clayton, Drury University
Lynn Clements, Florida Southern College
David Dahlberg, The College of St. Catherine
Patricia Davis, Keystone College
David Doyon, Southern New Hampshire University
John Dupuy, Southwestern College
Thomas Edmonds, Regis University
Charles Fazzi, Saint Vincent College
Roger Flint, Oklahoma Baptist University
Margaret Garnsey, Siena College
Sheri Geddes, Andrews University
Gary Gibson, Lindsey Wilson College
Bonnie Givens, Avila University
Steve Hall, University of Nebraska at Kearney
Matthew Henry, University of Arkansas at Pine Bluff
Judith Harris, Nova Southeastern University
Joyce Hicks, Saint Mary's College
Marianne James, California State University, Los Angeles
Patricia Johnson, Canisius College
Stephen Kerr, Hendrix College
Thomas Largay, Thomas College
Stephani Mason, Hunter College

Mike Metzcar, Indiana Wesleyan University
Dianne R. Morrison, University of Wisconsin, La Crosse
David O'Dell, McPherson College
Bruce Oliver, Rochester Institute of Technology
Pamela Ondeck, University of Pittsburgh at Greensburg
Anne Oppegard, Augustana College
Larry Ozzello, University of Wisconsin, Eau Claire
Glenda Partridge, Spring Hill College
Thomas Purcell, Creighton University
Abe Qastin, Lakeland College
Donna Randolph, National American University
Frederick Richardson, Virginia Tech
John Rossi, Moravian College
Angela Sandberg, Jacksonville State University
Mary Jane Sauceda, University of Texas at Brownville and Texas Southmost College
John Schatzel, Stonehill College
Michael Schoderbeck, Rutgers University
Joann Segovia, Minnesota State University, Moorhead
Stanley Self, East Texas Baptist University
Ray Slager, Calvin College
Duane Smith, Brescia University
Keith Smith, George Washington University
Kimberly Smith, County College of Morris
Pam Smith, Northern Illinois University
Jeffrey Spear, Houghton College
Catherine Staples, Randolph-Macon College
Natalie Strouse, Notre Dame College
Zane Swanson, Emporia State University
Anthony Tanzola, Holy Family University

Christine Todd, Colorado State University, Pueblo

Ron Twedt, Concordia College

Barbara Uliss, Metropolitan State College of Denver

Joan Van Hise, Fairfield University

Dan Weiss, Tel Aviv University, Faculty of Management

Stephen Wheeler, Eberhardt School of Business

Deborah Williams, West Virginia State University

H. James Williams, Grand Valley State University

Joe Wilson, Muskingum College

Alex Yen, Suffolk University

Sung Wook Yoon, California State University, Northridge

Suzanne Alonso Wright, Penn State

Ronald Zhao, Monmouth University

# CHAPTER 1

# Business Combinations

- On November 23, 2015, *Pfizer* announced it would acquire *Allergan* for $160 billion, making Pfizer one of the world's largest healthcare firms.
- On December 31, 2008, *Wells Fargo & Company* acquired all of the outstanding shares of *Wachovia Corporation* for $23.1 billion, making Wells Fargo one of the largest U.S. commercial banks.
- In October 2001, *Chevron* and *Texaco* announced completion of their merger agreement valued in excess of $30 billion.
- In 1998, gasoline-producing rivals *Exxon* and *Mobil* merged to form *ExxonMobil* Corporation in a deal valued at $80 billion.

**W**elcome to the world of business combinations. There has been an unparalleled growth in merger and acquisition activities in both the United States and in international markets since the 1990s. The level of activities fluctuates with changes in stock markets, as many combinations are achieved through stock-for-stock exchanges, rather than outright cash purchases of another company.

Merger activities slowed with the stock market downturn in 2001, and again during the financial crisis of 2008, but when the market recovers, the pace picks up. The year 2015 saw stock values soar and an accompanying record level of mergers and acquisitions of over $5 trillion worldwide. Approximately half of these occurred in the United States. The following firms announced combinations in 2015. *Allergan* agreed to be acquired by *Pfizer* for $160 billion. *Anheuser-Busch InBev* announced the intent to acquire *SAB Miller* for $117.4 billion. *HJ Heinz* completed a purchase of *Kraft Foods* for $62.6 billion.

Firms strive to produce economic value added for shareholders. Related to this strategy, expansion has long been regarded as a proper goal of business entities. A business may choose to expand either internally (building its own facilities) or externally (acquiring control of other firms in business combinations). The focus in this chapter is on why firms often prefer external over internal expansion options and how financial reporting reflects the outcome of these activities.

In general terms, **business combinations** unite previously separate business entities. The overriding objective of business combinations must be increasing profitability; however, many firms can become more efficient by horizontally or vertically integrating operations or by diversifying their risks through conglomerate operations.

**Horizontal integration** is the combination of firms in the same business lines and markets. The combinations of Pfizer and Allergan, Chevron and Texaco, Exxon and Mobil, and Wells Fargo and

## NOTE 24: OPERATING SEGMENTS

**Revenues (in millions)**

| | Total Revenues | | |
| --- | --- | --- | --- |
| | 2015 | 2014 | 2013 |
| Power | $ 21,490 | $ 20,580 | $ 19,315 |
| Renewable Energy | 6,273 | 6,399 | 4,824 |
| Oil & Gas | 16,450 | 19,085 | 17,341 |
| Energy Management | 7,600 | 7,319 | 7,569 |
| Aviation | 24,660 | 23,990 | 21,911 |
| Healthcare | 17,639 | 18,299 | 18,200 |
| Transportation | 5,933 | 5,650 | 5,885 |
| Appliances & Lighting | 8,751 | 8,404 | 8,338 |
| Total industrial | 108,796 | 109,727 | 103,383 |
| Capital | 10,801 | 11,320 | 11,267 |
| Corporate items and eliminations | (2,211) | (3,863) | (1,405) |
| Total | $117,386 | $117,184 | $113,245 |

The note goes on to provide similar detailed breakdown of intersegment revenues; external revenues; assets; property, plant, and equipment additions; depreciation and amortization; interest and other financial charges; and the provision for income taxes.

Wachovia are examples of horizontal integration. The past 25 years have witnessed significant consolidation activity in banking and other industries. *Kimberly-Clark* acquired *Scott Paper*, creating a consumer paper and related products giant. *American Airlines* took control of its rival *U.S. Airways* in 2013 at a cost of $4.592 billion.

**Vertical integration** is the combination of firms with operations in different, but successive, stages of production or distribution, or both. In March 2007, *CVS Corporation* and *Caremark Rx, Inc.*, merged to form *CVS/Caremark Corporation* in a deal valued at $26 billion. The deal joined the nation's largest pharmacy chain with one of the leading healthcare/pharmaceuticals service companies.

**Conglomeration** is the combination of firms with unrelated and diverse products or service functions, or both. Firms may diversify to reduce the risk associated with a particular line of business or to even out cyclical earnings, such as might occur in a utility's acquisition of a manufacturing company. Several utilities combined with telephone companies after the 1996 Telecommunications Act allowed utilities to enter the telephone business.

The early 1990s saw tobacco maker *Phillip Morris Company* acquire food producer *Kraft* in a combination that included over $11 billion of recorded goodwill alone. Although all of us have probably purchased a light bulb manufactured by *General Electric Company*, the scope of the firm's operations goes well beyond that household product. Exhibit 1-1 excerpts Note 24 from General Electric's 2015 annual report on its major operating segments.

## REASONS FOR BUSINESS COMBINATIONS

LEARNING OBJECTIVE 1.1

If expansion is a proper goal of business enterprise, why would a business expand through combination rather than by building new facilities? Among the many possible reasons are the following:

**Cost Advantage.** It is frequently less expensive for a firm to obtain needed facilities through combination than through development. This is particularly true in periods of inflation. Reduction of the total cost for research and development activities was a prime motivation in *AT&T's* acquisition of *NCR*.

**Lower Risk.** The purchase of established product lines and markets is usually less risky than developing new products and markets. The risk is especially low when the goal is diversification. Scientists may discover that a certain product provides an environmental or health hazard. A single-product, nondiversified firm may be forced into bankruptcy by such a discovery, whereas a multiproduct, diversified company is more likely to survive. For companies in industries already plagued with excess manufacturing capacity, business combinations may be the only way to grow. When *Toys R Us* decided to diversify its operations to include baby furnishings and other related products, it purchased retail chain *Baby Superstore*.

**Fewer Operating Delays.** Plant facilities acquired in a business combination are operative and already meet environmental and other governmental regulations. The time to market is critical, especially in the technology industry. Firms constructing new facilities can expect numerous delays in construction, as well as in getting the necessary governmental approval to commence operations. Environmental impact studies alone can take months or even years to complete.

**Avoidance of Takeovers.** Many companies combine to avoid being acquired themselves. Smaller companies tend to be more vulnerable to corporate takeovers; therefore, many of them adopt aggressive buyer strategies to defend against takeover attempts by other companies.

**Acquisition of Intangible Assets.** Business combinations bring together both intangible and tangible resources. The acquisition of patents, mineral rights, research, customer databases, or management expertise may be a primary motivating factor in a business combination. When *IBM* purchased *Lotus Development Corporation*, $1.84 billion of the total cost of $3.2 billion was allocated to research and development in process.

**Other Reasons.** Firms may choose a business combination over other forms of expansion for business tax advantages (e.g., tax-loss carryforwards), for personal income and estate-tax advantages, or for personal reasons. One of several motivating factors in the combination of *Wheeling-Pittsburgh Steel*, a subsidiary of *WHX*, and *Handy & Harman* was Handy & Harman's overfunded pension plan, which virtually eliminated Wheeling-Pittsburgh Steel's unfunded pension liability. The egos of company management and takeover specialists may also play an important role in some business combinations.

## ANTITRUST CONSIDERATIONS

Federal antitrust laws prohibit business combinations that restrain trade or impair competition. The U.S. Department of Justice and the Federal Trade Commission (FTC) have primary responsibility for enforcing federal antitrust laws. For example, in 1997 the FTC blocked *Staples's* proposed $4.3 billion acquisition of *Office Depot*, arguing in federal court that the takeover would be anticompetitive. *Office Depot* acquired rival *OfficeMax* in 2013.

In 2004, the FTC conditionally approved *Sanofi-Synthelabo SA's* $64 billion takeover of *Aventis SA*, creating the world's third-largest drug manufacturer. Sanofi agreed to sell certain assets and royalty rights in overlapping markets in order to gain approval of the acquisition.

Business combinations in particular industries are subject to review by additional federal agencies. The Federal Reserve Board reviews bank mergers, the Department of Transportation scrutinizes mergers of companies under its jurisdiction, the Department of Energy has jurisdiction over some electric utility mergers, and the Federal Communications Commission (FCC) rules on the transfer of communication licenses. After the Justice Department cleared a $23 billion merger between *Bell Atlantic Corporation* and *Nynex Corporation*, the merger was delayed by the FCC because of its concern that consumers would be deprived of competition. The FCC later approved the merger. The merger of *U.S. Airways* and *American Airlines* faced delay and scrutiny over the reduced competitive environment, but was finally approved in December 2013.

In addition to federal antitrust laws, most states have some type of statutory takeover regulations. Some states try to prevent or delay hostile takeovers of the business enterprises incorporated within their borders. On the other hand, some states have passed antitrust exemption laws to protect hospitals from antitrust laws when they pursue cooperative projects.

Interpretations of antitrust laws vary from one administration to another, from department to department, and from state to state. Even the same department under the same administration can change its mind. A completed business combination can be re-examined by the FTC at any time. Deregulation in the banking, telecommunication, and utility industries permits business combinations that once would have been forbidden. In 1997, the Justice Department and the FTC jointly issued new guidelines for evaluating proposed business combinations that allow companies to argue that cost savings or better products could offset potential anticompetitive effects of a merger.

## LEGAL FORM OF BUSINESS COMBINATIONS

LEARNING OBJECTIVE **1.2**

*Business combination* is a general term that encompasses all forms of combining previously separate business entities. Such combinations are **acquisitions** when one corporation acquires the productive assets of another business entity and integrates those assets into its own operations. Business combinations are also acquisitions when one corporation obtains operating control over the productive facilities of another entity by acquiring a majority of its outstanding voting stock. The acquired company need not be dissolved; that is, the acquired company does not have to go out of existence.

The terms **merger** and, **consolidation** are often used as synonyms for acquisitions. However, legally and in accounting there is a difference. A merger entails the dissolution of all but one of the business entities involved. A consolidation entails the dissolution of all the business entities involved and the formation of a new corporation.

A *merger* occurs when one corporation takes over all the operations of another business entity, and that entity is dissolved. For example, Company A purchases the assets of Company B directly from Company B for cash, other assets, or Company A securities (stocks, bonds, or notes). This business combination is an acquisition, but it is not a merger unless Company B goes out of existence. Alternatively, Company A may purchase the stock of Company B directly from Company B's stockholders for cash, other assets, or Company A securities. This acquisition will give Company A operating control over Company B's assets. It will not give Company A legal ownership of the assets unless it acquires all the stock of Company B and elects to dissolve Company B (again, a merger).

A *consolidation* occurs when a new corporation is formed to take over the assets and operations of two or more separate business entities and dissolves the previously separate entities. For example, Company D, a newly formed corporation, may acquire the net assets of Companies E and F by issuing stock directly to Companies E and F. In this case, Companies E and F may continue to hold Company D stock for the benefit of their stockholders (an acquisition), or they may distribute the Company D stock to their stockholders and go out of existence (a consolidation). In either case, Company D acquires ownership of the assets of Companies E and F.

Alternatively, Company D could issue its stock directly to the stockholders of Companies E and F in exchange for a majority of their shares. In this case, Company D controls the assets of Company E and Company F, but it does not obtain legal title unless Companies E and F are dissolved. Company D must acquire all the stock of Companies E and F and dissolve those companies if their business combination is to be a consolidation. If Companies E and F are not dissolved, Company D will operate as a holding company, and Companies E and F will be its subsidiaries.

Future references in this chapter will use the term *merger* in the technical sense of a business combination in which all but one of the combining companies go out of existence. Similarly, the term *consolidation* will be used in its technical sense to refer to a business combination in which all the combining companies are dissolved, and a new corporation is formed to take over their net assets. *Consolidation* is also used in accounting to refer to the accounting process of combining parent and subsidiary financial statements, such as in the expressions "principles of consolidation," "consolidation procedures," and "consolidated financial statements." In future chapters, the meanings of the terms will depend on the context in which they are found.

Mergers and consolidations do not present special accounting problems or issues after the initial combination, apart from those discussed in intermediate accounting texts. This is because only one legal and accounting entity survives in a merger or consolidation.

## ACCOUNTING CONCEPT OF BUSINESS COMBINATIONS

Generally accepted accounting principles (GAAP) define the accounting concept of a business combination as:

> *A transaction or other event in which an acquirer obtains control of one or more businesses. Transactions sometimes referred to as true mergers or mergers of equals also are business combinations.* (ASC 805-10)[1]

Note that the accounting concept of a business combination emphasizes the creation of a single entity and the independence of the combining companies before their union. Although one or more of the companies may lose its separate legal identity, dissolution of the legal entities is not necessary within the accounting concept.

Previously separate businesses are brought together into one entity when their business resources and operations come under the control of a single management team. Such control within one business entity is established in business combinations in which:

1. One or more corporations become subsidiaries;
2. One company transfers its net assets to another; or
3. Each company transfers its net assets to a newly formed corporation.

A corporation becomes a **subsidiary** when another corporation acquires a majority (more than 50 percent) of its outstanding voting stock. Thus, one corporation need not acquire all of the stock of another corporation to consummate a business combination. In business combinations in which less than 100 percent of the voting stock of other combining companies is acquired, the combining companies necessarily retain separate legal identities and separate accounting records even though they have become one entity for financial reporting purposes.

Business combinations in which one company transfers its net assets to another can be consummated in a variety of ways, but the acquiring company must acquire substantially all the net assets in any case. Alternatively, each combining company can transfer its net assets to a newly formed corporation. Because the newly formed corporation has no net assets of its own, it issues its stock to the other combining companies or to their stockholders or owners.

### A Brief Background on Accounting for Business Combinations

Accounting for business combinations is one of the most important and interesting topics of accounting theory and practice. At the same time, it is complex and controversial. Business combinations involve financial transactions of enormous magnitudes, business empires, success stories and personal fortunes, executive genius, and management fiascos. By their nature, they affect the fate of entire companies. Each is unique and must be evaluated in terms of its economic substance, irrespective of its legal form.

Historically, much of the controversy concerning accounting requirements for business combinations involved the **pooling of interests method**, which became generally accepted in 1950. Although there are conceptual difficulties with the pooling method, the underlying problem that arose was the introduction of alternative methods of accounting for business combinations (pooling versus purchase). Numerous financial interests are involved in a business combination, and alternate accounting procedures may not be neutral with respect to different interests. That is, the individual financial interests and the final plan of combination may be affected by the method of accounting.

Until 2001, accounting requirements for business combinations recognized both the pooling and purchase methods of accounting for business combinations. In August 1999, the Financial Accounting Standards Board (FASB) issued a report supporting its proposed decision to eliminate pooling. Principal reasons cited included the following:

- Pooling provides less relevant information to statement users.
- Pooling ignores economic value exchanged in the transaction and makes subsequent performance evaluation impossible.
- Comparing firms using the alternative methods is difficult for investors.

Pooling creates these problems because it uses historical book values to record combinations, rather than recognizing fair values of net assets at the transaction date. GAAP generally require recording asset acquisitions at fair values.

---

[1]FASB ASC 805-10. Originally Statement of Financial Accounting "Business Combinations." Stamford, CT: Financial Accounting Standards Board, 2016.

Further, the FASB believed that the economic notion of a pooling of interests rarely exists in business combinations. More realistically, virtually all combinations are acquisitions, in which one firm gains control over another.

GAAP eliminated the pooling of interests method of accounting for all transactions initiated after June 30, 2001. (ASC 805) Combinations initiated subsequent to that date must use the acquisition method. Because the new standard prohibited the use of the pooling method only for combinations initiated after the issuance of the revised standard, prior combinations accounted for under the pooling of interests method were grandfathered; that is, both the acquisition and pooling methods continue to exist as acceptable financial reporting practices for past business combinations.

Therefore, one cannot ignore the conditions for reporting requirements under the pooling approach. On the other hand, because no new poolings are permitted, this discussion focuses on the acquisition method. More detailed coverage of the pooling of interests method is relegated to the Appendix to this chapter.

**INTERNATIONAL ACCOUNTING** Elimination of pooling made GAAP more consistent with international accounting standards. Most major economies prohibit the use of the pooling method to account for business combinations. International Financial Reporting Standards (IFRS) require business combinations to be accounted for using the acquisition method, and specifically prohibit the pooling of interests method. In introducing the new standard, International Accounting Standards Board (IASB) Chairman Sir David Tweedie noted:

> *Accounting for business combinations diverged substantially across jurisdictions. IFRS 3 marks a significant step toward high quality standards in business combination accounting, and in ultimately achieving international convergence in this area.* (IFRS 3)[2]

Accounting for business combinations was a major joint project between the FASB and IASB. As a result, accounting in this area is now generally consistent between GAAP and IFRS. Some differences remain, and we will point them out in later chapters as appropriate.

## ACCOUNTING FOR COMBINATIONS AS ACQUISITIONS

**LEARNING OBJECTIVE 1.3**

GAAP requires that all business combinations initiated after December 15, 2008, be accounted for as acquisitions. (ASC 810-10) The **acquisition method** follows the same GAAP for recording a business combination as we follow in recording the purchase of other assets and the incurrence of liabilities. We record the combination using the fair-value principle. In other words, we measure the cost to the purchasing entity of acquiring another company in a business combination by the amount of cash disbursed or by the fair value of other assets distributed or securities issued.

We expense the direct costs of a business combination (such as accounting, legal, consulting, and finder's fees) other than those for the registration or issuance of equity securities. We charge registration and issuance costs of equity securities issued in a combination against the fair value of securities issued, usually as a reduction of additional paid-in capital. We expense indirect costs such as management salaries, depreciation, and rent under the acquisition method. We also expense indirect costs incurred to close duplicate facilities.

**NOTE TO THE STUDENT**

The topics covered in this text are sometimes complex and involve detailed exhibits and illustrative examples. Understanding the exhibits and illustrations is an integral part of the learning experience, and you should study them in conjunction with the related text. Carefully review the exhibits as they are introduced in the text. Exhibits and illustrations are designed to provide essential information and explanations for understanding the concepts presented.

Understanding the financial statement impact of complex business transactions is an important element in the study of advanced financial accounting topics. To assist you in this learning endeavor, this book depicts journal entries that include the types of accounts being affected and the directional impact of the event. Conventions used throughout the text are as follows: A parenthetical reference added to each account affected by a journal entry indicates the type of account and the effect of the entry. For example, an increase in accounts receivable, an asset account, is denoted as "Accounts receivable (+ A)." A decrease in this account is denoted as "Accounts receivable(– A)." The symbol (A) stands for assets, (L) for liabilities, (SE) for stockholders' equity accounts, (R) for revenues, (E) for expenses, (Ga) for gains, and (Lo) for losses.

---

[2]© IFRS 3. "Business Combinations." London, UK: International Accounting Standards Board, 2004.

To illustrate, assume that Pop Corporation issues 100,000 shares of $10 par common stock for the net assets of Son Corporation in a business combination on July 1, 2016. The market price of Pop common stock on this date is $16 per share. Additional direct costs of the combination consist of Securities and Exchange Commission (SEC) fees of $5,000, accountants' fees in connection with the SEC registration statement of $10,000, costs for printing and issuing the common stock certificates of $25,000, and finder's and consultants' fees of $80,000.

Pop records the issuance of the 100,000 shares on its books as follows (in thousands):

| | | |
|---|---|---|
| Investment in Son (+A) | 1,600 | |
| Common stock, $10 par (+SE) | | 1,000 |
| Additional paid-in capital (+SE) | | 600 |

To record issuance of 100,000 shares of $10 par
common stock with a market price of $16 per share
in a combination with Son Corporation.

Pop records additional direct costs of the business combination as follows:

| | | |
|---|---|---|
| Investment expense (E, −SE) | 80 | |
| Additional paid-in capital (−SE) | 40 | |
| Cash (or other net assets) (−A) | | 120 |

To record additional direct costs of combining with Son
Corporation: $80,000 for finder's and consultants' fees and
$40,000 for registering and issuing equity securities.

We treat registration and issuance costs of $40,000 as a reduction of the fair value of the stock issued and charge these costs to Additional paid-in capital. We expense other direct costs of the business combination ($80,000). The total cost to Pop of acquiring Son is $1,600,000, the amount entered in the Investment in Son account.

We accumulate the total cost incurred in purchasing another company in a single-investment account, regardless of whether the other combining company is dissolved or the combining companies continue to operate in a parent–subsidiary relationship. If we dissolve Son Corporation, we record its identifiable net assets on Pop's books at fair value and record any excess of investment cost over fair value of net assets as goodwill. In this case, we allocate the balance recorded in the Investment in Son account by means of an entry on Pop's books. Such an entry might appear as follows (in thousands):

| | | |
|---|---|---|
| Receivables (+A) | XXX | |
| Inventories (+A) | XXX | |
| Plant assets (+A) | XXX | |
| Goodwill (+A) | XXX | |
| Accounts payable (+L) | | XXX |
| Notes payable (+L) | | XXX |
| Investment in Son (−A) | | 1,600 |

To record allocation of the $1,600,000 cost of acquiring
Son Corporation to identifiable net assets according to
their fair values and to goodwill.

If we dissolve Son Corporation, we formally retire the Son Corporation shares. The former Son shareholders are now shareholders of Pop.

If Pop and Son Corporations operate as parent company and subsidiary, Pop will not record the entry to allocate the Investment in Son balance. Instead, Pop will account for its investment in Son by means of the Investment in Son account, and we will make the assignment of fair values to identifiable net assets required in the consolidation process.

Because of the additional complications of accounting for parent–subsidiary operations, the remainder of this chapter is limited to business combinations in which a single acquiring entity receives the net assets of the other combining companies. Subsequent chapters cover parent–subsidiary operations and the preparation of consolidated financial statements.

<table>
<tr><td>LEARNING OBJECTIVE</td><td>1.4</td></tr>
</table>

## Recording Fair Values in an Acquisition

The first step in recording an acquisition is to determine the fair values of all identifiable tangible and intangible assets acquired and liabilities assumed in the combination. This can be a monumental task, but much of the work is done before and during the negotiating process for the proposed merger. Companies generally retain independent appraisers and valuation experts to determine fair values. GAAP provides guidance on the determination of fair values. There are three levels of reliability for fair-value estimates. (ASC 820-10) Level 1 is fair value based on established market prices. Level 2 uses the present value of estimated future cash flows, discounted based on an observable measure such as the prime interest rate. Level 3 includes other internally derived estimations. Throughout this text, we assume that total fair value is equal to the total market value, unless otherwise noted.

We record identifiable assets acquired, liabilities assumed, and any noncontrolling interest using fair values at the acquisition date. We determine fair values for all identifiable assets and liabilities, regardless of whether they are recorded on the books of the acquired company. For example, an acquired company may have expensed the costs of developing patents, blueprints, formulas, and the like. However, we assign fair values to such identifiable intangible assets of an acquired company in a business combination accounted for as an acquisition. (ASC 750-10)

Assets acquired and liabilities assumed in a business combination that arise from contingencies should be recognized at fair value if fair value can be reasonably estimated. If the fair value of such an asset or liability cannot be reasonably estimated, the asset or liability should be recognized in accordance with general FASB guidelines to *account for contingencies*. It is expected that most litigation contingencies assumed in an acquisition will be recognized only if a loss is probable and the amount of the loss can be reasonably estimated. (ASC 450)

There are few exceptions to the use of fair value to record assets acquired and liabilities assumed in an acquisition. Deferred tax assets and liabilities arising in a combination, pensions and other employee benefits, and leases should be accounted for in accordance with normal guidance for these items. (ASC 740)

We assign no value to the goodwill recorded on the books of an acquired subsidiary because such goodwill is an unidentifiable asset and because we value the goodwill resulting from the business combination directly: (ASC 715 and ASC 840-10)

> *The acquirer shall recognize goodwill as of the acquisition date, measured as the excess of (a) over (b):*
>
> **a.** *The aggregate of the following:*
>   1. *The consideration transferred measured in accordance with this Section, which generally requires acquisition-date fair value (ASC 805-30-30-7)*
>   2. *The fair value of any noncontrolling interest in the acquiree*
>   3. *In a business combination achieved in stages, the acquisition-date fair value of the acquirer's previously held equity interest in the acquiree*
> **b.** *The net of the acquisition-date [fair value] amounts of the identifiable assets acquired and the liabilities assumed measured in accordance with this Topic*[3]

**RECOGNITION AND MEASUREMENT OF OTHER INTANGIBLE ASSETS**   GAAP (ASC 805-20) clarifies the recognition of intangible assets in business combinations under the acquisition method. Firms should recognize intangibles separate from goodwill only if they fall into one of two categories. Recognizable intangibles must meet either a separability criterion or a contractual-legal criterion.

GAAP defines intangible assets as either current or noncurrent assets (excluding financial instruments) that lack physical substance. Per GAAP:

> *The acquirer shall recognize separately from goodwill the identifiable intangible assets acquired in a business combination. An intangible asset is identifiable if it meets either*

---

[3]FASB ASC 805-30-30-1 Originally Statement of Financial Accounting "Business Combinations." Stamford, CT: Financial Accounting Standards Board, 2010.

*the separability criterion or the contractual-legal criterion described in the definition of identifiable.*

*The separability criterion means that an acquired intangible asset is capable of being separated or divided from the acquiree and sold, transferred, licensed, rented, or exchanged, either individually or together with a related contract, identifiable asset, or liability. An intangible asset that the acquirer would be able to sell, license, or otherwise exchange for something else of value meets the separability criterion even if the acquirer does not intend to sell, license, or otherwise exchange it. . . .*

*An acquired intangible asset meets the separability criterion if there is evidence of exchange transactions for that type of asset or an asset of a similar type, even if those transactions are infrequent and regardless of whether the acquirer is involved in them. . . .*

*An intangible asset that is not individually separable from the acquiree or combined entity meets the separability criterion if it is separable in combination with a related contract, identifiable asset, or liability. (ASC 805-30)[4]*

Intangible assets that are not separable should be included in goodwill. For example, acquired firms will have a valuable employee workforce in place, but this asset cannot be recognized as an intangible asset separately from goodwill. GAAP (reproduced in part in Exhibit 1-2) provides more detailed discussion and an illustrative list of intangible assets that firms can recognize separately from goodwill.

**CONTINGENT CONSIDERATION IN AN ACQUISITION**    A business combination may provide for additional payments to the previous stockholders of the acquired company, contingent on future events or transactions. The contingent consideration may include the distribution of cash or other assets or the issuance of debt or equity securities.

Contingent consideration in an acquisition must be measured and recorded at fair value as of the acquisition date as part of the consideration transferred in the acquisition. In practice, this requires the acquirer to estimate the amount of consideration it will be liable for when the contingency is resolved in the future.

The contingent consideration can be classified as equity or as a liability. An acquirer may agree to issue additional shares of stock to the acquiree if the acquiree meets an earnings goal in the future. Then, the contingent consideration is in the form of equity. At the date of acquisition, the Investment and Paid-in Capital accounts are increased by the fair value of the contingent consideration. Alternatively, an acquirer may agree to pay additional cash to the acquiree if the acquiree meets an earnings goal in the future. Then, the contingent consideration is in the form of a liability. At the date of the acquisition, the Investment and Liability accounts are increased by the fair value of the contingent consideration.

The accounting treatment of subsequent changes in the fair value of the contingent consideration depends on whether the contingent consideration is classified as equity or as a liability. If the contingent consideration is in the form of equity, the acquirer does not remeasure the fair value of the contingency at each reporting date until the contingency is resolved. When the contingency is settled, the change in fair value is reflected in the equity accounts. If the contingent consideration is in the form of a liability, the acquirer measures the fair value of the contingency at each reporting date until the contingency is resolved. Changes in the fair value of the contingent consideration are reported as a gain or loss in earnings, and the liability is also adjusted. (ASC 805-30)

**COST AND FAIR VALUE COMPARED**    After assigning fair values to all identifiable assets acquired and liabilities assumed, we compare the investment cost with the total fair value of identifiable assets less liabilities. If the investment cost exceeds net fair value, we first assign the excess to identifiable net assets according to their fair values and then assign the rest of the excess to goodwill.

In some business combinations, the total fair value of identifiable assets acquired over liabilities assumed may exceed the cost of the acquired company. The gain from such a **bargain purchase** is recognized as an ordinary gain by the acquirer.

---

[4]FASB ASC 805-20-55-11 through 55-38. Originally Statement of Financial Accounting Standards No. 141(R). "Business Combinations." Appendix A. Norwalk, CT: Financial Accounting Standards Board, 2007.

EXHIBIT 1-2

**Intangible Assets That Are Identifiable (ASC 805-20)**

*Source:* FASB ASC 805-20-55-11 through 55-38. Originally Statement of Financial Accounting Standards No. 141(R). "Business Combinations." Norwalk, CT: Financial Accounting Standards Board, 2007.

The following guidance presents examples of identifiable intangible assets acquired in a business combination. Some of the examples may have characteristics of assets other than intangible assets. The acquirer should account for those assets in accordance with their substance. The examples are not intended to be all-inclusive.

Intangible assets designated with the symbol # are those that arise from contractual or other legal rights. Those designated with the symbol * do not arise from contractual or other legal rights but are separable. Intangible assets designated with the symbol # might also be separable, but separability is not a necessary condition for an asset to meet the contractual-legal criterion.

**Marketing-Related Intangible Assets**
a. Trademarks, trade names, service marks, collective marks, certification marks #
b. Trade dress (unique color, shape, package design) #
c. Newspaper mastheads #
d. Internet domain names #
e. Noncompetition agreements #

**Customer-Related Intangible Assets**
a. Customer lists *
b. Order or production backlog #
c. Customer contracts and related customer relationships #
d. Noncontractual customer relationships *

**Artistic-Related Intangible Assets**
a. Plays, operas, ballets #
b. Books, magazines, newspapers, other literary works #
c. Musical works such as compositions, song lyrics, advertising jingles #
d. Pictures, photographs #
e. Video and audiovisual material, including motion pictures or films, music videos, television programs #

**Contract-Based Intangible Assets**
a. Licensing, royalty, standstill agreements #
b. Advertising, construction, management, service or supply contracts #
c. Lease agreements (whether the acquiree is the lessee or the lessor) #
d. Construction permits #
e. Franchise agreements #
f. Operating and broadcast rights #
g. Servicing contracts such as mortgage servicing contracts #
h. Employment contracts #
i. Use rights such as drilling, water, air, timber cutting, and route authorities #

**Technology-Based Intangible Assets**
a. Patented technology #
b. Computer software and mask works #
c. Unpatented technology *
d. Databases, including title plants *

## Illustration of an Acquisition

Pam Corporation acquires the net assets of Sun Company in an acquisition consummated on December 27, 2016. Sun Company is dissolved. The assets and liabilities of Sun Company on this date, at their book values and at fair values, are as follows (in thousands):

|  | Book Value | Fair Value |
|---|---|---|
| *Assets* | | |
| Cash | $   50 | $   50 |
| Net receivables | 150 | 140 |
| Inventories | 200 | 250 |
| Land | 50 | 100 |
| Buildings—net | 300 | 500 |
| Equipment—net | 250 | 350 |
| Patents | — | 50 |
| Total assets | $1,000 | $1,440 |
| *Liabilities* | | |
| Accounts payable | $ 60 | $ 60 |
| Notes payable | 150 | 135 |
| Other liabilities | 40 | 45 |
| Total liabilities | $  250 | $  240 |
| Net assets | $  750 | $1,200 |

# CASE 1: GOODWILL

Pam Corporation pays $400,000 cash and issues 50,000 shares of Pam Corporation $10 par common stock with a market value of $20 per share for the net assets of Sun Company. The following entries record the acquisition on the books of Pam Corporation on December 27, 2016 (in thousands).

| | | |
|---|---|---|
| Investment in Sun Company (+A) | 1,400 | |
| Cash (−A) | | 400 |
| Common stock, $10 par (+SE) | | 500 |
| Additional paid-in capital (+SE) | | 500 |

To record issuance of 50,000 shares of $10 par common stock plus $400,000 cash in a business combination with Sun Company.

| | | |
|---|---|---|
| Cash (+A) | 50 | |
| Net receivables (+A) | 140 | |
| Inventories (+A) | 250 | |
| Land (+A) | 100 | |
| Buildings (+A) | 500 | |
| Equipment (+A) | 350 | |
| Patents (+A) | 50 | |
| Goodwill (+A) | 200 | |
| Accounts payable (+L) | | 60 |
| Notes payable (+L) | | 135 |
| Other liabilities (+L) | | 45 |
| Investment in Sun Company (−A) | | 1,400 |

To assign the cost of Sun Company to identifiable assets acquired and liabilities assumed on the basis of their fair values and to goodwill.

We assign the amounts to the assets and liabilities based on fair values, except for goodwill. We determine goodwill by subtracting the $1,200,000 fair value of identifiable net assets acquired from the $1,400,000 purchase price for Sun Company's net assets.

# CASE 2: FAIR VALUE EXCEEDS INVESTMENT COST (BARGAIN PURCHASE)

Pam Corporation issues 40,000 shares of its $10 par common stock with a market value of $20 per share, and it also gives a 10 percent, five-year note payable for $200,000 for the net assets of Sun Company. Pam's books record the Pam/Sun business combination on December 27, 2016, with the following journal entries (in thousands):

| | | |
|---|---|---|
| Investment in Sun Company (+A) | 1,000 | |
| Common stock, $10 par (+SE) | | 400 |
| Additional paid-in capital (+SE) | | 400 |
| 10% Note payable (+L) | | 200 |

To record issuance of 40,000 shares of $10 par common stock plus a $200,000, 10% note in a business combination with Sun Company.

| | | |
|---|---|---|
| Cash (+A) | 50 | |
| Net receivables (+A) | 140 | |
| Inventories (+A) | 250 | |
| Land (+A) | 100 | |
| Buildings (+A) | 500 | |
| Equipment (+A) | 350 | |
| Patents (+A) | 50 | |
| Accounts payable (+L) | | 60 |
| Notes payable (+L) | | 135 |
| Other liabilities (+L) | | 45 |
| Investment in Sun Company (−A) | | 1,000 |
| Gain from bargain purchase (Ga, +SE) | | 200 |

To assign the cost of Sun Company to identifiable assets acquired and liabilities assumed on the basis of their fair values and to recognize the gain from a bargain purchase.

(*continued*)

We assign fair values to the individual asset and liability accounts in the last entry in accordance with GAAP provisions for an acquisition. (ASC 805) The $1,200,000 fair value of the identifiable net assets acquired exceeds the $1,000,000 purchase price by $200,000, so Pam recognizes a $200,000 gain from a bargain purchase. Bargain purchases are infrequent, but may occur even for very large corporations.

## The Goodwill Controversy

GAAP (ASC 350-20) defines *goodwill* as the excess of the investment cost over the fair value of net assets received. Theoretically, it is a measure of the present value of the combined company's projected future excess earnings over the normal earnings of a similar business. Estimating it requires considerable speculation. Therefore, the amount that we capitalize as goodwill is the portion of the purchase price left over after all other identifiable tangible and intangible assets and liabilities have been valued at fair value. Errors in the valuation of other assets will affect the amount capitalized as goodwill.

Under current GAAP, goodwill is not amortized. There are also income tax controversies relating to goodwill. In some cases, firms can deduct goodwill amortization for tax purposes over a 15-year period.

## Current GAAP for Goodwill and Other Intangible Assets

GAAP dramatically changed accounting for goodwill in 2001. (ASC 350-20) GAAP maintained the basic computation of goodwill, but the revised standards mitigate many of the previous controversies. Current GAAP provides clarification and more detailed guidance on when previously unrecorded intangibles should be recognized as assets, which can affect the amount of goodwill that firms recognize.

Under current GAAP (ASC 350-20), firms record goodwill but do *not* amortize it. Instead, GAAP requires that firms periodically assess goodwill for impairment in its value. An impairment occurs when the recorded value of goodwill is greater than its fair value. We calculate the fair value of goodwill in a manner similar to the original calculation at the date of the acquisition. Should such impairment occur, firms will write down goodwill to a new estimated amount and will record an offsetting loss in calculating net income for the period.

Firms no longer amortize goodwill or other intangible assets that have indefinite useful lives. Instead, firms will periodically review these assets (at least annually) and adjust for value impairment. GAAP provides detailed guidance for determining and measuring impairment of goodwill and other intangible assets.

GAAP also defines the reporting entity in accounting for intangible assets. Under prior rules, firms treated the acquired entity as a stand-alone reporting entity. GAAP now recognizes that many acquirees are integrated into the operations of the acquirer. GAAP treats goodwill and other intangible assets as assets of the business reporting unit, which is discussed in more detail in a later chapter on segment reporting. A reporting unit is a component of a business for which discrete financial information is available, and its operating results are regularly reviewed by management.

Firms report intangible assets, other than those acquired in business combinations, based on their fair values at the acquisition date. Firms allocate the cost of a group of assets acquired (which may include both tangible and intangible assets) to the individual assets based on relative fair values and "shall not give rise to goodwill."

GAAP is specific on accounting for internally developed intangible assets:

> *Costs of internally developing, maintaining, or restoring intangible assets that are not specifically identifiable, that have indeterminate lives, or that are inherent in a continuing business and related to the entity as a whole, shall be recognized as an expense when incurred.* (ASC 350-20)[5]

**RECOGNIZING AND MEASURING IMPAIRMENT LOSSES** The goodwill impairment test is a two-step process. (ASC 350-20) Firms first compare carrying values (book values) to fair values at the business reporting unit level. Carrying value includes the goodwill amount. If fair value is less than the carrying amount, then firms proceed to the second step, measurement of the impairment loss.

---

[5]FASB ASC 350-20. Originally Statement of Financial Accounting Standards No. 142. "Goodwill and Other Intangible Assets." Stamford, CT: Financial Accounting Standards Board, 2001.

The second step requires a comparison of the carrying amount of goodwill to its implied fair value. Firms should again make this comparison at the business reporting unit level. If the carrying amount exceeds the implied fair value of the goodwill, the firm must recognize an impairment loss for the difference. The loss amount cannot exceed the carrying amount of the goodwill. Firms cannot reverse previously recognized impairment losses.

Firms should determine the implied fair value of goodwill in the same manner used to originally record the goodwill at the business combination date. Firms allocate the fair value of the reporting unit to all identifiable assets and liabilities as if they purchased the unit on the measurement date. Any excess fair value is the implied fair value of goodwill.

Fair value of assets and liabilities is the value at which they could be sold, incurred, or settled in a current arm's-length transaction. GAAP considers quoted market prices as the best indicators of fair values, although these are often unavailable. When market prices are unavailable, firms may determine fair values using market prices of similar assets and liabilities or other commonly used valuation techniques. For example, firms may employ present value techniques to value estimated future cash flows or earnings. Firms may also employ techniques based on multiples of earnings or revenues.

Firms should conduct the impairment test for goodwill at least annually. GAAP (ASC 350-20) requires more-frequent impairment testing if any of the following events occurs:

a. *A significant adverse change in legal factors or in the business climate*

b. *An adverse action or assessment by a regulator*

c. *Unanticipated competition*

d. *A loss of key personnel*

e. *A more-likely-than-not expectation that a reporting unit or a significant portion of a reporting unit will be sold or otherwise disposed of*

f. *The testing for recoverability under the Impairment or Disposal of Long-Lived Assets Subsections of Subtopic 360-10 of a significant asset group within a reporting unit*

g. *Recognition of a goodwill impairment loss in the financial statements of a subsidiary that is a component of a reporting unit*[6]

The goodwill impairment testing is complex and may have significant financial statement impact. An entire industry has sprung up to assist companies in making goodwill valuations.

**AMORTIZATION VERSUS NON-AMORTIZATION**    Firms must amortize intangibles with a definite useful life over that life. GAAP defines *useful life* as estimated useful life to the reporting entity. The method of amortization should reflect the expected pattern of consumption of the economic benefits of the intangible. If firms cannot determine a pattern, then they should use straight-line amortization.

If intangibles with an indefinite life later have a life that can be estimated, they should be amortized at that point. Firms should periodically review intangibles that are not being amortized for possible impairment loss.

## DISCLOSURE REQUIREMENTS

GAAP requires significant disclosures about a business combination. FASB requires specific disclosures that are categorized by: (1) disclosures for the reporting period that includes a business combination, (2) disclosures when a business combination occurs after a reporting period ends, but before issuance of the financial statements, (3) disclosures about provisional amounts related to the business combination, and (4) disclosures about adjustments related to business combinations.

The specific information that must be disclosed in the financial statements for the period in which a business combination occurs can be categorized as follows:

1. General information about the business combination such as the name of the acquired company, a description of the acquired company, the acquisition date, the portion of the acquired company's voting stock acquired, the acquirer's reasons for the acquisition, and the manner in which the acquirer obtained control of the acquiree;

---

[6]FASB ASC 350-20-35-30. Originally Statement of Financial Accounting Standards No. 142. "Goodwill and Other Intangible Assets." Stamford, CT: Financial Accounting Standards Board, 2001.

2. Information about goodwill or a gain from a bargain purchase that results from the business combination;

3. Nature, terms, and fair value of consideration transferred in a business combination;

4. Details about specific assets acquired, liabilities assumed, and any noncontrolling interest recognized in connection with the business combination;

5. Reduction in acquirer's pre-existing deferred tax asset valuation allowance due to the business combination;

6. Information about transactions with the acquiree accounted for separately from the business combination;

7. Details about step acquisitions;

8. If the acquirer is a public company, additional disclosures are required such as pro forma information.

GAAP (ASC 350-20) requires firms to report material aggregate amounts of goodwill as a separate balance sheet line item. Likewise, firms must show goodwill impairment losses separately in the income statement, as a component of income from continuing operations (unless the impairment relates to discontinued operations). GAAP also provides increased disclosure requirements for intangible assets (which are reproduced in Exhibit 1-3).

---

**EXHIBIT 1-3**

**INTANGIBLE ASSETS DISCLOSURE REQUIREMENTS (ASC 350-20)**

*Source:* FASB ASC 350-20. Originally Statement of Financial Accounting Standards No. 142. "Goodwill and Other Intangible Assets." Stamford, CT: Financial Accounting Standards Board, 2001.

---

For intangible assets acquired either individually or as part of a group of assets (in either an asset acquisition or business combination), all of the following information shall be disclosed in the notes to financial statements in the period of acquisition:

a. For intangible assets subject to amortization, all of the following:
   1. The total amount assigned and the amount assigned to any major intangible asset class
   2. The amount of any significant residual value, in total and by major intangible asset class
   3. The weighted-average amortization period, in total and by major intangible asset class

b. For intangible assets not subject to amortization, the total amount assigned and the amount assigned to any major intangible asset class.

c. The amount of research and development assets acquired in a transaction other than a business combination and written off in the period and the line item in the income statement in which the amounts written off are aggregated.

d. For intangible assets with renewal or extension terms, the weighted-average period before the next renewal or extension (both explicit and implicit), by major intangible asset class.

This information also shall be disclosed separately for each material business combination or in the aggregate for individually immaterial business combinations that are material collectively if the aggregate fair values of intangible assets acquired, other than goodwill, are significant.

The following information shall be disclosed in the financial statements or the notes to financial statements for each period for which a statement of financial position is presented:

a. For intangible assets subject to amortization, all of the following:
   1. The gross carrying amount and accumulated amortization, in total and by major intangible asset class
   2. The aggregate amortization expense for the period
   3. The estimated aggregate amortization expense for each of the five succeeding fiscal years

b. For intangible assets not subject to amortization, the total carrying amount and the carrying amount for each major intangible asset class

c. The entity's accounting policy on the treatment of costs incurred to renew or extend the term of a recognized intangible asset

d. For intangible assets that have been renewed or extended in the period for which a statement of financial position is presented, both of the following:
   1. For entities that capitalize renewal or extension costs, the total amount of costs incurred in the period to renew or extend the term of a recognized intangible asset, by major intangible asset class
   2. The weighted-average period before the next renewal or extension (both explicit and implicit), by major intangible asset class

For each impairment loss recognized related to an intangible asset, all of the following information shall be disclosed in the notes to financial statements that include the period in which the impairment loss is recognized:

**a.** A description of the impaired intangible asset and the facts and circumstances leading to the impairment

**b.** The amount of the impairment loss and the method for determining fair value

**c.** The caption in the income statement or the statement of activities in which the impairment loss is aggregated

**d.** If applicable, the segment in which the impaired intangible asset is reported under Topic 280

Before completing the chapter, let's take a look at a summary example of required disclosures from a real-world company. In February, 2014, **Google Inc.** completed its acquisition of **Nest Labs, Inc.** Exhibit 1-4 provides Note 5 highlights from Google's 2014 annual report related to this and other acquisitions. Note, in particular, that $430 million of the $2.6 billion price tag relates to intangible assets, and another $2.3 billion is allocated to goodwill.

**EXHIBIT 1-4**

**Note 5. Acquisitions
2014 Acquisitions**

*Source:* From Google's 2014 Annual Report, Note 5. Acquisitions © 2015 Alphabet Inc.

### Nest

In February 2014, we completed the acquisition of Nest Labs, Inc. (Nest), a company whose mission is to reinvent devices in the home such as thermostats and smoke alarms. Prior to this transaction, we had an approximately 12% ownership interest in Nest. The acquisition is expected to enhance Google's suite of products and services and allow Nest to continue to innovate upon devices in the home, making them more useful, intuitive, and thoughtful, and to reach more users in more countries.

Of the total $2.6 billion purchase price and the fair value of our previously held equity interest of $152 million, $51 million was cash acquired, $430 million was attributed to intangible assets, $2.3 billion was attributed to goodwill, and $84 million was attributed to net liabilities assumed. The goodwill of $2.3 billion is primarily attributable to synergies expected to arise after the acquisition. Goodwill is not expected to be deductible for tax purposes.

This transaction is considered a "step acquisition" under GAAP whereby our ownership interest in Nest held before the acquisition was remeasured to fair value at the date of the acquisition. Such fair value was estimated by using discounted cash flow valuation methodologies. Inputs used in the methodologies primarily included projected future cash flows, discounted at a rate commensurate with the risk involved. The gain of $103 million as a result of remeasurement is included in interest and other income, net on our Consolidated Statements of Income for the year ended December 31, 2014.

### Dropcam

In July 2014, Nest completed the acquisition of Dropcam, Inc. (Dropcam), a company that enables consumers and businesses to monitor their homes and offices via video, for approximately $517 million in cash. With Dropcam on board, Nest expects to continue to reinvent products that will help shape the future of the connected home. Of the total purchase price of $517 million, $11 million was cash acquired, $55 million was attributed to intangible assets, $452 million was attributed to goodwill, and $1 million was attributed to net liabilities assumed. The goodwill of $452 million is primarily attributable to synergies expected to arise after the acquisition. Goodwill is not expected to be deductible for tax purposes.

### Skybox

In August 2014, we completed the acquisition of Skybox Imaging, Inc. (Skybox), a satellite imaging company, for approximately $478 million in cash. We expect the acquisition to keep Google Maps accurate with up-to-date imagery and, over time, improve internet access and disaster relief. Of the total purchase price of $478 million, $6 million was cash acquired, $69 million was attributed to intangible assets, $388 million was attributed to goodwill, and $15 million was attributed to net assets acquired. The goodwill of $388 million is primarily attributable to the synergies expected to arise after the acquisition. Goodwill is not expected to be deductible for tax purposes.

### Other Acquisitions

During the year ended December 31, 2014, we completed other acquisitions and purchases of intangible assets for total consideration of approximately $1,466 million, which includes the fair value of our previously held equity interest of $33 million. In aggregate, $65 million was cash acquired, $405 million was attributed to intangible assets, $1,045 million was attributed to goodwill, and $49 million was attributed to net liabilities assumed. These acquisitions generally enhance the breadth and depth of our offerings, as well as expanding our expertise in engineering and other functional areas. The amount of goodwill expected to be deductible for tax purposes is approximately $55 million.

Pro forma results of operations for these acquisitions have not been presented because they are not material to the consolidated results of operations, either individually or in aggregate.

For all acquisitions completed during the year ended December 31, 2014, patents and developed technology have a weighted-average useful life of 5.1 years, customer relationships have a weighted-average useful life of 4.5 years, and trade names and other have a weighted-average useful life of 6.9 years.

## THE SARBANES-OXLEY ACT

You have likely heard about Sarbanes-Oxley and are wondering why we haven't mentioned it yet. The financial collapse of **Enron Corporation** and **WorldCom** (among others) and the demise of public accounting firm **Arthur Andersen and Company** spurred Congress to initiate legislation intended to prevent future financial reporting and auditing abuse. The result was the *Sarbanes-Oxley Act of 2002* (SOX). For the most part, the rules focus on corporate governance, auditing, and internal-control issues, rather than the details of financial reporting and statement presentation that are the topic of this text. However, you should recognize that the law will impact all of the types of companies that we study. Here are a few of the important areas covered by SOX:

- Establishes the independent Public Company Accounting Oversight Board (PCAOB) to regulate the accounting and auditing profession
- Requires greater independence of auditors and clients, including restrictions on the types of consulting and advisory services provided by auditors to their clients
- Requires greater independence and oversight responsibilities for corporate boards of directors, especially for members of audit committees
- Requires management (CEO and CFO) certification of financial statements and internal controls
- Requires independent auditor review and attestation on management's internal-control assessments
- Increases disclosures about off–balance sheet arrangements and contractual obligations
- Increases types of items requiring disclosure on Form 8-K and shortens the filing period

Enforcement of Sarbanes-Oxley is under the jurisdiction of the SEC. The SEC treats violations of SOX or rules of the PCAOB the same as violations of the Securities Exchange Act of 1934. Congress also increased the SEC's budget to permit improved review and enforcement activities. SEC enforcement actions and investigations have increased considerably since the Enron collapse. One example is **Krispy Kreme Doughnuts, Inc.** A January 4, 2005, press release on the company's Web site announced that earnings for fiscal 2004, and the last three quarters of 2004, were being restated. Apparently the company did not make as much "dough" as originally reported. Pre-tax income was reduced by between $6.2 million and $8.1 million. Another example appeared in a *Reuters Limited* story on January 6, 2005, which noted that former directors of **WorldCom** agreed to a $54 million settlement in a class-action lawsuit brought by investors. This included $18 million from personal funds, with the remainder being covered by insurance.

Exhibit 1-5 provides an example of the required management responsibilities under SOX from the 2012 annual report of Chevron Corporation (p. 29). Notice that management's statement reads much like a traditional independent auditor's report. Management takes responsibility for preparation of the financial reports, explicitly notes compliance with GAAP, and declares amounts to be fairly presented. Management also takes explicit responsibility for designing and maintaining internal controls. Finally, the statement indicates the composition and functioning of the Audit Committee, which is designed to comply with SOX requirements. The statement is signed by the CEO, CFO, and comptroller of the company.

**MANAGEMENT'S RESPONSIBILITY FOR FINANCIAL STATEMENTS TO THE STOCKHOLDERS OF CHEVRON CORPORATION**

Management of Chevron is responsible for preparing the accompanying consolidated financial statements and the related information appearing in this report. The statements were prepared in accordance with accounting principles generally accepted in the United States of America and fairly represent the transactions and financial position of the company. The financial statements include amounts that are based on management's best estimates and judgment.

As stated in its report included herein, the independent registered public accounting firm of Pricewater-houseCoopers LLP has audited the company's consolidated financial statements in accordance with the standards of the Public Company Accounting Oversight Board (United States).

The Board of Directors of Chevron has an Audit Committee composed of directors who are not officers or employees of the company. The Audit Committee meets regularly with members of management, the internal auditors, and the independent registered public accounting firm to review accounting, internal control, auditing, and financial reporting matters. Both the internal auditors and the independent registered public accounting firm have free and direct access to the Audit Committee without the presence of management.

**MANAGEMENT'S REPORT ON INTERNAL CONTROL OVER FINANCIAL REPORTING**

The company's management is responsible for establishing and maintaining adequate internal control over financial reporting, as such term is defined in Exchange Act Rule 13a-15(f). The company's management, including the Chief Executive Officer and Chief Financial Officer, conducted an evaluation of the effectiveness of the company's internal control over financial reporting based on the Internal Control – Integrated Framework issued by the Committee of Sponsoring Organizations of the Treadway Commission. Based on the results of this evaluation, the company's management concluded that internal control over financial reporting was effective as of December 31, 2012.

   The effectiveness of the company's internal control over financial reporting as of December 31, 2012, has been audited by PriceWaterhouseCoopers LLP, an independent registered public accounting firm, as stated in its report included herein.

JOHN S. WATSON
Chairman of the Board and
Chief Executive Officer

PATRICIA E. YARRINGTON
Vice President and
Chief Financial Officer

MATTHEW J. FOEHR
Vice President and
Comptroller

*February 22, 2013*

We will note other relevant material from Sarbanes-Oxley throughout the text, as applicable. For example, transactions with related parties and variable interest entities are included in Chapter 11.

## SUMMARY

A business combination occurs when two or more separate businesses join into a single accounting entity. All combinations initiated after December 15, 2008, must be accounted for as acquisitions. Acquisition accounting requires the recording of assets acquired and liabilities assumed at their fair values at the date of the combination.

   The illustrations in this chapter are for business combinations in which there is only one surviving entity. Later chapters cover accounting for parent–subsidiary operations in which more than one of the combining companies continue to exist as separate legal entities.

## APPENDIX:  POOLING OF INTERESTS ACCOUNTING

LEARNING
OBJECTIVE **1.5**

Pooling of interests accounting for business combinations is a thing of the past under U.S. GAAP (ASC 805). No new pooling combinations may be recorded after 2001. Many of the detailed issues related to poolings concern the original recording of the combination. The information in this Appendix relates to the initial recording of poolings. Existing poolings were grandfathered in. Grandfathering of prior poolings makes it useful to understand the recording of past poolings, but you will not need this accounting detail for transactions that will not recur in the future.

**CONDITIONS FOR POOLING**    The pooling of interests concept was based on the assumption that it was possible to unite ownership interests through the exchange of equity securities without an acquisition of one combining company by another. Accordingly, application of the concept was limited to those business combinations in which the combining entities exchanged equity securities and the operations and ownership interests continued in a new accounting entity.

   The third condition for pooling was that *none of the combining companies changed the equity interest* of the voting common stock in contemplation of effecting the combination within two years before initiation of the plan of combination or between the dates of initiation and consummation.

   A fourth condition was that each of the combining companies *reacquired shares of voting common stock only for purposes other than business combination*, and that no company reacquired more than a normal number of shares between the dates the plan was initiated and consummated. This restriction on treasury stock transactions generally did not apply to shares purchased for stock option or compensation plans.

   The fifth condition required that the proportionate interest of each individual common stock–holder in each of the combining companies remain the same as a result of the exchange of stock to effect the combination. For example, if Stockholder A held 100 shares in the other combining company and Stockholder B held 200 shares, then Stockholder B's interest in the pooled entity must have been twice that of A's for the combination to be a pooling of interests.

Condition 6 specified that the voting rights in the combined corporation be immediately exercisable by the stockholders. The final condition required resolution of the combination on the date of consummation, with no provisions pending that related to the issue of securities or other considerations.

**ABSENCE OF PLANNED TRANSACTIONS**  The last group of conditions for a pooling of interests focused on planned transactions of the combined entity. First, the combined corporation must *not* have retired or reacquired stock issued to effect the combination. Second, the combined corporation must *not* have entered into financial arrangements (such as long guarantees) for the benefit of former stockholders of a combining company. Finally, the combined corporation must *not* have planned to dispose of a significant part of the assets of the combining companies within two years after the combination. Plans to dispose of assets that represented duplicate facilities were permissible.

If all 12 of these conditions were met, the business combination was accounted for as a pooling of interests; otherwise, the acquisition method was used. Exhibit 1A-1 reviews the 12 conditions for a pooling of interests.

In a pooling of interests, the recorded assets and liabilities of the separate companies became the assets and liabilities of the surviving (combined) corporation. Because total assets and liabilities equal the sum of the combining entities, so must the total equities.

These relationships can be shown through a series of illustrations. Assume that immediately before their pooling of interests business combination, the stockholders' equity accounts for Pam Corporation and Sun Corporation were as follows (all amounts are in thousands):

|  | Pam Corporation | Sun Corporation | Total |
|---|---|---|---|
| Capital stock, $10 par | $100 | $ 50 | $150 |
| Additional paid-in capital | 10 | 20 | 30 |
| Total paid-in capital | 110 | 70 | 180 |
| Retained earnings | 50 | 30 | 80 |
| Net assets and equity | $160 | $100 | $260 |

In cases A1 and A2 that follow, the pooling was in the form of a *merger*, in which Pam Corporation was the issuing corporation and the surviving entity. In cases A3, A4, and A5, the pooling was in the form of a *consolidation*, and Pop Corporation was formed to take over the net assets of Pam and Sun. Pam and Sun Corporations were dissolved.

---

**EXHIBIT 1A-1**

**Twelve Conditions for Pooling (*APB Opinion No. 16*)**

*Source:* © Financial Accounting Standards Board (FASB)

**Attributes of Combining Companies**

1. Autonomous (two-year rule)
2. Independent (10% rule)

**Manner of Combining Interests**

1. Single transaction (or completed within one year after initiation)
2. Exchange of common stock (the "substantially all" rule: 90% or more)
3. No equity changes in contemplation of combination (two-year rule)
4. Shares reacquired only for purposes other than combination
5. No change in proportionate equity interests
6. Voting rights immediately exercisable
7. Combination resolved at consummation (no pending provisions)

**Absence of Planned Transactions**

1. Issuing company cannot reacquire shares
2. Issuing company cannot make deals to benefit former stockholders
3. Issuing company cannot plan to dispose of assets within two years

## CASE A1: MERGER; PAID-IN CAPITAL EXCEEDS STOCK ISSUED

Pam, the surviving corporation, issued 7,000 shares of its stock for the net assets of Sun. In this case, the $180,000 total paid in capital of the combining companies exceeded the $170,000 capital stock of Pam by $10,000. As a result, Pam had capital stock of $170,000, additional paid-in capital of $10,000, and retained earnings of $80,000, for a total equity of $260,000. Observe that the net assets of the surviving entity still were equal to the total recorded assets of the combining companies. Pam recorded the pooling as follows (in thousands):

| | | |
|---|---|---|
| Net assets (+A) | 100 | |
|     Capital stock, $10 par (+SE) | | 70 |
|     Retained earnings (+SE) | | 30 |
| To record issuance of 7,000 shares in a | | |
|   pooling with Sun Corporation. | | |

## CASE A2: MERGER; STOCK ISSUED EXCEEDS PAID-IN CAPITAL

Pam, the surviving entity, issued 9,000 shares of its stock for the net assets of Sun. In this case, the $190,000 capital stock of Pam exceeded the $180,000 total paid-in capital of the combining companies by $10,000. The result was that Pam would have capital stock of $190,000, no additional paid-in capital, and retained earnings of $70,000. Notice that the maximum retained earnings that can be combined ($80,000) has been reduced by the $10,000 excess of capital stock over paid-in capital. The entry on Pam's books was as follows (in thousands):

| | | |
|---|---|---|
| Net assets (+A) | 100 | |
| Additional paid-in capital (−SE) | 10 | |
|     Capital stock $10 par (+SE) | | 90 |
|     Retained earnings (+SE) | | 20 |
| To record issuance of 9,000 shares in a | | |
|   pooling with Sun Corporation. | | |

The previous cases illustrated accounting procedures for a merger accounted for as a pooling of interests. Accounting procedures for consolidation of Pam and Sun are illustrated by assuming that Pop Corporation was formed to take over the net assets of Pam and Sun Corporations.

## CASE A3: CONSOLIDATION; PAID-IN CAPITAL EXCEEDS STOCK ISSUED

Pop Corporation issued 15,000 shares of $10 par capital stock, 10,000 to Pam and 5,000 to Sun, for their net assets. Pop opened its books with the following entry (in thousands):

| | | |
|---|---|---|
| Net assets (+A) | 260 | |
|     Capital stock, $10 par (+SE) | | 150 |
|     Additional paid-in capital (+SE) | | 30 |
|     Retained earnings (+SE) | | 80 |
| To record issuance of 10,000 shares to | | |
|   Pam and 5,000 shares to Sun in a business | | |
|   combination accounted for as a pooling of | | |
|   interests. | | |

The $180,000 combined paid-in capital of Pam and Sun exceeded the $150,000 capital stock of Pop, the surviving entity, so the $30,000 excess was the additional paid-in capital of the pooled entity. Also, the $80,000 maximum retained earnings was pooled.

## CASE A4: CONSOLIDATION; PAID-IN CAPITAL EXCEEDS STOCK ISSUED

Pop Corporation issued 17,000 shares of $10 par capital stock, 11,000 to Pam and 6,000 to Sun, for their net assets. The stockholders' equity of Pop in this case was the same as Pam's stockholders' equity in Case A1. Pop recorded the consolidation as follows (in thousands):

| | | |
|---|---|---|
| Net assets (+A) | 260 | |
| Capital stock, $10 par (+SE) | | 170 |
| Additional paid-in capital (+SE) | | 10 |
| Retained earnings (+SE) | | 80 |

To record issuance of 11,000 shares to Pam and 6,000 shares to Sun in a business combination accounted for as a pooling of interests.

The $180,000 total paid-in capital of the combining entities exceeded the $170,000 capital stock of Pop; therefore, the $10,000 excess was the additional paid-in capital of the pooled entity, and the $80,000 maximum retained earnings was pooled.

## CASE A5: CONSOLIDATION; STOCK ISSUED EXCEEDS PAID-IN CAPITAL

Pop Corporation issued 19,000 shares of $10 par capital stock, 12,000 to Pam and 7,000 to Sun, for their net assets. Pop's stockholders' equity in this case was the same as Pam's stockholders' equity in Case A2. The entry on Pop's books to record the pooling was as follows (in thousands):

| | | |
|---|---|---|
| Net assets (+A) | 260 | |
| Capital stock, $10 par (+SE) | | 190 |
| Retained earnings (+SE) | | 70 |

To record issuance of 12,000 shares to Pam and 7,000 shares to Sun in a business combination accounted for as a pooling of interests.

The $190,000 capital stock of Pop, the surviving entity, exceeded the $180,000 total paid-in capital of Pam and Sun, so the maximum pooled retained earnings was reduced by the $10,000 excess to $70,000, and the pooled entity had no additional paid-in capital.

SUMMARY BALANCE SHEETS    A summary balance sheet for the surviving entity in each of the five pooling of interests business combinations is shown in Exhibit 1A-2.

EXPENSES RELATED TO POOLING COMBINATIONS    The costs incurred to effect a business combination and to integrate the operations of the combining companies in a pooling were expenses of the combined corporation. For example, costs of registering and issuing securities, providing stockholders with information, paying accountants' and consultants' fees, and paying finder's fees to those who discovered the "combinable" situation were recorded as expenses of the combined entity in the

**EXHIBIT 1A-2**

Summary Balance Sheets for the Five Pooling of Interests Cases

| | Merger Pam's Books | | Consolidation Pop's Books | | |
|---|---|---|---|---|---|
| | Case A1 | Case A2 | Case A3 | Case A4 | Case A5 |
| Net assets | $260 | $260 | $260 | $260 | $260 |
| Capital stock, $10 par | $170 | $190 | $150 | $170 | $190 |
| Additional paid-in capital | 10 | — | 30 | 10 | — |
| Retained earnings | 80 | 70 | 80 | 80 | 70 |
| Stockholders' equity | $260 | $260 | $260 | $260 | $260 |

period in which they were incurred. If Pam or Pop Corporation in the preceding cases had incurred accountants' fees, consultants' fees, costs of security registration, and other costs of combining, the combined net assets of the surviving entity would have been less and combined expenses would have been greater. However, the capital stock recorded at the time of merger or consolidation would have been the same.

Financial statements of a pooled entity for the year of combination should have been presented as if the combination had been consummated at the beginning of the period. In addition, if comparative financial statements for prior years were presented, they must have been restated on a combined basis with disclosure of the fact that the statements of previously separate companies had been combined.

## QUESTIONS

Items marked with an asterisk are based on Appendix materials.

1. What is the accounting concept of a business combination?
2. Is dissolution of all but one of the separate legal entities necessary in order to have a business combination? Explain.
3. What are the legal distinctions between a business combination, a merger, and a consolidation?
4. When does goodwill result from a business combination? How does goodwill affect reported net income after a business combination?
5. What is a bargain purchase? Describe the accounting procedures necessary to record and account for a bargain purchase.

## EXERCISES

### E1-1
### General questions

1. A business combination in which a new corporation is formed to take over the assets and operations of two or more separate business entities, with the previously separate entities being dissolved, is a/an:
   a  *Consolidation*
   b  *Merger*
   c  *Pooling of interests*
   d  *Acquisition*

2. In a business combination, the direct costs of registering and issuing equity securities are
   a  *Added to the parent/investor company's investment account*
   b  *Charged against other paid-in capital of the combined entity*
   c  *Deducted from income in the period of combination*
   d  *None of the above*

3. An excess of the fair value of net assets acquired in a business combination over the price paid is
   a  *Reported as a gain from a bargain purchase*
   b  *Applied to a reduction of noncash assets before negative goodwill may be reported*
   c  *Applied to reduce noncurrent assets other than marketable securities to zero before negative goodwill may be reported*
   d  *Applied to reduce goodwill to zero before negative goodwill may be reported*

4. Cork Corporation acquires Dart Corporation in a business combination. Which of the following would be excluded from the process of assigning fair values to assets and liabilities for purposes of recording the acquisition? (Assume Dart Corporation is dissolved.)
   a  *Patents developed by Dart because the costs were expensed under GAAP*
   b  *Dart's mortgage payable because it is fully secured by land that has a market value far in excess of the mortgage*
   c  *An asset or liability amount for over- or underfunding of Dart's defined-benefit pension plan*
   d  *None of the above*

## E1-2
## [Based on AICPA] General problems

1. Pop Corporation paid $100,000 cash for the net assets of Son Company, which consisted of the following:

|  | Book Value | Fair Value |
| --- | --- | --- |
| Current assets | $ 40,000 | $ 56,000 |
| Plant and equipment | 160,000 | 220,000 |
| Liabilities assumed | (40,000) | (36,000) |
|  | $160,000 | $240,000 |

Assume Son Company is dissolved. The plant and equipment acquired in this business combination should be recorded at:

a $220,000

b $200,000

c $183,332

d $180,000

2. On April 1, Pam Company paid $1,600,000 for all the issued and outstanding common stock of Sun Corporation in a transaction properly accounted for as an acquisition. Sun Corporation is dissolved. The recorded assets and liabilities of Sun Corporation on April 1 follow:

| | |
| --- | --- |
| Cash | $160,000 |
| Inventory | 480,000 |
| Property and equipment (net of accumulated depreciation of $640,000) | 960,000 |
| Liabilities | (360,000) |

On April 1, it was determined that the inventory of Sun had a fair value of $380,000, and the property and equipment (net) had a fair value of $1,120,000. What is the amount of goodwill resulting from the acquisition?

a 0

b $100,000

c $300,000

d $360,000

## E1-3
## Prepare stockholders' equity section

The stockholders' equities of Pop Corporation and Son Corporation at January 1 were as follows (in thousands):

|  | Pop | Son |
| --- | --- | --- |
| Capital stock, $10 par | $3,000 | $1,600 |
| Other paid-in capital | 400 | 800 |
| Retained earnings | 1,200 | 600 |
| Stockholders' equity | $4,600 | $3,000 |

On January 2, Pop issued 300,000 of its shares with a market value of $20 per share for all of Son's shares, and Son was dissolved. On the same day, Pop paid $10,000 to register and issue the shares and $20,000 for other direct costs of combination.

**REQUIRED:** Prepare the stockholders' equity section of Pop Corporation's balance sheet immediately after the acquisition on January 2. (*Hint:* Prepare the journal entry.)

## E1-4
## Journal entries to record an acquisition

Pam Company issued 480,000 shares of $10 par common stock with a fair value of $10,200,000 for all the voting common stock of Sun Company. In addition, Pam incurred the following costs:

| | |
| --- | --- |
| Legal fees to arrange the business combination | $100,000 |
| Cost of SEC registration, including accounting and legal fees | 48,000 |
| Cost of printing and issuing net stock certificates | 12,000 |
| Indirect costs of combining, including allocated overhead and executive salaries | 80,000 |

Immediately before the acquisition in which Sun Company was dissolved, Sun's assets and equities were as follows (in thousands):

|  | Book Value | Fair Value |
|---|---|---|
| Current assets | $ 4,000 | $ 4,400 |
| Plant assets | 6,000 | 8,800 |
| Liabilities | 1,200 | 1,200 |
| Common stock | 8,000 |  |
| Retained earnings | 800 |  |

**REQUIRED:** Prepare all journal entries on Pam's books to record the acquisition.

## E1-5
## Journal entries to record an acquisition with direct costs and fair value/book value differences

On January 1, Pop Corporation pays $400,000 cash and also issues 36,000 shares of $10 par common stock with a market value of $660,000 for all the outstanding common shares of Son Corporation. In addition, Pop pays $60,000 for registering and issuing the 36,000 shares and $140,000 for the other direct costs of the business combination, in which Son Corporation is dissolved. Summary balance sheet information for the companies immediately before the merger is as follows (in thousands):

|  | Pop Book Value | Son Book Value | Son Fair Value |
|---|---|---|---|
| Cash | $ 700 | $ 80 | $ 80 |
| Inventories | 240 | 160 | 200 |
| Other current assets | 60 | 40 | 40 |
| Plant assets—net | 520 | 360 | 560 |
| Total assets | $1,520 | $640 | $880 |
| Current liabilities | $ 320 | $ 60 | $ 60 |
| Other liabilities | 160 | 100 | 80 |
| Common stock, $10 par | 840 | 400 |  |
| Retained earnings | 200 | 80 |  |
| Total liabilities and owners' equity | $1,520 | $640 |  |

**REQUIRED:** Prepare all journal entries on Pop's books to account for the acquisition.

## E1-6
## [Appendix] Journal entries to record business combinations

Pop Company issued 120,000 shares of $10 par common stock with a fair value of $2,550,000 for all the voting common stock of Son Company. In addition, Pop incurred the following additional costs:

| | |
|---|---|
| Legal fees to arrange the business combination | $25,000 |
| Cost of SEC registration, including accounting and legal fees | 12,000 |
| Cost of printing and issuing new stock certificates | 3,000 |
| Indirect costs of combining including allocated overhead and executive salaries | 20,000 |

Immediately before the business combination in which Son Company was dissolved, Son's assets and equities were as follows (in thousands):

|  | Book Value | Fair Value |
|---|---|---|
| Current assets | $1,000 | $1,100 |
| Plant assets | 1,500 | 2,200 |
| Liabilities | 300 | 300 |
| Common stock | 2,000 |  |
| Retained earnings | 200 |  |

**REQUIRED:** Assume that the business combination is a pooling of interests. Prepare all journal entries on Pop's books to record the business combination.

## E1-7
### [Appendix] Journal entries to record a pooling

On January 1, 2000, Pam Corporation held 2,000 shares of Sun Corporation common stock acquired at $15 per share several years earlier. On this date, Pam issued 1.5 of its $10 par value shares for each of the other 98,000 outstanding shares of Sun in a pooling of interests in which Sun Corporation was dissolved. Sun Corporation's after-closing trial balance on December 31, 1999, consisted of the following (in thousands):

| | | |
|---|---:|---:|
| Current assets | $ 800 | |
| Plant and equipment—net | 1,500 | |
| Liabilities | | $ 200 |
| Capital stock, $5 par | | 500 |
| Additional paid-in capital | | 1,000 |
| Retained earnings | | 600 |
| | $2,300 | $2,300 |

**REQUIRED:** Prepare a journal entry (or entries) on Pam's books to account for the pooling of interests. (*Hint*: Do not forget to consider the 2,000 shares of Sun held by Pam on January 1, 2000.)

## PROBLEMS

## P1-1
### Prepare balance sheet after acquisition

Comparative balance sheets for Pop and Son Corporations at December 31, 2015, are as follows (in thousands):

| | Pop | Son |
|---|---:|---:|
| Current assets | $2,080 | $ 960 |
| Land | 800 | 1,600 |
| Buildings—net | 4,800 | 1,600 |
| Equipment—net | 3,520 | 3,840 |
| Total assets | $11,200 | $8,000 |
| | | |
| Current liabilities | $ 800 | $ 960 |
| Capital stock, $10 par | 8,000 | 3,200 |
| Additional paid-in capital | 800 | 2,240 |
| Retained earnings | 1,600 | 1,600 |
| Total equities | $11,200 | $8,000 |

On January 2, 2016, Pop issues 240,000 shares of its stock with a market value of $40 per share for all the outstanding shares of Son Corporation in an acquisition. Son is dissolved. The recorded book values reflect fair values, except for the buildings of Pop, which have a fair value of $6,400,000, and the current assets of Son, which have a fair value of $1,600,000.

Pop pays the following expenses in connection with the business combination:

| | |
|---|---:|
| Costs of registering and issuing securities | $240,000 |
| Other direct costs of combination | $400,000 |

**REQUIRED:** Prepare the balance sheet of Pop Corporation immediately after the acquisition.

## P1-2
### Prepare balance sheet after an acquisition

On January 2, 2016, Pop Corporation enters into a business combination with Son Corporation in which Son is dissolved. Pop pays $1,650,000 for Son, the consideration consisting of 66,000 shares of Pop $10 par common stock with a market value of $25 per share. In addition, Pop pays the following expenses in cash at the time of the merger:

| | |
|---|---:|
| Finder's fee | $ 70,000 |
| Accounting and legal fees | 130,000 |
| Registration and issuance costs of securities | 80,000 |
| | $280,000 |

Balance sheet and fair value information for the two companies on December 31, 2015, immediately before the merger, is as follows (in thousands):

| | Pop Book Value | Son Book Value | Son Fair Value |
|---|---:|---:|---:|
| Cash | $ 300 | $ 60 | $ 60 |
| Accounts receivable—net | 460 | 100 | 80 |
| Inventories | 1,040 | 160 | 240 |
| Land | 800 | 200 | 300 |
| Buildings—net | 2,000 | 400 | 600 |
| Equipment—net | 1,000 | 600 | 500 |
| Total assets | $5,600 | $1,520 | $1,780 |
| | | | |
| Accounts payable | $ 600 | $ 80 | $ 80 |
| Note payable | 1,200 | 400 | 360 |
| Capital stock, $10 par | 1,600 | 600 | |
| Other paid-in capital | 1,200 | 100 | |
| Retained earnings | 1,000 | 340 | |
| Total liabilities and owners' equity | $5,600 | $1,520 | |

**REQUIRED:** Prepare a balance sheet for Pop Corporation as of January 2, 2016, immediately after the merger, assuming the merger is treated as an acquisition.

## P1-3
## Journal entries and balance sheet for an acquisition

On January 2, 2016, Pam Corporation issues its own $10 par common stock for all the outstanding stock of Sun Corporation in an acquisition. Sun is dissolved. In addition, Pam pays $40,000 for registering and issuing securities and $60,000 for other costs of combination. The market price of Pam's stock on January 2, 2016, is $60 per share. Relevant balance sheet information for Pam and Sun Corporations on December 31, 2015, just before the combination, is as follows (in thousands):

| | Pam Historical Cost | Sun Historical Cost | Sun Fair Value |
|---|---:|---:|---:|
| Cash | $ 240 | $ 20 | $ 20 |
| Inventories | 100 | 60 | 120 |
| Other current assets | 200 | 180 | 200 |
| Land | 160 | 40 | 200 |
| Plant and equipment—net | 1,300 | 400 | 700 |
| Total assets | $2,000 | $700 | $1,240 |
| Liabilities | $ 400 | $100 | $ 100 |
| Capital stock, $10 par | 1,000 | 200 | |
| Additional paid-in capital | 400 | 100 | |
| Retained earnings | 200 | 300 | |
| Total liabilities and owners' equity | $2,000 | $700 | |

## REQUIRED

1. Assume that Pam issues 25,000 shares of its stock for all of Sun's outstanding shares.
   a. Prepare journal entries to record the acquisition of Sun.
   b. Prepare a balance sheet for Pam Corporation immediately after the acquisition.

2. Assume that Pam issues 15,000 shares of its stock for all of Sun's outstanding shares.
   a. Prepare journal entries to record the acquisition of Sun.
   b. Prepare a balance sheet for Pam Corporation immediately after the acquisition.

## P1-4
## Allocation schedule and balance sheet

The balance sheets of Pop Corporation and Son Corporation at December 31, 2015, are summarized with fair-value information as follows (in thousands):

| | Pop Corporation | | Son Corporation | |
|---|---|---|---|---|
| | **Book Value** | **Fair Value** | **Book Value** | **Fair Value** |
| *Assets* | | | | |
| Cash | $115 | $115 | $ 10 | $ 10 |
| Receivables—net | 40 | 40 | 20 | 20 |
| Inventories | 120 | 150 | 50 | 30 |
| Land | 45 | 100 | 30 | 100 |
| Buildings—net | 200 | 300 | 100 | 150 |
| Equipment—net | 180 | 245 | 90 | 150 |
| Total assets | $700 | $950 | $300 | $460 |
| *Equities* | | | | |
| Accounts payable | $ 90 | $ 90 | $ 30 | $ 30 |
| Other liabilities | 100 | 90 | 60 | 70 |
| Capital stock, $10 par | 300 | | 100 | |
| Other paid-in capital | 100 | | 80 | |
| Retained earnings | 110 | | 30 | |
| Total equities | $700 | | $300 | |

On January 1, 2016, Pop Corporation acquired all of Son's outstanding stock for $300,000. Pop paid $100,000 cash and issued a five-year, 12 percent note for the balance. Son was dissolved.

---

**REQUIRED**

1. Prepare a schedule to show how the investment cost is allocated to identifiable assets and liabilities.
2. Prepare a balance sheet for Pop Corporation on January 1, 2016, immediately after the acquisition.

---

## P1-5
## Journal entries and balance sheet for an acquisition

Pam Corporation paid $10,000,000 for Sun Corporation's voting common stock on January 2, 2016, and Sun was dissolved. The purchase price consisted of 200,000 shares of Pam's common stock with a market value of $8,000,000, plus $2,000,000 cash. In addition, Pam paid $200,000 for registering and issuing the 200,000 shares of common stock and $400,000 for other costs of combination. Balance sheet information for the companies immediately before the acquisition is summarized as follows (in thousands):

| | Pam | Sun | |
|---|---|---|---|
| | **Book Value** | **Book Value** | **Fair Value** |
| Cash | $ 12,000 | $ 960 | $ 960 |
| Accounts receivable—net | 5,200 | 1,440 | 1,440 |
| Notes receivable—net | 6,000 | 1,200 | 1,200 |
| Inventories | 10,000 | 1,680 | 2,000 |
| Other current assets | 2,800 | 720 | 800 |
| Land | 8,000 | 400 | 800 |
| Buildings—net | 36,000 | 2,400 | 4,800 |
| Equipment—net | 40,000 | 3,200 | 2,400 |
| Total assets | $120,000 | $12,000 | $14,400 |
| Accounts payable | $ 4,000 | $ 1,200 | $ 1,200 |
| Mortgage payable—10% | 20,000 | 2,800 | 2,400 |
| Capital stock, $10 par | 40,000 | 4,000 | |
| Other paid-in capital | 32,000 | 2,400 | |
| Retained earnings | 24,000 | 1,600 | |
| Total equities | $120,000 | $12,000 | |

**REQUIRED**

1. Prepare journal entries for Pam Corporation to record its acquisition of Sun Corporation, including all allocations to individual asset and liability accounts.
2. Prepare a balance sheet for Pam Corporation on January 2, 2016, immediately after the acquisition and dissolution of Sun.

## P1-6
## [Appendix] Prepare balance sheets of pooled companies

Pop Corporation issued its own common stock for all the outstanding shares of Son Corporation in a pooling of interests business combination on January 1, 2000. The balance sheets of the two companies at December 31, 1999, were as follows (in thousands):

|  | Pop | Son |
|---|---|---|
| Current assets | $15,000 | $ 4,000 |
| Plant assets—net | 40,000 | 6,000 |
| Total assets | $55,000 | $10,000 |
|  |  |  |
| Liabilities | $10,000 | $ 3,000 |
| Common stock, $10 par | 30,000 | 4,000 |
| Additional paid-in capital | 3,000 | 2,000 |
| Retained earnings | 12,000 | 1,000 |
| Total equities | $55,000 | $10,000 |

**REQUIRED:** Prepare balance sheets for Pop Corporation on January 1, 2000, immediately after the pooling of interests in which Son was dissolved under the following assumptions:

1. Pop issued 800,000 of its common shares for all of Son's outstanding shares.
2. Pop issued 1,000,000 of its common shares for all of Son's outstanding shares.

## P1-7
## [Appendix] Journal entries to record pooling business combinations

Pam and Sun Corporations entered into a business combination accounted for as a pooling of interests in which Sun was dissolved. Net assets and stockholders' equities of the two companies immediately before the pooling follow (in thousands):

|  | Pam | Sun |
|---|---|---|
| Net assets | $1,000 | $800 |
| Capital stock, $10 par | $ 400 | $200 |
| Additional paid-in capital | 200 | 300 |
| Total paid-in capital | 600 | 500 |
| Retained earnings | 400 | 300 |
| Total stockholders' equity | $1,000 | $800 |

**REQUIRED**

1. Prepare the journal entry on Pam Corporation's books to record the pooling with Sun if Pam issued 35,000, $10 par common shares in exchange for all of Sun common shares.
2. Prepare the journal entry on Pam Corporation's books to record the pooling with Sun if Pam issued 77,000, $10 par common shares in exchange for all of Sun common shares.

## P1-8
## [Appendix] Journal entries and balance sheet for a pooling of interests

On January 2, 2000, Pop and Son Corporation merged their operations through a business combination accounted for as a pooling of interests. The $300,000 direct costs of combination were paid in cash by the surviving entity on January 2, 2000. At December 31, 1999, Son held 25,000 shares of Pop stock acquired at $20 per share. Summary balance sheet information for Pop and Son Corporations at December 31, 1999, was as follows (in thousands):

|  | Pop Corporation | Son Corporation |
| --- | --- | --- |
| Current assets | $ 6,500 | $ 4,500 |
| Plant and equipment—net | 10,000 | 10,000 |
| Investment in Pop |  | 500 |
| Total assets | $16,500 | $15,000 |
| Liabilities | $ 1,500 | $ 3,000 |
| Common stock, $10 par | 10,000 | 8,000 |
| Additional paid-in capital | 2,000 | 3,000 |
| Retained earnings | 3,000 | 1,000 |
| Total equities | $16,500 | $15,000 |

**REQUIRED:** Assume that the surviving corporation was Pop Corporation and that Pop issued 1,000,000 shares of its own stock for all the outstanding shares of Son Corporation.

**a.** Prepare journal entries on the books of Pop Corporation to record the business combination.

**b.** Prepare a balance sheet for Pop Corporation on January 2, 2000, immediately after the business combination.

# PROFESSIONAL RESEARCH ASSIGNMENTS

Answer the following questions by reference to the FASB Codification of Accounting Standards. Include the appropriate reference in your response.

**PR 1-1** What are the required disclosures related to goodwill included in the consolidated balance sheet?

**PR 1-2** Does current GAAP provide any exceptions to the fair-value measurement principle for business combinations?

# CHAPTER 2

# Stock Investments—Investor Accounting and Reporting

Chapter 1 illustrated business combinations in which one surviving entity acquired the net assets of other companies. A single legal accounting entity, with one record-keeping system, integrated the net assets and operations of all combining companies. In Chapter 1, we recorded the business combination in an investment account and immediately eliminated the account through allocation to individual asset and liability accounts.

This chapter focuses on equity investments in which the investor maintains the investment account on a continuous basis. It includes accounting for investments under the fair value/cost (fair value for marketable securities and cost for nonmarketable securities) method, in which the investor does not have the ability to influence the activities of the investee, as well as the equity method of accounting, in which an investor can exercise significant influence over the investee's operations. Generally accepted accounting principles (GAAP) generally prescribe equity method accounting for investments that represent a 20 percent ownership through a 50 percent ownership in the investee.

Investors also use the equity method for parent-company accounting for investments in subsidiaries. This situation arises when the investor controls the operating, investing, and financing decisions of the investee through ownership of more than 50 percent of the voting stock of the investee as the result of a combination in which one or more companies became subsidiaries. For financial-reporting purposes, business combinations require preparation of consolidated financial statements.

This chapter covers parent-company accounting for its investments in subsidiaries under the acquisition method, but it does *not* cover consolidated financial statements. Consolidated financial statement preparation is covered in Chapter 3 and subsequent chapters.

## ACCOUNTING FOR STOCK INVESTMENTS

Generally accepted accounting principles (GAAP) for recording common stock acquisitions requires that the investor record the investment at cost (which is equal to fair value at acquisition). The basic guidelines measure investment costs by including cash disbursed; the fair value of other assets given or securities issued; and additional direct costs of obtaining the investment, other than the costs of registering and issuing equity securities, which GAAP charges to additional paid-in capital.

One of the two basic methods of accounting for common stock investments generally applies— the **fair value (cost) method** (ASC 320-10) or the **equity method**. (ASC 323-10)

### Concepts Underlying Fair Value/Cost and Equity Methods

Under the fair value/cost method, we record investments in common stock at cost and report dividends received as dividend income. There is an exception. Dividends received in excess of the

---

**LEARNING OBJECTIVES**

**2.1** Recognize investors' varying levels of influence or control, based on the level of stock ownership.

**2.2** Understand how accounting adjusts to reflect the economics underlying varying levels of investor influence.

**2.3** Identify factors beyond stock ownership that affect an investor's ability to exert influence or control over an investee.

**2.4** Apply the fair value/ cost and equity methods of accounting for stock investments.

**2.5** Apply the equity method to stock investments.

**2.6** Learn how to test goodwill for impairment.

LEARNING OBJECTIVE **2.1**

LEARNING OBJECTIVE **2.2**

29

investor's share of earnings after the stock is acquired are considered a return of capital (or liquidating dividend) and recorded as reductions in the investment account. We classify equity securities that have a readily determinable fair value as either trading securities (securities bought and held principally for the purpose of resale in the near term) or available-for-sale securities (investments not classified as trading securities). (ASC 320-10-35)

Both classifications use fair values to report the investments at the end of each reporting period and report realized gains, losses, and dividends in net income. GAAP also includes unrealized gains and losses (changes in fair value) from the trading-securities classification in net income. However, we report unrealized gains and losses from the available-for-sale securities classification at a net amount as a separate line item under other comprehensive income. GAAP allows other comprehensive income to be reported either on the income statement, or as (ASC 220-10-45) a separate statement of comprehensive income. These amounts accumulate in the equity section of the balance sheet in the account titled *Accumulated other comprehensive income.* This treatment does not apply to investments in equity securities accounted for under the equity method or to investments in consolidated subsidiaries. (ASC 220)

The equity method of accounting is essentially accrual accounting for equity investments that enable the investor to exercise significant influence over the investee. Under the equity method, we record the investments at cost (which is equal to acquisition date fair value) and adjust for earnings, losses, and dividends. The investor reports its share of investee earnings as investment income and its share of the investee losses as investment loss. We increase the investment account for investment income and decrease it for investment losses. Dividends received from investees are disinvestments under the equity method, and they are recorded as decreases in the investment account. Thus, investment income under the equity method reflects the investor's share of the net income of the investee, and the investment account reflects the investor's share of investee net assets.

We account for an investment in voting stock that gives the investor the ability to exercise significant influence over the financial and operating policies of the investee using the equity method of accounting. GAAP requires the equity method of accounting for an investment in common stock by an investor whose investment in common stock gives the investor the ability to exercise significant influence over operating and financial policies of an investee even though the investor holds 50 percent or less of the voting shares. (ASC 323-10-15)

GAAP bases the ability to exert significant influence on a 20 percent ownership test:

> *An investment (direct or indirect) of 20 percent or more of the voting stock of an investee shall lead to a presumption that in the absence of predominant evidence to the contrary an investor has the ability to exercise significant influence over an investee. Conversely, an investment of less than 20 percent of the voting stock of an investee shall lead to a presumption that an investor does not have the ability to exercise significant influence unless such ability can be demonstrated.* (ASC 325)[1]

**LEARNING OBJECTIVE 2.3**

GAAP (ASC 323-10-15) cites (1) opposition by the investee that challenges the investor's influence, (2) surrender of significant stockholder rights by agreement between the investor and investee, (3) concentration of majority ownership in another group rather than the investor, (4) inadequate or untimely information to apply the equity method, and (5) failure to obtain representation on the investee's board of directors as indicators of an investor's inability to exercise significant influence. Application of the equity method is discontinued when the investor's share of losses reduces the carrying amount of the investment to zero.

The equity method is important for several reasons. First, these investments represent a significant component of total assets, net income, or both for some firms. Second, corporate joint ventures and other special-purpose entities widely use the equity method. Third, the equity method is used in the discussion of the preparation of consolidated financial statements in later chapters.

Many well-known firms report using the equity method for investments in other companies. *AT&T* reports investments in equity method affiliates of $250 million in its 2014 Annual Report. Net income was $6.224 billion in 2014, including $175 million from these equity method investments. *Chevron's* 2014 Annual Report discloses income from equity method investments of $7.098 billion (36.9 percent of total net income).

---

[1]FASB ASC 325. Originally Accounting Principles Board Opinion No. 18. "The Equity Method of Accounting for Investments in Common Stock." New York © 1971 American Institute of Certified Public Accountants.

A parent may use the equity method to account for investments even though the financial statements of the subsidiaries will be subsequently included in the consolidated financial statements. In other words, the parent maintains the "investment in subsidiary account" by taking up its share of subsidiary income and reducing the investment account for its share of subsidiary dividends declared. Under the equity method, the parent's net income and parent's share of consolidated net income are equal. The consolidated income statement reflects the income of the parent and its subsidiaries as a single economic entity.

GAAP requires that all majority-owned subsidiaries be consolidated, except when control does not lie with the majority interest. Examples of control of a subsidiary not resting with the parent include a subsidiary in legal reorganization or in bankruptcy, or a subsidiary operating under severe foreign-exchange restrictions or other governmentally imposed uncertainties. (ASC 323-10-15) An investment in an unconsolidated subsidiary is reported in the parent's financial statements by either the fair value/cost or the equity method. Chapter 3 discusses situations in which certain subsidiaries should not be consolidated.

## Fair Value/Cost and Equity Method Accounting Procedures

LEARNING OBJECTIVE **2.4**

Assume that Pop Corporation acquires 2,000 of the 10,000 outstanding shares of Son Corporation at $25 per share on July 1. Assume the book value and fair value of Son's assets and liabilities are equal. Further, the cash paid equals 20 percent of the fair value of Son's net assets. Son's net income for the fiscal year ending December 31 is $25,000, and dividends of $10,000 are paid on November 1. If there is evidence of an inability to exercise significant influence, Pop should apply the fair value/cost method, revaluing the investment account to fair market value at the end of the accounting period. Otherwise, the equity method is required. Accounting by Pop under the two methods is as follows:

**Entry on July 1 to Record the Investment:**

| *Fair Value/Cost Method* | | | *Equity Method* | | |
|---|---|---|---|---|---|
| Investment in Son (+A) | 50,000 | | Investment in Son (+A) | 50,000 | |
| Cash (−A) | | 50,000 | Cash (−A) | | 50,000 |

**Entry on November 1 to Record Dividends:**

| *Fair Value/Cost Method* | | | *Equity Method* | | |
|---|---|---|---|---|---|
| Cash (+A) | 2,000 | | Cash (+A) | 2,000 | |
| Dividend income (R, +SE) | | 2,000 | Investment in Son (−A) | | 2,000 |

**Entry on December 31 to Recognize Earnings:**

| *Fair Value/Cost Method* | | *Equity Method* | | |
|---|---|---|---|---|
| None (Assume that the stock is either nonmarketable or has a market *price* = $25 per share so that no revaluing is needed.) | | Investment in Son (+A) | 2,500 | |
| | | Income from Son (R, +SE) | | 2,500 |
| | | (25,000 × 1/2 year × 20%) | | |

Under the fair value/cost method, Pop recognizes income of $2,000 and reports its investment in Son at its $50,000 cost at December 31. Under the equity method, Pop recognizes $2,500 in income and reports the investment in Son at $50,500 at December 31. Here is a summary of Pop's equity method investment account activity:

| July 1 | Initial cost | $50,000 |
|---|---|---|
| November 1 | Dividends received | (2,000) |
| December 31 | Recognize 20% of Son's net income for 1/2 year | 2,500 |
| December 31 | Ending balance | $50,500 |

The entries to illustrate the fair value/cost method reflect the usual situation in which the investor records dividend income equal to dividends actually received. An exception arises when dividends received exceed the investor's share of earnings after the investment has been acquired. From the investor's point of view, the excess dividends since acquisition of the investment are a return of capital, or liquidating dividends. For example, if Son's net income for the year had been $15,000, Pop's share would have been $1,500 ($15,000 × 1/2 year × 20%). The $2,000 dividend received exceeds the $1,500 equity in Son's income, so the $500 excess would be considered a return of capital and credited to the Investment in Son account. Assuming that Pop records the $2,000 cash received on November 1 as dividend income, a year-end entry to adjust dividend income and the investment account is needed. Pop would record as follows:

| | | |
|---|---|---|
| Dividend income (−R, − SE) | 500 | |
| Investment in Son (−A) | | 500 |

To adjust dividend income and
investment accounts for dividends
received in excess of earnings.

This entry reduces dividend income to Pop's $1,500 share of income earned after July 1 and reduces the investment in Son to $49,500, the new fair value/cost basis for the investment. If, after the liquidating dividend, the stock (classified as an available-for-sale security) had a fair value of $60,000 at December 31, then another entry would be required to increase the investment to fair value:

| | | |
|---|---|---|
| Allowance to adjust available-for-sale securities to market value (+A) | 10,500 | |
| Unrealized gain on available-for-sale securities (+SE) | | 10,500 |

The unrealized gain on available-for-sale securities is included in reporting other comprehensive income for the period.

## Economic Consequences of Using the Fair Value/Cost and Equity Methods

The different methods of accounting (fair value/cost and equity) result in different investment amounts in the balance sheet of the investor and different income amounts in the income statement. When the investor can significantly influence or control the operations of the investee, including dividend declarations, the fair value/cost method is unacceptable. By influencing or controlling investee dividend decisions, the investor could manipulate reported investment income. The possibility of income manipulation does not exist when the financial statements of a parent company/investor are consolidated with the statements of a subsidiary/investee because the consolidated statements are the same, regardless of which method of accounting is used.

Although the equity method is not a substitute for consolidation, the income reported by a parent in its separate income statement under the equity method is generally the same as the parent's share of consolidated net income reported in consolidated financial statements.

## EQUITY METHOD—A ONE-LINE CONSOLIDATION

**LEARNING OBJECTIVE 2.5**

The equity method of accounting is often called a **one-line consolidation**. This is because the investment is reported in a single amount on one line of the investor's balance sheet, and investment income is reported in a single amount on one line of the investor's income statement (except when the investee has discontinued operations items that require separate disclosure). "One-line consolidation" also means that a parent-company/investor's income and stockholders' equity are the same when a subsidiary company/investee is accounted for under a complete and correct application of the equity method and when the financial statements of a parent and subsidiary are consolidated. Consolidated financial statements show the same income and the same net assets but include the details of revenues and expenses and assets and liabilities.

The equity method creates many complexities; in fact, it requires the same computational complexities encountered in preparing consolidated financial statements. For this reason, the equity method is the standard of parent-company accounting for subsidiaries, and the one-line consolidation is integrated throughout the consolidation chapters of this book. This parallel one-line consolidation/consolidation coverage permits you to check your work just as practitioners do, by making alternative computations of such key financial statement items as consolidated net income and consolidated retained earnings.

Basic accounting procedures for applying the equity method are the same whether the investor has the ability to exercise significant influence over the investee (20 percent to 50 percent ownership) or the ability to control the investee (more than 50 percent ownership). This is important because investments of more than 50 percent are business combinations and require preparation of consolidated financial statements. Thus, the accounting principles that apply to the acquisition method of accounting for business combinations also apply to accounting for investments of 50 percent or greater under the equity method. The difference between the way combination provisions are applied in this chapter and the way they are applied in Chapter 1 arises because:

1. Both the investor and investee continue to exist as separate legal entities with their own accounting systems (an acquisition).

2. The equity method applies to only one of the entities—the investor.

3. The investor's equity interest may range from 20 percent to 100 percent.

## Equity Investments at Acquisition[2]

Equity investments in voting common stock of other entities measure the investment cost by the cash disbursed or the fair value of other assets distributed or securities issued. Similarly, we charge direct costs of registering and issuing equity securities against additional paid-in capital, and we expense other direct costs of acquisition. We enter the total investment cost in an investment account under the one-line consolidation concept.

Assume that Pam Company purchases 30 percent of Sun Company's outstanding voting common stock on January 1 from existing stockholders for $2,000,000 cash plus 200,000 shares of Pam Company $10 par common stock with a market value of $15 per share. Additional cash costs of the equity interest consist of $50,000 for registration of the shares and $100,000 for consulting and advisory fees. Pam Company records these events with the following journal entries (in thousands):

*January 1*

| | | |
|---|---|---|
| Investment in Sun (+A) | 5,000 | |
|     Common stock (+SE) | | 2,000 |
|     Additional paid-in capital (+SE) | | 1,000 |
|     Cash (−A) | | 2,000 |
|     To record acquisition of a 30% equity investment in Sun Company. | | |

*January 1*

| | | |
|---|---|---|
| Investment expense (E, − SE) | 100 | |
| Additional paid-in capital (−SE) | 50 | |
|     Cash (−A) | | 150 |
|     To record additional direct costs of purchasing the 30% equity | | |
|     interest in Sun. | | |

Under a one-line consolidation, these entries can be made without knowledge of book value or fair value of Sun Company's assets and liabilities.

## Assignment of Excess Investment Cost over Underlying Book Value of Equity

Information about the individual assets and liabilities of Sun Company at acquisition is important because subsequent accounting under the equity method requires accounting for any differences between the investment cost and the underlying book value of equity in the net assets of the investee.

Assume that the following book value and fair value information for Sun Company at January 1 is available (in thousands):

| | Book Value | Fair Value |
|---|---|---|
| Cash | $ 1,500 | $ 1,500 |
| Receivables—net | 2,200 | 2,200 |
| Inventories | 3,000 | 4,000 |
| Other current assets | 3,300 | 3,100 |
| Equipment—net | 5,000 | 8,000 |
| Total assets | $15,000 | $18,800 |
| | | |
| Accounts payable | $ 1,000 | $ 1,000 |
| Note payable, due in five years | 2,000 | 1,800 |
| Common stock | 10,000 | |
| Retained earnings | 2,000 | |
| Total liabilities and stockholders' equity | $15,000 | |

---

[2]GAAP differs in equity method accounting for 20 percent to 50 percent ownership versus ownership greater than 50 percent, which will require preparation of consolidated financial statements. Our remaining discussion of equity method accounting focuses on application of the acquisition method for investments greater than 50 percent owned, unless otherwise noted.

### PAM COMPANY AND ITS 30 PERCENT-OWNED EQUITY INVESTEE, SUN COMPANY (IN THOUSANDS)

| | | | | |
|---|---|---|---|---|
| Investment in Sun | | | | $5,000 |
| Book value of the interest acquired (30% × $12,000,000 equity of Sun) | | | | (3,600) |
| Total excess of cost over book value acquired | | | | $1,400 |

Assignment to Identifiable Net Assets and Goodwill

| | Fair Value | − Book Value | × % Interest Acquired | = Amount Assigned |
|---|---|---|---|---|
| Inventories | $4,000 | $3,000 | 30% | $300 |
| Other current assets | 3,100 | 3,300 | 30 | (60) |
| Equipment | 8,000 | 5,000 | 30 | 900 |
| Note payable | 1,800 | 2,000 | 30 | 60 |
| Total assigned to identifiable net assets | | | | 1,200 |
| Remainder assigned to goodwill | | | | 200 |
| Total excess of cost over book value acquired | | | | $1,400 |

The underlying book value of equity in the net assets of Sun Company is $3,600,000 (30 percent of the $12,000,000 book value of Sun's net assets), and the difference between the investment cost and the underlying book value of equity is $1,400,000. The investor assigns this difference to identifiable assets and liabilities, based on their fair values and assigns the remaining difference to goodwill. Exhibit 2-1 illustrates the assignment to identifiable net assets and goodwill.

Pam Company does not record separately the asset and liability information given in Exhibit 2-1. The $1,400,000 excess of cost over the underlying book value of equity is already reflected in Pam's Investment in Sun account. Under the equity method of accounting, we eliminate this difference by periodic charges (debits) and credits to income from the investment and by equal charges or credits to the investment account. Thus, the original difference between investment cost and book value acquired disappears over the remaining lives of identifiable assets and liabilities. Exceptions arise for land, goodwill, and intangible assets having an indefinite life, which are not amortized under GAAP.

We determined the $200,000 assigned to goodwill in Exhibit 2-1 as a remainder of the total excess of cost/fair value over book value acquired ($1,400,000) over amounts assigned to identifiable assets and liabilities ($1,200,000). However, we can also compute goodwill as the excess of the investment cost of $5,000,000 over the $4,800,000 fair value of Sun's identifiable net assets acquired (30 percent × $16,000,000). We consider the difference as goodwill if it cannot be related to identifiable assets and liabilities.

Recall from our discussion in Chapter 1 that, under current GAAP, firms do not amortize goodwill and other intangible assets that have an indefinite life. Instead, we review such assets for impairment on a periodic basis, and write down the assets when impairment losses become evident.

The same procedure also applies to investments that will be reported under the equity method. However, the impairment test differs. When evaluating an equity method investment for impairment, we recognize impairment losses in the value of the investment as a whole. (ASC 350-20-35)

### Accounting for Excess of Investment Cost over Book Value

Assume that Sun pays dividends of $1,000,000 on July 1 and reports net income of $3,000,000 for the year. The excess cost over book value is amortized as follows:

| | **Amortization Rates** |
|---|---|
| Excess allocated to: | |
| Inventories—sold in the current year | 100% |
| Other current assets—disposed of in the current year | 100% |
| Equipment—depreciated over 20 years | 5% |
| Note payable—due in 5 years | 20% |

Pam makes the following entries under a one-line consolidation to record its dividends and income from Sun (in thousands):

*July 1*

| | | |
|---|---|---|
| Cash (+A) | 300 | |
|     Investment in Sun (−A) | | 300 |
|   To record dividends received from Sun ($1,000,000 × 30%). | | |

*December 31*

| | | |
|---|---|---|
| Investment in Sun (+A) | 900 | |
|     Income from Sun (R, +SE) | | 900 |
|   To record equity in income of Sun ($3,000,000 × 30%). | | |

*December 31*

| | | |
|---|---|---|
| Income from Sun (−R, −SE) | 300 | |
|     Investment in Sun (−A) | | 300 |
|   To record write-off of excess allocated to inventory items that were sold in the current year. | | |

*December 31*

| | | |
|---|---|---|
| Investment in Sun (+A) | 60 | |
|     Income from Sun (R, +SE) | | 60 |
|   To record income credit for overvalued other current assets disposed of in the current year. | | |

*December 31*

| | | |
|---|---|---|
| Income from Sun (−R, − SE) | 45 | |
|     Investment in Sun (−A) | | 45 |
|   To record depreciation on excess allocated to undervalued equipment with a 20-year remaining useful life ($900,000 ÷ 20). | | |

*December 31*

| | | |
|---|---|---|
| Income from Sun (−R, −SE) | 12 | |
|     Investment in Sun (−A) | | 12 |
|   To amortize the excess allocated to the overvalued note payable over the remaining life of the note ($60,000 ÷ 5 years). | | |

The last five journal entries involve the income and investment accounts, so Pam could record its income from Sun in a single entry at December 31, as follows:

| | | |
|---|---|---|
| Investment in Sun (+A) | 603 | |
|     Income from Sun (R, +SE) | | 603 |
|   To record equity income from 30% investment in Sun calculated as follows: | | |
|   Equity in Sun's reported income ($3,000,000 × 30%) | | $900 |
|     Amortization of excess cost over book value: | | |
|     Inventories sold in the current year ($300,000 × 100%) | | (300) |
|     Other current assets sold in the current year ($60,000 × 100%) | | 60 |
|     Equipment ($900,000 × 5% depreciation rate) | | (45) |
|     Note payable ($60,000 × 20% amortization rate) | | (12) |
|   Total investment income from Sun | | $603 |

Pam reports its investment in Sun at December 31 on one line of its balance sheet at $5,303,000 (see the following summary) and its income from Sun at $603,000 on one line of its income statement. Sun's book value of net assets (stockholders' equity) increased by $2,000,000 to $14,000,000, and Pam's share of this underlying equity is 30 percent, or $4,200,000. The $1,103,000 difference between the investment balance and the underlying book value of equity at December 31 represents the unamortized excess of investment cost/fair value over book value acquired. Confirm this amount by subtracting the $297,000 net amortization from the original excess of $1,400,000.

Here is a summary of Pam's equity method investment account activity (in thousands):

| | | |
|---|---|---|
| January 1 | Initial cost | $5,000 |
| July 1 | Dividends received | (300) |
| December 31 | Recognize 30% of Sun's net income | 900 |
| December 31 | Write off excess allocated to inventory | (300) |
| December 31 | Record income from Sun's overvalued current assets sold in the current year | 60 |
| December 31 | Additional equipment depreciation | (45) |
| December 31 | Amortize note payable excess | (12) |
| December 31 | Ending balance | $5,303 |

When the full $1,400,000 excess has been amortized (or written off as an impairment loss in the case of goodwill), the investment balance will equal its underlying book value, which is 30 percent of the stockholders' equity of Sun. A summary of these observations follows (in thousands):

| | Stockholders' Equity of Sun (A) | Underlying Equity (30% of Sun's Equity) (B) | Investment in Sun Account Balance (C) | Unamortized Cost/Book Value (C – B) |
|---|---|---|---|---|
| January 1 | $12,000 | $3,600 | $5,000 | $1,400 |
| Dividends, July | (1,000) | (300) | (300) | — |
| Income | 3,000 | 900 | 900 | — |
| Amortization | — | — | (297) | (297) |
| December 31 | $14,000 | $4,200 | $5,303 | $1,103 |

## Excess of Book Value over Cost

The book value of the interest acquired in an investee may be greater than the investment cost or fair value. This indicates that the identifiable net assets of the investee are overvalued or that the interest was acquired at a bargain price. The bargain purchase gain is recorded as an ordinary gain, as explained in Chapter 1.

To illustrate, assume that Pop Corporation purchases 50 percent of the outstanding voting common stock of Son Corporation on January 1 for $40,000 in cash. A summary of the changes in Son's stockholders' equity during the year appears as follows (in thousands):

| | |
|---|---|
| Stockholders' equity January 1 | $100 |
| Add: Income | 20 |
| Deduct: Dividends paid July 1 | (5) |
| Stockholders' equity December 31 | $115 |

The $10,000 excess of book value acquired over investment cost ($100,000 $\times$ 50%) − $40,000 was due to inventory items and equipment that were overvalued on Son's books. Son's January 1 inventory was overvalued by $2,000 and was sold in December. The remaining $18,000 overvaluation related to equipment with a 10-year remaining useful life from January 1. No goodwill results because the $40,000 cost is equal to the fair value of the net assets acquired (50% $\times$ $80,000).

The assignment of the difference between book value acquired and investment cost is as follows (in thousands):

| | |
|---|---|
| Cost of the investment in Son | $ 40 |
| Less: Underlying book value of Pop's 50% interest in Son ($100,000 stockholders' equity $\times$ 50%) | (50) |
| Excess book value over cost | $(10) |
| Excess assigned to: | |
| Inventories ($2,000 overvaluation $\times$ 50% owned) | $ (1) |
| Equipment ($18,000 overvaluation $\times$ 50% owned) | (9) |
| Excess book value over cost | $(10) |

Journal entries to account for Pop's investment in Son are as follows (in thousands):

*January 1*
| | | |
|---|---|---|
| Investment in Son (+A) | 40 | |
| Cash (−A) | | 40 |

To record purchase of 50% of Son's outstanding voting stock.

*July 1*
| | | |
|---|---|---|
| Cash (+A) | 2.5 | |
| Investment in Son (−A) | | 2.5 |

To record dividends received (5,000 $\times$ 50%).

*December 31*
| | | |
|---|---|---|
| Investment in Son (+A) | 10 | |
| Income from Son (R, +SE) | | 10 |

To recognize equity in the income of Son (20,000 $\times$ 50%).

*December 31*

| | | |
|---|---|---|
| Investment in Son (+A) | 1.9 | |
| Income from Son (R, +SE) | | 1.9 |

To amortize excess of book value over investment cost assigned to:

| | |
|---|---|
| Inventory (1,000 × 100%) | $1.0 |
| Equipment (9,000 × 10%) | .9 |
| Total | $1.9 |

Because assets were purchased at less than book value, Pop reports investment income from Son of $11,900 ($10,000 + $1,900) and an Investment in Son balance at December 31 of $49,400. Amortization of the excess of book value over investment cost increases Pop's Investment in Son balance by $1,900 during the year.

Here is a summary of the equity method investment account activity:

| | | |
|---|---|---|
| January 1 | Initial cost | $40,000 |
| July 1 | Dividends received | (2,500) |
| December 31 | Recognize 50% of Son's net income | 10,000 |
| December 31 | Amortization of excess of book value over investment cost | 1,900 |
| December 31 | Ending balance | $49,400 |

## Bargain Purchase

Assume that Pop also acquires a 25 percent interest in Sax Corporation for $110,000 on January 1, at which time Sax's net assets consist of the following (in thousands):

| | Book Value | Fair Value | Excess Fair Value |
|---|---|---|---|
| Inventories | $240 | $260 | $20 |
| Other current assets | 100 | 100 | |
| Equipment—net | 50 | 50 | |
| Buildings—net | 140 | 200 | 60 |
| | 530 | 610 | |
| Less: Liabilities | 130 | 130 | |
| Net assets | $400 | $480 | $80 |

Sax's net income and dividends for the year are $60,000 and $40,000, respectively. The undervalued inventory items were sold during the year, and the undervalued buildings had a four-year remaining useful life when Pop acquired its 25 percent interest. Exhibit 2-2 illustrates the assignment of the excess cost over book value.

In reviewing Exhibit 2-2, notice that the excess cost over book value is first assigned to fair values of identifiable net assets. Because the fair value of the net assets acquired exceeds the cost of the investment, the difference is a bargain purchase gain. This bargain purchase gain is recognized as an ordinary gain on the books of the investor.

**POP CORPORATION AND ITS 25 PERCENT–OWNED EQUITY INVESTEE, SAX CORPORATION (IN THOUSANDS)**

| | | |
|---|---|---|
| Investment cost | $110 | |
| Book value acquired ($400,000 × 25%) | (100) | |
| Excess cost over book value acquired | $ 10 | |

| | Assignment to Fair Value | Negative Excess | Final Assignment |
|---|---|---|---|
| Inventory ($20,000 × 25%) | $ 5 | | $ 5 |
| Buildings—net ($60,000 × 25%) | 15 | | 15 |
| Gain from bargain purchase | | $10 | (10) |
| Excess | $20 | $10 | $10 |

Journal entries for Pop to account for its investment in Sax follow (in thousands):

*January 1*

| | | |
|---|---|---|
| Investment in Sax (+A) | 120 | |
|     Cash (−A) | | 110 |
|     Gain on bargain purchase (Ga, +SE) | | 10 |
| To record purchase of a 25% interest in Sax's voting stock. | | |

*Throughout the year*

| | | |
|---|---|---|
| Cash (+A) | 10 | |
|     Investment in Sax (−A) | | 10 |
| To record dividends received ($40,000 × 25%). | | |

*December 31*

| | | |
|---|---|---|
| Investment in Sax (+A) | 6.25 | |
|     Income from Sax (R, +SE) | | 6.25 |
| To recognize investment income from Sax computed as follows: | | |
|     25% of Sax's $60,000 net income | $15,000 | |
|     Excess allocated to inventories | (5,000) | |
|     Excess allocated to buildings ($15,000 ÷ 4 years) | (3,750) | |
| | $ 6,250 | |

Pop's investment in Sax balance at December 31 is $116,250, and the underlying book value of the investment is $105,000 ($420,000 × 25%) on that same date. The $11,250 difference is due to the $11,250 unamortized excess assigned to buildings.

## Interim Acquisitions of Investment Interest

Accounting for equity investments becomes more specific when a firm makes acquisitions within an accounting period (interim acquisitions). Additional computations determine the underlying equity at the time of acquisition and the investment income for the year. We compute stockholders' equity of the investee by adding income earned since the last statement date to the date of purchase to the beginning stockholders' equity and subtracting dividends declared since the last statement date to the date of purchase. In accounting for interim acquisitions, we assume that income of the investee is earned proportionately throughout the year unless there is evidence to the contrary.

Assume that Pop Corporation acquires 40 percent of the voting common stock of Son Company for $80,000 on October 1. Son's net assets (owners' equity) at January 1 are $150,000, and it reports net income of $25,000 for the year ended December 31 and declares $15,000 dividends on July 1. The book values of Son's assets and liabilities are equal to fair values on October 1, except for a building with a fair value of $60,000 and recorded at $40,000. The building has a 20-year remaining useful life from October 1. GAAP requires application of the equity method and assignment of any difference between investment cost and book value acquired first to identifiable assets and liabilities and then to goodwill.

The excess of Pop's investment cost over book value of its 40 percent interest in Son is computed and assigned to identifiable assets and goodwill, as shown in Exhibit 2-3.

| **EXHIBIT 2-3** | **POP CORPORATION AND ITS 40 PERCENT–OWNED EQUITY INVESTEE, SON CORPORATION** | | |
|---|---|---|---|
| Schedule for Allocating the Excess of Investment Cost (Fair Value) over Book Value of Interest Acquired | Investment cost | | $80,000 |
| | Less: Share of Fair equity on October 1 | | |
| |     Beginning equity | $150,000 | |
| |     Add: Income to October 1 | 18,750 | |
| |     Less: Dividends | (15,000) | |
| | | 153,750 | |
| |     Times: Interest purchased | 40% | (61,500) |
| | Excess cost over book value | | $18,500 |
| | Excess assigned to: | | |
| |     Buildings [($60,000 − $40,000) × 40%] | | $ 8,000 |
| |     Goodwill (remainder) | | 10,500 |
| | Excess cost over book value | | $18,500 |

Journal entries on Pop's books to account for the 40 percent interest in Son for the current year are as follows (in thousands):

*October 1*

| | | |
|---|---|---|
| Investment in Son (+A) | 80 | |
|     Cash (−A) | | 80 |
| To record acquisition of 40% of Son's voting stock. | | |

*December 31*

| | | |
|---|---|---|
| Investment in Son (+A) | 2.5 | |
|     Income from Son (R, +SE) | | 2.5 |
| To record equity in Son's income | | |
| (40% × $25,000 × 1/4 year). | | |

*December 31*

| | | |
|---|---|---|
| Income from Son (−R, −SE) | .1 | |
|     Investment in Son (−A) | | .1 |
| To record amortization of excess of cost over book value | | |
| allocated to the undervalued building | | |
| ($8,000 ÷ 20 years) × 1/4 year. | | |

At December 31, after the entries are posted, Pop's Investment in Son account will have a balance of $82,400 ($80,000 cost + $2,400 income). This investment account balance is $18,400 more than the $64,000 underlying book value of Pop's interest in Son on that date (40% × $160,000). The $18,400 consists of the original excess cost over book value of $18,500 less the $100 amortized in the current year.

Here is a summary of Pop's equity method Investment in Son account activity:

| | | |
|---|---|---|
| October 1 | Initial cost | $80,000 |
| December 31 | Recognize 40% of Son's net income for 1/4 year | 2,500 |
| December 31 | Amortization of excess of cost over book value for 1/4 year | (100) |
| December 31 | Ending balance | $82,400 |

Notice that we do not recognize 40 percent of the dividends declared and paid by Son. The dividends were paid on July 1, prior to Pop's investment. Under the equity method, investors recognize dividends received, not their proportional share of total dividends declared and/or paid. Of course, if the investment is owned for the entire year, these amounts will be the same.

## INVESTMENT IN A STEP-BY-STEP ACQUISITION

An investor may acquire significant influence over the operating and financial policies of an investee in a series of stock acquisitions, rather than in a single purchase. For example, the investor may acquire a 10 percent interest in an investee and later acquire another 10 percent interest. We account for the original 10 percent interest by the fair value/cost method until we reach a 20 percent interest. Then we adopt the equity method and adjust the investment and retained earnings accounts retroactively.

Assume that Pop Corporation acquires a 10 percent interest in Son Corporation for $750,000 on January 2, 2016, and another 10 percent interest for $850,000 on January 2, 2017. The stockholders' equity of Son Corporation on the dates of these acquisitions is as follows (in thousands):

| | January 2, 2016 | January 2, 2017 |
|---|---|---|
| Capital stock | $5,000 | $5,000 |
| Retained earnings | 2,000 | 2,500 |
| Total stockholders' equity | $7,000 | $7,500 |

Pop Corporation is not able to relate the excess of investment cost over book value to identifiable net assets. Accordingly, the excess of cost over book value from each acquisition is goodwill.

On January 2, 2017, when the second 10 percent is acquired, Pop adopts the equity method of accounting for its 20 percent interest. This requires converting the carrying value of the original 10 percent interest from its $750,000 cost to its correct carrying value on an equity basis. The entry to adjust the investment account of Pop is as follows (in thousands):

*January 2, 2017*

| | | |
|---|---|---|
| Investment in Son (+A) | 50 | |
|     Retained earnings (+SE) | | 50 |

To adjust the Investment in Son account from a cost to an
    equity basis as follows: Share of Son's retained earnings increase during
    2016 of $50,000 [$500,000 × 10% interest held during the year] equals
    the retroactive adjustment from accounting change of $50,000.

Son's $500,000 retained earnings increase for 2016 represents its income less dividends for 2016. Pop reports its share of dividends received from Son as income under the cost method; therefore, Pop's income for 2016 under the equity method is greater by 10 percent of Son's retained earnings increase for 2016.

Changes in the cost, equity, and consolidation methods of accounting for subsidiaries and investments are changes in the reporting entity that require restatement of prior-period financial statements if the effect is material. (ASC 250-10-45)

## SALE OF AN EQUITY INTEREST

When an investor sells a portion of an equity investment that reduces its interest below 20 percent or to less than a level necessary to exercise significant influence, the equity method of accounting is no longer appropriate for the remaining interest. We account for the investment under the fair value/cost method from this time forward, and the investment account balance after the sale becomes the new basis. We require no other adjustment, and the investor accounts for the investment under the fair value/cost method in the usual manner. Gain or loss from the equity interest sold is the difference between the selling price and the book value of the equity interest immediately before the sale.

To illustrate, Pam Industries acquires 320,000 shares (a 40 percent interest) in Sun Corporation on January 1, 2016, for $580,000. Sun's stockholders' equity is $1,200,000, and the book values of its assets and liabilities equal their fair values. Pam accounts for its investment in Sun under the equity method during the years 2016 through 2017. At December 31, 2017, the balance of the investment account is $700,000, equal to 40 percent of Sun's $1,500,000 stockholders' equity plus $100,000 goodwill.

On January 1, 2018, Pam sells 80 percent of its holdings in Sun (256,000 shares) for $600,000, reducing its interest in Sun to 8 percent (40% × 20%). The book value of the interest sold is $560,000, or 80 percent of the $700,000 balance of the Investment in Sun account. Pam recognizes a gain on the sale of its interest in Sun of $40,000 ($600,000 selling price less $560,000 book value of the interest sold). The balance of the Investment in Sun account after the sale is $140,000 ($700,000 less $560,000 interest sold). Pam determines that it can no longer exercise significant influence over Sun, and accordingly, it switches to the fair value/cost method and accounts for its investment with the $140,000 balance becoming the new basis of the investment. (ASC 320-10-30)

## STOCK PURCHASES DIRECTLY FROM THE INVESTEE

We have assumed up to now that the investor purchased its shares from existing stockholders of the investee. In that situation, the interest acquired was equal to the shares acquired divided by the investee's outstanding shares. If an investor purchases shares directly from the issuing corporation, however, we determine the investor's interest by the shares acquired divided by the shares outstanding after the investee issues the new shares.

Assume that Pop Corporation purchases 20,000 shares of previously unissued common stock directly from Son Corporation for $450,000 on January 1, 2016. Son's stockholders' equity at December 31, 2015, consists of $200,000 of $10 par common stock and $150,000 retained earnings.

We compute Pop's 50 percent interest in Son as follows:

| A | Shares purchased by Pop | | 20,000 shares |
|---|---|---|---|
| B | Shares outstanding after new shares are issued: | | |
| | Outstanding December 31, 2015 | 20,000 | |
| | Issued to Pop | 20,000 | 40,000 shares |
| | Pop's interest in Son: A/B = 50% | | |

The book value of the interest acquired by Pop is $400,000, which is determined by multiplying the 50 percent interest acquired by Son's $800,000 stockholders' equity immediately after the issuance of the additional 20,000 shares. Computations are as follows:

| | |
|---|---|
| Son's stockholders' equity before issuance | $350,000 |
| ($200,000 capital stock + $150,000 retained earnings) | |
| Sale of 20,000 shares to Pop | 450,000 |
| Son's stockholders' equity after issuance | 800,000 |
| Pop's percentage ownership | 50% |
| Book value acquired by Pop | $400,000 |

## INVESTEE CORPORATION WITH PREFERRED STOCK

The equity method applies to investments in common stock, and some adjustments are necessary when an investee has both preferred and common stock outstanding. These adjustments require the following:

1. Allocation of the investee's stockholders' equity into preferred and common equity components upon acquisition in order to determine the book value of the common stock investment

2. Allocation of the investee's net income into preferred and common income components to determine the investor's share of the investee's income to common stockholders

Assume that Sun Corporation's stockholders' equity is $6,000,000 at the beginning of the year and $6,500,000 at the end of the year. Its net income and dividends for the year are $700,000 and $200,000, respectively.

| (Amounts in Thousands) | January 1 | December 31 |
|---|---|---|
| 10% cumulative preferred stock, $100 par | $1,000 | $1,000 |
| Common stock, $10 par | 3,000 | 3,000 |
| Other paid-in capital | 500 | 500 |
| Retained earnings | 1,500 | 2,000 |
| | $6,000 | $6,500 |

If Pam Corporation pays $2,500,000 on January 2 for 40 percent of Sun's outstanding common stock, the investment is evaluated as follows (in thousands):

| | | |
|---|---|---|
| Cost of 40% common interest in Sun | | $2,500 |
| Book value (and fair value) acquired: | | |
| Stockholders' equity of Sun | $6,000 | |
| Less: Preferred stockholders' equity | 1,000 | |
| Common stockholders' equity | 5,000 | |
| Percent acquired | × 40% | 2,000 |
| Goodwill | | $ 500 |

The equity of preferred stockholders is equal to the par value of outstanding preferred stock, increased by the greater of any call or liquidating premium and by preferred dividends in arrears. We assume Sun's preferred stock has no dividends in arrears and no call or liquidation premium.

Pam's income from Sun for the year from its 40 percent interest is computed as follows (in thousands):

| | |
|---|---:|
| Sun's net income | $700 |
| Less: Preferred income ($1,000,000 × 10%) | 100 |
| Income to common | $600 |
| Share of Sun's common income ($600,000 × 40%) | 240 |

GAAP provides that when an investee has cumulative preferred stock outstanding, an investor in common stock computes its share of earnings or losses after deducting preferred dividends, whether or not preferred dividends are declared. Additional coverage of accounting matters related to investees with preferred stock outstanding is provided in Chapter 10.

## DISCONTINUED OPERATIONS AND OTHER CONSIDERATIONS

In accounting for an investment under the equity method, the investor reports its share of the ordinary income of an investee on one line of its income statement. However, the one-line consolidation does not apply to the reporting of investment income when the investee's income includes discontinued operations. In this case, the investment income must be separated into its ordinary and discontinued operations components and reported accordingly.

Assume that Pop Corporation owns 40 percent of the outstanding stock of Son Corporation and that Son's income consists of the following (in thousands):

| | |
|---|---:|
| Income from continuing operations | $500 |
| Discontinued operations—loss (less applicable income taxes of $25,000) | (50) |
| Net income | $450 |

Pop records its investment income from Son as follows (in thousands):

| | | |
|---|---:|---:|
| Investment in Son (+A) | 180 | |
| Discontinued operations loss—Son (E, −SE) | 20 | |
| Income from Son (R, +SE) | | 200 |
| To record investment income from Son. | | |

Pop reports the $200,000 income from Son as investment income and reports the $20,000 discontinued operations loss along with any discontinued operations that Pop may have had during the year. A gain on an investee's disposal of a segment of a business would be treated similarly.

## Other Requirements of the Equity Method

In reporting earnings and losses of an investee under the equity method, an investor must eliminate the effect of profits and losses on transactions between the investor and investee until they are realized. This means adjusting the investment and investment income accounts as we have illustrated to amortize over- or undervalued identifiable net assets. Transactions of an investee that change the investor's share of the net assets of the investee also require adjustments under the equity method of accounting. These and other complexities of the equity method are covered in subsequent chapters, along with related consolidation procedures. Chapter 10 covers preferred stock, earnings per share, and income tax considerations.

## DISCLOSURES FOR EQUITY INVESTEES

The extent to which separate disclosure should be provided for equity investments depends on the significance (materiality) of such investments to the financial position and results of operations of the investor. If equity investments are significant, the investor should disclose the following information, parenthetically or in financial statement notes or schedules:

1. The name of each investee and percentage of ownership in common stock
2. The accounting policies of the investor with respect to investments in common stock

**3.** The difference, if any, between the amount at which an investment is carried and the amount of underlying equity in net assets, including the accounting treatment of the difference (ASC 323-10-50)

Additional disclosures for material equity investments include the aggregate value of each identified investment for which quoted market prices are available and summarized information regarding the assets, liabilities, and results of operations of the investees. An excerpt from The **Dow Chemical Company and Subsidiaries' 2014** annual report is presented in Exhibit 2-4 to illustrate the disclosure requirements. Financial information is separately presented for all significant equity investees as a group. Dow includes its share of the underlying net assets of these investees as "Investments" in the balance sheet and includes its share of the investees' net income in the income statement as "Equity in income of investees." The operating-activities section of Dow's consolidated statement of cash flows shows both "Equity in income of investees" and "Cash distributions from equity investees" as adjustments to net income.

## NOTE 8—NONCONSOLIDATED AFFILIATES AND RELATED COMPANY TRANSACTIONS (EXCERPT)

Sales to and purchases from nonconsolidated affiliates were not material to the consolidated financial statements. Balances due to or due from nonconsolidated affiliates at December 31, 2014 and 2013 are as follows:

### BALANCES DUE TO OR DUE FROM NONCONSOLIDATED AFFILIATES AT DECEMBER 31

| In millions | 2014 | 2013 |
|---|---|---|
| Accounts and notes receivable—other | $511 | $ 512 |
| Noncurrent receivables | 212 | 5 |
| Total assets | $723 | $ 517 |
| Notes payable | $189 | $ 137 |
| Accounts payable—other | 274 | 221 |
| Total current liabilities | $463 | $ 358 |

**Principal Nonconsolidated Affiliates**
Dow had an ownership interest in 59 nonconsolidated affiliates at December 31, 2014 (63 at December 31, 2013). The Company's principal nonconsolidated affiliates and its ownership interest (direct or indirect) for each at December 31, 2014, 2013, and 2012 are as follows:

### PRINCIPAL NONCONSOLIDATED AFFILIATES AT DECEMBER 31

| | Ownership Interest | | |
|---|---|---|---|
| | 2014 | 2013 | 2012 |
| Dow Corning Corporation | 50% | 50% | 50% |
| EQUATE Petrochemical Company K.S.C. | 42.5% | 42.5% | 42.5% |
| The Kuwait Olefins Company K.S.C. | 42.5% | 42.5% | 42.5% |
| The Kuwait Styrene Company K.S.C. | 42.5% | 42.5% | 42.5% |
| Map Ta Phut Olefins Company Limited (3) | 32.77% | 32.77% | 32.77% |
| MEGlobal (1) | 50% | 50% | 50% |
| Sadara Chemical Company | 35% | 35% | 35% |
| The SCG-Dow Group: | | | |
| Siam Polyethylene Company Limited | 50% | 50% | 50% |
| Siam Polystyrene Company Limited | 50% | 50% | 50% |
| Siam Styrene Monomer Co., Ltd. | 50% | 50% | 50% |
| Siam Synthetic Latex Company Limited | 50% | 50% | 50% |
| Univation Technologies LLC | 50% | 50% | 50% |

The Company's investment in its principal nonconsolidated affiliates was $3,487 million at December 31, 2014, and $3,625 million at December 31, 2013. Equity earnings from these companies were $845 million in 2014, $951 million in 2013, and $479 million in 2012. Equity earnings from principal nonconsolidated affiliates decreased in 2014 compared with 2013, primarily due to lower equity earnings at EQUATE Petrochemical Company K.S.C., The Kuwait Styrene Company K.S.C., and MEGlobal as well as increased equity losses from Sadara which were partially offset by increased earnings from Dow Corning. In 2014, Dow Corning's equity earnings were unfavorably impacted by an impairment charge related to the abandonment of a polycrystalline silicon plant expansion in Clarksville, Tennessee, which was partially offset by a reduction to its implant liability reserve. In 2012, Dow Corning's equity earnings were negatively impacted by asset impairment and restructuring charges.

**EXHIBIT 2-4**

**The Dow Chemical Company and Subsidiaries Notes to the Consolidated Financial Statements**

*Source:* From The Dow Chemical Company 2014 Annual Report © The Dow Chemical Company (1995-2015)

*(continued)*

The summarized financial information that follows represents the combined accounts (at 100 percent) of the principal nonconsolidated affiliates.

## SUMMARIZED BALANCE SHEET INFORMATION AT DECEMBER 31

| In millions | 2014 | 2013 |
|---|---|---|
| Current assets | $ 9,611 | $ 8,675 |
| Noncurrent assets | 27,025 | 24,166 |
| Total assets | $ 36,636 | $32,841 |
| Current liabilities | $ 6,321 | $ 5,972 |
| Noncurrent liabilities | 21,047 | 17,129 |
| Total liabilities | $27,368 | $23,101 |
| Noncontrolling interests | $ 666 | $ 624 |

## SUMMARIZED INCOME STATEMENT INFORMATION

| In millions | 2014 | 2013 | 2012 |
|---|---|---|---|
| Sales | $19,333 | $18,257 | $17,668 |
| Gross profit | $ 1,673 | $ 3,403 | $ 2,911 |
| Net income | $ 1,673 | $ 1,906 | $ 872 |

## Related-Party Transactions

There is no presumption of arm's-length bargaining between related parties. GAAP identifies material transactions between affiliated companies as related-party transactions requiring financial statements disclosure. (ASC 850-10-50) Related-party transactions arise when one of the transacting parties has the ability to influence significantly the operations of the other. The required disclosures include the following:

1. The nature of the relationship
2. A description of the transaction
3. The dollar amounts of the transaction and any change from the previous period in the method used to establish the terms of the transaction for each income statement presented
4. Amounts due to or due from related parties at the balance sheet date for each balance sheet presented

LEARNING
OBJECTIVE **2.6**

## TESTING GOODWILL FOR IMPAIRMENT

Chapter 1 introduced the rules for goodwill and other intangible assets. This section provides additional discussion and examples of impairment tests.

Goodwill and certain other intangible assets having an indefinite useful life are not amortized. Recorded intangible assets having a definite useful life continue to be amortized over that life. If an intangible asset has a definite, but unknown, useful life, firms should amortize over the best estimate of useful life.

Those intangibles (including goodwill) having an indefinite life are not amortized but are subject to annual review and testing for impairment. The focus here is impairment testing and reporting for goodwill.

*Time Warner, Inc.* (formerly *AOL Time Warner)* provides an example of significant goodwill and intangible asset impairment write-offs. In its 2003 annual report, the consolidated income statement includes "Impairment of goodwill and other intangible assets" of $318 million in calculating income from operations. This amount pales in comparison to the 2002 amounts. Operating income for 2002 included an impairment loss for goodwill and intangibles of $44.039 billion. Net income for 2002 included an additional cumulative effect of accounting changes of ($54.235) billion, due mostly to goodwill write-offs, and this number is net of tax.

Add up the numbers and you discover that total goodwill impairments (including the discontinued operations) were $98.884 billion in 2002, and an additional $1.418 billion in 2003. The note for 2002 also discloses an $853 million impairment write-off for brands and trademarks for the music

## NOTE 9. GOODWILL AND OTHER INTANGIBLE ASSETS

### Goodwill Impairments

The Company performs an impairment test for goodwill annually during the fourth quarter. Qualitative factors may be assessed by the Company to determine whether it is more likely than not that the fair value of a reporting unit is less than its carrying value. The qualitative factors assessed at the Company level include, but are not limited to, GDP growth rates, long-term hydrocarbon and energy prices, equity and credit market activity, discount rates, foreign exchange rates and overall financial performance. Qualitative factors assessed at the reporting unit level include, but are not limited to, changes in industry and market structure, competitive environments, planned capacity and new product launches, cost factors such as raw material prices, and financial performance of the reporting unit.

### 2014 Goodwill Impairment Testing

In 2014, the Company assessed qualitative factors for 9 of the 14 reporting units carrying goodwill. The qualitative assessment indicated that it was more likely than not that the fair value exceeded carrying value for those reporting units included in the qualitative test. The Company performed the first step of the quantitative testing for the remaining five reporting units. The Company utilized a discounted cash flow methodology to calculate the fair value of the reporting units. Based on the fair value analysis, management concluded that fair value exceeded carrying value for all reporting units. As a result, no additional quantitative testing was required for the reporting units.

### 2013 Goodwill Impairment Testing

In 2013, the Company assessed qualitative factors for 14 of the 19 reporting units carrying goodwill. The qualitative assessment indicated that it was more likely than not that the fair value exceeded carrying value for those reporting units included in the qualitative test. The Company performed the first step of the quantitative testing for the remaining five reporting units. The Company utilized a discounted cash flow methodology to calculate the fair value of the reporting units. Based on the fair value analysis, management concluded that fair value exceeded carrying value for all reporting units. As a result, no additional quantitative testing was required for the reporting units.

### 2012 Goodwill Impairment Testing

In 2012, the Company assessed qualitative factors for 11 of the 20 reporting units carrying goodwill. The qualitative assessment indicated that it was more likely than not that the fair value exceeded carrying value for those reporting units included in the qualitative test. The Company performed the first step of the quantitative testing for the remaining nine reporting units. The Company utilized a discounted cash flow methodology to calculate the fair value of the reporting units. Based on the fair value analysis, management concluded that fair value exceeded carrying value for all reporting units except Dow Formulated Systems. Management completed the second step of the quantitative test for Dow Formulated Systems which compared the implied fair value of the reporting unit's goodwill to the carrying value. As a result, the Company recorded an impairment loss of $220 million in the fourth quarter of 2012, which is included in "Goodwill and other intangible asset impairment losses" in the consolidated statements of income and reflected in the Performance Materials & Chemicals segment. The goodwill impairment loss represented the total amount of goodwill that was carried by the Dow Formulated Systems reporting unit.

**EXHIBIT 2-5**

**Excerpts from Dow Chemical Company 2014 Annual Report (pp. 86-87)**

*Source:* From The Dow Chemical Company 2014 Annual Report (P 86-87) © The Dow Chemical Company (1995-2015)

---

segment. To put this in perspective, Time Warner's total assets at December 31, 2001, were $208.5 billion; the impairment write-offs in 2002 represent almost 50 percent of that amount. Time Warner points out, correctly, that these are noncash charges; however, this is still a lot of shareholders' value wiped off the books.

Exhibit 2-5 provides a more recent example of goodwill impairment charges for ***Dow Chemical Company*** in the 2014 annual report. ***Dow Chemical Company*** recorded goodwill impairment charges of $220 million in 2012. Total remaining goodwill on the December 31, 2014 balance sheet was $12.632 billion.

## Recognizing and Measuring Impairment Losses

The goodwill impairment test is a two-step process. (ASC 350-20-35) Firms must first compare carrying values (book values) to fair values of all assets and liabilities at the business-reporting-unit level. Carrying value includes the goodwill amount. For purposes of applying the standard, GAAP (ASC 280-10-55-47) defines the reporting unit as an operating segment or one level below an operating segment. The definition of business reporting units is discussed in Chapter 15 on segment reporting.

If the reporting unit's fair value exceeds its carrying value, goodwill is unimpaired. No further action is needed.

If fair value is less than the carrying amount, then firms proceed to step 2, measurement and recognition of the impairment loss. Step 2 requires a comparison of the carrying amount of goodwill to its implied fair value. Firms should again make this comparison at the business-reporting-unit level. If the carrying amount exceeds the implied fair value of the goodwill, the firm must recognize an impairment loss for the difference. The loss amount cannot exceed the carrying amount of the goodwill. Firms cannot reverse previously recognized impairment losses.

A 2011 amendment issued by the FASB may allow some companies to avoid the two-step impairment testing. The amendment gives companies an option of making a qualitative evaluation to determine whether or not they must take the first step of calculating a reporting unit's fair value. If a company concludes that it is not more likely than not that the fair value of the reporting unit is less than the carrying amount, it need not perform the two-step impairment test.

## Implied Fair Value of Goodwill

Firms should determine the implied fair value of goodwill in the same manner used to originally record the goodwill at the business combination date. Firms allocate the fair value of the reporting unit to all identifiable assets and liabilities, as if they had purchased the unit on the measurement date. Any excess fair value is the implied fair value of goodwill.

Assume that Pam Corporation owns 80 percent of Sun Corporation, which qualifies as a business reporting unit. The consolidated balance sheet carries goodwill of $6.3 million related to the investment in Sun. Pam assesses the implied fair value of goodwill as follows.

Pam first estimates that if it purchased its investment in Sun today, the total fair value of Sun would be $36.25 million, based on current market prices for Sun's shares. Pam allocates the total fair value to the identifiable assets and liabilities of Sun as shown (figures are in millions):

|  | Book Value | Fair Value |
|---|---|---|
| Current assets | $11.10 | $12.85 |
| Property, plant, and equipment | 45.00 | 48.00 |
| Patents | 4.00 | 5.40 |
| Current liabilities | (9.00) | (9.00) |
| Long-term liabilities | (26.00) | (26.00) |
| Net | $25.10 | $31.25 |
| Total fair value | | 36.25 |
| Implied fair value of goodwill | | $ 5.00 |

The fair value of Sun's identifiable assets and liabilities is $31.25 million. Therefore, goodwill has an implied fair value of $5 million ($36.25 million less $31.25 million). Notice that goodwill applies to the entire business reporting unit.

Because the current carrying value for goodwill is $6.3 million and its implied fair value is only $5 million, Pam must record a goodwill impairment loss of $1.3 million. The carrying value of goodwill is adjusted to $5 million for purposes of future impairment testing. (If the carrying value for goodwill had been less than $5 million, no impairment loss would be recognized.)

## Determining the Fair Value of the Reporting Unit

Fair values of assets and liabilities are the amounts at which they could be exchanged in an arm's-length transaction. Therefore, the fair value of a reporting unit is the amount for which it could be purchased or sold in a current transaction. The previous example assumed that a current quoted market price was available for Sun's shares. GAAP considers current market prices (in an active market) to be the most reliable indicator of fair value for a reporting unit.

Of course, these values will not always be available. If Pam owned 100 percent of Sun's common stock, there would be no active market for Sun's shares. The same situation holds if Sun's shares are not publicly traded. In these cases, GAAP suggests estimating fair values by using prices for similar assets and liabilities or by applying other valuation techniques. For example, Pam might estimate future cash flows from Sun's operations and apply present value techniques to estimate the value of the reporting unit. Pam might also employ earnings or revenue multiples techniques to estimate the fair value of Sun.

Firms must conduct the impairment test for goodwill at least annually. GAAP requires more-frequent impairment testing if any of the following events occurs:

- Significant adverse changes in legal factors or business climate
- Adverse regulatory actions or assessments
- New and unanticipated competition

- Loss of key personnel
- A more likely than not expectation that a reporting unit or a significant portion of a reporting unit will be sold or disposed of
- Testing for the recoverability of a significant asset group within a reporting unit
- Recognition of a goodwill impairment loss of a subsidiary that is a component of the reporting unit (ASC 350-20-35-30)[3]

## Fair-Value Option for Equity Method Investments

Historically, equity method investments were not adjusted for changes in fair market value, but GAAP (ASC 825-10-25) now provides firms with an option to record equity method investments at fair value. The option may be elected on an investment-by-investment basis. Firms taking the fair-value option would calculate fair values using methods described earlier. The option must continue as long as the investment is owned. Fair value is recalculated annually. Changes in fair value are reflected in the investor's net income, and the offsetting cumulative amount will be recorded in a valuation allowance. (ASC 820-10-5)

Assume that Pop Corporation purchased a 30 percent interest in Son Company on July 1. Applying the equity procedures described previously, Pop's investment account has a balance of $202,000 on December 31. Pop elects the fair-value option for this investment. Based on market prices, Son Company is valued at $700,000 on December 31. Therefore, the fair value of Pop's 30 percent interest is $210,000. Pop would record the following adjusting entry:

| | | |
|---|---|---|
| Allowance to adjust equity method investment to fair value (+A) | 8,000 | |
| Unrealized gain on equity method investment (Ga, +SE) | | 8,000 |

Under GAAP, investors must separately disclose equity method investments using the fair-value option.

## Reporting and Disclosures

GAAP requires firms to report material aggregate amounts of goodwill as a separate line item on the balance sheet. Likewise, firms must show goodwill impairment losses separately in the income statement, as a component of income from continuing operations (unless the impairment relates to discontinued operations). Goodwill impairments from discontinued operations should be reported separately (net of income tax effects) in the discontinued operations section of the income statement.

## Equity Method Investments

The previous discussion on goodwill impairment applies only to goodwill arising from business combinations (i.e., a parent company acquires a controlling interest in a subsidiary). Impairment testing also applies to goodwill reflected in investments reported under the equity method of accounting when the investor has a significant influence, but a noncontrolling interest.

Once again, GAAP eliminates amortization of goodwill, replacing that treatment with periodic tests for impairment. However, impairment tests for equity method investments do not follow the same guidelines. Impairment tests for equity method investments are performed based on fair value versus book value of the investment taken as a whole. An impairment loss may be recognized for the equity method investment as a whole. Goodwill arising from an equity method investment is not separately tested for impairment.

## Potential Problems

The GAAP rules are straightforward in concept, but practical application may be difficult, especially in those cases in which quoted market prices are unavailable to value business reporting units. Alternative valuation methods are highly subjective.

The rules also pose considerable problems for auditors. Fair-value estimations may be very difficult to verify objectively. Auditors may also be faced with earnings-management issues for some clients. If a firm chooses to take a big bath by writing off large amounts of goodwill, the conservative nature of financial reporting makes it difficult to challenge managers' estimates.

---

[3]FASB ASC 350-20-35-30. Originally Statement of Financial Accounting Standards No. 121. "Accounting for the Impairment of Long-lived Assets and for long-lived Assets to be Disposed Of." Stamford, CT. © 1995 Financial Accounting Standards Board.

## SUMMARY

Exhibit 2-6 is a flowchart summary of accounting procedures for business investments. Investments in the voting common stock of an investee are accounted for under the fair value/cost method if the investment does not give the investor an ability to exercise significant influence over the investee. Otherwise, investors should normally use the equity method (a one-line consolidation). In the absence of evidence to the contrary, a 20 percent–ownership test determines whether the investor has significant influence over the investee.

**EXHIBIT 2-6**

**Accounting for Equity Investments Generally**

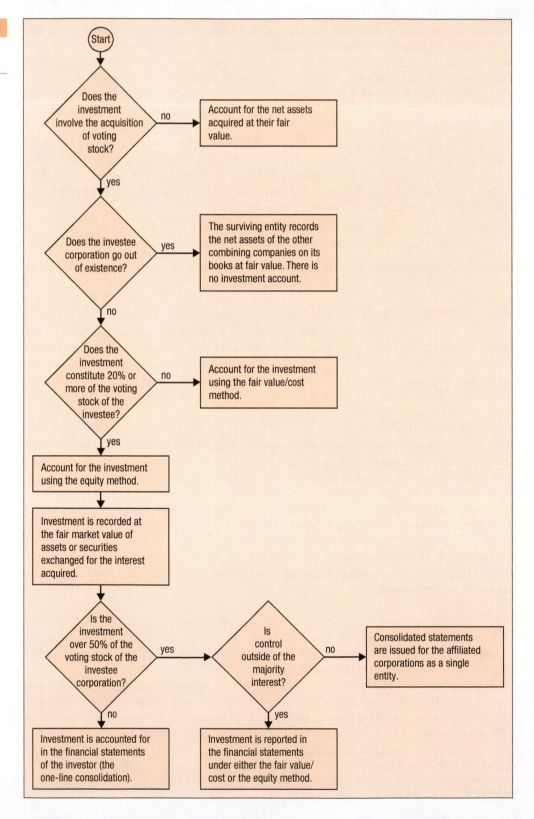

The equity method is referred to as a one-line consolidation because its application produces the same net income and stockholders' equity for the investor as would result from consolidation of the financial statements of the investor and investee corporations. Under the one-line consolidation, the investment is reflected in a single amount on one line of the investor's balance sheet, and the investor reports income from the investee on one line of the investor's income statement, except when the investee's income includes discontinued operations.

As you can see in the flowchart in Exhibit 2-6, the equity method can be used to account for investments that follow the acquisition method for business combinations. The flowchart also indicates that consolidated statements are generally required for investments in excess of 50 percent of the voting stock of the investee and that the one-line consolidation (equity method) is used in reporting investments of 20 percent to 50 percent in the investor's financial statements.

---

NOTE TO THE STUDENT

In solving problems in the areas of business combinations, equity investments, and consolidations, we frequently must make assumptions about the nature of the difference between investment cost (fair value) and book value of the net assets acquired, the timing of income earned within an accounting period, the period in which inventory items affecting intercompany investments are sold, and the source from which an equity interest is acquired. In the absence of evidence to the contrary, you should make the following assumptions:

1. An excess of investment cost (fair value) over book value of the net assets acquired is goodwill.
2. Goodwill is not amortized.
3. Income is earned evenly throughout each accounting period.
4. Inventory items on hand at the end of an accounting period are sold in the immediately succeeding fiscal period.
5. An equity interest is purchased from the stockholders of the investee rather than directly from the investee (that is, the total outstanding stock of the investee does not change).

---

## QUESTIONS

1. How are the accounts of investor and investee companies affected when the investor acquires stock from stockholders of the investee (e.g., a New York Stock Exchange purchase)? Does this differ if the investor acquires previously unissued stock directly from the investee?

2. Should goodwill arising from an equity investment of more than 20 percent be recorded separately on the books of the investor? Explain.

3. Under the fair value/cost method of accounting for stock investments, an investor records dividends received from earnings accumulated after the investment is acquired as dividend income. How does an investor treat dividends received from earnings accumulated before an investment is acquired?

4. Describe the equity method of accounting.

5. Why is the equity method referred to as a "one-line consolidation"?

6. Is there a difference between the amount of a parent's net income under the equity method and the consolidated net income for the same parent and its subsidiaries?

7. What is the difference in reporting income from a subsidiary in the parent's separate income statement and in consolidated financial statements?

8. Cite the conditions under which you would expect the balance of an equity investment account on a balance sheet date subsequent to acquisition to be equal to the underlying book value represented by that investment.

9. What accounting procedures or adjustments are necessary when an investor uses the cost method of accounting for an investment in common stock and later increases the investment such that the equity method is required?

10. Ordinarily, the income from an investment accounted for by the equity method is reported on one line of the investor's income statement. When would more than one line of the income statement of the investor be required to report such income?

11. Describe the accounting adjustments needed when a 25 percent equity interest in an investee is decreased to a 15 percent equity interest.

12. Does cumulative preferred stock in the capital structure of an investee affect the way that an investor accounts for its 30 percent common stock interest? Explain.

13. Briefly outline the steps to calculate a goodwill impairment loss.

14. Is there any difference in computing goodwill impairment losses for a controlled subsidiary versus an equity method investment?

## EXERCISES

### E2-1
### General questions

1. GAAP provides indicators of an investor's inability to exercise significant influence over an investee. Which of the following is *not* included among those indicators?
   a *Surrender of significant stockholder rights by agreement*
   b *Concentration of majority ownership in another group rather than the investor*
   c *Failure to obtain representation on the investee's board of directors*
   d *Inability to control the investee's operating policies*

2. A 20 percent common stock interest in an investee:
   a *Must be accounted for under the equity method*
   b *Is accounted for by the cost method because over 20 percent is required for the application of the equity method*
   c *Is presumptive evidence of an ability to exercise significant influence over the investee*
   d *Enables the investor to apply either the cost or the equity method*

3. The cost of a 25 percent interest in the voting stock of an investee that is recorded in the investment account includes:
   a *Cash disbursed and the book value of other assets given or securities issued, other than the cost of registering and issuing equity securities*
   b *Cash disbursed and the book value of other assets given or securities issued*
   c *Cash disbursed and the fair value of other assets given or securities issued, other than the cost of registering and issuing equity securities*
   d *Cash disbursed and the fair value of other assets given or securities issued*

4. The underlying equity of an investment at acquisition:
   a *Is recorded in the investment account under the equity method*
   b *Minus the cost of the investment is assigned to goodwill*
   c *Is equal to the fair value of the investee's net assets times the percentage acquired*
   d *Is equal to the book value of the investee's net assets times the percentage acquired*

5. Son Corporation is a 25 percent–owned equity investee of Pop Corporation. During the current year, Pop receives $12,000 in dividends from Son. How does the $12,000 dividend affect Pop's financial position and results of operations?
   a *Increases assets*
   b *Decreases investment*
   c *Increases income*
   d *Decreases income*

### E2-2
### [Based on AICPA] General problems

1. Pam Company owns 25 percent of Sun Corporation. During the year, Sun had net earnings of $450,000 and paid dividends of $28,000. Pam mistakenly recorded these transactions using the cost method rather than the equity method. What effect would this have on the investment account, net earnings, and retained earnings, respectively?
   a *Understate, overstate, overstate*
   b *Overstate, understate, understate*
   c *Overstate, overstate, overstate*
   d *Understate, understate, understate*

2. A corporation exercises control over an affiliate in which it holds a 25 percent common stock interest. If its affiliate completed a fiscal year profitably but paid *no* dividends, how would this affect the investor?
   a *Result in an increased current ratio*
   b *Result in increased earnings per share*
   c *Increase several turnover ratios*
   d *Decrease book value per share*

3. An investor uses the cost method to account for an investment in common stock. A portion of the dividends received this year were in excess of the investor's share of investee's earnings after the date of the investment. The amount of dividends revenue that should be reported in the investor's income statement for this year would be:

   a   Zero

   b   The total amount of dividends received this year

   c   The portion of the dividends received this year that were in excess of the investor's share of investee's earnings after the date of investment

   d   The portion of the dividends received this year that were not in excess of the investor's share of investee's earnings after the date of investment

4. On January 1, Pop Company paid $600,000 for 20,000 shares of Son Company's common stock, which represents a 15 percent investment in Son. Pop *does not* have the ability to exercise significant influence over Son. Son declared and paid a dividend of $2 per share to its stockholders during the year. Son reported net income of $520,000 for the year ended December 31. The balance in Pop's balance sheet account "Investment in Son Company" at December 31 should be:

   a   $560,000

   b   $600,000

   c   $638,000

   d   $678,000

5. On January 2, 2016, Pam Corporation bought 15 percent of Sun Corporation's capital stock for $30,000. Pam accounts for this investment using the cost method. Sun's net income for the years ended December 31, 2016, and December 31, 2017, were $10,000 and $50,000, respectively. During 2017 Sun declared a dividend of $70,000. No dividends were declared in 2016. How much should Pam report on its 2017 income statement as income from this investment?

   a   $1,575

   b   $7,500

   c   $9,000

   d   $10,500

6. Pam purchased 10 percent of Sun Company's 100,000 shares of common stock on January 2 for $100,000. On December 31, Pam purchased an additional 20,000 shares of Sun for $300,000. There was no goodwill as a result of either acquisition, and Sun had not issued any additional stock during the year. Sun reported earnings of $600,000 for the year. What amount should Pam report in its December 31 balance sheet as investment in Sun?

   a   $340,000

   b   $400,000

   c   $460,000

   d   $580,000

7. On January 1, Pop purchased 10 percent of Son Company's common stock. Pop purchased additional shares, bringing its ownership up to 40 percent of Son's common stock outstanding, on August 1. During October, Son declared and paid a cash dividend on all of its outstanding common stock. How much income from the Son investment should Pop report for the year ended December 31?

   a   10 percent of Son's income for January 1 to July 31, plus 40 percent of Son's income for August 1 to December 31

   b   40 percent of Son's income for August 1 to December 31 only

   c   40 percent of Son's income

   d   Amount equal to dividends received from Son

8. On January 2, Pam Company purchased a 30 percent interest in Sun Company for $250,000. On this date, the book value of Sun's stockholders' equity was $500,000. The carrying amounts of Sun's identifiable net assets approximated fair values, except for land, whose fair value exceeded its carrying amount by $200,000. Sun reported net income of $100,000 and paid no dividends. Pam accounts for this investment using the equity method. In its December 31 balance sheet, what amount should Pam report for this investment?

   a   $210,000

   b   $220,000

   c   $270,000

   d   $280,000

## E2-3
## Calculate percentage ownership and goodwill on investment acquired directly from investee

Son Corporation's stockholders' equity at December 31, 2015, consisted of the following (in thousands):

| | |
|---|---|
| Capital stock, $10 par, 60,000 shares issued and outstanding | $600 |
| Additional paid-in capital | 150 |
| Retained earnings | 250 |
| Total stockholders' equity | $1,000 |

On January 1, 2016, Pop Corporation purchased 20,000 previously unissued shares of Son stock directly from Son Corporation for $500,000.

### REQUIRED

1. Calculate Pop Corporation's percentage ownership in Son.

2. Determine the goodwill (if any) from Pop's investment in Son. Assume book values of all identifiable assets and liabilities equal the fair values.

## E2-4
## Calculate income for a midyear investment

Pam Corporation pays $300,000 for a 30 percent interest in Sun Corporation on July 1, 2016, when the book value of Sun's identifiable net assets equals fair value. Information relating to Sun follows (in thousands):

|  | December 31, 2015 | December 31, 2016 |
|---|---|---|
| Capital stock, $1 par | $ 300 | $ 300 |
| Retained earnings | 200 | 250 |
| Total stockholders' equity | $ 500 | $ 550 |
| Sun's net income earned evenly throughout 2016 |  | $ 100 |
| Sun's dividends for 2016 (paid $25,000 on March 1 and $25,000 on September 1) |  | $ 50 |

**REQUIRED:** Calculate Pam's income from Sun for 2016.

## E2-5
## Calculate income and investment balance allocation of excess to undervalued assets

Pop Company acquired a 30 percent interest in Son on January 1 for $500,000 cash. Assume the cost of the investment equals the fair value of Son's net assets. Pop assigned the $125,000 excess of fair value over book value of the interest acquired to the following assets:

| | |
|---|---|
| Inventories | $25,000 (sold in the current year) |
| Building | $50,000 (4-year remaining life at January 1) |
| Goodwill | $50,000 |

During the year Son reported net income of $200,000 and paid $50,000 dividends.

### REQUIRED

1. Determine Pop's income from Son for the year.

2. Determine the December 31 balance of the Investment in Son account.

## E2-6
## Journal entry to record income from investee with loss from discontinued operations

Pam Corporation purchased a 40 percent interest in Sun Corporation for $2,000,000 on January 1, at book value, when Sun's assets and liabilities were recorded at fair values. During the year, Sun reported net income of $1,200,000 as follows (in thousands):

| | |
|---|---|
| Income from continuing operations | $1,400 |
| Less: Loss from discontinued operations | (200) |
| Net income | $1,200 |

**REQUIRED:** Prepare the journal entry on Pam's books to recognize income from the investment in Sun for the year.

## E2-7
## General problems

1. On January 3, 2016, Pop Company purchases a 15 percent interest in Son Corporation's common stock for $50,000 cash. Pop accounts for the investment using the cost method. Son's net income for 2016 is $20,000, but it declares

no dividends. In 2017, Son's net income is $80,000, and it declares dividends of $120,000. What is the correct balance of Pop's Investment in Son account at December 31, 2017?

a  $47,000

b  $50,000

c  $62,000

d  $65,000

2. Son Corporation's stockholders' equity at December 31, 2016, follows (in thousands):

| | |
|---|---:|
| Capital stock, $100 par | $3,000 |
| Additional paid-in capital | 500 |
| Retained earnings | 500 |
| Total stockholders' equity | $4,000 |

On January 3, 2017, Son sells 10,000 shares of previously unissued $100 par common stock to Pop Corporation for $1,400,000. On this date the recorded book values of Son's assets and liabilities equal fair values. Goodwill from Pop's investment in Son at the date of purchase is:

a  $0

b  $50,000

c  $300,000

d  $400,000

3. On January 1, Pop Company paid $300,000 for a 20 percent interest in Son Corporation's voting common stock, at which time Son's stockholders' equity consisted of $600,000 capital stock and $400,000 retained earnings. Pop was not able to exercise any influence over the operations of Son and accounted for its investment using the cost method. During the year, Son had net income of $200,000 and paid dividends of $150,000. The balance of Pop's Investment in Son account at December 31 is:

a  $330,000

b  $310,000

c  $307,500

d  $300,000

4. Pop Corporation owns a 40 percent interest in Son Products acquired several years ago at book value. Son's income statement contains the following information (in thousands):

| | |
|---|---:|
| Income from continuing operations | $200 |
| Discontinued operations loss | (50) |
| Net income | $150 |

Pop should report income from Son in its income from continuing operations at:

a  $20,000

b  $60,000

c  $80,000

d  $100,000

# E2-8
## Calculate investment balance four years after acquisition

Pam Corporation owns a 40 percent interest in the outstanding common stock of Sun Corporation, having acquired its interest for $2,400,000 on *January 1, 2016*, when Sun's stockholders' equity was $4,000,000. The fair value/book value differential was assigned to inventories that were undervalued by $100,000 and sold in 2016, to equipment with a four-year remaining life that was undervalued by $200,000, and to goodwill for the remainder.
The balance of Sun's stockholders' equity at *December 31, 2019*, is $5,500,000, and all changes therein are the result of income earned and dividends paid.

REQUIRED: Determine the balance of Pam's investment in Sun at December 31, 2019.

# E2-9
## Calculate income and investment balance when investee capital structure includes preferred stock

Son Company had net income of $400,000 and paid dividends of $200,000 during 2017. Son's stockholders' equity on December 31, 2016, and December 31, 2017, is summarized as follows (in thousands):

| | December 31, 2016 | December 31, 2017 |
|---|---|---|
| 10% cumulative preferred stock, $100 par | $ 300 | $ 300 |
| Common stock, $1 par | 1,000 | 1,000 |
| Additional paid-in capital | 2,200 | 2,200 |
| Retained earnings | 500 | 700 |
| Total stockholders' equity | $4,000 | $4,200 |

On January 2, 2017, Pop Corporation purchased 300,000 common shares of Son at $4 per share. Pop also paid $50,000 in cash for direct costs of acquiring the investment.

**REQUIRED:** Determine (1) Pop's income from Son for 2017 and (2) the balance of the investment in the Son account at December 31, 2017. Assume the fair values of Son's assets and liabilities equal book values.

## E2-10
## Calculate income and investment balance for midyear investment

Pam Corporation acquired 25 percent of Sun Corporation's outstanding common stock on October 1, for $300,000. A summary of Sun's adjusted trial balances on this date and at December 31 follows (in thousands):

| | December 31 | October 1 |
|---|---|---|
| *Debits* | | |
| Current assets | $ 250 | $ 125 |
| Plant assets—net | 750 | 775 |
| Expenses (including cost of goods sold) | 400 | 300 |
| Dividends (paid in July) | 100 | 100 |
| | $1,500 | $1,300 |
| *Credits* | | |
| Current liabilities | $ 150 | $ 100 |
| Capital stock (no change during the year) | 500 | 500 |
| Retained earnings January 1 | 250 | 250 |
| Sales | 600 | 450 |
| | $1,500 | $1,300 |

Pam uses the equity method of accounting. No information is available concerning the fair values of Sun's assets and liabilities.

### REQUIRED

1. Determine Pam's investment income from Sun Corporation for the year ended December 31.
2. Compute the correct balance of Pam's investment in Sun account at December 31.

## E2-11
## Adjust investment account and determine income when additional investment qualifies for equity method of accounting

Summary balance sheet and income information for Son Company for two years is as follows (in thousands):

| | January 1, 2016 | December 31, 2016 | December 31, 2017 |
|---|---|---|---|
| Current assets | $ 50 | $ 60 | $ 75 |
| Plant assets | 200 | 240 | 250 |
| | $250 | $300 | $325 |
| Liabilities | $ 40 | $ 50 | $50 |
| Capital stock | 150 | 150 | 150 |
| Retained earnings | 60 | 100 | 125 |
| | $250 | $300 | $325 |

| | 2016 | 2017 |
|---|---|---|
| Net income | $100 | $50 |
| Dividends | 60 | 25 |

On January 2, 2016, Pop Company purchases 10 percent of Son Company for $25,000 cash, and it accounts for its investment (classified as an available-for-sale security) in Son using the fair-value method. On December 31, 2016, the fair value of all of Son's stock is $500,000. On January 2, 2017, Pop purchases an additional 10 percent interest in Son stock for $50,000 and adopts the equity method to account for the investment. The fair values of Son's assets and liabilities were equal to book values as of the time of both stock purchases.

### REQUIRED

1. Prepare a journal entry to adjust the Investment in Son account to the equity method on January 2, 2017.
2. Determine Pop's income from Son for 2017.

## E2-12
## Journal entries (investment in previously unissued stock)

The stockholders' equity of Sun Corporation at December 31, 2016, was $380,000, consisting of the following (in thousands):

| | |
|---|---|
| Capital stock, $10 par (24,000 shares outstanding) | $240 |
| Additional paid-in capital | 60 |
| Retained earnings | 80 |
| Total stockholders' equity | $380 |

On January 1, 2017, Sun Corporation, which was in a tight working capital position, sold 12,000 shares of previously unissued stock to Pam Corporation for $250,000. All of Sun's identifiable assets and liabilities were recorded at fair values on this date except for a building with a 10-year remaining useful life that was undervalued by $60,000. During 2017, Sun Corporation reported net income of $120,000 and paid dividends of $90,000.

**REQUIRED:** Prepare all journal entries necessary for Pam Corporation to account for its investment in Sun for 2017.

## E2-13
## Prepare journal entries and income statement, and determine investment account balance

Pop Corporation paid $780,000 for a 30 percent interest in Son Corporation on December 31, 2016, when Son's stockholders' equity consisted of $2,000,000 capital stock and $800,000 retained earnings. The price paid by Pop reflected the fact that Son's inventory (on an FIFO basis) was overvalued by $200,000. The overvalued inventory items were sold in 2017.

During 2017 Son paid dividends of $400,000 and reported income as follows (in thousands):

| | |
|---|---|
| Income from continuing operations | $680 |
| Discontinued operations loss (net of tax effect) | (80) |
| Net income | $600 |

### REQUIRED

1. Prepare all journal entries necessary to account for Pop's investment in Son for 2017.
2. Determine the correct balance of Pop's Investment in Son account at December 31, 2017.
3. Assume that Pop's net income for 2017 consists of $4,000,000 sales, $2,800,000 expenses, and its investment income from Son. Prepare an income statement for Pop Corporation for 2017.

## E2-14
## Calculate income and investment account balance (investee has preferred stock)

Pam Corporation paid $290,000 for 40 percent of the outstanding common stock of Sun Corporation on January 2, 2017. During 2017, Sun paid dividends of $48,000 and reported net income of $108,000. A summary of Sun's stockholders' equity at December 31, 2016 and 2017 follows (in thousands):

| December 31, | 2016 | 2017 |
|---|---|---|
| 8% cumulative preferred stock, $100 par | $100 | $100 |
| Common stock, $10 par | 300 | 300 |
| Premium on preferred stock | 10 | 10 |
| Other paid-in capital | 90 | 90 |
| Retained earnings | 100 | 160 |
| Total stockholders' equity | $600 | $660 |

**REQUIRED:** Calculate Pam Corporation's income from Sun for 2017 and its Investment in Sun account balance at December 31, 2017. Assume the book values of all of Sun's assets and liabilities equal fair values.

### E2-15
### Goodwill impairment

Pop Corporation recorded goodwill in the amount of $200,000 in its acquisition of Son Company in 2016. Pop paid a total of $700,000 to acquire Son. In preparing its 2017 financial statements, Pop estimates that identifiable net assets still have a fair value of $500,000, but the total fair value of Son is now $640,000. Calculate the implied value of goodwill at December 31, 2017, and indicate how the change in value (if any) will affect Pop's 2017 income statement.

### E2-16
### Goodwill impairment

Pam, Inc. has two primary business reporting units: Alfa and Beta. In preparing its 2017 financial statements, Pam conducts the required annual impairment review of goodwill. Alfa has recorded goodwill of $35,000 that has an estimated fair value of $30,000. Beta has recorded goodwill of $65,000 that has an estimated fair value of $80,000. What amount of impairment loss, if any, must Pam report in its 2017 income statement? Where in the income statement should this appear?

## PROBLEMS

### P2-1
### Computations for a midyear purchase (investee has a discontinued operations gain)

Pop Corporation paid $686,000 for a 30 percent interest in Son Corporation's outstanding voting stock on April 1, 2016. At December 31, 2015, Son had net assets of $2,000,000 and only common stock outstanding. During 2016, Son declared and paid dividends of $40,000 each quarter on March 15, June 15, September 15, and December 15 ($160,000 in total). At April 1, 2016, the book value of assets and liabilities equals the fair value. Son's 2016 income was reported as follows:

| | |
|---|---|
| Income from continuing operations | $240,000 |
| Discontinued operations gain, December 2016 | 80,000 |
| Net income | $320,000 |

**REQUIRED:** Determine the following items for Pop:
1. Goodwill from the investment in Son
2. Income from Son for 2016
3. Investment in Son account balance at December 31, 2016
4. Pop's equity in Son's net assets at December 31, 2016
5. The amount of discontinued operations gain that Pop will show on its 2016 income statement

### P2-2
### Journal entries for midyear investment (cost and equity methods)

Pam Company paid $440,000 for an 80 percent interest in Sun Company on July 1, 2016, when Sun had total equity of $220,000. Sun Company reported earnings of $20,000 for 2016 and declared dividends of $32,000 on November 1, 2016.

**REQUIRED:** Give the entries to record these facts on the books of Pam Company:
1. Assuming that Pam Company uses the cost method of accounting for its subsidiaries.
2. Assuming that Pam Company uses the equity method of accounting for its subsidiaries. (Any difference between investment cost and book value acquired is to be assigned to equipment and amortized over a 10-year period.)

### P2-3
### Computations for investee when excess allocated to inventories, building, and goodwill

Pop Company acquired a 30 percent interest in the voting stock of Son Company for $331,000 on January 1, 2016, when Son's stockholders' equity consisted of capital stock of $600,000 and retained earnings of

$400,000. At the time of Pop's investment, Son's assets and liabilities were recorded at fair values, except for inventories that were undervalued by $30,000 and a building with a 10-year remaining useful life that was overvalued by $60,000. Son has income for 2016 of $100,000 and pays dividends of $50,000. Assume undervalued inventories are sold in 2016.

**REQUIRED**

1. Compute Pop's income from Son for 2016.
2. What is the balance of Pop's Investment in Son account at December 31, 2016?
3. What is Pop's share of Son's recorded net assets at December 31, 2016?

## P2-4
## Journal entries for midyear investment (excess allocated to land, equipment, and goodwill)

Pam Corporation paid $190,000 for 40 percent of Sun Corporation's outstanding voting common stock on July 1, 2016. Sun's stockholders' equity on January 1, 2016, was $250,000, consisting of $150,000 capital stock and $100,000 retained earnings.

During 2016, Sun reported net income of $50,000, and on November 1, 2016, Sun declared dividends of $25,000.

Sun's assets and liabilities were stated at fair values on July 1, 2016, except for land that was undervalued by $15,000 and equipment with a five-year remaining useful life that was undervalued by $25,000.

**REQUIRED:** Prepare all the journal entries (other than closing entries) on the books of Pam Corporation during 2016 to account for the investment in Sun.

## P2-5
## Prepare an allocation schedule; compute income and the investment balance

Pop Corporation paid $1,680,000 for a 30 percent interest in Son Corporation's outstanding voting stock on January 1, 2016. The book values and fair values of Son's assets and liabilities on January 1, along with amortization data, are as follows (in thousands):

|  | Book Value | Fair Value |
|---|---|---|
| Cash | $ 400 | $ 400 |
| Accounts receivable—net | 700 | 700 |
| Inventories (sold in 2016) | 1,000 | 1,200 |
| Other current assets | 200 | 200 |
| Land | 900 | 1,700 |
| Buildings—net (10-year remaining life) | 1,500 | 2,000 |
| Equipment—net (7-year remaining life) | 1,200 | 500 |
| Total assets | $5,900 | $6,700 |
| Accounts payable | $ 800 | $ 800 |
| Other current liabilities | 200 | 200 |
| Bonds payable (due January 1, 2021) | 1,000 | 1,100 |
| Capital stock, $10 par | 3,000 |  |
| Retained earnings | 900 |  |
| Total equities | $5,900 |  |

Son Corporation reported net income of $1,200,000 for 2016 and paid dividends of $600,000.

**REQUIRED**

1. Prepare a schedule to allocate the investment fair values/book value differentials relating to Pop's investment in Son.
2. Calculate Pop's income from Son for 2016.
3. Determine the balance of Pop's Investment in Son account at December 31, 2016.

## P2-6
## Computations for a midyear acquisition

Pam Corporation purchased for cash 6,000 shares of voting common stock of Sun Corporation at $16 per share on July 1, 2016. On this date, Sun's equity consisted of $100,000 of $10 par capital stock, $20,000 retained earnings from prior periods, and $10,000 current earnings (for one-half of 2016).

Sun's income for 2016 was $20,000, and it paid dividends of $12,000 on November 1, 2016.

All of Sun's assets and liabilities had book values equal to fair values at July 1, 2016, and any differences between investment cost and book value acquired should be assigned to equipment and amortized over a 10-year period.

**REQUIRED:** Compute the correct amounts for each of the following items using the equity method of accounting for Pam's investment:

1. Pam's income from its investment in Sun for the year ended December 31, 2016.
2. The balance of Pam's Investment in Sun account at December 31, 2016.

(*Note:* Assumptions on page 49 are needed for this problem.)

## P2-7
## Partial income statement with a discontinued operations

Pop Corporation acquired 30 percent of the voting stock of Son Company at book value on July 1, 2016. During 2018, Son paid dividends of $160,000 and reported income of $500,000 as follows:

| | |
|---|---|
| Income from continuing operations | $300,000 |
| Discontinued operations gain | 200,000 |
| Net income | $500,000 |

**REQUIRED:** Show how Pop's income from Son should be reported for 2018 by means of a partial income statement for Pop Corporation.

## P2-8
## Computations and journal entries with excess of book value over fair value

Sun Corporation became a subsidiary of Pam Corporation on July 1, 2016, when Pam paid $1,980,000 cash for 90 percent of Sun's outstanding common stock. The price paid by Pam reflected the fact that Sun's inventories were undervalued by $50,000, and Sun's plant assets were overvalued by $500,000. Sun sold the undervalued inventory items during 2016 but continues to hold the overvalued plant assets that had a remaining useful life of nine years from July 1, 2016.

During the years 2016 through 2018, Sun's paid-in capital consisted of $1,500,000 capital stock and $500,000 additional paid-in capital. Sun's retained earnings statements for 2016, 2017, and 2018 were as follows (in thousands):

| | Year Ended December 31, 2016 | Year Ended December 31, 2017 | Year Ended December 31, 2018 |
|---|---|---|---|
| Retained earnings January 1 | $525 | $600 | $700 |
| Add: Net income | 250 | 300 | 200 |
| Deduct: Dividends (declared in December) | (175) | (200) | (150) |
| Retained earnings December 31 | $600 | $700 | $750 |

Pam uses the equity method in accounting for its investment in Sun.

**REQUIRED**

1. Compute Pam's income from its investment in Sun for 2016.
2. Determine the balance of Pam's Investment in Sun account at December 31, 2017.
3. Prepare the journal entries for Pam to account for its investment in Sun for 2018.

## P2-9
## Prepare allocation schedules under different stock price assumptions (bargain purchase)

Pop Corporation exchanged 40,000 previously unissued no par common shares for a 40 percent interest in Son Corporation on January 1, 2016. The assets and liabilities of Son on that date (after the exchange) were as follows (in thousands):

|  | Book Value | Fair Value |
|---|---|---|
| Cash | $ 200 | $ 200 |
| Accounts receivable—net | 400 | 400 |
| Inventories | 1,000 | 1,200 |
| Land | 200 | 600 |
| Buildings—net | 1,200 | 800 |
| Equipment—net | 800 | 1,000 |
| Total assets | $3,800 | $4,200 |
|  |  |  |
| Liabilities | $1,800 | $1,800 |
| Capital stock | 1,400 |  |
| Retained earnings | 600 |  |
| Total equities | $3,800 |  |

The direct cost of issuing the shares of stock was $20,000, and other direct costs of combination were $80,000.

### REQUIRED

1. Assume that the January 1, 2016, market price for Pop's shares is $24 per share. Prepare a schedule to allocate the investment cost/book value differentials.

2. Assume that the January 1, 2016, market price for Pop's shares is $16 per share. Prepare a schedule to allocate the investment cost/book value differentials. Assume that other direct costs were $0.

## P2-10
## Computations for a piecemeal acquisition

Pam Corporation made three investments in Sun during 2016 and 2017, as follows:

| Date Acquired | Shares Acquired | Cost |
|---|---|---|
| July 1, 2016 | 3,000 | $ 48,750 |
| January 1, 2017 | 6,000 | 99,000 |
| October 1, 2017 | 9,000 | 162,000 |

Sun's stockholders' equity on January 1, 2016, consisted of 20,000 shares of $10 par common stock and retained earnings of $100,000. Pam's intention was to buy a controlling interest in Sun, so it never considered its investment in Sun as a trading security. Sun stock had a market value of $16.50 on December 31, 2016, and $19.00 on December 31, 2017.

Sun had net income of $40,000 and $60,000 in 2016 and 2017, respectively, and paid dividends of $15,000 on May 1 and November 1, 2016 and 2017 ($60,000 total for the two years).

Pam Corporation accounts for its investment in Sun using the equity method. It does not amortize differences between investment cost and book value acquired.

### REQUIRED: Compute the following amounts:

1. Pam's income from its investment in Sun for 2016
2. The balance of Pam's Investment in Sun account at December 31, 2016
3. Pam's income from its investments in Sun for 2017
4. The balance of Pam's Investment in Sun account at December 31, 2017

## P2-11
## Computations and a correcting entry (errors)

Pam Corporation purchased 40 percent of the voting stock of Sun Corporation on July 1, 2016, for $600,000. On that date, Sun's stockholders' equity consisted of capital stock of $1,000,000, retained earnings of $300,000, and current earnings (just half of 2016) of $100,000. Income is earned proportionately throughout each year.

The Investment in Sun account of Pam Corporation and the retained earnings account of Sun Corporation for 2016 through 2019 are summarized as follows (in thousands):

### RETAINED EARNINGS (SUN)

| | | | |
|---|---|---|---|
| Dividends November 1, 2016 | $80 | Balance January 1, 2016 | $300 |
| Dividends November 1, 2017 | 80 | Earnings 2016 | 200 |
| Dividends November 1, 2018 | 100 | Earnings 2017 | 160 |
| Dividends November 1, 2019 | 100 | Earnings 2018 | 260 |
| | | Earnings 2019 | 240 |

### INVESTMENT IN SUE (PAM)

| | | | |
|---|---|---|---|
| Investment July 1, 2016 40% | $600 | Dividends 2016 | $32 |
| Income 2016 | 80 | Dividends 2017 | 32 |
| Income 2017 | 64 | Dividends 2018 | 40 |
| Income 2018 | 104 | Dividends 2019 | 40 |
| Income 2019 | 96 | | |

### REQUIRED

1. Determine the correct amount of the investment in Sun that should appear in Pam's December 31, 2019, balance sheet. Assume any difference between investment cost and book value acquired is due to goodwill.
2. Prepare any journal entry (entries) on Pam's books to bring the Investment in Sun account up to date on December 31, 2019, assuming that the books have not been closed at year-end 2019.

## P2-12
## Allocation schedule and computations (excess cost over fair value)

Pop Corporation acquired a 70 percent interest in Son Corporation on April 1, 2016, when it purchased 14,000 of Son's 20,000 outstanding shares in the open market at $13 per share. Additional costs of acquiring the shares consisted of $10,000 legal and consulting fees. Son Corporation's balance sheets on January 1 and April 1, 2016, are summarized as follows (in thousands):

| | January 1 (per books) | April 1 (per books) | April 1 (fair values) |
|---|---|---|---|
| Cash | $ 40 | $ 45 | $ 45 |
| Inventories | 35 | 60 | 50 |
| Other current assets | 25 | 20 | 20 |
| Land | 30 | 30 | 50 |
| Equipment—net | 100 | 95 | 135 |
| Total assets | $230 | $250 | $300 |
| Accounts payable | $ 45 | $ 40 | $ 40 |
| Other liabilities | 15 | 20 | 20 |
| Capital stock, $5 par | 100 | 100 | |
| Retained earnings January 1 | 70 | 70 | |
| Current earnings | | 20 | |
| Total liabilities and equity | $230 | $250 | |

### ADDITIONAL INFORMATION

1. The overvalued inventory items were sold in September 2016.
2. The undervalued items of equipment had a remaining useful life of four years on April 1, 2016.
3. Son's net income for 2016 was $80,000 ($60,000 from April to December 31, 2016).
4. On December 1, 2016, Son declared dividends of $2 per share, payable on January 10, 2017.
5. Any unidentified assets of Son are not amortized.

**REQUIRED**

1. Prepare a schedule showing how the difference between Pop's investment cost and book value acquired should be allocated to identifiable and/or unidentifiable assets.
2. Calculate Pop's investment income from Son for 2016.
3. Determine the correct balance of Pop's Investment in Son account at December 31, 2016.

## PROFESSIONAL RESEARCH ASSIGNMENTS

Answer the following questions by reference to the FASB Codification of Accounting Standards. Include the appropriate reference in your response.

**PR 2-1**  The equity method of accounting is often referred to as a one-line consolidation. Since the net impact on the balance sheet and income statement is the same under both consolidation and the equity method, is it acceptable to report a noncontrolling investment using the simpler equity method?

**PR 2-2**  A firm sells a part of its investment interest, reducing its holding from 30% to 10%. The firm decides, correctly, that the equity method is no longer appropriate. What is the basis for the investment in applying the new accounting method?

# CHAPTER 3

# An Introduction to Consolidated Financial Statements

This chapter contains material necessary to understand consolidated financial statements and provides an overview of the consolidation process. The acquisition method of accounting for business combinations is applied in the chapter. We assume the parent company/investor uses the complete equity method of accounting for subsidiary investments. All further discussions of business combinations in this book assume acquisition accounting.

Required consolidated financial statements include a consolidated balance sheet; a consolidated income statement; a consolidated retained earnings statement, or consolidated statement of changes in stockholders' equity; and a consolidated statement of cash flows.[1] The consolidated balance sheet and consolidated income and retained earnings statements in this chapter are prepared from the separate financial statements of the parent company and its subsidiaries. We prepare the consolidated statement of cash flows (introduced in Chapter 4) from consolidated income statements and consolidated balance sheets.

## BUSINESS COMBINATIONS CONSUMMATED THROUGH STOCK ACQUISITIONS

The accounting concept of a business combination under generally accepted accounting principles (GAAP) (ASC 805) includes combinations in which one or more companies become subsidiaries of a parent corporation. A corporation becomes a subsidiary when another corporation acquires a controlling interest in its outstanding voting stock. Ordinarily, one company gains control of another directly by acquiring a majority (more than 50 percent) of its voting stock. An investor may also gain control through indirect stock ownership, which is covered in Chapter 9 of this book. Until then, assume that direct ownership of a majority of the voting stock is required for control and to have a parent–subsidiary relationship.

Once a parent–subsidiary relationship is established, the purchase of additional subsidiary stock is not a business combination. In other words, separate entities can combine only once. Increasing a controlling interest is the same as simply making an additional investment. Under GAAP (ASC 810-10), acquisition of additional subsidiary stock is recorded by increasing the investment account and reducing the noncontrolling interest, based on the carrying amount of the noncontrolling interest at the additional acquisition date. (The increase in the investment account presumes that the fair value of the subsidiary increases after the additional investment.) Any difference between the

---

[1]GAAP (ASC 220) also requires a statement of comprehensive income. We ignore that statement, except in instances where it is particularly relevant to the material being discussed.

### LEARNING OBJECTIVES

**3.1** Recognize the benefits and limitations of consolidated financial statements.

**3.2** Understand requirements for including a subsidiary in consolidated financial statements.

**3.3** Apply consolidation concepts to parent company recording of an investment in a subsidiary company at the date of acquisition.

**3.4** Record the fair value of a subsidiary at the date of acquisition.

**3.5** Learn the concept of noncontrolling interest when a parent company acquires less than 100 percent of a subsidiary's outstanding common stock.

**3.6** Prepare consolidated balance sheets subsequent to the acquisition date, including preparation of eliminating entries.

**3.7** Amortize the excess of the fair value over the book value in periods subsequent to the acquisition.

LEARNING OBJECTIVE **3.2**

acquisition price and the carrying amount of the noncontrolling interest plus the increase in the investment account is an adjustment to additional paid-in capital of the parent company.

## The Reporting Entity

An acquisition brings two previously separate corporations under the control of a single management team. Although both corporations continue to exist as separate legal entities, the acquisition creates a new reporting entity that encompasses all operations controlled by management of the parent company.

When an investment in voting stock creates a parent–subsidiary relationship, the purchasing entity (parent) and the entity acquired (subsidiary) continue to function as separate entities and maintain accounting records on a separate basis. Separate parent and subsidiary financial statements are converted into consolidated financial statements to reflect the financial position and the results of operations of the combined entities. The new reporting entity is responsible for reporting to the stockholders and creditors of the parent and to other interested parties.

This chapter introduces combining the separate accounting records of the parent and subsidiary into a more meaningful set of consolidated financial statements. As you continue through the remaining chapters on acquisitions, you may at times feel that companies maintain separate legal entities and accounting systems only to make life difficult for advanced accounting students. In fact, there are sound business reasons for keeping these separate identities.

A parent may acquire a subsidiary in a different industry from its own as a means of diversifying its overall business risk. In such cases, the management experience and skills required in the subsidiary's line of business are already in place and are preserved within the separate entity. Further, the subsidiary may have established supply-chain and distribution systems different from its parent's. The subsidiary also may have established customer loyalties, which are easier to maintain with a separate identity.

Brand names and trademarks associated with the subsidiary represent extremely valuable intangible assets. If *Quicken Loans* were to purchase *Coca-Cola Company*, it likely would not be a great strategic move to rename it as *Quicken Loans and Cola!*

There are also compelling legal reasons for maintaining separate identities. In a typical investment, the parent buys the common stock of the subsidiary. Under the U.S. legal system, stockholders enjoy limited legal liability. If a lawsuit against a subsidiary results in a significant loss (e.g., from an environmental catastrophe), the parent cannot be held accountable for more than the loss of its investment.

## The Parent–Subsidiary Relationship

We presume that a corporation that owns more than 50 percent of the voting stock of another corporation controls that corporation through its stock ownership, and a parent–subsidiary relationship exists. When parent–subsidiary relationships exist, the companies are affiliated. Often the term **affiliate** is used to mean subsidiary, and the two terms are used interchangeably in this book. In many annual reports, however, the term *affiliate* is used to include all investments accounted for by the equity method. The following excerpt from the ***Deere & Company*** 2015 annual report (p. 46) is an example of this latter usage of the term *affiliate*: "Unconsolidated affiliated companies are companies in which Deere & Company generally owns 20 percent to 50 percent of the outstanding voting shares. Deere & Company does not control these companies and accounts for its investments in them on the equity basis. . . . Deere & Company's share of the income or loss of these companies is reported in the consolidated income statement under 'Equity in income (loss) of unconsolidated affiliates.' The investment in these companies is reported in the consolidated balance sheet under 'investments in unconsolidated affiliates.'"[2]

Exhibit 3-1 illustrates an affiliation structure with two subsidiaries, with Percy Company owning 90 percent of the voting stock of San Del Corporation and 80 percent of the voting stock of Saltz Corporation. Percy Company owns 90 percent of the voting stock of San Del, and stockholders outside the affiliation structure own the other 10 percent. These outside stockholders are the noncontrolling stockholders, and their interest is referred to as a **noncontrolling interest**.[3] Outside stockholders have a 20 percent noncontrolling interest in Saltz Corporation.

---

[2]From Deere & Company Annual Report 2015 (P46) © 2015 Deere & Company.

[3]GAAP prefers the term *noncontrolling interest* to minority interest (ASC 810-10). Some companies retain the more-traditional *minority interest* designation in their annual reports, but we use *noncontrolling* throughout this text.

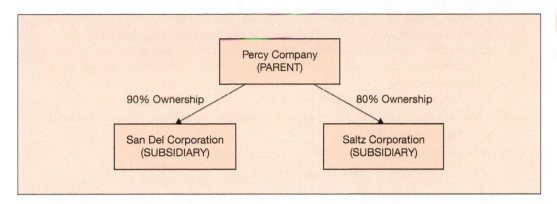

Percy Company and its subsidiaries are separate legal entities that maintain separate accounting records. In its separate records, Percy Company uses the equity method described in Chapter 2 to account for its investments in San Del and Saltz Corporations. For reporting purposes, however, the equity method of reporting usually does not result in the most meaningful financial statements. The parent, through its stock ownership, is able to elect subsidiary directors and control subsidiary decisions, including dividend declarations. Although affiliated companies are separate legal entities, there is really only one economic entity because all resources are under control of a single management—the directors and officers of the parent.

Under GAAP (ASC 810-10-10-1):

> *The purpose of consolidated financial statements is to present, primarily for the benefit of the owners and creditors of the parent, the results of operations and the financial position of a parent and all its subsidiaries as if the consolidated group were a single economic entity. There is a presumption that consolidated financial statements are more meaningful than separate financial statements and that they are usually necessary for a fair presentation when one of the entities in the consolidated group directly or indirectly has a controlling financial interest in the other entities.*[4]

Consolidated statements are intended primarily for the parent's investors, rather than for the noncontrolling stockholders and subsidiary creditors. The subsidiary, as a separate legal entity, continues to report the results of its own operations to the noncontrolling shareholders.

## Consolidation Policy

Consolidated financial statements provide information that is not included in the separate statements of the parent, and are usually required for fair presentation of the financial position and results of operations for the affiliated companies. The usual condition for consolidation is ownership of more than 50 percent of the voting stock of another company. Under current GAAP (ASC 810-10-65), a subsidiary can be excluded from consolidation in some situations: (1) when control does not rest with the majority owner, (2) formation of joint ventures, (3) the acquisition of an asset or group of assets that does not constitute a business, (4) acquiring financial assets and liabilities of a consolidated variable interest entity that is a collateralized financing entity, and (5) a combination between not-for-profit entities or the acquisition of a for-profit business by a not-for-profit entity. Control does not rest with the majority owner if the subsidiary is in legal reorganization or bankruptcy or is operating under severe foreign-exchange restrictions, controls, or other governmentally imposed uncertainties.

**DISCLOSURE OF CONSOLIDATION POLICIES**    GAAP (ASC 235-10) requires a description of significant accounting policies for financial reporting and traditionally, consolidation-policy disclosures were among the most frequent of all policy disclosures. Consolidation-policy disclosures are needed to report exceptions (e.g., inability to control) to the required consolidation of all majority-owned subsidiaries. In addition, GAAP requires an extensive list of disclosures. Disclosures are required for:

1. the reporting period that includes a business combination
   a. general information about the business combination such as name of target and acquisition date
   b. information about goodwill or bargain purchase gain

---

[4]FASB ASC 810-10-10-1. Originally Statement of Financial Accounting Standards No. 160."Noncontrolling Interests." Norwalk, CT © 2007 Financial Accounting Standards Board.

    **c.** nature, terms, and fair value of consideration transferred

    **d.** details about specific assets, liabilities, and any noncontrolling interest

    **e.** reduction in buyer's pre-existing deferred tax asset valuation allowance

    **f.** information about transactions accounted for separately from the business combination

    **g.** information about step acquisitions

**2.** a business combination that occurs after the reporting period but before the financial statements are issued

**3.** provisional amounts related to business combinations

**4.** adjustments related to business combinations.

The SEC requires publicly held companies to report their consolidation policies under Regulation S-X, Rule 3A-03. Consolidation policy is usually presented under a heading such as "principles of consolidation" or "basis of consolidation." The ***Deere & Company*** 2015 annual report contains a typical "principles of consolidation" policy note (p. 36):

> *The consolidated financial statements represent primarily the consolidation of all companies in which Deere & Company has a controlling interest. Certain variable interest entities (VIEs) are consolidated since the company has both the power to direct the activities that most significantly impact the VIEs' economic performance and the obligation to absorb losses or the right to receive benefits that could potentially be significant to the VIEs'.*[5]

### Parent and Subsidiary with Different Fiscal Periods

When the fiscal periods of the parent and its subsidiaries differ, we prepare consolidated statements for and as of the end of the parent's fiscal period. If the difference in fiscal periods is not in excess of three months, it usually is acceptable to use the subsidiary's statements for its fiscal year for consolidation purposes, with disclosure of the effect of intervening events that materially affect the financial position or results of operations. Otherwise, the statements of the subsidiary should be adjusted so that they correspond as closely as possible to the fiscal period of the parent company.

### Financing the Acquisition

There are many avenues available for financing an acquisition. As students, you are well aware that sufficient cash isn't always available for the things you'd like to buy; companies face the same problem in making significant purchases. The investor may pay cash, sell shares of authorized but previously unissued common stock, issue preferred shares, sell debt securities (bonds), or utilize some combination of these financial instruments.

The financing decision can be important strategically. Common shares are accompanied by voting rights, and an especially large acquisition may cost management its voting control. Nonvoting preferred shares or other financing alternatives are useful in cases in which keeping voting control is an important consideration.

---

**LEARNING OBJECTIVE 3.3**

## CONSOLIDATED BALANCE SHEET AT DATE OF ACQUISITION

A consolidated entity is a fictitious (conceptual) reporting entity. It is based on the assumption that the separate legal and accounting entities of a parent and its subsidiaries can be combined into a single meaningful set of financial statements for external reporting purposes. Note that the consolidated entity does not have transactions and does not maintain a consolidated ledger of accounts.

**LEARNING OBJECTIVE 3.4**

### Parent Acquires 100 Percent of Subsidiary at Book Value

Exhibit 3-2 shows the basic differences between separate-company and consolidated balance sheets. Pop Corporation acquires 100 percent of Son Corporation at its book value and fair value of $80,000 in an acquisition on January 1, 2016. Exhibit 3-2 shows the balance sheets prepared immediately after the investment. Pop's "Investment in Son" appears in the separate balance sheet of Pop, but

---

[5]From Deere & Company Annual Report 2015 (P36) © 2015 Deere & Company.

| (in thousands) | Separate Balance Sheets Pop | Son | Consolidated Balance Sheet: Pop and Subsidiary |
|---|---|---|---|
| **Assets** | | | |
| Current assets | | | |
| Cash | $ 40 | $ 20 | $ 60 |
| Other current assets | 90 | 30 | 120 |
| Total current assets | 130 | 50 | 180 |
| Plant assets | 150 | 90 | 240 |
| Less: Accumulated depreciation | (30) | (10) | (40) |
| Total plant assets | 120 | 80 | 200 |
| Investment in Son—100% | 80 | — | — |
| Total assets | $330 | $130 | $380 |
| **Liabilities and Stockholders' Equity** | | | |
| Current liabilities | | | |
| Accounts payable | $ 40 | $ 30 | $ 70 |
| Other current liabilities | 50 | 20 | 70 |
| Total current liabilities | 90 | 50 | 140 |
| Stockholders' equity | | | |
| Capital stock | 200 | 60 | 200 |
| Retained earnings | 40 | 20 | 40 |
| Total stockholders' equity | 240 | 80 | 240 |
| Total liabilities and stockholders' equity | $330 | $130 | $380 |

not in the consolidated balance sheet for Pop and Subsidiary. When preparing the balance sheet, we eliminate the Investment in Son account (Pop's books) and the stockholders' equity accounts (Son's books) because they are reciprocal—both representing the net assets of Son at January 1, 2016. We combine the nonreciprocal accounts of Pop and Sun and include them in the consolidated balance sheet of Pop Corporation and Subsidiary. Note that the consolidated balance sheet is not merely a summation of account balances of the affiliates. We eliminate reciprocal accounts in the process of consolidation and combine only nonreciprocal accounts. The capital stock that appears in a consolidated balance sheet is the capital stock of the parent, and the consolidated retained earnings are the retained earnings of the parent company.

## Parent Acquires 100 Percent of Subsidiary—With Goodwill

Exhibit 3-2 presented the consolidated balance sheet prepared for a parent company that acquired all the stock of Son Corporation at book value. If, instead, Pop acquires all of Son's stock for $100,000, there will be a $20,000 excess of investment cost over book value acquired ($100,000 investment cost less $80,000 stockholders' equity of Son). The $20,000 appears in the consolidated balance sheet at acquisition as an asset of $20,000. In the absence of evidence that identifiable net assets are undervalued, this asset is assumed to be goodwill. Exhibit 3-3 illustrates procedures for preparing a consolidated balance sheet for Pop Corporation, assuming that Pop pays $100,000 for the outstanding stock of Son.

We need only one workpaper entry to consolidate the balance sheets of Pop and Son at acquisition. Take a few minutes to review the format of the workpaper in Exhibit 3-3. The first two columns provide information from the separate balance sheets of Pop and Son. The third column records adjustments and eliminations, subdivided into debits and credits. The last column presents the totals that will appear in the consolidated balance sheet. We calculate amounts in the Consolidated Balance Sheet column by adding together amounts from the first two columns and then adding or subtracting the adjustments and eliminations, as appropriate. This basic workpaper format is used throughout the discussions of acquisitions and preparation of consolidated financial statements in this book. The elimination entry is reproduced in general journal form for convenient reference:

| | | | |
|---|---|---:|---:|
| a | Capital stock—Son ( − SE) | 60 | |
| | Retained earnings—Son ( − SE) | 20 | |
| | Goodwill ( + A) | 20 | |
| |     Investment in Son ( − A) | | 100 |

To eliminate reciprocal investment and equity accounts and to assign the excess of investment cost (fair value) over book value to goodwill.

Entries such as those shown in Exhibit 3-3 are only workpaper adjustments and eliminations and *are not recorded in the accounts of the parent or subsidiary corporations*. The entries will never be journalized or posted. Their only purpose is to facilitate completion of the workpapers to consolidate a parent and subsidiary at and for the period ended on a particular date. In this book, workpaper entries are shaded in orange to avoid confusing them with actual journal entries that are recorded in the accounts of the parent and subsidiary companies.

In future periods, the difference between the investment account balance and the subsidiary equity will decline *if, and only if, goodwill is written down due to impairment.*

LEARNING
OBJECTIVE **3.5**

## Parent Acquires 90 Percent of Subsidiary—With Goodwill

Assume that instead of acquiring all of Son's outstanding stock, Pop acquires 90 percent of it for $90,000. GAAP requires the acquisition method to record business combinations and subsequent issuance of consolidated financial statements. Essentially, the acquisition method uses the entity theory of consolidations. Under the acquisition method, all assets and liabilities of the subsidiary are reported using 100 percent of fair values at the combination date, based on the price paid by the parent for its controlling interest, even when the parent acquires less than a 100 percent interest. Thus, both the controlling and noncontrolling interests will be reported based on fair values at the acquisition date. GAAP provides guidance for measuring fair values (ASC 820-10). Fair values are not recalculated at future reporting dates, with two exceptions. Impairments of assets must be recorded, including goodwill impairments. In addition, financial assets and liabilities may be revalued under GAAP (ASC 825-10), but this revaluation is optional.

There are also two major exceptions to the initial recording of fair values for assets and liabilities. Deferred tax assets and liabilities and employee benefit amounts will be recorded at book values consistent with existing GAAP standards (presumably already recorded by the subsidiary). However, recognize that since the subsidiary is recorded at its fair value, differences in fair values and book values of these accounts are reflected in goodwill. They are not separately identified.

We can assume that the acquisition is an "arm's-length" transaction. Pop paid $90,000 for a 90 percent interest. This implies that the total fair value of Son is $100,000 ($90,000/90 percent). In this case, the excess of total fair value over book value of Son's net identifiable assets and liabilities is $20,000, and there is a noncontrolling interest of $10,000 (10 percent of the $100,000 fair value of Son's equity). The $20,000 excess of fair value over book value is goodwill. The workpapers in Exhibit 3-4 illustrate procedures for preparing the consolidated balance sheet for Pop and Son under the 90 percent ownership assumption.

Workpaper entry a eliminates the reciprocal accounts of Pop and Son and recognizes goodwill and the noncontrolling interest in Son at the date of acquisition:

| | | | |
|---|---|---:|---:|
| a | Capital stock—Son ( − SE) | 60 | |
| | Retained earnings—Son ( − SE) | 20 | |
| | Goodwill ( + A) | 20 | |
| |     Investment in Son ( − A) | | 90 |
| |     Noncontrolling interest ( + SE) | | 10 |

To eliminate reciprocal investment and equity balances, to assign the $20,000 excess of investment fair value ($100,000) over book value ($80,000) to goodwill, and to recognize a $10,000 noncontrolling interest in the net assets of Son ($100,000 equity × 10% noncontrolling interest).

**POP CORPORATION AND SUBSIDIARY CONSOLIDATED BALANCE SHEET WORKPAPERS JANUARY 1, 2016 (IN THOUSANDS)**

| | Pop | 100% Son | Adjustments and Eliminations Debits | Adjustments and Eliminations Credits | Consolidated Balance Sheet |
|---|---|---|---|---|---|
| **Assets** | | | | | |
| Cash | $ 20 | $ 20 | | | $ 40 |
| Other current assets | 90 | 30 | | | 120 |
| Plant assets | 150 | 90 | | | 240 |
| Accumulated depreciation | (30) | (10) | | | (40) |
| Investment in Son | 100 | | | a 100 | |
| Goodwill | | | a 20 | | 20 |
| Total assets | $330 | $130 | | | $380 |
| **Liabilities and Equity** | | | | | |
| Accounts payable | $ 40 | $ 30 | | | $ 70 |
| Other current liabilities | 50 | 20 | | | 70 |
| Capital stock—Pop | 200 | | | | 200 |
| Retained earnings—Pop | 40 | | | | 40 |
| Capital stock—Son | | 60 | a 60 | | |
| Retained earnings—Son | | 20 | a 20 | | |
| Total liabilities and stockholders' equity | $330 | $130 | 100 | 100 | $380 |

a. To eliminate reciprocal investment and equity accounts and to assign the excess of investment cost (fair value) over book value to goodwill.

## Noncontrolling Interest

We include all assets and liabilities of the subsidiary in the consolidated balance sheet and record the noncontrolling interest's share of subsidiary net assets based on fair values separately in stockholders' equity.

Workpapers provide the basis of preparing formal financial statements, and the question arises about how the $10,000 noncontrolling interest that appears in Exhibit 3-4 would be reported in a formal balance sheet. Historically, practice varied with respect to classification. The noncontrolling interest in subsidiaries was generally shown in a single amount in the liability section of the consolidated balance sheet, frequently under the heading of noncurrent liabilities. Conceptually, the classification of noncontrolling stockholder interests as liabilities was inconsistent because the interests of noncontrolling stockholders represent equity investments in the subsidiary net assets by stockholders outside the affiliation structure.

Current GAAP requires:

■ A noncontrolling interest in a subsidiary should be displayed and labeled in the consolidated balance sheet as a separate component of equity.

■ Income attributable to the noncontrolling interest is not an expense or a loss but a deduction from consolidated net income to compute income attributable to the controlling interest.

■ Both components of consolidated net income (net income attributable to noncontrolling interest and net income attributable to controlling interest) should be disclosed on the face of the consolidated income statement.

EXHIBIT 3-4

90 Percent Ownership,
Fair Value Greater Than
Book Value

## POP CORPORATION AND SUBSIDIARY CONSOLIDATED BALANCE SHEET WORKPAPERS JANUARY 1, 2016 (IN THOUSANDS)

| | Pop | 90% Son | Adjustments and Eliminations Debits | Adjustments and Eliminations Credits | Consolidated Balance Sheet |
|---|---|---|---|---|---|
| **Assets** | | | | | |
| Cash | $ 30 | $ 20 | | | $ 50 |
| Other current assets | 90 | 30 | | | 120 |
| Plant assets | 150 | 90 | | | 240 |
| Accumulated depreciation | (30) | (10) | | | (40) |
| Investment in Son | 90 | | | a 90 | |
| Goodwill | | | a 20 | | 20 |
| Total assets | $330 | $130 | | | $390 |
| **Liabilities and Equity** | | | | | |
| Accounts payable | $ 40 | $ 30 | | | $ 70 |
| Other current liabilities | 50 | 20 | | | 70 |
| Capital stock—Pop | 200 | | | | 200 |
| Retained earnings—Pop | 40 | | | | 40 |
| Capital stock—Son | | 60 | a 60 | | |
| Retained earnings—Son | | 20 | a 20 | | |
| | $330 | $130 | | | |
| Noncontrolling interest | | | | a 10 | 10 |
| Total liabilities and stockholders' equity | | | 100 | 100 | $390 |

a. To eliminate reciprocal investment and equity balances, assign the $20,000 excess of investment fair value ($100,000) over book value ($80,000) to goodwill, and recognize a $10,000 noncontrolling interest in the fair value of net assets of Son ($100,000 equity × 10% noncontrolling interest).

LEARNING OBJECTIVE **3.6**

## CONSOLIDATED BALANCE SHEETS AFTER ACQUISITION

The account balances of both parent and subsidiary change to reflect their separate operations after the parent–subsidiary relationship has been established. Subsequently, we make additional adjustments to eliminate other reciprocal balances. If a consolidated balance sheet is prepared between the date a subsidiary declares and the date it pays dividends, the parent's books will show a dividend receivable account that is the reciprocal of a dividends payable account on the books of the subsidiary. Such balances do not represent amounts receivable or payable outside the affiliated group; therefore, they must be reciprocals that we eliminate in preparing consolidated statements. We also eliminate other intercompany receivables and payables, such as accounts receivable and accounts payable, in preparing consolidated statements.

The balance sheets of Pop and Son Corporations at December 31, 2016, one year after acquisition, contain the following (in thousands):

| | Pop | Son |
|---|---|---|
| Cash | $ 54.8 | $30 |
| Dividends receivable | 18 | — |
| Other current assets | 82 | 56 |
| Plant assets | 150 | 90 |
| Accumulated depreciation | (40) | (16) |
| Investment in Son (90%) | 108 | — |
| Total assets | $ 372.8 | $160 |

|  | Pop | Son |
|---|---|---|
| Accounts payable | $ 60 | $30 |
| Dividends payable | — | 20 |
| Other current liabilities | 40 | 10 |
| Capital stock | 200 | 60 |
| Retained earnings | 72.8 | 40 |
| Total equities | $372.8 | $160 |

## Assumptions

1. Pop acquired a 90 percent interest in Son for $90,000 on January 1, 2016, when Son's stockholders' equity at book value was $80,000 (see Exhibit 3-4).

2. The accounts payable of Son include $10,000 owed to Pop.

3. During 2016 Son had income of $40,000 and declared $20,000 in dividends.

Exhibit 3-5 presents consolidated balance sheet workpapers reflecting this information. We determine the balance in the Investment in Son account at December 31, 2016, using the equity method of accounting. Calculations of the December 31, 2016, investment account balance are as follows:

| Original investment January 1, 2016 | $90,000 |
|---|---|
| Add: 90% of Son's $40,000 net income for 2016 | 36,000 |
| Deduct: 90% of Son's $20,000 dividends for 2016 | (18,000) |
| Investment account balance December 31, 2016 | $108,000 |

Even though the amounts involved are different, the *process* of consolidating balance sheets after acquisition is basically the same as at acquisition. In all cases, we eliminate the amount of the

---

**POP CORPORATION AND SUBSIDIARY CONSOLIDATED BALANCE SHEET WORKPAPERS DECEMBER 31, 2016 (IN THOUSANDS)**

|  | Pop | 90% Son | Adjustments and Eliminations Debits | Adjustments and Eliminations Credits | Consolidated Balance Sheet |
|---|---|---|---|---|---|
| **Assets** | | | | | |
| Cash | $ 54.8 | $ 30 | | | $ 84.8 |
| Dividends receivable | 18 | | | b 18 | |
| Other current assets | 82 | 56 | | c 10 | 128 |
| Plant assets | 150 | 90 | | | 240 |
| Accumulated depreciation | (40) | (16) | | | (56) |
| Investment in Son | 108 | | | a 108 | |
| Goodwill | | | a 20 | | 20 |
| Total assets | $372.8 | $ 160 | | | $416.8 |
| **Liabilities and Equity** | | | | | |
| Accounts payable | $ 60 | $ 30 | c 10 | | $ 80 |
| Dividends payable | | 20 | b 18 | | 2 |
| Other current liabilities | 40 | 10 | | | 50 |
| Capital stock—Pop | 200 | | | | 200 |
| Retained earnings—Pop | 72.8 | | | | 72.8 |
| Capital stock—Son | | 60 | a 60 | | |
| Retained earnings—Son | | 40 | a 40 | | |
| | $372.8 | $160 | | | |
| Noncontrolling interest | | | | a 12 | 12 |
| Total liabilities and stockholders' equity | | | 148 | 148 | $416.8 |

---

a. To eliminate reciprocal investment and equity balances, record goodwill, and enter the noncontrolling interest ($120,000 × 10%).

b. To eliminate reciprocal dividends receivable and payable amounts (90 percent of $20,000 dividends payable of Son).

c. To eliminate intercompany accounts receivable and accounts payable.

subsidiary investment account and the equity accounts of the subsidiary. We enter the excess of fair value over book value (goodwill in this illustration) in the workpapers during the process of eliminating reciprocal investment and equity balances. Goodwill does not appear on the books of the parent; we add it to the asset listing when preparing the workpapers. The noncontrolling interest is equal to the percentage of noncontrolling ownership times the fair value of the equity of the subsidiary at the balance sheet date. Consolidated retained earnings equal the parent company's retained earnings.

The workpaper entries necessary to consolidate the balance sheets of Pop and Son are reproduced in general journal form for convenient reference:

| | | | |
|---|---|---|---|
| a | Capital stock—Son (−SE) | 60 | |
| | Retained earnings—Son (−SE) | 40 | |
| | Goodwill (+A) | 20 | |
| | Investment in Son (−A) | | 108 |
| | Noncontrolling interest (+SE) | | 12 |
| | To eliminate reciprocal investment and equity balances, record goodwill, and enter the noncontrolling interest ($120,000 × 10%). | | |
| b | Dividends payable (−L) | 18 | |
| | Dividends receivable (−A) | | 18 |
| | To eliminate reciprocal dividends receivable and payable amounts (90% of $20,000 dividends payable of Son). | | |
| c | Accounts payable (−L) | 10 | |
| | Other current assets (−A) | | 10 |
| | To eliminate intercompany accounts receivable and accounts payable. | | |

## ASSIGNING EXCESS TO IDENTIFIABLE NET ASSETS AND GOODWILL

We assigned the excess of fair value over the book value in the Pop–Son illustration to goodwill. An underlying assumption of that assignment of the excess is that the book values and fair values of identifiable assets and liabilities are equal. When the evidence indicates that fair values exceed book values or book values exceed fair values, however, we assign the excess accordingly.

### Effect of Assignment on Consolidated Balance Sheet at Acquisition

The separate books of the affiliated companies do not record the fair value/book value differentials in acquisitions that create parent–subsidiary relationships. We use workpaper procedures to adjust subsidiary book values to reflect the fair value/book value differentials, and the adjusted amounts appear in the consolidated balance sheet. We determine the amount of the adjustment to individual assets and liabilities using the one-line consolidation approach presented in Chapter 2.

On December 31, 2016, Pam purchases 90 percent of Sun Corporation's outstanding voting common stock directly from Sun Corporation's stockholders for $5,200,000 cash plus 100,000 shares of Pam Corporation $10 par common stock with a market value of $5,000,000. Additional costs of combination are $200,000. Pam pays these additional costs in cash. Pam and Sun must continue to operate as parent company and subsidiary because 10 percent of Sun's shares are outstanding and held by noncontrolling stockholders. We expense the $200,000 costs in recording the investment.

Comparative book value and fair value information for Pam and Sun immediately before the acquisition on December 31, 2016, appear in Exhibit 3-6. Pam records the acquisition on its books with the following journal entries in thousands:

| | | |
|---|---|---|
| Investment in Sun (+A) | 10,200 | |
| Common stock (+SE) | | 1,000 |
| Additional paid-in capital (+SE) | | 4,000 |
| Cash (−A) | | 5,200 |
| To record acquisition of 90% of Sun Corporation's outstanding stock for $5,200,000 in cash and 100,000 shares of Pam common stock with a market value of $5,000,000. | | |
| Investment expense (E, −SE) | 200 | |
| Cash (−A) | | 200 |
| To record additional costs of combining with Sun. | | |

These are the only entries on Pam's books to record the combination. Sun records no entries because Pam acquired its 90 percent interest directly from Sun's stockholders. We do not use the balance sheet information given in Exhibit 3-6 in recording the acquisition on Pam's books; we use it in preparing the consolidated balance sheet for the combined entity immediately after the acquisition.

**RECORDING THE FAIR VALUE/BOOK VALUE DIFFERENTIAL**    We determine the adjustments necessary to combine the balance sheets of parent and subsidiary corporations by *assigning* the difference between fair value and book value to undervalued or overvalued identifiable assets and liabilities and any remainder to goodwill. The schedule in Exhibit 3-7 illustrates the adjustment necessary to consolidate the balance sheets of Pam and Sun at December 31, 2016.

| (in thousands) | Pam Corporation | | Sun Corporation | |
|---|---|---|---|---|
| | Per Books | Fair Values | Per Books | Fair Values |
| **Assets** | | | | |
| Cash | $ 6,600 | $ 6,600 | $ 200 | $ 200 |
| Receivables—net | 700 | 700 | 300 | 300 |
| Inventories | 900 | 1,200 | 500 | 600 |
| Other current assets | 600 | 800 | 400 | 400 |
| Land | 1,200 | 11,200 | 600 | 800 |
| Buildings—net | 8,000 | 15,000 | 4,000 | 5,000 |
| Equipment—net | 7,000 | 9,000 | 2,000 | 1,700 |
| Total assets | $25,000 | $44,500 | $8,000 | $9,000 |
| **Liabilities and Equity** | | | | |
| Accounts payable | $ 2,000 | $ 2,000 | $ 700 | $ 700 |
| Notes payable | 3,700 | 3,500 | 1,400 | 1,300 |
| Common stock, $10 par | 10,000 | | 4,000 | |
| Additional paid-in capital | 5,000 | | 1,000 | |
| Retained earnings | 4,300 | | 900 | |
| Total liabilities and stockholders' equity | $25,000 | | $8,000 | |

**EXHIBIT 3-6**

**Preacquisition Book and Fair Value Balance Sheets**

**PAM CORPORATION AND ITS 90%-OWNED SUBSIDIARY, SUN CORPORATION (IN THOUSANDS)**

| | | |
|---|---|---|
| Fair value (purchase price) of 90% interest acquired | | $ 10,200 |
| Implied fair value of Sun ($10,200/90%) | | $ 11,333 |
| Book value of Sun's net assets | | (5,900) |
| Total excess of fair value over book value | | $ 5,433 |

**Allocation to Identifiable Assets and Liabilities**

| | Fair Value | Book Value | Excess Allocated |
|---|---|---|---|
| Inventories | $ 600 | $ 500 | $ 100 |
| Land | 800 | 600 | 200 |
| Buildings | 5,000 | 4,000 | 1,000 |
| Equipment | 1,700 | 2,000 | (300) |
| Notes payable | 1,300 | 1,400 | 100 |
| Total allocated to identifiable net assets | | | $1,100 |
| Remainder allocated to goodwill | | | 4,333 |
| Total excess of fair value over book value | | | $5,433 |

**EXHIBIT 3-7**

**Schedule for Allocating the Excess of Investment Fair Value over the Book Value**

Although we do not use the book values of assets and liabilities in determining fair values for individual assets and liabilities, we use book values in the mechanical process of combining the balance sheets of parent and subsidiary.

The underlying book value of Sun Corporation is $5,900,000 (as shown in Exhibit 3-7), and the excess of fair value over book value is $5,433,000. We assign this excess first to the identifiable assets and liabilities and then assign the remainder to goodwill. The amounts assigned to identifiable assets and liabilities are for 100 percent of the fair value and book value difference. The other 10 percent interest in Sun's identifiable net assets relates to the interests of noncontrolling stockholders adjusted to their fair values on the basis of the price paid by Pam for its 90 percent interest.[6]

**WORKPAPER PROCEDURES TO ENTER ALLOCATIONS IN CONSOLIDATED BALANCE SHEET**  We incorporate the excess fair value over book value as determined in Exhibit 3-7 into a consolidated balance sheet through workpaper procedures. Exhibit 3-8 illustrates these procedures for Pam and Sun as of the date of acquisition.

| EXHIBIT 3-8 |
| --- |
| 90 Percent Ownership, Excess Allocated to Identifiable Net Assets and Goodwill |

**PAM CORPORATION AND SUBSIDIARY CONSOLIDATED BALANCE SHEET WORKPAPERS AFTER COMBINATION ON DECEMBER 31, 2016 (IN THOUSANDS)**

| | Pam | 90% Sun | Adjustments and Eliminations Debits | Credits | Consolidated Balance Sheet |
| --- | --- | --- | --- | --- | --- |
| **Assets** | | | | | |
| Cash | $ 1,200 | $ 200 | | | $ 1,400 |
| Receivables—net | 700 | 300 | | | 1,000 |
| Inventories | 900 | 500 | b 100 | | 1,500 |
| Other current assets | 600 | 400 | | | 1,000 |
| Land | 1,200 | 600 | b 200 | | 2,000 |
| Buildings—net | 8,000 | 4,000 | b 1,000 | | 13,000 |
| Equipment—net | 7,000 | 2,000 | | b 300 | 8,700 |
| Investment in Sun | 10,200 | | | a 10,200 | |
| Goodwill | | | b 4,333 | | 4,333 |
| Unamortized excess | | | a 5,433 | b 5,433 | |
| Total assets | $29,800 | $8,000 | | | $32,933 |
| **Liabilities and Equity** Accounts payable | $ 2,000 | $ 700 | | | $ 2,700 |
| Notes payable | 3,700 | 1,400 | b 100 | | 5,000 |
| Common stock—Pam | 11,000 | | | | 11,000 |
| Additional paid-in capital—Pam | 9,000 | | | | 9,000 |
| Retained earnings—Pam | 4,100 | | | | 4,100 |
| Common stock—Sun | | 4,000 | a 4,000 | | |
| Additional paid-in capital—Sun | | 1,000 | a 1,000 | | |
| Retained earnings—Sun | | 900 | a 900 | | |
| | $29,800 | $8,000 | | | |
| Noncontrolling interest | | | | a 1,133 | 1,133 |
| Total liabilities and stockholders' equity | | | 17,066 | 17,066 | $32,933 |

a. To eliminate reciprocal subsidiary investment and equity balances, establish noncontrolling interest, and enter the unamortized excess.
b. To allocate the unamortized excess to identifiable assets, liabilities, and goodwill.

---

[6]Revaluation of all assets and liabilities of a subsidiary on the basis of the price paid by the parent for its controlling interest is supported by the entity theory of consolidation. Entity theory is covered in more detail in Chapter 11.

The consolidated balance sheet workpapers show two workpaper entries for the consolidation. Entry a in general journal form follows:

| a | Unamortized excess (+ A) | 5,433 | |
|---|---|---|---|
| | Common stock, $10 par—Sun (− SE) | 4,000 | |
| | Additional paid-in capital—Sun (− SE) | 1,000 | |
| | Retained earnings—Sun (− SE) | 900 | |
| | Investment in Sun (− A) | | 10,200 |
| | Noncontrolling interest—10% (+ SE) | | 1,133 |

This workpaper entry eliminates reciprocal investment in Sun and stockholders' equity amounts of Sun, establishes the noncontrolling interest in Sun, and enters the total unamortized excess from Exhibit 3-7.

A second workpaper entry assigns the unamortized excess to individual assets and liabilities and to goodwill:

| b | Inventories (+ A) | 100 | |
|---|---|---|---|
| | Land (+ A) | 200 | |
| | Buildings—net (+ A) | 1,000 | |
| | Goodwill (+ A) | 4,333 | |
| | Notes payable (− L) | 100 | |
| | Equipment—net (− A) | | 300 |
| | Unamortized excess (− A) | | 5,433 |

We add a step and employ an unamortized excess account to simplify workpaper entries when assigning the fair value/book value differential to numerous assets and liabilities. We skip this step when assigning the total excess to goodwill, as in Exhibit 3-4 and Exhibit 3-5. Workpaper entries a and b enter equal debits and credits equal to the unamortized excess, so the account has no final effect on the consolidated balance sheet.

We combine debit and credit workpaper amounts with the line items shown in the separate statements of Pam and Sun to produce the amounts shown in the Consolidated Balance Sheet column. Sun is a partially owned subsidiary, but we record its assets and liabilities in the consolidated balance sheet at 100 percent of fair values.

## Effect of Amortization on Consolidated Balance Sheet After Acquisition

The effect of amortizing the $5,433,000 excess on the December 31, 2017, consolidated balance sheet is based on the following assumptions about the operations of Pam and Sun during 2017 and about the relevant amortization periods of the assets and liabilities to which we allocate the excess in Exhibit 3-7. These assumptions are as follows:

LEARNING OBJECTIVE **3.7**

**Income for 2017 (in thousands)**

| | |
|---|---|
| Sun's net income | $ 800 |
| Pam's income excluding income from Sun | 2,523.5 |

**Dividends Paid in 2017**

| | |
|---|---|
| Sun | $ 300 |
| Pam | 1,500 |

**Amortization of Excess**

Undervalued inventories—sold in 2017
Undervalued land—still held by Sun; no amortization
Undervalued buildings—useful life 40 years from January 1, 2017
Overvalued equipment—useful life 5 years from January 1, 2017
Overvalued notes payable—retired in 2017
Goodwill—no amortization

At December 31, 2017, Pam's Investment in Sun account has a balance of $10,501,500, consisting of the original $10,200,000 cost, increased by $571,500 investment income from Sun and decreased by $270,000 dividends received from Sun. Pam's income from Sun for 2017 is calculated under a one-line consolidation as follows (in thousands):

| | | |
|---|---|---|
| 90% of Sun's reported net income ($800) | | $720 |
| Add: Pam's 90% share of amortization on overvalued equipment (($300,000/5 years) × 90%) | | 54 |
| Deduct: Amortization of Pam's share of excess allocated to: | | |
| Inventories (sold in 2017) ($100,000 × 90%) | $90 | |
| Land | — | |
| Buildings (($1,000,000/40 years) × 90%) | 22.5 | |
| Notes payable (retired in 2017) ($100,000 × 90%) | 90 | (202.5) |
| Income from Sun | | $571.5 |

Alternatively, we can calculate income from Sun as 90 percent of Sun's "adjusted" net income:

| | | |
|---|---|---|
| Sun's net income | | $800 |
| Add: Amortization of overvalued equipment ($300,000/5 years) | | 60 |
| Deduct: Amortization of excess allocated to: | | |
| Inventories (sold in 2017) | $100 | |
| Land | — | |
| Buildings ($1,000,000/40 years) | 25 | |
| Notes payable (retired in 2017) | 100 | (225) |
| Sun's adjusted net income | | $635 |
| 90% of Sun's adjusted net income | | $571.5 |

We can also verify the noncontrolling interest at December 31, 2017, as follows:

| | |
|---|---|
| Noncontrolling interest at December 31, 2016 | $1,133 |
| Add: 10% of Sun's 2017 net income | 80 |
| Less: 10% of 2017 amortization of excess fair value | (16.5) |
| Less: 10% of 2017 dividends | (30) |
| Noncontrolling interest at December 31, 2017 | $1,166.5 |

Pam's net income for 2017 is $3,095,000, consisting of income from its own operations of $2,523,500, plus $571,500 income from Sun. Sun's stockholders equity increased $500,000 during 2017, from $5,900,000 to $6,400,000. Pam's retained earnings increased $1,795,000, from $4,100,000 at December 31, 2016, to $5,895,000 at December 31, 2017. Pam's retained earnings decreased from $4,300,000 to $4,100,000 at the acquisition date due to the expensing of the costs of the combination. We reflect this information in a consolidated balance sheet workpaper for Pam and Subsidiary at December 31, 2017, in Exhibit 3-9.

We reproduce the workpaper entries as follows:

| | | | |
|---|---|---|---|
| a | Common stock—Sun (−SE) | 4,000 | |
| | Additional paid-in capital—Sun (−SE) | 1,000 | |
| | Retained earnings—Sun (−SE) | 1,400 | |
| | Unamortized excess (+A) | 5,268 | |
| | Investment in Sun (−A) | | 10,501.5 |
| | Noncontrolling interest (+SE) | | 1,166.5 |
| | To eliminate reciprocal subsidiary investment and equity accounts, establish noncontrolling interest, and enter the unamortized excess. | | |
| b | Land (+A) | 200 | |
| | Buildings—net (+A) | 975 | |
| | Goodwill (+A) | 4,333 | |
| | Equipment—net (−A) | | 240 |
| | Unamortized excess (−A) | | 5,268 |
| | To assign the unamortized excess to identifiable assets and goodwill. | | |

**EXHIBIT 3-9**

90 Percent Ownership, Unamortized Excess One Year after Acquisition

## PAM CORPORATION AND SUBSIDIARY CONSOLIDATED BALANCE SHEET WORKPAPERS ON DECEMBER 31, 2017 (IN THOUSANDS)

| | Pam | 90% Sun | Debits | Credits | Consolidated Balance Sheet |
|---|---|---|---|---|---|
| | | | Adjustments and Eliminations | | |
| **Assets** | | | | | |
| Cash | $ 253.5 | $ 100 | | | $ 353.5 |
| Receivables—net | 540 | 200 | | | 740 |
| Inventories | 1,300 | 600 | | | 1,900 |
| Other current assets | 800 | 500 | | | 1,300 |
| Land | 1,200 | 600 | b 200 | | 2,000 |
| Buildings—net | 9,500 | 3,800 | b 975 | | 14,275 |
| Equipment—net | 8,000 | 1,800 | | b 240 | 9,560 |
| Investment in Sun | 10,501.5 | | | a 10,501.5 | |
| Goodwill | | | b 4,333 | | 4,333 |
| Unamortized excess | | | a 5,268 | b 5,268 | |
| Total assets | $32,095 | $7,600 | | | $34,461.5 |
| **Liabilities and Equity** | | | | | |
| Accounts payable | $ 2,300 | $1,200 | | | $ 3,500 |
| Notes payable | 4,000 | | | | 4,000 |
| Common stock—Pam | 11,000 | | | | 11,000 |
| Additional paid-in capital—Pam | 8,900 | | | | 8,900 |
| Retained earnings—Pam | 5,895 | | | | 5,895 |
| Common stock—Sun | | 4,000 | a 4,000 | | |
| Additional paid-in capital—Sun | | 1,000 | a 1,000 | | |
| Retained earnings—Sun | | 1,400 | a 1,400 | | |
| | $32,095 | $7,600 | | | |
| Noncontrolling Interest | | | | a 1,166.5 | 1,166.5 |
| Total liabilities and stockholders' equity | | | 17,176 | 17,176 | $34,461.5 |

a. To eliminate reciprocal subsidiary investment and equity balances, establish noncontrolling interest, and enter the unamortized excess.
b. To allocate the unamortized excess to identifiable assets and goodwill.

The differences in the adjustments and eliminations in Exhibit 3-8 and Exhibit 3-9 result from changes that occurred between December 31, 2016, acquisition, and December 31, 2017, when the investment had been held for one year. The following schedule provides the basis for the workpaper entries that appear in Exhibit 3-9 (in thousands).

| | Unamortized Excess December 31, 2016 | Amortization | Unamortized Excess December 31, 2017 |
|---|---|---|---|
| Inventories | $ 100 | $100 | $ — |
| Land | 200 | — | 200 |
| Buildings—net | 1,000 | 25 | 975 |
| Equipment—net | (300) | (60) | (240)* |
| Notes payable | 100 | 100 | — |
| Goodwill | 4,333 | — | 4,333 |
| | $5,433 | $165 | $5,268 |

*Excess book value over fair value.

The following summarizes the transactions recorded by Pam in its Investment in Sun account (in thousands):

| | |
|---|---:|
| Initial cost—December 31, 2016 | $10,200 |
| 90% of Sun's 2017 net income | 720 |
| 90% of Sun's 2017 dividends | (270) |
| Amortization of the fair value/book value differential (90% × 165) | (148.5) |
| Balance—December 31, 2017 | $10,501.5 |

The consolidated balance sheet workpaper adjustments in Exhibit 3-9 show elimination of reciprocal stockholders' equity and Investment in Sun balances. This elimination, entry a, involves debits to Sun's stockholders' equity accounts of $6,400, a credit to the noncontrolling interest in Sun of $1,166.5, and a credit to the Investment in Sun account of $10,501.5. The difference between these debits and credits totals $5,268, representing the unamortized excess of investment fair value over book value acquired on December 31, 2017, and we enter it in the workpapers as unamortized excess.

The undervalued inventory items and the overvalued notes payable on Sun's books at December 31, 2016, were fully amortized in 2017 (the inventory was sold and the notes payable were retired); therefore, these items do not require balance sheet adjustments at December 31, 2017. We enter the remaining items—land, $200; buildings, $975; equipment, $240 (overvaluation); and goodwill, $4,333 (which account for the $5,268 unamortized excess)—in the consolidated balance sheet workpapers through workpaper entry b, which assigns the unamortized excess as of the balance sheet date. The workpaper entries shown in Exhibit 3-9 are combination adjustment and elimination entries, because we eliminate the Investment in Sun and stockholders' equity accounts of Sun, reclassify the noncontrolling interest into a single amount representing 10 percent of the fair value of Sun's stockholders' equity, and adjust the asset accounts.

## CONSOLIDATED INCOME STATEMENT

LEARNING
OBJECTIVE **3.8**

Exhibit 3-10 presents comparative separate-company and consolidated income and retained earnings statements for Pam Corporation and Subsidiary. These statements reflect the previous assumptions and amounts that were used in preparing the consolidated balance sheet workpapers for Pam and Sun. Detailed revenue and expense items have been added to illustrate the consolidated income statement, but all assumptions and amounts are completely compatible with those already introduced. Adjustments and elimination entries have not been included in the illustration. These entries are covered extensively in Chapter 4.

*The difference between a consolidated income statement and an unconsolidated income statement of the parent company lies in the detail presented.* You can see this in Exhibit 3-10 by comparing the separate income statement of Pam with the consolidated income statement of Pam and Subsidiary. Under GAAP (ASC 810-10), consolidated net income is the net income of the consolidated group. The consolidated income statement must clearly separate income attributable to the controlling and noncontrolling interests. Throughout the remainder of this text, we label these as the controlling and noncontrolling interest shares of net income

Pam's separate income statement shows the revenues and expenses from Pam's own operations plus its investment income from Sun.[4] By contrast, the consolidated income statement column shows the revenues and expenses of both Sun and Pam but does not show the investment income from Sun. The $571,500 investment income is excluded because the consolidated income statement includes the detailed revenues ($2,200,000), expenses ($1,400,000), net amortization of the excess ($165,000), and the noncontrolling interest ($63,500) that account for the investment income.

We reflect the net amortization in the consolidated income statement by increasing cost of goods sold for the $100,000 undervalued inventories that were sold in 2017, increasing depreciation expense on undervalued buildings for the $25,000 amortization on the excess allocated to buildings, decreasing depreciation expense on equipment for the $60,000 amortization of the excess allocated to overvalued equipment, and increasing interest expense for the $100,000 allocated to overvalued notes payable that were retired in 2017.

---

[7]A parent's income from subsidiary investments is referred to as income from subsidiary, equity in subsidiary earnings, investment income from subsidiary, or other descriptive captions.

| PAM AND SUN CORPORATIONS SEPARATE COMPANY AND CONSOLIDATED STATEMENTS OF INCOME AND RETAINED EARNINGS FOR THE YEAR ENDED DECEMBER 31, 2017 (IN THOUSANDS) | Separate Company | | Consolidated |
|---|---|---|---|
| | Pam | Sun | |
| Sales | $9,523.5 | $2,200 | $11,723.5 |
| Investment income from Sun | 571.5 | | |
| Total revenue | 10,095 | 2,200 | 11,723.5 |
| Less: Operating expenses Cost of sales | 4,000 | 700 | 4,800 |
| Depreciation expense—buildings | 200 | 80 | 305 |
| Depreciation expense—equipment | 700 | 360 | 1,000 |
| Other expenses | 1,800 | 120 | 1,920 |
| Total operating expense | 6,700 | 1,260 | 8,025 |
| Operating income | 3,395 | 940 | 3,698.5 |
| Nonoperating item: Interest expense | 300 | 140 | 540 |
| **Net income** | **$3,095** | **$ 800** | |
| Consolidated net income | | | 3,158.5 |
| Less: Noncontrolling interest share | | | 63.5 |
| **Controlling interest share** | | | **$ 3,095** |
| Retained earnings December 31, 2016 | 4,300 | 900 | 4,300 |
| | 7,395 | 1,700 | 7,395 |
| Deduct: Dividends | 1,500 | 300 | 1,500 |
| Retained earnings December 31, 2017 | $5,895 | $1,400 | $ 5,895 |

**EXHIBIT 3-10**

Separate Company and Consolidated Income and Retained Earnings Statements

Consolidated income statements, like consolidated balance sheets, are more than summations of the income accounts of the affiliates. A summation of all income statement items for Pam and Sun would result in a combined income figure of $3,895,000, whereas consolidated net income is only $3,158,500. The $736,500 difference between these two amounts lies in the investment income of $571,500 and the $165,000 amortization.

Note that consolidated net income represents income to the stockholders of the consolidated group. Income of noncontrolling stockholders is a deduction in the determination of income of the controlling shareholders.

If the parent sells merchandise to a subsidiary, or vice versa, there will be intercompany purchases and sales on the separate books of the parent and the subsidiary. Intercompany purchases and sales balances are reciprocals that must be eliminated in preparing consolidated income statements because they do not represent purchases and sales to parties outside the consolidated entity. Intercompany inventory transactions are discussed in greater detail in Chapter 5. Adjustments for intercompany sales and purchases reduce revenue (sales) and expenses (cost of goods sold) by the same amount and therefore have no effect on consolidated net income. Reciprocal rent income and expense amounts are likewise eliminated without affecting consolidated net income.

Observe that Pam's separate retained earnings are identical to consolidated retained earnings. As expected, the $5,895,000 ending consolidated retained earnings in Exhibit 3-10 is the same amount that appears in the consolidated balance sheet for Pam and Subsidiary at December 31, 2017 (see Exhibit 3-9).

## PUSH-DOWN ACCOUNTING

LEARNING OBJECTIVE **3.9**

In the Pam and Sun illustration, we recorded the investment on the books of Pam at cost and assign the purchase price to identifiable assets and liabilities and goodwill through workpaper adjusting entries. In some instances, the assignment of the purchase price may be recorded in the subsidiary accounts—in other words, pushed down to the subsidiary records. **Push-down accounting** is the process of recording the effects of the purchase price assignment directly on the books of the subsidiary. Push-down accounting affects the books of the subsidiary and separate subsidiary financial statements. It does not alter consolidated financial statements and, in fact, simplifies the consolidation process. Current GAAP (ASC 805-25) provides an acquiree the option to apply push-down accounting. The decision to apply push-down accounting is irrevocable. The SEC requires push-down accounting for SEC filings when a subsidiary is substantially wholly owned (approximately 90 percent) with no publicly held debt or preferred stock outstanding.

Pop Corporation gives 5,000 shares of Pop $10 par common stock and $100,000 cash for all the capital stock of Son Company, a closely held company, on January 3, 2016. At this time, Pop's stock is quoted on a national exchange at $55 a share. We summarize Son's balance sheet and fair value information on January 3 as follows (in thousands):

|  | Book Value | Fair Value |
|---|---|---|
| Cash | $ 30 | $ 30 |
| Accounts receivable—net | 90 | 90 |
| Inventories | 130 | 150 |
| Land | 30 | 70 |
| Buildings—net | 150 | 130 |
| Equipment—net | 80 | 120 |
| Total assets | $510 | $590 |
| Current liabilities | $100 | $100 |
| Long-term debt | 150 | 150 |
| Capital stock, $10 par | 150 | |
| Retained earnings | 110 | |
| Total liabilities and stockholders' equity | $510 | |

Under push-down accounting, Pop records its investment in Son in the usual manner (in thousands):

| | | |
|---|---|---|
| Investment in Son (+A) | 375 | |
| Cash (−A) | | 100 |
| Capital stock, $10 par (+SE) | | 50 |
| Additional paid-in capital (+SE) | | 225 |

To record acquisition of Son Company.

An entry must also be made on Son's books on January 3 to record the new asset bases, including goodwill, in its accounts. Because Son is considered similar to a new entity, it also has to reclassify retained earnings. Son makes the following entry to record the push-down values (in thousands):

| | | |
|---|---|---|
| Inventories (+A) | 20 | |
| Land (+A) | 40 | |
| Equipment—net (+A) | 40 | |
| Goodwill (+A) | 35 | |
| Retained earnings (−SE) | 110 | |
| Building—net (−A) | | 20 |
| Push-down capital (+SE) | | 225 |

Son records this entry on its separate accounting records when using push-down accounting.

A separate balance sheet prepared for Son Company immediately after the combination on January 3 includes the following accounts and amounts (in thousands):

| | |
|---|---|
| Cash | $ 30 |
| Accounts receivable—net | 90 |
| Inventories | 150 |
| Land | 70 |
| Buildings—net | 130 |
| Equipment—net | 120 |
| Goodwill | 35 |
| Total assets | $625 |
| Current liabilities | $100 |
| Long-term debt | 150 |
| Capital stock, $10 par | 150 |
| Push-down capital | 225 |
| Total liabilities and stockholders' equity | $625 |

In consolidating the balance sheets of Pop and Son at January 3, 2016, after the push-down entries are made on Son's books, we eliminate the investment in Son account on Pop's books against Son's capital stock and push-down capital and combine the other accounts.

## PREPARING A CONSOLIDATED BALANCE SHEET WORKSHEET

LEARNING OBJECTIVE **3.10**

In this section you will learn how to set up a worksheet to prepare a consolidated balance sheet. Refer to Exhibit 3-11. We have two columns to record the balance sheet information for a parent company and (in our example) a 90 percent–owned subsidiary company. The numbers in these two columns are simply copied from the individual-company balance sheets. We include two columns to record the debits and credits for consolidation adjustments and eliminations. The final column provides calculations of the correct consolidated balance sheet totals.

Exhibit 3-11 shows spreadsheet formulae used in preparing the worksheet. Notice that most of these can be input using the COPY command *available in the spreadsheet software*. In the first two columns, total assets and total equities are simple summations of the relevant balances. The adjustments and eliminations columns each contain a single summation formula for the column totals. This is useful in verifying the equality of debits and credits—that in other words, you have not made any errors in posting your consolidation entries.

There are lots of formulae in the consolidated balance sheet column, but again most of these can be entered with the COPY command. Let's look at the formula for Cash (=B7+C7+D7−E7). We simply sum parent-company cash plus subsidiary-company cash and then make any needed adjustments and eliminations. Notice that cash has a normal debit balance, so we add the debit adjustments (+D7) and subtract credits (−E7) to arrive at the consolidated total. We can copy our formula for all accounts having normal debit balances (i.e., all assets).

Let's review the formula for accounts payable (=B15+C15−D15+E15). We sum parent-company plus subsidiary-company accounts payable and then make adjustments and eliminations. Notice that accounts payable has a normal credit balance, so we subtract debit adjustments (−D15)

---

**EXHIBIT 3-11**

Worksheet for Consolidated Balance Sheet

### PARENT CORPORATION AND SUBSIDIARY CONSOLIDATED BALANCE SHEET WORKPAPER DECEMBER 31, 2016

| (in thousands) | Parent | Subsidiary | Adjustments and Eliminations Debits | Credits | Consolidated Balance Sheet |
|---|---|---|---|---|---|
| Cash | 420 | 200 | | | =B7+C7+D7−E7 |
| Receivables—net | 500 | 1,300 | | | =B8+C8+D8−E8 |
| Inventories | 3,500 | 500 | | | =B9+C9+D9−E9 |
| Land | 1,500 | 2,000 | | | =B10+C10+D10−E10 |
| Equipment—net | 6,000 | 1,000 | | | =B11+C11+D11−E11 |
| Investment in Subsidiary | 4,590 | | | | =B12+C12+D12−E12 |
| | | | | | =B13+C13+D13−E13 |
| Total assets | =SUM(B7:B13) | =SUM(C7:C13) | | | =SUM(F7:F13) |
| Accounts payable | 4,100 | 800 | | | =B15+C15−D15+E15 |
| Dividends payable | 600 | 100 | | | =B16+C16−D16+E16 |
| Capital stock | 10,000 | 3,000 | | | =B17+C17−D17+E17 |
| Retained earnings | 1,810 | 1,100 | | | =B18+C18−D18+E18 |
| Total equities | =SUM(B15:B18) | =SUM(C15:C18) | | | |
| | | | | | =SUM(F15:F21) |
| | | | =SUM(D7:D22) | =SUM(E7:E22) | |

and add credits (+E15) to arrive at the consolidated total. We can copy our formula for all accounts having normal credit balances (i.e., all liabilities and equities).

We will discuss the completion of the worksheet by working through a sample problem. Separate company balance sheets for Parent Corporation and Subsidiary Company at December 31, 2016, are summarized as follows (in thousands):

|  | Parent Corporation | Subsidiary Company |
|---|---|---|
| Cash | $ 420 | $ 200 |
| Receivables—net | 500 | 1,300 |
| Inventories | 3,500 | 500 |
| Land | 1,500 | 2,000 |
| Equipment—net | 6,000 | 1,000 |
| Investment in Subsidiary | 4,590 | |
| Total assets | $16,510 | $5,000 |
| Accounts payable | $ 4,100 | $ 800 |
| Dividends payable | 600 | 100 |
| Capital stock | 10,000 | 3,000 |
| Retained earnings | 1,810 | 1,100 |
| Total equities | $16,510 | $5,000 |

Parent Corporation acquired 90 percent of the outstanding voting shares of Subsidiary Company for $4,500,000 on January 1, 2016, when Subsidiary's stockholders' equity was $4,000,000. All of the assets and liabilities of Subsidiary were recorded at their fair values (equal to book values) when Parent acquired its 90 percent interest. During 2016, Subsidiary reported net income of $200,000 and declared a dividend of $100,000. The dividend remained unpaid on December 31. Because the fair value of Parent's 90 percent interest is $4,500,000, the implied total fair value of the subsidiary is $5,000,000 on the acquisition date. Because subsidiary book value equals $4,000,000, goodwill must be $1,000,000.

We enter the data into our worksheet in Exhibit 3-11. We record balance sheet amounts picked up from the parent and the subsidiary. Total assets and total equities are simple summation functions. Next, we will review the required consolidation adjustments and eliminations. We provide a separate Exhibit 3-12 to show the final worksheet, after posting the adjustments and eliminations. This is simply Exhibit 3-11 updated to reflect the entries that follow. Notice that we have added some new accounts. We create noncontrolling interest and goodwill and copy the relevant formulae. The first workpaper entry in Exhibit 3-12 is the following:

| a | Capital stock (− SE) | 3,000 | |
|---|---|---|---|
| | Retained earnings (− SE) | 1,100 | |
| | Goodwill (+ A) | 1,000 | |
| | Investment in Subsidiary (− A) | | 4,590 |
| | Noncontrolling interest (+ SE) | | 510 |

To enter goodwill and the noncontrolling interest and to eliminate subsidiary capital accounts and the parent-company investment account.

Here is a journal entry for workpaper entry b for Exhibit 3-12:

| b | Dividends payable (− L) | 90 | |
|---|---|---|---|
| | Receivables—net (− A) | | 90 |

To eliminate the intercompany receivable and payable for dividends.

Our spreadsheet formulae compute the consolidated totals for us in the final column, completing the worksheet. Practice creating the spreadsheet for a few problems to be certain you understand the mechanics. However, you will not need to create your own spreadsheet for all problem assignments. We eliminate the drudgery, and allow you to focus on learning the concepts, by providing spreadsheet templates for many assignments on the *Advanced Accounting* Web site. The templates include the data for the parent and subsidiary companies and the formulae for calculating the consolidated balances.

**EXHIBIT 3-12**

Final Worksheet

## PARENT CORPORATION AND SUBSIDIARY CONSOLIDATED BALANCE SHEET WORKPAPER
## DECEMBER 31, 2016

| (in thousands) | Parent | Subsidiary | Adjustments and Eliminations Debits | Credits | Consolidated Balance Sheet |
|---|---|---|---|---|---|
| Cash | 420 | 200 | | | 620 |
| Receivables—net | 500 | 1,300 | | b 90 | 1,710 |
| Inventories | 3,500 | 500 | | | 4,000 |
| Land | 1,500 | 2,000 | | | 3,500 |
| Equipment—net | 6,000 | 1,000 | | | 7,000 |
| Investment in Subsidiary | 4,590 | | | a 4,590 | 0 |
| Goodwill | | | a 1,000 | | 1,000 |
| Total assets | 16,510 | 5,000 | | | 17,830 |
| Accounts payable | 4,100 | 800 | | | 4,900 |
| Dividends payable | 600 | 100 | b   90 | | 610 |
| Capital stock | 10,000 | 3,000 | a 3,000 | | 10,000 |
| Retained earnings | 1,810 | 1,100 | a 1,100 | | 1,810 |
| Total equities | 16,510 | 5,000 | | | |
| Noncontrolling interest | | | | a 510 | 510 |
| | | | | | 17,830 |
| | | | 5,190 | 5,190 | |

## SUMMARY

GAAP usually requires consolidated financial statements for the fair presentation of financial position and the results of operations of a parent company and its subsidiaries. Consolidated financial statements are not merely summations of parent-company and subsidiary financial statement items. Consolidated statements eliminate reciprocal amounts and combine and include only nonreciprocal amounts. We eliminate the investment in subsidiary and the subsidiary stockholders' equity accounts in the preparation of consolidated financial statements because they are reciprocal, both representing the net assets of the subsidiary. Sales and borrowing transactions between parent and subsidiaries also give rise to reciprocal amounts that we eliminate in the consolidating process.

The stockholders' equity amounts that appear in the consolidated balance sheet are those of the parent company, except for the equity of noncontrolling stockholders, which we report as a separate item within consolidated stockholders' equity. Consolidated net income is a measurement of income to the stockholders of the consolidated group. Incomes accruing to the benefit of controlling and noncontrolling stockholders are components of consolidated net income. Parent-company net income and retained earnings are equal to the controlling share of net income and consolidated retained earnings, respectively.

## QUESTIONS

**1.** When does a corporation become a subsidiary of another corporation?

**2.** In allocating the excess of investment fair value over book value of a subsidiary, are the amounts assigned to identifiable assets and liabilities (land and notes payable, for example) recorded separately in the accounts of the parent? Explain.

**3.** If the fair value of a subsidiary's land was $100,000 and its book value was $90,000 when the parent acquired its 100 percent interest for cash, at what amount would the land be included in the consolidated balance sheet immediately after the acquisition? Would your answer be different if the parent had acquired an 80 percent interest?

4. Define or explain the terms *parent company, subsidiary company, affiliates,* and *associates.*

5. What is a noncontrolling interest?

6. Describe the circumstances under which the accounts of a subsidiary would not be included in the consolidated financial statements.

7. Who are the primary users for which consolidated financial statements are intended?

8. What amount of capital stock is reported in a consolidated balance sheet?

9. In what general ledger would you expect to find the account "goodwill from consolidation"?

10. How should the parent's investment in subsidiary account be classified in a consolidated balance sheet? In the parent's separate balance sheet?

11. Name some reciprocal accounts that might be found in the separate records of a parent and its subsidiaries.

12. Why are reciprocal amounts eliminated in preparing consolidated financial statements?

13. How does the stockholders' equity of the parent that uses the equity method of accounting differ from the consolidated stockholders' equity of the parent and its subsidiaries?

14. Is there a difference in the amounts reported in the statement of retained earnings of a parent that uses the equity method of accounting and the amounts that appear in the consolidated retained earnings statement?

15. Is noncontrolling interest share an expense? Explain.

16. Describe how total noncontrolling interest at the end of an accounting period is determined.

17. What special procedures are required to consolidate the statements of a parent that reports on a calendar-year basis and a subsidiary whose fiscal year ends on October 31?

18. Does the acquisition of shares held by noncontrolling shareholders constitute a business combination?

---

**NOTE:** Don't forget the assumptions on page 49 when working exercises and problems in this chapter.

---

## EXERCISES

### E3-1
### General questions

1. A 75 percent–owned subsidiary should not be consolidated when:
   *a   Its operations are dissimilar from those of the parent company*
   *b   Control of the subsidiary does not lie with the parent company*
   *c   There is a dominant noncontrolling interest in the subsidiary*
   *d   Consolidation would not provide the most meaningful financial statements*

2. An 80 percent–owned subsidiary that cannot be consolidated must be accounted for:
   *a   Under the equity method*
   *b   Under the cost method*
   *c   Under the equity method if the parent exercises significant influence*
   *d   At market value if the subsidiary is in bankruptcy*

3. Consolidated statements for Pop Corporation and its 60 percent–owned investee, Son Company, will not be prepared under current GAAP if:
   *a   The fiscal periods of Pop and Son are more than three months apart*
   *b   Pop is a major manufacturing company and Son is an insurance company*
   *c   Son is a foreign company*
   *d   Pop Corporation and Son Company form a joint venture*

4. Pop Industries owns 7,000 shares of Son Corporation's outstanding common stock (a 70 percent interest). The remaining 3,000 outstanding common shares of Son are held by Ott Insurance Company. On Pop Industries' consolidated financial statements, Ott Insurance Company is considered:
   *a   An investee*
   *b   An associated company*
   *c   An affiliated company*
   *d   A noncontrolling interest*

5. On January 1, Pop Company purchased 75 percent of the outstanding shares of Son Company at a cost exceeding the book value and fair value of Son's net assets. Using the following notations, describe the amount at which the

plant assets will appear in a consolidated balance sheet of Pop Company and Subsidiary prepared immediately after acquisition:

$P_{by}$ = book value of Pop's plant assets
$P_{fv}$ = fair value of Pop's plant assets
$S_{bv}$ = book value of Son's plant assets
$S_{fv}$ = fair value of Son's plant assets

a  $P_{bv} + S_{bv} \pm (S_{fv} - S_{bv})$
b  $P_{bv} + 0.75(S_{bv}) \pm 0.75(S_{fv} - S_{bv})$
c  $P_{bv} + 0.75(S_{fv})$
d  $P_{bv} + S_{bv} \pm 0.75(S_{fv} - S_{bv})$

## E3-2
## General questions

1. Under GAAP, a parent company should exclude a subsidiary from consolidation if:
   a  *It measures income from the subsidiary under the equity method*
   b  *The subsidiary is in a regulated industry*
   c  *The subsidiary is a foreign entity whose books are recorded in a foreign currency*
   d  *The parent does not have control of the subsidiary*

2. The FASB's primary motivation for requiring consolidation of all majority-owned subsidiaries was to:
   a  *Ensure disclosure of all loss contingencies*
   b  *Prevent the use of off–balance sheet financing*
   c  *Improve comparability of the statements of cash flows*
   d  *Establish criteria for exclusion of finance and insurance subsidiaries from consolidation*

3. Parent-company and consolidated financial statement amounts would not be the same for:
   a  *Capital stock*
   b  *Retained earnings*
   c  *Investments in unconsolidated subsidiaries*
   d  *Investments in consolidated subsidiaries*

4. Noncontrolling interest, as it appears in a consolidated balance sheet, refers to:
   a  *Owners of less than 50 percent of the parent company's stock*
   b  *Parent's interest in subsidiary companies*
   c  *Interest expense on subsidiary's bonds payable*
   d  *Equity in the subsidiary's net assets held by stockholders other than the parent*

5. Pam Corporation acquired an 80 percent interest in Sun Corporation on January 1, 2016, and issued consolidated financial statements at and for the year ended December 31, 2016. Pam and Sun had issued separate-company financial statements in 2015.
   a  *The change in reporting entity is reported by restating the financial statements of all prior periods presented as consolidated statements.*
   b  *The cumulative effect of the change in reporting entity is shown in a separate category of the income statement net of tax.*
   c  *The income effect of the error is charged or credited directly to beginning retained earnings.*
   d  *The income effect of the accounting change is spread over the current and future periods.*

6. The noncontrolling interest share that appears in the consolidated income statement is computed as follows:
   a  *Consolidated net income is multiplied by the noncontrolling interest percentage.*
   b  *The subsidiary's income less amortization of fair/book value differentials is multiplied by the noncontrolling interest percentage.*
   c  *Subsidiary net income is subtracted from consolidated net income.*
   d  *Subsidiary income determined for consolidated statement purposes is multiplied by the noncontrolling interest percentage.*

7. The retained earnings that appear on the consolidated balance sheet of a parent company and its 60 percent–owned subsidiary are:
   a  *Parent company's retained earnings plus 100 percent of the subsidiary's retained earnings*
   b  *Parent company's retained earnings plus 60 percent of the subsidiary's retained earnings*
   c  *Parent company's retained earnings*
   d  *Pooled retained earnings*

## E3-3
## [Based on AICPA] General problems

1. Cobb Company's current receivables from affiliated companies at December 31, 2016, are (1) a $75,000 cash advance to Hill Corporation (Cobb owns 30 percent of the voting stock of Hill and accounts for the investment by the equity method), (2) a receivable of $260,000 from Vick Corporation for administrative and selling services (Vick is 100 percent owned by Cobb and is included in Cobb's consolidated financial statements), and (3) a receivable of $200,000 from Ward Corporation for merchandise sales on credit (Ward is a 90 percent–owned, unconsolidated subsidiary of Cobb accounted for by the equity method). In the current assets section of its December 31, 2016, consolidated balance sheet, Cobb should report accounts receivable from investees in the amount of:

   a  *$180,000*
   b  *$255,000*
   c  *$275,000*
   d  *$535,000*

Use the following information in answering questions 2 and 3.

On January 1, 2016, Pop Corporation purchased all of Son Corporation's common stock for $2,400,000. On that date, the fair values of Son's assets and liabilities equaled their carrying amounts of $2,640,000 and $640,000, respectively. Pop's policy is to amortize intangibles other than goodwill over 10 years. During 2016, Son paid cash dividends of $40,000.

Selected information from the separate balance sheets and income statements of Pop and Son as of December 31, 2016, and for the year then ended follows (in thousands):

|                                  | Pop      | Son      |
|----------------------------------|----------|----------|
| *Balance Sheet Accounts*         |          |          |
| Investment in subsidiary         | $2,640   | —        |
| Retained earnings                | 2,480    | $ 1,120  |
| Total stockholders' equity       | 5,240    | 2,240    |
| *Income Statement Accounts*      |          |          |
| Operating income                 | $ 840    | $ 400    |
| Equity in earnings of Son        | 280      | —        |
| Net income                       | 800      | 280      |

2. In Pop's 2016 consolidated income statement, what amount should be reported for amortization of goodwill?

   a  *$0*
   b  *$24,000*
   c  *$36,000*
   d  *$40,000*

3. In Pop's December 31, 2016, consolidated balance sheet, what amount should be reported as total retained earnings?

   a  *$2,480,000*
   b  *$2,720,000*
   c  *$2,760,000*
   d  *$3,600,000*

## E3-4
## Correction of consolidated net income

Pop Corporation paid $3,600,000 for a 90 percent interest in Son Corporation on January 1, 2016; Son's total book value was $3,600,000. The excess was allocated as follows: $120,000 to undervalued equipment with a three-year remaining useful life and $280,000 to goodwill. The income statements of Pop and Son for 2016 are summarized as follows (in thousands):

|                      | Pop      | Son      |
|----------------------|----------|----------|
| Sales                | $8,000   | $3,200   |
| Income from Son      | 360      |          |
| Cost of sales        | (4,000)  | (1,600)  |
| Depreciation expense | (800)    | (480)    |
| Other expenses       | (1,600)  | (720)    |
| Net income           | $ 1,960  | $ 400    |

## REQUIRED

1. Calculate the goodwill that should appear in the consolidated balance sheet of Pop and Subsidiary at December 31, 2016.

2. Calculate consolidated net income for 2016.

## E3-5
## Disclosure of consolidated dividends

On December 31, 2016, the separate-company financial statements for Pam Corporation and its 70 percent-owned subsidiary, Sun Corporation, had the following account balances related to dividends (in thousands):

|  | Pam | Sun |
|---|---|---|
| Dividends for 2016 | $2,400 | $1,600 |
| Dividends payable at December 31, 2016 | 1,200 | 400 |

### REQUIRED

1. At what amount will dividends be shown in the consolidated retained earnings statement?

2. At what amount should dividends payable be shown in the consolidated balance sheet?

## E3-6
## Prepare journal entries and balance sheet under push-down accounting

Book values and fair values of Son Corporation's assets and liabilities on December 31, 2015, are as follows (in thousands):

|  | Book Value | Fair Value |
|---|---|---|
| Cash | $ 560 | $ 560 |
| Accounts receivable—net | 640 | 640 |
| Inventories | 640 | 800 |
| Land | 1,200 | 1,600 |
| Buildings—net | 2,800 | 4,000 |
| Equipment—net | 1,760 | 2,400 |
|  | $7,600 | $10,000 |
| Accounts payable | $ 800 | $ 800 |
| Note payable | 1,120 | 1,200 |
| Capital stock | 4,000 |  |
| Retained earnings | 1,680 |  |
|  | $7,600 |  |

On January 1, 2016, Pop Corporation acquires all of Son's capital stock for $10,000,000 cash. The acquisition is recorded using push-down accounting.

### REQUIRED

1. Prepare the January 1 journal entry on Son's books to record push-down values.
2. Prepare a balance sheet for Son Corporation immediately after the acquisition on January 1 under push-down accounting.

## E3-7
## Prepare consolidated income statements with and without fair value/book value differentials

Summary income statement information for Pam Corporation and its 70 percent–owned subsidiary, Sun, for the year 2017 is as follows (in thousands):

|  | Pam | Sun |
|---|---|---|
| Sales | $4,000 | $ 1,600 |
| Income from Sun | 196 | — |
| Cost of sales | (2,400) | (800) |
| Depreciation expense | (200) | (160) |
| Other expenses | (796) | (360) |
| Net income | $ 800 | $ 280 |

### REQUIRED

1. Assume that Pam acquired its 70 percent interest in Sun at book value on January 1, 2016, when the fair value of Sun's assets and liabilities were equal to recorded book values. There were no intercompany transactions during 2016 and 2017. Prepare a consolidated income statement for Pam Corporation and Subsidiary for 2017.

**2.** Assume that Pam acquired its 70 percent interest in Sun on January 1, 2016, for $560,000. $120,000 *was allocated* to a reduction of overvalued equipment with a five-year remaining useful life and the remainder was allocated to goodwill. Sun's book value was $640,000. There were no intercompany transactions during 2016 and 2017. Prepare a consolidated income statement for Pam Corporation and Subsidiary for 2017.

## E3-8
## Calculate consolidated balance sheet amounts with goodwill and noncontrolling interest

Pop Corporation acquired an 80 percent interest in Son Corporation on January 2, 2016, for $1,400,000. On this date the capital stock and retained earnings of the two companies were as follows (in thousands):

|  | Pop | Son |
|---|---|---|
| Capital stock | $3,600 | $1,000 |
| Retained earnings | 1,600 | 200 |

The assets and liabilities of Son were stated at fair values equal to book values when Pop acquired its 80 percent interest. Pop uses the equity method to account for its investment in Son.

Net income and dividends for 2016 for the affiliated companies were as follows (in thousands):

|  | Pop | Son |
|---|---|---|
| Net income | $600 | $180 |
| Dividends declared | 360 | 100 |
| Dividends payable December 31, 2016 | 180 | 50 |

**REQUIRED:** Calculate the amounts at which the following items should appear in the consolidated balance sheet on December 31, 2016.

**1.** Capital stock

**2.** Goodwill

**3.** Consolidated retained earnings

**4.** Noncontrolling interest

**5.** Dividends payable

## E3-9
## Prepare stockholders' equity section of consolidated balance sheet one year after acquisition

Pam and Sun Corporations' balance sheets at December 31, 2015, are summarized as follows (in thousands):

|  | Pam | Sun |
|---|---|---|
| Cash | $1,020 | $240 |
| Other assets | 800 | 700 |
| Total assets | $1,820 | $940 |
| Liabilities | $280 | $ 140 |
| Capital stock, par $10 | 1,200 | 700 |
| Additional paid-in capital | 200 | 60 |
| Retained earnings | 140 | 40 |
| Total equities | $1,820 | $940 |

Pam acquired 80 percent of the voting stock of Sun on January 2, 2016, at a cost of $640,000. The fair values of Sun's net assets were equal to book values on January 2, 2016.

During 2016, Pam reported earnings of $220,000, including income from Sun of $64,000, and paid dividends of $100,000. Sun's earnings for 2016 were $80,000, and its dividends were $60,000.

**REQUIRED** Prepare the stockholders' equity section of the December 31, 2016, consolidated balance sheet for Pam Corporation and Subsidiary.

## E3-10
## Prepare consolidated income statement three years after acquisition

Comparative income statements of Pop Corporation and Son Corporation for the year ended December 31, 2018, are as follows (in thousands):

|  | Pop | Son |
|---|---|---|
| Sales | $3,200 | $1,000 |
| Income from Son | 261 | — |
| Total revenue | 3,461 | 1,000 |
| Less: Cost of goods sold | 1,800 | 400 |
| Operating expenses | 800 | 300 |
| Total expenses | 2,600 | 700 |
| Net income | $ 861 | $ 300 |

## ADDITIONAL INFORMATION

1. Son is a 90 percent–owned subsidiary of Pop, acquired by Pop for $1,620,000 on January 1, 2016, when Son's stockholders' equity at book value was $1,400,000.

2. The excess of the cost of Pop's investment in Son over book value acquired was allocated $60,000 to undervalued inventories that were sold in 2016, $40,000 to undervalued equipment with a four-year remaining useful life, and the remainder to goodwill.

REQUIRED: Prepare a consolidated income statement for Pop Corporation and Subsidiary for the year ended December 31, 2018.

## PROBLEMS

### P3-1
### Prepare a consolidated balance sheet at acquisition and compute consolidated net income one year later

On December 31, 2016, Pam Corporation purchased 80 percent of the stock of Sun Company at book value. The data reported on their separate balance sheets immediately after the acquisition follow. At December 31, 2016, Pam Corporation owes Sun $20,000 on accounts payable. (All amounts are in thousands.)

|  | Pam | Sun |
|---|---|---|
| *Assets* |  |  |
| Cash | $ 128 | $ 72 |
| Accounts receivable | 180 | 136 |
| Inventories | 572 | 224 |
| Investment in Sun | 800 |  |
| Equipment—net | 1,520 | 700 |
|  | $3,200 | $1,132 |
| *Liabilities and Stockholders' Equity* |  |  |
| Accounts payable | $ 160 | $ 132 |
| Common stock, $20 par | 1,840 | 600 |
| Retained earnings | 1,200 | 400 |
|  | $3,200 | $1,132 |

### REQUIRED

1. Prepare a consolidated balance sheet for Pam Corporation and Subsidiary at December 31, 2016.
2. Compute consolidated net income for 2017 assuming that Pam Corporation reported separate income of $680,000 and Sun Company reported net income of $360,000. (Separate incomes do *not* include income from the investment in Sun.)

### P3-2
### Allocation schedule for fair value/book value differential and consolidated balance sheet at acquisition

Pop Corporation acquired 70 percent of the outstanding common stock of Son Corporation on January 1, 2016, for $350,000 cash. Immediately after this acquisition the balance sheet information for the two companies was as follows (in thousands):

| | Pop Book Value | Son Book Value | Son Fair Value |
|---|---|---|---|
| *Assets* | | | |
| Cash | $ 70 | $ 40 | $ 40 |
| Receivables—net | 160 | 60 | 60 |
| Inventories | 140 | 60 | 100 |
| Land | 200 | 100 | 120 |
| Buildings—net | 220 | 140 | 180 |
| Equipment—net | 160 | 80 | 60 |
| Investment in Son | 350 | — | — |
| Total assets | $1,300 | $480 | $ 560 |
| *Liabilities and Stockholders' Equity* | | | |
| Accounts payable | $ 180 | $160 | $160 |
| Other liabilities | 20 | 100 | 80 |
| Capital stock, $20 par | 1,000 | 200 | |
| Retained earnings | 100 | 20 | |
| Total equities | $1,300 | $480 | |

### REQUIRED

1. Prepare a schedule to assign the difference between the fair value of the investment in Son and the book value of the interest to identifiable and unidentifiable net assets.

2. Prepare a consolidated balance sheet for Pop Corporation and Subsidiary at January 1, 2016.

## P3-3
## Prepare assignment schedule with book value greater than fair value

Pam Corporation pays $10,800,000 for an 80 percent interest in Sun Corporation on January 1, 2016, at which time the book value and fair value of Sun's net assets are as follows (in thousands):

| | Book Value | Fair Value |
|---|---|---|
| Current assets | $ 4,000 | $ 6,000 |
| Equipment—net | 8,000 | 12,000 |
| Other plant assets—net | 4,000 | 4,000 |
| Liabilities | (6,000) | (6,000) |
| Net assets | $10,000 | $16,000 |

**REQUIRED:** Prepare a schedule to assign the fair value/book value differentials to Sun's net assets.

## P3-4
## Given separate and consolidated balance sheets, reconstruct the schedule to assign the fair value/book value differential

Pam Corporation purchased a block of Sun Company common stock for $1,040,000 cash on January 1, 2016. Separate-company and consolidated balance sheets prepared immediately after the acquisition are summarized as follows (in thousands):

### Pam Corporation and Subsidiary Consolidated Balance Sheet at January 1, 2016

| | Pam | Sun | Consolidated |
|---|---|---|---|
| *Assets* | | | |
| Current assets | $ 760 | $ 400 | $ 1,160 |
| Investment in Sun | 1,040 | — | — |
| Plant assets—net | 2,200 | 800 | 3,040 |
| Goodwill | — | — | 220 |
| Total assets | $4,000 | $1,200 | $4,420 |
| *Equities* | | | |
| Liabilities | $1,600 | $ 160 | $1,760 |
| Capital stock, $20 par | 2,000 | 800 | 2,000 |
| Retained earnings | 400 | 240 | 400 |
| Noncontrolling interest | — | — | 260 |
| Total equities | $4,000 | $1,200 | $4,420 |

**REQUIRED:** Reconstruct the schedule to assign the fair value/book value differential from Pam's investment in Sun.

## P3-5
## Prepare a consolidated balance sheet one year after acquisition

Adjusted trial balances for Pop and Son Corporations at December 31, 2016, are as follows (in thousands):

|  | Pop | Son |
|---|---|---|
| *Debits* | | |
| Current assets | $ 1,920 | $ 800 |
| Plant assets—net | 4,000 | 2,400 |
| Investment in Son | 3,360 | — |
| Cost of sales | 2,400 | 2,400 |
| Other expenses | 800 | 400 |
| Dividends | 400 | — |
|  | $12,880 | $6,000 |
| *Credits* | | |
| Liabilities | $ 3,600 | $ 1,680 |
| Capital stock | 2,400 | 400 |
| Retained earnings | 2,720 | 720 |
| Sales | 4,000 | 3,200 |
| Income from Son | 160 | — |
|  | $12,880 | $6,000 |

Pop purchased all the stock of Son for $3,200,000 cash on January 1, 2016, when Son's stockholders' equity consisted of $400,000 capital stock and $720,000 retained earnings. Son's assets and liabilities were fairly valued except for inventory that was undervalued by $160,000 and sold in 2016, and plant assets that were undervalued by $320,000 and had a remaining useful life of four years from the date of the acquisition.

**REQUIRED:** Prepare a consolidated balance sheet for Pop Corporation and Subsidiary at December 31, 2016.

## P3-6
## Consolidated balance sheet workpapers with goodwill and dividends

Pam Corporation paid $1,800,000 cash for 90 percent of Sun Corporation's common stock on January 1, 2016, when Sun had $1,200,000 capital stock and $400,000 retained earnings. The book values of Sun's assets and liabilities were equal to fair values. During 2016, Sun reported net income of $80,000 and declared $40,000 in dividends on December 31. Balance sheets for Pam and Sun at December 31, 2016, are as follows (in thousands):

|  | Pam | Sun |
|---|---|---|
| *Assets* | | |
| Cash | $ 168 | $ 80 |
| Receivables—net | 200 | 520 |
| Inventories | 1,400 | 200 |
| Land | 600 | 800 |
| Equipment—net | 2,400 | 400 |
| Investment in Sun | 1,836 | — |
|  | $6,604 | $2,000 |
| *Equities* | | |
| Accounts payable | $1,640 | $ 320 |
| Dividends payable | 240 | 40 |
| Capital stock | 4,000 | 1,200 |
| Retained earnings | 724 | 440 |
|  | $6,604 | $2,000 |

**REQUIRED:** Prepare consolidated balance sheet workpapers for Pam Corporation and Subsidiary for December 31, 2016.

## P3-7
## Calculate items that may appear in consolidated statements two years after acquisition

Pop Corporation acquired 80 percent of the outstanding stock of Son Corporation for $1,120,000 cash on January 3, 2016, on which date Son's stockholders' equity consisted of capital stock of $800,000 and retained earnings of $200,000.

There were no changes in the outstanding stock of either corporation during 2016 and 2017. At December 31, 2017, the adjusted trial balances of Pop and Son are as follows (in thousands):

|  | Pop | Son |
|---|---|---|
| *Debits* | | |
| Current assets | $ 816 | $ 300 |
| Plant assets—net | 1,600 | 1,200 |
| Investment in Son—80% | 1,360 | — |
| Cost of goods sold | 1,000 | 480 |
| Other expenses | 200 | 120 |
| Dividends | 240 | 100 |
|  | $5,216 | $2,200 |
| *Credits* | | |
| Current liabilities | $ 648 | $ 200 |
| Capital stock | 2,000 | 800 |
| Retained earnings | 808 | 400 |
| Sales | 1,600 | 800 |
| Income from Son | 160 | — |
|  | $5,216 | $2,200 |

### ADDITIONAL INFORMATION

1. All of Son's assets and liabilities were recorded at fair values equal to book values on January 3, 2016.
2. The current liabilities of Son at December 31, 2017, include dividends payable of $40,000.

**REQUIRED** Determine the amounts that should appear in the consolidated statements of Pop Corporation and Subsidiary at December 31, 2017, for each of the following:

1. Noncontrolling interest share
2. Current assets
3. Income from Son
4. Capital stock
5. Investment in Son
6. Excess of investment fair value over book value
7. Consolidated net income for the year ended December 31, 2017
8. Consolidated retained earnings, December 31, 2016
9. Consolidated retained earnings, December 31, 2017
10. Noncontrolling interest, December 31, 2017

## P3-8
## [Based on AICPA] Prepare journal entries to account for investments, and compute noncontrolling interest, consolidated retained earnings, and investment balances

On January 1, 2016, Pop Corporation made the following investments:

1. Acquired for cash, 80 percent of the outstanding common stock of Son Corporation at $280 per share. The stockholders' equity of Son on January 1, 2016, consisted of the following:

| Common stock, par value $100 | $200,000 |
|---|---|
| Retained earnings | 80,000 |

2. Acquired for cash, 70 percent of the outstanding common stock of Sam Corporation at $160 per share. The stockholders' equity of Sam on January 1, 2016, consisted of the following:

| Common stock, par value $40 | $240,000 |
|---|---|
| Capital in excess of par value | 80,000 |
| Retained earnings | 160,000 |

**3.** After these investments were made, Pop was able to exercise control over the operations of both companies.

An analysis of the retained earnings of each company for 2016 is as follows:

|  | Pop | Son | Sam |
|---|---|---|---|
| Balance January 1 | $ 960,000 | $ 80,000 | $160,000 |
| Net income (loss) | 418,400 | 144,000 | (48,000) |
| Cash dividends paid | (160,000) | (64,000) | (36,000) |
| Balance December 31 | $1,218,400 | $160,000 | $ 76,000 |

## REQUIRED

**1.** What entries should have been made on the books of Pop during 2016 to record the following?
   **a.** Investments in subsidiaries
   **b.** Subsidiary dividends received
   **c.** Parent's share of subsidiary income or loss

**2.** Compute the amount of noncontrolling interest in each subsidiary's stockholders' equity at December 31, 2016.

**3.** What amount should be reported as consolidated retained earnings of Pop Corporation and subsidiaries as of December 31, 2016?

**4.** Compute the correct balances of Pop's Investment in Son and Investment in Sam accounts at December 31, 2016, before consolidation.

## P3-9
## Consolidated balance sheet workpapers (excess allocated to equipment and goodwill)

Pam Corporation purchased 90 percent of Sun Corporation's outstanding stock for $14,400,000 cash on January 1, 2016, when Sun's stockholders' equity consisted of $8,000,000 capital stock and $2,800,000 retained earnings. The excess was allocated $3,200,000 to undervalued equipment with an eight-year remaining useful life and $2,000,000 to goodwill. Sun's net income and dividends for 2016 were $2,000,000 and $800,000, respectively. Comparative balance sheet data for Pam and Sun Corporations at December 31, 2016, are as follows (in thousands):

|  | Pam | Sun |
|---|---|---|
| Cash | $ 1,200 | $ 800 |
| Receivables—net | 2,400 | 1,600 |
| Dividends receivable | 360 | — |
| Inventory | 2,800 | 2,400 |
| Land | 2,400 | 2,800 |
| Buildings—net | 8,000 | 4,000 |
| Equipment—net | 6,000 | 3,200 |
| Investment in Sun | 15,120 | — |
|  | $38,280 | $14,800 |
| Accounts payable | $ 1,200 | $ 2,400 |
| Dividends payable | 2,000 | 400 |
| Capital stock | 28,000 | 8,000 |
| Retained earnings | 7,080 | 4,000 |
|  | $38,280 | $14,800 |

**REQUIRED** Prepare consolidated balance sheet workpapers for Pam Corporation and Subsidiary on December 31, 2016.

## P3-10
## Calculate investment cost and account balances from a consolidated balance sheet five years after acquisition

The consolidated balance sheet of Pam Corporation and its 80 percent subsidiary, Sun Corporation, contains the following items on December 31, 2020 (in thousands):

| | |
|---|---:|
| Cash | $ 160 |
| Inventories | 1,536 |
| Other current assets | 560 |
| Plant assets—net | 2,160 |
| Goodwill | 480 |
| | $4,896 |
| | |
| Liabilities | $ 960 |
| Capital stock | 3,200 |
| Retained earnings | 240 |
| Noncontrolling interests | 496 |
| | $4,896 |

Pam Corporation uses the equity method of accounting for its investment in Sun. Sun Corporation stock was acquired by Pam on January 1, 2016, when Sun's capital stock was $1,600,000 and its retained earnings were $160,000. Fair values of Sun's net assets were equal to book values on January 1, 2016, and there have been no changes in outstanding stock of either Pam or Sun since January 1, 2016.

**REQUIRED** Determine the following:

1. The purchase price of Pam's investment in Sun stock on January 1, 2016.
2. The total of Sun's stockholders' equity on December 31, 2020.
3. The balance of Pam's Investment in Sun account at December 31, 2020.
4. The balances of Pam's Retained earnings and Capital stock accounts on December 31, 2020.

## P3-11
## Consolidated balance sheet workpapers (fair value/book value differentials and noncontrolling interest)

Pop Corporation acquired a 70 percent interest in Son Corporation on January 1, 2016, for $2,800,000, when Son's stockholders' equity consisted of $2,000,000 capital stock and $1,200,000 retained earnings. On this date, the book value of Son's assets and liabilities was equal to the fair value, except for inventories that were undervalued by $80,000 and sold in 2016, and plant assets that were undervalued by $320,000 and had a remaining useful life of eight years from January 1. Son's net income and dividends for 2016 were $280,000 and $40,000, respectively.

Separate-company balance sheet information for Pop and Son Corporations at December 31, 2016, follows (in thousands):

| | Pop | Son |
|---|---:|---:|
| Cash | $ 240 | $ 80 |
| Accounts receivable—customers | 1,760 | 800 |
| Accounts receivable from Pop | — | 40 |
| Dividends receivable | 28 | — |
| Inventories | 2,000 | 1,280 |
| Land | 400 | 600 |
| Plant assets—net | 2,800 | 1,400 |
| Investment in Son | 2,884 | — |
| | $10,112 | $4,200 |
| Accounts payable—suppliers | $ 1,200 | $ 320 |
| Accounts payable to Son | 40 | — |
| Dividends payable | 160 | 40 |
| Long-term debt | 2,400 | 400 |
| Capital stock | 4,000 | 2,000 |
| Retained earnings | 2,312 | 1,440 |
| | $10,112 | $4,200 |

**REQUIRED** Prepare consolidated balance sheet workpapers for Pop Corporation and Subsidiary at December 31, 2016.

## P3-12
## Calculate separate company and consolidated statement items given investment account for three years

A summary of changes in Pam Corporation's Investment in Sun account from January 1, 2016, to December 31, 2018, follows (in thousands):

| INVESTMENT IN SUN (80%) | | | |
|---|---|---|---|
| January 1, 2016 | 6,080 | | |
| Income—2016 | 512 | Dividends—2016 | 256 |
| 2017 | 640 | 2017 | 320 |
| 2018 | 768 | 2018 | 384 |
| | | to balance | 7,040 |
| | 8,000 | | 8,000 |
| December 31, 2018 | | | |
| Balance forward | 7,040 | | |

### ADDITIONAL INFORMATION

1. Pam acquired its 80 percent interest in Sun Corporation when Sun had capital stock of $4,800,000 and retained earnings of $2,400,000.

2. Dividends declared by Sun Corporation in each of the years 2016, 2017, and 2018 were equal to 50 percent of Sun Corporation's reported net income.

3. Sun Corporation's assets and liabilities were stated at fair values equal to book values on January 1, 2016.

**REQUIRED** Compute the following amounts:
1. Sun Corporation's dividends declared in 2017
2. Sun Corporation's net income for 2017
3. Goodwill at December 31, 2017
4. Noncontrolling interest share for 2018
5. Noncontrolling interest at December 31, 2018
6. Consolidated net income for 2018, assuming that Pam's separate income for 2018 is $2,240,000, without investment income from Sun

# PROFESSIONAL RESEARCH ASSIGNMENTS

Answer the following questions by reference to the FASB Codification of Accounting Standards. Include the appropriate reference in your response.

**PR 3-1**  Throughout this chapter we typically indicate that acquisitions take place on January 2. At what date should a business combination be recorded?

**PR 3-2**  What disclosures are required for a parent company with a less than wholly owned subsidiary?

# CHAPTER 4

# Consolidation Techniques and Procedures

This chapter discusses procedures to consolidate the financial statements of parent and subsidiary companies. Some differences in the consolidation process result from different methods of parent-company accounting for subsidiary investments. Consolidation workpapers for a parent company/investor that uses the complete equity method of accounting are illustrated in the chapter to set the standard for good consolidation procedures. The chapter examines additional complexities that arise from errors and omissions in the separate-company records and detailed recording of fair values of a subsidiary's net assets. Appendix A illustrates the trial balance workpaper format, which is an alternative to the financial statement format used in other sections of the chapter. Appendix B illustrates procedures to prepare consolidated statements when the parent company uses either the cost method or an incomplete (partial) equity method for internal accounting purposes.

Chapter 3 presented a balance sheet workpaper to organize the information needed for a consolidated balance sheet. This chapter presents a workpaper that develops the information needed for consolidated balance sheets and income and retained earnings statements. A consolidated statement of cash flows (SCF) is illustrated in a later section of this chapter.

## CONSOLIDATION UNDER THE EQUITY METHOD

The following example of a parent that uses the complete equity method of accounting for its subsidiary explains basic procedures used to consolidate the financial statements of affiliated companies.

### Equity Method—Year of Acquisition

LEARNING OBJECTIVE **4.1**

Pop Corporation pays $176,000 for 80 percent of the outstanding voting stock of Son Corporation on January 1, 2016, when Son Corporation's stockholders' equity consists of $120,000 capital stock and $60,000 retained earnings. This implies that the total fair value of Son is $220,000 ($176,000 ÷ 80%). We assign the $40,000 excess fair value to previously unrecorded patents with a 10-year useful life. Son's net income and dividends are as follows:

|            | 2016     | 2017     |
|------------|----------|----------|
| Net income | $50,000  | $60,000  |
| Dividends  | 30,000   | 30,000   |

Financial statements for Pop and Son Corporations for 2016 are presented in the first three columns of Exhibit 4-1. Pop's $36,800 income from Son for 2016 consists of 80 percent of Son's

## LEARNING OBJECTIVES

**4.1** Prepare a consolidation workpaper for the year of acquisition when the parent uses the complete equity method to account for its investment in a subsidiary.

**4.2** Prepare a consolidation workpaper for the years subsequent to an acquisition.

**4.3** Locate errors in a consolidation workpaper.

**4.4** Record fair values of identifiable net assets acquired.

**4.5** Prepare a consolidated statement of cash flows.

**4.6** **For the Students:** Create an electronic spreadsheet to prepare a consolidation workpaper.

**4.7** Appendix A: Understand the alternative trial balance workpaper format.

**4.8** Appendix B: Prepare a consolidation workpaper when parent company uses either the cost method or incomplete equity method.

**EXHIBIT 4-1**

Equity Method—
Workpaper for Year of
Acquisition

## POP CORPORATION AND SUBSIDIARY CONSOLIDATION WORKPAPER FOR THE YEAR ENDED DECEMBER 31, 2016 (IN THOUSANDS)

| | Pop | 80% Son | Adjustments and Eliminations Debits | Adjustments and Eliminations Credits | Consolidated Statements |
|---|---|---|---|---|---|
| *Income Statement* | | | | | |
| Revenue | $ 500 | $130 | | | $ 630 |
| Income from Son | 36.8 | | a  36.8 | | |
| Expenses | (400) | (80) | d  4 | | (484) |
| Noncontrolling interest share ($46,000 × 20%) | | | b  9.2 | | (9.2 ) |
| **Controlling share of net income** | **$ 136.8** | **$ 50** | | | **$  136.8** |
| *Retained Earnings Statement* | | | | | |
| Retained earnings—Pop | $  10 | | | | $ 10 |
| Retained earnings—Son | | $ 60 | c  60 | | |
| **Add: Controlling share of net income** | **136.8** | **50** | | | **136. 8** |
| Deduct: Dividends | (60) | (30) | | a 24 | |
| | | | | b  6 | (60) |
| **Retained earnings— December 31** | **$  86.8** | **$ 80** | | | **$    86.8** |
| *Balance Sheet* | | | | | |
| Cash | $ 78 | $ 20 | | | $ 98 |
| Other current assets | 180 | 100 | | | 280 |
| Investment in Son | 188.8 | | | a  12.8 | |
| | | | | c 176 | |
| Plant and equipment | 600 | 200 | | | 800 |
| Accumulated depreciation | (100) | (60) | | | (160) |
| Patents | | | c  40 | d 4 | 36 |
| | $ 946.8 | $260 | | | $1,054 |
| Liabilities | $ 160 | $ 60 | | | $ 220 |
| Capital stock | 700 | 120 | c 120 | | 700 |
| **Retained earnings** | **86.8** | **80** | | | **86.8** |
| | $ 946.8 | $260 | | | |
| Noncontrolling interest January 1 ($220,000 fair value × 20%) | | | | c 44 | |
| Noncontrolling interest December 31 | | | | b  3.2 | 47.2 |
| | | | 270 | 270 | $1,054 |

$50,000 net income for 2016 less $3,200 [($40,000 ÷ 10 yrs.) × 80%] patent amortization. Its $188,800 investment in Son account at December 31, 2016, consists of $176,000 investment cost plus $36,800 income from Son, less $24,000 dividends received from Son during 2016.

Numerous consolidation approaches and any number of different adjustment and elimination combinations will result in correct amounts for the consolidated financial statements. The adjustment and elimination entries that appear in the workpapers *do not affect the general ledger accounts of either the parent or its subsidiaries.* Adjusting or eliminating accounts or balances simply mean that the amounts listed in the separate-company columns of the workpapers are either (1) adjusted before inclusion in the consolidated statement column or (2) eliminated and do not appear in the consolidated statement column. A single workpaper entry often adjusts some items and eliminates others. Labeling the workpaper entries as either adjusting or eliminating entries is not important. It is important that you understand the consolidation process and develop your workpaper skills.

Take a few minutes to review the consolidation workpaper in Exhibit 4-1. This format is used extensively throughout the chapters on consolidated financial statements. The worksheet rows for controlling share of consolidated net income and ending retained earnings are in boldface to highlight that we do not make adjustments or eliminations directly on these lines. We do this because consolidated net income consists of consolidated revenues less consolidated expenses, and if we require adjustments, they will be made to the individual revenue and expense accounts, not directly to net income.

Similarly, the consolidated balance sheet reflects consolidated retained earnings. We calculate the balance sheet amount for consolidated retained earnings as follows:

| |
| --- |
| Beginning consolidated retained earnings |
| Plus: Controlling share of consolidated net income (or<br>        minus a controlling share of consolidated net loss) |
| Less: Parent-company dividends |
| Ending consolidated retained earnings |

In our workpaper format, we carry the controlling share of net income line down to the *Retained Earnings Statement* section of the worksheet without adjustment. We similarly carry the ending retained earnings row down to the *Balance Sheet* section, again without adjustments or eliminations. Notice too that each row in the workpaper generates the consolidated amounts by adding together the parent and subsidiary account balances and then adding or subtracting the adjustments and eliminations as appropriate.

Parent-retained earnings under the complete equity method of accounting are equal to consolidated retained earnings. Because Pop Corporation (Exhibit 4-1) correctly applies the equity method, its net income of $136,800 equals its controlling share of consolidated net income. Its beginning and ending retained earnings balances equal the $10,000 and $86,800 consolidated retained earnings amounts, respectively.

The first workpaper entry in Exhibit 4-1 is as follows:

| a | Income from Son( − R, − SE) | 36,800 | |
|---|---|---|---|
| | Dividends ( +SE) | | 24,000 |
| | Investment in Son ( − A) | | 12,800 |
| | **To eliminate income and dividends from Son and return<br>the investment account to its beginning-of-the-period balance.** | | |

Recall that throughout this text workpaper entries are shaded to avoid confusion with journal entries that are recorded by parents and subsidiaries. We eliminate investment income because the consolidated income statement shows the details of revenues and expenses rather than the one-line consolidation reflected in the Income from Son account. We eliminate dividends received from Son because they are mere transfers within the consolidated entity.

The difference between income from a subsidiary recognized on the books of the parent and dividends received represents the change in the investment account for the period. The $12,800 credit to the Investment in Son account reduces that account to its $176,000 beginning-of-the-period balance and establishes reciprocity between the investment in Son and Son's stockholders' equity at January 1, 2016.

Here is a journal entry for workpaper entry b from Exhibit 4-1:

| b | Noncontrolling interest share ( − SE) | 9,200 | |
|---|---|---|---|
| | Dividends( + SE) | | 6,000 |
| | Noncontrolling interest( + SE) | | 3,200 |
| | **To enter noncontrolling interest share of subsidiary income and<br>dividends.** | | |

Entry b incorporates the noncontrolling interest in a subsidiary's net income and the noncontrolling interest's share of dividends declared by the subsidiary directly into the consolidation workpaper. This approach explains all noncontrolling interest components through consolidation workpaper entries.

The portion of a subsidiary's net income not accruing to the parent is referred to as *noncontrolling interest share* throughout this text. Minority interest (income or expense) is the more-traditional term still sometimes found in published financial statements.

In this book, the term *noncontrolling interest* is used to reflect the balance sheet amount. Note that often noncontrolling interest or noncontrolling interest share does not appear in published, consolidated balance sheets or income statements because the amounts are immaterial.

Generally accepted accounting principles (GAAP) recommend noncontrolling interest as better reflecting the complexities of the modern business world. Many firms create *special purpose entities* (SPEs), not surprisingly created for a special business purpose. For example, SPEs may be created to facilitate leasing activities, loan securitizations, research and development activities, hedging transactions, or other business arrangements. SPEs gained fame (or infamy) with ***Enron Corporation***, which used these as a vehicle to set up energy futures trading and related business ventures. By excluding such ventures from consolidation, Enron was able to keep billions of dollars of debt off its balance sheet, hiding significant business risk from investors.

GAAP clarifies rules defining a *variable interest entity* as a subset of SPEs that should be included in preparing consolidated financial statements. Under GAAP, "The usual condition for a controlling financial interest is ownership of a majority voting interest."[1] GAAP further clarifies, adding: "However, application of the majority voting interest requirement to certain types of entities may not identify the party with a controlling financial interest because the controlling financial interest may be achieved through arrangements that do not involve voting interests."[2] (ASC 810-10-05) It is possible to achieve financial control of an entity with only a small equity voting interest through other contractual arrangements.[3] Chapter 11 discusses variable interest entities in greater detail. These voting, non–majority control situations are consistent with the GAAP preference for the controlling and noncontrolling versus majority and minority interests, terminology.

Workpaper entry c in journal entry form is as follows:

| c | | | |
|---|---|---|---|
| Retained earnings—Son (beginning) (− SE) | 60,000 | |
| Capital stock—Son (− SE) | 120,000 | |
| Patents (+ A) | 40,000 | |
|     Investment in Son (− A) | | 176,000 |
|     Noncontrolling interest (+ SE) | | 44,000 |

**To eliminate reciprocal equity and investment balances, establish beginning noncontrolling interest, and enter unamortized patents.**

This entry eliminates reciprocal investment and equity balances, enters the unamortized patents as of the beginning of the year, and records beginning noncontrolling interest ($220,000 × 20%) at fair value as a separate item. Observe that entry c eliminates reciprocal investment and equity balances as of the beginning of the period and enters noncontrolling interest as of the same date. The patents portion of the entry is also a beginning-of-the-period unamortized amount.

Many accountants prefer to eliminate only the parent's percentage of the capital stock and retained earnings of the subsidiary and to transfer the amount not eliminated directly to the noncontrolling interest. Although the difference is solely a matter of preference, the approach used here emphasizes that we eliminate all stockholders' equity accounts of a subsidiary in the process of consolidation.

Entry d in the workpapers of Exhibit 4-1 enters the current year's patent amortization as an expense of the consolidated entity and reduces unamortized patents from its $40,000 unamortized balance at January 1 to its $36,000 amortized balance at December 31, 2016.

---

[1]From Investor's Accounting for an Investee When the Investor Has a Majority of the Voting Interest but the Noncontrolling Shareholder or Shareholders Have Certain Approval or Veto Rights, EITF ABSTRACTS., Issue No. 96-16, © 2010 FASB.

[2]FASB ASC 810. Originally Statement of Financial Accounting "Consolidation." Stamford, CT: Financial Accounting Standards Board, 2016

[3]For example, if an acquirer becomes the primary beneficiary in a variable interest entity.

| d | Expenses (E, −SE) | 4,000 | |
|---|---|---|---|
| | Patents (−A) | | 4,000 |
| | To enter current amortization of patents. | | |

We need this workpaper entry to adjust consolidated expenses even though Pop amortized patents on its separate books under the equity method. Pop reflects amortization of the patents in its Income from Son account, and workpaper entry a eliminated that account for consolidation purposes in order to disaggregate the revenue and expense components in reporting consolidated income.

## Sequence of Workpaper Entries

The sequence of the workpaper entries in Exhibit 4-1 is both logical and necessary. Entry a adjusts the investment in Son for changes during 2016, and entry c eliminates the investment in Son after adjustment to its beginning-of-the-period balance in entry a. Entry c also enters unamortized patents in the workpaper as of the beginning of the period. Subsequently, entry d amortizes the patents for the current period and reduces the patents account to its amortized amount at the balance sheet date. As we encounter additional complexities of consolidation, the sequence of workpaper adjustments and eliminations expands to the following:

1. Adjustments for errors and omissions in the separate parent and subsidiary statements

2. Adjustments to eliminate intercompany profits and losses

3. Adjustment to eliminate income and dividends from subsidiary and adjust the investment in subsidiary to its beginning-of-the-period balance

4. Adjustment to record the noncontrolling interest in subsidiary's earnings and dividends

5. Eliminate reciprocal investment in subsidiary and subsidiary equity balances

6. Record and amortize fair-value differentials (from step 5)

7. Eliminate other reciprocal balances (intercompany receivables and payables, revenues and expenses, and so on)

Although other sequences of workpaper entries may be adequate in a given consolidation, the sequence just presented will always work. You should learn and apply it throughout your study of consolidations.

We compute the noncontrolling interest reflected in the consolidated balance sheet as beginning noncontrolling interest plus noncontrolling interest share less noncontrolling interest dividends. If ownership in a subsidiary increases during a period, the noncontrolling interest computation will reflect the noncontrolling interest at the balance sheet date, with noncontrolling interest share and dividends also reflecting the ending noncontrolling interest percentages. Note that the noncontrolling interest reflects fair value.

Note that we always eliminate the investment in subsidiary balances when a subsidiary is consolidated. Although the investment account may be adjusted to establish reciprocity, it never appears in a consolidated balance sheet. Likewise, we always eliminate investment income from consolidated subsidiaries. We compute consolidated net income by deducting consolidated expenses from consolidated revenues. It is *not* determined by adjusting the separate net incomes of parent and subsidiary. We then allocate consolidated net income into the shares attributable to the controlling (parent) and noncontrolling interests.

Capital stock and other paid-in capital accounts appearing in a consolidated balance sheet are those of the parent. Under GAAP (ASC 810-10-05) the noncontrolling interest must be reported as a component of consolidated stockholders' equity.

## Equity Method—Year Subsequent to Acquisition

LEARNING OBJECTIVE **4.2**

Pop Corporation maintains its 80 percent ownership interest in Son throughout 2017, recording income from Son of $44,800 for the year (80 percent of Son's $60,000 net income less $4,000 patents amortization). At December 31, 2017, Pop's Investment in Son account has a balance of $209,600, determined as follows:

| | |
|---|---:|
| Investment cost January 1, 2016 | $176,000 |
| Income from Son—2016 | 36,800 |
| Dividends from Son—2016 | −24,000 |
| Investment in Son December 31, 2016 | 188,800 |
| Income from Son—2017 | 44,800 |
| Dividends from Son—2017 | −24,000 |
| Investment in Son December 31, 2017 | $209,600 |

The only intercompany transaction between Pop and Son during 2017 was a $20,000 non-interest-bearing loan to Son during the third quarter of the year.

Consolidation workpapers for Pop Corporation and Subsidiary for 2017 are presented in Exhibit 4-2.

There were no errors or omissions or intercompany profits relating to the consolidation, so the first workpaper entry is to eliminate income and dividends from Son as follows:

| | | | |
|---|---|---:|---:|
| a | Income from Son (− R, − SE) | 44,800 | |
| | Dividends (+ SE) | | 24,000 |
| | Investment in Son (− A) | | 20,800 |
| | To eliminate income and dividends from Son and return the investment account to its beginning-of-the-period balance. | | |

This entry adjusts the Investment in Son account to its $188,800 December 31, 2016, balance and establishes reciprocity with Son's stockholders' equity at December 31, 2016.

Entry b incorporates the noncontrolling interest in Son's net income and the noncontrolling interest's share of Son's dividends:

| | | | |
|---|---|---:|---:|
| b | Noncontrolling interest share (− SE) | 11,200 | |
| | Dividends (+ SE) | | 6,000 |
| | Noncontrolling interest (+ SE) | | 5,200 |
| | To enter noncontrolling interest share of subsidiary income and dividends. | | |

Entry c eliminates Investment in Son and stockholders' equity of Son as follows:

| | | | |
|---|---|---:|---:|
| c | Retained earnings—Son (− SE) | 80,000 | |
| | Capital stock—Son (− SE) | 120,000 | |
| | Patents (+ A) | 36,000 | |
| | Investment in Son (− A) | | 188,800 |
| | Noncontrolling interest (+ SE) | | 47,200 |
| | To eliminate reciprocal investment and equity balances, establish beginning noncontrolling interest, and enter unamortized patents. | | |

Entry c eliminates the Investment in Son and stockholders' equity of Son amounts at December 31, 2016, and enters the noncontrolling interest at December 31, 2016; therefore, the $36,000 investment's fair-value difference reflects unamortized patents at December 31, 2016. Entry d amortizes this amount to the $32,000 balance at December 31, 2017:

| | | | |
|---|---|---:|---:|
| d | Expenses (E, − SE) | 4,000 | |
| | Patents (− A) | | 4,000 |
| | To enter current amortization. | | |

**EXHIBIT 4-2**

Equity Method—
Workpaper for Year
Subsequent to
Acquisition

## POP CORPORATION AND SUBSIDIARY CONSOLIDATION WORKPAPER FOR THE YEAR ENDED DECEMBER 31, 2017 (IN THOUSANDS)

| | Pop | 80% Son | Adjustments and Eliminations Debits | Adjustments and Eliminations Credits | Consolidated Statements |
|---|---|---|---|---|---|
| *Income Statement* | | | | | |
| Revenue | $600 | $150 | | | $ 750 |
| Income from Son | 44.8 | | a 44.8 | | |
| Expenses | (488) | (90) | d 4 | | (582) |
| Noncontrolling interest share ($56,000 × 20%) | | | b 11.2 | | (11.2) |
| **Controlling share of net income** | **$ 156.8** | **$ 60** | | | **$ 156.8** |
| *Retained Earnings Statement* | | | | | |
| Retained earnings—Pop | $ 86.8 | | | | $ 86.8 |
| Retained earnings—Son | | $ 80 | c 80 | | |
| **Add: Controlling share of net income** | **156.8** | **60** | | | **156.8** |
| Deduct: Dividends | (90) | (30) | | a  24 | |
| | | | | b   6 | (90) |
| **Retained earnings— December 31** | **$153.6** | **$110** | | | **$ 153.6** |
| *Balance Sheet* | | | | | |
| Cash | $ 90 | $ 40 | | | $ 130 |
| Note receivable—Son | 20 | | | e  20 | |
| Other current assets | 194 | 140 | | | 334 |
| Investment in Son | 209.6 | | | a  20.8 | |
| | | | | c 188.8 | |
| Plant and equipment | 600 | 200 | | | 800 |
| Accumulated depreciation | (120) | (80) | | | (200) |
| Patents | | | c 36 | d   4 | 32 |
| | **$993.6** | **$300** | | | **$1,096** |
| Note payable—Pop | | $ 20 | e 20 | | |
| Liabilities | $140 | 50 | | | $ 190 |
| Capital stock | 700 | 120 | c 120 | | 700 |
| **Retained earnings** | **153.6** | **110** | | | **153.6** |
| | **$993.6** | **$300** | | | |
| Noncontrolling interest January 1 ($236,000 × 20%) | | | | c 47.2 | |
| Noncontrolling interest December 31 | | | | b  5.2 | 52.4 |
| | | | **316** | **316** | **$1,096** |

The final workpaper entry eliminates intercompany notes payable and notes receivable balances because the amounts are not assets and liabilities of the consolidated entity:

| e   Note payable—Pop (− L) | 20,000 | |
|---|---|---|
| Note receivable—Son (− A) | | 20,000 |
| To eliminate reciprocal receivable and payable balances. | | |

The intercompany loan was not interest bearing, so the note receivable and payable are the only reciprocal balances created by the intercompany transaction. We would need additional eliminations for reciprocal interest income and interest expense and interest receivable and interest payable balances if the loan had been interest bearing.

Compare the consolidation workpaper of Exhibit 4-2 with that of Exhibit 4-1. Notice that the December 31, 2016, noncontrolling interest from Exhibit 4-1 is the beginning noncontrolling interest in Exhibit 4-2. Note that the unamortized patents amount in the consolidated balance sheet of Exhibit 4-1 is the beginning-of-the-period unamortized patents in Exhibit 4-2.

## LOCATING ERRORS

The last part of a consolidation workpaper to be completed is the consolidated balance sheet section. Most errors made in consolidating the financial statements will show up when the consolidated balance sheet does not balance. If the consolidated balance sheet fails to balance after recomputing totals, we should then check individual items to ensure that all items have been included. Omissions involving the noncontrolling interest share in the consolidated income statement and noncontrolling interest equity in the consolidated balance sheet occur because these items do not appear on the separate-company statements. We check the equality of debits and credits in the workpaper entries by totaling the adjustment and elimination columns. Although proper coding of each workpaper entry minimizes this type of error, many accountants prefer to total the adjustment and elimination columns as a regular workpaper procedure to protect against errors.

## EXCESS ASSIGNED TO IDENTIFIABLE NET ASSETS

GAAP (ASC 805-10-55) requires firms to provide at least summary disclosures regarding the allocation of the purchase price of an acquired subsidiary, especially as related to acquired goodwill and other intangible assets. GAAP specifically requires firms to disclose, in the year of acquisition, the fair value of the acquired enterprise, a condensed balance sheet showing amounts assigned to major classes of assets and liabilities, the amount of purchased research and development in process acquired, and total amounts assigned to major intangible asset categories. GAAP (ASC 350-10-05) further requires that the amount of goodwill be shown as a separate balance sheet line item (assuming it is material). Firms must also disclose material noncontrolling interests on the balance sheet and report noncontrolling interests' share of consolidated net income.

For example, in 2014, *GE* reported $76.553 billion of goodwill and $14.156 billion of other intangible assets. The separate listing of goodwill versus other intangible assets reflects new disclosure requirements for these assets under GAAP. (ASC 350-10-05) GE also reported a noncontrolling interest on the balance sheet of $8.674 billion.

The discussions thus far assume that firms assign any excess fair value to previously unrecorded patents. Consolidation workpaper procedures for allocating an excess fair value to specific assets and liabilities are similar to those illustrated for patents. The workpaper entries are more complex, however, because they affect more accounts and require additional allocation, amortization, and depreciation schemes. We illustrate these additional workpaper complexities here for Pam Corporation and its 90 percent–owned subsidiary, Sun Corporation.

Pam acquired its equity interest in Sun on December 31, 2016, for $360,000 cash, when Sun's stockholders' equity consisted of $200,000 capital stock and $50,000 retained earnings. This price implies a total fair value of $400,000 for Sun ($360,000 ÷ 90%). On the date that Sun became a subsidiary of Pam, the following assets of Sun had book values different from their fair values (amounts in thousands):

|  | Fair Value | Book Value | Undervaluation (Overvaluation) |
|---|---|---|---|
| Inventories | $ 60 | $ 50 | $ 10 |
| Land | 60 | 30 | 30 |
| Buildings—net | 180 | 100 | 80 |
| Equipment—net | 70 | 90 | (20) |
|  | $370 | $270 | $100 |

Based on this information, Pam assigns the $150,000 excess fair value to identifiable assets and goodwill, as shown in the following schedule (in thousands):

| | Undervaluation (Overvaluation) | Excess Allocation | Amortization Period |
|---|---|---|---|
| Inventories | $10 | $ 10 | Sold in 2017 |
| Land | 30 | 30 | None |
| Buildings—net | 80 | 80 | 20 years |
| Equipment—net | (20) | (20) | 10 years |
| Goodwill—remainder | | 50 | None |
| | | $150 | |

The schedule also shows the amortization periods assigned to the undervalued and overvalued assets.

## Consolidation at Acquisition

Exhibit 4-3 shows a consolidated balance sheet workpaper for Pam Corporation and Subsidiary immediately after the business combination on December 31, 2016. The excess fair-value allocation is reasonably complex, so we use an unamortized excess account in the workpaper.

The first workpaper entry eliminates reciprocal Investment in Sun and stockholders' equity accounts of Sun, enters the 10 percent noncontrolling interest in Sun (based on fair value), and debits the unamortized excess account for the $150,000 excess fair value over book value. A second workpaper entry assigns the excess to identifiable net assets and goodwill. The amounts assigned in the second workpaper entry are the original amounts because Pam and Sun are being consolidated immediately after the acquisition date.

**EXHIBIT 4-3**

Consolidation at Acquisition

**PAM CORPORATION AND SUBSIDIARY CONSOLIDATED BALANCE SHEET WORKPAPER ON DECEMBER 31, 2016 (IN THOUSANDS)**

| | Pam | 90% Sun | Adjustments and Eliminations Debits | Adjustments and Eliminations Credits | Consolidated Balance Sheet |
|---|---|---|---|---|---|
| **Assets** | | | | | |
| Cash | $ 25 | $ 5 | | | $ 30 |
| Receivables—net | 90 | 25 | | | 115 |
| Inventories | 80 | 50 | b 10 | | 140 |
| Land | 60 | 30 | b 30 | | 120 |
| Buildings—net | 200 | 100 | b 80 | | 380 |
| Equipment—net | 135 | 90 | | b 20 | 205 |
| Investment in Sun | 360 | | | a 360 | |
| Goodwill | | | b 50 | | 50 |
| Unamortized excess | | | a 150 | b 150 | |
| Totals | $950 | $300 | | | $1,040 |
| **Liabilities and Equity** | | | | | |
| Accounts payable | $130 | $ 50 | | | $ 180 |
| Capital stock—Pam | 700 | | | | 700 |
| Retained earnings—Pam | 120 | | | | 120 |
| Capital stock—Sun | | 200 | a 200 | | |
| Retained earnings—Sun | | 50 | a 50 | | |
| Noncontrolling interest | | | | a 40 | 40 |
| Totals | $950 | $300 | 570 | 570 | $1,040 |

## Consolidation After Acquisition

Sun reports $60,000 net income for 2017 and declares dividends of $10,000 on June 1 and December 1 ($20,000 total for 2017). Sun pays the June 1 dividend on July 1, but the December 1 dividend remains unpaid at December 31, 2017. During 2017, Sun sells the undervalued inventory items, but the undervalued land and buildings and overvalued equipment are still in use by Sun at December 31, 2017. On the date of acquisition, the buildings had a remaining useful life of 20 years, and the equipment, 10 years.

During 2017, Sun borrows $20,000 from Pam on a non-interest-bearing note. Sun repays the note on December 30, but the repayment check to Pam was in transit and was not reflected in Pam's separate balance sheet at December 31, 2017.

Pam made the following journal entries in 2017 to account for its investment in Sun:

*July 1*

| | | |
|---|---|---|
| Cash (+A) | 9,000 | |
|     Investment in Sun (−A) | | 9,000 |
| To record dividends from Sun | | |
| ($10,000 × 90%). | | |

*December 31*

| | | |
|---|---|---|
| Investment in Sun (+A) | 43,200 | |
|     Income from Sun (R, +SE) | | 43,200 |
| To record investment income from Sun, | | |
| determined as follows: | | |

| | |
|---|---|
| Sun's net income | $60,000 |
| Amortization of excess assigned to: | |
| Inventories (100% recognized) | −10,000 |
| Buildings ($80,000 ÷ 20 years) | −4,000 |
| Equipment ($20,000 ÷ 10 years) | +2,000 |
| Adjusted Income from Sun for 2017 | $48,000 |
| Pam's Share ($48,000 × 90%) | $43,200 |

These entries show that Pam has used a one-line consolidation in accounting for its $43,200 income from Sun for 2017, but it has failed to recognize Sun's December 1 dividend declaration. Accordingly, Pam has overstated its investment in Sun at December 31, 2017, by $9,000 (90 percent of Sun's $10,000 December 1 dividend declaration). The consolidation workpaper for Pam and Subsidiary for 2017 in Exhibit 4-4 shows Pam's investment in Sun at $394,200 ($360,000 cost plus $43,200 income less $9,000 dividends received), whereas the correct amount is $385,200. The overstatement is corrected in workpaper entry a of Exhibit 4-4:

| | | | |
|---|---|---|---|
| a | **Dividends receivable (+A)** | **9,000** | |
| |     **Investment in Sun (−A)** | | **9,000** |
| | **To correct investment balance for unrecorded dividends receivable.** | | |

This entry is different from previous workpaper entries because it represents a real adjustment that should also be recorded on Pam's books.

Workpaper entry b adjusts for the $20,000 cash in transit from Sun to Pam at December 31, 2017:

| | | | |
|---|---|---|---|
| b | **Cash (+A)** | **20,000** | |
| |     **Note receivable—Sun (−A)** | | **20,000** |
| | **To enter receipt of intercompany note receivable.** | | |

Workpaper entry b is also a real adjustment. Pam records this entry on its separate books, as well as in the consolidation workpaper. If Pam fails to record entries a and b as correcting entries on its separate books, it will record them in the normal course of events in 2018 when Pam receives the $9,000 dividend and the $20,000 note repayment checks from Sun. It is important that we always review year-end transactions between affiliates to make sure that both parent and subsidiary records properly reflect these events.

**PAM CORPORATION AND SUBSIDIARY CONSOLIDATION WORKPAPER FOR THE YEAR ENDED DECEMBER 31, 2017 (IN THOUSANDS)**

**EXHIBIT 4-4**

Consolidation One Year After Acquisition

| | Pam | 90% Sun | Adjustments and Eliminations Debits | Adjustments and Eliminations Credits | Consolidated Statements |
|---|---|---|---|---|---|
| *Income Statement* | | | | | |
| Sales | $900 | $300 | | | $1,200 |
| Income from Sun | 43.2 | | c  43.2 | | |
| Cost of goods sold | (600) | (150) | f  10 | | (760) |
| Operating expenses | (190) | (90) | g  4 | h  2 | (282) |
| Noncontrolling interest share ($48,000 × 10%) | | | d  4.8 | | (4.8) |
| **Controlling share of net income** | **$ 153.2** | **$ 60** | | | **$ 153.2** |
| *Retained Earnings Statement* Retained earnings—Pam | $ 120 | | | | $ 120 |
| Retained earnings—Sun | | $ 50 | e  50 | | |
| **Controlling share of net income** | **153.2** | **60** | | | **153.2** |
| Dividends | (100) | (20) | | c  18 | (100) |
| | | | | d  2 | |
| **Retained earnings—December 31** | **$173.2** | **$ 90** | | | **$ 173.2** |
| *Balance Sheet* Cash | $ 13 | $ 15 | b  20 | | $  48 |
| Accounts receivable—net | 76 | 25 | | | 101 |
| Note receivable—Sun | 20 | | | b  20 | |
| Inventories | 90 | 60 | | | 150 |
| Land | 60 | 30 | f  30 | | 120 |
| Buildings—net | 190 | 110 | f  80 | g  4 | 376 |
| Equipment—net | 150 | 120 | h  2 | f  20 | 252 |
| Investment in Sun | 394.2 | | | a  9 | |
| | | | | c  25.2 | |
| | | | | e 360 | |
| Dividends receivable | | | a  9 | i  9 | |
| Goodwill | | | f  50 | | 50 |
| Unamortized excess | | | e 150 | f 150 | |
| | $993.2 | $360 | | | $1,097 |
| Accounts payable | $120 | $ 60 | | | $  180 |
| Dividends payable | | 10 | i 9 | | 1 |
| Capital stock | 700 | 200 | e 200 | | 700 |
| **Retained earnings** | **173.2** | **90** | | | **173.2** |
| | $ 993.2 | $360 | | | |
| Noncontrolling interest January 1 | | | | e  40 | |
| Noncontrolling interest December 31 | | | | d  2.8 | 42.8 |
| | | | 662 | 662 | $1,097 |

Entry c eliminates the income from Sun and 90 percent of Sun's dividends, and it adjusts the Investment in Sun account to its $360,000 beginning-of-the-period balance. Entry d incorporates the noncontrolling interest in Sun's net income and the noncontrolling share of Sun's dividends. Entry e eliminates the reciprocal Investment in Sun account and the stockholders' equity accounts of Sun, records the 10 percent noncontrolling interest at the beginning of the period, and enters the $150,000 unamortized excess:

| | | | |
|---|---|---:|---:|
| c | Income from Sun (−R, −SE) | 43,200 | |
| |     Dividends (+SE) | | 18,000 |
| |     Investment in Sun (−A) | | 25,200 |
| | To eliminate income and dividends of Sun and return Investment account to beginning-of-the-period balance. | | |
| d | Noncontrolling interest share (−SE) | 4,800 | |
| |     Dividends (+SE) | | 2,000 |
| |     Noncontrolling interest (+SE) | | 2,800 |
| | To enter noncontrolling interest share of subsidiary income and dividends. | | |
| e | Retained earnings—Sun (−SE) | 50,000 | |
| | Capital stock—Sun (−SE) | 200,000 | |
| | Unamortized excess (+A) | 150,000 | |
| |     Investment in Sun (−A) | | 360,000 |
| |     Noncontrolling interest—January 1 (+SE) | | 40,000 |
| | To eliminate reciprocal investment and equity amounts, establish beginning noncontrolling interest, and enter unamortized excess. | | |

We assign the unamortized excess entered in workpaper entry e to identifiable assets and goodwill as of December 31, 2016, in entry f and amortize it in entries g and h. It is convenient to prepare a schedule to support these allocations and amortizations in preparing the workpaper entries and to provide documentation for subsequent consolidations:

| | Unamortized Excess December 31, 2016 | Amortization 2017 | Unamortized Excess December 31, 2017 |
|---|---:|---:|---:|
| Inventories | $ 10,000 | $10,000 | $    — |
| Land | 30,000 | — | 30,000 |
| Buildings—net | 80,000 | 4,000 | 76,000 |
| Equipment—net | (20,000) | (2,000) | (18,000) |
| Goodwill | 50,000 | — | 50,000 |
| | $150,000 | $12,000 | $138,000 |

With the exception of the $10,000 excess assigned to cost of goods sold, the allocation in workpaper entry f of Exhibit 4-4 is the same as the allocation in workpaper entry b in the consolidated balance sheet workpapers of Exhibit 4-3. We assign the $10,000 excess assigned to inventories to cost of goods sold because the related undervalued inventories from December 31, 2016, were sold in 2017, thus increasing cost of goods sold in the 2017 consolidated income statement. We journalize workpaper entry f as follows:

| | | | |
|---|---|---:|---:|
| f | Cost of goods sold (E, −SE) | 10,000 | |
| |     Land (+A) | 30,000 | |
| |     Building—net (+A) | 80,000 | |
| |     Goodwill (+A) | 50,000 | |
| |         Equipment—net (−A) | | 20,000 |
| |         Unamortized excess (−A) | | 150,000 |
| | To assign unamortized excess to identifiable assets and goodwill. | | |

Workpaper entries g and h are necessary to increase operating expenses for depreciation on the $80,000 excess assigned to undervalued buildings and to decrease operating expenses for excessive depreciation on the $20,000 assigned to overvalued equipment. Entry g for recording depreciation on the excess assigned to buildings is procedurally the same as the adjustment for patents shown previously, except that we credit buildings—net of depreciation. We can also show the credit to accumulated depreciation. The $2,000 debit to equipment—net and credit to operating expenses in workpaper entry h corrects for excessive depreciation on the overvalued equipment. Procedurally, this adjustment is the exact opposite of entry g, which corrects for underdepreciation on the buildings:

| | | | |
|---|---|---|---|
| g | Operating expenses (E, − SE) | 4,000 | |
| | Buildings—net (− A) | | 4,000 |
| | To enter current depreciation on excess assigned to buildings. | | |
| h | Equipment—net (+ A) | 2,000 | |
| | Operating expenses ( − E, + SE) | | 2,000 |
| | To adjust current depreciation for excess assigned to reduce equipment. | | |

Workpaper entry i eliminates reciprocal dividends payable and dividends receivable amounts:

| | | | |
|---|---|---|---|
| i | Dividends payable (− L) | 9,000 | |
| | Dividends receivable (− A) | | 9,000 |
| | To eliminate reciprocal receivables and payables. | | |

The $1,000 dividends payable of Sun that is not eliminated belongs to the noncontrolling interest. We include it among consolidated liabilities because it represents an amount payable outside the consolidated entity.

## CONSOLIDATED STATEMENT OF CASH FLOWS

LEARNING OBJECTIVE **4.5**

We prepare the consolidated statement of cash flows (SCF) from consolidated income statements and consolidated balance sheets, rather than from the separate parent and subsidiary statements. With minor exceptions, the preparation of a consolidated SCF involves the same analysis and procedures that are used in preparing the SCF for separate entities.

Exhibit 4-5 presents consolidated balance sheets at December 31, 2016 and 2017, and the 2017 consolidated income statement for Pop Corporation and its 80 percent–owned subsidiary, Son Corporation. We use consolidated balance sheets at the beginning and end of the year to calculate the year's changes, which must be explained in the SCF. Other information pertinent to the preparation of Pop's consolidated SCF is as follows:

1. During 2017, Son sold land that cost $20,000 to outside entities for $10,000 cash.
2. Pop issued a $300,000, two-year note on January 8, 2017, for new equipment.
3. Patents amortization from the Pop-Sun business combination is $10,000 per year.
4. Pop received $10,000 in dividends from its investments in equity investees.
5. Changes in plant assets not explained earlier are due to provisions for depreciation.

We prepare the SCF using a single concept: cash and cash equivalents. GAAP permits two presentations for reporting net cash flows from operations. The indirect method begins with the controlling share of consolidated net income and includes adjustments for items not providing or using cash to arrive at net cash flows from operations. The direct method offsets cash received from customers and investment income against cash paid to suppliers, employees, governmental units, and so on to arrive at net cash flows from operations. Although the GAAP has expressed a preference for the direct method of reporting net cash flows from operations (ASC 230-10-45), most companies present a SCF using the indirect method.

EXHIBIT 4-5

Consolidated Balance
Sheets and Income
Statement for Pop and
Subsidiary

## POP CORPORATION AND SUBSIDIARY COMPARATIVE CONSOLIDATED BALANCE SHEETS AT DECEMBER 31, 2016 AND 2017 (IN THOUSANDS)

| | 2017 | 2016 | Year's Change: Increase (Decrease) |
|---|---|---|---|
| Cash | $ 255 | $ 180 | $ 75 |
| Accounts receivable—net | 375 | 270 | 105 |
| Inventories | 250 | 205 | 45 |
| Equity investments | 100 | 95 | 5 |
| Land | 80 | 100 | (20) |
| Buildings—net | 200 | 220 | (20) |
| Equipment—net | 800 | 600 | 200 |
| Patents | 90 | 100 | (10) |
| | $2,150 | $1,770 | $380 |
| Accounts payable | $ 250 | 270 | $ (20) |
| Dividends payable | 20 | 20 | — |
| Note payable due 2019 | 300 | — | 300 |
| Common stock | 500 | 500 | — |
| Other paid-in capital | 300 | 300 | — |
| Retained earnings | 670 | 600 | 70 |
| Noncontrolling interest—20% | 110 | 80 | 30 |
| | $2,150 | $1,770 | $380 |

## CONSOLIDATED INCOME STATEMENT FOR THE YEAR ENDED DECEMBER 31, 2017 (IN THOUSANDS)

| | | | |
|---|---|---|---|
| Sales | | | $750 |
| Income from equity investees | | | 15 |
| Total revenue | | | 765 |
| Less expenses: | | | |
| Cost of goods sold | | $300 | |
| Depreciation expense | | 120 | |
| Patents amortization | | 10 | |
| Wages and salaries | | 54 | |
| Other operating expenses | | 47 | |
| Interest expense | | 24 | |
| Loss on sale of land | | 10 | (565) |
| Total consolidated net income | | | 200 |
| Less: Noncontrolling interest share | | | (50) |
| Controlling share of consolidated net income | | | 150 |
| Consolidated Retained Earnings January 1 | | | 600 |
| Less: Cash dividends paid | | | (80) |
| Consolidated Retained Earnings December 31 | | | $670 |

## Consolidated Statement of Cash Flows—Indirect Method

Exhibit 4-6 presents a consolidated SCF for Pop Corporation and Subsidiary under the indirect method. This statement is based on the consolidated balance sheet changes and the 2017 consolidated income statement that appears in Exhibit 4-5 for Pop Corporation and Subsidiary. Exhibit 4-7 presents an SCF worksheet that organizes the information for statement preparation using the

| POP CORPORATION AND SUBSIDIARY CONSOLIDATED STATEMENT OF CASH FLOWS FOR THE YEAR ENDED DECEMBER 31, 2017 (IN THOUSANDS) | | |
|---|---:|---:|
| *Cash Flows from Operating Activities* | | |
| Controlling share of consolidated net income | | $150 |
| Adjustments to reconcile controlling share of consolidated net income to net cash provided by operating activities: | | |
| Noncontrolling interest share | $ 50 | |
| Undistributed income—equity investees | (5) | |
| Loss on sale of land | 10 | |
| Depreciation on equipment | 100 | |
| Depreciation on buildings | 20 | |
| Amortization of patents | 10 | |
| Increase in accounts receivable | (105) | |
| Increase in inventories | (45) | |
| Decrease in accounts payable | (20) | 15 |
| Net cash flows from operating activities | | 165 |
| *Cash Flows from Investing Activities* | | |
| Proceeds from sale of land | $ 10 | |
| Net cash flows from investing activities | | 10 |
| *Cash Flows from Financing Activities* | | |
| Payment of cash dividends—controlling interest | $ (80) | |
| Payment of cash dividends—noncontrolling interest | (20) | |
| Net cash flows from financing activities | | (100) |
| Increase in cash for 2017 | | 75 |
| Cash on January 1, 2017 | | 180 |
| Cash on December 31, 2017 | | $255 |
| *Listing of Noncash Investing and Financing Activities* Equipment purchased for $300,000 by issuing a two-year note payable | | |

**EXHIBIT 4-6**

**Consolidated Statement of Cash Flows—Indirect Method**

schedule approach. We prepare the consolidated SCF directly from the Cash Flow from Operations, Cash Flow—Investing Activities, and Cash Flow—Financing Activities columns of the worksheet in Exhibit 4-7.

Noncontrolling interest share of consolidated net income is an increase in the cash flow from operating activities because noncontrolling interest share increases consolidated assets and liabilities in exactly the same manner as controlling interest share of consolidated net income. Similarly, we deduct noncontrolling interest dividends in reporting the cash flows from financing activities.

## Income and Dividends from Investees Under the Indirect and Direct Methods

Income from equity investees is an item that requires special attention in the consolidated SCF when using the indirect method. Income from equity investees increases income without increasing cash because the investment account reflects the increase. Conversely, dividends received from equity investees increase cash but do not affect income because the investment account reflects the decrease.

We deduct (or add) the net amount of these items from controlling share of net income in the Cash Flows from Operating Activities section of the SCF under the indirect method. We add an excess of dividends received over equity income. We would deduct an excess of equity income over

**EXHIBIT 4-7**

Worksheet for Consolidated SCF—Indirect Method

## POP CORPORATION AND SUBSIDIARY WORKPAPERS FOR THE STATEMENT OF CASH FLOWS (INDIRECT METHOD) FOR THE YEAR ENDED DECEMBER 31, 2017 (IN THOUSANDS)

| | Year's Change | Reconciling Items Debit | Reconciling Items Credit | Cash Flow from Operations | Cash Flow—Investing Activities | Cash Flow—Financing Activities |
|---|---|---|---|---|---|---|
| *Asset Changes* | | | | | | |
| Cash | 75 | | | | | |
| Accounts receivable—net | 105 | | k 105 | | | |
| Inventories | 45 | | l 45 | | | |
| Equity investments | 5 | | e 5 | | | |
| Land | (20) | f 20 | | | | |
| Buildings—net | (20) | i 20 | | | | |
| Equipment—net* | 200 | h 100 | g 300 | | | |
| Patents | (10) | j 10 | | | | |
| Total asset changes | 380 | | | | | |
| *Equity Changes* | | | | | | |
| Accounts payable | (20) | | m 20 | | | |
| Dividends payable | 0 | | | | | |
| Note payable due 2019* | 300 | g 300 | | | | |
| Common stock | 0 | | | | | |
| Other paid-in capital | 0 | | | | | |
| Retained earnings | 70 | a 150 | b 80 | | | |
| Noncontrolling interest | 30 | c 50 | d 20 | | | |
| Total equity changes | 380 | | | | | |
| Controlling share of consolidated net income | | | a 150 | 150 | | |
| Noncontrolling interest share | | | c 50 | 50 | | |
| Income—equity investees | | e 5 | | (5) | | |
| Loss of sale of land | | | f 10 | 10 | | |
| Depreciation on equipment | | | h 100 | 100 | | |
| Depreciation on buildings | | | i 20 | 20 | | |
| Amortization of patents | | | j 10 | 10 | | |
| Increase in accounts receivable | | k 105 | | (105) | | |
| Increase in inventories | | l 45 | | (45) | | |
| Decrease in accounts payable | | m 20 | | (20) | | |
| Proceeds from sale of land | | | f 10 | | 10 | |
| Payment of dividends—controlling | | b 80 | | | | (80) |
| Payment of dividends—noncontrolling | | d 20 | | | | (20) |
| | | 925 | 925 | 165 | 10 | (100) |
| Net cash flows from operating activities | | | | $165 | | |
| Net cash flows from investing activities | | | | 10 | | |
| Net cash flows from financing activities | | | | (100) | | |
| Increase in cash for 2017 = cash change above | | | | $ 75 | | |

*Noncash investing and financing transaction: equipment purchased for $300,000 by issuing a two-year note payable.

dividends received. We simply report dividends received from equity investees as cash inflows from operating activities when using the direct method to prepare the SCF.

## Consolidated Statement of Cash Flows—Direct Method

Exhibit 4-8 presents a consolidated SCF for Pop Corporation and Subsidiary under the direct method. This statement is identical to the one presented in Exhibit 4-6, except for cash flows from

**EXHIBIT 4-8**

Consolidated Statement of Cash Flows—Direct Method

## POP CORPORATION AND SUBSIDIARY CONSOLIDATED STATEMENT OF CASH FLOWS FOR THE YEAR ENDED DECEMBER 31, 2017 (IN THOUSANDS)

*Cash Flows from Operating Activities*

| | | |
|---|---|---|
| Cash received from customers | | $ 645 |
| Dividends received from equity investees | | 10 |
| Less: Cash paid to suppliers | $ 365 | |
| Cash paid to employees | 54 | |
| Paid for other operating items | 47 | |
| Cash paid for interest expense | 24 | (490) |
| Net cash flows from operating activities | | 165 |

*Cash Flows from Investing Activities*

| | | |
|---|---|---|
| Proceeds from sale of land | $ 10 | |
| Net cash flows from investing activities | | 10 |

*Cash Flows from Financing Activities*

| | | |
|---|---|---|
| Payment of cash dividends—controlling interests | $ (80) | |
| Payment of cash dividends—noncontrolling interests | (20) | |
| Net cash flows from financing activities | | (100) |
| Increase in cash for 2017 | | 75 |
| Cash on January 1, 2017 | | 180 |
| Cash on December 31, 2017 | | $ 255 |

*Listing of Noncash Investment and Financing Activities*
Equipment was purchased for $300,000 through the issuance of a two-year note payable

*Reconciliation of Controlling share of Consolidated Net Income to Net Cash from operating activities*

| | | |
|---|---|---|
| Controlling share of consolidated net income | | $ 150 |
| Adjustments to reconcile controlling share of consolidated net income to net cash provided by operating activities: | | |
| Noncontrolling interest share | $ 50 | |
| Undistributed income—equity investees | (5) | |
| Loss on sale of land | 10 | |
| Depreciation on equipment | 100 | |
| Depreciation on buildings | 20 | |
| Amortization of patents | 10 | |
| Increase in accounts receivable | (105) | |
| Increase in inventories | (45) | |
| Decrease in accounts payable | (20) | 15 |
| Net cash flows from operating activities | | $ 165 |

operating activities. Under the direct method, we convert the consolidated income statement items that involve cash flows from the accrual to the cash basis, and we explain those items that do not involve cash in notes or schedules supporting the cash flow statement. Exhibit 4-9 shows a worksheet that organizes information for a consolidated SCF under the direct method. We prepare the SCF from the last three columns of the worksheet.

If you compare the cash flow statements in Exhibits 4-6 and 4-8, you should observe that the cash flows from investing and financing activities are identical. The significant differences lie in the presentation of cash flows from operating activities and the additional schedule to reconcile the controlling share of consolidated net income to net cash flows from operating activities under the direct method. Although the presentation in Exhibit 4-8 under the direct method may be less familiar, it is somewhat easier to interpret.

## EXHIBIT 4-9

**Worksheet for Consolidated SCF—Direct Method**

### POP CORPORATION AND SUBSIDIARY WORKPAPERS FOR THE STATEMENT OF CASH FLOWS (DIRECT METHOD) FOR THE YEAR ENDED DECEMBER 31, 2017 (IN THOUSANDS)

| | Year's Change | Reconciling Items Debit | Reconciling Items Credit | Cash Flow from Operations | Cash Flow—Investing Activities | Cash Flow—Financing Activities |
|---|---|---|---|---|---|---|
| **Asset Changes** | | | | | | |
| Cash | 75 | | | | | |
| Accounts receivable—net | 105 | | a 105 | | | |
| Inventories | 45 | | c  45 | | | |
| Equity investments | 5 | | b   5 | | | |
| Land | (20) | h  20 | | | | |
| Buildings—net | (20) | f  20 | | | | |
| Equipment—net* | 200 | e 100 | d 300 | | | |
| Patents | (10) | g  10 | | | | |
| Total asset changes | 380 | | | | | |
| **Equity Changes** | | | | | | |
| Accounts payable | (20) | | c  20 | | | |
| Dividends payable | 0 | | | | | |
| Note payable due 2019* | 300 | d 300 | | | | |
| Common stock | 0 | | | | | |
| Other paid-in capital | 0 | | | | | |
| Retained earnings** | 70 | | | | | |
| Noncontrolling interest | 30 | i  50 | j  20 | | | |
| Total equity changes | 380 | | | | | |
| **Retained Earnings Changes*** | | | | | | |
| Sales | 750 | a 105 | | 645 | | |
| Income—equity investees | 15 | b   5 | | 10 | | |
| Cost of goods sold | (300) | c  65 | | (365) | | |
| Depreciation on equipment | (100) | | e 100 | | | |
| Depreciation on buildings | (20) | | f  20 | | | |
| Patents amortization | (10) | | g  10 | | | |
| Wages and salaries | (54) | | | (54) | | |
| Other operating expenses | (47) | | | (47) | | |
| Interest expense | (24) | | | (24) | | |
| Loss on sale of land | (10) | | h  10 | | | |
| Noncontrolling interest share | (50) | | i  50 | | | |
| Dividends paid by Pop | (80) | | k  80 | | | |
| Change in retained earnings | 70 | | | | | |
| Payment of dividends—controlling | | k  80 | | | | (80) |
| Payment of dividends—noncontrolling | | j  20 | | | | (20) |
| Proceeds from the land sale | | | h  10 | | 10 | |
| | | 775 | 775 | 165 | 10 | (100) |

*Noncash investing and financing transaction: equipment purchased for $300,000 by issuing a two-year note payable.
**Retained earnings changes replace the retained earnings account for reconciling purposes.

## PREPARING A CONSOLIDATION WORKSHEET

In this section, you learn how to set up a three-part worksheet to prepare a consolidated income statement, retained earnings statement, and balance sheet. This worksheet follows the same basic pattern as that described in Chapter 3 to prepare a consolidated balance sheet at acquisition. Refer to Exhibit 4-10. We have two columns to record trial balance information for a parent company and

---

**EXHIBIT 4-10**

Preparing a Complete Consolidation Worksheet

---

### PARENT AND SUBSIDIARY CONSOLIDATION WORKSHEET FOR THE YEAR ENDED DECEMBER 31, 2016 (IN THOUSANDS)

| | Parent | 70% Subsidiary | Adjustments and Eliminations | | Consolidated Statements |
| | | | Debits | Credits | |
| --- | --- | --- | --- | --- | --- |
| *Income Statement* | | | | | |
| Sales | | | | | = B6 + C6 − D6 + E6 |
| Income from Subsidiary | | | | | = B7 + C7 − D7 + E7 |
| Cost of goods sold | | | | | = B8 + C8 − D8 + E8 |
| Operating expenses | | | | | = B9 + C9 − D9 + E9 |
| Noncontrolling interest share | | | | | = B10 + C10 − D10 + E10 |
| **Controlling share of NI** | = SUM(B6:B10) | = SUM(C6:C10) | | | = SUM(F6:F10) |
| *Retained Earnings Statement* | | | | | |
| Retained earnings—Parent | | | | | = B13 + C13 − D13 + E13 |
| Retained earnings—Subsidiary | | | | | = B14 + C14 − D14 + E14 |
| Controlling share of NI | = B11 | = C11 | | | = F11 |
| Dividends | | | | | = B16 + C16 − D16 + E16 − D17 + E17 |
| **Retained earnings—ending** | = SUM(B13:B16) | = SUM(C13:C16) | | | = SUM(F13:F17) |
| *Balance Sheet* | | | | | |
| Cash | | | | | = B20 + C20 + D20 − E20 |
| Receivables—net | | | | | = B21 + C21 + D21 − E21 |
| Inventories | | | | | = B22 + C22 + D22 − E22 |
| Plant & equipment—net | | | | | = B23 + C23 + D23 − E23 |
| Investment in Subsidiary | | | | | = B24 + C24 + D24 − E24 + D25 − E25 = B26 + C26 + D26 − E26 |
| **Total assets** | = SUM(B20:B26) | = SUM(C20:C26) | | | = SUM(F20:F26) |
| Accounts payable | | | | | = B28 + C28 − D28 + E28 |
| Other liabilities | | | | | = B29 + C29 − D29 + E29 |
| Capital stock, $10 par | | | | | = B30 + C30 − D30 + E30 |
| Other paid-in capital | | | | | = B31 + C31 − D31 + E31 |
| Retained earnings | = B18 | = C18 | | | = F18 |
| **Total equities** | = SUM(B28:B32) | = SUM(C28:C32) | | | |
| Noncontrolling interest | | | | | = B34 + C34 − D34 + E34 − D35 + E35 |
| | | | = SUM(D6:D35) | = SUM(E6:E35) | = SUM(F28:F35) |

EXHIBIT 4-11

Building the Worksheet

## POP AND SUBSIDIARY CONSOLIDATION WORKSHEET FOR THE YEAR ENDED DECEMBER 31, 2016 (IN THOUSANDS)

| | Pop | 70% Son | Adjustments and Eliminations | | Consolidated Statements* |
| --- | --- | --- | --- | --- | --- |
| | | | Debits | Credits | |
| *Income Statement* | | | | | |
| Sales | 3,100 | 1,000 | | | 4,100 |
| Income from Son | 105 | 0 | | | 105 |
| Cost of goods sold | (2,000) | (650) | | | (2,650) |
| Operating expenses | (770) | (200) | | | (970) |
| **Net income** | **435** | **150** | | | **585** |
| *Retained Earnings Statement* | | | | | |
| Retained earnings—Pop | 650 | | | | 650 |
| Retained earnings—Son | | 110 | | | 110 |
| Net income | 435 | 150 | | | 585 |
| Dividends | (300) | (100) | | | (400) |
| **Retained earnings—ending** | **785** | **160** | | | **945** |
| *Balance Sheet* | | | | | |
| Cash | 455 | 150 | | | 605 |
| Accounts receivable—net | 600 | 300 | | | 900 |
| Inventories | 240 | 200 | | | 440 |
| Plant & equipment—net | 1,200 | 350 | | | 1,550 |
| Investment in Son | 490 | | | | 490 |
| | | | | | 0 |
| **Total assets** | **2,985** | **1,000** | | | **3,985** |
| Accounts payable | 300 | 180 | | | 480 |
| Other liabilities | 200 | 120 | | | 320 |
| Capital stock, $10 par | 1,500 | 500 | | | 2,000 |
| Other paid-in capital | 200 | 40 | | | 240 |
| Retained earnings | 785 | 160 | | | 945 |
| **Total equities** | **2,985** | **1,000** | | | **3,985** |

*Note the Consolidated statements column is before adjustments and eliminations.

(in our example) a 70 percent–owned subsidiary. Most of the numbers in these two columns are simply copied from the individual company trial balances. Note that we record 100 percent of amounts from the subsidiary, even though the parent owns only 70 percent of the common stock. We will adjust for the 30 percent of the subsidiary not controlled by the parent (the noncontrolling interest) in computing our consolidated totals. We include two columns to record the debits and credits for consolidation adjustments and eliminations. The final column provides calculations of the correct consolidated financial statement balances. Vertically, we divide the worksheet into three separate parts for the three financial statements we want to prepare. Notice the boldfaced items: **controlling share of net income**, retained earnings (ending), total assets, and total equities. No amounts are input for these items. They are calculated.

Exhibit 4-10 shows spreadsheet formulae used in preparing the worksheet. Notice that most of these can be input using the COPY command available in the spreadsheet software. In the first two columns, controlling share of net income, retained earnings—ending, total assets, and total equities—are simple summations of the relevant balances. Notice, too, that controlling share of net income in the retained earnings section of the worksheet and retained earnings in the balance sheet section are simple amount carryforwards from the income statement and retained earnings sections, respectively. The adjustments and eliminations columns each contain a single summation formula for the column totals. This is useful in verifying the equality of debits and credits (in other words, that you have not made any errors in posting your consolidation entries).

There are lots of formulae in the final consolidated statements column, but again most of these can be entered with the COPY command. As in the first two columns, controlling share of net income, retained earnings—ending, total assets, and total equities—are simple summations of the relevant balances, and controlling share of net income in the retained earnings section and retained earnings in the balance sheet section are simply amount carryforwards from the income statement and retained earnings sections, respectively. Let's look at the formula for Sales ($= B6 + C6 - D6 + E6$). We simply sum parent-company sales plus subsidiary-company sales and then make any needed adjustments and eliminations. Notice that sales has a normal credit balance, so we subtract the debit adjustments ($-D6$) and add credits ($+E6$) to arrive at the consolidated total. We can simply copy our formula for all accounts having normal credit balances (i.e., revenues, liabilities, and stockholders' equity).

We keep the same basic formula for cost of goods sold and any other expenses in the income statement portion of the worksheet. We do so because we enter the expenses as negative amounts.

If you look to the balance sheet section, our formula for consolidated cash ($= B20 + C20 + D20 - E20$) reflects the fact that cash has a normal debit balance that is increased by debit adjustments and decreased by credits. Formulae for the remaining asset balances are entered using the COPY command. Before leaving Exhibit 4-10, pay attention to the formula for the investment in subsidiary. This is a bit longer than the cash formula, and it simply illustrates how to adjust the formula when we have multiple debit and credit adjustments to the same account.

We will discuss the completion of the worksheet by working through a sample problem. Separate-company trial balances for Pop Corporation and Son Company at December 31, 2016, are summarized as follows (in thousands):

|  | Pop Corporation | Son Company |
|---|---|---|
| Sales | $3,100 | $1,000 |
| Income from Son | 105 | — |
| Accounts payable | 300 | 180 |
| Other liabilities | 200 | 120 |
| Capital stock, $10 par | 1,500 | 500 |
| Other paid-in capital | 200 | 40 |
| Retained earnings—January 1 | 650 | 110 |
|  | $6,055 | $1,950 |
| Cash | $ 455 | $ 150 |
| Accounts receivable—net | 600 | 300 |
| Cost of sales | 2,000 | 650 |
| Dividends | 300 | 100 |
| Inventory | 240 | 200 |
| Investment in Son—70% | 490 | — |
| Operating expenses | 770 | 200 |
| Plant & equipment—net | 1,200 | 350 |
|  | $6,055 | $1,950 |

Pop Corporation acquired 70 percent of the outstanding voting shares of Son Company for $455,000 on January 1, 2016, when Son's stockholders' equity at book value was $650,000. Note that the acquisition price implies that the total fair value of Son is $650,000 ($455,000 ÷ 70%). All of the assets and liabilities of Son were stated at fair values (equal to book values) when Pop acquired its 70 percent interest.

We enter the data into our worksheet in Exhibit 4-11. Exhibit 4-11 is our template worksheet from Exhibit 4-10, but we have added the example data in columns one and two. We begin with the income statement accounts. Note that we record revenues as positive amounts and expenses as negatives. Net income is then a simple summation of revenues and expenses. We carry the calculated Net income down to the *Retained Earnings* section of the worksheet with no further adjustment required.

Beginning-of-the-year retained earnings amounts come from the Pop and Son trial balances. We record dividends as negative amounts because they reduce retained earnings. Ending retained earnings is now a simple summation. We carry the calculated ending retained earnings down to the *Balance Sheet* section of the worksheet with no further adjustment required.

We record balance sheet amounts picked up from the Pop and Son trial balances. Notice that we record assets, liabilities, and equities as positive amounts. Total assets and total equities are simple summation functions.

Pop's $105,000 income from Son for 2016 consists of 70 percent of Son's $150,000 net income for 2016. Its $490,000 Investment in Son account balance at December 31, 2016, consists of the $455,000 investment cost plus $105,000 income from Son, less $70,000 dividends received from Son during 2016.

In our workpaper format, we carry the controlling share of net income line down to the retained earnings section of the worksheet without any further adjustment. We similarly carry the ending retained earnings row down to the balance sheet section, again without further adjustments or eliminations. Notice, too, that each row in the workpaper generates the consolidated amounts by adding together the Pop and Son account balances and then adding or subtracting the adjustments and eliminations as appropriate.

Finally, we are going to review the required consolidation adjustments and eliminations. We provide a separate Exhibit 4-12 to show the final consolidation worksheet, after posting the adjustments and eliminations. This is simply Exhibit 4-11, updated to reflect the entries that follow. Notice, too, that we have added some new accounts. We create noncontrolling interest share in the income statement section and noncontrolling interest in the balance sheet section and copy the relevant formulae for expense accounts and stockholders' equity. The first workpaper entry in Exhibit 4-12 is the following:

| | | | |
|---|---|---|---|
| a | Income from Son ($-$ R, $-$ SE) | 105,000 | |
| | Dividends ($+$ SE) | | 70,000 |
| | Investment in Son ($-$ A) | | 35,000 |
| | To eliminate income and dividends from Son and return the investment account to its beginning-of-the-period balance. | | |

The difference between income from a subsidiary recognized on the books of the parent and the dividends received represents the change in the investment account for the period. The $35,000 credit to the Investment in Son account reduces that account to its $455,000 beginning-of-the-period balance and thereby establishes reciprocity between the Investment in Son and Son's stockholders' equity at January 1, 2016.

Here is a journal entry for workpaper entry b for Exhibit 4-12:

| | | | |
|---|---|---|---|
| b | Noncontrolling interest share ($-$ SE) | 45,000 | |
| | Dividends ($+$ SE) | | 30,000 |
| | Noncontrolling interest ($+$ SE) | | 15,000 |
| | To enter noncontrolling interest share of subsidiary income and dividends. | | |

Entry b incorporates the noncontrolling interest in Son's net income and the noncontrolling interest's share of dividends declared by Son directly into the consolidation workpapers.

Workpaper entry c in journal entry form is as follows:

| | | | |
|---|---|---|---|
| c | Retained earnings—Son (beginning) ($-$ SE) | 110,000 | |
| | Capital stock—Son ($-$ SE) | 500,000 | |
| | Other paid-in capital—Son ($-$ SE) | 40,000 | |
| | Investment in Son ($-$ A) | | 455,000 |
| | Noncontrolling interest ($+$ SE) | | 195,000 |
| | To eliminate reciprocal equity and investment balances, and establish beginning noncontrolling interest. | | |

**EXHIBIT 4-12**

Completing the Worksheet

## POP CORPORATION AND SUBSIDIARY CONSOLIDATION WORKSHEET FOR THE YEAR ENDED DECEMBER 31, 2016 (IN THOUSANDS)

| | Pop | 70% Son | Adjustments and Eliminations Debits | Credits | Consolidated Statements |
|---|---|---|---|---|---|
| *Income Statement* | | | | | |
| Sales | 3,100 | 1,000 | | | 4,100 |
| Income from Son | 105 | | a 105 | | 0 |
| Cost of goods sold | (2,000) | (650) | | | (2,650) |
| Operating expenses | (770) | (200) | | | (970) |
| Noncontrolling interest share | | | b 45 | | (45) |
| **Controlling share of net income** | **435** | **150** | | | **435** |
| *Retained Earnings Statement* | | | | | |
| Retained earnings—Pop | 650 | | | | 650 |
| Retained earnings—Son | | 110 | c 110 | | 0 |
| Controlling share of net income | 435 | 150 | | | 435 |
| Dividends | (300) | (100) | | a 70 | |
| | | | | b 30 | (300) |
| **Retained earnings—ending** | **785** | **160** | | | **785** |
| *Balance Sheet* | | | | | |
| Cash | 455 | 150 | | | 605 |
| Receivables—net | 600 | 300 | | | 900 |
| Inventories | 240 | 200 | | | 440 |
| Plant and equipment—net | 1,200 | 350 | | | 1,550 |
| Investment in Son | 490 | | | a 35 | 0 |
| | | | | c 455 | |
| **Total assets** | **2,985** | **1,000** | | | **3,495** |
| Accounts payable | 300 | 180 | | | 480 |
| Other liabilities | 200 | 120 | | | 320 |
| Capital stock, $10 par | 1,500 | 500 | c 500 | | 1,500 |
| Other paid-in capital | 200 | 40 | c 40 | | 200 |
| Retained earnings | 785 | 160 | | | 785 |
| **Total equities** | **2,985** | **1,000** | | | |
| Noncontrolling interest | | | | c 195 | 210 |
| | | | | b 15 | |
| | | | **800** | **800** | **3,495** |

This entry eliminates reciprocal investment and equity balances, enters the unamortized excess of investment fair value over book value acquired as of the beginning of the year (zero in this example), and constructs beginning noncontrolling interest ($650,000 × 30%) as a separate item. Observe that entry c eliminates reciprocal investment and equity balances as of the beginning of the period and enters noncontrolling interest as of the same date.

Parent-retained earnings under the complete equity method of accounting are equal to consolidated retained earnings. Because Pop correctly applies the equity method, its net income of $435,000 equals the controlling share of consolidated net income. Its beginning and ending retained earnings balances equal the $650,000 and $785,000 consolidated retained earnings amounts, respectively.

Our spreadsheet formulae compute the final consolidated statement totals for us in the final column. The worksheet is complete. You may want to practice creating the worksheet for a few problems to be certain you understand the mechanics. However, you will not need to create your own worksheets for all problem assignments. We eliminate the mechanical drudgery, and allow you to focus on learning the advanced accounting concepts, by providing worksheet templates for many assignments. The templates already include the data from the problem for the parent and subsidiary and the formulae for calculating consolidated balances. You can find the templates on the *Advanced Accounting* Web site.

## SUMMARY

We use workpapers to prepare meaningful financial reports for a consolidated business entity. Preparation of meaningful consolidated financial statements is the objective. The workpapers are tools for organizing and manipulating data. If you clearly understand the objective, you can determine the proper amounts for the consolidated statements without preparing the workpapers.

Throughout the chapter, it was assumed that the parent uses the complete equity method to account for its investment in the subsidiary. The consolidated SCF can be prepared from the consolidated balance sheets and income statements.

## APPENDIX A

**LEARNING OBJECTIVE 4.7**

### TRIAL BALANCE WORKPAPER FORMAT

The main text of this chapter discusses preparation of consolidated statements using a workpaper format called the financial statement approach. This appendix presents an alternative workpaper format using parent and subsidiary-company trial balances.

The trial balance approach to consolidation workpapers brings together the adjusted trial balances for affiliated companies. Both the financial statement approach and the trial balance approach generate the same information, so the selection is based on user preference. If completed financial statements are available, the financial statement approach is easier to use because it provides measurements of parent and subsidiary income, retained earnings, assets, and equities that are needed in the consolidating process. If the accountant is given adjusted trial balances to consolidate, the trial balance approach may be more convenient.

Workpaper entries illustrated in this chapter are designed for convenient switching between the financial statement and trial balance approaches for consolidation workpapers. Recall that we adjust or eliminate account balances. Net income is not an account balance, so it is not subject to adjustment. We assume all nominal accounts are open to permit adjustment. The only retained earnings amount that appears in an adjusted trial balance is the beginning retained earnings amount. Therefore, the adjustments and eliminations are exactly the same whether we use the trial balance approach or the financial statement approach. This is so because we are working with beginning retained earnings and adjusting actual account balances.

### CONSOLIDATION EXAMPLE—TRIAL BALANCE FORMAT AND EQUITY METHOD

Exhibit 4-13 illustrates consolidation workpapers using the trial balance format for Pop Corporation and its 90 percent–owned subsidiary, Son Corporation. Pop acquired its interest in Son on January 1, 2016, at a price $20,000 in excess of Son's total $40,000 book value, and it assigned the excess to patents with a 10-year amortization period.

A summary of changes in Pop's Investment in Son account from the date of acquisition to December 31, 2017, the report date, is as follows:

| | |
|---|---:|
| Investment cost January 1, 2016 | $54,000 |
| Add: Income—2016 (90% of Son's $10,000 net income less $2,000 amortization of patents) | 7,200 |
| Investment balance December 31, 2016 | 61,200 |
| Add: Income—2017 (90% of Son's $20,000 net income less $2,000 amortization of patents) | 16,200 |
| Deduct: Dividends received from Son (90% × $10,000) | −9,000 |
| Investment balance December 31, 2017 | $68,400 |

The workpapers presented in Exhibit 4-13 reflect the additional assumptions that Pop sold merchandise to Son during 2017 for $14,000, and that, as of December 31, 2017, Son owed Pop $5,000 from the sale. Son sold the merchandise to its customers, so the consolidated entity realized all profit from the sale during 2017.

Separate adjusted trial balances are presented in the first three columns of Exhibit 4-13. As shown in the exhibit, debit-balance accounts are presented first and totaled, and credit-balance accounts are presented and totaled below the debit-balance accounts. Separate lines are added at the bottom of the list of accounts for Noncontrolling Interest Beginning of Year, Noncontrolling Interest Share, Controlling Share of Consolidated Net Income, Consolidated Retained Earnings End of Year, and Noncontrolling Interest End of Year.

The workpaper entries to prepare consolidated financial statements using the trial balance are the same as those for the financial statement approach. However, we classify the accounts in a trial

## EXHIBIT 4-13

**Trial Balance Approach for Workpapers**

### POP CORPORATION AND SUBSIDIARY CONSOLIDATION WORKPAPER FOR THE YEAR ENDED DECEMBER 31, 2017 (IN THOUSANDS)

| | Pop | 90% Son | Adjustments and Eliminations | | Income Statement | Retained Earnings | Balance Sheet |
|---|---|---|---|---|---|---|---|
| **Debits** | | | | | | | |
| Cash | $ 6.8 | $ 20 | | | | | $ 26.8 |
| Accounts receivable | 30 | 15 | | f 5 | | | 40 |
| Inventories | 50 | 25 | | | | | 75 |
| Plant and equipment | 75 | 45 | | | | | 120 |
| Investment in Son | 68.4 | | | b 7.2 | | | |
| | | | | d 61.2 | | | |
| Cost of goods sold | 80 | 30 | | a 14 | $(96) | | |
| Operating expenses | 19.6 | 20 | e 2 | | (41.6) | | |
| Dividends | 15 | 10 | | b 9 | | $(15) | |
| | | | | c 1 | | | |
| Patents | | | d 18 | e 2 | | | 16 |
| | $344.8 | $165 | | | | | $277.8 |
| **Credits** | | | | | | | |
| Accumulated depreciation | $ 25 | $ 11 | | | | | $ 36 |
| Accounts payable | 45 | 34 | f 5 | | | | 74 |
| Common stock | 100 | 30 | d 30 | | | | 100 |
| Retained earnings | 38.6 | 20 | d 20 | | | 38.6 | |
| Sales | 120 | 70 | a 14 | | 176 | | |
| Income from Son | 16.2 | | b 16.2 | | | | |
| | $344.8 | $165 | | | | | |
| Noncontrolling interest January 1 | | | | d 6.8 | | | |
| Noncontrolling Interest Share ($18,000 × 10%) | | | c 1.8 | | (1.8) | | |
| Controlling share of Consolidated net income | | | | | $ 36.6 | 36.6 | |
| Consolidated retained earnings December 31 | | | | | | $ 60.2 | 60.2 |
| Noncontrolling interest December 31 (6.8 + .8) | | | | c 0.8 | | | 7.6 |
| | | | 107 | 107 | | | $277.8 |

balance according to their debit and credit balances, so the locations of the accounts vary from those found in the financial statement format. Also, the trial balance includes only beginning-of-the-period retained earnings amounts.

Workpaper entries to consolidate the trial balances of Pop and Subsidiary at December 31, 2017, are as follows:

| | | Debit | Credit |
|---|---|---|---|
| a | Sales ($-R$, $-SE$) | 14,000 | |
| |     Cost of goods sold ($-E$, $+SE$) | | 14,000 |
| | To eliminate reciprocal sales and cost of sales from intercompany purchases. | | |
| b | Income from Son ($-R$, $-SE$) | 16,200 | |
| |     Dividends ($+SE$) | | 9,000 |
| |     Investment in Son ($-A$) | | 7,200 |
| | To eliminate income and dividends from Son and adjust the investment account to its beginning-of-the-year amount. | | |
| c | Noncontrolling interest share ($-SE$) | 1,800 | |
| |     Dividends ($+SE$) | | 1,000 |
| |     Noncontrolling interest ($+SE$) | | 800 |
| | To enter noncontrolling interest share of subsidiary income and dividends. | | |
| d | Common stock—Son ($-SE$) | 30,000 | |
| | Retained earnings—Son ($-SE$) | 20,000 | |
| | Patents ($+A$) | 18,000 | |
| |     Investment in Son ($-A$) | | 61,200 |
| |     Noncontrolling interest (10%) ($+SE$) | | 6,800 |
| | To eliminate reciprocal investment in Son and equity amounts of Son, record beginning noncontrolling interest, and enter unamortized patents. | | |
| e | Operating expenses ($E$, $-SE$) | 2,000 | |
| |     Patents ($-A$) | | 2,000 |
| | To record current amortization of patents as an expense. | | |
| f | Accounts payable ($-L$) | 5,000 | |
| |     Accounts receivable ($-A$) | | 5,000 |
| | To eliminate reciprocal accounts payable and receivable balances. | | |

After entering all adjustments and eliminations in the workpapers, we carry items not eliminated to the Income Statement, Retained Earnings Statement, or Balance Sheet columns. Next, we take noncontrolling interest share from entry c and include it in the Income Statement column as a deduction.

Here we can see an inconvenience of the trial balance workpaper approach. We must compute Son's $20,000 net income from the revenue and expense data and adjust for the patent amortization of $2,000 before multiplying by the noncontrolling interest percentage. We computed noncontrolling interest share directly when we used the financial statement workpaper approach.

We total the Consolidated Income Statement column and carry the total to the Consolidated Retained Earnings Statement column. We calculate noncontrolling interest at December 31 (6.8 + .8 = 7.6), and carry it to the Balance Sheet column. We next total the consolidated Retained Earnings Statement column and carry that total to the consolidated Balance Sheet column. Finally, we total the consolidated Balance Sheet debits and credits and complete the workpaper. We prepare the consolidated financial statements directly from the consolidated Income Statement, consolidated Retained Earnings Statement, and consolidated Balance Sheet columns.

## APPENDIX B

# PREPARING CONSOLIDATED STATEMENTS WHEN PARENT USES EITHER THE INCOMPLETE EQUITY METHOD OR THE COST METHOD

GAAP governs financial reporting for consolidated business entities, but does not mandate day-to-day internal record keeping by a parent company. Consolidation procedures for a parent company that uses the complete equity method were discussed throughout this chapter. Those earlier illustrations are repeated here for a parent company that uses either the incomplete equity method (sometimes called the partial equity method) or the cost method for internal record keeping.

## CONSOLIDATION UNDER AN INCOMPLETE EQUITY METHOD

When the complete equity method is applied, the parent company's net income equals the controlling share of consolidated net income, and the parent company's retained earnings equal consolidated retained earnings. This equality of parent-company and consolidated income and retained earnings amounts does not always exist. It is absent when the incomplete equity method is applied or when the cost method of accounting for subsidiary investment is applied. For example, a parent company, in applying the equity method of accounting, may not amortize the difference between investment fair value and book value acquired on its separate books, or it may not eliminate intercompany profits or losses. Such omissions result in an incomplete application of the equity method of accounting.

The problem of an incomplete equity method or use of the cost method in accounting for subsidiary investments may not be as serious as it first appears, because the accountant must prepare correct consolidated financial statements regardless of how the parent company accounts for its subsidiary investment. There is no violation of generally accepted accounting principles as long as the consolidated financial statements prepared for issuance to stockholders are correct and the parent/investor company issues no other audited financial statements.

### Incomplete Equity Method—Year of Acquisition

To illustrate consolidation procedures under an incomplete equity method, assume the same information from the Pop–Son illustration in the beginning of this chapter, except that Pop has not amortized patents on its separate books. Pop's income statement for 2016 would show income from Son of $40,000 and net income of $140,000, rather than the $36,800 and $136,800 shown under the equity method in Exhibit 4-1. This same $3,200 difference is reflected in Pop's Investment in Son account ($192,000 rather than $188,800) and Pop's retained earnings ($90,000 instead of $86,800) at December 31, 2016.

One of the first things that the accountant does in consolidating the financial statements of affiliated companies is determine how the parent company has accounted for its subsidiary investment(s). A simple check of the relationship between the parent company's equity in the subsidiary's net income and the income and the income recognized by the subsidiary will usually reveal the parent company's method of accounting. The fact that Pop's $40,000 income from Son is equal to 80% of Son's $50,000 net income for 2016 provides evidence of an incomplete equity method. Further evidence lies in the fact that Pop's Investment in Son account of $192,000 at December 31, 2016 is $3,200 greater than the underlying equity on that date, indicating that no patent amortization has occurred.

**CONVERSION TO EQUITY METHOD APPROACH**   A simple approach to preparing consolidation working papers when the parent company has not accounted for its subsidiary by the equity method is to convert the parent company's accounts to the equity method as the first working paper entry. The remaining working paper entries would be the same as if the firm had used the equity method. If Pop uses an incomplete equity method, the first entry in the working papers is a conversion to the equity method:

| | | |
|---|---|---|
| **Income from Son ( − R, − SE)** | 3,200 | |
| Investment in Son ( − A) | | 3,200 |
| **To correct for the omission of patents amortization on Pop's books.** | | |

This entry converts the parent company's accounts to the complete equity method, after which the other working paper entries for 2016 would be the same as those illustrated in Exhibit 4-1. The working paper entry illustrated above could also be recorded on Pop's separate records to adjust to the equity method as a one-line consolidation. If Pop's books have been closed for 2016, the correcting entry on Pop's books would be a debit to retained earnings and a credit to Investment in Son for $3,200.

## Incomplete Equity Method—Year Subsequent to Acquisition

Application of the incomplete equity method has a greater effect on consolidation working paper procedures in years subsequent to the year of acquisition, because the omissions affect beginning investment and retained earnings amounts on the parent company's books. Pop's Investment in Son account at December 31, 2017, is $216,000, compared with $209,600 in Exhibit 4-2 under the equity method. This $6,400 difference reflects the omission of patent amortization for both 2016 and 2017. The omissions affect Pop's beginning retained earnings in 2017 by $3,200 and ending retained earnings in 2017 by $6,400.

**CONVERSTION TO THE EQUITY METHOD APPROACH**  We can prepare consolidation working papers for 2017 by converting the parent company's accounts to the equity method as the first entry in the consolidation process. A first working paper entry corrects for the omissions on Pop's books as follows.

| | | | |
|---|---|---|---|
| a | Income from Son ( − R, − SE) | 3,200 | |
| | Retained earnings—Pop ( − SE) | 3,200 | |
| | Investment in Son ( − A) | | 6,400 |

To correct income from Son for the omission of the current year's patent amorilzation and correct Pop's beginning retained earnings for prior year's patent amortization.

The remaining eliminations would be the same as those shown in Exhibit 4-2, resulting in a correct set of consolidated financial statements.

## CONSOLIDATION UNDER THE COST METHOD

The cost method of accounting for subsidiary investments emphasizes the concept of legal entity, as opposed to the equity method, which emphasizes the economic entity under control of a single management team. Under the cost method, we recognize income only when the subsidiary declares dividends. The investment account remains unchanged except when dividends reduce subsidiary retained earnings below retained earnings at the date of acquisition of the investment, or when significant and permanent subsidiary losses impair subsidiary capital. Dividend income rather than investment income appears on the parent company's income statement when the cost method is used.

Differences from applying the cost, incomplete equity, and equity methods appear in the parent company's investment in subsidiary (assets) and retained earnings (equities) balances. No other balance sheet accounts are affected.

A simple approach to accomplish consolidation under the cost method is the conversion to equity method. The first consolidation working paper entry converts the statements to the complete equity method, after which the remaining working paper entries are the same as under the equity method.

## Cost Method—Conversion to Equity Approach

**YEAR OF ACQUISITION**  We can prepare a consolidation under the cost method by converting to the equity method in the first entry in the working papers. The remaining working paper entries are then the same as under the equity method. The cost-to-equity conversion in the year of acquisition is simplified by the fact that the investment is recorded at its cost. The entry on Pop's separate books in 2016 to record dividend income of $24,000 fails to recognize its equity in Son's undistributed income [80% × ($50,000 income − $30,000 dividends)] or to provide for the $4,000 patent amortization. Thus, Pop's dividend income from Son of $24,000 and net income of $124,000 under the cost method are each understated by Pop's $12,800 equity in Son's undistributed income less amortization for 2016. Conversion to the equity method requires the following working paper entry:

| a | Dividend income ($-$ R, $-$ SE) | 24,000 | |
|---|---|---|---|
| | Investment in Son ($+$ A) | 12,800 | |
| |    Income from Son (R, $+$ SE) | | 36,800 |
| | *To correct income and investment accounts for the cost method.* | | |

**YEAR SUBSEQUENT TO ACQUISITION**    The cost-to-equity conversion in the consolidation working papers is more complex in periods after the year in which the subsidiary investment is acquired. This is so because the cost method misstated the parent's prior-year income and failed to recognize the parent's equity in any undistributed income of the subsidiary or to provide for amortization of fair value/book value differentials. The balance sheet effect of the cost method is to misstate the investment in subsidiary and retained earnings balances at year-end by equal amounts. Thus, the cost-to-equity conversion in years after acquisition requires adjustments for prior-year effects to the investment in subsidiary and the parent's beginning retained earnings accounts. It also requires adjustment for those effects occurring in the year of consolidation (current period) to the investment in subsidiary and the income from subsidiary accounts. We analyze the cost-to-equity conversion in the working papers for the Pop-Son example for 2017 in terms of the components needed for conversion. Amounts that decrease the accounts are in parentheses.

| | Pop's Retained Earnings 12/31/16 | Investment in Son | Income from Son | Dividend Income |
|---|---|---|---|---|
| *Prior-Year Effect* | | | | |
| 80% of Son's $20,000 undistributed income for 2016 (see note) | $16,000 | $ 16,000 | | |
| Patent amortization (80%)—2016 | (3,200) | (3,200) | | |
| *Current-Year Effect* | | | | |
| Reclassify dividend income as investment decrease ($30,000 dividend $\times$ 80%) Equity in 2017 | | (24,000) | | $(24,000) |
| income of Son ($60,000 $\times$ 80%) | | 48,000 | $ 48,000 | |
| Parent amortization (80%)—2017 | | (3,200) | (3,200) | |
| 2017 working paper adjustments | $12,800 | $ 33,600 | $ 44,800 | $(24,000) |

*Note:* A corporation's undistributed earnings are reflected in its retained earnings balances. Therefore, the changes in a subsidiary's retained earnings from the date of its acquisition to a subsequent evaluation date are ordinarily the changes in a subsidiary's undistributed earnings for cost-to-equity conversions. In this example, the computation is 80% $\times$ ($80,000 retained earnings at December 31, 2016, less $60,000 retained earnings at January 1, 2016).

This analysis provides the basis for working paper entry a in the consolidation working papers of Pop Corporation and Subsidiary for 2017:

| a | Dividend income ($-$ R, $-$ SE) | 24,000 | |
|---|---|---|---|
| | Investment in Son ($+$ A) | 33,600 | |
| |    Income from Son (R, $+$ SE) | | 44,800 |
| |    Retained earnings—Pop ($+$ SE) | | 12,800 |
| | *To correct income and investment amounts to the equity basis.* | | |

The other working paper entries for 2017 are the same as those illustrated for the equity method in Exhibit 4-2. If the corporation chooses to convert from the cost to the equity method of parent company accounting, it can record entry a on its separate books before closing in 2017. Alternatively, the entry to convert to the equity method after the books are closed at December 31, 2017, would be a debit to the Investment in Son account and a credit to retained earnings for $33,600.

1. If a parent in accounting for its subsidiary amortizes patents on its separate books, why do we include an adjustment for patents amortization in the consolidation workpaper?

2. How is noncontrolling interest share entered in consolidation workpapers?

3. How are the workpaper procedures for the investment in subsidiary, income from subsidiary, and subsidiary's stockholders' equity accounts alike?

4. If a parent uses the equity method but does not amortize the difference between fair value and book value on its separate books, its net income and retained earnings will not equal its share of consolidated net income and consolidated retained earnings. How does this affect consolidation workpaper procedures?

5. Are workpaper adjustments and eliminations entered on the parent's books? The subsidiary's books? Explain.

6. The financial statement and trial balance workpaper approaches illustrated in the chapter generate comparable information, so why learn both approaches?

7. In what way do the adjustment and elimination entries for consolidation workpapers differ for the financial statement and trial balance approaches?

8. When is it necessary to adjust the parent's retained earnings account in the preparation of consolidation workpapers? In answering this question, explain the relationship between parent-retained earnings and consolidated retained earnings.

9. What approach would you use to check the accuracy of the consolidated retained earnings and noncontrolling interest amounts that appear in the balance sheet section of completed consolidation workpapers?

10. Explain why noncontrolling interest share is added to the controlling share of consolidated net income in determining cash flows from operating activities.

11. Controlling share of consolidated net income is a measurement of income to the stockholders of the parent, but does a change in cash as reflected in a statement of cash flows also relate to other stockholders of the parent?

12. Can the method used by a parent company in accounting for its subsidiary investments be determined by examining the separate financial statements of the parent and subsidiary companies?

13. How is reciprocity established between a parent company's investment account and the equity accounts of its subsidiary when the cost method is used?

## EXERCISES

### E 4-1
### General questions

1. Consolidation workpaper entries normally:
   a  Are posted to the general ledger accounts of one or more of the affiliates
   b  Are posted to the general ledger accounts only when the financial statement approach is used
   c  Are posted to the general ledger accounts only when the trial balance approach is used
   d  Do not affect the general ledger accounts of any of the affiliates

2. Consolidation workpaper techniques assume that nominal accounts are:
   a  Open when the financial statement approach is used
   b  Open when the trial balance approach is used
   c  Open in all cases
   d  Closed

3. Most errors made in consolidating financial statements will appear when:
   a  The consolidated balance sheet does not balance
   b  Consolidated net income does not equal parent net income
   c  The retained earnings amount on the balance sheet does not equal the amount on the retained earnings statement
   d  Adjustment and elimination column totals do not equal

4. Net income on consolidation workpapers is:
   a  Adjusted when the parent uses the cost method
   b  Adjusted when the parent uses the equity method
   c  Adjusted in all cases
   d  Not an account balance and not subject to adjustment

5. On consolidation workpapers, individual stockholders' equity accounts of a subsidiary are:
   - a  *Added to parent stockholders' equity accounts*
   - b  *Eliminated*
   - c  *Eliminated only to the extent of noncontrolling interest*
   - d  *Eliminated to the extent of the parent's interest*

6. On consolidation workpapers, investment income from a subsidiary is:
   - a  *Added to the investment account*
   - b  *Added to the parent's beginning retained earnings*
   - c  *Allocated between controlling and noncontrolling stockholders*
   - d  *Eliminated*

7. On consolidation workpapers, the investment in subsidiary account balances are:
   - a  *Allocated between controlling and noncontrolling interests*
   - b  *Always eliminated*
   - c  *Carried forward to the consolidated balance sheet*
   - d  *Eliminated when the financial statement approach is used*

8. On consolidation workpapers, the controlling share of consolidated net income is determined by:
   - a  *Adding net income of the parent and subsidiary*
   - b  *Deducting consolidated expenses and noncontrolling interest share from consolidated revenues*
   - c  *Making adjustments to the parent's income*
   - d  *Subtracting noncontrolling interest share from parent net income*

9. On consolidation workpapers, consolidated ending retained earnings is determined by:
   - a  *Adding beginning consolidated retained earnings and the controlling share of consolidated net income and subtracting parent dividends*
   - b  *Adding end-of-the-period retained earnings of the affiliates*
   - c  *Adjusting beginning parent-retained earnings for subsidiary profits and dividends*
   - d  *Adjusting the parent's retained earnings account balance*

10. Under the trial balance approach to consolidation workpapers, which of the following is used?
   - a  *Unadjusted trial balances*
   - b  *Adjusted trial balances*
   - c  *Postclosing trial balances*
   - d  *Either a or b, depending on the circumstances*

## E 4-2
## Consolidated statement items with equity method

Pop Corporation purchased 80 percent of the outstanding voting common stock of Son Corporation on January 2, 2016, for $1,200,000 cash. Son's balance sheets on this date and on December 31, 2016, are as follows:

### SON CORPORATION BALANCE SHEETS

|  | January 2 | December 31 |
|---|---|---|
| Inventory | $  200,000 | $   80,000 |
| Other current assets | 200,000 | 320,000 |
| Plant assets—net | 800,000 | 880,000 |
| Total assets | $1,200,000 | $1,280,000 |
| Liabilities | $  200,000 | $  240,000 |
| Capital stock | 600,000 | 600,000 |
| Retained earnings | 400,000 | 440,000 |
| Total equities | $1,200,000 | $1,280,000 |

### ADDITIONAL INFORMATION

1. Pop uses the equity method of accounting for its investment in Son.
2. Son's 2016 net income and dividends were $280,000 and $240,000, respectively.
3. Son's inventory, which was sold in 2016, was undervalued by $50,000 at January 2, 2016.

### REQUIRED

1. What is Pop's income from Son for 2016?
2. What is the noncontrolling interest share for 2016?

3. What is the total noncontrolling interest at December 31, 2016?

4. What will be the balance of Pop's Investment in Son account at December 31, 2016, if investment income from Son is $200,000? *Ignore* your answer to 1.

5. What is consolidated net income for Pop Corporation and Subsidiary if Pop's net income for 2016 is $720,800? (Assume investment income from Son is $200,000, and it is included in the $720,800.)

## E 4-3
## General problems

1. Pam Corporation owns a 70 percent interest in Sun Corporation, acquired several years ago at book value. On December 31, 2016, Sun mailed a check for $80,000 to Pam in part payment of an $160,000 account with Pam. Pam had not received the check when the books were closed on December 31. Pam had accounts receivable of $1,200,000 (including the $160,000 from Sun), and Sun had accounts receivable of $1,760,000 at year-end. In the consolidated balance sheet of Pam Corporation and Subsidiary at December 31, 2016, accounts receivable will be shown at what amount?

Use the following information in answering questions 2 and 3.

Pam Corporation purchased a 70 percent interest in Sun Corporation on January 1, 2016, for $112,000, when Sun's stockholders' equity consisted of $24,000 common stock, $80,000 additional paid-in capital, and $16,000 retained earnings. Income and dividend information for Sun is as follows:

|  | 2016 | 2017 | 2018 |
|---|---|---|---|
| Net income (or loss) | $8,000 | $1,600 | $(4,000) |
| Dividends | 3,200 | 800 | — |

2. Pam reported income of $96,000 for 2018. This does not include income from Sun. What is consolidated net income for 2018?

3. What is Pam's Investment in Sun balance at December 31, 2018, under the equity method?

## E 4-4
## Equity method

The stockholder's equity accounts of Pop Corporation and Son Corporation at December 31, 2015, were as follows (in thousands):

|  | Pop Corporation | Son Corporation |
|---|---|---|
| Capital stock | $1,200 | $500 |
| Retained earnings | 500 | 100 |
| Total | $1,700 | $600 |

On January 1, 2016, Pop Corporation acquired an 80 percent interest in Son Corporation for $580,000. The excess fair value was due to Son's equipment being undervalued by $50,000 and unrecorded patents. The undervalued equipment had a five-year remaining useful life when Pop acquired its interest. Patents are amortized over 10 years. The income and dividends of Pop and Son are as follows (in thousands):

|  | Pop | | Son | |
|---|---|---|---|---|
|  | 2016 | 2017 | 2016 | 2017 |
| Net income | $340 | $350 | $120 | $150 |
| Dividends | 240 | 250 | 80 | 90 |

**REQUIRED:** Assume that Pop Corporation uses the equity method of accounting for its investment in Son.

1. Determine consolidated net income for Pop Corporation and Subsidiary for 2016.

2. Compute the balance of Pop's Investment in Son account at December 31, 2016.

3. Compute noncontrolling interest share for 2016.

4. Compute noncontrolling interest at December 31, 2017.

## E 4-5
## General questions on statement of cash flows

1. In preparing a statement of cash flows, the cost of acquiring a subsidiary is reported:
   a  *As an operating activity under the direct method*
   b  *As an operating activity under the indirect method*
   c  *As an investing activity*
   d  *As a financing activity*

2. In computing cash flows from operating activities under the direct method, the following item is an addition:
   a  *Cash dividends from equity investees*
   b  *Collection of principal on a loan made to a subsidiary*
   c  *Noncontrolling interest dividends*
   d  *Noncontrolling interest share*

3. In computing cash flows from operating activities under the indirect method, the following item is an addition to the controlling share of consolidated net income:
   a  *Noncontrolling interest dividends*
   b  *Noncontrolling interest share*
   c  *Income from equity investees in excess of dividends received*
   d  *Write-off of negative goodwill*

4. In computing cash flows from operating activities under the direct method, the following item is an addition:
   a  *Sales*
   b  *Noncontrolling interest share*
   c  *Cash received from customers*
   d  *Depreciation expense*

5. Dividends paid as presented in a consolidated cash flow statement are:
   a  *Parent dividends*
   b  *Subsidiary dividends*
   c  *Parent and subsidiary dividends*
   d  *Parent and noncontrolling interest dividends*

## E 4-6
## Prepare cash flows from operating activities section

Information needed to prepare the Cash Flow from Operating Activities section of Pam Corporation's consolidated statement of cash flows is included in the following list:

| | |
|---|---|
| Amortization of patents | $ 16,000 |
| Consolidated net income | 150,000 |
| Decrease in accounts payable | 20,000 |
| Depreciation expense | 120,000 |
| Increase in accounts receivable | 105,000 |
| Increase in inventories | 45,000 |
| Loss on sale of land | 100,000 |
| Noncontrolling interest share | 50,000 |
| Noncontrolling interest dividends | 24,000 |
| Undistributed income of equity investees | 5,000 |

**REQUIRED:** Prepare the Cash Flows from Operating Activities section of Pam's consolidated statement of cash flows under the indirect method.

## E 4-7
## Prepare cash flows from operating activities section

The information needed to prepare the Cash Flow from Operating Activities section of Pop Corporation's consolidated statement of cash flows is included in the following list (in thousands):

| | |
|---|---|
| Cash received from customers | $1,290 |
| Cash paid to suppliers | 730 |
| Cash paid to employees | 108 |

| Cash paid for other operating items | 94 |
|---|---|
| Cash paid for interest expense | 48 |
| Cash proceeds from sale of land | 240 |
| Noncontrolling interest dividends | 40 |
| Dividends received from equity investees | 28 |

**REQUIRED:** Prepare the Cash Flows from Operating Activities section of Pop's consolidated statement of cash flows under the direct method.

## E 4-8
## (APPENDIX B) Journal entries and computations (cost and equity methods)

Son Corporation's outstanding capital stock (and paid in capital) has been $200,000 since the company was organized in 2016. Son's retained earnings account since 2016 is summarized as follows:

### RETAINED EARNINGS

| Dividends December 1, 2016 | $20,000 | Net income 2016 | $50,000 |
|---|---|---|---|
| Dividends December 1, 2017 | 20,000 | Net income 2017 | 70,000 |
| Dividends December 1, 2018 | 30,000 | Net income 2018 | 10,000 |
| Dividends December 1, 2019 | 40,000 | Net income 2019 | 60,000 |

Pop Corporation purchased 75% of Son's outstanding stock on January 1, 2018, for $300,000. During 2019. Pop's income, excluding the investment income from Son, was $90,000.

### REQUIRED

1. Prepare the journal entries, other than closing entries, on Pop's books to account for its investment in Son during 2019 under the *cost method*.
2. Determine the balance of Pop's Investment in Son account at December 31, 2019, under the *cost method*.
3. Prepare the journal entries, other than closing entries, on Pop's books to account for its investment in Son for 2019 under the *equity method*.
4. Determine the balance of Pop's Investment in Son account at December 31, 2019, under the *equity method*.
5. Compute consolidated net income for Pop Corporation and subsidiary for 2019.

## PROBLEMS

## P4-1
## Calculations five years after acquisition

Pam Corporation purchased 75 percent of the outstanding voting stock of Sun Corporation for $4,800,000 on January 1, 2016. Sun's stockholders' equity on this date consisted of the following (in thousands):

| Capital stock, $10 par | $2,000 |
|---|---|
| Additional paid-in capital | 1,200 |
| Retained earnings December 31, 2015 | 1,600 |
| Total stockholders' equity | $4,800 |

The excess fair value of the net assets acquired was assigned 10 percent to undervalued inventory (sold in 2016), 40 percent to undervalued plant assets with a remaining useful life of eight years, and 50 percent to goodwill.

Comparative trial balances of Pam Corporation and Sun at December 31, 2020, are as follows (in thousands):

| | Pam | Sun |
|---|---|---|
| Other assets—net | $7,530 | $5,200 |
| Investment in Sun—75% | 4,680 | — |
| Expenses (including cost of sales) | 6,370 | 1,200 |
| Dividends | 1,000 | 400 |
| | $19,580 | $6,800 |

| | Pam | Sun |
|---|---|---|
| Capital stock, $10 par | $6,000 | $2,000 |
| Additional paid-in capital | 1,700 | 1,200 |
| Retained earnings | 3,340 | 1,600 |
| Sales | 8,000 | 2,000 |
| Income from Sun | 540 | — |
| | $19,580 | $6,800 |

**REQUIRED:** Determine the amounts that would appear in the consolidated financial statements of Pam Corporation and Subsidiary for each of the following items:

1. Goodwill at December 31, 2020
2. Noncontrolling interest share for 2020
3. Consolidated retained earnings at December 31, 2019
4. Consolidated retained earnings at December 31, 2020
5. Consolidated net income for 2020
6. Noncontrolling interest at December 31, 2019
7. Noncontrolling interest at December 31, 2020

## P4-2
## Workpapers and financial statements in year of acquisition

Pop Corporation acquired 70 percent of the outstanding voting stock of Son Corporation for $182,000 cash on January 1, 2016, when Son's stockholders' equity was $260,000. All the assets and liabilities of Son were stated at fair values (equal to book values) when Pop acquired its 70 percent interest.

Financial statements of the two corporations at and for the year ended December 31, 2016, are summarized as follows (in thousands):

| | Pop | Son |
|---|---|---|
| **Combined Income and Retained Earnings Statements for the Year Ended December 31** | | |
| Sales | $1,240 | $400 |
| Income from Son | 42 | — |
| Cost of goods sold | (800) | (260) |
| Operating expenses | (308) | (80) |
| Net income | 174 | 60 |
| Add: Retained earnings January 1 | 260 | 44 |
| Deduct: Dividends | (120) | (40) |
| Retained earnings December 31 | $ 314 | $ 64 |
| **Balance Sheet at December 31** | | |
| Cash | $ 182 | $ 60 |
| Receivables—net | 240 | 120 |
| Inventories | 96 | 80 |
| Plant and equipment—net | 480 | 140 |
| Investment in Son | 196 | — |
| Total assets | $1,194 | $400 |
| Accounts payable | $ 120 | $ 72 |
| Other liabilities | 80 | 48 |
| Capital stock, $10 par | 600 | 200 |
| Other paid-in capital | 80 | 16 |
| Retained earnings | 314 | 64 |
| Total equities | $1,194 | $400 |

**REQUIRED**

1. Prepare consolidation workpapers for Pop Corporation and Subsidiary for 2016.
2. Prepare a consolidated income statement and a consolidated balance sheet for Pop Corporation and Subsidiary.

## P4-3
## Workpapers in year of acquisition (goodwill and intercompany transactions)

Pam Corporation acquired a 75 percent interest in Sun Corporation on January 1, 2016. Financial statements of Pam and Sun Corporations for the year 2016 are as follows (in thousands):

| | Pam | Sun |
|---|---|---|
| **Combined Income and Retained Earnings** | | |
| **Statements for the Year Ended December 31** | | |
| Sales | $1,600 | $400 |
| Income from Sun | 55.2 | — |
| Cost of sales | (1,000) | (200) |
| Other expenses | (388) | (104) |
| Net income | 267.2 | 96 |
| Add: Retained earnings January 1 | 720 | 136 |
| Deduct: Dividends | (200) | (64) |
| Retained earnings December 31 | $ 787.2 | $168 |
| | | |
| **Balance Sheet at December 31** | | |
| Cash | $ 212 | $ 60 |
| Accounts receivable—net | 344 | 80 |
| Dividends receivable from Sun | 24 | — |
| Inventories | 380 | 40 |
| Note receivable from Pam | — | 20 |
| Land | 260 | 120 |
| Buildings—net | 680 | 320 |
| Equipment—net | 520 | 200 |
| Investment in Sun | 727.2 | — |
| Total assets | $3,147.2 | $840 |
| | | |
| Accounts payable | $ 340 | $ 40 |
| Note payable to Sun | 20 | — |
| Dividends payable | — | 32 |
| Capital stock, $10 par | 2,000 | 600 |
| Retained earnings | 787.2 | 168 |
| Total equities | $3,147.2 | $840 |

**REQUIRED:** Prepare consolidation workpapers for Pam Corporation and Subsidiary for the year ended December 31, 2016. Only the information provided in the financial statements is available; accordingly, your solution will require some standard assumptions. Sun owned unrecorded patents having a fair value of $224,000, and a useful life of 10 years.

## P4-4
## Consolidation workpapers from separate financial statements

Pop Corporation acquired a 75 percent interest in Son Corporation on January 1, 2016, for $720,000 in cash. Financial statements of Pop and Son Corporations for 2016 are as follows (in thousands):

| | Pop | Son |
|---|---|---|
| **Combined Income and Retained Earnings** | | |
| **Statements for the Year Ended December 31** | | |
| Sales | $1,600 | $400 |
| Income from Son | 72 | — |
| Cost of sales | (1,000) | (200) |
| Other expenses | (388) | (104) |
| Net income | 284 | 96 |
| Add: Retained earnings January 1 | 720 | 136 |
| Deduct: Dividends | (200) | (64) |
| Retained earnings December 31 | $ 804 | $168 |

|  | Pop | Son |
|---|---|---|
| **Balance Sheet at December 31** | | |
| Cash | $ 236 | $ 60 |
| Accounts receivable—net | 320 | 80 |
| Dividends receivable from Son | 24 | — |
| Inventories | 380 | 40 |
| Note receivable from Pop | — | 20 |
| Land | 260 | 120 |
| Buildings—net | 680 | 320 |
| Equipment—net | 520 | 200 |
| Investment in Son | 744 | — |
| Total assets | $3,164 | $840 |
| Accounts payable | $ 340 | $ 40 |
| Note payable to Son | 20 | — |
| Dividends payable | — | 32 |
| Capital stock, $10 par | 2,000 | 600 |
| Retained earnings | 804 | 168 |
| Total equities | $3,164 | $840 |

**REQUIRED:** Prepare consolidation workpapers for Pop Corporation and Subsidiary for the year ended December 31, 2016. Only the information provided in the financial statements is available; accordingly, your solution will require some standard assumptions.

## P4-5
## Workpapers in year of acquisition (excess recorded for inventory, building, equipment, trademarks, and goodwill)

Pam Corporation acquired a 70 percent interest in Sun Corporation's outstanding voting common stock on January 1, 2016, for $980,000 cash. The stockholders' equity (book value) of Sun on this date consisted of $1,000,000 capital stock and $200,000 retained earnings. The differences between the fair value of Sun and the book value of Sun were assigned $10,000 to Sun's undervalued inventory, $28,000 to undervalued buildings, $42,000 to undervalued equipment, and $80,000 to previously unrecorded trademarks. Any remaining excess is goodwill.

The undervalued inventory items were sold during 2016, and the undervalued buildings and equipment had remaining useful lives of seven years and three years, respectively. The trademarks have a 40-year life. Depreciation is straight line.

At December 31, 2016, Sun's accounts payable include $20,000 owed to Pam. This $20,000 account payable is due on January 15, 2017. Separate financial statements for Pam and Sun for 2016 are summarized as follows (in thousands):

|  | Pam | Sun |
|---|---|---|
| **Combined Income and Retained Earnings** | | |
| **Statements for the Year Ended December 31** | | |
| Sales | $ 1,600 | $1,400 |
| Income from Sun | 119 | — |
| Cost of sales | (600) | (800) |
| Depreciation expense | (308) | (120) |
| Other expenses | (320) | (280) |
| Net income | 491 | 200 |
| Add: Retained earnings January 1 | 600 | 200 |
| Deduct: Dividends | (400) | (100) |
| Retained earnings December 31 | $ 691 | $ 300 |

| | Pam | Sun |
|---|---|---|
| **Balance Sheet at December 31** | | |
| Cash | $ 172 | $ 120 |
| Accounts receivable—net | 200 | 140 |
| Dividends receivable | 28 | — |
| Inventories | 300 | 200 |
| Other current assets | 140 | 60 |
| Land | 100 | 200 |
| Buildings—net | 280 | 320 |
| Equipment—net | 1,140 | 660 |
| Investment in Sun | 1,029 | — |
| Total assets | $ 3,389 | $1,700 |
| | | |
| Accounts payable | $ 400 | $ 170 |
| Dividends payable | 200 | 40 |
| Other liabilities | 98 | 190 |
| Capital stock, $20 par | 2,000 | 1,000 |
| Retained earnings | 691 | 300 |
| Total equities | $ 3,389 | $1,700 |

**REQUIRED:** Prepare consolidation workpapers for Pam Corporation and Subsidiary for the year ended December 31, 2016. Use an unamortized excess account.

## P4-6
## Workpapers (determine ownership interest, year after acquisition, excess assigned to land and patents)

Separate company financial statements for Pop Corporation and its subsidiary, Son Company, at and for the year ended December 31, 2017, are summarized as follows (in thousands):

| | Pop | Son |
|---|---|---|
| **Combined Income and Retained Earnings Statements for the Year Ended December 31** | | |
| Sales | $ 1,600 | $400 |
| Income from Son | 72 | — |
| Cost of sales | (1,000) | (200) |
| Other Expenses | (402.4) | (104) |
| Net income | 269.6 | 96 |
| Add: Retained earnings January 1 | 708 | 136 |
| Deduct: Dividends | (200) | (64) |
| Retained earnings December 31 | $ 777.6 | $16 8 |
| | | |
| **Balance Sheet at December 31** | | |
| Cash | $ 72 | $ 60 |
| Accounts receivable—net | 320 | 80 |
| Dividends receivable from Son | 28.8 | — |
| Note receivable from Pop | — | 20 |
| Inventory | 380 | 40 |
| Investment in Son | 878.4 | — |
| Land | 260 | 120 |
| Buildings—net | 680 | 320 |
| Equipment—net | 520 | 200 |
| Total assets | $3,139.2 | $840 |
| | | |
| Accounts payable | $ 341.6 | $ 40 |
| Note payable to Son | 20 | — |
| Dividends payable | — | 32 |
| Capital stock, $40 par | 2,000 | 600 |
| Retained earnings | 777.6 | 168 |
| Total equities | $3,139.2 | $840 |

## ADDITIONAL INFORMATION

1. Pop Corporation acquired 13,500 shares of Son Company stock for $60 per share on January 1, 2016, when Son's stockholders' equity consisted of $600,000 capital stock and $60,000 retained earnings.

2. Son Company's land was undervalued when Pop acquired its interest, and accordingly, $80,000 of the fair value/book value differential was assigned to land. Any remaining differential is assigned to unrecorded patents with a 10-year remaining life.

3. Son Company owes Pop $20,000 on account, and Pop owes Son $20,000 on a note payable.

**REQUIRED:** Prepare consolidated workpapers for Pop Corporation and Subsidiary for the year ended December 31, 2017.

## P4-7
### Workpapers (year of acquisition, excess recorded for inventory, building equipment, and goodwill, intercompany balances)

Pam Corporation acquired a 70 percent interest in Sun Corporation's outstanding voting common stock on January 1, 2016, for $490,000 cash. The stockholders' equity of Sun on this date consisted of $500,000 capital stock and $100,000 retained earnings. The difference between the fair value of Sun and the underlying equity acquired in Sun was assigned $5,000 to Sun's undervalued inventory, $14,000 to undervalued buildings, $21,000 to undervalued equipment, and $60,000 to goodwill.

The undervalued inventory items were sold during 2016, and the undervalued buildings and equipment had remaining useful lives of seven years and three years, respectively. Depreciation is straight line.

At December 31, 2016, Sun's accounts payable include $10,000 owed to Pam. This $10,000 account payable is due on January 15, 2017. Pam sold equipment with a book value of $15,000 for $25,000 on June 1, 2016. This is not an intercompany sale transaction. Separate financial statements for Pam and Sun for 2016 are summarized as follows (in thousands):

|  | Pam | Sun |
|---|---|---|
| **Combined Income and Retained Earnings** | | |
| **Statements for the Year Ended December 31** | | |
| Sales | $ 800 | $700 |
| Income from Sun | 60.2 | — |
| Gain on equipment | 10 | — |
| Cost of sales | (300) | (400) |
| Depreciation expense | (155) | (60) |
| Other expenses | (160) | (140) |
| Net income | 255.2 | 100 |
| Add: Retained earnings January 1 | 300 | 100 |
| Deduct: Dividends | (200) | (50) |
| Retained earnings December 31 | $ 355.2 | $150 |
| **Balance Sheet at December 31** | | |
| Cash | $ 96 | $ 60 |
| Accounts receivable—net | 100 | 70 |
| Dividends receivable | 14 | — |
| Inventories | 150 | 100 |
| Other current assets | 70 | 30 |
| Land | 50 | 100 |
| Buildings—net | 140 | 160 |
| Equipment—net | 570 | 330 |
| Investment in Sun | 515.2 | — |
| Total assets | $1,705.2 | $850 |
| Accounts payable | $ 200 | $ 85 |
| Dividends payable | 100 | 20 |
| Other liabilities | 50 | 95 |
| Capital stock, $10 par | 1,000 | 500 |
| Retained earnings | 355.2 | 150 |
| Total equities | $1,705.2 | $850 |

REQUIRED: Prepare consolidation workpapers for Pam Corporation and Sun for the year ended December 31, 2016. Use an unamortized excess account.

## P4-8
## Workpapers (excess due to undervalued land and goodwill)

Separate-company financial statements for Pop Corporation and its subsidiary, Son Company, at and for the year ended December 31, 2017, are summarized as follows (in thousands):

|  | Pop | Son |
|---|---|---|
| ***Combined Income and Retained Earnings*** | | |
| ***Statement for the Year Ended December 31*** | | |
| Sales | $400 | $100 |
| Income from Son | 21.6 | — |
| Cost of sales | (250) | (50) |
| Expenses | (100.6) | (26) |
| Net income | 71 | 24 |
| Add: Retained earnings January 1 | 181 | 34 |
| Deduct: Dividends | (50) | (16) |
| Retained earnings December 31 | $202 | $ 42 |
| | | |
| ***Balance Sheet at December 31*** | | |
| Cash | $ 18 | $ 15 |
| Accounts receivable—net | 80 | 20 |
| Dividends receivable from Son | 7.2 | — |
| Note receivable from Pop | — | 5 |
| Inventory | 95 | 10 |
| Investment in Son | 226.8 | — |
| Land | 65 | 30 |
| Buildings—net | 170 | 80 |
| Equipment—net | 130 | 50 |
| Total assets | $792 | $210 |
| | | |
| Accounts payable | $ 85 | $ 10 |
| Note payable to Son | 5 | — |
| Dividends payable | — | 8 |
| Capital stock, $10 par | 500 | 150 |
| Retained earnings | 202 | 42 |
| Total equities | $792 | $210 |

### ADDITIONAL INFORMATION

1. Pop Corporation acquired 13,500 shares of Son Company stock for $15 per share on January 1, 2016, when Son's stockholders' equity consisted of $150,000 capital stock and $15,000 retained earnings.
2. Son Company's land was undervalued when Pop acquired its interest, and accordingly, $20,000 of the fair value/book value differential was assigned to land. Any remaining differential is goodwill.
3. Son Company owes Pop $5,000 on account, and Pop owes Son $5,000 on a note payable.

REQUIRED: Prepare consolidation workpapers for Pop Corporation and Subsidiary for the year ended December 31, 2017.

## P4-9
## Workpapers (year of acquisition, excess recorded for inventory, equipment and patents, intercompany transactions)

Pam Corporation acquired 80 percent of Sun Corporation's common stock on January 1, 2016, for $840,000 cash. The stockholders' equity of Sun at this time consisted of $600,000 capital stock and

$200,000 retained earnings. The difference between the fair value of Sun and the underlying equity acquired in Sun was due to a $50,000 undervaluation of Sun's inventory, a $100,000 undervaluation of Sun's equipment, and unrecorded patents with a 20-year remaining life.

The undervalued inventory was sold by Sun during 2016, and the undervalued equipment had a remaining useful life of five years. Straight-line depreciation is used.

Sun owed Pam $16,000 on accounts payable at December 31, 2016.

The separate financial statements of Pam and Sun Corporations at and for the year ended December 31, 2016, are as follows (in thousands):

|  | Pam | Sun |
|---|---|---|
| **Combined Income and Retained Earnings Statements for the Year Ended December 31** | | |
| Sales | $ 800 | $ 440 |
| Income from Sun | 68 | — |
| Cost of sales | (320) | (160) |
| Depreciation expense | (160) | (80) |
| Other expenses | (102) | (40) |
| Net income | 286 | 160 |
| Add: Retained earnings January 1 | 300 | 200 |
| Deduct: Dividends | (160) | (80) |
| Retained earnings December 31 | $ 426 | $ 280 |
| **Balance Sheet at December 31** | | |
| Cash | $ 118 | $ 120 |
| Trade receivables—net | 112 | 160 |
| Dividends receivable | 32 | — |
| Inventories | 160 | 120 |
| Land | 60 | 120 |
| Buildings—net | 260 | 280 |
| Equipment—net | 800 | 400 |
| Investment in Sun | 844 | — |
| Total assets | $2,386 | $1,200 |
| Accounts payable | $ 160 | $200 |
| Dividends payable | 400 | 40 |
| Other liabilities | 200 | 80 |
| Capital stock, $10 par | 1,200 | 600 |
| Retained earnings | 426 | 280 |
| Total equities | $2,386 | $1,200 |

**REQUIRED:** Prepare consolidation workpapers for Pam Corporation and Subsidiary at and for the year ended December 31, 2016.

## P4-10
### Workpapers (year of acquisition, fair value/book value differentials, intercompany balances)

Pop Corporation acquired 80 percent of Son Corporation's common stock on January 1, 2016, for $420,000 cash. The stockholders' equity of Son at this time consisted of $300,000 capital stock and $100,000 retained earnings. The difference between the fair value of Son and the underlying equity acquired in Son was due to a $25,000 undervaluation of Son's inventory, a $50,000 undervaluation of Son's equipment, and goodwill.

The undervalued inventory was sold by Son during 2016, and the undervalued equipment had a remaining useful life of five years. Straight-line depreciation is used.

Son owed Pop $8,000 on accounts payable at December 31, 2016.

The separate financial statements of Pop and Son Corporations at and for the year ended December 31, 2016, are as follows (in thousands):

|  | Pop | Son |
|---|---|---|
| **Combined Income and Retained Earnings Statements for the Year Ended December 31** | | |
| Sales | $ 400 | $220 |
| Income from Son | 36 | — |
| Cost of sales | (160) | (80) |
| Depreciation expense | (80) | (40) |
| Other expenses | (51) | (20) |
| Net income | 145 | 80 |
| Add: Retained earnings January 1 | 150 | 100 |
| Deduct: Dividends | (80) | (40) |
| Retained earnings December 31 | $ 215 | $140 |
| **Balance Sheet at December 31** | | |
| Cash | $ 59 | $ 60 |
| Trade receivables—net | 56 | 80 |
| Dividends receivable | 16 | — |
| Inventories | 80 | 60 |
| Land | 30 | 60 |
| Buildings—net | 130 | 140 |
| Equipment—net | 400 | 200 |
| Investment in Son | 424 | — |
| Total assets | $1,195 | $600 |
| Accounts payable | $ 80 | $100 |
| Dividends payable | 200 | 20 |
| Other liabilities | 100 | 40 |
| Capital stock, $10 par | 600 | 300 |
| Retained earnings | 215 | 140 |
| Total equities | $1,195 | $600 |

**REQUIRED:** Prepare consolidation workpapers for Pop Corporation and Son at and for the year ended December 31, 2016.

## P4-11
### Balance sheet (four years after acquisition, fair value/book value differentials)

Pam Corporation paid $170,000 for an 80 percent interest in Sun Corporation on December 31, 2016, when Sun's stockholders' equity consisted of $100,000 capital stock and $50,000 retained earnings. A summary of the changes in Pam's Investment in Sun account from December 31, 2016, to December 31, 2020, follows (in thousands):

| | | |
|---|---|---|
| Investment cost December 31, 2016 | | $170 |
| *Increases* | | |
| 80% of Sun's net income 2017 through 2020 | | 112 |
| | | 282 |
| *Decreases* | | |
| 80% of Sun's dividends 2017 through 2020 | $56 | |
| 80% of Amortization of excess fair value over book value: | | |
| Assigned to inventories, $8,750 (sold in 2017) | 7 | |
| Assigned to plant assets, $22,500 (depreciated over a nine-year period) 2017 through 2020 | 8 | |
| Assigned to patents, $31,250 (amortized over a five-year period) 2017 through 2020 | 20 | 91 |
| Investment balance December 31, 2020 | | $191 |

Financial statements for Pam and Sun at and for the year ended December 31, 2020, are summarized as follows (in thousands):

| | Pam | Sun |
|---|---|---|
| ***Combined Income and Retained Earnings*** | | |
| ***Statements for the Year Ended December 31*** | | |
| Sales | $300 | $200 |
| Income from Sun | 25 | — |
| Cost of sales | (180) | (140) |
| Other expenses | (50) | (20) |
| Net income | 95 | 40 |
| Add: Retained earnings January 1 | 255 | 100 |
| Deduct: Dividends | (50) | (20) |
| Retained earnings December 31 | $300 | $120 |
| | | |
| ***Balance Sheet at December 31*** | | |
| Cash | $ 41 | $ 35 |
| Trade receivables—net | 60 | 55 |
| Dividends receivable | 8 | — |
| Advance to Sun | 25 | — |
| Inventories | 125 | 35 |
| Plant assets—net | 300 | 175 |
| Investment in Sun | 191 | — |
| Total assets | $750 | $300 |
| | | |
| Accounts payable | $ 50 | $ 45 |
| Dividends payable | — | 10 |
| Advance from Pam | — | 25 |
| Capital stock | 400 | 100 |
| Retained earnings | 300 | 120 |
| Total equities | $750 | $300 |

## ADDITIONAL INFORMATION

1. The accounts payable of Sun at December 31, 2020, include $5,000 owed to Pam.
2. Pam advanced $25,000 to Sun during 2018. This advance is still outstanding.
3. Half of Sun's 2020 dividends will be paid in January 2021.

**REQUIRED:** Prepare workpapers to consolidate the balance sheets only of Pam and Sun Corporations at December 31, 2020.

## P4-12
## Workpapers (two years after acquisition, fair value/book differentials, adjustments)

Pop Corporation acquired an 80 percent interest in Son Corporation for $240,000 on January 1, 2016, when Son's stockholders' equity consisted of $200,000 capital stock and $25,000 retained earnings. The excess fair value over book value acquired was assigned to plant assets that were undervalued by $50,000 and to goodwill. The undervalued plant assets had a four-year useful life.

## ADDITIONAL INFORMATION

1. Pop's account receivable includes $5,000 owed by Son.
2. Son mailed its check for $20,000 to Pop on December 30, 2017, in settlement of the advance.
3. A $10,000 dividend was declared by Son on December 30, 2017, but was not recorded by Pop.
4. Financial statements for Pop and Son Corporations for 2017 follow (in thousands):

|  | Pop | Son |
|---|---|---|
| **Statements of Income and Retained Earnings** | | |
| **for the Year Ended December 31** | | |
| Sales | $ 900 | $300 |
| Income from Son | 38 | — |
| Cost of sales | (600) | (150) |
| Operating expenses | (190) | (90) |
| Net Income | 148 | 60 |
| Add: Retained earnings January 1 | 122 | 50 |
| Less: Dividends | (100) | (20) |
| Retained earnings December 31 | $ 170 | $ 90 |
| **Balance Sheet at December 31** | | |
| Cash | $ 6 | $ 15 |
| Accounts receivable—net | 26 | 20 |
| Inventories | 82 | 60 |
| Advance to Son | 20 | — |
| Other current assets | 80 | 5 |
| Land | 160 | 30 |
| Plant assets—net | 340 | 230 |
| Investment in Son | 280 | — |
| Total assets | $ 994 | $360 |
| Accounts payable | $ 24 | $ 15 |
| Dividends payable | — | 10 |
| Other liabilities | 100 | 45 |
| Capital stock | 700 | 200 |
| Retained earnings | 170 | 90 |
| Total liabilities and stockholders' equity | $ 994 | $360 |

**REQUIRED:** Prepare consolidation workpapers for Pop Corporation and Subsidiary for 2017.

## P4-13
### [Appendix A] Workpapers for two successive years (equity method misapplied in second year)

Comparative adjusted trial balances for Pam Corporation and Sun Corporation are given here. Pam Corporation acquired an 80 percent interest in Sun Corporation on January 1, 2016, for $80,000 cash. Except for inventory items that were undervalued by $1,000 and equipment that was undervalued by $4,000, all of Sun's identifiable assets and liabilities were stated at their fair values on December 31, 2015. The remaining excess was assigned to previously unrecorded intangibles, which had a 40-year remaining life.

Sun sold the undervalued inventory items during 2016 but continues to own the equipment, which had a four-year remaining useful life as of December 31, 2015. (All amounts are in thousands.)

|  | December 31, 2015 | | December 31, 2016 | | December 31, 2017 | |
|---|---|---|---|---|---|---|
|  | Pam | Sun | Pam | Sun | Pam | Sun |
| Cash | $100 | $ 30 | $ 24.7 | $ 15 | $ 26.7 | $ 20 |
| Trade receivables—net | 30 | 15 | 25 | 20 | 45 | 30 |
| Dividends receivable | — | — | 4 | — | 4 | — |
| Inventories | 50 | 20 | 40 | 30 | 40 | 30 |
| Plant and equipment—net | 90 | 60 | 100 | 55 | 95 | 60 |
| Investment in Sun | — | — | 86.3 | — | 94.3 | — |
| Cost of sales | 100 | 40 | 105 | 35 | 110 | 35 |
| Operating expenses | 20 | 30 | 35 | 30 | 30 | 35 |
| Dividends | 10 | 5 | 10 | 5 | 15 | 10 |
|  | $400 | $200 | $430 | $190 | $460 | $220 |
| Accounts payable | $ 30 | $ 35 | $ 20.7 | $ 15 | $ 17.7 | $ 25 |
| Dividends payable | 10 | — | 9 | 5 | 6 | 5 |
| Capital stock | 100 | 40 | 100 | 40 | 100 | 40 |
| Other paid-in capital | 60 | 20 | 60 | 20 | 60 | 20 |
| Retained earnings | 50 | 25 | 70 | 30 | 90.3 | 40 |
| Sales | 150 | 80 | 160 | 80 | 170 | 90 |
| Income from Sun | — | — | 10.3 | — | 16 | — |
|  | $400 | $200 | $430 | $190 | $460 | $220 |

**REQUIRED:** Prepare consolidation workpapers for Pam Corporation and Subsidiary for 2016 and 2017 using the financial statement approach. (*Hint:* Pam Corporation's accountant applied the equity method correctly for 2016 but misapplied the equity method for 2017.)

## P4-14
### [Appendix A] Investment account analysis and trial balance workpapers

Pop Company paid $198,000 for a 90 percent interest in Son on January 5, 2016, when Son's capital stock was $120,000 and its retained earnings $40,000. Trial balances for the companies at December 31, 2019, are as follows (in thousands):

|  | Pop | Son |
|---|---|---|
| Cash | $ 22 | $ 30 |
| Accounts receivable | 30 | 50 |
| Plant assets | 440 | 360 |
| Investment in Son | 273.6 | — |
| Cost of goods sold | 100 | 60 |
| Operating expenses | 50 | 80 |
| Dividends | 40 | 20 |
|  | $ 955.6 | $ 600 |
| Accumulated depreciation | $ 180 | $ 100 |
| Liabilities | 160 | 60 |
| Capital stock | 200 | 120 |
| Paid-in excess | 40 | — |
| Retained earnings | 143.2 | 140 |
| Sales | 200 | 180 |
| Income from Son | 32.4 | — |
|  | $955.6 | $ 600 |

The excess fair value over book value acquired was assigned $20,000 to undervalued inventory items that were sold in 2016 and the remainder to patents having a remaining useful life of 10 years from January 1, 2016.

### REQUIRED
1. Summarize the changes in Pop Company's Investment in Son account from January 5, 2016, through December 31, 2019.
2. Prepare consolidation workpapers for Pop Company and Son for 2019 using the trial balance approach for your workpapers.

## P4-15
### [Appendix A] Trial balance workpapers and financial statements in year of acquisition

Pam Corporation owns 90 percent of the voting stock of Sun Corporation and 25 percent of the voting stock of Ell Corporation.

The 90 percent interest in Sun was acquired for $36,000 cash on January 1, 2016, when Sun's stockholders' equity was $40,000 ($36,000 capital stock and $4,000 retained earnings).

Pam's 25 percent interest in Ell was purchased for $14,000 cash on July 1, 2016, when Ell's stockholders' equity was $48,000 ($30,000 capital stock, $12,000 retained earnings, and $6,000 current earnings—first half of 2016).

The difference between fair value and book value is due to unrecorded patents and is amortized over 10 years.

Adjusted trial balances of the three associated companies at December 31, 2016, are as follows:

| | Pam | Sun | Ell |
|---|---|---|---|
| Cash | $ 37,900 | $ 8,000 | $ 2,000 |
| Other current assets | 80,000 | 22,000 | 20,000 |
| Plant assets—net | 240,000 | 28,000 | 40,000 |
| Investment in Sun—90 percent | 39,600 | — | — |
| Investment in Ell—25% | 12,900 | — | — |
| Cost of sales | 120,000 | 32,000 | 30,000 |
| Other expenses | 50,000 | 14,000 | 18,000 |
| Dividends (paid in November) | 20,000 | 6,000 | 10,000 |
| Total Debits | $600,400 | $110,000 | $120,000 |
| Current liabilities | $ 50,000 | $ 14,000 | $ 18,000 |
| Capital stock | 300,000 | 36,000 | 30,000 |
| Retained earnings | 40,000 | 4,000 | 12,000 |
| Sales | 200,000 | 56,000 | 60,000 |
| Income from Sun | 9,000 | — | — |
| Income from Ell | 1,400 | — | — |
| Total credits | $600,400 | $110,000 | $120,000 |

## REQUIRED

1. Reconstruct the journal entries that were made by Pam Corporation during 2016 to account for its investments in Sun and Ell Corporations.
2. Prepare an income statement, a retained earnings statement, and a balance sheet for Pam Corporation for December 31, 2016.
3. Prepare consolidation workpapers (trial balance format) for Pam and Subsidiaries for 2016.
4. Prepare consolidated financial statements other than the cash flows statement for Pam Corporation and Subsidiaries for the year ended December 31, 2016.

## P4-16
## Prepare cash flows from operating activities section (direct method)

The accountant for Pop Corporation collected the following information that he thought might be useful in the preparation of the company's consolidated statement of cash flows (in thousands):

| | |
|---|---|
| Cash paid for purchase of equipment | $1,080 |
| Cash paid for other expenses | 1,800 |
| Cash paid to suppliers | 2,520 |
| Cash received from customers | 6,400 |
| Cash received from sale of land | 2,000 |
| Cash received from treasury stock sold | 1,600 |
| Dividends from equity investees | 160 |
| Dividends paid to noncontrolling stockholders | 80 |
| Dividends paid to Pop's stockholders | 200 |
| Gain on sale of land | 800 |
| Income from equity investees | 320 |
| Interest received from short-term loan | 20 |
| Noncontrolling interest share | 180 |

**REQUIRED:** Prepare the Cash Flows from Operating Activities section of the consolidated statement of cash flows for Pop Corporation and Subsidiaries using the *direct method* of presentation.

## P4-17
## Prepare consolidated statement of cash flows using the direct method or indirect method

Comparative consolidated financial statements for Pam Corporation and its 90 percent–owned subsidiary, Sun Corporation, at and for the years ended December 31 are as follows:

## PAM CORPORATION AND SUBSIDIARY COMPARATIVE CONSOLIDATED FINANCIAL STATEMENTS (IN THOUSANDS)

| | Year 2016 | Year 2015 | 2016–2015 |
|---|---|---|---|
| *Income and Retained Earnings* | | | |
| *Statements for the Year* | | | *Change* |
| Sales | $ 1,350 | $1,200 | $ 150 |
| Cost of sales | (700) | (649) | 51 |
| Depreciation expense | (102) | (102) | 0 |
| Other operating expenses | (278) | (241) | 37 |
| Noncontrolling interest share | (10) | (8) | 2 |
| Controlling share of income | 260 | 200 | 60 |
| Add: Beginning retained earnings | 380 | 260 | 120 |
| Less: Dividends | (80) | (80) | 0 |
| Ending Retained Earnings | $ 560 | $ 380 | $ 180 |
| | | | |
| *Balance Sheets at December 31* | | | |
| Assets | | | |
| Cash | $ 111 | $ 130 | $ (19) |
| Accounts receivable—net | 170 | 160 | 10 |
| Inventories | 280 | 240 | 40 |
| Other current assets | 200 | 162 | 38 |
| Plant and equipment—net | 1,348 | 1,200 | 148 |
| Patents | 38 | 39 | (1) |
| Total assets | $ 2,147 | $1,931 | $ 216 |
| | | | |
| Equities | | | |
| Accounts payable | $ 170 | $ 126 | $ 44 |
| Dividends payable | 42 | 34 | 8 |
| Long-term liabilities | 70 | 92 | (22) |
| Capital stock | 1,000 | 1,000 | 0 |
| Other paid-in capital | 240 | 240 | 0 |
| Retained earnings | 560 | 380 | 180 |
| Noncontrolling interest—10% | 65 | 59 | 6 |
| Total equities | $ 2,147 | $1,931 | $ 216 |

**REQUIRED:** Prepare a consolidated statement of cash flows for Pam Corporation and Subsidiary for the year ended December 31, 2016, using either the indirect method or the direct method. All changes in plant assets are due to asset acquisitions with cash and depreciation. Sun's net income and dividends for 2016 are $100,000 and $40,000, respectively.

## P4-18
### [Based on AICPA] Prepare consolidated statement of cash flows

The consolidated workpaper balances of Pop, Inc., and its subsidiary, Son Corporation, as of December 31 are as follows (in thousands):

| | 2016 | 2015 | Net Change Increase (Decrease) |
|---|---|---|---|
| *Assets* | | | |
| Cash | $ 313 | $ 195 | $118 |
| Marketable equity securities at cost (MES) | 175 | 175 | — |
| Allowance to reduce MES to market | (13) | (24) | (11) |
| Accounts receivable—net | 418 | 440 | (22) |
| Inventories | 595 | 525 | 70 |
| Land | 385 | 170 | 215 |
| Plant and equipment | 755 | 690 | 65 |
| Accumulated depreciation | (199) | (145) | 54 |
| Patents—net | 57 | 60 | (3) |
| Total assets | $2,486 | $2,086 | $400 |

| | 2016 | 2015 | Net Change Increase (Decrease) |
|---|---|---|---|
| *Liabilities and Stockholders' Equity* | | | |
| Note payable, current portion | $ 150 | $ 150 | $ — |
| Accounts and accrued payables | 595 | 474 | 121 |
| Note payable, long-term portion | 300 | 450 | (150) |
| Deferred income taxes | 44 | 32 | 12 |
| Noncontrolling interest in Son | 179 | 161 | 18 |
| Common stock—$10 par | 580 | 480 | 100 |
| Additional paid-in capital | 303 | 180 | 123 |
| Retained earnings | 335 | 195 | 140 |
| Treasury stock at cost | — | (36) | 36 |
| Total equities | $2,486 | $2,086 | $400 |

### ADDITIONAL INFORMATION

1. On January 20, 2016, Pop issued 10,000 shares of its common stock for land having a fair value of $215,000.
2. On February 5, 2016, Pop reissued all of its treasury stock for $44,000.
3. On May 15, 2016, Pop paid a cash dividend of $58,000 on its common stock.
4. On August 8, 2016, equipment was purchased for $127,000 with cash.
5. On September 30, 2016, equipment was sold for $40,000. The equipment cost $62,000 and had a carrying amount of $34,000 on the date of sale.
6. On December 15, 2016, Son Corporation paid a cash dividend of $50,000 on its common stock.
7. Deferred income taxes represent temporary differences relating to the use of accelerated depreciation methods for income tax reporting and the straight-line method for financial reporting.
8. Controlling share of net income for 2016 was $198,000. Son's net income was $110,000.
9. Pop owns 70 percent of its subsidiary, Son Corporation. There was no change in the ownership interest in Son during 2015 and 2016. There were no intercompany transactions other than the dividend paid to Pop by its subsidiary.
10. Assume the marketable equity securities are classified as trading securities.

**REQUIRED:** Prepare a consolidated statement of cash flows for Pop and Subsidiary for the year ended December 31, 2016. Use the *indirect method*.

### P4-19
### Prepare consolidated statement of cash flows using either the direct or indirect method

Comparative consolidated financial statements for Pam Corporation and its 80 percent–owned subsidiary at and for the years ended December 31 are summarized as follows:

**PAM CORPORATION AND SUBSIDIARY COMPARATIVE CONSOLIDATED FINANCIAL STATEMENTS AT AND FOR THE YEAR ENDED DECEMBER 31 (IN THOUSANDS)**

| | Year 2016 | Year 2015 | Year's Change 2016–2015 |
|---|---|---|---|
| *Income and Retained Earnings Statements* | | | |
| Sales | $5,200 | $4,800 | $ 400 |
| Income—equity investees | 120 | 100 | 20 |
| Cost of sales | (2,900) | (2,816) | 84 |
| Depreciation expense | (400) | (300) | 100 |
| Other operating expenses | (940) | (924) | 16 |
| Noncontrolling interest share | (80) | (60) | 20 |
| Controlling share of income | 1,000 | 800 | 200 |
| Retained earnings, January 1 | 2,000 | 1,400 | 600 |
| Dividends | (300) | (200) | 100 |
| Retained earnings, December 31 | $2,700 | $2,000 | $ 700 |

| | Year 2016 | Year 2015 | Year's Change 2016–2015 |
|---|---|---|---|
| **Balance Sheet** | | | |
| Cash | $ 860 | $ 720 | $ 140 |
| Accounts receivable—net | 1,500 | 1,080 | 420 |
| Inventories | 1,400 | 1,400 | 0 |
| Plant and equipment—net | 3,600 | 3,000 | 600 |
| Equity investments | 860 | 800 | 60 |
| Patents | 380 | 400 | (20) |
| Total assets | $8,600 | $7,400 | $1,200 |
| | | | |
| Accounts payable | $ 984 | $ 950 | $ 34 |
| Dividends payable | 76 | 50 | 26 |
| Long-term note payable | 1,200 | 800 | 400 |
| Capital stock | 2,000 | 2,000 | 0 |
| Other paid-in capital | 1,200 | 1,200 | 0 |
| Retained earnings | 2,700 | 2,000 | 700 |
| Noncontrolling interest—20% | 440 | 400 | 40 |
| Total equities | $8,600 | $7,400 | $1,200 |

**REQUIRED:** Prepare a consolidated statement of cash flows for Pam Corporation and Subsidiary for the year ended December 31, 2016. Assume that all changes in plant assets are due to asset acquisitions with cash and depreciation. Income and dividends from 20 percent– to 50 percent–owned investees for 2016 were $120,000 and $60,000, respectively. Pam's only subsidiary reported $400,000 net income for 2016 and declared $200,000 in dividends during the year. Patent amortization for 2016 is $20,000.

## P4-20
### (Appendix B) Consolidated financial statements (cost method)

Pop Company paid $88,000 for an 80% interest in Son Company on January 5, 2016, when Son's capital stock was $60,000 and its retained earnings $40,000. Trial balances for the companies at December 31, 2016, are as follows (in thousands):

| | Pop | Son |
|---|---|---|
| Cash | $ 2.5 | $ 15 |
| Accounts receivable | 15 | 25 |
| Other assets | 120 | 100 |
| Investment in Son | 88 | — |
| Cost of goods sold | 50 | 30 |
| Operating expenses | 25 | 40 |
| Dividends | 20 | 10 |
| | $320.5 | $220 |
| | | |
| Liabilities | $ 80 | $ 30 |
| Capital Stock | 100 | 60 |
| Paid-in excess | 10 | — |
| Retained earnings | 22.5 | 40 |
| Sales | 100 | 90 |
| Dividend income | 8 | — |
| | $320.5 | $220 |

The only entries that Pop Company made in regard to the investment in Son Company are as follows:

| | | |
|---|---|---|
| *January 5, 2016* | | |
| Investment in Son (+A) | 88,000 | |
|    Cash (−A) | | 88,000 |
| *November 15, 2016* | | |
| Cash (+A) | 8,000 | |
|    Dividend income (R, +SE) | | 8,000 |

Assets and liabilities of Son are stated at their fair values.

**REQUIRED:**

1. Prepare a balance sheet for Pop Company at December 31, 2016.
2. Prepare a consolidated income statement for Pop Company and Subsidiary for 2016.
3. Prepare a consolidated balance sheet for Pop Company and Subsidiary at December 31, 2016.

---

## PROFESSIONAL RESEARCH ASSIGNMENTS

Answer the following questions by reference to the FASB Codification of Accounting Standards. Include the appropriate reference in your response.

**PR 4-1**   In preparing a consolidated statement of cash flows, is a firm required to disclose cash flow per share?

**PR 4-2**   Firms adopting the direct method to prepare the statement of cash flows often include a reconciliation of net income to net cash flows from operating activities. Is this required, and, if so, how should it be presented?

# CHAPTER 5

# Intercompany Profit Transactions—Inventories

W e prepare consolidated statements to show the financial position and the results of operations of two or more affiliates as if they were one entity. We eliminate the effects of transactions between the affiliates (referred to as *intercompany transactions*) from consolidated financial statements.

Intercompany transactions may result in reciprocal account balances on the books of the affiliates. For example, intercompany sales transactions produce reciprocal sales and purchases (or cost of goods sold) balances, as well as reciprocal balances for accounts receivable and accounts payable. Intercompany transactions are intracompany transactions from the viewpoint of the consolidated entity; therefore, we eliminate their effects in the consolidation process.

Generally accepted accounting principles (GAAP) concisely summarize consolidation procedures:

> *In the preparation of consolidated financial statements, intercompany balances and transactions shall be eliminated. This includes intercompany open account balances, security holdings, sales and purchases, interest, dividends, etc. As consolidated financial statements are based on the assumption that they represent the financial position and operating results of a single economic entity, such statements should not include gain or loss on transactions among the entities in the consolidated group. Accordingly, any intercompany income or loss on assets remaining within the consolidated group shall be eliminated; the concept usually applied for this purpose is profit or loss. (ASC 810-10-45)[1]*

The reason we eliminate intercompany profits and losses is that the management of the parent controls all intercompany transactions, including authorization and pricing, without arm's-length bargaining between the affiliates. In eliminating the effect of intercompany profits and losses from consolidated statements, however, the issue is not whether the intercompany transactions were or were not at arm's length. *The objective is to show the income and financial position of the consolidated entity as they would have appeared if the intercompany transactions had never taken place,* irrespective of the amounts involved in such transactions. The same reasoning applies to the measurement of the investment account and investment income under a one-line consolidation. In the case of a one-line consolidation, however, evidence that intercompany transactions were not at arm's length may necessitate additional adjustments for fair presentation of the parent's income and financial position in separate parent financial statements (ASC 323-10-15).

Most intercompany transactions creating gains and losses can be grouped as inventory items, plant assets, and bonds. Consolidation procedures for inventory items are discussed in this chapter, and those for plant assets and bonds are covered in subsequent chapters. Although the discussion

[1]From Deere & Company Annual Report 2015 (P36) © 2015 Deere & Company

---

**LEARNING OBJECTIVES**

**5.1** Understand the impact of intercompany inventory profit on consolidation workpapers.

**5.2** Apply the concepts of upstream versus downstream inventory transfers.

**5.3** Defer unrealized inventory profits remaining in the ending inventory.

**5.4** Recognize realized, previously deferred inventory profits in the beginning inventory.

**5.5** Adjust noncontrolling interest amounts in the presence of intercompany inventory profits.

and illustrations in this chapter relate to intercompany profit situations, the examples also provide a basis for analyzing and accounting for intercompany losses. Tax considerations are covered in Chapter 10.

## INTERCOMPANY INVENTORY TRANSACTIONS

Firms recognize revenue when it is realized, that is, when it is earned. For revenue to be earned from the viewpoint of the consolidated entity, there must be a sale to outside entities. Revenue on sales between affiliates cannot be recognized until merchandise is sold outside of the consolidated entity. No consolidated income results from transfers among affiliates. The sale of inventory items by one company to an affiliate produces reciprocal sales and purchases accounts when the purchaser has a periodic inventory system, and reciprocal sales and cost of goods sold accounts when the purchaser uses a perpetual inventory system. We eliminate reciprocal sales and cost of goods sold (or purchases) amounts in preparing a consolidated income statement in order to report sales and cost of goods sold for the consolidated entity; eliminating equal sales and cost of goods sold has no effect on consolidated net income.

As mentioned in Chapter 1, vertical integration of operating activities is often a prime motivation for business combinations. Segment information presented in the AT&T 2014 annual report (p. 51) discloses elimination of intersegment net revenues of $12.686 billion. Similarly, *Chevron* Corporation discloses elimination of intersegment sales of $48.9 billion (2014 annual report, p. 47).

### Elimination of Intercompany Purchases and Sales

We eliminate intercompany sales and purchases (or cost of goods sold) in the consolidation process in order to report consolidated sales and purchases (or cost of goods sold) at amounts purchased from and sold to outside entities. When a periodic inventory system is used, the workpaper entry to eliminate intercompany sales and purchases is simply a debit to sales and a credit to purchases. The workpaper elimination under a perpetual inventory system (used throughout this book) is a debit to sales and a credit to cost of goods sold. The reason is that a perpetual inventory system includes intercompany purchases in a separate cost of goods sold account of the purchasing affiliate when it is sold to outside third parties. These observations are illustrated for Pop Corporation and its subsidiary, Son Corporation.

Pop Corporation formed a subsidiary, Son Corporation, in 2016 to retail a special line of Pop's merchandise. All Son's purchases are made from Pop Corporation at 20 percent above Pop's cost. During 2016, Pop sold merchandise that cost $40,000 to Son for $48,000, and Son sold all the merchandise to its customers for $60,000. Both Pop and Son record journal entries relating to the merchandise on their separate books, as follows:

POP'S BOOKS

| | | |
|---|---|---|
| Inventory (+A) | 40,000 | |
| Accounts payable (+L) | | 40,000 |
| To record purchases on account from other entities. | | |
| Accounts receivable—Son (+A) | 48,000 | |
| Sales (R, +SE) | | 48,000 |
| To record intercompany sales to Son. | | |
| Cost of sales (E, −SE) | 40,000 | |
| Inventory (−A) | | 40,000 |
| To record cost of sales to Son. | | |

SON'S BOOKS

| | | |
|---|---|---|
| Inventory (+A) | 48,000 | |
| Accounts payable—Pop (+L) | | 48,000 |
| To record intercompany purchases from Pop. | | |
| Accounts receivable (+A) | 60,000 | |
| Sales (R, +SE) | | 60,000 |
| To record sales to customers outside the consolidated entity. | | |
| Cost of sales (E, −SE) | 48,000 | |
| Inventory (−A) | | 48,000 |
| To record cost of sales to customers. | | |

At year-end 2016, Pop's sales include $48,000 sold to Son, and cost of sales includes the $40,000 cost of merchandise transferred to Son. Son's sales consist of $60,000 in merchandise sold to other entities, and its cost of sales is the $48,000 transfer price from Pop. Pop and Son are considered one entity for reporting purposes, so combined sales and cost of sales are overstated by $48,000. We eliminate that overstatement in the consolidation workpapers. The elimination is as follows:

|  | Pop | 100% Son | Adjustments and Eliminations | | Consolidated |
|---|---|---|---|---|---|
| Sales | $48,000 | $60,000 | a 48,000 | | $60,000 |
| Cost of sales | 40,000 | 48,000 | | a 48,000 | 40,000 |
| Gross profit | $ 8,000 | $12,000 | | | $20,000 |

*The workpaper elimination has no effect on consolidated net income because it eliminates equal sales and cost of sales amounts, and combined gross profit equals consolidated gross profit.* However, the elimination is necessary to reflect merchandising activity accurately for the consolidated entity that purchased merchandise for $40,000 (Pop) and sold it for $60,000 (Son). The fact that Pop's separate records include $8,000 gross profit on the merchandise and Son's records show $12,000 is irrelevant in reporting the consolidated results of operations. In addition to eliminating intercompany profit items, it is necessary to eliminate intercompany receivables and payables in consolidation.

## Elimination of Unrealized Profit in Ending Inventory

The consolidated entity realizes and recognizes the full amount of intercompany profit on sales between affiliates in the period in which the merchandise is resold to outside entities. Until reselling the merchandise, any profit or loss on intercompany sales is unrealized, and we must eliminate its effect in the consolidation process. The *ending inventory of the purchasing affiliate* reflects any unrealized profit or loss on intercompany sales because that inventory reflects the intercompany transfer price rather than cost to the consolidated entity. The elimination is a debit to cost of goods sold and a credit to the ending inventory for the amount of unrealized profit. The credit reduces the inventory to its cost basis to the consolidated entity; and the debit to cost of goods sold increases cost of goods sold to its cost basis. These relationships are illustrated by continuing the Pop and Son example for 2017.

During 2017 Pop sold merchandise that cost $60,000 to Son for $72,000, and Son sold all but $12,000 of this merchandise to its customers for $75,000. Journal entries relating to the merchandise transferred intercompany during 2017 are as follows:

### POP'S BOOKS

| | | |
|---|---|---|
| Inventory (+A) | 60,000 | |
|     Accounts payable (+L) | | 60,000 |
| To record purchase on account from other entities. | | |
| Accounts receivable—Son (+A) | 72,000 | |
|     Sales (R, +SE) | | 72,000 |
| To record intercompany sales to Son. | | |
| Cost of sales (E, −SE) | 60,000 | |
|     Inventory (−A) | | 60,000 |
| To record cost of sales to Son. | | |

### SON'S BOOKS

| | | |
|---|---|---|
| Inventory (+A) | 72,000 | |
|     Accounts payable—Pop (+L) | | 72,000 |
| To record intercompany purchases from Pop. | | |
| Accounts receivable (+A) | 75,000 | |
|     Sales (R, +SE) | | 75,000 |
| To record sales to customers outside the consolidated entity. | | |
| Cost of sales (E, −SE) | 60,000 | |
|     Inventory (−A) | | 60,000 |
| To record cost of sales to outside entities. | | |

Pop's sales for 2017 include $72,000 sold to Son, and its cost of sales reflects the $60,000 cost of merchandise transferred to Son. Son's $75,000 sales for 2017 consist of merchandise acquired from Pop, and its $60,000 cost of sales equals 5/6, or $60,000/$72,000, of the $72,000 transfer price of merchandise acquired from Pop. The remaining merchandise acquired from Pop in 2017 stays in Son's December 31, 2017, inventory at the $12,000 transfer price, which includes $2,000 unrealized profit.

**WORKPAPER ENTRIES**  The consolidated entity views this as an intercompany transfer of merchandise that costs $60,000:

- $50,000 (or 5/6) of this merchandise was then sold to outside entities for $75,000.
- $10,000 (or 1/6) remains in inventory at year-end.
- The consolidated entity realizes a gross profit of $25,000.

We accomplish the consolidated results through workpaper entries that eliminate the effects of intercompany transactions from sales, cost of sales, and inventory. Although a single entry can be made to reduce combined sales by $72,000, combined cost of sales by $70,000, and inventory by $2,000, two entries are ordinarily used in order to separate the elimination of intercompany sales and cost of sales from the elimination (deferral) of unrealized profit.

The eliminations follow:

|  | Pop | Son | Adjustments and Eliminations | | Consolidated |
| --- | --- | --- | --- | --- | --- |
| *Income Statement* | | | | | |
| Sales | $72,000 | $75,000 | a 72,000 | | $75,000 |
| Cost of sales | 60,000 | 60,000 | b 2,000 | a 72,000 | 50,000 |
| Gross profit | $12,000 | $15,000 | | | $25,000 |
| *Balance Sheet* | | | | | |
| Inventory | | $12,000 | | b 2,000 | $10,000 |

The first entry eliminates intercompany sales and cost of sales, journalized as follows:

| a | Sales (− R, − SE) | 72,000 | |
| --- | --- | --- | --- |
| | Cost of sales (− E, + SE) | | 72,000 |
| | To eliminate intercompany sales and cost of sales. | | |

This entry is procedurally the same as the one made in 2016 to eliminate intercompany cost of sales and sales.

A secondary entry defers the $2,000 intercompany profit that remains unrealized ($27,000 combined gross profit − $25,000 consolidated gross profit) and reduces the ending inventory from $12,000 to its $10,000 cost to the consolidated entity:

| b | Cost of sales (E, − SE) | 2,000 | |
| --- | --- | --- | --- |
| | Inventory (− A) | | 2,000 |
| | To eliminate intercompany profit from cost of sales and inventory. | | |

The debit to cost of sales reduces profit by increasing consolidated cost of sales, and the credit reduces the valuation of inventory for consolidated statement purposes from the intercompany transfer price to cost. From the viewpoint of the consolidated entity, Son overstated its ending inventory by the $2,000 unrealized profit. An overstated ending inventory understates cost of sales and overstates gross profit, so we correct the error with entry b, which increases (debits) cost of sales and decreases (credits) the overstated ending inventory. This elimination reduces consolidated gross profit by $2,000 (income effect) and consolidated ending inventory by $2,000 (balance sheet effect).

These two workpaper entries should be learned at this time because they are always the same, regardless of additional complexities introduced later.

**EQUITY METHOD**   On December 31, 2017, Pop computes its investment income in the usual manner, except that Pop defers $2,000 intercompany profit. Pop's one-line consolidation entry reduces income from Son by the $2,000 unrealized profit in the ending inventory and accordingly reduces the Investment in Son account by $2,000.

## Recognition of Unrealized Profit in Beginning Inventory

Unrealized profit in an ending inventory is realized for consolidated statement purposes when the merchandise is sold outside the consolidated entity. Ordinarily, realization occurs in the immediately succeeding fiscal period, so firms simply defer recognition for consolidated statement purposes until the following year. Recognition of the previously unrealized profit requires a workpaper credit to cost of goods sold because the amount of the beginning inventory is reflected in cost of goods sold when the perpetual system is used. The direction of the sale, noncontrolling ownership percentage, and parent method of accounting for the subsidiary may complicate the related workpaper debits. These complications do not affect consolidated gross profit, however, and we extend the previous example to reflect 2018 operations for Pop and Son.

During 2018, Pop Corporation sold merchandise that cost $80,000 to Son for $96,000, and Son sold 75 percent of the merchandise for $90,000. Son also sold the items in the beginning inventory with a transfer price of $12,000 to its customers for $15,000. Journal entries relating to the merchandise transferred intercompany follow:

POP'S BOOKS

| | | |
|---|---|---|
| Inventory (+A) | 80,000 | |
|     Accounts payable (+L) | | 80,000 |
| To record purchase on account from other entities. | | |
| Accounts receivable—Son (+A) | 96,000 | |
|     Sales (R, +SE) | | 96,000 |
| To record intercompany sales to Son. | | |
| Cost of sales (E, −SE) | 80,000 | |
|     Inventory (−A) | | 80,000 |
| To record cost of sales to Son. | | |

SON'S BOOKS

| | | |
|---|---|---|
| Inventory (+A) | 96,000 | |
|     Accounts payable—Pop (+L) | | 96,000 |
| To record intercompany purchases from Pop. | | |
| Accounts receivable (+A) | 105,000 | |
|     Sales (R, +SE) | | 105,000 |
| To record sales of $90,000 and $15,000 to outside entities. | | |
| Cost of sales (E, −SE) | 84,000 | |
|     Inventory (−A) | | 84,000 |
| To record cost of sales ($96,000 transfer price × 75% sold) and $12,000 from beginning inventory. | | |

Son sold 75 percent of the merchandise purchased from Pop, so its ending inventory in 2018 is $24,000 ($96,000 × 25%) and that inventory includes $4,000 unrealized profit [$24,000 − ($24,000/1.2 transfer price)].

**WORKPAPER ENTRIES**   From the viewpoint of the consolidated entity, merchandise that cost $80,000 was transferred intercompany:

- $60,000 of this merchandise, plus $10,000 beginning inventory, was sold for $105,000.
- $20,000 remained in inventory at year-end 2018.
- The consolidated entity realized a gross profit of $35,000.

The workpapers that eliminate the effects of intercompany transactions from sales, cost of sales, and inventory reflect these consolidated results. Three workpaper entries eliminate intercompany cost of sales and sales, recognize previously deferred profit from beginning inventory, and defer unrealized profit in the ending inventory, as follows:

| | Pop | Son | Adjustments and Eliminations | | Consolidated |
|---|---|---|---|---|---|
| *Income Statement* | | | | | |
| Sales | $96,000 | $105,000 | a 96,000 | | $105,000 |
| Cost of sales | 80,000 | 84,000 | c  4,000 | a 96,000 | |
| | | | | b  2,000 | 70,000 |
| Gross profit | $16,000 | $ 21,000 | | | $ 35,000 |
| *Balance Sheet* | | | | | |
| Inventory | | $ 24,000 | | c  4,000 | $ 20,000 |
| Investment in Son | XXX | | b  2,000 | | |

Journal entries to eliminate the effects of intercompany transactions between Pop and Son for 2018 follow:

| | | | |
|---|---|---|---|
| a | Sales (− R, − SE) | 96,000 | |
| | Cost of sales (− E, + SE) | | 96,000 |
| | To eliminate intercompany cost of sales and sales. | | |
| b | Investment in Son (+ A) | 2,000 | |
| | Cost of sales (−E, + SE) | | 2,000 |
| | To recognize previously deferred profit from beginning inventory. | | |
| c | Cost of sales (E, −SE) | 4,000 | |
| | Inventory (− A) | | 4,000 |
| | To defer unrealized profit in ending inventory. | | |

Workpaper entries a and c are procedurally the same as the entries for 2017. Their purpose is to eliminate intercompany cost of sales and sales and defer unrealized profit in the ending inventory. From the consolidated viewpoint, the $2,000 overstated beginning inventory overstates cost of sales in 2018. Entry b recognizes previously deferred profit from 2017 by reducing consolidated cost of sales and thereby increasing consolidated gross profit. (Note, of course, that entry b is made only in those cases in which the inventory has subsequently been sold to a customer outside the consolidated entity.) The related debit to the Investment in Son account adjusts for the one-line consolidation entry that reduced the Investment in Son account in 2017 to defer unrealized profit in the ending inventory of that year. Although the credit side of this entry is always the same, additional complexities sometimes arise with the debit side of the entry.

The Pop–Son example illustrates the effects of intercompany inventory transactions on consolidated sales, cost of sales, and gross profit, and these effects are always the same. But the example did not cover the effects of intercompany inventory transactions on noncontrolling interest computations or on parent accounting under the equity method. These ramifications are discussed and illustrated next.

## DOWNSTREAM AND UPSTREAM SALES

LEARNING OBJECTIVE 5.2

A **downstream sale** is a sale by a parent to a subsidiary. A sale by a subsidiary to a parent is an **upstream sale**. The upstream and downstream designations relate to the usual diagram of affiliation structures that places the parent at the top. Thus, sales from top to bottom are downstream, and sales from bottom to top are upstream.

Consolidated statements eliminate reciprocal sales and cost of goods sold amounts for both upstream and downstream sales. We also eliminate unrealized gross profit in ending inventory in its entirety for both downstream and upstream sales. However, the effect of unrealized profits in ending inventory on separate parent statements (as investor) and on consolidated financial statements (which show income to the controlling and noncontrolling stockholders) is determined by both the direction of the intercompany sales activity and the percentage ownership of the subsidiary, except for 100 percent–owned subsidiaries that have no noncontrolling ownership.

In the case of downstream sales, the parent's separate income includes the full amount of unrealized profit (included in sales and cost of sales accounts), and the subsidiary's income is unaffected. When sales are upstream, the subsidiary's net income includes the full amount of any unrealized profit (included in sales and cost of sales accounts), and the parent's separate income is unaffected. The consolidation process eliminates the full amount of intercompany sales and cost of sales for both downstream and upstream sales. However, the noncontrolling interest share *may be affected* if the subsidiary's net income includes unrealized profit (the upstream situation). It *is not affected* if the parent's separate income includes unrealized profit (the downstream situation) because the non-controlling shareholders have an interest only in the income of the subsidiary. When subsidiary net income is overstated (from the viewpoint of the consolidated entity) because it includes unrealized profit, the income allocated to noncontrolling interests should be based on the *realized income of the subsidiary*. A subsidiary's realized income is its reported net income adjusted for intercompany profits from upstream sales.

Noncontrolling interest share *may be affected* by unrealized profit from upstream sales because accounting standards are not definitive with respect to the computation. GAAP provides that elimination of intercompany profit or loss may be allocated proportionately between controlling and noncontrolling interests but does not require such allocation (ASC 810-10-45). The alternative to allocation is to eliminate intercompany profits and losses from upstream sales in the same manner as for downstream sales, debiting (crediting) the full amount of unrealized gain (loss) to the parent's income.

The approach that allocates unrealized profits and losses from upstream sales proportionately between noncontrolling and controlling interests is conceptually superior because it applies the viewpoint of the consolidated entity consistently to both controlling and noncontrolling interests. That is, both controlling share of consolidated income and noncontrolling interest share are computed on the basis of income that is realized from the viewpoint of the consolidated entity. In addition, material amounts of unrealized profits and losses from upstream sales may be allocated between controlling and noncontrolling interests in accounting practice. *Accordingly, unrealized profits and losses from upstream sales are allocated proportionately between consolidated net income (controlling interests) and noncontrolling interest share (noncontrolling interests) throughout this* book. Using the same allocation approach in accounting for the parent/investor's interest under the equity method accomplishes a consistent treatment between consolidation procedures and equity method accounting (the one-line consolidation).

## Downstream and Upstream Effects on Income Computations

Assume that the separate incomes of a parent and its 80 percent–owned subsidiary for 2016 are as follows (in thousands):

|  | Parent | Subsidiary |
|---|---|---|
| Sales | $600 | $300 |
| Cost of sales | 300 | 180 |
| Gross profit | 300 | 120 |
| Expenses | 100 | 70 |
| Parent's separate income | $200 | |
| Subsidiary's net income | | $ 50 |

Intercompany sales during the year are $100,000, and the December 31, 2016, inventory includes $20,000 unrealized profit.

NONCONTROLLING INTEREST SHARE COMPUTATION   If the intercompany sales are downstream, the parent's sales and cost of sales accounts reflect the $20,000 unrealized profit, and the subsidiary's $50,000 net income is equal to its realized income. In this case, the noncontrolling interest share computation is unaffected by the intercompany transactions and is computed as

$$\$50,000 \text{ net income of subsidiary} \times 20\% = \$10,000$$

If the intercompany sales are upstream, the subsidiary's sales and cost of sales accounts reflect the $20,000 unrealized profit, and the subsidiary's realized income is $30,000. In this case, the noncontrolling interest share computation is

$$(\$50,000 \text{ net income of subsidiary} - \$20,000 \text{ unrealized profit}) \times 20\% = \$6,000$$

**CONSOLIDATED NET INCOME COMPUTATION** Exhibit 5-1 shows comparative consolidated income statements for the parent and its 80 percent–owned subsidiary under the two assumptions. In examining the exhibit, note that the only difference in the computation of controlling interest share of consolidated net income under the two assumptions lies in the computation of noncontrolling interest share. This is so because the eliminations for intercompany cost of sales and sales and intercompany inventory profits are the same regardless of whether the sales are downstream or upstream. Parent net income under the equity method is equal to the controlling share of consolidated net income, so the approach used in computing income from subsidiary must be consistent with the approach used in determining consolidated net income. For downstream sales, the full amount of unrealized profit is charged against the income from subsidiary, but for upstream sales, only the parent's proportionate share is charged against its investment income from subsidiary. Computations are as follows (in thousands):

|  | Downstream | Upstream |
|---|---|---|
| Parent's separate income | $200 | $200 |
| Add: Income from subsidiary |  |  |
| *Downstream* |  |  |
| Equity in subsidiary's reported income less unrealized profit [($50,000 × 80%) − $20,000] | 20 |  |
| *Upstream* |  |  |
| Equity in subsidiary realized income [($50,000 − $20,000) × 80%] |  | 24 |
| Parent net income | $220 | $224 |

Recognize that affiliates may engage in simultaneous upstream and downstream inventory transactions. In such cases, it is necessary to eliminate both the upstream and downstream sales/cost of sales. These transactions do not simply offset one another, due to the deferral of unrealized intercompany inventory profits.

For example, assume that the parent sells $100,000 of inventory to its wholly owned subsidiary at a profit of $20,000. The entire inventory remains unsold at year-end. The subsidiary company likewise sells $100,000 of inventory to the parent, including an identical intercompany inventory profit of $20,000. This inventory also remains unsold at year-end.

We could simply assume that the two transactions are offsetting. However, this would distort both the consolidated balance sheet and income statement. The combined parent and subsidiary balance sheets include the inventory at the total intercompany transfer price of $200,000. However, $40,000 of this total is intercompany profit. The correct consolidated balance sheet inventory should be the cost of $160,000.

We would also overstate consolidated net income by $40,000. The intercompany profit must be deferred until the affiliates realize the gains through sales to parties outside the consolidated entity.

| EXHIBIT 5-1 | | |
|---|---|---|
| Consolidated Income Effect of Downstream and Upstream Sales | | |

**PARENT CORPORATION AND SUBSIDIARY CONSOLIDATED INCOME STATEMENT (IN THOUSANDS) FOR THE YEAR ENDED DECEMBER 31, 2016**

|  | Downstream Sales | Upstream Sales |
|---|---|---|
| Sales ($900 − $100) | $800 | $800 |
| Cost of sales (480 + $20 − $100) | 400 | 400 |
| Gross profit | 400 | 400 |
| Expenses ($100 + $70) | 170 | 170 |
| Consolidated net income | 230 | 230 |
| Less: Noncontrolling interest share | 10 | 6 |
| Controlling interest share of consolidated net income | $220 | $224 |

We can avoid these misstatements only if we separately eliminate the effects of all upstream and downstream transactions. Notice that intercompany inventory transactions provide a convenient means of managing reported consolidated net income if the impact of simultaneous upstream and downstream sales is not properly eliminated.

## UNREALIZED PROFITS FROM DOWNSTREAM SALES

LEARNING OBJECTIVE **5.3**

Sales by a parent to its subsidiaries increase parent sales, cost of goods sold, and gross profit, but do not affect the income of subsidiaries until the merchandise is resold to outside parties. The full amount of gross profit on merchandise sold downstream and remaining in subsidiary inventories increases parent income, so the full amount must be eliminated from the parent's income statement under the equity method of accounting. Consistent with a one-line consolidation concept, this is done by reducing investment income and the investment account. Consolidated financial statements eliminate unrealized gross profit by increasing consolidated cost of goods sold and reducing merchandise inventory to its cost basis to the consolidated entity. The overstatement of the ending inventory from the consolidated viewpoint understates consolidated cost of goods sold.

## Deferral of Intercompany Profit in Period of Intercompany Sale

The following example illustrates the deferral of unrealized profits on downstream sales. Pam Corporation owns 90 percent of the voting stock of Sun Corporation. Separate income statements of Pam and Sun for 2016, before consideration of unrealized profits, are as follows (in thousands):

|  | Pam | Sun |
|---|---|---|
| Sales | $100 | $50 |
| Cost of goods sold | 60 | 35 |
| Gross profit | 40 | 15 |
| Expenses | 15 | 5 |
| Operating income | 25 | 10 |
| Income from Sun | 9 | — |
| Net income | $ 34 | $10 |

Pam's sales include $15,000 to Sun at a profit of $6,250, and Sun's December 31, 2016, inventory includes 40 percent of the merchandise from the intercompany transaction. Pam's operating income reflects the $2,500 unrealized profit in Sun's inventory ($6,000 transfer price less $3,500 cost). On its separate books, Pam records its share of Sun's income and defers recognition of the unrealized profit with the following entries:

| | | |
|---|---|---|
| Investment in Sun (+A) | 9,000 | |
|     Income from Sun (R, +SE) | | 9,000 |
|   To record share of Sun's income. | | |
| Income from Sun (−R, −SE) | 2,500 | |
|     Investment in Sun (−A) | | 2,500 |
|   To eliminate unrealized profit on sales to Sun. | | |

The second entry on Pam's books reduces Pam's income from Sun from $9,000 to $6,500. Reciprocal sales and cost of goods sold, as well as all unrealized profit, must be eliminated in consolidated financial statements. These adjustments are shown in the partial workpaper in Exhibit 5-2.

Entry a deducts the full amount of intercompany sales from sales and cost of goods sold. Entry b then corrects cost of goods sold for the unrealized profit at year-end and reduces the inventory to its cost basis to the consolidated entity. Note that entries a and b are equivalent to a single debit to sales for $15,000, a credit to cost of goods sold for $12,500, and a credit to inventory for $2,500.

In examining Exhibit 5-2, observe that Pam's net income on an equity basis is equal to the controlling share of consolidated net income. This equality would not have occurred without the equity method journal entry that reduced Pam's income from $34,000 to $31,500. The $1,000 noncontrolling interest share shown in Exhibit 5-2 is not affected by the unrealized profit on Pam's sales because noncontrolling stockholders share only in subsidiary profit and Sun's reported income for 2016 (equal to its realized income) is unaffected by the unrealized profit in its ending inventory.

## PAM AND SUBSIDIARY, SUN, PARTIAL WORKPAPER FOR THE YEAR ENDED DECEMBER 31, 2016 (IN THOUSANDS)

| | Pam | 90% Sun | Adjustments and Eliminations Debits | Credits | Consolidated Statements |
|---|---|---|---|---|---|
| *Income Statement* | | | | | |
| Sales | $100 | $50 | a 15 | | $135 |
| Income from Sun | 6.5 | | c 6.5 | | |
| Cost of goods sold | (60) | (35) | b 2.5 | a 15 | (82.5) |
| Expenses | (15) | (5) | | | (20) |
| Consolidated net income | | | | | $ 32.5 |
| Noncontrolling interest share ($10,000 × 10%) | | | | | (1) |
| Controlling interest share | $ 31.5 | $10 | | | $ 31.5 |
| *Balance Sheet* | | | | | |
| Inventory | | $ 6 | | b 2.5 | $ 3.5 |
| Investment in Sun | XXX | | | c 6.5 | |

a. Eliminates reciprocal sales and cost of goods sold.
b. Adjusts cost of goods sold and ending inventory to a cost basis to the consolidated entity.
c. Eliminates investment income and adjusts the Investment in Sun account to the January 1, 2016, balance.

## Recognition of Intercompany Profit upon Sale to Outside Entities

Now assume that the merchandise acquired from Pam during 2016 is sold by Sun during 2017, and there are no intercompany transactions between Pam and Sun during 2017. Separate income statements for 2017 before consideration of the $2,500 unrealized profit in Sun's beginning inventory are as follows (in thousands):

| | Pam | Sun |
|---|---|---|
| Sales | $120 | $60 |
| Cost of goods sold | 80 | 40 |
| Gross profit | 40 | 20 |
| Expenses | 20 | 5 |
| Operating income | 20 | 15 |
| Income from Sun | 13.5 | — |
| Net income | $ 33.5 | $15 |

Pam's operating income for 2017 is unaffected by the unrealized profit in Sun's December 31, 2016, inventory. But Sun's 2017 profit is affected because the $2,500 overstatement of Sun's beginning inventory overstates cost of goods sold from a consolidated viewpoint. From Pam's viewpoint, the unrealized profit from 2016 is realized in 2017, and its investment income is recorded and adjusted as follows:

| | | |
|---|---|---|
| Investment in Sun (+A) | 13,500 | |
| Income from Sun (R, +SE) | | 13,500 |
| To record investment income from Sun. | | |
| Investment in Sun (+A) | 2,500 | |
| Income from Sun (R, +SE) | | 2,500 |
| To record realization of profit from 2016 intercompany sales to Sun. | | |

The last entry increases Pam's investment from $13,500 to $16,000 and Pam's net income from $33,500 to $36,000. The partial workpaper for Pam and Sun for 2017 reflects the adjusted amounts as shown in Exhibit 5-3.

In examining Exhibit 5-3, note that entry a debits the Investment in Sun account and credits cost of goods sold for $2,500. The beginning inventory of Sun has already been closed to cost of goods sold under a perpetual inventory system, so the inventory cannot be adjusted. The adjustment to the investment account is necessary to increase the investment account at the beginning of the year to

**PAM AND SUBSIDIARY, SUN, PARTIAL WORKPAPER FOR THE YEAR ENDED DECEMBER 31, 2017 (IN THOUSANDS)**

| | Pam | 90% Sun | Adjustments and Eliminations Debits | Credits | Consolidated Statements |
|---|---|---|---|---|---|
| **Income Statement** | | | | | |
| Sales | $120 | $60 | | | $180 |
| Income from Sun | 16 | | b 16 | | |
| Cost of goods sold | (80) | (40) | | a 2.5 | (117.5) |
| Expenses | (20) | (5) | | | (25) |
| Consolidated net income | | | | | $ 37.5 |
| Noncontrolling interest share ($15,000 × 10%) | | | | | (1.5) |
| Controlling interest share | $ 36 | $15 | | | $ 36 |
| **Balance Sheet** | | | | | |
| Investment in Sun | XXX | | a 2.5 | b 16 | |

a. Adjusts cost of goods sold to a cost basis and adjusts the Investment in Sun account balance to reestablish reciprocity with the beginning subsidiary equity accounts.
b. Eliminates investment income and adjusts the Investment in Sun account to the January 1, 2017, balance.

reflect realization during 2017 of the unrealized profit that was deferred at the end of 2016. *This adjustment reestablishes reciprocity between the investment balance at January 1, 2017, and the subsidiary equity accounts at the same date. It is important to record this adjustment before eliminating reciprocal investment and equity balances.* The computation of noncontrolling interest share in Exhibit 5-3 is unaffected because the sales are downstream.

Unrealized inventory profits in consolidated financial statements are self-correcting over any two accounting periods and are subject to the same type of analysis as inventory errors. Total consolidated net income for Pam and Sun for 2016 and 2017 is unaffected by the $2,500 deferral in 2016 and recognition in 2017. The significance of the adjustments lies in the accurate statement of the consolidated income for each period.

## UNREALIZED PROFITS FROM UPSTREAM SALES

Sales by a subsidiary to its parent increase the sales, cost of goods sold, and gross profit of the subsidiary, but they do not affect the operating income of the parent until the merchandise is resold by the parent to outside entities. The parent's net income is affected in the year of transfer from the subsidiary, however, because the parent recognizes its share of the subsidiary's income on an equity basis. If the selling subsidiary is a 100 percent–owned affiliate, the parent defers 100 percent of any unrealized profit in the year of intercompany sale. If the subsidiary is a partially owned affiliate, the parent defers only its proportionate share of the unrealized subsidiary profit.

### Deferral of Intercompany Profit in Period of Intercompany Sale

LEARNING OBJECTIVE 5.5

Assume that Son Corporation (subsidiary) sells merchandise that it purchased for $7,500 to Pop Corporation (parent) for $20,000 during 2016 and that Pop Corporation sold 60 percent of the merchandise to outsiders during the year for $15,000. At year-end the unrealized inventory profit is $5,000 (cost $3,000, but included in Pop's inventory at $8,000). If Son reports net income of $50,000 for 2016, Pop recognizes its proportionate share as shown in Exhibit 5-4. The exhibit compares parent-company accounting for a one-line consolidation of a 100 percent–owned subsidiary and a 75 percent–owned subsidiary.

As the illustration shows, if Pop records 100 percent of Son's income under the equity method, it must eliminate 100 percent of any unrealized profit included in that income. However, if Pop records only 75 percent of Son's income under the equity method, it must eliminate only 75 percent

*Part A*
*If Son Is a 100%-Owned Subsidiary*

| | | |
|---|---|---|
| Investment in Son (+A) | 50,000 | |
| Income from Son (R, +SE) | | 50,000 |
| To record 100% of Son's reported income as income from subsidiary. | | |
| Income from Son (−R, −SE) | 5,000 | |
| Investment in Son (−A) | | 5,000 |
| To defer 100% of the unrealized inventory profits reported by Son until realized. | | |

A single entry for $45,000 [($50,000 − $5,000) × 100%] is equally acceptable.

*Part B*
*If Son Is a 75%-Owned Subsidiary*

| | | |
|---|---|---|
| Investment in Son (+A) | 37,500 | |
| Income from Son (R, +SE) | | 37,500 |
| To record 75% of Son's reported income as income from subsidiary. | | |
| Income from Son (−R, −SE) | 3,750 | |
| Investment in Son (−A) | | 3,750 |
| To defer 75% of the unrealized inventory profits reported by Son until realized. | | |

A single entry for $33,750 [($50,000 − $5,000) × 75%] is equally acceptable.

of any unrealized profit included in Son's income. In both cases, Pop eliminates all the unrealized profit from its income and investment accounts.

The elimination of unrealized inventory profits from upstream sales in consolidated financial statements results in the elimination of 100 percent of all unrealized inventory profits from consolidated sales and cost of goods sold accounts. However, because the controlling share of consolidated net income is a measurement of income to the stockholders of the parent, noncontrolling interest share is reduced for its proportionate share of any unrealized profit of the subsidiary. This requires deducting the noncontrolling interest's share of unrealized profits from the noncontrolling interest's share of the subsidiary's reported net income. Thus, the effect on consolidated net income of unrealized profits from upstream sales is the same as the effect on parent income under the equity method of accounting.

Exhibit 5-5 illustrates partial consolidation workpapers for Pop Corporation and its 75 percent–owned subsidiary, Son Corporation. Although the amounts for sales, cost of goods sold, and expenses

**POP AND SUBSIDIARY, SON, PARTIAL WORKPAPER FOR THE YEAR ENDED DECEMBER 31, 2016 (IN THOUSANDS)**

| | Pop | 75% Son | Adjustments and Eliminations Debits | Adjustments and Eliminations Credits | Consolidated Statements |
|---|---|---|---|---|---|
| *Income Statement* | | | | | |
| Sales | $250 | $150 | a 20 | | $380 |
| Income from Son | 33.75 | | c 33.75 | | |
| Cost of goods sold | (100) | (80) | b 5 | a 20 | (165) |
| Expenses | (50) | (20) | | | (70) |
| Consolidated net income | | | | | $145 |
| Noncontrolling interest share [($50,000 − $5,000) × 25%] | | | | | (11.25) |
| Controlling interest share | $133.75 | $ 50 | | | $133.75 |
| *Balance Sheet* | | | | | |
| Inventory | $ 8 | | | b 5 | |
| Investment in Son | XXX | | | c 33.75 | |

a. Eliminates reciprocal sales and cost of goods sold.
b. Adjusts cost of goods sold and ending inventory to a cost basis to the consolidated entity.
c. Eliminates investment income and adjusts the Investment in Son account to the January 1, 2016, balance.

are presented without explanation, the data provided are consistent with previous assumptions for Pop and Son Corporations.

Part B of Exhibit 5-4 explains the $33,750 income from Son that appears in Pop's separate income statement in Exhibit 5-5. Noncontrolling interest share is computed by subtracting unrealized profit from Son's reported income and multiplying by the noncontrolling interest percentage. Failure to adjust the noncontrolling interest share for unrealized profit will result in a lack of equality between parent net income on an equity basis and the controlling share of consolidated net income. This potential problem is, of course, absent in the case of a 100 percent–owned subsidiary because there is no noncontrolling interest.

## Recognition of Intercompany Profit upon Sale to Outside Entities

The effect of unrealized profits in a beginning inventory on parent and consolidated net incomes is just the opposite of the effect of unrealized profits in an ending inventory. That is, the relationship between unrealized profits in ending inventories (year of intercompany sale) and consolidated net income is direct, whereas the relationship between unrealized profit in beginning inventories (year of sale to outside entities) and consolidated net income is inverse. This is illustrated by continuing the Pop and Son example to show realization during 2017 of the $5,000 unrealized profit in the December 31, 2016, inventories. Assume that there are no intercompany transactions between Pop and Son during 2017, that Son is a 75 percent–owned subsidiary of Pop, and that Son reports income of $60,000 for 2017. Pop records its share of Son's income under the equity method as follows:

| | | |
|---|---|---|
| Investment in Son (+A) | 45,000 | |
|     Income from Son (R, +SE) | | 45,000 |
|   To record 75% of Son's reported income as income | | |
|     from subsidiary. | | |
| Investment in Son (+A) | 3,750 | |
|     Income from Son (R, +SE) | | 3,750 |
|   To record realization during 2017 of 75% of the $5,000 unrealized | | |
|     inventory profits of Son from 2016. | | |

Exhibit 5-6 illustrates consolidation procedures for unrealized profits in beginning inventories from upstream sales for Pop and Subsidiary. Several of the items in Exhibit 5-6 differ from those

**EXHIBIT 5-6**

Inventory Profit on Upstream Sales in Year After Intercompany Sales

**POP AND SUBSIDIARY, SON, PARTIAL WORKPAPER FOR THE YEAR ENDED DECEMBER 31, 2017 (IN THOUSANDS)**

| | Pop | 75% Son | Adjustments and Eliminations Debits | Adjustments and Eliminations Credits | Consolidated Statements |
|---|---|---|---|---|---|
| *Income Statement* | | | | | |
| Sales | $275 | $160 | | | $435 |
| Income from Son | 48.75 | | b 48.75 | | |
| Cost of goods sold | (120) | (85) | | a 5 | (200) |
| Expenses | (60) | (15) | | | (75) |
| Consolidated net income | | | | | $160 |
| Noncontrolling interest share [($60,000 + $5,000) × 25%] | | | | | (16.25) |
| Controlling interest share | $143.75 | $ 60 | | | $143.75 |
| *Balance Sheet* | | | | | |
| Investment in Son | XXX | | a 3.75 | b 48.75 | |
| Noncontrolling interest: January 1, 2017 | | | | a 1.25 | |

a. Adjusts cost of goods sold to a cost basis and adjusts the Investment in Sal account balance to reestablish reciprocity with the beginning subsidiary equity accounts. We also adjust noncontrolling interest in entry (a).
b. Eliminates investment income and adjusts the Investment in Son account to the January 1, 2017, balance.

for upstream sales with unrealized profit in the ending inventory (Exhibit 5-5). In particular, cost of goods sold is overstated (because of the overstated beginning inventory) and requires a worksheet adjustment to reduce it to its cost basis. This is shown in entry a, which also adjusts the investment account and beginning noncontrolling interest. *Consolidated statements require the allocation between the investment balance (75%) and the noncontrolling interest (25%) for unrealized profits in beginning inventories from upstream sales to correct for prior-year effects on the investment account and the noncontrolling interest.*

## CONSOLIDATION EXAMPLE—INTERCOMPANY PROFITS FROM DOWNSTREAM SALES

Sun Corporation is a 90 percent–owned subsidiary of Pam Corporation, acquired for $94,500 cash on July 1, 2016, when Sun's net assets consisted of $100,000 capital stock and $5,000 retained earnings. The cost of Pam's 90 percent interest in Sun was equal to book value and fair value of the interest acquired ($105,000 × 90%), and accordingly, no allocation to identifiable and unidentifiable assets was necessary.

Pam sells inventory items to Sun on a regular basis, and the intercompany transaction data for 2019 are as follows:

| | |
|---|---:|
| Sales to Sun in 2019 (cost $15,000), selling price | $20,000 |
| Unrealized profit in Sun's inventory at December 31, 2018 (inventory was sold during 2019) | 2,000 |
| Unrealized profit in Sun's inventory at December 31, 2019 | 2,500 |
| Sun's accounts payable to Pam at December 31, 2019 | 10,000 |

### Equity Method

At December 31, 2018, Pam's Investment in Sun account had a balance of $128,500. This balance consisted of Pam's 90 percent equity in Sun's $145,000 net assets on that date less $2,000 unrealized profit in Sun's December 31, 2018, inventory.

During 2019, Pam made the following entries on its books for its investment in Sun under the equity method:

| | | |
|---|---:|---:|
| Cash (+A) | 9,000 | |
|     Investment in Sun (−A) | | 9,000 |
|   To record dividends from Sun ($10,000 × 90%) | | |
| Investment in Sun (+A) | 26,500 | |
|     Income from Sun (R, +SE) | | 26,500 |
|   To record income from Sun for 2019 computed as follows: | | |
|   Equity in Sun's net income ($30,000 × 90%) | | $27,000 |
|   Add: 2018 inventory profit recognized in 2019 | | 2,000 |
|   Less: 2019 inventory profit deferred at year-end | | −2,500 |
| | | $26,500 |

The intercompany sales that led to the unrealized inventory profits were downstream, so we recognize the full amount of profit deferred in 2018 in 2019, and the full amount of the unrealized inventory profit originating in 2019 is deferred at December 31, 2019. Pam's Investment in Sun account increased from $128,500 at January 1, 2019, to $146,000 at December 31, 2019, the entire change consisting of $26,500 income less $9,000 dividends for the year. Exhibit 5-7 shows these amounts in the separate-company columns of the consolidation workpaper for Pam Corporation and Subsidiary for the year ended December 31, 2019.

**EXHIBIT 5-7**

Intercompany Profits on Downstream Sales— Equity Method

## PAM CORPORATION AND SUBSIDIARY CONSOLIDATION WORKPAPER FOR THE YEAR ENDED DECEMBER 31, 2019 (IN THOUSANDS)

| | Pam | 90% Sun | Adjustments and Eliminations Debits | Adjustments and Eliminations Credits | Consolidated Statements |
|---|---|---|---|---|---|
| *Income Statement* Net sales | $1,000 | $300 | a 20 | | $1,280 |
| Income from Sun | 26.5 | | d 26.5 | | |
| Cost of goods sold | (550) | (200) | c 2.5 | a 20 b 2 | (730.5) |
| Other expenses | (350) | (70) | | | (420) |
| Consolidated net income | | | | | 129.5 |
| Noncontrolling interest share ($30,000 × 10%) | | | e 3 | | (3) |
| **Controlling share of net income** | **$ 126.5** | **$ 30** | | | **$ 126.5** |
| *Retained Earnings Statement* Retained earnings—Pam | $ 194 | | | | $ 194 |
| Retained earnings—Sun | | $ 45 | f 45 | | |
| **Controlling share of net income** | 126.5 | 30 | | | 126.5 |
| Dividends | (50) | (10) | | d 9 e 1 | (50) |
| **Retained earnings—December 31** | **$ 270.5** | **$ 65** | | | **$ 270.5** |
| *Balance Sheet* Cash | $ 30 | $ 5 | | | $ 35 |
| Accounts receivable | 70 | 20 | | g 10 | 80 |
| Inventory | 90 | 45 | | c 2.5 | 132.5 |
| Other current assets | 64 | 10 | | | 74 |
| Plant and equipment | 800 | 120 | | | 920 |
| Investment in Sun | 146 | | b 2 | d 17.5 f 130.5 | |
| | $1,200 | $200 | | | $1,241.5 |
| Accounts payable | $ 80 | $ 15 | g 10 | | $ 85 |
| Other liabilities | 49.5 | 20 | | | 69.5 |
| Capital stock | 800 | 100 | f 100 | | 800 |
| **Retained earnings** | 270.5 | 65 | | | 270.5 |
| | $1,200 | $200 | | | |
| Noncontrolling interest January 1 | | | | f 14.5 | |
| Noncontrolling interest December 31 | | | | e 2 | 16.5 |
| | | | $209 | $209 | $1,241.5 |

The entries in Exhibit 5-7 are presented in journal form as follows:

| | | | |
|---|---|---|---|
| a | Sales (− R, − SE) | 20,000 | |
| |     Cost of goods sold (− E, + SE) | | 20,000 |
| | To eliminate intercompany sales and related cost of goods sold amounts. | | |
| b | Investment in Sun (+ A) | 2,000 | |
| |     Cost of goods sold (− E, + SE) | | 2,000 |
| | To adjust cost of goods sold and the beginning investment balance for unrealized profits in the beginning inventory. | | |
| c | Cost of goods sold (E, − SE) | 2,500 | |
| |     Inventory (− A) | | 2,500 |
| | To eliminate unrealized profits in the ending inventory and to increase cost of goods sold to the consolidated entity. | | |
| d | Income from Sun (− R, − SE) | 26,500 | |
| |     Dividends (+ SE) | | 9,000 |
| |     Investment in Sun (− A) | | 17,500 |
| | To eliminate the investment income and 90 percent of the dividends of Sun and to reduce the investment account to its beginning-of-the-period balance, plus the $2,000 from entry b. | | |
| e | Noncontrolling interest share (− SE) | 3,000 | |
| |     Dividends (+ SE) | | 1,000 |
| |     Noncontrolling interest (+ SE) | | 2,000 |
| | To enter noncontrolling interest share of subsidiary income and dividends. | | |
| f | Capital stock—Sun (− SE) | 100,000 | |
| | Retained earnings—Sun (− SE) | 45,000 | |
| |     Investment in Sun (− A) | | 130,500 |
| |     Noncontrolling interest (+ SE) | | 14,500 |
| | To eliminate reciprocal investment and equity balances and record beginning noncontrolling interest. | | |
| g | Accounts payable (− L) | 10,000 | |
| |     Accounts receivable (− A) | | 10,000 |
| | To eliminate reciprocal payables and receivables from intercompany sales. | | |

In the workpaper of Pam Corporation and Subsidiary in Exhibit 5-7, note that Pam's net income ($126,500) is equal to the controlling share of consolidated net income, and Pam's retained earnings amount ($270,500) equals consolidated retained earnings. These equalities are expected from a correct application of the equity method of accounting. The sales that gave rise to the intercompany profits in Sun's inventories were downstream, so neither beginning noncontrolling interest ($14,500) nor noncontrolling interest share ($3,000) was affected by the intercompany transactions.

## CONSOLIDATION EXAMPLE—INTERCOMPANY PROFITS FROM UPSTREAM SALES

Son Corporation is an 80 percent–owned subsidiary of Pop Corporation, acquired for $480,000 on January 2, 2016, when Son's stockholders' equity consisted of $500,000 capital stock and $100,000 retained earnings. The investment cost was equal to the book value and fair value of Son's net assets acquired, so no fair value/book value differential resulted from the acquisition.

Son Corporation sells inventory items to Pop Corporation on a regular basis. The intercompany transaction data for 2017 are as follows:

| | |
|---|---|
| Sales to Pop in 2017 | $300,000 |
| Unrealized profit in Pop's inventory, December 31, 2016 | 40,000 |
| (inventory was sold during 2017) | |
| Unrealized profit in Pop's inventory, December 31, 2017 | 30,000 |
| Intercompany accounts receivable and payable at December 31, 2017 | 50,000 |

## Equity Method

At December 31, 2016, Pop's Investment in Son account had a balance of $568,000, consisting of $600,000 underlying equity in Son's net assets ($750,000 × 80%) less 80 percent of the $40,000 unrealized profit in Pop's December 31, 2016, inventory from upstream sales. During 2017, Pop made the following entries to account for its investment in Sit under the equity method:

| | | |
|---|---|---|
| Cash (+A) | 40,000 | |
| Investment in Son (−A) | | 40,000 |
| To record dividends from Son ($50,000 × 80%). | | |
| Investment in Son (+A) | 88,000 | |
| Income from Son (R, +SE) | | 88,000 |
| To record income from Son for 2017, computed as follows: | | |
| Equity in Son's net income ($100,000 × 80%) | | $ 80,000 |
| Add: 80% of $40,000 unrealized profit deferred in 2016 | | 32,000 |
| Less: 80% of $30,000 unrealized profit at December 31, 2017 | | −24,000 |
| | | $ 88,000 |

The intercompany sales that led to the unrealized inventory profits in 2016 and 2017 were upstream, and, accordingly, only 80 percent of the $40,000 unrealized profit from 2016 is recognized by Pop in 2017. Similarly, only 80 percent of the $30,000 unrealized profit from 2017 sales is deferred by Pop at December 31, 2017. Pop's Investment in Son account was increased by the $88,000 income from Son during 2017 and decreased by $40,000 dividends received from Son. Thus, the $568,000 Investment in Son account at December 31, 2016, increased to $616,000 at December 31, 2017. These amounts, combined with other compatible information to provide complete separate-company financial statements, are shown in the separate-company columns of the consolidation workpaper for Pop Corporation and Subsidiary in Exhibit 5-8.

The entries in Exhibit 5-8 in journal form for convenient reference are as follows:

| | | | |
|---|---|---|---|
| a | Sales (− R, − SE) | 300,000 | |
| | Cost of goods sold (− E, + SE) | | 300,000 |
| | To eliminate reciprocal sales and cost of goods sold amounts. | | |
| b | Investment in Son (+ A) | 32,000 | |
| | Noncontrolling interest (− SE) | 8,000 | |
| | Cost of goods sold (− E, + SE) | | 40,000 |
| | To adjust cost of goods sold for unrealized profit in beginning inventory and to allocate the unrealized profit 80% to the parent's investment account and 20% to noncontrolling interest. | | |
| c | Cost of goods sold (E, − SE) | 30,000 | |
| | Inventory (− A) | | 30,000 |
| | To eliminate unrealized profit from ending inventory and increase cost of goods sold. | | |
| d | Income from Son (− R, − SE) | 88,000 | |
| | Dividends (+ SE) | | 40,000 |
| | Investment in Son (− A) | | 48,000 |
| | To eliminate investment income and 80% of the dividends paid by Son and to reduce the investment account to its beginning balance. | | |

| e | Noncontrolling interest share (− SE) | 22,000 | |
|---|---|---|---|
| | Dividends (+ SE) | | 10,000 |
| | Noncontrolling interest (+ SE) | | 12,000 |
| | To enter noncontrolling interest share of subsidiary income and dividends. | | |
| f | Retained earnings—Son (− SE) | 250,000 | |
| | Capital stock—Son (− SE) | 500,000 | |
| | Investment in Son (− A) | | 600,000 |
| | Noncontrolling interest (+ SE) | | 150,000 |
| | To eliminate reciprocal investment and equity balances and to enter beginning noncontrolling interest. | | |
| g | Accounts payable (− L) | 50,000 | |
| | Accounts receivable (− A) | | 50,000 |
| | To eliminate reciprocal accounts receivable and payable. | | |

The consolidation workpaper entries shown in Exhibit 5-8 are similar to those in the Pam–Sun illustration in Exhibit 5-7. Only entry b, which allocates the unrealized profit in Pop's beginning inventory between investment in Son (80%) and noncontrolling interest (20%), differs significantly. Allocation is necessary because the unrealized profit arises from an upstream sale and was included in Son's reported income for 2016. Pop's share of the $40,000 unrealized profit is only 80 percent. The other 20 percent relates to noncontrolling interests, and, accordingly, the $8,000 debit is necessary to reduce beginning noncontrolling interest from $150,000 (20% of Son's reported equity of $750,000) to $142,000—20 percent of Son's realized equity of $710,000 ($750,000 − $40,000) at December 31, 2016.

**NONCONTROLLING INTEREST**   In computing noncontrolling interest share for 2017, it is necessary to adjust Son's reported net income for unrealized profits before multiplying by the noncontrolling interest percentage. The computation is:

| | |
|---|---|
| Reported net income of Son | $100,000 |
| Add: Inventory profits from 2016 realized in 2017 | +40,000 |
| Deduct: Unrealized inventory profits at December 31, 2017 | (30,000) |
| Son's realized income for 2017 | 110,000 |
| Noncontrolling interest percentage | × 20% |
| Noncontrolling interest share | $ 22,000 |

The $154,000 noncontrolling interest at December 31, 2017, is determined in the workpapers by adding noncontrolling interest share of $22,000 to beginning noncontrolling interest of $142,000 and subtracting noncontrolling interest dividends. An alternative computation that may be used as a check is to deduct unrealized profit in the December 31, 2017, inventory from Son's equity at December 31, 2017, and multiply the resulting realized equity of Son by the 20 percent noncontrolling interest [($800,000 − $30,000) × 20% = $154,000]. The advantage of this approach is that only unrealized profits at the balance sheet date need to be considered in the computation.

## POP CORPORATION AND SUBSIDIARY CONSOLIDATION WORKPAPER FOR THE YEAR ENDED DECEMBER 31, 2017 (IN THOUSANDS)

**EXHIBIT 5-8**

Intercompany Profits on Upstream Sales—Equity Method

| | Pop | 80% Son | Adjustments and Eliminations Debits | Credits | Consolidated Statements |
|---|---|---|---|---|---|
| *Income Statement* | | | | | |
| Sales | $3,000 | $1,500 | a 300 | | $4,200 |
| Income from Son | 88 | | d 88 | | |
| Cost of goods sold | (2,000) | (1,000) | c 30 | a 300 b 40 | (2,690) |
| Other expenses | (588) | (400) | | | (988) |
| Consolidated net income | | | | | 522 |
| Noncontrolling interest share* | | | e 22 | | (22) |
| **Controlling share of net income** | **$ 500** | **$ 100** | | | **$ 500** |
| *Retained Earnings Statement* | | | | | |
| Retained earnings—Pop | $1,000 | | | | $1,000 |
| Retained earnings—Son | | $ 250 | f 250 | | |
| **Add: Controlling share of net income** | **500** | **100** | | | **500** |
| Deduct: Dividends | (400) | (50) | | d 40 e 10 | (400) |
| **Retained earnings—December 31** | **$1,100** | **$ 300** | | | **$1,100** |
| *Balance Sheet* | | | | | |
| Cash | $ 200 | $ 50 | | | $ 250 |
| Accounts receivable | 700 | 100 | | g 50 | 750 |
| Inventory | 1,100 | 200 | | c 30 | 1,270 |
| Other current assets | 384 | 150 | | | 534 |
| Plant and equipment—net | 2,000 | 500 | | | 2,500 |
| Investment in Son | 616 | | b 32 | d 48 f 600 | |
| | $5,000 | $1,000 | | | $5,304 |
| Accounts payable | $ 500 | 150 | g 50 | | $ 600 |
| Other liabilities | 400 | 50 | | | 450 |
| Capital stock | 3,000 | 500 | f 500 | | 3,000 |
| **Retained earnings** | **1,100** | **300** | | | **1,100** |
| | $5,000 | $1,000 | | | |
| Noncontrolling interest January 1 | | | b 8 | f 150 | |
| Noncontrolling interest December 31 | | | | e 12 | 154 |
| | | | $1,280 | $1,280 | $5,304 |

*Noncontrolling interest share ($100,000 + $40,000 − $30,000) × 20% = $22,000

## SUMMARY

Intercompany sales and purchases of inventory items result in reciprocal sales and cost of goods sold amounts that do not reflect merchandising activity of the consolidated entity. These intercompany transactions also give rise to unrealized intercompany profits. The consolidated entity defers recognition of these profits until they can be realized by subsequent sales to parties outside the consolidated entity.

The direction of intercompany sales is important, except for consolidated companies with only 100 percent–owned subsidiaries. We deduct the full amount of the unrealized intercompany profit from downstream sales against parent and consolidated net income. In the case of upstream sales, however, we deduct unrealized profits from consolidated net income and noncontrolling interest share on the basis of controlling and noncontrolling ownership. Intercompany profits that are deferred in one period are subsequently recognized in the period in which the related inventory items are sold to nonaffiliated entities. Exhibit 5-9 presents a summary illustration of the effect of intercompany profit eliminations on parent and consolidated net income.

Under the assumption that Parent (P) sells to Subsidiary (S), P's net income and the controlling share of consolidated net income are exactly the same as if the sales had never taken place. In that case, P's separate income would have been $95,000 ($100,000 + $5,000 − $10,000), and P's income from S would have been $45,000 ($50,000 × 90%), for a total of $140,000. Under the assumption that S sells to P, P's net income and the controlling share of consolidated net income are exactly the same as if the intercompany sales had never taken place. In that case, P's income would have been $100,000 (as given), and S's net income would have been $45,000 ($50,000 + $5,000 − $10,000). P's $100,000 separate income plus P's income from S of $40,500 ($45,000 × 90%) is equal to P's net income and the controlling share of consolidated net income.

| EXHIBIT 5-9 | Assumptions | | |
|---|---|---|---|
| Summary Illustration—Unrealized Inventory Profits | 1. Parent company's income, excluding income from subsidiary, is $100,000. 2. 90%-owned subsidiary reports net income of $50,000. 3. Unrealized profit in beginning inventory is $5,000. (Sold in current year.) 4. Unrealized profit in ending inventory is $10,000. | | |

| | Downstream: Assume That P Sells to S | Upstream: Assume That S Sells to P |
|---|---|---|
| **P's Net Income—Equity Method** | | |
| P's separate income | $100,000 | $100,000 |
| P's share of S's reported net income: | | |
| ($50,000 × 90%) | 45,000 | 45,000 |
| Add: Unrealized profit in beginning inventory: | | |
| ($5,000 × 100%) | 5,000 | |
| ($5,000 × 90%) | | 4,500 |
| Deduct: Unrealized profit in ending inventory: | | |
| ($10,000 × 100%) | (10,000) | |
| ($10,000 × 90%) | | (9,000) |
| P's net income | $140,000 | $140,500 |
| **Controlling Share of Consolidated Net Income** | | |
| P's separate income plus S's net income | $150,000 | $150,000 |
| Adjustments for unrealized profits: | | |
| Beginning inventory ($5,000 × 100%) | 5,000 | 5,000 |
| Ending inventory ($10,000 × 100%) | (10,000) | (10,000) |
| Total realized income | 145,000 | 145,000 |
| Less: Noncontrolling interest share: | | |
| ($50,000 × 10%) | (5,000) | |
| ($50,000 + $5,000 − $10,000) × 10% | | (4,500) |
| Controlling share of consolidated net income | $140,000 | $140,500 |

## QUESTIONS

1. The effect of unrealized profits and losses on sales between affiliated companies is eliminated in preparing consolidated financial statements. When are profits and losses on such sales realized for consolidated statement purposes?

2. In eliminating unrealized profit on intercompany sales of inventory items, should gross profit or net profit be eliminated?

3. Is the amount of intercompany profit to be eliminated from consolidated financial statements affected by the existence of a noncontrolling interest? Explain.

4. What effect does the elimination of intercompany sales and cost of goods sold have on consolidated net income?

5. What effect does the elimination of intercompany accounts receivable and accounts payable have on consolidated working capital?

6. Explain the designations *upstream sales* and *downstream sales*. Of what significance are these designations in computing parent and consolidated net income?

7. Would failure to eliminate unrealized profit in inventories at December 31, 2016, have any effect on consolidated net income in 2017? 2018?

8. Under what circumstances is noncontrolling interest share affected by intercompany sales activity?

9. How does a parent adjust its investment income for unrealized profit on sales it makes to its subsidiaries (a) in the year of the sale and (b) in the year in which the subsidiaries sell the related merchandise to outsiders?

10. How is the combined cost of goods sold affected by unrealized profit in (a) the beginning inventory of the subsidiary and (b) the ending inventory of the subsidiary?

11. Is the effect of unrealized profit on consolidated cost of goods sold influenced by (a) the existence of a noncontrolling interest and (b) the direction of intercompany sales?

12. Unrealized profit in the ending inventory is eliminated in consolidation workpapers by increasing cost of sales and decreasing the inventory account. How is unrealized profit in the beginning inventory reflected in the consolidation workpapers?

13. Describe the computation of noncontrolling interest share in a year in which there is unrealized inventory profit from upstream sales in both the beginning and ending inventories of the parent.

14. Consolidation workpaper procedures are usually based on the assumption that any unrealized profit in the beginning inventory of one year is realized through sales in the following year. If the related merchandise is not sold in the succeeding period, would the assumption result in an incorrect measurement of consolidated net income?

---

**NOTE:** Don't forget the assumptions on page 49 when working exercises and problems in this chapter.

---

## EXERCISES

### E 5-1
### General Questions

1. Intercompany profit elimination entries in consolidation workpapers are prepared in order to:
   a  *Nullify the effect of intercompany transactions on consolidated statements*
   b  *Defer intercompany profit until realized*
   c  *Allocate unrealized profits between controlling and noncontrolling interests*
   d  *Reduce consolidated income*

2. The direction of intercompany sales (upstream or downstream) does not affect consolidation workpaper procedures when the intercompany sales between affiliates are made:
   a  *At fair value*
   b  *Above market value*
   c  *At book value*
   d  *To a 100 percent–owned subsidiary*

3. Pop Corporation sells inventory items for $500,000 to Son Corporation, its 80 percent–owned subsidiary. The consolidated workpaper entry to eliminate the effect of this intercompany sale will include a debit to sales for:
   a  *$500,000*
   b  *$400,000*
   c  *The amount remaining in Son's ending inventory*
   d  *80 percent of the amount remaining in Son's ending inventory*

4. Sun Corporation, a 90 percent–owned subsidiary of Pam Corporation, buys half of its raw materials from Pam. The transfer price is exactly the same price as Sun pays to buy identical raw materials from outside suppliers and the same price as Pam sells the materials to unrelated customers. In preparing consolidated statements for Pam Corporation and Subsidiary:

    *a*   *The intercompany transactions can be ignored because the transfer price represents arm's-length bargaining*

    *b*   *Any unrealized profit from intercompany sales remaining in Pam's ending inventory must be offset against the unrealized profit in Pam's beginning inventory*

    *c*   *Any unrealized profit on the intercompany transactions in Sun's ending inventory is eliminated in its entirety*

    *d*   *Only 90 percent of any unrealized profit on the intercompany transactions in Sun's ending inventory is eliminated*

5. Pop Corporation sells an inventory item to its subsidiary, Son Company, to be used as a plant asset by Son. The workpaper entry to eliminate intercompany profits in the year of sale will *not* include:

    *a*   *A debit to sales*

    *b*   *A credit to cost of sales*

    *c*   *A credit to inventories*

    *d*   *A credit to plant assets*

6. Sun Corporation regularly sells inventory items to its parent, Pam Corporation. In preparing the consolidated income statement, which of the following items would *not* be affected by the direction (upstream or downstream) of these intercompany sales?

    *a*   *Consolidated gross profit*

    *b*   *Noncontrolling interest share*

    *c*   *Controlling interest share of consolidated net income*

    *d*   *Consolidated retained earnings*

7. Pop Corporation regularly sells inventory items to its subsidiary, Son Corporation. If unrealized profits in Son's 2016 year-end inventory exceed the unrealized profits in its 2017 year-end inventory:

    *a*   *Combined cost of sales will be greater than consolidated cost of sales in 2016*

    *b*   *Combined cost of sales will be less than consolidated cost of sales in 2016*

    *c*   *Combined gross profit will be greater than consolidated gross profit in 2016*

    *d*   *Combined sales will be less than consolidated sales in 2016*

8. Sun Corporation is a 90 percent–owned subsidiary of Pam Corporation, acquired on January 1, 2016, at a price equal to book value and fair value. Pam accounts for its investment in Sun using the equity method of accounting. The only intercompany transactions between the two affiliates in 2016 and 2017 are as follows:

| | |
|---|---|
| 2016 | Pam sold inventory items that cost $400 to Sun for $500. One-fourth of this merchandise remains unsold at December 31, 2016 |
| 2017 | Pam sold inventory items that cost $600 to Sun for $750. One-third of this merchandise remains unsold at December 31, 2017 |

At December 31, 2017, Pam's Investment in Sun account:

    *a*   *Will equal its underlying equity in Sun*

    *b*   *Will be $25 greater than its underlying equity in Sun*

    *c*   *Will be $50 less than its underlying equity in Sun*

    *d*   *Will be $25 less than its underlying equity in Sun*

## E 5-2
## [Based on AICPA] General problems

1. Pop, Inc., owns 80 percent of Son, Inc. During 2016, Pop sold goods with a 40 percent gross profit to Son. Son sold all of these goods in 2016. For 2016 consolidated financial statements, how should the summation of Pop and Son income statement items be adjusted?

    *a*   *Sales and cost of goods sold should be reduced by the intercompany sales.*

    *b*   *Sales and cost of goods sold should be reduced by 80 percent of the intercompany sales.*

    *c*   *Net income should be reduced by 80 percent of the gross profit on intercompany sales.*

    *d*   *No adjustment is necessary.*

2. Car Company had the following transactions with affiliated parties during 2016.

    ■   Sales of $180 to Den, with $60 gross profit. Den had $45 of this inventory on hand at year-end. Car owns a 15 percent interest in Den and does not exert significant influence.

    ■   Purchases of raw materials totaling $720 from Ken Corporation, a wholly owned subsidiary. Ken's gross profit on the sale was $144. Car had $180 of this inventory remaining on December 31, 2016.

Before eliminating entries, Car had consolidated current assets of $960. What amount should Car report in its December 31, 2016, consolidated balance sheet for current assets?

a $960
b $951
c $924
d $303

3. Pam Corporation owns 80 percent of Sun's common stock. During 2016, Pam sold Sun $750 of inventory on the same terms as sales made to third parties. Sun sold 100 percent of the inventory purchased from Pam in 2016. The following information pertains to Sun's and Pam's sales for 2016:

|  | Pam | Sun |
| --- | --- | --- |
| Sales | $3,000 | $2,100 |
| Cost of sales | 1,200 | 1,050 |
|  | $1,800 | $1,050 |

What amount should Pam report as cost of sales in its 2016 consolidated income statement?

a $2,250
b $2,040
c $1,500
d $1,290

# E 5-3
# Downstream sales

1. The separate incomes of Pop Corporation and Son Corporation, a 100 percent–owned subsidiary of Pop, for 2017 are $2,000 and $1,000, respectively. Pop sells all of its output to Son at 150 percent of Pop's cost of production. During 2016 and 2017, Pop's sales to Son were $9,000 and $7,000, respectively. Son's inventory at December 31, 2016, included $3,000 of the merchandise acquired from Pop, and its December 31, 2017, inventory included $2,400 of such merchandise. Assume Son sells the inventory purchased from Pop in the following year.

   A consolidated income statement for Pop Corporation and Subsidiary for 2017 should show controlling interest share of consolidated net income of:

a $2,200
b $2,800
c $3,000
d $3,200

---

**USE THE FOLLOWING INFORMATION IN ANSWERING QUESTIONS 2 AND 3:**

Pam Corporation owns 75 percent of the voting common stock of Sun Corporation, acquired at book value during 2016. Selected information from the accounts of Pam and Sun for 2017 are as follows:

|  | Pam | Sun |
| --- | --- | --- |
| Sales | $1,800 | $1,000 |
| Cost of sales | 980 | 380 |

During 2017 Pam sold merchandise to Sun for $100, at a gross profit to Pam of $40. Half of this merchandise remained in Sun's inventory at December 31, 2017. Sun's December 31, 2016, inventory included unrealized profit of $8 on goods acquired from Pam.

---

2. In a consolidated income statement for Pam Corporation and Subsidiary for the year 2017, consolidated sales should be:

a $2,900
b $2,800
c $2,725
d $2,700

3. In a consolidated income statement for Pam Corporation and Subsidiary for the year 2017, consolidated cost of sales should be:

a $1,372
b $1,360
c $1,272
d $1,248

## E 5-4
## Upstream sales

Pop Corporation owns an 80 percent interest in Son Corporation and at December 31, 2016, Pop's investment in Son on an equity basis was equal to 80 percent of Son's stockholders' equity. During 2017, Son sells merchandise to Pop for $200,000, at a gross profit to Son of $40,000. At December 31, 2017, half of this merchandise is included in Pop's inventory. Separate incomes for Pop and Son for 2017 are summarized as follows:

|  | Pop | Son |
|---|---|---|
| Sales | $1,000,000 | $600,000 |
| Cost of sales | (500,000) | (400,000) |
| Gross profit | 500,000 | 200,000 |
| Operating expenses | (250,000) | (80,000) |
| Separate incomes | $ 250,000 | $120,000 |

1. Pop's income from Son for 2017 is:
   a  $96,000
   b  $80,000
   c  $76,000
   d  $56,000

2. Consolidated cost of sales for 2017 is:
   a  $920,000
   b  $900,000
   c  $880,000
   d  $720,000

3. Noncontrolling interest share for 2017 is:
   a  $24,000
   b  $20,000
   c  $8,000
   d  $4,000

## E 5-5
## Upstream sales

Pam Corporation owns an 80 percent interest in Sun Corporation acquired several years ago. Sun regularly sells merchandise to Pam at 125 percent of Sun's cost. Gross profit data of Pam and Sun for 2017 are as follows:

|  | Pam | Sun |
|---|---|---|
| Sales | $1,000 | $800 |
| Cost of goods sold | 800 | 640 |
| Gross profit | $ 200 | $160 |

During 2017, Pam purchased inventory items from Sun at a transfer price of $400. Pam's December 31, 2016 and 2017, inventories included goods acquired from Sun of $100 and $125, respectively. Assume Pam sells the inventory purchased from Sun in the following year.

1. Consolidated sales of Pam Corporation and Subsidiary for 2017 were:
   a  $1,800
   b  $1,425
   c  $1,400
   d  $1,240

2. The unrealized profits in the year-end 2016 and 2017 inventories were:
   a  $100 and $125, respectively
   b  $80 and $100, respectively
   c  $20 and $25, respectively
   d  $16 and $20, respectively

3. Consolidated cost of goods sold of Pam Corporation and Subsidiary for 2017 was:
   a  $1,024
   b  $1,045
   c  $1,052.8
   d  $1,056

## E 5-6
## Upstream and downstream sales

1. Pam Corporation owns 70 percent of Sun Company's common stock, acquired January 1, 2017. Patents from the investment are being amortized at a rate of $20,000 per year. Sun regularly sells merchandise to Pam at 150 percent of Sun's cost. Pam's December 31, 2017, and 2018 inventories include goods purchased intercompany of $112,500 and $33,000, respectively. The separate incomes (do not include investment income) of Pam and Sun for 2018 are summarized as follows:

|  | Pam | Sun |
|---|---|---|
| Sales | $1,200,000 | $800,000 |
| Cost of sales | (600,000) | (500,000) |
| Other expenses | (400,000) | (100,000) |
| Separate incomes | $ 200,000 | $200,000 |

Total consolidated income should be allocated to controlling and noncontrolling interest shares in the amounts of:

a  *$344,550 and $61,950, respectively*
b  *$358,550 and $60,000, respectively*
c  *$346,500 and $60,000, respectively*
d  *$346,500 and $67,950, respectively*

2. Pop acquired a 60 percent interest in Son on January 1, 2016, for $360,000, when Son's net assets had a book value and fair value of $600,000. During 2016, Pop sold inventory items that cost $600,000 to Son for $800,000, and Son's inventory at December 31, 2016, included one-fourth of this merchandise. Pop reported separate income from its own operations (excludes investment income) of $300,000, and Son reported a net loss of $150,000 for 2016. Controlling share of consolidated net income for Pop Corporation and Subsidiary for 2016 is:

a  *$260,000*
b  *$180,000*
c  *$160,000*
d  *$100,000*

3. Sun Corporation, a 75 percent–owned subsidiary of Pam Corporation, sells inventory items to its parent at 125 percent of cost. Inventories of the two affiliates for 2016 are as follows:

|  | Pam | Sun |
|---|---|---|
| Beginning inventory | $400,000 | $250,000 |
| Ending inventory | 500,000 | 200,000 |

Pam's beginning and ending inventories include merchandise acquired from Sun of $150,000 and $200,000, respectively, which is sold in the following year. If Sun reports net income of $300,000 for 2016, Pam's income from Sun will be:

a  *$255,000*
b  *$217,500*
c  *$215,000*
d  *$195,000*

## E 5-7
## Determine consolidated net income with downstream intercompany sales

Pam Corporation owns an 80 percent interest in the common stock of Sun Corporation, acquired several years ago at book value. Pam regularly sells merchandise to Sun. Information relevant to the intercompany sales and profits of Pam and Sun for 2016, 2017, and 2018 is as follows:

|  | 2016 | 2017 | 2018 |
|---|---|---|---|
| Sales to Sun | $600 | $720 | $1,200 |
| Unrealized profit in Sun's inventory at December 31 | 180 | 240 | 120 |
| Sun's separate income | 3,000 | 3,300 | 2,850 |
| Pam's separate income (does not include investment income) | 1,800 | 2,400 | 2,100 |

**REQUIRED:** Prepare a schedule showing consolidated net income for each year.

## E 5-8
### Consolidated income statement with downstream sales

The separate incomes (which do not include investment income) of Pop Corporation and Son Corporation, its 80 percent–owned subsidiary, for 2016 were determined as follows (in thousands):

|  | Pop | Son |
|---|---|---|
| Sales | $3,200 | $800 |
| Less: Cost of sales | 1,600 | 320 |
| Gross profit | 1,600 | 480 |
| Other expenses | 800 | 240 |
| Separate incomes | $ 800 | $240 |

During 2016, Pop sold merchandise that cost $160,000 to Son for $320,000, and at December 31, 2016, half of these inventory items remained unsold by Son.

**REQUIRED:** Prepare a consolidated income statement for Pop Corporation and Subsidiary for the year ended December 31, 2016.

## E 5-9
### Compute noncontrolling interest and consolidated cost of sales (upstream sales)

Income statement information for 2016 for Pam Corporation and its 60 percent–owned subsidiary, Sun Corporation, is as follows:

|  | Pam | Sun |
|---|---|---|
| Sales | $900 | $350 |
| Cost of sales | 400 | 250 |
| Gross profit | 500 | 100 |
| Operating expenses | 250 | 50 |
| Sun's net income |  | $ 50 |
| Pam's separate income | $250 |  |

Intercompany sales for 2016 are upstream (from Sun to Pam) and total $100,000. Pam's December 31, 2015, and December 31, 2016, inventories contain unrealized profits of $5,000 and $10,000, respectively.

### REQUIRED

1. Compute noncontrolling interest share for 2016.

2. Compute consolidated sales, cost of sales, and total consolidated net income for 2016.

## E 5-10
### Consolidated income statement (upstream sales)

Pop Corporation purchased an 80 percent interest in Son Corporation for $1,200,000 on January 1, 2017, at which time Son's stockholders' equity consisted of $1,000,000 common stock and $400,000 retained earnings. The excess fair value over book value was goodwill. Comparative income statements for the two corporations for 2018 are as follows:

|  | Pop | Son |
|---|---|---|
| Sales | $2,000 | $1,000 |
| Income from Son | 224 | — |
| Cost of sales | (800) | (500) |
| Depreciation expense | (260) | (80) |
| Other expenses | (180) | (120) |
| Net income | $ 984 | $ 300 |

Dividends of Pop and Son for all of 2018 were $600,000 and $200,000, respectively. During 2017 Son sold inventory items to Pop for $160,000. This merchandise cost Son $100,000, and one-third of it remained in Pop's December 31, 2017, inventory. During 2018 Son's sales to Pop were $180,000. This merchandise cost Son $120,000, and one-half of it remained in Pop's December 31, 2018, inventory.

**REQUIRED:** Prepare a consolidated income statement for Pop Corporation and Subsidiary for the year ended December 31, 2018.

## E 5-11
## Upstream sales

On January 1, 2009, Pam Corporation acquired 60 percent of the voting common shares of Sun Corporation at an excess of fair value over book value of $1,000,000. This excess was attributed to plant assets with a remaining useful life of five years. For the year ended December 31, 2016, Sun prepared *condensed* financial statements as follows (in thousands):

**Condensed Balance Sheet at December 31, 2016**

| | |
|---|---|
| Current assets (except inventory) | $   600 |
| Inventories | 300 |
| Plant assets—net | 5,000 |
| Total assets | $ 5,900 |
| Liabilities | $   400 |
| Capital stock | 3,400 |
| Retained earnings | 2,100 |
| Total equities | $5,900 |

**Condensed Statement of Income and Retained Earnings**

| | |
|---|---|
| Sales | $1,000 |
| Cost of sales | (500) |
| Other expenses | (300) |
| Net income | 200 |
| Add: Retained earnings January 1, 2016 | 2,000 |
| Less: Dividends | (100) |
| Retained earnings December 31, 2016 | $ 1,900 |

Sun regularly sells inventory items to Pam at a price of 120 percent of cost. In 2015 and 2016, sales from Sun to Pam are as follows:

| | 2015 | 2016 |
|---|---|---|
| Sales at selling price | $840 | $960 |
| Inventory unsold by Pam on December 31 | 120 | 360 |

1. Under the equity method, Pam reports investment income from Sun for 2016 of:
   a  $120
   b  $96
   c  $80
   d  $104 loss

2. Noncontrolling interest on December 31, 2016, is:
   a  $2,200
   b  $2,184
   c  $2,176
   d  $2,140

3. On the books of Pam Corporation, the investment account is properly reflected on December 31, 2016, at:
   a  $3,240
   b  $3,264
   c  $3,276
   d  Not enough information is given.

## E 5-12
## Consolidated income statement (intercompany sales correction)

The consolidated income statement of Pop and Son for 2016 was as follows (in thousands):

| | |
|---|---|
| Sales | $5,520 |
| Cost of sales | (3,680) |
| Operating expenses | (640) |
| Income to 20 percent noncontrolling interest in Son | (160) |
| Consolidated net income | $ 1,040 |

After the consolidated income statement was prepared, it was discovered that intercompany sales transactions had not been considered and that unrealized profits had not been eliminated. Information concerning these items follows (in thousands):

| | Cost | Selling Price | Unsold at Year-End |
|---|---|---|---|
| 2015 Sales—Pop to Son | $640 | $720 | 25% |
| 2016 Sales—Son to Pop | 360 | 480 | 40 |

**REQUIRED:** Prepare a corrected consolidated income statement for Pop and Son for the year ended December 31, 2016.

## PROBLEMS

### P 5-1
### Consolidated income and retained earnings (upstream sales, noncontrolling interest)

Pam Corporation acquired its 90 percent interest in Sun Corporation at its book value of $3,600,000 on January 1, 2016, when Sun had capital stock of $3,000,000 and retained earnings of $1,000,000.

The December 31, 2016 and 2017, inventories of Pam included merchandise acquired from Sun of $300,000 and $400,000, respectively. Sun realizes a gross profit of 40 percent on all merchandise sold. During 2016 and 2017, sales by Sun to Pam were $600,000 and $800,000, respectively.

Summary adjusted trial balances for Pam and Sun at December 31, 2017, follow (in thousands):

| | Pam | Sun |
|---|---|---|
| Cash | $ 1,000 | $    200 |
| Receivables—net | 2,000 | 500 |
| Inventories | 2,400 | 1,000 |
| Plant assets—net | 2,500 | 4,800 |
| Investment in Sun—90% | 4,356 | — |
| Cost of sales | 8,000 | 3,900 |
| Other expenses | 3,400 | 1,600 |
| Dividends | 1,000 | 500 |
| | $24,656 | $ 12,500 |

| | Pam | Sun |
|---|---|---|
| Accounts payable | $ 1,500 | $    900 |
| Other liabilities | 600 | 600 |
| Capital stock, $10 par | 5,000 | 3,000 |
| Retained earnings | 3,692 | 1,500 |
| Sales | 13,000 | 6,500 |
| Income from Sun | 864 | — |
| | $24,656 | $12,500 |

**REQUIRED:** Prepare a combined consolidated income and retained earnings statement for Pam Corporation and Subsidiary for the year ended December 31, 2017.

### P 5-2
### Computations (upstream sales)

Pop Corporation acquired a 90 percent interest in Son Corporation at book value on January 1, 2016. Intercompany purchases and sales and inventory data for 2016, 2017, and 2018, are as follows:

| | Sales by Son to Pop | Intercompany Profit in Pop's Inventory at December 31 |
|---|---|---|
| 2016 | $200,000 | $15,000 |
| 2017 | 150,000 | 12,000 |
| 2018 | 300,000 | 24,000 |

Selected data from the financial statements of Pop and Son at and for the year ended December 31, 2018, are as follows:

| | Pop | Son |
|---|---|---|
| *Income Statement* | | |
| Sales | $900,000 | $600,000 |
| Cost of sales | 625,000 | 300,000 |

| | Pop | Son |
|---|---|---|
| Expenses | 225,000 | 150,000 |
| Income from Son | 124,200 | — |
| **Balance Sheet** | | |
| Inventory | $150,000 | $ 80,000 |
| Retained earnings December 31, 2018 | 425,000 | 220,000 |
| Capital stock | 500,000 | 300,000 |

**REQUIRED:** Prepare well-organized schedules showing computations for each of the following:

1. Consolidated cost of sales for 2018
2. Noncontrolling interest share for 2018
3. Consolidated net income for 2018
4. Noncontrolling interest at December 31, 2018

## P 5-3
### Computations (parent buys from one subsidiary and sells to the other)

Pam Company owns controlling interests in Sun and Toy Corporations, having acquired an 80 percent interest in Sun in 2016, and a 90 percent interest in Toy on January 1, 2017. Pam's investments in Sun and Toy were at book value equal to fair value.

Inventories of the affiliated companies at December 31, 2017, and December 31, 2018, were as follows:

| | December 31, 2017 | December 31, 2018 |
|---|---|---|
| Pam inventories | $120,000 | $108,000 |
| Sun inventories | 77,500 | 62,500 |
| Toy inventories | 48,000 | 72,000 |

Pam sells to Sun at a 25 percent markup based on cost, and Toy sells to Pam at a 20 percent markup based on cost. Pam's beginning and ending inventories for 2018 consisted of 40 percent and 50 percent, respectively, of goods acquired from Toy. All of Sun's inventories consisted of merchandise acquired from Pam.

### REQUIRED

1. Calculate the inventory that should appear in the December 31, 2017, consolidated balance sheet.
2. Calculate the inventory that should appear in the December 31, 2018, consolidated balance sheet.

## P 5-4
### Computations (upstream and downstream sales)

Comparative income statements of Son Corporation for the calendar years 2016, 2017, and 2018 are as follows (in thousands):

| | 2016 | 2017 | 2018 |
|---|---|---|---|
| Sales | $48,000 | $51,000 | $57,000 |
| Cost of sales | 25,200 | 26,400 | 30,000 |
| Gross profit | 22,800 | 24,600 | 27,000 |
| Operating expenses | 18,000 | 19,200 | 22,800 |
| Net income | $ 4,800 | $ 5,400 | $ 4,200 |

### ADDITIONAL INFORMATION

1. Son was a 75 percent–owned subsidiary of Pop Corporation throughout the 2016–2018 period. Pop's separate income (excludes income from Son) was $21,600,000, $20,400,000, and $24,000,000 in 2016, 2017, and 2018, respectively. Pop acquired its interest in Son at its underlying book value, which was equal to fair value on July 1, 2015.

2. Pop sold inventory items to Son during 2016 at a gross profit to Pop of $2,400,000. Half the merchandise remained in Son's inventory at December 31, 2016. Total sales by Pop to Son in 2016 were $6,000,000. The remaining merchandise was sold by Son in 2017.

**3.** Pop's inventory at December 31, 2017, included items acquired from Son on which Son made a profit of $1,200,000. Total sales by Son to Pop during 2017 were $4,800,000.

**4.** There were no unrealized profits in the December 31, 2018, inventories of either company.

**5.** Pop uses the equity method of accounting for its investment in Son.

**REQUIRED:**

1. Prepare a schedule showing Pop's income from Son for the years 2016, 2017, and 2018.
2. Compute Pop's net income for the years 2016, 2017, and 2018.
3. Prepare a schedule of consolidated net income for Pop Corporation and Subsidiary for the years 2016, 2017, and 2018, beginning with the separate incomes of the two affiliates and including noncontrolling interest computations.

## P 5-5
### Workpapers (100 percent owned, downstream sales, year after acquisition)

Pam Corporation acquired 100 percent of Sun Corporation's outstanding voting common stock on January 1, 2016, for $660,000 cash. Sun's stockholders' equity on this date consisted of $300,000 capital stock and $300,000 retained earnings. The difference between the price paid by Pam and the underlying equity acquired in Sun was allocated $30,000 to Sun's undervalued inventory and the remainder to patents with a five-year write-off period. The undervalued inventory items were sold by Sun during 2016.

Pam made sales of $100,000 to Sun at a gross profit of $40,000 during 2016; during 2017, Pam made sales of $120,000 to Sun at a gross profit of $48,000. One-half the 2016 sales were inventoried by Sun at year-end 2016, and one-fourth the 2017 sales were inventoried by Sun at year-end 2017. Sun owed Pam $17,000 on account at December 31, 2017.

The separate financial statements of Pam and Sun Corporations at and for the year ended December 31, 2017, are summarized as follows (in thousands):

|  | Pop | Son |
|---|---|---|
| ***Combined Income and Retained Earnings*** | | |
| ***Statements for the Year Ended December 31, 2017*** | | |
| Sales | $ 800 | $400 |
| Income from Sun | 102 | — |
| Cost of sales | (400) | (200) |
| Depreciation expense | (110) | (40) |
| Other expenses | (192) | (60) |
| Net income | 200 | 100 |
| Beginning retained earnings | 600 | 380 |
| Less: Dividends | (100) | (50) |
| Retained earnings December 31, 2017 | $ 700 | $430 |
| ***Balance Sheet at December 31, 2017*** | | |
| Cash | $ 54 | $ 37 |
| Receivables—net | 90 | 60 |
| Inventories | 100 | 80 |
| Other assets | 70 | 90 |
| Land | 50 | 50 |
| Buildings—net | 200 | 150 |
| Equipment—net | 500 | 400 |
| Investment in Sun | 736 | — |
| Total assets | $1,800 | $867 |
| Accounts payable | $ 160 | $ 47 |
| Other liabilities | 340 | 90 |
| Common stock, $10 par | 600 | 300 |
| Retained earnings | 700 | 430 |
| Total equities | $1,800 | $867 |

**REQUIRED:** Prepare workpapers to consolidate the financial statements of Pam Corporation and Subsidiary at and for the year ended December 31, 2017.

## P 5-6
### Workpapers (noncontrolling interest, downstream sales, year after acquisition)

Pop Corporation acquired a 75 percent interest in Son Corporation for $600,000 on January 1, 2016, when Son's equity consisted of $300,000 capital stock and $100,000 retained earnings. The fair values of Son's assets and liabilities were equal to book values on this date, and any goodwill is not amortized. Pop uses the equity method of accounting for its investment in Son.

During 2016, Pop sold inventory items to Son for $160,000, and at December 31, 2016, Son's inventory included items on which there were $20,000 unrealized profits. During 2017, Pop sold inventory items to Son for $260,000, and at December 31, 2017, Son's inventory included items on which there were $40,000 unrealized profits.

On December 31, 2017, Son owed Pop $30,000 on account for merchandise purchases. The financial statements of Pop and Son Corporations at and for the year ended December 31, 2017, are summarized as follows (in thousands):

|  | Pop | Son |
|---|---|---|
| **Combined Income and Retained Earnings Statements for the Year Ended December 31, 2017** | | |
| Sales | $ 1,200 | $ 800 |
| Income from Son | 205 | — |
| Cost of sales | (540) | (420) |
| Operating expenses | (290) | (80) |
| Net income | 575 | 300 |
| Beginning retained earnings | 365 | 180 |
| Deduct: Dividends | (300) | (100) |
| Retained earnings December 31, 2017 | $ 640 | $ 380 |
| **Balance Sheet at December 31, 2017** | | |
| Cash | $ 170 | $ 60 |
| Accounts receivable | 330 | 200 |
| Dividends receivable | 30 | — |
| Inventories | 120 | 160 |
| Land | 160 | 100 |
| Buildings—net | 460 | 200 |
| Equipment—net | 400 | 280 |
| Investment in Son | 770 | — |
| Total assets | $ 2,440 | $1,000 |
| Accounts payable | $ 450 | $ 200 |
| Dividends payable | 140 | 40 |
| Other liabilities | 310 | 80 |
| Common stock, $10 par | 900 | 300 |
| Retained earnings | 640 | 380 |
| Total equities | $ 2,440 | $1,000 |

**REQUIRED:** Prepare consolidation workpapers for Pop Corporation and Subsidiary for the year ended December 31, 2017.

## P 5-7
### Consolidation workpapers (upstream sales, noncontrolling interest)

Pam Corporation purchased a 90 percent interest in Sun Corporation on December 31, 2015, for $2,700,000 cash, when Sun had capital stock of $2,000,000 and retained earnings of $500,000. All Sun's assets and liabilities were recorded at fair values when Pam acquired its interest. The excess of fair value over book value is due to previously unrecorded patents and is being amortized over a 10-year period.

The Pam–Sun affiliation is a vertically integrated merchandising operation, with Sun selling all of its output to Pam Corporation at 140 percent of its cost. Pam sells the merchandise acquired from Sun at 150 percent of its purchase price from Sun. All of Pam's December 31, 2016, and December 31, 2017, inventories of $280,000 and $420,000, respectively, were acquired from Sun. Sun's December 31, 2016, and December 31, 2017, inventories were $800,000 each.

Pam's accounts payable at December 31, 2017, includes $100,000 owed to Sun from 2017 purchases.

Comparative financial statements for Pam and Sun Corporations at and for the year ended December 31, 2017, are as follows (in thousands):

| | Pam | Sun |
|---|---|---|
| **Combined Income and Retained Earnings Statement for the Year Ended December 31, 2017** | | |
| Sales | $8,190 | $5,600 |
| Income from Sun | 819 | — |
| Cost of sales | (5,460) | (4,000) |
| Other expenses | (1,544) | (600) |
| Net income | 2,005 | 1,000 |
| Add: Beginning retained earnings | 1,200 | 700 |
| Deduct: Dividends | (1,000) | (500) |
| Retained earnings December 31, 2017 | $2,205 | $1,200 |
| **Balance Sheet at December 31, 2017** | | |
| Cash | $ 753 | $ 500 |
| Inventory | 420 | 800 |
| Other current assets | 600 | 200 |
| Plant assets—net | 3,000 | 3,000 |
| Investment in Sun | 3,132 | — |
| Total assets | $7,905 | $4,500 |
| Current liabilities | $1,700 | $1,300 |
| Capital stock | 4,000 | 2,000 |
| Retained earnings | 2,205 | 1,200 |
| Total equities | $7,905 | $4,500 |

**REQUIRED:** Prepare consolidation workpapers for Pam Corporation and Subsidiary for the year ended December 31, 2017.

## P 5-8
### Consolidated workpapers (downstream sales)

Pop Corporation acquired 100 percent of Son Corporation's outstanding voting common stock on January 1, 2016, for $660,000 cash. Son's stockholders' equity on this date consisted of $300,000 capital stock and $300,000 retained earnings. The difference between the fair value of Son and the underlying equity acquired in Son was allocated $30,000 to Son's undervalued inventory and the remainder to goodwill. The undervalued inventory items were sold by Son during 2016.

Pop made sales of $100,000 to Son at a gross profit of $40,000 during 2016; during 2017, Pop made sales of $120,000 to Son at a gross profit of $48,000. One-half the 2016 sales were inventoried by Son at year-end 2016, and one-fourth the 2017 sales were inventoried by Son at year-end 2017. Son owed Pop $17,000 on account at December 31, 2017.

The separate financial statements of Pop and Son Corporations at and for the year ended December 31, 2017, are summarized as follows:

| | Pop | Son |
|---|---|---|
| **Combined Income and Retained Earnings Statement for the Year Ended December 31, 2017 (in thousands)** | | |
| Sales | $ 800 | $400 |
| Income from Son | 108 | — |
| Cost of sales | (400) | (200) |
| Depreciation expense | (110) | (40) |
| Other expenses | (192) | (60) |
| Net income | 206 | 100 |
| Beginning retained earnings | 606 | 380 |
| Less: Dividends | (100) | (50) |
| Retained earnings December 31, 2017 | $ 712 | $430 |

|  | **Pop** | **Son** |
|---|---|---|
| **Balance Sheet at December 31, 2017** | | |
| Cash | $ 54 | $ 37 |
| Receivables—net | 90 | 60 |
| Inventories | 100 | 80 |
| Other assets | 70 | 90 |
| Land | 50 | 50 |
| Buildings—net | 200 | 150 |
| Equipment—net | 500 | 400 |
| Investment in Son | 748 | — |
| Total assets | $1,812 | $867 |
| Accounts payable | $ 160 | $ 47 |
| Other liabilities | 340 | 90 |
| Common stock, $10 par | 600 | 300 |
| Retained earnings | 712 | 430 |
| Total equities | $1,812 | $867 |

**REQUIRED:** Prepare workpapers to consolidate the financial statements of Pop Corporation and Subsidiary at and for the year ended December 31, 2017.

## P 5-9
## Consolidated workpaper (noncontrolling interest, upstream sales, intercompany receivables/payables)

Pop Corporation purchased a 90 percent interest in Son Corporation on December 31, 2016, for $5,400,000 cash, when Son had capital stock of $4,000,000 and retained earnings of $1,000,000. All Son's assets and liabilities were recorded at fair values when Pop acquired its interest. The excess of fair value over book value is goodwill.

The Pop–Son affiliation is a vertically integrated merchandising operation, with Son selling all of its output to Pop Corporation at 140 percent of its cost. Pop sells the merchandise acquired from Son at 150 percent of its intercompany purchase price. All of Pop's December 31, 2018, and December 31, 2019, inventories of $560,000 and $840,000, respectively, were acquired from Son. Son's December 31, 2018, and December 31, 2019, inventories were $1,600,000 each.

Pop's accounts payable at December 31, 2019, includes $200,000 owed to Son from 2019 purchases.

Comparative financial statements for Pop and Son Corporations at and for the year ended December 31, 2019, are as follows:

|  | **Pop** | **Son** |
|---|---|---|
| **Combined Income and Retained Earnings Statement for the Year Ended December 31, 2019 (in thousands)** | | |
| Sales | $ 16,380 | $11,200 |
| Income from Son | 1,728 | — |
| Cost of sales | (10,920) | (8,000) |
| Other expenses | (3,088) | (1,200) |
| Net income | 4,100 | 2,000 |
| Add: Beginning retained earnings | 2,500 | 1,400 |
| Deduct: Dividends | (2,000) | (1,000) |
| Retained earnings December 31, 2019 | $ 4,600 | $ 2,400 |

| | Pop | Son |
|---|---|---|
| *Balance Sheet at December 31, 2019* | | |
| Cash | $ 1,516 | $ 1,000 |
| Inventory | 840 | 1,600 |
| Other current assets | 1,200 | 400 |
| Plant assets—net | 6,000 | 6,000 |
| Investment in Son | 6,444 | — |
|    Total assets | $ 16,000 | $ 9,000 |
| Current liabilities | $ 3,400 | $ 2,600 |
| Capital stock | 8,000 | 4,000 |
| Retained earnings | 4,600 | 2,400 |
|    Total equities | $ 16,000 | $ 9,000 |

**REQUIRED:** Prepare a consolidation workpaper for Pop Corporation and Subsidiary for the year ended December 31, 2019.

---

## PROFESSIONAL RESEARCH ASSIGNMENTS

Answer the following questions by reference to the FASB Codification of Accounting Standards. Include the appropriate reference in your response.

**PR 5-1** Should the consolidated financial statements include the subsidiary's retained earnings at the acquisition date?

**PR 5-2** Does noncontrolling interest represent a liability or an equity in the consolidated balance sheet?

# APPENDIX

# SEC Influence on Accounting

Accountants recognize the influence of the Securities and Exchange Commission (SEC) on the development of accounting and reporting principles. Congress gave the SEC authority to establish accounting principles when it passed the Securities Exchange Act of 1934, which created the SEC. Initially, Congress assigned the administration of the Securities Act of 1933 to the Federal Trade Commission. But a year later, the 1934 act created the Securities and Exchange Commission and made it responsible for establishing regulations over accounting and auditing matters for firms under its jurisdiction. The SEC has the authority to prescribe accounting principles for entities that fall under its jurisdiction.[2]

A combination of inadequate regulation of securities at the federal and state levels, the stock market crash of 1929, and the Great Depression of the 1930s contributed to the enactment of new securities legislation in the early 1930s. Similar circumstances surrounding the collapse of Enron Corporation, *WorldCom*, and others led to passage of the Sarbanes-Oxley Act and related legislation in recent years.

## THE 1933 SECURITIES ACT

A primary objective of the Securities Act of 1933 was "to provide full and fair disclosure of the character of securities sold in interstate and foreign commerce and the mails, and to prevent fraud in the sale thereof"[3] (Securities Act of 1933). Another objective was to protect investors against fraud, deceit, and misrepresentation. There have been many amendments, but these objectives still constitute the primary thrust of the 1933 Act.

The Securities Act of 1933 is often called the "Truth in Securities Act." This is because the SEC's objective is to prevent the issuers of securities from disclosing false, incomplete, or otherwise misleading information to prospective buyers of their securities. The SEC emphasizes that its objective is not to pass judgment on the merits of any firm's securities. The SEC imposes severe penalties on firms and individuals that violate disclosure requirements.

### Issuance of Securities in Public Offerings

The Securities Act of 1933 regulates the issuance of specific securities to investors in public offerings. Public offerings of securities must be registered with the SEC and advertised in a prospectus before being offered for sale to the public.

EXEMPT SECURITY ISSUES   Certain security issuances are exempt from the 1933 Act. A partial list of exempt securities includes those issued by governmental units, not-for-profit organizations, firms in bankruptcy and subject to court order, firms in stock splits or in direct sales to existing shareholders (private placements), and firms issuing intrastate securities with sales limited to residents of that state.

---

[2]For example, in 1993 the SEC issued *Staff Accounting Bulletin No. 93*, which requires discontinued operations that have not been divested within one year of their measurement dates to be accounted for prospectively as investments held for sale.

[3]US Securities Exchange Commission

**Issues of $5,000,000 or Less**   *Regulation A* provides less-restrictive registration procedures for security issuances not exceeding $5,000,000. Regulation A permits firms to use an *offering circular* rather than the prospectus required for full registration.

**The Prospectus**   A **prospectus** is a part of the registration statement that provides detailed information about the background of the registrant firm, including its development, its business, and its financial statements. An **offering circular** is like a prospectus but has fewer disclosure requirements. A copy of the prospectus must be presented to prospective buyers before the securities are offered for sale. A **preliminary prospectus** (also known as a *red herring prospectus*) is a communication that identifies the nature of the securities to be issued, states that they have not been approved or disapproved by the SEC, and explains how to obtain the prospectus when it becomes available.

## THE SECURITIES EXCHANGE ACT OF 1934

The Securities Exchange Act of 1934 created the Securities and Exchange Commission and gave it authority to administer the 1933 Act as well as to regulate trading of securities on national exchanges. Subsequently, the 1934 Act was amended to include securities traded in over-the-counter markets, provided that the firms have total assets of more than $10 million and at least 500 stockholders. Firms that want their securities traded on the national exchanges or in over-the-counter markets subject to the net-asset and stockholder limitations must file **registration statements** with the SEC. Form 10 is the primary form used for registering securities on national stock exchanges or in over-the-counter markets. This registration for trading purposes is required in addition to the registration prepared for new security issuances under the 1933 Act.

**Additional Periodic Reporting Requirements**   Companies covered by the 1934 Act also have periodic reporting responsibilities. These include filing 10-K annual reports, 10-Q quarterly reports, and 8-K current "material event" reports with the SEC. The information in these reports is publicly available so that company officers, directors, and major stockholders (insiders) will not be able to use it to gain an unfair advantage over the investing public. The objective is to provide full disclosure of all material facts about the company and contribute to a more efficient and ethical securities market.

**The SEC and National Exchanges**   In addition to registration and periodic reporting rules for publicly traded companies, the Securities Exchange Act contains registration and reporting requirements for the national securities exchanges. The SEC has responsibility for monitoring the activities of the national exchanges and ensuring compliance with applicable legal provisions. The 1934 Act also gave the SEC broad enforcement powers over stockbrokers and dealers and over accountants involved in SEC work.

## THE SARBANES-OXLEY ACT

The passage of Sarbanes-Oxley and related legislation provides the SEC with even broader powers and an increased budget for enforcement activities. SEC inquiries and enforcement actions against public companies have increased substantially since 2000. Many firms, for example, *Krispy Kreme Doughnuts* in January 2005, have restated earnings as a result of SEC investigations. Such activity is likely to continue.

Among SEC pronouncements, one of the most far-reaching is *Staff Accounting Bulletin (SAB) No. 101, Revenue Recognition in Financial Statements*, issued in December 1999. Here the SEC addresses and clarifies revenue recognition issues commonly encountered in the modern and increasingly complex business world. Current common practices of selling bundled products and services and how to separate and recognize the components of revenue in such contracts are some of the SEC's many concerns. *SAB No. 101* represents the SEC's response to a research study on fraudulent reporting practices conducted by the Committee of Sponsoring Organizations (COSO) of the Treadway Commission in March 1999. That report indicated that more than one-half of the reporting frauds reviewed involved overstatement of revenues.

## Additional Responsibilities of the SEC

Subsequent to the Securities Exchange Act of 1934, the SEC acquired regulatory and administrative responsibilities under the Public Utilities Holding Company Act of 1935, the Trust Indenture Act of 1939, the Investment Company Act of 1940, the Investment Advisers Act of 1940, the Securities Investor Protection Act of 1970, and the Foreign Corrupt Practices Act of 1977. These acts are listed solely for identification purposes, and not discussed further here.

## THE REGISTRATION STATEMENT FOR SECURITY ISSUES

The Securities Act of 1933 requires firms issuing securities to the public to provide full and fair disclosure of all material facts about those securities. The disclosures are provided in a registration statement filed with the SEC at least 20 days before the securities are offered for sale to the public. The SEC may extend the 20-day waiting period if it finds deficient or misleading information in the registration statement. In addition, if a firm files an amendment to the registration statement, the SEC treats the amended statement as a new registration for purposes of applying the 20-day rule.

### Security Registration

The registration of securities with the SEC is a major undertaking for the registrant. The process includes developing a registration team consisting of financial managers, legal counsel, security underwriters, public accountants, and other professionals as needed. The team plans the registration process in detail, assigns responsibility for each task, coordinates the efforts of all team members, and maintains a viable time throughout each phase of the project. Because of its complexity, the coordination of efforts is sometimes referred to as a balancing act.

REGISTERING SECURITIES UNDER THE INTEGRATED DISCLOSURE SYSTEM    In 1980 the SEC changed the process of registering securities when it adopted an integrated disclosure system for most reports required by the 1933 and 1934 Securities Acts. The integrated system revised the registration forms and streamlined the process for filing with the SEC. As a result, the registration statement is now completed in accordance with instructions for the particular registration form deemed appropriate for a specific registrant.

For example, Form S-1 is a general form to be used by firms going public (issuing securities to the public for the first time) and by firms that have been SEC registrants for fewer than three years. It is also a default form to be used unless another form is specified. Forms S-2 and S-3 are forms with fewer disclosure requirements than S-1. They are used primarily for registrations of established firms that have been SEC registrants for more than three years and that meet certain other criteria. Form S-4 is used for registering securities issued in a business combination. Firms issuing securities under Regulation A use Form 1-A. A number of other registration forms are applicable to selected types of security issues and firm situations.

## THE INTEGRATED DISCLOSURE SYSTEM

The basic regulations of the SEC are found in *Regulation S-X*, which prescribes rules for the form and content of financial statements filed with the SEC, and *Regulation S-K*, which covers the non-financial statement disclosures of the registration statements and other periodic SEC filings. Before the 1980s, the two regulations sometimes had conflicting requirements, and firms often had difficulty in identifying the appropriate rules and procedures for reporting to the SEC.

From 1933 to 1980 the SEC issued numerous *Accounting Series Releases* (ASRs)—official supplements to AICPA and FASB pronouncements—and *Staff Accounting Bulletins* (SABs)—informal interpretations by the SEC staff on GAAP and S-X provisions. The issuance of these ASRs and SABs often increased the difficulty of complying with SEC regulations because their provisions were sometimes inconsistent with GAAP or other SEC regulations.

### Codification of SABs and ASRs

In implementing the integrated disclosure system, the SEC issued *SAB No. 40* to codify *SABs 1 through 38*. This revised the content of the SABs to conform to GAAP, to eliminate duplicate material contained in some SABs, and in some cases to recognize FASB pronouncements as meeting the

SEC's requirements. The SEC also codified the relevant accounting-related ASRs into *Financial Reporting Release (FRR) No. 1*. Thus, the current series consists of FRRs rather than ASRs.

## Objectives of Integrated Disclosure System

The objectives of the integrated disclosure system are to simplify the registration process, to reduce the cost of compliance, and to improve the quality of information provided to investors and other parties. Under the integrated system, the disclosure included in SEC filings and those distributed to investors via prospectuses, proxy statements, and annual reports are essentially the same.

## Standardization of Audited Financial Statements

The integrated disclosure system amended Regulation S-X in order to standardize the financial statement requirements in most SEC filings. Regulation S-X, which prescribes the form and content of financial statements filed with the SEC, was amended in 1992 to conform certain of its accounting and disclosure requirements to those contained in the FASB Standards (now the Codification). This permits financial statements included in annual reports to shareholders to be the same as those included in the prospectus, the 10-K, and other reports filed with the SEC.

Note that the SEC's proxy rules govern the content of annual reports to shareholders. Under current rules, the content of the annual report to shareholders is the same as in 10-K filings. **Form 10-K** is the general form for the annual report that registrants file with the SEC. It is required to be filed within 90 days after the end of the registrant company's fiscal year. The 10-K report must be signed by the chief executive officer, the chief financial officer, the chief accounting officer, and a majority of the company's board of directors.

Exhibit A-1 summarizes the 10-K disclosures required by the SEC for public companies. As shown in the exhibit, the SEC divides the disclosures into four groups. This is done to distinguish the information required to be disclosed in annual reports to shareholders from the complete 10-K information package required for filings with the SEC. The information included in Part II of the exhibit is primarily accounting information that is required for annual reports filed with the SEC as well as the annual reports distributed to the company's shareholders. The disclosure requirements

---

**EXHIBIT A-1**

Summary of Required Disclosures Under SEC Form 10-K

### SUMMARY OF REQUIRED DISCLOSURES UNDER SEC FORM 10-K

**Part I**
Item 1: Business (nature and history of the business, industry segments, etc.)
Item 2: Properties (location, description, and use of property, etc.)
Item 3: Legal proceedings (details of pending legal proceedings)
Item 4: Voting by security holders (items submitted to shareholders for voting)
**Part II**
Item 5: Market for common equity (place traded, shares, dividends, etc.)
Item 6: Selected financial data (five-year trend data for net sales, income from continuing operations including EPS, total assets, long-term debt, cash dividends, etc.)
Item 7: Management's discussion and analysis (discussion of the firm's liquidity, capital resources, operations, financial condition, etc.)
Item 8: Financial statements and supplementary data (requirements include audited balance sheets for two years and audited income statements and statements of cash flows for three years; three-year and five-year summaries are required for selected statement items)
Item 9: Changes in accountants and disagreements on accounting matters (changes in accountants and accounting changes, disagreements, disclosures, etc.)
**Part III**
Item 10: Directors and executive officers (names, ages, positions, etc.)
Item 11: Executive compensation (names, positions, salaries, stock options, etc.)
Item 12: Security ownership of beneficial owners and management (listing of insider owners of securities)
Item 13: Certain relationships (business relations and transactions with management, etc.)
**Part IV**
Item 14: Exhibits, financial statement schedules, and 8-K reports (supporting schedules of securities, borrowings, subsidiaries, ratios, etc.)

summarized in Parts I, III, and IV of the exhibit are only required for SEC filings, but they may be included in annual reports to shareholders.

In implementing its integrated disclosure system, the SEC eliminated a number of differences between reports filed with the SEC and those contained in annual reports to shareholders. This permitted public companies to meet many of the SEC filing requirements by reference to disclosures made in the annual reports to shareholders. That is, companies can include copies of their annual shareholder reports in 10-K filings and satisfy many SEC disclosure requirements with one report. The SEC encourages incorporation of information by reference to other reports and does not require that information to be duplicated. This "incorporation by reference" ruling resulted in a substantial increase in the size of corporate annual reports and a corresponding decrease in the size of 10-K reports filed with the SEC.

**FORM 8-K** **Form 8-K** is a report that requires registrants to inform the SEC about significant changes that take place regarding firm policies or financial condition. Firms must submit the report within 15 days (5 days in some cases) of the occurrence. Items that might be disclosed in Form 8-K include changes in management, major acquisitions or disposals of assets, lawsuits, bankruptcy filings, and unexpected changes in directors.

**FORM 10-Q** **Form 10-Q** contains quarterly data prepared in accordance with GAAP and must be filed within 45 days of the end of each of the registrant's first three quarters. Chapter 14 of this text describes and illustrates the SEC requirements for quarterly reports. The SEC Web site (www.sec.gov) provides access to details of various SEC forms and filing requirements under the Securities Acts of 1933 and 1934, as well as subsequent legislation. The Web site also provides access to all SEC rules and pronouncements.

## SEC DEVELOPMENTS

**INTERNATIONAL REGISTRANTS** The SEC also regulates international firms that list their shares for trading on U.S. securities exchanges. Historically, the SEC required these firms to either convert to U.S. GAAP or to prepare financial statements in accordance with either their home nation's GAAP or International Financial Reporting Standards (IFRS). Those firms choosing to use non-U.S. GAAP were required to provide supplemental disclosures, notably including a reconciliation of their financial statements to U.S. GAAP. In November 2007, the SEC voted to change the rules for international registrants. The SEC permits these firms to provide IFRS-based financial statements. Reconciliations to U.S. GAAP are no longer necessary if the registrant prepares statements under IFRS.

This change may mark the demise of the FASB. There will likely be a domino effect. U.S. firms with significant international operations are likely to request similar treatment (i.e., preparation of IFRS-based financials), arguing for fairness. If the SEC permits these firms to use IFRS, all U.S. firms are likely to follow suit and request the same option. If these arguments succeed, the FASB may cease to exist or, at a minimum, see a dramatic reduction in its authority. A potential new role for the FASB would be to carve out a subset of IFRS deemed appropriate for U.S. financial reporting. For example, the United States would likely still permit firms to use the LIFO (Last In First Out) inventory method due to its significant tax ramifications. Most other nations ban LIFO.

**REGULATION S** The SEC issued **Regulation S** in 1990 to clarify the applicability of U.S. securities laws across national boundaries. Generally, the regulation provides that sales of securities outside the United States are not subject to the 1933 Securities Act. The regulation also provides "safe harbor" rules to exempt any U.S. companies that sell securities offshore from SEC registration requirements.

**THE EDGAR SYSTEM** The Securities and Exchange Commission introduced a massive new computerized system to facilitate the process of filing, reviewing, and disseminating corporate information to the public in 1984 [www.sec.gov/edaux/searches.htm][4]. **EDGAR** is an abbreviation for the SEC's system, titled Electronic Data Gathering Analysis and Retrieval System. One of the SEC's goals under the integrated disclosure system is to provide investors, analysts, and other interested parties with instant access to corporate information on file with the SEC.

---

[4]US Securities Exchange Commission

**Small Business**    Although most SEC registrants are large public companies, the capital needs of small business issuers (under $25 million in both revenue and public float) have been addressed by the SEC, and new financial rules for small business enterprises were adopted in 1992 and 1993. Those rules provide new opportunities for small firms to raise capital to start or expand their businesses. Rule 504 relating to certain tax-exempt private offerings was amended to allow issuers other than development-stage enterprises to raise up to $1,000,000 in any 12-month period without registering under the 1933 Securities Act. Also, safe-harbor rules for information or trends and future events that may affect future operating results have been revised.

## SUMMARY

This appendix provides an overview of securities legislation related to financial accounting and reporting. It also explains the function of the Securities and Exchange Commission and its authority to prescribe accounting principles. SEC requirements that are relevant to particular topics are integrated into the chapters throughout this book. For example, Chapters 3 and 11 discuss and illustrate the SEC's requirement to push down the purchase price of a subsidiary to the subsidiary's financial statements. Chapter 8 discusses the SEC's position on recognizing gain on a subsidiary's stock sales, and Chapter 15 traces the history of the SEC's efforts in requiring segment disclosures and SEC requirements for interim reports.

# CHAPTER 6

# Intercompany Profit Transactions—Plant Assets

Transactions among affiliates for sales and purchases of plant assets create unrealized profits and losses to the consolidated entity. The consolidated entity eliminates (defers) such profits and losses in reporting the results of operations and financial position. We also eliminate these in reporting the financial position and results of operations of a parent under the equity method. The adjustments to eliminate the effects of intercompany profits on plant assets are similar to, but not identical with, those for unrealized inventory profits. Unrealized inventory profits self-correct over any two accounting periods, but unrealized profits or losses on plant assets affect the financial statements until the related assets are sold outside the consolidated entity or are exhausted through use by the purchasing affiliate. This chapter covers concepts and procedures for eliminating unrealized profits on plant assets in one-line consolidations under the equity method and in consolidated statements.

## LEARNING OBJECTIVES

**6.1** Assess the impact of intercompany profit on transfers of plant assets on consolidated financial statements.

**6.2** Defer unrealized profits on plant asset transfers by either the parent or subsidiary.

**6.3** Recognize realized, previously deferred profits on plant asset transfers.

**6.4** Adjust the calculations of noncontrolling interest share in the presence of intercompany profits on plant asset transfers.

## INTERCOMPANY PROFITS ON NONDEPRECIABLE PLANT ASSETS

LEARNING OBJECTIVE **6.1**

The transfer of nondepreciable plant assets between affiliates at a price other than book value gives rise to unrealized profit or loss to the consolidated entity. These transactions might include intercompany sales of land or of intangible assets that have an indefinite life, and are therefore not amortized. An intercompany gain or loss appears in the income statement of the selling affiliate in the year of sale. However, such gain or loss is unrealized and must be eliminated from investment income in a one-line consolidation by the parent. We also eliminate its effects in preparing consolidated financial statements.

Intercompany transfers of plant assets are much less frequent than intercompany inventory transfers. They most likely occur when mergers are completed, as a part of a reorganization of the combined companies.

The direction of intercompany sales of plant assets, like intercompany sales of inventory items, is important in evaluating the effect of unrealized profit on parent and consolidated financial statements. A gain or loss on sales downstream from parent to subsidiary is initially included in parent income and must be eliminated. The amount of elimination is 100 percent, regardless of the noncontrolling interest percentage. Subsidiary accounts include any profit or loss from upstream sales from subsidiary to parent. The parent recognizes only its share of the subsidiary's income, so only the parent's proportionate share of unrealized profits should be eliminated. The effect on consolidated net income is the same as for the parent.

This section of the chapter discusses and illustrates accounting practices for intercompany sales of land, covering both downstream and upstream sales. Accounting for intercompany sales of any non-amortizable asset will receive similar treatment.

**187**

## Downstream Sale of Land

Son Corporation is a 90 percent–owned subsidiary of Pop Corporation, acquired for $540,000 on January 1, 2016. Investment cost was equal to book value and fair value of the interest acquired. Son's net income for 2016 was $140,000, and Pop's income, excluding income from Son, was $180,000. Pop's income includes a $20,000 unrealized gain on land that cost $80,000 and was sold to Son for $100,000. Accordingly, Pop makes the following entries in accounting for its investment in Son at December 31, 2016:

| | | |
|---|---|---|
| Investment in Son (+A) | 126,000 | |
|     Income from Son (R, +SE) | | 126,000 |
|     To record 90% of Son's $140,000 reported income. | | |
| Income from Son (−R, −SE) | 20,000 | |
|     Investment in Son (−A) | | 20,000 |
|     To eliminate unrealized profit on land sold to Son. | | |

Exhibit 6-1 presents a consolidation workpaper for Pop and Subsidiary for 2016. Separate summary financial statements for Pop and Son appear in the first three columns.

Gain on the sale of land should not appear in the consolidated income statement, and the land should be included in the consolidated balance sheet at its original cost of $80,000. Entry a eliminates the gain on sale of land and reduces the land account to $80,000—its cost to the consolidated entity. This is the only entry that is significantly different from previous chapters.

| | | |
|---|---|---|
| a  **Gain on sale of land (−Ga, −SE)** | **20,000** | |
|     **Land (− A)** | | **20,000** |
| **To eliminate gain on intercompany sale of land and reduce land to its cost basis.** | | |

The overvalued land will continue to appear in the separate balance sheet of Son in subsequent years until it is sold outside of the consolidated entity, but the gain on land does not appear in the separate income statements of Pop in subsequent years. Therefore, entry a as shown in Exhibit 6-1 applies only in the year of the intercompany sale.

**YEARS SUBSEQUENT TO INTERCOMPANY SALE**   Here is the adjustment to reduce land to its cost to the consolidated entity in years subsequent to the year of the intercompany downstream sale:

| | | |
|---|---|---|
| **Investment in Son (+ A)** | **20,000** | |
|     **Land (− A)** | | **20,000** |
| **To reduce land to its cost basis and adjust the investment account to establish reciprocity with Son's equity accounts at the beginning of the period.** | | |

The debit to the investment account adjusts its balance to establish reciprocity with the subsidiary equity accounts at the beginning of each subsequent period in which the land is held. For example, the investment account balance at December 31, 2016, is $646,000. This is $20,000 less than Pop's underlying equity in Son of $666,000 on that date ($740,000 × 90%) The difference arises from the entry on Pop's books to reduce investment income and the investment account for the intercompany profit in the year of sale.

## Sale in Subsequent Year to Outside Entity

Assume that Son uses the land for four years and sells it for $130,000 in 2020. In the year of sale, Son reports a $30,000 gain ($130,000 proceeds less $100,000 cost), but the gain to the consolidated entity is $50,000 ($130,000 proceeds less $80,000 cost to Pop).

Pop recognizes its gain on the land in 2020 under the equity method by adjusting its investment income. The entry on Pop's books is:

| | | |
|---|---|---|
| Investment in Son (+A) | 20,000 | |
|     Income from Son (R, +SE) | | 20,000 |
|     To recognize previously deferred profit on sale of land to Son. | | |

## POP CORPORATION AND SUBSIDIARY CONSOLIDATION WORKPAPER FOR THE YEAR ENDED DECEMBER 31, 2016 (IN THOUSANDS)

EXHIBIT 6-1

Intercompany Profit from Downstream Sale of Land

| | Pop | 90% Son | Adjustments and Eliminations Debits | Adjustments and Eliminations Credits | Consolidated Statements |
|---|---|---|---|---|---|
| *Income Statement* | | | | | |
| Sales | $ 760 | $ 440 | | | $1,200 |
| Income from Son | 106 | | b 106 | | |
| Gain on sale of land | 20 | | a 20 | | |
| Expenses (including cost of goods sold) | (600) | (300) | | | (900) |
| Noncontrolling interest share ($140,000 × 10%) | | | c 14 | | (14) |
| **Controlling Share of Net Income** | $ 286 | $ 140 | | | $ 286 |
| *Retained Earnings Statement* | | | | | |
| Retained earnings—Pop | $ 414 | | | | $ 414 |
| Retained earnings—Son | | $ 200 | d 200 | | |
| Add: Controlling Share of Net Income | 286 | 140 | | | 286 |
| Retained earnings—December 31 | $ 700 | $ 340 | | | $ 700 |
| *Balance Sheet* | | | | | |
| Current assets | $ 954 | $ 700 | | | $1,654 |
| Land | | 100 | | a 20 | 80 |
| Investment in Son | 646 | | | b 106 / d 540 | |
| | $1,600 | $ 800 | | | $1,734 |
| Liabilities | $ 100 | $ 60 | | | $ 160 |
| Capital stock | 800 | 400 | d 400 | | 800 |
| Retained earnings | 700 | 340 | | | 700 |
| | $1,600 | $ 800 | | | |
| Noncontrolling interest | | | | c 14 / d 60 | 74 |
| | | | 740 | 740 | $1,734 |

a. Eliminates gain on sale of land and reduces land to a cost basis.
b. Eliminates investment income and reduces the investment account to its January 1 balance.
c. Records the noncontrolling interest in subsidiary earnings for the current period.
d. Eliminates reciprocal equity and investment amounts and establishes beginning noncontrolling interest.

This entry on Pop's books reestablishes equality between the investment account and 90 percent of the equity of Son on the same date.

The following workpaper entry adjusts the $30,000 gain to Son to the $50,000 consolidated gain on the land:

| Investment in Son (+A) | 20,000 | |
| Gain on land (Ga, +SE) | | 20,000 |
| To adjust gain on land to the $50,000 gain to the consolidated entity. | | |

This entry in the year of sale is almost the same as the entry in each of the years 2017, 2018, and 2019 to eliminate the unrealized profit from the land account. The difference is that the credit is to the gain account because the land no longer appears on the separate books of Pop or Son.

## Upstream Sale of Land

To illustrate the accounting for upstream sales of nondepreciable plant assets, assume that Pop purchases the land referred to in the previous section during 2016 from its 90 percent–owned affiliate, Son. As before, Son's net income for 2016 is $140,000, and Pop's income, excluding income from Son, is $180,000. However, the $20,000 unrealized profit on the intercompany sale of land is now reflected in the income of Son, rather than Pop. In accounting for its investment in Son at year-end 2016, Pop makes the following entries:

| | | |
|---|---|---|
| Investment in Son (+A) | 126,000 | |
|     Income from Son (R, +SE) | | 126,000 |
|       To record 90% of Son's reported net income. | | |
| | | |
| Income from Son (−R, −SE) | 18,000 | |
|     Investment in Son (−A) | | 18,000 |
|       To eliminate 90% of the $20,000 unrealized profit on | | |
|       land purchased from Son. | | |

These entries record Pop's investment income for 2016 in the amount of $108,000 ($126,000 − $18,000). Note that the $108,000 investment income consists of 90 percent of Son's $120,000 realized income for 2016 ($140,000 reported income less $20,000 unrealized gain on land). Pop's net income for 2016 is $288,000 ($180,000 separate income plus $108,000 investment income), as compared with $286,000 in the case of the downstream sale. The difference lies in the $2,000 unrealized gain attributed to noncontrolling interest and deducted from noncontrolling interest share.

Exhibit 6-2 presents a consolidation workpaper for Pop Corporation and Subsidiary for 2016. The workpaper uses the same information as in Exhibit 6-1 except for minor changes necessary to switch to the upstream sale situation.

The adjustments reflected in the consolidation workpaper in Exhibit 6-2 are the same as those in Exhibit 6-1 except for the amount of entry b, which is $108,000 rather than $106,000 and the amount of entry c, which is discussed next. Entry a eliminates the full amount of the gain on the sale of land and reduces the land to its cost basis to the consolidated entity whether the intercompany sale is upstream or downstream.

NONCONTROLLING INTEREST SHARE    Noncontrolling interest share is $14,000 in Exhibit 6-1 but only $12,000 in Exhibit 6-2. We reduce the noncontrolling interest share with its share of the unrealized gain on Son's sale of land to Pop. We do this in the consolidation workpaper by converting Son's reported net income into realized income and multiplying by the noncontrolling interest percentage. The $12,000 noncontrolling interest share is 10 percent of Son's $120,000 realized income.

YEARS SUBSEQUENT TO INTERCOMPANY SALE    While Pop continues to hold the land in subsequent years, consolidation will require an adjustment to reduce the land account to its cost basis to the consolidated entity. The entry to eliminate unrealized profit from the land account is:

| | | |
|---|---|---|
| **Investment in Son (+ A)** | **18,000** | |
| **Noncontrolling interest (− SE)** | **2,000** | |
|     **Land (− A)** | | **20,000** |
|     **To reduce land to its cost basis and adjust the investment account and** | | |
|       **beginning noncontrolling interest to establish reciprocity with Son's** | | |
|       **equity accounts at the beginning of the period.** | | |

We enter noncontrolling interest in the workpaper at the noncontrolling interest share of *reported* subsidiary equity when reciprocal investment and subsidiary equity accounts are eliminated, so we need the foregoing adjustment to reduce noncontrolling interest to its *realized* amount each time we prepare consolidation workpapers. This adjustment makes beginning noncontrolling interest in 2017 equal to ending noncontrolling interest in 2016, and so on.

| POP CORPORATION AND SUBSIDIARY CONSOLIDATION WORKPAPER FOR THE YEAR ENDED DECEMBER 31, 2016 (IN THOUSANDS) | | | | | |
|---|---|---|---|---|---|
| | | | Adjustments and Eliminations | | |
| | Pop | 90% Son | Debits | Credits | Consolidated Statements |
| **Income Statement** | | | | | |
| Sales | $ 780 | $ 420 | | | $1,200 |
| Income from Son | 108 | | b 108 | | |
| Gain on sale of land | | 20 | a 20 | | |
| Expenses (including cost of goods sold) | (600) | (300) | | | (900) |
| Noncontrolling interest share [($140,000 − $20,000) × 10%] | | | c 12 | | (12) |
| **Controlling Share of Net Income** | $ 288 | $ 140 | | | $ 288 |
| **Retained Earnings Statement** | | | | | |
| Retained earnings—Pop | $ 414 | | | | $ 414 |
| Retained earnings—Son | | $ 200 | d 200 | | |
| **Add: Controlling Share of Net Income** | 288 | 140 | | | 288 |
| **Retained earnings—December 31** | $ 702 | $ 340 | | | $ 702 |
| **Balance Sheet** | | | | | |
| Current assets | $ 854 | $ 800 | | | $1,654 |
| Land | 100 | | | a 20 | 80 |
| Investment in Son | 648 | | | b 108 d 540 | |
| | $1,602 | $ 800 | | | $1,734 |
| Liabilities | $ 100 | $ 60 | | | $ 160 |
| Capital stock | 800 | 400 | d 400 | | 800 |
| **Retained earnings** | 702 | 340 | | | 702 |
| | $1,602 | $ 800 | | | |
| Noncontrolling interest | | | | c 12 d 60 | 72 |
| | | | 740 | 740 | $1,734 |

a. Eliminates gain on sale of land and reduces land to a cost basis.
b. Eliminates investment income and reduces the investment account to its January 1 balance.
c. Records the noncontrolling interest in subsidiary earnings for the current period.
d. Eliminates reciprocal equity and investment amounts and establishes beginning noncontrolling interest.

**EXHIBIT 6-2**

Intercompany Profit from Upstream Sale of Land

## Sale in Subsequent Year to Outside Entity

Assume that Pop uses the land for four years and sells it for $130,000 in 2020. In the year of sale, Pop will report a $30,000 gain ($130,000 proceeds less $100,000 cost), but the gain to the consolidated entity is $50,000, allocated $48,000 [$30,000 + ($20,000 × 0.9)] to controlling stockholders and $2,000 to noncontrolling stockholders.

Pop adjusts its investment income from Son in 2020 with the following entry:

| | | |
|---|---|---|
| Investment in Son (+A) | 18,000 | |
|     Income from Son (R, +SE) | | 18,000 |
|     To recognize previously deferred intercompany profits on land. | | |

The $30,000 gain on the sale of land plus the $18,000 increase in investment income on Pop's books equals the $48,000 effect on consolidated net income in 2020.

In the consolidation workpaper, the adjustment of the $30,000 gain of Pop to the $50,000 consolidated gain requires the following entry:

| | | |
|---|---|---|
| Investment in Son ( + A) | 18,000 | |
| Noncontrolling interest ( − SE) | 2,000 | |
| Gain on land (Ga, + SE) | | 20,000 |
| To adjust gain on land to the $50,000 gain to the consolidated entity. | | |

This entry allocates the $20,000 gain between the Investment in Son (90%) and noncontrolling interest (10%).

LEARNING
OBJECTIVE
6.2

## INTERCOMPANY PROFITS ON DEPRECIABLE PLANT ASSETS

The accounts of the selling affiliate may reflect intercompany sales of plant assets subject to depreciation, depletion, or amortization that result in unrealized gains or losses. Firms must eliminate the effects of these gains and losses from parent and consolidated financial statements until the consolidated entity realizes them *through sale to other entities or through use within the consolidated entity*. Adjustments to eliminate the effects of unrealized gains and losses on parent and consolidated financial statements are more complex than in the case of nondepreciable assets. This additional complexity stems from the depreciation (or depletion or amortization) process that affects parent and consolidated income in each year in which the related assets are held by affiliates.

The discussion of intercompany sales of plant assets in this section is limited to depreciable assets, but the analysis and procedures illustrated apply equally to assets subject to depletion or amortization. Intercompany gains and losses from downstream sales of depreciable plant assets are considered initially, and the upstream-sale situation is covered next.

### Downstream Sales of Depreciable Plant Assets

The initial effect of unrealized gains and losses from downstream sales of depreciable assets is the same as for nondepreciable assets. Gains or losses appear in the parent's accounts in the year of sale and must be eliminated in determining its investment income under the equity method. Similarly, we eliminate such gains or losses from consolidated statements by removing each gain or loss and reducing the plant assets to their depreciated cost to the consolidated entity.

DOWNSTREAM SALE AT THE END OF A YEAR    Assume that Pam Corporation sells machinery to its 80 percent–owned subsidiary, Sun Corporation, on December 31, 2016. The machinery has an undepreciated cost of $50,000 on this date (cost, $90,000, and accumulated depreciation, $40,000), and it is sold to Sun for $80,000. Journal entries to record the sale and purchase on Pam's and Sun's books are as follows:

PAM'S BOOKS

| | | |
|---|---|---|
| Cash (+A) | 80,000 | |
| Accumulated depreciation (+A) | 40,000 | |
| Machinery (−A) | | 90,000 |
| Gain on sale of machinery (Ga, +SE) | | 30,000 |

SUN'S BOOKS

| | | |
|---|---|---|
| Machinery (+A) | 80,000 | |
| Cash (−A) | | 80,000 |

There is an unrealized gain on Pam's books at December 31, 2016, and, accordingly, Pam adjusts its equity method investment income for 2016 for the full amount of the unrealized gain:

| | | |
|---|---|---|
| Income from Sun (−R, −SE) | 30,000 | |
| Investment in Sun (−A) | | 30,000 |

The gain on machinery should not appear in the consolidated income statement for 2016, and Pam should include the machinery in the consolidated balance sheet at $50,000, its depreciated cost to the consolidated entity. A consolidation adjustment accomplishes this effect:

| Gain on sale of machinery ($-$ Ga, $-$ SE) | 30,000 | |
| Machinery ($-$ A) | | 30,000 |

We could also record this effect by debiting Gain on sale of machinery for $30,000, debiting Machinery for $10,000, and crediting Accumulated depreciation—machinery for $40,000. Conceptually, this entry is superior because it results in reporting plant assets and accumulated depreciation at the amounts that would have been shown if the intercompany sale had not taken place. From a practical viewpoint, however, the additional detail is usually not justified because the same net asset amounts are obtained without the additional recordkeeping costs. The examples in this book reflect the more practical approach.

No adjustment of the noncontrolling interest is necessary, because the intercompany sale does not affect Sun's income. Note that the analysis up to this point is equivalent to the one for the intercompany sale of land discussed earlier in this chapter.

**DOWNSTREAM SALE AT THE BEGINNING OF A YEAR**   If the sale from Pam to Sun had occurred on January 1, 2016, the machinery would have been depreciated by Sun during 2016, and any depreciation on the unrealized gain would be considered a piecemeal recognition of the gain during 2016. Assume that on January 1, 2016, the date of the intercompany sale, the machinery has a five-year remaining useful life and no expected residual value at December 31, 2020. Straight-line depreciation is used. The entries to record the sale and purchase are the same as for the December 31 sale; however, Sun also records depreciation expense of $16,000 for 2016 ($80,000 ÷ 5 years). Of this $16,000 depreciation, $10,000 is based on cost to the consolidated entity ($50,000 cost ÷ 5 years), and $6,000 is based on the $30,000 unrealized gain ($30,000 ÷ 5 years). The $6,000 is considered a piecemeal recognition of one-fifth of the $30,000 unrealized gain on the intercompany transaction. Conceptually, this is equivalent to the sale to other entities of one-fifth of the services remaining in the machinery.[1]

In eliminating the effect of the intercompany sale from its Investment in Sun account for 2016, Pam makes the following entries:

| Income from Sun ($-$R, $-$SE) | 30,000 | |
| Investment in Sun ($-$A) | | 30,000 |
| Investment in Sun ($+$A) | 6,000 | |
| Income from Sun (R, $+$SE) | | 6,000 |

Thus, elimination of the effect of the intercompany sale reduces Pam's investment income in 2016 by $24,000 ($30,000 unrealized gain less $6,000 realized through depreciation). Although Sun's income decreases by the $6,000 excess depreciation during 2016, the $6,000 is considered realized through use, and, accordingly, no adjustment of the noncontrolling interest share is necessary.

**EFFECT OF DOWNSTREAM SALE ON A CONSOLIDATION WORKPAPER**   A partial consolidation workpaper illustrates the effects of the January 1 intercompany sale of machinery on the consolidated financial statements at December 31, 2016 as follows (in thousands):

LEARNING OBJECTIVE **6.3**

| | Pam | 80% Sun | Adjustments and Eliminations | | Consolidated Statements |
|---|---|---|---|---|---|
| *Income Statement* | | | | | |
| Gain on sale of machinery | $30 | | a 30 | | |
| Depreciation expense | | $16 | | b 6 | $10 |
| *Balance Sheet* | | | | | |
| Machinery | | $80 | | a 30 | $50 |
| Accumulated depreciation | | 16 | b 6 | | 10 |

The first entry eliminates the $30,000 unrealized gain and reduces machinery to its cost basis to the consolidated entity at the time of intercompany sale. The second entry reduces depreciation

---

[1]We assume that the machine services have entered the cost of goods delivered to customers during the current period. If, instead, they are included in inventory, realization has not yet occurred and appropriate adjustments should be made. This additional refinement is not justified when the amounts involved are immaterial.

expense and accumulated depreciation to adjust these items to the depreciated cost basis to the consolidated entity at December 31, 2016. Noncontrolling interest computations are not affected by the workpaper adjustments because the sale was downstream.

In each of the years 2017 through 2020, Pam adjusts its investment income for the piecemeal recognition of the previously unrecognized gain on the machinery with the following entry:

| | | |
|---|---|---|
| 2017, 2018, 2019, and 2020 | | |
| Investment in Sun (+A) | 6,000 | |
| Income from Sun (R, +SE) | | 6,000 |

By December 31, 2020, the end of the useful life of the machinery, Pam will have recognized the full $30,000 gain as investment income. Its investment account balance will reflect the elimination and piecemeal recognition of the unrealized gain as follows:

| Year | Elimination of Gain on Machinery | Piecemeal Recognition of Gain through Depreciation | Effect on Investment Balance at December 31 |
|---|---|---|---|
| 2016 | $-30,000 | $+6,000 | $-24,000 |
| 2017 | | +6,000 | -18,000 |
| 2018 | | +6,000 | -12,000 |
| 2019 | | +6,000 | -6,000 |
| 2020 | | +6,000 | 0 |

In a consolidation workpaper, it is necessary to establish reciprocity between the investment and subsidiary equity accounts at the beginning of the period before eliminating reciprocal balances. We eliminate the effect of the unrealized gain on the December 31, 2016, investment account in the 2017 consolidation workpaper with the following entry:

| | | |
|---|---|---|
| **Investment in Sun ( + A)** | **24,000** | |
| **Accumulated depreciation ( + A)** | **6,000** | |
| **Machinery ( − A)** | | **30,000** |

The partial consolidation workpaper shown in Exhibit 6-3 for Pam and Sun includes the entry for 2017. The exhibit shows eliminations for each subsequent year in which the unrealized gain would require adjustment.

The partial workpaper in Exhibit 6-3 shows two adjustments for each of the years 2017 through 2020. We use two entries for each year to isolate the effect on beginning-of-the-period balances and current-year changes. Current-year changes affect depreciation expense and accumulated depreciation in equal amounts, so the entries can be combined in subsequent illustrations and in problem solutions.

## Upstream Sales of Depreciable Plant Assets

Upstream sales of depreciable assets from a subsidiary to a parent result in unrealized gains or losses in the subsidiary accounts in the year of sale (unless the assets are sold at book values). In computing investment income in the year of sale, the parent adjusts its share of the reported income of the subsidiary for (1) its share of any unrealized gain on the sale and (2) its share of any piecemeal recognition of such unrealized gain through depreciation.

EFFECT OF UPSTREAM SALE ON THE AFFILIATES' SEPARATE BOOKS    The effect of a gain on an upstream sale is illustrated by the following example. Pop Corporation purchases a truck from its 80 percent–owned subsidiary, Son Corporation, on January 1, 2016. Other information is as follows:

| | |
|---|---|
| Son's reported net income for 2016 | $50,000 |
| Remaining useful life of the truck at January 1, 2016 | 3 years |
| Depreciation method | Straight line |
| Trade-in value of the truck at December 31, 2018 | $ 3,000 |
| Cost of truck to Son | $14,000 |
| Accumulated depreciation on truck at December 31, 2015 | $ 5,000 |

**PAM CORPORATION AND SUBSIDIARY PARTIAL CONSOLIDATION WORKPAPERS FOR THE YEARS 2017, 2018, 2019, AND 2020 (IN THOUSANDS)**

| | Pam | 80% Sun | Adjustments and Eliminations Debits | Adjustments and Eliminations Credits | Consolidated Statements |
|---|---|---|---|---|---|
| **2017** | | | | | |
| *Income Statement* | | | | | |
| Depreciation expense | | $16 | | b 6 | $10 |
| *Balance Sheet—December 31* | | | | | |
| Machinery | | 80 | | a 30 | 50 |
| Accumulated depreciation | | 32 | a 6 / b 6 | | 20 |
| Investment in Sun | XXX* | | a 24 | | |
| **2018** | | | | | |
| *Income Statement* | | | | | |
| Depreciation expense | | $16 | | b 6 | $10 |
| *Balance Sheet—December 31* | | | | | |
| Machinery | | 80 | | a 30 | 50 |
| Accumulated depreciation | | 48 | a 12 / b 6 | | 30 |
| Investment in Sun | XXX* | | a 18 | | |
| **2019** | | | | | |
| *Income Statement* | | | | | |
| Depreciation expense | | $16 | | b 6 | $10 |
| *Balance Sheet—December 31* | | | | | |
| Machinery | | 80 | | a 30 | 50 |
| Accumulated depreciation | | 64 | a 18 / b 6 | | 40 |
| Investment in Sun | XXX* | | a 12 | | |
| **2020** | | | | | |
| *Income Statement* | | | | | |
| Depreciation expense | | $16 | | b 6 | $10 |
| *Balance Sheet—December 31* | | | | | |
| Machinery | | 80 | | a 30 | 50 |
| Accumulated depreciation | | 80 | a 24 / b 6 | | 50 |
| Investment in Sun | XXX* | | a 6 | | |

*Whatever the balance of the investment account, it will be less than the underlying book value of the investment at the beginning of the year by the amount of the unrealized profit.

a. Eliminates unrealized profit from machinery and accumulated depreciation as of the beginning of the year and adjusts the Investment in Sun account to establish reciprocity with Sun's equity accounts at the beginning of the period.

b. Eliminates the current year's effect of unrealized profit from depreciation expense and accumulated depreciation.

If Son sells the truck to Pop for $12,000 cash, Son and Pop make the following journal entries on their separate books for 2016:

### SON'S BOOKS

*January 1 (sale of truck)*

| | | |
|---|---:|---:|
| Cash (+A) | 12,000 | |
| Accumulated depreciation (+A) | 5,000 | |
|     Trucks (−A) | | 14,000 |
|       Gain on sale of truck (Ga, +SE) | | 3,000 |
|   To record sale of truck. | | |

### POP'S BOOKS

*January 1 (purchase of truck)*

| | | |
|---|---:|---:|
| Trucks (+A) | 12,000 | |
|     Cash (−A) | | 12,000 |
|   To record purchase of truck. | | |

*December 31 (depreciation expense)*

| | | |
|---|---:|---:|
| Depreciation expense (E, −SE) | 3,000 | |
|     Accumulated depreciation (−A) | | 3,000 |
|   To record depreciation for one year. | | |
|     [($12,000 − $3,000 scrap) ÷ 3 years] | | |

*December 31 (investment income)*

| | | |
|---|---:|---:|
| Investment in Son (+A) | 38,400 | |
|     Income from Son (R, +SE) | | 38,400 |
|   To record investment income for 2016 computed as follows: | | |
|     Share of Son's reported net income ($50,000 × 80%) | | $40,000 |
|     Less: Unrealized gain on truck ($3,000 × 80%) | | −2,400 |
|     Add: Piecemeal recognition of gain | | |
|       [($3,000 gain ÷ 3 years) × 80%] | | + 800 |
|     Investment income | | $38,400 |

The deferral of the intercompany gain decreases Pop's investment income for 2016 by $1,600 (from $40,000 to $38,400). This is 80 percent of the unrealized gain at December 31, 2016 [($3,000 unrealized gain from sale − $1,000 piecemeal recognition through depreciation) × 80%] Pop will recognize the remaining $1,600 during 2017 and 2018 at the rate of $800 per year.

---

**LEARNING OBJECTIVE 6.4**

**EFFECT OF UPSTREAM SALE ON CONSOLIDATION WORKPAPERS**    To illustrate the workpaper procedures for Pop and Son, we include the following investment and equity balances—and changes in them—as additional assumptions:

| | Investment in Son 80% | 80% of the Equity of Son | 100% of the Equity of Son |
|---|---:|---:|---:|
| December 31, 2015 | $400,000 | $400,000 | $500,000 |
| Income—2016 | +38,400 | +40,000 | +50,000 |
| December 31, 2016 | 438,400 | 440,000 | 550,000 |
| Income—2017 | +40,800 | +40,000 | +50,000 |
| December 31, 2017 | 479,200 | 480,000 | 600,000 |
| Income—2018 | +40,800 | +40,000 | +50,000 |
| December 31, 2018 | $520,000 | $520,000 | $650,000 |

Pop's Investment in Son account at December 31, 2016, is $1,600 below its underlying book value ($438,400, compared with $440,000), and at December 31, 2017, it is $800 below its underlying book value ($479,200, compared with $480,000). By December 31, 2018, the $3,000 gain has been realized through depreciation. Pop's share of that gain ($2,400) has been recognized at the rate of $800 per year in 2016, 2017, and 2018. Thus, reciprocity between Pop's investment account and its underlying book value is reestablished at the end of 2018.

A partial consolidation workpaper for 2016, the year of sale, appears next, followed by the workpaper entries in journal form.

**2016: Year of Sale (in Thousands)**

| | Pop | 80% Son | Adjustments and Eliminations Debits | Adjustments and Eliminations Credits | Consolidated Statements |
|---|---|---|---|---|---|
| *Income Statement* | | | | | |
| Income from Son | $38.4 | | c  38.4 | | |
| Gain on sale of truck | | $ 3 | b  3 | | |
| Depreciation expense | 3 | | | a  1 | $2 |
| Noncontrolling interest share | | | d  9.6 | | 9.6 |
| *Balance Sheet* | | | | | |
| Trucks | $12 | | | b  3 | $9 |
| Accumulated depreciation | 3 | | a  1 | | 2 |
| Investment in Son | 438.4 | | | c  38.4 | |
| | | | | e 400 | |
| Equity of Son—January 1 | | $500 | e 500 | | |
| Noncontrolling interest | | | | d  9.6 | |
| | | | | e 100 | 109.6 |

| a | Accumulated depreciation (+ A) | 1,000 | |
|---|---|---|---|
| | Depreciation expense (− E, + SE) | | 1,000 |

To eliminate the current year's effect of unrealized gain from depreciation accounts.

| b | Gain on sale of truck (− Ga, − SE) | 3,000 | |
|---|---|---|---|
| | Trucks (− A) | | 3,000 |

To eliminate unrealized gain and to reduce trucks to a cost basis.

| c | Income from Son (− R, − SE) | 38,400 | |
|---|---|---|---|
| | Investment in Son (− A) | | 38,400 |

To eliminate investment income and to adjust the investment account to its beginning-of-the-period balance.

| d | Noncontrolling interest share (− SE) | 9,600 | |
|---|---|---|---|
| | Noncontrolling interest (+ SE) | | 9,600 |

To enter noncontrolling interest share of Son's income.

| e | Equity of Son January 1, 2016 (− SE) | 500,000 | |
|---|---|---|---|
| | Investment in Son (− A) | | 400,000 |
| | Noncontrolling interest January 1, 2016 (+ SE) | | 100,000 |

To eliminate reciprocal investment and equity accounts and to establish beginning noncontrolling interest.

We compute noncontrolling interest share of $9,600 for 2016 as 20 percent of Son's realized income of $48,000 [($50,000 − $3,000 + $1,000) × 20%]. A partial consolidation workpaper and the workpaper entries in journal form for 2017, the first subsequent year after the upstream sale, are as follows:

**2017: First Subsequent Year (in Thousands)**

| | Pop | 80% Son | Adjustments and Eliminations Debits | Adjustments and Eliminations Credits | Consolidated Statements |
|---|---|---|---|---|---|
| *Income Statement* | | | | | |
| Income from Son | $40.8 | | c  40.8 | | |
| Depreciation expense | 3 | | | a   1 | $2 |
| Noncontrolling interest share | | | d  10.2 | | 10.2 |
| *Balance Sheet* | | | | | |
| Trucks | $12 | | | b   3 | $9 |
| Accumulated depreciation | 6 | | a   1 <br> b   1 | | 4 |
| Investment in Son | 479.2 | | b   1.6 | c  40.8 <br> e 440 | |
| Equity of Son—January 1 | | $550 | e 550 | | |
| Noncontrolling interest | | | b   0.4 | d  10.2 | |
| | | | | e 110 | 119.8 |

<table>
<tr><td>a</td><td colspan="2">Accumulated depreciation (+ A)</td><td align="right">1,000</td><td></td></tr>
<tr><td></td><td colspan="2">Depreciation expense (− E, + SE)</td><td></td><td align="right">1,000</td></tr>
</table>

a  **Accumulated depreciation (+ A)**  —  **1,000**
  **Depreciation expense (− E, + SE)**  —  **1,000**
To eliminate the effect of the 2016 unrealized gain from
current depreciation accounts.

b  **Accumulated depreciation (+ A)**  —  **1,000**
 **Investment in Son (+ A)**  —  **1,600**
 **Noncontrolling interest January 1, 2017 (− SE)**  —  **400**
  **Trucks (− A)**  —  **3,000**
To eliminate the effect of 2016 unrealized gain
from accumulated depreciation and truck accounts and
to assign the unrealized gain of $2,000 at January 1 to the
investment account (80%) and noncontrolling interest (20%).

c  **Income from Son (− R, − SE)**  —  **40,800**
 **Investment in Son (− A)**  —  **40,800**
To eliminate investment income and to adjust the
investment account to its beginning-of-the-period balance.

d  **Noncontrolling interest share (− SE)**  —  **10,200**
 **Noncontrolling interest (+ SE)**  —  **10,200**
To enter noncontrolling interest share of subsidiary income.

e  **Equity of Son January 1, 2017 (− SE)**  —  **550,000**
 **Investment in Son (− A)**  —  **440,000**
 **Noncontrolling interest January 1, 2017 (+ SE)**  —  **110,000**
To eliminate reciprocal investment and equity accounts
and to establish beginning noncontrolling interest.

Noncontrolling interest share of $10,200 for 2017 consists of 20 percent of Son's reported net income of $50,000 plus 20 percent of the $1,000 gain realized through depreciation in 2017. In 2018 the computation of noncontrolling interest share is the same as in 2017.

Noncontrolling interest share in 2016 (the year of sale) is decreased by $400, the noncontrolling interest's share of the $2,000 gain not realized through depreciation in 2016. The 2016 beginning equity of Son is not affected by the intercompany sale in 2016, so beginning noncontrolling interest is unaffected and does not require adjustment. Depreciation expense for each of the years 2016,

2017, and 2018 of $3,000 is reduced to $2,000 by a workpaper adjustment of $1,000. The $2,000 depreciation expense that appears in the consolidated income statement is simply one-third of the book value less residual value of the truck at the time of intercompany sale [($9,000 − $3,000) ÷ 3 years].

**EFFECT OF UPSTREAM SALE ON SUBSEQUENT YEARS**    In 2017, the first year subsequent to the intercompany sale, the unrealized gain affects both the beginning investment account and the noncontrolling interest. Entry b allocates the $2,000 unrealized gain 80 percent to the Investment in Son account and 20 percent to beginning noncontrolling interest. The debit to the Investment in Son account adjusts for the $1,600 difference between the investment account and 80 percent of Son's equity at December 31, 2016. The $400 debit to noncontrolling interest is necessary to adjust beginning noncontrolling interest in 2017 to $109,600, equal to the ending noncontrolling interest in 2016.

In the partial consolidation workpaper for 2018, the second subsequent year after the upstream sale, the amounts allocated in entry b are $800 to the investment account and $200 to noncontrolling interest because only $1,000 of the initial $3,000 unrealized gain is unrealized at January 1, 2018. No further adjustments are necessary in 2019 because the full amount of the unrealized gain has been realized through depreciation. Observe that the truck account less accumulated depreciation on the consolidated statements at December 31, 2018, is equal to the $3,000 residual value of the truck on that date (trucks, $9,000, less accumulated depreciation, $6,000).

**2018: Second Subsequent Year (in Thousands)**

| | Pop | 80% Son | Adjustments and Eliminations Debits | Adjustments and Eliminations Credits | Consolidated Statements |
|---|---|---|---|---|---|
| *Income Statement* | | | | | |
| Income from Son | $40.8 | | c  40.8 | | |
| Depreciation expense | 3 | | | a  1 | $2 |
| Noncontrolling interest share | | | d  10.2 | | 10.2 |
| *Balance Sheet* | | | | | |
| Trucks | $12 | | | b  3 | $9 |
| Accumulated depreciation | 9 | | a  1 <br> b  2 | | 6 |
| Investment in Son | 520 | | b  .8 | c  40.8 <br> e  480 | |
| Equity of Son—January 1 | | $600 | e  600 | | |
| Noncontrolling interest | | | b  .2 | d  10.2 <br> e  120 | 130 |

| | | | | |
|---|---|---|---|---|
| **a** | **Accumulated depreciation (+ A)** | | 1,000 | |
| | Depreciation expense (− E, + SE) | | | 1,000 |
| | To eliminate the effect of the 2016 unrealized gain from current depreciation accounts. | | | |
| **b** | **Accumulated depreciation (+ A)** | | 2,000 | |
| | **Investment in Son (+ A)** | | 800 | |
| | **Noncontrolling interest January 1, 2018 (− SE)** | | 200 | |
| | Trucks (− A) | | | 3,000 |
| | To eliminate the effect of 2016 unrealized gain from accumulated depreciation and truck accounts and to assign the unrealized gain of $1,000 at January 1 to the investment account (80%) and noncontrolling interest (20%). | | | |

*(continued)*

| | | | |
|---|---|---|---|
| c | Income from Son ($-$R, $-$SE) | 40,800 | |
| | Investment in Son ($-$A) | | 40,800 |
| | To eliminate investment income and to adjust the investment account to its beginning-of-the-period balance. | | |
| d | Noncontrolling interest share ($-$SE) | 10,200 | |
| | Noncontrolling interest ($+$SE) | | 10,200 |
| | To enter noncontrolling interest share of subsidiary income. | | |
| e | Equity of Son January 1, 2018 ($-$SE) | 600,000 | |
| | Investment in Son ($-$A) | | 480,000 |
| | Noncontrolling interest January 1, 2018 ($+$SE) | | 120,000 |
| | To eliminate reciprocal investment and equity accounts and to establish beginning noncontrolling interest. | | |

## PLANT ASSETS SOLD AT OTHER THAN FAIR VALUE

An intercompany sale of plant assets at a loss requires special evaluation to make sure that the loss is not one that the seller should have recognized on its separate books prior to the intercompany sale (or in the absence of an intercompany sale). For example, if a parent sells a machine with a book value of $30,000 to its 90 percent–owned subsidiary for $20,000 on January 1, 2016, a question should arise as to the fair value of the asset at the time of sale. If the fair value is in fact $20,000, then the parent should have written the asset down to its $20,000 fair value before the sale and recognized the actual loss on its separate books. If the fair value is $30,000, then the propriety of the parent's action is suspect because the controlling stockholders lose and the noncontrolling stockholders gain on the exchange. Parent officers and directors may be charged with improper stewardship.

Similar suspicions arise if a subsidiary sells an asset to the parent at less than its fair value, because the transaction would have been approved by parent officials who also serve as directors of the subsidiary.

Intercompany sales at prices above fair value also create inequities. The Federal Trade Commission charged Nynex Corporation with overcharging its own telephone subsidiaries for equipment, supplies, and services. The telephone companies were fined $1.4 million for passing the costs of the overpayments along to customers.[2]

### Consolidation with Loss on Intercompany Sale

Consolidation procedures to eliminate intercompany unrealized losses are essentially the same as those to eliminate unrealized gains. Assume that a machine had a remaining useful life of five years when it was sold on January 1, 2016, to Son Corporation (a 90 percent–owned subsidiary of Pop Corporation) for $20,000. Pop's book value was $30,000. Pop has a $10,000 unrealized loss that is recognized on a piecemeal basis over five years. If Son's net income for 2016 is $200,000 and there are no other intercompany transactions, Pop records its income from Son as follows:

| | | |
|---|---|---|
| Investment in Son ($+$A) | 188,000 | |
| Income from Son (R, $+$SE) | | 188,000 |
| To record income for 2016 determined as follows: | | |
| Equity in Son's income ($200,000 \times 90\%$) | | $180,000 |
| Add: Unrealized loss on machine | | 10,000 |
| Less: Piecemeal recognition of loss ($10,000 \div 5$ years) | | (2,000) |
| | | $188,000 |

---

[2]*The Wall Street Journal,* February 21, 1990, p. B8.

Consolidation workpaper entries relating to the intercompany loss for 2016 would be as follows:

| | | |
|---|---:|---:|
| Machinery ( + A) | 10,000 | |
|     Loss on sale of machinery ( − Lo, + SE) | | 10,000 |
|   To eliminate unrealized intercompany loss on downstream sale. | | |
| Depreciation expense (E, − SE) | 2,000 | |
|     Accumulated depreciation ( − A) | | 2,000 |
|   To increase depreciation expense to reflect depreciation on a cost basis. | | |

In the years 2017 through 2020, Pop's income from Son will be reduced by $2,000 each year under the equity method. Consolidated net income is also reduced by $2,000 each year through entries to eliminate the effect of the intercompany loss. The elimination reduces consolidated income by increasing depreciation expense to a cost basis for consolidated statement purposes. In 2017 the entry would be as follows:

| | | |
|---|---:|---:|
| Machinery ( + A) | 10,000 | |
| Depreciation expense (E, − SE) | 2,000 | |
|     Accumulated depreciation ( − A) | | 4,000 |
|     Investment in Son ( − A) | | 8,000 |
|   To eliminate the effects of intercompany sale at a loss. | | |

An upstream sale of plant assets at a loss would be accounted for in similar fashion, except that the intercompany loss and its piecemeal recognition would be allocated proportionately to controlling stockholders and noncontrolling interests.

## CONSOLIDATION EXAMPLE—UPSTREAM AND DOWNSTREAM SALES OF PLANT ASSETS

Pam Corporation acquired a 90 percent interest in Sun Corporation at its underlying book value (equal to fair value) of $450,000 on January 3, 2016. Since Pam Corporation acquired its interest in Sun, the two corporations have participated in the following transactions involving plant assets:

1. On July 1, 2016, Pam sold land to Sun at a gain of $5,000. Sun resold the land to outside entities during 2018 at a loss to Sun of $1,000.

2. On January 2, 2017, Sun sold equipment with a five-year remaining useful life to Pam at a gain of $20,000. This equipment was still in use by Pam at December 31, 2018.

3. On January 5, 2018, Pam sold a building to Sun at a gain of $32,000. The remaining useful life of the building on this date was eight years, and Sun still owned the building at December 31, 2018.

Exhibit 6-4 shows comparative financial statements for Pam and Sun Corporations for 2018 in the separate-company columns of the consolidation workpaper.

### Equity Method

An examination of the consolidation workpaper in Exhibit 6-4 shows that Pam uses the equity method. The fact that Pam's net income of $300,000 is equal to the controlling share as well as the equality of Pam's retained earnings and consolidated retained earnings are evidence of the use of

EXHIBIT 6-4

Intercompany Sales of Plant Assets—Equity Method

## PAM CORPORATION AND SUBSIDIARY CONSOLIDATION WORKPAPER FOR THE YEAR ENDED DECEMBER 31, 2018 (IN THOUSANDS)

| | Pam | 90% Sun | Adjustments and Eliminations Debits | Adjustments and Eliminations Credits | Consolidated Statements |
|---|---|---|---|---|---|
| **Income Statement** | | | | | |
| Sales | $2,000 | $700 | | | $2,700 |
| Gain on building | 32 | | c 32 | | |
| **Gain or (loss) on land** | | (1) | | a 5 | 4 |
| Income from Sun | 52.6 | | d 52.6 | | |
| Cost of goods sold | (1,000) | (320) | | | (1,320) |
| Depreciation expense | (108) | (50) | b 4 / c 4 | | (150) |
| Other expenses | (676.6) | (249) | | | (925.6) |
| **Noncontrolling interest share** | | | e 8.4 | | (8.4) |
| **Controlling Share of Net Income** | $ 300 | $ 80 | | | $ 300 |
| **Retained Earnings Statement** | | | | | |
| Retained earnings—Pam | $ 400 | | | | $ 400 |
| **Retained earnings—Sun** | | $200 | f 200 | | |
| **Controlling Share of Net Income** | 300 | 80 | | | 300 |
| Dividends | (200) | (30) | | d 27 / e 3 | (200) |
| **Retained earnings—December 31** | $ 500 | $250 | | | $ 500 |
| **Balance Sheet** | | | | | |
| Cash | $ 131.8 | $ 32 | | | $ 163.8 |
| Other current assets | 200 | 150 | | | 350 |
| Land | 160 | 40 | | | 200 |
| Buildings | 500 | 232 | | c 32 | 700 |
| Accumulated depreciation—buildings | (200) | (54) | c 4 | | (250) |
| Equipment | 620 | 400 | | b 20 | 1,000 |
| Accumulated depreciation—equipment | (258) | (100) | b 8 | | (350) |
| Investment in Sun | 546.2 | | a 5 / b 14.4 | d 25.6 / f 540 | |
| | $1,700 | $700 | | | $1,813.8 |
| Current liabilities | $200 | $ 50 | | | $ 250 |
| Capital stock | 1,000 | 400 | f 400 | | 1,000 |
| **Retained earnings** | 500 | 250 | | | 500 |
| | $1,700 | $700 | | | |
| **Noncontrolling interest** | | | b 1.6 | e 5.4 / f 60 | 63.8 |
| | | | 726 | 726 | $1,813.8 |

the equity method. A reconciliation of Pam's Investment in Sun account at December 31, 2017, and December 31, 2018, follows:

| | |
|---|---:|
| Underlying equity in Sun December 31, 2017 | $540,000 |
| ($600,000 equity of Sun × 90%) | |
| Less: Unrealized profit on land | (5,000) |
| Less: 90% of unrealized profit on equipment ($16,000 × 90%) | (14,400) |
| Investment in Sun December 31, 2017 | 520,600 |
| Add: Income from Sun 2018 [(90% of Sun's $80,000 net | 52,600 |
| income) + $5,000 gain on land + $3,600 piecemeal recognition | |
| of gain on equipment − $28,000 unrealized profit on building] | |
| Less: Dividends received 2018 | (27,000) |
| Investment in Sun December 31, 2018 | $546,200 |

Pam sold land to Sun in 2016 at a gain of $5,000. This gain was realized in 2018 when Sun sold the land to an outside entity. However, Sun sold the land at a $1,000 loss based on the transfer price, and the net result is a $4,000 gain for the consolidated entity during 2018. Workpaper entry a converts the $1,000 loss included in Sun's separate income to a $4,000 consolidated gain:

| | | | |
|---|---|---:|---:|
| a | Investment in Sun (+ A) | 5,000 | |
| | Gain on land (Ga, + SE) | | 5,000 |
| | To recognize previously deferred gain on land. | | |

Entry b relates to the $20,000 intercompany profit on Sun's sale of equipment to Pam at the beginning of 2017. The adjustment is:

| | | | |
|---|---|---:|---:|
| b | Investment in Sun (+ A) | 14,400 | |
| | Noncontrolling interest January 1, (− SE) | 1,600 | |
| | Accumulated depreciation—equipment (+ A) | 8,000 | |
| | Depreciation expense (− E, + SE) | | 4,000 |
| | Equipment (− A) | | 20,000 |
| | To eliminate unrealized profit on upstream sale of equipment and eliminate current year's effect of unrealized gain from depreciation accounts. | | |

Depreciation on the unrealized gain is $4,000 per year ($20,000 ÷ 5 years), and the portion unrealized at the beginning of 2018 was $16,000, the original gain less piecemeal recognition of $4,000 through depreciation in 2017. The sale was upstream, so the $16,000 unrealized profit is allocated 90 percent and 10 percent to investment in Sun ($14,400) and beginning noncontrolling interest ($1,600), respectively. The $14,400 is debited to the Investment in Sun account because Pam used the equity method.

Entry c eliminates intercompany profit on the buildings that Pam sold to Sun in 2018 at a gain of $32,000:

| | | | |
|---|---|---:|---:|
| c | Gain on buildings (− Ga, − SE) | 32,000 | |
| | Accumulated depreciation—buildings (+ A) | 4,000 | |
| | Buildings (− A) | | 32,000 |
| | Depreciation expense (− E, + SE) | | 4,000 |
| | To eliminate unrealized gain on the downstream sale of buildings and eliminate current year's effect of unrealized gain from depreciation accounts. | | |

The transaction occurred at the beginning of the year, so the sale did not affect prior-period balances. We eliminate the $32,000 gain and reduce buildings to reflect their cost to the consolidated entity. We also eliminate depreciation expense and accumulated depreciation relating to the unrealized gain.

Entry d in the consolidation workpaper eliminates income from Sun and 90 percent of Sun's dividends, and it credits Investment in Sun for the $25,600 difference in order to establish reciprocity between investment and equity accounts at the beginning of the year. Entry f eliminates reciprocal investment and equity accounts and establishes the noncontrolling interest at the beginning of the year:

| | | | |
|---|---|---|---|
| d | Income from Sun (− R, − SE) | 52,600 | |
| |     Dividends (+ SE) | | 27,000 |
| |     Investment in Sun (− A) | | 25,600 |
| | To eliminate income and dividends from subsidiary. | | |
| e | Noncontrolling interest share (− SE) | 8,400 | |
| |     Dividends (+ SE) | | 3,000 |
| |     Noncontrolling interest (+ SE) | | 5,400 |
| | To enter noncontrolling interest share of subsidiary income and dividends. | | |
| f | Retained earnings—Sun (− SE) | 200,000 | |
| | Capital stock—Sun (− SE) | 400,000 | |
| |     Investment in Sun (− A) | | 540,000 |
| |     Noncontrolling interest—beginning (+ SE) | | 60,000 |
| | To eliminate reciprocal investment and equity balances and establish noncontrolling interest at beginning of year. | | |

The $8,400 deduction for noncontrolling interest in the consolidated income statement of Exhibit 6-4 is equal to 10 percent of Sun's reported income for 2018 plus the piecemeal recognition of the gain in 2018 from Sun's sale of equipment to Pam [(80,000 + $4,000) × 10 percent]. At December 31, 2018, the noncontrolling interest's share of the unrealized gain on the equipment is $1,200. This $1,200 is reflected in the $63,800 noncontrolling interest that is shown in the consolidated balance sheet. If the effect of the unrealized gain applicable to noncontrolling interest had not been eliminated, noncontrolling interest in the consolidated balance sheet would be $65,000, 10 percent of Sun's reported equity at December 31, 2018.

## INVENTORY PURCHASED FOR USE AS AN OPERATING ASSET

Intercompany asset transactions do not always fall neatly into the categories of inventory items or plant assets. For example, inventory items may be sold for use in the operations of an affiliate. In this case, any gross profit on the sale will be realized for consolidated statement purposes as the purchaser depreciates the property.

Assume that Pop Company sells a computer that it manufactures at a cost of $150,000 to Son Corporation, its 100 percent–owned subsidiary, for $200,000. The computer has a five-year expected useful life, and straight-line depreciation is used. Pop's separate income statement includes $200,000 intercompany sales, but Son's cost of sales does *not* include intercompany purchases, because the purchase price is reflected in its plant assets, and the $50,000 gross profit is reflected in its equipment account. Workpaper entries to consolidate the financial statements of Pop and Son in the year of sale are:

| | | |
|---|---|---|
| Sales (− R, − SE) | 200,000 | |
|     Cost of sales (− E, + SE) | | 150,000 |
|     Equipment (− A) | | 50,000 |
| To eliminate intercompany sales and to reduce cost of sales and equipment for the cost and gross profit, respectively. | | |
| | | |
| Accumulated depreciation—equipment (+ A) | 10,000 | |
|     Depreciation expense (− E, + SE) | | 10,000 |
| To eliminate depreciation on the gross profit from the sale ($50,000 ÷ 5 years). | | |

Recognition of the remaining $40,000 unrealized profit will occur as Son depreciates the computer over its remaining four-year useful life. Assuming that Pop adjusts its Investment in Son account for the unrealized profit on the sale under the equity method, the workpaper entry for the second year will be:

| | | |
|---|---|---|
| Investment in Son (+ A) | 40,000 | |
| Accumulated depreciation—equipment (+ A) | 20,000 | |
|     Equipment (− A) | | 50,000 |
|     Depreciation expense (− E, + SE) | | 10,000 |
| To reduce equipment to its cost basis to the consolidated entity, to eliminate the effects of the intercompany sale from depreciation expense and accumulated depreciation, and to establish reciprocity between beginning-of-the-period equity and investment amounts. | | |

Workpaper entries for the remaining three years of the computer's useful life will include the same debit and credit items, but the accumulated depreciation debit will increase by $10,000 in each subsequent year to a maximum of $50,000, and the debits to Investment in Son will decrease by $10,000 in each subsequent year as the gross profit is realized. The credit amounts are the same every year.

## SUMMARY

The effects of intercompany gains and losses on plant assets must be eliminated from consolidated financial statements until the consolidated entity realizes the gains and losses through use or sale of the assets. Realization through use results from the depreciation, depletion, or amortization recorded by the purchaser. Although all unrealized profit must be eliminated from the consolidated statements, we adjust consolidated net income for all unrealized gains and losses in the case of downstream sales. For upstream sales, however, we allocate the total amount of unrealized gains and losses between the controlling and noncontrolling interest shares. One-line consolidation procedures for parent financial statements must be compatible with consolidation procedures in order to maintain the equality of parent income under the equity method and the controlling share of consolidated net income (see Exhibit 6-5).

**EXHIBIT 6-5**

Summary Illustration—
Unrealized Profit from
Plant Assets

**Assumptions**

1. Parent's (P) net income, excluding income from Subsidiary (S), is $100,000.
2. 90 percent–owned Subsidiary reported net income of $50,000.
3. An intercompany sale of land in the current year resulted in a gain of $5,000.
4. The land is still held within the consolidated entity.

| | Downstream<br>Assume that P sells to S | Upstream<br>Assume that S sells to P |
|---|---|---|
| **P's Net Income—Equity Method** | | |
| P's separate income | $100,000 | $100,000 |
| P's share of S's reported net income | 45,000 | 45,000 |
| Deduct: Unrealized gain from land | | |
| ($5,000 × 100%) | (5,000) | |
| ($5,000 × 90%) | | (4,500) |
| P's Net Income | $140,000 | $140,500 |
| **Controlling Share of Consolidated Net Income** | | |
| P's separate income plus S's net income | $150,000 | $150,000 |
| Less: Unrealized gain on land | (5,000) | (5,000) |
| Total realized income | 145,000 | 145,000 |
| Less: Noncontrolling interest share | | |
| ($50,000 × 10%) | (5,000) | |
| ($50,000 − $5,000) × 10% | | (4,500) |
| Controlling share of net income | $140,000 | $140,500 |

Note that P's net income and controlling share of consolidated net income are the same as if the intercompany transaction had never taken place. In the downstream example, P's separate income would have been $95,000 ($100,000 − $5,000 gain) without the intercompany transaction, and S's reported income would have remained at $50,000. P's separate income of $95,000 plus P's $45,000 income from S ($50,000 × 90%) equals $140,000.

In the upstream example, P's separate income would have been unchanged at $100,000 in the absence of the intercompany transaction, but S's reported income would have been only $45,000 ($50,000 − $5,000 gain). P's separate income of $100,000 plus P's $40,500 income from S ($45,000 × 90%) equals $140,500. Although helpful in understanding the nature of accounting procedures, these assumptions concerning what the incomes would have been without the intercompany transactions lack economic realism because they ignore the productive use of the land.

## QUESTIONS

1. What is the objective of eliminating the effects of intercompany sales of plant assets in preparing consolidated financial statements?

2. In accounting for unrealized profits and losses from intercompany sales of plant assets, does it make any difference if the parent is the purchaser or the seller? Would your answer be different if the subsidiary were 100 percent owned?

3. When are unrealized gains and losses from intercompany sales of land realized from the viewpoint of the selling affiliate?

4. How is the computation of noncontrolling interest share affected by downstream sales of land? By upstream sales of land?

5. Consolidation workpaper entries are made to eliminate 100 percent of the unrealized profit from the land account in downstream sales of land. Is 100 percent also eliminated for upstream sales of land?

6. How are unrealized gains and losses from intercompany transactions involving depreciable assets eventually realized?

7. Describe the computation of noncontrolling interest share in the year of an upstream sale of depreciable plant assets.

8. How does a parent eliminate the effects of unrealized gains on intercompany sales of plant assets under the equity method?

9. What is the effect of intercompany sales of plant assets on the parent and consolidated net income in years subsequent to the year of sale?

10. Explain the sequence of workpaper adjustments and eliminations for unrealized gains and losses on depreciable plant assets. Is your answer affected by whether the intercompany transaction occurred in the current year or in prior years?

# EXERCISES

## E 6-1
## General Questions

Use the following information in answering questions 1 and 2:

Pop Company sells land with a book value of $5,000 to Son Company for $6,000 in 2016. Son is a wholly owned subsidiary of Pop. Son Company holds the land during 2017. Son Company sells the land for $8,000 to an outside entity in 2018.

**1.** In 2016 the unrealized gain:

   a  **To be eliminated is affected by the noncontrolling interest percentage**

   b  **Is initially included in Son's accounts and must be eliminated from Pop Company's income from Son Company under the equity method**

   c  **Is eliminated from consolidated net income by a workpaper entry that includes a credit to the land account for $1,000**

   d  **Is eliminated from consolidated net income by a workpaper entry that includes a credit to the land account for $6,000**

**2.** Which of the following statements is true?

   a  **Under the equity method, Pop Company's Investment in Son account will be $1,000 less than its underlying equity in Son throughout 2017.**

   b  **No workpaper adjustments for the land are required in 2017 if Pop Company has applied the equity method correctly.**

   c  **A workpaper entry debiting gain on sale of land and crediting land will be required each year until the land is sold outside the consolidated entity.**

   d  **In 2018, the year of Son's sale to an outside entity, the workpaper adjustment for the land will include a debit to gain on sale of land for $2,000.**

Use the following information in answering questions 3 and 4:

Pop Corporation sold machinery to its 80 percent–owned subsidiary, Son Corporation, for $100,000 on December 31, 2016. The cost of the machinery to Pop was $80,000, the book value at the time of sale was $60,000, and the machinery had a remaining useful life of five years.

**3.** How will the intercompany sale affect Pop's income from Son and Pop's net income for 2016?

|   | Pop's Income from Son | Pop's Net Income |
|---|---|---|
| a | No effect | No effect |
| b | Increased | No effect |
| c | Decreased | No effect |
| d | No effect | Decreased |

**4.** How will the consolidated assets and consolidated net income for 2016 be affected by the intercompany sale?

|   | Consolidated Net Assets | Consolidated Net Income |
|---|---|---|
| a | No effect | Decreased |
| b | Decreased | Decreased |
| c | Increased | No effect |
| d | No effect | No effect |

## E 6-2
## Discuss effect of intercompany sale of land

Sun Corporation is a 90 percent–owned subsidiary of Pam Corporation, acquired in 2016. During 2019 Pam sells land to Sun for $100,000 for which it paid $50,000. Sun still owns this land at December 31, 2019.

### REQUIRED

**1.** How and in what amount will the sale of land affect Pam's income from Sun and net income for 2019 and the balance of Pam's Investment in Sun account on December 31, 2019?

**2.** How will the consolidated financial statements of Pam Corporation and Subsidiary for 2019 be affected by the intercompany sale of land?

**3.** If Sun still owns the land at December 31, 2020, how will Pam's income from Sun and net income for 2020 be affected, and what will be the effect on Pam's Investment in Sun account on December 31, 2020?

**4.** If Sun sells the land during 2021 for $100,000, how will Pam's income from Sun and total consolidated income for 2021 be affected?

## E 6-3
## Computations for downstream and upstream sales of land

Son Company is a 90 percent–owned subsidiary of Pop Corporation, acquired several years ago at book value equal to fair value. For 2016 and 2017, Pop and Son report the following:

|  | 2016 | 2017 |
|---|---|---|
| Pop's separate income (excludes income from Son) | $150,000 | $200,000 |
| Son's Net Income | 40,000 | 30,000 |

The only intercompany transaction between Pop and Son during 2016 and 2017 was the January 1, 2016, sale of land. The land had a book value of $10,000 and was sold intercompany for $15,000, its appraised value at the time of sale.

**1.** Assume that the land was sold by Pop to Son and that Son still owns the land at December 31, 2017.
   **a** *Calculate controlling share of consolidated net income for 2016 and 2017.*
   **b** *Calculate noncontrolling interest share for 2016 and 2017.*

**2.** Assume that the land was sold by Son to Pop and Pop still holds the land at December 31, 2017.
   **a** *Calculate controlling share of consolidated net income for 2016 and 2017.*
   **b** *Calculate noncontrolling interest share for 2016 and 2017.*

## E 6-4
## Journal entries and consolidated income statement (downstream sale of building)

Sun is a 90 percent–owned subsidiary of Pam Corporation, acquired at book value several years ago. Comparative separate-company income statements for the affiliates for 2016 are as follows:

|  | Pam Corporation | Sun Corporation |
|---|---|---|
| Sales | $750,000 | $350,000 |
| Income from Sun | 54,000 | — |
| Gain on building | 15,000 | — |
| Income credits | 819,000 | 350,000 |
| Cost of sales | 500,000 | 200,000 |
| Operating expenses | 150,000 | 75,000 |
| Income debits | 650,000 | 275,000 |
| Net income | $169,000 | $ 75,000 |

On January 5, 2016, Pam sold a building with a 10-year remaining useful life to Sun at a gain of $15,000. Sun paid dividends of $50,000 during 2016.

### REQUIRED

**1.** Reconstruct the journal entries made by Pam during 2016 to account for its investment in Sun. Explanations of the journal entries are required.

**2.** Prepare a consolidated income statement for Pam Corporation and Subsidiary for 2016.

## E 6-5
## General questions [Based on AICPA]

**1.** On January 1, 2016, Pam Company sold equipment to its wholly owned subsidiary, Sun Company, for $1,800. The equipment cost Pam $2,000. Accumulated depreciation at the time of sale was $500. Pam was depreciating the equipment on the straight-line method over 20 years with no salvage value, a procedure that Sun continued. On the consolidated balance sheet at December 31, 2016, the cost and accumulated depreciation, respectively, should be:
   **a** *$1,500 and $600*
   **b** *$1,800 and $100*
   **c** *$1,800 and $500*
   **d** *$2,000 and $600*

**2.** In the preparation of consolidated financial statements, intercompany items for which eliminations will not be made are:

*a*  *Purchases and sales where the parent employs the equity method*
*b*  *Receivables and payables where the parent employs the cost method*
*c*  *Dividends received and paid where the parent employs the equity method*
*d*  *Dividends receivable and payable where the parent employs the equity method*

**3.** Pam Corporation owns 100 percent of Sun Corporation's common stock. On January 2, 2016, Pam sold to Sun for $40,000 machinery with a carrying amount of $30,000. Sun is depreciating the acquired machinery over a five-year life by the straight-line method. The net adjustments to compute 2016 and 2017 consolidated income before income tax would be an increase (decrease) of:

|   | 2016 | 2017 |
|---|---|---|
| a | $ (8,000) | $2,000 |
| b | $ (8,000) | $  0 |
| c | $(10,000) | $2,000 |
| d | $(10,000) | $  0 |

**4.** Pam Company owns 100 percent of Sun Company. On January 1, 2016, Pam sold Sun delivery equipment at a gain. Pam had owned the equipment for two years and used a five-year straight-line depreciation rate with no residual value. Sun is using a three-year straight-line depreciation rate with no residual value for the equipment. In the consolidated income statement, Sun's recorded depreciation expense on the equipment for 2016 will be decreased by:

*a*  *20% of the gain on sale*
*b*  *33.33% of the gain on sale*
*c*  *50% of the gain on sale*
*d*  *100% of the gain on sale*

## E 6-6
## General problems

**1.** Son Corporation is an 80 percent–owned subsidiary of Pop Corporation. In 2016, Son sold land that cost $15,000 to Pop for $25,000. Pop held the land for eight years before reselling it in 2024 to Roy Company, an unrelated entity, for $55,000. The 2024 consolidated income statement for Pop and its subsidiary, Son, will show a gain on the sale of land of:

*a*  *$40,000*
*b*  *$32,000*
*c*  *$30,000*
*d*  *$24,000*

**2.** On January 3, 2016, Pop Corporation sells equipment with a book value of $90,000 to its 100 percent–owned subsidiary, Son Corporation, for $120,000. The equipment has a remaining useful life of three years with no salvage at the time of transfer. Son uses the straight-line method of depreciation. As a result of this intercompany transaction, Pop's Investment in Son account balance at December 31, 2016, will be:

*a*  *$20,000 greater than its underlying equity interest*
*b*  *$20,000 less than its underlying equity interest*
*c*  *$30,000 less than its underlying equity interest*
*d*  *$10,000 greater than its underlying equity interest*

**3.** Pop Corporation sells equipment with a book value of $80,000 to Son Company, its 75 percent–owned subsidiary, for $100,000 on January 1, 2016. Son determines that the remaining useful life of the equipment is four years and that straight-line depreciation is appropriate. The December 31, 2016, separate financial statements of Pop and Son show equipment—net of $500,000 and $300,000, respectively. Consolidated equipment—net will be:

*a*  *$800,000*
*b*  *$785,000*
*c*  *$780,000*
*d*  *$650,000*

**4.** Pop Corporation sold equipment with a remaining three-year useful life and a book value of $14,500 to its 80 percent–owned subsidiary, Son Corporation, for $16,000 on January 2, 2016. A consolidated workpaper entry on December 31, 2016, to eliminate the unrealized profits from the intercompany sale of equipment will include:

*a*  *A debit to gain on sale of equipment for $1,000*
*b*  *A debit to gain on sale of equipment for $1,500*
*c*  *A credit to depreciation expense for $1,500*
*d*  *A debit to machinery for $1,500*

5. Son Company, a subsidiary, sells equipment with a four-year remaining useful life to Pop Corporation at a $12,000 gain on January 1, 2016. The effect of this intercompany transaction on the Pop's investment income from Son for 2016 will be:
   a   **An increase of $12,000 if Son is 100% owned**
   b   **An increase of $9,000 if Son is 100% owned**
   c   **A decrease of $9,000 if Son is 100% owned**
   d   **A decrease of $3,600 if Son is 60% owned**

6. On January 1, 2016, Son Corporation, a 60 percent–owned subsidiary of Pop Company, sells a building with a book value of $300,000 to Pop for $350,000. At the time of sale, the building has an estimated remaining life of 10 years with no salvage value. Pop uses straight-line depreciation. If Son reports net income of $1,000,000 for 2016, noncontrolling interest share will be:
   a   **$450,000**
   b   **$400,000**
   c   **$382,000**
   d   **$355,000**

## E 6-7
### Consolidated income statement (sale of asset sold upstream 2 years earlier)

A summary of the separate income of Pam Corporation and the net income of its 75 percent–owned subsidiary, Sun Corporation, for 2016 is as follows:

|  | Pam | Sun |
|---|---|---|
| Sales | $125,000 | $75,000 |
| Gain on sale of machinery | 2,500 | |
| Cost of good sold | (50,000) | (32,500) |
| Depreciation expense | (12,500) | (7,500) |
| Other expenses | (20,000) | (10,000) |
| Separate income (excludes investment income) | $ 45,000 | $ 25,000 |

Sun Corporation sold machinery with a book value of $10,000 to Pam Corporation for $16,250 on January 2, 2014. At the time of the intercompany sale, the machinery had a remaining useful life of five years. Pam uses straight-line depreciation. Pam used the machinery until December 28, 2016, when it was sold to an outside entity for $9,000.

**REQUIRED:** Prepare a consolidated income statement for Pam Corporation and Subsidiary for 2016.

## E 6-8
### Investment income from 40 percent investee (upstream and downstream sales)

Pop Corporation owns 40 percent of the outstanding voting stock of Son Corporation, acquired for $200,000 on July 1, 2016, when Son's common stockholders' equity was $400,000. The excess of investment fair value over book value acquired was due to valuable patents owned by Son that were expected to give Son a competitive advantage until July 1, 2021.

Son's net income for 2016 was $80,000 (for the entire year), and for 2017, Son's net income was $120,000. Pop's December 31, 2016 and 2017, inventories included unrealized profit on goods acquired from Son in the amounts of $8,000 and $12,000, respectively. At December 31, 2016, Pop sold land to Son at a gain of $4,000. This land is still owned by Son at December 31, 2017.

### REQUIRED
1. Compute Pop's investment income from Son for 2016 on the basis of a one-line consolidation.
2. Compute Pop's investment income from Son for 2017 on the basis of a one-line consolidation.

## E 6-9
### Upstream sale of equipment, noncontrolling interest

Pam Corporation has an 80 percent interest in Sun Corporation, its only subsidiary. The 80 percent interest was acquired on July 1, 2016, for $800, at which time Sun's equity consisted of $600 capital stock and $200 retained earnings. The excess of fair value over book value was assigned to buildings with a 20-year remaining useful life.

On December 31, 2018, Sun sold equipment with a remaining useful life of four years to Pam at a gain of $40. Pam Corporation had separate income for 2018 of $1,000 and for 2019 of $1,200.

Income and retained earnings data for Sun Corporation for 2018 and 2019 are as follows:

|                              | 2018   | 2019   |
|------------------------------|--------|--------|
| Retained earnings January 1  | $300   | $400   |
| Add: Net income              | 200    | 220    |
| Deduct: Dividends            | − 100  | − 120  |
| Retained earnings December 31| $400   | $500   |

### REQUIRED

1. Compute Pam Corporation's income from Sun, net income, and consolidated net income for each of the years 2018 and 2019.

2. Compute the correct balances of Pam's investment in Sun at December 31, 2018 and 2019, assuming no changes in Sun's outstanding stock since Pam acquired its interest.

## E 6-10
## Inventory items of parent capitalized by subsidiary

Pop Industries manufactures heavy equipment used in construction and excavation. On January 3, 2016, Pop sold a piece of equipment from its inventory that cost $360,000 to its 60 percent–owned subsidiary, Son Corporation, at Pop's standard price of twice its cost. Son is depreciating the equipment over six years using straight-line depreciation and no salvage value.

### REQUIRED

1. Determine the net amount at which this equipment will be included in the consolidated balance sheets for Pop Industries and Subsidiary at December 31, 2016 and 2017.

2. Pop accounts for its investment in Son as a one-line consolidation. Prepare the consolidation workpaper entries related to this intercompany sale that are necessary to consolidate the financial statements of Pop and Son at December 31, 2016 and 2017.

## E 6-11
## Consolidated net income (upstream and downstream sales)

Income data from the records of Pam Corporation and Sun Corporation, Pam's 80 percent–owned subsidiary, for 2016 through 2019 follow (in thousands):

|                       | 2016  | 2017  | 2018 | 2019  |
|-----------------------|-------|-------|------|-------|
| Pam's separate income | $200  | $150  | $40  | $120  |
| Sun's net income      | 60    | 70    | 80   | 90    |

Pam acquired its interest in Sun on January 1, 2016, at a price of $40,000 less than book value. The $40,000 was assigned to a reduction of plant assets with a remaining useful life of 10 years.

On July 1, 2016, Sun sold land that cost $25,000 to Pam for $30,000. This land was resold by Pam for $35,000 in 2019.

Pam sold machinery to Sun for $100,000 on January 2, 2017. This machinery had a book value of $75,000 at the time of sale and is being depreciated by Sun at the rate of $20,000 per year.

Pam's December 31, 2018, inventory included $8,000 unrealized profit on merchandise acquired from Sun during 2018. This merchandise was sold by Pam during 2019.

**REQUIRED:** Prepare a schedule to calculate the consolidated net income of Pam Corporation and Subsidiary for each of the years 2016, 2017, 2018, and 2019.

## PROBLEMS

### P6-1
### Consolidated workpaper (downstream sales, intercompany receivable/payable)

Son Corporation, a 90 percent–owned subsidiary of Pop Corporation, was acquired on January 1, 2016, at a price of $90,000 in excess of underlying book value. The excess was due to goodwill. Separate financial statements for Pop and Son for 2017 follow (amounts in thousands):

|  | Pop | Son |
|---|---|---|
| **Combined Income and Retained Earnings Statement for the Year Ended December 31, 2017** | | |
| Sales | $ 600 | $ 200 |
| Income from Son | 62 | — |
| Gain on sale of equipment | 18 | — |
| Cost of sales | (280) | (100) |
| Operating expenses | (120) | (20) |
| Net income | 280 | 80 |
| Add: Beginning retained earnings | 314 | 140 |
| Less: Dividends | (120) | (40) |
| Retained earnings, December 31 | $ 474 | $ 180 |
| **Balance Sheet at December 31, 2017** | | |
| Cash | $ 200 | $ 34 |
| Accounts receivable | 180 | 100 |
| Dividends receivable | 18 | — |
| Inventories | 40 | 16 |
| Land | 80 | 30 |
| Buildings—net | 270 | 100 |
| Equipment—net | 330 | 120 |
| Investment in Son | 316 | — |
| Total assets | $1,434 | $ 400 |
| Accounts payable | $ 196 | $ 60 |
| Dividends payable | 30 | 20 |
| Other liabilities | 134 | 40 |
| Capital stock | 600 | 100 |
| Retained earnings | 474 | 180 |
| Total equities | $1,434 | $ 400 |

### ADDITIONAL INFORMATION

1. Pop sold inventory items to Son during 2016 and 2017 as follows (in thousands):

|  | 2016 | 2017 |
|---|---|---|
| Sales | $60 | $40 |
| Cost of sales to Pop | 30 | 20 |
| Unrealized profit at December 31 | 10 | 8 |

2. Pop sold land that cost $14,000 to Son for $20,000 during 2016. The land is still owned by Son.

3. In January 2017, Pop sold equipment with a book value of $42,000 to Son for $60,000. The equipment is being depreciated by Son over a three-year period using the straight-line method.

4. On December 30, 2017, Son remitted $4,000 to Pop for merchandise purchases. The remittance was not recorded by Pop until January 5, 2018, and it is not reflected in Pop's financial statements at December 31, 2017.

**REQUIRED:** Prepare a consolidation workpaper for Pop Corporation and Subsidiary for the year ended December 31, 2017.

## P6-2
### Consolidated workpaper (downstream sales, intercompany receivable/payable)

Pam Corporation acquired a 90 percent interest in Sun Corporation on January 1, 2016, for $540,000, at which time Sun's capital stock and retained earnings were $300,000 and $180,000, respectively. The entire fair value/book value differential is goodwill. Financial statements for Pam and Sun for 2017 are as follows (in thousands):

|  | Pam | Sun |
| --- | --- | --- |
| ***Combined Income and Retained Earnings Statement*** | | |
| ***for the Year Ended December 31, 2017*** | | |
| Sales | $ 900 | $380 |
| Income from Sun | 80 | — |
| Gain on land | 10 | — |
| Cost of sales | (400) | (200) |
| Operating expenses | (226) | (80) |
| Net income | 364 | 100 |
| Add: Retained earnings January 1 | 404 | 240 |
| Less: Dividends | (300) | (40) |
| Retained earnings, December 31 | $ 468 | $300 |
| ***Balance Sheet at December 31, 2017*** | | |
| Cash | $ 266 | $ 28 |
| Accounts receivable | 360 | 200 |
| Dividends receivable | 36 | — |
| Inventories | 120 | 72 |
| Land | 200 | 60 |
| Buildings—net | 560 | 160 |
| Machinery—net | 660 | 280 |
| Investment in Sun | 606 | — |
|  | $2,808 | $800 |
| Accounts payable | $ 400 | $100 |
| Dividends payable | 60 | 40 |
| Other liabilities | 280 | 60 |
| Capital stock | 1,600 | 300 |
| Retained earnings | 468 | 300 |
|  | $2,808 | $800 |

### ADDITIONAL INFORMATION

1. Pam sold inventory items to Sun for $120,000 during 2016 and $144,000 during 2017. Sun's inventories at December 31, 2016 and 2017, included unrealized profits of $20,000 and $24,000, respectively.

2. On July 1, 2016, Pam sold machinery with a book value of $56,000 to Sun for $70,000. The machinery had a useful life of 3.5 years at the time of sale, and straight-line depreciation is used.

3. During 2017, Pam sold land with a book value of $30,000 to Sun for $40,000.

4. Pam's accounts receivable on December 31, 2017, includes $20,000 due from Sun.

5. Pam uses the equity method for its 90 percent interest in Sun.

**REQUIRED:** Prepare a consolidation workpaper for Pam Corporation and Subsidiary for the year ended December 31, 2017.

## P6-3
### Workpaper in year of acquisition (downstream and upstream sales)

Pop Corporation acquired a 90 percent interest in Son Corporation's outstanding voting common stock on January 1, 2016, for $630,000 cash. The stockholders' equity of Son on this date consisted of $500,000 capital stock and $200,000 retained earnings.

The financial statements of Pop and Son at and for the year ended December 31, 2016, are summarized as follows (in thousands):

|  | Pop | Son |
|---|---|---|
| ***Combined Income and Retained Earnings Statement for the Year Ended December 31, 2016*** | | |
| Sales | $ 700 | $ 500 |
| Income from Son | 70 | — |
| Gain on land | — | 10 |
| Gain on equipment | 20 | — |
| Cost of sales | (300) | (300) |
| Depreciation expense | (90) | (35) |
| Other expenses | (200) | (65) |
| Net income | 200 | 110 |
| Beginning retained earnings | 600 | 200 |
| Dividends | (100) | (50) |
| Retained earnings December 31 | $ 700 | $ 260 |
| ***Balance Sheet at December 31, 2016*** | | |
| Cash | $ 35 | $ 30 |
| Accounts receivable—net | 90 | 110 |
| Inventories | 100 | 80 |
| Other current items | 70 | 40 |
| Land | 50 | 70 |
| Buildings—net | 200 | 150 |
| Equipment—net | 500 | 400 |
| Investment in Son | 655 | — |
|  | $1,700 | $ 880 |
| Accounts payable | $ 160 | $ 50 |
| Other liabilities | 340 | 70 |
| Capital stock, $10 par | 500 | 500 |
| Retained earnings | 700 | 260 |
|  | $1,700 | $ 880 |

During 2016, Pop made inventory sales of $50,000 to Son at a gross profit of $15,000. One-third of these sales were inventoried by Son at year-end. Son owed Pop $10,000 on open account at December 31, 2016.

Son sold land that cost $20,000 to Pop for $30,000 on July 1, 2016. Pop still owns the land. On January 1, 2016, Pop sold equipment with a book value of $20,000 and a remaining useful life of four years to Son for $40,000. Son uses straight-line depreciation and assumes no salvage value on this equipment.

**REQUIRED:** Prepare a consolidation workpaper for Pop and Subsidiary for the year ended December 31, 2016.

### P6-4
### Workpaper (downstream sales, two years)

Pam Corporation acquired a 90 percent interest in Sun Corporation on January 1, 2016, for $2,700,000, at which time Sun's capital stock and retained earnings were $1,500,000 and $900,000, respectively. The fair value cost/book value differential is due to a patent with a 10-year amortization period. Financial statements for Pam and Sun for 2017 are as follows (in thousands):

|  | Pam | Sun |
|---|---|---|
| ***Combined Income and Retained Earnings Statement for the Year Ended December 31, 2017*** | | |
| Sales | $ 4,500 | $ 1,900 |
| Income from Sun | 346 | — |
| Gain on land | 50 | — |
| Cost of sales | (2,000) | (1,000) |
| Operating expenses | (1,130) | (400) |
| Net income | 1,766 | 500 |
| Add: Retained earnings January 1 | 2,000 | 1,200 |
| Less: Dividends | (1,500) | (200) |
| Retained earnings, December 31 | $ 2,266 | $ 1,500 |

| | Pam | Sun |
|---|---|---|
| **Balance Sheet at December 31, 2017** | | |
| Cash | $ 1,364 | $ 140 |
| Accounts receivable | 1,800 | 1,000 |
| Dividends receivable | 180 | — |
| Inventories | 600 | 360 |
| Land | 1,000 | 300 |
| Buildings—net | 2,800 | 800 |
| Machinery—net | 3,300 | 1,400 |
| Investment in Sun | 2,922 | — |
| | $13,966 | $ 4,000 |
| Accounts payable | $ 2,000 | $ 500 |
| Dividends payable | 300 | 200 |
| Other liabilities | 1,400 | 300 |
| Capital stock | 8,000 | 1,500 |
| Retained earnings | 2,266 | 1,500 |
| | $13,966 | $ 4,000 |

### ADDITIONAL INFORMATION

1. Pam sold inventory to Sun for $600,000 during 2016 and $720,000 during 2017; Sun's inventories at December 31, 2016 and 2017, included unrealized profits of $100,000 and $120,000, respectively.

2. On July 1, 2016, Pam sold machinery with a book value of $280,000 to Sun for $350,000. The machinery had a useful life of 3.5 years at the time of intercompany sale, and straight-line depreciation is used.

3. During 2017, Pam sold land with a book value of $150,000 to Sun for $200,000.

4. Pam's accounts receivable on December 31, 2017, includes $100,000 due from Sun.

5. Pam uses the equity method for its 90 percent interest in Sun.

**REQUIRED:** Prepare a consolidation workpaper for Pam and Subsidiary for the year ended December 31, 2017.

## P6-5
### Workpaper (fair value/book value differential, upstream sales)

Financial statements for Pop and Son Corporations for 2016 are as follows (in thousands):

| | Pop | Son |
|---|---|---|
| **Combined Income and Retained Earnings Statement** | | |
| **for the Year Ended December 31, 2016** | | |
| Sales | $ 420 | $ 260 |
| Income from Son | 63.8 | — |
| Gain on sale of land | — | 20 |
| Depreciation expense | (80) | (60) |
| Other expenses | (220) | (120) |
| Net income | 183.8 | 100 |
| Add: Beginning retained earnings | 280.8 | 100 |
| Deduct: Dividends | (60) | |
| Retained earnings December 31 | $ 404.6 | $ 200 |
| **Balance Sheet at December 31, 2016** | | |
| Current assets | $ 400 | $ 340 |
| Plant assets | 1,100 | 700 |
| Accumulated depreciation | (240) | (140) |
| Investment in Son | 644.6 | — |
| Total assets | $1,904.6 | $ 900 |
| Current liabilities | $ 300 | $ 100 |
| Capital stock | 1,200 | 600 |
| Retained earnings | 404.6 | 200 |
| Total equities | $1,904.6 | $ 900 |

## ADDITIONAL INFORMATION

1. Pop acquired an 80 percent interest in Son on January 2, 2014, for $580,000, when Son's stockholders' equity consisted of $600,000 capital stock and no retained earnings. The excess of investment fair value over book value of the net assets acquired related 50 percent to undervalued inventories (subsequently sold in 2014) and 50 percent to a patent with a 10-year amortization period.

2. Son sold equipment to Pop for $50,000 on January 1, 2015, at which time the equipment had a book value of $20,000 and a five-year remaining useful life (included in plant assets in the financial statements).

3. During 2016, Son sold land to Pop at a profit of $20,000 (included in plant assets in the financial statements).

4. Pop uses the equity method to accounting for its investment in Son.

**REQUIRED:** Prepare a consolidation workpaper for Pop Corporation and Subsidiary for the year ended December 31, 2016.

## P6-6
## Workpaper (downstream and upstream sales)

Pam Corporation acquired all the outstanding stock of Sun Corporation on April 1, 2016, for $15,000,000, when Sun's stockholders' equity consisted of $5,000,000 capital stock and $2,000,000 retained earnings. The price reflected a $500,000 undervaluation of Sun's inventory (sold in 2016) and a $3,500,000 undervaluation of Sun's buildings (remaining useful life seven years from April 1, 2016).

During 2017, Sun sold land that cost $1,000,000 to Pam for $1,500,000. Pam resold the land for $2,200,000 during 2020.

Pam sells inventory items to Sun on a regular basis, as follows (in thousands):

|  | Sales to Sun | Cost to Pam | Percentage Unsold by Sun at Year End | Percentage Unpaid by Sun at Year End |
|---|---|---|---|---|
| 2016 | $ 500 | $300 | 0% | 0% |
| 2017 | 1,000 | 600 | 30 | 50 |
| 2018 | 1,200 | 720 | 18 | 30 |
| 2019 | 1,000 | 600 | 25 | 20 |
| 2020 | 1,500 | 900 | 20 | 20 |

Sun sold equipment with a book value of $800,000 to Pam on January 3, 2020, for $1,600,000. This equipment had a remaining useful life of four years at the time of sale.

Pam uses the equity method to account for its investment in Sun. The financial statements for Pam and Sun are summarized as follows (in thousands):

|  | Pam | Sun |
|---|---|---|
| ***Combined Income and Retained Earnings Statement for the Year Ended December 31, 2020*** |  |  |
| Sales | $26,000 | $11,000 |
| Gain on land | 700 | — |
| Gain on equipment | — | 800 |
| Income from Sun | 1,380 | — |
| Cost of sales | (15,000) | (5,000) |
| Depreciation expense | (3,700) | (2,000) |
| Other expenses | (4,280) | (2,800) |
| Net income | 5,100 | 2,000 |
| Add: Beginning retained earnings | 12,375 | 4,000 |
| Deduct: Dividends | (3,000) | (1,000) |
| Retained earnings December 31 | $14,475 | $ 5,000 |
| ***Balance Sheet at December 31, 2020*** |  |  |
| Cash | $ 1,170 | $ 500 |
| Accounts receivable—net | 2,000 | 1,500 |
| Inventories | 5,000 | 2,000 |
| Land | 4,000 | 1,000 |
| Buildings—net | 15,000 | 4,000 |
| Equipment—net | 10,000 | 4,000 |
| Investment in Sun | 14,405 | — |
| Total assets | $51,575 | $13,000 |

|  | Pam | Sun |
|---|---|---|
| Accounts payable | $ 4,100 | $ 1,000 |
| Other liabilities | 7,000 | 2,000 |
| Capital stock | 26,000 | 5,000 |
| Retained earnings | 14,475 | 5,000 |
| Total equities | $51,575 | $13,000 |

**REQUIRED:** Prepare a consolidation workpaper for Pam Corporation and Subsidiary for the year ended December 31, 2020.

## P6-7
## Workpaper (upstream sales current and previous years)

Pam Corporation acquired an 80 percent interest in Sun Corporation on January 1, 2016, for $108,000 cash, when Sun's capital stock was $100,000 and retained earnings were $10,000. The difference between investment fair value and book value acquired is due to a patent being amortized over a 10-year period.

Separate financial statements for Pam and Sun on December 31, 2019, are summarized as follows (in thousands):

|  | Pam | Sun |
|---|---|---|
| ***Combined Income and Retained Earnings Statement*** | | |
| ***for the Year Ended December 31, 2019*** | | |
| Sales | $ 650 | $120 |
| Income from Sun | 42 | — |
| Cost of sales | (390) | (40) |
| Other expenses | (170) | (30) |
| Net income | 132 | 50 |
| Add: Beginning retained earnings | 95.6 | 20 |
| Deduct: Dividends | (70) | (20) |
| Retained earnings December 31 | $157.6 | $ 50 |
| ***Balance Sheet at December 31, 2019*** | | |
| Cash | $ 58 | $ 20 |
| Accounts receivable | 40 | 20 |
| Inventories | 60 | 35 |
| Plant assets | 290 | 205 |
| Accumulated depreciation | (70) | (100) |
| Investment in Sun | 121.6 | — |
| Total assets | $ 499.6 | $180 |
| Accounts payable | $ 42 | $ 30 |
| Capital stock | 300 | 100 |
| Retained earnings | 157.6 | 50 |
| Total equities | $499.6 | $180 |

### ADDITIONAL INFORMATION

1. Sun's sales include intercompany sales of $8,000, and Pam's December 31, 2019, inventory includes $1,000 profit on goods acquired from Sun. Pam's December 31, 2018, inventory contained $2,000 profit on goods acquired from Sun.

2. Pam owes Sun $4,000 on account.

3. On January 1, 2018, Sun sold plant assets to Pam for $60,000. These assets had a book value of $40,000 on that date and are being depreciated by Pam over five years.

4. Pam uses the equity method to account for its investment in Sun.

**REQUIRED:** Prepare a consolidation workpaper for Pam Corporation and Subsidiary for 2019.

### P6-8
### Consolidation workpaper (upstream sales)

Financial statements for Pam and Sun Corporations for 2016 are as follows (in thousands):

| | Pam | Sun |
|---|---|---|
| **Combined Income and Retained Earnings Statement for the Year Ended December 31, 2016** | | |
| Sales | $210 | $130 |
| Income from Sun | 34.4 | — |
| Gain on sale of land | — | 10 |
| Depreciation expense | (40) | (30) |
| Other expenses | (110) | (60) |
| Net income | 94.4 | 50 |
| Add: Beginning retained earnings | 145.4 | 50 |
| Deduct: Dividends | (30) | — |
| Retained earnings December 31 | $209.8 | $100 |
| **Balance Sheet at December 31, 2016** | | |
| Current assets | $200 | $170 |
| Plant assets | 550 | 350 |
| Accumulated depreciation | (120) | (70) |
| Investment in Sun | 329.8 | — |
| Total assets | $959.8 | $450 |
| Current liabilities | $150 | $ 50 |
| Capital stock | 600 | 300 |
| Retained earnings | 209.8 | 100 |
| Total equities | $959.8 | $450 |

### ADDITIONAL INFORMATION

1. Pam acquired an 80 percent interest in Sun on January 2, 2014, for $290,000, when Sun's stockholders' equity consisted of $300,000 capital stock and no retained earnings. The excess of investment fair value over book value of the net assets acquired related 50 percent to undervalued inventories (subsequently sold in 2014) and 50 percent to goodwill.

2. Sun sold equipment to Pam for $25,000 on January 1, 2015, when the equipment had a book value of $10,000 and a five-year remaining useful life (included in plant assets).

3. During 2016, Sun sold land to Pam at a profit of $10,000 (included in plant assets).

4. Pam uses the equity method to account for its investment in Sun.

**REQUIRED:** Prepare a consolidation workpaper for Pam and Subsidiary for the year ended December 31, 2016.

### P6-9
### Analyze provided separate company and consolidated statements

Separate company and consolidated financial statements for Pop Corporation and its only subsidiary, Son Corporation, for 2017 are summarized here. Pop acquired its interest in Son on January 1, 2016, at a price in excess of book value, which was due to an unrecorded patent.

**POP CORPORATION AND SUBSIDIARY SEPARATE COMPANY AND CONSOLIDATED FINANCIAL STATEMENTS AT AND FOR THE YEAR ENDED DECEMBER 31, 2017 (IN THOUSANDS)**

| | Pop | Son | Consolidated |
|---|---|---|---|
| **Income Statement** | | | |
| Sales | $ 500 | $300 | $ 716 |
| Income from Son | 17.4 | — | — |
| Gain on equipment | 20 | — | — |
| Cost of sales | (200) | (150) | (275) |
| Depreciation expense | (60) | (40) | (95) |
| Other expenses | (77) | (60) | (141) |
| Noncontrolling interest share | — | — | (4.6) |
| Controlling share of net income | $ 200.4 | $ 50 | $ 200.4 |

|  | **Pop** | **Son** | **Consolidated** |
|---|---|---|---|
| ***Retained Earnings Statement*** | | | |
| Retained earnings | $  250 | $120 | $   250 |
| Net income | 200.4 | 50 | 200.4 |
| Dividends | (100) | (30) | (100) |
| Retained earnings | $  350.4 | $140 | $   350.4 |
| ***Balance Sheet*** | | | |
| Cash | $     21.1 | $ 35 | $      56.1 |
| Accounts receivable—net | 50 | 30 | 70 |
| Dividends receivable | 13.5 | — | — |
| Inventories | 90 | 60 | 136 |
| Other current assets | 70 | 40 | 110 |
| Land | 50 | 20 | 70 |
| Buildings—net | 100 | 50 | 150 |
| Equipment—net | 300 | 265 | 550 |
| Investment in Son | 305.8 | — | — |
| Patents | — | — | 32 |
| Total assets | $1,000.4 | $500 | $1,174.1 |
| Accounts payable | $     60 | $ 50 | $   100 |
| Dividends payable | — | 15 | 1.5 |
| Other liabilities | 90 | 95 | 185 |
| Capital stock, $10 par | 500 | 200 | 500 |
| Retained earnings | 350.4 | 140 | 350.4 |
| Noncontrolling interest December 31, 2017 | — | — | 37.2 |
| Total equities | $1,000.4 | $500 | $1,174.1 |

**REQUIRED:** Answer the following questions about the financial statements of Pop and Son.

1. What is Pop's percentage interest in Son Corporation? Provide a computation to explain your answer.
2. Does Pop use a one-line consolidation in accounting for its investment in Son? Explain your answer.
3. Were there intercompany sales between Pop and Son in 2017? If so, show computations.
4. Are there unrealized inventory profits on December 31, 2017? If so, show computations.
5. Provide computations to explain the difference between the combined separate cost of sales and consolidated cost of sales.
6. Explain the difference between combined separate and the consolidated "equipment—net" line item by reconstructing the workpaper entry(s) that was (were) apparently made.
7. Are there intercompany receivables and payables? If so, identify them and state the amounts.
8. Beginning with the noncontrolling interest at January 1, 2017, provide calculations of the $37,200 noncontrolling interest at December 31, 2017.
9. What was the amount of patents at December 31, 2016? Show computations.
10. Provide computations to explain the $305,800 Investment in Son account balance on December 31, 2017.

# PROFESSIONAL RESEARCH ASSIGNMENTS

Answer the following questions by reference to the FASB Codification of Accounting Standards. Include the appropriate reference in your response.

**PR 6-1**  How should a company treat intercompany sales of assets in the consolidated financial statements?

**PR 6-2**  What information should be disclosed about property, plant, and equipment in the consolidated financial statements?

# 7

# Intercompany Profit Transactions—Bonds

Companies frequently hold the debt instruments of affiliates and justify such intercompany borrowing and lending activity on the basis of convenience, efficiency, and flexibility. Even though each affiliate is a separate legal entity, the parent is in a position to negotiate all loans between affiliates, and a decision to borrow from or loan directly to affiliates is really only a decision to transfer funds among affiliates. Direct loans among affiliates produce reciprocal receivable and payable accounts for principal and interest, as well as reciprocal income and expense accounts. Companies eliminate these reciprocal accounts in preparing consolidated financial statements because the intercompany receivables and payables do not reflect assets or obligations of the consolidated entity.

Special problems of accounting for intercompany bonds and notes arise when a company purchases debt instruments of an affiliate from outside entities. Such purchases constitute a retirement of debt from a consolidated viewpoint, even though the debt remains outstanding from the viewpoint of the debtor as a separate legal entity. The issuing affiliate (debtor) accounts for its debt obligations as if they were held by unaffiliated entities, and the purchasing affiliate accounts for its investment in the affiliate's obligations as if they were the obligations of unaffiliated entities. Consolidated statements, however, show the financial position and results of operations as if the issuing corporation had purchased and retired its own debt.

Intercompany debt transactions are not uncommon. For example, Note 16 of the **Dow Chemical Company** annual report discloses $189 million of notes payable to related companies in 2014 (p.108).

Prior experience teaching this material indicates that students often have difficulty with this chapter due to a lack of familiarity with the basics of accounting for bond transactions. You may want to review the bond accounting information included in an Intermediate Accounting textbook before continuing this chapter.

## LEARNING OBJECTIVES

**7.1** Differentiate between intercompany receivables and payables, and assets or liabilities of the consolidated reporting entity.

**7.2** Demonstrate how a consolidated reporting entity constructively retires debt.

**7.3** Defer unrealized gains/losses and later recognize realized gains/losses on bond transfers between parent and subsidiary.

**7.4** Calculate noncontrolling interest share in the presence of intercompany gains/losses on debt transfers.

## INTERCOMPANY BOND TRANSACTIONS

At the time a company issues bonds, its bond liability will reflect the current market rate of interest. However, subsequent changes in the market rate of interest create a disparity between the book value and the market value of that liability. If the market rate of interest increases, the market value of the liability decreases. Unless the fair value option for liabilities is elected, the gain is *not recognized* on the issuer's books under generally accepted accounting principles (GAAP). Similarly, a decline in the market rate of interest gives rise to an *unrealized* loss that is *not recognized*. These unrecognized gains and losses are disclosed in the financial statements or footnotes in accordance with GAAP. (ASC 825-10-55) GAAP offers a fair value option for liabilities, which, if elected, permits recognition of gains and losses due to changes in market values.

LEARNING OBJECTIVE **7.1**

If the fair value option is not used, an issuing firm can recognize previously unrecognized gains or losses on outstanding bonds by retiring the outstanding bonds. The parent, which controls all debt retirement and other decisions for the consolidated entity, has the following options:

1. The *issuer* (parent or subsidiary) can use its available resources to purchase and *retire its own bonds*.

2. The *issuer* (parent or subsidiary) can borrow money from unaffiliated entities at the market rate of interest and use the proceeds to *retire its own bonds*. (This option constitutes refunding.)

3. The *issuer* can borrow money from an affiliate and use the proceeds to *retire its own bonds*.

4. An *affiliate* (parent or subsidiary) can purchase the bonds of the issuer from outside entities, in which case the bonds are *constructively retired*.

The first three options result in an **actual retirement** of the bonds. If the issuer is not using the fair value option, the issuer recognizes the previously unrecognized gain or loss in these three situations and includes it appropriately in measuring consolidated net income. The fourth option results in a **constructive retirement**. This means that the bonds are retired for consolidated statement purposes because the bond investment and payable items of the parent and the subsidiary are reciprocals that must be eliminated in consolidation. The difference between the book value of the bond liability and the purchase price of the bond investment is a gain or loss for consolidated statement purposes. It is also a gain or loss for parent accounting under the equity method. The gain or loss is not recognized on the books of the issuer, whose bonds are held as an investment by the purchasing affiliate.

Although the constructive retirement is different in form, the substance of the debt extinguishment is the same as for the other three options from the consolidated viewpoint. The effect of a constructive retirement on consolidated statements is the same as for an actual retirement. The gain or loss on constructive retirement of bonds payable is a gain or loss of the issuer that has been realized by changes in the market rate of interest after the bonds were issued, and it is recognized for consolidated statement purposes when the bonds are repurchased and held within the consolidated entity.

## CONSTRUCTIVE GAINS AND LOSSES ON INTERCOMPANY BONDS

If the price paid by an affiliate to acquire the debt of another is greater than the book value of the liability (par value plus unamortized premium or less unamortized discount and issuance costs), a constructive loss on retirement of debt occurs. Alternatively, if the price paid is less than the book value of the debt, a constructive gain results. The gain or loss is referred to as *constructive* because it is a gain or loss that is realized and recognized from the viewpoint of the consolidated entity, but it is not recorded on the separate books of the affiliates at the time of purchase.

Constructive gains and losses on bonds are (1) realized gains and losses from the consolidated viewpoint (2) that arise when a company purchases the bonds of an affiliate (3) from other entities (4) at a price other than the book value of the bonds. No gains or losses result from the purchase of an affiliate's bonds at book value or from direct lending and borrowing between affiliates.

Some accounting theorists argue that constructive gains and losses on intercompany bond transactions should be allocated between the purchasing and issuing affiliates according to the par value of the bonds. For example, if Parent pays $99,000 for $100,000 par of Subsidiary's outstanding bonds with $2,000 unamortized premium, they would allocate the $3,000 constructive gain ($102,000 less $99,000) $1,000 to Parent and $2,000 to Subsidiary. This is known as **par value theory**.

The alternative to the par value theory is **agency theory**, under which the affiliate that purchases the intercompany bonds acts as agent for the issuer, under directions from Parent management. Agency theory assigns the $3,000 constructive gain to the subsidiary (the issuer), and the consolidated statement effect is the same as if the subsidiary had purchased its own bonds for

$99,000. Although not supported by a separate theory, constructive gains and losses are sometimes assigned 100 percent to the parent on the basis of expediency. The accounting is less complicated.

Changes in market interest rates generate gains or losses for a debt issuer, so accounting procedures should assign such gains and losses to the issuer, irrespective of the form of the transaction (direct retirement by the issuer or purchase by an affiliate). Failure to assign the full amount of a constructive gain or loss to the issuer results in recognizing form over substance in debt retirement transactions. The substance of a transaction should be considered over its form (incidentally, this is what consolidation is all about); therefore, agency theory is conceptually superior, and, accordingly, we assign constructive gains and losses to the issuer throughout this text.

Most long-term corporate debt is in the form of outstanding bonds, so the analysis in this chapter relates to bonds even though it also applies to long-term notes and other types of debt instruments. Straight-line rather than effective interest amortization of premiums and discounts is used in the illustrations throughout the chapter to make the illustrations easier to follow and to help students learn the concepts involved without the added complexity of effective interest computations. It should be understood that the *effective interest method is generally superior* to the straight-line method.[1] This discussion of intercompany bond transactions among affiliates also applies to investments accounted for under the equity method.

The first illustration in this section assumes that a subsidiary purchases parent bonds (the parent company is the bond issuer) and assigns the constructive gain or loss to the parent. In the second illustration, the parent purchases bonds issued by a subsidiary, and we assign the constructive gain or loss to the subsidiary.

## Subsidiary Acquisition of Parent Bonds

LEARNING OBJECTIVE **7.2**

Son Corporation is an 80 percent–owned affiliate of Pop Corporation, and Pop issues $2,000,000 par of 10 percent, 10-year bonds at par value to the public on December 30, 2015. On December 31, 2016, Son purchases $200,000 of the bonds for $209,000 in the open market. Son's purchase results in the constructive retirement of $200,000 of Pop bonds and a constructive loss of $9,000 ($209,000 paid to retire bonds with a book value of $200,000).

Pop adjusts investment income and investment accounts at December 31, 2016 to record the constructive loss under the equity method. The entry on Pop's books is:

| | | |
|---|---|---|
| Income from Son (−R, −SE) | 9,000 | |
|     Investment in Son (−A) | | 9,000 |
|     To adjust income from Son for the constructive loss on bonds. | | |

Without this entry, the income of Pop on an equity basis would not equal its share of consolidated net income.

We charge the $9,000 constructive loss against Pop's share of Son's reported income because Pop is the bond issuer. Agency theory assigns the full amount of any constructive gain or loss on bonds to the issuer. The parent is the issuer, so the analysis is similar to one for a downstream sale, and we charge the full amount to Pop.

The $9,000 constructive loss appears in the consolidated income statement of Pop and Subsidiary for 2016, and the 10 percent bond issue is reported at $1,800,000 in the consolidated balance sheet at December 31, 2016. The following workpaper adjustment accomplishes this:

| | | |
|---|---|---|
| **Loss on constructive retirement of bonds (Lo, −SE)** | **9,000** | |
| **10% bonds payable (−L)** | **200,000** | |
|     **Investment in bonds (−A)** | | **209,000** |
| **To enter loss and eliminate reciprocal bond investment and liability amounts.** | | |

---

[1]GAAP (ASC 835-30-15) generally requires the effective interest method of amortization, but it does not apply to transactions between parent and subsidiary companies and between subsidiaries of a common parent.

## Parent Acquisition of Subsidiary Bonds

Assume that Son sold $2,000,000 par of 10 percent, 10-year bonds to the public at par on December 30, 2015, and that Pop acquires $200,000 par of these bonds for $209,000 on December 31, 2016, in the open market. The purchase by Pop results in a constructive retirement of $200,000 par of Son bonds and a constructive loss of $9,000 to the consolidated entity. We assign only 80 percent of the constructive loss to controlling stockholders because the purchase of subsidiary bonds is equivalent to an upstream sale, in which the intercompany transactions affect noncontrolling interest share.

In accounting for its investment in Son under the equity method, Pop recognizes 80 percent of the constructive loss at December 31, 2016 with the following entry:

| | | |
|---|---|---|
| Income from Son (−R, −SE) | 7,200 | |
| Investment in Son (−A) | | 7,200 |
| Recognize the constructive loss on acquisition of Son's bonds. | | |

The workpaper adjustment in the year of intercompany bond purchase is the same as that illustrated for the intercompany purchase of Pop's bonds. However, the $7,200 decrease in consolidated net income consists of the $9,000 constructive loss less the $1,800 noncontrolling interest share of the loss, which reduces noncontrolling interest share.

To summarize, when the parent is the issuer, no allocation of gains and losses from intercompany bond transactions is necessary. When the subsidiary is the issuer, intercompany gains and losses on bonds must be allocated between controlling and noncontrolling interest shares in the consolidated income statement. In a one-line consolidation, the parent company recognizes only its proportionate share of the constructive gain or loss on purchases of bonds issued by a subsidiary.

## PARENT BONDS PURCHASED BY SUBSIDIARY

A constructive retirement of parent bonds occurs when an affiliate purchases outstanding bonds of the parent. The purchaser records the amount paid as an investment in bonds. This is the only entry made by either the purchaser or the issuer at the time of the intercompany purchase. The separate accounts of the affiliates do *not* record any gain or loss that results from the constructive retirement, although it is included in investment income on the parent's books under the equity method. The difference between the bond liability and bond investment accounts on the books of the parent and subsidiary reflects the constructive gain or loss.

To illustrate, assume that Sun is a 70 percent–owned subsidiary of Pam, acquired at a fair value equal to its $6,300,000 book value on December 31, 2016, when Sun had capital stock of $5,000,000 and retained earnings of $4,000,000.

Pam has $10,000,000 par of 10 percent bonds outstanding with a $100,000 unamortized premium on January 2, 2017, at which time Sun purchases $1,000,000 par of these bonds for $950,000 from an investment broker. The purchase results in a constructive retirement of 10 percent of Pam's bonds and a $60,000 constructive gain, computed as follows (in thousands):

| | |
|---|---|
| Book value of bonds purchased | $1,010 |
| [10% × ($10,000,000 par + $100,000 premium)] | |
| Less: Purchase price | (950) |
| Constructive gain on bond retirement | $ 60 |

The only entry Sun makes when purchasing the Pam bonds is (in thousands):

| | | |
|---|---|---|
| Investment in Pam bonds (+A) | 950 | |
| Cash (−A) | | 950 |
| To record acquisition of Pam bonds at 95, and classify as a held to maturity investment. | | |

## Equity Method

If we prepare consolidated financial statements immediately after the constructive retirement, the workpaper entry to eliminate the intercompany bond investment and liability balances[2] includes the $60,000 gain as follows (in thousands):

| *January 2, 2017* | | |
|---|---|---|
| 10% bonds payable (− L) | 1,010 | |
|     Investment in Pam bonds (− A) | | 950 |
|     Gain on retirement of bonds (Ga, + SE) | | 60 |

As a result of this workpaper entry, the Investment in Pam bonds is eliminated, the consolidated income statement reflects the gain and the consolidated balance sheet shows the bond liability to holders outside the consolidated entity at $9,090,000 ($9,000,000 par plus $90,000 unamortized premium).

During 2017, Pam amortizes the bond premium on its books and Sun amortizes the discount on its bond investment. Assuming that interest is paid on January 1 and July 1, that the bonds mature on January 1, 2022 (five years after purchase), and that straight-line amortization is used at year end, Pam amortizes 20 percent of the bond premium annually and Sun amortizes 20 percent of the discount annually as follows (in thousands):

### PAM'S BOOKS

| *July 1* | | |
|---|---|---|
| Interest expense (E, −SE) | 500 | |
|     Cash (−A) | | 500 |
|     ($10,000,000 par × 10% × 1/2 year) | | |
| *December 31* | | |
| Interest expense (E, −SE) | 500 | |
|     Interest payable (+L) | | 500 |
|     ($10,000,000 par × 10% × 1/2 year) | | |
| *December 31* | | |
| Bonds payable (−L) | 20 | |
|     Interest expense (−E, +SE) | | 20 |
|     ($100,000 premium ÷ 5 years) | | |

### SUN'S BOOKS

| *July 1* | | |
|---|---|---|
| Cash (+A) | 50 | |
|     Interest income (R, +SE) | | 50 |
|     ($1,000,000 par × 10% × 1/2 year) | | |
| *December 31* | | |
| Interest receivable (+A) | 50 | |
|     Interest income (R, +SE) | | 50 |
|     ($1,000,000 par × 10% × 1/2 year) | | |
| *December 31* | | |
| Investment in Pam bonds (+A) | 10 | |
|     Interest income (R, +SE) | | 10 |
|     ($50,000 discount ÷ 5 years) | | |

At December 31, 2017, after posting the foregoing entries, the ledgers of Pam and Sun show the following balances (in thousands):

| **Pam's Books** | |
|---|---|
| 10% bonds payable (including $80,000 unamortized premium) | $10,080 |
| Interest expense | 980 |
| **Sun's Books** | |
| Investment in Pam bonds | $  960 |
| Interest income | $  110 |

---

[2]We employ the net method in accounting for bonds throughout the chapter. We do not separately record premiums and discounts.

The difference between the bond investment ($960,000) and 10 percent of Pam's bond liability ($1,008,000) is now $48,000 rather than $60,000. The reason is that there has been a piecemeal realization and recognition of the constructive gain on the separate books of Pam and Sun. This piecemeal recognition occurred during 2017 as Pam amortized the $2,000 premium and Sun amortized the $10,000 discount on bonds that were constructively retired on January 2, 2017. This difference is reflected in interest expense and income accounts relating to the constructively retired bonds. That is, interest income of $110,000 less 10 percent of $980,000 interest expense equals $12,000, or 20 percent of the original constructive gain. The workpaper entries to eliminate reciprocal bond accounts at December 31, 2017, are (in thousands):

| | | | |
|---|---|---|---|
| a | 10% bonds payable (−L) | 1,008 | |
| | Investment in Pam bonds (−A) | | 960 |
| | Gain on retirement of bonds (Ga, +SE) | | 48 |
| b | Interest income (−R, −SE) | 110 | |
| | Interest expense (−E, +SE) | | 98 |
| | Gain on retirement of bonds (Ga, +SE) | | 12 |
| f | Interest payable (−L) | 50 | |
| | Interest receivable (−A) | | 50 |

Because 2017 is the year in which the bonds are constructively retired, the combined gain that is entered by the workpaper entries is $60,000, the original gain. If the workpaper entries were combined, the gain would appear as a single amount. Note that the amount of piecemeal recognition of a constructive gain or loss is always the difference between the intercompany interest expense and income amounts that are eliminated. The fact that the piecemeal recognition was 20 percent of the $60,000 gain is the result of straight-line amortization, a relationship that would not hold under the effective interest method.

The first three columns of the consolidation workpaper in Exhibit 7-1 include financial statements for Pam and Sun. Except for the Investment in Sun and the Income from Sun accounts, the amounts shown reflect all previous assumptions and computations.

We compute Pam's investment income of $202,000 as follows (in thousands):

| | |
|---|---|
| 70% of Sun's reported income of $220,000 | $154 |
| Add: Constructive gain on bonds | 60 |
| | 214 |
| Less: Piecemeal recognition of constructive gain ($60,000 ÷ 5 years) | 12 |
| Income from Sun | $202 |

On December 31, 2017, separate entries on the books of Pam to record the investment income from Sun under a one-line consolidation are as follows (in thousands):

| | | |
|---|---|---|
| Investment in Sun (+A) | 154 | |
| Income from Sun (R, +SE) | | 154 |

To record investment income from Sun ($220,000 × 70%)

| | | |
|---|---|---|
| Investment in Sun (+A) | 60 | |
| Income from Sun (R, +SE) | | 60 |

To adjust income from Sun for 100% of the $60,000 constructive gain on bonds.

| | | |
|---|---|---|
| Income from Sun (−R, −SE) | 12 | |
| Investment in Sun (−A) | | 12 |

To adjust income from Sun for the piecemeal recognition of the constructive gain on bonds that occurred during 2017. (Either $60,000 gain ÷ 5 years or $110,000 interest income − $98,000 interest expense)

We add the $60,000 constructive gain to Pam's share of the reported income of Sun because it is realized from the consolidated viewpoint. We recognize this constructive gain on the books of the

**EXHIBIT 7-1**

Parent-Company Bonds
Held by Subsidiary

**PAM CORPORATION AND SUBSIDIARY CONSOLIDATION WORKPAPER FOR THE YEAR ENDED DECEMBER 31, 2017 (IN THOUSANDS)**

| | Pam | 70% Sun | Adjustments and Eliminations Debits | Adjustments and Eliminations Credits | Consolidated Statements |
|---|---|---|---|---|---|
| *Income Statement* Sales | $ 4,000 | $ 2,000 | | | $ 6,000 |
| Income from Sun | 202 | | c   202 | | |
| Gain on retirement of bonds | | | | a    48 b    12 | 60 |
| Interest income | | 110 | b   110 | | |
| Expenses including cost of sales | (1,910) | (1,890) | | | (3,800) |
| Interest expense | (980) | | | b    98 | (882) |
| Noncontrolling interest share ($220 × 30%) | | | d    66 | | (66) |
| **Controlling interest share** | **$ 1,312** | **$   220** | | | **$ 1,312** |
| *Retained Earnings Statement* Retained earnings—Pam | $ 4,900 | | | | $ 4,900 |
| Retained earnings—Sun | | $ 4,000 | e 4,000 | | |
| **Add: Controlling interest share** | 1,312 | 220 | | | 1,312 |
| **Retained earnings—December 31** | **$ 6,212** | **$ 4,220** | | | **$ 6,212** |
| *Balance Sheet* Other assets | $39,880 | $19,100 | | | $58,980 |
| Interest receivable | | 50 | | f    50 | |
| Investment in Sun | 6,502 | | | c   202 e 6,300 | |
| Investment in Pam bonds | | 960 | | a   960 | |
| | $46,382 | $20,110 | | | $58,980 |
| Other liabilities | $ 9,590 | $10,890 | | | $20,480 |
| Interest payable | 500 | | f    50 | | 450 |
| 10% bond payable | 10,080 | | a 1,008 | | 9,072 |
| Common stock | 20,000 | 5,000 | e 5,000 | | 20,000 |
| **Retained earnings** | 6,212 | 4,220 | | | 6,212 |
| | $46,382 | $20,110 | | | |
| Noncontrolling interest | | | | d    66 e 2,700 | 2,766 |
| | | | 10,436 | 10,436 | $58,980 |

affiliates as they continue to account for the $1,000,000 par of bonds constructively retired on January 2, 2017.

Pam's investment income for 2017 increases by $48,000 from the constructive retirement of the bonds ($60,000 constructive gain less $12,000 piecemeal recognition of the gain). In the years 2018, 2019, 2020, and 2021, Pam's investment income will be reduced $12,000 each year as the constructive gain is recognized on the books of Pam and Sun. In other words, in addition to recording its share of the reported income of Sun in each of these four years, Pam makes the following entry to adjust its income from Sun for the piecemeal recognition of the constructive gain (in thousands):

$$\text{Income from Sun } (-R, -SE) \quad 12$$
$$\text{Investment in Sun } (-A) \qquad 12$$

At January 1, 2022, the maturity date of the bonds, the full amount of the constructive gain will have been recognized, and Pam's Investment in Sun account will equal 70 percent of the equity of Sun.

The following workpaper entries consolidate the financial statements of Pam Corporation and Subsidiary at December 31, 2017 (see Exhibit 7-1) (in thousands):

| | | | |
|---|---|---|---|
| a | **10% bonds payable ($-$L)** | 1,008 | |
| | Gain on retirement of bonds (Ga, $+$SE) | | 48 |
| | Investment in Pam bonds ($-$A) | | 960 |
| | To enter gain and eliminate reciprocal bond investment and bond liability amounts, including unamortized premium. | | |
| b | **Interest income ($-$R, $-$SE)** | 110 | |
| | Interest expense ($-$E, $+$SE) | | 98 |
| | Gain on retirement of bonds (Ga, $+$SE) | | 12 |
| | To eliminate reciprocal interest income and interest expense amounts. | | |
| c | **Income from Sun ($-$R, $-$SE)** | 202 | |
| | Investment in Sun ($-$A) | | 202 |
| | To establish reciprocity, eliminate investment income and adjust the investment account to its beginning of the period balance. | | |
| d | **Noncontrolling interest share ($-$SE)** | 66 | |
| | Noncontrolling interest ($+$SE) | | 66 |
| | To enter noncontrolling interest share of Sun's income. | | |
| e | **Retained earnings—Sun ($-$SE)** | 4,000 | |
| | **Common stock—Sun ($-$SE)** | 5,000 | |
| | Investment in Sun ($-$A) | | 6,300 |
| | Noncontrolling interest January 1, 2017 ($+$SE) | | 2,700 |
| | To eliminate reciprocal investment and equity accounts and set up beginning noncontrolling interest. | | |
| f | **Interest payable ($-$L)** | 50 | |
| | Interest receivable ($-$A) | | 50 |
| | To eliminate reciprocal interest payable and interest receivable amounts. | | |

The first workpaper entry eliminates 10 percent of Pam's bond liability and 100 percent of Sun's bond investment and also enters $48,000 of the gain on retirement of bonds. This $48,000 is that part of the $60,000 constructive gain not recognized on the separate books of Pam and Sun as of December 31, 2017.

Entry b eliminates reciprocal interest expense and income. The difference between the interest expense and income amounts represents that part of the constructive gain recognized on the books of Pam and Sun through amortization in 2017. This amount is $12,000, and when credited to the gain on retirement of bonds, it brings the gain up to the original $60,000. As mentioned earlier, if entries a and b had been combined, we would enter the constructive gain in the workpaper as one amount.

Workpaper entry c eliminates investment income and adjusts the Investment in Sun account to its beginning-of-the-period balance. Entry d enters the noncontrolling interest share of Sun's net income. Entry e eliminates Pam's Investment in Sun and the equity accounts of Sun and establishes the beginning-of-the-period noncontrolling interest.

Entry f of the consolidation workpaper eliminates reciprocal interest payable and receivable amounts on the intercompany bonds. This results in showing interest payable in the consolidated balance sheet at $450,000, the nominal interest payable for one-half year on the $9,000,000 par of bonds held outside of the consolidated entity. Noncontrolling interest share computations in Exhibit 7-1 are not affected by the intercompany bond holdings. This is because Pam issued the bonds, and the full amount of the constructive gain is assigned to the issuer.

## Effect on Consolidated Statements in Subsequent Years

LEARNING OBJECTIVE **7.3**

In subsequent years until the actual maturity of the bonds, Pam and Sun continue to account for the bonds on their separate books—reporting interest expense (Pam) of $98,000 and interest income (Sun) of $110,000. The $12,000 difference is recognized on Pam's books as an adjustment of investment income. Consolidated financial statements for 2018 through 2021 eliminate all balances related to the intercompany bonds. Exhibit 7-2 shows the year-end balances related to the intercompany bonds on the books of Pam and Sun.

A single adjusting and eliminating entry in the consolidation workpaper at December 31, 2018, could be used for items relating to the intercompany bonds (in thousands):

| | | |
|---|---:|---:|
| Interest income ($-$R, $-$SE) | 110 | |
| Interest payable ($-$L) | 50 | |
| 10% bonds payable ($-$L) | 1,006 | |
|     Interest expense ($-$E, $+$SE) | | 98 |
|     Interest receivable ($-$A) | | 50 |
|     Investment in Pam bonds ($-$A) | | 970 |
|     Investment in Sun ($-$A) | | 48 |

This entry eliminates reciprocal interest income and expense amounts, reciprocal interest receivable and payable amounts, and reciprocal bond investment and liability amounts. We credit the remaining difference of $48,000 to the Investment in Sun account to establish reciprocity between Pam's Investment in Sun and the equity accounts of Sun at the beginning of 2018. This is necessary because Pam increased its investment account in 2017 when it adjusted its investment income account for the constructive gain. In other words, Pam's Investment in Sun account exceeded its underlying book value in Sun by $48,000 at December 31, 2017. The 2018 workpaper entry to adjust the Investment in Sun account establishes reciprocity with the equity accounts of Sun and is entered in the consolidation workpaper before eliminating reciprocal investment and equity amounts.

Similar workpaper adjustments are necessary in 2019, 2020, and 2021. For example, the consolidation workpaper credit to the Investment in Sun account will be $36,000 in 2019, $24,000 in 2020, and $12,000 in 2021.

| Pam's Books (in Thousands) | | | | | | | |
|---|---|---|---|---|---|---|---|
| | | | | December 31, | | | |
| | | 2018 | | 2019 | | 2020 | 2021 |
| Interest expense | $ | 980 | $ | 980 | $ | 980 | $ 980 |
| Interest payable | | 500 | | 500 | | 500 | 500 |
| Bonds payable | | 10,060 | | 10,040 | | 10,020 | 10,000 |

| Sun's Books (in Thousands) | | | | | | | |
|---|---|---|---|---|---|---|---|
| | | | | December 31, | | | |
| | | 2018 | | 2019 | | 2020 | 2021 |
| Interest income | $ | 110 | $ | 110 | $ | 110 | $ 110 |
| Interest receivable | | 50 | | 50 | | 50 | 50 |
| Investment in Pam bonds | | 970 | | 980 | | 990 | 1,000 |

**EXHIBIT 7-2**

**Year-End Account Balances Relating to Intercompany Bonds**

## PARENT PURCHASES SUBSIDIARY BONDS

The illustration in this section is similar to that for Pam and Sun, except that the subsidiary is the issuer and the constructive retirement of bonds results in a loss to the consolidated entity.

Pop Corporation owns 90 percent of the voting common stock of Son Corporation. Pop purchased its interest in Son a number of years ago at its book value of $9,225,000. Son's capital stock was $10,000,000 and its retained earnings were $250,000 on the acquisition date.

At December 31, 2016, Son had $10,000,000 par of 10 percent bonds outstanding with an unamortized discount of $300,000. The bonds pay interest on January 1 and July 1 of each year, and they mature in five years on January 1, 2022.

On January 2, 2017, Pop purchases 50 percent of Son's outstanding bonds for $5,150,000 cash and classifies the bonds as a held-to-maturity investment. This is a constructive retirement and results in a loss of $300,000 from the viewpoint of the consolidated entity. The consolidated entity retires a liability of $4,850,000 (50% of the $9,700,000 book value of the bonds) at a cost of $5,150,000. We assign the loss to Son Corporation under the theory that the parent acts as agent for Son, the issuer, in all intercompany transactions.

During 2017, Son Corporation records interest expense on the bonds of $1,060,000 [($10,000,000 par $\times$ 10%) + $60,000 discount amortization]. Of this interest expense, $530,000 relates to the intercompany bonds. Pop Corporation records interest income from its investment in bonds during 2017 of $470,000 [($5,000,000 par $\times$ 10%) − $30,000 premium amortization]. The $60,000 difference between the interest expense and the income on the intercompany bonds reflects recognition of one-fifth of the constructive loss during 2017. At December 31, 2017, the books of Pop and Son have not recognized $240,000 of the constructive loss through premium amortization (Pop's books) and discount amortization (Son's books).

### Equity Method

Son reports net income of $750,000 for 2017, and Pop computes its $459,000 income from Son as follows (in thousands):

| | |
|---|---:|
| 90% of Son's $750,000 reported income | $ 675 |
| Deduct: $300,000 constructive loss $\times$ 90% | (270) |
| Add: $60,000 recognition of constructive loss $\times$ 90% | 54 |
| Investment income from Son | $ 459 |

The journal entries Pop makes to account for its investment in Son during 2017 follow (in thousands):

*December 31, 2017*

| | | |
|---|---:|---:|
| Investment in Son (+A) | 675 | |
|     Income from Son (R, +SE) | | 675 |

   To record 90% of Son's reported income for 2017.

*December 31, 2017*

| | | |
|---|---:|---:|
| Income from Son (−R, −SE) | 270 | |
|     Investment in Son (−A) | | 270 |

   To adjust investment income from Son for 90% of the
    loss on the constructive retirement of Son's bonds.
    (This entry could be made on January 2, 2017.)

*December 31, 2017*

| | | |
|---|---:|---:|
| Investment in Son (+A) | 54 | |
|     Income from Son (R, +SE) | | 54 |

   To adjust investment income from Son for 90% of the
    $60,000 piecemeal recognition of the constructive loss
    on Son bonds during 2017.

In future years until the bonds mature, Pop computes income from Son by adding $54,000 annually to its share of the reported income of Son.

Pop's Investment in Son account at December 31, 2017, has a balance of $10,584,000. This balance equals the underlying book value of Pop's investment in Son at January 1, 2017, plus $459,000 investment income from Son for 2017 (in thousands):

| | |
|---|---|
| Investment in Son January 1 ($11,250,000 × 90%) | $10,125 |
| Add: Income from Son | 459 |
| Investment in Son December 31 | $10,584 |

Exhibit 7-3 presents a consolidated financial statement workpaper for Pop and Subsidiary. The constructive loss of $300,000 on the intercompany bonds appears in the consolidated income

**POP CORPORATION AND SUBSIDIARY CONSOLIDATION WORKPAPER FOR THE YEAR ENDED DECEMBER 31, 2017 (IN THOUSANDS)**

**EXHIBIT 7-3**

Subsidiary Bonds Held by Parent

| | Pop | 90% Son | Adjustments and Eliminations Debits | Credits | Consolidated Statements |
|---|---|---|---|---|---|
| *Income Statement* | | | | | |
| Sales | $25,750 | $14,250 | | | $40,000 |
| Income from Son | 459 | | c 459 | | |
| Interest income | 470 | | b 470 | | |
| Expenses including cost of sales | (21,679) | (12,440) | | | (34,119) |
| Interest expense | | (1,060) | | b 530 | (530) |
| Loss on retirement of bonds | | | a 240, b 60 | | (300) |
| Noncontrolling interest share ($750 − $300 + $60) × 10% | | | f 51 | | (51) |
| **Controlling interest share** | **$ 5,000** | **$ 750** | | | **$ 5,000** |
| *Retained Earnings Statement* | | | | | |
| Retained earnings—Pop | $13,000 | | | | $13,000 |
| Retained earnings—Son | | $ 1,250 | d 1,250 | | |
| **Add: Controlling interest share** | **5,000** | **750** | | | **5,000** |
| **Retained earnings—December 31** | **$18,000** | **$ 2,000** | | | **$18,000** |
| *Balance Sheet* | | | | | |
| Other assets | $34,046 | $25,000 | | | $59,046 |
| Interest receivable | 250 | | | e 250 | |
| Investment in Son | 10,584 | | | c 459, d 10,125 | |
| Investment in Son bonds | 5,120 | | | a 5,120 | |
| | $50,000 | $25,000 | | | $59,046 |
| Other liabilities | $12,000 | $ 2,740 | | | $14,740 |
| Interest payable | | 500 | e 250 | | 250 |
| 10% bonds payable | | 9,760 | a 4,880 | | 4,880 |
| Capital stock | 20,000 | 10,000 | d 10,000 | | 20,000 |
| **Retained earnings** | **18,000** | **2,000** | | | **18,000** |
| | $50,000 | $25,000 | | | |
| Noncontrolling interest | | | | f 51, d 1,125 | 1,176 |
| | | | 17,660 | 17,660 | $59,046 |

statement for 2017. Because $5,000,000 par of Son's bonds have been constructively retired, the consolidated balance sheet reports bonds payable of $4,880,000 ($5,000,000 par less the unamortized discount of $120,000) related to the bonds held outside of the consolidated entity.

<table>
<tr><td>LEARNING<br>OBJECTIVE</td><td>7.4</td></tr>
</table>

**EFFECT OF CONSTRUCTIVE LOSS ON NONCONTROLLING INTEREST SHARE AND CONSOLIDATED NET INCOME**   Noncontrolling interest share for 2017 is $51,000 [($750,000 − $300,000 + $60,000) × 10%]. We assign the constructive loss to Son. We charge the noncontrolling interest for 10 percent of the $300,000 constructive loss and credit it for 10 percent of the $60,000 piecemeal recognition of the constructive loss during 2017. Accordingly, noncontrolling interest share for 2017 is 10 percent of Son's $510,000 realized income, and not 10 percent of Son's $750,000 reported net income.

The constructive retirement of bonds payable reduces the controlling interest share of consolidated net income for 2017 by $216,000. We reflect this reduction in the consolidated income statement through the inclusion of the $300,000 loss on the constructive retirement of the bonds, elimination of interest income of $470,000 and interest expense of $530,000, and reduction of noncontrolling interest share by $24,000 (from $75,000 based on reported net income of Son to $51,000 noncontrolling interest share for the year). An analysis of the effect follows (in thousands):

**Controlling Interest Share of Consolidated Net Income—2017**

| | |
|---|---:|
| *Decreased by:* | |
| Constructive loss | $300 |
| Elimination of interest income | 470 |
| Total decreases | $770 |
| *Increased by:* | |
| Elimination of interest expense | $530 |
| Reduction of noncontrolling interest share ($75,000 − $51,000) | 24 |
| Total increases | $554 |
| Effect on controlling interest share for 2017 | $216 |

The reduction of noncontrolling interest share is similar to the reduction of other expenses.

**CONSOLIDATION WORKPAPER ENTRIES**   The entries shown in the consolidation workpaper of Exhibit 7-3 are similar to those in the Pam–Sun illustration in Exhibit 7-1 except for the amounts and the shift to a constructive loss situation. As in the previous illustration, workpaper entries a, b, and e are separated for illustrative purposes, but they could be combined into a single entry as follows (in thousands):

| | | |
|---|---:|---:|
| Loss on retirement of bonds (Lo, −SE) | 300 | |
| Interest payable (−L) | 250 | |
| Interest income (−R, −SE) | 470 | |
| 10% bonds payable (−L) | 4,880 | |
|     Investment in Son bonds (−A) | | 5,120 |
|     Interest receivable (−A) | | 250 |
|     Interest expense (−E, +SE) | | 530 |

## Effect on Consolidated Statements in Subsequent Years

The loss on the retirement of bonds only appears in the consolidated income statement in the year in which we constructively retire the bonds. In subsequent years, we allocate the unrecognized portion of the constructive loss between the investment account (the controlling interest) and noncontrolling interest. For example, the combined workpaper entry to eliminate the bond investment and bonds payable and the interest income and interest expense amounts at December 31, 2018, would be as follows (in thousands):

| | | | |
|---|---|---|---|
| Investment in Son (+A) | 216 | | |
| Noncontrolling interest (−SE) | 24 | | |
| Interest income (−R, −SE) | 470 | | |
| 10% bonds payable (−L) | 4,910 | | |
|     Investment in Son bonds (−A) | | | 5,090 |
|     Interest expense (−E, +SE) | | | 530 |

The assignment of the constructive loss to Son dictates allocation of the unrecognized loss between the investment in Son ($216,000) and noncontrolling interest ($24,000). The loss is a subsidiary loss, so noncontrolling interest must share in the loss. In computing noncontrolling interest share for 2018, we add 10 percent of the $60,000 constructive loss recognized in 2018 to the noncontrolling interest share of income reported by Son. We require this adjustment of noncontrolling interest share each year through 2021. By December 31, 2021, the bond investment will decrease to $5,000,000 through premium amortization, and the intercompany bond liability will increase to $5,000,000 through discount amortization.

The intercompany bond holdings increase the controlling share of consolidated net income by $54,000 each year for 2018 through 2021. Under the equity method, Pop's income from Son and net income also increase by $54,000 in each of the years. Computations of the controlling share of consolidated net income effect follow (in thousands):

**Controlling Share of Consolidated Net Income—2018 through 2021**

| | |
|---|---|
| *Increased by:* | |
| Elimination of interest expense | $530 |
| *Decreased by:* | |
| Elimination of interest income | $470 |
| Increase in noncontrolling interest share<br>    ($60,000 piecemeal recognition × 10%) | 6 |
| Total decreases | $476 |
| Annual effect on controlling share | $ 54 |

Exhibit 7-4 summarizes the intercompany bond account balances that appear on the books of Pop and Son at year-end 2018 through 2021. The exhibit also summarizes the required workpaper

**SUMMARY OF INTERCOMPANY BOND ACCOUNT BALANCES ON SEPARATE BOOKS**

| December 31, | 2018 | 2019 | 2020 | 2021 |
|---|---|---|---|---|
| **Pop's Books (in Thousands)** | | | | |
| Investment in Son bonds | $5,090 | $5,060 | $5,030 | $ 5,000 |
| Interest income | 470 | 470 | 470 | 470 |
| Interest receivable | 250 | 250 | 250 | 250 |
| **Son's Books (in Thousands)** | | | | |
| 10% bonds payable | $9,820 | $9,880 | $9,940 | $10,000 |
| Interest expense | 1,060 | 1,060 | 1,060 | 1,060 |
| Interest payable | 500 | 500 | 500 | 500 |

*(continued)*

## SUMMARY OF CONSOLIDATION WORKPAPER ADJUSTMENTS

| December 31, | 2018 | 2019 | 2020 | 2021 |
|---|---|---|---|---|
| *Debits (in Thousands)* | | | | |
| Investment in Son (90%)* | $ 216 | $ 162 | $ 108 | $  54 |
| Noncontrolling interest (10%)* | 24 | 18 | 12 | 6 |
| Interest income | 470 | 470 | 470 | 470 |
| 10% bonds payable** | 4,910 | 4,940 | 4,970 | 5,000 |
| Interest payable | 250 | 250 | 250 | 250 |
| *Credits (in Thousands)* | | | | |
| Investment in Son bonds | 5,090 | 5,060 | 5,030 | 5,000 |
| Interest expense** | 530 | 530 | 530 | 530 |
| Interest receivable | 250 | 250 | 250 | 250 |

*The unrecognized portion of the constructive loss at the beginning of the year is charged 90% to the Investment in Son account and 10% to noncontrolling interest.

**Elimination of 50% of Son's bonds (including 50% of the unamortized discount on the bonds) and 50% of the current interest expense on the bonds.

adjustments to consolidate the financial statements of Pop and Son for years subsequent to the year of intercompany purchase of Son bonds. Because the Investment in Son account is involved, we make the workpaper entries shown in Exhibit 7-4 before eliminating reciprocal investment and subsidiary equity amounts.

The workpaper entries shown in Exhibit 7-4 eliminate those amounts that would have been eliminated from the separate statements of Pop and Son if the bonds had in fact been retired in 2017. The objective is to produce the consolidated financial statements as if Son had purchased and retired its own bonds.

## SUMMARY

Transactions in which a corporation acquires the outstanding bonds of an affiliate on the open market result in constructive gains and losses except when an affiliate purchases bonds at book value. The consolidated entity realizes constructive gains and losses when an affiliate purchases another affiliate's bonds. The constructive gains and losses should be reflected in the income of the parent (under the equity method) and consolidated net income in the year of purchase.

Constructive gains and losses on parent bonds purchased by a subsidiary are similar to unrealized gains and losses on downstream sales and do not require allocation between noncontrolling and controlling interests. However, constructive gains and losses on subsidiary bonds purchased by the parent company should be allocated between the controlling and noncontrolling interests. Constructive gains or losses on intercompany bonds are recognized on the books of the purchaser and issuer as they amortize differences between the book value and par value of bonds.

A summary illustration comparing effects of constructive gains and losses from intercompany bond transactions on parent and consolidated net incomes is presented in Exhibit 7-5.

## QUESTIONS

**1.** What reciprocal accounts arise when one company borrows from an affiliate?

**2.** Do direct lending and borrowing transactions between affiliates give rise to unrealized gains or losses and unrecognized gains or losses?

**3.** What are constructive gains and losses? Describe a transaction having a constructive gain.

**4.** A company has a $1,000,000 bond issue outstanding with unamortized premium of $10,000 and unamortized issuance cost of $5,300. What is the book value of its liability? If an affiliate purchases half the bonds in the market at 98, what is the gain or loss? Is the gain or loss actual or constructive?

**Assumptions**

1. Parent (P) Company's net income, excluding income from Subsidiary (S), was $100,000 for 2016.
2. 90%-owned Subsidiary reported net income of $50,000 for 2016.
3. $100,000 of 10% bonds payable are outstanding with $6,000 unamortized premium as of January 1, 2016.
4. $50,000 par of the bonds were purchased for $51,500 on January 2, 2016.
5. The bonds mature on January 1, 2019.

| | S Acquires P's Bonds (Similar to Downstream) | P Acquires S's Bonds (Similar to Upstream) |
|---|---|---|
| **P's Net Income—Equity Method** | | |
| P's separate income | $100,000 | $100,000 |
| P's share of S's reported net income | 45,000 | 45,000 |
| Add: Constructive gain on bonds | | |
| ($53,000 − $51,500) × 100% | 1,500 | |
| ($53,000 − $51,500) × 90% | | 1,350 |
| Deduct: Piecemeal recognition of constructive gain | | |
| ($1,500 gain ÷ 3 years) × 100% | (500) | |
| ($1,500 gain ÷ 3 years) × 90% | | (450) |
| P's net income | $146,000 | $145,900 |
| | | |
| **Controlling Interest Share of Consolidated Net Income** | | |
| P's separate income plus S's net income | $150,000 | $150,000 |
| Add: Constructive gain on bonds | 1,500 | 1,500 |
| Eliminate: Interest expense (increase) | 4,000 | 4,000 |
| Interest income (decrease) | (4,500) | (4,500) |
| Total realized income | 151,000 | 151,000 |
| Less: Noncontrolling interest share | | |
| ($50,000 × 10%) | (5,000) | |
| ($50,000 + $1,500 − $500 × 10%) | | (5,100) |
| Controlling interest share of consolidated net income | $146,000 | $145,900 |

P's net income and controlling share of consolidated net income of $146,000 when S acquires P's bonds are the same as if the bonds were retired by P at the end of 2016. In that case, P's separate income would have been $101,000 ($100,000 plus $1,000 constructive gain), and S's net income would be unchanged. P's $101,000 plus P's $45,000 share of S's reported net income equals $146,000. An assumption of retirement at year-end is necessary because interest expense of P and interest income of S are both realized and recognized during 2016. The amount of the gain is $1,000 ($1,500 less $500 realized and recognized during the current year).

P's net income and controlling share of consolidated net income of $145,900 when P acquires S's bonds are the same as if the bonds were retired by S at the end of 2016. In that case, P's separate income would be unchanged at $100,000, and S's reported net income would be $51,000 ($50,000 plus $1,000 constructive gain). P's $100,000 separate income plus P's $45,900 share of S's reported income ($51,000 × 90%) equals $145,900. Again, the assumption of retirement at year-end is necessary because interest income of P and interest expense of S are realized and recognized during the current year.

5. Compare a constructive gain on intercompany bonds with an unrealized gain on the intercompany sale of land.

6. Describe the process by which constructive gains on intercompany bonds are realized and recognized on the books of the affiliates. Does recognition of a constructive gain in consolidated financial statements precede or succeed recognition on the books of affiliates?

7. If a subsidiary purchases parent bonds at a price in excess of recorded book value, is the gain or loss attributed to the parent or the subsidiary? Explain.

8. The following information related to intercompany bond holdings was taken from the adjusted trial balances of a parent and its 90 percent–owned subsidiary four years before the bond issue matured:

| | Parent | Subsidiary |
|---|---|---|
| Investment in S bonds, $50,000 par | $49,000 | |
| Interest receivable | 2,500 | |
| Interest expense | | $9,000 |
| 10% bonds payable, $100,000 par | | 100,000 |
| Bond premium | | 4,000 |
| Interest income | 5,250 | |
| Interest payable | | 5,000 |

Construct the consolidation workpaper entries necessary to eliminate reciprocal balances (a) assuming that the parent acquired its intercompany bond investment at the beginning of the current year, and (b) assuming that the parent acquired its intercompany bond investment two years prior to the date of the adjusted trial balance.

9. Prepare a journal entry (or entries) to account for the parent's investment income for the current year if the reported income of its 80 percent–owned subsidiary is $50,000 and the consolidated entity has a $4,000 constructive gain from the subsidiary's acquisition of parent bonds.

10. Calculate the parent's income from its 75 percent–owned subsidiary if the reported net income of the subsidiary for the period is $100,000 and the consolidated entity has a constructive loss of $8,000 from the parent's acquisition of subsidiary bonds.

11. If a parent reports interest expense of $4,300 with respect to bonds held intercompany and the subsidiary reports interest income of $4,500 for the same bonds: (a) Was there a constructive gain or loss on the bonds? (b) Is the gain or loss attributed to the parent or the subsidiary? And (c) what does the $200 difference between interest income and expense represent?

## EXERCISES

### E 7-1
### General questions

1. Which of the following is not a characteristic of a constructive retirement of bonds from an intercompany bond transaction?
   a  *Bonds are retired for consolidated statement purposes only.*
   b  *The reciprocal intercompany bond investment and liability amounts are eliminated in the consolidation process.*
   c  *Any gain or loss from the intercompany bond transaction is recognized on the books of the issuer.*
   d  *For consolidated statement purposes, the gain or loss on the constructive retirement of bonds is the difference between the book value of the bond liability and the purchase price of the bond investment.*

2. When bonds are purchased in the market by an affiliate, the book value of the intercompany bond liability is:
   a  *The par value of the bonds less unamortized issuance costs and less unamortized discount or plus unamortized premium.*
   b  *The par value of the bonds less issuance costs, less unamortized discount or plus unamortized premiums, and less the costs incurred to purchase the bond investment.*
   c  *The par value of the bonds.*
   d  *The par value of the bonds less the discount or plus the premium at issuance.*

3. Constructive gains and losses on bonds payable:
   a  *Arise when one company purchases the bonds of an affiliate or lends money directly to the affiliate to repurchase its own bonds*
   b  *Are realized gains and losses from the viewpoint of the issuer affiliate*
   c  *Are always assigned to the parent because its management makes the decisions for intercompany transactions*
   d  *Are realized and recognized from the viewpoint of the consolidated entity*

4. Straight-line interest amortization of bond premiums and discounts is used as an expedient in this book. However, the effective interest rate method is generally required under GAAP. When using the effective interest rate method:
   a  *The amount of the piecemeal recognition of a constructive gain or loss is the difference between the intercompany interest expense and income that is eliminated.*
   b  *The piecemeal recognition of a constructive gain or loss is recorded in the separate accounts of the affiliates.*
   c  *No piecemeal recognition of the constructive gain or loss is required for consolidated statement purposes.*
   d  *The issuing and the purchasing affiliates do not amortize the discounts and premiums on their separate books because the bonds are retired.*

### E 7-2
### General problems

Son Corporation is a 70 percent–owned subsidiary of Pop Corporation. On January 2, 2016, Son purchased $600,000 par of Pop's $900,000 outstanding bonds for $602,000 in the bond market. Pop's bonds have an 8 percent interest rate, pay interest on January 1 and July 1, and mature on January 1, 2020. There was $48,000 unamortized premium on the bond issue on January 1, 2016. Assume straight-line amortization.

1. The constructive gain or loss that should appear in the consolidated income statement of Pop Corporation and Subsidiary for 2016 is:
   a  *$30,000 gain*
   b  *$46,000 gain*
   c  *$2,000 loss*
   d  *$30,000 loss*

2. Interest expense that should appear in the 2016 consolidated income statement for Pop's bond issue is:
   a  *$28,000*
   b  *$24,000*
   c  *$20,800*
   d  *$20,000*

## E 7-3
## Constructive gain on purchase of parent bonds

Pam Corporation's long-term debt on January 1, 2016, consists of $400,000 par value of 10 percent bonds payable due on January 1, 2020, with an unamortized discount of $8,000. On January 2, 2016, Sun Corporation, Pam's 90 percent-owned subsidiary, purchased $80,000 par of Pam's 10 percent bonds for $76,000. Interest payment dates are January 1 and July 1, and straight-line amortization is used.

1. On the consolidated income statement of Pam Corporation and Subsidiary for 2016, a gain or loss should be reported in the amount of:
   a  *$5,600 loss*
   b  *$4,000 gain*
   c  *$2,400 gain*
   d  *$2,000 loss*

2. Bonds payable of Pam less unamortized discount appears in the consolidated balance sheet at December 31, 2016, in the amount of:
   a  *$392,000*
   b  *$394,000*
   c  *$320,000*
   d  *$315,200*

3. The amount of the constructive gain or loss that is unrecognized on the separate books of Pam and Sun at December 31, 2016, is:
   a  *$2,400*
   b  *$2,200*
   c  *$1,800*
   d  *$0*

4. Interest expense on Pam bonds appears in the consolidated income statement for 2016 at:
   a  *$42,000*
   b  *$40,000*
   c  *$33,600*
   d  *$32,000*

5. Consolidated net income for 2017 will be affected by the intercompany bond transactions as follows:
   a  *Increased by 100 percent of the constructive gain from 2016*
   b  *Decreased by 25 percent of the constructive gain from 2016*
   c  *Increased by 25 percent of the constructive loss from 2016*
   d  *Decreased by (25% × 90%)of the constructive loss from 2016*

## E 7-4
## Subsidiary purchases parent bonds

Pop Company acquired an 80 percent interest in Son Company on January 1, 2016, for $1,600,000 in excess of book value and fair value. On January 1, 2019, Pop had $4,000,000 par, 8 percent bonds outstanding with a $160,000 unamortized discount. On January 2, 2019, Son purchased $1,600,000 par of Pop's bonds at par. The bonds mature on January 1, 2023, and pay interest on January 1 and July 1. Pop's separate income, not including investment income, for 2019 is $3,200,000, and Son's reported net income is $2,000,000.

**REQUIRED:** Determine the following:

1. Controlling interest share of consolidated net income for Pop and Subsidiary for 2019
2. Noncontrolling interest share for 2019

## E 7-5
## Consolidated income statement (constructive gain on purchase of parent's bonds)

Comparative income statements for Pam Corporation and its 100 percent–owned subsidiary, Sun Corporation, for the year ended December 31, 2024, are summarized as follows:

|  | Pam | Sun |
|---|---|---|
| Sales | $1,000,000 | $500,000 |
| Income from Sun | 226,000 | — |
| Bond interest income (includes discount amortization) | — | 22,000 |
| Cost of sales | (670,000) | (200,000) |
| Operating expenses | (150,000) | (100,000) |
| Bond interest expense | (50,000) | — |
| Net income | $356,000 | $222,000 |

Pam purchased its interest in Sun at fair value equal to book value on January 1, 2016. On January 1, 2017, Pam sold $500,000 par of 10 percent, 10-year bonds to the public at par, and on January 2, 2024, Sun purchased $200,000 par of the bonds at 97. The companies use straight-line amortization. There are no other intercompany transactions between the affiliates.

**REQUIRED:** Prepare a consolidated income statement for Pam Corporation and Subsidiary for the year ended December 31, 2024.

## E 7-6
## Parent purchases subsidiary bonds

Pop Corporation owns a 70 percent interest in Son Corporation acquired several years ago at book value equal to fair value. On January 1, 2016, Son had outstanding $1,000,000 of 9 percent bonds with a book value of $990,000. On January 2, 2016, Pop purchased $500,000 of Son's 9 percent bonds for $503,000. The bonds are due on January 1, 2020, and pay interest on January 1 and July 1.

**REQUIRED**

1. Determine the gain or loss on the constructive retirement of Son's bonds.
2. Son reports net income of $14,000 for 2016. Determine Pop's income from Son.

## E 7-7
## Constructive gain purchase of subsidiary's bonds

Comparative balance sheets of Pam and Sun Corporations at December 31, 2016, follow:

|  | Pam | Sun |
|---|---|---|
| *Assets* |  |  |
| Accounts receivable—net | $ 2,048,600 | $ 600,000 |
| Interest receivable | 20,000 | — |
| Inventories | 6,000,000 | 1,000,000 |
| Other current assets | 197,000 | 400,000 |
| Plant assets—net | 7,680,000 | 5,000,000 |
| Investment in Sun stock | 3,661,600 | — |
| Investment in Sun bonds | 392,800 | — |
| Total assets | $20,000,000 | $7,000,000 |
| *Liabilities and Stockholders' Equity* |  |  |
| Accounts payable | $ 800,000 | $ 278,000 |
| Interest payable | — | 100,000 |
| 10% bonds payable | — | 2,072,000 |
| Capital stock | 16,000,000 | 4,000,000 |
| Retained earnings | 3,200,000 | 550,000 |
| Total equities | $20,000,000 | $7,000,000 |

Pam acquired 80 percent of Sun's capital stock for $3,320,000 on January 1, 2014, when Sun's capital stock was $4,000,000 and Sun's retained earnings was $150,000.

On January 2, 2016, Pam acquired $400,000 par of Sun's 10 percent bonds in the market for $391,000, on which date the unamortized premium for bonds payable on Sun's books was $90,000. The bonds pay interest on January 1 and July 1 and mature on January 1, 2021. (Assume straight-line amortization.)

1. The gain or loss on the constructive retirement of $400,000 of Sun bonds on January 2, 2016, is reported in the consolidated income statement in the amount of:

   a  $27,000
   b  $23,000
   c  $21,000
   d  $14,000

2. The portion of the constructive gain or loss on Sun bonds that remains unrecognized on the separate books of Pam and Sun at December 31, 2016, is:

   a  $24,000
   b  $21,600
   c  $21,000
   d  $18,400

3. Consolidated bonds payable at December 31, 2016, should be reported at:

   a  $2,072,000
   b  $2,000,000
   c  $1,657,600
   d  $1,600,000

# E 7-8
## Midyear purchase of parent's bonds

The consolidated balance sheet of Pop Corporation and Son (an 80 percent–owned subsidiary) at December 31, 2016, includes the following items related to an 8 percent, $500,000 outstanding bond issue:

| | |
|---|---:|
| *Current Liabilities* | |
| Bond interest payable (6 months' interest due January 1, 2017) | $ 20,000 |
| *Long-Term Liabilities* | |
| 8% bonds payable (maturity date January 1, 2021, net of $15,000 unamortized discount) | $485,000 |

Pop Corporation is the issuer, and straight-line amortization is applicable. Son purchases $300,000 par of the outstanding bonds of Pop on July 2, 2017, for $287,400.

---

### REQUIRED

1. Calculate the following:
   a. The gain or loss on constructive retirement of the bonds
   b. The consolidated bond interest expense for 2017
   c. The consolidated bond liability at December 31, 2017
2. How would the amounts determined in part 1 differ if Pop purchased Sun's bonds?

---

# E 7-9
## Different assumptions for purchase of parent's bonds and subsidiary's bonds

The balance sheets of Pam and Sun Corporations, an 80 percent–owned subsidiary of Pam, at December 31, 2016, are as follows (in thousands):

| | Pam | Sun |
|---|---:|---:|
| *Assets* | | |
| Cash | $ 2,440 | $2,500 |
| Accounts receivable—net | 3,000 | 300 |
| Other current assets | 8,000 | 1,200 |
| Plant assets—net | 15,000 | 5,500 |
| Investment in Sun | 6,560 | — |
| Total assets | $35,000 | $9,500 |

| | Pam | Sun |
|---|---|---|
| *Liabilities and Stockholders' Equity* | | |
| Accounts payable | $ 750 | $ 230 |
| Interest payable | 250 | 50 |
| 10% bonds payable (due January 1, 2022) | 4,900 | 1,020 |
| Capital stock | 25,000 | 7,000 |
| Retained earnings | 4,100 | 1,200 |
| Total liabilities and stockholders' equity | $35,000 | $9,500 |

The book value of Pam's bonds reflects a $100,000 unamortized discount. The book value of Sun's bonds reflects a $20,000 unamortized premium.

---

### REQUIRED

1. Assume that Sun purchases $2,000,000 par of Pam's bonds for $1,900,000 on January 2, 2017, and that semiannual interest is paid on July 1 and January 1. Determine the amounts at which the following items should appear in the consolidated financial statements of Pam and Sun at and for the year ended December 31, 2017.
   a. Gain or loss on bond retirement
   b. Interest payable
   c. Bonds payable at par value
   d. Investment in Pam bonds

2. Disregard 1 above and assume that Pam purchases $1,000,000 par of Sun's bonds for $1,030,000 on January 2, 2017, and that semiannual interest on the bonds is paid on July 1 and January 1. Determine the amounts at which the following items will appear in the consolidated financial statements of Pam and Sun for the year ended December 31, 2017.
   a. Gain or loss on bond retirement
   b. Interest expense (assume straight-line amortization)
   c. Interest receivable
   d. Bonds payable at book value

### E 7-10
### Constructive retirement of parent's bonds

Pop Corporation has $8,000,000 of 12 percent bonds outstanding on December 31, 2016, with unamortized premium of $240,000. These bonds pay interest semiannually on July 1 and January 1 and mature on January 1, 2022.

On January 2, 2017, Son Corporation, an 80 percent–owned subsidiary of Pop, purchases $2,000,000 par of Pop's outstanding bonds in the market for $1,960,000.

---

### ADDITIONAL INFORMATION

1. Pop and Son use the straight-line method of amortization.
2. The financial statements are consolidated.
3. Pop's bonds are the only outstanding bonds of the affiliated companies.
4. Son's net income for 2017 is $800,000 and for 2018, $1,200,000.

---

### REQUIRED

1. Compute the constructive gain or loss that will appear in the consolidated income statement for 2017.
2. Prepare a consolidation entry (entries) at December 31, 2017, to eliminate the effect of the intercompany bondholdings.
3. Compute the amounts that will appear in the consolidated income statement for 2018 for the following:
   a. Constructive gain or loss
   b. Noncontrolling interest share
   c. Bond interest expense
   d. Bond interest income
4. Compute the amounts that will appear in the consolidated balance sheet at December 31, 2018, for the following:
   a. Investment in Pop bonds
   b. Book value of bonds payable
   c. Bond interest receivable
   d. Bond interest payable

## E 7-11
### Consolidated income statement (constructive retirement of all subsidiary bonds)

Comparative income statements for Pam Corporation and its 80 percent–owned subsidiary, Sun Corporation, for the year ended December 31, 2017, are summarized as follows:

|  | Pam | Sun |
|---|---|---|
| Sales | $1,200,000 | $600,000 |
| Income from Sun | 260,800 | — |
| Bond interest income (includes discount amortization) | 91,000 | — |
| Cost of sales | (750,000) | (200,000) |
| Operating expenses | (200,000) | (200,000) |
| Bond interest expense | — | (60,000) |
| Net income | $ 601,800 | $140,000 |

Pam purchased its 80 percent interest in Sun at book value on January 1, 2016, when Sun's assets and liabilities were equal to their fair values.

On January 1, 2017, Pam paid $783,000 to purchase all of Sun's $1,000,000, 6 percent outstanding bonds. The bonds were issued at par on January 1, 2015, pay interest semiannually on June 30 and December 31, and mature on December 31, 2023.

**REQUIRED:** Prepare a consolidated income statement for Pam Corporation and Subsidiary for the year ended December 31, 2017.

## E 7-12
### Computations and entries (parent purchases subsidiary bonds)

Pop Corporation, which owns an 80 percent interest in Son Corporation, purchases $100,000 of Son's 8 percent bonds at 106 on July 2, 2016. The bonds pay interest on January 1 and July 1 and mature on July 1, 2019. Pop uses the equity method for its investment in Son. Selected data from the December 31, 2016, adjusted trial balances of the two companies are as follows:

|  | Pop | Son |
|---|---|---|
| Interest receivable | $ 4,000 | $ — |
| Investment in Son 8% bonds | 105,000 | — |
| Interest payable | — | 40,000 |
| 8% bonds payable ($1,000,000 par) | — | 985,000 |
| Interest income | 3,000 | — |
| Interest expense | — | 86,000 |
| Gain or loss on retirement of intercompany bonds | | |

### REQUIRED

1. Determine the amounts for each of the foregoing items that will appear in the consolidated financial statements on or for the year ended December 31, 2016.
2. Prepare in general journal form the workpaper adjustments and eliminations related to the foregoing bonds that are required to consolidate the financial statements of Pop and Son Corporations for the year ended December 31, 2016.
3. Prepare in general journal form the workpaper adjustments and eliminations related to the bonds that are required to consolidate the financial statements of Pop and Son Corporations for the year ended December 31, 2017.

## E 7-13
### Computations and entries (constructive gain on purchase of parent bonds)

Pop Corporation acquired an 80 percent interest in Son Corporation at book value equal to fair value on January 1, 2017, at which time Son's capital stock and retained earnings were $200,000 and $80,000, respectively. On January 2, 2018, Son purchased $100,000 par of Pop's 8 percent, $200,000 par bonds for $97,600 three years before maturity. Interest payment dates are January 1 and July 1. During 2018, Son reports interest income of $8,800 from the bonds, and Pop reports interest expense of $16,000.

## ADDITIONAL INFORMATION

1. Pop's separate income for 2018 is $400,000.
2. Son's net income for 2018 is $100,000.
3. Pop accounts for its investment using the equity method.
4. Straight-line amortization is applicable.

## REQUIRED

1. Determine the gain or loss on the bonds.
2. Prepare the journal entries for Son to account for its bond investment during 2018.
3. Prepare the journal entries for Pop to account for its bonds payable during 2018.
4. Prepare the journal entry for Pop to account for its 80 percent investment in Son for 2018.
5. Calculate noncontrolling interest share and consolidated net income for 2018.

## PROBLEMS

### P7-1
### Computations and entries (constructive retirement of parent's bonds)

Partial adjusted trial balances for Pam Corporation and its 90 percent–owned subsidiary, Sun Corporation, for the year ended December 31, 2016, are as follows:

|  | Pam Corporation Debit (Credit) | Sun Corporation Debit (Credit) |
|---|---|---|
| Interest receivable | $ — | $ 2,000 |
| Investment in Pam bonds | — | 105,400 |
| Interest payable | (4,000) | — |
| 8% bonds payable, due April 1, 2019 | (196,400) | — |
| Interest income | — | (4,200) |
| Interest expense | 17,600 | — |

Sun Corporation acquired $100,000 par of Pam's bonds on April 2, 2016, for $107,200. The bonds pay interest on April 1 and October 1 and mature on April 1, 2019.

## REQUIRED

1. Compute the gain or loss on the bonds that will appear in the 2016 consolidated income statement.
2. Determine the amounts of interest income and expense that will appear in the 2016 consolidated income statement.
3. Determine the amounts of interest receivable and payable that will appear in the December 31, 2016, consolidated balance sheet.
4. Prepare in general journal form the consolidation workpaper entries needed to eliminate the effects of the intercompany bonds for 2016.

### P7-2
### Four-year income schedule (several intercompany transactions)

Intercompany transactions between Pop Corporation and Son Corporation, its 80 percent–owned subsidiary, from January 2016, when Pop acquired its controlling interest, to December 31, 2019, are summarized as follows:

| 2016 | Pop sold inventory items that cost $30,000 to Son for $40,000. Son sold $30,000 of these inventory items in 2016 and $10,000 of them in 2017. |
|---|---|
| 2017 | Pop sold inventory items that cost $15,000 to Son for $20,000. All of these items were sold by Son during 2018. |
| 2018 | Son sold land with a book value of $20,000 to Pop at its fair market value of $27,500. This land is to be used as a future plant site by Pop. |

| | |
|---|---|
| 2018 | Pop sold equipment with a four-year remaining useful life to Son on January 1 for $40,000. This equipment had a book value of $25,000 at the time of sale and was still in use by Son at December 31, 2019. |
| 2019 | Son purchased $50,000 par of Pop's 10% bonds in the bond market for $53,000 on January 2, 2019. These bonds had a book value of $49,000 when acquired by Son and mature on January 1, 2023. |

The separate income of Pop (excludes income from Son) and the reported net income of Son for 2016 through 2019 were:

| | 2016 | 2017 | 2018 | 2019 |
|---|---|---|---|---|
| Separate income of Pop | $250,000 | $187,500 | $230,000 | $255,000 |
| Net income of Son | 50,000 | 60,000 | 55,000 | 60,000 |

**REQUIRED:** Compute Pop's net income (and the controlling share of consolidated net income) for each of the years 2016 through 2019. A schedule with columns for each year is suggested as the most efficient approach to solve this problem. (Use straight-line depreciation and amortization and take a full year's depreciation on the equipment sold to Son in 2018.)

## P7-3
## Workpapers (constructive retirement of bonds, intercompany sales)

Financial statements for Pam Corporation and its 75 percent–owned subsidiary, Sun Corporation, for 2016 are summarized as follows (in thousands):

| | Pam | Sun |
|---|---|---|
| ***Combined Income and Retained Earnings Statement*** | | |
| ***for the Year Ended December 31, 2016*** | | |
| Sales | $2,520 | $2,000 |
| Gain on land | 40 | — |
| Gain on building | 80 | — |
| Income from Sun | 208 | — |
| Cost of goods sold | (1,400) | (1,200) |
| Depreciation expense | (304) | (160) |
| Interest expense | (80) | — |
| Other expenses | (184) | (240) |
| Net income | 880 | 400 |
| Add: Retained earnings, January 1 | 600 | 400 |
| Deduct: Dividends | (640) | (320) |
| Retained earnings, December 31 | $ 840 | $ 480 |
| ***Balance Sheet at December 31, 2016*** | | |
| Cash | $ 108 | $ 324 |
| Bond interest receivable | — | 20 |
| Other receivables—net | 160 | 120 |
| Inventories | 320 | 200 |
| Land | 360 | 280 |
| Buildings—net | 600 | 720 |
| Equipment—net | 560 | 360 |
| Investment in Sun | 1,372 | — |
| Investment in Pam Bonds | — | 376 |
| Total assets | $3,480 | $2,400 |
| Accounts payable | $ 200 | $ 320 |
| Bond interest payable | 40 | — |
| 10% bonds payable | 800 | — |
| Common stock | 1,600 | 1,600 |
| Retained earnings | 840 | 480 |
| Total equities | $3,480 | $2,400 |

Pam acquired its interest in Sun at book value during 2013, when the fair values of Sun's assets and liabilities were equal to their recorded book values.

## ADDITIONAL INFORMATION

1. Pam uses the equity method for its investment in Sun.

2. Intercompany merchandise sales totalled $200,000 during 2016. All intercompany balances have been paid except for $40,000 in transit at December 31, 2016.

3. Unrealized profits in Sun's inventory of merchandise purchased from Pam were $48,000 on December 31, 2015, and $60,000 on December 31, 2016.

4. Sun sold equipment with a six-year remaining life to Pam on January 3, 2014, at a gain of $96,000. Pam still uses the equipment in its operations.

5. Pam sold land to Sun on July 1, 2016, at a gain of $40,000.

6. Pam sold a building to Sun on July 1, 2016, at a gain of $80,000. The building has a 10-year remaining life and is still used by Sun.

7. Sun purchased $400,000 par value of Pam's 10 percent bonds in the open market for $376,000 plus $20,000 accrued interest on December 31, 2016. Interest is paid semiannually on January 1 and July 1. The bonds mature on December 31, 2021.

**REQUIRED:** Prepare consolidation workpapers for Pam and Subsidiary for the year ended December 31, 2016.

## P7-4
## Computations of separate and consolidated statements given

Pop Corporation acquired an 80 percent interest in Son Corporation on January 1, 2016, for $640,000, at which time Son had capital stock of $400,000 outstanding and retained earnings of $200,000. The price paid reflected a $200,000 undervaluation of Son's plant and equipment. The plant and equipment had a remaining useful life of eight years when Pop acquired its interest.

Separate and consolidated financial statements for Pop and its subsidiary, Son Corporation, for the year ended December 31, 2018, are as follows (in thousands):

|  | Pop | Son | Consolidated |
|---|---|---|---|
| ***Combined Income and Retained Earnings Statement for the Year Ended December 31, 2018*** |  |  |  |
| Sales | $  360 | $200 | $  460 |
| Income from Son | 40 | — | — |
| Interest income | — | 16 | — |
| Cost of goods sold | (220) | (120) | (220) |
| Operating expenses | (60) | (36) | (116) |
| Interest expense | (36) | — | (18) |
| Loss | — | — | (6) |
| Noncontrolling interest share | — | — | (16) |
| Controlling share of net income | 84 | 60 | 84 |
| Add: Beginning retained earnings | 588 | 270 | 588 |
| Deduct: Dividends | (40) | (30) | (40) |
| Ending retained earnings | $  632 | $300 | $  632 |
| ***Balance Sheet at December 31, 2018*** |  |  |  |
| Cash | $  120 | $ 52 | $  172 |
| Accounts receivable | 240 | 120 | 330 |
| Inventories | 200 | 100 | 280 |
| Plant and equipment | 1,000 | 400 | 1,560 |
| Accumulated depreciation | (200) | (100) | (360) |
| Investment in Son stock | 640 | — | — |
| Investment in Pop bonds | — | 208 | — |
| Total assets | $2,000 | $780 | $1,982 |
| Accounts payable | $  160 | $ 80 | $  210 |
| 10% bonds payable | 408 | — | 204 |
| Common stock | 800 | 400 | 800 |
| Retained earnings | 632 | 300 | 632 |
| Noncontrolling interest | — | — | 136 |
| Total equities | $2,000 | $780 | $1,982 |

Son sells merchandise to Pop but never purchases inventory from Pop. On January 1, 2018, Son purchased $200,000 par of 10 percent Pop Corporation bonds for $212,000. These bonds mature on December 31, 2020, and Son expects to hold the bonds until maturity. Both Son and Pop use straight-line amortization. Interest is payable on December 31.

**REQUIRED:** Show computations for each of the following items:

1. The $6,000 loss in the consolidated income statement
2. The $460,000 consolidated sales
3. Consolidated cost of goods sold of $220,000
4. Intercompany profit in beginning inventories
5. Intercompany profit in ending inventories
6. Consolidated accounts receivable of $330,000
7. Noncontrolling interest share of $16,000 (Hint: The amount $16,000 may be incorrect.)
8. Noncontrolling interest at December 31, 2018
9. Investment in Son stock at December 31, 2017
10. Investment income account of $40,000 (Pop's books)

## P7-5
## [Based on AICPA] Computations (constructive retirement of subsidiary bonds)

Selected amounts from the separate unconsolidated financial statements of Pam Corporation and its 90 percent–owned subsidiary, Sun Company, at December 31, 2016, are as follows (in thousands).

|  | Pam | Sun |
|---|---|---|
| ***Selected Income Statement Amounts*** | | |
| Sales | $710 | $530 |
| Cost of goods sold | 490 | 370 |
| Gain on sale of equipment | — | 21 |
| Earnings from investment in subsidiary | 63 | — |
| Interest expense | — | 16 |
| Depreciation | 25 | 20 |
| ***Selected Balance Sheet Amounts*** | | |
| Cash | $ 50 | $ 15 |
| Inventories | 229 | 150 |
| Equipment | 440 | 360 |
| Accumulated depreciation | (200) | (120) |
| Investment in Sun | 189 | — |
| Investment in bonds | 91 | — |
| Bonds payable | — | (200) |
| Common stock | (100) | (10) |
| Additional paid-in capital | (250) | (40) |
| Retained earnings | (402) | (140) |
| ***Selected Statement of Retained Earnings Amounts*** | | |
| Beginning balance December 31, 2015 | $272 | $100 |
| Net income | 212 | 70 |
| Dividends paid | 80 | 30 |

**ADDITIONAL INFORMATION**

1. On January 2, 2016, Pam purchased 90 percent of Sun's 100,000 outstanding common stock for cash of $153,000. On that date, Sun's stockholders' equity equaled $150,000 and the fair values of Sun's assets and liabilities equaled their carrying amounts. Pam correctly accounted for the combination as an acquisition. The difference between fair value and book value was due to goodwill.

2. On September 4, 2016, Sun paid cash dividends of $30,000.

3. On December 31, 2016, Pam recorded its equity in Sun's earnings.

4. On January 3, 2016, Sun sold equipment with an original cost of $30,000 and a carrying value of $15,000 to Pam for $36,000. The equipment had a remaining life of three years and was depreciated using the straight-line method by both companies.

**5.** During 2016, Sun sold merchandise to Pam for $60,000, which included a profit of $20,000. At December 31, 2016, half of this merchandise remained in Pam's inventory.

**6.** On December 31, 2016, Pam paid $91,000 to purchase half of the outstanding bonds issued by Sun. The bonds mature on December 31, 2022, and were originally issued at par. These bonds pay interest annually on December 31 of each year, and the interest was paid to the prior investor immediately before Pam's purchase of the bonds.

**REQUIRED:** Determine the amounts at which the following items will appear in the consolidated financial statements of Pam Corporation and Subsidiary for the year ended December 31, 2016.

**1.** Cash
**2.** Equipment less accumulated depreciation
**3.** Investment in Sun
**4.** Bonds payable
**5.** Common stock
**6.** Beginning retained earnings
**7.** Dividends declared
**8.** Gain on retirement of bonds
**9.** Cost of goods sold
**10.** Interest expense
**11.** Depreciation expense

### P7-6
### Workpapers (constructive retirement of bonds, intercompany sales)

Financial statements for Pop Corporation and its 75 percent–owned subsidiary, Son Corporation, for 2017 are summarized as follows (in thousands):

|  | Pop | Son |
|---|---|---|
| **Combined Income and Retained Earnings Statement for the Year Ended December 31, 2017** | | |
| Sales | $1,260 | $1,000 |
| Gain on plant | 60 | — |
| Income from Son | 104 | — |
| Cost of goods sold | (700) | (600) |
| Depreciation expense | (152) | (80) |
| Interest expense | (40) | — |
| Other expenses | (92) | (120) |
| Net income | 440 | 200 |
| Add: Beginning retained earnings | 300 | 200 |
| Deduct: Dividends | (320) | (160) |
| Retained earnings December 31 | $ 420 | $ 240 |
| **Balance Sheet at December 31, 2017** | | |
| Cash | $ 54 | $ 162 |
| Bond interest receivable | — | 10 |
| Other receivables—net | 80 | 60 |
| Inventories | 160 | 100 |
| Land | 180 | 140 |
| Buildings—net | 300 | 360 |
| Equipment—net | 280 | 180 |
| Investment in Son | 686 | — |
| Investment in Pop bonds | — | 188 |
| Total assets | $1,740 | $1,200 |
| Accounts payable | $ 100 | $ 160 |
| Bond interest payable | 20 | — |
| 10% bonds payable | 400 | — |
| Common stock | 800 | 800 |
| Retained earnings | 420 | 240 |
| Total equities | $1,740 | $1,200 |

Pop Corporation acquired its interest in Son at book value during 2014, when the fair values of Son's assets and liabilities were equal to recorded book values.

## ADDITIONAL INFORMATION

1. Pop uses the equity method for its investment in Son.

2. Intercompany sales of merchandise between the two affiliates totalled $100,000 during 2017. All intercompany balances have been paid except for $20,000 in transit from Son to Pop at December 31, 2017.

3. Unrealized profits in Son's inventories of merchandise acquired from Pop were $24,000 at December 31, 2016, and $30,000 at December 31, 2017.

4. Son sold equipment with a six-year remaining useful life to Pop on January 2, 2015, at a gain of $48,000. The equipment is still in use by Pop.

5. Pop sold a plant to Son on July 1, 2017. The land was sold at a gain of $20,000 and the building, which had a remaining useful life of 10 years, at a gain of $40,000.

6. Son purchased $200,000 par of Pop's 10 percent bonds in the open market for $188,000 plus $10,000 accrued interest on December 31, 2017. Interest is paid semiannually on January 1 and July 1, and the bonds mature on January 1, 2022.

**REQUIRED:** Prepare a consolidation workpaper for Pop Corporation and Subsidiary for the year ended December 31, 2017.

# PROFESSIONAL RESEARCH ASSIGNMENTS

Answer the following questions by reference to the FASB Codification of Accounting Standards. Include the appropriate reference in your response.

**PR 7-1**  How should a company determine the fair value of long-term debt?

**PR 7-2**  A firm issues mandatorily redeemable preferred stock. Should this be classified as debt or equity in the consolidated financial statements?

# CHAPTER 8

# Consolidations—Changes in Ownership Interests

This chapter discusses changes in parent/investor ownership interests. These topics include accounting and consolidation procedures for interim acquisitions of stock, piecemeal acquisitions of a controlling interest, sales of ownership interests, and changes in ownership interests through investee stock issuances or treasury stock transactions.

## ACQUISITIONS DURING AN ACCOUNTING PERIOD

LEARNING OBJECTIVES

**8.1** Apply consolidation procedures to interim (midyear) acquisitions.

**8.2** Prepare consolidated statements when the parent company's ownership percentage increases or decreases during the reporting period.

**8.3** Record subsidiary/ investee stock issuances and treasury stock transactions.

Previous chapters illustrated consolidations for subsidiary acquisitions at the beginning of an accounting period. Acquisitions often take place within an accounting period. When the parent acquires a subsidiary during an accounting period, some adjustments must be made to account for the income of the subsidiary that was earned prior to the acquisition date and included in the purchase price. Such income is referred to as **preacquisition earnings** to distinguish it from income of the consolidated entity. Similarly, **preacquisition dividends** are dividends paid on stock before the acquisition date that require additional adjustments. Interim acquisitions are common transactions. In fact, acquisitions on January 2 are unlikely. These beginning of period acquisitions have been used so far in the text to help simplify understanding of the process.

### Preacquisition Earnings

Conceptually, we can eliminate preacquisition earnings from consolidated income by either of two methods. We could exclude the revenues and expenses of the subsidiary prior to the acquisition date from consolidated revenues and expenses. Or we could include the revenues and expenses of the subsidiary in the consolidated income statement for the full year and deduct preacquisition income as a separate item.

Assume, for example, that Pop Corporation purchases a 90 percent interest in Son Company on April 1, 2016, for $427,500. Son's income, dividends, and equity for 2016 are as follows:

|  | January 1 to March 31 | April 1 to December 31 | January 1 to December 31 |
|---|---|---|---|
| *Income* |  |  |  |
| Sales | $50,000 | $150,000 | $ 200,000 |
| Cost of sales and expenses | 25,000 | 75,000 | 100,000 |
| Net income | $25,000 | $ 75,000 | $ 100,000 |
| *Dividends* | $20,000 | $ 30,000 | $ 50,000 |
|  | **January 1** | **April 1** | **December 31** |
| *Stockholders' Equity* |  |  |  |
| Capital stock | $400,000 | $400,000 | $400,000 |
| Retained earnings | 70,000 | 75,000 | 120,000 |
| Stockholders' equity | $470,000 | $475,000 | $520,000 |

Son's income from January 1 to March 31 is $25,000 ($50,000 sales − $25,000 expenses), and Son's equity at April 1 is $475,000. Therefore, the book value acquired by Pop ($475,000 × 90% interest) is equal to the $427,500 purchase price of Son's stock.

In recording income from its investment in Son at year-end, Pop makes the following entry:

| | | |
|---|---|---|
| Investment in Son (+A) | 67,500 | |
|     Income from Son (R, +SE) | | 67,500 |
|   To record income from the last three quarters | | |
|     of 2016 ($75,000 × 90%). | | |

Recording investment income on an equity basis increases Pop's income by $67,500, so the effect on Pop's controlling share of consolidated net income must also be $67,500. Conceptually, the consolidated income statement is affected as follows:

| | |
|---|---|
| Sales (last three quarters of 2016) | $150,000 |
| Expenses (last three quarters of 2016) | (75,000) |
| Noncontrolling interest share (last three quarters of 2016) | (7,500) |
|     Effect on controlling share of consolidated net income | $ 67,500 |

This solution poses two practical problems. First, the 10 percent noncontrolling interest share for 2016 is $10,000 for the full year, even though it is only $7,500 for the last nine months. Second, by consolidating revenues and expenses for only nine months of the year, the consolidated income statement does not provide a basis for projecting future annual revenues and expenses for the consolidated entity.

Historically, generally accepted accounting principles (GAAP) (ASC 810-10-45) held that the most meaningful consolidated income statement presentation results from including the revenues and expenses in the consolidated income statement for the full year and deducting preacquisition income as a separate item. GAAP recommended consolidating subsidiary accounts in the following manner:

| | |
|---|---|
| Sales (full year) | $200,000 |
| Expenses (full year) | (100,000) |
| Preacquisition income | (22,500) |
| Noncontrolling interest share | (10,000) |
|     Effect on controlling share of consolidated net income | $ 67,500 |

GAAP (ASC 810-10-65) changed in 2007, indicating that an acquirer purchases control of the assets and assumes the liabilities of a subsidiary at a price that reflects fair values at the combination date. The acquirer does not purchase earnings. Under current GAAP, consolidated net income should only reflect subsidiary earnings subsequent to the acquisition date. Preacquisition earnings should not appear as a reduction of consolidated net income. Under this approach, we essentially close the books of the subsidiary at the acquisition date. So, our Pop Corporation example reverts to the first presentation given previously under current GAAP, calculating the controlling share of consolidated net income as follows:

| | |
|---|---|
| Sales (last three quarters of 2016) | $150,000 |
| Expenses (last three quarters of 2016) | (75,000) |
| Noncontrolling interest share (last three quarters of 2016) | (7,500) |
| Controlling share of consolidated net income | $ 67,500 |

## Preacquisition Dividends

We eliminate dividends paid on a stock prior to the acquisition date (preacquisition dividends) in the consolidation process because they are not part of the equity acquired. Son paid $50,000 dividends during 2016, but it paid $20,000 of this amount before the acquisition by Pop. Accordingly, Pop makes the following entry to account for dividends received (after the acquisition):

| | | |
|---|---|---|
| Cash (+A) | 27,000 | |
|     Investment in Son (−A) | | 27,000 |
|   Record dividends received from Son. | | |

We eliminate preacquisition dividends relating to the 90 percent interest acquired by Pop in the consolidation process along with preacquisition revenues and expenses. We include these eliminations in the workpaper entry that eliminates reciprocal investment in subsidiary and subsidiary equity balances in order to compensate for the fact that subsidiary equity balances are eliminated as of the beginning of the period, and the investment account balance is eliminated as of the acquisition date within the period. Son's allocations of income and dividends are as follows:

| | Controlling Interest (Pop) | Noncontrolling Interest (10%) | Preacquisition Eliminations | Total |
|---|---|---|---|---|
| Son's net income | $67,500 | $7,500 | $25,000 | $100,000 |
| Son's dividends | 27,000 | 5,000 | 18,000 | 50,000 |

## Consolidation

Exhibit 8-1 illustrates consolidation procedures for the midyear acquisition of the Subsidiary by Pop Corporation. The $468,000 Investment in Son balance in Pop's balance sheet consists of the $427,500 cost plus $67,500 income less $27,000 dividends received. Although other amounts in the statements of Pop and Son are introduced for the first time in the consolidation workpapers, they are entirely compatible with previous assumptions and data for Pop and Son Corporations.

Workpaper entry a eliminates the income from Son and dividends received from Son and returns the Investment in Son account to its $427,500 balance at acquisition on April 1, 2016:

| | | |
|---|---|---|
| a | Income from Son ($-R, -SE$) | 67,500 | |
| | Dividends—Son ($+SE$) | | 27,000 |
| | Investment in Son ($-A$) | | 40,500 |
| | To eliminate investment income and the dividends received from Son and to adjust the investment in Son to its fair value on April 1, 2016. | | |

This entry does not reflect new procedures, but we must be careful to eliminate only dividends actually received by the parent company (90% $\times$ $30,000).

The second entry in Exhibit 8-1 reflects new workpaper procedures because it contains items from preacquisition sales and cost of sales and expenses and dividends. We journalize it as follows:

| | | | |
|---|---|---|---|
| b | Sales ($-R, -SE$)* | 50,000 | |
| | Cost of sales and expenses ($-E, +SE$)* | | 25,000 |
| | Capital stock—Son ($-SE$) | 400,000 | |
| | Retained earnings—Son ($-SE$) | 70,000 | |
| | Dividends—Son ($+SE$)* | | 18,000 |
| | Investment in Son ($-A$) | | 427,500 |
| | Noncontrolling interest—beginning ($+SE$) | | 49,500 |

To eliminate reciprocal investment and equity balances, preacquisition income, and preacquisition dividends and to record the beginning noncontrolling interest. The * items represent the preacquisition income and dividends. Note that the beginning noncontrolling interest is the amount at the acquisition date. It represents 10% of the January 1 beginning capital stock plus retained earnings, plus the preacquisition earnings [10% $\times$ (400,000 + $70,000 + $25,000)].

| | | | |
|---|---|---|---|
| c | Noncontrolling interest share ($-SE$) | 7,500 | |
| | Dividends—Son ($+SE$) | | 5,000 |
| | Noncontrolling interest ($+SE$) | | 2,500 |

To enter noncontrolling interest share of subsidiary's postacquisition earnings and dividends. The dividends also include preacquisition dividends for noncontrolling interest.

In cases of *increases* in ownership interests during a period, we compute noncontrolling interest for the noncontrolling shares outstanding at year-end. Midyear acquisitions do not affect consolidation workpapers in subsequent accounting periods.

## POP CORPORATION AND SUBSIDIARY CONSOLIDATION WORKPAPER FOR THE YEAR ENDED DECEMBER 31, 2016

| | Pop | 90% Son | Adjustments and Eliminations Debits | Adjustments and Eliminations Credits | Consolidated Statements |
|---|---|---|---|---|---|
| *Income Statement*<br>Sales | $ 600,000 | $ 200,000 | b  50,000 | | $ 750,000 |
| Income from Son | 67,500 | | a  67,500 | | |
| Expenses including cost of sales | (400,000) | (100,000) | | b  25,000 | (475,000) |
| Consolidated net income | | | | | 275,000 |
| Noncontrolling interest share<br>(10% × $75,000) | | | | c  7,500 | (7,500) |
| **Controlling share of Consolidated Net Income** | **$  267,500** | **$ 100,000** | | | **$  267,500** |
| *Retained Earnings Statement*<br>Retained earnings—Pop | $  532,500 | | | | $  532,500 |
| Retained earnings—Son | | $  70,000 | b  70,000 | | |
| **Controlling share of Consolidated Net Income** | **267,500** | **100,000** | | | **267,500** |
| Dividends | (200,000) | (50,000) | | a  27,000<br>b  18,000<br>c   5,000 | (200,000) |
| **Retained earnings—Dec. 31** | **$  600,000** | **$ 120,000** | | | **$  600,000** |
| *Balance Sheet*<br>Other assets | $ 1,132000 | $ 520,000 | | | $1,652,000 |
| Investment in Son | 468,000 | | | a  40,500<br>b 427,500 | |
| | $1,600,000 | $ 520,000 | | | $1,652,000 |
| Capital stock | $1,000,000 | $ 400,000 | b 400,000 | | $1,000,000 |
| **Retained earnings** | **600,000** | **120,000** | | | **600,000** |
| | $1,600,000 | $ 520,000 | | | |
| Noncontrolling interest | | | | b  49,500<br>c   2,500 | 52,000 |
| | | | 595,000 | 595,000 | $1,652,000 |

Son's 10 percent ending noncontrolling interest at December 31, 2016 (reported on the balance sheet), is held outside of the consolidated entity for the entire year, so the noncontrolling interest computation is simply 10 percent of Son's equity at the beginning of the year plus 10 percent of Son's net income for the year less 10 percent of the dividends declared by Son during the year.

## PIECEMEAL ACQUISITIONS

A corporation may acquire an interest in another corporation in a series of separate stock purchases over a period of time. For example, *Dow Chemical Company's* Note 4 in its 2014 annual report discloses a plan to acquire *Exxon-Mobil's* shares of a 50/50 joint venture in *Univation Technologies LLC* in 2015, making Univation a wholly owned subsidiary (pending necessary regulatory approval).

For another example, *USX Corporation's* Note 28 to its 2000 annual report discloses that:

> On February 7, 2001, Marathon acquired 87 percent of the outstanding common stock of Pennaco Energy, Inc., a natural gas producer. Marathon plans to acquire the remaining Pennaco shares through a merger.[1]

---

[1]From The 2000 U.S. Steel Group Annual Report (P72) © USX Corporation.

These **piecemeal acquisitions** require the previously held investment to be remeasured at fair value at the date control of the subsidiary is obtained. Piecemeal acquisitions increase the details of computing investment income and consolidated net income. This section discusses these details and illustrates accounting for them.

Pop Corporation acquires a 90 percent interest in Son Corporation in a series of separate stock purchases between July 1 and October 1, 2018. Data concerning the acquisitions and interests acquired are as follows:

| Date | Interest Acquired | Investment Cost | Equity at Acquisition Date |
|------|-------------------|-----------------|----------------------------|
| July 1 | 5% | $ 7,000 | |
| August 1 | 5% | 8,000 | |
| October 1 | 80% | 210,000 | $220,000 |

The net identifiable assets of Son have fair values equal to book values. Any excess of investment cost over fair value/book value is due to goodwill. Pop's acquired interests during July and August are less than 20 percent, so Pop appropriately records these investments using the cost method. The additional investment on October 1, 2018 increases the investment account balance to $225,000 and increases Pop's ownership interest to 90 percent. An acquisition has now taken place, and Son must be consolidated. The $210,000 price paid for the 80 percent interest implies a total fair value for Son of $262,500. The fair value of identifiable net assets is $220,000, implying total goodwill of $42,500 for the Son acquisition. The original 10 percent investment must be adjusted to reflect the fair value on October 1, 2018. The fair value of the 10 percent interest is 10 percent of $262,500. Pop records a gain from revaluation of the investment in Son of $11,250. The gain is calculated by $26,250 − ($7,000 + $8,000). October 1 makes this a midyear acquisition. The consolidated income statement should only include Son's revenues and expenses for the last three months of 2018. Exhibit 8-2 shows consolidation workpapers for Pop and Subsidiary for 2018. Additional data, compatible with previous information, is provided for illustrative purposes. Son earned income during the year as follows: January 1 through September 30—$30,000 and October 1 through December 31—$10,000.

The workpaper entries are reproduced here for convenient reference:

| | | | |
|---|---|---|---|
| a | Income from Son (− R, − SE) | 9,000 | |
| | Investment in Son (− A) | | 9,000 |

To eliminate investment income and return the investment account to its beginning-of-the-period (i.e., acquisition date) balance.

| | | | |
|---|---|---|---|
| b | Sales (− R, − SE)* | 112,500 | |
| | Cost of sales and expenses (− E, + SE)* | | 82,500 |
| | Capital stock—Son (− SE) | 100,000 | |
| | Retained earnings—Son (− SE) | 90,000 | |
| | Goodwill (+ A) | 42,500 | |
| | Investment in Son (− A) | | 236,250 |
| | Noncontrolling interest—beginning (+ SE) | | 26,250 |

To eliminate reciprocal investment and equity balances, and preacquisition income, and record the beginning noncontrolling interest and goodwill. The * items represent the preacquisition revenues and expenses. Note that the beginning noncontrolling interest is the amount at the acquisition date of October 1, 2018. It represents 10% of the January 1 beginning capital stock plus retained earnings, plus implied goodwill, plus the revenues and expenses prior to the acquisition date. [10% × ($100,000 + $90,000 + $42,500 + $30,000)].

| | | | |
|---|---|---|---|
| c | Noncontrolling interest share (− SE) | 1,000 | |
| | Noncontrolling interest (+ SE) | | 1,000 |

To enter noncontrolling interest share of subsidiary's postacquisition earnings (10% × $10,000).

| EXHIBIT 8-2 |
|---|
| Piecemeal Acquisition of a Controlling Interest |

## POP CORPORATION AND SUBSIDIARY CONSOLIDATION WORKPAPER FOR THE YEAR ENDED DECEMBER 31, 2018

| | Pop | 90% Son | Adjustments and Eliminations Debits | Adjustments and Eliminations Credits | Consolidated Statements |
|---|---|---|---|---|---|
| *Income Statement* Sales | $274,875 | $150,000 | b 112,500 | | $312,375 |
| Income from Son | 9,000 | | a   9,000 | | |
| Gain from revaluation of prior investment in Son | 11,250 | | | | 11,250 |
| Expenses including cost of sales | (220,000) | (110,000) | | b   82,500 | (247,500) |
| Consolidated net income | | | | | 76,125 |
| Noncontrolling interest share (10% × $10,000) | | | c   1,000 | | (1,000) |
| **Controlling share of Consolidated Net Income** | **$ 75,125** | **$ 40,000** | | | **$75,125** |
| *Retained Earnings Statement* Retained earnings—Pop | $221,500 | | | | $221,500 |
| Retained earnings—Son | | $ 90,000 | b  90,000 | | |
| **Controlling share of Consolidated Net Income** | **75,125** | **40,000** | | | **75,125** |
| **Retained earnings—Dec. 31** | **$296,625** | **$130,000** | | | **$296,625** |
| *Balance Sheet* Other assets | $451,375 | $300,000 | | | $751,375 |
| Investment in Son | 245,250 | | | a     9,000 b 236,250 | |
| Goodwill | | | b  42,500 | | 42,500 |
| | $696,625 | $300,000 | | | $793,875 |
| Liabilities | $100,000 | $70,000 | | | $170,000 |
| Capital stock | 300,000 | 100,000 | b 100,000 | | 300,000 |
| **Retained earnings** | **296,625** | **130,000** | | | **296,625** |
| | $696,625 | $300,000 | | | |
| Noncontrolling interest | | | | b   26,250 c    1,000 | 27,250 |
| | | | 355,000 | 355,000 | $793,875 |

Except for the adjustment for preacquisition earnings, the consolidation workpaper procedures are equivalent to those used in previous chapters.

## SALE OF OWNERSHIP INTERESTS

When an investor sells an ownership interest, we normally compute a gain or loss on the sale as the difference between the sales proceeds and the carrying value of the investment interest sold. The carrying value of the investment should reflect the equity method when the investor is able to exercise significant influence over the investee. If the investor acquired its interest in several different purchases, the shares sold must be identified with particular acquisitions. This is usually done on the basis of specific identification or the first-in, first-out flow assumption.

GAAP changed the rules for consolidated groups of firms in 2007 (ASC 810-10-65). When a parent/investor sells an ownership interest, computation of a gain or loss on the sale is dependent on the nature and size of the transaction. We record a gain or loss only in those cases where the interest sold leads to deconsolidation of a former subsidiary. In other words, gains and losses are only recorded when a parent no longer holds a controlling interest after the sale.

If control is maintained, the sale of subsidiary shares is treated as an equity transaction. No gain or loss is recorded. There will be no recognized changes in recorded amounts for the subsidiary's assets and liabilities.

The following information illustrates sale of ownership interests, both at the beginning of the period and during the period. Sun Corporation is a 90 percent–owned subsidiary of Pam Corporation. Pam's Investment in Sun account at January 1, 2017, has a balance of $288,000, consisting of its underlying equity in Sun plus $18,000 goodwill. (Implied total goodwill is therefore $20,000.) Sun's stockholders' equity at January 1, 2017, consists of $200,000 capital stock and $100,000 retained earnings. During 2017, Sun reports income of $36,000, earned proportionately throughout the year, and it pays dividends of $20,000 on July 1.

## Sale of an Interest at the Beginning of the Period

If Pam sells a 10 percent interest in Sun (one-ninth of its holdings) on January 1, 2017, for $40,000, we record no gain or loss on the sale. Pam maintains an 80 percent controlling interest in Sun, and the noncontrolling interest increases to 20 percent. Recorded assets and liabilities of Sun, including goodwill, are unaffected. Pam makes the following entry to record the sale:

| | | |
|---|---|---|
| Cash (+A) | 40,000 | |
|     Investment in Sun (−A) | | 32,000 |
|     Additional paid-in capital—Pam (+SE) | | 8,000 |
| To record sale of a 10% interest in Sun. | | |

The consolidation workpaper entries increase the noncontrolling interest balance to reflect the transfer from the controlling (parent) to the noncontrolling interest.

During 2017, Pam accounts for its 80 percent interest under the equity method and records income of $28,800 ($36,000 net income of Sun × 80%) and a reduction in its investment account for dividends received. At December 31, 2017, Pam's Investment in Sun account has a balance of $268,800, computed as follows:

| | |
|---|---|
| Investment balance January 1, 2017 | $288,000 |
| Less: Book value of interest sold | 32,000 |
| | 256,000 |
| Add: Income less dividends ($28,800 − $16,000) | 12,800 |
| Investment balance December 31, 2017 | $268,800 |

The investment balance at year-end consists of Pam's underlying equity in Sun of $252,800 ($316,000 × 80%) plus $16,000 goodwill on the 80 percent retained interest. Consolidation workpapers for Pam and Subsidiary as shown in Exhibit 8-3 illustrate the effect of a decrease in ownership interest on workpaper procedures.

The sale of the interest was at the beginning of the period, so the effect of the sale on consolidation procedures for 2017 is minimal. The workpaper entries from Exhibit 8-3 are in general journal form:

| | | | |
|---|---|---|---|
| a | Income from Sun (−R, −SE) | 28,800 | |
| |     Dividends—Sun (+SE) | | 16,000 |
| |     Investment in Sun (−A) | | 12,800 |
| | To eliminate income and dividends from Sun and return the investment account to its beginning-of-the-period balance after the sale of the 10% interest. | | |

**EXHIBIT 8-3**

Sale of a 10% Interest
at the Beginning of the
Period

**PAM CORPORATION AND SUBSIDIARY CONSOLIDATION WORKPAPER FOR THE YEAR ENDED DECEMBER 31, 2017**

| | Pam | 80% Sun | Adjustments and Eliminations Debits | Credits | Consolidated Statements |
|---|---|---|---|---|---|
| *Income Statement* Sales | $600,000 | $136,000 | | | $ 736,000 |
| Income from Sun | 28,800 | | a 28,800 | | |
| Expenses including cost of sales | (508,800) | (100,000) | | | (608,800) |
| Consolidated net income | | | | | 127,200 |
| Noncontrolling interest share | | | c 7,200 | | (7,200) |
| **Controlling share of Net Income** | **$120,000** | **$ 36,000** | | | **$ 120,000** |
| *Retained Earnings Statement* Retained earnings—Pam | $210,000 | | | | $ 210,000 |
| Retained earnings—Sun | | $100,000 | b 100,000 | | |
| **Controlling share of Net Income** | 120,000 | 36,000 | | | 120,000 |
| Dividends | (80,000) | (20,000) | | a 16,000 / c 4,000 | (80,000) |
| **Retained earnings — Dec. 31** | **$250,000** | **$116,000** | | | **$ 250,000** |
| *Balance Sheet* Other assets | $639,200 | $350,000 | | | $ 989,200 |
| Investment in Sun | 268,800 | | | a 12,800 / b 256,000 | |
| Goodwill | | | b 20,000 | | 20,000 |
| | $908,000 | $350,000 | | | $ 1,009,200 |
| Liabilities | $150,000 | $ 34,000 | | | $ 184,000 |
| Capital stock | 500,000 | 200,000 | b 200,000 | | 500,000 |
| Other paid-in capital | 8,000 | | | | 8,000 |
| **Retained earnings** | 250,000 | 116,000 | | | 250,000 |
| | $908,000 | $350,000 | | | |
| Noncontrolling interest | | | | b 64,000 / c 3,200 | 67,200 |
| | | | 356,000 | 356,000 | $1,009,200 |

| b | Capital stock—Sun (−SE) | 200,000 | |
|---|---|---|---|
| | Retained earnings—Sun (−SE) | 100,000 | |
| | Goodwill (+A) | 20,000 | |
| | Investment in Sun (−A) | | 256,000 |
| | Noncontrolling interest (20%) (+SE) | | 64,000 |

To eliminate reciprocal investment and equity balances, and to record goodwill and beginning noncontrolling interest.

| c | Noncontrolling interest share (−SE) | 7,200 | |
|---|---|---|---|
| | Dividends—Sun (+SE) | | 4,000 |
| | Noncontrolling interest (+SE) | | 3,200 |

To enter noncontrolling interest share of subsidiary income and dividends.

Workpaper entry a reduces the investment in Sun to its $256,000 beginning balance after sale of the 10 percent interest, and entry b enters goodwill and noncontrolling interest based on amounts immediately after the 10 percent interest was sold. The last entry records the noncontrolling interest share of Sun Corporation's income and dividends.

## Sale of an Interest During an Accounting Period

If Pam sells the 10 percent interest in Sun on April 1, 2017, for $40,000, the sale may be recorded as of April 1, 2017, or, as an expedient, as of January 1, 2017. Assuming that Pam records the sale as of January 1, 2017, Pam records the $8,000 stockholders' equity effect the same as in the beginning-of-the-year sale situation and makes the same one-line consolidation entries as those previously illustrated. Consistency with the one-line consolidation requires that we prepare the consolidated financial statements using the same beginning-of-the-period sale assumption. That is, we compute noncontrolling interest share for a 20 percent noncontrolling interest outstanding throughout 2017, and we base beginning and ending noncontrolling interest amounts on a 20 percent noncontrolling interest. This alternative beginning-of-the-period sale assumption affects the parent's controlling share of consolidated net income and any difference in the additional paid-in capital is offset by differences in computing the income from subsidiary under a one-line consolidation and in computing noncontrolling interest share amounts in the consolidated financial statements.[2]

If the sale is recorded as of April 1, 2017, the stockholders' equity effect will be $7,100, computed as:

| | | |
|---|---|---|
| Selling price of 10% interest | | $40,000 |
| Less: Book value of the interest sold: | | |
| Investment balance January 1 | $288,000 | |
| Equity in income $36,000 × 1/4 year × 90% | 8,100 | |
| | 296,100 | |
| Portion of investment sold | × 1/9 | 32,900 |
| Stockholders' equity effect | | $ 7,100 |

Journal entries on Pam's books during 2017 to account for the 10 percent interest sold and its investment in Sun are as follows:

| | | |
|---|---|---|
| *April 1, 2017* | | |
| Investment in Sun (+A) | 8,100 | |
|     Income from Sun (R, +SE) | | 8,100 |
|   To record income for first quarter | | |
|     ($8,100 equity in income). | | |
| Cash (+A) | 40,000 | |
|     Investment in Sun (−A) | | 32,900 |
|     Additional paid-in Capital (+SE) | | 7,100 |
|   To record sale of a 10% interest in Sun. | | |
|   (See earlier computations.) | | |
| *July 1, 2017* | | |
| Cash (+A) | 16,000 | |
|     Investment in Sun (−A) | | 16,000 |
|   To record dividends received ($20,000 × 80%). | | |
| *December 31, 2017* | | |
| Investment in Sun (+A) | 21,600 | |
|     Income from Sun (R, +SE) | | 21,600 |
|   To record income for last three quarters of 2017. | | |

The income from Sun for 2017 is $29,700, consisting of $8,100 the first quarter and $21,600 the last three quarters. At year-end, the Investment in Sun account has the same $268,800 balance as in the beginning-of-the-period sale, but the balance includes different amounts:

| | |
|---|---|
| Investment balance January 1 | $288,000 |
| Less: Book value of interest sold | 32,900 |
| | 255,100 |
| Add: Income less dividends | 13,700 |
| Investment balance December 31 | $268,800 |

---

[2]If recorded as of the beginning of the period, we must consider dividends received on the interest sold prior to sale and adjust consolidation procedures accordingly.

The investment balance at year-end is the same as before because Pam holds the same ownership interest as under the beginning-of-the-year sale assumption. Further, Pam has received the same cash inflow from the investment ($40,000 proceeds from the sale and $16,000 dividends). We explain the effects under the different assumptions as follows:

|  | Sale at or Assumed at Beginning of Period | Sale within the Accounting Period |
|---|---|---|
| Equity effect on sale of investment | $ 8,000 | $ 7,100 |
| Income from Sun | 28,800 | 29,700 |
| Total equity effect | $36,800 | $36,800 |

The total equity effect of the two different assumptions is the same, but the effect on the consolidated financial statements differs. Both the controlling and noncontrolling interest shares of consolidated net income differ. Consolidation workpapers for a sale within an accounting period are illustrated in Exhibit 8-4.

We journalize workpaper entries to consolidate financial statements as follows:

| | | | |
|---|---|---|---|
| a | Income from Sun (−R, −SE) | 29,700 | |
| | Dividends—Sun (+SE) | | 16,000 |
| | Investment in Sun (−A) | | 13,700 |
| b | Capital stock—Sun (−SE) | 200,000 | |
| | Retained earnings—Sun (−SE) | 100,000 | |
| | Goodwill (+A) | 20,000 | |
| | Investment in Sun (−A) | | 255,100 |
| | Noncontrolling interest January 1 (+SE) | | 32,000 |
| | Noncontrolling interest April 1 (+SE) | | 32,900 |
| c | Noncontrolling interest share (−SE) | 6,300 | |
| | Dividends—Sun (+SE) | | 4,000 |
| | Noncontrolling interest (+SE) | | 2,300 |

**NONCONTROLLING INTEREST COMPUTATIONS**  We separate the noncontrolling interest amounts entered in entry b for illustrative purposes, but this is not required. We based one part of the noncontrolling interest calculation on the 10 percent noncontrolling interest at the beginning of the period. We calculate this as [($300,000 equity of Sun at January 1 plus goodwill of $20,000) × 10%]. The other part reflects the book value of the 10 percent increase in noncontrolling interest from the April 1 sale [($309,000 equity of Sun at April 1 plus goodwill of $20,000) × 10%]. Note that we also need a dual calculation for noncontrolling interest share of $6,300 [($36,000 × 10% × 1/4 year) + ($36,000 × 20% × 3/4 year)] for midyear sale situations. The investment in Sun decreased when the interest was sold on April 1; therefore, the $255,100 credit in workpaper entry b reflects the $288,000 beginning investment balance less the $32,900 book value of the interest sold on April 1.

Except for the items discussed, the workpapers in Exhibits 8-3 and 8-4 are similar, and the resulting consolidated financial statements are equivalent in all material respects. Because of the additional complexity involved when recording a sale as of the actual sale date, it is more efficient to use the beginning-of-the-period sale assumption. Use of a beginning-of-the-period assumption is also practical because current earnings information is not always available during an accounting period.

## Sale of an Interest Resulting in Deconsolidation

Whenever a parent ceases to have a controlling interest, the subsidiary should be deconsolidated (i.e., eliminated from the consolidated financial statements and recorded as either an equity method or cost method investment). Typically, this would result from a sale of an interest in the subsidiary, which reduces the parent share to less than 50 percent. In such cases, a gain or loss is calculated. The gain or loss is included in net income attributable to the parent. GAAP (ASC 810-10-65) measures the gain or loss as the difference between:

| | | | Adjustments and Eliminations | | |
|---|---|---|---|---|---|
| | Pam | 80% Sun | Debits | Credits | Consolidated Statements |
| **Income Statement** | | | | | |
| Sales | $600,000 | $136,000 | | | $ 736,000 |
| Income from Sun | 29,700 | | a  29,700 | | |
| Expenses including cost of sales | (508,800) | (100,000) | | | (608,800) |
| Consolidated net income | | | | | 127,200 |
| Noncontrolling interest share | | | c    6,300 | | (6,300) |
| **Controlling share of Net Income** | **$120,900** | **$ 36,000** | | | **$ 120,900** |
| **Retained Earnings Statement** Retained earnings—Pam | $210,000 | | | | $ 210,000 |
| Retained earnings—Sun | | $100,000 | b 100,000 | | |
| **Controlling share of Net Income** | 120,900 | 36,000 | | | 120,900 |
| Dividends | (80,000) | (20,000) | | a  16,000 c   4,000 | (80,000) |
| **Retained earnings—Dec. 31** | **$250,900** | **$116,000** | | | **$ 250,900** |
| **Balance Sheet** Other assets | $639,200 | $350,000 | | | $ 989,200 |
| Investment in Sun | 268,800 | | | a  13,700 b 255,100 | |
| Goodwill | | | b  20,000 | | 20,000 |
| | $908,000 | $350,000 | | | $1,009,200 |
| Liabilities | $150,000 | $ 34,000 | | | $ 184,000 |
| Capital stock | 500,000 | 200,000 | b 200,000 | | 500,000 |
| Other paid-in capital | 7,100 | | | | 7,100 |
| **Retained earnings** | 250,900 | 116,000 | | | 250,900 |
| | $908,000 | $350,000 | | | |
| Noncontrolling interest — Jan. 1                                   Apr. 1                                   Dec. 31 | | | | b  32,000 b  32,900 c   2,300 | 67,200 |
| | | | 356,000 | 356,000 | $1,009,200 |

**EXHIBIT 8-4**

Sale of a 10 percent Interest within an Accounting Period

**PAM CORPORATION AND SUBSIDIARY CONSOLIDATION WORKPAPER FOR THE YEAR ENDED DECEMBER 31, 2017**

**a.** The aggregate of:
  **1.** The fair value of consideration received
  **2.** The fair value of any retained noncontrolling investment in the former subsidiary at the date the subsidiary is deconsolidated
  **3.** The carrying amount of the noncontrolling interest in the former subsidiary (including any accumulated other comprehensive income attributable to the noncontrolling interest) at the date the subsidiary is deconsolidated

**b.** The carrying amount of the former subsidiary's assets and liabilities.

Assume that Pop Corporation sells its entire 90 percent interest in Son Corporation for $550,000 in cash. Pop uses the carrying amount of its investment to determine the gain or loss on the sale. If the carrying value equals $530,000, then Pop deconsolidates Son and records a gain of $20,000. Pop records the transaction as follows:

| | | |
|---|---:|---:|
| Cash (+A) | 550,000 | |
|     Investment in Son (−A) | | 530,000 |
|     Gain on sale (Ga, +SE) | | 20,000 |

**LEARNING OBJECTIVE 8.3**

## CHANGES IN OWNERSHIP INTERESTS FROM SUBSIDIARY STOCK TRANSACTIONS

Subsidiary stock issuances provide a means of expanding the operations of a subsidiary through external financing. Both the expansion and the financing decisions are, of course, controlled by the parent. Parent management may decide to construct a new plant for the subsidiary and to finance the construction by advising the subsidiary to sell additional subsidiary stock to the parent.

Subsidiary operations may also be expanded through the issuance of subsidiary stock to the public. A parent may even issue shares of one subsidiary to acquire another.

In the case of a partially owned subsidiary, noncontrolling stockholders may exercise their preemptive rights to subscribe to additional stock issuances in proportion to their existing holdings.

Subsidiary operations may be curtailed if the parent management decides to have the subsidiary reacquire its own shares.

A parent/investor's ownership in a subsidiary/investee may change as a result of subsidiary sales of additional shares or through subsidiary purchases of its own shares. The effect of such activities on the parent/investor depends on the price at which additional shares are sold or treasury stock is purchased and on whether the parent is directly involved in transactions with the subsidiary. In accounting for an equity investment under a one-line consolidation, GAAP (ASC 323-10-35) stipulates that transactions of an investee of a capital nature that affect the investor's share of stockholders' equity of the investee should be accounted for as if the investee were a consolidated subsidiary.

### Sale of Additional Shares by a Subsidiary

Assume that Pam Corporation owns an 80 percent interest in Sun Corporation and that Pam's investment in Sun is $180,000 on January 1, 2017, equal to 80 percent of Sun's $200,000 stockholders' equity plus $20,000 of goodwill (total goodwill is $25,000). Sun's equity on this date consists of:

| | |
|---|---:|
| Capital stock, $10 par | $100,000 |
| Additional paid-in capital | 60,000 |
| Retained earnings | 40,000 |
| Total stockholders' equity | $200,000 |

**SUBSIDIARY SELLS SHARES TO PARENT**    If Sun sells an additional 2,000 shares of stock to Pam *at book value of $20 per share* on January 2, 2017, Pam's investment in Sun will increase by $40,000 to $220,000, and its interest in Sun will increase from 80 percent (8,000 ÷ 10,000 shares) to 83-1/3 percent (10,000 ÷ 12,000 shares). The amount paid for the 2,000 additional shares is equal to book value, so Pam's investment in Sun still reflects the $20,000 goodwill:

| | January 1<br>Before Sale | January 2<br>After Sale |
|---|---:|---:|
| Sun's stockholders' equity | $200,000 | $240,000 |
| Pam's interest | × 80% | ×83 1/3% |
| Pam's equity in Sun | 160,000 | 200,000 |
| Goodwill | 20,000 | 20,000 |
|     Investment in Sun Balance | $180,000 | $220,000 |

If Sun sells the 2,000 shares to Pam *at $35 per share*, Pam's investment in Sun will increase to $250,000 ($180,000 + $70,000 additional investment), and its ownership interest will increase from 80 percent to 83-1/3 percent. Now Pam's investment in Sun reflects a $25,000 excess of investment balance over underlying book value. The additional $5,000 excess is the result of Pam's $70,000 payment to increase its equity in Sun by $65,000, which we analyze as follows:

| | | |
|---|---|---|
| Price paid by Pam (2,000 shares × $35) | | $70,000 |
| Book value acquired: | | |
| Underlying book value after purchase | $225,000 | |
| ($200,000 + $70,000) × 83-1/3% | | |
| Underlying book value before purchase | 160,000 | |
| ($200,000 × 80%) | | |
| Book value acquired | | 65,000 |
| Excess cost over book value acquired | | $ 5,000 |

We assign the $5,000 excess to identifiable assets or goodwill as appropriate and amortize over the remaining life of undervalued assets.

Now assume that Sun sells the 2,000 shares to Pam at *$15 per share* (or $5 per share below book value). Pam's ownership interest increases from 80 percent to 83-1/3 percent as before, and its investment in Sun increases by $30,000 to $210,000. As a result of paying less than book value for the shares, however, book value acquired exceeds investment cost:

| | | |
|---|---|---|
| Price paid by Pam (2,000 shares × $15) | | $30,000 |
| Book value acquired: | | |
| Underlying book value after purchase | $191,667 | |
| ($200,000 + $30,000) × 83-1/3% | | |
| Underlying book value before purchase | 160,000 | |
| ($200,000 × 80%) | | |
| Book value acquired | | 31,667 |
| Excess book value acquired over cost | | $ 1,667 |

Conceptually, the $1,667 excess book value acquired over cost should be assigned to reduce overvalued identifiable net assets. The practical solution, however, is to charge the excess book value to goodwill from investments in the same company's stock. In this example, reduce goodwill from $20,000 to $18,333. (Total goodwill is reduced to $23,000.)

**SUBSIDIARY SELLS SHARES TO OUTSIDE ENTITIES** Assume that Sun sells the 2,000 additional shares to other entities (noncontrolling stockholders). Pam's ownership interest declines from 80% (8,000 ÷ 10,000 shares) to 66-2/3 percent (8,000 ÷ 12,000 shares), regardless of the selling price of the shares. But the effect on Pam's Investment in Sun account depends on the selling price. The effect of the sale on Pam's underlying book value in Sun under each of three issuance assumptions ($20, $35, and $15 per share) is:

| | January 2, 2017, After Sale | | |
|---|---|---|---|
| | **Sale at $20** | **Sale at $35** | **Sale at $15** |
| Sun's stockholders' equity | $240,000 | $270,000 | $ 230,000 |
| Interest owned | × 66 2/3% | × 66 2/3% | × 66 2/3% |
| Pam's equity in Sun after issuance | 160,000 | 180,000 | 153,333 |
| Pam's equity in Sun before issuance | 160,000 | 160,000 | 160,000 |
| Increase (Decrease) in Pam's Equity in Sun | $ 0 | $ 20,000 | $ (6,667) |

Sale to outside entities at $20 per share does not affect Pam's equity in Sun because the selling price equals book value. If Sun sells the stock at $35 per share (above book value), Pam's equity in Sun will increase by $20,000, and if Sun sells at $15 per share (below book value), Pam's equity in Sun will decrease by $6,667.

GAAP (ASC 810-10-65) requires that we account for the effect of the decreased ownership percentage as an equity transaction. We adjust the parent's investment and additional paid-in capital account balances; we do not record a gain or loss on these types of transactions. Entries to record the changes in underlying equity on Pam's books under this approach are:

*Sale at $20 per Share (Book Value)*
None

*Sale at $35 per Share (Above Book Value)*

| | | |
|---|---|---|
| Investment in Sun (+A) | 20,000 | |
| Additional paid-in capital (+SE) | | 20,000 |

*Sale at $15 per Share (Below Book Value)*

| | | |
|---|---|---|
| Additional paid-in capital[3] (−SE) | 6,667 | |
| Investment in Sun (−A) | | 6,667 |

Under this method, we do not adjust unamortized fair value/book value differentials for the decreased ownership percentage.

**SUMMARY OF SUBSIDIARY STOCK SALES CONCEPTS**   Sales of stock by a subsidiary to its parent do not result in gain or loss recognition or adjustments to additional paid-in capital, but they do result in fair value/book value differentials equal to the difference between the cost of the additional shares and the parent's share of the difference in the subsidiary's stockholders' equity immediately before and after the stock sale.

GAAP considers sales of stock by a subsidiary to outside parties as capital transactions and requires adjustment of the parent's investment and additional paid-in capital accounts except when the shares are sold at book value. The amount of adjustment is the difference between the underlying book value of the interest in subsidiary's stockholders' equity held immediately before and after the additional shares are issued to outsiders.

If a parent and outside investors purchase shares of a subsidiary in relation to existing stock ownership (ratably), no adjustments to additional paid-in capital will be necessary, regardless of whether the stock is sold at book value, below book value, or above book value. Similarly, no excess or deficiency of investment cost over book value for the parent can result from this situation. This is true because the increased investment is necessarily equal to the parent's increase (decrease) in underlying book value from the ratable purchase of additional shares.

## Treasury Stock Transactions by a Subsidiary

The acquisition of treasury stock by a subsidiary decreases subsidiary equity and shares outstanding. If the subsidiary acquires treasury stock from noncontrolling shareholders at book value, no change in the parent's share of subsidiary equity results even though the parent's percentage ownership increases. A subsidiary's purchase of its own shares from noncontrolling stockholders at an amount above or below book value decreases or increases the parent's share of subsidiary book value and at the same time increases the parent's ownership percentage. This latter situation requires an entry on the parent's books to adjust the investment in subsidiary balance and to debit or credit additional paid-in capital for the difference in the parent's share of subsidiary book value before and after the treasury stock transaction. Once again, no gain or loss is recognized on these types of transactions.

Assume that Son Company is an 80 percent subsidiary of Pop and that Son has 10,000 shares of common stock outstanding at December 31, 2017. On January 1, 2018, Son purchases 400 shares of its stock from noncontrolling stockholders. Exhibit 8-5 summarizes the effect of this treasury stock acquisition on Pop's share of Son's book value under three different assumptions regarding the purchase price of the treasury shares.

Pop's equity in Son before the purchase of the 400 shares of treasury stock by Son was $160,000, and its ownership interest was 80 percent, as shown in Column 1 of Exhibit 8-5. The purchase of the 400 treasury shares by Son increases Pop's ownership percentage to 83-1/3 percent (or 8,000 of 9,600 outstanding shares), regardless of the price paid by Son. If Son purchases the 400 shares at their $20-per-share book value, Pop's share of Son's equity remains at $160,000, as shown in Column 2 of Exhibit 8-5, even though its interest increases to 83-1/3 percent. This requires no adjustment.

---

[3]This debit is to retained earnings when the parent's additional paid-in capital is insufficient to stand the debit.

**EXHIBIT 8-5**

Purchase of Treasury
Stock by Subsidiary

**EQUITY OF SON COMPANY**

| | Column 1:<br>Before<br>Purchase of<br>Treasury Stock | Column 2:<br>After<br>Purchase of 400<br>Shares at $20 | Column 3:<br>After<br>Purchase of 400<br>Shares at $30 | Column 4:<br>After<br>Purchase of 400<br>Shares at $15 |
|---|---|---|---|---|
| Capital stock, $10 par | $100,000 | $100,000 | $100,000 | $100,000 |
| Retained earnings | 100,000 | 100,000 | 100,000 | 100,000 |
| | 200,000 | 200,000 | 200,000 | 200,000 |
| Less: Treasury stock (cost) | — | 8,000 | 12,000 | 6,000 |
| Total equity | $200,000 | $192,000 | $188,000 | $194,000 |
| Pop's interest | × 4/5* | × 5/6** | × 5/6** | × 5/6** |
| Pop's share of<br>Son's book value | $160,000 | $160,000 | $156,667 | $161,667 |

*8,000 out of 10,000 outstanding shares.
**8,000 out of 9,600 outstanding shares.

If Son purchases the 400 shares of treasury stock at $30 per share, Pop's equity decreases by $3,333 to $156,667, as shown in Column 3 of Exhibit 8-5. Pop records the decrease with the following entry:

| | | |
|---|---|---|
| Additional paid-in capital (−SE) | 3,333 | |
|     Investment in Son (−A) | | 3,333 |
|       To record an investment decrease from Son's purchase<br>      of treasury stock at a price in excess of book value. | | |

This entry reduces Pop's Investment in Son to its share of the underlying book value in Son and also reduces additional paid-in capital. Treasury stock transactions are of a capital nature, so they do not affect gain or loss.

The third situation illustrated in Exhibit 8-5 (Column 4) assumes that Son purchases 400 shares of treasury stock at a price of $15 per share ($5 per share below book value). As a result of Son's acquisition of its own shares, Pop's share of Son's equity increases from $160,000 to $161,667. This increase of $1,667 requires the following adjustment on Pop's books:

| | | |
|---|---|---|
| Investment in Son (+A) | 1,667 | |
|     Additional paid-in capital (+SE) | | 1,667 |
|       To record an investment increase from Son's purchase<br>      of treasury shares at a price below book value. | | |

Current GAAP supports the parent adjustments illustrated here for changes resulting from subsidiary treasury stock transactions. GAAP prohibits the recognition of gain or loss from treasury stock transactions but, at the same time, requires the equity method with amortization of any differences between the investment fair value and its underlying book value, unless the difference is due to an intangible asset with an indeterminate life, such as goodwill. The parent bases accounting from subsidiary treasury stock transactions on the book value of net assets. During the time treasury shares are held, the book value of net assets would change due to the subsidiary's operations. If the treasury shares are eventually resold, the parent would account for this change on the basis of the book value of the assets at the time of sale. It should be understood, however, that *frequent and insignificant treasury stock transactions by a subsidiary tend to be offsetting with respect to purchases and sales and do not require the adjustments illustrated.*

## STOCK DIVIDENDS AND STOCK SPLITS BY A SUBSIDIARY

Stock dividends and stock splits by substantially owned subsidiaries are not common unless the noncontrolling interest actively trades in the security markets. This is because the parent controls such actions, and there is ordinarily no advantage to the consolidated entity or the parent from increasing the number of subsidiary shares outstanding through stock splits or stock dividends. Even if a subsidiary splits its stock or issues a stock dividend, the effect of such actions on consolidation procedures is minimal.

A stock split by a subsidiary increases the number of shares outstanding, but it does not affect either the net assets of the subsidiary or the individual equity accounts. Also, parent and noncontrolling interest ownership percentages are unaffected by subsidiary stock splits; accordingly, parent accounting and consolidation procedures are unaffected.

These same observations apply to stock dividends by subsidiaries except that the individual subsidiary equity accounts are changed in the case of stock dividends. This change occurs because retained earnings equal to par or stated value or to the market price of the additional shares issued is transferred to paid-in capital. Although capitalization of retained earnings does not affect parent accounting, it does change the amounts of capital stock, additional paid-in capital, and retained earnings to be eliminated in consolidation.

Pam Corporation owns 80 percent of the outstanding stock of Sun Corporation acquired on January 1, 2016, for $160,000. Sun's stockholders' equity on that date was as follows:

| | |
|---|---|
| Capital stock, $10 par | $100,000 |
| Additional paid-in capital | 20,000 |
| Retained earnings | 80,000 |
| Total stockholders' equity | $200,000 |

During 2016, Sun had net income of $30,000 and paid cash dividends of $10,000. Pam increased its investment in Sun for its investment income of $24,000 ($30,000 × 80%) and decreased it for dividends received of $8,000 ($10,000 × 80%). Thus, Pam's Investment in Sun account at December 31, 2016, was $176,000.

On the basis of the information given, the consolidation workpaper for Pam Corporation and Subsidiary at December 31, 2016 would include the following adjustments and eliminations:

| | | |
|---|---|---|
| Income from Sun (−R, −SE) | 24,000 | |
|   Dividends (+SE) | | 8,000 |
|   Investment in Sun (−A) | | 16,000 |
| Capital stock—Sun (−SE) | 100,000 | |
| Additional paid-in capital—Sun (−SE) | 20,000 | |
| Retained earnings—Sun (−SE) | 80,000 | |
|   Investment in Sun (−A) | | 160,000 |
|   Noncontrolling interest—beginning (+SE) | | 40,000 |

If Sun had also declared and issued a 10 percent stock dividend on December 31, 2016, when its stock was selling at $40 per share, Sun Corporation would record the stock dividend as follows:

| | | |
|---|---|---|
| Stock dividend on common (−SE) | 40,000 | |
|   Capital stock, $10 par (+SE) | | 10,000 |
|   Additional paid-in capital (+SE) | | 30,000 |

This stock dividend does not affect Pam's accounting for its investment in Sun (although now there are more shares and a different cost per share), but it does affect the consolidation workpaper, because Sun's capital stock has increased to $110,000 ($100,000 + $10,000) and its additional paid-in capital has increased to $50,000 ($20,000 + $30,000). Consolidation workpaper adjustment and elimination entries at December 31, 2016, would be as follows:

| | | |
|---|---|---|
| Income from Sun (−R, −SE) | 24,000 | |
|   Dividends (+SE) | | 8,000 |
|   Investment in Sun (−A) | | 16,000 |
| Capital stock—Sun (−SE) | 110,000 | |
| Additional paid-in capital—Sun (−SE) | 50,000 | |
| Retained earnings—Sun (−SE) | 80,000 | |
|   Investment in Sun (−A) | | 160,000 |
|   Noncontrolling interest—beginning (+SE) | | 40,000 |
|   Stock dividend on common (+SE) | | 40,000 |

We eliminate the $40,000 stock dividend account along with the reciprocal investment and equity balances because it is really an offset to $10,000 of the capital stock and $30,000 of the additional paid-in capital. In 2017 and subsequent years, retained earnings will reflect the $40,000 decrease from the stock dividend, and no further complications will result.

## SUMMARY

When a parent purchases a subsidiary during an accounting period, we do not include preacquisition earnings in computing consolidated net income. Both the controlling share and consolidated net income should only reflect postacquisition revenues and expenses. We also eliminate preacquisition dividends on an interest acquired during an accounting period in the consolidation process.

The acquisition of a controlling interest through a series of separate stock purchases over a period of time increases the detail involved in accounting for the total investment under the equity method. It also complicates the preparation of consolidated financial statements because the original investments must be adjusted to reflect the fair value on the date of the acquisition (i.e., when a controlling interest is achieved).

When a parent/investor sells an ownership interest in a subsidiary/investee, the gain or loss on sale is equal to the difference between the selling price and the book value of the investment interest sold. The gain or loss is recorded only when the parent no longer holds a controlling interest after the sale. If control is maintained by the parent after the sale, no gain or loss is recorded, and we adjust the additional paid-in capital instead. The sale of an interest during an accounting period increases the noncontrolling interest and necessitates changes in the computation of noncontrolling interest share.

The sale of additional shares by a subsidiary changes the parent's percentage ownership in the subsidiary unless the shares are sold to the parent and noncontrolling shareholders in proportion to their holdings. The direct sale of additional shares to the parent increases the parent's interest and decreases the noncontrolling shareholders' interest. The issuance of additional shares to noncontrolling stockholders or outside entities by the subsidiary decreases the parent's percentage interest and increases the noncontrolling shareholders' interests. Such changes require special care in accounting for a parent's investment under the equity method and in preparing consolidated financial statements.

Parent accounting and consolidation procedures are not affected by subsidiary stock splits. However, subsidiary stock dividends may lead to changes in the consolidation workpapers.

## QUESTIONS

1. Explain the terms *preacquisition earnings* and *preacquisition dividends*.

2. How are preacquisition earnings accounted for by a parent under the equity method? How are they accounted for in the consolidated income statement?

3. Assume that an 80 percent investor of Sub Company acquires an additional 10 percent interest in Sub halfway through the current fiscal period. Explain the effect of the 10 percent acquisition by the parent on noncontrolling interest share for the period and on total noncontrolling interest at the end of the current period.

4. Isn't preacquisition income really noncontrolling interest share?

5. How is the gain or loss determined for the sale of part of an investment interest that is accounted for as a one-line consolidation? Is the amount of gain or loss affected by the accounting method used by the investor?

6. When a parent sells a part of its interest in a subsidiary during an accounting period, is the income applicable to the interest sold up to the time of sale included in consolidated net income and parent income under the equity method? Explain.

7. Assume that a subsidiary has 10,000 shares of stock outstanding, of which 8,000 shares are owned by the parent. What equity method adjustment will be necessary on the parent books if the subsidiary sells 2,000 additional shares of its own stock to outside interests at book value? At an amount in excess of book value?

8. Assume that a subsidiary has 10,000 shares of stock outstanding, of which 8,000 shares are owned by the parent. If the parent purchases an additional 2,000 shares of stock directly from the subsidiary at book value, how should the parent record its additional investment? Would your answer have been different if the purchase of the 2,000 shares had been made above book value? Explain.

9. How do the treasury stock transactions of a subsidiary affect the parent's accounting for its investment under the equity method?

10. Can gains or losses to a parent/investor result from a subsidiary's/investee's treasury stock transactions? Explain.

11. Do common stock dividends and stock splits by a subsidiary affect the amounts that appear in the consolidated financial statements? Explain, indicating the items, if any, that would be affected.

## EXERCISES

### E 8-1
### Allocate income and dividends to controlling, noncontrolling, and preacquisition interests

Pop Corporation increases its ownership interest in its subsidiary, Son Corporation, from 70 percent on January 1, 2016, to 90 percent at July 1, 2016. Son's net income for 2016 is $200,000, and it declares $60,000 dividends on March 1 and $60,000 on September 1.

**REQUIRED:** Show the allocation of Son's net income and dividends among controlling interests, noncontrolling interests, and preacquisition interests.

### E 8-2
### Piecemeal acquisition of controlling interest with preacquisition income and dividends

On January 1, 2016, Pam Corporation purchased a 40 percent interest in Sun Corporation for $1,600,000, when Sun's stockholders' equity consisted of $2,000,000 capital stock and $2,000,000 retained earnings. On September 1, 2016, Pam purchased an additional 20 percent interest in Sun for $840,000. Both purchases were made at book value equal to fair value.

Sun had income for 2016 of $480,000, earned evenly throughout the year, and it paid dividends of $120,000 in April and $120,000 in October.

**REQUIRED:** Compute the following:
1. Pam's income from Sun for 2016
2. Preacquisition income that will appear on the consolidated income statement for 2016
3. Noncontrolling interest share for 2016

### E 8-3
### Journal entries (sale of an interest—beginning-of-year assumption)

Pop Corporation owns 100 percent (300,000 shares) of the outstanding shares of Son Corporation's common stock on January 1, 2016. Its Investment in Son account on this date is $4,400,000, equal to Son's $4,000,000 stockholders' equity plus $400,000 goodwill. During 2016, Son reports net income of $600,000 and pays no dividends.

On April 1, 2016, Pop sells a 15 percent interest (45,000 shares) in Son for $750,000, thereby reducing its holdings to 85 percent.

**REQUIRED:** Prepare the journal entries needed for Pop to account for its investment in Son for 2016, using a beginning-of-the-period sales assumption.

### E 8-4
### Sale of equity interest—beginning-of-year or actual sale date assumption

The balance of Pam Corporation's investment in Sun Company account at December 31, 2015, was $436,000, consisting of 80 percent of Sun's $500,000 stockholders' equity on that date and $36,000 goodwill.

On May 1, 2016, Pam sold a 20 percent interest in Sun (one-fourth of its holdings) for $130,000. During 2016, Sun had net income of $150,000, and on July 1, 2016, Sun declared dividends of $80,000.

**REQUIRED:** (Solve using both the actual date of sale assumption and the beginning-of-the-year sale assumption.)
1. Determine the gain or loss on sale of the 20 percent interest.
2. Calculate Pam's income from Sun for 2016.
3. Determine the balance of Pam's Investment in Sun account at December 31, 2016.

## E 8-5
### Computations and workpaper entries (midyear acquisition)

Pop Corporation paid $2,548,000 cash for 70 percent of the common stock of Son Corporation on June 1, 2016. The assets and liabilities of Son were fairly valued, and any fair value/book value differential is goodwill. Data related to the stockholders' equity of Son are as follows:

**Stockholders' Equity December 31, 2015**

| | |
|---|---|
| Common stock, $10 par | $2,000,000 |
| Retained earnings | 960,000 |
| Total stockholders' equity | $2,960,000 |

*Income and Dividends—2016*

| | |
|---|---|
| Net income (earned evenly throughout the year) | $ 480,000 |
| Dividends (declared and paid in equal | 240,000 |
| amounts in January, April, July, and October) | |

### REQUIRED

1. Determine the following:
   a. Goodwill from the investment in Son
   b. Pop's income from Son for 2016
   c. The Investment in Son account balance at December 31, 2016
2. Prepare the workpaper entries needed to consolidate the financial statements for 2016. Add the preacquisition income to Retained Earnings—Son.

## E 8-6
### Additional stock issued by subsidiary directly to parent

The stockholders' equities of Pam Corporation and its 80 percent–owned subsidiary, Sun Corporation, on December 31, 2016, are as follows (in thousands):

| | Pam | Sun |
|---|---|---|
| Common stock, $10 par | $10,000 | $6,000 |
| Retained earnings | 4,000 | 3,000 |
| Total Stockholders' Equity | $14,000 | $9,000 |

Pam's Investment in Sun account balance on December 31, 2016, is equal to its underlying book value. On January 2, 2017, Sun issued 60,000 previously unissued common shares directly to Pam at $25 per share.

### REQUIRED

1. Calculate the balance of Pam's Investment in Sun account on January 2, 2017, after the new investment is recorded.
2. Determine the goodwill, if any, from Pam's purchase of the 60,000 new shares.

## E 8-7
### Additional stock issued by subsidiary under different assumptions

The stockholders' equities of Pop Corporation and its 80 percent–owned subsidiary, Son Corporation, on December 31, 2016, appear as follows (in thousands):

| | Pop | Son |
|---|---|---|
| Common stock, $10 par | $5,000 | $2,200 |
| Retained earnings | 2,000 | 1,000 |
| Total | $7,000 | $3,200 |

Pop's Investment in Son account on this date is equal to its underlying book value. On January 1, 2017, Son issues 30,000 previously unissued common shares for $20 per share.

**REQUIRED**

1. If Pop purchases the 30,000 shares directly from Son, what is Pop's percentage ownership in Son after the new shares are acquired?
2. If Son sells the 30,000 previously unissued common shares to the public, what is Pop's percentage ownership in Son after the new issuance?
3. If Son sells the 30,000 shares to the public, prepare the journal entry on Pop's books to account for the effect of the issuance on its Investment in Son account assuming that *no* gain or loss is recognized.

## E 8-8
## Subsidiary issues additional stock under different assumptions

Pam Corporation owns two-thirds (600,000 shares) of the outstanding $1 par common stock of Sun Company on January 1, 2016. In order to raise cash to finance an expansion program, Sun issues an additional 100,000 shares of its common stock for $5 per share on January 3, 2016. Sun's stockholders' equity before and after the new stock issuance is as follows (in thousands):

|  | Before Issuance | After Issuance |
| --- | --- | --- |
| Common stock, $1 par | $ 900 | $1,000 |
| Additional paid-in capital | 600 | 1,000 |
| Retained earnings | 600 | 600 |
| Total stockholders' equity | $2,100 | $2,600 |

**REQUIRED**

1. Assume that Pam purchases all 100,000 shares of common stock directly from Sun.
   a. What is Pam's percentage ownership interest in Sun after the purchase?
   b. Calculate goodwill from Pam's acquisition of the 100,000 shares of Sun.

2. Assume that the 100,000 shares of common stock are sold to Van Company, one of Sun's noncontrolling stockholders.
   a. What is Pam's percentage ownership interest after the new shares are sold to Van?
   b. Calculate the change in underlying book value of Pam's investment after the sale.
   c. Prepare the journal entry on Pam's books to recognize the increase or decrease in underlying book value computed in b above assuming that gain or loss is *not* recognized.

## E 8-9
## Midyear piecemeal acquisition with goodwill

The stockholder's equity of Son Corporation at December 31, 2015, 2016, and 2017, is as follows (in thousands):

|  | December 31, | | |
| --- | --- | --- | --- |
|  | 2015 | 2016 | 2017 |
| Capital stock, $10 par | $200 | $200 | $200 |
| Retained earnings | 80 | 160 | 220 |
|  | $280 | $360 | $420 |

Son reported income of $80,000 in 2016 and paid no dividends. In 2017, Son reported net income of $80,000 and declared and paid dividends of $10,000 on May 1 and $10,000 on November 1. Income was earned evenly in both years.

Pop Corporation acquired 4,000 shares of Son common stock on April 1, 2016, for $64,000 cash and another 8,000 shares on July 1, 2017, for $164,000. Any fair value/book value differential is goodwill.

**REQUIRED:** Determine the following:

1. Pop's income from Son for 2016 and 2017
2. Noncontrolling interest at December 31, 2017
3. Preacquisition income in 2017
4. Balance of the Investment in Son account at December 31, 2017

## E 8-10
## Computations for sale of an interest

Pam Corporation acquired a 90 percent interest in Sun Corporation on July 1, 2017, for $675,000. The stockholders' equity of Sun at December 31, 2016, was as follows (in thousands):

|  |  |
|---|---|
| Capital stock | $500 |
| Retained earnings | 200 |
| Total | $700 |

During 2017 and 2018, Sun reported income and declared dividends as follows:

|  | **2017** | **2018** |
|---|---|---|
| Net income | $100,000 | $80,000 |
| Dividends (December) | 50,000 | 30,000 |

On July 1, 2018, Pam sold a 10 percent interest (or one-ninth of its investment) in Sun for $85,000.

### REQUIRED

1. Determine Pam's investment income for 2017 and 2018, and its investment balance on December 31, 2017 and 2018.

2. Determine noncontrolling interest share for 2017 and 2018, and the total of noncontrolling interest on December 31, 2017 and 2018.

## E 8-11
## Changes in subsidiary's outstanding shares

Pop Corporation purchased a 75 percent interest in Son Corporation in the open market on January 1, 2017, for $690,000. A summary of Son's stockholders' equity on December 31, 2016 and 2017, is as follows (in thousands):

|  | *December 31,* | |
|---|---|---|
|  | **2016** | **2017** |
| Capital stock, $10 par | $400 | $ 400 |
| Additional paid-in capital | 300 | 300 |
| Retained earnings | 100 | 300 |
| Total stockholders' equity | $800 | $1,000 |

On January 1, 2018, Son Corporation sold an additional 10,000 shares of its own $10 par stock for $30 per share. Pop assigns any excess/deficiency of fair value over book value to goodwill.

### REQUIRED: Compute the following:

1. The underlying book value of the interest in Son held by Pop on December 31, 2017.

2. Pop's percentage ownership interest in Son on January 3, 2018, assuming that Pop purchased the 10,000 additional shares directly from Son.

3. Pop's investment in Son on January 3, 2018, assuming that Pop purchased the additional shares directly from Son.

4. Pop's percentage ownership interest in Son on January 3, 2018, assuming that Son sold the 10,000 additional shares to investors outside the consolidated entity.

5. Pop's investment in Son on January 3, 2018, assuming that Son sold the 10,000 additional shares to investors outside the consolidated entity and no gain or loss is recognized.

## E 8-12
## Journal entries when subsidiary issues additional shares directly to parent

Pam Corporation's Investment in Sun Company account had a balance of $475,000 at December 31, 2016. This balance consisted of goodwill of $35,000 and 80 percent of Sun's $550,000 stockholders' equity.

On January 2, 2017, Sun increased its outstanding shares from 10,000 to 12,000 shares by selling 2,000 additional shares directly to Pam at $80 per share. Sun's net income for 2017 was $90,000, and in December 2017 it paid $60,000 dividends.

### REQUIRED: Prepare all journal entries other than closing entries to account for Pam's investment in Sun during 2017. Any difference between fair value and book value is goodwill.

## E 8-13
## Computations and entries (subsidiary issues additional shares to outside entities)

Pop Corporation paid $1,800,000 for 90,000 shares of Son Company's 100,000 outstanding shares on January 1, 2016, when Son's equity consisted of $1,000,000 of $10 par common stock and $500,000 retained earnings. The excess fair value over book value was goodwill. On January 2, 2018, Son sold an additional 20,000 shares to the public for $600,000, and its equity before and after issuance of the additional 20,000 shares was as follows (in thousands):

| | January 1, 2018<br>(Before Issuance) | January 2, 2018<br>(After Issuance) |
|---|---|---|
| $10 par common stock | $1,000 | $1,200 |
| Additional paid-in capital | — | 400 |
| Retained earnings | 800 | 800 |
| Total stockholders' equity | $1,800 | $2,400 |

### REQUIRED

1. Determine Pop's Investment in Son account balance on January 1, 2018.
2. Prepare the entry on Pop's books to account for its decreased ownership interest if gain or loss is not recognized.

# PROBLEMS

## P8-1
## Midyear acquisition and purchase of additional shares

A summary of changes in the stockholders' equity of Sun Corporation from January 1, 2016, to December 31, 2017, appears as follows (in thousands):

| | Capital Stock $10 Par | Additional Paid-in Capital | Retained Earnings | Total Equity |
|---|---|---|---|---|
| Balance January 1, 2016 | $500 | — | $50 | $550 |
| Dividends, December 2016 | — | — | (50) | (50) |
| Income, 2016 | — | — | 100 | 100 |
| Balance December 31, 2016 | $500 | — | $100 | $600 |
| Sale of stock January 1, 2017 | 100 | $ 62 | — | 162 |
| Dividends, December 2017 | — | — | (60) | (60) |
| Income, 2017 | — | — | 150 | 150 |
| Balance December 31, 2017 | $600 | $ 62 | $190 | $852 |

Pam Corporation purchases 40,000 shares of Sun's outstanding stock on July 1, 2016, in the open market for $620,000 and an additional 10,000 shares directly from Sun for $162,000 on January 1, 2017. Any excess of investment fair value over book value is due to goodwill.

### REQUIRED

1. Determine the balance of Pam's Investment in Sun account on December 31, 2016.
2. Compute Pam's investment income from Sun for 2017.
3. Determine the balance of Pam's Investment in Sun account on December 31, 2017.

## P8-2
## Computations and entries (subsidiary issues additional shares to public)

Pop Corporation purchased 480,000 shares of Son Corporation's common stock (an 80 percent interest) for $10,600,000 on January 1, 2016. The $1,000,000 excess of investment fair value over book value acquired was attributed to goodwill.

On January 1, 2018, Son sold 200,000 previously unissued shares of common stock to the public for $30 per share. Son's stockholders' equity on January 1, 2016, when Pop acquired its interest, and on January 1, 2018, immediately before and after the issuance of additional shares, was as follows (in thousands):

| | January 1, 2016 | January 1, 2018 Before Issuance | January 1, 2018 After Issuance |
|---|---|---|---|
| Common stock, $10 par | $ 6,000 | $ 6,000 | $ 8,000 |
| Other paid-in capital | 2,000 | 2,000 | 6,000 |
| Retained earnings | 4,000 | 5,000 | 5,000 |
| Total | $12,000 | $13,000 | $19,000 |

### REQUIRED

1. Calculate the balance of Pop's Investment in Son account on January 1, 2018, before the additional stock issuance.
2. Determine Pop's percentage interest in Son on January 1, 2018, immediately after the additional stock issuance.
3. Prepare a journal entry on Pop's books to adjust for the additional share issuance on January 1, 2018, if gain or loss is not recognized.

## P8-3
## Journal entries for sale of an interest

Pam Corporation owned a 90 percent interest in Sun Corporation, and during 2015 the following changes occurred in Sun's equity and Pam's investment in Sun (in thousands):

| | Sun's Stockholders' Equity | Goodwill | Investment in Sun (90%) |
|---|---|---|---|
| Balance, January 1, 2015 | $1,000 | $49.5 | $ 949.5 |
| Income—2015 | 250 | — | 225 |
| Dividends—2015 | (150) | — | (135) |
| Balance, December 31, 2015 | $1,100 | $49.5 | $1,039.5 |

During 2016, Sun's net income was $280,000, and it declared $40,000 dividends each quarter of the year.

Pam reduced its interest in Sun to 80 percent on July 1, 2016, by selling Sun shares for $120,000.

### REQUIRED

1. Prepare the journal entry on Pam's books to record the sale of Sun shares as of the actual date of sale.
2. Prepare the journal entry on Pam's books to record the sale of Sun shares as of January 1, 2016.
3. Prepare a schedule to reconcile the answers to parts 1 and 2.

## P8-4
## Reduction of interest owned under three options

Pop Corporation owns 300,000 of 360,000 outstanding shares of Son Corporation, and its $8,700,000 Investment in Son account balance on December 31, 2016, is equal to the underlying equity interest in Son. Son's stockholders' equity at December 31, 2016, is as follows (in thousands):

| | |
|---|---|
| Common stock, $10 par, 500,000 shares authorized, 400,000 shares issued, of which 40,000 are treasury shares | $ 4,000 |
| Additional paid-in capital | 2,500 |
| Retained earnings | 5,500 |
| | 12,000 |
| Less: Treasury shares at cost | 1,560 |
| Total stockholder's equity | $10,440 |

Because of a cash shortage, Pop decided to reduce its ownership interest in Son from a 5/6 interest to a 3/4 interest and is considering the following options:

Option 1. Sell 30,000 of the 300,000 shares held in Son.
Option 2. Instruct Son to issue 40,000 shares of previously unissued stock to the public.
Option 3. Instruct Son to reissue the 40,000 shares of treasury stock to the public.

Assume that the shares can be sold at the current market price of $50 per share under each of the three options and that any tax consequences can be ignored. Pop's stockholders' equity at

December 31, 2016, consists of $10,000,000 par value of common stock, $3,000,000 additional paid-in capital, and $7,000,000 retained earnings.

**REQUIRED:** Compare the consolidated stockholders' equity on January 1, 2017, under each of the three options. (*Hint:* Prepare journal entries on Pop's books as an initial step to your solution.)

## P8-5
### Subsidiary issues additional shares

Pam Corporation purchased 9,000 shares of Sun Corporation's $50 par common stock at $90 per share on January 1, 2016, when Sun had capital stock of $500,000 and retained earnings of $300,000. During 2016, Sun Corporation had net income of $50,000 but declared no dividends.

On January 1, 2017, Sun Corporation sold an additional 5,000 shares of stock at $100 per share. Sun's net income for 2017 was $70,000, and no dividends were declared.

**REQUIRED:** Determine each of the following:

1. The balance of Pam Corporation's Investment in Sun account on December 31, 2016
2. The goodwill that should appear in the consolidated balance sheet at December 31, 2017, assuming that Pam Corporation purchased the 5,000 shares issued on January 1, 2017
3. Additional paid-in capital from consolidation at December 31, 2017, assuming that Sun sold the 5,000 shares issued on January 1, 2017, to outside entities
4. Noncontrolling interest at December 31, 2017, assuming that Sun sold the 5,000 shares issued on January 1, 2017, to outsiders

## P8-6
### Midyear purchase of additional interest, preacquisition income

Pop Corporation purchased a 70 percent interest in Son Corporation on January 2, 2016, for $98,000, when Son had capital stock of $100,000 and retained earnings of $20,000. On June 30, 2017, Pop purchased an additional 20 percent interest for $37,000.

Comparative financial statements for Pop and Son Corporations at and for the year ended December 31, 2017, are as follows (in thousands):

|  | Pop | Son |
|---|---|---|
| **Combined Income and Retained Earnings** | | |
| **Statement for the Year Ended December 31** | | |
| Sales | $400 | $200 |
| Income from Son | 24 | — |
| Cost of sales | (250) | (150) |
| Expenses | (50) | (20) |
| Net income | 124 | 30 |
| Add: Beginning retained earnings | 200 | 50 |
| Less: Dividends, December 1 | (64) | (10) |
| Retained earnings, December 31 | $260 | $ 70 |
| | | |
| **Balance Sheet at December 31** | | |
| Other assets | $429 | $200 |
| Investment in Son | 171 | — |
| Total assets | $600 | $200 |
| Liabilities | $ 40 | $30 |
| Common stock | 300 | 100 |
| Retained earnings | 260 | 70 |
| Total equities | $600 | $200 |

**REQUIRED**

1. Prepare a schedule explaining the $171,000 balance in Pop's Investment in Son account at December 31, 2017.
2. Compute goodwill that will appear in the December 31, 2017, consolidated balance sheet.
3. Prepare a schedule computing consolidated net income for 2017.
4. Compute consolidated retained earnings on December 31, 2017.
5. Compute noncontrolling interest on December 31, 2017.

## P8-7
## Consolidated income statement (midyear purchase of additional interest)

Comparative separate-company and consolidated balance sheets for Pam Corporation and its 70 percent–owned subsidiary, Sun Corporation, at year-end 2016, were as follows (in thousands):

|  | Pam | Sun | Consolidated |
|---|---|---|---|
| Cash | $ 100 | $ 70 | $ 170 |
| Inventories | 800 | 100 | 900 |
| Other current assets | 500 | 130 | 630 |
| Plant assets—net | 3,500 | 800 | 4,300 |
| Investment in Sun | 600 | — | — |
| Goodwill | — | — | 40 |
| Total assets | $5,500 | $1,100 | $6,040 |
| Current liabilities | $ 500 | $ 300 | $ 800 |
| Capital stock, $10 par | 3,000 | 500 | 3,000 |
| Other paid-in capital | 1,000 | 100 | 1,000 |
| Retained earnings | 1,000 | 200 | 1,000 |
| Noncontrolling interest | — | — | 240 |
| Total equities | $5,500 | $1,100 | $6,040 |

Sun's net income for 2017 was $150,000, and its dividends for the year were $80,000 ($40,000 on March 1, and $40,000 on September 1). On April 1, 2017, Pam increased its interest in Sun to 80 percent by purchasing 5,000 shares in the market at $19 per share.

Separate incomes of Pam and Sun for 2017 are computed as follows:

|  | Pam | Sun |
|---|---|---|
| Sales | $2,000 | $1,200 |
| Cost of sales | (1,200) | (700) |
| Gross profit | 800 | 500 |
| Depreciation expense | (400) | (300) |
| Other expenses | (100) | (50) |
| Separate incomes | $ 300 | $ 150 |

### REQUIRED

1. Prepare a consolidated income statement for the year ended December 31, 2017.
2. Prepare a schedule to show how Sun's net income and dividends for 2017 are allocated among noncontrolling interests and controlling interests.

## P8-8
## Workpaper (midyear acquisition of 80% interest, downstream inventory sales)

Pop Corporation acquired an 80 percent interest in Son Corporation on October 1, 2016, for $82,400, equal to 80 percent of the underlying equity of Son on that date plus $16,000 goodwill (total goodwill is $20,000). Financial statements for Pop and Son Corporations for 2016 are as follows (in thousands):

|  | Pop | Son |
|---|---|---|
| ***Combined Income and Retained Earnings Statement for the Year Ended December 31*** |  |  |
| Sales | $112 | $ 50 |
| Income from Son | 3.8 | — |
| Cost of sales | (60) | (20) |
| Operating expenses | (25.1) | (6) |
| Net income | 30.7 | 24 |
| Retained earnings January 1 | 30 | 20 |
| Dividends | (20) | (10) |
| Retained earnings December 31 | $ 40.7 | $ 34 |

*(continued)*

| | Pop | Son |
|---|---|---|
| **Balance Sheet at December 31** | | |
| Cash | $   5.1 | $   7 |
| Accounts receivable | 10.4 | 17 |
| Note receivable | 5 | 10 |
| Inventories | 30 | 16 |
| Plant assets—net | 88 | 60 |
| Investment in Son | 82.2 | — |
| Total assets | $220.7 | $110 |
| Accounts payable | $ 15 | $ 16 |
| Notes payable | 25 | 10 |
| Capital stock | 140 | 50 |
| Retained earnings | 40.7 | 34 |
| Total equities | $220.7 | $110 |

---

## ADDITIONAL INFORMATION

1. In November 2016, Pop sold inventory items to Son for $12,000 at a gross profit of $3,000. One-third of these items remained in Son's inventory at December 31, 2016, and $6,000 remained unpaid.

2. Son's dividends were declared in equal amounts on March 15 and November 15, and its income was earned in proportionate amounts throughout each quarter of the year.

3. Pop applies the equity method such that its net income is equal to the controlling share of consolidated net income.

**REQUIRED:** Prepare a workpaper to consolidate the financial statements of Pop Corporation and Subsidiary for the year ended December 31, 2016.

## P8-9
## Workpaper (noncontrolling interest, preacquisition income, downstream sale of equipment, upstream sale of land, subsidiary holds parent's bonds)

Pam Corporation paid $175,000 for a 70 percent interest in Sun Corporation's outstanding stock on April 1, 2016. Sun's stockholders' equity on January 1, 2016, consisted of $200,000 capital stock and $50,000 retained earnings.

Accounts and balances at and for the year ended December 31, 2016, follow (in thousands):

| | Pam | Sun |
|---|---|---|
| **Combined Income and Retained Earnings** | | |
| **Statement for the Year Ended December 31** | | |
| Sales | $287.1 | $150 |
| Income from Sun | 12.3 | — |
| Gain | 12 | 2 |
| Interest income | — | 5.85 |
| Expenses (includes cost of goods sold) | (200) | (117.85) |
| Interest expense | (11.4) | — |
| Net income | 100 | 40 |
| Add: Beginning retained earnings | 250 | 50 |
| Less: Dividends | (50) | (20) |
| Retained earnings December 31 | $300 | $ 70 |
| **Balance Sheet at December 31** | | |
| Cash | $ 17 | $ 4 |
| Interest receivable | — | 6 |
| Inventories | 140 | 60 |
| Other current assets | 110 | 20 |
| Plant assets—net | 502.7 | 107.3 |
| Investment in Sun common | 180.3 | — |
| Investment in Pam bonds | — | 102.7 |
| Total assets | $950 | $300 |

| | Pam | Sun |
|---|---|---|
| Interest payable | $   6 | $   — |
| Other current liabilities | 38.6 | 30 |
| 12% bonds payable | 105.4 | — |
| Common stock | 500 | 200 |
| Retained earnings | 300 | 70 |
| Total equities | $950 | $300 |

## ADDITIONAL INFORMATION

**1.** Sun Corporation paid $102,850 for all of Pam's outstanding bonds on July 1, 2016. These bonds were issued on January 1, 2016, bear interest at 12 percent, have interest payment dates of July 1 and January 1, and mature 10 years from the date of issue. The $6,000 premium on the issue is being amortized under the straight-line method.

**2.** Other current liabilities of Sun Corporation on December 31, 2016, include $10,000 dividends declared on December 15 and unpaid at year-end. Sun also declared $10,000 dividends on March 15, 2016.

**3.** Pam Corporation sold equipment to Sun on July 1, 2016, for $30,000. This equipment was purchased by Pam on July 1, 2013, for $36,000 and is being depreciated over a six-year period using the straight-line method (no salvage value). Sun still owns the equipment.

**4.** Sun sold land that cost $8,000 to Pam for $10,000 on October 15, 2016. Pam still owns the land.

**5.** Pam uses the equity method for its 70 percent interest in Sun.

**REQUIRED:** Prepare a consolidation workpaper for the year ended December 31, 2016.

## P8-10
### Workpaper (midyear purchase of 10% interest, downstream sales)

Pop Corporation acquired a 70 percent interest in Son Corporation on January 1, 2016, for $420,000 cash, when Son's equity consisted of $300,000 capital stock and $200,000 retained earnings. On July 1, 2017, Pop acquired an additional 10 percent interest in Son for $67,500, to bring its interest in Son to 80 percent. The financial statements of Pop and Son Corporations at and for the year ended December 31, 2017, are as follows (in thousands):

| | Pop | Son |
|---|---|---|
| **Combined Income and Retained Earnings** | | |
| **Statement for the Year Ended December 31** | | |
| Sales | $  900 | $500 |
| Income from Son | 38 | — |
| Gain on machinery | 40 | — |
| Cost of sales | (400) | (300) |
| Depreciation expense | (90) | (60) |
| Other expenses | (160) | (40) |
| Net income | 328 | 100 |
| Add: Beginning retained earnings | 155 | 250 |
| Less: Dividends | (200) | (50) |
| Retained earnings December 31 | $  283 | $300 |
| | | |
| **Balance Sheet at December 31** | | |
| Cash | $    20 | $  80 |
| Accounts receivable | 130 | 30 |
| Dividends receivable | 20 | — |
| Inventories | 90 | 70 |
| Other current items | 20 | 80 |
| Land | 50 | 40 |
| Buildings—net | 60 | 105 |
| Machinery—net | 100 | 320 |
| Investment in Son | 510 | — |
| Total assets | $1,000 | $725 |
| Accounts payable | $  177 | $  40 |
| Dividends payable | 100 | 25 |
| Other liabilities | 140 | 60 |
| Capital stock, $10 par | 300 | 300 |
| Retained earnings | 283 | 300 |
| Total equities | $1,000 | $725 |

## ADDITIONAL INFORMATION

1. The fair value/book value differential from Pop's two purchases of Son was goodwill.

2. Pop Corporation sold inventory items to Son during 2016 for $60,000, at a gross profit of $10,000. During 2017, Pop's sales to Son were $48,000, at a gross profit of $8,000. Half of the 2016 intercompany sales were inventoried by Son at year-end 2016, and three-fourths of the 2017 sales remained unsold by Son at year-end 2017. Son owes Pop $25,000 from 2017 purchases.

3. At year-end 2016, Son purchased land from Pop for $20,000. The cost of this land to Pop was $12,000.

4. Pop sold machinery with a book value of $40,000 to Son for $80,000 on July 8, 2017. The machinery had a five-year useful life at that time. Son uses straight-line depreciation without considering salvage value on the machinery.

5. Pop uses a one-line consolidation in accounting for Son. Both Pop and Son Corporations declared dividends for 2017 in equal amounts in June and December.

**REQUIRED:** Prepare a workpaper to consolidate the financial statements of Pop Corporation and Subsidiary for the year ended December 31, 2017.

## P8-11
### Workpaper (midyear acquisition, preacquisition income and dividends, upstream sale of inventory, downstream sale of inventory item used by subsidiary as plant asset)

Pam Corporation acquired an 85 percent interest in Sun Corporation on August 1, 2016, for $522,750, equal to 85 percent of the underlying equity of Sun on that date.

In August 2016, Sun sold inventory items to Pam for $60,000 at a gross profit of $15,000. One-third of these items remained in Pam's inventory at December 31, 2016.

On September 30, 2016, Pam sold an inventory item (equipment) to Sun for $50,000 at a gross profit to Pam of $10,000. When this equipment was placed in service by Sun, it had a five-year remaining useful life and no expected salvage value.

Sun's dividends were declared in equal amounts on June 15 and December 15, and its income was earned in relatively equal amounts throughout each quarter of the year. Pam applies the equity method, such that its net income is equal to the controlling share of consolidated net income. Financial statements for Pam and Sun are as follows (in thousands):

| | Pam | Sun |
|---|---|---|
| **Combined Income and Retained Earnings** | | |
| **Statement for the Year Ended December 31, 2016** | | |
| Sales | $ 910 | $400 |
| Income from Sun | 7.5 | — |
| Cost of sales | (500) | (250) |
| Operating expenses | (200) | (90) |
| Net income | 217.5 | 60 |
| Add: Beginning retained earnings | 192.5 | 100 |
| Deduct: Dividends | (100) | (40) |
| Retained earnings December 31 | $ 310 | $120 |
| | | |
| **Balance Sheet at December 31, 2016** | | |
| Cash | $ 33.75 | $10 |
| Dividends receivable | 17 | — |
| Accounts receivable—net | 120 | 70 |
| Inventories | 300 | 150 |
| Plant assets—net | 880 | 500 |
| Investment in Sun—85% | 513.25 | — |
| Total assets | $1,864 | $730 |
| Accounts payable | $ 154 | $ 90 |
| Dividends payable | — | 20 |
| Capital stock | 1,400 | 500 |
| Retained earnings | 310 | 120 |
| Total equities | $1,864 | $730 |

**REQUIRED:** Prepare a consolidation workpaper for the year ended December 31, 2016.

## P8-12
### Consolidated statement of cash flows–indirect method (sale of an interest)

Comparative consolidated financial statements for Pop Corporation and its subsidiary, Son Corporation, at and for the years ended December 31, 2017 and 2016 follow (in thousands).

**Pop Corporation and Subsidiary Comparative Consolidated Financial Statements At and For the Years Ended December 31, 2017 and 2016**

|  | Year 2017 | Year 2016 | Year's Change 2017–2016 |
|---|---|---|---|
| *Income Statement* |  |  |  |
| Sales | $3,050.0 | $2,850.0 | $ 200.0 |
| Gain on 10% interest | 5.7 | — | 5.7 |
| Cost of sales | (1,750.7) | (1,690.0) | 60.7 |
| Depreciation expense | (528.0) | (508.0) | 20.0 |
| Other expenses | (455.0) | (392.0) | 63.0 |
| Noncontrolling interest share | (22.0) | (10.0) | 12.0 |
| Net income | $ 300.0 | $250.0 | $ 50.0 |
| *Retained Earnings Statement* |  |  |  |
| Retained earnings—beginning | $1,000.0 | $ 950.0 | $50.0 |
| Net income | 300.0 | 250.0 | 50.0 |
| Dividends | (200.0) | (200.0) | — |
| Retained earnings—ending | $1,100.0 | $1,000.0 | $ 100.0 |
| *Balance Sheet* |  |  |  |
| Cash | $ 46.5 | $50.5 | $(4.0) |
| Accounts receivable—net | 87.5 | 90.0 | (2.5) |
| Inventories | 377.5 | 247.5 | 130.0 |
| Prepaid expenses | 68.0 | 88.0 | (20.0) |
| Equipment | 2,970.0 | 2,880.0 | 90.0 |
| Accumulated depreciation | (1,542.0) | (1,044.0) | 498.0 |
| Land and buildings | 960.0 | 960.0 | — |
| Accumulated depreciation | (300.0) | (272.0) | 28.0 |
| Total assets | $2,667.5 | $3,000.0 | $(332.5) |
| Accounts payable | $ 140.0 | $ 343.5 | $(203.5) |
| Dividends payable | 52.5 | 52.5 | — |
| Long-term notes payable | 245.0 | 545.0 | (300.0) |
| Capital stock, $10 par | 1,000.0 | 1,000.0 | — |
| Retained earnings | 1,100.0 | 1,000.0 | 100.0 |
| Noncontrolling interest | 130.0 | 59.0 | 71.0 |
| Total equities | $2,667.5 | $3,000.0 | $(332.5) |

**REQUIRED:** Prepare a consolidated statement of cash flows for the year ended December 31, 2017. The changes in equipment are due to a $100,000 equipment acquisition for cash, current depreciation, and the sale of one-ninth of the fair value/book value differential allocated to equipment ($10,000) and related accumulated depreciation ($2,000). This reduction in the unamortized fair value/book value differential results from selling a 10 percent interest in Son for $72,700 and thereby reducing its interest from 90 percent to 80 percent. Son's net income and dividends for 2017 were $110,000 and $50,000, respectively. Dividends were declared and paid on December 31. Use the indirect method.

## PROFESSIONAL RESEARCH ASSIGNMENTS

Answer the following questions by reference to the FASB Codification of Accounting Standards. Include the appropriate reference in your response.

**PR 8-1**  Pop Corporation has owned a 30 percent interest in Son Corporation for ten years, and has properly recorded this investment using the equity method of accounting. On July 1 of the current year Pop purchased an additional 40 percent interest in Son. Is it permissible for Pop to include all current year earnings of Son in the consolidated income statement for the current year?

**PR 8-2**  Again, consider the facts presented in PR 8-1 above. Is it acceptable for Pop to continue to account for its investment in Son for the current year, using the equity method of accounting and delaying consolidation until the following year?

# CHAPTER 9

# Indirect and Mutual Holdings

Previous chapters presented situations in which an investor or parent directly owned some or all of the voting stock of an investee. The equity method is appropriate in those situations and equally appropriate when an investor indirectly owns 20 percent or more of an investee's voting stock. Consolidation is appropriate when one corporation, directly or indirectly, owns a majority of the outstanding voting stock of another. (ASC 325-20-35)

This chapter discusses parent company accounting and consolidation procedures for indirect ownership situations under the heading of "Indirect Holdings." The chapter also considers additional complexities that arise when affiliates hold the voting stock of each other. Affiliation structures of this type are covered under the heading of "Mutual Holdings." Discussion of **mutual holding** relationships logically follows the coverage of indirect holdings because such relationships are a special type of indirect holdings in which affiliates indirectly own themselves.

Although consolidation procedures for indirectly and mutually held affiliates are more complex than for directly held affiliates, the basic consolidation objectives remain the same. Most of the problems require measuring the realized income of the separate entities and allocating it between controlling and noncontrolling interests.

## AFFILIATION STRUCTURES

The potential complexity of corporate affiliation structures is limited only by one's imagination. Even so, the general types of affiliations are not difficult to identify. Exhibit 9-1 illustrates the more basic types of affiliations.

Although Exhibit 9-1 illustrates affiliation structures for parent and subsidiary corporations, the diagrams also apply to investor and investee corporations associated through the direct or indirect ownership of 20 percent or more of the voting stock of an investee. **Direct holdings** result from direct investments in the voting stock of one or more investees. **Indirect holdings** are investments that enable the investor to control or significantly influence the decisions of an investee not directly owned through an investee that is directly owned. Exhibit 9-1 illustrates two types of indirect ownership structures—the **father-son-grandson relationship** and the **connecting affiliates relationship**.

In the father-son-grandson diagram, the parent directly owns an 80 percent interest in Subsidiary A and indirectly owns a 56 percent interest (80% × 70%) in Subsidiary B. Noncontrolling shareholders own the other 44 percent of B—the 30 percent held directly by noncontrolling holders of B stock plus 14 percent held by the 20 percent noncontrolling holders of A stock (20% × 70%). The parent indirectly holds 56 percent of Subsidiary B stock, so consolidation of Subsidiary B is clearly appropriate. It is not the direct and indirect ownership of the parent, however, that determines whether an affiliate should be consolidated. The decision to consolidate is based on whether a

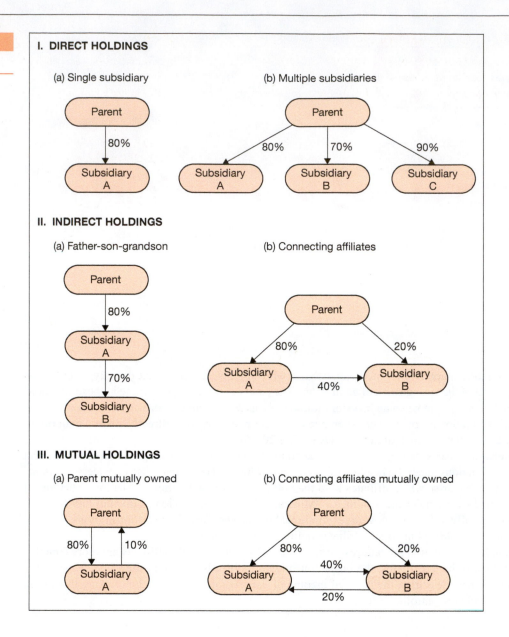

I. DIRECT HOLDINGS

(a) Single subsidiary

(b) Multiple subsidiaries

II. INDIRECT HOLDINGS

(a) Father-son-grandson

(b) Connecting affiliates

III. MUTUAL HOLDINGS

(a) Parent mutually owned

(b) Connecting affiliates mutually owned

controlling interest in an affiliate is held within the affiliation structure, thus giving the parent an ability to control the operations of the affiliate.

If Subsidiary A in the father-son-grandson diagram of Exhibit 9-1 had owned 60 percent of the stock of Subsidiary B, the parent's indirect ownership in Subsidiary B would have been 48 percent (80% × 60%), and the noncontrolling shareholders' interest would have been 52 percent [40% + (20% × 60%)]. Consolidation of Subsidiary B would still be appropriate, because 60 percent of B's stock would be held within the affiliation structure.

In the illustration of connecting affiliates, the parent company owns 20 percent of Subsidiary B stock directly and 32 percent (80% × 40%) indirectly, for a total direct and indirect ownership of 52 percent. The other 48 percent of Subsidiary B is held 40 percent by B's noncontrolling shareholders and 8 percent (20% × 40%) indirectly by A's noncontrolling shareholders.

In the first affiliation diagram for mutual holdings, the parent owns 80 percent of the stock of Subsidiary A, and Subsidiary A owns 10 percent of the stock of the parent. Thus, 10 percent of the parent's stock is held within the affiliation structure and 90 percent is outstanding. In diagram b for mutual holdings, the parent is not a party to the mutual holding relationship, but Subsidiary A owns 40 percent of Subsidiary B, and Subsidiary B owns 20 percent of Subsidiary A. The complexity involved in this latter case requires the use of simultaneous equations or other appropriate mathematical procedures to allocate incomes and equities among the affiliates.

LEARNING OBJECTIVE **9.1**

# INDIRECT HOLDINGS—FATHER-SON-GRANDSON STRUCTURE

The major problems encountered with indirect control situations are the determination of earnings and equities of the affiliates on an equity basis. Once we adjust the income and equity accounts of the affiliates to an equity basis, the consolidation procedures are the same for indirect as for direct ownership situations. The mechanics of the consolidation process may be cumbersome, however, because of the additional detail required to consolidate the operations of multiple entities.

Assume that Pop Corporation acquires 80 percent of the stock of Son Corporation on January 1, 2016, and that Son acquires 70 percent of the stock of Toy Corporation on January 1, 2017. Both Pop's investment in Son and Son's investment in Toy are made at fair value equal to book value. Trial balances for the three corporations on January 1, 2017, immediately after Son acquires its 70 percent interest in Toy, are as follows (in thousands):

|  | Pop | Son | Toy |
|---|---|---|---|
| Other assets | $400 | $195 | $190 |
| Investment in Son (80%) | 200 | — | — |
| Investment in Toy (70%) | — | 105 | — |
|  | $600 | $300 | $190 |
| Liabilities | $100 | $ 50 | $ 40 |
| Capital stock | 400 | 200 | 100 |
| Retained earnings | 100 | 50 | 50 |
|  | $600 | $300 | $190 |

Separate earnings of the three corporations (excluding investment income) and dividends for 2017 are (in thousands):

|  | Pop | Son | Toy |
|---|---|---|---|
| Separate earnings | $100 | $50 | $40 |
| Dividends | 60 | 30 | 20 |

## Equity Method of Accounting for Father-Son-Grandson Affiliates

In accounting for investment income for 2017 on an equity basis, Son determines its investment income from Toy before Pop determines its investment income from Son. Son Corporation accounts for its investment in Toy Corporation for 2017 with the following entries:

SON'S BOOKS

| Cash (+A) | 14,000 | |
| Investment in Toy (−A) | | 14,000 |
| To record dividends received from Toy ($20,000 × 70%). | | |
| Investment in Toy (+A) | 28,000 | |
| Income from Toy (R, +SE) | | 28,000 |
| To record income from Toy ($40,000 × 70%). | | |

Son's net income for 2017 is $78,000 ($50,000 separate income plus $28,000 income from Toy), and its Investment in Toy account balance at December 31, 2017, is $119,000 ($105,000 beginning balance, plus $28,000 income, less $14,000 dividends).

Pop's entries to account for its investment in Son Corporation for 2017 are as follows:

POP'S BOOKS

| Cash (+A) | 24,000 | |
| Investment in Son (−A) | | 24,000 |
| To record dividends received from Son ($30,000 × 80%). | | |
| Investment in Son (+A) | 62,400 | |
| Income from Son (R, +SE) | | 62,400 |
| To record income from Son ($78,000 × 80%). | | |

Pop's net income for 2017 is $162,400 ($100,000 separate income plus $62,400 income from Son), and its Investment in Son account balance at December 31, 2017, is $238,400 ($200,000 beginning balance, plus $62,400 income, less $24,000 dividends). The controlling share of consolidated net income for 2017 is $162,400, equal to Pop's equity method income.

## Computational Approaches for Consolidated Net Income

We determine Pop's income and consolidated net income independently by alternative methods. Computation in terms of the definition of consolidated net income is:

| | |
|---|---:|
| Pop's separate earnings | $100,000 |
| Add: Pop's share of Son's separate earnings ($50,000 × 80%) | 40,000 |
| Add: Pop's share of Toy's separate earnings ($40,000 × 80% × 70%) | 22,400 |
| Pop's net income and controlling share of consolidated net income | $162,400 |

We compute parent and controlling share of consolidated net income in terms of the consolidated income statement presentation by deducting noncontrolling interest share from combined separate earnings:

| | | |
|---|---:|---:|
| Combined separate earnings: | | |
| Pop Corporation | $100,000 | |
| Son Corporation | 50,000 | |
| Toy Corporation | 40,000 | $190,000 |
| Less: Noncontrolling interest shares: | | |
| Direct noncontrolling interest in Toy's income | $ 12,000 | |
| ($40,000 × 30%) | | |
| Indirect noncontrolling interest in Toy's income | 5,600 | |
| ($40,000 × 70% × 20%) | | |
| Direct noncontrolling interest in Son's income | | |
| ($50,000 × 20%) | 10,000 | 27,600 |
| Pop's net income and controlling share of net income | | $162,400 |

Still another computational approach uses a schedule such as the following:

| | Pop | Son | Toy |
|---|---:|---:|---:|
| Separate earnings | $100,000 | $ 50,000 | $ 40,000 |
| Allocate Toy's income to Son | | | |
| ($40,000 × 70%) | — | +28,000 | −28,000 |
| Allocate Son's income to Pop | | | |
| ($78,000 × 80%) | + 62,400 | −62,400 | — |
| Controlling share of net income | $162,400 | | |
| Noncontrolling interest share | | $ 15,600 | $ 12,000 |

Schedules are often helpful in making allocations for complex affiliations. This is particularly true when there are intercompany profits and when the equity method is not used or is applied incorrectly. The schedule illustrated here shows parent and controlling share of consolidated net income, as well as noncontrolling interest share. It also shows Son's investment income from Toy Corporation ($28,000) and Pop's investment income from Son Corporation ($62,400).

## Consolidation Workpaper—Equity Method

Exhibit 9-2 illustrates a consolidation workpaper for the year 2017. The workpaper shows that no new consolidation procedures have been introduced. Consolidation workpaper entries a and b eliminate investment income, dividends, and investment and equity balances for Son's investment in Toy. Entries c and d eliminate investment income, dividends, and investment and equity balances for Pop's investment in Son. Entry e records noncontrolling interests in the earnings and dividends of Toy and Son.

| | | | |
|---|---|---:|---:|
| e | Noncontrolling interest share—Son (−SE) | 15,600 | |
| | Noncontrolling interest share—Toy (−SE) | 12,000 | |
| | Dividends (+SE) | | 12,000 |
| | Noncontrolling interest—Son (+SE) | | 9,600 |
| | Noncontrolling interest—Toy (+SE) | | 6,000 |
| | To enter noncontrolling interest shares of subsidiary income and dividends. | | |

| POP CORPORATION AND SUBSIDIARIES CONSOLIDATION WORKPAPER FOR THE YEAR ENDED DECEMBER 31, 2017 (IN THOUSANDS) | | | | Adjustments and Eliminations | | |
|---|---|---|---|---|---|---|
| | Pop | 80% Son | 70% Toy | Debits | Credits | Consolidated Statements |
| *Income Statement* Sales | $ 200 | $140 | $100 | | | $440 |
| Income from Son | 62.4 | | | c  62.4 | | |
| Income from Toy | | 28 | | a  28 | | |
| Expenses including cost of sales | (100) | (90) | (60) | | | (250) |
| Noncontrolling interest share—Son | | | | e  15.6 | | (15.6) |
| Noncontrolling interest share—Toy | | | | e  12 | | (12) |
| **Controlling share of Net income** | **$ 162.4** | **$ 78** | **$ 40** | | | **$162.4** |
| *Retained Earnings Statement* Retained earnings—Pop | $ 100 | | | | | $100 |
| Retained earnings—Son | | $ 50 | | d  50 | | |
| Retained earnings—Toy | | | $ 50 | b  50 | | |
| **Controlling share of Net income** | 162.4 | 78 | 40 | | | 162.4 |
| Dividends | (60) | (30) | (20) | | a  14 c  24 e  12 | (60) |
| **Retained earnings—December 31** | **$ 202.4** | **$ 98** | **$ 70** | | | **$202.4** |
| *Balance Sheet* Other assets | $ 461.6 | $231 | $ 200 | | | $892.6 |
| Investment in Son | 238.4 | | | | c  38.4 d 200 | |
| Investment in Toy | | 119 | | | a  14 b 105 | |
| | $ 700 | $350 | $ 200 | | | $892.6 |
| Liabilities | $  97.6 | $ 52 | $  30 | | | $179.6 |
| Capital stock—Pop | 400 | | | | | 400 |
| Capital stock—Son | | 200 | | d 200 | | |
| Capital stock—Toy | | | 100 | b 100 | | |
| **Retained earnings** | 202.4 | 98 | 70 | | | 202.4 |
| | $ 700 | $350 | $ 200 | | | |
| Noncontrolling interest in Toy, January 1 Noncontrolling interest in Son, January 1 Noncontrolling interest in Son, December 31 Noncontrolling interest in Toy, December 31 | | | | | b  45 d  50 e  9.6 e  6 | 110.6 |
| | | | | 518 | 518 | $892.6 |

**EXHIBIT 9-2**

Indirect Holdings— Father-Son-Grandson Type (Equity Method)

Toy's $45,000 beginning noncontrolling interest is simply the 30 percent direct noncontrolling interest percentage times Toy's $150,000 equity at the beginning of 2017. Noncontrolling interest share of Toy is 30 percent of Toy's $40,000 reported income. Similarly, the $50,000 beginning noncontrolling interest in Son is 20 percent of Son's $250,000 equity at January 1, 2017, and the $15,600 noncontrolling interest share of Son is 20 percent of Son's reported net income. The controlling share of net income and consolidated retained earnings of $162,400 and $202,400, respectively, are equal to Pop's net income and retained earnings, respectively.

## INDIRECT HOLDINGS—CONNECTING AFFILIATES STRUCTURE

Pet Corporation owns a 70 percent interest in Sal Corporation and a 60 percent interest in Tie Corporation. In addition, Sal Corporation owns a 20 percent interest in Tie. We diagram the affiliation structure of Pet Corporation and Subsidiaries as follows:

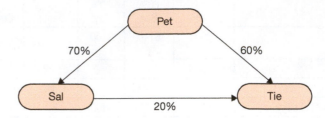

The following table summarizes data relevant to the investments of Pet and Sal.

|  | Pet's Investment in Sal (70%) Acquired January 1, 2017 | Pet's Investment in Tie (60%) Acquired January 1, 2016 | Sal's Investment in Tie (20%) Acquired January 1, 2013 |
|---|---|---|---|
| Fair value/Cost | $176,400 | $ 97,200 | $22,400 |
| Less: Book value | (164,400) | (85,200) | (22,400) |
| Goodwill | $ 12,000 | $ 12,000 | — |
| *Investment Balance December 31, 2017* |  |  |  |
| Cost | $176,400 | $ 97,200 | $22,400 |
| Add: Share of investees' pre-2018 income less dividends | 7,000 | 18,000 | 16,000 |
| Balance December 31, 2017 | $183,400 | $115,200 | $38,400 |

During 2018, Pet, Sal, and Tie had earnings from their own operations of $70,000, $35,000, and $20,000, respectively, and declared dividends of $40,000, $20,000, and $10,000, respectively. Pet's separate earnings of $70,000 included an unrealized gain of $10,000 from the sale of land to Sal during 2018. Sal's separate earnings of $35,000 included an unrealized profit of $5,000 on inventory items sold to Pet for $15,000 during 2018 that remained in Pet's December 31, 2018, inventory. A schedule computing controlling interest share and noncontrolling interest share of consolidated net income for the Pet-Sal-Tie affiliation for 2018 is shown in Exhibit 9-3.

| EXHIBIT 9-3 |  | Pet | Sal | Tie |
|---|---|---|---|---|
| **Income Allocation Schedule** | Separate earnings | $ 70,000 | $ 35,000 | $20,000 |
|  | Deduct: Unrealized profit | −10,000 | −5,000 | — |
|  | Separate realized earnings | 60,000 | 30,000 | 20,000 |
|  | Allocate Tie's income: |  |  |  |
|  | 20% to Sal | — | +4,000 | −4,000 |
|  | 60% to Pet | +12,000 | — | −12,000 |
|  | Allocate Sal's income: |  |  |  |
|  | 70% to Pet | +23,800 | −23,800 | — |
|  | Pet's net income and controlling share of consolidated net income | $ 95,800 |  |  |
|  | Noncontrolling interest share |  | $ 10,200 | $  4,000 |

## Equity Method of Accounting for Connecting Affiliates

Before allocating the separate earnings of Sal and Tie to Pet, we eliminate any unrealized profits included in earnings. Exhibit 9-3 shows the allocation of Tie's income as 20 percent to Sal and 60 percent to Pet. This allocation must precede the allocation of Sal's income to Pet because Sal's income includes $4,000 investment income from Tie.

In accounting for its investment in Tie for 2018, Sal makes the following entries:

| | | |
|---|---|---|
| Cash (+A) | 2,000 | |
|     Investment in Tie (−A) | | 2,000 |
|     To record dividends received from Tie ($10,000 × 20%). | | |
| Investment in Tie (+A) | 4,000 | |
|     Income from Tie (R, +SE) | | 4,000 |
|     To record income from Tie ($20,000 × 20%). | | |

Sal's Investment in Tie account at December 31, 2018, has a balance of $40,400—the $38,400 balance at December 31, 2017, plus $4,000 investment income, less $2,000 dividends. We do not reduce Sal's income from Tie for the $5,000 unrealized profit on inventory items sold to Pet because Tie is not a party in the intercompany sale. Sal's $39,000 net income includes $5,000 unrealized profit, which we eliminate when allocating Sal's realized income to Pet and Sal's noncontrolling stockholders.

Pet makes the following entries to account for its investments during 2018:

| | | |
|---|---|---|
| *Investment in Tie* | | |
| Cash (+A) | 6,000 | |
|     Investment in Tie (−A) | | 6,000 |
|     To record dividends received from Tie ($10,000 × 60%). | | |
| Investment in Tie (+A) | 12,000 | |
|     Income from Tie (R, +SE) | | 12,000 |
|     To record income from Tie. | | |
| *Investment in Sal* | | |
| Cash (+A) | 14,000 | |
|     Investment in Sal (−A) | | 14,000 |
|     To record dividends received from Sal ($20,000 × 70%). | | |
| Investment in Sal (+A) | 13,800 | |
|     Income from Sal (R, +SE) | | 13,800 |
|     To record income from Sal computed as follows: | | |
|     70% of Sal's reported income of $39,000 | | $27,300 |
|     Less: 70% of Sal's unrealized inventory profit of $5,000 | | −3,500 |
|     Less: 100% of unrealized gain on land | | −10,000 |
| | | $ 13,800 |

Pet's investment accounts at December 31, 2018, show the following balances:

| | Investment in Sal (70%) | Investment in Tie (60%) |
|---|---|---|
| Balance December 31, 2017 | $183,400 | $115,200 |
| Add: Investment income | 13,800 | 12,000 |
| Deduct: Dividends | −14,000 | − 6,000 |
| Balance December 31, 2018 | $183,200 | $121,200 |

## Consolidation Workpaper—Equity Method

Exhibit 9-4 presents a consolidation workpaper for Pet Corporation and Subsidiaries for 2018.

EXHIBIT 9-4

Connecting Affiliates
with Intercompany
Profits

## PET CORPORATION AND SUBSIDIARIES CONSOLIDATION WORKPAPER FOR THE YEAR ENDED DECEMBER 31, 2018 (IN THOUSANDS)

| | Pet | Sal | Tie | Adjustments and Eliminations Debits | Adjustments and Eliminations Credits | Consolidated Statements |
|---|---|---|---|---|---|---|
| *Income Statement* Sales | $200 | $150 | $100 | a  15 | | $435 |
| Income from Sal | 13.8 | | | g  13.8 | | |
| Income from Tie | 12 | 4 | | d  16 | | |
| Gain on land | 10 | | | c  10 | | |
| Cost of sales | (100) | (80) | (50) | b   5 | a  15 | (220) |
| Other expenses | (40) | (35) | (30) | | | (105) |
| Noncontrolling interest share—Sal [($39 − $5) × 30%] | | | | | i  10.2 | (10.2) |
| Noncontrolling interest share—Tie ($20 × 20%) | | | | | f   4 | (4) |
| **Controlling share of Net income** | **$ 95.8** | **$ 39** | **$ 20** | | | **$ 95.8** |
| *Retained Earnings Statement* Retained earnings—Pet | $223 | | | | | $223 |
| Retained earnings—Sal | | $ 50 | | h  50 | | |
| Retained earnings—Tie | | | $ 80 | e  80 | | |
| **Controlling share of net income** | **95.8** | **39** | **20** | | | **95.8** |
| Dividends | | | | | d   8<br>f   2<br>g  14<br>i   6 | |
| | (40) | (20) | (10) | | | (40) |
| **Retained earnings—December 31** | **$278.8** | **$ 69** | **$ 90** | | | **$278.8** |
| *Balance Sheet* Other assets | $ 50.6 | $ 19.6 | $ 85 | | | $155.2 |
| Inventories | 50 | 40 | 15 | | b   5 | 100 |
| Plant assets—net | 400 | 200 | 100 | | c  10 | 690 |
| Investment in Sal (70%) | 183.2 | | | g    .2 | h 183.4 | |
| Investment in Tie (60%) | 121.2 | | | | d   6<br>e 115.2 | |
| Investment in Tie (20%) | | 40.4 | | | d   2<br>e  38.4 | |
| Goodwill | | | | e  12<br>h  12 | | 24 |
| | $805 | $300 | $200 | | | $969.2 |
| Liabilities | $126.2 | $ 31 | $ 10 | | | $167.2 |
| Capital stock—Pet | 400 | | | | | 400 |
| Capital stock—Sal | | 200 | | h 200 | | |
| Capital stock—Tie | | | 100 | e 100 | | |
| **Retained earnings** | **278.8** | **69** | **90** | | | **278.8** |
| | $805 | $300 | $200 | | | |
| Noncontrolling interest in Tie, January 1<br>Noncontrolling interest in Sal, January 1<br>Noncontrolling interest in Tie, December 31<br>Noncontrolling interest in Sal, December 31 | | | | | e  38.4<br>h  78.6<br>f   2<br>i   4.2 | 123.2 |
| | | | | 528.2 | 528.2 | $969.2 |

The adjustment and elimination entries are reproduced in journal form.

| | | | |
|---|---|---|---|
| a | Sales (− R, − SE) | 15,000 | |
| |     Cost of sales (− E, + SE) | | 15,000 |
| | To eliminate reciprocal sales and cost of sales. | | |
| b | Cost of sales (E, − SE) | 5,000 | |
| |     Inventory (− A) | | 5,000 |
| | To eliminate unrealized intercompany profit from inventory at December 31, 2018. | | |
| c | Gain on land (− Ga, − SE) | 10,000 | |
| |     Plant assets—net (− A) | | 10,000 |
| | To eliminate unrealized profit from intercompany sale of land. | | |
| d | Income from Tie (− R, − SE) | 16,000 | |
| |     Dividends (Tie's) (+ SE) | | 8,000 |
| |     Investment in Tie (60%) (− A) | | 6,000 |
| |     Investment in Tie (20%) (− A) | | 2,000 |
| | To eliminate income from Tie and dividends from Tie and to adjust the Investment in Tie account. | | |
| e | Retained earnings—Tie, January 1, 2018 (− SE) | 80,000 | |
| | Goodwill (+ A) | 12,000 | |
| | Capital stock—Tie (− SE) | 100,000 | |
| |     Investment in Tie (60%) (− A) | | 115,200 |
| |     Investment in Tie (20%) (− A) | | 38,400 |
| |     Noncontrolling interests—Tie (+ SE) | | 38,400 |
| | To eliminate reciprocal investment and equity amounts of Tie and to establish goodwill and noncontrolling interest at January 1, 2018. | | |
| f | Noncontrolling interest share—Tie (− SE) | 4,000 | |
| |     Dividends (+ SE) | | 2,000 |
| |     Noncontrolling interest—Tie (+ SE) | | 2,000 |
| | To enter noncontrolling interest share of subsidiary income and dividends. | | |
| g | Income from Sal (− R, − SE) | 13,800 | |
| | Investment in Sal (+ A) | 200 | |
| |     Dividends (Sal's) (+ SE) | | 14,000 |
| | To eliminate income from Sal and dividends from Sal and to adjust the Investment in Sal account. | | |
| h | Retained earnings—Sal, January 1, 2018 (− SE) | 50,000 | |
| | Goodwill (+ A) | 12,000 | |
| | Capital stock—Sal (− SE) | 200,000 | |
| |     Investment in Sal (− A) | | 183,400 |
| |     Noncontrolling interest—Sal (+ SE) | | 78,600 |
| | To eliminate reciprocal investment and equity amounts in Sal and to establish goodwill and noncontrolling interest at January 1, 2018. | | |
| i | Noncontrolling interest share—Sal (− SE) | 10,200 | |
| |     Dividends (+ SE) | | 6,000 |
| |     Noncontrolling interest—Sal (+ SE) | | 4,200 |
| | To enter noncontrolling interest share of subsidiary income and dividends. | | |

A check on the $123,200 noncontrolling interest at December 31, 2018, as shown in Exhibit 9-4 may be helpful at this point. We can confirm the noncontrolling interest as follows:

|  | Noncontrolling Interest in Sal (30%) | Noncontrolling Interest in Tie (20%) | Total Noncontrolling Interest |
|---|---|---|---|
| Fair value* at December 31, 2018: |  |  |  |
| Sal (($269,000 + $12,000) × 30%) | $84,300 | — | $ 84,300 |
| Tie (($190,000 + $12,000) × 20%) | — | $40,400 | 40,400 |
| Less: Unrealized profit of Sal ($5,000 × 30%) | (1,500) | — | (1,500) |
| Noncontrolling interest December 31, 2018 | $82,800 | $40,400 | $123,200 |

*Book value plus implied total goodwill (i.e., goodwill associated with the 70% investment for Sal and the 60% investment for Tie).

Except for the deduction of 30 percent of the $5,000 unrealized inventory profit on Sal's sale to Pet, the noncontrolling interest is stated at its underlying fair value at December 31, 2018.

## MUTUAL HOLDINGS—PARENT STOCK HELD BY SUBSIDIARY

When affiliates hold ownership interests in each other, a mutual holding situation exists. Parent stock held by the subsidiary is not outstanding from the consolidated viewpoint and should not be reported as outstanding stock in a consolidated balance sheet. (ASC 810-10-45)

For example, if Pam Corporation owns a 90 percent interest in Sun Corporation and Sun owns a 10 percent interest in Pam, the 10 percent interest held by Sun is not outstanding for consolidation purposes, nor is the 90 percent interest in Sun held by Pam. Consolidation practice requires the exclusion of both the 10 percent and the 90 percent interests from consolidated statements, and the question is not whether the 10 percent interest in Pam should be excluded, but rather how we eliminate it in the consolidation process. The elimination procedures depend on the method used in accounting for the investment.

There are two generally accepted methods of accounting for parent stock held by a subsidiary—the treasury stock approach and the conventional approach. The **treasury stock approach** considers parent stock held by a subsidiary to be treasury stock of the consolidated entity. Accordingly, we maintain the investment in parent account on the books of the subsidiary on a cost basis and deduct it at cost from stockholders' equity in the consolidated balance sheet. The **conventional approach** is to account for the subsidiary investment in parent stock on an equity basis and to eliminate the subsidiary investment account against the parent equity accounts in the usual manner. Although both approaches are acceptable, they do not result in equivalent consolidated financial statements. In particular, the consolidated retained earnings and noncontrolling interest amounts usually differ under the two methods.

### Treasury Stock Approach

Assume that Pam Corporation acquired a 90 percent interest in Sun Corporation on January 1, 2016, for $540,000, when Sun's capital stock was $400,000 and its retained earnings $200,000. In addition, Sun purchased a 10 percent interest in Pam on January 5, 2016, for $140,000, when Pam's capital stock was $1,000,000 and its retained earnings $400,000. Trial balances for Pam and Sun on December 31, 2016, before either company recorded its investment income, were as follows (in thousands):

|  | Pam | Sun |
|---|---|---|
| *Debits* |  |  |
| Other assets | $ 960 | $520 |
| Investment in Sun (90%) | 540 | — |
| Investment in Pam (10%) | — | 140 |
| Expenses including cost of goods sold | 140 | 100 |
|  | $1,640 | $760 |
| *Credits* |  |  |
| Capital stock, $10 par | $1,000 | $400 |
| Retained earnings | 400 | 200 |
| Sales | 240 | 160 |
|  | $1,640 | $760 |

**CONSOLIDATION IN YEAR OF ACQUISITION**    If we use the treasury stock approach, Sun Corporation has no investment income for 2016, and Pam's share of Sun's $60,000 income ($160,000 sales − $100,000 expenses) is $54,000. Exhibit 9-5 shows a consolidation workpaper for Pam and Subsid-

| PAM CORPORATION AND SUBSIDIARY CONSOLIDATION WORKPAPER FOR THE YEAR ENDED DECEMBER 31, 2016 (IN THOUSANDS) | | | Adjustments and Eliminations | | Consolidated Statements |
|---|---|---|---|---|---|
| | Pam | 90% Sun | Debits | Credits | |
| *Income Statement* Sales | $ 240 | $ 160 | | | $ 400 |
| Investment income | 54 | | a  54 | | |
| Expenses including cost of sales | (140) | (100) | | | (240) |
| Noncontrolling interest share | | | d  6 | | (6) |
| **Controlling share of Net income** | $ 154 | $ 60 | | | $ 154 |
| *Retained Earnings Statement* Retained earnings—Pam | $ 400 | | | | $400 |
| Retained earnings—Sun | | $ 200 | b 200 | | |
| **Controlling share of net income** | 154 | 60 | | | 154 |
| **Retained earnings—December 31** | $ 554 | $ 260 | | | $ 554 |
| *Balance Sheet* Other assets | $ 960 | $ 520 | | | $1,480 |
| Investment in Sun (90%) | 594 | | | a  54 | |
| | | | | b 540 | |
| Investment in Pam (10%) | | 140 | | c 140 | |
| | $1,554 | $ 660 | | | $1,480 |
| Capital stock—Pam | $1,000 | | | | $1,000 |
| Capital stock—Sun | | $ 400 | b 400 | | |
| **Retained earnings** | 554 | 260 | | | 554 |
| | $1,554 | $ 660 | | | |
| Treasury stock | | | c 140 | | (140) |
| Noncontrolling interest | | | | b  60 | |
| | | | | d   6 | 66 |
| | | | 800 | 800 | $1,480 |

iary for 2016. In examining the workpaper, notice that Sun's investment in Pam is reclassified as treasury stock and deducted from stockholders' equity in the consolidated balance sheet.

**CONSOLIDATION IN SUBSEQUENT YEARS**    The 2017 earnings and dividends are as follows:

| | Pam | Sun |
|---|---|---|
| Separate earnings | $120,000 | $80,000 |
| Dividends | 60,000 | 40,000 |

Under the treasury stock approach, Sun Corporation records dividend income of $6,000 from Pam (10% of Pam's $60,000 dividends) and reports its net income for 2017 under the cost method in the amount of $86,000.

Pam Corporation accounts for its investment in Sun under the equity method as follows:

| | | |
|---|---|---|
| Cash (+A) | 36,000 | |
| Investment in Sun (−A) | | 36,000 |
| To record 90% of $40,000 dividends paid by Sun. | | |
| Investment in Sun (+A) | 77,400 | |
| Income from Sun (R, +SE) | | 77,400 |
| To record 90% of Sun's $86,000 income for 2017. | | |

| | | |
|---|---|---|
| Income from Sun (−R, −SE) | 6,000 | |
|     Dividends (+SE) | | 6,000 |

To eliminate intercompany dividends of $6,000
(10% of Pam's $60,000 dividends paid to Sun) and
to adjust investment income for Pam's dividends
that are included in Sun's income.

Thus, Pam records investment income from Sun of $71,400 ($77,400 − $6,000) and an investment account increase of $41,400 during 2017 ($77,400 − $36,000). The increase of $41,400 in Pam's Investment in Sun account is equal to 90 percent of Sun's $80,000 separate earnings, plus 90 percent of the $6,000 dividends paid to Sun that accrued to the benefit of Pam, less 90 percent of Sun's $40,000 dividends. Pam's investment income from Sun consists of 90 percent of Sal's $80,000 separate earnings, less $600 (the 10 percent of the $6,000 dividends from Pam that accrues to the benefit of Sun's noncontrolling stockholders).

Exhibit 9-6 shows a consolidation workpaper for Pam Corporation and Subsidiary for 2017. We compute the $635,400 balance in Pam's Investment in Sun account as follows:

| | |
|---|---|
| Investment in Sun (90%) December 31, 2016 | $594,000 |
| Add: 90% of Sun's reported income | 77,400 |
| Deduct: 90% of Sun's dividends | (36,000) |
| Investment in Sun (90%) December 31, 2017 | $635,400 |

Pam's investment in Sun was acquired at fair value equal to book value, so we can also compute the Investment in Sun account balance as 90 percent of Sun's equity at December 31, 2017 ($706,000 × 90% = $635,400)

Entry a in the consolidation working paper shown in Exhibit 9-6 is affected by the $6,000 dividend adjustment under the equity method and is reproduced here for convenient reference:

| | | | |
|---|---|---|---|
| a | Income from Sun (− R, − SE) | 71,400 | |
| | Dividend income (− R, − SE) | 6,000 | |
| |     Dividends (+ SE) | | 36,000 |
| |     Investment in Sun (− A) | | 41,400 |

This entry is unusual because we eliminate both Pam's investment income from Sun and Sun's dividend income from Pam in adjusting the Investment in Sun account to its $594,000 beginning-of-the-period balance. Other workpaper adjustments are similar to those in Exhibit 9-5.

Although Pam paid dividends of $60,000 during 2017, only $54,000 was paid to outside stockholders. Thus, Pam's retained earnings statement and the consolidated retained earnings statement show $54,000 dividends rather than $60,000. The consolidated balance sheet shows a $140,000 equity deduction for the cost of Sun's investment in Pam. This amount is the same as was shown in the workpaper in Exhibit 9-5.

## Conventional Approach

The consolidated balance sheets in Exhibits 9-5 and 9-6 for the treasury stock approach consolidated 100 percent of Pam Corporation's capital stock and retained earnings and deducted the cost of Sun's 10 percent investment in Pam from the consolidated stockholders' equity. Under the conventional approach, we consider parent stock held by a subsidiary as constructively retired, and the capital stock and retained earnings applicable to the interest held by the subsidiary do not appear in the consolidated financial statements.

We consider Sun's acquisition of Pam stock under the conventional procedure a constructive retirement of 10 percent of Pam's capital stock. A consolidated balance sheet for Pam and Subsidiary at acquisition shows capital stock and retained earnings applicable to the 90 percent of Pam Corporation's equity held outside the consolidated entity as follows (in thousands):

| | *January 1, 2016* | |
|---|---|---|
| | **Pam** | **Consolidated** |
| Capital stock | $1,000 | $900 |
| Retained earnings | 400 | 360 |
| Total stockholders' equity | $1,400 | $1,260 |

**PAM CORPORATION AND SUBSIDIARY CONSOLIDATION WORKPAPER FOR THE YEAR ENDED DECEMBER 31, 2017 (IN THOUSANDS)**

| | Pam | 90% Sun | Adjustments and Eliminations Debits | Credits | Consolidated Statements |
|---|---|---|---|---|---|
| *Income Statement* | | | | | |
| Sales | $280 | $200 | | | $480 |
| Income from Sun | 71.4 | | a 71.4 | | |
| Dividend income | | 6 | a 6 | | |
| Expenses including cost of sales | (160) | (120) | | | (280) |
| Noncontrolling interest share | | | d 8.6 | | (8.6) |
| **Controlling share of net income** | **$ 191.4** | **$ 86** | | | **$ 191.4** |
| *Retained Earnings Statement* | | | | | |
| Retained earnings—Pam | $554 | | | | $554 |
| Retained earnings—Sun | | $260 | b 260 | | |
| **Controlling share of net income** | **191.4** | **86** | | | **191.4** |
| Dividends | (54) | (40) | | a  36 | |
| | | | | d   4 | (54) |
| **Retained earnings—December 31** | **$ 691.4** | **$306** | | | **$ 691.4** |
| *Balance Sheet* | | | | | |
| Other assets | $1,056 | $566 | | | $1,622 |
| Investment in Sun (90%) | 635.4 | | | a  41.4 b 594 | |
| Investment in Pam (10%) | | 140 | | c 140 | |
| | $1,691.4 | $706 | | | $1,622 |
| Capital stock—Pam | $1,000 | | | | $1,000 |
| Capital stock—Sun | | $400 | b 400 | | |
| **Retained earnings** | **691.4** | **306** | | | **691.4** |
| | $1,691.4 | $706 | | | |
| Treasury stock | | | c 140 | | (140) |
| Noncontrolling interest | | | | b  66 d   4.6 | 70.6 |
| | | | 886 | 886 | $1,622 |

Accountants generally agree that the consolidated balance sheet should show the capital stock and retained earnings applicable to controlling stockholders outside the consolidated entity. However, this treatment raises a question concerning the applicability of the equity method to mutual holdings involving parent stock. Specifically, is the equity method applicable to affiliation structures that involve investments in the parent? If so, the parent's (investor's) share of consolidated net income for the period and its stockholders' equity at the end of the period are the same regardless of whether an investment in a subsidiary is accounted for under the equity method or the subsidiary is consolidated.

In spite of some reservations that have been expressed about the applicability of the equity method to mutually held parent stock, the position taken in this book is that the equity method applies and is, in fact, required by GAAP. (ASC 323-10-35) Transactions of an investee of a capital nature that affect the investor's share of stockholders' equity of the investee should be accounted for as if the investee were a consolidated subsidiary. In accounting for Pam's investment in Sun, we apply this requirement as follows:

*January 1, 2016*
Investment in Sun (90%) (+A)                              540,000
    Cash (−A)                                        540,000
To record acquisition of a 90% interest in Sun at book value.

*January 5, 2016*

| | | |
|---|---|---|
| Capital stock, $10 par (−SE) | 100,000 | |
| Retained earnings (−SE) | 40,000 | |
|     Investment in Sun (−A) | | 140,000 |

    To record the constructive retirement of 10% of Pam's
      outstanding stock as a result of Sun's purchase of Pam stock.

These entries reduce parent capital stock and retained earnings to reflect amounts applicable to controlling stockholders outside the consolidated entity. We base the reduction of the Investment in Sun account on the theory that parent stock purchased by a subsidiary is, in effect, returned to the parent and constructively retired.

By recording the constructive retirement of the parent stock on the parent's books, parent equity reflects the equity of stockholders outside the consolidated entity. These are the shareholders for which the consolidated statements are intended. In addition, recording the constructive retirement as indicated establishes consistency between capital stock and retained earnings for the parent's outside stockholders (90%) and parent net income, dividends, and earnings per share, which also relate to the 90 percent outside stockholders of the parent. Financial statement notes should explain the details of the constructive retirement.

**ALLOCATION OF MUTUAL INCOME**    When we use the conventional method of accounting for mutually held stock, the income of the parent on an equity basis cannot be determined until the income of the subsidiary has been determined on an equity basis, and vice versa. This is because the incomes are mutually related. The solution to the problem of determining parent and subsidiary incomes lies in the use of some mathematical procedure, the most common procedure being the use of simultaneous equations and substitution. We accomplish the allocation of income to the affiliates and to outside stockholders in two steps. First, we compute the incomes of Pam and Sun on a consolidated basis, which includes the mutual income held by the affiliates. Next, we multiply these amounts by the percentage ownership held within the affiliated group and the noncontrolling interest percentage to determine consolidated net income on an equity basis and noncontrolling interest share, respectively.

In the first step, we determine the incomes of Pam and Sun on a consolidated basis for 2016 mathematically as follows:

        $P$ = the income of Pam on a consolidated basis (including mutual income)

        $S$ = the income of Sun on a consolidated basis (including mutual income)

Then,

        $P$ = Pam's separate earnings of $100,000 + 90% $S$

        $S$ = Sun's separate earnings of $60,000 + 10% $P$

By substitution,

$$P = \$100,000 + 0.9(\$60,000 + 0.1P)$$
$$P = \$100,000 + \$54,000 + 0.09P$$
$$\underline{P = \$169,231}$$
$$S = \$60,000 + (\$169,231 \times 0.1)$$
$$\underline{S = \$76,923}$$

These are not final solutions because some of the income (mutual income) has been double-counted. The combined separate earnings of Pam and Sun are only $160,000, but $P$ plus $S$ equals $246,154. In the next step, we determine Par's net income on an equity basis by multiplying the value determined for $P$ in the equation by the 90 percent interest outstanding, and we determine noncontrolling interest share by multiplying the value determined for $S$ by the noncontrolling interest percentage. In other words, *Pam's net income on an equity basis is 90 percent of $169,231, or $152,308, and the noncontrolling interest share is 10 percent of $76,923, or $7,692.* Pam's net income (and controlling share of consolidated net income) of $152,308 plus noncontrolling interest share of $7,692, is equal to the $160,000 separate earnings of Pam and Sun.

**ACCOUNTING FOR MUTUAL INCOME UNDER THE EQUITY METHOD**    Pam Corporation records its investment income for 2016 on an equity basis as follows:

| | | |
|---|---|---|
| Investment in Sun (+A) | 52,308 | |
|     Income from Sun (R, +SE) | | 52,308 |

    To record income from Sun.

The $52,308 income from Sun equals 90 percent of Sun's $76,923 income on a consolidated basis, less 10 percent of Pam's $169,231 income on a consolidated basis. This represents Pam's 90 percent interest in Sun's income less Sun's 10 percent interest in Pam's income. An alternative calculation that gives the same result deducts Pam's separate earnings from its net income ($152,308 − $100,000).

Assume that Sun Corporation accounts for its investment in Pam on a cost basis because its interest in Pam is only 10 percent. Pam did not declare dividends during 2016, so Sun would have no investment income for the year, and its investment account would remain at the $140,000 original cost of the 10 percent interest.

**CONSOLIDATION UNDER THE EQUITY METHOD**    Exhibit 9-7 presents a consolidation workpaper for Pam and Subsidiary under the conventional procedure for 2016. The workpaper shows the investment in Sun (90%) at $452,308 (the $540,000 initial investment, plus $52,308 investment income, less the $140,000 reduction for the constructive retirement of Pam's stock). Entry a in the workpaper eliminates the $140,000 investment in Pam (Sun's books) and increases Pam's Investment in Sun account to $592,308. This entry reflects the constructive retirement of Pam stock that was credited to Pam's Investment in Sun account. Entry b eliminates investment income of $52,308 and reduces the investment account to its $540,000 cost at January 5, 2016. Entry c eliminates the reciprocal investment in Sun and equity of Sun amounts and establishes the noncontrolling interest in Sun at $60,000 (10% of $600,000) at the beginning of 2016.

## PAM CORPORATION AND SUBSIDIARY CONSOLIDATION WORKPAPER FOR THE YEAR ENDED DECEMBER 31, 2016

| | Pam | 90% Sun | Adjustments and Eliminations Debits | Adjustments and Eliminations Credits | Consolidated Statements |
|---|---|---|---|---|---|
| *Income Statement* | | | | | |
| Sales | $ 240,000 | $160,000 | | | $ 400,000 |
| Investment income | 52,308 | | b 52,308 | | |
| Expenses including cost of sales | (140,000) | (100,000) | | | (240,000) |
| Noncontrolling interest share | | | d 7,692 | | (7,692) |
| **Controlling share of net income** | **$ 152,308** | **$ 60,000** | | | **$ 152,308** |
| *Retained Earnings Statement* | | | | | |
| Retained earnings—Pam | $ 360,000 | | | | $ 360,000 |
| Retained earnings—Sun | | $200,000 | c 200,000 | | |
| **Controlling share of net income** | 152,308 | 60,000 | | | 152,308 |
| **Retained earnings—December 31** | **$ 512,308** | **$260,000** | | | **$ 512,308** |
| *Balance Sheet* | | | | | |
| Other assets | $ 960,000 | $520,000 | | | $1,480,000 |
| Investment in Sun (90%) | 452,308 | | a 140,000 | b 52,308<br>c 540,000 | |
| Investment in Pam (10%) | | 140,000 | | a 140,000 | |
| | $1,412,308 | $660,000 | | | $1,480,000 |
| Capital stock—Pam | $ 900,000 | | | | $ 900,000 |
| Capital stock—Sun | | $400,000 | c 400,000 | | |
| **Retained earnings** | 512,308 | 260,000 | | | 512,308 |
| | $1,412,308 | $660,000 | | | |
| Noncontrolling interest | | | | c 60,000<br>d 7,692 | 67,692 |
| | | | 800,000 | 800,000 | $1,480,000 |

**EXHIBIT 9-7**

**Parent Stock Held by Subsidiary— Conventional Approach (Year of Acquisition)**

In examining the workpaper in Exhibit 9-7, observe that the net income, capital stock, and retained earnings in the separate statements of Pam Corporation are equal to the controlling share of consolidated net income, consolidated capital stock, and consolidated retained earnings, respectively. This equality would not have existed without the entry to record the constructive retirement of stock on Pam's books.

**CONSOLIDATION IN SUBSEQUENT YEARS**   The separate earnings and dividends of Pam and Sun for 2017 are as follows:

|  | Pam | Sun |
|---|---|---|
| Separate earnings | $120,000 | $80,000 |
| Dividends | 60,000 | 40,000 |

Application of the conventional method of accounting requires the following mathematical computations for Pam and Sun for 2017:

$P$ = the income of Pam on a consolidated basis (including mutual income)

$S$ = the income of Sun on a consolidated basis (including mutual income)

Basic equations:

$$P = \$120,000 + 0.9S$$

$$S = \$80,000 + 0.1P$$

Substitution:

$$P = \$120,000 + 0.9(\$80,000 + 0.1P)$$
$$0.91P = \$192,000$$
$$P = \$210,989$$
$$S = \$80,000 + 0.1(\$210,989)$$
$$S = \$101,099$$

These computed amounts for $P$ and $S$ include mutual income that we must then eliminate. We use these amounts to determine the controlling share of consolidated net income and noncontrolling interest share as follows:

| | |
|---|---|
| Pam's net income (and controlling share) | $189,890 |
| ($210,989 × 90% outside ownership) | |
| Noncontrolling interest share ($101,099 × 10%) | 10,110 |
| Total separate earnings of Pam and Sun | $200,000 |

If Sun accounts for its investment in Pam under the cost method, it will record dividend income from Pam of $6,000 for 2017 (10% of Pam's dividends). Alternatively, Sun will record income from Pam of $21,099 ($210,989 × 10%) if it uses the equity method.

Pam accounts for its investment in Sun on an equity basis as follows:

| | | |
|---|---|---|
| Cash (+A) | 36,000 | |
|     Investment in Sun (−A) | | 36,000 |
|   To record 90% of Sun's $40,000 dividend for 2017. | | |
| Investment in Sun (+A) | 69,890 | |
|     Income from Sun (R, +SE) | | 69,890 |

To record investment income computed as follows: $189,890 Pam's net income less $120,000 Pam's separate earnings = $69,890. An alternative computation: 90% of Sun's income on a consolidated basis ($101,099 × 90%), less 10% of Pam's income on a consolidated basis ($210,989 × 10%) = $69,890.

| | | |
|---|---|---|
| Investment in Sun (+A) | 6,000 | |
|     Dividends (+SE) | | 6,000 |

To eliminate parent dividends paid to Sun and to adjust the investment in Sun account.

Pam's Investment in Sun account at December 31, 2017, will have a balance of $492,198 under the equity method. This balance is computed as follows:

| | |
|---|---:|
| Investment in Sun, December 31, 2016 | $452,308 |
| Add: Investment income | 69,890 |
| Add: Dividends paid to Sun | 6,000 |
| Deduct: Dividends received from Sun | −36,000 |
| Investment in Sun, December 31, 2017 | $492,198 |

Exhibit 9-8 presents a consolidation workpaper for Pam and Subsidiary for 2017. We assume that Sun accounts for its investment in Pam using the cost method. The equity method has been applied by Pam. Therefore, parent net income of $189,890 is equal to the controlling share of consolidated net income. Parent capital stock and retained earnings amounts also equal their corresponding consolidated amounts. The workpaper adjustments in Exhibit 9-8 are procedurally equivalent to those shown earlier in the chapter.

**PAM CORPORATION AND SUBSIDIARY CONSOLIDATION WORKPAPER FOR THE YEAR ENDED DECEMBER 31, 2017**

| | Pam | 90% Sun | Adjustments and Eliminations Debits | Adjustments and Eliminations Credits | Consolidated Statements |
|---|---|---|---|---|---|
| *Income Statement* | | | | | |
| Sales | $ 280,000 | $200,000 | | | $ 480,000 |
| Income from Sun | 69,890 | | b  69,890 | | |
| Dividend income | | 6,000 | b  6,000 | | |
| Expenses including cost of sales | (160,000) | (120,000) | | | (280,000) |
| Noncontrolling interest share | | | d  10,110 | | (10,110) |
| **Controlling share of net income** | **$ 189,890** | **$ 86,000** | | | **$ 189,890** |
| *Retained Earnings Statement* | | | | | |
| Retained earnings—Pam | $ 512,308 | | | | $ 512,308 |
| Retained earnings—Sun | | $260,000 | c 260,000 | | |
| **Controlling share of net income** | **189,890** | **86,000** | | | **189,890** |
| Dividends | (54,000) | (40,000) | | b  36,000 | |
| | | | | d   4,000 | (54,000) |
| **Retained earnings—December 31** | **$ 648,198** | **$306,000** | | | **$ 648,198** |
| *Balance Sheet* | | | | | |
| Other assets | $1,056,000 | $566,000 | | | $1,622,000 |
| Investment in Sun (90%) | 492,198 | | a 140,000 | b  39,890 | |
| | | | | c 592,308 | |
| Investment in Pam (10%) | | 140,000 | | a 140,000 | |
| | $1,548,198 | $706,000 | | | $1,622,000 |
| Capital stock—Pam | $ 900,000 | | | | $900,000 |
| Capital stock—Sun | | $400,000 | c 400,000 | | |
| **Retained earnings** | **648,198** | **306,000** | | | **648,198** |
| | $1,548,198 | $706,000 | | | |
| Noncontrolling interest | | | | c  67,692 | 73,802 |
| | | | | d   6,110 | |
| | | | 886,000 | 886,000 | $1,622,000 |

**EXHIBIT 9-8**

**Parent Stock Held by Subsidiary— Conventional Approach (Year After Acquisition)**

Once we determine the net asset increases, the simultaneous equations used earlier for determining income allocations allocate the separate net asset increases to consolidated retained earnings and to noncontrolling interest. The computations for Pam and Sun are:

P = increase in net assets of Pam on a consolidated basis since purchase by Sun

S = increase in net assets of Sun on a consolidated basis since acquisition by Pam

Basic equations:

$$P = \$196{,}000 + 0.9S$$
$$S = \$106{,}000 + 0.1P$$

By substitution:

$$P = \$196{,}000 + 0.9\,(\$106{,}000 + 0.1P)$$
$$P = \$196{,}000 + \$95{,}400 + 0.09P$$
$$0.91P = \$291{,}400$$
$$P = \underline{\$320{,}220}$$
$$S = \overline{\$106{,}000} + (0.1 \times \$320{,}220)$$
$$S = \underline{\$138{,}022}$$

These computations (which still include mutual amounts) can be used to allocate the $302,000 net asset increase to consolidated retained earnings and noncontrolling interest as follows:

| | |
|---|---|
| Pam's retained earnings increase (or increase in consolidated retained earnings) = $320,220 × 90% | $288,198 |
| Noncontrolling interest's retained earnings increase = $138,022 × 10% | 13,802 |
| Total net asset increase | $302,000 |

At acquisition, Pam's retained earnings were $400,000, and they were adjusted downward to $360,000 for the constructive retirement of 10 percent of Pam's stock. We compute the correct amount of consolidated retained earnings at December 31, 2017, as $360,000 + $288,198, or $648,198. This computation provides a convenient check on the $648,198 retained earnings shown in the consolidated balance sheet in Exhibit 9-8.

Noncontrolling interest in Sun Corporation at January 1, 2016, was $60,000 ($600,000 equity × 10%). We compute the noncontrolling interest at December 31, 2017, as $60,000 + $13,802 or $73,802. This computation confirms the $73,802 noncontrolling interest that appears in the consolidation workpaper of Exhibit 9-8.

## SUBSIDIARY STOCK MUTUALLY HELD

Parent stock held within an affiliation structure is not outstanding and is not reported as outstanding stock either in the parent statements under the equity method or in consolidated financial statements. Two generally accepted approaches for eliminating the effect of mutually held parent stock—the treasury stock approach and the conventional approach—were explained and illustrated in the previous section of this chapter. In this section, *the mutually held stock involves subsidiaries holding the stock of each other, and the treasury stock approach is not applicable.*

Consider the following diagram of the affiliation structure of Pal, Set, and Ton. Pal owns an 80 percent interest in Set directly. Set has a 70 percent interest in Ton, and Ton has a 10 percent interest in Set. There is a 10 percent noncontrolling interest in Set and a 30 percent noncontrolling interest in Ton.

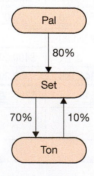

The acquisitions of Pal, Set, and Ton were as follows:

1. Pal acquired its 80 percent interest in Set Corporation on January 2, 2016, for $260,000, when the stockholders' equity of Set consisted of capital stock of $200,000 and retained earnings of $100,000 ($25,000 implied total goodwill).

2. Set acquired its 70 percent interest in Ton Corporation for $112,000 on January 3, 2017, when the stockholders' equity of Ton consisted of $100,000 capital stock and $50,000 retained earnings ($10,000 implied total goodwill).

3. Ton acquired its 10 percent interest in Set for $40,000 on December 31, 2017, when the stockholders' equity of Set consisted of $200,000 capital stock and $200,000 retained earnings (no goodwill).

## Accounting Prior to Mutual Holding Relationship

Assume that the recorded net assets from the investments described were equal to their fair values at acquisition and that any excess was goodwill. Post-closing trial balances for Pal, Set, and Ton at December 31, 2017, are as follows (in thousands):

|  | Pal | Set | Ton |
|---|---|---|---|
| Cash | $  64 | $ 42 | $ 20 |
| Other current assets | 200 | 85 | 80 |
| Plant and equipment—net | 500 | 240 | 110 |
| Investment in Set (80%) | 340 | — | — |
| Investment in Ton (70%) | — | 133 | — |
| Investment in Set (10%) | — | — | 40 |
|  | $1,104 | $500 | $250 |
| Liabilities | $  200 | $100 | $ 70 |
| Capital stock | 500 | 200 | 100 |
| Retained earnings | 404 | 200 | 80 |
|  | $1,104 | $500 | $250 |

The balance in Pal's Investment in Set account at December 31, 2017, is $340,000:

| | |
|---|---|
| Cost | $260,000 |
| Add: 80% of Set's $40,000 income less dividends—2016 | 32,000 |
| 80% of Set's $60,000 income less dividends—2017 | 48,000 |
| | $340,000 |

The balance of Ton's 10 percent Investment in Set account at December 31, 2017, is equal to the $40,000 cost of the investment on that date. Assume that Ton accounts for this 10 percent investment in Set on a cost basis, even though the equity method might be used because absolute control lies with the parent.

We compute Set's $133,000 investment in Ton at December 31, 2017, as follows:

| | |
|---|---|
| Investment in Ton January 3, 2017—cost | $112,000 |
| Add: 70% of Ton's $30,000 income less dividends—2017 | 21,000 |
| | $133,000 |

## Accounting for Mutually Held Subsidiaries

During 2018, the affiliates had income from operations and dividends as follows (in thousands):

|  | Pal | Set | Ton | Total |
|---|---|---|---|---|
| Income from separate operations | $112 | $51 | $40 | $203 |
| Dividends declared | 50 | 30 | 20 | 100 |

We allocate the incomes of the three companies under the conventional approach.

**INCOME ALLOCATION COMPUTATIONS**   Income allocation computations for the affiliates follow:

$$P = \text{separate income of Pal} + 0.8S$$
$$S = \text{separate income of Set} + 0.7U$$
$$U = \text{separate income of Ton} + 0.1S$$
$$P = \$112{,}000 + 0.8S$$
$$S = \$51{,}000 + 0.7U$$
$$U = \$40{,}000 + 0.1S$$

Solve for $S$ (amounts are rounded to nearest \$1):

$$S = \$51{,}000 + 0.7(\$40{,}000 + 0.1S) = \$79{,}000 + 0.07S$$
$$0.93S = \$79{,}000$$
$$S = \$84{,}946$$
$$U = \$40{,}000 + 0.1(\$84{,}946)$$
$$U = \$48{,}495$$
$$P = \$112{,}000 + 0.8(\$84{,}946)$$
$$P = \$179{,}957$$

We allocate total income for the affiliated group to:

| | |
|---|---:|
| Controlling share of consolidated net income (equal to Pal's net income) | $179,957 |
| Noncontrolling interest share in Set's income ($84,946 × 10%) | 8,495 |
| Noncontrolling interest share in Ton's income ($48,495 × 30%) | 14,548 |
| Total separate income | $203,000 |

**COMPUTATIONS OF INVESTMENT ACCOUNT BALANCES**   A summary of the investment account balances at December 31, 2018, is as follows:

| | Pal (Equity Method) | Set (Equity Method) | Ton (Cost Method)* |
|---|---:|---:|---:|
| Investment balances December 31, 2017 | $340,000 | $133,000 | $40,000 |
| Add: Investment income | | | |
| Pal ($84,946 × 0.8) | 67,957 | — | — |
| Set ($48,495 × 0.7) | — | 33,946 | — |
| Deduct: Dividends received: | | | |
| Pal ($30,000 × 0.8) | (24,000) | — | — |
| Set ($20,000 × 0.7) | — | (14,000) | — |
| Investment balance December 31, 2018 | $383,957 | $152,946 | $40,000 |

*\$3,000 dividend income and dividends received amounts for Ton's 10 percent investment in Set do not affect the investment account because Ton uses the cost method.

**CONSOLIDATION WORKPAPER—EQUITY METHOD**   Exhibit 9-9 reflects the investment incomes and balances in the consolidation workpaper. We show financial statements of Pal, Set, and Ton in the first four columns of the workpaper. Consolidation workpaper entries a, b, and c eliminate investment income (including dividend income of Ton) and intercompany dividends, and adjust the investment accounts to their beginning-of-the-period balances. Workpaper entry d eliminates reciprocal equity and investment balances for Ton, records the $10,000 beginning-of-the-period goodwill from Set's investment in Ton, and establishes the $57,000 beginning noncontrolling interest in Ton (computed as $190,000 × 30%). Entry e eliminates reciprocal equity and investment balances for Set (both Pal's 80% and Ton's 10%), records the $25,000 beginning-of-the-period goodwill from Pal's investment in Set, and establishes the $45,000 beginning noncontrolling interest in Set. Although there are two Investment in Set accounts and therefore two eliminations could have been made, *it is convenient to prepare one entry for each entity* (Set in this case) *rather than for each investment account.*

**EXHIBIT 9-9**

Consolidation Involving Mutually Held Subsidiary Stock

## PAL CORPORATION AND SUBSIDIARIES CONSOLIDATION WORKPAPER FOR THE YEAR ENDED DECEMBER 31, 2018

| | Pal | Set | Ton | Adjustments and Eliminations Debits | Adjustments and Eliminations Credits | Consolidated Statements |
|---|---|---|---|---|---|---|
| *Income Statement* | | | | | | |
| Sales | $ 412,000 | $ 161,000 | $100,000 | | | $ 673,000 |
| Income from Set (80%) | 67,957 | | | c 67,957 | | |
| Income from Ton (70%) | | 33,946 | | b 33,946 | | |
| Dividend income (10%) | | | 3,000 | a 3,000 | | |
| Cost of sales | (220,000) | (70,000) | (40,000) | | | (330,000) |
| Expenses | (80,000) | (40,000) | (20,000) | | | (140,000) |
| Noncontrolling interest share—Set | | | | f 8,495 | | (8,495) |
| Noncontrolling interest share—Ton | | | | g 14,548 | | (14,548) |
| **Controlling share of net Income** | **$ 179,957** | **$ 84,946** | **$ 43,000** | | | **$ 179,957** |
| *Retained Earnings Statement* | | | | | | |
| Retained earnings—Pal | $ 404,000 | | | | | $ 404,000 |
| Retained earnings—Set | | $ 200,000 | | e 200,000 | | |
| Retained earnings—Ton | | | $ 80,000 | d 80,000 | | |
| **Controlling share of net income** | 179,957 | 84,946 | 43,000 | | | 179,957 |
| Dividends | (50,000) | (30,000) | (20,000) | | a 3,000 | |
| | | | | | b 14,000 | |
| | | | | | c 24,000 | |
| | | | | | f 3,000 | |
| | | | | | g 6,000 | (50,000) |
| **Retained earnings—December 31** | **$ 533,957** | **$ 254,946** | **$103,000** | | | **$ 533,957** |
| *Balance Sheet* | | | | | | |
| Cash | $ 60,000 | $ 33,000 | $ 43,000 | | | $ 136,000 |
| Other current assets | 250,000 | 80,000 | 70,000 | | | 400,000 |
| Plant assets—net | 550,000 | 300,000 | 130,000 | | | 980,000 |
| Investment in Set (80%) | 383,957 | | | | c 43,957 e 340,000 | |
| Investment in Ton (70%) | | 152,946 | | | b 19,946 d 133,000 | |
| Investment in Set (10%) | | | 40,000 | | e 40,000 | |
| Goodwill—Pal | | | | e 25,000 | | 25,000 |
| Goodwill—Set | | | | d 10,000 | | 10,000 |
| | $1,243,957 | $ 565,946 | $283,000 | | | $1,551,000 |
| Liabilities | $ 210,000 | $ 111,000 | $ 80,000 | | | $ 401,000 |
| Capital stock—Pal | 500,000 | | | | | 500,000 |
| Capital stock—Set | | 200,000 | | e 200,000 | | |
| Capital stock—Ton | | | 100,000 | d 100,000 | | |
| **Retained earnings** | 533,957 | 254,946 | 103,000 | | | 533,957 |
| | $1,243,957 | $ 565,946 | $283,000 | | | |
| Noncontrolling interest in Ton, January 1 | | | | | d 57,000 | 116,043 |
| Noncontrolling interest in Set, January 1 | | | | | e 45,000 | |
| Noncontrolling interest in Set, December 31 | | | | | f 5,495 | |
| Noncontrolling interest in Ton, December 31 | | | | | g 8,548 | |
| | | | | 742,946 | 742,946 | $1,551,000 |

Pal accounts for its investment in Set as a one-line consolidation, so the controlling share of consolidated net income of $179,957 for 2018 and consolidated retained earnings of $533,957 at December 31, 2018, equal the corresponding amounts in the separate financial statements of Pal. We determine noncontrolling interest share by equation, as demonstrated earlier.

## SUMMARY

A corporation may control another through direct or indirect ownership of its voting stock. Indirect holdings give an investor the ability to control or significantly influence the operations of the investee not directly owned through an investee that is directly owned. The major problem encountered in consolidating the financial statements of companies in indirect control situations lies in allocating income and equities among controlling and noncontrolling stockholders. Several computational approaches are available for such allocations, but the schedule approach is probably the best overall approach because of its simplicity and because it provides a step-by-step reference of all allocations made.

When affiliates own the stock of each other, the stock is not outstanding from the viewpoint of the consolidated entity. We eliminate the effect of mutually held parent stock from consolidated financial statements by either the treasury stock approach or the conventional approach. The treasury stock approach deducts the investment in parent stock on a cost basis from consolidated stockholders' equity. Under the conventional approach, we treat the investment in parent stock as constructively retired by adjusting the parent's investment in subsidiary and the parent's equity accounts to reflect a one-line consolidation. Then we eliminate the subsidiary's investment in parent account against the parent's investment in subsidiary account.

We account for mutual investments by subsidiaries in the stock of each other under the conventional method of eliminating reciprocal investment and equity balances. The treasury stock approach is not applicable to such mutually held investments because only parent stock and retained earnings appear in the consolidated financial statements. Under the conventional method, we use simultaneous equations to allocate income and equities among mutually held companies.

## QUESTIONS

*(Questions 1 through 7 cover indirect holdings, and 8 through 15 cover mutual holdings.)*

1. What is an indirect holding of the stock of an affiliate?

2. P owns a 60 percent interest in S, and S owns a 40 percent interest in T. Should T be consolidated? If not, how should T be included in the consolidated statements of P and Subsidiaries?

3. Distinguish between indirect holding affiliation structures and mutual holding affiliation structures.

4. Parent Company owns 70 percent of the voting stock of Subsidiary A, and Subsidiary A owns 70 percent of the stock of Subsidiary B. Is the inside ownership of Subsidiary B more than 50 percent? Should Subsidiary B be included in the consolidated statements? Explain.

5. Pat Corporation owns 80 percent of the stock of Sam Corporation, and Sam owns 70 percent of the stock of Stan Corporation. Separate earnings of Pat, Sam, and Stan are $200,000, $160,000, and $100,000, respectively. Compute controlling and noncontrolling interest shares of consolidated net income under two different approaches.

6. In using the schedule approach for allocating income of subsidiaries to controlling and noncontrolling stockholders in an indirect holding affiliation structure, why is it necessary to begin with the lowest subsidiary in the affiliation tier?

7. P owns 80 percent of S1, and S1 owns 70 percent of S2. Separate incomes of P, S1, and S2 are $20,000, $10,000, and $5,000, respectively, for 2016. During 2016, S1 sold land to P at a gain of $1,000. Compute S1's income on an equity basis. Discuss why you did or did not adjust S1's investment in S2's account for the unrealized gain.

8. If a parent owns 80 percent of the voting stock of a subsidiary, and the subsidiary in turn owns 20 percent of the stock of the parent, what kind of affiliation structure is involved? Explain.

9. How is the treasury stock approach applied to the elimination of mutually held stock?

10. Are the treasury stock and conventional approaches equally applicable to all mutual holdings? Explain.

11. Under the treasury stock approach, a mutually held subsidiary accounts for its investment in the parent on a cost basis. Are dividends received by the subsidiary from the parent included in investment income of the parent under the equity method?

12. Describe the concept of a constructive retirement of parent stock. Should the parent adjust its equity accounts when its stock is constructively retired?

13. P's separate earnings are $100,000, and S's separate earnings are $40,000. P owns an 80 percent interest in S, and S owns a 10 percent interest in P. What is the controlling share of consolidated net income?

14. How do consolidation procedures for mutual holdings involving the father-son-grandson type of affiliation structure differ from those for mutually held parent stock?

15. If companies in an affiliation structure account for investments on an equity basis, how can noncontrolling interests be determined without the use of simultaneous equations?

## EXERCISES

*(Exercises 9-1 through 9-8 cover indirect holdings, and 9-9 through 9-13 cover mutual holdings.)*

### E 9-1
### Calculate consolidated net income

On January 1, 2016, Pop Corporation purchased a 60 percent interest in Son Corporation at book value (equal to fair value). At that time, Son owned a 60 percent interest in Tip Corporation (acquired at book value equal to fair value) and a 15 percent interest in Win Company. The four companies had the following separate incomes and dividends for 2016 (all amounts are in thousands of dollars and separate income does not include investment income or dividend income):

|  | Separate Income | Dividends |
|---|---|---|
| Pop Corporation | $3,200 | $1,200 |
| Son Corporation | 2,000 | 800 |
| Tip Corporation | 800 | 400 |
| Win Company | 1,200 | 400 |

**REQUIRED:** Determine the controlling and noncontrolling interest shares of consolidated net income.

### E 9-2
### Allocate investment income and loss

Pam Corporation owns 60 percent of Sun Corporation and 80 percent of Tim Corporation. Tim owns 20 percent of Sun. Separate income and loss data (not including investment income) for the three affiliates for 2016 are as follows:

| | |
|---|---|
| Pam | $800,000 separate income |
| Sun | $300,000 separate income |
| Tim | ($400,000) separate loss |

There are no differentials or unrealized profits to consider in measuring 2016 income.

**REQUIRED:** Calculate the controlling share of consolidated net income for 2016.

### E 9-3
### Prepare an income allocation schedule (includes unrealized profit on land)

The affiliation structure for Place Corporation and its affiliates is as follows:

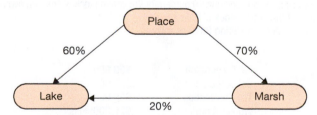

During 2016 the separate incomes of the affiliates were as follows:

| | |
|---|---|
| Place | $400,000 |
| Lake | $160,000 |
| Marsh | $140,000 |

Lake's income includes $40,000 unrealized profit on land sold to Marsh during 2016.

**REQUIRED:** Prepare a schedule that shows the allocation of income among the affiliates and also shows controlling and noncontrolling interest shares of consolidated net income for 2016.

### E 9-4
### Determine equation to compute income from subsidiary, noncontrolling interest share, and controlling interest share of consolidated net income

The affiliation structure for Pin Corporation and its subsidiaries is as follows:

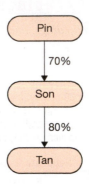

Separate incomes of Pin, Son, and Tan Corporations for 2016 are $360,000, $160,000, and $100,000, respectively.

1. The equation for determining Pin's income from Son on a one-line consolidation basis for 2016 is:
   a **$160,000 × 70%**
   b **($160,000 × 70%) + ($100,000 × 80%)**
   c **($160,000 × 70%) + ($100,000 × 56%)**
   d **70% × ($160,000 × $100,000)**

2. Noncontrolling interest share for Pin and Subsidiaries for 2016 is determined as follows:
   a **$30% × $160,000**
   b **(30% × $160,000) + (20% × $100,000)**
   c **(30% × $160,000) + (24% × $100,000)**
   d **(30% × $160,000) + (44% × $100,000)**

3. Controlling share of consolidated net income can be determined by the following equation:
   a **$620,000 − ($160,000 × 30%)**
   b **$620,000 − ($160,000 × 30%) − ($100,000 × 20%)**
   c **$620,000 − ($160,000 × 30%) − ($100,000 × 20%) − ($100,000 × 30% × 90%)**
   d **$620,000 − ($160,000 × 30%) − ($100,000 × 44%)**

### E 9-5
### Prepare income allocation schedule

Pal Corporation owns 80 percent each of the voting common stock of Sal and Tea Corporations. Sal owns 60 percent of the voting common stock of Won Corporation and 10 percent of the voting stock of Tea. Tea owns 70 percent of the voting stock of Val and 10 percent of the voting stock of Won.

The affiliates had separate incomes during 2016 as follows:

| | |
|---|---|
| Pal Corporation | $50,000 |
| Sal Corporation | $30,000 |
| Tea Corporation | $35,000 |
| Won Corporation | ($20,000) loss |
| Val Corporation | $40,000 |

The only intercompany profits included in the separate incomes of the affiliates consisted of $5,000 on merchandise that Pal acquired from Tea, and it remained in Pal's December 31, 2016, inventory.

**REQUIRED:** Compute controlling and noncontrolling interest shares of consolidated net income.

## E 9-6
## Calculate controlling interest share and noncontrolling interest share of consolidated net income

Pet Company owns 90 percent of the stock of Man Corporation and 70 percent of the stock of Nun Company. Man owns 70 percent of the stock of Oak Corporation and 10 percent of the stock of Nun Company. Nun Company owns 20 percent of the stock of Oak Corporation.

Separate incomes for the year ended December 31, 2016, are as follows:

| | |
|---|---|
| Pet | $130,000 |
| Man | $ 36,000 |
| Nun | $ 56,000 |
| Oak | $ 18,000 |

During 2016, Man sold land to Nun at a profit of $8,000. Oak sold inventory items to Pet at a profit of $16,000, half of which remains in Pet's inventory. Pet purchased for $30,000 Nun's bonds, which had a book value of $34,000 on December 31, 2016.

**REQUIRED:** Calculate controlling and noncontrolling interest shares of consolidated net income for 2016.

## E 9-7
## No intercompany profits

The affiliation structure for a group of interrelated companies is diagrammed as follows:

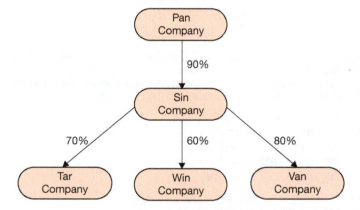

The investments were acquired at fair value equal to book value in 2016, and there are no unrealized or constructive profits or losses.

Separate incomes and dividends for the companies for 2016 are:

| | Separate Income (Loss) | Dividends |
|---|---|---|
| Pan | $1,240,000 | $400,000 |
| Sin | 350,000 | 200,000 |
| Tar | 400,000 | 160,000 |
| Win | (100,000) | — |
| Van | 240,000 | 120,000 |

1. The direct noncontrolling interest share of Tar Company's net income for 2016 is:
   a  $120,000
   b  $148,000
   c  $252,000
   d  $280,000

2. The direct noncontrolling interest share of Van Company's net income for 2016 is:
   a  $48,000
   b  $96,000
   c  $110,400
   d  $144,000

3. The total noncontrolling interest share that should appear in the consolidated income statement for 2016 is:
   a  *$244,200*
   b  *$210,200*
   c  *$204,200*
   d  *$76,200*

4. Controlling share of consolidated net income for Pan Company and Subsidiaries for 2016 is:
   a  *$1,925,800*
   b  *$1,881,800*
   c  *$1,240,000*
   d  *$685,800*

5. Pan's Investment in Sin account should reflect a net increase for 2016 in the amount of:
   a  *$762,000*
   b  *$685,800*
   c  *$625,800*
   d  *$505,800*

## E 9-8
## Correcting net income for unrealized profits

Pat Corporation owns an 80 percent interest in Sam Corporation and a 70 percent interest in Ten Corporation. Ten owns a 10 percent interest in Sam. These investment interests were acquired at fair value equal to book value.
   The net incomes of the affiliates for 2016 were as follows:

| | |
|---|---|
| Pat | $240,000 |
| Sam | $ 80,000 |
| Ten | $ 40,000 |

On December 31, 2016, Pat's inventory included $10,000 of unrealized profits on merchandise purchased from Sam during 2016, and Sam's land account reflected $15,000 unrealized profit on land purchased from Ten during 2016. These unrealized profits have not been eliminated from the net income amounts shown. Except for adjustments related to unrealized profits, the net income amounts were determined on a correct equity basis.

1. The separate incomes of Pat, Sam, and Ten for 2016 were:
   a  *$240,000, $80,000, and $32,000, respectively*
   b  *$148,000, $80,000, and $32,000, respectively*
   c  *$148,000, $72,000, and $40,000, respectively*
   d  *$240,000, $72,000, and $40,000, respectively*

2. The separate realized incomes of Pat, Sam, and Ten for 2016 were:
   a  *$138,000, $80,000, and $25,000, respectively*
   b  *$138,000, $70,000, and $25,000, respectively*
   c  *$123,000, $80,000, and $17,000, respectively*
   d  *$148,000, $70,000, and $17,000, respectively*

3. Controlling share of consolidated net income for Pat Corporation and Subsidiaries for 2016 was:
   a  *$220,800*
   b  *$215,900*
   c  *$214,400*
   d  *$212,400*

4. Noncontrolling interest share that should appear in the consolidated income statement for Pat Corporation and Subsidiaries for 2016 is:
   a  *$23,600*
   b  *$21,200*
   c  *$19,100*
   d  *$14,200*

## E 9-9
## Calculate consolidated net income (conventional method, no complications)

Pan Corporation owns an 80 percent interest in Sol Company and Sol owns a 30 percent interest in Pan, both acquired at a fair value equal to book value. Separate incomes (not including investment income) of the two affiliates for 2016 are:

| | |
|---|---|
| Pan | $6,000,000 |
| Sol | $3,000,000 |

**REQUIRED:** Compute controlling share of consolidated net income for 2016 using the conventional (equation) approach.

## E 9-10
### Prepare computations (subsidiary stock mutually held, no unrealized profits)

Intercompany investment percentages and 2016 earnings for three affiliates are as follows:

|  | Percentage Interest in Sad | Percentage Interest in Two | Separate Earnings |
|---|---|---|---|
| Pad Corporation | 70% | — | $400,000 |
| Sad Corporation | — | 80% | 240,000 |
| Two Corporation | 10% | — | 160,000 |

**REQUIRED:** Compute controlling share of consolidated net income and noncontrolling interest share for 2016.

## E 9-11
### [Based on AICPA] Mutually held parent-company stock

Pin, Inc., owns 80 percent of the capital stock of Son Company and 70 percent of the capital stock of Tin, Inc. Son owns 15 percent of the capital stock of Tin. Tin owns 25 percent of the capital stock of Pin. These ownership interrelationships are illustrated in the following diagram:

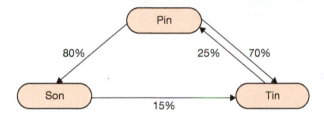

Income before adjusting for interests in intercompany income for each corporation follows:

| Pin, Inc. | $190,000 |
|---|---|
| Son Company | $170,000 |
| Tin, Inc. | $230,000 |

The following notations relate to the following questions:

$A$ = Pin's consolidated income − its separate income plus its share of the consolidated incomes of Son and Tin
$B$ = Son's consolidated income − its separate income plus its share of the consolidated income of Tin
$C$ = Tin's consolidated income − its separate income plus its share of the consolidated income of Pin

**1.** The equation, in a set of simultaneous equations, that computes **A** is:
a  $A = 0.75(190,000 + 0.8B + 0.7C)$
b  $A = 190,000 + 0.8B + 0.7C$
c  $A = 0.75(190,000) + 0.8(170,000) + 0.7(230,000)$
d  $A = 0.75(190,000) + 0.8B + 0.7C$

**2.** The equation, in a set of simultaneous equations, that computes **B** is:
a  $B = 170,000 + 0.15C + 0.75A$
b  $B = 170,000 + 0.15C$
c  $B = 0.2(170,000) + 0.15(230,000)$
d  $B = 0.2(170,000) + 0.15C$

**3.** Tin's noncontrolling interest share of consolidated income is:
a  $0.15(230,000)$
b  $230,000 + 0.25A$
c  $0.15(230,000) + 0.25A$
d  $0.15C$

4. Son's noncontrolling interest share of consolidated income is:
   - a  $34,316
   - b  $25,500
   - c  $45,755
   - d  $30,675

## E 9-12
## Mutually held parent stock

Pet Corporation owns 90 percent of Sod Corporation's common stock and Sod owns 15 percent of Pet, both acquired at fair value equal to book value. Separate incomes and dividends of the affiliates for 2016 are as follows:

|                 | Separate Incomes | Dividends |
|-----------------|------------------|-----------|
| Pet Corporation | $100,000         | $50,000   |
| Sod Corporation | 60,000           | 30,000    |

1. If the treasury stock approach is used, Pet's income and controlling share of consolidated net income for 2016 will be computed:
   - a  $100,000 + (90% × $60,000)
   - b  $100,000 + (90% × $67,500)
   - c  $100,000 + (90% × $67,500) − (90% × $30,000)
   - d  ($100,000 + $60,000) − (10% × $67,500)

2. If the conventional approach is used, Pet's income on a consolidated basis is denoted $P = \$100,000 + \$0.9S$ and Sod's income on a consolidated basis is denoted $S = \$60,000 + 0.15P$. Given these equations, the controlling share of consolidated net income is equal to:
   - a  $P$
   - b  $0.85P$
   - c  $P - 0.1S$
   - d  $P + S - 0.15S$

## E 9-13
## Computations (treasury stock and conventional)

Pug Corporation acquired a 70 percent interest in Sat Corporation for $238,000 on January 2, 2015, when Sat's equity consisted of $200,000 capital stock and $50,000 retained earnings. The excess is due to a patent amortized over a 10-year period, at $9,000 per year. Pug accounted for its investment in Sat during 2015 as follows:

| | |
|---|---|
| Investment cost January 2, 2015 | $238,000 |
| Income from Sat [($40,000 − $9,000) × 70%] | 21,700 |
| Dividends from Sat ($20,000 × 70%) | (14,000) |
| Investment balance December 31, 2015 | $245,700 |

On January 3, 2016, Sat acquired a 10 percent interest in Pug at a $60,000 fair value equal to book value. No intercompany profit transactions have occurred. Incomes and dividends for 2016 were as follows:

|                 | Pug       | Sat      |
|-----------------|-----------|----------|
| Separate income | $120,000  | $50,000  |
| Dividends       | 60,000    | 30,000   |

## REQUIRED

1. Determine the balance of Pug's Investment in Sat account on December 31, 2016, if the treasury stock approach is used for Sat's investment in Pug.
2. Compute controlling and noncontrolling interest shares of consolidated net income if the conventional approach is used for Sat's investment in Pug. Also determine the amount of Pug's income from Sat and the balance in Pug's Investment in Sat account at December 31, 2016.

# PROBLEMS

*(Problems 9-1 through 9-3 cover indirect holdings, and 9-4 through 9-7 cover mutual holdings.)*

## P9-1
## Schedule for allocating income (unrealized profits and goodwill)

The affiliation structure for Pad Corporation and its subsidiaries is diagrammed as follows:

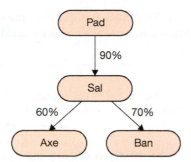

The incomes and dividends for the affiliates for 2016 are (in thousands):

|  | Pad | Sal | Axe | Ban |
|---|---|---|---|---|
| Separate income (loss) | $500 | $300 | $150 | $(20) |
| Dividends | 200 | 140 | 50 | — |

### ADDITIONAL INFORMATION

**1.** Axe sold land to Sal during 2016 at a $20,000 gain. The land is still held by Sal.

**2.** Sal is amortizing a previously unrecorded patent of Axe at the rate of $12,000 per year. (Total amortization is $20,000.)

**3.** Pad is amortizing a previously unrecorded patent acquired from Sal with a book value of $360,000 over its remaining nine-year life.

**REQUIRED:** Prepare a schedule to compute controlling and noncontrolling interest shares of consolidated net income for each subsidiary for 2016.

## P9-2
## Prepare journal entries, computations, and a financial position summary (unrealized profits)

A summary of the assets and equities of Pot Corporation and its 80 percent–owned subsidiary, Sea Corporation, at December 31, 2016, is given as follows (in thousands):

|  | Pot | Sea |
|---|---|---|
| Assets | $3,200 | $1,400 |
| Investment in Sea (80%) | 800 | — |
| Total assets | $4,000 | $1,400 |
|  |  |  |
| Liabilities | $ 600 | $ 400 |
| Capital stock | 2,400 | 800 |
| Retained earnings | 1,000 | 200 |
| Total equities | $4,000 | $1,400 |

On January 2, 2017, Sea acquired a 70 percent interest in Toy Corporation for $588,000. Toy's net assets of $800,000 were recorded at fair values on this date. The equity of Toy on December 31, 2016, consisted of $600,000 capital stock and $200,000 retained earnings.

Data on operations of the affiliates for 2017 are as follows (in thousands):

| | Separate Earnings | Dividends | Unrealized Profit Included in Separate Earnings |
|---|---|---|---|
| Pot | $600 | $200 | $40 |
| Sea | 200 | 120 | — |
| Toy | 120 | 40 | 20 |

Pot Corporation's $40,000 unrealized profit resulted from the sale of land to Toy. Toy's unrealized profit is from sales of merchandise items to Sea and is included in Sea's inventory at December 31, 2017.

### REQUIRED

1. Prepare all journal entries required on the books of Pot and Sea to account for their investments for 2017 on an equity basis. The excess of fair value over book value is goodwill.
2. Compute the net incomes of Pot and Sea, and total noncontrolling interest share for 2017.
3. Prepare a schedule showing the assets and equities of Pot, Sea, and Toy on December 31, 2017, assuming liabilities of $600,000, $400,000, and $200,000 for Pot, Sea, and Toy, respectively.

### P9-3
### Financial statement workpaper (goodwill and unrealized profits)

Comparative financial statements for Pen Corporation and its subsidiaries, Sir and Tip Corporations, for the year ended December 31, 2016, are as follows (in thousands):

| | Pen | Sir | Tip |
|---|---|---|---|
| **Income and Retained Earnings Statement for the Year Ended December 31** | | | |
| Sales | $500 | $300 | $100 |
| Income from Sir | 72 | — | — |
| Income from Tip | 12.5 | 10 | — |
| Cost of sales | (240) | (150) | (60) |
| Other expenses | (160) | (70) | (15) |
| Net income | 184.5 | 90 | 25 |
| Add: Beginning retained earnings | 115.5 | 160 | 45 |
| Deduct: Dividends | (80) | (40) | (10) |
| Ending retained earnings | $220 | $210 | $60 |
| **Balance Sheet at December 31** | | | |
| Cash | $67 | $36 | $10 |
| Accounts receivable—net | 70 | 50 | 20 |
| Inventories | 110 | 75 | 35 |
| Plant and equipment—net | 140 | 425 | 115 |
| Investment in Sir (80%) | 508 | — | — |
| Investment in Tip (50%) | 95 | — | — |
| Investment in Tip (40%) | — | 74 | — |
| Total assets | $990 | $660 | $180 |
| Accounts payable | $70 | $40 | $15 |
| Other liabilities | 100 | 10 | 5 |
| Capital stock | 600 | 400 | 100 |
| Retained earnings | 220 | 210 | 60 |
| Total equities | $990 | $660 | $180 |

### ADDITIONAL INFORMATION

1. Pen acquired its 80 percent interest in Sir Corporation for $420,000 on January 2, 2014, when Sir had capital stock of $400,000 and retained earnings of $100,000. The excess fair value over book value acquired relates to equipment that had a remaining useful life of four years from January 1, 2014.
2. Pen acquired its 50 percent interest in Tip Corporation for $75,000 on July 1, 2014, when Tip's equity consisted of $100,000 capital stock and $20,000 retained earnings. Sir acquired its 40 percent interest in

Tip on December 31, 2015, for $68,000, when Tip's capital stock was $100,000 and its retained earnings were $45,000. The difference between fair value and book value acquired is due to goodwill.

3. Although Pen and Sir use the equity method in accounting for their investments, they do not apply the method to intercompany profits or to differences between fair value and book value acquired.

4. At December 31, 2015, the inventory of Sir included inventory items acquired from Pen at a profit of $8,000. This merchandise was sold during 2016.

5. Tip sold merchandise that had cost $30,000 to Sir for $50,000 during 2016. All of this merchandise is held by Sir at December 31, 2016. Sir owes Tip $10,000 on this merchandise.

**REQUIRED:** Prepare a consolidation workpaper for the year ended December 31, 2016.

## P9-4
### Computations for mutually held subsidiaries

A schedule of intercompany investment interests and separate earnings for Par Corporation, Sit Corporation, and Tot Corporation is presented as follows:

| | Percentage Interest in Sit | Percentage Interest in Tot | Separate Earnings Current Year |
|---|---|---|---|
| Par Corporation | 80% | 50% | $400,000 |
| Sit Corporation | — | 20 | 200,000 |
| Tot Corporation | 10 | — | 100,000 |

### REQUIRED

1. Compute controlling interest share and noncontrolling interest share of consolidated net income assuming no investment differences between fair value and book value or unrealized profits.

2. Compute controlling interest share and noncontrolling interest share assuming $20,000 unrealized inventory profits on Tot's sales to Sit and a $40,000 gain on Par's sale of land to Sit.

## P9-5
### Financial statement workpaper (treasury stock approach)

Pin Corporation acquired a 90 percent interest in Sun Corporation for $360,000 cash on January 2, 2014, when Sun had capital stock of $200,000 and retained earnings of $150,000. Sun purchased its 10 percent interest in Pin in 2015 for $80,000. The excess of Pin's investment fair value over book value acquired is due to goodwill.

Financial statements for the year ended December 31, 2018, are as follows (in thousands):

| | Pin | Sun |
|---|---|---|
| ***Combined Income and Retained Earnings Statement for the Year Ended December 31*** | | |
| Sales | $400 | $100 |
| Investment income | 27 | — |
| Dividend income | — | 10 |
| Cost of goods sold | (200) | (50) |
| Expenses | (50) | (30) |
| Net income | 177 | 30 |
| Add: Beginning retained earnings | 300 | 200 |
| Deduct: Dividends | (100) | (20) |
| Retained earnings December 31 | $377 | $210 |
| ***Balance Sheet at December 31*** | | |
| Other assets | $486 | $420 |
| Investment in Sun (90%) | 414 | — |
| Investment in Pin (10%) | — | 80 |
| Total assets | $900 | $500 |
| Liabilities | $123 | $90 |
| Capital stock | 400 | 200 |
| Retained earnings | 377 | 210 |
| Total equities | $900 | $500 |

**REQUIRED:** Prepare a consolidation workpaper using the treasury stock approach.

## P9-6
## Consolidation workpaper second year (conventional approach)

Par Corporation acquired an 80 percent interest in Sip Corporation for $180,000 cash on January 1, 2016, when Sip had capital stock of $50,000 and retained earnings of $150,000. The excess of fair value over book value acquired is due to a patent, which is being amortized over five years. Sip purchased its 20 percent interest in Par at book value on January 2, 2016, for $100,000.

Financial statements for the year ended December 31, 2017, are summarized as follows:

|  | Par | Sip |
|---|---|---|
| ***Combined Income and Retained Earnings*** | | |
| ***Statement for the Year Ended December 31*** | | |
| Sales | $140,000 | $100,000 |
| Income from Sip | 28,000 | — |
| Dividend income | — | 4,000 |
| Gain on sale of land | — | 3,000 |
| Expenses | (80,000) | (60,000) |
| Net income | 88,000 | 47,000 |
| Add: Beginning retained earnings | 405,710 | 180,000 |
| Deduct: Dividends | (16,000) | (20,000) |
| Retained earnings December 31 | $477,710 | $207,000 |
| ***Balance Sheet at December 31*** | | |
| Other assets | $448,000 | $157,000 |
| Investment in Sip (80%) | 109,710 | — |
| Investment in Par (20%) | — | 100,000 |
| Total assets | $557,710 | $257,000 |
| Capital stock | $ 80,000 | $ 50,000 |
| Retained earnings | 477,710 | 207,000 |
| Total equities | $557,710 | $257,000 |

### ADDITIONAL INFORMATION

1. Par's separate earnings and dividends for 2017 were $60,000 and $20,000, respectively. Sip's separate earnings and dividends in 2017 were $40,000 and $20,000, respectively.

2. Sip sold land to an outside interest for $7,000 on January 3, 2017, that it purchased from Par on January 3, 2016, for $4,000. The land had originally cost Par $2,000.

**REQUIRED:** Prepare consolidation workpaper entries and a consolidation workpaper for Par Corporation and Subsidiary at December 31, 2017, using the conventional approach for the mutual holding.

## P9-7
## Computations and entries (parent stock mutually held)

Pop Corporation purchased an 80 percent interest in Son Corporation for $170,000 on January 1, 2016, when Son's stockholders' equity was $200,000. The excess of fair value over book value is due to goodwill.

At December 31, 2017, the balance of Pop's Investment in Son account is $208,000, and the stockholders' equity of the two corporations is as follows:

|  | Pop | Son |
|---|---|---|
| Capital stock | $600,000 | $150,000 |
| Retained earnings | 200,000 | 100,000 |
| Total | $800,000 | $250,000 |

On January 2, 2018, Son acquires a 10 percent interest in Pop for $80,000. Earnings and dividends for 2018 are:

|  | **Pop** | **Son** |
|---|---|---|
| Separate earnings | $100,000 | $40,000 |
| Dividends | 50,000 | 20,000 |

### REQUIRED

1. Compute controlling and noncontrolling interest shares of consolidated net income for 2018 using the conventional approach.
2. Prepare journal entries to account for Pop's investment in Son for 2018 under the equity method (conventional approach).
3. Prepare journal entries on Son's books to account for its investment in Pop under the equity method (conventional approach).
4. Compute Pop's and Son's net incomes for 2018.
5. Determine the balances of Pop's and Son's investment accounts on December 31, 2018.
6. Determine the total stockholders' equity of Pop and Son on December 31, 2018.
7. Compute the noncontrolling interest in Son on December 31, 2018.
8. Prepare the adjusting and eliminating entries needed to consolidate the financial statements of Pop and Son for the year ended December 31, 2018.

# PROFESSIONAL RESEARCH ASSIGNMENTS

Answer the following questions by reference to the FASB Codification of Accounting Standards. Include the appropriate reference in your response.

**PR 9-1**  Par Corporation owns a 30 percent interest in Sox Corporation, which Par properly accounts for using the equity method. Sox is in need of capital and decides to issue an additional 10,000 shares of common stock to the public. After issuance, Par's ownership interest will decline to 25 percent. How will the share issuance impact Par's financial statements?

**PR 9-2**  Pop Corporation owns 80 percent of Son Corporation, and properly included Son as a subsidiary in preparing consolidated financial statements for the year ended December 31, 2016. Pop issued the financial statements on March 1, 2017. In May of 2017, Son had an explosion that severely damaged one of its major manufacturing operations. The cost of replacement will require Son to issue additional shares of stock, which will reduce Pop's ownership to 60 percent. Will Pop be required to restate the December 31, 2016 financial statements for this subsequent event?

# 10

# Subsidiary Preferred Stock, Consolidated Earnings per Share, and Consolidated Income Taxation

T his chapter covers three additional topics related to consolidation: consolidation of a subsidiary with preferred stock in its capital structure, calculation of consolidated earnings per share (EPS), and financial accounting for income taxes of consolidated entities. These topics tend to be detailed and technical, and the illustrations often use simplifying assumptions to minimize details and emphasize significant concepts and relationships. An intermediate accounting background in all three areas is assumed.

## SUBSIDIARIES WITH PREFERRED STOCK OUTSTANDING

LEARNING OBJECTIVE **10.1**

Modern corporations often have complex capital structures, including various categories of preferred stock issued by the parent, a subsidiary, or both. For example, the 2014 annual report of ***Dow Chemical Company*** discloses $4 billion of preferred stock outstanding versus $3.1 billion of common stock (p.70). ***Bank of America Corporation's*** 2014 balance sheet discloses $19.309 billion of preferred stock (p.143). Reviewing Note 13 to the financial statements indicates that there are 20 different series of preferred shares (p.221).

The existence of preferred stock in the capital structure of a subsidiary complicates the consolidation process, but the basic procedures do not change. Parent/investor accounting under the equity method is also affected when an investee has preferred stock outstanding. The complications stem from the need to consider the contractual rights of preferred stockholders in allocating the investee's equity and income between preferred and common stock components.

Most preferred stock issues are cumulative, nonparticipating, and nonvoting. In addition, preferred stocks usually have preference rights in liquidation and frequently are callable at prices in excess of the par or liquidating values. We allocate net income of an investee with preferred stock outstanding first to preferred stockholders based on the preferred stock contract and then the remainder to common stockholders. Similarly, we first allocate the stockholders' equity of an investee to preferred stockholders based on the preferred stock contract, and then allocate the remainder to common stockholders.

When preferred stock has a call or redemption price, we use this amount in allocating the investee's equity to preferred stockholders. In the absence of a redemption provision, we base the equity allocated to preferred stock on par value of the stock plus any liquidation premium. In addition, we include any dividends in arrears on cumulative preferred stock in the equity allocated to preferred stockholders. For nonparticipating preferred stock, we assign income to preferred stockholders on the basis of the preference rate or amount. If the preferred stock is cumulative and nonparticipating, the current year's income assigned to the preferred stockholders is the current year's dividend requirement, irrespective of whether the directors declare only current-year dividends, current-year

## LEARNING OBJECTIVES

**10.1** Modify consolidation procedures for subsidiaries with outstanding preferred stock.

**10.2** Calculate basic and diluted earnings per share for a consolidated entity.

**10.3** Understand the complexities of accounting for income taxes by consolidated entities.

dividends plus prior-year arrearages, or no dividends at all. We assign income to noncumulative, nonparticipating preferred stock only if dividends are declared and only in the amount declared.

## Subsidiary with Preferred Stock Not Held by Parent

Assume that Pop Corporation purchases 90 percent of Son Corporation's outstanding common stock for $396,000 on January 1, 2017, and that Son Corporation's stockholders' equity on December 31, 2016, was as follows (in thousands):

| | |
|---|---|
| $10 preferred stock, $100 par, cumulative, nonparticipating, callable at $105 per share | $100 |
| Common stock, $10 par | 200 |
| Other paid-in capital | 40 |
| Retained earnings | 160 |
| Total stockholders' equity | $500 |

There were no preferred dividends in arrears as of January 1, 2017. During 2017, Son reported net income of $50,000 and paid dividends of $30,000 ($20,000 on common and $10,000 on preferred). Son's assets and liabilities were stated at fair values equal to book values when Pop acquired its interest, so any excess of fair value over book value is goodwill.

In comparing the price paid for the 90 percent interest in Son with the book value of the interest acquired, we separate Son's December 31, 2016, equity into its preferred and common stock components (in thousands):

| | |
|---|---|
| Stockholders' equity of Son | $500 |
| Less: Preferred stockholders' equity (1,000 shares × $105 per share call price) | 105 |
| Common stockholders' equity | $395 |

We compare the price paid for 90 percent of the common equity of Son with the book value (and fair value) acquired to determine goodwill. The implied total fair value is $440,000 ($396,000 ÷ 90%) (in thousands):

| | |
|---|---|
| Fair value | $440 |
| Less: book value | 395 |
| Goodwill | $ 45 |

Son's $50,000 net income for 2017 is allocated $10,000 to preferred stock (1,000 shares × 10 per share) and $40,000 to common stock. The entries to account for Pop's investment in Son for 2017 are:

*January 1*
| | | |
|---|---|---|
| Investment in Son common (+A) | 396,000 | |
| Cash (−A) | | 396,000 |
| To record acquisition of 90% of Son's common stock. | | |

*During Year*
| | | |
|---|---|---|
| Cash (+A) | 18,000 | |
| Investment in Son common (−A) | | 18,000 |
| To reduce Investment in Son for dividends received ($20,000 × 90%). | | |

*December 31*
| | | |
|---|---|---|
| Investment in Son common (+A) | 36,000 | |
| Income from Son (R, +SE) | | 36,000 |
| To record equity in Son's income. | | |

In consolidating the financial statements for 2017 (see Exhibit 10-1), we assign Son's $520,000 equity at December 31, 2017, to preferred and common components as follows (in thousands):

| | |
|---|---|
| Total stockholders' equity | $520 |
| Less: Preferred stockholders' equity (1,000 shares × $105 call price per share) | 105 |
| Common stockholders' equity | $415 |

| POP CORPORATION AND SUBSIDIARY CONSOLIDATION WORKPAPER FOR THE YEAR ENDED DECEMBER 31, 2017 (IN THOUSANDS) | | | | | |
|---|---|---|---|---|---|
| | | | Adjustments and Eliminations | | Consolidated Statements |
| | Pop | 90% Son | Debits | Credits | |
| *Income Statement* | | | | | |
| Sales | $ 618 | $300 | | | $ 918 |
| Income from Son (common) | 36 | | b 36 | | |
| Expenses including cost of sales | (450) | (250) | | | (700) |
| Noncontrolling interest share (common) ($40 × 10%) | | | d 4 | | (4) |
| Noncontrolling interest share (preferred) ($10 × 100%) | | | e 10 | | (10) |
| **Controlling share of net income** | **$ 204** | **$ 50** | | | **$ 204** |
| *Retained Earnings Statement* | | | | | |
| Retained earnings—Pop | $ 300 | | | | $ 300 |
| Retained earnings—Son | | $160 | a 5 c 155 | | |
| **Controlling share of net income** | **204** | **50** | | | **204** |
| Dividends (common) | (100) | (20) | | b 18 d 2 | (100) |
| Dividends (preferred) | | (10) | | e 10 | |
| **Retained earnings—December 31** | **$ 404** | **$180** | | | **$ 404** |
| *Balance Sheet* | | | | | |
| Other assets | $1,290 | $600 | | | $1,890 |
| Investment in Son (common) | 414 | | | b 18 c 396 | |
| Goodwill | | | c 45 | | 45 |
| | $1,704 | $600 | | | $1,935 |
| Liabilities | $ 200 | $ 80 | | | $ 280 |
| Preferred stock—Son | | 100 | a 100 | | |
| Common stock | 1,000 | 200 | c 200 | | 1,000 |
| Other paid-in capital | 100 | 40 | c 40 | | 100 |
| **Retained earnings** | **404** | **180** | | | **404** |
| | $1,704 | $600 | | | |
| Noncontrolling interest: Preferred, January 1 Noncontrolling interest: Common, January 1 Noncontrolling interest: Common, December 31 | | | | a 105 c 44 d 2 | 151 |
| | | | 595 | 595 | $1,935 |

**EXHIBIT 10-1**

Preferred and Common Stock in the Affiliation Structure

**NONCONTROLLING INTEREST IN PREFERRED STOCK**   The *noncontrolling interest* in Son at December 31, 2017, consists of 100 percent of the preferred stockholders' equity and 10 percent of the common stockholders' equity, or $146,500 [($105,000 × 100%) + ($415,000 × 10%)] plus 10 percent of the implied $45,000 goodwill. Similarly, *noncontrolling interest share* for 2017 consists of 100 percent of the income to preferred stockholders and 10 percent of the income to common stockholders, or $14,000 [($10,000 × 100%) + ($40,000 × 10%)]. This information is reflected in the consolidation workpaper for Pop Corporation and Subsidiary in Exhibit 10-1.

Except for workpaper entries a and e the entries are similar to those encountered in earlier chapters. Entry a is reproduced in journal form as follows:

| a | Preferred stock—Son (− SE) | 100,000 | |
|---|---|---|---|
| | Retained earnings—Son (− SE) | 5,000 | |
| | Noncontrolling interest—preferred (+ SE) | | 105,000 |

Entry a reclassifies the preferred stockholders' equity as a noncontrolling interest. The $105,000 preferred equity at the beginning of the period exceeded the $100,000 par value, so we debit the $5,000 excess to Son's retained earnings. We make this debit to Son's retained earnings because the preferred stockholders have a maximum claim on Son's retained earnings for the $5,000 call premium.

The consolidated income statement of Exhibit 10-1 shows separate deductions for noncontrolling interest share applicable to preferred ($10,000) and common stock ($4,000). This division is helpful in preparing a workpaper, but a consolidated income statement prepared from the workpaper would ordinarily show noncontrolling interest share as one amount. Also, Exhibit 10-1 shows total noncontrolling interest in Son at December 31, 2017, on one line of the consolidated balance sheet in the single amount of $151,000. Although the consolidation workpaper contains the information to separate this amount into preferred and common components, the separation is ordinarily not used for financial reporting, because we eliminate all individual subsidiary equity accounts in the consolidation process.[1] Consolidated financial statements are intended primarily for the stockholders and creditors of the parent, and we do not expect that the noncontrolling stockholders could benefit significantly from the information contained in them.

## Subsidiary Preferred Stock Acquired by Parent

A parent's purchase of the outstanding subsidiary preferred stock results in a retirement of the stock purchased from the viewpoint of the consolidated entity. The stock is retired for consolidated statement purposes because its book value no longer appears as a noncontrolling interest in the consolidated balance sheet. However, the retirement is really a constructive retirement because we report the investment in preferred (parent) and the preferred stock equity (subsidiary) as outstanding in the separate financial statements of the parent and subsidiary.

We report the **constructive retirement of subsidiary preferred stock** through purchase by the parent as an actual retirement in the consolidated statements. That is, we eliminate the equity related to the preferred stock held by the parent and the investment in preferred stock, and we debit or credit any difference to the additional paid-in capital that would otherwise be reported in the consolidated balance sheet.[2] Parent stockholders' equity in a one-line consolidation is equal to consolidated stockholders' equity, so comparable accounting requires that the parent adjust its investment in subsidiary preferred stock to its book value at acquisition and debit or credit its additional paid-in capital for the difference between the price paid for the investment and its underlying book value. We account for the investment in preferred stock on the basis of its book value, not on the basis of the cost or equity method.

CONSTRUCTIVE RETIREMENT OF SUBSIDIARY PREFERRED STOCK  Son Corporation experiences a net loss of $40,000 in 2018 and pays no dividends. Stockholders' equity decreases from $520,000 at December 31, 2017 (see Exhibit 10-1), to $480,000 at December 31, 2018. Pop's 90 percent investment in Son decreases from $414,000 at year-end 2017 to $369,000 at year-end 2018.

---

[1]Noncontrolling interest in a subsidiary's preferred stock is sometimes reported as outstanding stock of the consolidated entity with notation of the name of the issuing corporation. This reporting practice is usually confined to regulated companies.

[2]Parent's retained earnings are reduced when additional paid-in capital is insufficient to absorb an excess of purchase price over book value.

The $45,000 decrease in Pop's Investment in Son common account is as follows:[3]

| | |
|---|---:|
| Net loss of Son | $40,000 |
| Add: Income to preferred (1,000 shares × $10) | 10,000 |
| Loss to common | 50,000 |
| Pop's ownership interest | ×90% |
| Loss from Son for 2018 | $45,000 |

We verify the $369,000 investment in Son common at December 31, 2018, as follows:

| | |
|---|---:|
| Stockholders' equity of Son, December 31, 2018 | $480,000 |
| Less: Preferred stockholders' equity [1,000 shares × ($105 per share call price + $10 per share dividend arrearage)] | 115,000 |
| Common stockholders' equity, December 31, 2018 | 365,000 |
| Pop's ownership interest | ×90% |
| Share of Son's common stockholders' equity | 328,500 |
| Add: Goodwill ($45,000 × 90%) | 40,500 |
| Investment in Son common, December 31, 2018 | $369,000 |

On January 1, 2019, Pop responded to the depressed price of Son's preferred stock and purchased 800 shares (an 80% interest) at $100 per share. The $80,000 price paid is less than the $92,000 book value of the stock that is constructively retired ($115,000 × 80%), so Pop records the investment in Son preferred as follows:

| | | |
|---|---:|---:|
| Investment in Son preferred (+A) | 80,000 | |
|     Cash (−A) | | 80,000 |
| To record purchase of 80% of Son's preferred stock. | | |
| Investment in Son preferred (+A) | 12,000 | |
|     Other paid-in capital (+SE) | | 12,000 |
| To adjust other paid-in capital to reflect the constructive retirement. | | |

Son reports net income of $20,000 for 2019, but it again passes dividends for the year. Pop accounts for its investments during 2019 as follows:

| | | |
|---|---:|---:|
| Investment in Son preferred (+A) | 8,000 | |
|     Income from Son preferred (R, +SE) | | 8,000 |
| To record 80% of the $10,000 increase in Son's preferred dividend arrearage. | | |
| Investment in Son common (+A) | 9,000 | |
|     Income from Son common (R, +SE) | | 9,000 |
| To record equity in Son's income to common [($20,000 net income − $10,000 preferred income) × 90%]. | | |

A summary of Son's preferred and common stockholders' equity and Pop's investment-account balances at the end of 2019 follows:

| | |
|---|---:|
| *Son's Stockholders' Equity, December 31, 2019* | |
| Total stockholders' equity ($480,000 on January 1 plus $20,000 net income) | $500,000 |
| Less: Preferred stockholders' equity [1,000 shares × ($105 call price + $20 dividends in arrears)] | 125,000 |
| Common stockholders' equity | $375,000 |
| | |
| *Pop's Investment Accounts, December 31, 2019* | |
| Investment in Son preferred ($125,000 preferred *equity* × 80% owned) | $100,000 |
| Investment in Son common [($375,000 common equity × 90%) + ($45,000 goodwill × 90%)] | $378,000 |

---

[3]A deduction of cumulative preferred dividends in computing income to common stockholders is required by GAAP, (ASC 323-10-35) regardless of whether such dividends are declared.

This information for 2019 is reflected in a consolidation workpaper for Pop and Son Corporations in Exhibit 10-2.

## POP CORPORATION AND SUBSIDIARY CONSOLIDATION WORKPAPER FOR THE YEAR ENDED DECEMBER 31, 2019 (IN THOUSANDS)

| | Pop | 90% Son | Adjustments and Eliminations Debits | Adjustments and Eliminations Credits | Consolidated Statements |
|---|---|---|---|---|---|
| **Income Statement** | | | | | |
| Sales | $ 690 | $280 | | | $ 970 |
| Income from Son (common) | 9 | | c 9 | | |
| Income from Son (preferred) | 8 | | a 8 | | |
| Expenses including cost of sales | (583) | (260) | | | (843) |
| Noncontrolling interest share (common) ($10 × 10%) | | | e 1 | | (1) |
| Noncontrolling interest share (preferred) ($10 × 20%) | | | f 2 | | (2) |
| **Controlling share of net income** | **$ 124** | **$ 20** | | | **$ 124** |
| **Retained Earnings Statement** Retained earnings—Pop | $ 458 | | | | $ 458 |
| Retained earnings—Son | | $140 | b 15 d 125 | | |
| **Controlling share of net income** | 124 | 20 | | | 124 |
| Dividends (common) | (70) | — | | | (70) |
| **Retained earnings—December 31** | **$ 512** | **$160** | | | **$ 512** |
| **Balance Sheet** Other assets | $1,334 | $600 | | | $1,934 |
| Investment in Son (common) | 378 | | | c 9 d 369 | |
| Investment in Son (preferred) | 100 | | | a 8 b 92 | |
| Goodwill (common) | | | d 45 | | 45 |
| | $1,812 | $600 | | | $1,979 |
| Liabilities | $ 188 | $100 | | | $ 288 |
| Preferred stock—Son | | 100 | b 100 | | |
| Common stock | 1,000 | 200 | d 200 | | 1,000 |
| Other paid-in capital | 112 | 40 | d 40 | | 112 |
| **Retained earnings** | **512** | **160** | | | **512** |
| | $1,812 | $600 | | | |
| Noncontrolling interest: Preferred, January 1 Noncontrolling interest: Common, January 1 Noncontrolling interest: Common, December 31 Noncontrolling interest: Preferred, December 31 | | | | b 23 d 41 e 1 f 2 | 67 |
| | | | 545 | 545 | $1,979 |

The workpaper entries for 2019 are similar to those in Exhibit 10-1 for 2017, except for items related to the investment in Son's preferred stock. Procedures to eliminate the preferred equity and investment accounts parallel those for common stock. First, we eliminate Pop's income from Son preferred against the investment in Son preferred. This workpaper entry (entry a) reduces the Investment in Son preferred account to its $92,000 adjusted balance at January 1, 2019. Next, we eliminate the investment in Son preferred and the preferred equity of Son as of January 1, 2019, in workpaper entry b. This entry also enters the preferred noncontrolling interest as of the beginning of the year. Entries a and b in journal form follow:

| | | | |
|---|---|---|---|
| a | Income from Son preferred ($-R$, $-SE$) | 8,000 | |
| | Investment in Son preferred ($-A$) | | 8,000 |
| b | Preferred stock—Son ($-SE$) | 100,000 | |
| | Retained earnings—Son ($-SE$) | 15,000 | |
| | Investment in Son preferred ($-A$) | | 92,000 |
| | Noncontrolling interest in Son preferred ($+SE$) | | 23,000 |

The only difference between Exhibits 10-1 and 10-2 is that we now have entries for the investment in Son's preferred stock. Entries c through e are similar to those for consolidations involving common stock only. Entry f records the noncontrolling interest share for preferred stock.

The workpaper in Exhibit 10-2 shows Pop Corporation's net income equal to the controlling share of consolidated net income and its stockholders' equity equal to consolidated stockholders' equity. These equalities result from parent entries to adjust the preferred stock investment account to its underlying equity at acquisition and to accrue dividend arrearages on cumulative preferred stock.

**PREFERRED STOCK INVESTMENT MAINTAINED ON COST BASIS**   If the constructive retirement were *not* recorded by Pop at the time of purchase, the Investment in Son preferred account would remain at its $80,000 cost throughout 2019, and we would recognize no preferred income. In this case, the consolidation workpaper entry to eliminate the preferred investment and equity amounts would be:

| | | |
|---|---|---|
| Retained earnings—Son ($-SE$) | 15,000 | |
| Preferred stock—Son ($-SE$) | 100,000 | |
| Investment in Son preferred ($-A$) | | 80,000 |
| Noncontrolling interest in Son preferred ($+SE$) | | 23,000 |
| Other paid-in capital—Pop ($+SE$) | | 12,000 |

To eliminate reciprocal preferred equity and investment amounts, establish noncontrolling interest at the beginning of the period (20% $\times$ $115,000 beginning book value of preferred), and adjust Pop's other paid-in capital account for the difference between the purchase price and underlying book value of the preferred stock.

**COMPARISON OF COST METHOD AND CONSTRUCTIVE RETIREMENT**   The consolidated financial statements will be the same whether the investment in preferred stock remains at its original cost or is adjusted to book value in the parent's books. However, by adjusting the parent's additional paid-in capital for the constructive retirement of subsidiary preferred stock, we avoid further paid-in capital adjustments in the consolidation process. Under the cost method, we need a workpaper entry to adjust additional paid-in capital each time we consolidate parent and subsidiary statements.

## PARENT AND CONSOLIDATED EARNINGS PER SHARE

LEARNING OBJECTIVE **10.2**

Generally accepted accounting principles (GAAP) require that firms calculate and report both basic and diluted (where applicable) earnings per share (EPS). Consolidated entities disclose EPS on a consolidated basis. For example, the consolidated statement of income included in the 2014 annual report (p. 45) of *The Hershey Company* reports:

**The Hershey Company**[4]

| | |
|---|---|
| Net income per share—Basic—Class B Common Stock | $3.77 |
| Net income per share—Diluted—Class B Common Stock | $3.52 |
| Net income per share—Basic—Common Stock | $3.91 |
| Net income per share—Diluted—Common Stock | $3.54 |

Note 14 to the statements is titled "Earnings per Share," and it describes the calculations in detail (p. 83).

[4]From Proxy Statement and 2014 Annual Report to Stockholders (Part 1, Item 6, P 16) © 2015 Hersheys Food Corporation.

Similarly, the ***Coca-Cola Company*** 2014 annual report (p. 73) discloses basic earnings per common share of $1.62 and diluted earnings per common share of $1.60. Both amounts appear on the face of the income statement, and Coke reports these amounts on a consolidated basis.

A parent's net income and EPS under the equity method are equal to the controlling share of consolidated net income and consolidated basic EPS, respectively. However, the computational differences in determining parent and consolidated net income (i.e., one-line consolidation versus consolidation) do not extend to EPS calculations. Parent EPS and consolidated basic EPS calculations are identical. EPS procedures for equity investors who are able to exercise significant influence over investees are the same as those for parent investors.[5]

Parent procedures for computing consolidated diluted EPS depend on the subsidiary's capital structure. When the subsidiary has *no* potentially dilutive securities, the procedures applied in computing consolidated EPS are the same as those for separate entities. When the subsidiary does have potentially dilutive securities outstanding, however, the potential dilution has to be considered in computing the parent's (and consolidated) diluted EPS.

We compute basic EPS the same way for a consolidated entity as for separate entities (assuming the equity method is used). For consolidated diluted EPS, the adjustment to parent EPS calculations depends on whether the subsidiary's potentially dilutive securities are convertible into subsidiary or parent common stock. If convertible into subsidiary common stock, we reflect the potential dilution in subsidiary EPS computations, which are then used in determining parent (and consolidated) EPS. If the dilutive securities of the subsidiary are convertible into parent company common stock, we treat them as parent dilutive securities and include them directly in computing the parent (and consolidated) EPS. (ASC 260-10-55) In this latter case, we do not need (or use) subsidiary EPS computations in parent EPS computations.

General formats for EPS calculations in these situations are summarized in Exhibit 10-3 for diluted EPS. The first column of Exhibit 10-3 shows parent computations for diluted EPS when the subsidiary has no potentially dilutive securities. In this case, EPS computations are the same as those for unrelated entities, and no adjustments are necessary for subsidiary income included in parent income, provided that the parent applies the equity method correctly.

## Dilutive Securities of Subsidiary Convertible into Subsidiary Shares

The second column of Exhibit 10-3 summarizes parent EPS computations when subsidiary potentially dilutive securities are convertible into subsidiary common shares. We adjust diluted earnings of the parent (the numerators of the EPS calculations) by excluding the parent's **equity in subsidiary realized income** and replacing that equity with the parent's share of diluted earnings of the subsidiary.

Parent's equity in subsidiary's realized income is the parent's percentage interest in reported income of the subsidiary adjusted for the effects of intercompany profits from upstream sales and constructive gains or losses of the subsidiary. This adjustment to remove the potential dilution from the parent's diluted earnings is based on separate EPS computations for the subsidiary. We make these computations of subsidiary EPS only for the purpose of calculating the parent's EPS, and they are not necessarily the same as those prepared by the subsidiary for its own external reporting.

Note that "parent's equity in subsidiary's realized income" in column 2 of Exhibit 10-3 differs from "parent's income from subsidiary," which includes amortization of valuation differentials and the income effects of all intercompany transactions. The parent's investment valuation differentials, unrealized profits from downstream sales, and constructive gains and losses assigned to the parent do not affect the equity of the subsidiary's security holders; therefore, we exclude these items from the replacement calculation.

We use the subsidiary's diluted EPS in determining diluted earnings of the parent (see column 2 of Exhibit 10-3), so EPS computations for the subsidiary (based on subsidiary's realized income)

---

[5]The provisions of GAAP (ASC 260-10-05) on earnings per share that apply to subsidiaries also apply to investments accounted for by the equity method.

**EXHIBIT10-3**

**Parent-Company and Consolidated Diluted EPS Calculations**

| | Subsidiary Does Not Have Potentially Dilutive Securities Outstanding | Subsidiary Has Potentially Dilutive Securities Convertible into Subsidiary Common Stock | Subsidiary Has Potentially Dilutive Securities Convertible into Parent-Company Common Stock |
|---|---|---|---|
| *Numerator in Dollars ($)* | | | |
| Income to parent's common stockholders | $$$ | $$$ | $$$ |
| Add: Adjustments for parent's dilutive securities | +$ | +$ | +$ |
| Add: Adjustments for subsidiary's potentially dilutive securities convertible into parent-company stock | NA | NA | +$ |
| Replacement calculation (must result in a net decrease) | | | |
| Deduct: Parent's equity in subsidiary's realized income | NA | −$ | NA |
| Add: Parent's equity in subsidiary's diluted earnings | NA | +$ | NA |
| Parent's diluted earnings = a | $$$ | $$$ | $$$ |
| *Denominator in Shares (Y)* | | | |
| Parent's common shares outstanding | YYY | YYY | YYY |
| Add: Shares represented by parent's potentially dilutive securities | +Y | +Y | +Y |
| Add: Shares represented by subsidiary's potentially dilutive securities convertible into parent-company common shares | NA | NA | +Y |
| Parent's common shares and common share equivalents = b | YYY | YYY | YYY |
| *Parent-Company and Consolidated Diluted EPS* | a/b | a/b | a/b |
| NA—Not applicable. | | | |

are made as a first step in computing the parent's EPS. In computing the subsidiary's diluted earnings, we eliminate unrealized profits of the subsidiary and include constructive gains and losses of the subsidiary. We reflect the resulting EPS calculations of the subsidiary in the parent EPS calculation by replacing the "parent's equity in subsidiary's realized income" with the "parent's equity in subsidiary's diluted earnings." We determine the parent's equity in the subsidiary's diluted earnings by multiplying the subsidiary shares owned by the parent by the subsidiary's diluted EPS. This replacement allocates the subsidiary's realized income for EPS purposes to holders of the subsidiary's common stock and potentially dilutive securities, rather than only to the subsidiary's common stockholders.

## Diluted Securities of Subsidiary Convertible into Parent Shares

Parent common shares (the denominators of EPSs) are identical in columns 1 and 2 of Exhibit 10-3 but increase in column 3 for subsidiary securities that are convertible into parent common stock. This adjustment in column 3 is necessary when the subsidiary's potentially dilutive securities are potentially dilutive securities of the parent rather than of the subsidiary. When potentially dilutive securities of a subsidiary are convertible into parent common stock, income attributable to these securities under the if-converted method must be added back in calculating the parent's diluted earnings. Thus, column 3 of Exhibit 10-3 includes the item "adjustment for subsidiary's dilutive securities convertible into parent common stock," which is not applicable when the subsidiary does not have potentially dilutive securities (column 1) or when such securities are convertible into subsidiary common stock (column 2).

## SUBSIDIARY WITH CONVERTIBLE PREFERRED STOCK

Pop Corporation purchases 90 percent of Son Corporation's outstanding voting common stock for $328,000 on January 1, 2016. On this date, the stockholders' equity of the two corporations consists of the following (in thousands):

|  | Pop | Son |
|---|---|---|
| Common stock, $5 par, 200,000 shares issued and outstanding | $1,000 | |
| Common stock, $10 par, 20,000 shares outstanding | | $200 |
| 10% cumulative, convertible preferred stock, $100 par, 1,000 shares outstanding | | 100 |
| Retained earnings | 500 | 120 |
| Total stockholders' equity | $1,500 | $420 |

During 2016, Son reports $50,000 net income and pays $25,000 dividends, $10,000 to preferred and $15,000 to common. Pop's net income for 2016 is $186,000, determined as follows:

| | |
|---|---|
| Income from Pop's operations | $150,000 |
| Income from Son | 36,000 |
| [($50,000 net income − $10,000 preferred income) × 90%] | |
| Pop's net income | $186,000 |

### Subsidiary Preferred Stock Convertible into Subsidiary Common Stock

Assume that Son's preferred stock is convertible into 12,000 shares of Son's common stock and that neither Pop nor Son has other potentially dilutive securities outstanding. Son's realized net income is $40,000. Son's diluted EPS is $1.5625 [$50,000 earnings ÷ (20,000 common shares + 12,000 share dilution)], and Pop's diluted EPS is $0.89, computed as follows:

| | |
|---|---|
| Net income of Pop (equal to income to common) | $186,000 |
| Replacement of Pop's equity in Son's realized income ($40,000 × 90%) | (36,000) |
| with Pop's equity in Son's diluted earnings (18,000 shares of Son × Son's $1.5625 diluted EPS) | 28,125 |
| Pop's diluted earnings = a | $178,125 |
| Pop's outstanding shares = b | 200,000 |
| Pop's diluted EPS = a/b | $    0.89 |

The $7,875 potential dilution reflected in Pop's diluted earnings results from replacing Pop's equity in Son's realized income with Pop's equity in Son's diluted EPS. Note that Pop's equity in Son's realized income is $36,000, which is the same as Pop's income from Son.

### Subsidiary Preferred Stock Convertible into Parent Common Stock

Assume that Son's preferred stock is convertible into 24,000 shares of Pop's common stock and that neither Pop nor Son has other potentially dilutive securities outstanding. Son's diluted EPS (not used in Pop's EPS computations) is $2 per share ($40,000 income to common ÷ 20,000 common *shares outstanding*) because the preferred stock is not a dilutive security of Son Corporation. Pop's diluted EPS is computed as follows:

| | |
|---|---|
| Net income of Pop (equal to income to common) | $186,000 |
| Add: Income to preferred stockholders of Son assumed to be converted (90%) | 9,000 |
| Pop's diluted earnings = a | $195,000 |
| Pop's outstanding shares | 200,000 |
| Add: Son's preferred shares assumed converted | 24,000 |
| Pop's common shares and common stock equivalents = b | 224,000 |
| Pop's diluted EPS = a/b | $    0.87 |

Preferred income is added to Pop's net income because we allocated no income to the preferred stock assumed to be converted.

## SUBSIDIARY WITH OPTIONS AND CONVERTIBLE BONDS

Pad Corporation has $1,500,000 income from its own operations for 2016 and $300,000 income from Syd Corporation, its 80 percent–owned subsidiary. The $300,000 income from Syd consists of 80 percent of Syd's $450,000 net income for 2016, less 80 percent of a $50,000 unrealized gain on land purchased from Syd, less $20,000 amortization of the excess of fair value over the book value of Syd. The excess was assigned to a previously unrecognized patent. Assume the tax rate is 34 percent. Outstanding securities of the two corporations throughout 2016 are:

| | |
|---|---|
| Pad: | Common stock, 1,000,000 shares |
| Syd: | Common stock, 400,000 shares |
| | Options to purchase 60,000 shares of stock at $10 per share (average market price is $15 per share) |
| | 7% convertible bonds, $1,000,000 par outstanding, convertible into 80,000 shares of common stock |

### Options and Bonds Convertible into Subsidiary Common Stock

Assume that the options are exercisable and the bonds are convertible into Syd's common stock. Exhibit 10-4 shows computations for Syd's diluted EPS. Under the treasury stock approach for options and warrants, the effect of options on EPS is dilutive when the average market price of the shares to which the options apply exceeds the exercise price. If holders of Syd's options had exercised rights to acquire 60,000 shares of Syd's common stock at $10 per share, Syd would have received $600,000 cash. Under the treasury stock approach, we assume Syd uses this cash to reacquire 40,000 shares of its own stock ($600,000 ÷ $15 average market price). This assumed exercise and repurchase of treasury shares increase Syd's outstanding common stock for EPS computations by 20,000 shares.

The convertible bonds must also be included in Syd's diluted EPS computations. Under the if-converted method, we include $46,200 net-of-tax interest in Syd's diluted earnings and include the 80,000 shares issuable upon conversion in calculating Syd's diluted common shares.

We use Syd's $0.89 diluted EPS in the EPS computations for Pad Corporation. Exhibit 10-5 shows computations for Pad's diluted EPS.

In the computation of Pad's diluted earnings, we replace Pad's equity in Syd's realized income ($320,000) with Pad's share of Syd's diluted earnings ($284,800). This replacement decreases Pad's diluted earnings by $35,200. This dilution results from allocating Syd's $400,000 realized income plus $46,200 net-of-tax interest effect from the convertible bonds to holders of Syd's common shares, options, and convertible bonds, rather than just to Syd's common stockholders.

| | Syd's Diluted EPS |
|---|---|
| Syd's income to common stockholders | $450,000 |
| Less: Unrealized profit on sale of land | (50,000) |
| Add: Net-of-tax interest expense assuming subsidiary bonds converted into subsidiary shares ($1,000,000 × 7% × 66% assumed net-of-tax effect) | 46,200 |
| Subsidiary adjusted earnings = a | $446,200 |
| Syd's common shares outstanding | 400,000 |
| Incremental shares assuming exercise of options [60,000 shares − ($600,000 proceeds from exercise of options ÷ $15 market price)] | 20,000 |
| Additional shares assuming bonds converted into subsidiary shares | 80,000 |
| Syd's adjusted shares = b | 500,000 |
| Syd's Diluted EPS = a ÷ b | $    0.89 |

**EXHIBIT 10-4**

**Subsidiary's Diluted EPS Computations**

| EXHIBIT 10-5 | | Pad's Diluted EPS |
|---|---|---|
| **Parent's Diluted EPS Computations—Dilution Relates to Subsidiary Shares** | Pad's income to common stockholders | $1,800,000 |
| | Replacement of Pad's $320,000 equity in Syd's realized income [($450,000 − $50,000 unrealized profit) × 80%] | (320,000) |
| | with Pad's $284,800 equity in Syd's diluted EPS (320,000 shares × Syd's $0.89 diluted EPS) | 284,800 |
| | Pad's adjusted earnings = a | $1,764,800 |
| | Pad's outstanding common shares = b | 1,000,000 |
| | Pad's Diluted EPS = a ÷ b | $        1.76 |

| EXHIBIT 10-6 | | Pad's Diluted EPS |
|---|---|---|
| **Parent's Diluted EPS Computations—Dilution Relates to Parent Shares** | Pad's income to common stockholders | $1,800,000 |
| | Add: Net-of-tax interest assuming subsidiary bonds converted into parent's common stock ($1,000,000 × 7% × 66% net-of-tax effect) | 46,200 |
| | Pad's adjusted earnings = a | $1,846,200 |
| | Pad's outstanding shares | 1,000,000 |
| | Incremental shares assuming options converted into Pad's shares [60,000 shares − ($600,000 proceeds from exercise of options ÷ $15 market price)] | 20,000 |
| | Additional shares assuming subsidiary bonds are converted into Pad shares | 80,000 |
| | Pad's adjusted shares = b | 1,100,000 |
| | Pad's Diluted EPS = a ÷ b | $        1.68 |

## Options and Bonds Convertible into Parent's Common Stock

Exhibit 10-6 presents computations for Pad's diluted EPS under the assumptions that Syd Corporation's options can be used to purchase 60,000 shares of Pad Corporation's common stock (a net new 20,000 shares under the Treasury Stock method as discussed earlier) and that Syd Corporation's bonds are convertible into 80,000 shares of Pad Corporation's common stock. Under these assumptions, we do not need Syd's diluted EPS in determining Pad's diluted EPS because we only use subsidiary EPS computations for replacement computations when subsidiary dilutive securities are convertible into subsidiary shares. The subsidiary dilutive securities are convertible into parent shares in this example, so we only need parent EPS computations.

**LEARNING OBJECTIVE 10.3**

## INCOME TAXES OF CONSOLIDATED ENTITIES

This section on accounting for income taxes of consolidated entities begins with a discussion of which companies may file consolidated tax returns, the advantages and disadvantages of filing a consolidated tax return, and the status of accounting pronouncements on income taxes. Temporary differences in consolidated and separate tax returns are discussed, and income tax allocation procedures are illustrated for a parent and subsidiary that file separate tax returns. Next, four cases compare consolidation procedures when a parent and subsidiary file separate tax returns with those necessary when filing a consolidated tax return. A final section looks at the tax basis of assets and liabilities acquired in an acquisition.

Some consolidated entities prepare consolidated income tax returns and pay taxes on consolidated taxable income. Others prepare income tax returns for each affiliate and pay taxes on the taxable income included in the separate returns. The right of a consolidated entity to file a consolidated income tax return is contingent upon classification as an *affiliated group* under Sections 1501 through

1504 of the U.S. Internal Revenue Code (USIRC). An affiliated group exists when a common parent owns at least 80 percent of the voting power of all classes of stock and 80 percent or more of the total value of all outstanding stock of each of the includable corporations. The common parent must meet the 80 percent requirements directly for at least one includable corporation (USIRC 1504[a]).

A consolidated entity that is an affiliated group may elect to file consolidated income tax returns. All other consolidated entities *must* file separate income tax returns for each affiliate.

Note 1 to **Home Depot's** 2014 consolidated financial statements discusses its filing status as follows:

> *The Company and its eligible subsidiaries file a consolidated U.S. federal income tax return. Non-U.S. subsidiaries and certain U.S. subsidiaries, which are consolidated for financial reporting purposes, are not eligible to be included in the Company's consolidated U.S. federal income tax return. Separate provisions for income taxes have been determined for these entities. The Company intends to reinvest substantially all of the unremitted earnings of its non-U.S. subsidiaries and postpone their remittance indefinitely. Accordingly, no provision for U.S. income taxes on these earnings was recorded in the accompanying Consolidated Statements of Earnings.*[6]

## Advantages of Filing Consolidated Tax Returns

The primary advantages of filing a consolidated return are as follows:

1. Losses of one affiliate are offset against income of other members of the group. However, loss carryforwards at the time of acquisition of an affiliate can be offset only against taxable income of the affiliate.

2. Intercompany dividends are excluded from taxable income.

3. Intercompany profits are deferred from income until realized (but unrealized losses are also deferred until realized).

Exclusion of intercorporate dividends is not a unique advantage of filing a consolidated tax return, because a consolidated entity that is classified as an affiliated group is allowed a 100 percent exclusion on dividends received from members of the same group even if it elects not to file consolidated tax returns. In addition, corporate taxpayers can deduct 80 percent of the dividends received from domestic corporations that are 20 to 80 percent owned and can deduct 70 percent of the dividends received from domestic corporations that are less than 20 percent owned.

## Disadvantages of Filing Consolidated Tax Returns

Consolidated entities that file consolidated tax returns lose some of the flexibility of entities that file separate returns. For example, each subsidiary included in a consolidated tax return must use the parent's taxable year. Different years can be used when filing separate returns. The election to file a consolidated return commits an entity to consolidated returns year after year. It is difficult to obtain permission from the IRS to stop filing consolidated returns. Also, deconsolidated corporations cannot rejoin the affiliated group for five years.

## INCOME TAX ALLOCATION

The objectives of accounting for income taxes under current GAAP (ASC 740-10-05) are to recognize the amount of taxes payable or refundable for the current year and to recognize deferred tax liabilities and assets for the future tax consequences of events that have been recognized in the financial statements or tax returns.

Events that have future tax consequences are designated *temporary differences* to separate them from events that do not have tax consequences, such as interest income on municipal bond obligations. The tax consequences of temporary differences must be considered in the measurement of income for a period. Some accounting/income tax differences are the same, regardless of whether the affiliates file separate-entity or consolidated tax returns, whereas others depend on the kind of return filed. For example, unrealized and constructive gains and losses from

---

[6]From 2014 Annual Report (P 38) © 2015 Home Depot, Inc

intercompany transactions are temporary differences when filing separate returns because the individual entities are taxed on the income included in the separate returns. However, these items are *not* temporary differences when filing consolidated returns because adjustments to defer intercompany profits until realized are reflected in both the consolidation workpaper and the consolidated tax return.

Dividends received from members of an affiliated group are excluded from taxation regardless of whether affiliates file separate or consolidated returns, but dividends received from affiliates that are not members of an affiliated group are taxed currently, subject to the 80 percent dividends-received deduction.

## Temporary Differences from Undistributed Earnings of Subsidiaries and Equity Investees

Accounting requirements under the equity method of accounting are generally the same for investments of 20 to 50 percent of the voting stock of an investee as for subsidiary investments. Investors pay income taxes currently on dividends received (distributed income) from equity investees and subsidiaries that are not members of an affiliated group, and GAAP requires investors to provide for deferred income taxes on their shares of undistributed income of their investees. That is, a temporary difference results when an investor's equity in its investees' income exceeds dividends received.

Under prior GAAP (ASC 740-30-25), the parent/investor could avoid the general presumption that all undistributed earnings will be transferred to the parent by showing that undistributed earnings of the subsidiary had been invested indefinitely. Current GAAP (ASC 740-10-05) amends prior standards to remove the exception and require the parent/investor to treat the undistributed income of their domestic subsidiaries as temporary differences unless the tax law provides a means by which the investment can be recovered tax free. An exception for undistributed earnings of foreign subsidiaries and foreign joint ventures remains.

In accounting for the *tax effect* of a temporary difference relating to income from equity investees, we do not use the one-line consolidation concept because we include investment income in the investor's income *before* income taxes—in other words, on a pretax basis. If the undistributed earnings of an investee are the only temporary differences, a parent or equity investor provides for income taxes on its share of undistributed income by debiting income tax expense and crediting a deferred tax liability. The temporary difference related to undistributed earnings is, of course, only one of several possible differences that interact to produce the combined tax impact.

## Accounting for Distributed and Undistributed Income

Assume that Pop Corporation owns a 30 percent interest in Son Corporation, a domestic corporation. Son reports $1,200,000 net income for the current year and pays dividends of $400,000. An income tax rate of 34 percent applies. (The 34% tax rate is the *only* enacted tax rate applicable throughout this illustration.) We analyze Pop's share of Son's distributed and undistributed income as follows:

| | |
|---|---:|
| Share of distributed earnings (dividends) ($400,000 × 30%) | $120,000 |
| Share of undistributed earnings (retained earnings increase) ($800,000 × 30%) | 240,000 |
| Equity in Son's earnings ($1,200,000 × 30%) | $360,000 |

Pop is taxed currently on 20 percent of the $120,000 dividends received because Son is a domestic corporation that qualifies for the 80 percent dividends-received deduction. The income tax expense equals income tax liability for this part of Pop's income from Son. The current tax liability is $8,160 ($120,000 dividends received × 20% taxable × 34% tax rate)

No income tax is due currently on Pop's share of Son's undistributed earnings, but accounting standards require that we recognize income taxes attributable to that temporary difference as if the earnings had been remitted as dividends during the current period. Assuming that undistributed earnings are the only temporary difference, Pop makes the following entry to provide for income taxes on its share of Son's undistributed earnings:

*December 31*
| | | |
|---|---|---|
| Income tax expense (E, −SE) | 16,320 | |
|     Deferred tax liability (+L) | | 16,320 |
| To provide for taxes on undistributed earnings of | | |
|     Son ($240,000 × 20% taxable × 34% tax rate). | | |

The same procedures for income taxes on undistributed earnings apply to parent/investors, but not to dividends received from members of an affiliated group because we exclude 100 percent of those dividends from taxable income of the group.

## Unrealized Gains and Losses from Intercompany Transactions

Unrealized and constructive gains and losses from intercompany transactions create temporary differences that may affect deferred tax calculations when filing separate income tax returns. (This is *not* true when filing consolidated tax returns.) In the case of an unrealized gain, the selling entity includes the gain in its separate tax return and pays the tax due on the transaction. We eliminate the unrealized gain in the consolidation process, so we defer the income taxes related to the gain. An unrealized loss is treated similarly.

We include the tax effects of temporary differences from unrealized gains and losses on intercompany transactions in measuring the income tax expense of the selling affiliate. Under this approach, the consolidated income tax expense is equal to the combined income tax expense of the consolidated entities, and we eliminate intercompany profit items on a gross basis. Similarly, this approach permits the parent/investor to eliminate intercompany profits on a gross, rather than a net-of-tax, basis. (When eliminating intercompany profits on a net-of-tax basis by the parent/investor, we need a consolidation workpaper entry to convert the combined income tax expense of the affiliates into consolidated income tax expense and to adjust the deferred tax asset or liability amounts to a consolidated basis.)

Assume that Pam Corporation sells merchandise that cost $200,000 to Sun Corporation, its 75 percent–owned subsidiary, for $400,000, and that Sun still holds 70 percent of this merchandise at year-end. A 34 percent tax rate is applicable, and Pam pays $68,000 income tax on the transaction during the current year. Sun is a 75 percent–owned subsidiary, so we file separate tax returns. (Again, assume that the intercompany transaction is the only temporary difference and that the 34 percent tax rate is the only enacted rate.) Relevant consolidation and one-line consolidation entries are as follows:

**Consolidation Workpaper Entries—Year of Sale**
| | | |
|---|---|---|
| Sales (− R, − SE) | 400,000 | |
|     Cost of sales (− E, + SE) | | 400,000 |
|   To eliminate intercompany sales and cost of sales. | | |
| Cost of sales (E, − SE) | 140,000 | |
|     Inventory (− A) | | 140,000 |
|   To eliminate unrealized profit on intercompany merchandise | | |
|     remaining in inventory (($400,000 − $200,000) × 70%). | | |

*Pam's One-Line Consolidation Entry—Year of Sale*
| | | |
|---|---|---|
| Income from Sun (−R, −SE) | 140,000 | |
|     Investment in Sun (−A) | | 140,000 |
|   To eliminate unrealized profit on sales to Sun | | |
| ($140,000 unrealized profit × 100%). | | |

If Sun sells the merchandise in the next period, the consolidation and one-line consolidation entries in that year will be:

| | | |
|---|---:|---:|
| **Consolidation Workpaper Entry—Year of Realization** | | |
| **Investment in Sun ( + A)** | **140,000** | |
| **Cost of sales ( − E, +SE)** | | **140,000** |
| **To recognize previously deferred profit on inventory and to adjust** | | |
| **Pam's beginning Investment in Sun account to reflect realization.** | | |

| | | |
|---|---:|---:|
| *Pam's One-Line Consolidation Entry—Year of Realization* | | |
| Investment in Sun (+A) | 140,000 | |
| Income from Sun (R, +SE) | | 140,000 |
| To reinstate previously deferred profit | | |
| on intercompany sales. | | |

If the sale had been upstream from Sun to Pam, the $68,000 tax on the intercompany profit would have been paid by Sun, but Sun would show $47,600 ($140,000 × 34%) of that amount as a deferred tax asset, rather than as income tax expense for the year. The consolidation workpaper entry to eliminate the intercompany profit in the year of sale would be for $140,000, the same amount as in the downstream example. Noncontrolling interest share in the year of sale would decrease by $35,000 ($140,000 unrealized gain × 25%), and the amount of the one-line consolidation entry to eliminate the effect of the unrealized profit on Pam's books would be for $105,000 ($140,000 × 75%) rather than $140,000 as in the downstream example.

## SEPARATE-COMPANY TAX RETURNS WITH INTERCOMPANY GAIN

This section provides an extended illustration of income tax allocation for a parent and its subsidiary that file separate tax returns. Pop Corporation paid $375,000 cash for a 75 percent interest in Son Corporation on January 1, 2016, when Son's equity consisted of $300,000 capital stock and $200,000 retained earnings. At the time Pop acquired its interest in Son, Pop had a deferred income tax liability of $10,200, consisting of $30,000 tax/book depreciation differences that reverse in equal ($7,500) amounts over the years 2017 through 2020.

On January 8, 2016, Pop sold equipment to Son at a gain of $20,000. Son Corporation is depreciating the equipment on a straight-line basis over five years. Comparative income and retained earnings data for 2016 are as follows:

| | Pop | Son |
|---|---:|---:|
| Sales | $380,000 | $300,000 |
| Gain on equipment sale | 20,000 | — |
| Income from Son | 23,600 | — |
| Cost of sales | (200,000) | (180,000) |
| Operating expenses | (100,000) | (40,000) |
| Income tax expense | (31,253) | (27,200) |
| Net income | 92,347 | 52,800 |
| Add: Beginning retained earnings | 357,653 | 200,000 |
| Deduct: Dividends (December) | (50,000) | (28,000) |
| Retained earnings December 31 | $400,000 | $224,800 |

GAAP (ASC 740-10-05) requires Pop to provide for income taxes on its share of Son's $24,800 undistributed earnings ($52,800 net income less $28,000 dividends). The 80 percent dividends-received deduction is applicable to dividends received from Son Corporation. We assume a flat 34 percent income tax rate for both Pop and Son. Pop's deferred tax computation on the undistributed earnings is therefore $1,265 [($24,800 × 75% owned × 20% taxable) = $3,720 × 34% tax rate].

## One-Line Consolidation

Pop makes the following journal entries to account for its investment in Son during 2016:

| | | |
|---|---|---|
| *January 1* | | |
| Investment in Son (+A) | 375,000 | |
|     Cash (−A) | | 375,000 |
|   To record purchase of a 75% interest in Son. | | |
| *December* | | |
| Cash (+A) | 21,000 | |
|     Investment in Son (−A) | | 21,000 |
|   To record dividends received from Son ($28,000 × 75%). | | |
| *December 31* | | |
| Investment in Son (+A) | 23,600 | |
|     Income from Son (R, +SE) | | 23,600 |
|   To record income from Son computed as follows: | | |
|     Pop's share of Son's net income ($52,800 × 75%) | | $ 39,600 |
|     Less: Unrealized profit on sale of equipment | | (20,000) |
|     Add: Piecemeal recognition of gain ($20,000 ÷ 5 years) | | 4,000 |
|     Income from Son | | $ 23,600 |

Note that in computing its investment income from Son, Pop takes up its share of Son's income on which taxes have been paid by Son.

At December 31, 2016, Pop's Investment in Son account has a balance of $377,600 ($375,000 beginning balance + $23,600 income from Son − $21,000 dividends), and Pop's share of Son's equity is $393,600 ($524,800 × 75%). The $16,000 difference ($377,600 − $393,600) is the $16,000 unrealized profit from downstream sale of equipment.

## Income Tax Expense Based on Separate Returns

Son's $27,200 income tax expense is simply 34 percent of Son's $80,000 pretax accounting income, but Pop's income tax expense of $31,253 requires further analysis. In accordance with GAAP (ASC 740-10-05), we calculate Pop's income tax expense as follows:

| | |
|---|---|
| Tax on Pop's operating income [(380,000 sales − $200,000 cost of sale − $100,000 operating expenses) × 34%] | $27,200 |
| Tax on gain from sale of equipment ($20,000 × 34%) | 6,800 |
| Tax on dividends received [($21,000 × 20% taxable) × 34%] | 1,428 |
| Income taxes currently payable | 35,428 |
| *Less:* Decrease in deferred tax liability [($16,000 unrealized gain on equipment at year-end − $3,720 taxable share of Son's undistributed earnings)] × 34% | ($4,175) |
| Income tax expense | $31,253 |

Exhibit 10-7 provides a schedule to support the computation of Pop's income tax expense. Only one tax rate (34%) is applicable, so the schedule approach is not necessary, but it may be helpful. The calculation for future dividends in the schedule is $3,720 ($52,800 net income − $28,000 dividends) × 75 percent owned × 20 percent taxable portion, which reverses in 2021 when dividends are distributed.

Pop's interest in Son is only 75 percent, so it must file separate tax returns and pay income taxes on the $20,000 intercompany gain on the equipment sold to Son. Pop also pays income taxes on dividends received from Son, less an 80 percent dividends-received deduction. The multiplication of dividends received and undistributed income by 20 percent in calculating Pop's income tax expense effectively takes the 80 percent dividends-received deduction into account without calculating the amount of the deduction and subtracting it from distributed dividends or undistributed earnings.

EXHIBIT 10-7

Schedule of Deferred
Income Tax Liability at
December 31, 2016

| Temporary Difference | 2016 | 2017 | 2018 | 2019 | 2020 | Future Years |
|---|---|---|---|---|---|---|
| Depreciation | | $7,500 | $7,500 | $7,500 | $7,500 | |
| Gain on equipment | $20,000 | | | | | |
| Piecemeal recognition | (4,000) | (4,000) | (4,000) | (4,000) | (4,000) | |
| Future dividends | (3,720) | — | — | — | — | $3,720 |
| Taxable in future years | | 3,500 | 3,500 | 3,500 | 3,500 | 3,720 |
| Enacted tax rate | | ×34% | ×34% | ×34% | ×34% | ×34% |
| Deferred tax liability | | $1,190 | $1,190 | $1,190 | $1,190 | $ 1,265 |

Son's $27,200 income tax expense is equal to the tax liability indicated on its separate return because it has no temporary differences. Pop's income tax expense of $31,253 consists of $35,428 currently payable, less a $4,175 decrease in deferred tax liability for the year. The balance of Pop's deferred tax liability at December 31 is $6,025 ($10,200 beginning balance −$4,175 decrease for the year). Son and Pop record income tax expenses as follows:

*Son's Books—December 31, 2016*
| | | |
|---|---|---|
| Income tax expense (E, −SE) | 27,200 | |
|     Income taxes currently payable (+L) | | 27,200 |
|   To accrue income taxes for 2016. | | |

*Pop's Books—December 31, 2016*
| | | |
|---|---|---|
| Income tax expense (E, −SE) | 31,253 | |
| Deferred tax liability (−L) | 4,175 | |
|     Income taxes currently payable (+L) | | 35,428 |
|   To accrue income taxes for 2016. | | |

## Consolidation Workpaper

Exhibit 10-8 presents a consolidation workpaper for Pop Corporation and Subsidiary. The workpaper entries are the same as those encountered in earlier chapters except for the inclusion of income tax considerations. Observe that Pop's income tax expense plus Son's income tax expense equal the $58,453 consolidated income tax expense.

Pop paid income taxes on the $20,000 gain on the intercompany sale of equipment. We do not recognize this gain for consolidated statement purposes, so a temporary difference exists for which we require income tax allocation procedures.

## Workpaper Entry for 2017

The workpaper entry for 2017 to eliminate the effect of the unrealized profit from the intercompany sale of equipment is as follows:

| | | |
|---|---|---|
| **Investment in Son ( + A)** | **16,000** | |
| **Accumulated depreciation ( + A)** | **8,000** | |
|     **Equipment ( − A)** | | **20,000** |
|     **Depreciation expense ( − E, + SE)** | | **4,000** |
|   **To eliminate unrealized profit from downstream sale of equipment.** | | |

The income tax expense in 2017 will be equal to the income tax currently payable, adjusted for the change in the deferred tax asset or liability that occurs in 2017.

## POP CORPORATION AND SUBSIDIARY CONSOLIDATION WORKPAPER FOR THE YEAR ENDED DECEMBER 31, 2016

**EXHIBIT 10-8**

Parent and Subsidiary Companies File Separate Tax Returns

| | Pop | 75% Son | Adjustments and Eliminations Debits | Adjustments and Eliminations Credits | Consolidated Statements |
|---|---|---|---|---|---|
| *Income Statement* | | | | | |
| Sales | $380,000 | $300,000 | | | $680,000 |
| Gain on equipment | 20,000 | | a 20,000 | | |
| Income from Son | 23,600 | | c 23,600 | | |
| Cost of sales | (200,000) | (180,000) | | | (380,000) |
| Operating expense | (100,000) | (40,000) | | b 4,000 | (136,000) |
| Income tax expense | (31,253) | (27,200) | | | (58,453) |
| Noncontrolling interest share | | | e 13,200 | | (13,200) |
| **Controlling share of net income** | **$ 92,347** | **$ 52,800** | | | **$ 92,347** |
| *Retained Earnings Statement* | | | | | |
| Retained earnings—Pop | $357,653 | | | | $357,653 |
| Retained earnings—Son | | $200,000 | d 200,000 | | |
| **Controlling share of net income** | 92,347 | 52,800 | | | 92,347 |
| Dividends | (50,000) | (28,000) | | c 21,000 <br> e 7,000 | (50,000) |
| **Retained earnings— December 31** | **$400,000** | **$224,800** | | | **$400,000** |
| *Balance Sheet* | | | | | |
| Other assets | $362,400 | $432,000 | | | $794,400 |
| Equipment | 120,000 | 200,000 | | a 20,000 | 300,000 |
| Accumulated depreciation | (60,000) | (50,000) | b 4,000 | | (106,000) |
| Investment in Son | 377,600 | | | c 2,600 <br> d 375,000 | |
| | $800,000 | $582,000 | | | $988,400 |
| Deferred tax liability | $ 6,025 | | | | $6,025 |
| Income tax liability | 35,428 | $ 27,200 | | | 62,628 |
| Other liabilities | 58,547 | 30,000 | | | 88,547 |
| Capital stock | 300,000 | 300,000 | d 300,000 | | 300,000 |
| **Retained earnings** | **400,000** | **224,800** | | | **400,000** |
| | $800,000 | $582,000 | | | |
| Noncontrolling interest | | | | d 125,000 <br> e 6,200 | 131,200 |
| | | | 560,800 | 560,800 | $988,400 |

## EFFECT OF CONSOLIDATED AND SEPARATE-COMPANY TAX RETURNS ON CONSOLIDATION PROCEDURES

This section compares consolidation procedures for a parent and its subsidiary when separate-company and consolidated tax returns are filed. Under GAAP (ASC 740-10-05), the income tax expense and the income from subsidiary are the same in both cases. When firms file consolidated tax returns, we allocate the tax liability among the parent and its subsidiaries.

### Allocation of Consolidated Income Tax to Affiliates

A subsidiary that is part of a group filing a consolidated tax return is required to disclose its current and deferred income tax expense and any tax-related balances due to or from affiliates in its separate financial statements. Although GAAP provides no single method of allocating consolidated income tax expense among affiliates, firms must disclose the method used.

Four methods currently used in the allocation of consolidated income taxes to affiliates are as follows:

- **Separate return method.** Each subsidiary computes income taxes as if it were filing a separate return.

- **Agreement method.** Tax expense is allocated by agreement between parent and subsidiaries.

- **With-or-without method.** The income tax provision is computed for the group with and without the pretax income of the subsidiary. The subsidiary's income tax expense is the difference.

- **Percentage allocation method.** Consolidated income tax expense is allocated to a subsidiary on the basis of its pretax income as a percentage of consolidated pretax income.

The percentage allocation method is used for the illustrations throughout this text.

### Background Information for Consolidated and Separate Tax Return Illustrations

The following illustrations for Pal Corporation and its 90 percent–owned subsidiary, Sal Corporation, compare consolidation procedures used when filing consolidated tax returns with consolidation procedures necessary when filing separate-company tax returns. Tax effects of intercompany profits from both upstream and downstream inventory sales are also illustrated.

On January 1, 2016, Pal acquired 90 percent of the outstanding voting stock of Sal for $432,000, when Sal had $300,000 capital stock and $100,000 retained earnings. The $432,000 purchase price implies that Sal's total fair value is $480,000 ($432,000/90%). Sal's book value is $400,000, implying goodwill of $80,000. Goodwill is not amortized for either financial reporting or tax purposes. Additional information follows:

1. A flat 34 percent enacted income tax rate applies to all years.

2. Pal and Sal are an affiliated group entitled to the 100 percent dividend exclusion.

3. Sal pays dividends of $20,000 during 2016.

4. Intercompany sales are $40,000, of which $10,000 represents unrealized profits at year-end 2016.

5. Pretax operating incomes for the two affiliates are:

|  | Pal | Sal |
|---|---|---|
| Sales | $900,000 | $500,000 |
| Cost of sales | (500,000) | (350,000) |
| Expenses | (250,000) | (100,000) |
| Pretax operating income | $150,000 | $ 50,000 |

Cases 1 and 2 illustrate a temporary difference for unrealized profits from downstream sales that originates in the current year and reverses in the succeeding year. Subsequently, Cases 3 and 4 repeat illustrations 1 and 2 using an upstream-sale assumption as the only temporary difference.

## Case 1: Consolidated Tax Return With Downstream Sales

Assume that a consolidated tax return is filed and that the intercompany sales are downstream. The consolidated tax return includes the $200,000 combined operating income (Pal's $150,000 operating income plus Sal's $50,000 operating income) less $10,000 unrealized profit. The consolidated tax expense will be $64,600 ($190,000 × 34%). The $64,600 income tax expense is equal to the $64,600 consolidated income tax liability because we eliminate the unrealized profits in the consolidation workpaper and in the consolidated tax return. In addition, no tax is assessed on the $18,000 dividends that Pal receives from Sal.

We allocate the $64,600 consolidated income tax liability to Pal and Sal based on the amounts of their income included in the $190,000 consolidated taxable income. The intercompany sales are downstream in this case, so the allocation is:

$$Pal = \frac{\$150,000 - \$10,000}{\$190,000} \times \$64,600 = \$47,600$$

$$Sal = \frac{\$50,000}{\$190,000} \times \$64,600 = \$17,000$$

Pal and Sal record the 2016 income tax expense amounts determined in this allocation as follows:

| | | |
|---|---|---|
| *Pal's Books—December 31* | | |
| Income tax expense (E, −SE) | 47,600 | |
|     Income taxes currently payable (+L) | | 47,600 |
|   To record share of the consolidated income tax liability. | | |
| *Sal's Books—December 31* | | |
| Income tax expense (E, −SE) | 17,000 | |
|     Income taxes currently payable (+L) | | 17,000 |
|   To record share of the consolidated income tax liability. | | |

After entering this tax allocation, Sal's net income will be $33,000 ($50,000 − $17,000 income tax), and Pal records income from Sal as follows:

| | | |
|---|---|---|
| *December 31* | | |
| Investment in Sal (+A) | 19,700 | |
|     Income from Sal (R, +SE) | | 19,700 |
|   To record investment income from Sal computed as follows: | | |
|   Share of Sal's net income ($33,000 × 90%) | | $29,700 |
|   Less: Unrealized profit in inventory | | (10,000) |
|   Income from Sal | | $19,700 |

We deduct the full amount of the unrealized inventory profit because the sale is downstream, and no tax is assessed on unrealized profits when filing consolidated income tax returns. Exhibit 10-9 presents a consolidation workpaper for Pal and Subsidiary.

Related workpaper entries, presented in general journal form, are:

| | | | |
|---|---|---|---|
| a | **Sales (−R, −SE)** | **40,000** | |
| |     **Cost of goods sold (−E, +SE)** | | **40,000** |
| |   **To eliminate intercompany sales and cost of sales.** | | |
| b | **Cost of goods sold (E, −SE)** | **10,000** | |
| |     **Inventory (−A)** | | **10,000** |
| |   **To eliminate intercompany profits from downstream sale.** | | |
| c | **Income from Sal (−R, −SE)** | **19,700** | |
| |     **Investment in Sal (−A)** | | **1,700** |
| |     **Dividends (+SE)** | | **18,000** |
| |   **To eliminate investment income and dividends and adjust the Investment in Sal account to its beginning-of-the-period balance.** | | |

*(continued)*

| d | Capital stock—Sal (−SE) | 300,000 | |
|---|---|---|---|
| | Retained earnings—Sal (−SE) | 100,000 | |
| | Goodwill (+A) | 80,000 | |
| | Investment in Sal (−A) | | 432,000 |
| | Noncontrolling interest—beginning (+SE) | | 48,000 |

To eliminate reciprocal beginning-of-the-period investment and equity amounts, establish beginning-of-the-period goodwill and noncontrolling interest.

| e | Noncontrolling interest share (−SE) | 3,300 | |
|---|---|---|---|
| | Dividends (+SE) | | 2,000 |
| | Noncontrolling interest (+SE) | | 1,300 |

To enter noncontrolling interest shares of subsidiary income and dividends.

## Case 2: Separate Tax Returns with Downstream Sales

Assume that the intercompany sales are downstream and that they file separate tax returns. Sal has an income tax liability of $17,000 and reports net income of $33,000. Pal records income from Sal of $19,700, computed as follows:

| | |
|---|---|
| Share of Sal's net income ($33,000 × 90%) | $29,700 |
| Less: Unrealized profit | (10,000) |
| Income from Sal | $19,700 |

Pal's income tax currently payable is 34 percent of its $150,000 operating income, or $51,000. Pal's income tax expense is $47,600, computed as follows:

| | |
|---|---|
| Income tax currently payable | $51,000 |
| Less: Increase in deferred tax asset from temporary difference ($10,000 unrealized *profit* × 34% tax rate) | (3,400) |
| Income tax expense | $47,600 |

Exhibit 10-10 reflects these observations in the consolidation workpaper.

Income taxes currently payable that will appear in the consolidated balance sheet are $68,000 ($51,000 for Pal Corporation plus $17,000 for Sal Corporation). The difference between the consolidated income tax expense ($64,600) and income taxes currently payable ($68,000) is the $3,400 deferred tax asset for the $10,000 unrealized profit. The $64,600 income tax expense appearing in the consolidated income statement can be computed independently as follows:

| | |
|---|---|
| Consolidated income before income taxes and noncontrolling interest share ($1,360,000 sales − $820,000 cost *of goods sold* − $350,000 expenses) | $190,000 |
| Tax rate | ×34% |
| Income tax expense | $ 64,600 |

Compare Exhibits 10-9 and 10-10. Income tax expense and income from subsidiary are the same whether we file separate tax returns or consolidated tax returns. However, there is a difference in income tax currently payable and in the deferred tax asset.

When filing a consolidated tax return, income tax expense is equal to income tax currently payable because no tax is assessed on the unrealized intercompany profit. Consolidated income tax expense is the same whether we file separate-company or consolidated income tax returns. However, with separate tax returns, Pal's income tax expense consists of $51,000 income tax currently payable, less the $3,400 deferred tax asset related to the $10,000 temporary difference.

**PAL CORPORATION AND SUBSIDIARY CONSOLIDATION WORKPAPER FOR THE YEAR ENDED DECEMBER 31, 2016 (IN THOUSANDS)**

| | Pal | Sal | Adjustments and Eliminations Debits | Credits | Consolidated Statements |
|---|---|---|---|---|---|
| *Income Statement* | | | | | |
| Sales | $900 | $500 | a  40 | | $ 1,360 |
| Income from Sal | 19.7 | | c  19.7 | | |
| Cost of goods sold | (500) | (350) | b  10 | a  40 | (820) |
| Expenses (excluding income taxes) | (250) | (100) | | | (350) |
| Income tax expense | (47.6) | (17) | | | (64.6) |
| Noncontrolling interest share | | | e   3.3 | | (3.3) |
| **Controlling share of net income** | **$122.1** | **$ 33** | | | **$   122.1** |
| *Retained Earnings Statement* | | | | | |
| Retained earnings—Pal | $352.9 | | | | $   352.9 |
| Retained earnings—Sal | | $100 | d 100 | | |
| **Controlling share of net income** | 122.1 | 33 | | | 122.1 |
| Dividends | (80) | (20) | | c  18 / e  2 | (80) |
| **Retained earnings—December 31** | **$395** | **$113** | | | **$   395** |
| *Balance Sheet* | | | | | |
| Inventory | $183.3 | $ 80 | | b  10 | $253.3 |
| Other assets | 378 | 520 | | | 898 |
| Investment in Sal | 433.7 | | | c   1.7 / d 432 | |
| Goodwill | | | d  80 | | 80 |
| | $995 | $600 | | | $ 1,231.3 |
| Income tax payable | $ 47.6 | $ 17 | | | $ 64.6 |
| Other liabilities | 152.4 | 170 | | | 322.4 |
| Capital stock | 400 | 300 | d 300 | | 400 |
| **Retained earnings** | 395 | 113 | | | 395 |
| | $995 | $600 | | | |
| Noncontrolling interest | | | | d  48 / e   1.3 | 49.3 |
| | | | 553 | 553 | $ 1,231.3 |

**EXHIBIT 10-9**

Consolidated Tax Return—Unrealized Profit from Downstream Sales

Subsidiary Preferred Stock, Consolidated Earnings per Share, and Consolidated Income

**EXHIBIT 10-10**

Separate Tax Returns—
Unrealized Profit from
Downstream Sales

### PAL CORPORATION AND SUBSIDIARY CONSOLIDATION WORKPAPER FOR THE YEAR ENDED DECEMBER 31, 2016 (IN THOUSANDS)

| | Pal | Sal | Adjustments and Eliminations Debits | Adjustments and Eliminations Credits | Consolidated Statements |
|---|---|---|---|---|---|
| *Income Statement* Sales | $900 | $500 | a 40 | | $1,360 |
| Income from Sal | 19.7 | | c 19.7 | | |
| Cost of goods sold | (500) | (350) | b 10 | a 40 | (820) |
| Expenses (excluding income taxes) | (250) | (100) | | | (350) |
| Income tax expense | (47.6) | (17) | | | (64.6) |
| Noncontrolling interest share | | | e 3.3 | | (3.3) |
| **Controlling share of net income** | **$122.1** | **$ 33** | | | **$ 122.1** |
| *Retained Earnings Statement* Retained earnings—Pal | $352.9 | | | | $ 352.9 |
| Retained earnings—Sal | | $100 | d 100 | | |
| **Controlling share of net income** | **122.1** | **33** | | | **122.1** |
| Dividends | (80) | (20) | | c 18 e 2 | (80) |
| **Retained earnings— December 31** | **$395** | **$113** | | | **$ 395** |
| *Balance Sheet* Inventory | $183.3 | $ 80 | | b 10 | $ 253.3 |
| Deferred tax asset | 3.4 | | | | 3.4 |
| Other assets | 378 | 520 | | | 898 |
| Investment in Sal | 433.7 | | | c 1.7 d 432 | |
| Goodwill | | | d 80 | | 80 |
| | $998.4 | $600 | | | $1,234.7 |
| Income tax payable | $ 51 | $ 17 | | | $ 68 |
| Other liabilities | 152.4 | 170 | | | 322.4 |
| Capital stock | 400 | 300 | d 300 | | 400 |
| **Retained earnings** | **395** | **113** | | | **395** |
| | $998.4 | $600 | | | |
| Noncontrolling interest | | | | d 48 e 1.3 | 49.3 |
| | | | 553 | 553 | $1,234.7 |

## Case 3: Consolidated Tax Return with Upstream Sales

Now assume that intercompany sales are upstream (from Sal to Pal). If we file a consolidated return, the consolidated tax expense will be $64,600, the same as in the downstream example, but the allocation to Pal and Sal changes because we exclude $10,000 of Sal's $50,000 pretax income from consolidated taxable income. The allocation is:

$$\text{Pal} = \frac{\$150,000}{\$190,000} \times \$64,600 = \$51,000$$

$$\text{Sal} = \frac{\$50,000 - \$10,000}{\$190,000} \times \$64,600 = \$13,600$$

We record these amounts in the separate company books as follows:

| | | |
|---|---|---|
| *Pal's Books—December 31* | | |
| Income tax expense (E, −SE) | 51,000 | |
|     Income taxes currently payable (+L) | | 51,000 |
|   To record share of consolidated income taxes | | |
| *Sal's Books—December 31* | | |
| Income tax expense (E, −SE) | 13,600 | |
|     Income taxes currently payable (+L) | | 13,600 |
|   To record share of consolidated income taxes. | | |

Sal's net income is $36,400 ($50,000 pretax income less $13,600 income tax expense), and Pal determines income from Sal as follows:

| | |
|---|---|
| Share of Sal's net income ($36,400 × 90%) | $32,760 |
| Less: Unrealized profit from upstream sales ($10,000 × 90%) | (9,000) |
| Income from Sal | $23,760 |

Consolidation workpapers to illustrate the effect of the upstream-sale example appear in Exhibit 10-11. We compute noncontrolling interest share of $2,640 as 10 percent of Sal's realized income of $26,400 ($36,400 net income − $10,000 unrealized profit). The consolidated tax expense of $64,600 is the same as in the downstream-sale example, but controlling share of consolidated net income is $660 greater because we attribute the $10,000 unrealized gain and the related $3,400 tax allocation effect to subsidiary operations. Thus, noncontrolling interest share is $660 less than in the downstream-sale examples, and controlling share of consolidated net income is $660 more ($122,760 instead of $122,100 in Exhibits 10-9 and 10-10). The noncontrolling interest share computation in Exhibit 10-11 eliminates 100 percent of the $10,000 unrealized profit because no tax is paid on unrealized profits when filing consolidated returns.

## Case 4: Separate Tax Returns with Upstream Sales

Assume that intercompany sales are upstream and that they file separate tax returns. Sal's income tax currently payable, as determined from its separate tax return, is $17,000, because income taxes are assessed on Sal's $50,000 pretax income, which includes the $10,000 unrealized profit. However, Sal's income tax expense is only $13,600, computed as follows:

| | |
|---|---|
| Income tax currently payable | $17,000 |
| Less: Increase in deferred tax asset from temporary difference ($10,000 unrealized profit × 34% tax rate) | (3,400) |
| Income tax expense | $13,600 |

*(continued)*

## PAL CORPORATION AND SUBSIDIARY CONSOLIDATION WORKPAPER FOR THE YEAR ENDED DECEMBER 31, 2016 (IN THOUSANDS)

| | Pal | 90% Sal | Adjustments and Eliminations Debits | Adjustments and Eliminations Credits | Consolidated Statements |
|---|---|---|---|---|---|
| *Income Statement* | | | | | |
| Sales | $ 900 | $500 | a  40 | | $ 1,360 |
| Income from Sal | 23.76 | | c  23.76 | | |
| Cost of goods sold | (500) | (350) | b  10 | a  40 | (820) |
| Expenses (excluding income taxes) | (250) | (100) | | | (350) |
| Income tax expense | (51) | (13.6) | | | (64.6) |
| Noncontrolling interest share | | | e  2.64 | | (2.64) |
| **Controlling share of net income** | **$ 122.76** | **$ 36.4** | | | **$  122.76** |
| *Retained Earnings Statement* | | | | | |
| Retained earnings—Pal | $ 352.9 | | | | $  352.9 |
| Retained earnings—Sal | | $100 | d 100 | | |
| **Controlling share of net income** | 122.76 | 36.4 | | | 122.76 |
| Dividends | (80) | (20) | | c  18 <br> e  2 | (80) |
| **Retained earnings— December 31** | **$ 395.66** | **$116.4** | | | **$  395.66** |
| *Balance Sheet* | | | | | |
| Inventory | $ 183.3 | $ 80 | | b  10 | $  253.3 |
| Other assets | 378 | 520 | | | 898 |
| Investment in Sal | 437.76 | | | c  5.76 <br> d 432 | |
| Goodwill | | | d  80 | | 80 |
| | $ 999.06 | $600 | | | $ 1,231.3 |
| Income tax payable | $  51 | $ 13.6 | | | $ 64.6 |
| Other liabilities | 152.4 | 170 | | | 322.4 |
| Capital stock | 400 | 300 | d 300 | | 400 |
| **Retained earnings** | 395.66 | 116.4 | | | 395.66 |
| | $ 999.06 | $600 | | | |
| Noncontrolling interest | | | | d  48 <br> e   0.64 | 48.64 |
| | | | 556.4 | 556.4 | $ 1,231.3 |

Sal's net income is $36,400, as in Case 3, and Pal records its income from Sal at $23,760, determined as follows:

| | |
|---|---|
| Pal's share of Sal's net income ($36,400 × 90%) | $32,760 |
| Less: Unrealized profit from upstream sales | (9,000) |
| ($10,000 × 90% owned) | |
| Pal's income from Sal | $23,760 |

Exhibit 10-12 shows a workpaper when separate returns are filed and unrealized inventory profit results from upstream sales.

In comparing Exhibits 10-11 and 10-12, note that the income tax expense and the income from the subsidiary are the same whether we file separate or consolidated tax returns. There is, however, a difference in income tax currently payable and in the deferred tax asset. When filing separate tax returns, consolidated tax expense consists of the following:

| | Pal | Sal | Consolidated |
|---|---|---|---|
| Income taxes currently payable | $51,000 | $17,000 | $68,000 |
| Deferred tax asset | — | (3,400) | (3,400) |
| Income tax expense | $51,000 | $13,600 | $64,600 |

Thus, the consolidated income statement will show income tax expense of $64,600, and the consolidated balance sheet will show a liability for income tax currently payable of $68,000 and a current asset for the $3,400 deferred tax asset.

## BUSINESS COMBINATIONS

For income tax purposes, the term *reorganization* refers to certain corporate restructurings or combinations that are tax free under Internal Revenue Code Section 368. Reorganization transactions include mergers, recapitalizations, and divisions of corporations. Failure to meet any of the required conditions specified in the code may disqualify a reorganization so that the transaction loses its tax-free status. Although the code describes seven types of transactions (Type A through Type G) as reorganizations, only three are discussed here:

- **Merger or consolidation.** A merger occurs when one corporation acquires another corporation, primarily for the acquiring company's stock (but some other consideration may be given), and the acquired corporation is dissolved. Its assets and liabilities are taken over by the acquiring corporation. A consolidation occurs when two or more companies combine to form a new corporation and the original corporations are dissolved.[7]

- **Acquiring another corporation's stock.** If a corporation exchanges any of its voting stock *(and no other consideration is given)* for stock of another corporation and it controls the second corporation immediately after the exchange, the transaction is a reorganization. Control means ownership of at least 80 percent of the voting stock and at least 80 percent of all other classes of stock.

- **Acquiring another corporation's assets.** If a corporation exchanges any of its voting stock (and generally nothing else) for substantially all of another corporation's property, the transaction is a reorganization. The assumption of liabilities does not disqualify this transaction as a tax-free reorganization.

These summaries are brief and nontechnical. The point is the qualifications under the tax code for an exchange of shares to be a tax-free reorganization are *not identical* to the qualifications under accounting principles for the former pooling of interests business combination. Purchase business combinations may be either taxable or tax free, and structuring a transaction to meet the goals of both buyer and seller is an important part of the negotiating process for any business combination. As you would expect, firms often structure combinations to be tax free.

---

[7]The accounting concepts of mergers and consolidations were discussed in Chapter 1.

**EXHIBIT10-12**

Separate Tax Returns—
Unrealized Profit from
Upstream Sales

## PAL CORPORATION AND SUBSIDIARY CONSOLIDATION WORKPAPER FOR THE YEAR ENDED DECEMBER 31, 2016 (IN THOUSANDS)

| | Pal | Sal | Adjustments and Eliminations Debits | Adjustments and Eliminations Credits | Consolidated Statements |
|---|---|---|---|---|---|
| *Income Statement*<br>Sales | $900 | $500 | a  40 | | $1,360 |
| Income from Sal | 23.76 | | c  23.76 | | |
| Cost of goods sold | (500) | (350) | b  10 | a  40 | (820) |
| Expenses (excluding income taxes) | (250) | (100) | | | (350) |
| Income tax expense | (51) | (13.6) | | | (64.6) |
| Noncontrolling interest share | | | e  2.64 | | (2.64) |
| **Controlling share of net income** | **$122.76** | **$ 36.4** | | | **$ 122.76** |
| *Retained Earnings Statement*<br>Retained earnings—Pal | $352.9 | | | | $ 352.9 |
| Retained earnings—Sal | | $100 | d 100 | | |
| **Controlling share of net income** | **122.76** | **36.4** | | | **122.76** |
| Dividends | (80) | (20) | | c  18<br>e  2 | (80) |
| **Retained earnings— December 31** | **$395.66** | **$116.4** | | | **$ 395.66** |
| *Balance Sheet*<br>Inventory | $183.3 | $ 80 | | b  10 | $ 253.3 |
| Deferred tax asset | | 3.4 | | | 3.4 |
| Other assets | 378 | 520 | | | 898 |
| Investment in Sal | 437.76 | | | c   5.76<br>d 432 | |
| Goodwill | | | d  80 | | 80 |
| | $999.06 | $603.4 | | | $1,234.7 |
| Income tax payable | $ 51 | $ 17 | | | $ 68 |
| Other liabilities | 152.4 | 170 | | | 322.4 |
| Capital stock | 400 | 300 | d 300 | | 400 |
| **Retained earnings** | **395.66** | **116.4** | | | **395.66** |
| | $999.06 | $603.4 | | | |
| Noncontrolling interest | | | | d  48<br>e  0.64 | 48.64 |
| | | | 556.4 | 556.4 | $1,234.7 |

In a taxable business combination, we revalue the assets and liabilities of the acquired corporation to reflect the fair value acquired. The seller recognizes gain or loss equal to the fair value of the consideration received, less the tax basis of the assets or stock sold. In a tax-free reorganization, the tax basis of the assets and liabilities are carried forward with no revaluation.

The Revenue Recognition Act of 1993 allows a tax deduction for amortization of goodwill (which is no longer amortized under GAAP (ASC 350-20-35)) and other intangible assets (called Section 197 intangible assets). This deduction is only allowed when taxes have been paid (gain or loss recognized) by the seller on the purchase transaction.[8] All Section 197 intangible assets are amortized for tax purposes over a 15-year period, regardless of their useful lives.

## Acquisitions

GAAP (ASC 740-10-05) requires that firms recognize a deferred tax liability or deferred tax asset for the difference between the book values (tax bases) and the assigned values of the assets and liabilities (except goodwill and leveraged leases) acquired in an acquisition. In other words, we record the assets and liabilities acquired at their gross fair values and record a deferred tax asset or liability for the related tax effect.

A difference between book value and tax value only occurs when the assets are not written up to fair value for tax purposes as they are for book purposes. When the assets are written up for tax purposes, the only differences between written-up book value and tax basis should have already been accounted for in the acquirer's separate books as a deferred tax asset or liability (due to an original difference between book and tax value at the point of purchase).

The tax-free business combination of Pat and Sad is used to illustrate the computation of a deferred tax liability for the book value/fair value differentials and for the determination of goodwill. On January 1, 2016, Pat Corporation paid $400,000 for 60 percent of the outstanding voting stock of Sad Corporation, when Sad's stockholders' equity consisted of $300,000 capital stock and $200,000 retained earnings. Book values were equal to fair values of Sad's assets and liabilities, except for a building and land. The building had a book value of $80,000, a fair value of $120,000, and a remaining useful life of eight years. The land had a book value of $50,000 and a fair value of $150,000. Any goodwill is not amortized. The tax rate applicable to both companies is 34 percent, and an 80 percent dividends deduction applies.

We assign the $100,000 excess of cost over book value acquired [$400,000 cost − ($500,000 book value of net assets × 60% interest)] as follows:

|  | Book Value | Pretax Fair Value | Difference | Pat's 60% Interest × The Difference |
|---|---|---|---|---|
| Building | $80,000 | $120,000 | $ 40,000 | $ 24,000 |
| Land | 50,000 | 150,000 | 100,000 | 60,000 |
| Revaluation of assets (gross amount) |  |  |  | 84,000 |
| Less: Deferred tax on revaluation ($84,000 × 34%) |  |  |  | (28,560) |
| Net differential from revaluation of assets |  |  |  | 55,440 |
| Goodwill |  |  |  | 44,560 |
| Excess cost over book value acquired |  |  |  | $100,000 |

The $24,000 assigned to the building and the $8,160 related deferred tax liability ($24,000 × 34%) will be written off over the building's remaining eight-year useful life at the annual amounts of $3,000 and $1,020, respectively. Thus, consolidated net income will be decreased by $1,980 each year on an after-tax basis. The $60,000 revaluation of the land and the $20,400 deferred tax liability on the revalued land will remain on the books until the land is sold to outside entities.

GAAP (ASC 805-740-45) does not assign a deferred tax liability to the goodwill account (when the goodwill is not deductible), due to the difficulty in the simultaneous calculation of the residual

---

[8]The company's liabilities may or may not be assumed in the transaction.

account, goodwill, and a deferred tax assignment to this residual account. The FASB decided that very little incremental information would be added by this calculation.

## Equity Method of Accounting for Acquisitions

During 2016, Sad has net income of $100,000 and pays dividends of $40,000. Pat makes the following entries on its separate books to account for its investment in Sad:

| | | |
|---|---:|---:|
| Investment in Sad (+A) | 400,000 | |
|     Cash (−A) | | 400,000 |
| To record acquisition of a 60% interest in Sad Corporation. | | |
| Cash (+A) | 24,000 | |
|     Investment in Sad (−A) | | 24,000 |
| To record receipt of dividends from Sad ($40,000 × 60%). Note that Pat must also provide for income taxes on its share of the $60,000 undistributed earnings of Sad ($36,000 × 20% taxable × 34% tax *rate* = $2,448 deferred taxes). | | |
| Investment in Sad (+A) | 58,020 | |
|     Income from Sad (R, +SE) | | 58,020 |
| To record income from Sad and the related amortization of deferred tax liability on the building computed as follows: | | |

| | |
|---|---:|
| Share of Sad's income ($100,000 × 60%) | $60,000 |
| Less: Depreciation on excess allocated to building | (3,000) |
| Add: Amortization of deferred taxes on building | 1,020 |
| Income from Sad | $58,020 |

The stockholders' equity of Sad at December 31, 2016, consists of $300,000 capital stock and $260,000 retained earnings. The balance of Pat's Investment in Sad account at December 31, 2016, is $434,020. An analysis of the investment account balance shows the following:

| | January 1, 2016 | 2016 Change | December 31, 2016 |
|---|---:|---:|---:|
| Book value of investment | $300,000 | $36,000 | $336,000 |
| Unamortized excess: | | | |
|     Building | 24,000 | (3,000) | 21,000 |
|     Land | 60,000 | | 60,000 |
|     Deferred income taxes | (28,560) | 1,020 | (27,540) |
|     Goodwill | 44,560 | | 44,560 |
| Investment balance | $400,000 | $34,020 | $434,020 |

## Workpaper Entries

When Pat prepares a consolidation workpaper at December 31, 2016, the Investment in Sad account will have a balance of $434,020 ($400,000 original investment + $58,020 income from Sad−$24,000 dividends). The workpaper entries in general journal form follow:

| | | | |
|---|---|---:|---:|
| a | Income from Sad (−R, −SE) | 58,020 | |
| |     Dividends (+SE) | | 24,000 |
| |     Investment in Sad (−A) | | 34,020 |
| | To eliminate income and dividends from Sad and adjust the Investment in Sad account to its beginning-of-the-period balance. | | |

| b | Capital stock—Sad (−SE) | 300,000 | |
|---|---|---|---|
| | Retained earnings—Sad (−SE) | 200,000 | |
| | Building (+A) | 24,000 | |
| | Land (+A) | 60,000 | |
| | Goodwill (+A) | 44,560 | |
| | Investment in Sad (−A) | | 400,000 |
| | Deferred taxes on revaluation (+L) | | 28,560 |
| | Noncontrolling interest—beginning (+SE) | | 200,000 |

To eliminate reciprocal investment and equity balances, establish beginning noncontrolling interest, enter beginning-of-the-period cost/book value differentials, and enter deferred taxes on revaluation.

| c | Depreciation expense (E, −SE) | 3,000 | |
|---|---|---|---|
| | Accumulated depreciation—building (−A) | | 3,000 |

To record depreciation on excess allocated to building.

| d | Deferred taxes on revaluation (−L) | 1,020 | |
|---|---|---|---|
| | Income tax expense (−E, +SE) | | 1,020 |

To record amortization of deferred taxes.

| e | Noncontrolling interest share (−SE) | 40,000 | |
|---|---|---|---|
| | Dividends (+SE) | | 16,000 |
| | Noncontrolling interest (+SE) | | 24,000 |

To enter noncontrolling interest shares of subsidiary income and dividends.

## Income Tax Uncertainties

In June 2006, the FASB revised GAAP to clarify accounting for uncertainty in income taxes recognized in financial statements. GAAP prescribes both a recognition threshold and measurement attribute for tax positions taken in tax returns.

Evaluation of tax positions is a two-step process. The first step is recognition, where the reporting entity determines whether it is more likely than not that a tax position will be sustained on examination. Entities should presume that the tax position will be examined by the appropriate taxing authority. The second step is measurement, where a tax position that meets the recognition threshold is measured to determine the amount to recognize in the financial statements. Per GAAP (ASC 740-30-7):

> A tax position that meets the more-likely-than-not recognition threshold shall initially and subsequently be measured as the largest amount of tax benefit that is greater than 50 percent likely of being realized upon settlement with a taxing authority that has full knowledge of all relevant information. Measurement of a tax position that meets the more-likely-than-not recognition threshold shall consider the amounts and probabilities of the outcomes that could be realized upon settlement using the facts, circumstances, and information available at the reporting date.[9]

Exhibit 10-13 provides an example of the measurement process.

Since the 2006 GAAP revision, more companies are now required to adjust and report a valuation allowance on recognized deferred tax assets. For example, *The Hershey Company* reported a $147.223 million valuation allowance in Note 4 to their 2014 annual report (p. 66). Note 4 also reports the details about Hershey's federal, state, and international income tax positions. *General Electric* discloses in Note 14 to its annual report that it has recorded a valuation allowance for *GE* of $2.015 billion, and an additional allowance of $880 million for *GECC* (p. 185). *Coca Cola* reported a valuation allowance of $649 million in Note 14 to its 2014 annual report (p. 118).

---

[9]FASB ASC 740-30-7. Originally Financial Accounting Standards Board Interpretation No. 48. "Accounting for Uncertainty in Income Taxes: An interpretation of FASB Statement No. 109." Norwalk, CT © 2006 Financial Accounting Standards Board.

This example demonstrates an application of the measurement requirements of paragraph 740-10-30-7 for a tax position that meets the paragraph 740-10-25-6 requirements for recognition. Measurement in this example is based on identified information about settlement.

In applying the recognition criterion of this subtopic for tax positions, an entity has determined that a tax position resulting in a benefit of $100 qualifies for recognition and should be measured. The entity has considered the amounts and probabilities of the possible estimated outcomes as follows.

| Possible Estimated Outcome | Individual Probability of Occurring (%) | Cumulative Probability of Occurring (%) |
|---|---|---|
| $100 | 5 | 5 |
| 80 | 25 | 30 |
| 60 | 25 | 55 |
| 50 | 20 | 75 |
| 40 | 10 | 85 |
| 20 | 10 | 95 |
| 0 | 5 | 100 |

Because $60 is the largest amount of benefit that is greater than 50 percent likely of being realized upon settlement, the entity would recognize a tax benefit of $60 in the financial statements.[10]

Source: FASB Accounting Standards Codification 740-10-55-102–104.

## FINANCIAL STATEMENT DISCLOSURES FOR INCOME TAXES

Historically, GAAP divided deferred tax assets or liabilities into two categories, a current amount and a noncurrent amount, for balance sheet presentation. GAAP classified deferred tax liabilities and assets as current or noncurrent based on the classification of the related asset or liability for financial reporting. If the deferred item was not related to an asset or liability for financial reporting, its classification depended on the reversal date of the temporary difference. For financial reporting periods beginning after December 15, 2016, GAAP no longer classifies deferred tax assets and liabilities as current or noncurrent. All amounts will be reported as noncurrent. The firm will report a single net amount as either a net noncurrent deferred tax asset or liability (ASC 740-10-45-4).

The significant components of income tax expense or benefit are disclosed in the financial statements or notes to the financial statements. GAAP also requires disclosures for income tax expense and benefits allocated to continuing operations, discontinued operations, and prior-period adjustments.

*The Hershey Company's* 2014 annual report provides an example of required disclosures for income taxes. Note 7 offers a detailed description of its income tax calculations for the year.

## SUMMARY

When the capital structure of a subsidiary or equity investee includes outstanding preferred stock, we allocate the investee's equity and income to the preferred stockholders based on the preferred contract and then allocate to common stockholders. If the subsidiary's preferred stock is not held by the parent, we include the preferred income in noncontrolling interest share and the preferred equity in noncontrolling interest. The viewpoint of the consolidated entity considers any of the subsidiary's preferred stock held by the parent as retired for consolidated statement purposes.

Consolidated and parent EPS computations are identical, and the procedures used in computing parent EPS also apply to investor accounting under the equity method. Parent/investor relationships do not affect EPS computations unless the subsidiary/investee has outstanding potentially dilutive securities. When a subsidiary has potentially dilutive securities outstanding, the computational adjustments for EPS differ according to whether the subsidiary's potentially dilutive securities are convertible into subsidiary common stock or parent common stock.

A consolidated entity classified as an affiliated group may elect to file consolidated tax returns. All other consolidated entities file separate tax returns. In determining taxable income, consolidated

[10]Based on ASC 740-10-55-102–104 © Anthony H Joseph

entities that are members of an affiliated group can exclude all dividends received from group members. Affiliated groups that elect to file consolidated tax returns avoid paying taxes on unrealized profits and can offset losses of one group member against income of other group members.

Investors with equity investees and subsidiaries that are not members of an affiliated group pay income taxes currently on a portion of dividends received and provide for deferred income taxes on their share of undistributed income of their investees.

Unrealized and constructive gains and losses from intercompany transactions create temporary differences that may affect deferred tax calculations when filing separate-company tax returns.

An acquisition of another company for accounting purposes may be a taxable combination or a tax-free reorganization under the Internal Revenue Code. In a tax-free business combination, we allocate the fair value/book value differential to the assets and liabilities acquired at fair values and record a deferred tax asset or deferred tax liability for the related tax effect.

## QUESTIONS

1. Son Corporation has 100,000 outstanding shares of $10 par common stock and 5,000 outstanding shares of $100 par, cumulative, 10 percent preferred stock. Son's net income for the year is $300,000, and its stockholders' equity at year-end is as follows:

| | |
|---|---|
| 10% cumulative preferred stock, $100 par | $ 500,000 |
| Common stock, $10 par | 1,000,000 |
| Additional paid-in capital | 600,000 |
| Retained earnings | 400,000 |
| Total Stockholders' Equity | $2,500,000 |

Pop Corporation owns 60 percent of the outstanding common stock of Son, acquired at a fair value equal to book value several years ago. Compute Pop's investment income for the year and the balance of its Investment in Son account at the end of the year.

2. Refer to the information in question 1. Assume that Son pays two years' preferred dividend requirements during the current year. Would this affect your computation of Pop's investment income for the current year? If so, recompute Pop's investment income.

3. How should preferred stock of a subsidiary be shown in a consolidated balance sheet in each case?
   *a.* If it is held 100 percent by the parent
   *b.* If it is held 50 percent by the parent and 50 percent by outside interests
   *c.* If it is held 100 percent by outside interests

4. Describe the computation of noncontrolling interest share for an 80 percent–owned subsidiary with both preferred and common stock outstanding.

5. How does controlling share of consolidated earnings per share differ from parent earnings per share?

6. Do investments in nonconsolidated subsidiaries and 20 to 50 percent–owned investees affect the nature of the investor's EPS calculations?

7. Under what conditions will the procedures used in computing a parent's EPS be the same as those for a company without equity investments?

8. It may be necessary to compute the earnings per share for subsidiaries and equity investees before parent (and consolidated) earnings per share can be determined. When are the subsidiary EPS computations used in calculating parent earnings per share?

9. Potentially dilutive securities of a subsidiary may be converted into parent common stock or subsidiary common stock. Describe how these situations affect the parent's EPS procedures.

10. In computing diluted earnings for a parent, it may be necessary to replace the parent's equity in subsidiary's realized income with the parent's equity in the subsidiary's diluted earnings. Does this replacement calculation involve unrealized profits that are included in the parent's income from subsidiary?

11. Are consolidated income tax returns required for all consolidated entities? Discuss.

12. Can a consolidated entity that is classified as an "affiliated group" under the IRS code elect to file separate tax returns for each affiliate?

13. What are the primary advantages of filing a consolidated tax return?

14. Some or all of the dividends received by a corporation from domestic affiliates may be excluded from federal income taxation. When are all of the dividends excluded?

15. Describe the nature of the tax effect of temporary differences that arise from use of the equity method of accounting.

16. Does a parent/investor provide for income taxes on the undistributed earnings of a subsidiary by adjusting investment and investment income accounts? Explain.

17. When do unrealized and constructive gains and losses create temporary differences for a consolidated entity?

## EXERCISES

### E 10-1
### [Based on AICPA] Preferred stock and income tax

1. [Preferred stock] During 2017, Pop Corporation owns 20 percent of Son Corporation's preferred stock and 80 percent of its common stock. Son's stock outstanding on December 31, 2017, is as follows:

| | |
|---|---|
| 10% cumulative preferred stock | $   400,000 |
| Common stock | 2,800,000 |

Son reported net income of $240,000 for the year ended December 31, 2017. What amount should Pop record as equity in earnings of Son for the year ended December 31, 2017?

a  **$168,000**
b  **$192,000**
c  **$193,600**
d  **$200,000**

2. [Tax] Pop Corporation uses the equity method to account for its 25% investment in Son Corporation. During 2016, Pop received dividends of $60,000 from Son and recorded $360,000 as its equity in the earnings of Son. Additional information follows:

■ The dividends received from Son are eligible for the 80 percent dividends-received deduction.
■ There are no other temporary differences.
■ Enacted income tax rates are 30 percent for 2016 and thereafter.

In its December 31, 2016, balance sheet, what amount should Pop report for deferred income tax liability?

a  **$18,000**
b  **$21,600**
c  **$90,000**
d  **$108,000**

3. [Tax] In 2016, Pop Corporation received $600,000 in dividends from Son Corporation, its 80 percent–owned subsidiary. What net amount of dividend income should Pop include in its 2016 consolidated tax return?

a  **$600,000**
b  **$480,000**
c  **$420,000**
d  **$0**

4. [Tax] Pop Corporation and Son Corporation filed consolidated tax returns. In January 2016, Pop sold land, with a basis of $120,000 and a fair value of $150,000, to Son for $200,000. Son sold the land in December 2017 for $250,000. In its 2017 and 2016 tax returns, what amount of gain should be reported for these transactions in the consolidated return?

| | 2017 | 2016 |
|---|---|---|
| a | $50,000 | $80,000 |
| b | $100,000 | 0 |
| c | $100,000 | $50,000 |
| d | $130,000 | 0 |

### E 10-2
### [Preferred stock] Subsidiary preferred stock with dividends in arrears

The stockholders' equity of Sun Corporation at December 31, 2016, was as follows (in thousands):

| | |
|---|---|
| 10% cumulative preferred stock, $100 par, callable at $105, 20,000 shares issued and outstanding, with one year's dividends in arrears | $2,000 |
| Common stock, $10 par, 200,000 shares issued and outstanding | 2,000 |
| Additional paid-in capital | 4,000 |
| Retained earnings | 8,000 |
| Total stockholders' equity | $16,000 |

On January 1, 2017, Pam Corporation purchased 90 percent of Sun Corporation's common stock at $90 per share. Sun's assets and liabilities were recorded at their fair values when Pam acquired its 90 percent interest. Any fair value/book value differential is assigned to goodwill and is not amortized. During 2017, Sun Corporation reported net income of $2,400,000 and paid dividends of $1,200,000.

**REQUIRED:** Calculate the following:

1. The fair value/book value differential from Pam's investment in Sun.
2. Pam's income from Sun for 2017.
3. The balance of Pam's investment in Sun at December 31, 2017.
4. Total noncontrolling interest in Sun Corporation on December 31, 2017.

## E 10-3
### [Preferred stock] Goodwill and investment income—subsidiary preferred stock

The stockholders' equity of Son Corporation at December 31, 2015, was as follows (in thousands):

| | |
|---|---:|
| 12% preferred stock, cumulative, nonparticipating, $100 par, callable at $105 | $1,200 |
| Common stock, $10 par | 2,000 |
| Other paid-in capital | 280 |
| Retained earnings | 1,520 |
| Total stockholders' equity | $5,000 |

Pop Corporation purchased 80 percent of Son's common stock on January 2, 2016, for $3,072,000. During 2016, Son reported a $200,000 net loss and paid no dividends. During 2017, Son Corporation reported $1,000,000 net income and declared dividends of $688,000. Any excess fair value is due to goodwill.

**REQUIRED:**

1. Compute the fair value/book value differential from Pop's investment in Son.
2. Determine Pop's income (loss) from Son for 2016.
3. Determine Pop's income (loss) from Son for 2017.
4. Compute the balance of Pop's Investment in Son account on December 31, 2017.

## E 10-4
### [Preferred stock] Investment cost and net income—subsidiary preferred stock

Pam Corporation owns 80 percent of Sun Corporation's common stock, having acquired the interest at a fair value equal to book value on December 31, 2016. During 2017, Pam's separate income is $6,000,000 and Sun Corporation's net income is $1,000,000. Pam and Sun declare dividends in 2017 of $2,000,000 and $600,000, respectively.

The stockholders' equity of Sun consists of the following (in thousands):

| | December 31, 2016 | December 31, 2017 |
|---|---:|---:|
| 12% cumulative preferred stock, $100 par, callable at $105 per share | $2,000 | $2,000 |
| Common stock, $10 par | 4,000 | 4,000 |
| Other paid-in capital | 600 | 600 |
| Retained earnings | 1,400 | 1,800 |
| Total stockholders' equity | $8,000 | $8,400 |

**REQUIRED:**

1. Determine the cost of Pam's investment in Sun on December 31, 2016, if Sun has one year's preferred dividends in arrears on that date.
2. Calculate Pam's net income and noncontrolling interest share for 2017.
3. Calculate the underlying book value of Pam's investment in Sun on December 31, 2017.

## E 10-5
### [Preferred stock] Journal entries—parent owns both common and preferred stock of subsidiary

The stockholders' equity of Son Corporation on December 31, 2016, was as follows (in thousands):

| | |
|---|---:|
| 15% preferred stock, $100 par, cumulative, nonparticipating, with one year's dividends in arrears | $1,000 |
| Common stock, $10 par | 2,000 |
| Other paid-in capital | 200 |
| Retained earnings | 300 |
| Total stockholders' equity | $3,500 |

Pop Corporation acquired 50 percent of Son's preferred stock for $600,000 and 80 percent of its common stock for $2,000,000 on January 1, 2017. Son reported net income of $400,000 and paid dividends of $300,000 in 2017.

### REQUIRED:

1. Prepare the journal entries to record Pop's 50 percent investment in Son's preferred stock.
2. Calculate the excess fair value/book value differential from Pop's 80 percent investment in Son common. Assume the differential is goodwill.
3. Compute Pop's income from Son—preferred for 2017.
4. Compute Pop's income from Son—common for 2017.
5. Calculate the noncontrolling interest in Son that will appear in the consolidated balance sheet of Pop Corporation and Subsidiary on December 31, 2017.

## E 10-6
### [Preferred stock] Fair value/book value differentials for preferred and common stock

Pam Corporation purchased 60 percent of Sun Corporation's outstanding preferred stock for $6,500,000 and 70 percent of its outstanding common stock for $35,000,000 on January 1, 2017. Sun's stockholders' equity on December 31, 2016, consisted of the following (in thousands):

| | |
|---|---:|
| 10% cumulative, $100 par, preferred stock, callable at $105 (100,000 shares issued and outstanding with one year's dividends in arrears) | $10,000 |
| Common stock, $10 par | 30,000 |
| Other paid-in capital | 5,000 |
| Retained earnings | 15,000 |
| Total stockholders' equity | $60,000 |

### REQUIRED:

1. Determine the fair value/book value differentials from Pam's investments in Sun.
2. Without bias on your part, assume that the fair value/book value differential applicable to the preferred investment is a negative $400,000. Describe the accounting treatment of the preferred differential if the preferred investment is treated as a constructive retirement for consolidation purposes.

## E 10-7
### [EPS] General questions

1. A parent company and its 100 percent–owned subsidiary have only common stock outstanding (10,000 shares for the parent and 3,000 shares for the subsidiary), and neither company has issued other potentially dilutive securities. The equation to compute consolidated EPS for the parent company and its subsidiary is:
   a  (Net income of parent + Net income of subsidiary) ÷ 13,000 shares
   b  (Net income of parent + Net income of subsidiary) ÷ 10,000 shares
   c  Net income of parent ÷ 13,000 shares
   d  Net income of parent ÷ 10,000 shares

2. A parent company has a 90 percent interest in a subsidiary that has no potentially dilutive securities outstanding. In computing consolidated EPS:

    a  *Subsidiary common shares are added to parent common shares and common share equivalents*

    b  *Subsidiary EPS and parent EPS amounts are combined*

    c  *Subsidiary EPS computations are not needed*

    d  *Subsidiary EPS computations are used in computing basic earnings*

3. In computing a parent company's diluted EPS, it may be necessary to subtract the parent's equity in subsidiary realized income and replace it with the parent's equity in subsidiary diluted earnings. The subtraction in this replacement computation is affected by:

    a  *Constructive gain from purchase of parent bonds*

    b  *Current amortization from investment in the subsidiary*

    c  *Unrealized profits from downstream sales*

    d  *Unrealized profits from upstream sales*

## E 10-8
## [EPS] Consolidated EPS with goodwill, noncontrolling interest, and warrants

Pop Corporation's net income for 2016 is $316,000, including $160,000 income from Son Corporation, its 80 percent–owned subsidiary. The income from Son consists of $176,000 equity in income less $16,000 patent amortization. Pop has 300,000 shares of $10 par common stock outstanding, and Son has 50,000 shares of $10 par common stock outstanding throughout 2016. In addition, Son has 10,000 outstanding warrants to acquire 10,000 shares of Son common stock at $10 per share. The average market price of Son's common stock was $20 per share during 2016.

1. For purposes of calculating Pop Corporation's (and consolidated) diluted earnings per share, Son's diluted earnings are:

    a  *$220,000*

    b  *$200,000*

    c  *$176,000*

    d  *$160,000*

2. For purposes of calculating Pop Corporation's (and consolidated) diluted earnings per share, Son's outstanding common shares and common share equivalents are:

    a  *60,000 shares*

    b  *56,000 shares*

    c  *55,000 shares*

    d  *50,000 shares*

3. For purposes of calculating Pop Corporation's (and consolidated) earnings per share, assume that Son's diluted EPS is $4 per share. Pop Corporation's (and consolidated) diluted earnings will be:

    a  *$316,000*

    b  *$300,000*

    c  *$156,000*

    d  *$140,000*

4. If Son's diluted earnings for 2016 are $4 per share, Pop Corporation's (and consolidated) diluted earnings per share will be:

    a  *$1.64*

    b  *$1.59*

    c  *$1.04*

    d  *$1.00*

## E 10-9
## [EPS] Consolidated basic and diluted EPS

The following information is available regarding Pam Corporation and its 80 percent–owned subsidiary, Sun Corporation, at and for the year ended December 31, 2016:

|  | Pam | Sun |
| --- | --- | --- |
| Outstanding common stock | 8,000 shares | 5,000 shares |
| Warrants to purchase 1,000 shares of Sun common stock at $9 per share (average market price is $15) |  | 1,000 warrants |
| Net income (includes income from Sun) | $20,000 | $18,000 |
| Income from Sun ($14,400 − $2,400 amortization of excess cost over book value acquired) | $12,000 |  |

**REQUIRED:** Determine consolidated earnings per share (both basic and diluted).

### E 10-10
### [EPS] Consolidated EPS with unrealized profit from upstream sale

The income statements of Pop Corporation and its 80 percent–owned subsidiary, Son Corporation, for 2016 are as follows:

|  | Pop | Son |
|---|---|---|
| Sales | $1,270,000 | $ 740,000 |
| Income from Son (see note) | 13,920 | — |
| Cost of sales | (700,000) | (470,000) |
| Expenses | (462,000) | (230,000) |
| Income before taxes | 121,920 | 40,000 |
| Provision for income taxes | (41,453) | (13,600) |
| Net income | $ 80,467 | $ 26,400 |

*Note:* Income from Son is computed as [($26,400 reported income × 80%) − $2,000 patent amortization −$5,200 unrealized profit in Son's inventory].

Pop had 10,000 shares of common stock and 1,200 shares of $100 par, 10 percent cumulative preferred stock outstanding throughout 2016. Son had 20,000 shares of common stock and warrants to purchase 5,000 shares of Son common stock at $24 outstanding throughout 2016. The average market price of Son common stock was $30 per share.

**REQUIRED:** Compute Pop's (and consolidated) basic and diluted EPS.

### E 10-11
### [EPS] Subsidiary EPS and consolidated EPS with goodwill and warrants

Pow Corporation owns an 80 percent interest in Soy Corporation. Pow does not have common stock equivalents or other potentially dilutive securities outstanding, so it calculated its EPS for 2016 as follows:

$$\frac{\$1,000,000 \text{ separate income} + \$480,000 \text{ Income from Soy}}{1,000,000 \text{ outstanding common shares of Pow}} = \$1.48$$

An examination of Pow's income from Soy shows that it is determined correctly as 80 percent of Soy's $630,000 net income less $24,000 patent amortization. Pow's EPS computation is in error, however, because it fails to consider outstanding warrants of Soy that permit their holders to acquire 10,000 shares of Soy common stock at $24 per share and increase Soy's outstanding common stock to 60,000 shares. The average price of Soy common stock during 2016 was $40.

**REQUIRED:**
1. Compute Soy Corporation's diluted EPS for use in determining consolidated EPS.
2. Compute consolidated EPS for 2016 (both basic and diluted).

### E 10-12
### [Tax] General questions

1. Income taxes are currently due on intercompany profits when:
   a *Profits originate from upstream sales*
   b *Separate-company tax returns are filed*
   c *Consolidated tax returns are filed*
   d *Affiliates are accounted for as consolidated subsidiaries*

2. The right of a consolidated entity to file a consolidated tax return is contingent upon:
   a *Ownership by a common parent of all the voting stock of group members*
   b *Ownership by a common parent of 90% of the voting stock of group members*
   c *Classification as an affiliated group*
   d *Direct or indirect ownership of a majority of the outstanding stock of all group members*

3. When affiliates are classified as an affiliated group for tax purposes, the group:
   a *Excludes unrealized profits from intercompany transactions from taxable income*
   b *Must file a consolidated income tax return*
   c *May file separate income tax returns*
   d *Pays lower income taxes*

**4.** Deferred income taxes are provided for unrealized profits from intercompany transactions when:

 a  *A consolidated tax return is filed*

 b  *Separate-company tax returns are filed*

 c  *The unrealized profits are from upstream sales*

 d  *The consolidated entity is an affiliated group*

# E 10-13
## [Tax] Asset allocation in business combination, tax effect from equity investees

**1.** When Pop Corporation acquired its 100 percent interest in Son Corporation in a tax-free reorganization, Son's equipment had a fair value of $12,000,000 and a book value and tax basis of $8,000,000. If Pop's effective tax rate is 34 percent, how much of the purchase price should be allocated to equipment and to deferred income taxes?

 a  *$8,000,000 and $0, respectively*

 b  *$10,640,000 and $1,360,000, respectively*

 c  *$12,000,000 and $1,360,000, respectively*

 d  *$12,000,000 and $4,080,000, respectively*

**2.** Pop Corporation, whose effective income tax rate is 34 percent, received $400,000 dividends from its 30 percent–owned domestic equity investee during the current year and recorded $1,000,000 equity in the investee's income. Pop's income tax expense for the year should include taxes on the investment of:

 a  *$27,200*

 b  *$40,800*

 c  *$68,000*

 d  *$136,000*

**3.** During 2016, Pop Corporation reported $120,000 investment income from Son Corporation, its 30 percent–owned investee, and it received $60,000 dividends from Son. Pop's effective income tax rate is 34 percent, and it is entitled to an 80 percent dividends-received deduction on dividends received from Son. On the basis of this information, Pop should:

 a  *Report investment income from Son of $115,920*

 b  *Increase its investment in Son for 2016 in the amount of $55,920*

 c  *Credit its deferred tax liability in the net amount of $4,080 for 2016*

 d  *Debit its deferred tax liability in the net amount of $4,080 for 2016*

**4.** Pop Corporation owns 35 percent of the voting stock of Son Corporation, a domestic corporation. During 2016, Son reports net income of $200,000 and pays dividends of $100,000. Pop's effective income tax rate is 34 percent. What amounts should Pop record as income taxes currently payable and as deferred income taxes from its investment in Son?

 a  *$34,000 and $0, respectively*

 b  *$11,900 and $11,900, respectively*

 c  *$6,800 and $6,800, respectively*

 d  *$2,380 and $2,380, respectively*

**5.** Pop Corporation and its 100 percent–owned domestic subsidiary, Son Corporation, are classified as an affiliated group for tax purposes. During the current year, Son pays $160,000 in cash dividends. Assuming a 34 percent income tax rate, how much income tax expense on this dividend should be reported in the consolidated income statement of Pop Corporation and Subsidiary?

 a  *$0*

 b  *$54,400*

 c  *$10,880*

 d  *$5,440*

# E 10-14
## [Tax] Compare separate and consolidated tax filings

The pretax accounting incomes of Pam Corporation and its 100 percent–owned subsidiary, Sun Company, for 2016 are as follows (in thousands):

|                          | Pam      | Sun      |
|--------------------------|----------|----------|
| Sales                    | $4,000   | $2,000   |
| Gain on land             | 800      | —        |
| Total revenue            | 4,800    | 2,000    |
| Cost of sales            | 2,000    | 1,200    |
| Gross profit             | 2,800    | 800      |
| Operating expenses       | 1,600    | 400      |
| Pretax accounting income | $ 1,200  | $ 400    |

The only intercompany transaction during 2016 was a gain on land sold to Sun. Assume a 34 percent flat income tax rate. The land remains unsold at year-end.

**REQUIRED:**

1. What amount should be shown on the consolidated income statement as income tax expense if separate-company tax returns are filed?
2. Compute the consolidated income tax expense if a consolidated tax return is filed.
3. What will be the income taxes currently payable if separate income tax returns are filed? If a consolidated return is filed?

## E 10-15
### [Tax] Consolidated income statement (downstream gain on sale of equipment)

Pop Corporation and its 70 percent–owned subsidiary, Son Corporation, have pretax operating incomes for 2016 as follows (in thousands):

|  | **Pop** | **Son** |
|---|---|---|
| Sales | $8,000 | $4,000 |
| Gain on equipment | 200 | — |
| Cost of sales | (5,000) | (2,000) |
| Other expenses | (1,800) | (1,200) |
| Pretax income | $1,400 | $ 800 |

Pop received $280,000 dividends from Son during 2016. A previously unrecorded patent from Pop's investment in Son is being amortized at a rate of $50,000 per year (the same time horizon is used for both book and tax purposes).

On January 1, 2016, Pop sold equipment to Son at a $200,000 gain. Son is depreciating the equipment at a rate of 20 percent per year. A flat 34 percent tax rate is applicable to both companies.

**REQUIRED:** Prepare a consolidated income statement for Pop Corporation and Subsidiary for 2016. (Assume no deferred tax balance on January 1, 2016.)

## E 10-16
### [Tax] Journal entries for unrealized profit with separate and consolidated tax returns

Sun Corporation is a 100 percent–owned subsidiary of Pam Corporation. During the current year, Pam sold merchandise that cost $200,000 to Sun for $400,000. A 34 percent income tax rate is applicable, and 80 percent of the merchandise remains unsold by Sun at year-end.

**REQUIRED:**

1. Prepare comparative one-line consolidation entries relating to the unrealized profit when separate and consolidated income tax returns are filed.
2. Prepare comparative consolidation workpaper entries in general journal form relating to the intercompany sales transaction and the related income tax effect when separate and consolidated income tax returns are filed.

## E 10-17
### [Tax] Journal entries for unrealized profit from upstream sale and separate tax returns

Son Corporation, an 80 percent–owned subsidiary of Pop Corporation, sold equipment with a book value of $600,000 to Pop for $1,000,000 at December 31, 2016. Separate income tax returns are filed, and a 34 percent income tax rate is applicable to both Pop and Son.

**REQUIRED:**

1. Prepare a one-line consolidation entry for Pop to eliminate the effect of the intercompany transaction.
2. Prepare workpaper entries in general journal form to eliminate the unrealized profit.
3. Assume that the reported net income of Son is $3,200,000 and that the sale of equipment is the only intercompany transaction between Pop and Son. What is the noncontrolling interest's share of total consolidated income?

## E 10-18
### [Tax] Valuation Allowance

Pam Corporation recognizes a deferred tax asset (benefit) of $1,000,000 related to its acquisition of Sun Company. Pam has determined that the tax position qualifies for recognition and should be measured. Pam has determined the amounts and the probabilities of the possible outcomes, as follows:

| Possible Estimated Outcome | Probability of Occurring (%) |
|---|---|
| $1,000,000 | 10 |
| 800,000 | 25 |
| 600,000 | 25 |
| 400,000 | 20 |
| 200,000 | 10 |
| 0 | 10 |

**REQUIRED:** Calculate the tax benefit to be recognized by Pam.

## E 10-19
### [Tax] Valuation Allowance

Pop Corporation recognizes a deferred tax asset (benefit) of $150,000 related to its acquisition of Son Company. Pop has determined that the tax position qualifies for recognition and should be measured. Pop has determined the amounts and the probabilities of the possible outcomes, as follows:

| Possible Estimated Outcome | Probability of Occurring (%) |
|---|---|
| $150,000 | 50 |
| 125,000 | 20 |
| 100,000 | 10 |
| 50,000 | 10 |
| 0 | 10 |

**REQUIRED:** Calculate the tax benefit to be recognized by Pop.

## PROBLEMS

## P 10-1
### [Preferred stock] Investment in common stock (subsidiary preferred stock)

Pam Corporation paid $7,200,000 for 360,000 shares of Sun Corporation's outstanding voting common stock on January 1, 2016, when the stockholders' equity of Sun consisted of (in thousands):

| | |
|---|---|
| 10% cumulative, preferred stock, $100 par. Liquidation preference is $105 per share, and 20,000 shares are issued and outstanding with one year's dividends in arrears | $2,000 |
| Common stock, $10 par, 400,000 shares issued and outstanding | 4,000 |
| Other paid-in capital | 1,000 |
| Retained earnings | 1,300 |
| Total stockholders' equity | $8,300 |

During 2016, Sun reported net income of $1,000,000 and declared dividends of $800,000. Any excess of fair value over book value is goodwill, which is not amortized.

**REQUIRED:** Calculate the following:

1. Goodwill from Pam's acquisition of Sun
2. Pam's income from Sun for 2016
3. Noncontrolling interest share for 2016
4. Noncontrolling interest in Sun at December 31, 2016
5. Pam's Investment in Sun account balance at December 31, 2016

## P 10-2
### [Preferred stock] Consolidation entries—investments in preferred and common stock—midyear purchases

Pop Corporation acquired 80 percent of Son Corporation's preferred stock for $175,000 and 90 percent of Son's common stock for $630,000 on July 1, 2016. Son's stockholders' equity on December 31, 2016, was as follows (in thousands):

| *Stockholders' Equity* | |
|---|---|
| 9% preferred stock, cumulative, nonparticipating, $100 par, call price $105 | $200 |
| Common stock, $10 par | 500 |
| Paid-in capital in excess of par | 40 |
| Retained earnings | 160 |
| Total stockholders' equity | $900 |

Son had net income of $24,000 in 2015 and $46,000 in 2016, but declared no dividends in either year. Assume that preferred dividends accrue ratably throughout each year and that Son Corporation's net assets were fairly valued on July 1, 2016.

**REQUIRED:**

1. Determine the account balances of Pop Corporation's investments in Son's preferred and common stocks at December 31, 2016, on the basis of a one-line consolidation.
2. Prepare workpaper entries to consolidate the balance sheets of Pop and Son at December 31, 2016.

## P 10-3
### [Preferred stock] Consolidation workpaper (subsidiary preferred stock, equity method, midyear purchase)

Financial statements for Pam and Sun Corporations for 2016 are summarized as follows (in thousands):

| | Pam | Sun |
|---|---|---|
| ***Combined Income and Retained Earnings Statements for the Year Ended December 31*** | | |
| Sales | $1,233 | $700 |
| Income from Sun | 68 | — |
| Cost of sales | (610) | (400) |
| Other expenses | (390) | (210) |
| Net income | 301 | 90 |
| Add: Retained earnings January 1 | 501 | 200 |
| Less: Dividends | (200) | (50) |
| Retained earnings December 31 | $ 602 | $240 |

|                              | Pam      | Sun    |
|------------------------------|----------|--------|
| **Balance Sheet at December 31** |      |        |
| Cash                         | $  191   | $ 50   |
| Other current assets         | 200      | 300    |
| Plant assets—net             | 900      | 600    |
| Investment in Sun            | 711      | —      |
| Total assets                 | $2,002   | $950   |
|                              |          |        |
| Current liabilities          | $  200   | $ 60   |
| $10 preferred stock          | —        | 100    |
| Common stock                 | 1,200    | 500    |
| Other paid-in capital        | —        | 50     |
| Retained earnings            | 602      | 240    |
| Total equities               | $2,002   | $950   |

Pam owns 90,000 shares of Sun's outstanding voting common stock at December 31, 2016. These shares were acquired in two lots as follows:

|        | Date            | Shares  | Purchase Price |
|--------|-----------------|---------|----------------|
| Lot 1  | January 1, 2015 | 70,000  | $490,000       |
| Lot 2  | April 1, 2016   | 20,000  | 152,000        |

The stockholders' equity of Sun at year-end 2014, 2015, and 2016 was as follows (in thousands):

|                                                                | December 31 |       |       |
|----------------------------------------------------------------|-------------|-------|-------|
|                                                                | 2014        | 2015  | 2016  |
| $10 preferred stock, $100 par, cumulative with no dividends in arrears | $100 | $100  | $100  |
| Common stock, $5 par                                           | 500         | 500   | 500   |
| Other paid-in capital                                          | 50          | 50    | 50    |
| Retained earnings                                              | 150         | 200   | 240   |
| Total stockholders' equity                                     | $800        | $850  | $890  |

Sun's net income for 2016 is $90,000, earned proportionately throughout the year, and its quarterly dividends of $12,500 are declared on March 15, June 15, September 15, and December 15. (Quarterly dividends of $12,500 include dividends on common stock and preferred stock.) There are no intercompany receivables or payables at December 31, 2016, and there have been no intercompany transactions other than dividends.

---

**REQUIRED:** Prepare a consolidation workpaper for Pam and Subsidiary for 2016.

---

## P 10-4
### [Preferred stock] Consolidation workpaper (subsidiary preferred stock, downstream inventory sales, upstream sale of land, subsidiary bonds)

Pop Corporation acquired an 80 percent interest in Son Corporation common stock for $240,000 on January 1, 2015, when Son's stockholders' equity consisted of $200,000 common stock, $100,000 preferred stock, and $25,000 retained earnings. The excess was due to goodwill.

Intercompany sales of inventory items from Pop to Son were $50,000 in 2015 and $60,000 in 2016. The cost of these items to Pop was 60 percent of the selling price to Son, and Son inventoried $30,000 of the intercompany sales items at December 31, 2015, and $40,000 at December 31, 2016. Intercompany receivables and payables from these sales were $10,000 at December 31, 2015, and $5,000 at December 31, 2016.

Son sold land that cost $10,000 to Pop for $20,000 during 2015. During 2016, Pop resold the land outside the consolidated entity for $30,000.

On July 1, 2016, Pop purchased all of Son's bonds payable in the open market for $91,000. These bonds were issued at par, have interest payment dates of June 30 and December 31, and mature on June 30, 2019.

Son declared and paid dividends of $10,000 on its cumulative preferred stock and $10,000 on its common stock in each of the years 2015 and 2016.

Financial statements for Pop and Son Corporations at and for the year ended December 31, 2016, are summarized as follows (in thousands):

| | Pop | Son |
|---|---|---|
| **Combined Income and Retained Earnings Statement for the Year Ended December 31** | | |
| Sales | $ 900 | $ 300 |
| Gain on land | 10 | — |
| Interest income | 6.5 | — |
| Income from Son | 50 | — |
| Cost of sales | (600) | (140) |
| Operating expenses | (208.5) | (90) |
| Interest expense | — | (10) |
| Net income | 158 | 60 |
| Add: Beginning retained earnings | 132 | 50 |
| Deduct: Dividends | (100) | (20) |
| Retained earnings December 31 | $ 190 | $ 90 |
| **Balance Sheet at December 31** | | |
| Cash | $ 5.5 | $ 15 |
| Accounts receivable | 26 | 20 |
| Inventories | 80 | 60 |
| Other current assets | 100 | 5 |
| Land | 160 | 30 |
| Plant and equipment—net | 268 | 420 |
| Investment in Son—bonds | 92.5 | — |
| Investment in Son—stock | 282 | — |
| Total assets | $1,014 | $ 550 |
| Accounts payable | $ 24 | $ 15 |
| 10% bonds payable | — | 100 |
| Other liabilities | 100 | 45 |
| 10% preferred stock | — | 100 |
| Common stock | 700 | 200 |
| Retained earnings | 190 | 90 |
| Total equities | $1,014 | $ 550 |

**REQUIRED:** Prepare a consolidation workpaper for Pop Corporation and Subsidiary for the year ended December 31, 2016.

## P 10-5
## [EPS] Computing EPS with convertible debentures

Pam Corporation has $108,000 income from its own operations for 2016, and $42,000 income from Sun Corporation, its 70 percent–owned subsidiary. Sun's net income of $60,000 consists of $66,000 operating income less $6,000 net-of-tax interest on its outstanding 10 percent convertible debentures. Throughout 2016, Pam has 100,000 shares of common stock outstanding, and Sun has 50,000 outstanding common shares.

**REQUIRED:**

1. Compute Pam's diluted earnings per share for 2016, assuming that Sun's bonds are convertible into 10,000 shares of Sun's common stock.
2. Compute Pam's diluted earnings per share for 2016, assuming that Sun's bonds are convertible into 10,000 shares of Pam's common stock.

## P 10-6
### [EPS] Compute basic and diluted EPS (options; preferred stock)

Pop Corporation owns an 80 percent interest in Son Corporation. Throughout 2016, Pop had 20,000 shares of common stock outstanding. Son had the following securities outstanding:

- 10,000 shares of common stock

- Options to purchase 2,000 shares of Son Corporation common at $15 per share

- 1,000 shares of 10%, $100 par, convertible, preferred stock that are convertible into 3,000 shares of Son common stock

    Income data for the affiliates for 2016 are as follows:

|  | Pop | Son |
|---|---|---|
| Separate incomes | $120,000 | $ 55,000 |
| Income from Son ($45,000 income to common × 80%) − $6,000 patent amortization | 30,000 | — |
|  | $150,000 | $ 55,000 |

**REQUIRED:** Compute basic and diluted earnings per share for Pop Corporation and Subsidiary for 2016, assuming an average market price for Son Corporation common stock of $30 per share.

## P 10-7
### [EPS] Convertible preferred stock and amortization of excess

Pam Corporation owns 80 percent of Sun Corporation's outstanding common stock. The 80 percent interest was acquired in 2016 at $40,000 in excess of book value due to undervalued equipment with an eight-year remaining useful life. Outstanding securities of the two companies throughout 2017 and at December 31, 2017, are:

|  | Pam | Sun |
|---|---|---|
| Common stock, $5 par | 20,000 shares | — |
| Common stock, $10 par | — | 6,000 shares |
| 14% cumulative, convertible, preferred stock, $100 par | — | 1,000 shares |

Sun Corporation's net income is $50,000 for 2017, and Pam's net income consists of $70,000 separate income and $23,800 income from Sun.

### REQUIRED:
1. Compute consolidated basic and diluted earnings per share, assuming that the preferred stock is convertible into 4,000 shares of Sun Corporation's common stock.
2. Compute consolidated basic and diluted earnings per share, assuming that the preferred stock is convertible into 5,000 shares of Pam's common stock.

## P 10-8
### [EPS] Compute consolidated EPS; subsidiary diluted

Pop Company owns 40,000 of 50,000 outstanding shares of Son Company, and during 2016, it recognizes income from Son as follows:

| | |
|---|---|
| Share of Son net income ($500,000 × 80%) | $ 400,000 |
| Patent amortization | (50,000) |
| Unrealized profit—downstream sales | (40,000) |
| Unrealized profit—upstream sales ($60,000 × 80%) | (48,000) |
| Income from Son | $262,000 |

Pop's net income for 2016 is $1,262,000, consisting of separate income from Pop of $1,000,000 and $262,000 income from Son. Pop has 100,000 shares of common stock outstanding, but no common stock equivalents or other potentially dilutive securities.

Son has $100,000 par of 10 percent convertible bonds outstanding that are convertible into 10,000 shares of Son common stock. The net-of-tax interest on the bonds is $6,400, and Son's diluted earnings per share for purposes of computing consolidated earnings per share are determined as follows:

| | |
|---|---:|
| Net income | $500,000 |
| Add: Net-of-tax interest on convertible bonds | 6,400 |
| Less: Unrealized profit on upstream sales | (60,000) |
| a  Diluted earnings | $446,400 |
| Common shares outstanding | 50,000 |
| Shares issuable on conversion of bonds | 10,000 |
| b  Common shares and equivalents | 60,000 |
| Diluted earnings per share (a ÷ b) | $7.44 |

**REQUIRED:** Compute Pop Company's and consolidated diluted earnings per share for 2016.

## P 10-9
### [EPS] Computations (subsidiary preferred stock and warrants)

Pam Corporation's net income for 2016 consists of the following:

| | | |
|---|---:|---:|
| Separate income | | $320,000 |
| Income from Sun Corporation: | | |
| 80% of Sun's income to common | $160,000 | |
| Less: Patent amortization | (4,000) | |
| Less: Unrealized profits on equipment sold to Sun | (10,000) | |
| Less: 80% of unrealized profit on land purchased from Sun | (16,000) | 130,000 |
| Net income | | $450,000 |

### ADDITIONAL INFORMATION

1. Pam has 100,000 shares of common stock, and Sun has 50,000 shares of common and 10,000 shares of $10 cumulative, convertible, preferred stock outstanding throughout 2016. The preferred stock is convertible into 30,000 shares of Sun stock.

2. Sun has warrants outstanding that permit their holders to purchase 10,000 shares of Sun Corporation common stock at $15 per share (average market price $20).

3. Sun's reported net income for 2016 is $300,000, allocated $100,000 to preferred stockholders and $200,000 to common stockholders.

4. Pam owned 40,000 shares of Sun common stock throughout 2016.

**REQUIRED:** Compute Pam Corporation's (and consolidated) basic and diluted EPS.

## P 10-10
### [Tax] Comparative income statements (consolidated and separate tax returns)

Pop Corporation and its 100 percent–owned subsidiary, Son Corporation, are members of an affiliated group with pretax accounting incomes as follows (in thousands):

|                          | Pop       | Son       |
|--------------------------|-----------|-----------|
| Sales                    | $9,600    | $5,600    |
| Gain on sale of land     | 400       | —         |
| Cost of sales            | (4,800)   | (2,400)   |
| Operating expenses       | (2,800)   | (2,000)   |
| Pretax accounting income | $2,400    | $1,200    |

The gain reported by Pop relates to land sold to Son during the current year. A flat 34 percent income tax rate is applicable. The land remains unsold at year-end.

**REQUIRED:** Prepare income statements for Pop Corporation assuming (a) that separate income tax returns are filed and (b) that a consolidated income tax return is filed. (*Note:* Pop applies the equity method as a one-line consolidation.)

## P 10-11
### [Tax] Computations and income statement (upstream sales)

Pam Corporation paid $1,155,000 cash for a 70 percent interest in Sun Corporation's outstanding common stock on January 2, 2016, when the equity of Sun consisted of $1,000,000 common stock and $600,000 retained earnings. The excess fair value is due to goodwill.

In December 2016, Sun sold inventory items to Pam at a gross profit of $100,000 (selling price $240,000 and cost $140,000), and all these items were included in Pam's inventory at December 31, 2016.

Sun paid dividends of $100,000 in 2016, and an 80 percent dividends-received deduction applies. A flat 34 percent income tax rate applies to both companies.

Separate pretax incomes of Pam and Sun for 2016 are as follows (in thousands):

|                    | Pam       | Sun       |
|--------------------|-----------|-----------|
| Sales              | $8,000    | $2,000    |
| Cost of sales      | (4,000)   | (1,100)   |
| Operating expenses | (3,000)   | (500)     |
| Pretax income      | $ 1,000   | $ 400     |

**REQUIRED:**
1. Determine 2016 income tax currently payable and income tax expense for Pam and Sun.
2. Calculate Pam's income from Sun for 2016.
3. Prepare a consolidated income statement for Pam and Sun for 2016.

## P 10-12
### [Tax] Consolidated income statement (downstream sales)

Taxable incomes for Pop Corporation and Son Corporation, its 70 percent–owned subsidiary, for 2016 are as follows (in thousands):

|                            | Pop       | Son       |
|----------------------------|-----------|-----------|
| Sales                      | $1,000    | $600      |
| Dividends received from Son| 56        | —         |
| Total revenue              | 1,056     | 600       |
| Cost of sales              | 500       | 240       |
| Operating expenses         | 156       | 160       |
| Total deductions           | 656       | 400       |
| Taxable income             | $ 400     | $200      |

## ADDITIONAL INFORMATION

1. Pop acquired its interest in Son at a fair value equal to book value on December 31, 2015.

2. Son paid dividends of $80,000 in 2016.

3. Pop sold $180,000 in merchandise to Son during 2016, and there was $20,000 in unrealized profit from the sales at year-end.

4. A flat 34 percent income tax rate is applicable.

5. Pop is eligible for the 80 percent dividends-received deduction.

**REQUIRED:** Prepare a consolidation income statement workpaper for Pop Corporation and Subsidiary for 2016.

## P 10-13
### [Tax] Reconstruct workpaper (separate and consolidated income statements)

Pam Corporation acquired a 90 percent interest in Sun Corporation in a taxable transaction on January 1, 2016, for $900,000, when Sun had $500,000 capital stock and $400,000 retained earnings. The $100,000 excess cost over book value is due to goodwill. Pam and Sun are an affiliated group for tax purposes.

During 2016, Pam sold land to Sun at a $20,000 profit. Sun still holds the land. Sun paid dividends of $50,000. A flat 34 percent tax rate applies to Pam and Sun. Income statements for Pam and Sun, and a consolidated income statement for Pam and Subsidiary, are summarized as follows:

|  | Pam | Sun | Consolidated |
|---|---|---|---|
| Sales | $ 800,000 | $200,000 | $1,000,000 |
| Gain on sale of land | 20,000 | — | — |
| Income from Sun | 36,430 | — | — |
| Cost of sales | (400,000) | (75,000) | (475,000) |
| Other expenses | (150,000) | (30,000) | (180,000) |
| Income tax expense | (85,000) | (32,300) | (117,300) |
| Noncontrolling interest share | — | — | (6,270) |
| Net income | $ 221,430 | $ 62,700 | $ 221,430 |

**REQUIRED:** Reconstruct all the workpaper entries needed to consolidate the financial statements of Pam Corporation and Subsidiary for 2016.

## P 10-14
### [Tax] Allocate fair value/book value differentials in a taxable purchase combination

Pop Corporation acquired all the stock of Son Corporation on January 1, 2016, for $280,000 cash, when the book values and fair values of Son's assets and liabilities were as follows (in thousands):

|  | Book Values (Tax Bases) | Fair Values |
|---|---|---|
| Current assets | $100 | $100 |
| Land | 20 | 60 |
| Buildings—net | 80 | 110 |
| Equipment—net | 60 | 70 |
| Total Assets | $260 | $340 |
| Liabilities | $ 90 | $ 90 |
| Capital stock | 150 | |
| Retained earnings | 20 | |
| Total Equities | $260 | |

Son's buildings have a remaining life of 10 years, and the equipment has a useful life of 2 years from the date of the combination. During 2016, Son had income of $50,000 and paid dividends of $20,000. Pop and Son are subject to a 35 percent tax rate.

**REQUIRED:**

1. Prepare a schedule to allocate the excess fair value over book value to Son's assets, liabilities, deferred taxes, and goodwill at January 1, 2016, assuming the purchase was a taxable transaction.
2. Prepare a schedule to allocate the excess fair value over book value to Son's assets, liabilities, deferred taxes, and goodwill at January 1, 2016, assuming the purchase was a tax-free reorganization.
3. Compute Pop's income from Son for 2016 under both options.

## P 10-15
### [Tax] Consolidated income statement (separate returns and intercompany equipment)

The pretax operating incomes of Pop Corporation and Son Corporation, its 70 percent–owned subsidiary, for 2016 are as follows (in thousands):

|  | Pop | Son |
|---|---|---|
| Sales | $8,000 | $4,000 |
| Gain on equipment | 500 | — |
| Cost of sales | (5,000) | (2,000) |
| Other expenses | (2,100) | (1,200) |
| Pretax income (excluding Pop's income from Son) | $1,400 | $ 800 |

**ADDITIONAL INFORMATION**

1. Pop received $280,000 dividends from Son during 2016.
2. Goodwill from Pop's investment in Son is not amortized.
3. Pop sold equipment to Son at a gain of $500,000 on January 1, 2016. Son is depreciating the equipment at a rate of 20 percent per year.
4. A flat 34 percent tax rate is applicable.
5. Pop provides for income taxes on undistributed income from Son.

**REQUIRED:**

1. Determine the separate income tax expenses for Pop and Son.
2. Determine Pop's income from Son on an equity basis.
3. Prepare a consolidated income statement for Pop Corporation and Subsidiary for the year ended December 31, 2016.

## P 10-16
### [Tax] Computations (separate tax returns with goodwill, downstream inventory sales, and upstream land sale)

On January 3, 2016, Pam Corporation purchased a 90% interest in Sun Corporation at a price $120,000 in excess of book value and fair value. The excess is goodwill. During 2016, Pam sold inventory items to Sun for $100,000, and $15,000 in profit from the sale remained unrealized at year-end. Sun sold land to Pam during the year at a gain of $30,000.

## ADDITIONAL INFORMATION

1. The companies are an affiliated group for tax purposes.
2. Sun declared and paid dividends of $100,000 in 2016.
3. Pam and Sun file separate income tax returns, and a 34 percent tax rate is applicable to both companies.
4. Pam uses the complete equity method to account for its investment in Sun.
5. Pretax accounting incomes, excluding Pam's income from Sun, are as follows (in thousands):

|  | Pam | Sun |
|---|---|---|
| Sales | $ 3,815 | $ 2,000 |
| Gain on land | — | 30 |
| Cost of sales | (2,200) | (1,200) |
| Other expenses | (1,000) | (400) |
| Pretax accounting income | $ 615 | $ 430 |

**REQUIRED:** Calculate the following:

1. Sun's net income
2. Pam's income from Sun
3. Pam's net income

# PROFESSIONAL RESEARCH ASSIGNMENTS

Answer the following questions by reference to the FASB Codification of Accounting Standards. Include the appropriate reference in your response.

**PR 10-1** Your CEO called you into his office to discuss an article he had read over the weekend. The article stated that the FASB had changed accounting for deferred taxes such that all deferred tax assets and liabilities would be treated as noncurrent items. The article continued noting that this would save companies money and would be required for years beginning after December 15, 2016. Your CEO doesn't know much about accounting or deferred taxes, but he does like saving money. He asks if it would be possible to adopt the new rules immediately. Is this permitted?

**PR 10-2** What are the required disclosures related to EPS calculations when preparing consolidated financial statements?

# 11

# Consolidation Theories, Push-Down Accounting, and Corporate Joint Ventures

## LEARNING OBJECTIVES

**11.1** Compare and contrast the elements of consolidation approaches under parent-company and contemporary/entity theories.

**11.2** Adjust subsidiary assets and liabilities to fair values using push-down accounting.

**11.3** Account for corporate and unincorporated joint ventures.

**11.4** Identify variable interest entities.

**11.5** Consolidate a variable interest entity.

Previous chapters have described practices used in the preparation of consolidated financial statements and have explained the rationale for those practices. The concepts and procedures discussed in earlier chapters reflect the **contemporary theory** of consolidated statements. Contemporary theory has evolved from accounting practice and is essentially an entity theory approach to the preparation of consolidated financial statements.

**Traditional theory,** generally accepted accounting principles (GAAP) prior to 2001 (ASC 810-10), reflected parts of both parent-company theory and entity theory. **Parent-company theory** assumes that consolidated financial statements are an extension of parent statements and should be prepared from the viewpoint of parent stockholders. Under parent-company theory, we prepare consolidated statements for the benefit of the stockholders of the parent, and we do not expect that noncontrolling stockholders can benefit significantly from the statements. Consolidated net income under parent-company theory is a measurement of income to the parent stockholders.

Certain problems and inconsistencies in accounting procedures under parent-company theory arise in the case of less-than-100 percent–owned subsidiaries. For example, the noncontrolling interest is a liability from the viewpoint of parent stockholders. Similarly, noncontrolling interest share is an expense from the viewpoint of controlling stockholders. However, shareholder interests, whether controlling or noncontrolling, are not liabilities under any of the accepted concepts of a liability, and income to shareholders does not meet the requirements for expense recognition.

**Entity theory** represents an alternative view of consolidation. It was developed by Professor Maurice Moonitz and published by the American Accounting Association in 1944 under the title *The Entity Theory of Consolidated Statements.* The focal point of entity theory is that the consolidated statements reflect the viewpoint of the total business entity, under which all resources controlled by the entity are valued consistently. Under entity theory, the income of noncontrolling interests is a distribution of the total income of the consolidated entity, and the interests of noncontrolling stockholders are a part of consolidated stockholders' equity.

Entity theory requires that the income and equity of a subsidiary be determined for all stockholders, so that the total amounts can be allocated between controlling and noncontrolling shareholders in a consistent manner. Entity theory accomplishes this by imputing a total fair value for the subsidiary on the basis of the price paid by the parent for its controlling interest. We assign 100 percent of the excess of total fair value of the subsidiary over the book value of subsidiary net assets to identifiable assets and to goodwill. In this manner, entity theory consolidates subsidiary assets (including goodwill) and liabilities at fair values, which are applicable to both noncontrolling and controlling interests.

## COMPARISON OF CONSOLIDATION THEORIES

Exhibit 11-1 compares the basic differences between parent-company and contemporary/entity theories. Parent-company theory adopts the viewpoint of parent stockholders, and entity theory focuses on the total consolidated entity. By contrast, traditional theory identifies the primary users of consolidated financial statements as the stockholders and creditors of the parent, but it assumes the objective of reporting financial position and results of operations of a single business entity. Thus, the viewpoint of traditional theory (ASC 810-10-15) was a compromise between the parent-company and entity theories. We will focus our discussion here on a comparison of parent company and contemporary/entity theories.

### Income Reporting

Consolidated net income is a measurement of income to parent stockholders under the parent-company theory. Entity theory, however, requires a computation of income to all equity holders, which we label "total consolidated net income." Entity theory then assigns total consolidated net income to noncontrolling and controlling stockholders, with appropriate disclosure on the face of the income statement.

Under current GAAP (ASC 805-10-65), a noncontrolling interest in a subsidiary should be labeled and displayed as a separate component of equity in the consolidated balance sheet. Income attributable to the noncontrolling interest is not an expense or a loss, but it is a deduction from consolidated net income in computing income attributable to the controlling interest. The consolidated income statement should disclose the portions of consolidated net income attributable to the controlling interest and noncontrolling interests.

### Asset Valuation

The greatest difference between parent-company theory and entity theory lies in the valuation of subsidiary net assets. Parent-company theory initially consolidates subsidiary assets at their book values, plus the parent's share of any excess fair value over book value. In other words, we revalue subsidiary assets only to the extent of the net assets (including goodwill) acquired by the parent. We consolidate the noncontrolling interest in subsidiary net assets at book value. Although this approach reflects the cost principle from the viewpoint of the parent, it leads to inconsistent treatment of controlling and noncontrolling interests in the consolidated financial statements and to a balance sheet valuation that reflects neither historical cost nor fair value.

Entity theory consolidates subsidiary assets and liabilities at fair values and accounts for the controlling and noncontrolling interests in those net assets consistently. However, this consistent treatment is obtained through the practice of imputing a total subsidiary valuation on the basis of the price paid by the parent for its controlling interest. Conceptually, this valuation approach has considerable appeal when the parent acquires essentially all of the subsidiary's stock for cash. It has less appeal when the parent acquires a slim majority of subsidiary outstanding stock for noncash assets or through an exchange of shares. An investor may be willing to pay a premium for the rights to *control* an investee (an investment of more than 50%), but not willing to purchase the remaining stock at the inflated price.

Additional problems with the imputed total valuation of a subsidiary under entity theory develop after the parent acquires its interest. *Once the parent is able to exercise absolute control over the subsidiary, the shares held by noncontrolling stockholders do not represent equity ownership in the usual sense.* Typically, the stock of a subsidiary will be "delisted" after an acquisition, leaving the parent as the only viable purchaser for noncontrolling shares. In this case, noncontrolling shareholders are at the mercy of the parent. In this sense, a noncontrolling share does not have the same equity characteristics as a controlling share.

### Unrealized Gains and Losses

A difference between the parent-company and entity theories also exists in the treatment of unrealized gains and losses from intercompany transactions (see Exhibit 11-1). Although there is general agreement that 100 percent of all unrealized gains and losses from downstream sales should be eliminated, we accord gains and losses arising from upstream sales different treatment under parent-company and entity theories. Under parent-company theory, we eliminate unrealized gains and losses

EXHIBIT 11-1

Alternative consolidation theories

| COMPARISON OF CONSOLIDATION THEORIES | | |
|---|---|---|
| | Parent-Company Theory | Contemporary/Entity Theory |
| Basic purposes and users of consolidated financial statements | Consolidated statements are an extension of parent statements, prepared for the benefit and from the viewpoint of the stockholders of the parent. | Consolidated statements are prepared from the viewpoint of the total consolidated entity, intended for all parties having an interest in the entity. |
| Consolidated net income | Consolidated net income is income to the stockholders of the parent. | Total consolidated net income is income to all equity holders of the consolidated entity. |
| Noncontrolling interest share | Noncontrolling interest share is an expense from the viewpoint of the parent stockholders measured on the basis of the subsidiary as a separate legal entity. | Noncontrolling interest share is an allocation of total consolidated net income to noncontrolling stockholders. |
| Equity of noncontrolling interests | Equity of noncontrolling stockholders is a liability from the viewpoint of the parent stockholders; it is measured based on the subsidiary's legal entity. | Equity of noncontrolling stockholders is a part of consolidated stockholders' equity equivalent to the presentation accorded the equity of controlling stockholders. |
| Consolidation of subsidiary net assets | Parent's share of subsidiary net assets is consolidated on the basis of the price paid by the parent for its interest. The noncontrolling interest's share is consolidated at book value. | All net assets of a subsidiary are consolidated at their fair values imputed on the basis of the price paid by the parent for its interest. Thus, controlling and noncontrolling interests in net assets are valued consistently. |
| Unrealized gains and losses from intercompany transactions | 100% elimination from consolidated net income for downstream sales and elimination of the parent's share for upstream sales. | 100% elimination in determining total consolidated net income with allocation between controlling and noncontrolling interests for upstream sales. |
| Constructive gains and losses on debt retirement | 100% recognition in consolidated net income on retirement of parent debt, and recognition of the parent's share for retirement of subsidiary debt. | 100% recognition in total consolidated net income with allocation between controlling and noncontrolling interests for retirement of subsidiary debt. |

from upstream sales to the extent of the parent's ownership percentage in the subsidiary. The portion of unrealized gains and losses not eliminated relates to the noncontrolling interest and, from the parent viewpoint, is considered to be realized by noncontrolling shareholders.

We eliminate unrealized gains and losses in determining total consolidated net income under entity theory. In the case of upstream sales, however, we allocate the eliminated amounts between income to noncontrolling and controlling stockholders according to their respective ownership percentages.

GAAP (ASC 810-45-1) requires that all unrealized gains and losses be eliminated, but the elimination of the intercompany profit or loss may be allocated proportionately between the controlling and noncontrolling interests in the case of upstream sales. Presumably, the assignment of the full amount of unrealized gains and losses from upstream sales to controlling interests would also be acceptable. This latter approach was not used in earlier chapters because of its inherent inconsistency for consolidation purposes and because its use seems incompatible with requirements for the equity method of accounting. If unrealized gains and losses from upstream sales are not allocated between controlling and noncontrolling interests, the parent's income and equity will not equal the controlling share of consolidated net income and consolidated equity unless the same inconsistency is applied under the equity method.

## Constructive Gains and Losses

The pattern of accounting for constructive gains and losses from intercompany debt acquisitions under the two theories parallels the pattern of accounting for unrealized gains and losses from intercompany transactions (see Exhibit 11-1).

## Consolidated Stockholders' Equity

Current GAAP differs from pure entity theory in reporting consolidated stockholders' equity. Under entity theory, both controlling and noncontrolling interests are components of consolidated equity. Further, entity theory would show the components of each interest, that is, breaking the controlling and noncontrolling interests into their respective shares of contributed capital and retained earnings. Under GAAP (ASC 805-10-65), the noncontrolling interest is shown as a single, combined amount under consolidated stockholders' equity.

## ILLUSTRATION—CONSOLIDATION UNDER PARENT-COMPANY AND ENTITY THEORIES

Differences among the various consolidation theories may be more comprehensible when shown in numerical examples. The following section relates to the acquisition of Son by Pop Corporation on January 1, 2016. Assume that Pop Corporation acquires a 90 percent interest in Son Corporation for $198,000 cash on January 1, 2016. Comparative balance sheets of the two companies immediately before the acquisition are as follows (in thousands):

|  | Pop | | Son | |
| --- | --- | --- | --- | --- |
|  | **Book Value** | **Fair Value** | **Book Value** | **Fair Value** |
| Cash | $220 | $220 | $ 5 | $ 5 |
| Accounts receivable—net | 80 | 80 | 30 | 35 |
| Inventories | 90 | 100 | 40 | 50 |
| Other current assets | 20 | 20 | 10 | 10 |
| Plant assets—net | 220 | 300 | 60 | 80 |
| Total assets | $630 | $720 | $145 | $180 |
| Liabilities | $ 80 | $ 80 | $ 25 | $ 25 |
| Capital stock, $10 par | 400 | | 100 | |
| Retained earnings | 150 | | 20 | |
| Total equities | $630 | | $145 | |

The $198,000 purchase price for the 90 percent interest implies a $220,000 total value for Son's net assets ($198,000 ÷ 90%). Under entity theory, we revalue all subsidiary assets and liabilities and reflect these values in the consolidated statements on the basis of the $220,000 implied total valuation. Under parent-company theory, we do not reflect the total implied value of the subsidiary in the consolidated financial statements; therefore, only 90 percent of the subsidiary's net assets are revalued. Although *the different theories do not affect parent accounting under the equity method*, they do result in different amounts for consolidated assets, liabilities, and noncontrolling interests.

**ENTITY THEORY**   In the Pop–Son example, entity theory assigns the $100,000 excess of implied value over the $120,000 book value of Son's net assets to identifiable net assets and goodwill as follows (in thousands):

|  | **Fair Value** | | **Book Value** | | **Excess Fair Value** |
| --- | --- | --- | --- | --- | --- |
| Accounts receivable—net | $35 | − | $30 | = | $ 5 |
| Inventories | 50 | − | 40 | = | 10 |
| Plant assets—net | 80 | − | 60 | = | 20 |
| Goodwill (remainder) | | | | | 65 |
| Total implied fair value over book value | | | | | $100 |

**PARENT-COMPANY THEORY**   Amounts assigned to identifiable net assets and goodwill under parent-company theory would be 90 percent of the foregoing amounts:

| | |
| --- | --- |
| Accounts receivable—net | $ 5,000 × 90% = $ 4,500 |
| Inventories | 10,000 × 90% = 9,000 |
| Plant assets—net | 20,000 × 90% = 18,000 |
| Goodwill | 65,000 × 90% = 58,500 |
| Total purchase price over book value acquired | $90,000 |

**GOODWILL**   Goodwill under the two theories can be determined independently. Under entity theory, the $65,000 goodwill is equal to the total implied value of Son's net assets over the fair value of Son's identifiable net assets ($220,000 − $155,000). Under parent-company theory, the $58,500 goodwill is equal to the investment cost less 90 percent of the fair value of Son's identifiable net assets ($198,000 − $139,500). Entity theory reflects the $10,000 additional amount assigned to identifiable assets and goodwill ($100,000 − $90,000) in the noncontrolling interest classification in a consolidated balance sheet.

## Consolidation at Acquisition

Exhibit 11-2 compares consolidated balance sheet workpapers for Pop Corporation and Subsidiary under parent-company and entity theories. The comparative workpapers in Exhibit 11-2 begin with separate balance sheets of the affiliates and use established procedures for consolidation. Although the workpapers could be modified under parent-company theory to reflect the noncontrolling interest among the liabilities, this modification does not seem necessary. Such classification differences can be reflected in the consolidated statements without changing workpaper procedures.

Parent-company theory allocates 90 percent of the excess of fair value over book value of identifiable net assets to identifiable assets and liabilities, and it allocates the $58,500 excess of investment cost over fair value of net assets acquired to goodwill. Noncontrolling interest of $12,000 for parent-company theory is equal to 10 percent of the $120,000 book value of Son's net assets at the time of acquisition.

Entity theory assigns the full excess of fair value over book value to identifiable net assets, and it enters the excess of implied total fair value over fair value of net identifiable assets as goodwill. The $22,000 noncontrolling interest is 10 percent of the implied fair value of Son's net assets (including goodwill).

Consolidated assets under parent-company theory consist of the book value of combined assets plus 90 percent of the excess of fair value of Son's assets over their book value. Under entity theory, consolidated assets consist of the book value of Pop's assets plus the fair value of Son's assets. Although entity theory consolidates all assets of Son at their fair values, total consolidated assets do not reflect fair values under either theory because we never revalue the assets of the parent at the time of an acquisition.

## Consolidation After Acquisition

Differences between parent-company theory and entity theory can be explained further by examining the operations of Pop Corporation and Son Corporation for 2016. The following assumptions are made:

1. Son's net income and dividends for 2016 are $35,000 and $10,000, respectively.

2. The excess of fair value over book value of Son's accounts receivable and inventories at January 1, 2016, is realized during 2016.

3. Son's plant assets are being depreciated over 20 years, using the straight-line method (i.e., at a 5% annual rate).

EQUITY METHOD    Under these assumptions, Pop records $17,100 investment income from Son for 2016, computed under the equity method as follows:

| | |
|---|---|
| Share of Son's net income ($35,000 × 90%) | $31,500 |
| Less: Realization of excess allocated to receivables ($5,000 × 90%) | (4,500) |
| Realization of excess allocated to inventories ($10,000 × 90%) | (9,000) |
| Depreciation on excess allocated to plant assets ($20,000 × 90%) ÷ 20 years | (900) |
| Income from Son for 2016 | $17,100 |

Pop's Investment in Son account under the equity method has a balance of $206,100 at December 31, 2016. This consists of the $198,000 investment cost, plus $17,100 investment income for 2016, less $9,000 dividends received from Son during 2016. Equity method accounting is not affected by the viewpoint adopted for consolidating the financial statements of affiliates; therefore, *the separate statements of Pop and Son will be the same at December 31, 2016, regardless of the theory adopted.*

EXHIBIT  11-2

Balance Sheet
Workpaper Comparisons

## POP CORPORATION AND SUBSIDIARY CONSOLIDATED BALANCE SHEET WORKPAPER AT JANUARY 1, 2016 (IN THOUSANDS)

| | Pop | 90% Son | Adjustments and Eliminations Debits | Adjustments and Eliminations Credits | Consolidated Statements |
|---|---|---|---|---|---|
| **Parent-Company Theory** | | | | | |
| *Assets* | | | | | |
| Cash | $ 22 | $ 5 | | | $ 27 |
| Accounts receivable—net | 80 | 30 | b    4.5 | | 114.5 |
| Inventories | 90 | 40 | b    9 | | 139 |
| Other current assets | 20 | 10 | | | 30 |
| Plant assets—net | 220 | 60 | b   18 | | 298 |
| Investment in Son | 198 | | | a 198 | |
| Goodwill | | | b   58.5 | | 58.5 |
| Unamortized excess | | | a   90 | b   90 | |
| Total assets | $630 | $145 | | | $667 |
| *Liabilities and Equity* | | | | | |
| Liabilities | $ 80 | $ 25 | | | $105 |
| Capital stock | 400 | 100 | a 100 | | 400 |
| Retained earnings | 150 | 20 | a   20 | | 150 |
| Noncontrolling interest | | | | a   12 | 12 |
| Total equities | $630 | $145 | 300 | 300 | $667 |
| **Entity Theory** | | | | | |
| *Assets* | | | | | |
| Cash | $ 22 | $ 5 | | | $ 27 |
| Accounts receivable—net | 80 | 30 | b    5 | | 115 |
| Inventories | 90 | 40 | b   10 | | 140 |
| Other current assets | 20 | 10 | | | 30 |
| Plant assets—net | 220 | 60 | b   20 | | 300 |
| Investment in Son | 198 | | | a 198 | |
| Goodwill | | | b   65 | | 65 |
| Unamortized excess | | | a 100 | b 100 | |
| Total assets | $630 | $145 | | | $677 |
| *Liabilities and Equity* | | | | | |
| Liabilities | $ 80 | $ 25 | | | $105 |
| Capital stock | 400 | 100 | a 100 | | 400 |
| Retained earnings | 150 | 20 | a   20 | | 150 |
| Noncontrolling interest | | | | a   22 | 22 |
| Total equities | $630 | $145 | 320 | 320 | $677 |

**CONSOLIDATION PROCEDURES**    Consolidated net income under parent-company theory is the same as the income allocated to parent stockholders under entity theory. Therefore, the differences between the parent-company and entity theories lie solely in the manner of consolidating parent and subsidiary financial statements and in reporting the financial position and results of operations in the consolidated financial statements. Consolidation workpapers for Pop Corporation and Subsidiary under parent-company theory in Exhibit 11-3 and under entity theory in Exhibit 11-4 reflect these differences. Again, workpaper procedures have not been modified to reflect differences in financial statement classification. Exhibits 11-5 and 11-6 illustrate differences in financial statement presentation for Pop Corporation and Subsidiary and show financial statements prepared from the workpapers.

**POP CORPORATION AND SUBSIDIARY CONSOLIDATION WORKPAPER FOR THE YEAR ENDED DECEMBER 31, 2016 (IN THOUSANDS)**

**EXHIBIT 11-3**

**Parent-Company Theory**

| | Pop | 90% Son | Adjustments and Eliminations — Debits | Adjustments and Eliminations — Credits | Consolidated Statements |
|---|---|---|---|---|---|
| *Income Statement* | | | | | |
| Sales | $600 | $ 200 | | | $800 |
| Income from Son | 17.1 | | a  17.1 | | |
| Cost of sales | (300) | (120) | c  9 | | (429) |
| Operating expenses | (211.25) | (45) | c  4.5<br>d  .9 | | (261.65) |
| Noncontrolling interest share ($35 × 10%) | | | e  3.5 | | (3.5) |
| **Controlling share of net income** | **$105.85** | **$  35** | | | **$105.85** |
| *Retained Earnings Statement* | | | | | |
| Retained earnings | $150 | $  20 | b  20 | | $150 |
| **Controlling share of net income** | 105.85 | 35 | | | 105.85 |
| Dividends | (80) | (10) | | a  9<br>e  1 | (80) |
| **Retained earnings—December 31** | **$175.85** | **$  45** | | | **$175.85** |
| *Balance Sheet* | | | | | |
| Cash | $ 29.75 | $  13 | | | $ 42.75 |
| Accounts receivable—net | 90 | 32 | | | 122 |
| Inventories | 100 | 48 | | | 148 |
| Other current assets | 30 | 17 | | | 47 |
| Plant assets—net | 200 | 57 | c  18 | d  .9 | 274.1 |
| Investment in Son | 206.1 | | | a  8.1<br>b 198 | |
| Goodwill | | | c  58.5 | | 58.5 |
| Unamortized excess | | | b  90 | c  90 | |
| | $655.85 | $ 167 | | | $692.35 |
| Liabilities | $ 80 | $  22 | | | $102 |
| Capital stock | 400 | 100 | b 100 | | 400 |
| **Retained earnings** | 175.85 | 45 | | | 175.85 |
| | $655.85 | $ 167 | | | |
| Noncontrolling interest | | | | b  12<br>e  2.5 | 14.5 |
| | | | 321.5 | 321.5 | $692.35 |

EXHIBIT 11-4

Entity Theory

# POP CORPORATION AND SUBSIDIARY CONSOLIDATION WORKPAPER FOR THE YEAR ENDED DECEMBER 31, 2016 (IN THOUSANDS)

| | Pop | 90% Son | Adjustments and Eliminations Debits | Credits | Consolidated Statements |
|---|---|---|---|---|---|
| *Income Statement* Sales | $600 | $200 | | | $800 |
| Income from Son | 17.1 | | a 17.1 | | |
| Cost of sales | (300) | (120) | c 10 | | (430) |
| Operating expenses | (211.25) | (45) | c 5 d 1 | | (262.25) |
| Noncontrolling interest share* | | | e 1.9 | | (1.9) |
| **Controlling share of net income** | **$105.85** | **$ 35** | | | **$105.85** |
| *Retained Earnings Statement* Retained earnings | $150 | $ 20 | b 20 | | $150 |
| **Controlling share of net income** | 105.85 | 35 | | | 105.85 |
| Dividends | (80) | (10) | | a 9 e 1 | (80) |
| **Retained earnings— December 31** | **$175.85** | **$ 45** | | | **$175.85** |
| *Balance Sheet* Cash | $ 29.75 | $ 13 | | | $ 42.75 |
| Accounts receivable—net | 90 | 32 | | | 122 |
| Inventories | 100 | 48 | | | 148 |
| Other current assets | 30 | 17 | | | 47 |
| Plant assets—net | 200 | 57 | c 20 | d 1 | 276 |
| Investment in Son | 206.1 | | | a 8.1 b 198 | |
| Goodwill | | | c 65 | | 65 |
| Unamortized excess | | | b 100 | c 100 | |
| | $655.85 | $167 | | | $700.75 |
| Liabilities | $ 80 | $ 22 | | | $102 |
| Capital stock | 400 | 100 | b 100 | | 400 |
| **Retained earnings** | 175.85 | 45 | | | 175.85 |
| | $655.85 | $167 | | | |
| Noncontrolling interest | | | | b 22 e .9 | 22.9 |
| | | | 340 | 340 | $700.75 |

*Noncontrolling interest share = ($35 − $16) × 10%.

**EXHIBIT 11-5**

Consolidated Income
Statements Under
Alternative Theories

**POP CORPORATION AND SUBSIDIARY CONSOLIDATED INCOME STATEMENTS FOR THE YEAR ENDED DECEMBER 31, 2016 (IN THOUSANDS)**

| | | |
|---|---:|---:|
| *Parent-Company Theory* | | |
| Sales | | $800.00 |
| Less: Cost of sales | $429.00 | |
| Operating expenses | 261.65 | |
| Noncontrolling interest share | 3.50 | |
| Total expenses | | 694.15 |
| Consolidated net income | | $105.85 |
| *Entity Theory* | | |
| Sales | | $800.00 |
| Less: Cost of sales | $430.00 | |
| Operating expenses | 262.25 | |
| Total expenses | | 692.25 |
| Total consolidated net income | | $107.75 |
| Attributable: to noncontrolling stockholders | $ 1.90 | |
| to controlling stockholders | $105.85 | |

**EXHIBIT 11-6**

Consolidated Balance
Sheets Under
Alternative Theories

**POP CORPORATION AND SUBSIDIARY CONSOLIDATED BALANCE SHEETS AT DECEMBER 31, 2016 (IN THOUSANDS)**

| | Parent-Company Theory | Entity Theory |
|---|---:|---:|
| *Assets* | | |
| Cash | $ 42.75 | $ 42.75 |
| Accounts receivable—net | 122.00 | 122.00 |
| Inventories | 148.00 | 148.00 |
| Other current assets | 47.00 | 47.00 |
| Total current assets | 359.75 | 359.75 |
| Plant assets—net | 274.10 | 276.00 |
| Goodwill | 58.50 | 65.00 |
| Total noncurrent assets | 332.60 | 341.00 |
| Total assets | $692.35 | $700.75 |
| *Liabilities and Equity* | | |
| Liabilities | $102.00 | $102.00 |
| Noncontrolling interest | 14.50 | — |
| Total liabilities | 116.50 | 102.00 |
| Capital stock | 400.00 | 400.00 |
| Retained earnings | 175.85 | 175.85 |
| Noncontrolling interest | — | 22.90 |
| Total stockholders' equity | 575.85 | 598.75 |
| Total equities | $692.35 | $700.75 |

In comparing the consolidation workpapers under parent-company theory in Exhibit 11-3 with those under entity theory in Exhibit 11-4, note that the workpaper adjustment and elimination entries have the same debit and credit items, but the amounts differ for all workpaper entries other than entry a. Accounting for the subsidiary under the equity method is the same for both consolidation theories, so the entry to eliminate investment income and intercompany dividends and to adjust the investment account to its beginning-of-the-period balance (entry a) is exactly the same under parent-company theory as under entity theory.

The remaining adjustment and elimination entries in Exhibit 11-3 under parent-company theory differ from those under the contemporary theory used in earlier chapters. Entry b eliminates reciprocal subsidiary equity and investment amounts, establishes beginning noncontrolling interest at book value ($120,000 × 10%), and enters the unamortized excess. Entry c then allocates the excess of investment cost over book value acquired: $9,000 to cost of sales (for undervalued inventory items realized during 2016), $4,500 to operating expense (for undervalued receivables realized during 2016), $18,000 to plant assets (for undervalued plant assets at the beginning of 2016), and $58,500 to goodwill. Entries d and e reflect current depreciation on the excess allocated to plant assets ($18,000 × 5%) and the noncontrolling interest in subsidiary income and dividends, respectively. Noncontrolling interest share of $3,500 is simply 10 percent of Son's $35,000 reported net income.

Entries b, c, d, and e in Exhibit 11-4 under entity theory have the same objective as those for the same items under parent-company theory, except for amounts that relate to the noncontrolling interest. Beginning noncontrolling interest under entity theory is $22,000, equal to 10 percent of the $220,000 implied total value of Son Corporation at January 1, 2016. Beginning noncontrolling interest under entity theory is $10,000 greater than beginning noncontrolling interest of $12,000 under parent-company theory. The additional $10,000 relates to the allocation of 100 percent of the excess fair value over book value of Son's net assets at acquisition under entity theory. In other words, workpaper entry b under entity theory is equivalent to entry b under parent-company theory, plus the additional $10,000 unamortized excess applicable to noncontrolling interest:

| b | Unamortized excess (+A) | 100,000 | |
|---|---|---|---|
| | Capital stock (−SE) | 100,000 | |
| | Retained earnings January 1, 2016 (−SE) | 20,000 | |
| | Investment in Son (−A) | | 198,000 |
| | Noncontrolling interest January 1, 2016 (+SE) | | 22,000 |

To eliminate reciprocal investment and equity balances, establish beginning noncontrolling interest, and enter the unamortized excess amount.

Entry c under entity theory is equivalent to entry c under parent-company theory, plus the additional excess fair value over book value amounts:

| c | Cost of sales (E, −SE) | 10,000 | |
|---|---|---|---|
| | Operating expenses (E, −SE) | 5,000 | |
| | Plant assets (+A) | 20,000 | |
| | Goodwill (+A) | 65,000 | |
| | Unamortized excess (−A) | | 100,000 |

To allocate unamortized excess to identifiable assets and goodwill.

Workpaper entry d for depreciation on the excess allocated to plant assets is $1,000 under entity theory, compared with $900 under parent-company theory. The $100 difference is simply the 5 percent depreciation rate applied to the additional $2,000 allocated to plant assets under entity theory.

Noncontrolling interest share under entity theory is $1,900, consisting of 10 percent of Son's $35,000 income, less 10 percent of the $16,000 amortization on the $100,000 implied fair value/ book value differential. Alternatively, noncontrolling interest share can be computed as follows:

| | |
|---|---|
| Share of Son's reported income ($35,000 × 10%) | $3,500 |
| Less: Operating expenses for realization of excess allocated to receivables ($5,000 × 10%) | (500) |
| Cost of sales for realization of excess allocated to inventory ($10,000 × 10%) | (1,000) |
| Depreciation on excess allocated to plant assets ($20,000 ÷ 20 years × 10%) | (100) |
| Noncontrolling interest share | $1,900 |

**COMPARISON OF CONSOLIDATED INCOME STATEMENTS**   The additional expenses deducted in determining consolidated net income under entity theory can be summarized as follows:

| | Parent-Company Theory | Entity Theory |
|---|---|---|
| Operating expenses (for receivables) | $ 4,500 | $ 5,000 |
| Cost of sales (for inventory) | 9,000 | 10,000 |
| Operating expenses (for depreciation) | 900 | 1,000 |
| | $14,400 | $16,000 |

The $1,600 additional expenses ($16,000 − $14,400) under entity theory are exactly offset by the lower noncontrolling interest share ($3,500 − $1,900) under entity theory. Thus, income to the parent stockholders is the same under the two theories, even though there are differences in the amounts reported and in the way the amounts are disclosed in the consolidated income statements. These differences are shown in Exhibit 11-5, which compares consolidated income statements for Pop Corporation and Subsidiary under parent-company theory and entity theory. The reporting of income under entity theory shows a final amount for "total consolidated net income" of $107,750 and attribution of that income to noncontrolling and controlling stockholders.

**COMPARISON OF CONSOLIDATED BALANCE SHEETS**   Comparative balance sheets for Pop Corporation and Subsidiary at December 31, 2016, are illustrated in Exhibit 11-6 under both theories. The amount of total assets is greater under entity theory. The difference in total assets is $8,400 ($700,750 − $692,350), and consists of the unamortized excess of implied fair value over book value of Son's net assets. This difference relates to goodwill of $6,500 ($65,000 − $58,500) and plant assets of $1,900 ($276,000 − $274,100).

Total liabilities and equity are greater under entity theory. Liabilities are $14,500 greater under parent-company theory because noncontrolling interest is classified as a liability. Stockholders' equity is $22,900 greater under entity theory because noncontrolling interest is classified as a part of stockholders' equity.

**OTHER VIEWS OF NONCONTROLLING INTEREST**   Some accountants believe that noncontrolling interest should not appear as a separate line item in consolidated financial statements. One suggestion for eliminating noncontrolling interest from consolidated statements is to report total consolidated net income as the bottom line in the consolidated income statements, with separate footnote disclosure of controlling and noncontrolling interests. Consistent treatment in the consolidated balance sheet would require total consolidated equity to be reported as a single line item, with separate footnote disclosure of the equity of controlling and noncontrolling interests.

Another suggestion for excluding reference to noncontrolling interest in consolidated financial statements is to consolidate only the controlling interest portion of the revenues, expenses, assets, and liabilities of less-than-100 percent–owned subsidiaries. This is known as proportional consolidation and is discussed later in this chapter under accounting for corporate joint ventures.

## PUSH-DOWN ACCOUNTING AND OTHER BASIS CONSIDERATIONS

LEARNING OBJECTIVE **11.2**

Under the theories discussed in the first section of this chapter, we assigned fair values to the individual identifiable assets and liabilities and goodwill of the subsidiary by workpaper entries in the process of consolidating the financial statements of the parent and subsidiary. The books of the subsidiary were not affected by the price paid by the parent for its ownership interest.

In certain situations, the Securities and Exchange Commission (SEC) requires that the fair values of the acquired subsidiary's assets and liabilities, which represent the parent's fair value basis under GAAP (ASC 810-10-25), be recorded in the separate financial statements of the subsidiary. In other words, the values are "pushed down" to the subsidiary's statements.[1] The SEC requires the use of push-down accounting for SEC filings when a subsidiary is substantially wholly-owned (usually 90%) with no substantial publicly held debt or preferred stock outstanding.

The SEC's argument is that when the parent controls the form of ownership of an entity, the basis of accounting for purchased assets and liabilities should be the same regardless of whether the entity continues to exist or is merged into the parent's operations. However, when a subsidiary has outstanding public debt or preferred stock, or when a significant noncontrolling interest exists, the parent may not be able to control the form of ownership. The SEC encourages push-down accounting in these circumstances, but it does not require it.

The American Institute of Certified Public Accountants (AICPA) issues paper "Push-Down Accounting" (October 30, 1979) describes ***push-down accounting*** as:

> *The establishment of a new accounting and reporting basis for an entity in its separate financial statements, based on a purchase transaction in the voting stock of the entity that results in a substantial change of ownership of the outstanding voting stock of the entity.*[2]

---

[1]*SEC Staff Accounting Bulletin, No. 54*, 1983. For further clarification of the SEC's position, see *Staff Accounting Bulletin, No. 73*, 1987.

[2]FASB ASC 810-10-45-1. Originally 'Statement of Financial Accounting Standards No. 160.' "Noncontrolling Interests." Norwalk, CT © 2007 Financial Accounting Standards Board.

When we do not use push-down accounting in an acquisition, we assign the implied fair value/book value differential to identifiable net assets and goodwill in a consolidation workpaper. The consolidation process is simplified if the subsidiary records the fair values in its financial statements under push-down accounting.

Push-down accounting is controversial only in the separate-company statements of the subsidiary that are issued to noncontrolling interests, creditors, and other interested parties. Critics of push-down accounting argue that the transaction between the parent/investor and the subsidiary's old stockholders does not justify a new accounting basis for the subsidiary's assets and liabilities under historical cost principles. The subsidiary is not a party to the transaction—it receives no new funds; it sells no assets. Proponents counter that the price paid by the new owners provides the most relevant basis for measuring the subsidiary's assets, liabilities, and results of operations.

Push-down accounting is not consistently applied among the supporters of the concept, although, in practice, a subsidiary's assets are usually revalued on a proportional basis. What percentage of ownership constitutes a significant noncontrolling interest that would preclude the use of push-down accounting? Should the allocation be done on a proportional basis if less than a 100 percent change in ownership has occurred? These are questions in need of authoritative answers.

Current GAAP now permits companies the option to adopt push-down accounting following an acquisition.

In the illustration that follows, the Pop–Son example is extended using both a proportional allocation for the purchase of a 90 percent interest in Son and a 100 percent allocation, in which we impute the entity's market value as a whole from the acquisition price of the 90 percent interest.

## Push-Down Procedures in Year of Acquisition

Recall that Pop acquired its 90 percent interest for $198,000 cash on January 1, 2016. If we use push-down accounting and revalue only 90 percent of Son's identifiable net assets (parent-company theory), we allocate the $90,000 fair value/book value differential as follows (in thousands):

| | Book Value | Push-Down Adjustment | Book Value After Push-Down |
|---|---|---|---|
| Cash | $ 5 | — | $ 5 |
| Accounts receivable—net | 30 | $ 4.5 | 34.5 |
| Inventory | 40 | 9 | 49 |
| Other current assets | 10 | — | 10 |
| Plant assets—net | 60 | 18 | 78 |
| Goodwill | — | 58.5 | 58.5 |
| | $145 | $ 90 | $235 |
| Liabilities | $ 25 | — | $ 25 |
| Capital stock | 100 | — | 100 |
| Retained earnings | 20 | $(20) | — |
| Push-down capital | — | 110 | 110 |
| | $145 | $ 90 | $235 |

We record the push-down adjustment on Son's separate books as follows:

| | | |
|---|---|---|
| Accounts receivable (+A) | 4,500 | |
| Inventory (+A) | 9,000 | |
| Plant assets (+A) | 18,000 | |
| Goodwill (+A) | 58,500 | |
| Retained earnings (−SE) | 20,000 | |
| Push-down capital (+SE) | | 110,000 |

If we impute a total value of $220,000 from the price of the 90 percent interest in Son under entity theory ($198,000 cost ÷ 90%), we push down the $100,000 excess on Son's books as follows (in thousands):

| | Book Value | Push-Down Adjustment | Book Value After Push-Down |
|---|---|---|---|
| Cash | $  5 | — | $  5 |
| Accounts receivable—net | 30 | $  5 | 35 |
| Inventory | 40 | 10 | 50 |
| Other current assets | 10 | — | 10 |
| Plant assets—net | 60 | 20 | 80 |
| Goodwill | — | 65 | 65 |
| | $145 | $100 | $245 |
| Liabilities | $ 25 | — | $ 25 |
| Capital stock | 100 | — | 100 |
| Retained earnings | 20 | $ (20) | — |
| Push-down capital | — | 120 | 120 |
| | $145 | $100 | $245 |

The entry to record the 100 percent push-down adjustment on Son's separate books is:

| | | |
|---|---|---|
| Accounts receivable (+A) | 5,000 | |
| Inventory (+A) | 10,000 | |
| Plant assets (+A) | 20,000 | |
| Goodwill (+A) | 65,000 | |
| Retained earnings (−SE) | 20,000 | |
| Push-down capital (+SE) | | 120,000 |

Observe that we transfer the balance of Son's Retained Earnings account to push-down capital regardless of whether the push down is for 90 percent or 100 percent of the fair value. This treatment is basic to push-down accounting, which requires a new accounting and reporting basis for the acquired entity. Push-down capital is an additional paid-in capital account. It includes the revaluation of subsidiary identifiable net assets and goodwill, based on the acquisition price, and the subsidiary's Retained Earnings account balance, which we eliminate under the new entity concept of push-down accounting.

Exhibit 11-7 presents a consolidated balance sheet workpaper to illustrate the effect of the push-down adjustments. The balance sheet worksheet at the top of the exhibit reflects the 90 percent push-down adjustment (with parent-company theory), and the worksheet at the bottom reflects the 100 percent push-down adjustment (entity theory). Including the push-down adjustments in Son's separate balance sheets greatly simplifies consolidation procedures. The simplification results from not having to assign unamortized fair values in the workpaper under push-down accounting. The consolidated balance sheet amounts, however, are identical in Exhibit 11-7 under push-down accounting and in Exhibit 11-2, where we maintain the subsidiary balance sheets on an historical-cost basis.

## Push-Down Procedures in Year After Acquisition

Exhibits 11-8 and 11-9 illustrate consolidated financial statement workpapers for Pop and Son Corporations under push-down accounting procedures for the year ended December 31, 2016. Exhibit 11-8 reflects the 90 percent push-down adjustment (parent-company theory), and Exhibit 11-9 reflects the 100 percent push-down adjustment (entity theory). Both exhibits greatly simplify the consolidation procedures in relation to the comparable workpapers for Pop and Son shown in Exhibits 11-3 and 11-4.

In the consolidation workpaper of Exhibit 11-9 (entity theory), the noncontrolling interest share of $1,900 is equal to 10 percent of Son's $19,000 net income as measured under push-down accounting. Similarly, the $22,900 noncontrolling interest at December 31, 2016, is equal to 10 percent of Son's $229,000 stockholders' equity on that date. We determine these noncontrolling interest items under standard consolidation procedures. By contrast, in Exhibit 11-8 (parent-company theory), the $3,500 noncontrolling interest share for 2016 and the $14,500 noncontrolling interest at December 31, 2016, do not have a direct reference to the $20,600 net income of Son or the $220,600 stockholders' equity of Son, as shown in Son's separate income statement and balance sheet under 90 percent push-down accounting. This is a problem that arises in the use of push-down accounting for a

## POP CORPORATION AND SUBSIDIARY CONSOLIDATED BALANCE SHEET WORKPAPER AT JANUARY 1, 2016 (IN THOUSANDS)

| | Pop | 90% Son | Adjustments and Eliminations Debits | Adjustments and Eliminations Credits | Consolidated Statements |
|---|---|---|---|---|---|
| **Parent-Company Theory** | | | | | |
| *Assets* | | | | | |
| Cash | $ 22 | $ 5 | | | $ 27 |
| Accounts receivable—net | 80 | 34.5 | | | 114.5 |
| Inventories | 90 | 49 | | | 139 |
| Other current assets | 20 | 10 | | | 30 |
| Plant assets—net | 220 | 78 | | | 298 |
| Investment in Son | 198 | | | a 198 | |
| Goodwill | | 58.5 | | | 58.5 |
| Total assets | $ 630 | $235 | | | $667 |
| *Liabilities and Equity* | | | | | |
| Liabilities | $ 80 | $ 25 | | | $105 |
| Capital stock | 400 | 100 | a 100 | | 400 |
| Retained earnings | 150 | 0 | | | 150 |
| Push-down capital—Son | | 110 | a 110 | | |
| Noncontrolling interest | | | | a 12 | 12 |
| Total equities | $ 630 | $235 | 210 | 210 | $667 |
| **Entity Theory** | | | | | |
| *Assets* | | | | | |
| Cash | $ 22 | $ 5 | | | $ 27 |
| Accounts receivable—net | 80 | 35 | | | 115 |
| Inventories | 90 | 50 | | | 140 |
| Other current assets | 20 | 10 | | | 30 |
| Plant assets—net | 220 | 80 | | | 300 |
| Investment in Son | 198 | | | a 198 | |
| Goodwill | | 65 | | | 65 |
| Total assets | $ 630 | $245 | | | $677 |
| *Liabilities and Equity* | | | | | |
| Liabilities | $ 80 | $ 25 | | | $105 |
| Capital stock | 400 | 100 | a 100 | | 400 |
| Retained earnings | 150 | 0 | | | 150 |
| Push-down capital—Son | | 120 | a 120 | | |
| Noncontrolling interest | | | | a 22 | 22 |
| Total equities | $ 630 | $245 | 220 | 220 | $677 |

**EXHIBIT 11-8**

Push-Down Accounting—
Parent-Company Theory

**POP CORPORATION AND SUBSIDIARY CONSOLIDATION WORKPAPER FOR THE YEAR ENDED DECEMBER 31, 2016 (IN THOUSANDS)**

| | Pop | 90% Son | Adjustments and Eliminations Debits | Adjustments and Eliminations Credits | Consolidated Statements |
|---|---|---|---|---|---|
| *Income Statement* | | | | | |
| Sales | $600 | $200 | | | $800 |
| Income from Son | 17.1 | | a 17.1 | | |
| Cost of sales | (300) | (129) | | | (429) |
| Operating expenses | (211.25) | (50.4) | | | (261.65) |
| Noncontrolling interest share ($35 × 10%) | | | c 3.5 | | (3.5) |
| **Controlling share of net income** | **$105.85** | **$ 20.6** | | | **$105.85** |
| *Retained Earnings Statement* | | | | | |
| Retained earnings | $150 | $ 0 | | | $150 |
| **Controlling share of net income** | 105.85 | 20.6 | | | 105.85 |
| Dividends | (80) | (10) | | a 9 / c 1 | (80) |
| **Retained earnings— December 31** | **$175.85** | **$ 10.6** | | | **$175.85** |
| *Balance Sheet* | | | | | |
| Cash | $ 29.75 | $ 13 | | | $ 42.75 |
| Accounts receivable—net | 90 | 32 | | | 122 |
| Inventories | 100 | 48 | | | 148 |
| Other current assets | 30 | 17 | | | 47 |
| Plant assets—net | 200 | 74.1 | | | 274.1 |
| Investment in Son | 206.1 | | | a 8.1 / b 198 | |
| Goodwill | | 58.5 | | | 58.5 |
| | $655.85 | $242.6 | | | $692.35 |
| Liabilities | $ 80 | $ 22 | | | $102 |
| Capital stock | 400 | 100 | b 100 | | 400 |
| **Retained earnings** | 175.85 | 10.6 | | | 175.85 |
| Push-down capital—Son | | 110 | b 110 | | |
| | $655.85 | $242.6 | | | |
| Noncontrolling interest | | | | b 12 / c 2.5 | 14.5 |
| | | | 230.6 | 230.6 | $692.35 |

EXHIBIT 11-9

Push-Down
Accounting—Entity
Theory

## POP CORPORATION AND SUBSIDIARY CONSOLIDATION WORKPAPER FOR THE YEAR ENDED DECEMBER 31, 2016 (IN THOUSANDS)

| | Pop | 90% Son | Adjustments and Eliminations Debits | Adjustments and Eliminations Credits | Consolidated Statements |
|---|---|---|---|---|---|
| *Income Statement* | | | | | |
| Sales | $600 | $200 | | | $800 |
| Income from Son | 17.1 | | a 17.1 | | |
| Cost of sales | (300) | (130) | | | (430) |
| Operating expenses | (211.25) | (51) | | | (262.25) |
| Noncontrolling interest share* | | | c 1.9 | | (1.9) |
| **Controlling share of net income** | **$105.85** | **$ 19** | | | **$105.85** |
| *Retained Earnings Statement* | | | | | |
| Retained earnings | $150 | $ 0 | | | $150 |
| **Controlling share of net income** | 105.85 | 19 | | | 105.85 |
| Dividends | (80) | (10) | | a 9 | (80) |
| | | | | c 1 | |
| **Retained earnings— December 31** | **$175.85** | **$ 9** | | | **$175.85** |
| *Balance Sheet* | | | | | |
| Cash | $ 29.75 | $ 13 | | | $ 42.75 |
| Accounts receivable—net | 90 | 32 | | | 122 |
| Inventories | 100 | 48 | | | 148 |
| Other current assets | 30 | 17 | | | 47 |
| Plant assets—net | 200 | 76 | | | 276 |
| Investment in Son | 206.1 | | | a 8.1 | |
| | | | | b 198 | |
| Goodwill | | 65 | | | 65 |
| | $655.85 | $251 | | | $700.75 |
| Liabilities | $ 80 | $ 22 | | | $102 |
| Capital stock | 400 | 100 | b 100 | | 400 |
| **Retained earnings** | 175.85 | 9 | | | 175.85 |
| Push-down capital—Son | | 120 | b 120 | | |
| | $655.85 | $251 | | | |
| Noncontrolling interest | | | | b 22 | |
| | | | | c .9 | 22.9 |
| | | | 239 | 239 | $700.75 |

*Noncontrolling interest share = ($19 × 10%).

less-than-100 percent–owned subsidiary, where only the parent's percentage interest is pushed down on the subsidiary's books. The noncontrolling interest amount in Exhibit 11-8 can be determined directly from Son's separate cost-based statements as shown in Exhibit 11-3. Noncontrolling shareholders are not expected to get meaningful information from consolidated financial statements; therefore, the 100 percent push-down approach under entity theory may be preferable, especially when the affiliated group has multiple partially-owned subsidiaries.

## Leveraged Buyouts

In a **leveraged buyout** (LBO), an investor group (often including company management, an investment banker, and financial institutions) acquires a company (Company A) from the public shareholders in a transaction financed with very little equity and very large amounts of debt. Usually, the investor group raises the money for the buyout by investing perhaps 10 percent of their own money and borrowing the rest. A holding company may be formed to acquire the shares of Company A.

Usually debt raised by the investors to finance the LBO is partially secured by Company A's own assets and is serviced with funds generated by Company A's operations and/or the sale of its assets. Because the loans are secured by Company A's assets, banks lending money to the investors often require that the debt appear on Company A's financial statements.

If the previous owners were paid a high premium for their stock, which is often the case, and book values, rather than fair values, of the assets and liabilities are carried forward to the balance sheet of the new company (the acquired Company A), the debt incurred in the LBO may cause the new company's financial condition to look worse than it is. The popularity of LBOs is one reason many accountants support a change to push-down accounting for acquisitions, including LBOs, that would allow the assets of the acquired firm to be written up on its financial statements to reflect the acquisition price.

Both the late 1980s and 1990s witnessed significant LBO activities in U.S. markets. ***Kohlberg, Kravis, Roberts and Company (KKR)*** has been a major acquirer, buying out ***Beatrice Foods*** for $6.25 billion and ***Safeway Stores*** for $4.24 billion, both in 1986, and taking over ***RJR Nabisco*** in 1989 at a cost of $24.72 billion. In 1986, ***Macy Acquisitions Corporation*** was formed to effect an LBO of ***R. H. Macy & Company***, the department store chain, for $3.50 billion. LBO activity has cooled down in recent years due to problems in U.S. and worldwide credit markets.

The structure of a buyout influences the accounting basis for the new entity. For example, a holding company may be used to acquire the net assets of Company A, a holding company may be used to acquire the equity of Company A, or an investor group may acquire Company A without using a holding company. If there has been a change in control, a change in accounting basis for the new entity is generally appropriate, because the new entity has new controlling stockholders and is similar to an acquisition.

## Another Accounting Basis Solution

Corporations have tried to structure business combinations in ways to avoid recording goodwill. A corporation acquires a controlling interest in another company (the target), and, in the same transaction, the target issues additional shares to the parent in exchange for the parent's interest in a subsidiary. In substance, the parent sells its subsidiary to the target as part of the price of acquiring the target. The argument is that this is a combination of enterprises under common control. Therefore, the combination would not be an acquisition and the transaction would be accounted for using historical costs:

- The parent should account for the transfer of the subsidiary to the target as *an acquisition*. This would now be in accordance with GAAP. (ASC 810-10-25) Obtaining control of the target and the transfer of the subsidiary to the target cannot be separated and should be treated as one transaction.

- The parent should account for the transaction as a partial sale of the subsidiary (to the noncontrolling stockholders of the target) and a partial acquisition of the target. The parent should recognize gain or loss on the portion of the subsidiary sold.

- The parent should step up the target's assets and liabilities to the extent acquired by the parent and the subsidiary's assets and liabilities to the extent the ownership interest in the subsidiary was sold.

This structure for business combinations did not avoid acquisition accounting and the resulting goodwill. The pressure to search for ways to avoid recording goodwill diminished in 1993 because goodwill became tax deductible. The fact that goodwill will no longer be amortized (i.e., reducing reported earnings) under GAAP (ASC 350-20-35) eliminates the need to structure combinations to avoid recording goodwill.

## JOINT VENTURES

A *joint venture* is a form of partnership that originated with the maritime trading expeditions of the Greeks and Romans. The objective was to combine management participants and capital contributors in undertakings limited to the completion of specific trading projects. Today the joint venture takes many different forms, such as partnership and corporate, domestic and foreign, and temporary as well as relatively permanent.

A common type of temporary joint venture is the formation of syndicates of investment bankers to purchase securities from an issuing corporation and market them to the public. The joint venture enables several participants to share in the risks and rewards of undertakings that would be too large or too risky for a single venturer. It also enables them to combine technology, markets, and human resources to enhance the profit potential of all participants. Other areas in which joint ventures are common are land sales, oil exploration and drilling, and major construction projects.

New areas and uses for the joint venture form of organization continue to emerge. For example, nearly all major telecommunications companies use joint ventures to gain size and capital. The joint ventures amass capital in order to bid in the multibillion-dollar auction for personal communications services licenses and to build nationwide wireless telephone networks. One advantage of these joint ventures is avoidance of expensive acquisitions.

Joint ventures by U.S. firms are common. An old and well-known example is ***Dow Corning Corporation***, a corporate joint venture of the ***Dow Chemical Company*** and ***Corning Incorporated***. The joint venture allows for a spreading of risk between or among the venturers, making this business form appealing in the oil and gas and chemical industries, and for international investing. The limited liability enjoyed by shareholders makes the corporate form of joint venture especially appealing. Joint ventures are also common in the pharmaceuticals industry.

### Nature of Joint Ventures

A **joint venture** is a business entity that is owned, operated, and jointly controlled by a small group of investors (**venturers**) for the conduct of a specific business undertaking that provides mutual benefit for each of the venturers. It is common for each venturer to be active in management of the venture and to participate in important decisions that typically require the consent of each venturer irrespective of ownership interest. Ownership percentages vary widely, and unequal ownership interests in a specific venture are commonplace.

### Organizational Structures of Joint Ventures

Joint ventures may be organized as corporations, partnerships, or undivided interests. These forms are defined in the AICPA's statement of position, "Accounting for Investment in Real Estate Ventures" *(SOP 78-9)*, as follows:

> **Corporate joint venture.** A corporation owned and operated by a small group of venturers to accomplish a mutually beneficial venture or project.
>
> **General partnership.** An association in which each partner has unlimited liability.
>
> **Limited partnership.** An association in which one or more general partners have unlimited liability, and one or more partners have limited liability. A limited partnership is usually managed by the general partner or partners, subject to limitations, if any, imposed by the partnership agreement.
>
> **Undivided interest.** An ownership arrangement in which two or more parties jointly own property, and title is held individually to the extent of each party's interest.[3]

Financial reporting requirements for the investors in ventures differ according to the organizational structures.

---

[3]Statement of Position 78-9 Accounting for Investments in Real Estate Ventures, © AICPA

## Accounting for Corporate Joint Ventures

Investors who can participate in the overall management of a *corporate joint venture* should report their investments as equity investments (one-line consolidations) under GAAP. (ASC 323-10-15) The approach for establishing significant influence in corporate joint ventures is quite different from that for most common stock investments because *each venturer* usually has to consent to *each significant venture decision*, thus establishing an ability to exercise significant influence regardless of ownership interest. Even so, when a venturer cannot exercise significant influence over its joint venture for whatever reason we account for its investment in the venture by the *cost method*.

An investment in the common stock of a corporate joint venture that exceeds 50 percent of the venture's outstanding shares is a *subsidiary investment*, for which parent–subsidiary accounting and reporting requirements apply. A corporate joint venture that is more than 50 percent owned by another entity is not considered a joint venture, even though it continues to be described as a joint venture in financial releases. GAAP (ASC 323-10-15) describes corporate joint ventures as follows:

> *A corporation owned and operated by a small group of entities (the joint venturers) as a separate and specific business or project for the mutual benefit of the members of the group. A government may also be a member of the group. The purpose of a corporate joint venture frequently is to share risks and rewards in developing a new market, product or technology; to combine complementary technological knowledge; or to pool resources in developing production or other facilities. A corporate joint venture also usually provides an arrangement under which each joint venturer may participate, directly or indirectly, in the overall management of the joint venture. Joint venturers thus have an interest or relationship other than as passive investors. An entity that is a subsidiary of one of the joint venturers is not a corporate joint venture. The ownership of a corporate joint venture seldom changes, and its stock is usually not traded publicly. A noncontrolling interest held by public ownership, however, does not preclude a corporation from being a corporate joint venture.*[4]

Note that a subsidiary (more than 50 percent owned) of a joint venturer is *not* a corporate joint venture under GAAP. (ASC 323-10-15) Instead, we would consolidate it. (ASC 840-10-45)

GAAP concludes that investors in the common stock of corporate joint ventures should account for investments by the equity method in consolidated financial statements. The equity method best enables the investors to reflect the underlying nature of the venture.

Investments in the common stock of joint venturers, or other investments accounted for by the equity method, may be material in relation to the financial position or results of operations of the joint venture investor. If so, it may be necessary for the investor to provide summarized information about the assets, liabilities, and results of operations of its investees in its own financial statements. The required disclosures should be presented *individually* for investments in joint ventures that are material in relation to the financial position or results of operations of the investor. Alternatively, the required disclosures can be *grouped* for investments that are material as a group but are not material individually.

## Accounting for Unincorporated Joint Ventures

GAAP (ASC 323-10-15) also explains that many provisions of corporate joint venture accounting are appropriate in accounting for unincorporated entities. For example, partnership profits and losses accrued by investor-partners are generally reflected in the partners' financial statements. Elimination of intercompany profit in accounting for a partnership interest also seems appropriate, as does providing for deferred income tax liabilities on profits accrued by partner-investors.

The previous discussion of the applicability of GAAP to partnerships also applies to undivided interests in joint ventures, where the investor-venturer owns an undivided interest in each asset and is proportionately liable for its share of each liability. However, the provisions do not apply in some industries that have specialized industry practices. For example, the established industry practice in

---

[4]From Statement of Position on 78-9 Accounting for Investments in Real Estate Ventures December, Proposal to the Financial Accounting Standards Board Issued by Accounting Standards Division © 1978 American Institute of Certified Public Accountants.

oil and gas ventures is for the investor-venturer to account for the pro rata share of the assets, liabilities, revenues, and expenses of a joint venture in its own financial statements. This reporting procedure is referred to as *pro rata or proportionate consolidation.*

Alternatively, the SEC (ASC 323-10-15) recommends against proportionate consolidation for undivided interests in real estate ventures subject to joint control by the investors. A venture is subject to joint control if decisions regarding the financing, development, or sale of property require the approval of two or more owner-venturers. A 1979 AICPA issues paper titled "Joint Venture Accounting" recommended that a venture that is not subject to joint control because its liabilities are several rather than joint be required to use proportionate consolidation.

## One-Line Consolidation and Proportionate Consolidation

To illustrate the reporting alternatives for unincorporated joint ventures, assume that Pam Corporation has a 50 percent undivided interest in Sun Company, a merchandising joint venture. Comparative financial statements under the two assumptions (accounting under the equity method and proportionate consolidation) appear in Exhibit 11-10. Column 1 presents a summary of Pam's income statement and balance sheet, assuming that it uses the equity method of accounting for its investment in Sun, an unconsolidated joint venture company. Sun's income statement and balance sheet are summarized in column 2. In column 3, Pam has consolidated its share (50 percent) of Sun's assets, liabilities, revenues, and expenses (from column 2)—in other words, a proportionate consolidation.

Note that we eliminate Sun's $1,000,000 venture capital in its entirety against the $500,000 Investment in Sun balance, the $100,000 Income from Sun and against half of Sun's asset, liability, revenue, and expense account balances in the proportionate consolidation.

| | Equity Method— Pam Corporation | Sun Unincorporated | Proportionate Consolidation— Pam and Sun |
|---|---|---|---|
| **(All amounts in thousands)** | | | |
| *Income Statement* | | | |
| Revenues | | | |
| Sales | $2,000 | $ 500 | $2,250 |
| Income from Sun | 100 | — | — |
| Total revenue | 2,100 | 500 | 2,250 |
| Expenses | | | |
| Cost of sales | 1,200 | 200 | 1,300 |
| Other expenses | 400 | 100 | 450 |
| Total expenses | 1,600 | 300 | 1,750 |
| Net income | $ 500 | $ 200 | $ 500 |
| *Balance Sheet* | | | |
| Cash | $ 200 | $ 50 | $ 225 |
| Accounts receivable | 300 | 150 | 375 |
| Inventory | 400 | 300 | 550 |
| Plant assets | 800 | 800 | 1,200 |
| Investment in Sun | 500 | — | — |
| Total assets | $2,200 | $ 1,300 | $2,350 |
| Accounts payable | $ 400 | $ 200 | $ 500 |
| Other liabilities | 500 | 100 | 550 |
| Capital stock | 1,000 | — | 1,000 |
| Retained earnings | 300 | — | 300 |
| Venture capital | — | 1,000 | — |
| Total equities | $2,200 | $ 1,300 | $2,350 |

**EXHIBIT 11-10**

**The Equity Method and Proportionate Consolidation Compared**

## ACCOUNTING FOR VARIABLE INTEREST ENTITIES

Companies create special-purpose entities for a variety of valid business reasons. For example, companies separately account for employee benefit plans (pension funds or other postretirement-benefit plans) and do not include such plan accounting as a part of the consolidated financial statements. GAAP (ASC 860-10-05) sets accounting and disclosure rules for these plans.

These special-purpose entities are afforded off-balance-sheet treatment under GAAP. Companies record transactions with these entities, but they do not include the entities in the consolidated financial statements. For example, payments to a pension fund are recorded by the sponsor, but the assets and liabilities of the fund are not included in consolidated balance sheet asset and liability totals. We report the net pension asset or liability on the balance sheet.

However, *Enron Corporation* provides an example in which exclusion of special-purpose entities from the consolidated financial statements gave investors a distorted picture of the company's financial health and business risks. The SEC has alleged financial reporting fraud against Enron in that many of the entities were created primarily to mislead investors, rather than to serve a legitimate business purpose. We will leave discussion of the alleged Enron fraud to other texts and courses on auditing, business law, and business ethics. Our goal here is to provide an introduction to accounting considerations for these special-purpose entities.

In 2003, GAAP (ASC 860-10-60) addressed perceived abuses in accounting for special-purpose entities, and continues to evolve the standard with amendments and clarifications. Both the Financial Accounting Standards Board (FASB) and IASB continue to work on consolidation policy for these entities.

The FASB coined the term *variable interest entities (VIEs)* to define those special-purpose entities that require consolidation. There are a few major issues and concepts to cover. First, does an entity meet the conditions for inclusion in consolidated financial statements? Second, if consolidation is required, how should consolidated amounts be determined? Prior rules for consolidation relied on voting control or percentage ownership of voting shares to decide both of the issues just noted. Current GAAP attempts to identify those entities in which financial control exists because of contractual and financial arrangements other than ownership of voting interests. Recall your early childhood. Your parents did not legally "own" you, but they clearly had financial control over your activities. GAAP now includes companies as VIEs in which the equity investors cannot provide financing for the entity's business risks and activities without additional financial support.

This change does not apply just to Enron. Many companies are required to consolidate VIEs under the new interpretation, even *Disney*. Note 6 to Disney's 2012 annual report (p. 83) discloses that its ownership interests in Disneyland Paris, Hong Kong Disneyland Resort, and Shanghai Disney Resort are all reported as consolidated VIEs, even though some are less than 50 percent owned. Note 6 also provides a condensed consolidated balance sheet and income statement summarizing amounts before and after consolidating these entities as of September 29, 2012. A few items are notable. Consolidated net income is unaffected by the consolidations. Total assets increase from $72,924 million to $74,898 million, primarily due to the reported increase in fixed assets upon consolidation.

### Identifying Variable Interest Entities

A VIE must be consolidated by the primary beneficiary. What is a variable interest? What is a VIE? Our goal here is to provide an understanding of the concepts embodied in current GAAP, not to cover all of the details. (ASC 810-10-15) This is a very complex topic, and identification of a VIE requires considerable judgment.

"Variable interests are contractual, ownership, or other pecuniary interests in a legal entity that change with changes in the fair value of the legal entity's net assets exclusive of variable interests."[5] (ASC 810-10-15) For example, an at-risk equity investment is a variable interest.

GAAP looks at all forms of business entities to identify VIEs. Therefore, a VIE might be another corporation, partnership, limited liability company, or trust-type arrangement. A potential VIE must be

---

[5]FASB ASC 810. Originally Statement of Financial Accounting Standards No. 160. "Noncontrolling Interests." Norwalk, CT © 2007 Financial Accounting Standards Board.

a separate entity, not a subset, branch, or division of another entity. Certain entities, such as pension plans, are specifically excluded, as they are covered by other reporting standards. GAAP defines VIEs requiring consolidation. "The total equity investment at risk is not sufficient to permit the entity to finance its activities without additional subordinated financial support provided by any parties, including equity holders."[6] For example, a company may own only a minimal voting equity interest in an entity, but be contractually required to provide additional financial support in the event of future operating losses.

"The investments or other interests that will absorb portions of a variable interest entity's expected losses or receive portions of the entity's expected residual returns are called variable interests."[7]

> *A variable interest entity's expected losses are the expected negative variability in the fair value of its net assets exclusive of variable interests. A variable interest entity's expected residual returns are the expected positive variability in the fair value of its net assets exclusive of variable interests. Expected variability in the fair value of net assets includes expected variability resulting from operating results of the entity. (ASC 810-10-15-14)*

GAAP offers a general guideline of an equity investment at risk of less than 10 percent of total assets to be indicative of an entity unable to finance operations without additional subordinated financial support. GAAP also describes situations in which an even greater equity interest may be insufficient to indicate financial independence.

Having identified VIEs, entities that will require consolidation, GAAP turns its attention to who will be required to consolidate the VIE. GAAP uses the term **primary beneficiary** to indicate the company that will include the VIE in consolidated statements. There can be only one primary beneficiary. It is possible that no entity is a primary beneficiary (in which case the special purpose entity is not a VIE).

> *All enterprises holding a significant interest in a VIE are required to make disclosures under GAAP. The primary beneficiary must disclose:*

**a.** The nature, purpose, size, and activities of the VIE.

**b.** The carrying amount and classification of consolidated assets that are collateral for the VIE's obligations.

**c.** Lack of recourse if creditors (or beneficial interest holders) of a consolidated VIE have no recourse to the general credit of the primary beneficiary.

Other enterprises, not the primary beneficiary, must disclose:

**a.** The nature of the involvement with the VIE and when that involvement began.

**b.** The nature, purpose, size, and activities of the VIE.

**c.** The enterprise's maximum exposure to loss as a result of its involvement with the VIE.[8]

The other entities (not the primary beneficiaries) account for their investment in the VIE under either the cost or equity methods of accounting.

Current GAAP provides two characteristics, which must both be met, to determine the primary beneficiary. The first is an economic power concept. Does the entity have power to direct the VIE activities that most significantly impact the VIE's economic performance? The second characteristic focuses on legal obligations. Does the entity have an obligation to absorb losses and/or a right to receive significant benefits from the VIE? If one or neither condition is met, the reporting entity is not the primary beneficiary.

Here is a simple example. Ten independent companies—Melanie, Troy, Matthew, Emily, Megan, Danielle, Ryan, Corinne, Tricia, and Lisa Corporations—decide to pool their financial resources for a new business venture investing in offshore oil leases, GetRichQuick Corporation.

---

[6]FASB ASC 810. Originally Statement of Financial Accounting Standards No. 160."Noncontrolling Interests." Norwalk, CT © 2007 Financial Accounting Standards Board.
[7]Statement of Financial Accounting  Standards No. 167. Amendments to FASB Interpretation No. 46(R), © FASB
[8]SUMMARY OF INTERPRETATION NO. 46, © FASB

There is no intent to publicly trade shares of the new company. If the concept is successful, GetRichQuick will provide the investors with enormous future returns, but the venture is not without risk. Each investor contributes $1 million and each receives 10 percent of the voting common stock of GetRichQuick. Additionally, each investor will have one member on the board of directors of the new company. However, the other investors agree that Corinne will have veto power over any business decisions. Under the business plan, GetRichQuick will borrow an additional $20 million to help finance acquisition of leasing rights and subsequent exploration, research, and development. Corinne Corporation agrees to assume 75 percent of losses if the venture is unsuccessful. Corinne believes that the risk is minimal, but offshore oil leasing could produce significant environmental liabilities, well beyond the initial $10 million equity capitalization. In exchange for Corinne's generous offer to absorb a majority of the downside risks, the investors agree that Corinne will receive a 28 percent share of all future profits. The remaining nine investors will each receive an 8 percent profit share.

How should the investors account for their investments in GetRichQuick? At first glance, it appears that all 10 investors would apply the cost method of accounting under current GAAP. No company holds a significant influence or controlling voting interest in the new venture. Assume that the investors correctly determine that GetRichQuick is a VIE under GAAP. One of the investors will be required to consolidate the new venture.

Corinne's contractual agreement makes Corinne the primary beneficiary. Corinne's veto gives the power to direct economic activities of the VIE. Corinne also has an obligation to absorb losses and a right to share benefits from VIE operations. Because both conditions are met, Corinne is the primary beneficiary and is required to consolidate GetRichQuick. The remaining nine investors do not consolidate; however, because GetRichQuick has been identified as a VIE, they are required to make GAAP disclosures and account for their investments using the cost method. (The equity method is not appropriate, because the VIE shares are not publicly traded.)

## Consolidation of a Variable Interest Entity

LEARNING OBJECTIVE **11.5**

We now consider the second issue: How the consolidation should be effected? The rules essentially follow those for any other consolidation. The primary beneficiary measures and consolidates based on the fair values of assets, liabilities, and noncontrolling interest at the date it becomes the primary beneficiary. If the primary beneficiary has transferred assets to the VIE, these should be transferred at the same amounts at which they were carried on the primary beneficiary's books (i.e., no gain or loss is recorded on the transfer). Thus, the primary beneficiary treats the initial valuation consistent with an application of GAAP for an acquisition.

After the initial measurement of fair values and consolidation, the primary beneficiary follows normal consolidation principles in subsequent accounting for the VIE. So the primary beneficiary uses voting interests to allocate future performance among the controlling and noncontrolling interests. All intercompany transactions and account balances must be eliminated. Income or expense due to fees between the primary beneficiary and the VIE must be eliminated against the net income of the VIE. None of these fees should be allocated to any noncontrolling interests.

Estimating the fair value of VIE assets will pose challenges for many firms. Often VIEs invest in unique assets for which fair market values cannot be found from simply looking up a current trading value on a stock exchange. Firms will often need to estimate expected future cash flows associated with VIE operations as a means of estimating fair values.

The 2014 annual report of The Dow Chemical Company provides an example of the company's consolidation policy for VIEs. Note 19 indicates that Dow holds a variable interest in eight joint ventures where Dow is the primary beneficiary. Dow consolidates these eight VIEs in the financial statements. The equity held by the other venturers is shown as noncontrolling interest in the consolidated financial statements.

Dow owns a variable interest in another joint venture where their partner is the primary beneficiary. Dow reports this as an "Investment in nonconsolidated affiliates" using the equity method of accounting. This VIE is not consolidated.[9]

---

[9]Based on The Dow Chemical Company 2014 Annual Report © Anthony H Joseph.

## SUMMARY

This chapter covers different theories related to consolidating the financial statements of a parent and its subsidiaries. It also examines "new basis accounting" for assets and liabilities in a subsidiary's separate financial statements under push-down accounting and describes accounting for corporate joint ventures.

We identify the concepts and procedures underlying current consolidation practices (i.e., current GAAP) to distinguish from accounting practices under parent-company theory. The basic differences between the two theories are compared in a matrix in Exhibit 11-1. Nearly all of the differences disappear when subsidiaries are wholly-owned.

Under push-down accounting, we record the fair values determined in an acquisition in the separate books of the subsidiary. Push-down accounting is ordinarily required by the SEC for combinations in which all or substantially all of the ownership interests in the acquired company change hands. GAAP also now gives companies an option to adopt push-down accounting following an acquisition. Some acquisitions can be structured to avoid push-down accounting.

A joint venture is a business entity that is owned, operated, and jointly controlled by a small group of investors for their mutual benefit. The joint venture investors are usually active in management of the venture, and each venturer usually has the ability to exercise significant influence over the joint venture investee. Investors account for investments in corporate joint ventures as one-line consolidations under the equity method. Similarly, investors account for investments in unincorporated joint ventures (partnerships and undivided interests) as one-line consolidations or proportionate consolidations, depending on the special accounting practices of the industries in which they operate.

Companies also create entities or relationships with other firms for a variety of special business purposes. Often these entities are structured such that an investor has effective economic control, even though the investor lacks voting control through a significant equity ownership interest. GAAP recognizes these situations and requires that the primary beneficiary consolidate these VIEs.

## QUESTIONS

1. Compare the parent-company and entity theories of consolidated financial statements.

2. Under the entity theory, a total valuation of the subsidiary is imputed on the basis of the price paid by the parent company for its controlling interest. Do you see any practical or conceptual problems with this approach?

3. Assume that Pop Corporation acquires 60 percent of the voting common stock of Son Corporation for $6,000,000 and that a consolidated balance sheet is prepared immediately after the acquisition. Would total consolidated assets be equal to their fair values if the parent-company theory were applied? If the entity theory were applied?

4. Cite the conditions under which consolidated net income under parent-company theory would equal income to controlling stockholders under entity theory.

5. If income from a subsidiary is measured under the equity method and the statements are consolidated under entity theory, will consolidated net income equal parent net income?

6. To what extent does push-down accounting facilitate the consolidation process?

7. What is a joint venture and how are joint ventures organized?

8. What accounting and reporting methods are used by investor-venturers in accounting for their joint venture investments?

## EXERCISES

### E 11-1
### Parent-company and entity theories

1. The classification of noncontrolling interest share as an expense and noncontrolling interest as a liability is preferred under:
    a  *Parent-company theory*
    b  *Entity theory*
    c  *Traditional theory*
    d  *None of the above*

2. Consolidated financial statement amounts and classifications should be identical under the entity and parent-company theories of consolidation if:
   a *All subsidiaries are acquired at book value*
   b *Only 100 percent–owned subsidiaries are consolidated*
   c *There are no intercompany transactions*
   d *All subsidiaries are acquired at book value and there are no intercompany transactions*

3. When the fair values of an acquired subsidiary's assets and liabilities are recorded in the subsidiary's accounts (push-down accounting), the subsidiary's retained earnings will be:
   a *Adjusted for the difference between the push-down capital and goodwill from the acquisition*
   b *Credited for the amount of the push-down capital*
   c *Transferred in its entirety to push-down capital*
   d *Credited for the difference between the total imputed value of the entity and the purchase price of the interest acquired*

4. The most consistent statement of assets in consolidated financial statements would result from applying:
   a *Traditional theory*
   b *Parent-company theory*
   c *Entity theory*
   d *None of the above*

# E 11-2
## Joint ventures

1. A joint venture would not be organized as a(an):
   a *Corporation*
   b *Proprietorship*
   c *Partnership*
   d *Undivided interest*

2. Corporate joint ventures should be accounted for by the equity method, provided that the joint venturer:
   a *Cannot exercise significant influence over the joint venture*
   b *Can participate in the overall management of the venture*
   c *Owns more than 50 percent of the joint venture*
   d *All of the above*

3. An investor in a corporate joint venture would be least likely to:
   a *Be active in the management of the venture*
   b *Have an ability to exercise significant influence*
   c *Consent to each significant venture decision*
   d *Hold title to a pro rata share of joint venture assets*

4. Investors account for investments in corporate joint ventures under the equity method if their individual ownership percentages are at least:
   a *10 percent*
   b *20 percent*
   c *50 percent*
   d *None of the above*

5. Far, Get, and Hog Corporations own 60 percent, 25 percent, and 15 percent, respectively, of the common stock of Pod Corporation, a joint venture that they organized for wholesaling fruits. Which of the corporations should report their joint venture interests under the equity method?
   a *Far, Get, and Hog*
   b *Far and Get*
   c *Get and Hog*
   d *Far and Hog*

# E 11-3
## Parent-company and entity theories

1. Pet Company pays $1,440,000 for an 80 percent interest in Sit Corporation on December 31, 2016, when Sit's net assets at book value and fair value are $1,600,000. Under entity theory, the noncontrolling interest at acquisition is:
   a *$288,000*
   b *$320,000*
   c *$360,000*
   d *$400,000*

**2.** Sat Corporation sold inventory items to its parent company, Pan Corporation, during 2016, and at December 31, 2016, Pan's inventory included items acquired from Sat at a gross profit of $100,000. If Sat is an 80 percent–owned subsidiary of Pan, the amount of unrealized inventory profits to be eliminated in preparing the consolidated income statements of Pan and Subsidiary for 2016 is $80,000 under:

a **Parent-company theory**
b **Traditional theory**
c **Entity theory**
d **The equity method of accounting**

**3.** A parent company that applies the entity theory of consolidation in preparing its consolidated financial statements computed income from its 90 percent–owned subsidiary under the equity method of accounting as follows:

| | |
|---|---|
| Equity in subsidiary income ($400,000 × 90%) | $360,000 |
| Patent amortization ($140,000 ÷ 10 years × 90%) | (12,600) |
| Income from subsidiary | $347,400 |

Given the foregoing information, noncontrolling interest share is:

a **$40,000**
b **$38,600**
c **$36,000**
d **$34,600**

**4.** Pad Corporation acquired an 80 percent interest in Sun Corporation on January 1, 2016, when Sun's total stockholders' equity was $1,680,000. The book values and fair values of Sun's assets and liabilities were equal on this date.

At December 31, 2016, the consolidated balance sheet of Pad and Subsidiary shows unamortized patents from consolidation of $108,000, with a note that the patents are being amortized over a 10-year period.

If the entity theory of consolidation was used, the purchase price of the 80 percent interest in Sun must have been:

a **$1,440,000**
b **$1,464,000**
c **$1,494,000**
d **$1,800,000**

## E 11-4
## Computations (parent-company and entity theories)

Balance sheet information of Pop and Son Corporations at December 31, 2015, is summarized as follows (in thousands):

| | Pop Book Value | Son Book Value | Son Fair Value |
|---|---|---|---|
| Current assets | $ 520 | $ 50 | $ 90 |
| Plant assets—net | 480 | 250 | 360 |
| | $1,000 | $300 | $450 |
| Current liabilities | $ 80 | $ 40 | $ 50 |
| Capital stock | 800 | 200 | |
| Retained earnings | 120 | 60 | |
| | $1,000 | $300 | |

On January 2, 2016, Pop purchases 80 percent of Son's outstanding shares for $500,000 cash.

**REQUIRED**

**1.** Determine goodwill from the acquisition under (a) parent-company theory and (b) entity theory.

**2.** Determine noncontrolling interest at January 2, 2016, under (a) parent-company theory and (b) entity theory.

**3.** Determine the amount of total assets that would appear on a consolidated balance sheet prepared at January 2, 2016, under (a) parent-company theory and (b) entity theory.

## E 11-5
## Computations under parent-company and entity theories (fair value/book value differentials)

On January 1, 2017, Pam Corporation pays $600,000 for an 80 percent interest in Sun Company, when Sun's net assets have a book value of $550,000 and a fair value of $700,000. The $150,000 excess fair value is due to undervalued equipment with a five-year remaining useful life. Any goodwill is not amortized.

Separate incomes of Pam and Sun for 2017 are $1,000,000 and $100,000, respectively.

### REQUIRED

1. Calculate consolidated net income and noncontrolling interest share under (a) parent-company theory and (b) entity theory.
2. Determine goodwill at December 31, 2017, under (a) parent-company theory and (b) entity theory.

## E 11-6
## Computations under parent-company and entity theories (midyear acquisition)

Son Corporation's recorded assets and liabilities are equal to their fair values on July 1, 2017, when Pop Corporation purchases 36,000 shares of Son common stock for $900,000. Identifiable net assets of Son on this date are $855,000, and Son's stockholders' equity consists of $400,000 of $10 par common stock and $455,000 retained earnings.

Son has net income for 2017 of $40,000 earned evenly throughout the year and declares no dividends.

### REQUIRED

1. Determine the total value of Son's net assets at July 1, 2017, under entity theory.
2. Determine goodwill that would appear in a consolidated balance sheet of Pop Corporation and Subsidiary at July 1, 2017, under (a) entity theory and (b) parent-company theory.
3. Determine Pop's investment income from Son on an equity basis for 2017.
4. Determine noncontrolling interest in Son that will be reported in the consolidated balance sheet at December 31, 2017, under entity theory.

## E 11-7
## Computations under parent-company and entity theories (upstream sales)

Pam Company acquired an 80 percent interest in Sun Corporation at book value equal to fair value on January 1, 2016. During the year, Sun sold $50,000 inventory items to Pam, and at December 31, 2016, unrealized profits amounted to $15,000. Separate incomes of Pam and Sun for 2016 were $250,000 and $150,000, respectively.

### REQUIRED

1. Determine consolidated net income for Pam Company and Subsidiary under the parent-company theory of consolidation.
2. Determine total consolidated income for Pam Company and Subsidiary, income to controlling stockholders, and income to noncontrolling stockholders under the entity theory of consolidation.

## E 11-8
## Compute consolidated net income under two theories (upstream and downstream sales)

Pop Corporation acquired an 80 percent interest in Son Company at book value a number of years ago.

Separate incomes of Pop and Son for 2016 were $120,000 and $60,000, respectively. The only transactions between Pop and Son during 2016 were as follows:

1. Pop sold inventory items to Son for $60,000. These items cost Pop $30,000, and half the items were still inventoried at $30,000 by Son at December 31, 2016.
2. Son sold land that cost $70,000 to Pop for $96,000 during 2016. The land was still held by Pop at December 31, 2016.
3. Son paid $24,000 dividends to Pop during 2016.

**REQUIRED:** Compute consolidated net income for Pop Corporation and Subsidiary for 2016 under:

1. Parent-company theory
2. Entity theory

## E 11-9
## Journal entries for push-down accounting

On January 1, 2016, Pam Corporation acquired a 90 percent interest in Sun Corporation for $1,260,000. The book values and fair values of Sun's assets and equities on this date are as follows (in thousands):

| | Book Value | Fair Value |
|---|---|---|
| Cash | $ 100 | $ 100 |
| Accounts receivable—net | 150 | 150 |
| Inventories | 250 | 300 |
| Land | 150 | 400 |
| Buildings—net | 350 | 500 |
| Equipment—net | 400 | 300 |
| | $1,400 | $1,750 |
| Accounts payable | $ 275 | $ 275 |
| Other liabilities | 225 | 275 |
| Capital stock | 500 | |
| Retained earnings | 400 | |
| | $1,400 | |

**REQUIRED**

1. Prepare the journal entries on Sun Corporation's books to push down the values reflected in the acquisition price under *parent-company theory*.

2. Prepare the journal entries on Sun Corporation's books to push down the values reflected in the acquisition price under *entity theory*.

## E 11-10
## Determine investment income for corporate joint venturers

Sun Corporation is a corporate joint venture that is jointly controlled and operated by five investor-venturers, four with 15 percent interests each and one with a 40 percent interest. Each of the five venturers is active in venture management. Land sales and other important venture decisions require the consent of each venturer. All venturers paid $15 per share for their investments on January 1, 2016, and no changes in ownership interests have occurred since that time. During 2017, Sun reported net income of $500,000 and paid dividends of $100,000. The stockholders' equity of Sun at December 31, 2017, is as follows (in thousands):

**Sun Corporation Stockholders' Equity at December 31, 2017**

| | |
|---|---|
| Common stock $10 par, 500,000 shares authorized, issued, and outstanding | $5,000 |
| Additional paid-in capital | 2,500 |
| Total paid-in capital | 7,500 |
| Retained earnings | 1,000 |
| Total stockholders' equity | $8,500 |

**REQUIRED:** Determine the investment income for 2017 and the investment account balance at December 31, 2017, for the 40 percent venturer and for one of the 15 percent venturers.

## E 11-11
## Accounting for a VIE beyond the initial measurement date

Pop Corporation is the primary beneficiary in a VIE, even though Pop owns only 10 percent of the outstanding voting shares. In the year following the initial consolidation, the VIE earns net income of $2,000,000. Included in income is a fee paid by Pop for $160,000. What amount of noncontrolling interest share will appear in the consolidated income statement?

## E 11-12
## VIE reporting and disclosure requirements

Pam, Inc., holds an interest in Sun Corporation. Pam has determined that Sun qualifies as a VIE and that Pam's contractual position makes Pam the primary beneficiary. Den Corporation also holds a significant financial interest in Sun. What are the financial reporting and disclosure requirements for both Pam and Den?

## E 11-13
### Determining the primary beneficiary in a VIE

Pop Corporation and Son Company participate in a business classified as a VIE. Under terms of their contractual arrangement, Pop and Son share equally in expected residual returns of the VIE. However, expected losses are allocated 70 percent to Son and 30 percent to Pop. Son serves as CEO and has the final decision on all operating and financing matters. Which of the Investors is the primary beneficiary in this VIE?

## PROBLEMS

## P 11-1
### Consolidated balance sheets (parent-company and entity theories)

The adjusted trial balances of Pop Corporation and its 80 percent–owned subsidiary, Son Corporation, at December 31, 2017, are as follows (in thousands):

|                      | Pop      | Son      |
|----------------------|----------|----------|
| Cash                 | $   64   | $    40  |
| Receivables—net      | 240      | 360      |
| Inventories          | 600      | 300      |
| Plant assets—net     | 2,400    | 1,500    |
| Investment in Son    | 1,504    | —        |
| Cost of sales        | 2,600    | 1,200    |
| Depreciation         | 450      | 150      |
| Other expenses       | 542      | 350      |
| Dividends            | 400      | 100      |
|                      | $8,800   | $4,000   |
| Accounts payable     | $  408   | $  200   |
| Other liabilities    | 600      | 400      |
| Capital stock        | 2,000    | 1,000    |
| Retained earnings    | 1,600    | 400      |
| Sales                | 4,000    | 2,000    |
| Income from Son      | 192      | —        |
|                      | $8,800   | $4,000   |

Pop acquired its interest in Son for $1,280,000 on January 1, 2016, when Son's stockholders' equity consisted of $1,000,000 capital stock and $200,000 retained earnings. The excess cost was due to a $200,000 undervaluation of plant assets with a 5-year remaining useful life and to previously unrecorded patents with a 10-year amortization period. Pop uses a one-line consolidation in accounting for its investment in Son.

---

**REQUIRED:** Prepare comparative consolidated balance sheets at December 31, 2017, for Pop Corporation and Subsidiary under (a) parent-company theory and (b) entity theory.

---

## P 11-2
### Consolidated balance sheet and income statement under entity theory

Pam Corporation acquires an 80 percent interest in Sun Company on January 3, 2016, for $640,000. On this date Sun's stockholders' equity consists of $400,000 capital stock and $280,000 retained earnings. The fair value/book value differential is assigned to undervalued equipment with a 6-year remaining life. Immediately after acquisition, Sun sells equipment with a 10-year remaining useful life to Pam at a gain of $20,000.

Adjusted trial balances of Pam and Sun at December 31, 2016, are as follows (in thousands):

|                      | Pam      | Sun      |
|----------------------|----------|----------|
| Current assets       | $  606.4 | $  360   |
| Plant and equipment  | 1,600    | 800      |
| Investment in Sun    | 673.6    | —        |
| Cost of sales        | 1,000    | 520      |
| Depreciation         | 200      | 100      |
| Other expenses       | 240      | 80       |
| Dividends            | 200      | 40       |
|                      | $4,520   | $1,900   |

*(continued)*

|                          | Pam     | Sun    |
|--------------------------|---------|--------|
| Accumulated depreciation | $  600  | $200   |
| Liabilities              | 400     | 200    |
| Capital stock            | 1,200   | 400    |
| Retained earnings        | 654.4   | 280    |
| Sales                    | 1,600   | 800    |
| Gain on plant assets     | —       | 20     |
| Income from Sun          | 65.6    | —      |
|                          | $4,520  | $1,900 |

## REQUIRED

**1.** Prepare a consolidated income statement for 2016 using entity theory.

**2.** Prepare a consolidated balance sheet at December 31, 2016, using entity theory.

## P 11-3
## Computations (parent-company and entity theories)

Pop Corporation paid $1,190,000 cash for 70 percent of the outstanding voting stock of Son Corporation on January 2, 2017, when Son Corporation's stockholders' equity consisted of $1,000,000 of $10 par common stock and $500,000 retained earnings. The book values of Son's assets and liabilities were equal to their fair values on this date.

During 2017, Pop Corporation had separate income of $600,000 and paid dividends of $300,000. Son Corporation's net income for 2017 was $180,000 and its dividends were $100,000. At December 31, 2017, the stockholders' equities of Pop and Son were as follows (in thousands):

|                            | Pop      | Son      |
|----------------------------|----------|----------|
| Common stock ($10 par)     | $2,800   | $1,000   |
| Retained earnings          | 900      | 580      |
| Total stockholders' equity | $3,700   | $1,580   |

There were no intercompany transactions between Pop Corporation and Son Corporation during 2017. Pop uses the equity method of accounting for its investment in Son.

## REQUIRED

**1.** Assume that Pop Corporation uses parent-company theory for preparing consolidated financial statements for 2017. Determine the following amounts:
   a. Pop Corporation's income from Son for 2017
   b. Goodwill that will appear in the consolidated balance sheet at December 31, 2017
   c. Consolidated net income for 2017
   d. Noncontrolling interest expense for 2017
   e. Noncontrolling interest at December 31, 2017

**2.** Assume that Pop Corporation uses entity theory for preparing consolidated financial statements for 2017. Determine the following amounts:
   a. Pop Corporation's income from Son for 2017
   b. Goodwill that will appear in the consolidated balance sheet at December 31, 2017
   c. Total consolidated income for 2017
   d. Noncontrolling interest share for 2017
   e. Noncontrolling interest at December 31, 2017

## P 11-4
## Comparative consolidated statements under alternative theories

At December 31, 2016, when the fair values of Sun Corporation's net assets were equal to their book values of $2,400,000, Pam Corporation acquired an 80 percent interest in Sun for $2,240,000. One year later, at December 31, 2017, the comparative adjusted trial balances of the two corporations appear as follows (in thousands):

|  | Pam Corporation | Sun Corporation |
|---|---|---|
| Cash | $    408 | $   700 |
| Accounts receivable | 900 | 300 |
| Inventory | 1,600 | 400 |
| Land | 2,000 | 800 |
| Buildings | 9,000 | 2,000 |
| Investment in Sun | 2,400 | — |
| Cost of sales | 3,750 | 2,000 |
| Expenses | 1,500 | 500 |
| Dividends | 1,200 | 300 |
| Total debits | $22,758 | $ 7,000 |
| Accumulated depreciation | $ 2,000 | $   600 |
| Accounts payable | 1,758 | 1,000 |
| Capital stock | 8,000 | 2,000 |
| Retained earnings | 3,600 | 400 |
| Sales | 7,000 | 3,000 |
| Income from Sun | 400 | — |
| Total credits | $22,758 | $ 7,000 |

### ADDITIONAL INFORMATION:

During 2017, Sun Corporation sold inventory items costing $150,000 to Pam for $230,000. Half of these inventory items remain unsold at December 31, 2017.

**REQUIRED:** Prepare comparative consolidated financial statements for Pam Corporation and Subsidiary at and for the year ended December 31, 2017, under

1. Parent-company theory
2. Entity theory

## P 11-5
## Comparative balance sheets under entity theory

Balance sheets for Pop Corporation and its 80 percent–owned subsidiary, Son Company, at December 31, 2017, are summarized as follows (in thousands):

|  | Pop | Son |
|---|---|---|
| *Assets* | | |
| Cash | $   100 | $ 40 |
| Receivables—net | 150 | 70 |
| Inventories | 220 | 60 |
| Plant assets—net | 430 | 170 |
| Investment in Sit | 288 | — |
| Total assets | $1,188 | $340 |
| *Liabilities and Stockholders' Equity* | | |
| Accounts payable | $   160 | $ 30 |
| Other liabilities | 40 | 10 |
| Total liabilities | 200 | 40 |
| Capital stock | 600 | 200 |
| Retained earnings | 388 | 100 |
| Stockholders' equity | 988 | 300 |
| Total equities | $1,188 | 340 |

### ADDITIONAL INFORMATION

1. Pop Corporation paid $256,000 for its 80 percent interest in Son on January 1, 2016, when Son had capital stock of $200,000 and retained earnings of $20,000.
2. At December 31, 2017, Pop's inventory included items on which Son had recorded gross profit of $40,000.

**REQUIRED:** Prepare a consolidated balance sheet for Pop Corporation and Subsidiary at December 31, 2017, under the entity theory of consolidation.

## P 11-6
### [Based on AICPA] Separate and consolidated financial statements—entity theory

The individual and consolidated balance sheets and income statements of P and S Companies for the current year are presented in the accompanying table. The entity theory is used.

### ADDITIONAL INFORMATION

1. P Company purchased its interest in S Company several years ago.

2. P Company sells products to S Company for further processing and also sells to firms outside the affiliated entity. The inventories of S Company include an intercompany profit at both the beginning and the end of the year.

3. At the beginning of the current year, S Company purchased bonds of P Company having a maturity value of $100,000. These bonds are being held as available-for-sale securities and are, correspondingly, carried at fair value. No change in fair value has occurred over the course of the year. S Company has agreed to offer P Company the option of reacquiring the bonds at S's cost before deciding to dispose of them on the open market.

**P and S Companies' Individual and Consolidated Balance Sheets as of the End of the Current Year (in thousands)**

|  | P Company | S Company | Consolidated |
|---|---|---|---|
| *Assets* | | | |
| Cash and receivables | $ 35 | $108 | $ 97.4 |
| Inventories | 40 | 90 | 122 |
| Plant (net) | 460 | 140 | 600 |
| Patents | — | — | 30 |
| Investment in S | 245 | — | — |
| P bonds owned | — | 103 | — |
| Total assets | $780 | $441 | $849.4 |
| *Liabilities and Equity* | | | |
| Current payables | $ 70 | $ 23 | $ 53 |
| Dividends payable | 10 | 8 | 12.4 |
| Mortgage bonds (5%) | 200 | 50 | 150 |
| Capital stock | 300 | 200 | 300 |
| Retained earnings | 200 | 160 | 217 |
| Noncontrolling interest | — | — | 117 |
| Total liabilities and equity | $780 | $441 | $849.4 |

**Individual and Consolidated Income Statements for the Current Year**

|  | P Company | S Company | Consolidated |
|---|---|---|---|
| Sales | $600 | $400 | $760 |
| Cost of sales | (360) | (280) | (403) |
| Gross profit | 240 | 120 | 357 |
| Operating expenses | (130) | (54) | (189) |
| Operating profit | 110 | 66 | 168 |
| Interest revenue | 1.8 | 5 | 1.8 |
| Dividend revenue | 11.2 | — | — |
|  | 123 | 71 | 169.8 |
| Interest expense | (10) | (3) | (8) |
| Provision for income tax | (56) | (34) | (90) |
| Nonrecurring loss | — | — | (3) |
| Noncontrolling share | — | — | (60.1) |
| Net income | $ 57 | $ 34 | $ 8.7 |
| Dividends | (20) | (16) | (24.8) |
| Transfer to retained earnings | $ 37 | $ 18 | $ (16.1) |

**REQUIRED:** Answer the following questions on the basis of the preceding information.

1. Does P Company carry its investment in S Company on the cost or the equity basis? Explain the basis of your answer.

2. If S Company's common stock has a stated value of $100 per share, how many shares does P Company own? How did you determine this?

3. When P acquired its interest in S Company, the assets and liabilities of S Company were recorded at their fair values. The $30,000 patents represent unamortized patents at the end of the current year. The unrecorded patents were $50,000 under entity theory, and the amortization is over a 10-year period. What was the amount of S's retained earnings at the date that P Company acquired its interest in S Company?

4. What is the nature of the nonrecurring loss appearing on the consolidated income statement? Reproduce the consolidating entry from which this figure originated and explain.

5. What is the amount of intercompany sales during the current year by P Company to S Company?

6. Are there any intercompany debts other than the intercompany bondholdings? Identify any such debts, and state which company is the debtor and which is the creditor in each case. Explain your reasoning.

7. What is the explanation for the difference between the consolidated cost of goods sold and the combined cost of goods sold of the two affiliated companies? Prepare a schedule reconciling combined and consolidated cost of goods sold, showing the amount of intercompany profit in the beginning and ending inventories of S Company and demonstrating how you determined the amount of intercompany profit. (*Hint:* A well-organized and labeled T-account for cost of goods sold will be an acceptable approach.)

8. Show how the $8,700 noncontrolling interest share in total consolidated net income was determined.

9. Show how the total noncontrolling interest on the balance sheet ($117,000) was determined.

10. Beginning with the $200,000 balance in P Company's retained earnings at the end of the current year, prepare a schedule in which you derive the $217,000 balance of consolidated retained earnings at the end of the current year.

## P 11-7
### Journal entry to record push-down, subsidiary balance sheet, and investment income

Pam Corporation paid $960,000 cash for a 100 percent interest in Sun Corporation on January 1, 2017, when Sun's stockholders' equity consisted of $400,000 capital stock and $160,000 retained earnings. Sun's balance sheet on December 31, 2016, is summarized as follows (in thousands):

|  | Book Value | Fair Value |
|---|---|---|
| Cash | $ 60 | $ 60 |
| Accounts receivable—net | 140 | 140 |
| Inventories | 120 | 160 |
| Land | 100 | 150 |
| Buildings—net | 200 | 380 |
| Equipment—net | 180 | 150 |
| Total assets | $ 800 | $1,040 |
| Accounts payable | $ 100 | $ 100 |
| Other liabilities | 140 | $ 120 |
| Capital stock | 400 | |
| Retained earnings | 160 | |
| Total equities | $ 800 | |

Pam uses the equity method to account for its interest in Sun. The amortization periods for the fair value/book value differentials at the time of acquisition were as follows:

| $ 40,000 | Undervalued inventories (sold in 2017) |
|---|---|
| 50,000 | Undervalued land |
| 180,000 | Undervalued buildings (10-year useful life remaining) |
| (30,000) | Overvalued equipment (5-year useful life remaining) |
| 20,000 | Other liabilities (2 years before maturity) |
| 140,000 | Goodwill |

### REQUIRED

1. Prepare a journal entry on Sun's books to push down the values reflected in the purchase price. Use entity theory.

2. Prepare a balance sheet for Sun Corporation on January 1, 2017.

3. Sun's net income for 2017 under the new push-down accounting system is $180,000. What is Pam's income from Sun for 2017?

### P 11-8
### Journal entries and calculations for push-down accounting

Pop Corporation paid $3,000,000 for an 80 percent interest in Son Corporation on January 1, 2016, when the book values and fair values of Son's assets and liabilities were as follows (in thousands):

|  | Book Value | Fair Value |
|---|---|---|
| Cash | $ 300 | $ 300 |
| Accounts receivable—net | 600 | 600 |
| Inventories | 800 | 2,400 |
| Land | 200 | 200 |
| Buildings—net | 600 | 600 |
| Equipment—net | 1,000 | 500 |
|  | $3,500 | $4,600 |
| Accounts payable | $ 500 | $ 500 |
| Long-term debt | 1,000 | 1,000 |
| Capital stock, $1 par | 800 |  |
| Retained earnings | 1,200 |  |
|  | $3,500 |  |

#### REQUIRED

1. Prepare a journal entry on Son's books to push down 80 percent of the values reflected in the purchase price (the parent-company-theory approach).
2. Prepare a journal entry on Son's books to push down 100 percent of the values reflected in the purchase price (the entity-theory approach).
3. Calculate the noncontrolling interest in Son on January 1, 2016, under parent-company theory.
4. Calculate the noncontrolling interest in Son on January 1, 2016, under entity theory.

### P 11-9
### Journal entries and comparative balance sheets at acquisition for push-down

Pam Corporation paid $180,000 cash for a 90 percent interest in Sun Corporation on January 1, 2017, when Sun's stockholders' equity consisted of $100,000 capital stock and $20,000 retained earnings. Sun Corporation's balance sheets at book value and fair value on December 31, 2016, are as follows (in thousands):

|  | Book Value | Fair Value |
|---|---|---|
| Cash | $ 20 | $ 20 |
| Accounts receivable—net | 50 | 50 |
| Inventories | 40 | 30 |
| Land | 15 | 15 |
| Buildings—net | 30 | 50 |
| Equipment—net | 70 | 100 |
| Total assets | $225 | $265 |
| Accounts payable | $ 45 | $ 45 |
| Other liabilities | 60 | 60 |
| Capital stock | 100 |  |
| Retained earnings | 20 |  |
| Total equities | $225 |  |

#### ADDITIONAL INFORMATION

1. The amortization periods for the fair value/book value differentials at the time of acquisition are as follows:

| | |
|---|---|
| Overvalued inventories (sold in 2017) | $10,000 |
| Undervalued buildings (10-year useful lives) | 20,000 |
| Undervalued equipment (5-year useful lives) | 30,000 |
| Goodwill | Remainder |

2. Pam uses the equity method to account for its interest in Sun.

## REQUIRED

1. Prepare a journal entry on Sun Corporation's books to push down the values reflected in the purchase price under parent-company theory.
2. Prepare a journal entry on Sun Corporation's books to push down the values reflected in the purchase price under entity theory.
3. Prepare comparative balance sheets for Sun Corporation on January 1, 2017, under the approaches of (1) and (2).

## P 11-10
### Consolidation workpaper one year after acquisition under push-down accounting (both 90%- and 100%-ownership assumptions)

Use the information and assumptions from Problem P 11-9 for this problem. The accompanying financial statements are for Pam and Sun Corporations, one year after the acquisition. Note that Sun's statements are presented first under 90 percent push-down accounting, and then under 100 percent push-down accounting.

Sun mailed a check to Pam on December 31, 2017, to settle an account payable of $8,000. Pam received the check in 2018. The $8,000 amount is included in Pam's December 31, 2017, accounts receivable.

**Pam Corporation and Sun Corporation Comparative Financial Statements with Push-Down Accounting at and for the Year Ended December 31, 2017 (in Thousands)**

|  | Basic Accounting Pam | Push Down 90% Sun | Push Down 100% Sun |
|---|---|---|---|
| *Income Statement* |  |  |  |
| Sales | $310.8 | $110 | $110 |
| Income from Sun | 37.8 | — | — |
| Cost of sales | (140) | (33) | (32) |
| Depreciation expense | (29) | (24.2) | (25) |
| Other operating expenses | (45) | (11) | (11) |
| Net income | $134.6 | $ 41.8 | $ 42 |
| *Retained Earnings* |  |  |  |
| Retained earnings—beginning | $147 | $ — | $ — |
| Add: Net income | 134.6 | 41.8 | 42 |
| Deduct: Dividends | (60) | (10) | (10) |
| Retained earnings—ending | $221.6 | $ 31.8 | $ 32 |
| *Balance Sheet* |  |  |  |
| Cash | $ 63.8 | $ 27 | $ 27 |
| Accounts receivable | 90 | 40 | 40 |
| Dividends receivable | 9 | — | — |
| Inventories | 20 | 35 | 35 |
| Land | 40 | 15 | 15 |
| Buildings—net | 140 | 43.2 | 45 |
| Equipment—net | 165 | 77.6 | 80 |
| Investment in Sun | 208.8 | — | — |
| Goodwill | — | 36 | 40 |
| Total assets | $736.6 | $273.8 | $282 |
| Accounts payable | $125 | $ 20 | $ 20 |
| Dividends payable | 15 | 10 | 10 |
| Other liabilities | 75 | 20 | 20 |
| Capital stock | 300 | 100 | 100 |
| Push-down capital | — | 92 | 100 |
| Retained earnings | 221.6 | 31.8 | 32 |
| Total equities | $736.6 | $273.8 | $282 |

**REQUIRED:** Prepare consolidation workpapers for Pam Corporation and Subsidiary for the year ended December 31, 2017, under (a) 90 percent push-down accounting and (b) 100 percent push-down accounting.

## P 11-11
### Workpaper for proportionate consolidation (joint venture)

Pop Corporation owns a 40 percent interest in Son Company, a joint venture that is organized as an undivided interest. In its separate financial statements, Pop accounts for Son under the equity method, but for reporting purposes, the proportionate consolidation method is used.

Separate financial statements of Pop and Son at and for the year ended December 31, 2016, are summarized as follows (in thousands):

|  | Pop Corporation | Son Company |
|---|---|---|
| *Combined Income and Retained Earnings* | | |
| *Statements for the Year Ended December 31, 2016* | | |
| Sales | $ 800 | $300 |
| Income from Son | 20 | — |
| Cost of sales | (400) | (150) |
| Depreciation expense | (100) | (40) |
| Other expenses | (120) | (60) |
| Net income | 200 | 50 |
| Beginning retained earnings | 300 | — |
| Beginning venture equity | — | 250 |
| Dividends | (100) | — |
| Retained earnings/venture equity | $ 400 | $300 |
| *Balance Sheets at December 31, 2016* | | |
| Cash | $ 100 | $ 50 |
| Receivables—net | 130 | 30 |
| Inventories | 110 | 40 |
| Land | 140 | 60 |
| Buildings—net | 200 | 100 |
| Equipment—net | 300 | 180 |
| Investment in Son | 120 | — |
| Total assets | $1,100 | $460 |
| Accounts payable | $ 120 | $100 |
| Other liabilities | 80 | 60 |
| Common stock, $10 par | 500 | — |
| Retained earnings | 400 | — |
| Venture equity | — | 300 |
| Total equities | $1,100 | $460 |

**REQUIRED:** Prepare a workpaper for a proportionate consolidation of the financial statements of Pop Corporation and Son Company at and for the year ended December 31, 2016.

# PROFESSIONAL RESEARCH ASSIGNMENTS

Answer the following questions by reference to the FASB Codification of Accounting Standards. Include the appropriate reference in your response.

**PR 11-1** This chapter noted that an acquired firm may elect push-down accounting. If the transaction results in recognition of goodwill, should that goodwill also be reflected on the acquiree's financial statements?

**PR 11-2** What disclosures are required for a variable interest entity? Are the disclosures only required for VIEs that will be consolidated?

# CHAPTER 12

# Derivatives and Foreign Currency: Concepts and Common Transactions

This chapter covers the economics of derivatives and foreign currency transactions and how firms manage the risks they face. The next chapter covers hedge accounting, which will include the accounting for derivatives used for hedging risks. We first introduce some concepts about risk and how firms can manage risk with derivatives. Then we describe different types of derivatives. Finally, we discuss concepts and transactions involving foreign currency–denominated transactions.

## DERIVATIVES

### Definitions

**Derivative** is the name given to a broad range of financial securities. Their common characteristic is that the derivative contract's value to the investor has a direct relationship to fluctuations in price, rate, or some other variable that *underlies* it. Using a derivative contract can limit businesses' exposure to price or rate fluctuations. One party to the contract, in effect, bets that the underlying price or rate will move in the opposite direction to what the other party is expecting. A party trying to control its economic rate or price change risk is engaging in a derivative, or *hedge contract*. Contract structures and the accounting for such contracts vary across the types of risk managed.

Interest rates, commodity prices, foreign currency exchange rates, and stock prices are the most common types of price and rate risks that companies hedge. For example, *Starbucks* faces a variety of risks including interest rate risk, commodity price fluctuation, and foreign currency fluctuation. Because Starbucks forecasts future cash flows and earnings based on future rates and prices, it enters into derivative contracts to manage the risk of those future outcomes.[1] By entering into these types of agreements, Starbucks locks in exchange rates, interest rates, and commodity prices, reducing the effects of future changes in exchange rates, interest rates, and commodity prices, on its cash flow and income.

In 2014 the apparel and footwear company *Wolverine Worldwide* held an interest rate swap. This derivative, in effect, converts $405,400,000 of their $525,200,000 variable rate loans from variable-rate to fixed-rate agreements. Usually, firms negotiate interest rate swap agreements with financial institutions. Like Starbucks, Wolverine Worldwide is reducing the variability of its future cash flow streams and income by entering into this type of agreement.

Companies enter into derivative contracts to reduce the vulnerability of their cash flows, market values of assets and liabilities, and earnings to changes in the prices of goods, commodities, and

LEARNING OBJECTIVE **12.1**

### LEARNING OBJECTIVES

**12.1** Understand the definition of a derivative and the types of risks that derivatives can manage.

**12.2** Understand the structure, benefits, and costs of options, futures contracts, forward contracts, and swaps.

**12.3** Understand key concepts related to foreign currency exchange rates, such as indirect and direct quotes; floating, fixed, and multiple exchange rates; and spot, current, and historical exchange rates.

**12.4** Explain the difference between receivable or payable measurement and denomination.

**12.5** Record foreign currency–denominated sales/receivables and purchases/payables at the initial transaction date, period-end, and the receivable or payable settlement date.

---

[1] *Source:* Starbucks' fiscal 2015 annual report.

financial instruments that they purchase, sell, or invest in. Typical forms of derivative instruments are option contracts, forward contracts, futures contracts, and swaps.

## Hedge Transactions

*Hedge* is the term we use to describe a combined transaction of an existing position and a derivative contract designed to manage the risks the firm faces by holding the existing position alone. Most firms create hedges by using one of a few basic types of derivatives: forward contracts, futures contracts, options, or swaps.

**Forward contracts** are negotiated contracts between two parties for the delivery or purchase of a commodity or foreign currency at a preagreed price, quantity, and delivery date. The agreement may require actual physical delivery of the goods, or currency, or may allow a net settlement.

**Net settlement** allows the payment of money so that the parties are in the same economic condition as they would have been if delivery had occurred. For example, assume that BigOil wants to reduce its vulnerability to future oil-price changes and contracts with an oil-price speculator to buy 10,000 barrels of oil at $100 per barrel in three months. In three months, when the contract settles, oil is selling on the open market at $110 per barrel. Because BigOil has locked in a $100 per barrel price, the speculator could be required to either deliver 10,000 barrels of oil to BigOil in exchange for $100 per barrel or settle the contract net. In a net settlement situation, the speculator would not deliver 10,000 barrels of oil but would pay BigOil $100,000 (($110 − $100) × 10,000) to settle the contract. BigOil would then buy the oil in the open market at $110 per barrel ($100 from BigOil and $10 from the payment from the speculator). BigOil and the speculator are in the same position economically as they would have been if an actual exchange of oil had occurred between them. Companies plan many derivative transactions in a similar fashion; the derivative's value mimics a physical transaction and then settles in cash.

**Futures contracts** and forward contracts have essentially the same contracting characteristics, except futures differ from forward contracts in ways that allow them to easily trade in markets. Futures contracts are very standardized. A futures exchange, not the trading parties, determines the contract termination date, the exact quality and quantity of the goods to be delivered, and the delivery location. The exchange guarantees the performance of both clearing firms engaged in the trade, which in turn guarantee the performance of the traders they represent.

To get out of a futures position, one can simply purchase or sell an identical contract in the opposite direction. The exchange will then cancel the two positions, so the net position is zero. One need not take delivery of the commodity. At the end of each day, the exchange computes the gain or loss on the trader's position and charges or credits their account. In essence, the markets use a daily mark-to-market approach through these cash payments.

The cost of contracting in a futures market is generally lower than using a forward contract. In addition, the exchange and clearing houses guarantee performance or carrying out of the contract's terms. Firms must be careful about the possibility of nonperformance with forward contracts. Because individual companies contract with each other directly, if one company cannot pay when the contract settles, the other may be left absorbing the risk it was trying to hedge against. Futures contracts do not have this problem. However, forward contracts have their benefits also. Because the forward contract is a tailored contract, the exact quality of the goods to be delivered can be defined. Although this clearly is not crucial with currencies, it might be with respect to commodities such as oil, copper, and silver.

The parties in a forward contract can negotiate delivery quantities, prices, product quality, and delivery dates. Under a futures contract, the exchange defines the quantities, delivery dates, and product quality of each contract. The futures price is a market-determined amount.

For example, perhaps the only silver futures contracts available are for 25,000 troy ounces of silver to be delivered on January 6, 2016. If we wish to hedge a future purchase of 110,000 troy ounces of silver, either we underhedge by 10,000 (purchasing four contracts totaling 100,000) troy ounces or we overhedge by 15,000 (purchasing five contracts totaling 125,000) troy ounces. Either way, some of the hedge will be ineffective. In a forward contract, the exact amount can be negotiated. In a similar fashion, the delivery date can be negotiated.

**Options** are another commonly used hedging instrument structure. Option types are either calls or puts. A call gives the holder the right to buy an asset, and a put gives the holder the right to sell.

The holder of an option has the right, but not the obligation to carry out the transaction at the strike price, a predetermined amount. The writer or seller of an option is obligated to carry out the transaction, if the holder exercises their right to buy or sell. Only one side of the option contract is required to perform at the behest of the other. The other party to the option has the ability, but not the obligation, to perform.

Options are traded on equities, commodities, foreign currency, and interest rates. Option prices can be determined using a variety of option-pricing models. The most common is the Black-Scholes option pricing model. The Black-Scholes model uses probability parameters such as the variability of the underlying (the historical variability of the stock price, for an equity option), current price levels of the underlying (the stock's current market value), time to maturity, and the strike price to determine the price of the option. The option price will obviously be higher if the probability of exercise is higher. Two main classifications of options are American and European types, which differ in respect to the exercise date. A European-style option can only be exercised on the maturity date, while the American-style option can be exercised any time before the maturity date. If you compared two option contracts that were identical except for this distinction, the American-style option would have a higher value. The American-style option gives the holder many more chances to exercise the option at a profit.

Companies purchase options to manage risk—quite frequently, price risk. For example, a company may buy an option to purchase a commodity, say fuel, at a specified price. Assume that the option costs $1,000 and that the company can exercise its option to purchase 100,000 gallons of fuel at $1 per gallon. If the market fuel price is $1.10 at the time the company needs the fuel, then the company will exercise the option and purchase the fuel at the lower price. The total cost of the fuel is $1,000 + ($1.00 × 100,000) or $101,000. On the other hand, if the market fuel price is $0.90 per gallon, the company will allow the option to expire because it is cheaper to purchase the fuel at the market price. The company still incurs an expense of $1,000 related to the fuel option contract.

**Swaps** are contracts to exchange an ongoing stream of cash flows. The most common swap is an interest rate swap, but swaps can be designed around any underlying and corresponding price or rate. A common use for swaps is to lock in fixed rates on liabilities, as described in the Wolverine Worldwide example earlier. Like forwards, swaps are commonly negotiated on an individual basis, although there are some standardized swaps that are exchange traded. A firm that holds variable rate debt might not want the risk of increases in future interest payments and would enter into a receive-variable and pay-fixed swap. If the firm had $1 million in debt currently at 8 percent, but subject to fluctuation in future rates, they could enter into a swap that would receive (pay) the increase (decrease) from the original 8 percent rate and a variable rate.

| Date | Variable Rate | Interest Payment on Debt | Net Settlement of Swap Pay (Receive) | Net Interest Payment |
|---|---|---|---|---|
| At inception | 8% | | | |
| Period 1 | 7% | $70,000 | $10,000 | $80,000 |
| Period 2 | 8% | $80,000 | 0 | $80,000 |
| Period 3 | 9% | $90,000 | ($10,000) | $80,000 |

The firm entering into a swap will have to pay a fee or premium to the counterparty of the swap. The counterparty for most interest rate swaps will be a large bank, which ideally has offsetting positions and is primarily acting as a market maker in interest rate hedging.

## Examples of Derivative Use

To help you understand the economics underlying derivative contracting, we illustrate the effects on income of using both a forward contract and an option contract. Recall that forward contracts and futures contracts are very similar so the economic effects will be similar. Because of that similarity, we will not illustrate futures here.

FORWARD CONTRACT   Assume that Gre Company mines copper. It will mine and sell 2,000,000 pounds of copper during the next four quarters and will sell all the copper it produces at the end of that time. Gre's projected fixed costs are $2,400,000 and variable costs are $0.80 per pound. Based on these figures, Gre needs to cover $4,000,000 in costs in order to break even, $2,400,000 fixed costs plus $1,600,000 variable costs. The break-even revenue is $2.00 per pound.

The following table contains the profit and loss related to various per pound revenue points:

| Per Pound Revenue | Profit (Loss) |
|---|---|
| $2.20 | $400,000 |
| $2.10 | $200,000 |
| $2.00 | — |
| $1.90 | ($200,000) |
| $1.80 | ($400,000) |

Gre decides now to sell its future production by entering into a forward contract with Bro for delivery to Bro of 2,000,000 pounds of copper in one year at a price of $2.20 per pound.

Why would Gre decide to do this? If its projected costs are correct, Gre knows that the $2.20 price will generate a profit. In any event, the risk of fluctuation in sales price has been shifted to Bro. Bro might be a speculator who is willing to take the risk, hoping that the price will actually be higher in one year than $2.20, but willing to assume the risk that it could be lower than $2.20. Alternatively, Bro might use the copper in its own production and may be trying to manage its costs in the same way that Gre is trying to manage the risk on the revenue side.

Obviously, Gre is also giving up the possibility of making a larger profit, but there are several reasons that Gre might wish to manage its risk in this way. First, Gre might need to borrow money to finance its operation. By eliminating the selling price risk, Gre should be able to negotiate a lower interest rate and/or might now be able to find lenders from which to borrow, given the mitigation of this risk. Taxes are another reason that hedging might make sense. Losses are deductible to the extent of offsetting profits. However, losses must be carried forward to future years if there are insufficient profits to offset them. Thus the tax benefit of losses is smaller than the tax cost of profits because of time value of money concerns. As a result, because of the unequal treatment of income and loss, a company may be willing to forego some profit to avoid losses. Other reasons could include avoiding bankruptcy, or to maintain managerial bonus incentives.

The following table outlines what the impact on economic income—ignoring taxes—would be in an unhedged situation compared to if Gre hedges the transaction with a forward:

| Market Price per Pound | Forward Price per Pound | Unhedged Gain/(Loss) | Economic Gain/(Loss) on Forward | Economic Income with Hedge |
|---|---|---|---|---|
| $2.40 | $2.20 | $800,000 | ($400,000) | $400,000 |
| $2.20 | $2.20 | $400,000 | — | $400,000 |
| $2.00 | $2.20 | — | $400,000 | $400,000 |
| $1.80 | $2.20 | ($400,000) | $800,000 | $400,000 |

Gre's income of $400,000 can be decomposed into the gain/(loss) related to the forward contract and the gain/(loss) if no hedging exists at each price. The column headed Economic Gain/(Loss) on Forward is computed by taking the difference in the market price per pound at the date the contract is settled and the forward price per pound multiplied by 2,000,000 pounds. For example, if the market price per pound is $2.40 and Gre receives $2.20 per pound from the forward contract, there is an economic loss from Gre's perspective related to the forward contract of $0.20 per pound, or $400,000. If Gre had not hedged, it would have earned revenue of $2.40 per pound and profit of $800,000. The difference between the gain if no hedging had occurred, $800,000, and the loss on the hedging contract, $400,000, results in reported income of $400,000.

This example demonstrates that the forward's gain/(loss) moves in the opposite direction of the unhedged gain/(loss) and effectively eliminates the revenue price risk at any level of price. This is a completely effective hedge. Notice that at every revenue price point, the income is $400,000.

In the next chapter, we discuss the accounting for this situation during the year that the forward contract is in place. We will see that the accounting reflects the economic impact of this strategy.

**OPTION CONTRACT**    Another way that Gre might manage its risk is to use options. Options can be thought of as a type of insurance. When an individual buys homeowners' insurance, the insurance company will cover the homeowner's losses in the event of theft, fire, or many other events. Of course, this is not costless, and the amount that the homeowner pays for insurance depends on the risk of loss. For example, high-property-crime areas typically have higher homeowners' insurance premiums than low-property-crime areas because the risk assumed by the insurance company is higher.

In a similar fashion, Gre might buy a put option. A put option requires that the seller (or writer) of the put option must buy the asset at a fixed price, while the buyer of the put option has the option to sell the asset at market, and will sell if the market price is higher than the option price at the option's exercise date. Gre would have a right to exercise the option and require the writer of the option to buy the copper at a set price, say $2.30. Gre would exercise its option if the market price of copper were below $2.30 at the option's exercise date. Gre would let the option expire if the price were above $2.30. In this way, Gre shifts the risk of lower market prices to the writer of the option but still can benefit from higher prices if the market price is higher than the option exercise price of $2.30.

In order for the option writer to agree to write the option, the writer must be compensated. The seller would use a pricing model to determine the price at which they would write the option. The Black-Scholes model uses probability parameters such as the variability of the underlying (in this case, the historical copper price variability), current price levels of the underlying (in this case, copper), and time to maturity of the option to determine the price of the option. The option price will be higher if the probability of exercise is higher.

Let's assume that Gre has the same $4,000,000 total cost, or a breakeven price of $2.00 a pound. Further, assume the option price is $0.05 per pound and that the exercise price is $2.30. If the price of the copper is $2.30 or above at the exercise date, Gre will not exercise the option. Instead, Gre will sell the copper at the market price, say $2.40. But this is not a costless transaction, unlike the forward contract illustrated previously. The option cost to Gre is $0.05 per pound, so Gre will net only $2.35 revenue per pound after the option cost is considered. Gre's income is lower than it would have been if it had not hedged.

Using a table similar to the forward case, let us examine the impact on income of the option at various market prices:

| Market Price per Pound | Option Exercise Price | Option Exercise, Yes or No | Unhedged Profit/(Loss) | Economic Gain on Option Exercise | Cost of Option | Net Profit/ (Loss) |
|---|---|---|---|---|---|---|
| $2.45 | $2.30 | No | $900,000 | | $100,000 | $800,000 |
| $2.35 | $2.30 | No | $700,000 | | $100,000 | $600,000 |
| $2.30 | $2.30 | No | $600,000 | | $100,000 | $500,000 |
| $2.25 | $2.30 | Yes | $500,000 | $100,000 | $100,000 | $500,000 |
| $2.15 | $2.30 | Yes | $300,000 | $300,000 | $100,000 | $500,000 |

From this table we can see the impact of the exercise of the option on income. If no option was purchased, the company's profit varies greatly, and if the price fell below $2.00 the company would lose money. The income distribution is transformed into a much less risky one after the option is purchased. At all price points below $2.30, the company will have income of no less than $500,000 in total. Unlike a forward, the option preserves the higher profit of a price increase. If the price rises to $2.45, Gre would see income of $800,000.

In the next chapter, we will illustrate the accounting for the Gre situation. Accounting under generally accepted accounting principles (GAAP) (ASC 815) tries to capture the underlying economic substance of the hedging relationship. Clearly, intent is important. The reason that Gre enters into the option contract is to mitigate risk, while the option writer is possibly speculating. Should the accounting from both perspectives be identical? The answer is no.

## FOREIGN EXCHANGE CONCEPTS AND DEFINITIONS

Foreign business activity by U.S. corporations has expanded over time. In 2015, exports of U.S. goods and services were $2.230 trillion, and imports of foreign goods and services totaled $2.762 trillion.[2] The average yearly change in total import export activity since 1996 has been about 6%. As global trade continues to expand, we can expect continued growth in these trade figures.

The effect of international branch and subsidiary operations on U.S. companies' operating results is significant. In 2014, 59 percent of *The Coca-Cola Company's* operating revenues and 80 percent of its operating income came from operations outside of the United States. Also in 2014, 51 percent of *Apple's* net sales and 55 percent of its operating income came from Europe, Japan, and Asia-Pacific.

In this section, we discuss foreign currency concepts. Chapter 13 demonstrates the accounting for hedging foreign currency risks, while Chapter 14 discusses foreign currency financial statement translation.

Currencies provide a standard of value, a medium of exchange, and a unit of measure for economic transactions. Currencies of different countries perform the first two functions with varying degrees of efficiency, but essentially all currencies provide a unit of measure for the economic activities and resources of their respective countries.

For transactions to be included in financial records, they must be measured in a currency. Typically, the currency in which a transaction is recorded and the currency needed to settle the transaction are the same. For example, a Chicago pizza shop buys all its produce and other inputs and pays all of its employees and other bills using U.S. dollars. The pizza shop collects dollars from its customers. If a receivable or payable arises, it will require receiving or paying dollars for settlement. A receivable or payable is **denominated** in a currency when it must be paid in that currency. A receivable or payable is **measured** in a currency when it is recorded in the financial records in that currency. In this example, the pizza shop's receivables and payables are denominated and measured in the same currency, the U.S. dollar.

In the case of transactions between business entities of different countries, the amounts receivable and payable are ordinarily denominated in the local currency of either the buying entity or the selling entity.[3] For example, if a U.S. firm sells merchandise to a British firm, the transaction amount will be denominated (or paid) in either U.S. dollars or British pounds, even though the U.S. firm will measure and record its account receivable and sale in U.S. dollars and the British firm will measure and record its purchase and account payable in British pounds, regardless of the currency in which the transaction is denominated.

If the transaction is denominated in British pounds, the U.S. firm has to determine how many U.S. dollars the transaction represents in order to record it. If the transaction is denominated in U.S. dollars, the British firm has to determine how many British pounds the transaction represents. To measure transactions in their own currencies, businesses around the world rely on exchange rates negotiated on a continuous basis in world currency markets. Exchange rates are essentially prices for currencies expressed in units of other currencies.

### Direct and Indirect Quotation of Exchange Rates

An **exchange rate** is the ratio between a unit of one currency and the amount of another currency for which that unit can be exchanged at a particular time. The exchange rate can be computed directly or indirectly. Assume that $1.41 can be exchanged for 1 British pound (£1).

**Direct quotation** (U.S. dollar per one foreign currency unit):

$$\frac{\$1.41}{1} = \$1.41$$

---

[2]U.S. Department of Commerce, Bureau of Economic Analysis. *U.S. International Trade in Goods and Services Report,* February 5, 2016.

[3]Sometimes the amounts are denominated in the currency of a third country whose currency is relatively more stable than the currency of either the buyer or the seller.

**Indirect quotation** (the number of foreign currency units per U.S. dollar):

$$\frac{1}{\$1.41} = £\,0.709$$

The first approach is a *direct quotation* (from a U.S. viewpoint) because the rate is expressed in U.S. dollars: $1.41 is equivalent to one British pound (one unit of the foreign currency). The second approach is an *indirect quotation* (from a U.S. viewpoint) because the rate is expressed in British pounds (the foreign currency): £0.709 is equivalent to one U.S. dollar. A direct quote is the reciprocal of an indirect quote and vice versa.

## Floating, Fixed, and Multiple Exchange Rates

Exchange rates may be fixed by a governmental unit or may be allowed to fluctuate (float) with changes in the currency markets. **Official**, or **fixed, exchange rates** are set by a government and do not change as a result of changes in world currency markets. **Free**, or **floating, exchange rates** are those that reflect fluctuating market prices for a currency based on supply and demand and other factors in the world currency markets.

FLOATING EXCHANGE RATES    Theoretically a currency's value should reflect its buying power in world markets. For example, an increase in a country's inflation rate indicates that its currency's purchasing power is decreasing. The currency's value should fall in relation to other currencies. The technical term for this movement in currency value is **weakening**. A currency falls, or *weakens*, relative to another currency if it takes more of the weakening currency to purchase one unit of the other currency.

A large trade surplus (when the amount of exports exceeds imports) usually results in an increased demand for a country's currency because many of those export sales must be paid in the exporting country's currency. The exporting country's currency becomes more valuable relative to the importing countries' currencies, or it **strengthens**. A currency strengthens relative to another currency if it takes fewer units of the strengthening currency to purchase one unit of the other currency.

A large trade deficit (when the amount of imports exceeds exports) should lead to a decrease, or weakening, of the currency's value. Although inflation and net trade position (trade surplus or trade deficit) are common causes of changes in floating exchange rates, other factors have occasionally been more influential. Interest rate differences across countries influence supply and demand for a country's currency because many investors buy securities in the international securities markets. Speculative trading to take advantage of currency movements also affects exchange rates.

To reduce its trade deficit, the U.S. government has occasionally asked other countries (e.g., Taiwan and South Korea) to let their currencies strengthen against the U.S. dollar. A decline in value of the dollar in relation to other major currencies should increase the price of foreign products in the United States and lead to a reduction of imports to the United States. Similarly, U.S. goods can be sold in international markets for fewer foreign currency units when the dollar weakens against those currencies. Even so, a weakening U.S. dollar has often done little to abate U.S. consumers' demand for imported products, and changes in the exchange rates may have little effect on the trade deficit. Other factors that may affect a country's trade balance include interest rates and tax rates.

A mathematical example of strengthening and weakening of a currency relative to another currency follows. Initially, assume that one British pound can be purchased for $1.50. If the quote is indirect, $1 can be purchased for 0.6667 pound.

If the dollar weakens relative to the pound, each pound is more expensive in dollar terms. If the dollar weakens by 10 percent, each pound will now cost $1.65. If the dollar weakens by 10 percent, it takes fewer pounds to buy $1, so now $1 can be purchased for 0.6061 pound.

If the dollar strengthens relative to the pound, each pound is less expensive in dollar terms. If the dollar strengthens by 10 percent, each pound will now cost $1.35. If the quote is indirect, $1 can now be purchased for 0.7407 pound.

FIXED AND MULTIPLE EXCHANGE RATES    When exchange rates are fixed, the issuing government is able to set (fix) different rates for different kinds of transactions. For example, it may set a preferential rate for imports (or certain kinds of imports) and penalty rates for exports (or certain kinds of exports) in order to promote the economic objectives of the country. Such rates are referred to as **multiple exchange rates**.

### Spot, Current, and Historical Exchange Rates

The exchange rates that are used in accounting for foreign operations and transactions (other than forward contracts) are spot rates, current exchange rates, and historical exchange rates. Spot rate is a *market* term; current and historical rates are *accounting* terms. These are defined as follows:

> **Spot rate**—the exchange rate for immediate delivery of currencies exchanged.
>
> **Current rate**—the rate at which one unit of currency can be exchanged for another currency at the balance sheet date or the transaction date.
>
> **Historical rate**—the rate in effect at the date a specific transaction or event occurred.

Spot, current, and historical rates may be either fixed or floating rates, depending on the particular currency involved. Spot rates for foreign transactions between the United States and a country with fixed exchange rates will normally change in that foreign country only as a result of government action (except for transactions in the black market in the foreign country's currency). For example, the Argentine government can control the exchange rate in Buenos Aires, but not in New York. Spot rates for foreign transactions with a country that has floating exchange rates may change daily, or several times in a single day, depending on factors that influence the currency markets. However, only one spot rate exists for a given transaction.

The foreign currency transaction's current rate is the spot rate in effect for immediate settlement of the amounts denominated in foreign currency at the transaction date or at the balance sheet date. Historical rates are the spot rates that were in effect on the date that a particular event or transaction occurred.

### Foreign Exchange Quotations[4]

Major U.S. banks facilitate international trade by maintaining departments that provide bank transfer services between U.S. and non-U.S. companies, as well as currency exchange services.

Selected interbank transaction exchange rates on March 23, 2016, were:

|  | U.S. $ Equivalent | Currency per U.S. $ |
|---|---|---|
| Britain (pound) | $1.4096 | 0.7094 pounds |
| Canada (dollars) | $0.7574 | 1.3203 Canadian dollars |
| Euro | $1.1167 | 0.8955 euros |
| Japan (yen) | $0.0089 | 112.7300 yen |
| Mexico (peso) | $0.0570 | 17.5536 pesos |

A payment of $1,409,600 to a U.S. banker at 4 p.m. EST on March 23, 2016, would have entitled a U.S. corporation to purchase British goods selling for £1,000,000 or to settle an account payable denominated at £1,000,000. Similarly, a U.S. company could have purchased merchandise selling for 1,000,000 Canadian dollars for $757,400 at that time.

The U.S. bankers that provide foreign exchange services are, of course, paid for their services. The payment is the difference between the amount that they receive from U.S. corporations and the amount they pay out for the foreign currencies, or vice versa. For example, a bank that trades foreign currency may offer to sell British pounds for $1.42 or to buy them for $1.40 when the quoted rate for British pounds is $1.41. Thus, a firm can buy £1,000,000 from the bank for $1,420,000 or sell £1,000,000 to the bank for $1,400,000, and the bank realizes a $10,000 gain in either case.

---

<table>
<tr><td>LEARNING<br>OBJECTIVE</td><td>**12.4**</td></tr>
</table>

## FOREIGN CURRENCY TRANSACTIONS OTHER THAN FORWARD CONTRACTS

Transactions within a country that are measured and recorded in the currency of that country are **local transactions**. The transactions of a British subsidiary would be recorded in British pounds, and its financial statements would be stated in British pounds. However, its financial statements must

---

[4]*Source:* © 2016 Bloomberg L.P.

be converted into U.S. dollars before consolidation with a U.S. parent company. Translation of foreign currency financial statements is covered in Chapter 14.

This discussion of foreign currency transactions assumes the point of view of a U.S. firm whose functional currency is the U.S. dollar (which is also its local currency). An entity's *functional currency* is the currency of its primary economic environment. Normally, the predominant currency received or expended to complete transactions is the functional currency. Chapter 14 contains a more extensive discussion of the functional currency concept. **Foreign transactions** are transactions between countries or between enterprises in different countries. **Foreign currency transactions** are transactions whose terms are stated (denominated) in a currency other than an entity's functional currency. Thus, a foreign transaction may or may not be a foreign currency transaction.

The most common types of foreign transactions are imports and exports of goods and services. Import and export transactions are foreign transactions, but they are not foreign currency transactions unless their terms are denominated in a foreign currency—that is, a currency other than the entity's functional currency. An export sale by a U.S. company to a Canadian company is a foreign currency transaction from the viewpoint of the U.S. company only if the invoice is denominated (fixed) in Canadian dollars. Translation is required if the transaction is denominated in a foreign currency, but not if it is denominated in the entity's functional currency.

## FASB Requirements

Current GAAP (ASC 830) applies only to foreign currency transactions and to foreign currency financial statements. GAAP stipulates the following requirements for foreign currency transactions other than derivatives:

1.  At the date the transaction is recognized, each asset, liability, revenue, expense, gain, or loss arising from the transaction shall be measured and recorded in the functional currency of the recording entity by use of the exchange rate in effect at that date.

2.  At each balance sheet date, recorded balances that are denominated in a currency other than the functional currency of the recording entity shall be adjusted to reflect the current exchange rate.[5]

**TRANSLATION AT THE SPOT RATE**    The first requirement for recording foreign currency transactions is that they must be translated into U.S. dollars at the spot rate in effect at the *transaction date*. Each asset, liability, revenue, and expense account arising from the transaction is translated into dollars before it is recorded. The unit of measurement is changed from the foreign currency to the U.S. dollar.

Assume that a U.S. corporation imports inventory on account from a Canadian firm when the spot rate for Canadian dollars is $0.7000. The invoice calls for payment of 10,000 Canadian dollars in 30 days. (*Note:* The $ sign used for the spot rate indicates direct quotation—the U.S. dollar equivalent of one unit of foreign currency.) The U.S. importer records the transaction as follows:

| | | |
|---|---|---|
| Inventory (+A) | 7,000 | |
|     Accounts payable (fc) (+L) | | 7,000 |
|     (Translation: 10,000 Candian dollars × $0.7000 spot rate.) | | |

Except for the foreign currency (fc) notation, the entry is recorded in the usual manner. The notation is used here to indicate that the account payable is denominated in foreign currency. The inventory is measured in U.S. dollars, and no subsequent adjustment is made to the inventory account for foreign currency rate fluctuation.

If the account payable is paid when the spot rate is $0.6900, the payment is recorded as follows:

| | | |
|---|---|---|
| Accounts payable (fc) (−L) | 7,000 | |
|     Exchange gain (+Ga, +SE) | | 100 |
|     Cash (−A) | | 6,900 |
|     (Cash required equals 10,000 Canadian | | |
|     dollars × $0.6900 spot rate.) | | |

---

[5]FASB ASC 830. Originally 'Foreign Currency Matters.' Norwalk, CT: Financial Accounting Standards Board, 2015.

The $100 exchange gain results because a liability measured at $7,000 is settled for $6,900. This gain reflects a change in the exchange rate between the initial transaction date and the date of payment. If the exchange rate had changed to $0.7200, a $200 exchange loss would have resulted.

Exhibit 12-1 illustrates the accounting differences that arise when foreign transactions are denominated in an entity's functional currency (U.S. dollars) as opposed to a foreign currency. In examining the exhibit, keep in mind that a transaction must be denominated in a foreign currency to be a foreign currency transaction. When the billing for a U.S. company's sale or purchase is denominated in U.S. dollars, no translation is required.

---

**EXHIBIT 12-1**

Comparison of Purchase and Sale Transactions Denominated in U.S. Dollars versus British Pounds

---

**SALES TRANSACTION**

Assumption: U.S. Foods sells merchandise on account to London Industries Ltd. for $16,500, or £10,000 when the exchange rate is $1.65, and receives payment when the exchange rate is $1.64. Ignore Cost of Goods Sold.

**IF BILLING IS IN U.S. DOLLARS**

| | | |
|---|---|---|
| *(Date of sale)* | | |
| Accounts receivable (+A) | 16,500 | |
|     Sales (+R, +SE) | | 16,500 |
|   To record sale to London Industries; invoice is $16,500. | | |
| *(Date of receipt)* | | |
| Cash (+A) | 16,500 | |
|     Accounts receivable (−A) | | 16,500 |
|   To record collection in full from London Industries. | | |

**IF BILLING IS IN BRITISH POUNDS**

| | | |
|---|---|---|
| Accounts receivable (fc) (+A) | 16,500 | |
|     Sales (+R, +SE) | | 16,500 |
|   To record sale to London Industries; billing is for £10,000 (£10,000 × $1.65 = $16,500). | | |
| Cash (fc) (+A) | 16,400 | |
| Exchange loss (+Lo, −SE) | 100 | |
|     Accounts receivable (fc) (−A) | | 16,500 |
|   To record collection in full from London Industries (£10,000 × $1.64 = $16,400). | | |

**PURCHASE TRANSACTION**

Assumption: U.S. Foods purchases merchandise on account from London Industries Ltd. for $8,250, or £5,000 when the exchange rate is $1.65 and pays the account when the exchange rate is $1.67.

**IF BILLING IS IN U.S. DOLLARS**

| | | |
|---|---|---|
| *(Date of purchase)* | | |
| Inventory (+A) | 8,250 | |
|     Accounts payable (+L) | | 8,250 |
|   To record purchase from London Industries; billing is $8,250. | | |
| *(Date of payment)* | | |
| Accounts payable (−L) | 8,250 | |
|     Cash (−A) | | 8,250 |
|   To record payment in full to London Industries. | | |

**IF BILLING IS IN BRITISH POUNDS**

| | | |
|---|---|---|
| Inventory (+A) | 8,250 | |
|     Accounts payable (fc) (+L) | | 8,250 |
|   To record purchase from London Industries; billing is for £5,000 (£5,000 × $1.65 = $8,250). | | |
| Accounts payable (fc) (−L) | 8,250 | |
| Exchange loss (+Lo, −SE) | 100 | |
|     Cash (fc) (−A) | | 8,350 |
|   To record payment in full to London Industries (£5,000 × $1.67 = $8,350). | | |

The potential for exchange gains and losses arises only when the receivable or payable is billed in the foreign currency. However, no gain or loss on translation is recorded at the initial recording.

**BALANCE SHEET DATE ADJUSTMENTS**   Gains and losses on foreign currency transactions cannot be deferred until the foreign currency is converted into U.S. dollars or until related receivables are collected or payables are settled. Instead, these amounts are adjusted to reflect current exchange rates at the balance sheet date, and any exchange gains or losses that result from the adjustments are included in current-year income.

## Purchases Denominated in Foreign Currency

ATC, a U.S. corporation, purchased merchandise on account from Paris Company on December 1, 2016, for 10,000 euros, when the spot rate for euros was $0.6600. ATC closed its books at December 31, 2016, when the spot rate for euros was $0.6550, and it settled the account on January 30, 2017, when the spot rate was $0.6650. These transactions and events are recorded by ATC as follows:

LEARNING OBJECTIVE **12.5**

*December 1, 2016*
| | | |
|---|---|---|
| Inventory (+A) | 6,600 | |
|     Accounts payable (fc) (+L) | | 6,600 |
|   To record purchase of merchandise from | | |
|     Paris Company (10,000 euros × $0.6600 rate). | | |

*December 31, 2016*
| | | |
|---|---|---|
| Accounts payable (fc) (−L) | 50 | |
|     Exchange gain (+Ga, +SE) | | 50 |
|   To adjust accounts payable to exchange rate at year-end | | |
|     [10,000 euros × ($0.6550 − $0.6600)]. | | |

*January 30, 2017*
| | | |
|---|---|---|
| Accounts payable (fc) (−L) | 6,550 | |
| Exchange loss (+Lo, −SE) | 100 | |
|     Cash (fc) (−A) | | 6,650 |
|   To record payment in full to Paris Company | | |
|     (10,000 euros × 0.6650 spot rate). | | |

| Date | Spot Rate | Inventory | Accounts Payable (10,000 Euros) | Gain (Loss) |
|---|---|---|---|---|
| December 1, 2016 (initial transaction date) | $0.6600 | $6,600 | $6,600 | — |
| December 31, 2016 (financial statement date) | $0.6550 | $6,600 | $6,550 | $50 |
| January 30, 2017 (settled accounts payable by purchasing and distributing euros) | $0.6650 | $6,600 | $6,650 | ($100) |
| Overall | | | | ($50) |

The example shows that on December 1, 2016, ATC incurred a liability of $6,600 denominated in euros. On December 31, 2016, the liability is adjusted to reflect the current exchange rate, and a $50 exchange gain was included in ATC's 2016 income statement. The exchange gain is the product of multiplying 10,000 euros by the change in the spot rate for euros between December 1 and December 31, 2016. By January 30, 2017, when the liability was settled, the spot rate for euros had increased to $0.6650, and ATC recorded a $100 exchange loss. The actual total exchange loss is only $50 [10,000 euros × ($0.6650 − $0.6600)], but this loss is reported as a $50 exchange gain in 2016 and a $100 exchange loss in 2017.

In summary, foreign currency–denominated purchases must be measured in dollars at the purchase date using the foreign currency spot rate on that date.

If a balance sheet date occurs before the liability is paid, the accounts payable must be remeasured to reflect the spot rate at the financial statement date. A gain results if the dollar strengthens, because more euros can be purchased by one dollar than when the liability was first recorded. A loss results if the dollar weakens, because fewer euros can be purchased by one dollar than when the liability was first recorded.

When the liability is paid, a gain (when the liability is smaller since the last financial statement date) or loss (when the liability is larger than at the last financial statement date) is recorded because the liability is paid at the spot rate on the payment date. Typically, companies arrange with banks to handle the conversion. The bank charges the company's bank account in dollars (including a transaction fee) and transfers foreign currency to the payee's account.

## Sales Denominated in Foreign Currency

On December 15, 2016, ATC sold merchandise on account to Rome Company for 20,000 euros, when the spot rate for euros was $0.6625. (Ignore Cost of Goods Sold.) ATC closed its books on December 31, when the spot rate was $0.6550, collected the account on January 15, 2017, when the spot rate was $0.6700, and held the euros until January 20, when it converted the euros into U.S. dollars at the $0.6725 spot rate in effect on that date. ATC records the transactions as follows:

*December 15, 2016*

| | | |
|---|---|---|
| Accounts receivable (fc) (+A) | 13,250 | |
| Sales (+R, +SE) | | 13,250 |

To record sales to Rome
(20,000 euros × $0.6625 spot rate).

*December 31, 2016*

| | | |
|---|---|---|
| Exchange loss (+Lo, −SE) | 150 | |
| Accounts receivable (fc) (−A) | | 150 |

To adjust accounts receivable at year-end
[20,000 euros × ($0.6550 − $0.6625)].

*January 15, 2017*

| | | |
|---|---|---|
| Cash (fc) (+A) | 13,400 | |
| Accounts receivable (fc) (−A) | | 13,100 |
| Exchange gain (+Ga, +SE) | | 300 |

To record collection in full from Rome
(20,000 euros × $0.6700) and recognize exchange gain
for 2017 [20,000 euros × ($0.6700 − $0.6550)].

*January 20, 2017*

| | | |
|---|---|---|
| Cash (+A) | 13,450 | |
| Exchange gain (+Ga, +SE) | | 50 |
| Cash (fc) (−A) | | 13,400 |

To convert 20,000 euros into U.S. dollars
(20,000 euros × $0.6725).

| Date | Spot Rate | Accounts Receivable 20,000 Euros | Sales | Gain (Loss) |
|---|---|---|---|---|
| 12/15/16 (initial transaction date) | $0.6625 | $13,250 | $13,250 | — |
| 12/31/16* (financial statement date) | $0.6550 | $13,100 | Unchanged | ($150) |
| 1/15/17 (collection of accounts receivable in euros) | $0.6700 | $13,400 | Unchanged | $300 |
| 1/20/17 (conversion of euros to dollars) | $0.6725 | | Unchanged | $50 |
| Overall | | | | $200 |

*Sales are closed at period-end into retained earnings. The term *unchanged* here means that no further adjustment of the sales amount is necessary because the sales amount was "locked in" when the accounts receivable and related sales were first recorded.

In summary, foreign currency–denominated sales must be measured in dollars at the sales date using the foreign currency spot rate on that date.

If a financial statement date occurs before the receivable is paid, the accounts receivable must be remeasured to reflect the spot rate at the financial statement date. A gain results when the dollar has weakened because the foreign currency to be received is worth more dollars than when initially recorded. A loss results when the dollar has strengthened because the foreign currency to be received is worth less in dollars than when it was originally recorded.

When the receivable is paid, a gain or loss is recorded because the receivable will be paid at the spot rate on the payment date. If a company holds foreign currency for a period of time for speculative purposes after a receivable is paid instead of converting it into dollars, gains and losses continue to be reported at each financial statement date until the foreign currency is converted into dollars.

The following table shows the effect of foreign exchange rate changes on selected accounts.

**SUMMARY OF DIRECT RATE CHANGES ($ PER CURRENCY UNIT) ON THE CARRYING VALUE OF FOREIGN CURRENCY–DENOMINATED ACCOUNTS RECEIVABLE AND ACCOUNTS PAYABLE**

| Spot Rate Change | Effect on the Dollar Relative to the Foreign Currency | Impact on Foreign Currency–Denominated Account |
|---|---|---|
| Increases | Dollar weaker | Accounts Receivable Increases—Gain |
| Increases | Dollar weaker | Accounts Payable Increases—Loss |
| Decreases | Dollar stronger | Accounts Receivable Decreases—Loss |
| Decreases | Dollar stronger | Accounts Payable Decreases—Gain |

## International Accounting Standards

International Financial Reporting Standards (IFRS) (IASC IAS 21) address how to include foreign currency transactions and foreign operations in the financial statements. Like GAAP (ASC 830), IFRS requires that entities initially record transactions at the rate of exchange on the date of the transaction. At each subsequent balance sheet date, foreign currency monetary amounts (such as foreign currency–denominated accounts receivable and payable) should be marked to the spot rate at the balance sheet date. Again, similar to GAAP, gains and losses from differences between the initial amount recorded and the year-end value for these monetary assets and liabilities are included in current year income.

## SUMMARY

Derivatives are a widely used mechanism to manage various risks. Because of their flexibility to isolate one type of risk, and manage risks with low costs, they have become very popular tools for hedging strategies. This chapter explains the types and uses of derivatives, while Chapter 13 covers the accounting for derivatives and hedging activity.

International accounting is concerned with accounting for foreign currency transactions and operations. An entity's functional currency is the currency of the primary environment in which the entity operates. Foreign currency transactions are denominated in a currency other than an entity's functional currency.

Foreign currency transactions (other than forward contracts) are measured and recorded in U.S. dollars at the spot rate in effect at the transaction date. A change in the exchange rate between the date of the transaction and the settlement date results in an exchange gain or loss that is reflected in income for the period. At the balance sheet date, any remaining balances that are denominated in a currency other than the functional currency are adjusted to reflect the current exchange rate, and the gain or loss is reflected in income.

## QUESTIONS

1. Define the term *derivative* and provide examples of risks that derivative contracts are designed to reduce.
2. Explain the differences between forward contracts and futures contracts and the potential benefits and potential costs of each type of contract.
3. Explain the differences between options and swaps and the potential benefits and potential costs of each type of contract.
4. What does "Net Settlement" mean?
5. Distinguish between *measurement* and *denomination* in a particular currency.

6. Assume that one euro can be exchanged for 1.20 U.S. dollars. What is the exchange rate if the exchange rate is quoted directly? Indirectly?

7. What is the difference between official and floating foreign exchange rates? Does the United States have floating exchange rates?

8. What is a spot rate with respect to foreign currency transactions? Could a spot rate ever be a historical rate? Could a spot rate ever be a fixed exchange rate? Discuss.

9. Assume that a U.S. corporation imports electronic equipment from Japan in a transaction denominated in U.S. dollars. Is this transaction a foreign currency transaction? A foreign transaction? Explain the difference between these two concepts and their application here.

10. How are assets and liabilities denominated in foreign currency measured and recorded at the transaction date? At the balance sheet date?

11. Criticize the following statement: "Exchange losses arise from foreign import activities, and exchange gains arise from foreign export activities."

12. When are exchange gains and losses reflected in a business's financial statements?

13. A U.S. corporation imported merchandise from a British company for £1,000 when the spot rate was $1.45. It issued financial statements when the current rate was $1.47, and it paid for the merchandise when the spot rate was $1.46. What amount of exchange gain or loss will be included in the U.S. corporation's income statements in the period of purchase and in the period of settlement?

## EXERCISES

### E 12-1

1. What is a characteristic of a forward contract?
   - a *Traded on an exchange*
   - b *Negotiated with a counterparty*
   - c *Covers a stream of future payments*
   - d *Must be settled daily*

2. What is a characteristic of a swap?
   - a *Traded on an exchange*
   - b *Only interest rates can be the underlying*
   - c *Covers a stream of future payments*
   - d *Must be settled daily*

3. What is a characteristic of a futures contract?
   - a *Gives the holder the right but not the obligation to buy or sell*
   - b *Negotiated with a counterparty*
   - c *Covers a stream of future payments*
   - d *Must be settled daily*

4. What is a characteristic of an option?
   - a *Gives the holder the right but not the obligation to buy or sell*
   - b *Negotiated with a counterparty*
   - c *Covers a stream of future payments*
   - d *Must be settled daily*

### E 12-2

1. Which of the following is true about the seller of a put option?
   - a *They have the right to buy the underlying*
   - b *They have the right to sell the underlying*
   - c *They have the obligation to buy the underlying*
   - d *They have the obligation to sell the underlying*

2. Which of the following is true about the holder of a call option?
   - a *They have the right to buy the underlying*
   - b *They have the right to sell the underlying*
   - c *They have the obligation to buy the underlying*
   - d *They have the obligation to sell the underlying*

**3.** Which of the following is true about the seller of a call option?
 *a   They have the right to buy the underlying*
 *b   They have the right to sell the underlying*
 *c   They have the obligation to buy the underlying*
 *d   They have the obligation to sell the underlying*

**4.** Which of the following is true about the holder of a put option?
 *a   They have the right to buy the underlying*
 *b   They have the right to sell the underlying*
 *c   They have the obligation to buy the underlying*
 *d   They have the obligation to sell the underlying*

## E 12-3
## Quotation conventions, measurement versus denomination

**1.** If $1.5625 can be exchanged for 1 British pound, the direct and indirect exchange rate quotations are:
 *a   $1.5625 and 1 British pound, respectively*
 *b   $1.5625 and 0.64 British pounds, respectively*
 *c   $1.00 and 1.5625 British pounds, respectively*
 *d   $1.00 and 0.64 British pounds, respectively*

**2.** A U.S. firm purchases merchandise from a Canadian firm with payment due in 60 days and denominated in Canadian dollars. The U.S. firm will report an exchange gain or loss on settlement if the transaction is:
 *a   Recorded in U.S. dollars*
 *b   Measured in U.S. dollars*
 *c   Not hedged through a forward contract*
 *d   Settled after an exchange rate change has occurred*

**3.** Exchange gains and losses on accounts receivable and payable that are denominated in a foreign currency are:
 *a   Accumulated and reported upon settlement*
 *b   Deferred and treated as transaction price adjustments*
 *c   Reported as equity adjustments from translation*
 *d   Recognized in the periods in which exchange rates change*

## E 12-4
## Accounting for foreign currency–denominated purchases

Zip purchased merchandise from Tas of Japan on November 1, 2016, for 10,000,000 yen, payable on December 1, 2016. The spot rate for yen on November 1 was $0.0075, and on December 1 the spot rate was $0.0076.

**REQUIRED**

**1.** Did the dollar weaken or strengthen against the yen between November 1 and December 1, 2016? Explain.

**2.** On November 1, 2016, at what amount did Zip record the account payable to Tas?

**3.** On December 1, 2016, Zip paid the 10,000,000 yen to Tas. Prepare the journal entry to record settlement of the account on Zip's books.

**4.** If Zip had chosen to hedge its exposed net liability position on November 1, would it have entered a forward contract to purchase yen for future receipt or to sell yen for future delivery? Explain.

## E 12-5
## Accounting for foreign currency–denominated purchases settled in subsequent year

On December 16, 2016, Ava Corporation, a U.S. firm, purchased merchandise from Wig Company for 40,000 euros to be paid on January 15, 2017. Relevant exchange rates for euros are as follows:

| | |
|---|---|
| December 16, 2016 | $1.20 |
| December 31, 2016 | $1.25 |
| January 15, 2017 | $1.24 |

**REQUIRED:** Prepare all journal entries on Ava Corporation's books to account for the purchase on December 16, adjustment of the books on December 31, and payment of the account payable on January 15.

## E 12-6
### Accounting for foreign currency–denominated sales settled in subsequent year

On November 16, 2016, Wik of the United States sold inventory items to Can of Canada for 90,000 Canadian dollars, to be paid on February 14, 2017. Exchange rates for Canadian dollars on selected dates are as follows:

| | |
|---|---|
| November 16, 2016 | $0.80 |
| December 31, 2016 | $0.84 |
| February 14, 2017 | $0.83 |

**REQUIRED:** Determine the exchange gain or loss on the sale to Can to be included in Wik's income statement for the years 2016 and 2017.

## E 12-7
### Accounting for foreign currency–denominated sales

Dot, a U.S. company, sold inventory items on account to Roa of Great Britain for £200,000 on May 1, 2016, when the spot rate was 0.7000 pounds. The invoice was paid by Roa on May 30, 2016, when the spot rate was 0.7050 pounds.

**REQUIRED:** Prepare Dot's journal entries for the sale to Roa on May 1 and receipt of the £200,000 on May 30. Ignore Cost of Goods Sold.

## E 12-8
### [Based on AICPA] Various foreign currency–denominated transactions

1. On September 1, 2016, Ban received an order for equipment from a foreign customer for 300,000 euros, when the U.S. dollar equivalent was $400,000. Ban shipped the equipment on October 15, 2016, and billed the customer for 300,000 euros when the U.S. dollar equivalent was $420,000. Ban received the customer's remittance in full on November 16, 2016, and sold the 300,000 euros for $415,000. In its income statement for the year ended December 31, 2016, what should Ban report as a foreign exchange gain or loss?

2. On September 22, 2016, Yup purchased merchandise on account from an unaffiliated foreign company for 10,000 euros. On that date, the spot rate was $1.20. Yup paid the bill in full on March 20, 2017, when the spot rate was $1.30. The spot rate was $1.24 on December 31, 2016. What amount should Yup report as a foreign currency transaction gain or loss in its income statement for the year ended December 31, 2016?

3. On July 1, 2016, Cle borrowed 1,680,000 pesos from a foreign lender by signing an interest-bearing note due on July 1, 2017, which is denominated in pesos. The U.S. dollar equivalent of the note principal was as follows:

| | |
|---|---|
| July 1, 2016 (date borrowed) | $210,000 |
| December 31, 2016 (Cle's year-end) | 240,000 |
| July 1, 2017 (date paid) | 280,000 |

In its income statement for 2017, what amount should Cle include as a foreign exchange gain or loss?

4. On July 1, 2016, Set lent $120,000 to a foreign supplier by accepting an interest-bearing note due on July 1, 2017. The note is denominated in the currency of the borrower and was equivalent to 840,000 pesos on the loan date. The note principal was appropriately included at $140,000 in the receivables section of Set's December 31, 2016, balance sheet. The note principal was repaid to Set on the July 1, 2017, due date, when the exchange rate was 8 pesos to $1. In its income statement for the year ended December 31, 2017, what amount should Set include as a foreign currency transaction gain or loss?

## E 12-9
### Various foreign currency–denominated transactions settled in subsequent year

Meo imports merchandise from some Canadian companies and exports its own products to other Canadian companies. The *unadjusted* accounts denominated in Canadian dollars at December 31, 2016, are as follows:

| | |
|---|---|
| Account receivable from the sale of merchandise on December 16 to Cav. Billing is for 150,000 Canadian dollars and due January 15, 2017 | $103,500 |
| Account payable to Fot for merchandise received December 2 and payable on January 30, 2017. Billing is for 275,000 Canadian dollars. | $195,250 |

Exchange rates on selected dates are as follows:

| | |
|---|---|
| December 31, 2016 | $0.680 |
| January 15, 2017 | $0.675 |
| January 30, 2017 | $0.685 |

## REQUIRED

**1.** Determine the net exchange gain or loss from the two transactions that will be included in Meo's income statement for 2016.

**2.** Determine the net exchange gain or loss from settlement of the two transactions that will be included in Meo's 2017 income statement.

## E 12-10
## Various foreign currency–denominated transactions settled in subsequent year

ATV had two foreign currency transactions during December 2016, as follows:

| | |
|---|---|
| December 12 | Purchased electronic parts on account from Tok of Japan at an invoice price of 50,000,000 yen when the spot rate for yen was $0.00750. Payment is due on January 11, 2017. |
| December 15 | Sold television sets on account to BPL for 40,000 pounds when the spot rate for British pounds was $1.65. The invoice is denominated in pounds and is due on January 14, 2017. |

## REQUIRED

**1.** Prepare journal entries to record the foregoing transactions. Ignore Cost of Goods Sold.

**2.** Prepare journal entries to adjust the accounts of ATV at December 31, 2016, if the current exchange rates are $0.00760 and $1.60 for Japanese yen and British pounds, respectively.

**3.** Prepare journal entries to record payments to Tok on January 11, 2017, when the spot rate for Japanese yen is $0.00765, and to record receipt from BPL on January 14, 2017, when the spot rate for British pounds is $1.63.

## PROBLEMS

## P 12-1
## The economics of derivatives

On June 1, 2016, TCO enters into a forward agreement with XYZ to buy 100,000 gallons of fuel oil at $2.40 on December 31, 2016. At the time of inception of the forward, the price of fuel oil is $2.45. On December 31, 2016, the price of fuel oil is $2.48. The contract allows for net settlement.

## REQUIRED

**1.** What is the net settlement on the forward contract?

## P 12-2
## The economics of derivatives

In July of 2016, Sue enters into a forward agreement with Ann to lock in a sales price for wheat. Sue anticipates selling 300,000 bushels of wheat at the market in March of 2017. Ann agrees to a forward with Sue to buy 300,000 bushels at $5.20. Sue's cost for the wheat is $4.90 per bushel. The contract allows for net settlement.

## REQUIRED

**1.** Determine the economic income of the sales transaction at various price levels at maturity for the forward. Consider market prices of $5.00, $5.10, $5.20, $5.30, and $5.40. Make a table similar to the Gre copper example found in the chapter.

## P 12-3
## The economics of derivatives

Consider the same basic facts as in P12-2, but instead of a forward contract Sue purchases put options to sell 300,000 bushels at $5.20 per bushel. The options cost $0.05 a bushel.

### REQUIRED

1. Determine the economic income of the sales transaction at various price levels at maturity for the option. Consider market prices of $5.00, $5.10, $5.20, $5.30, and $5.40. Make a table similar to the Gre copper example.

## P 12-4
## Accounting for foreign currency–denominated receivables and payables—multiple years

The accounts of Lin, a U.S. corporation, show $81,300 accounts receivable and $38,900 accounts payable at December 31, 2016, before adjusting entries are made. An analysis of the balances reveals the following:

| | |
|---|---:|
| *Accounts Receivable* | |
| Receivable denominated in U.S. dollars | $28,500 |
| Receivable denominated in 20,000 Swedish krona | 11,800 |
| Receivable denominated in 25,000 British pounds | 41,000 |
| Total | $81,300 |
| *Accounts Payable* | |
| Payable denominated in U.S. dollars | $6,850 |
| Payable denominated in 10,000 Canadian dollars | 7,600 |
| Payable denominated in 15,000 British pounds | 24,450 |
| Total | $38,900 |

Current exchange rates for Swedish krona, British pounds, and Canadian dollars at December 31, 2016, are $0.52, $1.65, and $0.70, respectively.

### REQUIRED

1. Determine the net exchange gain or loss that should be reflected in Lin's income statement for 2016 from year-end exchange adjustments.
2. Determine the amounts at which the accounts receivable and accounts payable should be included in Lin's December 31, 2016, balance sheet.
3. Prepare journal entries to record collection of the receivables in 2017 when the spot rates for Swedish krona and British pounds are $0.55 and $1.63, respectively.
4. Prepare journal entries to record settlement of accounts payable in 2017 when the spot rates for Canadian dollars and British pounds are $0.69 and $1.62, respectively.

## P 12-5
## Foreign currency–denominated receivables and payables—multiple years

Sho of New York is an international dealer in jewelry and engages in numerous import and export activities. Sho's receivables and payables in foreign currency units before year-end adjustments on December 31, 2016, are summarized as follows:

| Foreign Currency | Currency Units | Rate on Date of Transaction | Per Books in U.S. Dollars | Current Rate on December 31, 2016 |
|---|---|---|---|---|
| *Accounts Receivable Denominated in Foreign Currency* | | | | |
| British pounds | 100,000 | $1.6500 | $165,000 | $1.6600 |
| Euros | 250,000 | $0.6600 | 165,000 | $0.6700 |
| Swedish krona | 160,000 | $0.6600 | 105,600 | $0.6400 |
| Japanese yen | 2,000,000 | $0.0075 | 15,000 | $0.0076 |
| | | | $450,600 | |

| Foreign Currency | Currency Units | Rate on Date of Transaction | Per Books in U.S. Dollars | Current Rate on December 31, 2016 |
|---|---|---|---|---|
| *Accounts Payable Denominated in Foreign Currency* | | | | |
| Canadian dollars | 150,000 | $0.7000 | $105,000 | $0.6900 |
| Mexican pesos | 220,000 | $0.1300 | 28,600 | $0.1350 |
| Japanese yen | 4,500,000 | $0.0074 | 33,300 | $0.0076 |
| | | | $166,900 | |

## REQUIRED

1. Determine the amount at which the receivables and payables should be reported in Sho's December 31, 2016, balance sheet.

2. Calculate individual gains and losses on each of the receivables and payables and the net exchange gain that should appear in Sho's 2016 income statement.

3. When the sale occurs, assume that Sho wants to hedge its exposure to amounts denominated in euros. Should it buy or sell euros for future delivery? In what amount or amounts?

## PROFESSIONAL RESEARCH ASSIGNMENTS

Answer the following questions by reference to the FASB Codification of Accounting Standards. Include the appropriate reference in your response.

**PR 12-1** What are the primary characteristics that define a derivative? How many paragraphs does it take the ASC to define a derivative completely?

# CHAPTER 13

# Accounting for Derivatives and Hedging Activities

## ACCOUNTING FOR DERIVATIVE INSTRUMENTS AND HEDGING ACTIVITIES

Evidence of derivative use has existed for more than 2500 years[1]. However, it was only recently that the Financial Accounting Standards Board (FASB) began to consider how to account for derivative instruments and hedges. The Board added the broad topic of accounting for financial instruments to its agenda in 1986. The late 1980s and early 1990s saw the development of many small steps toward the goal of accounting for all types of financial instruments. From that point until today, and into the future, the FASB continues to refine the accounting for Derivatives and Hedging (ASC 815), Fair Value Measurement (ASC 820), and Financial Instruments (ASC 825).

### Derivatives Not Designated as a Hedge

LEARNING OBJECTIVE **13.1**

A firm might hold a derivative for speculative or investment purposes. They might also hold a derivative for hedging purposes, but choose not to qualify the derivative for special hedge accounting. Any derivative a firm holds that does meet all the criteria to qualify for hedge accounting is accounted for as if it was a stand-alone asset or liability using fair-value accounting. These contracts are recorded at fair value at initial recognition and all subsequent balance sheet dates. Firms recognize any unrealized changes in the fair value during each accounting period in earnings. If a firm intends to use a derivative, or a pool of derivatives for hedging purposes, and they meet the criteria to qualify as a hedge, then the derivatives are accounted for in the manner explained in the following sections.

### Hedge Accounting

The objective of generally accepted accounting principles (GAAP) is to account for derivative instruments used to hedge risks so that the financial statements reflect their effectiveness in reducing a company's exposure to risk. For the financial statements to reflect the derivative contract's effectiveness, both changes in the hedged item's fair value and the hedging instrument's fair value resulting from the underlying change must be recorded in the same period. The investor can then clearly assess the effectiveness of the strategy. The term *hedge accounting* refers to accounting designed to record changes in the value of the hedged item, and in the value of the hedging instrument in the same accounting period.

---

[1]The story of Thales of Miletus buying options on olive presses is often cited as the first example of the use of a financial derivative.

## LEARNING OBJECTIVES

**13.1** Account for derivative instruments that are not designated as a hedge.

**13.2** Understand the definition of a cash-flow hedge and the circumstances in which a derivative is accounted for as a cash-flow hedge.

**13.3** Understand the definition of a fair-value hedge and the circumstances in which a derivative is accounted for as a fair-value hedge.

**13.4** Account for a cash-flow-hedge situation from inception through settlement and for a fair-value-hedge situation from inception through settlement.

**13.5** Understand the special derivative accounting related to hedges of existing foreign currency–denominated receivables and payables.

GAAP (ASC 815-10-15-83) establishes three broad defining characteristics for a derivative:

1. It has one or more underlyings and one or more notional amounts or payment provisions, or both.

2. It requires no initial net investment or an initial net investment that is smaller than would be required for other types of contracts that would be expected to have a similar response to changes in market factors.

3. Its terms require or permit net settlement, so it can readily be settled net by a means outside the contract, or it provides for delivery of an asset that puts the recipient in a position not substantially different from net settlement.[2]

The specific requirements of ASC Topic 815 are based on four fundamental decisions:

- Derivative instruments represent rights or obligations that meet the definitions of assets or liabilities and should be reported in the financial statements. At year-end, the derivative contract value is recorded on the books as an asset or liability.

- Fair value is the most relevant measure for financial instruments and the only relevant measure for derivative instruments. Derivative instruments should be measured at fair value, and adjustments to the carrying amounts of the hedged items should reflect changes in their fair value (i.e., gains or losses) that are attributable to the risk being hedged and that arise while the hedge is in effect.

- Only items that are assets or liabilities should be reported as such in financial statements.

- Special accounting for items designated as being hedged should be provided only for qualifying items. One aspect of qualification should be an assessment of the expectation of effective offsetting changes in fair values or cash flows during the term of the hedge for the risk being hedged.

For hedged items and the derivative instruments designated to hedge them to qualify for hedge accounting, formal documentation must be prepared defining:

- The relationship between the hedged item and the derivative instrument
- The risk-management objective and the strategy that the company is achieving through this hedging relationship, including identification of:

> The hedging instrument
> The hedged item
> The nature of the risk being hedged
> For fair-value hedges, how the hedging instrument's effectiveness in offsetting the exposure to changes in the hedged item's fair value will be assessed
> For cash-flow hedges, how the hedging instrument's effectiveness in hedging the hedged transaction's variability in cash flows attributable to the hedged risk will be assessed

In order to qualify for hedge accounting, management must demonstrate that the derivative is considered highly effective in mitigating an identified risk.

### Hedge Effectiveness

Once a type of risk is identified that qualifies for hedge accounting, the effectiveness of the hedge to offset gains or losses in the item being hedged must be assessed. The firm does this assessment when the hedge is first entered into, as well as during the life of the hedge.

In order for a hedge to qualify for hedge accounting, the derivative instrument must be considered highly effective in offsetting gains or losses in the item being hedged. ASC Topic 815 requires statistical or other numerical tests to assess hedge effectiveness, unless a specific exception exists. Companies must choose a methodology to be applied to assess hedge effectiveness. Two common approaches are critical term analysis and statistical analysis.

Critical term analysis involves examining the nature of the underlying variable, the notional amount of the derivative and the item being hedged, the delivery date for the derivative, and the

---

[2]FASB ASC 815. Originally 'Derivatives and Hedging' .Norwalk, CT: Financial Accounting Standards Board, 2016.

settlement date for the item being hedged. If the critical terms of the derivative and the hedged item are identical, then you can assume the hedge is effective. For example, in the Gre Copper forward contract example used in Chapter 12:

|  | Copper | Forward Contract Terms |
| --- | --- | --- |
| Amount | 2,000,000 pounds | 2,000,000 pounds |
| Underlying variable | Copper | |
| Hedge | | Copper |

This situation would be considered a highly effective hedge because the critical terms match exactly. Hedge accounting could be used for this situation.

However, real-world complications often exist when trying to structure hedges of a volatile underlying. A good example of why it might be difficult to hedge some types of risk comes from the airline industry. All airlines face the risk of increasing jet fuel prices. Some choose to live with the possible decreases in cash flow and income that would result from an increase in fuel costs. At the end of 2015, American Airlines chose to not hedge and they forecast that for each one-cent increase in the price of jet fuel they would have an increase of $44 million in costs. While millions of dollars might seem like a large risk, consider that American's net income for 2015 was $7,610 million. At the same time, Southwest Airlines did choose to hedge the projected cost of their jet fuel expense. The disclosure in their footnote about derivatives makes it clear that it is not always a straightforward task to hedge your risks.

> The Company endeavors to acquire jet fuel at the lowest possible cost and to reduce volatility in operating expenses through its fuel hedging program. Although the Company may periodically enter into jet fuel derivatives for short-term timeframes, because jet fuel is not widely traded on an organized futures exchange, there are limited opportunities to hedge directly in jet fuel for time horizons longer than approximately 24 months into the future. However, the Company has found that financial derivative instruments in other commodities, such as West Texas Intermediate ("WTI") crude oil, Brent crude oil, and refined products, such as heating oil and unleaded gasoline, can be useful in decreasing its exposure to jet fuel price volatility.[3]

Because Southwest uses commodities other than jet fuel to hedge the price of jet fuel, they will probably have to use statistical approaches to determine if their hedges are effective. A statistical approach such as correlation analysis or regression analysis can be used to show the relationship of jet-fuel prices to heating oil and crude oil prices over time. ASC Topic 815 does not define a specific benchmark correlation coefficient or an adjusted $R^2$; however, cash-flow offsets of between 80 percent and 125 percent are considered to reflect highly effective hedges. In addition to an initial assessment of a hedge's effectiveness, an ongoing assessment must occur to ensure that the hedge continues to be highly effective. Statistical methods again can be used to gauge ongoing effectiveness. If a derivative does not qualify as a highly effective hedge, then the derivative is marked to market at the end of each year regardless of when the gain or loss on the item that management is attempting to hedge is recognized. No offsetting changes in the fair value of the item being hedged are recorded until they are realized.

## Types of Hedge Accounting

LEARNING OBJECTIVE **13.2, 3**

One of three approaches must be used to account for the derivative and related hedged item that has qualified as a highly effective hedge:

**Fair-value hedge accounting.** The item being hedged is an existing asset or liability position or firm purchase or sale commitment. In this case, both the item being hedged and the derivative are marked to fair value at the end of the quarter or year-end on the books. The gain or loss on these items is reflected immediately in earnings. The risk being hedged is the variability in the fair value of the asset or liability.

**Cash-flow hedge accounting.** The derivative hedges the exposure to the variability in expected future cash flows associated with a risk. The exposure may be related to a recognized asset or liability (such as a variable-rate financial instrument) or to a forecasted

[3]From 10K form © 2015 South West Airlines.

transaction such as a forecasted purchase or sale. The derivative is marked to fair value at year-end and is recorded as an asset or liability. The effective portion of the related gain or loss's recognition is deferred until the forecasted transaction affects income. The gain or loss is included as a component of Accumulated Other Comprehensive Income (AOCI) in the balance sheet's stockholders' equity section.

**Hedge of net investment in a foreign subsidiary.** This will be discussed in Chapter 14.

GAAP allows the use of cash-flow hedge accounting for certain types of hedges of existing foreign currency–denominated receivables or payables. We will discuss this accounting later.

**LEARNING OBJECTIVE 13.4**

**CASH-FLOW HEDGES**  We will begin exploring how to account for derivatives using the Gre copper forward contract that we began in Chapter 12. Recall that Gre anticipates producing and selling copper in one year. The expected cost of the 2,000,000-pound production was $4,000,000. Gre enters into a forward contract with Bro that locks in a $2.20 per pound price for the copper. Gre will sell the copper in the open market at the prevailing price and will then either receive or pay the difference between the market price and $2.20 so that Gre nets $2.20 per pound. All of the variability in income resulting from the revenue side is eliminated by this contract. This forward contract is a highly effective hedge.

The forward contract is signed on October 1, 2016. The contract will be settled in one year, on September 30, 2017. Gre prepares quarterly financial reports. Assume that the market price of copper is $2.20 on October 1, 2016. At this time, no entry would be recorded because the contract value is $0.

On December 31, 2016, the company would need to record the estimated value of the contract. Recall that the purpose of this contract is to mitigate the risk of revenue price fluctuations related to an anticipated or a forecasted transaction—the production and sale of copper. The company has entered into a **cash-flow hedge** because it is attempting to control the impact of price fluctuations on its future cash flows and its sales. This is a hedge of an anticipated or a forecasted transaction. In order to reflect this strategy in the financial statements, the gain or loss on the contract will be recognized when the copper is actually sold, which is on September 30, 2017. We must defer recognition of the gain or loss of the contract until that time, and we use the other comprehensive income account to do so. Cash-flow hedge accounting always uses other comprehensive income to defer recognition of gains or losses until the item being hedged actually is recognized in income.

Recall that other comprehensive income is a type of stockholders' equity account. While changes in it are reflected in the statement of comprehensive income, the income statement does not include those changes.

The entries to account for the forward contract are as follows:

**October 1, 2016.** No Entry

**December 31, 2016.** Assume that the market price of copper is $2.30 on this date. If the market price stays the same, Gre would pay Bro $0.10 × 2,000,000 = $200,000 at the expiration of the contract in nine months. We will use this information to estimate the value of the forward contract at December 31, 2016. Because the $200,000 is our estimate of a payment to be paid in nine months, we must use present value concepts to estimate its fair value on December 31, 2016. Assuming that a discount rate of 1 percent per month is reasonable, the estimated fair value of this contract is $200,000/(1.01)^9 = $182,868, and the journal entry to record the change in fair value is:

| | | |
|---|---|---|
| Other comprehensive income (−SE) | 182,868 | |
| Forward contract (+L) | | 182,868 |

**March 31, 2017.** Assume that the market price of copper is $2.15. If this price remains constant, then the company can anticipate receiving $0.05 × 2,000,000 = $100,000 in six months. The estimated fair value of the forward is valued at $100,000/(1.01)^6 = $94,205 and we have moved from a liability situation to an asset situation. The entry to adjust the carrying value of the forward contract is:

| | | |
|---|---|---|
| Forward contract (+A) | 94,205 | |
| Forward contract (−L) | 182,868 | |
| Other comprehensive income (+SE) | | 277,073 |

Notice that the balance for other comprehensive income has moved from a debit balance of $182,868 to a credit balance of $94,205.

**June 30, 2017.** Assume that the market price of copper is $2.10. If this price remains constant, then the company can anticipate receiving $0.10 × 2,000,000 = $200,000 in three months. The estimated fair value of the forward contract is $200,000/(1.01)$^3$ = $194,118. We must increase the forward contract asset and other comprehensive income by $99,913 (the $194,118 desired balance less the $94,205 current balance). The entry to adjust the carrying value of the forward contract is:

| | | |
|---|---|---|
| Forward contract (+A) | 99,913 | |
| Other comprehensive income (+SE) | | 99,913 |

**September 30, 2017.** Assume that the company produced the copper this quarter and sold it on September 30, 2017. The cost was as expected at $4,000,000 for 2,000,000 pounds of copper. The market price of copper on this date is $2.30. Gre sells the copper in the market at $2.30 and will settle the forward contract by paying Bro $200,000 [($2.30 − $2.20) × 2,000,000)]. The journal entries to record the sale are:

| | | |
|---|---|---|
| Cash (+A) | 4,600,000 | |
| Sales (+R, +SE) | | 4,600,000 |
| Cost of goods sold (+E, −SE) | 4,000,000 | |
| Inventory (−A) | | 4,000,000 |

The journal entries to record the settlement of the forward contract are:

| | | |
|---|---|---|
| Sales (−R, −SE) | 200,000 | |
| Other comprehensive income (−SE) | 194,118 | |
| Cash (−A) | | 200,000 |
| Forward contract (−A) | | 194,118 |

The effect of this strategy is to report gross profit of $400,000. Sales are $4,400,000, and cost of goods sold is $4,000,000. Recall that this is the economic income with hedge for every market price realization and agrees with our earlier discussion of this contract. On your own, prepare the journal entries for September 30, 2017, using different realizations of market price to prove to yourself that each realization will result in exactly the same income amount.

The preceding example was accounted for as a cash-flow hedge because the hedge was of an anticipated or forecasted transaction. The unrealized gain or loss on the forward contract was deferred until the transaction being hedged (the copper sale) was reflected in the income statement.

Later, we will explore other types of situations in which cash-flow hedge accounting is appropriate, but now we turn to an example of a fair-value hedge.

**FAIR-VALUE HEDGES**    Fair-value hedge accounting is appropriate for highly effective hedges of either existing assets or liabilities or firm sales/purchase commitments.

Wav Company refines oil. Wav purchases raw crude from various producers and, after the refinement process, sells it to gasoline wholesalers. The price that Wav receives from a gasoline wholesaler depends on the raw crude market price as well as other factors. Typically, Wav refines the oil almost immediately after purchase; however, because of some factory breakdowns, it has about 100,000 barrels of oil that will not be processed for six months. Wav is concerned about how to maintain the value of that oil. While it would be nice if the oil was worth more in six months than it currently is worth, there are no guarantees, and it might be worth less. As a result, Wav is considering entering into a derivative contract that will help it maintain its net investment value.

Wav enters into a forward contract to sell the crude for $90 per barrel in six months. The contract will be settled net. Wav won't actually sell the crude because it intends to refine it, but this type of contract will allow it to maintain the fair value of the crude on its books.

How does the contract work? If the price of crude is $95 per barrel in six months, then Wav will pay the counterparty to the forward $5 per barrel. However, Wav will also have crude that is worth $95 (and therefore will be able to sell it, processed, for more). If, on the other hand, the price of crude is $70 per barrel, Wav will receive $20 per barrel from the counterparty, which will help to compensate it for the lower value of its crude inventory (which will be sold for less when processed).

The accounting for such a situation will reflect the offsetting movement of the derivative and its underlying crude oil price fluctuation. Under fair-value hedge accounting, Wav will write the derivative to market at each financial statement date and will be able to increase or decrease the value of the crude oil inventory by the change in its fair value from the date that the derivative contract is signed and the financial statement date. This is a significant departure from historical cost accounting; both the value of the derivative and the item it is hedging—the crude oil—will change over time.

Before we look at the journal entries to record this situation, we need to discuss one more aspect of hedging existing assets. The crude oil will not be marked to its fair value unless the fair value of the oil at the date the derivative contract is signed is equal to its original cost. If the values are different, the inventory will be changed only by the difference between its fair value and the fair value at the derivative contract signing date. This type of hybrid valuation is called a **mixed-attribute model**. The balance sheet value of the oil contains both historical cost and fair-value elements.

Again, let us assume that the forward contract price of $90 equals the spot price at the contract date. Wav's book value of the oil is $86, its historical cost. Again, the present value model will be used to measure the forward value.

We will now also need a market value for the crude oil because under hedge accounting, we will change the carrying value by the difference between the market value at the date of the hedge contract and subsequent balance sheet dates until the date the forward contract settles. We need to determine which spot crude oil price to use. All crude oil prices, even for oil of the same quality, are not the same. Oil is costly to transport and is produced in many places in the world. As a result, crude oil (and many other commodities) has different spot prices, depending on where it is produced. We will assume that Wav is located in West Texas and that it is located next door to a major West Texas producer. The appropriate spot rate would be West Texas Crude.

On November 1, 2016, the forward contract is signed. No entries are required on this date because no cash payment or receipt exists.

On December 31, 2016, the market price of crude oil is $92. We must record the value of the forward contract at this date and adjust the inventory value for changes in its spot price since the contract was signed.

**FORWARD CONTRACT** If the market price of crude stays at $92, then Wav will pay $2 \times 100,000 = \$200,000$ to settle the contract. That payment will occur in four months, so the estimated value of the contract at December 31, 2016, assuming 1 percent per month interest, is $\$200,0000/(1.01)^4 = \$192,196$. The adjusting entry related to the forward is:

| | | |
|---|---|---|
| Loss on Forward contract (+Lo, −SE) | 192,196 | |
| Forward contract (+L) | | 192,196 |

**INVENTORY** The change in the inventory market value from November 1, 2016 is also $2 per barrel ($92 − $90). So the inventory would be increased by $200,000:

| | | |
|---|---|---|
| Inventory (+A) | 200,000 | |
| Gain on Inventory (+Ga, +SE) | | 200,000 |

Notice that the inventory carrying value is now $8,600,000 + $200,000 = $8,800,000 compared to $9,200,000 for its market value. This is the result of using a mixed-attribute model.

On March 31, 2017, the spot price is $89. If the market price of crude remains at $89, then Wav will receive $100,000 in one month. The estimated value of the forward is $100,000/1.01 = $99,010.

The entry to record the forward contract is:

| | | |
|---|---|---|
| Forward contract (+A) | 99,010 | |
| Forward contract (−L) | 192,196 | |
| Gain on Forward contract (+Ga, +SE) | | 291,206 |

The inventory entry is ($92 − $89) × 100,000 = $300,000.

| | | |
|---|---|---|
| Loss on Inventory (+Lo, −SE) | 300,000 | |
| Inventory (−A) | | 300,000 |

The book value of the inventory is now $8,500,000 ($8,600,000 + $200,000 − $300,000).

On April 30, 2017, the contract settles. The spot price is $87.50. Wav will receive $250,000 [($90 − $87.50) × 100,000] to settle the contract.

### FORWARD CONTRACT

| | | |
|---|---|---|
| Cash (+A) | 250,000 | |
|     Forward contract (−A) | | 99,010 |
|     Gain on Forward contract (+Ga, +SE) | | 150,990 |

### INVENTORY

| | | |
|---|---|---|
| Loss on Inventory (+Lo, −SE) | 150,000 | |
|     Inventory (−A) | | 150,000 |

**Summary of Effect on Earnings**

| Date | Inventory Adjustment | Forward Contract Adjustment | Net Effect |
|---|---|---|---|
| December 31, 2016 | $200,000 | ($192,196) | $7,804 |
| March 31, 2017 | (300,000) | 291,206 | (8,794) |
| April 30, 2017 | (150,000) | 150,990 | 990 |
| Total | ($250,000) | $250,000 | $    0 |

This forward contract works for Wav. Wav's inventory value went down by $250,000 over the time of the production delay. Wav received $250,000 cash on the forward contract, which compensated it for the decline in the value of its inventory. Wav's economic condition would have been worse if it had not entered into the contract.

## Additional Cash-Flow Hedge Examples

**OPTION CONTRACTS**    Assume that a company signs a contract on January 15, 2016, the contract costs $1,000, the option price on that date is $1 per gallon on 100,000 gallons of fuel, and the option expires on May 31, 2016. Further assume that the option is a European one, in which the company can elect to exercise it only on the expiration date. The fuel option contract is a cash-flow hedge because it is designed to limit the company's exposure to price changes in forecasted purchases of fuel. Because the purchase of the fuel will occur in the future and the company purchases the option contract now, it initially records the option contract price as an asset. The company records the option as follows:

| | | |
|---|---|---|
| *January 15, 2016* | | |
| Fuel contract option (+A) | 1,000 | |
|     Cash (−A) | | 1,000 |

The company prepares its quarterly report on March 31, 2016. Assume that the market price of fuel on March 31, 2016, is $1.25. If the company could exercise the option on this date, it would save $0.25 per gallon on the fuel, or $25,000 in total. The estimate of the option payment is $25,000 if it could be paid on March 31, 2016. But the actual payment will occur on May 31, 2016, two months later. The fair value of the option at March 31 needs to be estimated by computing the present value of the option payment. If we assume that the appropriate discount rate is 6 percent per year, or 0.5 percent per month, then we can compute the present value:

$$\$25,000 \div (1.005)^2 = \$24,752$$

The estimate of the value of the option to the company on March 31 is $24,752. The company needs to record an adjusting entry on March 31 because the option must be recorded at fair value according to Topic 815. The fuel contract option account already has a debit balance of $1,000, so the required adjustment is $23,752 to that account.

The purpose of the option contract is to control the cost that the company will pay when purchasing the fuel, so the increase in the option's value should be recorded in income in the same period that the fuel is used. The gain is deferred by including it as a component of other comprehensive income in the stockholders' equity section of the balance sheet. The gain bypasses that quarter's income statement. The entry is as follows:

*March 31, 2016*

| | | |
|---|---|---|
| Fuel contract option (+A) | 23,752 | |
|     Other comprehensive income— | | 23,752 |
|       unrealized holding gain on fuel | | |
|       option contract (+SE) | | |

On May 31, 2016, we assume that the fuel price is $1.30 per gallon. The fuel's market value is $130,000. The writer of the fuel price option must pay the company $0.30 per gallon, or $30,000. An additional gain of $5,248 occurs as a result of the change in market value. The company makes the following entries:

*May 31, 2016*

| | | |
|---|---|---|
| Fuel inventory (+A) | 130,000 | |
|     Cash (−A) | | 130,000 |
| Cash (+A) | 30,000 | |
|     Fuel contract option (−A) | | 24,752 |
|     Other comprehensive income (+SE) | | 5,248 |

Notice that the gain on the contract is still not recognized in income, because the fuel remains in inventory. Once the fuel is used, the gain on the contract will be recognized as a reduction in cost of goods sold, so the net cost of goods sold is $101,000, not $130,000.

Assume that the fuel inventory is used on June 15, 2016. The entries to record Cost of Goods Sold are as follows:

*June 15, 2016*

| | | |
|---|---|---|
| Cost of goods sold (+E, −SE) | 130,000 | |
|     Fuel inventory (−A) | | 130,000 |
| Other comprehensive income (−SE) | 29,000 | |
|     Cost of goods sold (−E, +SE) | | 29,000 |

**FUTURES CONTRACTS—CASH-FLOW HEDGE OF FORECASTED TRANSACTION** Companies can also hedge forecasted transactions using futures contracts. Here is an illustration. On December 1, 2016, a utility enters into a futures contract to purchase 100,000 barrels of heating oil for delivery on January 31, 2017, at $1.4007 per gallon. Heating oil is traded on the NYMEX. Each contract is for 1,000 barrels (42,000 gallons). The utility must enter into 100 contracts. The exchange requires a margin of $100 per contract to be paid up front.

The utility enters into this contract so that it will have a supply of oil for delivery to customers in February and so it can lock in the $1.4007-per-gallon price. This is a forecasted purchase and therefore is accounted for as a cash-flow hedge. The entry is:

*December 1, 2016*

| | | |
|---|---|---|
| Futures contract (+A) | 10,000 | |
|     Cash (−A) | | 10,000 |

At year-end, the company must mark the futures contract to market. Unlike the option contract illustrated on page 425, which is not traded and which requires an estimate of its fair value, the futures contract has an observable market value at December 31, 2016. Assume that the NYMEX reported that the heating oil futures contract for delivery on January 31, 2017, is $1.4050 per gallon. This price already is adjusted for the time value of money because the market would have adjusted for it in the pricing. The contract's estimated value is $18,060 ([$1.4050 − $1.4007] × 4,200,000 gallons). We can now write the contracts to market:

*December 31, 2016*

| | | |
|---|---|---|
| Futures contract (+A) | 18,060 | |
|     Other comprehensive income (+SE) | | 18,060 |

On January 31, 2017, the spot and futures rates are the same, $1.3995 per gallon. The company settles the futures contract and buys 100,000 barrels (4,200,000 gallons) of oil on the open market for

$5,877,900 ($1.3995 per gallon × 4,200,000 gallons) for delivery to the utility's customers during the first week in February. The entry to mark the contract to market is:

*January 31, 2017*

| | | |
|---|---|---|
| Other comprehensive income (−SE) | 23,100 | |
|     Futures contract (−A) | | 23,100 |

100 contracts × 42,000 gallons per contract × ($1.3995 − $1.4050) = $23,100—
Accumulated other comprehensive income account

The balance in the Futures Contract account is a $4,960 debit ($10,000 margin + $18,060 December 31 adjustment − $23,100 January 31, 2017, adjustment). The company lost $5,040 ($23,100 − $18,060) on the contract, which is included in other comprehensive income as a debit balance. The entries to settle the futures contract and record the oil purchase are:

| | | |
|---|---|---|
| Cash (+A) | 4,960 | |
|     Futures contract (−A) | | 4,960 |
| Heating oil inventory (+A) | 5,877,900 | |
|     Cash (−A) | | 5,877,900 |

Assume that the company sells the oil for $2.00 per gallon to its customers during the first week in February. The impact of the gain or loss of the futures contract on earnings is deferred until the hedged transaction actually affects income. The entries at the date of sale are:

| | | |
|---|---|---|
| Cash (+A) | 8,400,000 | |
|     Sales (+R, +SE) | | 8,400,000 |
| Cost of goods sold (+E, −SE) | 5,877,900 | |
|     Heating oil inventory (−A) | | 5,877,900 |
| Cost of goods sold (+E, −SE) | 5,040 | |
|     Other comprehensive income (+SE) | | 5,040 |

The total cost of goods sold is $5,882,940 ($5,877,900 + $5,040), which is equal to 42,000 × 100 contracts × $1.4007 (the contract rate).

## Additional Fair-Value Hedge Example

A **fair-value hedge** is a derivative contract that attempts to reduce the price risk of an existing asset or firm purchase commitment. Fair-value-hedge accounting is used when a highly effective hedge is used to reduce the price risk of an existing asset or liability or a firm sale or purchase commitment contract. Both the item being hedged and the hedge contract are marked to market on an ongoing basis, and the gains and losses are recognized in income immediately. Even though firm sale and purchase commitments are usually not included on the balance sheet until they are executed, GAAP (ASC 815) requires the recognition of them on the balance sheet if they are the object of a hedging contract.

Assume that on January 1, 2016, a company agrees to take delivery of 100,000 liters of Scotch whiskey from a manufacturer in six months—on June 30, 2016—at $15 per liter, the price of Scotch on January 1. In order to take advantage of changes in the market price of whiskey over time, the company also enters into a pay variable/receive fixed forward contract with a speculator, with a fixed price of $15 per liter. The company has in essence unlocked the fixed element of the firm purchase commitment.

The following example illustrates a pay variable/receive fixed forward contract from the company's perspective. The terminology pay variable/receive fixed pertains to the forward contract and not to the contract between the company and the supplier. The exposure being hedged is between the company and the supplier. The hedge of that exposure is the contract between the company and the speculator. If the market price is $14, the company receives $1 in net settlement ($100,000 in total). Then the company pays $14 ($1,400,000 in total) out of its own money and the $1 ($100,000 in total) received from the speculator to settle the fixed price contract with the supplier for $15 ($1,500,000).

If the market price is $17 per liter, the company must pay the speculator $2 per liter and then pay the whiskey supplier $15 per liter. In each case, the whiskey costs the company the market price after considering both the hedge settlement and any additional amounts that must be paid to the supplier out of the company's pocket.

Notice that the company has a *firm purchase commitment* with the whiskey distiller that is non-cancellable, and it has also entered into a forward contract with the speculator. This transaction qualifies as a fair-value hedge because it is aimed at controlling the cost of an existing commitment, not a forecasted transaction.

As discussed earlier, a forward contract is negotiated between the parties, not through an exchange. This allows considerable flexibility in defining the quality, quantity, and delivery schedule.

On January 1, 2016, no entry would be required for either the firm purchase commitment or the forward contract.

On March 31, 2016, assume that the market price of Scotch whiskey is $13 per liter. The company has experienced an unrealized gain of $200,000 on the forward contract [($15 − $13) × 100,000]. It has also experienced an unrealized loss on the purchase commitment because the market price of the whiskey is now below the fixed contract price. The change in the firm purchase commitment fair value and the offsetting change in the forward contract value are recorded immediately in income at present value, assuming a 0.5 percent per month interest rate:

*March 31, 2016*

| | | |
|---|---|---|
| Forward contract (+A) | 197,030 | |
|     Unrealized gain on forward contract (+Ga, +SE) | | 197,030 |
|   To record the change in the fair value of the | | |
|     forward contract. [$200,000/(1.005)$^3$] | | |
| Unrealized loss on firm purchase commitment (+Lo, −SE) | 197,030 | |
|     Firm purchase commitment (+L) | | 197,030 |
|   To record the change in the firm purchase commitment. | | |

At June 30, 2016, both contracts are settled when the market price of whiskey is $14.50. The entries are as follows:

*June 30, 2016*

| | | |
|---|---|---|
| Cash (+A) | 50,000 | |
| Unrealized loss on forward contract (+Lo, −SE) | 147,030 | |
|     Forward contract (−A) | | 197,030 |
| Firm purchase commitment (−L) | 197,030 | |
| Whiskey inventory (+A) | 1,450,000 | |
|     Cash (−A) | | 1,500,000 |
|     Unrealized gain on firm purchase commitment (+Ga, +SE) | | 147,030 |

## ACCOUNTING FOR HEDGE CONTRACTS: ILLUSTRATIONS OF CASH FLOW AND FAIR-VALUE HEDGE ACCOUNTING USING INTEREST RATE SWAPS

We will use interest rate swaps to illustrate the differences in accounting for derivatives as fair-value and cash-flow hedges.

### Cash-Flow Hedge Accounting

We will assume that on January 1, 2016, Jac Company borrows $200,000 from State Bank. The three-year loan with interest paid annually is a variable-rate loan. The initial interest rate is set at 9 percent for year 1. The subsequent years' interest-rate formula is the London Interbank Offer Rate (LIBOR) + 2 percent, determined at the end of each year for the next year. The LIBOR rate at December 31, 2016, is used to set the loan interest rate for 2017. The LIBOR rate at December 31, 2017, is used to set the loan interest rate for 2018.

Because Jac does not wish to assume the risk that the interest rate could increase and therefore the cash paid for interest could increase, Jac decides to hedge this risk.

On January 1, 2016, Jac enters into a **pay-fixed, receive-variable interest rate swap** with Watson for the latter two interest payments. Jac agrees to pay a set rate of 9 percent to Watson and will in return receive LIBOR + 2 percent. The hedge will be settled net. The notional amount is $200,000. Jac or Watson will pay the other the difference between the variable rate and the 9 percent fixed rate depending on which is higher. For example, if the LIBOR rate is 4 percent on December 31, 2016, then Watson will receive $6,000 on December 31, 2017. LIBOR + 2 percent is 6 percent. Jac has agreed to pay 9 percent, so Watson benefits from the lower interest rate and receives the difference multiplied by $200,000. Jac will still end up paying 9 percent in total—3 percent to Watson and 6 percent to State Bank.

If the LIBOR rate on December 31, 2017, is 8 percent, then Jac will receive $2,000 from Watson. LIBOR + 2 percent is 10 percent. Jac will again end up paying 9 percent net. It will pay 10 percent to State Bank and then receive 1 percent from Watson. As you can see, this hedge eliminates the cash-flow variability related to this debt.

To determine the fair value of the interest rate swap to be recorded on Jac's books at December 31, 2016, Jac must make some assumptions about what the future LIBOR interest rates will be and, therefore, what its future cash receipts and future cash payments related to the hedge will be.

Assume that the LIBOR rate on December 31, 2016, is 6.5 percent. This means that Jac's interest payment on December 31, 2017, to State Bank will be 8.5 percent × $200,000, or $17,000. Jac has agreed to pay 9 percent to Watson. This means that, at this point in time, Jac knows it will pay $1,000 to Watson in one year. In order to measure the fair value of the swap arrangement, Jac will make an assumption about the payment that will be made on December 31, 2018. Assuming that a flat interest rate curve is expected, Jac will assume that the interest rate for 2018 will not change from the current rate, so it will expect to pay $1,000 at December 31, 2018, as well.

The interest rate swap fair-value computation at December 31, 2016 is:

Present value at December 31, 2016, of payment to be made to Watson on December 31, 2017:

$$\$1,000/(1.085) = \$922$$

Present value at December 31, 2016, of estimated payment to be paid to Watson on December 31, 2018:

$$\$1,000/(1.085)^2 = \$848$$

The total estimated value of the interest rate swap at December 31, 2016, is:

$$\$922 + \$848 = \$1,770$$

Because Jac anticipates paying this amount, the interest rate swap is recorded as a liability. Assume that at December 31, 2017, the LIBOR rate is 7.25 percent. Watson will now be required to pay Jac under the interest-rate-swap arrangement on December 31, 2018. Watson will pay $200,000 × (0.0925 − 0.0900) = $500. However, this payment will be received by Jac in one year. The fair value of the interest-rate-swap asset at December 31, 2017, is $500 ÷ (1.0925) = $458.

Because this hedge is designed to reduce the variability in the cash flows related to the debt, Jac designates it as a cash-flow hedge. This hedge is also expected to be effective because its terms match the terms of the underlying debt interest payments it is hedging. The notional amount of both is $200,000, the term length matches exactly, and initially the fair value of the hedge is zero (the fixed rate of 9% equals the LIBOR + 2% at the inception of the hedge).

**CASH-FLOW HEDGE ACCOUNTING ENTRIES**   Jac's journal entries to account for the debt, the interest, and the derivative under cash-flow hedge accounting follow:

*January 1, 2016*
Cash (+A)     200,000
     Loan payable (+L)     200,000
   To record receipt of loan proceeds on Jac's books.
*December 31, 2016*
Interest expense (+E, −SE)     18,000
     Cash (−A)     18,000
   To record the payment of interest to State Bank.
Other comprehensive income (−SE)     1,770
     Interest rate swap (+L)     1,770
   To record the fair value of the interest rate swap.
*December 31, 2017*
Interest expense (+E, −SE)     17,000
     Cash (−A)     17,000
   To record interest payment to State Bank,
     $200,000 × 0.085 = $17,000; the variable interest
     rate was determined as of January 1, 2017, as LIBOR + 2%.

| Interest expense (+E, −SE) | 1,000 | |
| Cash (−A) | | 1,000 |

To record payment to Watson of interest-rate-swap settlement.

| Interest rate swap (−L) | 1,770 | |
| Interest rate swap (+A) | 458 | |
| Other comprehensive income (+SE) | | 2,228 |

To adjust the interest rate swap to fair value at December 31, 2017; the other comprehensive income account now has a balance of $458 credit.

*December 31, 2018*

| Interest expense (+E, −SE) | 18,500 | |
| Cash (−A) | | 18,500 |

To record interest payment to State Bank, $200,000 × 0.0925 = $18,500; the variable interest rate was determined as of January 1, 2018, as LIBOR + 2%.

| Cash (+A) | 500 | |
| Interest expense (−E, +SE) | | 500 |

To record receipt of interest-rate-swap settlement from Watson.

| Other comprehensive income (−SE) | 458 | |
| Interest rate swap (−A) | | 458 |

To adjust the interest rate swap to fair value at December 31, 2018, which is zero; notice that the other comprehensive income account is also zero.

| Loan payable (−L) | 200,000 | |
| Cash (−A) | | 200,000 |

To record payment of loan agreement.

## Fair-Value Hedge Accounting

We will now assume that instead of initially borrowing $200,000 from State Bank using a variable-rate note, Jac borrows $200,000 for three years at a fixed rate of 9 percent on January 1, 2016. As a result, Jac enters into a **pay-variable, receive-fixed interest rate swap** with Watson. The notional amount is again $200,000, and the variable-rate formula is LIBOR + 2 percent. Assume that the LIBOR rate is 7 percent on January 1, 2016. The hedge will be settled net.

Jac designates this as a **fair-value hedge**. This is a fair-value hedge because the fair value of the fixed-rate loan fluctuates as a result of the changes in the market rate of interest. The hedge is designed to offset these changes in value.

In this case, both the loan and the interest rate swap will be marked to fair value at each year-end. Recording debt at fair value at year-end is a departure from the historical cost principle. Normally, a bond or loan is recorded initially at its fair value. In subsequent years, the interest expense is based on the market interest rate in effect at the initial borrowing date for the entire bond or loan's existence. Therefore, although amortization of a discount or premium may affect the loan's carrying value, the resulting carrying value is the present value of the cash flows using the original market rate, not the market rate in effect at each year-end.

In this case, the debt carrying value will be adjusted throughout its life for changes in the market interest rate.

### FAIR-VALUE HEDGE ACCOUNTING ENTRIES

*January 1, 2016*

| Cash (+A) | 200,000 | |
| Loan payable (+L) | | 200,000 |

To record the receipt of a loan from State Bank.

*December 31, 2016*

| Interest expense (+E, −SE) | 18,000 | |
| Cash (−A) | | 18,000 |

To record fixed rate interest payment to State Bank.

| Interest rate swap (+A) | 1,770 | |
| Loan payable (+L) | | 1,770 |

To mark both the swap and the loan to market to reflect the market rate of interest on the swap agreement at December 31, 2016, 8.5%. Because the market rate is below the fixed interest rate of 9%, the loan's fair value has increased. This is similar to a bond being sold at a premium.

*December 31, 2017*

| | | |
|---|---|---|
| Interest expense (+E, −SE) | 18,000 | |
|     Cash (−A) | | 18,000 |
| To record fixed-rate interest payment to State Bank. | | |
| Cash (+A) | 1,000 | |
|     Interest expense (−E, +SE) | | 1,000 |
| To record net settlement from Watson; | | |
|     the variable rate is 8.5%, so Watson owes Jac | | |
|     0.005 × $200,000 = $1,000. | | |
| Loan payable (−L) | 2,228 | |
|     Interest rate swap (−A) | | 1,770 |
|     Interest rate swap (+L) | | 458 |
| To mark both the swap and the loan to market; the | | |
|     carrying value of the loan is now $200,000 − $458 = | | |
|     $199,542, a discount. Remember that the variable rate, | | |
|     LIBOR + 2%, on December 31, 2017, is 9.25%. | | |

*December 31, 2018*

| | | |
|---|---|---|
| Interest Expense (+E, −SE) | 18,000 | |
|     Cash (−A) | | 18,000 |
| To record fixed-rate interest payment to State Bank. | | |
| Interest expense (+E, −SE) | 500 | |
|     Cash (−A) | | 500 |
| To record the payment of interest to Watson. | | |
| Interest rate swap (−L) | 458 | |
|     Loan payable (+L) | | 458 |
| To mark the swap and the loan to market; | | |
|     the carrying value of the loan is now $200,000, | | |
|     which will now be paid. | | |
| Loan payable (−L) | 200,000 | |
|     Cash (−A) | | 200,000 |
| To record payment of the loan. | | |

The following table summarizes the fair-value hedge transactions.

| Date | Interest Rate Swap Balance Sheet Debit—Asset; Credit—Liability | Loan Payable Balance Sheet | Interest Expense |
|---|---|---|---|
| January 1, 2016 | | $200,000 | |
| December 31, 2016 | $1,770 debit | $201,770 | $18,000 |
| December 31, 2017 | $458 credit | $199,542 | $17,000 |
| December 31, 2018 | | | $18,500 |

Notice that the fluctuation in the fair value of the loan is reflected in the liability. The company's strategy to hedge this risk is also reflected because the combination of the interest-rate-swap asset/liability value and the loan balance value at December 31, 2016, and December 31, 2017, is $200,000.

# FOREIGN CURRENCY DERIVATIVES AND HEDGING ACTIVITIES

## Foreign Currency–Denominated Receivables and Payables

LEARNING OBJECTIVE **13.5**

In Chapter 12, we discussed the accounting for foreign currency–denominated receivables and payables. Companies frequently hedge their exposure to foreign currency exchange risk for existing foreign currency–denominated assets and liabilities and anticipated foreign currency–denominated transactions. In this section, we will focus on hedge accounting when foreign currency transactions are involved. The accounting for such foreign currency hedges is a bit different than for the derivatives discussed already.

FASB ASC Topic 830 requires marking to fair-value (the current spot rate) foreign currency–denominated receivables and payables at period-end. The resulting gain or loss is recognized immediately in income. Under FASB ASC Topic 815, a company may be able to choose to account for hedges of such receivables and payables using either a fair-value hedge model or a cash-flow hedge model. The contract-term requirements for selecting a cash-flow hedge model are stringent, as we will discuss next.

The forward premium or discount is the difference between the contracted forward rate and the spot rate prevailing when the contract is entered into. This premium or discount is amortized into income over the life of the contract if the hedge is designated as a cash-flow hedge. The effective interest method is appropriate.

**CASH-FLOW HEDGES**  For a forward contract to qualify for **cash-flow hedge** accounting, the contract must have the following characteristics:

1. Cash-flow hedges can be used in recognized foreign currency–denominated asset and liability situations if the variability of the cash flows is completely eliminated by the hedge. This requirement is generally met if the settlement date, currency type, and currency amounts match the expected payment dates and amounts of the foreign currency–denominated receivable or payable. If any of these critical terms don't match between the hedged item and the hedging instrument, then the contract is designated a **fair-value hedge** with current earnings recognition of changes in the value of the hedging derivative and the hedged item. (This is illustrated later.)

2. According to GAAP, the transaction gain or loss arising from the remeasurement of the foreign currency–denominated asset or liability is offset by a related amount reclassified from other comprehensive income to earnings each period. Thus, the foreign currency–denominated asset or liability is marked to fair value at period-end, and the gain or loss is recognized in income. The cash-flow hedge is also marked to fair value at period-end. Like other cash-flow hedges, the gain or loss is included in other comprehensive income. At period-end, a portion of the gain or loss included in other comprehensive income is then recognized in income to offset the gain or loss on the foreign currency–denominated asset or liability.

3. Finally, the premium or discount related to the hedge is amortized to income using an effective interest rate.

### Example of Accounting for a Cash-Flow Hedge of an Existing Foreign Currency–Denominated Accounts Receivable

Assume that Win Corporation, a U.S. firm, sold hospital equipment to Howard Ltd. of Britain on November 2, 2016, for 100,000 British pounds, receivable in 90 days, on January 31, 2017. In addition, on November 2, Win enters into a 90-day forward contract with Ross Company to hedge its exposed net accounts receivable position. We will assume that the forward contract allows for net settlement. Assume that a reasonable incremental interest rate is 12 percent. Selected exchange rates of pounds are:

|  | November 2, 2016 | December 31, 2016 | January 31, 2017 |
|---|---|---|---|
| Spot rate | $1.650 | $1.660 | $1.665 |
| 90-day forward rate | $1.638 | | |
| 30-day forward rate | | $1.655 | |

The entry on November 2, 2016, to record the sale is:

| | | |
|---|---|---|
| Accounts receivable (fc) (+A) | 165,000 | |
| Sales (+R, +SE) | | 165,000 |

To record the sale of equipment to Howard Company, £100,000 × $1.6500, the spot rate at November 2, 2016.

Because Win entered into a forward contract that is to be settled net, no entry is necessary at the date that contract is entered into. Recall that if this were a futures or option contract, an entry would be necessary because some cash would have been paid by Win at the inception of these types of contracts.

Both the foreign currency–denominated accounts receivable and the forward contract must be marked to fair value at year-end, December 31, 2016.

### ACCOUNTS RECEIVABLE ADJUSTMENT

| | | |
|---|---|---|
| Accounts receivable (fc) (+A) | 1,000 | |
| Exchange gain (+Ga, +SE) | | 1,000 |
| To adjust accounts receivable to spot rate at year-end [£100,000 × ($1.660 − $1.650)]. | | |

**FORWARD CONTRACT ADJUSTMENT**   Win's 90-day forward contract expires on January 31, 2017, with Win set to receive $1.638 per pound. At December 31, 2016, a 30-day forward contract rate is $1.655. A 30-day forward contract entered into on December 31, 2016, would be settled on January 31, 2017. Based on the change in the forward rate, the estimated loss on the forward contract is £100,000 × ($1.655 − $1.638) = $1,700. However, this is the estimated loss to be realized in one month. To estimate the fair value of the forward contract on December 31, 2016, we must compute the present value of this amount:

| Date | Forward Contract Rate | Forward Contract Rate at This Date | Difference | × | 100,000 | Factor | Present Value at Date Below |
|---|---|---|---|---|---|---|---|
| December 31 | $1.638 | $1.655 | $0.017 | | $1,700 | $1.01^1$ | $1,683 |

The approximate fair value of the forward contract is $1,683. The December 31, 2016, entry is:

| | | |
|---|---|---|
| Other comprehensive income (−SE) | 1,683 | |
| Forward contract (+L) | | 1,683 |

**ENTRY TO OFFSET ACCOUNTS RECEIVABLE EXCHANGE GAIN**   Thus far at December 31, 2016, an exchange gain of $1,000 has been recorded as a result of marking the accounts receivable to fair value. The related forward contract has also been marked to market with the resulting loss recorded in other comprehensive income. We must now record an entry to offset the exchange gain in order to properly account for this cash-flow hedge. The entry is:

| | | |
|---|---|---|
| Exchange loss (+Lo, −SE) | 1,000 | |
| Other comprehensive income (+SE) | | 1,000 |

**DISCOUNT AMORTIZATION**   This situation qualifies for cash-flow hedge accounting because the forward contract completely eliminates the variability in cash flows related to the pound-denominated accounts receivable. Win has locked in a rate of $1.638. However, this is not a costless transaction. The spot rate on November 2, 2016, was $1.650. The company knows it will receive $1,200 less than the initial $165,000. This cost must be recognized in income over time. GAAP requires that an effective rate method be used to amortize the discount or premium. In this case, because the asset's ultimate amount to be received is less than the initial amount recorded, this is a discount. The formula to solve for the implicit interest rate is:

Hedged asset or liability fair value at the hedge date $\times (1 + r)^n$ = Hedge contract cash flow

Here the hedged accounts receivable fair value at November 2, 2016, is $165,000, the hedge contract cash flow is £100,000 × $1.638 = $163,800, and $n = 3$ because the contract will expire in 90 days, or three months. We will solve for $r$, the monthly implicit interest rate.

$$\$165,000(1 + r)^3 = \$163,800$$
$$(1 + r)^3 = 0.99273$$
$$\sqrt[3]{(1 + r)^3} = \sqrt[3]{(0.99273)}$$
$$(1 + r) = 0.99757$$
$$r = -0.00243, \text{ or } -0.243\% \text{ per month}$$

Here is the amortization table for this discount amortization:

|  | Discount Amortization: Balance × 0.00243 | Balance |
|---|---|---|
|  |  | $165,000 |
| November 30 | $401 | $164,599 |
| December 31 | $400 | $164,199 |
| January 31 | $399 | $163,800 |
| Total discount amortization | $1,200 |  |

The journal entry at December 31, 2016, to record November and December amortization is:

| | | |
|---|---|---|
| Exchange loss (+Lo, −SE) | 801 | |
|    Other comprehensive income (+SE) | | 801 |

At December 31, 2016, accounts receivable has a balance of $166,000 (the fair value of the British pound denominated receivable), the forward contract balance is $1,683 credit (its fair value), and other comprehensive income is $118 credit. Income has been reduced by the amortization of the discount, $801.

**ACCOUNTS RECEIVABLE FAIR-VALUE ADJUSTMENT AND SETTLEMENT**   On January 31, 2017, five journal entries must be made. Assume that the spot rate at January 31, 2017, is $1.665 and that Win collects the £100,000 accounts receivable and immediately converts it into dollars.

| | | |
|---|---|---|
| Cash (+A) | 166,500 | |
|    Accounts receivable (fc) (−A) | | 166,000 |
|    Exchange gain (+Ga, +SE) | | 500 |

**FORWARD CONTRACT FAIR-VALUE ADJUSTMENT AND NET SETTLEMENT**   Win must pay Ross $166,500 − $163,800 = $2,700 because the spot rate on the date the contract expires is $1.665 and the forward contract rate is $1.638. We will first record the forward contract gain or loss from December 31 to January 31 and then record the net settlement payment to Ross.

| | | |
|---|---|---|
| Other comprehensive income (−SE) | 1,017 | |
|    Forward contract (+L) | | 1,017 |

The contract loss is $2,700 (forward contract value at settlement date) − $1,683 (December 31, 2016, forward contract fair-value estimate) = $1,017.

| | | |
|---|---|---|
| Forward contract (−L) | 2,700 | |
|    Cash (−A) | | 2,700 |

**OFFSET GAIN ENTRY**   Next, we must record a loss to offset the exchange gain recorded related to the receivable:

| | | |
|---|---|---|
| Exchange loss (+Lo, −SE) | 500 | |
|    Other comprehensive income (+SE) | | 500 |

**DISCOUNT ENTRY**   From the previous table, $399 of the discount must be amortized for the period December 31, 2016, to January 31, 2017:

| | | |
|---|---|---|
| Exchange loss (+Lo, −SE) | 399 | |
|    Other comprehensive income (+SE) | | 399 |

Let's summarize what has happened to the accounts involved in this cash-flow-hedge situation:

**Accounts Receivable (Asset)**

| | |
|---|---|
| November 2, 2016—initial sale date | $165,000 |
| December 31, 2016—adjusted to spot rate | + 1,000 |
| Balance on December 31, 2016 (spot rate (spot rate $1.66 × £100,000) | $166,000 |
| January 31, 2017—adjusted to spot rate | + 500 |
| Balance on January 31, 2017, before settlement | $166,500 |

**Forward Contract**

| | |
|---|---|
| November 2, 2016—initial contract date | No entry—net settlement |
| December 31, 2016—adjusted to fair value estimate | +1,683—liability |
| Balance on December 31, 2016 | $1,683 credit—liability |
| January 31, 2017—adjusted to fair value | $1,017 credit |
| Balance before settlement | $2,700 credit |
| Settlement | $2,700 debit |
| Balance after settlement | $ 0 |

**Other Comprehensive Income (OCI)**

| | |
|---|---|
| November 2, 2016 | No entry |
| December 31, 2016—adjust forward contract to fair value estimate | $1,683 debit |
| Offset gain on hedged item—accounts receivable | 1,000 credit |
| Discount amortization for November and December | 801 credit |
| Balance on December 31, 2016 | $118 credit |
| January 31, 2017—adjust forward contract to fair-value estimate | $1,017 debit |
| Offset gain on hedged item—accounts receivable | 500 credit |
| Discount amortization for January | 399 credit |
| Balance on January 31, 2017 | $0 |

**Income Effect**

| | |
|---|---|
| *December 31, 2016* | |
| Gain on hedged item | $1,000 |
| Offsetting amount from OCI due to forward contract and cash-flow-hedge accounting | (1,000) |
| Discount amortization—exchange loss | (801) |
| Net exchange loss at December 31, 2016 | ($801) |
| *January 31, 2017* | |
| Gain on hedged item | $500 |
| Offsetting amount from OCI due to forward contract and cash-flow-hedge accounting | (500) |
| Discount amortization—exchange loss | (399) |
| Net exchange loss at January 31, 2017 | ($399) |

What has this accounting accomplished? Notice that the company knew on November 2, 2016, that it was going to lose $1,200 related to the foreign currency–denominated accounts receivable and the related hedging contract. The previous accounting reflects management's purpose in entering into this contract because the effect of changes in the exchange rate on the receivable value is exactly offset by reclassifying an offsetting amount from other comprehensive income. The actual cost of the cash-flow hedge to the company, $1,200, is rationally and systematically amortized to income. Finally, both the item being hedged and the hedge contract are valued at fair value at year-end.

Also notice something else. Recall that the amortized value of the hedged item on December 31, 2016, from the discount amortization table on page 434 is $164,199. How is this number reflected on the balance sheet at December 31?

| | |
|---|---|
| Accounts receivable—at fair value | $166,000 debit |
| Less: Forward contract—at estimated fair value | 1,683 credit |
| Less: Other comprehensive income | 118 credit |
| Net balance sheet effect of the cash flow hedge | $164,199 debit |

As illustrated previously, a company may incur losses (and garner gains) when the foreign exchange rate of foreign currency–denominated receivables or payables fluctuates between the date that the receivable (payable) is recorded and when it is ultimately received and converted into dollars (or dollars are used to buy the foreign currency used to settle the payable).

## Fair-Value Hedge Accounting: Foreign Currency–Denominated Receivable Example

**ILLUSTRATION: HEDGE AGAINST EXPOSED NET ASSET (ACCOUNTS RECEIVABLE) POSITIONS**   U.S. Oil Company sells oil to Monato Company of Japan for 15,000,000 yen on December 1, 2016. The billing date for the sale is December 1, 2016, and payment is due in 60 days, on January 30, 2017. Concurrent with the sale, U.S. Oil enters into a forward contract to deliver 15,000,000 yen to its exchange broker in

60 days. This transaction will not be settled net. The yen will be delivered to the broker. Exchange rates for Japanese yen are as follows:

|  | December 1, 2016 | December 31, 2016 | January 30, 2017 |
|---|---|---|---|
| Spot rate | **$0.007500** | **$0.007498** | **$0.007497** |
| 30-day forward rate | $0.007490 | **$0.007489** | $0.007488 |
| 60-day forward rate | **$0.007490** | $0.007488 | $0.007486 |

The bold rates are the relevant rates for accounting purposes. The forward contract is carried at market value, which is the forward rate. Journal entries on the books of U.S. Oil are as follows:

*December 1, 2016*

| | | |
|---|---|---|
| Accounts receivable (fc) (+A) | 112,500 | |
|     Sales (+R, +SE) | | 112,500 |
|     To record sales to Monato Company (15,000,000 | | |
|       yen × $0.007500 spot rate). | | |
| Contract receivable (+A) | 112,350 | |
|     Contract payable (fc) (+L) | | 112,350 |
|     To record forward contract to deliver 15,000,000 yen in | | |
|       60 days. Receivable: 15,000,000 yen × $0.007490 forward rate. | | |

At the time that the forward contract is entered into, the company can compute its total gain or loss on the hedged item and the hedge contract. Fluctuations in exchange rates subsequent to this will not affect the magnitude of this gain or loss. The net gain or loss is the difference between the contracted forward rate and the spot rate on the date the contract is entered into:

$$(\$0.007490 - \$0.00750) \times 15,000,000 = -\$0.00001 \times 15,000,000 = -\$150$$

The company will lose $150, because it has contracted to receive $0.00001 less than the spot rate at the time the contract was entered into.

At December 31, 2016, the accounts receivable from the sale is adjusted to reflect the current exchange rate, and a $30 exchange loss is recorded. Calculating the exchange gain on the forward contract is a bit more complex. On the surface, the gain would appear to be the initial forward rate of $0.007490 × 15,000,000 less the current forward rate of $0.007489 × 15,000,000 ($112,350 − $112,335), which is $15. However, the FASB has elected to discount this amount from the contract termination date to the financial statement date. If we assume that 12 percent is a reasonable discount rate, this would be a discount of $0.15. The present value of $15 to be received in one month is computed as $15 ÷ $(1.01)^1 = \$14.85$.

*December 31, 2016*

| | | |
|---|---|---|
| Exchange loss (+Lo, −SE) | 30 | |
|     Accounts receivable (fc) (−A) | | 30 |
|     To adjust accounts receivable to year-end spot exchange rate | | |
|       [15,000,000 yen × ($0.007500 − $0.007498) = $30]. | | |
| Contract payable (fc) (−L) | 14.85 | |
|     Exchange gain (+Ga, +SE) | | 14.85 |
|     To adjust contract payable to exchange broker to | | |
|       the year-end forward exchange rate. Payable: | | |
|       [15,000,000 yen × ($0.007490 − $0.007489)]/(1.01) | | |

The exchange gain or loss on the hedged underlying asset is not the same as the exchange gain or loss on the forward contract because the underlying asset is carried at the spot rate, and the forward contract is carried at the forward rate.

Over the contract period, the forward rate will approach the spot rate, exactly equaling it on the settlement date. In this example, the net change in the relative value was $15.15 ($30 loss − $14.85 gain) for 2016 and $134.85 ($15 loss + $119.85 loss) for 2017:

*January 30, 2017*

| | | |
|---|---|---|
| Cash (fc) (+A) | 112,455 | |
| Exchange loss (+Lo, −SE) | 15 | |
|     Accounts receivable (fc) (−A) | | 112,470 |
|     To record collection of receivable from | | |
|       Monato Company. Cash: 15,000,000 yen × $0.007497. | | |

| | | |
|---|---|---|
| Contract payable (fc) (+L) | 112,335.15 | |
| Exchange loss (+Lo, −SE) | 119.85 | |
|    Cash (fc) (−A) | | 112,455 |

To record delivery of 15,000,000 yen from Monato to
foreign exchange broker in settlement of liability.

| | | |
|---|---|---|
| Cash (+A) | 112,350 | |
|    Contract receivable (−A) | | 112,350 |

To record receipt of cash from exchange broker.

In the final analysis, U.S. Oil Company makes a sale in the amount of $112,500. It takes a $150 loss on the transaction in order to avoid the risks of foreign currency price fluctuations, and it collects $112,350 in final settlement of the sale transaction. The $150 reduces income over the term of the forward contract.

**HEDGE AGAINST EXPOSED NET LIABILITY POSITION**    Accounting procedures for hedging an exposed net liability position are comparable to those illustrated for U.S. Oil Company except that the objective is to hedge a liability denominated in foreign currency, rather than a receivable. Normally, the forward rate for buying foreign currency for future receipt is greater than the spot rate. For example, a forward contract to acquire 10,000 British pounds for receipt in 60 days might have a forward rate of $1.675 when the spot rate is $1.66. The forward contract is recorded as follows:

| | | |
|---|---|---|
| Contract receivable (fc) (+A) | 16,750 | |
|    Contract payable (+L) | | 16,750 |

The contract hedges any effect of changes in the exchange rate so that the net cost over the life of the contract will be the $150 differential between the spot and forward rates.

**RESULT OF HEDGING**    Forward rates are ordinarily set so that a cost is incurred related to the hedge. Occasionally, the rates for futures contracts result in hedges that increase income.

In summary, a forward contract is recorded at the forward rate, while the underlying asset or liability is recorded at the spot rate (and adjusted to these respective rates and values at the financial statement date). Over the life of the contract, the initial difference between the spot and the forward rates is the cost of hedging the exchange rate risk. Because the gains and losses on both the hedge and the underlying asset or liability are recorded in current earnings, the net cost reported in the income statement is the change in the relative values of the spot and forward rates.

If a firm enters a forward contract for foreign currency units in excess of the foreign currency units reflected in its exposed net asset or net liability position (a speculation in the currency), the difference ends up as a gain or loss. This is due to the difference in the change in the value of the derivative and the change in the value of the underlying item hedged both being reported in the income statement.

## Fair-Value Hedge of an Identifiable Foreign Currency Commitment

A **foreign currency commitment** is a contract or agreement denominated in foreign currency that will result in a foreign currency transaction at a later date. For example, a U.S. firm may contract to buy equipment from a Canadian firm at a future date with the invoice price denominated in Canadian dollars. The U.S. firm has an exposure to exchange rate changes because the future price in U.S. dollars may increase or decrease before the transaction is consummated.

An identifiable foreign currency commitment differs from an exposed asset or liability position because the commitment does not meet the accounting tests for recording the related asset or liability in the accounts. The risk of the exposure still may be avoided by hedging. This situation is special because the underlying transaction being hedged is not recorded as an asset or liability. Therefore, some method must be established to record the change in the value of the underlying unrecorded commitment in order to record the derivative instrument as a hedge of the commitment. Once this mechanism has been created, the change in both the derivative instrument and the underlying commitment are recorded—in effect, offsetting each other. Because a forward contract that is a hedge of a firm commitment is based on the forward rate, not the spot rate, any gain or loss on the derivative and underlying contract is based on the forward rate.

The forward contract accounting begins when the forward contract is designated as a hedge of a foreign currency commitment.

**ILLUSTRATION: HEDGE OF AN IDENTIFIABLE FOREIGN CURRENCY PURCHASE COMMITMENT**   On October 2, 2016, American Stores Corporation contracts with Canadian Distillers for purchase of 1,000 cases of bourbon at a price of 60,000 Canadian dollars, when the spot rate for Canadian dollars is $0.70. The bourbon is to be delivered in March and payment made in Canadian dollars on March 31, 2017. In order to hedge this future commitment, American Stores enters into a forward contract to purchase 60,000 Canadian dollars for delivery to American Stores in 180 days at a forward exchange rate of $0.725. Applicable forward rates on December 31, 2016, and March 31, 2017 (because the maturity is March 31, this rate is also the spot rate) are $0.71 and $0.68, respectively.

Assume that the derivative instrument (the forward contract) is designated as a hedge of this identifiable foreign currency commitment (the bourbon purchase). The purchase of the forward contract on October 2, 2016, is recorded as follows:

*October 2, 2016*

| | | |
|---|---:|---:|
| Contract receivable (fc) (+A) | 43,500 | |
|     Contract payable (+L) | | 43,500 |
|   To record forward contract to purchase 60,000 | | |
|     Canadian dollars for delivery in 180 days at a forward rate | | |
|     of $0.725. | | |

By December 31, 2016, the forward exchange rate for Canadian dollars decreases to $0.71, and American Stores adjusts its receivable to reflect the 60,000 Canadian dollars at the 90-day forward exchange rate. This adjustment creates a $900 exchange loss on the forward contract as follows:

*December 31, 2016*

| | | |
|---|---:|---:|
| Exchange loss (+Lo, −SE) | 900 | |
|     Contract receivable (fc) (−A) | | 900 |
|   To record exchange loss: 60,000 | | |
|     Canadian dollars × ($0.725 − $0.71). | | |

However, this loss is offset by the increase in the value of the underlying firm commitment:

*December 31, 2016*

| | | |
|---|---:|---:|
| Change in value of firm commitment in | 900 | |
|     Canadian dollars (fc) (+A) | | |
|         Exchange gain (+Ga, +SE) | | 900 |
|   To record exchange gain: 60,000 Canadian | | |
|     dollars × ($0.725 − $0.71). (Payment in Canadian | | |
|     dollars will cost fewer US$.) | | |

Journal entries on March 31, 2017, to account for the foreign currency transaction and related forward contract are as follows:

*March 31, 2017*

| | | |
|---|---:|---:|
| 1. Contract payable (−L) | 43,500 | |
|     Cash (−A) | | 43,500 |
|   To record settlement of forward contract with the | | |
|     exchange broker (denominated in U.S. dollars). | | |
| 2. Cash (fc) (+A) | 40,800 | |
|    Exchange loss (+Lo, −SE) | 1,800 | |
|     Contract receivable (fc) (−A) | | 42,600 |
|   To record receipt of 60,000 Canadian dollars from | | |
|     the exchange broker when the exchange rate is $0.68. | | |
| 3. Change in value of firm commitment in Canadian dollars (+A) | 1,800 | |
|     Exchange gain (+Ga, +SE) | | 1,800 |
|   To record the change in the value of the underlying | | |
|     firm commitment. | | |
| 4. Inventory (+A) | 43,500 | |
|     Change in value of firm commitment in Canadian | | 2,700 |
|       dollars (−A) | | |
|     Accounts payable (fc) (+L) | | 40,800 |
|   To record receipt of 1,000 cases of bourbon | | |
|     at a cost of 60,000 Canadian dollars × forward | | |
|     exchange rate of $0.725. | | |
| 5. Accounts payable (fc) (−L) | 40,800 | |
|     Cash (fc) (−A) | | 40,800 |
|   To record payment of 60,000 Canadian dollars to | | |
|     Canadian Distillers. | | |

Entry 1 records payment to the exchange broker for the 60,000 Canadian dollars at the contracted forward rate of $0.725. The second entry reflects collection of the 60,000 Canadian dollars from the broker and records an additional exchange loss on the further decline of the exchange rate from the forward rate of $0.71 at December 31, 2016, to the $0.68 spot rate (this is also the forward rate for the date of settlement) at March 31, 2017. The third entry records the gain on the change in the dollar cost of the firm commitment to buy the bourbon since December 31, 2016. The fourth entry on March 31 records receipt of the 1,000 cases of bourbon from Canadian Distillers and records the liability payable in Canadian dollars. It also incorporates the change in the firm commitment in the inventory value. In entry 5, Canadian Distillers is paid the 60,000 Canadian dollars in final settlement of the account payable.

**HEDGE OF AN IDENTIFIABLE FOREIGN CURRENCY SALES COMMITMENT**    Accounting procedures for hedging an identifiable foreign currency sales commitment are comparable to those illustrated for hedging a purchase commitment, except that the sales, rather than the inventory, account is adjusted for any deferred exchange gains or losses.

## Cash-Flow Hedge of an Anticipated Foreign Currency Commitment

Win Corporation, a U.S. corporation, anticipates a contract based on December 2, 2016, discussions to purchase heavy equipment from Smith Ltd. of Scotland for 500,000 British pounds. The equipment is anticipated to be delivered to Win and the amount paid to Smith on March 2, 2017, but nothing has been signed.

In order to hedge its anticipated commitment, Win enters into a forward contract with Sea Company to buy 500,000 British pounds for delivery on March 2. The contract is to be settled net. Assume that this qualifies as an effective hedge under GAAP and should be accounted for as a cash-flow hedge of an anticipated foreign currency commitment.

On December 2, 2016, the spot rate is $1.7000 and the 90-day forward rate is $1.6800 (for delivery on March 2, 2017). Because this is an anticipated commitment, there is no hedged item on the balance sheet that will be marked to fair value until the actual sale occurs, which will be in three months. However, the company has engaged in this forward contract. The contract must be recorded at estimated fair value at year-end. However, because this is considered a cash-flow hedge of an anticipated foreign currency commitment, the resulting gain or loss is deferred until the item being hedged actually affects income. The discount or premium related to the forward contract must be amortized to income over time.

**FORWARD CONTRACT ADJUSTMENT AT DECEMBER 31, 2016**    Assume that the 60-day forward rate at December 31, 2016, is $1.6900. We estimate the fair value of this forward contract as follows, assuming a 12 percent annual incremental borrowing rate:

| Date | Forward Contract Rate | Forward Contract Rate at this Date | Difference | × 500,000 | Factor | Present Value at Date Below |
|---|---|---|---|---|---|---|
| December 31 | $1.68 | $1.69 | $0.01 | $5,000 | $1.01^2$ | $4,901 |

The journal entry is:

| | | |
|---|---|---|
| Forward contract (+A) | 4,901 | |
|     Other comprehensive income (+SE) | | 4,901 |

**FORWARD DISCOUNT ADJUSTMENT**    The original forward discount was $1.70 - $1.68 = 0.02 × 500,000 = $10,000. Recall from our discussion of cash-flow hedges of existing foreign currency–denominated receivables and payables that the discount or premium resulting from the hedge must be amortized to income over the life of the contract. If the spot rate and forward rate on December 2, 2016, had been the same, there would be no discount or premium to amortize. Win would have just recorded the forward contract fair value at year-end as illustrated earlier. Income would not have been affected. However, in this case, the spot and forward rates were different, resulting in a discount that must be amortized to income over the contract's life. A discount arises when the contracted forward rate is lower than the spot rate at that date. A premium arises when the contracted forward rate is higher than the spot rate at the contract date. We again solve for the monthly implicit rate to be used to amortize the $10,000 discount. The rate is .3937 percent or .003937. The amortization table is presented below:

| | Discount Amortization | Balance |
|---|---|---|
| | | $850,000 |
| December 31 | $ 3,346 | $846,654 |
| January 31 | $ 3,333 | $843,321 |
| March 2 | $ 3,321 | $840,000 |
| Total discount amortization | $10,000 | |

The journal entry to record the discount amortization and related gain at December 31 is:

| | | |
|---|---|---|
| Other comprehensive income (−SE) | 3,346 | |
|     Exchange gain (+Ga, +SE) | | 3,346 |

There are four journal entries on March 2.

**FORWARD CONTRACT ADJUSTMENT AND EQUIPMENT PURCHASE**  Assume that the spot rate on March 2 is $1.72. The forward contract value on this date is ($1.72 − $1.68) × 500,000 = $20,000. The balance on December 31, 2016, was $4,901 debit, so we must increase the forward contract to its fair value by increasing the account by $15,099. Win will receive $20,000 from Sea because the spot rate is higher than the forward contract rate:

| | | |
|---|---|---|
| Forward contract (+A) | 15,099 | |
|     Other comprehensive income (+SE) | | 15,099 |
| Equipment (+A) | 860,000 | |
|     Cash (−A) | | 860,000 |
|     (1.72 × 500,000) | | |
| Cash (−A) | 20,000 | |
|     Forward contract (−A) | | 20,000 |

**DISCOUNT AMORTIZATION ENTRY**  We must record the amortization of the discount for January and February. From the amortization table earlier, the amortization for those two months is $3,333 + $3,321 = $6,654:

| | | |
|---|---|---|
| Other comprehensive income (−SE) | 6,654 | |
|     Exchange gain (+Ga, +SE) | | 6,654 |

This table presents a summary of account balances:

| | |
|---|---|
| **Forward contract** | |
| December 2, 2016—no entry required | $0 |
| December 31, 2016 | +4,901 debit |
| Balance on December 31, 2016 | $4,901 debit—asset |
| Fair value adjustment at March 2, 2017 | +15,099 debit |
| Balance before settlement on March 2, 2017 | $20,000 debit—asset |
| **Other Comprehensive Income** | |
| December 31, 2016, adjustment of forward contract to fair value | $ 4,901 credit |
| December 31, 2016, amortization of discount | 3,346 debit |
| Balance on December 31, 2016 | $ 1,555 credit |
| March 2, 2017, adjustment of forward contract to fair value | $15,099 credit |
| March 2, 2017, amortization of discount | 6,654 debit |
| Balance on March 2, 2017 | $10,000 credit |
| **Income** | |
| December 31, 2016—exchange gain resulting from amortizing discount | $ 3,346 |
| March 2, 2017—exchange gain resulting from amortizing discount | $ 6,654 |

On March 2, 2017, the equipment is recorded at $860,000. As the equipment is depreciated, the $10,000 balance in the other comprehensive income account will be amortized to reduce depreciation expense.

## Speculation

Exchange gains or losses on derivative instruments that speculate in foreign currency price movements are included in income in the periods in which the forward exchange rates change. Forward or future exchange rates for 30-, 90-, and 180-day delivery are quoted on a daily basis for the leading world currencies. A foreign currency derivative that is a speculation is valued at forward rates throughout the life of the contract (which is the fair value of the contract at that point in time). The basic accounting is illustrated in the following example.

On November 2, 2016, U.S. International enters into a 90-day forward contract (future) to purchase 10,000 euros when the current quotation for 90-day futures in euros is $0.5400. The spot rate for euros on November 2 is $0.5440. Exchange rates at December 31, 2016, and January 31, 2017, are as follows:

|  | December 31, 2016 | January 31, 2017 |
|---|---|---|
| 30-day forward | $0.5450 | $0.5480 |
| Spot rate | $0.5500 | $0.5530 |

Journal entries on the books of U.S. International to account for the speculation are as follows:

*November 2, 2016*

| | | |
|---|---|---|
| Contract receivable (fc) (+A) | 5,400 | |
|     Contract payable (+L) | | 5,400 |

    To record contract for 10,000 euros × $0.5400 exchange rate for 90-day futures.

*December 31, 2016*

| | | |
|---|---|---|
| Contract receivable (fc) (+A) | 50 | |
|     Exchange gain (+Ga, +SE) | | 50 |

    To adjust receivable from exchange broker and recognize exchange gain (10,000 euros × $0.5450 forward exchange rate for 30-day futures − $5,400 per books).

*January 31, 2017*

| | | |
|---|---|---|
| Cash (fc) (+A) | 5,530 | |
|     Exchange gain (+Ga, +SE) | | 80 |
|     Contract receivable (fc) (−A) | | 5,450 |

    To record receipt of 10,000 euros. The current spot rate for euros is $0.5530.

| | | |
|---|---|---|
| Contract payable (−L) | 5,400 | |
|     Cash (−A) | | 5,400 |

    To record payment of the liability to the exchange broker denominated in dollars.

The entry on November 2 records U.S. International's right to receive 10,000 euros from the exchange broker in 90 days. It also records U.S. International's liability to pay $5,400 to the exchange broker in 90 days. Both the receivable and the liability are recorded at $5,400 (10,000 euros × $0.5400 forward rate), but only the receivable is denominated in euros and is subject to exchange rate fluctuations.

At December 31, 2016, the forward contract has 30 days until maturity. Under GAAP, the receivable denominated in euros is adjusted to reflect the exchange rate of $0.5450 for 30-day futures on December 31, 2016. This is the fair value of the contract. The amount of the adjustment is included in U.S. International's income for 2016.

On January 31, 2017, U.S. International receives 10,000 euros with a current value of $5,530 (10,000 euros × $0.5530 spot rate). The translated value of the foreign currency received is $80 more than the recorded amount of the receivable, so an additional exchange gain results. U.S. International also settles its liability with the exchange broker on January 31.

A speculation involving the sale of foreign currency for future delivery is accounted for in a similar fashion, except that the receivable is fixed in U.S. dollars and the liability is denominated in the foreign currency.

## Derivative Accounting Summarized

The accounting required for a derivative depends primarily on management's intent when entering into the transaction. Exhibit 13-1 summarizes the types of derivatives and the purpose, required accounting, and effect on income of each.

EXHIBIT 13-1

**EXHIBIT 13-1**

**Summary of Types of Derivatives and Their Accounting**

| Classification | Purpose | Recognition | Expected Effect of Hedge and Related Item |
|---|---|---|---|
| Speculation | To speculate in exchange rate changes | Exchange gains and losses are recognized currently, based on forward exchange rate changes. | Income effect equals exchange gains and losses recognized. |
| Hedge of a net asset or liability position | To offset exposure to existing net asset or liability position | Exchange gains and losses are recognized currently, but they are offset by related gains or losses on net asset or liability position. | Income effect equals the amortization of premium or discount. (Gains and losses offset.) |
| Hedge of an identifiable firm commitment | To offset exposure to a future purchase or sale and thereby lock in the price of an existing contract in U.S. dollars | Exchange gains and losses are recognized currently, but they are offset by related gains or losses in the firm commitment. | Income effect equals the difference in the change in value of the hedge instrument versus the firm commitment. |
| Hedge of an anticipated transaction | To offset exposure of possible future purchase or sale | Exchange gains or losses on the hedge are counted in other comprehensive income until the underlying transaction is complete. | No immediate income effect. Adjusts underlying transaction. |
| Hedge of a net investment in a foreign entity (see Chapter 14) | To offset exposure to an existing net investment in a foreign entity | Exchange gains and losses are recognized as other comprehensive income and will offset translation adjustments recorded on the net investment. | Income effect equals the change in the future value of the hedge versus the value of the net investment. |

**LEARNING OBJECTIVE 13.6**

## Footnote-Disclosure Requirements

Disclosure requirements focus on how its derivatives fit into a company's overall risk-management objectives and strategy. The company should be specific about the types of risks being hedged and how they are being hedged. In addition, the company should describe initially how it determines hedge effectiveness and how it assesses continuing hedge effectiveness.

The disclosures related to fair-value hedges include reporting the net gain or loss included in earnings during the period and where in the financial statements the gain or loss is reported. This gain or loss is separated into the portion that represents the hedge's ineffectiveness and the portion of the gain or loss on the hedge instrument that was not included in the assessment of hedge effectiveness.

Cash-flow hedging instrument disclosures include reporting the amount of any hedge ineffectiveness gain or loss and any gain or loss from the derivative excluded from the assessment of hedge effectiveness. In addition, location of these gains and losses in the financial statements should be disclosed.

The disclosures for cash-flow hedges also include a description of the situations in which the gain or loss included in Accumulated Other Comprehensive Income is reclassified to income. An estimate of the amount of reclassification to occur within the next 12 months should also be reported.

Because cash-flow hedge accounting can be used for forecasted transactions, the company should report the maximum length of time that the entity is hedging its exposure to these forecasted transactions. This disclosure excludes transaction hedges of variable interest on existing financial instruments.

Finally, the company should report the amount of gains and losses that could be reclassified to income if the cash-flow hedges were discontinued because the original forecasted transactions did not occur.

**LEARNING OBJECTIVE 13.7**

## International Accounting Standards

International standards for accounting for hedging and derivatives are controlled by two companion standards. *International Accounting Standard (IAS) No. 32*, "Financial Instruments: Disclosure and Presentation" (revised in December 2003, originally issued in June 1995), and *International Accounting Standard No. 39*, "Financial Instruments: Recognition and Measurement" (a significant revision in December 2003, but also revised in March 2004; originally issued in December 1998) are both related to the ASC Topic 815. *IAS No. 32's* major points include clarifying when a financial instrument issued by a company should be classified as a liability or as equity and requiring a wide range of disclosures regarding financial instruments, including their fair values. In addition, the statement defines and provides examples of many terms, such as financial assets, financial liability, equity instrument, and fair values.

*IAS No. 39* addresses many of the same issues as ASC Topic 815, including defining and providing examples of derivatives as well as hedge accounting. In fact, the conditions that must be present to use hedge accounting, such as formally designating and documenting the corporation's risk-management objective and strategy for undertaking the hedge, as well as the need to assess hedge effectiveness initially and during the hedge's existence, are almost identical to GAAP. For example, the 80 percent to 125 percent range mentioned in ASC Topic 815 is also mentioned in *IAS 39* to assess effectiveness.

The definitions of fair-value hedges and cash-flow hedges and the general accounting are very similar. However, one difference between International Accounting Standards (IAS) and U.S. GAAP is how firm sale or purchase commitments are accounted for. Under U.S. GAAP, such firm sale or purchase commitments are accounted for as fair-value hedges, but under International Financial Reporting Standards (IFRS) they can be accounted for as either fair-value hedges or cash-flow hedges. Despite some differences, U.S. GAAP and IFRS standards relating to derivatives are converging.

## SUMMARY

Derivatives are a widely used mechanism to mitigate various risks. Hedge accounting is designed so that companies' strategies to control risk are more transparently disclosed in the financial statements.

International accounting is concerned with accounting for foreign currency transactions and operations. An entity's functional currency is the currency of the primary environment in which the entity operates. Foreign currency transactions are denominated in a currency other than an entity's functional currency.

Foreign currency transactions (other than forward contracts) are measured and recorded in U.S. dollars at the spot rate in effect at the transaction date. A change in the exchange rate between the date of the transaction and the settlement date results in an exchange gain or loss that is reflected in income for the period. At the balance sheet date, any remaining balances that are denominated in a currency other than the functional currency are adjusted to reflect the current exchange rate, and the gain or loss is reflected in income.

Corporations use forward exchange contracts and other derivatives to avoid the risks of exchange rate changes and to speculate on foreign currency exchange price movements. ASC Topic 815 prescribes different provisions for forward contracts (and other derivatives), depending on their nature and purposes.

## QUESTIONS

1. Explain the objective of hedge accounting and how this objective should improve the transparency of financial statements.

2. Explain the differences between options, forward contracts, and futures contracts and the potential benefits and potential costs of each type of contract.

3. Hedge effectiveness must be documented before a particular hedge qualifies for hedge accounting. Describe the most common approaches used to determine hedge effectiveness and when they are appropriate. In each of the approaches, when would a particular hedge *not* be considered effective?

4. A hedged firm purchase or sale commitment typically qualifies for fair-value hedge accounting if the hedge is documented to be effective. Compare the accounting for both the derivative and the firm purchase or sale commitment under each of these circumstances: (a) the hedge relationship is deemed to be effective and (b) the hedge relationship is *not* deemed to be effective.

5. Interest rate swaps were used in the chapter to highlight the differences between fair-value and cash-flow hedge accounting. Explain what type of risk is being hedged when a *pay-fixed, receive-variable swap* is used to hedge an existing variable-rate loan.

6. Interest rate swaps were used in the chapter to highlight the differences between fair-value and cash-flow hedge accounting. Explain what type of risk is being hedged when a *receive-fixed, pay-variable swap* is used to hedge an existing fixed-rate loan.

7. Explain the circumstances under which fair-value hedge accounting should be used and when cash-flow hedge accounting should be used.

8. ASC 815 allows companies to account for certain hedges of existing foreign currency–denominated receivables and payables as cash-flow hedges. Also in ASC 815, hedges of existing assets and liabilities must be accounted for as fair-value hedges. Explain the circumstances that must be present for a hedge of an existing foreign currency–denominated receivable or payable to be accounted for as a cash-flow hedge and how the accounting differs from cash-flow hedge accounting in more-general situations.

9. Briefly describe how derivatives are accounted for according to the International Accounting Standards Board. Is the accounting similar to U.S. GAAP? How is it different?

10. Describe how to account for a forward contract that is intended as a hedge of an identifiable foreign currency commitment.

## EXERCISES

### E 13-1
### Hedge of an anticipated purchase

On December 1, 2016, Jol Company enters into a 90-day forward contract with a rice speculator to purchase 500 tons of rice at $1,000 per ton. Jol enters into this contract in order to hedge an anticipated rice purchase. The contract is to be settled net. The spot price of rice at December 1, 2016, is $950.

On December 31, 2016, the forward rate on the contract is $980 per ton. The contract is settled and rice is purchased on February 28, 2017. The spot and forward rates when the contract is settled are $1,005. Assume that Jol purchases 500 tons of rice on the date of the forward contract's expiration. Assume that this contract has been documented to be an effective hedge. Also assume an appropriate interest rate is 6 percent.

1. Prepare the required journal entries to account for this hedge situation and the subsequent rice purchase on:
   a *December 1, 2016*
   b *December 31, 2016*
   c *The settlement date*

2. Assume that the rice is subsequently sold by Jol on June 1, 2017, for $1,200 per ton. What journal entries will Jol make on that date?

### E 13-2
### Hedge of a firm purchase commitment

Refer to Exercise E 13-1 and assume that Jol enters into the forward contract to hedge a firm purchase commitment. Repeat parts 1 and 2 under this assumption.

### E 13-3
### Firm sales commitment

Brk signs a firm sales commitment with Riv. The contract is to sell 100,000 widgets deliverable in three months, on January 31, 2017, at the prevailing market price of widgets at that date. On November 1, 2016, the current sales price of widgets is $5 each. Brk is concerned that the sales price could decrease by the time the delivery is to occur. On November 1, 2016, Brk contracts with Lyn to sell 100,000 widgets deliverable on January 31, 2017, for $5 each. The forward contract is to be settled net. Assume that 6 percent is a reasonable annual discount rate.

Prepare the journal entries to record the firm sales commitment and forward contract on the following dates:
   1  *November 1, 2016, assuming a sales price of $5.00 per widget*
   2  *December 31, 2016, assuming a sales price of $4.50 per widget*
   3  *January 31, 2017, assuming a sales price of $6 per widget*

### E 13-4
### Hedging of an Existing Asset

Wil has 100,000 units of widgets in its inventory on October 1, 2016. Wil purchased them for $1 per unit one month ago. It hedges the value of the widgets by entering into a forward contract to sell 100,000 widgets on January 31, 2017, for $2 each. The contract is to be settled net. Assume that a discount rate of 6 percent is reasonable.

Prepare the journal entries to properly account for this hedge of an existing asset on the following dates:
   1  *October 1, 2016, when the widget price is $1.50*
   2  *December 31, 2016, when the widget price is $2.50*
   3  *January 31, 2017, when the widget price is $2.30*

## E 13-5
## [Based on AICPA] Various foreign currency hedge situations

On December 12, 2016, Car entered into three forward exchange contracts, each to purchase 100,000 Canadian dollars in 90 days. Assume a 12 percent interest rate. The relevant exchange rates are as follows:

|  | **Spot Rate** | **Forward Rate (for March 11, 2017)** |
|---|---|---|
| December 12, 2016 | $0.91 | $0.90 |
| December 31, 2016 | $0.98 | $0.99 |

1. Car entered into the first forward contract to hedge a purchase of inventory in November 2016, payable in March 2017. At December 31, 2016, what amount of foreign currency transaction gain should Car include in income from this forward contract? Explain.
2. Car entered into the second forward contract to hedge a commitment to purchase equipment being manufactured to Car's specifications. At December 31, 2016, what amount of net gain or loss on foreign currency transactions should Car include in income from this forward contract? Explain.
3. Car entered into a third forward contract for speculation. At December 31, 2016, what amount of foreign currency transaction gain should Car include in income from this forward contract? Explain.

## E 13-6
## Firm sales commitment, foreign currency hedge

On April 1, 2016, Win of Canada ordered customized fittings from Ace, a U.S. firm, to be delivered on May 31, 2016, at a price of 50,000 Canadian dollars. The spot rate for Canadian dollars on April 1, 2016, was $0.71. Also on April 1, in order to fix the sale price of the fittings at $35,250, Ace entered into a 60-day forward contract with the exchange broker to hedge the Win contract. This derivative met the conditions set forth in ASC Topic 815 for a hedge of a foreign currency commitment. Exchange rates for Canadian dollars are as follows:

|  | **April 1** | **May 31** |
|---|---|---|
| Spot rate | $0.710 | $0.725 |
| 60-day forward rate | 0.705 | 0.715 |

**REQUIRED:** Prepare all journal entries on Ace's books to account for the commitment and related events on April 1 and May 31, 2016.

## E 13-7
## Firm purchase commitment, foreign currency hedge

On November 2, 2016, Baz, a U.S. retailer, ordered merchandise from Mat of Japan. The merchandise is to be delivered to Baz on January 31, 2017, at a price of 1,000,000 yen. Also on November 2, Baz hedged the foreign currency commitment with Mat by contracting with its exchange broker to buy 1,000,000 yen for delivery on January 31, 2017. Exchange rates for yen are:

|  | **11/2/16** | **12/31/16** | **1/31/17** |
|---|---|---|---|
| Spot rate | $0.0078 | $0.0076 | $0.0075 |
| 30-day forward rate | $0.0079 | $0.0078 | $0.0076 |
| 90-day forward rate | $0.0080 | $0.0079 | $0.0078 |

## REQUIRED
1. Prepare the entry (or entries) on Baz's books on November 2, 2016.
2. Prepare the adjusting entry on December 31, 2016.

## PROBLEMS

## P 13-1
## Cash-flow hedge, futures contract

NGW, a consumer gas provider, estimates a rather cold winter. As a result it decides to enter into a futures contract on the NYMEX for natural gas on November 2, 2016. The trading unit is 10,000 million British thermal units (MMBtu). The three-month futures contract rate is $7.00 per MMBtu, so each contract will cost NGW $70,000. In addition, the exchange requires a $5,000 deposit on each contract. NGW enters into 20 such contracts.

### REQUIRED

1. Why is this futures contract likely to be considered an effective hedge and therefore qualified for hedge accounting?
2. Why would this transaction be accounted for as a cash-flow hedge?
3. Assume that the December 31, 2016, futures contract rate is $6.75 for delivery on February 2, 2017, and the spot rate on February 2, 2017, is $6.85. Assume that NGW sells all of the gas on February 3, 2017, for $8.00 per MMBtu. Prepare all the necessary journal entries from November 2, 2016, through February 3, 2017, to account for this hedge situation.

### P 13-2
### Fair-value hedge, option

Ins makes sophisticated medical equipment. A key component of the equipment is Grade A silver. On May 1, 2016, Ins enters into a firm purchase agreement to buy 1,200,000 troy ounces (equal to 100,000 pounds) of Grade A silver from Sil, for delivery on February 1, 2017, at the market price on that date. To hedge against volatility in price, Ins also enters into an option contract with Cur to buy 1,200,000 troy ounces on February 1, 2017, for $14 per troy ounce, the market price on May 1, 2016. If the market price of silver is above $14 per troy ounce on May 1, then Ins will exercise the option. If it is below $14 per troy ounce, then Ins will let the option expire. The option is to be settled net. Cur will pay Ins the difference between the market price and the exercise price. The option costs Ins $1,000 initially. Assume that a 6 percent annual incremental borrowing rate is reasonable.

1. Why would you expect this situation to qualify for hedge accounting?
2. Why should this hedge be accounted for as a fair-value hedge instead of as a cash-flow hedge?
3. What entries should be made on May 1, 2016, to account for the firm commitment and the option?
4. Assume that the market price for Grade A silver is $15 per troy ounce on December 31, 2016. What are the required entries?
5. Assume that the market price of Grade A silver is $13.8 per troy ounce on February 1, 2017, when Ins receives the silver from Sil. Prepare the appropriate journal entries on February 1, 2017.

### P 13-3
### Cash-flow hedges, interest rate swap

On January 1, 2016, Cam borrows $400,000 from Ven. The five-year term note is a variable-rate one in which the 2016 interest rate is determined to be 8 percent, the LIBOR rate at January 1, 2016, +2%. Subsequent years' interest rates are determined in a similar manner, with the rate set for a particular year equal to the beginning-of-the-year LIBOR rate +2 percent. Interest payments are due on December 31 each year and are computed assuming annual compounding.

Also on January 1, 2016, Cam decides to enter into a pay-fixed, receive-variable interest rate swap arrangement with Gra. Cam will pay 8 percent.

Assume that the LIBOR rate on December 31, 2016, is 5 percent.

1. Why is this considered a cash-flow hedge instead of a fair-value hedge?
2. Do you think that this hedge would be considered effective and therefore would qualify for hedge accounting?
3. Assuming that this hedge relationship qualifies for hedge accounting:
   a. Determine the estimated fair value of the hedge at December 31, 2016. Recall that the hedge contract is in effect for the 2017, 2018, 2019, and 2020 interest payments.
   b. Prepare the entry at December 31, 2016, to account for this cash-flow hedge as well as the December 31, 2016, interest payment.
4. Assuming that the LIBOR rate is 5.5 percent on December 31, 2017, prepare all the necessary entries to account for the interest rate swap at December 31, 2017, including the 2017 interest payment.

## P 13-4
### Fair-value hedge, interest rate swap

Refer to Problem P 13-3 and assume that instead of initially signing a variable-rate loan, Cam receives a fixed rate of 8 percent on the loan on January 1, 2016. Instead of entering into a pay-fixed, receive-variable interest rate swap with Gra, Cam enters into a pay-variable, receive-fixed interest rate swap. The variable portion of the swap formula is LIBOR rate +2 percent, determined at the end of the year to set the rate for the following year. The first year that the swap will be in effect is for interest payments in 2017.

Assume that the LIBOR rate on December 31, 2016, is 7 percent.

1. Why is this considered a fair-value hedge instead of a cash-flow hedge?

2. Do you think that this hedge would be considered effective and therefore would qualify for hedge accounting?

3. Assuming that this hedge relationship qualifies for hedge accounting:
   a. Determine the estimated fair value of the hedge at December 31, 2016. Recall that the hedge contract is in effect for the 2017, 2018, 2019, and 2020 interest payments.
   b. Prepare the entry at December 31, 2016, to account for this fair-value hedge as well as the December 31, 2016, interest payment.

4. Assuming that the LIBOR rate is 6.5 percent on December 31, 2017, prepare all the necessary entries to account for the interest rate swap at December 31, 2017, including the 2017 interest payment.

## P 13-5
### Foreign currency hedge, existing receivable

On April 1, 2016, Bay delivers merchandise to Ram for 200,000 pesos when the spot rate for pesos is 6.0496 pesos. The receivable from Ram is due May 31. Also on April 1, Bay hedges its foreign currency asset and enters into a 60-day forward contract to sell 200,000 pesos at a forward rate of 6.019 pesos. The spot rate on May 31 was 5.992 pesos.

#### REQUIRED
1. Prepare journal entries to record the receivable from the sales transaction and the forward contract on April 1.
2. Prepare journal entries to record collection of the receivable and settlement of the forward contract on May 31.

## P 13-6
### Foreign currency hedge, firm purchase commitment

On October 2, 2016, Flx, a U.S. company, entered into a forward contract to purchase 50,000 euros for delivery in 180 days at a forward rate of $0.6350. The forward contract is a derivative instrument hedging an identifiable foreign currency purchase commitment for inventory as defined in ASC Topic 815. The spot rate for euros on October 2, 2016 was $0.6250. Spot rates and forward rates for euros on December 31, 2016, and March 31, 2017, are as follows:

|  | December 31, 2016 | March 31, 2017 |
|---|---|---|
| Spot rate | $0.6390 | $0.6560 |
| Forward rates |  |  |
| 30-day futures | $0.6410 | $0.6575 |
| 90-day futures | $0.6420 | $0.6615 |
| 180-day futures | $0.6450 | $0.6680 |

**REQUIRED:** Prepare journal entries to:
1. Record the forward contract on October 2, 2016
2. Adjust the accounts at December 31, 2016
3. Account for settlement of the forward contract and record and adjust the related cash purchase on March 31, 2017

## P 13-7
### Foreign currency hedge, anticipated sale

Bat, a U.S. corporation, anticipates a contract based on December 2, 2016, discussions to sell heavy equipment to Ram of Scotland for 500,000 British pounds. The equipment is likely to be delivered and the amount collected on March 1, 2017.

In order to hedge its anticipated commitment, Bat entered into a forward contract on December 2 to sell 500,000 British pounds for delivery on March 1. The forward contract meets all the conditions of ASC Topic 815 for a cash-flow hedge of an anticipated foreign currency commitment. A 6 percent interest rate is appropriate. The forward contract is settled net.

Exchange rates for British pounds on selected dates are as follows:

| British Pounds | 12/2/16 | 12/31/16 | 3/1/17 |
|---|---|---|---|
| Spot rate | $1.7000 | $1.7050 | $1.7100 |
| Forward rate for March 1, 2017, delivery | $1.6800 | $1.6900 | $1.7100 |

REQUIRED: Prepare the necessary journal entries on Bat's books to account for:
1. The forward contract on December 2, 2016.
2. Year-end adjustments relating to the forward contract on December 31, 2016.
3. The delivery of the equipment and settlement of all accounts with Ram and the exchange broker on March 1, 2017.

## P 13-8
### Foreign currency hedge, existing payable

Mar, a U.S. firm, purchased equipment for 400,000 British pounds from Thc on December 16, 2016. The terms were n/30, payable in British pounds.

On December 16, 2016, Mar also entered into a 30-day forward contract to hedge the account payable to Thc. The forward contract is settled net. Exchange rates for British pounds on selected dates are as follows:

| | 12/16/16 | 12/31/16 | 1/15/17 |
|---|---|---|---|
| Spot rate | $1.67 | $1.65 | $1.64 |
| Forward rate for 1/15/17 | $1.68 | $1.66 | $1.64 |

REQUIRED
1. Assuming this situation qualifies as a cash-flow hedge, prepare journal entries on December 16, 2016, to record Mar's purchase and the forward contract. A 6 percent interest rate is appropriate.
2. Prepare year-end journal entries for Mar as needed on December 31, 2016.
3. Prepare journal entries for Mar's settlement of its accounts payable and the forward contract on January 15, 2017.

# PROFESSIONAL RESEARCH ASSIGNMENTS

Answer the following questions by reference to the FASB Codification of Accounting Standards. Include the appropriate reference in your response.

**PR 13-1** What criteria are required for a hedged item to qualify for special accounting as a fair-value hedge?

**PR 13-2** What criteria are required for a hedged item to qualify for special accounting as a cash-flow hedge?

# Foreign Currency Financial Statements

If a foreign subsidiary does not keep its records in its parent's currency, then the foreign subsidiary's financial statements must be *translated* or *remeasured* into its parent's currency prior to consolidation of the financial statements. U.S. multinational corporations apply the provisions of ASC Topic 830 "Foreign Currency Matters" to convert the financial statements of their foreign subsidiaries and branches into U.S. dollars. This chapter covers the mechanics of preparing translated and remeasured financial statements as required by generally accepted accounting principles (GAAP).

## OBJECTIVES OF TRANSLATION AND THE FUNCTIONAL CURRENCY CONCEPT

The objectives of translation are to (a) provide "information that is generally compatible with the expected economic effects of a rate change on an enterprise's cash flows and equity" and (b) reflect "in consolidated statements the financial results and relationships of the individual consolidated entities as measured in their *functional currencies* in conformity with U.S. generally accepted accounting principles" (ASC 830). To decipher these objectives, one must first understand the functional currency concept.[1]

### Functional Currency Concept

LEARNING OBJECTIVE **14.1**

An entity's **functional currency** is the currency of the primary economic environment in which it operates. Normally, a foreign entity's functional currency is the currency it receives from its customers and spends to pay its liabilities. GAAP (ASC 830) only gives general guidance on determining the functional currency. Rather than a bright line rule, ASC 830 leaves the determination of the functional currency up to management's judgment. GAAP identifies the following factors management should consider when determining the functional currency of a subsidiary.

1. If *cash flows* related to the foreign entity's assets and liabilities are denominated and settled in the foreign currency rather than the parent's currency, then the foreign entity's local currency may be the functional currency.

2. If *sales prices* of the foreign entity's products are determined by local competition or local government regulation, rather than by short-run exchange rate changes or worldwide markets, then the foreign entity's local currency may be the functional currency.

3. A *sales market* that is primarily in the parent company's country, or sales contracts that are normally denominated in the parent's currency, may indicate that the parent's currency is the functional currency.

---

[1]FASB ASC 830. Originally 'Foreign Currency Matters.' Norwalk, CT: Financial Accounting Standards Board, 2015.

LEARNING
OBJECTIVE **14.2**

4. *Expenses* such as labor and materials that are primarily local costs provide some evidence that the foreign entity's local currency is the functional currency.

5. If *financing* is denominated primarily in the foreign entity's local currency and funds generated by its operations are sufficient to service existing and expected debt, then the foreign entity's local currency is likely to be the functional currency.

6. A high volume of *intercompany transactions and arrangements* indicates that the parent's currency may be the functional currency.

In the final analysis, management bases the choice of functional currency on their judgment, including weighing the preceding factors.

Several definitions from ASC Topic 830 are related to the functional currency concept. A **foreign currency** is a currency other than the entity's functional currency. If the functional currency of a German subsidiary is the euro, the U.S. dollar is a foreign currency of the German subsidiary. If the functional currency of the German subsidiary is the U.S. dollar, the euro is a foreign currency to the German subsidiary.

The **local currency** is the currency of the country to which reference is made. Thus, the Canadian dollar is the local currency of a Canadian subsidiary of a U.S. firm. The subsidiary's books and financial statements will be prepared in the local currency in nearly all cases involving foreign currency financial statements, regardless of the determination of the functional currency.

The **reporting currency** is the currency in which the consolidated financial statements are prepared. The reporting currency for the consolidated statements of a U.S. firm with foreign subsidiaries is the U.S. dollar. **Foreign currency statements** are statements prepared in a currency that is *not* the reporting currency (the U.S. dollar) of the U.S. parent-investor.

GAAP permits two different methods for converting the foreign subsidiary's financial statements into U.S. dollars, based on the foreign entity's functional currency. If the functional currency is the U.S. dollar, the foreign financial statements are remeasured into U.S. dollars using the **temporal method**. If the functional currency is the local currency of the foreign entity, the foreign financial statements are translated into U.S. dollars using the **current rate method**. A company should select the method that best reflects the nature of its foreign operations.

The designation of a functional currency for a foreign subsidiary is the criterion for choosing which method of foreign currency translation to use—the current rate method or the temporal method. Consolidated financial statement amounts, including net income, differ depending on which of these methods is used.

Recall that the purpose of translation or remeasurement of a foreign subsidiary's financial statements is to convert them to the parent's currency so that consolidation can occur. As a result, one must view the ultimate purpose behind the functional currency choice as being the generation of consolidated financial statements that will reflect the company's underlying economic condition.

Choosing the parent's currency as the functional currency means one should use the temporal method. Selecting this functional currency implies that the resulting consolidated financial statements will reflect the transactions engaged in by the subsidiary as if the parent had engaged in those transactions directly. For example, a company may choose to set up a sales subsidiary in a foreign country for legal or cultural convenience. The parent ships all of the goods to the subsidiary, which sells the goods in the foreign country. The subsidiary then remits the proceeds to the parent. If they remit foreign currency to the parent, the parent will report a foreign exchange gain or loss when they convert the foreign currency to dollars. If the subsidiary remits the functional currency to the parent, the result is the same as if the parent had directly engaged in transactions in the foreign country. The method used to translate the subsidiary's financial statements should result in consolidated financial statements that reflect this underlying similarity. The temporal method is designed to accomplish this. The gain or loss on remeasurement is included in current year consolidated income because the transactions of the subsidiary are assumed to have immediate or almost immediate cash implications for the parent.

In contrast, if the foreign subsidiary functions as a freestanding enterprise that engages in manufacturing and/or providing services within the foreign country, pays for most of its costs and receives proceeds from sales and services in the local currency, and reinvests these amounts back into the subsidiary operations, economically the subsidiary does not function as a channel for the parent's operations. The functional currency in this case is the subsidiary's local currency, and the firm would use the current rate method to translate the financial statements.

Presumably, the parent receives most of its cash flow from the subsidiary in the form of dividends. As a result, the impact of exchange rate changes on parent cash flows is limited to the parent's net investment in the subsidiary when distributed. If the parent were to liquidate its entire investment, it would be subject to realized exchange rate gains and losses that would make their way into the income statement. The current rate method measures the effect of exchange rate changes on this net investment. Typically, liquidation is not imminent, so under the current rate method, the effect of changes in the net investment due to exchange rate fluctuations is not included on the income statement, but as part of stockholders' equity, under accumulated other comprehensive income.

## APPLICATION OF THE FUNCTIONAL CURRENCY CONCEPT

A foreign subsidiary's foreign currency statements must be in conformity with U.S. GAAP before translation into U.S. dollars. They must adjust the recorded amounts to convert them to U.S. GAAP before translation. All account balances on the balance sheet date denominated in a foreign currency (from the foreign entity's point of view) are adjusted to reflect current exchange rates. For example, a French subsidiary must adjust a British-pound-denominated receivable to reflect the pound-to-euro exchange rate on the financial statement date.

Under the objectives of the functional currency concept, a foreign entity's assets, liabilities, and operations must be measured in its functional currency. Subsequently, the foreign entity's balance sheet and income statement are consolidated with those of the parent company in the reporting enterprise's currency.

The accounting procedures required to convert a foreign entity's financial statements into the currency of the parent depend on the foreign subsidiary's functional currency. Because the foreign entity maintains their books in its local currency, which may be its functional currency or a currency different from the functional currency, the combining or consolidating may require translation, remeasurement, or both.

### Translation

When the foreign entity's books are maintained in its functional currency, the statements are *translated* into the reporting entity's currency. **Translation** involves expressing functional currency measurements in the reporting currency.

A basic provision of ASC Topic 830 is that all elements of financial statements, except for stockholders' equity accounts, are translated using a current exchange rate. This is referred to as the *current rate method*. The functional currency is not the parent's; therefore, no direct impact on the reporting entity's cash flows from exchange rate changes is expected. They report the effects of exchange rate changes as a stockholders' equity adjustment in other comprehensive income. They accumulate the equity adjustments from translation until sale or liquidation of the foreign entity investment, at which time they are reported as adjustments of the gain or loss on sale.

### Remeasurement

When the foreign entity's books are not maintained in its functional currency, the foreign currency financial statements must be **remeasured** into the functional currency. If the foreign currency financial statements are remeasured into a U.S. dollar functional currency, no translation is necessary because the reporting currency of the parent-investor is the U.S. dollar.

The objective of remeasurement is to produce the same financial statements as if the books had been maintained in the functional currency. To accomplish this objective, both historical and current exchange rates are used in the remeasurement process. Under this method (the *temporal method*), monetary assets and liabilities are remeasured at current exchange rates, and other assets and equities are remeasured at historical rates. **Monetary assets and liabilities** are those in which the amounts to be received or paid are fixed in particular currency units. Examples of monetary assets and liabilities are cash, accounts receivable, and accounts payable. The remeasurement produces exchange rate adjustments that are included in income because a direct impact on the enterprise's cash flows is expected.

## Translation and Remeasurement of Foreign Currency Financial Statements

Patriot Corporation, a U.S. company, has a wholly owned subsidiary, Regal Corporation, which operates in England. The translation/remeasurement possibilities for the accounts of Regal are as follows:

|        | Functional Currency | Currency of Accounting Records | Required Procedures for Consolidating or Combining |
|--------|---------------------|--------------------------------|----------------------------------------------------|
| Case 1 | British pounds      | British pounds                 | Translation                                        |
| Case 2 | U.S. dollar         | British pounds                 | Remeasurement                                      |
| Case 3 | Euro                | British pounds                 | Remeasurement and translation                      |

Under Case 1, Regal Corporation keeps its books in its local currency, pounds (£), which is also the functional currency, and no remeasurement is needed. The accounts require translation into U.S. dollars (the currency of the reporting enterprise). GAAP (ASC 830) requires translation using the current rate method. The current exchange rate at the balance sheet date is used to translate all assets and liabilities. Theoretically, the exchange rates in effect at each transaction date should be used to translate all revenues, expenses, gains, and losses. As a practical matter, revenues and expenses are generally translated at appropriate weighted average exchange rates for the period. The adjustments from translation are reported in other comprehensive income, as required by GAAP.

In Case 2, Regal's books are maintained in pounds, but the functional currency is the U.S. dollar. Under GAAP, the accounts of Regal are remeasured into the functional currency, the dollar. In this case, no translation is needed because the dollar is also the ultimate reporting currency. The objective of remeasurement is to obtain the results that would have been produced if Regal's books of record had been maintained in the functional currency. Thus, remeasurement requires the use of historical exchange rates for some items and current rates for others and recognition in income of exchange gains and losses from measurement of all monetary assets and liabilities not denominated in the functional currency (the U.S. dollar, in this case).

In Case 3, Regal's books are maintained in pounds although the functional currency is the euro. (This situation could arise if the subsidiary is a holding company for operations in France.) The consolidation requires a remeasurement of all assets, liabilities, revenues, expenses, gains, and losses into euros (the functional currency) and recognition in income of exchange gains and losses from remeasurement of the monetary assets and liabilities not denominated in euros. After the remeasurement is completed and Regal's financial statements are stated in euros, the statements are translated into U.S. dollars using the current rate method. This translation from the functional currency to the currency of the reporting entity will create translation adjustments, but such adjustments are not recognized in current income. Instead, they are reported in other comprehensive income, in stockholders' equity.

Exhibit 14-1 summarizes the exchange rates to be used for remeasurement and translation. Once the functional currency has been determined, it should be "used consistently unless significant changes in economic facts and circumstances" indicate that the functional currency has changed. A change in functional currency is not considered a change in an accounting principle. (ASC 830)

## Intercompany Foreign Currency Transactions

Intercompany transactions are foreign currency transactions if they produce receivable or payable balances denominated in a currency other than the entity's (parent's or subsidiary's) functional currency. Such intercompany foreign currency transactions result in exchange gains and losses that generally are included in income. An exception exists when these transactions produce intercompany balances of a long-term investment nature, when settlement is not expected in the foreseeable future. In these cases, we report the translation adjustments in other comprehensive income as an equity adjustment from translation.

An intercompany transaction requires analysis to see if it is a foreign currency transaction for one, both, or neither of the affiliates. To illustrate, assume that a U.S. parent company borrows $1,600,000 (£1,000,000) from its British subsidiary. The following analysis shows that either the parent or the subsidiary will have a foreign currency transaction if the subsidiary's local currency (the pound) is its functional currency.

## EXHIBIT 14-1

### Summary of Exchange Rates Used for Remeasurement and Translation

| | Remeasurement to Functional Currency | Translation to Currency of Reporting Entity |
|---|---|---|
| *Assets* | | |
| Cash, demand deposits, and time deposits | Current | Current |
| Marketable securities carried at cost | | |
|   Equity securities | Historical | Current |
|   Debt securities | Historical | Current |
| Accounts and notes receivable and related unearned discounts | Current | Current |
| Accounts for uncollectible accounts and notes | Current | Current |
| Inventories | | |
|   Carried at cost | Historical | Current |
|   Carried at lower of cost or market | * | Current |
| Prepaid insurance, advertising, and rent | Historical | Current |
| Refundable deposits | Current | Current |
| Property, plant, and equipment | Historical | Current |
| Accumulated depreciation on property, plant, and equipment | Historical | Current |
| Cash surrender value of life insurance | Current | Current |
| Deferred income tax assets | Current | Current |
| Patents, trademarks, licenses, and formulas | Historical | Current |
| Goodwill | Historical | Current |
| Other intangible assets | Historical | Current |
| *Liabilities* | | |
| Accounts and notes payable and overdrafts | Current | Current |
| Accrued expenses | Current | Current |
| Deferred income tax liabilities | Current | Current |
| Deferred income | Historical | Current |
| Other deferred credits | Historical | Current |
| Bonds payable and other long-term debt | Current | Current |
| *Stockholders' Equity* | | |
| Common stock | Historical | Historical[†] |
| Preferred stock carried at issuance price | Historical | Historical[†] |
| Other paid-in capital | Historical | Historical[†] |
| Retained earnings | Not remeasured | Not translated |
| *Income Statement Items Related to Nonmonetary Items[‡]* | | |
| Cost of goods sold | Historical | Average (current-year) |
| Depreciation on property, plant, and equipment | Historical | Average (current-year) |
| Amortization of intangible items (patents, etc.) | Historical | Average (current-year) |
| Amortization of deferred charges and credits | Historical | Average (current-year) |

*When the books are not maintained in the functional currency and the lower-of-cost-or-market rule is applied to inventories, inventories at cost are remeasured using historical rates. Then the historical cost in the functional currency is compared to market in the functional currency.

†Translation at historical rates is necessary for elimination of reciprocal parent investment and subsidiary equity accounts. It should be noted that conversion of all asset, liability, and equity accounts at current exchange rates would obviate the "equity adjustment from translation" component.

‡Income statement items related to monetary items are translated or remeasured at weighted average exchange rates to approximate the exchange rates in existence at the time of the related transactions. Intercompany dividends are converted at the rate in effect at the time of payment under both the remeasurement and translation approaches. Translation of income statement items at current rates is implemented by using weighted average exchange rates.

| | Currency in Which Loan Is Denominated | Functional Currency of Subsidiary | Foreign Currency Transaction of | |
|---|---|---|---|---|
| | | | Subsidiary? | Parent? |
| Case 1 | British pound | British pound | No | Yes |
| Case 2 | British pound | U.S. dollar | Yes | Yes |
| Case 3 | U.S. dollar | British pound | Yes | No |
| Case 4 | U.S. dollar | U.S. dollar | No | No |

When the U.S. dollar is the functional currency of the subsidiary, either both affiliates have foreign currency transactions, which offset each other (Case 2), or the intercompany transaction is not a foreign currency transaction (Case 4). Only the cases in which the subsidiary's functional currency is its local currency (Cases 1 and 3) have the potential to affect consolidated income. In these cases, translation adjustments will be reported as equity adjustments from translation on the balance sheet if the loan is of a long-term investment nature; otherwise, they will be reported as exchange gains and losses on the income statement.

## Foreign Entities Operating in Highly Inflationary Economies

LEARNING OBJECTIVE **14.3**

In a highly inflationary economy, the local currency rapidly loses value, resulting in the escalation of goods and services' prices. Generally, the currency is weakening against other currencies as well. The lack of a stable measuring unit presents special problems for converting foreign currency statements into U.S. dollars.

For example, assume that at the end of year 1, $1 can be exchanged for 50 local currency units (LCU), a $0.02 exchange rate, but at the end of year 2, $1 can be exchanged for 200 LCU, a $0.005 exchange rate. An equity investment of 9,000,000 LCU at the end of year 1 is translated at $180,000 using the current exchange rate, but one year later, the same investment of 9,000,000 LCU is translated at $45,000 using the current exchange rate. Under the current rate method, translation gains and losses are accumulated and reported in other comprehensive income. They are not recognized in income until the investment is sold.

The Financial Accounting Standards Board (FASB) recognized that the current rate method of translation would pose a problem for foreign entities operating in countries with high rates of inflation. Price-level-adjusted financial statements are not basic financial statements under GAAP, so the FASB prescribed a practical alternative. Recall that inflation is a major determinant of exchange rates. In order to reflect the impact of hyperinflation in the consolidated financial statements, the reporting currency (the U.S. dollar) is used to remeasure the financial statements of foreign entities in highly inflationary economies. Exchange gains and losses from remeasuring the financial statements of the foreign entity are recognized in the income for the period, thus reflecting the impact of hyperinflation on the consolidated entity.

GAAP (ASC 830) defines a "highly inflationary economy" as one with a cumulative three-year inflation rate of approximately 100 percent or more. Consider a foreign country with inflation data for a three-year period as follows:

| | Index | Change in Index | Annual Rate of Inflation |
|---|---|---|---|
| January 1, 2016 | 120 | | |
| January 1, 2017 | 150 | 30 | 30 ÷ 120 (or 25%) |
| January 1, 2018 | 210 | 60 | 60 ÷ 150 (or 40%) |
| January 1, 2019 | 250 | 40 | 40 ÷ 210 (or 19%) |

The three-year inflation rate is 108.3 percent [(250−120) ÷ 120], *not* 84 percent (25% + 40% + 19%). The three-year inflation rate in this example exceeds 100 percent, so the usual criteria for identifying the functional currency are ignored, and the U.S. dollar (the functional currency of the reporting entity) is the functional currency for purposes of preparing consolidated financial statements.

## Business Combinations

LEARNING OBJECTIVE **14.4**

A foreign entity's assets and liabilities are translated into U.S. dollars using the current exchange rate in effect on the date of the business combination.

The identifiable assets and liabilities of the foreign operations are adjusted to their local currency fair values and are translated at the exchange rate in effect on the date of the business combination. Any difference between investment fair value and translated net assets acquired is accounted for as goodwill or as bargain purchase, as required by GAAP.

**FAIR VALUE/BOOK VALUE DIFFERENTIAL**   When the foreign entity's books are maintained in the functional currency, the excess of fair value over book value acquired is assigned to assets, liabilities, and goodwill in LCU and subsequently is *translated* at current exchange rates under the current rate method.

For example, assume that a 10,000 British-pound excess is allocated to equipment that has a five-year estimated life on January 1, 2016, when the exchange rate is $1.50. If the average exchange rate for 2016 is $1.45 and the year-end exchange rate is $1.40, depreciation on the excess for 2016 will be $2,900 (£2,000 × $1.45), and the undepreciated balance at December 31 will be $11,200 (£8,000 × $1.40). The unrealized translation loss of $900 [$15,000−($2,900 + $11,200)] will be recorded in other comprehensive income as an equity adjustment from translation.

When the foreign entity does not maintain their books in the functional currency, *remeasurement* is required and the excess allocated to equipment is amortized at the historical exchange rate in effect at the time of the business combination. Thus, the depreciation expense would be $3,000 (£2,000×$1.50), and the undepreciated balance would be $12,000 (£8,000 × $1.50).

**NONCONTROLLING INTEREST**   The computation of the amount of a noncontrolling interest in a foreign subsidiary must be based on the translated or remeasured financial statements of the subsidiary adjusted for fair value/book value differences. Similarly, the financial statements of a foreign investee must be translated or remeasured before the equity method of accounting is applied.

## ILLUSTRATION: TRANSLATION
## Background Information

Pat Corporation, a U.S. firm, paid $525,000 cash to acquire all the stock of the British firm Star Company when the book value of Star's net assets was equal to fair value. This business combination occurred on December 31, 2016, when the exchange rate for British pounds was $1.50. Star's assets and equities at acquisition on December 31, 2016, were as follows:

|  | British Pounds | Exchange Rate | U.S. Dollars |
|---|---|---|---|
| *Assets* | | | |
| Cash | £140,000 | $1.50 | $210,000 |
| Accounts receivable | 40,000 | 1.50 | 60,000 |
| Inventories (cost) | 120,000 | 1.50 | 180,000 |
| Plant assets | 100,000 | 1.50 | 150,000 |
| Less: Accumulated depreciation | (20,000) | 1.50 | (30,000) |
| Total assets | £380,000 | | $570,000 |
| *Equities* | | | |
| Accounts payable | £30,000 | $1.50 | $45,000 |
| Bonds payable | 100,000 | 1.50 | 150,000 |
| Capital stock | 200,000 | 1.50 | 300,000 |
| Retained earnings | 50,000 | 1.50 | 75,000 |
| Total equities | £380,000 | | $570,000 |

During 2017, the British pound weakened against the U.S. dollar, resulting in a year-end current exchange rate of $1.40. Average exchange rates for 2017 were $1.45. Star paid £30,000 dividends on December 1, 2017, when the exchange rate was $1.42 (U.S.) per British pound.

## Intercompany Transaction

The only intercompany transaction between the firms was an $84,000 (£56,000) noninterest-bearing advance by Star to Pat that happened on January 4, 2017, when the exchange rate was still $1.50. The advance is denominated in U.S. dollars. Assuming that Star's functional currency is determined to be the British pound, the advance to Pat is a foreign currency transaction from Star's perspective but not to Pat because it is denominated in dollars.

Star adjusts its advance to Pat account at year-end 2017 to reflect the $1.40 current exchange rate. Star records an exchange gain because there is no evidence that the advance is of a long-term investment nature. The entry on Star's books is as follows:

| | | |
|---|---|---|
| Advance to Pat (+A) | £4,000 | |
|     Exchange gain (+Ga, +SE) | | £4,000 |
|   To adjust receivable denominated in dollars | | |
|   [$84,000/$1.40 − £56,000 per books]. | | |

Star's adjusted trial balance at December 31, 2017, reflects the advance to Pat, £60,000, and the exchange gain, £4,000.

## LEARNING OBJECTIVE 14.5

## Translating the Foreign Subsidiary's Adjusted Trial Balance

Pat translates Star's adjusted trial balance at December 31, 2017, into U.S. dollars before it accounts for its investment under the equity method and consolidates its financial statements with those of Star. We show the translation of Star's accounts into U.S. dollars in Exhibit 14-2, which illustrates translation working paper procedures.

The *current rate method* is required for foreign subsidiaries whose functional currency is not the parent's reporting currency, here the U.S. dollar. All assets and liabilities are translated at the balance sheet date's exchange rates. All income statement items are translated at accounting-period average exchange rates. Average rates are applied to approximate the current exchange rates in effect when the revenue and expense transactions occurred during the period. We use the exchange rates in effect when dividends are paid to translate the foreign subsidiary's dividends.

The subsidiary's stockholders' equity accounts are not translated at current exchange rates. Capital stock and other paid-in capital accounts are translated at the exchange rate in effect when the subsidiary was acquired. The retained earnings ending balance is not translated after acquisition. The retained earnings account balance consists of retained earnings at acquisition, plus income, less dividends after acquisition, all in translated dollar amounts. In years subsequent to the year of

**EXHIBIT 14-2**

Translation of Foreign Subsidiary Accounts into U.S. Dollars

### STAR COMPANY LTD. TRANSLATION WORKSHEET FOR 2017 (BRITISH POUNDS FUNCTIONAL CURRENCY)

| | Trial Balance | Translation Rate | Trial Balance |
|---|---|---|---|
| *Debits* | | | |
| Cash | £110,000 | $1.40 | $ 154,000 |
| Accounts receivable | 80,000 | 1.40 | 112,000 |
| Inventories (FIFO) | 120,000 | 1.40 | 168,000 |
| Plant assets | 100,000 | 1.40 | 140,000 |
| Advance to Pat | 60,000 | 1.40 | 84,000 |
| Cost of sales | 270,000 | 1.45 | 391,500 |
| Depreciation expense | 10,000 | 1.45 | 14,500 |
| Wages and salaries expense | 120,000 | 1.45 | 174,000 |
| Other expenses | 60,000 | 1.45 | 87,000 |
| Dividends | 30,000 | 1.42 | 42,600 |
| Accumulated other comprehensive income | | | 28,600 |
| | £960,000 | | $1,396,200 |
| *Credits* | | | |
| Accumulated depreciation | £30,000 | $1.40 | $42,000 |
| Accounts payable | 36,000 | 1.40 | 50,400 |
| Bonds payable | 100,000 | 1.40 | 140,000 |
| Capital stock | 200,000 | 1.50 | 300,000 |
| Retained earnings | 50,000 | Computed | 75,000 |
| Sales | 540,000 | 1.45 | 783,000 |
| Exchange gain (advance) | 4,000 | 1.45 | 5,800 |
| | £960,000 | | $1,396,200 |

acquisition, translated beginning retained earnings of one period is simply the prior year's ending translated retained earnings from the financial statements.

After all financial statement items have been translated into dollars, the trial balance debits and credits are totaled and the amount needed to balance debits and credits is entered as an equity adjustment from translation and is included in other comprehensive income. For example, the $28,600 equity adjustment on translation in Exhibit 14-2 is measured by subtracting the $1,367,600 debits from the $1,396,200 credits in the U.S. dollar column. The resulting subsidiary's translated financial statements are illustrated in Exhibit 14-3 for Star Company.

## Equity Method of Accounting

LEARNING OBJECTIVE **14.6,7**

Pat records the investment in Star at its $525,000 fair value on December 31, 2016, in order to track the total value of their investment in Star prior to the consolidation process. Pat subsequently uses the equity method to account for its foreign subsidiary. Star's translated financial statements are used by Pat when applying the equity method. The entry to record receipt of the £30,000, or $42,600, dividend from Star on December 1, 2017, follows:

| | | |
|---|---|---|
| Cash (+A) | 42,600 | |
| Investment in Star (−A) | | 42,600 |

**EXHIBIT 14-3**

Translated Financial Statements—British Pounds Functional Currency

**STAR COMPANY LTD.**
**INCOME AND RETAINED EARNINGS STATEMENTS**
**FOR THE YEAR ENDED DECEMBER 31, 2017**
**(IN U.S. DOLLARS)**

| | | |
|---|---|---|
| Sales | | $783,000 |
| Less costs and expenses | | |
| Cost of sales | $391,500 | |
| Depreciation expense | 14,500 | |
| Wages and salaries expense | 174,000 | |
| Other expenses | 87,000 | |
| Total costs and expenses | | 667,000 |
| Operating income | | 116,000 |
| Exchange gain | | 5,800 |
| Net income | | 121,800 |
| Retained earnings January 1 | | 75,000 |
| | | 196,800 |
| Less: Dividends | | 42,600 |
| Retained earnings December 31, 2017 | | $154,200 |

**STAR COMPANY LTD.**
**BALANCE SHEET**
**AT DECEMBER 31, 2017**
**(IN U.S. DOLLARS)**

| | |
|---|---|
| *Assets* | |
| Cash | $154,000 |
| Accounts receivable | 112,000 |
| Inventories | 168,000 |
| Plant assets | 140,000 |
| Less: Accumulated depreciation | (42,000) |
| Advance to Pat | 84,000 |
| Total Assets | $616,000 |
| *Equities* | |
| Accounts payable | $50,400 |
| Bonds payable | 140,000 |
| Capital stock | 300,000 |
| Retained earnings | 154,200 |
| Accumulated other comprehensive income | (28,600) |
| Total Equities | $616,000 |

Pat received this dividend when the exchange rate was $1.42, so the dividends paid by Star also have to be translated into dollars at the current exchange rate in effect when the dividends were paid, $1.42 (see Exhibit 14-2).

Pat recognizes its equity in Star's income from 2017 in an entry that also recognizes Star's unrecognized loss on translation. The entry for 2017 is as follows:

| | | |
|---|---|---|
| Investment in Star (+A) | 93,200 | |
| Other comprehensive income: equity adjustment on translation (−SE) | 28,600 | |
| Income from Star (+R, +SE) | | 121,800 |

This entry recognizes 100 percent of Star's 2017 net income in dollars, as investment income, and it also includes the $28,600 loss from translation on Pat's books in other comprehensive income. The reported income of $121,800 less the $28,600 loss on translation equals the $93,200 investment increase from Star's operations.

### ILLUSTRATION OF AMORTIZATION WHEN EXCESS OF FAIR VALUE OVER BOOK VALUE IS ALLOCATED TO IDENTIFIABLE ASSETS AND LIABILITIES: PATENT AMORTIZATION

Pat paid $525,000 for its investment in Star. However, Star's book value and the fair value of its recorded net assets acquired were equal to $375,000. The $150,000 excess of cost over net asset book value is all allocable to a patent that has no book value on Star's books because it was internally developed with negligible legal costs. Under the current rate method, the patent-related calculations are based on LCU (British pounds), rather than U.S. dollar amounts. The first step to calculate patent amortization for Pat's investment in Star is to convert the $150,000 allocated to the patent at acquisition into its pound equivalent. Because the exchange rate at December 31, 2016, the acquisition date, is $1.50, the pound equivalent of $150,000 is £100,000.

The 2017 amortization of the excess on Pat's books is £100,000 ÷ 10 years × $1.45 average exchange rate for 2017, or $14,500. Patent amortization for 2017 is recorded on Pat's books as follows:

| | | |
|---|---|---|
| Income from Star (−R, −SE) | 14,500 | |
| Other comprehensive income: | | |
| Equity adjustment from translation (−SE) | 9,500 | |
| Investment in Star (−A) | | 24,000 |

The equity adjustment on translation of a patent that appears in the entry is the result of changes in exchange rates during 2017, and the $24,000 credit to the investment in Star reflects the decrease in unamortized patent during the year, $150,000 − (£90,000 × $1.40). These relationships are summarized as follows:

| | In Pounds | Exchange Rate | In Dollars |
|---|---|---|---|
| Beginning patent | £100,000 | $1.50 | $150,000 |
| Less: Amortization | 10,000 | 1.45 | 14,500 |
| | 90,000 | | 135,500 |
| Equity adjustment | — | | 9,500 |
| Ending patent | £ 90,000 | 1.40 | $126,000 |

Alternatively, the $9,500 equity adjustment can be computed as follows:

| | |
|---|---|
| £10,000 amortization × ($1.45−$1.50) exchange rate decline to midyear | $500 |
| £90,000 unamortized patent × ($1.40−$1.50) exchange rate decline for the year | 9,000 |
| Equity adjustment | $9,500 |

Notice that this equity adjustment is *only* recorded on Pat's books because the patent is not recorded on Star's books.

Similar adjustments are required when an excess of fair value over book value is allocated to other identifiable assets and liabilities and the current rate method is used.

**INVESTMENT IN FOREIGN SUBSIDIARY**    At this point, it may be helpful to summarize the changes in Pat's Investment in Star account during 2017:

| | |
|---|---|
| Investment cost December 31, 2016 | $525,000 |
| Less: Dividends received 2017 | (42,600) |
| Add: Equity in Star's net income | 121,800 |
| Less: Unrealized loss on translation | (28,600) |
| Less: Patent amortization | (14,500) |
| Less: Unrealized translation loss on patent | (9,500) |
| Investment balance December 31, 2017 | $551,600 |

## Consolidation

LEARNING OBJECTIVE **14.8**

Exhibit 14-4 contains the financial statement consolidation worksheet for Pat Corporation and Star Company for the year ended December 31, 2017. Pat reports income from Star of $107,300. This is its share of Star's reported income ($121,800) less the amortization of the unrecorded patent, $14,500. The Investment in Star account balance of $551,600 agrees with the reconciliation presented earlier. Pat also has a $38,100 equity adjustment balance that equals Star's equity adjustment of $28,600, recorded by Pat when it applied the equity method to account for its investment in Star and also included in Star's translated financial statements. The remaining $9,500 equity adjustment is related to the unrecorded patent, which was only recorded by Pat.

The procedures to consolidate a foreign subsidiary are the same as the procedures needed to consolidate a domestic subsidiary. The sequence of working paper entries is the same also. Working paper entry a, in Exhibit 14-4, is as follows:

| | | | |
|---|---|---|---|
| a | Income from Star (− R, − SE) | 107,300 | |
| | Dividends (+ SE) | | 42,600 |
| | Investment in Star (− A) | | 64,700 |

Entry b eliminates reciprocal equity and investment balances at beginning-of-the-period amounts and enters the beginning-of-the-period patent balance.

Entry c adjusts the Investment in Star account for unrealized translation losses, eliminates the unrealized translation loss for the patent, and eliminates Star's remaining stockholders' equity account—the equity adjustment from translation account:

| | | | |
|---|---|---|---|
| b | Retained earnings—Star (− SE) | 75,000 | |
| | Capital stock—Star (− SE) | 300,000 | |
| | Patent (+ A) | 150,000 | |
| | Investment in Star (− A) | | 525,000 |
| c | Investment in Star (+ A) | 38,100 | |
| | Patent (− A) | | 9,500 |
| | Other comprehensive income: equity adjustment from translation—Star (+ SE) | | 28,600 |

Working paper entry d, in Exhibit 14-4, enters the current patent-amortization expense (£10,000 × $1.45 average exchange rate) and reduces the patent to $126,000, the unamortized amount at year-end (£90,000 × $1.40 exchange rate).

The final working paper entry eliminates the reciprocal balances of advance to Pat and advance from Star.

Under the current rate method, the change in the accumulated other comprehensive income account from the beginning to the end of the year represents the change in the dollar amount of the investment in the net assets of the company during the year due to exchange rate changes. The

**EXHIBIT 14-4**

Working Papers Under
the British Pound
Functional Currency
Assumption

## PAT CORPORATION AND SUBSIDIARY CONSOLIDATION WORKING PAPERS TRANSLATION—FUNCTIONAL CURRENCY BRITISH POUND FOR THE YEAR ENDED DECEMBER 31, 2017

| | Pat | Star | Adjustments and Eliminations Debits | Adjustments and Eliminations Credits | Consolidated Statements |
|---|---|---|---|---|---|
| *Income Statement* | | | | | |
| Sales | $1,218,300 | $783,000 | | | $2,001,300 |
| Income from Star | 107,300 | | a 107,300 | | |
| Cost of sales | (600,000) | (391,500) | | | (991,500) |
| Depreciation expense | (40,000) | (14,500) | | | (54,500) |
| Wages and salaries expense | (300,000) | (174,000) | | | (474,000) |
| Other expenses | (150,000) | (87,000) | d 14,500 | | (251,500) |
| Exchange gain | | 5,800 | | | 5,800 |
| **Net income** | **$ 235,600** | **$121,800** | | | **$ 235,600** |
| *Retained Earnings* | | | | | |
| Retained earnings—Pat | $ 245,500 | | | | $ 245,500 |
| Retained earnings—Star | | $ 75,000 | b 75,000 | | |
| **Net income** | **235,600** | **121,800** | | | **235,600** |
| Dividends | (100,000) | (42,600) | | a 42,600 | (100,000) |
| **Retained earnings— December 31, 2017** | **$ 381,100** | **$154,200** | | | **$ 381,100** |
| *Balance Sheet* | | | | | |
| Cash | $ 317,600 | $154,000 | | | $ 471,600 |
| Accounts receivable | 150,000 | 112,000 | | | 262,000 |
| Inventories | 300,000 | 168,000 | | | 468,000 |
| Plant assets | 400,000 | 140,000 | | | 540,000 |
| Accumulated depreciation | (100,000) | (42,000) | | | (142,000) |
| Advance to Pat | | 84,000 | | e 84,000 | |
| Investment in Star | 551,600 | | c 38,100 | a 64,700 | |
| | | | | b 525,000 | |
| Patent | | | b 150,000 | c 9,500 | 126,000 |
| | | | | d 14,500 | |
| | $1,619,200 | $616,000 | | | $1,725,600 |
| Accounts payable | $ 142,200 | $ 50,400 | | | $ 192,600 |
| Advance from Star | 84,000 | | e 84,000 | | |
| Bonds payable | 250,000 | 140,000 | | | 390,000 |
| Capital stock | 800,000 | 300,000 | b 300,000 | | 800,000 |
| **Retained earnings** | **381,100** | **154,200** | | | **381,100** |
| Accumulated other comprehensive income | (38,100) | (28,600) | | c 28,600 | (38,100) |
| | $1,619,200 | $616,000 | 768,900 | 768,900 | $1,725,600 |

balance in the accumulated other comprehensive income account that represents the amount needed to balance the subsidiary's translated worksheet is the beginning accumulated other comprehensive income (AOCI) plus the change in that account resulting from exchange rate changes during the year.

To gain a better understanding of what the change in the accumulated other comprehensive income account balance represents, the change is computed directly for Star:

| | |
|---|---|
| Star's beginning accumulated other comprehensive income—translation loss | $0 |
| Increase in AOCI—translation loss | 28,600 |
| Ending AOCI—translation loss | $28,600 |

The impact of exchange rate changes on the book value of Star's net assets is shown here:

| | | Change in Exchange Rates | |
|---|---|---|---|
| Book value of beginning net assets | £250,000 | −0.10 ($1.40 − $1.50) | ($25,000) |
| Net income | £84,000 | −0.05 ($1.40 − $1.45) | (4,200) |
| −Dividends | − £30,000 | −0.02 ($1.40 − $1.42) | +600 |
| Effect of exchange rate changes on net assets | | | ($28,600) |

On a consolidated basis, the change in the AOCI account is a loss of $38,100; the $9,500 loss in excess of the $28,600 computed here is due to changes in the value of the unamortized patent account during the year. The patent is not recorded on Star's books, but here it is a part of the Investment in Star account according to Pat's books.

The computation of the change in the AOCI provides insight into the nature of the loss and why it is included in other comprehensive income instead of being reflected immediately in income. Because the functional currency of the subsidiary is the local currency, the parent will realize a loss due to exchange rate changes when the earnings of the subsidiary are distributed to the parent or when the parent liquidates its investment in the company. The latter occurrence is not an immediate probability, so the gain or loss on translation is not included in current income but is reflected directly in the stockholders' equity section and in the statement of comprehensive income.

## ILLUSTRATION: REMEASUREMENT

When the functional currency of a foreign entity is the U.S. dollar, the foreign entity's accounts are *remeasured* into its U.S. dollar functional currency, and the net exchange gains or losses that result from the remeasurement are recognized in current income. The objective of remeasurement is to produce the same results as if the books had been maintained in the U.S. dollar.

To enable you to compare the remeasurement (temporal method) and translation (current rate method) procedures, remeasurement procedures are applied to the Pat–Star example, assuming that Star's functional currency is the U.S. dollar and its books of record are maintained in British pounds.

Star's assets, liabilities, and stockholders' equity at acquisition on December 31, 2016, are all remeasured using the $1.50 exchange rate in effect on that date. The remeasurement at acquisition is exactly the same as translation at acquisition. The $525,000 investment cost to Pat over the $375,000 net assets acquired in Star results in $150,000 assigned to the patent. Unlike translation, under remeasurement procedures, the patent's value is not adjusted for subsequent changes in exchange rates. As a result, annual patent amortization over the 10-year period is $15,000.

The £56,000 ($84,000) advance to Pat is not a foreign currency transaction of either Pat or Star because the advance is denominated in dollars, and the functional currency of both Pat and Star is the U.S. dollar. As a result, Star does not adjust its advance to Pat to reflect the £60,000 equivalent and does not report a £4,000 exchange gain. Instead, the £56,000 advance to Pat is remeasured at its $84,000 reciprocal amount on Pat's books. Exhibit 14-5 is a remeasurement worksheet for Star Company for 2017. Except for the advance to Pat and the resulting £4,000 exchange gain under

EXHIBIT 14-5

Remeasurement of
Foreign Subsidiary
Accounts into U.S.
Dollars

## STAR COMPANY LTD. REMEASUREMENT WORKSHEET FOR 2017 (U.S. DOLLAR FUNCTIONAL CURRENCY)

| | Trial Balance in British Pounds | Exchange Rate | | Trial Balance in U.S. Dollars |
|---|---|---|---|---|
| **Debits** | | | | |
| Cash | £110,000 | C | $1.40 | $ 154,000 |
| Accounts receivable | 80,000 | C | 1.40 | 112,000 |
| Inventories (FIFO) | 120,000 | H | 1.42 | 170,400 |
| Plant assets | 100,000 | H | 1.50 | 150,000 |
| Advance to Pat | 56,000* | R | | 84,000 |
| Cost of sales | 270,000 | H | | 401,100 |
| Depreciation expense | 10,000 | H | 1.50 | 15,000 |
| Wages and salaries expense | 120,000 | A† | 1.45 | 174,000 |
| Other expenses | 60,000 | A† | 1.45 | 87,000 |
| Dividends | 30,000 | R | | 42,600 |
| Exchange loss on remeasurement | | | | 3,300 |
| | £956,000 | | | $1,393,400 |
| **Credits** | | | | |
| Accumulated depreciation | £30,000 | H | $1.50 | 45,000 |
| Accounts payable | 36,000 | C | 1.40 | 50,400 |
| Bonds payable | 100,000 | C | 1.40 | 140,000 |
| Capital stock | 200,000 | H | 1.50 | 300,000 |
| Retained earnings | 50,000 | Computed | | 75,000 |
| Sales | 540,000 | A | 1.45 | 783,000 |
| | £956,000 | | | $1,393,400 |

A, average exchange rate; C, current exchange rate; H, historical exchange rate; R, reciprocal of U.S. dollar amounts.

*A translation gain might need to be reported under British GAAP to the British government. However, no gain or loss is reported under U.S. GAAP, and the reciprocal rate is used.

†Assumed to be paid in cash during 2017.

translation, Star's December 31, 2017, trial balance in British pounds is the same as the one shown under the British-pound functional currency assumption in Exhibit 14-2.

Except for the intercompany advance, all of Star's monetary items are remeasured at current exchange rates. These monetary items include cash, accounts receivable, accounts payable, and bonds payable. The remeasurement produces the same amounts for the monetary items as translation under the current rate method. The advance to Pat and the dividends paid are translated at the dollar amounts that Pat recorded on its own books.

The cost of sales and inventory remeasurements shown in the worksheet assume first-in, first-out procedures and acquisition of the ending inventory items on December 1, 2017, when the exchange rate was $1.42. Historical exchange rates are used in the computations as follows:

| | Pounds | Exchange Rate | Dollars |
|---|---|---|---|
| Inventory December 31, 2016 | £120,000 | $1.50 H | $180,000 |
| Purchases 2017 | 270,000 | 1.45 A | 391,500 |
| Cost of goods available for sale | 390,000 | | 571,500 |
| Inventory December 31, 2017 | (120,000) | 1.42 H | (170,400) |
| Cost of sales | £270,000 | | $401,100 |

All of Star's plant assets were owned by Star when it became a subsidiary of Pat. Therefore, the plant assets, as well as the related depreciation expense and accumulated depreciation, are remeasured at the $1.50 exchange rate in effect at December 31, 2016. If Star had acquired additional plant assets during 2017, the additions and related depreciation would be remeasured at the exchange rates in effect when the additional assets were acquired.

Under GAAP (ASC 830), expenses are remeasured at average rates during the period if they relate to monetary items (cash, receivables, and payables), and at historical exchange rates, if they relate to **nonmonetary items** (such as plant assets, deferred charges, or intangibles). The wages and salaries and other expense items in Exhibit 14-5 are remeasured at average exchange rates, assuming they are related to monetary items. When a single expense account includes amounts related to both monetary and nonmonetary items, the remeasurement involves more computations than application of a single average rate. The same reasoning applies to the remeasurement of sales, even though it would be rather unusual for sales to relate to nonmonetary items.

Capital stock and other paid-in capital items are remeasured at historical exchange rates. No difference exists between the amounts that result from remeasurement and translation for these items. As explained earlier, the retained earnings balance is computed but not remeasured or translated. (Ending retained earnings is equal to beginning retained earnings plus remeasured income less remeasured dividends.)

After all items in the remeasurement worksheet, other than the exchange loss, are remeasured into the U.S. dollar functional currency, the trial balance debits and credits are totaled, and the difference between debits and credits is determined. If the credits are greater, the difference is entered in the remeasurement working papers as the exchange loss for the period. Thus, the $3,300 exchange loss in Exhibit 14-5 is computed by subtracting $1,390,100 debits, excluding the exchange loss, from $1,393,400 total credits.

ASC Topic 830 requires exchange gains and losses on remeasurement to be recognized in income. Exchange gains and losses on remeasurement and those arising from foreign currency transactions are combined for external reporting purposes. Separate disclosure of transaction and remeasurement gains and losses is provided in financial statement notes.

## The Equity Method and Consolidation

Similar to the translation example, Pat tracks the value of the investment account using the equity method prior to the consolidation of the remeasured statements. All remeasurement gains and losses are recognized in current income. The entries on Pat's books to account for its investment in Star are as follows:

| | | |
|---|---|---|
| Investment in Star (+A) | 525,000 | |
|     Cash (−A) | | 525,000 |
| To record acquisition on December 31, 2016. | | |
| Cash (+A) | 42,600 | |
|     Investment in Star (−A) | | 42,600 |
| To record dividends received on December 1, 2017. | | |
| Investment in Star (+A) | 87,600 | |
|     Income from Star (+R, +SE) | | 87,600 |
| To record investment income for 2017 equal to Star's | | |
|   $102,600 net income less $15,000 patent amortization. | | |

Pat's Investment in Star account at December 31, 2017, has a balance of $570,000 and is equal to Star's $435,000 net assets on that date plus $135,000 unamortized patent. These amounts are shown in the consolidation working papers of Exhibit 14-6.

The consolidation worksheet entries under remeasurement are listed here in journal entry form:

| | | | |
|---|---|---|---|
| a | Income from Star (−R, −SE) | 87,600 | |
| |   Dividends (+SE) | | 42,600 |
| |   Investment in Star (−A) | | 45,000 |
| b | Capital stock—Star (−SE)) | 300,000 | |
| |   Retained earnings—Star (−SE) | 75,000 | |
| |   Patent (+A) | 150,000 | |
| |     Investment in Star (−A) | | 525,000 |
| c | Other expenses (+E, −SE) | 15,000 | |
| |   Patent (−A) | | 15,000 |
| d | Advance from Star (−L) | 84,000 | |
| |   Advance to Pat (−A) | | 84,000 |

**PAT CORPORATION AND SUBSIDIARY CONSOLIDATION WORKING PAPERS REMEASUREMENT—FUNCTIONAL CURRENCY U.S. DOLLAR FOR THE YEAR ENDED DECEMBER 31, 2017**

| | Pat | Star | Adjustments and Eliminations Debits | Credits | Consolidated Statements |
|---|---|---|---|---|---|
| *Income Statement* | | | | | |
| Sales | $1,218,300 | $783,000 | | | $2,001,300 |
| Income from Star | 87,600 | | a 87,600 | | |
| Cost of sales | (600,000) | (401,100) | | | (1,001,100) |
| Depreciation expense | (40,000) | (15,000) | | | (55,000) |
| Wages and salaries expense | (300,000) | (174,000) | | | (474,000) |
| Other expenses | (150,000) | (87,000) | c 15,000 | | (252,000) |
| Exchange loss | | (3,300) | | | (3,300) |
| **Net income** | **$ 215,900** | **$102,600** | | | **$ 215,900** |
| *Retained Earnings* | | | | | |
| Retained earnings—Pat | $ 245,500 | | | | $ 245,500 |
| Retained earnings—Star | | $ 75,000 | b 75,000 | | |
| **Net income** | **215,900** | **102,600** | | | **215,900** |
| Dividends | (100,000) | (42,600) | | a 42,600 | (100,000) |
| **Retained earnings— December 31, 2017** | **$ 361,400** | **$135,000** | | | **$ 361,400** |
| *Balance Sheet* | | | | | |
| Cash | $ 317,600 | $154,000 | | | $ 471,600 |
| Accounts receivable | 150,000 | 112,000 | | | 262,000 |
| Inventories | 300,000 | 170,400 | | | 470,400 |
| Plant assets | 400,000 | 150,000 | | | 550,000 |
| Accumulated depreciation | (100,000) | (45,000) | | | (145,000) |
| Advance to Pat | | 84,000 | | d 84,000 | |
| Investment in Star | 570,000 | | | a 45,000 b 525,000 | |
| Patent | | | b 150,000 | c 15,000 | 135,000 |
| Total assets | $1,637,600 | $625,400 | | | $1,744,000 |
| Accounts payable | $ 142,200 | $ 50,400 | | | $ 192,600 |
| Advance from Star | 84,000 | | d 84,000 | | |
| Bonds payable | 250,000 | 140,000 | | | 390,000 |
| Capital stock | 800,000 | 300,000 | b 300,000 | | 800,000 |
| **Retained earnings** | **361,400** | **135,000** | | | **361,400** |
| Total equities | $1,637,600 | $625,400 | 711,600 | 711,600 | $1,744,000 |

Consolidation of a foreign subsidiary with a U.S. dollar functional currency is essentially the same as for a domestic subsidiary, once the foreign entity's financial statements have been remeasured in U.S. dollars. Although the remeasurement process is more complex than translation, the consolidation process is less complex because remeasurement does not produce unrealized translation gains and losses or equity adjustments from translation.

In a manner similar to the translation proof illustrated earlier, the gain or loss on remeasurement can also be computed directly. However, as one might expect given the complexity of the remeasurement procedure, the proof is more complicated than under the current rate method. All monetary assets and liabilities are remeasured using the year-end current exchange rate, whereas all nonmonetary assets and liabilities are remeasured using the historical exchange rate.

As previously disclosed on page 455, Star's December 31, 2016, net monetary assets in pounds were cash, 140,000; accounts receivable, 40,000; accounts payable, 30,000; and bonds payable, 100,000. Thus, a beginning net monetary asset (Monetary assets − Monetary liabilities) exists equal to 180,000 pounds − 130,000 pounds, or 50,000 pounds.

|  |  |  | Change in Exchange Rates |
|---|---|---|---|
| Beginning net monetary asset position | £50,000 | ($1.40 − $1.50) | ($5,000) |
| Sales (increases cash or accounts receivable during the year) | £540,000 | ($1.40 − $1.45) | (27,000) |
| Purchases (decreases cash or accounts receivable or increases accounts payable) | £270,000 | ($1.40 − $1.45) | 13,500 |
| Wages and salaries (assumed to be in cash) | £120,000 | ($1.40 − $1.45) | 6,000 |
| Other expenses (assumed to be in cash) | £60,000 | ($1.40 − $1.45) | 3,000 |
| Advance to Pat | £56,000 | ($1.40 − $1.50) | 5,600 |
| Dividends | £30,000 | ($1.40 − $1.42) | 600 |
| Total exchange loss | | | $(3,300) |

The exchange loss results from the effect of exchange rate changes on the monetary position of the firm during the year.

## Translation and Remeasurement Differences in Consolidated Statements

The consolidated financial statements of Pat Corporation and Subsidiary under the translation (current rate) and remeasurement (temporal) procedures are presented in comparative form in Exhibit 14-7.

**DISCLOSURE FOR CHANGES IN TRANSLATION ADJUSTMENTS** The Pat–Star illustration involves consolidation in the year of acquisition, so the impact of translation and remeasurement differences is relatively small. For many firms it can be substantial, however. For example, Ford reported after-tax losses relating to foreign currency translation of $521 million, $36 million, and $1,132 million in 2013, 2014, and 2015, respectively.

## HEDGING A NET INVESTMENT IN A FOREIGN ENTITY

LEARNING OBJECTIVE **14.9**

U.S. firms with foreign investees may enter into forward exchange contracts or other foreign currency transactions to offset the effects of foreign currency fluctuations on their net investments in the foreign investee. Gains and losses that arise from foreign currency transactions designated as, and effective as, economic **hedges of a net investment in a foreign subsidiary** are recorded as translation adjustments of stockholders' equity.

Classification as a **translation adjustment** means that these transaction gains and losses are included in comprehensive income (ASC 815) and are excluded from the determination of net income. This treatment is necessary because translation of the financial statements of a foreign subsidiary *with a functional currency other than the U.S. dollar* also produces translation adjustments, which are included in comprehensive income, rather than deductions or credits to net income. Thus, the adjustment from hedging a net investment in a foreign entity offsets the adjustment from translating the foreign investees' financial statements into U.S. dollars.

Procedures to hedge a net investment in a foreign entity are not applicable to investees with a U.S. dollar functional currency. Hedges of these investments are accounted for as speculations. Gains and losses from remeasuring foreign-investee financial statements into U.S. dollars are included in net income for the period if the U.S. dollar is the investee's functional currency. Therefore, the gains and losses resulting from the hedge of the net investment must be included in net income for the period. This means that the gain or loss on the hedge will offset the recognized gain or loss from the remeasurement.

EXHIBIT 14-7

Comparative
Consolidated Financial
Statements

## PAT CORPORATION AND BRITISH SUBSIDIARY
## CONSOLIDATED INCOME AND RETAINED EARNINGS STATEMENTS
## FOR THE YEAR ENDED DECEMBER 31, 2017

| | Translation (Current Rate Method) | Remeasurement (Temporal Method) |
|---|---|---|
| Sales | $2,001,300 | $2,001,300 |
| Less: Costs and expenses | | |
| Cost of sales | 991,500 | 1,001,100 |
| Wages and salaries expense | 474,000 | 474,000 |
| Other expenses | 237,000 | 237,000 |
| Depreciation expense | 54,500 | 55,000 |
| Patent amortization | 14,500 | 15,000 |
| Total costs and expenses | 1,771,500 | 1,782,100 |
| Operating income | 229,800 | 219,200 |
| Exchange gain (loss) | 5,800 | (3,300) |
| Net income | 235,600 | 215,900 |
| Retained earnings January 1, 2017 | 245,500 | 245,500 |
| | 481,100 | 461,400 |
| Less: Dividends | 100,000 | 100,000 |
| Retained earnings December 31, 2017 | $ 381,100 | $ 361,400 |

## PAT CORPORATION AND BRITISH SUBSIDIARY
## CONSOLIDATED BALANCE SHEETS
## AT DECEMBER 31, 2017

| | Translation (Current Rate Method) | Remeasurement (Temporal Method) |
|---|---|---|
| *Assets* | | |
| Cash | $471,600 | $471,600 |
| Accounts receivable | 262,000 | 262,000 |
| Inventories | 468,000 | 470,400 |
| Plant assets | 540,000 | 550,000 |
| Less: Accumulated depreciation | (142,000) | (145,000) |
| Patent | 126,000 | 135,000 |
| Total assets | $1,725,600 | $1,744,000 |
| *Liabilities* | | |
| Accounts payable | $192,600 | $192,600 |
| Bonds payable | 390,000 | 390,000 |
| Total liabilities | 582,600 | 582,600 |
| *Stockholders' Equity* | | |
| Capital stock | 800,000 | 800,000 |
| Retained earnings | 381,100 | 361,400 |
| Other comprehensive income: equity adjustment on translation | (38,100) | |
| Total stockholders' equity | 1,143,000 | 1,161,400 |
| Total liabilities and stockholders' equity | $1,725,600 | $1,744,000 |

## Illustration

To illustrate the hedge of a net investment of a foreign entity, assume that Pin, a U.S. company, has a 100 percent equity investment in a British company, Ben, acquired at book value equal to fair value. Ben's functional currency is the British pound. An investee's assets and liabilities hedge each other, so only the net assets are exposed to the risk of exchange rate fluctuations.

To hedge the foreign currency exposure, the translation adjustment from the hedging transaction must move in a direction opposite to the translation adjustment from the net assets of the investee. Thus, Pin borrows British pounds to hedge the equity investment. Any translation losses on the equity investment will be fully or partially offset by the translation gains on the loan, and vice versa.

The balance in Pin's Investment in Ben account at December 31, 2016, is $1,280,000, 100 percent of Ben's £800,000 times a $1.60 year-end current exchange rate. On this date, Pin has no translation adjustment balance relative to its investment in Ben. In order to hedge its net investment in Ben, Pin borrows £800,000 for one year at 12 percent interest on January 1, 2017, at a spot rate of $1.60. The loan is denominated in pounds, with principal and interest payable on January 1, 2018. Pin records its loan as follows:

*January 1, 2017*
| | | |
|---|---|---|
| Cash (+A) | 1,280,000 | |
| Loan payable (fc) (+L) | | 1,280,000 |
| To record loan denominated in British pounds | | |
| (£800,000 × $1.60 spot rate). | | |

On November 1, 2017, Ben declares and pays a £40,000 dividend. Pin records receipt of the dividend at the $1.75 spot rate on this date.

*November 1, 2017*
| | | |
|---|---|---|
| Cash (+A) | 70,000 | |
| Investment in Ben (−A) | | 70,000 |
| To record receipt of dividends from Ben | | |
| (£40,000 × $1.75 spot rate). | | |

For 2017, Ben reports net income of £160,000. The weighted average exchange rate for translation of Ben's revenue and expense items for the year is $1.70, and the current exchange rate at December 31, 2017, is $1.80. These changes in Ben's net assets are included in the following summary:

| | British Pounds | | U.S. Dollars |
|---|---|---|---|
| Net assets on January 1, 2017 | £800,000 | × $1.60 | $1,280,000 |
| Add: Net income for 2017 | 160,000 | × $1.70 | 272,000 |
| Less: Dividends | (40,000) | × $1.75 | (70,000) |
| Equity adjustment—change | | | 174,000 |
| Net assets on December 31, 2017 | £920,000 | × $1.80 | $1,656,000 |

Pin makes the following entry at December 31, 2017, to record its share of Ben's income:

*December 31, 2017*
| | | |
|---|---|---|
| Investment in Ben (+A) | 446,000 | |
| Income from Ben (+R, +SE) | | 272,000 |
| Other comprehensive income (+SE) | | 174,000 |
| To record 100% share of Ben's income (£160,000 × | | |
| $1.70 weighted average exchange rate) and to record 100% | | |
| share of translation adjustment. | | |

Also, Pin adjusts the loan payable and the equity investment to the current rate at December 31, 2017, and accrues interest on the loan:

| | | |
|---|---|---|
| Other comprehensive income (−SE) | 160,000 | |
| Loan payable (fc) (+L) | | 160,000 |
| To adjust loan payable denominated in British pounds to | | |
| the current rate at year-end [£800,000 × ($1.80 − $1.60)]. | | |
| Interest expense (+E, −SE) | 163,200 | |
| Exchange loss (+Lo, −SE) | 9,600 | |
| Interest payable (fc) (+L) | | 172,800 |
| To record interest expense (at weighted average exchange | | |
| rate) and accrue interest payable denominated in pounds at the | | |
| year-end current rate as follows: | | |
| Interest payable (£800,000 × 12% interest × 1 year × $1.80 current | | $172,800 |
| exchange rate) | | |
| Less: Interest expense (£800,000 × 12% interest × 1 year × $1.70 | | 163,200 |
| weighted average exchange rate) | | |
| Exchange loss | | $   9,600 |

On January 1, 2018, Pin pays the loan and interest at the $1.80 spot rate as follows:

*January 1, 2018*

| | | |
|---|---|---|
| Interest payable (fc) (−L) | 172,800 | |
| Loan payable (fc) (−L) | 1,440,000 | |
| Cash (−A) | | 1,612,800 |

To record payment of loan and interest denominated in
British pounds when the spot rate is $1.80.

As a result of the hedging operation, the changes in Pin's investment in Ben that were due to changing exchange rates were partially offset by its loan in British pounds. The equity adjustment from translation balance that appears in the stockholders' equity section of Pin's December 31, 2017, balance sheet is a $14,000 credit ($174,000 credit from the equity investment from translation, less $160,000 debit from adjustment of the loan denominated in British pounds).

### Limit on Gain or Loss from Translation Adjustment

The gain or loss on an after-tax basis from the **hedging operations** that can be considered a translation adjustment is limited in amount to the *current* translation adjustment from the equity investment. (ASC 830)

## SUMMARY

Before the results of foreign operations can be included in the financial statements of U.S. corporations, they have to be converted into U.S. dollars using procedures specified in ASC Topic 830 that are based on the foreign entity's functional currency.

If the U.S. dollar is determined to be the functional currency, the foreign entity's financial statements are remeasured into U.S. dollar financial statements using the temporal method, and the resulting exchange gain or loss is included in consolidated net income for the period.

If the functional currency is determined to be the local currency of the foreign entity, the financial statements of that entity must be translated into U.S. dollars using the current rate method. The effects of the exchange rate changes from translation are accumulated in an equity adjustment from translation account and are reported in other comprehensive income.

Foreign currency financial statements of subsidiaries operating in highly inflationary economies are remeasured as if the functional currency were the U.S. dollar.

Intercompany transactions between affiliated companies will result in a foreign currency transaction for either the parent or the subsidiary if the subsidiary's local currency is its functional currency. Alternatively, if the subsidiary's functional currency is the U.S. dollar, the intercompany transaction will be a foreign currency transaction to both affiliates or to neither affiliate.

On the date of a business combination, assets and liabilities are translated into U.S. dollars using the exchange rate at the date of the acquisition.

## QUESTIONS

1. Define the functional currency concept and briefly describe how a foreign entity's functional currency is determined. Why is this definition critical from a financial reporting perspective?
2. How does ASC Topic 830 define a highly inflationary economy? If the economy is deemed to be highly inflationary, which method for converting the financial statements to the reporting currency is used? How does the use of this method improve the economic representational faithfulness of the financial statements?
3. What procedure is used to allocate the investment purchase price at the date of acquisition of a foreign subsidiary?
4. Describe what the current rate method is and under what circumstances it should be used.
5. Describe what the temporal method is and under what circumstances it should be used.
6. If the current rate method is used, the gain or loss on translation is included under other comprehensive income. Explain why this makes sense economically.
7. The gain or loss on remeasurement is included in net income each year if the temporal method is used. Explain why this makes sense economically.

**8.** Under what circumstances would a foreign entity's financial statements need to be both remeasured and translated? Would this process have an effect on both the income statement and other comprehensive income? Explain.

**9.** If a company's sales were very seasonal—for example, a holiday-tree grower—would it be appropriate to use the annual average exchange rate to translate and remeasure sales and other expenses? Why or why not?

**10.** In the current-rate-method example in the chapter, the parent's other comprehensive income adjustment related to its investment in the subsidiary was larger than the other comprehensive income adjustment on the subsidiary's translated financial statements. Why?

**11.** Under the current rate method, all the expenses are translated using some form of current-period exchange rate. Under the temporal method, some expenses such as salaries and utilities are translated using current rates but others, such as cost of goods sold and depreciation expense, use historical rates. Why are different rates used between the two methods? After all, they are all expenses.

**12.** How does the choice of functional currency affect how the gain or loss on a hedge of a net investment in a foreign subsidiary is reported in the financial statements?

## EXERCISES

### E 14-1
### Translation/remeasurement differences

**1.** A German subsidiary of a U.S. firm has the British pound as its functional currency. Under the provisions of ASC Topic 830, the U.S. dollar from the subsidiary's viewpoint would be:
  *a* *Its local currency*
  *b* *Its recording currency*
  *c* *A foreign currency*
  *d* *None of the above*

**2.** Which of the following foreign subsidiary accounts will be converted into the same number of U.S. dollars, regardless of whether translation or remeasurement is used?
  *a* *Accounts receivable*
  *b* *Inventories*
  *c* *Machinery*
  *d* *Prepaid insurance*

**3.** Which one of the following items from the financial statements of a foreign subsidiary would be translated into dollars using the historical exchange rate?
  *a* *Accounts payable*
  *b* *Amortization of bond premium*
  *c* *Common stock*
  *d* *Inventories*

**4.** Average exchange rates are used to translate certain items from foreign income statements into U.S. dollars. Such averages are used to:
  *a* *Approximate the effects of using the current exchange rates in effect on the transaction dates*
  *b* *Avoid using different exchange rates for some revenue and expense accounts*
  *c* *Eliminate large and temporary fluctuations in exchange rates that may reverse in the near future*
  *d* *Smooth out large exchange gains and losses*

**5.** Pal, a U.S. Corporation, made a long-term, dollar-denominated loan of $600,000 to its British subsidiary on January 1, 2016, when the exchange rate for British pounds was $1.53. If the subsidiary's functional currency is its local currency, this transaction is a foreign currency transaction of:
  *a* *The parent company but not the subsidiary*
  *b* *The subsidiary company but not the parent*
  *c* *Both the subsidiary and the parent*
  *d* *Neither the subsidiary nor the parent*

**6.** Sum is a 100 percent–owned subsidiary of a U.S. corporation. The country in which Sum is located has been determined to have a highly inflationary economy. Given this information, the functional currency of Sum is:
  *a* *Its local currency*
  *b* *The U.S. dollar*
  *c* *Its recording currency*
  *d* *None of the above*

7. An exchange gain on a long-term loan of a U.S. parent company to its British subsidiary whose functional currency is the British pound is:
   a *Recognized in consolidated income currently*
   b *Deferred until the loan is settled*
   c *Treated as an equity adjustment from translation*
   d *Treated as an equity adjustment from remeasurement*

8. A U.S. firm has a $10,000,000 investment in a foreign subsidiary, and the U.S. dollar is weakening against the currency of the country in which the foreign entity is located, which is also the subsidiary's functional currency. On the basis of this information, one would expect the consolidated financial statements to show:
   a *Translation gains*
   b *Translation losses*
   c *Stockholders' equity increase from remeasurement adjustments*
   d *Stockholders' equity decrease from remeasurement adjustments*

9. Which one of the following would not give rise to changes in a parent company's equity adjustment from translation account?
   a *Remeasurement of a foreign subsidiary's statements*
   b *Hedge of a net investment in a foreign subsidiary*
   c *Long-term intercompany loans to its foreign subsidiary*
   d *Translation of a foreign subsidiary's statements*

### E 14-2
### Translation/remeasurement differences

1. When consolidated financial statements for a U.S. parent and its foreign subsidiary are prepared, the account balances expressed in foreign currency must be converted into the currency of the reporting entity. One objective of the translation process is to provide information that:
   a *Reflects current exchange rates*
   b *Reflects current monetary equivalents*
   c *Is compatible with the economic effects of rate changes on the firm's cash flows*
   d *Reflects each translated account at its unexpired historical cost*

2. A company is translating account balances from another currency into dollars for its December 31, 2016, statement of financial position and its calendar year 2016 earnings statement and statement of cash flows. The average exchange rate for 2016 should be used to translate:
   a *Cash at December 31, 2016*
   b *Land purchased in 2016*
   c *Retained earnings at January 1, 2016*
   d *Sales for 2016*

3. A subsidiary's functional currency is the local currency, which has not experienced significant inflation. The appropriate exchange rate for translating the depreciation expense on plant assets in the income statement of the foreign subsidiary is the:
   a *Exit rate*
   b *Historical exchange rate*
   c *Weighted average exchange rate over the economic life of each plant asset*
   d *Weighted average exchange rate for the current year*

4. The year-end balance of accounts receivable on the books of a foreign subsidiary should be translated by the parent company for consolidation purposes at the:
   a *Historical rate*
   b *Current rate*
   c *Negotiated rate*
   d *Average rate*

5. When remeasuring foreign currency financial statements into the functional currency, which of the following items would be remeasured using historical exchange rates?
   a *Inventories carried at cost*
   b *Marketable equity securities reported at market values*
   c *Bonds payable*
   d *Accrued liabilities*

## E 14-3
## Acquisition date effects

On January 1, 2016, Pai, a U.S. firm, purchases all the outstanding capital stock of Sta, a British firm, for $880,000, when the exchange rate for British pounds is $1.55. The book values of Sta's assets and liabilities are equal to fair values on this date, except for land that has a fair value of £200,000 and equipment with a fair value of £100,000.

Summarized balance sheet information for Pai in U.S. dollars and for Sta in pounds just before the business combination is as follows:

|  | Pai | Sta |
|---|---|---|
| Current assets | $3,000,000 | £100,000 |
| Land | 800,000 | 100,000 |
| Buildings—net | 1,200,000 | 250,000 |
| Equipment—net | 1,000,000 | 50,000 |
|  | $6,000,000 | £500,000 |
| Current liabilities | $600,000 | £50,000 |
| Notes payable | 1,000,000 | 150,000 |
| Capital stock | 3,000,000 | 200,000 |
| Retained earnings | 1,400,000 | 100,000 |
|  | $6,000,000 | £500,000 |

**REQUIRED:** Prepare a consolidated balance sheet for Pai and Subsidiary at January 1, 2016, immediately after the business combination.

## E 14-4
## Inventory remeasurement effect

Stadt Corporation of the Netherlands is a 100 percent–owned subsidiary of Port Corporation, a U.S. firm, and its functional currency is the U.S. dollar. Stadt's books of record are maintained in euros and its inventory is carried at cost.

The current exchange rate for euros at December 31, 2016, is $0.90.
The historical cost of the inventory is 10,000 euros.
The historical exchange rate is $0.85.

**REQUIRED:** Determine the amount at which the inventory will be carried on (a) the foreign currency statements, (b) the remeasured statements, and (c) the translated statements.

## E 14-5
## Acquisition—Excess allocation and amortization effect

On January 1, 2016, Pan acquired all the stock of Sim of Belgium for $1,200,000, when Sim had 20,000,000 euros (Eu) capital stock and 15,000,000 euros (Eu) retained earnings. Sim's net assets were fairly valued on this date and any cost/book value differential is due to a patent with a 10-year amortization period. Sim's functional currency is the euro. The exchange rates for euros for 2016 were as follows:

| January 1, 2016 | $.02 |
|---|---|
| Average for 2016 | $.022 |
| December 31, 2016 | $.025 |

### REQUIRED

1. Calculate the patent value from the business combination on January 1, 2016.
2. Determine patent amortization in U.S. dollars for 2016.
3. Prepare a journal entry on Pan's books to record the patent amortization for 2016.

## E 14-6
## Acquisition—Excess allocation and amortization effect

Pal acquired all the stock of Sta of Britain on January 1, 2016, for $163,800, when Sta had capital stock of £60,000 and retained earnings of £30,000. Sta's assets and liabilities were fairly valued, except for equipment with a three-year life that was undervalued by £6,000. Any remaining excess is due to a patent with a useful life of 10 years.

Sta's functional currency is the pound. Exchange rates for British pounds are as follows:

| | |
|---|---|
| January 1, 2016 | $1.66 |
| Average for the year 2016 | 1.65 |
| December 31, 2016 | 1.64 |

### REQUIRED

1. Determine the unrealized translation gain or loss at December 31, 2016, related to the cost/book value differential assigned to equipment.
2. Determine the unrealized translation gain or loss at December 31, 2016, related to the patent.

## E 14-7
### Acquisition—excess allocation

Pac of the United States purchased all the outstanding stock of Swi of Switzerland for $1,350,000 cash on January 1, 2016. The book values of Swi's assets and liabilities were equal to fair values on this date except for land, which was valued at 1,000,000 euros. Summarized balance sheet information in euros at January 1, 2016, is as follows:

| | | | |
|---|---|---|---|
| Current assets | €800,000 | Current liabilities | €400,000 |
| Land | 600,000 | Bonds payable | 500,000 |
| Buildings—net | 400,000 | Capital stock | 1,000,000 |
| Equipment—net | 500,000 | Retained earnings | 400,000 |
| | €2,300,000 | | €2,300,000 |

The functional currency of Swi is the euro. Exchange rates for euros for 2016 are as follows:

| | |
|---|---|
| Spot rate January 1, 2016 | $0.75 |
| Average rate 2016 | 0.76 |
| Current rate December 31, 2016 | 0.77 |

**REQUIRED:** Determine the unrealized translation gain or loss at December 31, 2016, relating to the excess allocated to the undervalued land.

## E 14-8
### Acquisition excess allocation effects, specific account translation, and remeasurement

1. Fay had a realized foreign exchange loss of $15,000 for the year ended December 31, 2016, and must determine whether the following items will require year-end adjustment:

   Fay had an $8,000 equity adjustment resulting from the translation of the accounts of its wholly owned foreign subsidiary for the year ended December 31, 2016.

   Fay had an account payable to an unrelated foreign supplier payable in the supplier's local currency. The U.S. dollar equivalent of the payable was $64,000 on the October 31, 2016, invoice date, and it was $60,000 on December 31, 2016. The invoice is payable on January 30, 2017.

   In Fay's 2016 consolidated income statement, what amount should be included as foreign exchange loss?
   a  $11,000
   b  $15,000
   c  $19,000
   d  $23,000

2. On January 1, 2016, the Ben Company formed a foreign subsidiary. On February 15, 2016, Ben's subsidiary purchased 100,000 local currency units (LCU) of inventory; 25,000 LCU of the original inventory made up the entire inventory on December 31, 2016. The subsidiary's functional currency is the U.S. dollar. The exchange rates were 2.2 LCU to $1 from January 1, 2016, to June 30, 2016, and 2 LCU to $1 from July 1, 2016, to December 31, 2016. The December 31, 2016, inventory balance for Ben's foreign subsidiary should be remeasured into U.S. dollars in the amount of:
   a  $10,500
   b  $11,364
   c  $11,905
   d  $12,500

3. The Dee Company owns a foreign subsidiary with 3,600,000 local currency units of property, plant, and equipment before accumulated depreciation at December 31, 2018. Of this amount, 2,400,000 LCU were acquired in 2016, when the rate of exchange was 1.6 LCU to $1, and 1,200,000 LCU were acquired in 2017, when the rate of exchange was 1.8 LCU to $1.

   The rate of exchange in effect at December 31, 2018, was 2 LCU to $1. The weighted average of exchange rates in effect during 2018 was 1.92 LCU to $1. The subsidiary's functional currency is the U.S. dollar.

   Assuming that the property, plant, and equipment are depreciated using the straight-line method over a 10-year period with no salvage value, how much depreciation expense relating to the foreign subsidiary's property, plant, and equipment should be charged in Dee's income statement for 2018?

   a  $180,000
   b  $187,500
   c  $200,000
   d  $216,667

4. The Clark Company owns a foreign subsidiary that had net income for the year ended December 31, 2016, of 4,800,000 local currency units, which was appropriately translated into $800,000.

   On October 15, 2016, when the rate of exchange was 5.7 LCU to $1, the foreign subsidiary paid a dividend to Clark of 2,400,000 LCU. The dividend represented the net income of the foreign subsidiary for the six months ended June 30, 2016, during which time the weighted average exchange rate was 5.8 LCU to $1.

   The rate of exchange in effect at December 31, 2016, was 5.9 LCU to $1. What rate of exchange should be used to translate the dividend for the December 31, 2016, financial statements?

   a  5.7 LCU to $1
   b  5.8 LCU to $1
   c  5.9 LCU to $1
   d  6.0 LCU to $1

5. The Jem Company used the current rate method when translating foreign currency amounts at December 31, 2016. At that time, Jem had foreign subsidiaries with 1,500,000 local currency units in long-term receivables and 2,400,000 LCU in long-term debt. The rate of exchange in effect when the specific transactions occurred involving those foreign currency amounts was 2 LCU to $1. The rate of exchange in effect at December 31, 2016, was 1.5 LCU to $1. The translation of these foreign currency amounts into U.S. dollars would result in long-term receivables and long-term debt, respectively, of:

   a  $750,000 and $1,200,000
   b  $750,000 and $1,600,000
   c  $1,000,000 and $1,200,000
   d  $1,000,000 and $1,600,000

6. Certain balance sheet accounts of a foreign subsidiary of Row at December 31, 2016, have been translated into U.S. dollars as follows:

|  | Translated at | |
|---|---|---|
|  | **Current Rates** | **Historical Rates** |
| Note receivable, long-term | $240,000 | $200,000 |
| Prepaid rent | 85,000 | 80,000 |
| Patent | 150,000 | 170,000 |
|  | $475,000 | $450,000 |

   The subsidiary's functional currency is the currency of the country in which it is located. What total amount should be included in Row's December 31, 2016, consolidated balance sheet for the three accounts?

   a  $450,000
   b  $455,000
   c  $475,000
   d  $495,000

7. Inflation data of a foreign country for three years are as follows:

| | Index | Change in Index | Annual Rate of Inflation |
|---|---|---|---|
| January 1, 2015 | 150 | — | |
| January 1, 2016 | 200 | 50 | $50 \div 150 = 33\%$ |
| January 1, 2017 | 250 | 50 | $50 \div 200 = 25\%$ |
| January 1, 2018 | 330 | 80 | $80 \div 250 = 32\%$ |

   The cumulative three-year inflation rate is:

   a  45%
   b  90%
   c  120%
   d  180%

## PROBLEMS

### P 14-1
### Parent accounting under the equity method

Pak purchased a 40 percent interest in Sco of Germany for $1,080,000 on January 1, 2016. The excess cost over book value is due to a patent with a 10-year amortization period. A summary of Sco's net assets at December 31, 2015, and at December 31, 2016, after translation into U.S. dollars, is as follows:

|  | Capital Stock | Retained Earnings | Equity Adjustment | Net Assets |
|---|---|---|---|---|
| December 31, 2015 | $2,000,000 | $400,000 |  | $2,400,000 |
| Net income |  | 310,000 |  | 310,000 |
| Dividends |  | (192,000) |  | (192,000) |
| Translation adjustment |  |  | $212,000 | 212,000 |
| December 31, 2016 | $2,000,000 | $518,000 | $212,000 | $2,730,000 |

Exchange rates for euros were $1.14 on January 1, 2016; $1.16 average for 2016; $1.15 when dividends were declared; and $1.18 at December 31, 2016. Sco had net assets of €4,000,000 at January 1, 2016; net income of €500,000 for 2016; and dividends of €300,000. It ended the year with net assets of €4,200,000. Sco's functional currency is the euro.

**REQUIRED**

1. Calculate Pak's income from Sco for 2016.
2. Determine the balance of Pak's Investment in Sco account at December 31, 2016.
3. Develop a proof of your calculation of the Investment in Sco account balance at December 31, 2016.

### P 14-2
### Parent accounting under the equity method

Pla purchased a 40 percent interest in Sor, a foreign company, on January 1, 2016, for $342,000, when Sor's stockholders' equity consisted of 3,000,000 LCU capital stock and 1,000,000 LCU retained earnings. Sor's functional currency is its local currency unit. The exchange rate at this time was $0.15 per LCU. Any excess allocated to patents is to be amortized over 10 years.

A summary of changes in the stockholders' equity of Sor during 2016 (including relevant exchange rates) is as follows:

|  | LCUs | Exchange Rate | U.S. Dollars |
|---|---|---|---|
| Stockholders' equity January 1, 2016 | 4,000,000 | $0.15 H | $600,000 |
| Net income | 800,000 | 0.14 A | 112,000 |
| Dividends | (400,000) | 0.14 A | (56,000) |
| Equity adjustment |  |  | (84,000) |
| Stockholders' equity December 31, 2016 | 4,400,000 | 0.13 C | $572,000 |

**REQUIRED:** Determine the following:

1. Excess patent from Pla's Investment in Sor on January 1, 2016
2. Excess patent amortization for 2016
3. Unamortized excess patent at December 31, 2016
4. Equity adjustment from patents for 2016
5. Income from Sor for 2016
6. Investment in Sor balance at December 31, 2016

## P 14-3
### Translation worksheet, parent accounting

Pyl acquired all the outstanding capital stock of Soo of London on January 1, 2016, for $800,000, when the exchange rate for British pounds was $1.50 and Soo's stockholders' equity consisted of £400,000 capital stock and £100,000 retained earnings. Soo's functional currency is the British pound. Balance sheet accounts for Soo at January 1, 2016, in British pounds and U.S. dollars are summarized as follows:

| | British Pounds | Exchange Rate | U.S. Dollars |
|---|---|---|---|
| Cash | £ 50,000 | $1.50 | $ 75,000 |
| Accounts receivable—net | 60,000 | 1.50 | 90,000 |
| Inventories | 40,000 | 1.50 | 60,000 |
| Equipment | 750,000 | 1.50 | 1,125,000 |
| | £900,000 | | $1,350,000 |
| Accumulated depreciation | £250,000 | $1.50 | $ 375,000 |
| Accounts payable | 150,000 | 1.50 | 225,000 |
| Capital stock | 400,000 | 1.50 | 600,000 |
| Retained earnings | 100,000 | 1.50 | 150,000 |
| | £900,000 | | $1,350,000 |

Exchange rates for 2016 are as follows:

| | |
|---|---|
| Current exchange rate, January 1, 2016 | $1.50 |
| Average exchange rate for 2016 | 1.53 |
| Rate for cash dividends | 1.62 |
| Current exchange rate, December 31, 2016 | 1.55 |

Soo's adjusted trial balance in British pounds at December 31, 2016, is as follows:

*Debits*

| | |
|---|---|
| Cash | £20,000 |
| Accounts receivable—net | 70,000 |
| Inventories | 50,000 |
| Equipment | 800,000 |
| Cost of sales | 350,000 |
| Depreciation expense | 80,000 |
| Operating expenses | 100,000 |
| Dividends | 30,000 |
| | £1,500,000 |

*Credits*

| | |
|---|---|
| Accumulated depreciation | £330,000 |
| Accounts payable | 70,000 |
| Capital stock | 400,000 |
| Retained earnings | 100,000 |
| Sales | 600,000 |
| | £1,500,000 |

### REQUIRED
1. Prepare a translation worksheet to convert Soo's December 31, 2016, adjusted trial balance into U.S. dollars.
2. Prepare journal entries on Pyl's books to account for the investment in Soo for 2016.
3. Directly compute the translation gain or loss.

## P 14-4
### Translation worksheet, parent accounting

Pet acquired 80 percent of the common stock of Sul for $4,000,000 on January 2, 2016, when the stockholders' equity of Sul consisted of 5,000,000 euros capital stock and 2,000,000 euros retained earnings. The spot rate for euros on this date was $0.50. Any cost/book value difference attributable to a patent is to be amortized over a 10-year period, and Sul's functional currency is the euro.

Accounts from Sul's adjusted trial balance in euros at December 31, 2016, are as follows:

| | |
|---|---:|
| *Debits* | |
| Cash | €1,000,000 |
| Accounts receivable | 2,000,000 |
| Inventories | 4,000,000 |
| Equipment | 8,000,000 |
| Cost of sales | 4,000,000 |
| Depreciation expense | 800,000 |
| Operating expenses | 2,700,000 |
| Dividends | 500,000 |
| | €23,000,000 |
| *Credits* | |
| Accumulated depreciation—equipment | €2,400,000 |
| Accounts payable | 3,600,000 |
| Capital stock | 5,000,000 |
| Retained earnings January 1 | 2,000,000 |
| Sales | 10,000,000 |
| | €23,000,000 |

Relevant exchange rates in U.S. dollars for euros are as follows:

| | |
|---|---:|
| Current exchange rate December 31, 2016 | $0.60 |
| Average exchange rate 2016 | 0.55 |
| Exchange rate applicable to dividends | 0.54 |

**REQUIRED**

1. Prepare a translation worksheet for Sul at December 31, 2016.
2. Calculate Pet's income from Sul for 2016 on the basis of a one-line consolidation.
3. Determine the correct balance of Pet's investment in Sul at December 31, 2016.

## P 14-5
## Remeasurement worksheet

Par of Chicago acquired all the outstanding capital stock of Sar of London on January 1, 2016, for $1,120,000. The exchange rate for British pounds was $1.40 and Sar's stockholders' equity was £800,000, consisting of £500,000 capital stock and £300,000 retained earnings. The functional currency of Sar is the U.S. dollar.

Exchange rates for British pounds for 2016 are as follows:

| | |
|---|---:|
| Current rate January 1, 2016 | $1.40 |
| Current rate December 31, 2016 | 1.50 |
| Average exchange rate for 2016 | 1.55 |
| Exchange rate for dividends | 1.54 |

Sar's cost of goods sold consists of £200,000 inventory on hand at January 1, 2016, and purchases of £600,000 less £150,000 inventory on hand at December 31, 2016, that was acquired at an exchange rate of $1.68.

All of Sar's plant assets were on hand when Par acquired Sar, and Sar's other expenses were paid in cash or relate to accounts payable.

Sar's adjusted trial balance at December 31, 2016, in British pounds is as follows:

| | |
|---|---:|
| *Debits* | |
| Cash | £50,000 |
| Accounts receivable | 200,000 |
| Short-term note receivable | 50,000 |
| Inventories | 150,000 |
| Land | 300,000 |
| Buildings—net | 400,000 |
| Equipment—net | 500,000 |
| Cost of sales | 650,000 |
| Depreciation expense | 200,000 |
| Other expenses | 400,000 |
| Dividends | 100,000 |
| | £3,000,000 |

*Credits*

| | |
|---|---|
| Accounts payable | £180,000 |
| Bonds payable—10% | 500,000 |
| Bond interest payable | 20,000 |
| Capital stock | 500,000 |
| Retained earnings | 300,000 |
| Sales | 1,500,000 |
| | £3,000,000 |

**REQUIRED:** Prepare a remeasurement worksheet to restate Sar's adjusted trial balance at December 31, 2016, in U.S. dollars.

## P 14-6
## Remeasurement worksheet

Phi, a U.S. firm, acquired 100 percent of Stu's outstanding stock at book value on January 1, 2016, for $112,000. Stu is a New Zealand–based company, and its functional currency is the U.S. dollar. The exchange rate for New Zealand dollars (NZ$) was $0.70 when Phi acquired its interest. Stu's stockholders' equity on January 1, 2016, consisted of NZ$150,000 capital stock and NZ$10,000 retained earnings. The adjusted trial balance for Stu at December 31, 2016, is as follows:

*Debits*

| | |
|---|---|
| Cash | NZ$15,000 |
| Accounts receivable—net | 60,000 |
| Inventories | 30,000 |
| Prepaid expenses | 10,000 |
| Land | 45,000 |
| Equipment | 60,000 |
| Cost of sales | 120,000 |
| Depreciation expense | 12,000 |
| Other operating expenses | 28,000 |
| Dividends | 20,000 |
| | NZ$400,000 |

*Credits*

| | |
|---|---|
| Accumulated depreciation | NZ$22,000 |
| Accounts payable | 18,000 |
| Capital stock | 150,000 |
| Retained earnings | 10,000 |
| Sales | 200,000 |
| | NZ$400,000 |

## ADDITIONAL INFORMATION

**1.** Prepaid expenses (supplies) of NZ$18,000 were on hand when Phi acquired Stu. Other operating expenses include NZ$8,000 of these supplies that were used in 2016. The remaining NZ$10,000 of supplies is on hand at year-end.

**2.** The NZ$120,000 cost of sales consists of NZ$50,000 inventory on hand at January 1, 2016, and NZ$100,000 in purchases during the year, less NZ$30,000 ending inventory that was acquired when the exchange rate was $0.66.

**3.** The NZ$60,000 of equipment consists of NZ$50,000 included in the business combination and NZ$10,000 purchased during 2016, when the exchange rate was $0.68. A depreciation rate of 20 percent is applicable to all equipment for 2016.

**4.** Exchange rates for 2016 are summarized as follows:

| | |
|---|---|
| Current exchange rate, January 1, 2016 | $0.70 |
| Exchange rate when new equipment was acquired | 0.68 |
| Average exchange rate for 2016 | 0.67 |
| Exchange rate for December 31, 2016, inventory | 0.66 |
| Exchange rate for dividends | 0.66 |
| Current exchange rate, December 31, 2016 | 0.65 |

**REQUIRED:** Prepare a worksheet to remeasure the adjusted trial balance of Stu Corporation into U.S. dollars at December 31, 2016.

## P 14-7
### Translation worksheet, parent accounting

Pel, a U.S. firm, paid $308,000 for all the common stock of Sar of Israel on January 1, 2016, when the exchange rate for sheqels was $0.35. Sar's equity on this date consisted of 500,000 sheqels common stock and 300,000 sheqels retained earnings. The $28,000 (80,000 sheqels) excess is attributable to a patent with a 10-year amortization period. Sar's functional currency is the sheqel.

Sar's adjusted trial balance at December 31, 2016, in sheqels is as follows:

| Debits | Sheqels | Credits | Sheqels |
|---|---|---|---|
| Cash | 40,000 | Accounts payable | 120,000 |
| Receivables—net | 50,000 | Other liabilities | 60,000 |
| Inventories | 150,000 | Advance from Pel | 140,000 |
| Land | 160,000 | Common stock | 500,000 |
| Equipment—net | 300,000 | Retained earnings 1/1 | 300,000 |
| Buildings—net | 500,000 | Sales | 600,000 |
| Expenses | 400,000 | | |
| Exchange loss (advance) | 20,000 | | |
| Dividends | 100,000 | | |
| | 1,720,000 | | 1,720,000 |

On January 2, 2016, Pel advanced $42,000 (120,000 sheqels) to Sar. This advance was short-term, denominated in U.S. dollars, and made when the exchange rate for sheqels was $0.35. In June 2016, Sar paid a 100,000-sheqel dividend when the exchange rate was $0.33. The average and year-end exchange rates for sheqels are $0.32 and $0.30, respectively.

### REQUIRED
1. Prepare a worksheet to translate Sar's adjusted trial balance at December 31, 2016, into U.S. dollars.
2. Prepare the necessary journal entries for Pel to account for its investment in Sar for 2016.

## P 14-8
### Parent accounting and consolidation under translation

PWA Corporation paid $1,710,000 for 100 percent of the stock of SAA Corporation on January 1, 2016, when the stockholders' equity of SAA consisted of 5,000,000 LCU capital stock and 3,000,000 LCU-retained earnings. SAA's functional currency is the local currency unit, and any cost/book value differential is attributable to a patent with a 10-year amortization period.

On July 1, 2016, PWA advanced $333,000 (1,800,000 LCU) to SAA when the exchange rate was $0.185. The advance is short-term and denominated in U.S. dollars.

Relevant exchange rates for LCUs for 2016 are as follows:

| | |
|---|---|
| Rate at acquisition on January 1 | $0.190 |
| Rate applicable to the advance on July 1 | 0.185 |
| Rate applicable to dividends on September 1 | 0.185 |
| Average rate for the year | 0.185 |
| Current rate at December 31 | 0.180 |

A translation worksheet for SAA's adjusted trial balance at December 31, 2016, is as follows:

| | LCUs | Exchange Rate | U.S. Dollars |
|---|---|---|---|
| *Debits* | | | |
| Cash | 550,000 | $0.180 C | $99,000 |
| Accounts receivable—net | 500,000 | 0.180 C | 90,000 |
| Inventories | 1,500,000 | 0.180 C | 270,000 |
| Land | 1,600,000 | 0.180 C | 288,000 |
| Equipment—net | 3,000,000 | 0.180 C | 540,000 |
| Buildings—net | 5,000,000 | 0.180 C | 900,000 |
| Expenses | 4,000,000 | 0.185 A | 740,000 |
| Exchange loss (advance) | 50,000 | 0.185 A | 9,250 |
| Dividends | 1,000,000 | 0.185 R | 185,000 |
| Equity adjustment from translation | — | | 84,750 |
| | 17,200,000 | | $3,206,000 |
| *Credits* | | | |
| Accounts payable | 750,000 | $0.180 C | $135,000 |
| Other liabilities | 600,000 | 0.180 C | 108,000 |
| Advance from PWA (short-term) | 1,850,000 | 0.180 C | 333,000 |
| Capital stock | 5,000,000 | 0.190 H | 950,000 |
| Retained earnings January 1 | 3,000,000 | 0.190 H | 570,000 |
| Sales | 6,000,000 | 0.185 A | 1,110,000 |
| | 17,200,000 | | $3,206,000 |

Financial statements for PWA and SAA at and for the year ended December 31, 2016, are summarized as follows:

| | PWA | SAA |
|---|---|---|
| **Combined Income and Retained Earnings Statement for the Year Ended December 31, 2016** | | |
| Sales | $ 569,500 | $1,110,000 |
| Income from SAA | 342,250 | — |
| Expenses | (400,000) | (740,000) |
| Exchange loss | — | (9,250) |
| Net income | 511,750 | 360,750 |
| Add: Beginning retained earnings | 856,500 | 570,000 |
| Less: Dividends | (300,000) | (185,000) |
| Retained earnings December 31 | $1,068,250 | $ 745,750 |
| **Balance Sheet at December 31, 2016** | | |
| Cash | $ 90,720 | $ 99,000 |
| Accounts receivable—net | 128,500 | 90,000 |
| Advance to SAA | 333,000 | — |
| Inventories | 120,000 | 270,000 |
| Land | 100,000 | 288,000 |
| Equipment—net | 600,000 | 540,000 |
| Buildings—net | 300,000 | 900,000 |
| Investment in SAA | 1,773,000 | — |
| | $3,445,220 | $2,187,000 |
| Accounts payable | $ 162,720 | $ 135,000 |
| Advance from PWA | — | 333,000 |
| Other liabilities | 308,500 | 108,000 |
| Common stock | 2,000,000 | 950,000 |
| Retained earnings | 1,068,250 | 745,750 |
| Equity adjustment from translation | (94,250) | (84,750) |
| | $3,445,220 | $2,187,000 |

## REQUIRED

1. Prepare journal entries on PWA's books to account for its investment in SAA for 2016.
2. Prepare consolidation working papers for PWA Corporation and Subsidiary for the year ended December 31, 2016.

**P 14-9**
**Translation worksheet, parent accounting, consolidation**

San is a 90 percent–owned foreign subsidiary of Par, acquired by Par on January 1, 2016, at book value equal to fair value, when the exchange rate for LCUs of San's home country was $0.24. San's functional currency is the LCU. Par made a 200,000 LCU loan to San on May 1, 2016, when the exchange rate for LCUs was $0.23. The loan is short-term and is denominated at $46,000. Adjusted trial balances of the affiliated companies at year-end 2016 are as follows:

| | Par in U.S. Dollars | San in LCU |
|---|---|---|
| *Debits* | | |
| Cash | $ 25,100 | 150,000 |
| Accounts receivable | 90,000 | 180,000 |
| Short-term loan to San | 46,000 | — |
| Inventories | 110,000 | 230,000 |
| Land | 150,000 | 250,000 |
| Buildings | 300,000 | 600,000 |
| Equipment | 220,000 | 800,000 |
| Investment in San (100%) | 230,000 | — |
| Cost of sales | 400,000 | 200,000 |
| Depreciation expense | 81,000 | 100,000 |
| Other expenses | 200,000 | 120,000 |
| Exchange loss | — | 30,000 |
| Dividends | 100,000 | 100,000 |
| Equity adjustment | 44,000 | — |
| | $1,996,100 | 2,760,000 |
| *Credits* | | |
| Accumulated depreciation—buildings | $ 120,000 | 300,000 |
| Accumulated depreciation—equipment | 60,000 | 400,000 |
| Accounts payable | 241,100 | 130,000 |
| Short-term loan from Par | — | 230,000 |
| Capital stock | 500,000 | 800,000 |
| Retained earnings January 1 | 220,000 | 200,000 |
| Sales | 800,000 | 700,000 |
| Income from San | 55,000 | — |
| | $1,996,100 | 2,760,000 |

San paid dividends in September, when the exchange rate was $0.21. The exchange rate for LCUs was $0.20 at December 31, 2016, and the average exchange rate for 2016 was $0.22.

**REQUIRED**

1. Prepare a worksheet to translate San's adjusted trial balance into U.S. dollars at December 31, 2016.
2. Prepare the necessary journal entries for Par to account for its investment in San for 2016 under the equity method.
3. Prepare consolidation working papers for Par Corporation and Subsidiary for the year ended December 31, 2016.

# PROFESSIONAL RESEARCH ASSIGNMENTS

Answer the following questions by reference to the FASB Codification of Accounting Standards. Include the appropriate reference in your response.

**PR 14-1** What is required to disclose concerning the changes in a firm's cumulative translation adjustment?

**PR 14-2** Should a firm readjust after the fiscal period end if before the release of their statements the exchange rate is materially different?

# CHAPTER 15

# Segment and Interim Financial Reporting

onsolidated financial statements enable investors to assess management's overall effectiveness in managing company resources by providing useful information for computing overall measures of profitability, liquidity, and efficiency. To help investors evaluate a company's business segments' performance, supplemental footnote disclosures are required. The first part of this chapter discusses business segment reporting.

Financial accounting courses typically focus on reporting company performance for a year—the annual report. Many companies are also required to issue financial reports covering shorter periods during the year, most notably on a quarterly basis. The second part of this chapter focuses on reporting guidelines for such interim reports.

## SEGMENT REPORTING

LEARNING OBJECTIVE **15.1**

Segment reporting under generally accepted accounting principles (GAAP) (ASC 280) applies to public business enterprises, which are defined as enterprises that have issued debt or equity securities that are traded in a public market, that are required to file financial statements with the Securities and Exchange Commission (SEC), or that provide financial statements for the purpose of issuing securities in a public market. Enterprises must report segment information in the same way that management organizes the enterprise into units for internal decision-making and performance-evaluation purposes. GAAP (ASC 280-10-50-5) refers to this approach as the *management approach* to segmentation. The management approach relies on the concept of a *chief operating decision maker* (CODM). The CODM identifies a function rather than a specific person or title. That function is allocating resources and assessing the performance of the segments of the firm. For some firms the CODM is the chief executive officer or chief operating officer, but it could be any combination of executives or other managers.

For example, *Intel Corporation's* CODM is its president and chief executive officer. The CODM allocated resources to, and evaluated the performance of, its operating segments using revenue and operating income before interest and taxes. According to its 2015 annual report, Intel's operating segments are the Client Computing Group, Data Center Group, Internet of Things, and software and services operating segments. Intel reports the remaining portions of their business as All Other.

The Client Computing and Data Center Groups are reportable segments because they meet one or more of the quantitative threshold tests (revenue, asset, and operating-profit tests) described later in the chapter. Intel has chosen to also report the remaining operating segments, even though they do not meet one of the threshold tests, because management believes that such disclosure is useful for the reader.

## LEARNING OBJECTIVES

**15.1** Understand how firms use the management approach to identify potentially reportable operating segments.

**15.2** Apply the threshold tests to identify reportable operating segments: the revenue test, the asset test, and the operating-profit test.

**15.3** Determine the reporting of any additional segments using the 75 percent external-revenue test.

**15.4** Understand the types of disclosure information for segments and the reasons that the levels of disclosure may vary across companies.

**15.5** Understand what segment disclosures are reconciled to the consolidated amounts.

**15.6** Know the required enterprise-wide disclosures with respect to products and services, geographic areas of operation, and major customers.

**15.7** Understand the similarities and

481

differences in the reporting of operations in an interim versus an annual reporting period.

**15.8** Compute interim-period income tax expense.

In contrast, *Apple Inc.,* manages its business primarily on a geographic basis. According to its 2015 annual report, its reported segments were the "Americas", "Europe", "Japan", and "Rest of Asia Pacific". Rather than reporting the remaining portions of their firm as "Other," Apple provides a reconciliation between segment totals and corporate totals.

If internal reporting and evaluation are geographically based, segment reporting should be geographically based. If internal reporting and evaluation are product-line or industry based, segment reporting should be similarly based.

LEARNING OBJECTIVE **15.2**

### Identifying Reportable Segments

Management-approach-based segments are called **operating segments**. GAAP (ASC 280-10-50-1) characterizes an operating segment as a component of an enterprise (1) that engages in business activities from which it may earn revenues and incur expenses, including intersegment revenues and expenses; (2) whose operating results are regularly reviewed by the enterprise's CODM; and (3) for which discrete financial information is available.

Some parts of an enterprise are not included in operating segments. Pension and other postretirement benefit plans are not operating segments. Likewise, corporate headquarters or functional departments that do not earn revenues are not operating segments. Intel reports that in addition to its reported operating segments, it also has sales and marketing, manufacturing, finance, and administration groups. The costs of these groups are allocated to the operating segments.

**AGGREGATION CRITERIA**  An enterprise may combine similar operating segments if aggregation is consistent with the objectives of the CODM and if the segments have similar economic characteristics. The segments also must be similar in each of the following areas: (1) the nature of the products and services, (2) the nature of the production processes, (3) the type or class of customer for their products and services, (4) the distribution method for products and services, and (5) if applicable, the nature of the regulatory environment (e.g., public utilities).

**QUANTITATIVE THRESHOLDS**  Operating segments are reportable if they meet materiality thresholds. A segment is considered material and separately reportable if one of the following three criteria is met:

1. Its reported revenue, including intersegment revenues, is 10 percent or more of the combined revenue of all operating segments.

2. The absolute value of its reported profit or loss is 10 percent or more of the greater of (a) the combined reported profit of all operating segments that reported a profit or (b) the absolute value of the combined reported loss of all operating segments that reported a loss.

3. Its assets are 10 percent or more of the combined assets of all operating segments.

Once reportable segments are identified, all other operating segments are combined with other business activities in an "all other" category for reporting purposes.

LEARNING OBJECTIVE **15.3**

**RECONSIDERATION OF REPORTABLE SEGMENTS**  Reported segments must include at least 75 percent of all external revenue. External revenue excludes intersegment revenue. If reportable segments do not meet this criterion, additional segments must be identified as reportable, even if they do not meet the quantitative thresholds. Two or more of the smaller segments that were not reportable on their own may be aggregated to form a **reportable operating segment** *only if* they meet a majority of the aggregation criteria.

GAAP (ASC 280-10-50-18) does not specify the number of segments that must be reported. However, too many segments would be considered overly detailed and therefore counterproductive. Although no firm limit was established, the standard encourages enterprises that identify more than 10 reportable segments to consider additional aggregation of their segments.

For some firms, GAAP (ASC 280-10-50-9) determines directly which operating segments will be reported. A firm whose CODM reviews multiple overlapping cross sections of their operations must present segments based on products and services. For example, a manufacturer who managed using geography, product line, and marketing channels, at both the unit and global level, is described as a matrix style of organizational management. A firm such as this would be required to present segments based on products.

## Illustration of the Tests for Reportable Operating Segments

Ace's CODM evaluates the company's operating results, organized by industry. We apply the three materiality-tests to determine which of Ace's operating segments (transportation, oil refining, insurance, and finance) are reportable segments.

**REVENUE TEST**    We apply the revenue test by comparing each operating segment's revenue (revenue to external customers plus intersegment revenue) with 10 percent of the combined revenue (both internal and external) of all operating segments. Ace's revenue test is as follows:

| Segment | Operating Segment Revenue | Intersegment Revenue | Total Segment Revenue | | Test Value | Reportable Segment Under Revenue Test? |
|---|---|---|---|---|---|---|
| Transportation | $ 360,000 | $ 0 | $ 360,000 | ≥ | $150,000 | Yes |
| Oil refining | 405,000 | 480,000 | 885,000 | ≥ | 150,000 | Yes |
| Insurance | 95,000 | 20,000 | 115,000 | ≤ | 150,000 | No |
| Finance | 140,000 | 0 | 140,000 | ≤ | 150,000 | No |
| Total | $1,000,000 | $500,000 | $1,500,000 | | | |

The revenue test value is $150,000 because the total revenue for all operating segments is $1,500,000. The transportation ($360,000) and oil refining ($885,000) segments are reportable segments under the revenue test because each of these segments' total revenue exceeds $150,000. The insurance and finance segments are not reportable segments under this criterion.

**ASSET TEST**    The asset test involves comparing the total amount of each operating segment's assets with 10 percent of the total assets of all operating segments. We define a segment's assets as those included in the measure of the segment's assets that the CODM reviews. General corporate assets may be included or excluded in the asset measurement, depending on the way management has organized the assets for operating decision-making purposes.

Assume that all assets of Ace are assigned to operating segments except those maintained for general corporate purposes:

| Segment | Operating Segment's Identifiable Assets | | Test Value | Reportable Segment Under Asset Test? |
|---|---|---|---|---|
| Transportation | $ 700,000 | ≥ | $300,000 | Yes |
| Oil refining | 950,000 | ≥ | 300,000 | Yes |
| Insurance | 180,000 | ≤ | 300,000 | No |
| Finance | 1,170,000 | ≥ | 300,000 | Yes |
| Total | $3,000,000 | | | |

The finance segment is added to the reportable-segment list because its identifiable assets exceed the $300,000 threshold.

**OPERATING PROFIT TEST**    No uniform definition of operating profit is required in applying this test. An operating segment's operating profit or loss depends on the revenues and expenses that management includes in the measurement reviewed by the CODM.

In applying the operating-profit test, the absolute amount of each segment's operating profit or loss is compared with 10 percent of the greater of the combined operating profits of all profitable operating segments or the absolute value of the combined operating losses of all unprofitable operating segments. Ace's test is as follows:

| Segment | Operating Segment's Operating Profit | Operating Segment's Operating Loss | | Test Value | Reportable Segment Under Operating Profit Test? |
|---|---|---|---|---|---|
| Transportation | | $(100,000) | ≥ | $27,000 | Yes |
| Oil refining | $200,000 | | ≥ | 27,000 | Yes |
| Insurance | 20,000 | | ≤ | 27,000 | No |
| Finance | 50,000 | | ≥ | 27,000 | Yes |
| Total | $270,000 | $(100,000) | | | |

Because the profitable segments' operating profit total of $270,000 exceeds the absolute value of the $100,000 total operating loss for loss segments, the test value is based on $270,000. After the $27,000 test value is determined, the test is applied to the absolute amounts of operating profit or loss for each segment. The transportation, oil refining, and finance segments are reportable segments under the 10 percent operating-profit test.

**REEVALUATION OF REPORTABLE SEGMENTS**   The insurance segment failed to meet any of the 10 percent tests for a reportable segment. The reportable segments are thus transportation, oil refining, and finance. In the revenue test, the test value is based on 10 percent of the total external and intersegment revenue. If intersegment revenue is very large, some segments that make up a large percentage of consolidated (or external) revenue may not qualify for reporting under the revenue test. If these segments do not qualify for reporting under either of the other two tests, then investors will not be provided with potentially relevant information. GAAP (ASC 280-10-50-14) requires that total external revenue from the reportable operating segments be equal to at least 75 percent of total consolidated revenue.

In the Ace example, total revenue of all segments is $1,500,000; $500,000 of this amount is intersegment, so $1,000,000 is revenue from external customers or consolidated revenue. The external revenue of the transportation, oil refining, and finance operating segments of $905,000 is greater than 75 percent of consolidated revenue, and thus no additional segments need to be reported. If the 75 percent test is not met, additional operating segments are added until the 75 percent criterion is met.

If the insurance segment had been a reportable segment in the previous period and Ace's management considered it still to be significant, Ace would report the insurance segment separately as a reportable operating segment, even though it failed all of the 10 percent tests for this period.

## Segment Disclosures

The basis of organization used by the CODM to determine operating segments (e.g., products and services, geographic areas, regulatory environments, or some combination of these factors) must be disclosed, as well as any aggregation of operating segments used in arriving at these reportable segments. Each reportable segment's types of products and services are disclosed. Required disclosures are made for each year for which financial statements are presented.

**PROFIT/LOSS AND ASSET INFORMATION**   A measure of *profit or loss* and *total assets* is reported for each reportable operating segment. In addition, GAAP (ASC 280-10-50-22) requires the following information for each reportable segment "if the specified amounts are included in the measure of segment profit or loss reviewed by the chief operating decision maker":

1. Amount of revenue from external customers
2. Amount of revenue from other operating segments of the same enterprise
3. Interest revenue
4. Interest expense (If a segment's revenues are primarily interest and the chief operating decision maker relies on net interest revenue to evaluate performance, the segment may report interest revenue net of interest expense.)
5. Depreciation, depletion, and amortization expense
6. Unusual items
7. Equity in the net income of investees accounted for by the equity method
8. Income tax expense or benefit
9. Significant noncash items other than depreciation, depletion, and amortization expense[1]

Other disclosures about assets are required if the specified amounts are included for review by the CODM. These include the amount of investment in equity investees, the total expenditures for additions to long-lived assets other than financial instruments and certain other items, and deferred tax assets.

---

[1]FASB ASC 280. Originally 'Segment Reporting.' Norwalk, CT: Financial Accounting Standards Board.

**MEASUREMENT**   The amounts reported in segment information disclosures depend on the amounts reported to the CODM. If allocations of revenues, expenses, gains, or losses are made to operating segments in determining the profit or loss measures used by the CODM, the allocations are also a part of the reported segment data. If assets are allocated to segments in internal reports, assets are allocated to segments for external reporting.

The enterprise also reports the accounting basis of intersegment transactions (e.g., cost or market). Any differences between segment profit or loss, asset measurements, and the consolidated amounts that are not apparent from the required reconciliation (described in the next section) are disclosed. Changes in measurement methods from prior periods are also disclosed.

**RECONCILIATION REQUIREMENTS**   In addition to the information provided for each segment, a reconciliation between the segment data and consolidated information must be provided for the following items:

> **LEARNING OBJECTIVE 15.5**

1. The total of the reportable segments' revenues and the reported consolidated revenues
2. The total reportable segments' profit or loss and consolidated income before taxes (however, if items such as taxes and unusual items are included in segment profit or loss, segment profit or loss can be reconciled to consolidated income after these items are included)
3. The total reportable segments' assets to consolidated assets
4. The total reportable segments' amounts for every other significant item of information disclosed, with their corresponding consolidated amount

## Enterprise-wide Disclosures

> **LEARNING OBJECTIVE 15.6**

Enterprises report limited information about products and services, geographic areas of operation, and major customers, regardless of the operating segmentation used. This additional information is only required if it is not provided as part of the reportable operating-segment information.

**PRODUCTS AND SERVICES**   Enterprises disclose revenues from each product or service, or group of similar products or services, or that it is impractical to provide this information.

**GEOGRAPHIC INFORMATION**   If practicable, enterprises disclose geographic information, including revenues from external customers attributed to the enterprise's home country and revenues attributed to all foreign countries in total. If revenue from one country is material (generally considered 10 percent), it is disclosed separately. Similarly, enterprises disclose long-lived assets by country of domicile and by all other foreign countries in total. Additionally, they make separate disclosures for any individual country where the assets are material.

**MAJOR CUSTOMERS**   Enterprises are required to disclose the existence of major customers. The fact that a single customer accounts for 10 percent or more of the enterprise's revenue must be disclosed, as well as the amount of revenue from each such customer and the segments reporting the revenue. Disclosure of the identity of the customer is not required. In calculating the 10 percent rule, a group of entities under common control count as a single customer. However, federal, state, and local governments count as different entities. In its 2015 annual report, for example, *Intel* reported that *Hewlett-Packard*, *Dell*, and *Lenovo* accounted for 18 percent, 15 percent, and 13 percent, respectively, of the company's revenue. The majority of sales to these customers were from the sale of platforms and other components by Client Computing Group and the Data Center Group operating segments.

## Segment Disclosure

Exhibit 15-1 presents segment disclosures *Brunswick Corporation* included in its 2015 annual report. The disclosures are required for each year for which a complete set of financial statements is presented. Brunswick is a manufacturer and marketer of leading consumer brands such as Mercury Marine and Boston Whaler and operates in three reportable segments: Marine Engine, Boat, and Fitness. The company's segments are defined by management's reporting structure and operating activities.

EXHIBIT 15-1

Brunswick Corporation
Notes to Consolidated
Financial Statements

*Source:* ©2015 Brunswick Corporation

## INFORMATION ABOUT THE OPERATIONS OF BRUNSWICK'S OPERATING SEGMENTS IS SET FORTH BELOW:

### Operating Segments

| (in millions) | Net Sales | | | Operating Earnings (Loss) | | | Total Assets [A] | |
|---|---|---|---|---|---|---|---|---|
| | 2015 | 2014 | 2013 | 2015 | 2014 | 2013 | 2015 | 2014 |
| Marine Engine | $ 2,314.3 | $ 2,189.4 | $ 2,088.1 | $ 350.4 | $ 309.1 | $ 284.2 | $ 981.8 | $ 908.3 |
| Boat | 1,274.6 | 1,135.8 | 1,032.0 | 37.6 | 17.2 | (21.8) | 379.7 | 376.5 |
| Marine eliminations | (277.8) | (255.8) | (236.4) | — | — | — | — | — |
| Total Marine | 3,311.1 | 3,069.4 | 2,883.7 | 388.0 | 326.3 | 262.4 | 1,361.5 | 1,284.8 |
| Fitness | 794.6 | 769.3 | 716.0 | 116.5 | 115.3 | 108.1 | 625.1 | 578.4 |
| Pension - non-service costs | — | — | — | (94.0) | (42.7) | (18.7) | — | — |
| Corporate/Other | — | — | — | (78.8) | (70.4) | (70.0) | 1,165.9 | 1,224.7 |
| Total | $ 4,105.7 | $ 3,838.7 | $ 3,599.7 | $ 331.7 | $ 328.5 | $ 281.8 | $ 3,152.5 | $ 3,087.9 |

| (in millions) | Depreciation | | | Amortization | | |
|---|---|---|---|---|---|---|
| | 2015 | 2014 | 2013 | 2015 | 2014 | 2013 |
| Marine Engine | $ 47.4 | $ 44.3 | $ 40.0 | $ 2.1 | $ 2.2 | $ 1.9 |
| Boat | 26.6 | 24.9 | 21.2 | 0.7 | 0.7 | 0.8 |
| Fitness | 9.1 | 6.9 | 6.0 | 0.2 | — | — |
| Corporate/Other | 2.8 | 2.2 | 1.5 | — | — | — |
| Total | $ 85.9 | $ 78.3 | $ 68.7 | $ 3.0 | $ 2.9 | $ 2.7 |

| (in millions) | Capital Expenditures | | | Research & Development Expense | | |
|---|---|---|---|---|---|---|
| | 2015 | 2014 | 2013 | 2015 | 2014 | 2013 |
| Marine Engine | $ 77.4 | $ 57.9 | $ 77.0 | $ 78.9 | $ 72.5 | $ 70.6 |
| Boat | 37.7 | 46.6 | 39.7 | 22.3 | 23.8 | 22.4 |
| Fitness | 16.9 | 19.6 | 8.4 | 24.7 | 23.3 | 21.8 |
| Corporate/Other | 0.5 | 0.7 | 1.4 | — | — | — |
| Total | $ 132.5 | $ 124.8 | $ 126.5 | $ 125.9 | $ 119.6 | $ 114.8 |

### Geographic Segments

| (in millions) | Net Sales | | | Long-Lived Assets | |
|---|---|---|---|---|---|
| | 2015 | 2014 | 2013 | 2015 | 2014 |
| United States | $ 2,727.8 | $ 2,400.0 | $ 2,214.6 | $ 429.3 | $ 367.5 |
| International | 1,377.9 | 1,438.7 | 1,385.1 | 62.7 | 72.9 |
| Corporate/Other | — | — | — | 13.2 | 19.9 |
| Total | $ 4,105.7 | $ 3,838.7 | $ 3,599.7 | $ 505.2 | $ 460.3 |

(A) For 2014, total assets reported on the Consolidated Balance Sheets includes $30.0 million of current assets held for sale and $12.6 million of longterm assets held for sale.

Brunswick reports the following information for each of its segments:

Net Sales

Operating Earnings (Loss)

Total Assets

Depreciation

Amortization

Capital Expenditures

Research & Development Expense

To reconcile the amount of revenue from external customers, Brunswick reports Marine eliminations that are intersegment sales from the Marine Engine to the Boat segment. The CODM evaluates these segments on many of the dimensions listed on page 484. It appears that income taxes, unusual items, and interest revenue are not allocated to the individual segments when internal financial statements are prepared for review by the CODM. In contrast to Brunswick, Intel reports only net revenue and operating income or loss for its segments. As we can observe from these two companies, considerable variety exists in the type of information reviewed by the CODM when evaluating segments.

## Segment Disclosures for Interim Reports

GAAP (ASC 280-10-50-32) requires limited segment information to be included in interim reports. These requirements are covered in the next section of this chapter.

## INTERIM FINANCIAL REPORTING

LEARNING OBJECTIVE **15.7**

Interim financial reports provide information about a firm's operations for less than a full year. They are commonly issued on a quarterly basis and typically include cumulative, year-to-date information, as well as comparative information for corresponding periods of the prior year. The guidelines for interim reporting are particularly applicable to publicly traded companies that are required to prepare quarterly reports according to SEC and New York Stock Exchange requirements. Even so, GAAP (ASC 270-10-05) guidelines apply whenever publicly traded companies issue interim financial information to their security holders.

## Nature of Interim Reports

**Interim financial reports** provide more timely, but less complete, information than annual financial reports. Interim reports reflect a trade-off between timeliness and reliability because estimates must replace many of the extensive reviews of receivables, payables, inventory, and the related income effects that support the measurements presented in annual financial reports, which have to meet audit requirements. Under current GAAP (ASC 270-10-45), interim financial statements only require a minimum level of disclosure. Therefore, interim financial statements are usually labeled *unaudited*.

Under GAAP, each interim period is considered an integral part of each annual period, rather than a basic accounting period unto itself. Generally, interim-period results should be based on the accounting principles and practices used in the latest annual financial statements. Some modifications may be needed, however, to relate the interim-period to annual-period results in a meaningful manner. For example, interim statements may modify the procedures used in annual statements for product costs and other expenses, as discussed in the next section.

## Product Costs

GROSS PROFIT METHOD   The gross profit method of estimating inventory and cost of goods sold was discussed in your intermediate accounting course. As you may recall, this method is not acceptable for annual financial statement purposes. However, a company can use the gross profit method for interim reporting purposes when it does not use the perpetual inventory method, and it is too costly to perform an inventory count to cost out the inventory. Obviously, the gross profit method must yield a reasonable estimate of the inventory and cost of goods sold in order to be used.

**LIFO INVENTORIES** One reason companies use the last in, first out (LIFO) method is to reduce taxable income, and therefore taxes paid, when prices are rising. The IRS requires the LIFO method's use for financial reporting purposes if it is used for tax purposes. To avoid paying taxes previously avoided, companies attempt to avoid LIFO layer liquidation that results in lower cost of goods sold, higher net income, and a higher tax bill.

LIFO inventory layers may be liquidated during an interim period but could be expected to be replaced by year-end. Cost of sales can include the replacement cost of the liquidated LIFO layer if the reduction is determined to be temporary. For example, a firm experiencing a temporary 100-unit LIFO inventory liquidation would expense the current cost of the 100 units, rather than the historical LIFO cost. The amount of current cost in excess of the historical cost is shown as a current liability on the interim balance sheet.

**INVENTORY MARKET DECLINES** Permanent inventory market declines are recognized in the interim period unless they are considered temporary (i.e., no loss is expected for the fiscal year as a whole).

**STANDARD COST SYSTEM** Planned variances under a standard cost system that are expected to be absorbed by year-end are usually deferred at the interim date.

## Expenses Other Than Product Costs

**ANNUAL EXPENSES IN INTERIM REPORTS** Annual expenses are allocated to the interim periods to which they relate. Major annual repair allowances are an example of this kind of allocation. Expenses arising in an interim period are not deferred unless they would be deferred at year-end. For example, property taxes accrued or deferred for annual purposes are also accrued or deferred for interim periods.

**ADVERTISING COSTS** Advertising costs are expensed in the interim period in which they are incurred unless the benefits clearly apply to subsequent interim periods.

**INCOME TAXES** Income taxes for interim reporting are divided into (1) those applicable to income from continuing operations before income taxes, excluding unusual or infrequently occurring items, and (2) those applicable to significant, unusual, or infrequently occurring items, and discontinued items.

Income tax expense for an interim period is based on an estimated effective annual tax rate that is applied to taxable income from continuing operations, excluding unusual and infrequently occurring items. The year-to-date tax expense, less the tax expense recognized in earlier interim periods, is the tax expense for the current interim period. The tax effects of unusual and infrequently occurring items are calculated separately and added to the tax expense of the interim period in which these items are reported. Gains and losses on discontinued operations are reported on a net-of-tax basis, as in annual reports.

## Computation of the Estimated Annual Effective Tax Rate

**LEARNING OBJECTIVE 15.8**

The following example shows how Small Corporation estimates its annual effective tax rate for the purpose of preparing quarterly financial reports. Small Corporation bases its estimate on the following *assumed* tax-rate schedule for corporations for the current year:

| If Taxable Income Is: | | The Tax Is: | | | |
|---|---|---|---|---|---|
| **Over** | **But Not Over** | **Pay** | **+** | **Excess** | **Of the Amount Over** |
| $0 | $50,000 | | | 15% | $0 |
| 50,000 | 75,000 | $7,500 | + | 25 | 50,000 |
| 75,000 | 100,000 | 13,750 | + | 34 | 75,000 |
| 100,000 | 335,000 | 22,250 | + | 39 | 100,000 |
| 335,000 | — | | | 34 | 0 |

Small Corporation estimates quarterly income for the calendar year 2016 as follows:

| Quarter | Estimated Income | | Rate (%) | Estimated Tax |
|---------|-----------------|---|----------|---------------|
| First   | $20,000   | × | 15 | $3,000 |
| Second  | 30,000    | × | 15 | 4,500 |
| Third   | 25,000    | × | 25 | 6,250 |
| Fourth  | 25,000    | × | 34 | 8,500 |
| Totals  | $100,000  | | | $22,250 |

The estimated quarterly income and income tax estimates assume that Small anticipates no accounting changes or discontinued operations for the year. Thus, the estimated annual effective tax rate is 22.25 percent, equal to the estimated tax divided by the estimated income for the year. This computation reflects the *integral theory*, such that each interim period is an essential part of an annual period, and not the *discrete theory* that each interim period is a basic, independent accounting period. The integral theory is required by GAAP. If no changes in the estimates occur during the year, the income by quarter would be estimated as follows:

|  | First Quarter | Second Quarter | Third Quarter | Fourth Quarter | Fiscal |
|---|---|---|---|---|---|
| Income year-to-date | $20,000 | $50,000 | $75,000 | $100,000 | $100,000 |
| Quarterly period income | 20,000 | 30,000 | 25,000 | 25,000 | 100,000 |
| Tax expense (22.25%) | (4,450) | (6,675) | (5,563) | (5,563) | (22,250) |
| Net income | $15,550 | $23,325 | $19,437 | $19,437 | $77,750 |

The estimated annual effective tax rate is applied to year-to-date income, and prior-quarter income taxes are deducted to compute the current quarterly income tax expense. For example, the third-quarter tax expense is calculated as follows: [($75,000 × 0.2225) − ($4,450 + $6,675)] = $5,563. This procedure provides for revision of the estimated annual effective tax rate to reflect changes in estimated income levels during the year. For example, if the $100,000 estimated income for the year had included $5,000 dividend income subject to an 80 percent dividend-received deduction, the annual effective tax rate would have been 20.89 percent. The calculation entails a $1,360 deduction for the tax savings on the dividends-received deduction: The estimated annual effective tax rate would have been calculated as follows: ($22,250−$1,360)/$100,000 = 0.2089.

## GUIDELINES FOR PREPARING INTERIM STATEMENTS

Current GAAP (ASC 270) summarizes both the consolidated and segment financial information to be disclosed in interim reports. At a minimum, publicly traded companies should report:

a. Sales or gross revenues, provision for income taxes, net income, and comprehensive income

b. Basic and diluted earnings per share data for each period presented

c. Seasonal revenue, costs, or expenses

d. Significant changes in estimates or provisions for income taxes

e. Disposal of a component of an entity and unusual or infrequently occurring items

f. Contingent items

g. Changes in accounting principles or estimates

h. Significant changes in financial position

i. All of the following information about reportable operating segments
   1. Revenues from external customers
   2. Intersegment revenues
   3. A measure of segment profit or loss
   4. Total assets for which there has been a material change from the amount disclosed in the last annual report

5. A description of differences from the last annual report in the basis of segmentation or in the measurement of segment profit or loss

6. A reconciliation of the total of the reportable segments' measures of profit or loss to the entity's consolidated income before income taxes, and discontinued operations. However, if, for example, an entity allocates items such as income taxes and unusual items to segments, the entity may choose to reconcile the total of the segments' measures of profit or loss to consolidated income after those items. Significant reconciling items shall be separately identified and described in that reconciliation.

j. All of the following information about defined benefit pension plans and other defined benefit postretirement benefit plans, disclosed for all periods presented:

1. The amount of net periodic benefit cost recognized, for each period for which a statement of income is presented, showing separately the service cost component, the interest cost component, the expected return on plan assets for the period, the gain or loss component, the prior service cost or credit component, the transition asset or obligation component, and the gain or loss recognized due to a settlement or curtailment

2. The total amount of the employer's contributions paid, and expected to be paid, during the current fiscal year, if significantly different from amounts previously disclosed. Estimated contributions may be presented in the aggregate combining all of the following:

   i. Contributions required by funding regulations or laws
   ii. Discretionary contributions
   iii. Noncash contributions

k. The information about the use of fair value to measure assets and liabilities recognized in the statement of financial position

l. The information about derivative instruments

m. The information about fair value of financial instruments

n. The information about certain investments in debt and equity securities

o. The information about other-than-temporary impairments[2]

Exhibit 15-2 displays the third quarter's report in 2012 for **Colgate-Palmolive**, including their segment report. The Income Statement reports comparative information for both the prior and current year's third quarter, and for the prior and current year's cumulative 9-month period. The Statement of Cash Flows reports only the prior and current year's cumulative 9-month period. The segment footnote disclosure displays the same time periods as the Income Statement.

## SEC Interim Financial Disclosures

The SEC requires that quarterly reports be prepared for the company's stockholders and for filing with the SEC. These reports are to be prepared using GAAP and are filed on Form 10-Q within 40 days after the end of a quarter for accelerated filers, and 45 days after the end of a quarter for all others. Fourth-quarter reports are not required, but SEC Rule 14a-3 requires inclusion of selected quarterly data in the annual report to shareholders. Quarterly reports are not audited, so the CPA's report states that a *review*, rather than an audit, has been performed.

A company's Form 10-Q report to the SEC includes additional information beyond the minimum reporting requirements under GAAP. SEC quarterly and annual reporting requirements are similar. For example, Part I of Form 10-Q contains the following summary contents:

Part 1—Financial Information

Item 1—Consolidated Balance Sheet
   Consolidated Statement of Income
   Consolidated Statement of Cash Flows
   Notes to Consolidated Financial Statements

Item 2—Management's Discussion of Financial Condition and Results of Operations

---

[2]FASB ASC 270-10-50-1. Originally Statement of Financial Accounting Standards No. 2016-01. "Financial Instruments—Overall ." Stamford, CT. © 2016 Financial Accounting Standards Board.

**EXHIBIT 15-2**

**Colgate-Palmolive Third Quarter 2012 Financial Statements**

*Source:* Colgate-Palmolive Third Quarter 2015 Financial Statements, Colgate-Palmolive Form 10-Q 2015, Colgate-Palmolive Company

**COLGATE-PALMOLIVE COMPANY CONDENSED CONSOLIDATED STATEMENTS OF INCOME (DOLLARS IN MILLIONS EXCEPT PER SHARE AMOUNTS) (UNAUDITED)**

| | Three Months Ended September 30, | | Nine Months Ended September 30, | |
|---|---|---|---|---|
| | 2015 | 2014 | 2015 | 2014 |
| Net sales | $3,999 | $4,379 | $12,135 | $13,056 |
| Cost of sales | 1,652 | 1,821 | 5,029 | 5,422 |
| Gross profit | 2,347 | 2,558 | 7,106 | 7,634 |
| Selling, general and administrative expenses | 1,347 | 1,497 | 4,178 | 4,548 |
| Other (income) expense, net | (136) | 113 | — | 524 |
| Operating profit | 1,136 | 948 | 2,928 | 2,562 |
| Interest (income) expense, net | 5 | 4 | 19 | 20 |
| Income before income taxes | 1,131 | 944 | 2,909 | 2,542 |
| Provision for income taxes | 361 | 364 | 940 | 869 |
| Net income including noncontrolling interests | 770 | 580 | 1,969 | 1,673 |
| Less: Net income attributable to noncontrolling interests | 44 | 38 | 127 | 121 |
| Net income attributable to Colgate-Palmolive Company | $726 | $542 | $1,842 | $1,552 |
| Earnings per common share, basic | $0.81 | $0.59 | $2.04 | $1.69 |
| Earnings per common share, diluted | $0.80 | $0.59 | $2.02 | $1.68 |
| Dividends declared per common share* | $0.38 | $0.36 | $1.50 | $1.42 |

**COLGATE-PALMOLIVE COMPANY CONDENSED CONSOLIDATED BALANCE SHEETS (DOLLARS IN MILLIONS) (UNAUDITED)**

| | September 30, 2015 | December 31, 2014 |
|---|---|---|
| **Assets** | | |
| **Current Assets** | | |
| Cash and cash equivalents | $1,445 | $1,089 |
| Receivables (net of allowances of $58 and $54, respectively) | 1,561 | 1,552 |
| Inventories | 1,277 | 1,382 |
| Other current assets | 806 | 840 |
| Total current assets | 5,089 | 4,863 |
| Property, plant and equipment: | | |
| Cost | 8,312 | 8,385 |
| Less: Accumulated depreciation | (4,353) | (4,305) |
| | 3,959 | 4,080 |
| Goodwill | 2,139 | 2,307 |
| Other intangible assets, net | 1,367 | 1,413 |
| Deferred income taxes | 137 | 76 |
| Other assets | 872 | 720 |
| Total assets | $13,563 | $13,459 |
| **Liabilities and Shareholders' Equity** | | |
| **Current Liabilities** | | |
| Notes and loans payable | $10 | $16 |
| Current portion of long-term debt | 226 | 488 |
| Accounts payable | 1,109 | 1,231 |
| Accrued income taxes | 340 | 294 |
| Other accruals | 2,252 | 1,917 |
| Total current liabilities | 3,937 | 3,946 |
| Long-term debt | 6,554 | 5,644 |
| Deferred income taxes | 234 | 261 |
| Other liabilities | 2,248 | 2,223 |
| Total liabilities | 12,973 | 12,074 |

*(continued)*

## COLGATE-PALMOLIVE COMPANY CONDENSED CONSOLIDATED BALANCE SHEETS (DOLLARS IN MILLIONS) (UNAUDITED)

|  | September 30, 2012 | December 31, 2011 |
|---|---|---|
| Shareholders' Equity |  |  |
| Common stock | 1,466 | 1,466 |
| Additional paid-in capital | 1,351 | 1,236 |
| Retained earnings | 19,323 | 18,832 |
| Accumulated other comprehensive income (loss) | (4,085) | (3,507) |
| Unearned compensation | (8) | (20) |
| Treasury stock, at cost | (17,792) | (16,862) |
| Total Colgate-Palmolive Company shareholders' equity | 255 | 1,145 |
| Noncontrolling interests | 335 | 240 |
| Total shareholders' equity | 590 | 1,385 |
| Total liabilities and shareholders' equity | $13,563 | $13,459 |

## COLGATE-PALMOLIVE COMPANY CONDENSED CONSOLIDATED STATEMENTS OF CASH FLOWS (DOLLARS IN MILLIONS) (UNAUDITED)

|  | Nine Months Ended September 30, | |
|---|---|---|
|  | 2015 | 2014 |
| **Operating Activities** |  |  |
| Net income including noncontrolling interests | $1,969 | $1,673 |
| Adjustments to reconcile net income including noncontrolling interests to net cash provided by operations: |  |  |
| Depreciation and amortization | 337 | 329 |
| Restructuring and termination benefits, net of cash | 68 | 69 |
| Voluntary benefit plan contributions | — | (2) |
| Venezuela remeasurement charges | 34 | 327 |
| Charge for a foreign tax matter | — | 66 |
| Stock-based compensation expense | 104 | 109 |
| Gain on sale of South Pacific laundry detergent business | (187) | — |
| Deferred income taxes | (42) | (35) |
| Cash effects of changes in: |  |  |
| Receivables | (172) | (222) |
| Inventories | 1 | (51) |
| Accounts payable and other accruals | (18) | 100 |
| Other non-current assets and liabilities | 14 | 29 |
| Net cash provided by operations | 2,108 | 2,392 |
| **Investing Activities** |  |  |
| Capital expenditures | (459) | (493) |
| Purchases of marketable securities and investments | (499) | (232) |
| Proceeds from sale of marketable securities and investments | 398 | 277 |
| Proceeds from sale of South Pacific laundry detergent business | 221 | — |
| Payment for acquisitions, net of cash acquired | (13) | (25) |
| Other | 8 | 18 |
| Net cash used in investing activities | (344) | (455) |
| **Financing Activities** |  |  |
| Principal payments on debt | (6,691) | (6,220) |
| Proceeds from issuance of debt | 7,293 | 6,597 |
| Dividends paid | (1,033) | (990) |
| Purchases of treasury shares | (1,196) | (1,119) |
| Proceeds from exercise of stock options and excess tax benefits | 301 | 295 |
| Net cash used in financing activities | (1,326) | (1,437) |
| Effect of exchange rate changes on Cash and cash equivalents | (82) | (107) |
| Net increase (decrease) in Cash and cash equivalents | 356 | 393 |
| Cash and cash equivalents at beginning of the period | 1,089 | 962 |
| Cash and cash equivalents at end of the period | $1,445 | $1,355 |
| **Supplemental Cash Flow Information** |  |  |
| Income taxes paid | 967 | 781 |

**COLGATE-PALMOLIVE COMPANY NOTES TO CONDENSED CONSOLIDATED FINANCIAL STATEMENTS (DOLLARS IN MILLIONS EXCEPT SHARE AND PER SHARE AMOUNTS) (UNAUDITED)**

Net sales and Operating profit by segment were as follows:

| | Three Months Ended September 30, | | Nine Months Ended September 30, | |
|---|---|---|---|---|
| | 2015 | 2014 | 2015 | 2011 |
| **Net sales** | | | | |
| Oral, Personal and Home Care | | | | |
| North America | $791 | $789 | $2,360 | $2,344 |
| Latin America | 1,064 | 1,194 | 3,277 | 3,577 |
| Europe/South Pacific | 728 | 886 | 2,200 | 2,624 |
| Asia | 624 | 634 | 1,908 | 1,916 |
| Africa/Eurasia | 246 | 310 | 754 | 916 |
| Total Oral, Personal and Home Care | 3,453 | 3,813 | 10,499 | 11,377 |
| Pet Nutrition | 546 | 566 | 1,636 | 1,679 |
| Total Net sales | $3,999 | $4,379 | $12,135 | $13,056 |
| **Operating profit** | | | | |
| Oral, Personal and Home Care | | | | |
| North America | $258 | $240 | $699 | $687 |
| Latin America | 300 | 330 | 929 | 931 |
| Europe/South Pacific | 206 | 237 | 573 | 681 |
| Asia | 195 | 187 | 569 | 558 |
| Africa/Eurasia | 44 | 60 | 128 | 177 |
| Total Oral, Personal and Home Care | 1,003 | 1,054 | 2,898 | 3,034 |
| Pet Nutrition | 157 | 149 | 450 | 439 |
| Corporate | (24) | (255) | (420) | (911) |
| Total Operating profit | $1,136 | $948 | $2,928 | $2,562 |

**COLGATE-PALMOLIVE COMPANY CONDENSED CONSOLIDATED STATEMENTS OF COMPREHENSIVE INCOME (DOLLARS IN MILLIONS) (UNAUDITED)**

| | Three Months Ended September 30, | | Nine Months Ended September 30, | |
|---|---|---|---|---|
| | 2015 | 2014 | 2015 | 2014 |
| Net income including noncontrolling interests | $770 | $580 | $1,969 | $1,673 |
| Other comprehensive income, (loss), net of tax | | | | |
| Cumulative translation adjustments | (350) | (367) | (635) | (386) |
| Retirement Plan and other retiree benefit adjustments | 25 | (17) | 52 | 4 |
| Gains (losses) on available-for-sale securities | — | (4) | (8) | (56) |
| Gains (losses) on cash flow hedges | 7 | 3 | 4 | (1) |
| Total Other comprehensive income, net of tax | (318) | (385) | (587) | (439) |
| Total Comprehensive income including noncontrolling interests | 452 | 195 | 1,382 | 1,234 |
| Less: Net income attributable to noncontrolling interests | 44 | 38 | 127 | 121 |
| Less: Cumulative translation adjustments attributable to noncontrolling interests | (9) | (2) | (9) | (3) |
| Total Comprehensive income attributable to noncontrolling interests | 35 | 36 | 118 | 118 |
| Total Comprehensive income attributable to Colgate-Palmolive Company | $417 | $159 | $1,264 | $1,116 |

Companies present comparative consolidated balance sheets as of the end of the current quarter and at the prior year-end. They present the comparative consolidated income statements for the current quarter and the same quarter of the prior year. Companies also present the current year-to-date and the prior year-to-date results on the consolidated income statement. Comparative consolidated statements of cash flows are presented for the current year-to-date and the prior year-to-date activity.

### International Accounting Standards

The current International Financial Reporting Standards (IFRS 8) for reporting operating segments was adopted in November 2006 and became effective on January 1, 2009. This update is a good example of the convergence process. The prior IFRS on operating segments dates to 1997, and had a number of differences from GAAP. The current IFRS is similar to GAAP in most respects, with few differences. The major similarities include using a management approach in defining reportable segments, and the same types and level of quantitative thresholds. Additionally, the 75 percent consolidated-revenue test is also applied to determine if additional segments must be disclosed.

IFRS (IAS 34) for interim reporting has one major difference with GAAP for interim reporting. IFRS uses the discrete theory, treating each interim period as an independent period.

### SUMMARY

Current GAAP requires disclosures about operating segments. The operating segments of a public business enterprise are determined by the structure of the enterprise's internal organization. This method of identifying segments is called the management approach. Aggregation criteria and materiality-tests determine which operating segments are reportable.

Disclosures required for each reportable operating segment include a description of the types of products and services sold, a profit or loss measure used internally to evaluate the segment, and total assets. Other disclosures on revenues, expenses, gains, losses, and assets may be made if these amounts are included in the profit or loss and segment-assets measures reviewed by the CODM. Reportable segment data are reconciled with the enterprise's consolidated amounts. Limited segment information is also disclosed in quarterly reports.

GAAP also requires disclosures on an enterprise-wide basis. A company must disclose information about its products and services, geographic areas, and major customers unless the information is included as part of the segment disclosures.

Segment information is important for effective analysis of financial statements because the opportunities for expansion and capital requirements differ by industry and geographic area.

GAAP for interim financial report disclosures helps to assure that interim financial reports provide timely information. However, much of the information is based on estimates, and the reports are unaudited. Each interim period is considered an integral part of the annual period. As a result, interim-period information is based on the accounting principles used in the last annual report. However, some modifications at the interim reporting date may be necessary so that the interim-period results complement the annual results of operations.

### QUESTIONS

1. What is an operating segment?
2. What is a reportable segment according to *FASB ASC Topic 280*? What criteria are used in determining what operating segments are also reportable segments?
3. How are the segments that are not reportable segments handled in the required disclosures of *FASB ASC Topic 280*?
4. Revenue information for Mahoney Corporation is as follows:

| | |
|---|---|
| Consolidated revenue (from the income statement) | $400,000 |
| Intersegment sales and transfers | 80,000 |
| Combined revenues of all industry segments | $480,000 |

Does the 10 percent revenue test for a reportable segment apply to 10 percent of the $400,000 or 10 percent of the $480,000?

5. Describe the 10 percent operating-profit test for determining reportable segments.

6. Describe the 10 percent asset test for determining reportable segments.

7. Describe the 10 percent revenue test for determining reportable segments.

8. Assume that an enterprise has 10 operating segments. Of these, five segments qualify as reportable segments by passing one of the 10 percent tests. However, their combined revenues from sales to unaffiliated customers total only 70 percent of the combined unaffiliated revenues from all operating segments. Should the remaining five operating segments be aggregated and shown as an "other segments" category? Explain.

9. What disclosures are required for the reportable segments and all remaining segments in the aggregate?

10. When is an enterprise required to include information in its financial statements about its foreign and domestic operations?

11. Must a major customer be identified by name?

12. Do the requirements of *FASB ASC Topic 280* apply to financial statements for interim periods? If so, how?

13. Explain how a company estimates its annual effective tax rate for interim reporting purposes.

14. What is the difference between the integral theory and the discrete theory with respect to interim financial reporting?

15. Describe the minimum financial information to be disclosed in interim reports under the provisions of *FASB ASC Topic 270*.

## EXERCISES

### E 15-1
### Segment disclosures

1. The disclosure requirements for an operating segment do not include:
   a *Unusual items*
   b *Income tax expense or benefit*
   c *Interest revenue*
   d *Cost of goods or services sold*

2. A reconciliation between the numbers disclosed in operating segments and consolidated numbers need not be provided for:
   a *Cost of goods sold*
   b *Profit or loss*
   c *Net assets*
   d *Revenues*

3. Each reportable segment is required to disclose the following information except for:
   a *Unusual items*
   b *Depreciation, depletion, and amortization*
   c *Capital expenditures*
   d *Gross profit or loss*

4. An enterprise is required to disclose information about its major customers if 10 percent or more of its revenue is derived from any single customer. This disclosure must include:
   a *The products or services generating the revenue from such sales*
   b *The operating segment or segments making such sales and the total revenue from the customer*
   c *The name of the customer to whom the sales were made*
   d *The dollar amounts of revenue and any profit or loss on the sales*

5. Which of the following is not a criterion for aggregating two or more operating segments?
   a *The segments should have similar products or services.*
   b *The segments should have similar production processes.*
   c *The distribution of products should be similar.*
   d *The segments should have similar amounts of revenue.*

6. Required segment disclosures in interim-period statements do not include:
   a *A measure of segment profit or loss*
   b *Net interest revenue*
   c *A description of a change in segmentation from the last annual report*
   d *Intersegment revenue*

## E 15-2
## Apply threshold tests—disclosure

Vic Corporation operates entirely in the United States but in different industries. It segments the business based on industry. Total sales of the segments, including intersegment sales, are as follows:

| | |
|---|---|
| Concrete and stone products | $400,000 |
| Construction | 1,000,000 |
| Lumber and wood products | 1,800,000 |
| Building materials | 1,000,000 |
| Other | 100,000 |

Further analysis reveals sales from one segment to another as follows:

| | |
|---|---|
| Lumber and wood products | $800,000 |
| Building materials | 400,000 |

### REQUIRED

1. Determine which segments are reportable segments under both the 10 percent and the 75 percent revenue tests.
2. Prepare a schedule suitable for disclosing revenue by industry segment for external reporting.
3. Prepare a reconciliation of segment revenue with consolidated revenue.

## E 15-3
## Apply threshold tests

Sur Corporation's internal divisions are based on industry. The revenues, operating profits, and assets of the operating segments of Sur are presented in thousands of dollars as follows:

| | Sales to Nonaffiliates | Intersegment Sales | Total Sales | Operating Profit (Loss) | Assets |
|---|---|---|---|---|---|
| Food service industry | $150,000 | $20,000 | $170,000 | $20,000 | $100,000 |
| Copper mine | 40,000 | — | 40,000 | (5,000) | 30,000 |
| Information systems | 10,000 | 7,500 | 17,500 | 2,500 | 20,000 |
| Chemical industry | 65,000 | 10,000 | 75,000 | 15,250 | 108,500 |
| Agricultural products | 24,000 | — | 24,000 | (7,750) | 25,000 |
| Pharmaceutical products | 10,000 | — | 10,000 | 4,000 | 9,000 |
| Foreign operations | 7,500 | — | 7,500 | 2,500 | 10,000 |
| Corporate assets* | | | | | 16,500 |
| | $306,500 | $37,500 | $344,000 | $31,500 | $319,000 |

*Corporate assets include equity investees of $5,000 and general assets of $11,500.

**REQUIRED:** Determine the reportable segments of Sur Corporation.

## E 15-4
## Segment and enterprise-wide disclosures

The sales in thousands of dollars of the segments of Wow Corporation (Wow is organized on a geographic basis) for 2016 are as follows:

| | Unaffiliated Sales | Intersegment Sales | Total |
|---|---|---|---|
| United States | $100,000 | $30,000 | $130,000 |
| Canada | 36,000 | 16,000 | 52,000 |
| Europe | 20,000 | 2,000 | 22,000 |
| Latin America | 14,000 | 6,000 | 20,000 |
| Japan | 6,000 | — | 6,000 |
| Korea | 2,000 | — | 2,000 |
| | $178,000 | $54,000 | $232,000 |

The $178,000 sales to unaffiliated customers is the amount of revenue reported in Wow's consolidated income statement.

**REQUIRED:** Illustrate the disclosure of Wow's domestic and foreign revenue in a form acceptable for external reporting, including reconciliation with consolidated revenue.

## E 15-5
## Apply threshold tests

1. Coy Corporation and its divisions are engaged solely in manufacturing operations. The following data (consistent with prior years' data) pertain to the industries in which operations were conducted for the year ended December 31, 2016 (in thousands):

| Industry | Total Revenue | Operating Profit | Assets at December 31, 2016 |
|---|---|---|---|
| A | $10,000 | $1,750 | $20,000 |
| B | 8,000 | 1,400 | 17,500 |
| C | 6,000 | 1,200 | 12,500 |
| D | 3,000 | 550 | 7,500 |
| E | 4,250 | 675 | 7,000 |
| F | 1,500 | 225 | 3,000 |
| | $32,750 | $5,800 | $67,500 |

In its segment information for 2016, how many reportable segments does Coy have?
a  *Three*
b  *Four*
c  *Five*
d  *Six*

2. Hen Corporation's revenues for the year ended December 31, 2016, are as follows (in thousands):

| | |
|---|---|
| Consolidated revenue per income statement | $1,200 |
| Intersegment sales | 180 |
| Intersegment transfers | 60 |
| Combined revenues of all segments | $1,440 |

Hen has a reportable segment if that segment's revenues exceed:
a  *$6*
b  *$24*
c  *$120*
d  *$144*

3. The following information pertains to Ari Corporation and its divisions for the year ended December 31, 2016 (in thousands):

| | |
|---|---|
| Sales to unaffiliated customers | $4,000 |
| Intersegment sales of products similar to those sold to unaffiliated customers | 1,200 |
| Interest earned on loans to other industry segments | 80 |

The intersegment interest is not reported by the divisions on internal reports reviewed by the chief operating officer. Ari and all of its divisions are engaged solely in manufacturing operations. Ari has a reportable segment if that segment's revenue exceeds:
a  *$528*
b  *$520*
c  *$408*
d  *$400*

**4.** The following information pertains to revenue earned by Wig Company's operating segments for the year ended December 31, 2016:

| Segment | Sales to Unaffiliated Customers | Intersegment Sales | Total Revenues |
|---------|-------------------------------:|-------------------:|---------------:|
| Ames | $ 10,000 | $6,000 | $ 16,000 |
| Beck | 16,000 | 8,000 | 24,000 |
| Cyns | 8,000 | — | 8,000 |
| DG | 86,000 | 32,000 | 118,000 |
| Combined | 120,000 | 46,000 | 166,000 |
| Elimination | — | (46,000) | (46,000) |
| Consolidated | $120,000 | — | $120,000 |

In conformity with the revenue test, Wig reportable segments were:

a   *Only DG*
b   *Beck and DG*
c   *Ames, Beck, and DG*
d   *Ames, Beck, Cyns, and DG*

Use the following information in answering questions 5 and 6:

Gum Corporation, a publicly owned corporation, is subject to the requirements for segment reporting. In its income statement for the year ended December 31, 2016, Gum reported revenues of $50,000,000, operating expenses of $47,000,000, and net payroll costs of $15,000,000. Gum's combined identifiable assets of all industry segments at December 31, 2016, were $40,000,000.

**5.** In its 2016 financial statements, Gum should disclose major customer data if sales to any single customer amount to at least:

a   *$300,000*
b   *$1,500,000*
c   *$4,000,000*
d   *$5,000,000*

**6.** In its 2016 financial statements, if Gum is organized on an industry basis, it should disclose foreign operations data on a specific country if revenues from that country's operations are at least:

a   *$5,000,000*
b   *$4,700,000*
c   *$4,000,000*
d   *$1,500,000*

**7.** Selected data for a segment of a business enterprise are to be separately reported in accordance with GAAP when the revenues of the segment exceed 10 percent of the:

a   *Combined net income of all segments reporting profits*
b   *Total revenues obtained in transactions with outsiders*
c   *Total revenues of all the enterprise's operating segments*
d   *Total combined revenues for all segments reporting profits*

**8.** In financial reporting of segment data, which of the following items is used in determining a segment's operating income?

a   *Income tax expense*
b   *Sales to other segments*
c   *General corporate expense*
d   *Gain or loss on discontinued operations*

## E 15-6
## Apply threshold tests

A summary of the segment operations of the Nog Corporation for the year ended December 31, 2016, follows:

| | United States | Canada | Germany | Japan | Mexico | Other Foreign | Consolidated |
|---|---:|---:|---:|---:|---:|---:|---:|
| Sales to unaffiliated customers | $35,000 | $6,000 | $3,000 | $3,500 | $1,500 | $1,000 | $50,000 |
| Interarea transfers | 10,000 | — | — | $3,000 | — | — | 13,000 |
| Total revenue | $45,000 | $6,000 | $3,000 | $6,500 | $1,500 | $1,000 | $63,000 |
| Operating profits | $8,000 | $1,000 | $1,500 | $1,000 | $500 | $500 | $12,500 |
| Segment assets | $50,000 | $7,500 | $8,500 | $9,000 | $2,000 | $1,500 | $78,500 |

1. For which of the following geographic areas will separate disclosures be required if only the 10 percent revenue test is considered?

   a  *United States, Canada, and Japan*
   b  *United States and Canada*
   c  *United States and Japan*
   d  *United States, Canada, Germany, and Japan*

2. For which of the following geographic areas will separate disclosures be required if only the 10 percent asset test is considered?

   a  *United States*
   b  *United States and Canada*
   c  *United States, Japan, and Germany*
   d  *United States, Canada, Germany, and Japan*

3. For which of the following geographic areas will separate disclosures be required if all relevant tests are considered?

   a  *United States, Canada, Germany, and Japan*
   b  *United States, Germany, and Japan*
   c  *United States, Canada, and Japan*
   d  *United States and Canada*

## E 15-7
## Interim accounting for various situations—tax

1. Interim reporting under *FASB ASC Topic 270* guidelines refers to financial reporting:

   a  *On a monthly basis*
   b  *On a quarterly basis*
   c  *On a regular basis*
   d  *For periods less than a year*

2. A liquidation of LIFO inventories for interim reporting purposes may create a problem in measuring cost of sales. Accordingly, cost of sales in interim periods should:

   a  *Be determined using the gross profit method*
   b  *Include the income effect of the LIFO liquidation*
   c  *Include the expected cost of replacing the liquidated LIFO base*
   d  *None of the above*

3. Bar Company's effective annual income tax rates for the first two quarters of 2016 are 34 percent and 30 percent for the first and second quarter, respectively. Assume that Bar's pretax income is $240,000 for the first quarter and $180,000 for the second quarter. Income tax expense for the second quarter is computed as:

   a  *$54,000*
   b  *$126,000*
   c  *$135,600*
   d  *$44,400*

4. Assume corporate tax rates of 15 percent on the first $50,000 of taxable income, 25 percent on taxable income between $50,000 and $75,000, 34 percent on taxable income between $75,000 and $100,000, and 39 percent on taxable income between $100,000 and $335,000. If a corporation estimates its pretax income at $20,000 for the first quarter, $25,000 for the second quarter, $30,000 for the third quarter, and $35,000 for the fourth quarter, its estimated annual effective tax rate is:

   a  *23.77 percent*
   b  *25 percent*
   c  *24.67 percent*
   d  *34 percent*

## E 15-8
## Interim tax

The estimated and actual pretax incomes of Ent Corporation by quarter for 2016 were as follows:

|  | 1st Quarter | 2nd Quarter | 3rd Quarter | 4th Quarter |
|---|---|---|---|---|
| Estimated pretax income | $30,000 | $30,000 | $40,000 | $50,000 |
| Actual pretax income | 30,000 | 40,000 | 40,000 | 40,000 |

Ent calculated its estimated annual effective income tax rate to be 27.8333 percent, based on estimated pretax income and existing income tax rates.

**REQUIRED:** Prepare a schedule to calculate Ent Corporation's net income by quarter.

## E 15-9
### Interim accounting for various situations—tax

1. An inventory loss from a market price decline occurred in the first quarter, and the decline was not expected to reverse during the fiscal year. However, in the third quarter, the inventory's market price recovery exceeded the market decline that occurred in the first quarter. For interim financial reporting, the dollar amount of net inventory should:

   a *Decrease in the first quarter by the amount of the market price decline and increase in the third quarter by the amount of the decrease in the first quarter*

   b *Decrease in the first quarter by the amount of the market price decline and increase in the third quarter by the amount of the market price recovery*

   c *Decrease in the first quarter by the amount of the market price decline and not be affected in the third quarter*

   d *Not be affected in either the first quarter or the third quarter*

2. Far Corporation had the following transactions during the quarter ended March 31, 2016:

   | | |
   |---|---|
   | Loss on early extinguishment of debt | $70,000 |
   | Payment of fire insurance premium for calendar year 2016 | 100,000 |

   What amount should be included in Far's income statement for the quarter ended March 31, 2016?

   | | Insurance Expense |
   |---|---|
   | a | $100,000 |
   | b | $25,000 |
   | c | $50,000 |
   | d | $70,000 |

3. An inventory loss from a permanent market decline of $360,000 occurred in May 2016. Cox Company appropriately recorded this loss in May 2016, after its March 31, 2016, quarterly report was issued. What amount of inventory loss should be reported in Cox's quarterly income statement for the three months ended June 30, 2016?

   a *$0*

   b *$90,000*

   c *$180,000*

   d *$360,000*

4. On July 1, 2016, Dol Corporation incurred an discontinued operations loss of $300,000, net of income tax saving. Dol's operating income for the full year ending December 31, 2016, is expected to be $500,000. In Dol's income statement for the quarter ended September 30, 2016, how much of this discontinued operations loss should be disclosed?

   a *$300,000*

   b *$150,000*

   c *$75,000*

   d *$0*

5. In January 2016, Pin Company paid property taxes of $80,000 covering the calendar year 2016. Also in January 2016, Pin estimated that its year-end bonuses to executives would amount to $320,000 for 2016. What is the total amount of expense relating to these two items that should be reflected in Pin's quarterly income statement for the three months ended June 30, 2016?

   a *$100,000*

   b *$80,000*

   c *$20,000*

   d *$0*

## E 15-10
### Interim accounting under LIFO

Tap Manufacturing Company records sales of $1,000,000 and cost of sales of $550,000 during the first quarter of 2016. Tap uses the LIFO inventory method, and its inventories are computed as follows:

| | | |
|---|---|---|
| Beginning LIFO inventory at January 1 | 10,000 units at $5 | $50,000 |
| Ending LIFO inventory at March 31 | 6,000 units at $5 | $30,000 |

Before year-end, Tap expects to replace the 4,000 units liquidated in the first quarter. The current cost of the inventory units is $7 each.

**REQUIRED:** At what amount will Tap report cost of sales in its first-quarter interim report?

## PROBLEMS

### P 15-1
### Apply threshold tests

The following information has been accumulated for use in preparing segment disclosures for Wod Corporation (in thousands):

| | Sales to Unaffiliated Customers | Sales to Affiliated Customers | Total Sales |
|---|---|---|---|
| Apparel | $164 | — | $164 |
| Construction | 112 | — | 112 |
| Furniture | 208 | $6 | 214 |
| Lumber and wood products | 175 | 90 | 265 |
| Paper | 90 | — | 90 |
| Textiles | 50 | 170 | 220 |
| Tobacco | 93 | — | 93 |
| Total | $892 | $266 | $1,158 |

### REQUIRED

1. Determine Wod's reportable segments under the 10 percent revenue test.
2. Are additional reportable segments required under the 75 percent revenue test?
3. Prepare a schedule to disclose revenue by operating segment for external reporting. Assume that the paper and tobacco segments, both sold in grocery stores, share similar operating characteristics on four of the five aggregation criteria.

### P 15-2
### Apply threshold tests

The following data for 2016 relate to Hay Industries, a worldwide conglomerate:

| | Sales to Unaffiliated Customers | Intersegment Sales | Operating Profit (Loss) | Assets |
|---|---|---|---|---|
| Food | $300,000 | $50,000 | $45,000 | $310,000 |
| Chemical | 110,000 | 40,000 | 23,000 | 150,000 |
| Textiles | 65,000 | 5,000 | (8,000) | 60,000 |
| Furniture | 48,000 | — | 9,000 | 40,000 |
| Beverage | 62,000 | 10,000 | 18,000 | 60,000 |
| Oil | 15,000 | — | (2,000) | 25,000 |
| Segment | 600,000 | 105,000 | 85,000 | 645,000 |
| Corporate | — | — | (7,000) | 15,000 |
| Consolidated | $600,000 | 0 | $78,000 | $660,000 |

### REQUIRED: Answer the following questions related to Hay's required segment disclosures and show computations:

1. Which segments are reportable segments under (a) the revenue test, (b) the operating-profit test, and (c) the asset test?
2. Do additional reportable segments have to be identified?

## P 15-3
## Apply threshold tests—Disclosure

DaP Corporation's home country is the United States, but it also has operations in Canada, Mexico, Brazil, and South Africa and reports internally on a geographic basis. Information relevant to DaP's operating-segment disclosure requirement for the year ended December 31, 2016, is presented in summary form as follows:

| | United States | Canada | Mexico | Brazil | South Africa | Consolidated |
|---|---|---|---|---|---|---|
| Sales to unaffiliated customers | $120,000 | $13,000 | $20,000 | $22,000 | $15,000 | $190,000 |
| Intersegment transfers | 29,000 | 11,000 | — | — | 10,000 | $50,000 |
| Total revenue | $149,000 | $24,000 | $20,000 | $22,000 | $25,000 | $240,000 |
| Operating profit | $ 24,000 | $ 6,000 | $ 8,000 | $ 5,000 | $ 7,000 | $ 50,000 |
| Identifiable assets | $150,000 | $30,000 | $19,000 | $20,000 | $31,000 | $250,000 |

### REQUIRED

1. Prepare schedules to show which of DaP's operating segments require separate disclosure under (a) the 10 percent revenue test, (b) the 10 percent asset test, and (c) the 10 percent profit test.
2. Which of DaP's operating segments meet at least one of the tests for segment reporting?
3. Prepare a schedule to disclose DaP's segment operations from the information given.

## P 15-4
## Apply threshold tests—Segment and enterprise-wide disclosure

Mer Corporation has five major operating segments and operates in both domestic and foreign markets. Mer is organized internally on an industry basis. Information about its revenue from operating segments and foreign operations for 2016 is as follows (in thousands):

SALES TO UNAFFILIATED CUSTOMERS

| | Domestic | Foreign | Total |
|---|---|---|---|
| Foods | $150 | $30 | $180 |
| Soft drinks | 650 | 250 | 900 |
| Distilled spirits | 500 | 50 | 550 |
| Cosmetics | 200 | — | 200 |
| Packaging | 110 | — | 110 |
| Other (four minor segments) | 240 | — | 240 |
| | $1,850 | $330 | $2,180 |

SALES TO AFFILIATED CUSTOMERS

| | Domestic | Foreign | Total |
|---|---|---|---|
| Foods | $30 | — | $30 |
| Soft drinks | 160 | — | 160 |
| Distilled spirits | — | $20 | 20 |
| Cosmetics | — | — | — |
| Packaging | 10 | — | 10 |
| Other (four minor segments) | — | — | — |
| | $200 | $20 | $220 |

A Japanese subsidiary of Mer operates exclusively in the soft drink market. All other foreign operations are carried out through Canadian subsidiaries, none of which are included in the soft drink business.

Only the soft drink and distilled spirits segments are reportable segments under the asset and operating-profit tests for segments.

## REQUIRED

**1.** Determine which industry segments are reportable segments under the revenue test for segment reporting. Assume no further aggregation is possible. Would the possible aggregation of smaller segments change your response?

**2.** Prepare a schedule suitable for disclosing Mer's revenue by segment for 2016, assuming no further aggregation is possible.

**3.** Prepare a schedule suitable for disclosing Mer's revenue by geographic area for 2016.

## P 15-5
## Apply threshold tests—Disclosure

Selected information, which is reported to the chief operating officer, for the five segments of Rad Company for the year ended December 31, 2016, is as follows:

| | Food | Tobacco | Lumber | Textiles | Furniture | General Corporate | Consolidated |
|---|---|---|---|---|---|---|---|
| *Revenue Data* | | | | | | | |
| Sales to unaffiliated customers | $12,000 | $10,000 | $7,000 | $18,000 | $7,000 | | $ 54,000 |
| Sales to affiliated customers | 5,000 | 7,000 | | 8,000 | | | 20,000 |
| Income from equity investees | | | | 3,000 | | $ 6,000 | 9,000 |
| Total revenue | $17,000 | $17,000 | $7,000 | $29,000 | $7,000 | $6,000 | $ 83,000 |
| *Expense Data* | | | | | | | |
| Cost of sales | $10,000 | $9,000 | $4,000 | $16,000 | $4,000 | | $ 43,000 |
| Depreciation expense | 1,000 | 2,000 | 2,500 | 3,000 | 500 | | 9,000 |
| Other operating expenses | 2,000 | 2,000 | 1,000 | 2,000 | 1,000 | | 8,000 |
| Interest expense | 2,000 | | | 2,000 | | $ 3,000 | 7,000 |
| Income taxes | 1,000 | 2,000 | (250) | 3,000 | 750 | 1,500 | 8,000 |
| Net income | $ 1,000 | $2,000 | $(250) | $ 3,000 | $ 750 | $ 1,500 | $ 8,000 |
| *Asset Data* | | | | | | | |
| Segment assets | $18,000 | $19,000 | $6,000 | $22,000 | $7,000 | | $72,000 |
| Investment in affiliates | | | | 20,000 | | $40,000 | 60,000 |
| General corporate assets | | | | | | 4,000 | 4,000 |
| Intersegment advances | 1,000 | 2,000 | | | | | |
| Total assets | $19,000 | $21,000 | $6,000 | $42,000 | $7,000 | $44,000 | $136,000 |

The lumber segment has not been a reportable segment in prior years and is not expected to be a reportable segment in future years.

## REQUIRED

**1.** Prepare schedules to show which of the segments are reportable segments under:
a. The 10 percent revenue test
b. The 10 percent operating-profit test
c. The 10 percent asset test

**2.** Which of the segments meet at least one of the tests for reportable segments?

**3.** Must additional reportable segments be identified?

**4.** Prepare a schedule for appropriate disclosure of the segmented data in the financial report of Rad Company for the year ended December 31, 2016.

## P 15-6
### Apply threshold tests—Disclosure

The consolidated income statement of Tut Company for 2016 is as follows (in thousands):

TUT CONSOLIDATED INCOME STATEMENT FOR
THE YEAR ENDED DECEMBER 31, 2016

| | |
|---|---:|
| Sales | $360 |
| Interest income | 10 |
| Income from equity investee | 30 |
| Total revenue | 400 |
| Cost of sales | $180 |
| General expenses | 40 |
| Selling expenses | 50 |
| Interest expense | 10 |
| Noncontrolling interest share | 15 |
| Income taxes | 45 |
| Total expenses | 340 |
| Income from continuing operations | $ 60 |
| Discontinued operations loss (net of income taxes) | 10 |
| Consolidated net income | $50 |

Tut's operations are conducted through three domestic operating segments with sales, expenses, and assets as follows (in thousands):

| | Chemical | Food | Drug | Corporate |
|---|---:|---:|---:|---:|
| Sales (including intersegment sales) | $160 | $140 | $120 | |
| Cost of sales (including intersegment cost of sales) | 80 | 70 | 60 | |
| General expenses | 15 | 10 | 10 | $5 |
| Selling expenses | 20 | 15 | 15 | |
| Interest expense (unaffiliated) | 5 | | 5 | |
| Identifiable assets | 200 | 180 | 150 | 200 |
| Investment in equity investee | | | | 300 |

The $10,000 interest income is not related to any industry segment. Consolidated total assets are $1,000,000. The chemical and food segments had intersegment sales of $35,000 and $25,000, respectively.

**REQUIRED:** Prepare a schedule of required disclosures for Tut's industry segments in a form acceptable for reporting purposes. Assume the CODM uses operating profit to evaluate segments.

## P 15-7
### Apply threshold tests—Disclosure

The information that follows is for Cob Company at and for the year ended December 31, 2016. Cob's operating segments are cost centers currently used for internal planning and control purposes. Amounts shown in the Total Consolidated column are amounts prepared under GAAP for external reporting. (Data are in thousands of dollars.)

| | Food Industry | Packing Industry | Textile Industry | Foreign Operations | All Other Industries | Corporate | Total Consolidated |
|---|---:|---:|---:|---:|---:|---:|---:|
| *Income Statement* | | | | | | | |
| Sales to unaffiliated customers | $950 | $500 | $300 | $250 | $400 | | $2,400 |
| Income from equity investees | | | | | | | 100 |
| Cost of sales to unaffiliated customers | (600) | (350) | (175) | (125) | (250) | | (1,500) |
| Operating expense | (200) | (75) | (150) | (75) | (75) | $(25) | (600) |
| Interest expense | | | | | | | (20) |
| Income taxes | | | | | | | (150) |
| Noncontrolling interest share | | | | | | | (30) |
| Net income (loss) | $150 | $ 75 | $ (25) | $ 50 | $ 75 | $(25) | $200 |

| | Food Industry | Packing Industry | Textile Industry | Foreign Operations | All Other Industries | Corporate | Total Consolidated |
|---|---|---|---|---|---|---|---|
| *Assets* | | | | | | | |
| Current assets | $300 | $100 | $ 75 | $100 | $225 | $   25 | $  825 |
| Plant assets—net | 400 | 400 | 250 | 100 | 175 | 25 | 1,350 |
| Advances | 50 | | 25 | | | 50 | |
| Equity investments | | | | | | 1,000 | 1,000 |
| Total assets | $750 | $500 | $350 | $200 | $400 | $1,100 | $3,175 |
| *Intersegment Transfers* | | | | | | | |
| Sales* | $ 60 | $ 60 | $ 30 | $ 50 | | | |
| Cost of Goods Sold* | $100 | $ 25 | | $ 75 | | | |

*Amounts have been eliminated from the income data given.

## REQUIRED

1. Prepare a schedule to determine which of Cob's operating segments are reportable segments under (a) the 10 percent revenue test, (b) the 10 percent operating-profit test, and (c) the 10 percent asset test.
2. Prepare a schedule to show how Cob's segment information would be disclosed under the provisions of *FASB ASC Topic 280*.

## P 15-8
## Interim reporting—tax

Tor Corporation is subject to income tax rates of 20 percent on its first $50,000 pretax income and 34 percent on amounts in excess of $50,000. Quarterly pretax accounting income for the calendar year is estimated by Tor to be as follows:

| Quarter | Estimated Pretax Income |
|---|---|
| First | $20,000 |
| Second | 30,000 |
| Third | 60,000 |
| Fourth | 50,000 |
| Total | $160,000 |

No changes in accounting principles, discontinued items, or unusual or infrequently occurring items are anticipated for the year. The fourth quarter's pretax income is, however, expected to include $20,000 in dividends from domestic corporations, for which an 80 percent dividend-received deduction is available.

## REQUIRED

1. Calculate the estimated annual effective tax rate for Tor Corporation for 2016.
2. Prepare a schedule showing Tor's estimated net income for each quarter and the calendar year 2016.

---

# PROFESSIONAL RESEARCH ASSIGNMENTS

Answer the following questions by reference to the FASB Codification of Accounting Standards. Include the appropriate reference in your response.

**PR 15-1** Does an entity need to disclose segment level information about depreciation and amortization (D&A) if the chief decision maker does not consider D&A in their assessment of the segments?

**PR 15-2** When preparing interim reports, does an entity need to use the same method to value inventory that they use at the annual report date? What options are accepted?

# 16

# Partnerships—Formation, Operations, and Changes in Ownership Interests

T his chapter and Chapter 17 focus on accounting for partnership entities. This chapter describes general matters involving the partnership form of business organization, including partnership formation, accounting for partnership operations, and accounting for changes in ownership interests. We describe the accounting for a limited partnership, commonly used by CPA firms, at the end of this chapter. Chapter 17 covers the dissolution and liquidation of partnerships.

Although accounting for partnerships differs from that of other types of business organizations, asset, liability, and income accounting usually follow GAAP.

## LEARNING OBJECTIVES

**16.1** Comprehend the legal characteristics of partnerships.

**16.2** Understand initial investment valuation and record keeping.

**16.3** Grasp the diverse nature of profit- and loss-sharing agreements and their computation.

**16.4** Value a new partner's investment in an existing partnership.

**16.5** Value a partner's share on retirement or death.

**16.6** Understand limited liability partnership characteristics.

## NATURE OF PARTNERSHIPS

Partnerships allow two or more people to share a business's risk and reward. Partners can contribute their expertise and their capital, either real assets or financial assets to the venture. Partnerships are common in many areas of business, including service industries, retail trade, wholesale and manufacturing operations, and the professions, particularly the legal, medical, and public accounting professions.

State statutes govern partnership formation, operation, and dissolution. In 1914, the National Conference of Commissioners on Uniform State Laws developed the Uniform Partnership Act (UPA) (1914), which was eventually adopted, with some variations, by all states except Louisiana. In 1992 and 1997, the Uniform Partnership Act (1914) was revised by the National Conference and has been adopted, with revision, by several states. The original Uniform Partnership Act still provides legal guidance for general partnerships in most states, and its provisions generally apply to the formation, operation, and dissolution of partnerships in the United States. The change in the Uniform Partnership Act (UPA) (1997) that is relevant to our discussion here is the adoption of the entity theory to define the nature of partnerships. Under the entity theory, partners own their share of the partnership but do not have ownership shares in the individual assets of the entity. The UPA (1914) applied an aggregate theory approach in which partners not only had an ownership interest in the partnership but also in the individual assets of the entity. Under UPA (1997), in most circumstances, partners can dissociate themselves from a partnership without an accompanying winding up of the business. Winding up the business requires selling off all assets, settling liabilities, and distributing the proceeds to the partners. This process is called **dissolution of a partnership**. Dissociation allows the other partners or other people to buy out the dissociating partner's share of the business without interrupting the business itself. This is similar to the way in which a corporation's stock can be traded.

We discuss dissociation in this chapter and dissolution with the resulting winding up of the business in Chapter 17. The 1997 UPA is included on this book's Web site. Remember, however, that each state has its own variation of partnership law.

## Partnership Characteristics

**Partnership** is defined in Section 101(6) of the UPA as "an association of two or more persons to carry on as co-owners a business for profit."[1] Partnership business operations frequently continue to run smoothly when new partners are admitted or old partners withdraw.

Under the legal concept of **mutual agency**, each partner is an agent for all partnership activities, with the power to bind all other partners by his or her actions on behalf of the partnership. The implications of mutual agency are particularly significant when considered in conjunction with the **unlimited liability** feature of partnerships. Each partner is liable for all partnership debts and, in case of insolvency, may be required to use personal assets to pay partnership debts authorized by any other partner.

## Articles of Partnership

A partnership may be formed by a simple oral agreement among two or more people to operate a business for profit. Even though oral agreements may be legal and binding, written **partnership agreements** are a sound business practice. Such agreements should specify:

1. The types of products and services to be provided and other details of the business's operations
2. Each partner's rights and responsibilities in conducting the business
3. Each partner's initial investment including the value assigned to noncash asset investments
4. Additional investment conditions
5. Asset withdrawal provisions
6. Profit- and loss-sharing formulas
7. Procedures for dissolving the partnership

When no specific agreement for dividing profits and losses exists, all partners share equally, irrespective of investments made or time devoted to the business (UPA Section 401[b]).

## Partnership Financial Reporting

The accounting reports of partnerships are designed to meet the needs of three user groups—the partners, the partnership's creditors, and the Internal Revenue Service (IRS). Partners need accounting information for planning and controlling partnership assets and activities and for making personal investment decisions with respect to their partnership investments. In the absence of an agreement to the contrary, every partner has access to the partnership books at all times (UPA Section 403[b]). Credit grantors such as banks and other financial institutions frequently require financial reports in support of loan applications and other credit matters relating to partnerships.

Although partnerships do not pay federal income taxes, partnerships are required to submit financial information to the IRS. This allows the IRS to verify that each partner pays income taxes on his or her share of partnership income. Partnerships are not required to prepare annual reports for public inspection.

## INITIAL INVESTMENTS IN A PARTNERSHIP

All property brought into the partnership or acquired by the partnership is partnership property (UPA Section 203). Initial investments in a partnership are recorded in capital accounts maintained for each partner. If Ash and Bec each invest $20,000 cash in a new partnership, they record the investments as follows:

| | | |
|---|---|---|
| Cash (+A) | 20,000 | |
|     Ash capital (+OE) * | | 20,000 |
|   To record Ash's original investment of cash. | | |
| Cash (+A) | 20,000 | |
|     Bec capital (+OE) | | 20,000 |
|   To record Bec's original investment of cash. | | |

---

\* Our journal entry notation in Chapters 16 and 17 uses OE to represent partnership equity instead of SE to represent shareholders' equity.

---

[1]© By National Conference of Commissioners on Uniform State Laws

## Noncash Investments

When property other than cash is invested in a partnership, the noncash property is recorded at the fair value of the property at the time of the investment. Conceptually, the fair value should be determined by independent valuations, but as a practical matter, the fair value of noncash property is determined by agreement of all partners. The amounts involved should be specified in the written partnership agreement.

Assume, for example, that Col and Cro enter into a partnership with the following investments:

| | Col<br>(Fair Value) | Cro<br>(Fair Value) |
|---|---|---|
| Cash | — | $7,000 |
| Land (cost to Col, $5,000) | $10,000 | — |
| Building (cost to Col, $30,000) | 40,000 | — |
| Inventory items (cost to Cro, $28,000) | — | 35,000 |
| Total | $50,000 | $42,000 |

After Col and Cro agree to the values assigned to the assets, they record the investments as follows:

| | | |
|---|---|---|
| Land (+A) | 10,000 | |
| Building (+A) | 40,000 | |
| Col capital (+OE) | | 50,000 |
| To record Col's original investment of land and building at fair value. | | |
| Cash (+A) | 7,000 | |
| Inventory (+A) | 35,000 | |
| Cro capital (+OE) | | 42,000 |
| To record Cro's original investment of cash and inventory items at fair value. | | |

## Bonus or Goodwill on Initial Investments

A valuation problem arises when partners agree on relative capital interests that are not aligned with their investments of identifiable assets. For example, Col and Cro could agree to divide initial partnership capital equally, even though Col contributed $50,000 in identifiable assets and Cro contributed $42,000. Such an agreement implies that Cro is contributing an unidentifiable asset such as individual talent, established clientele, or banking connections to the partnership. The dollar amount of the implied unidentifiable asset can be inferred from Col's fair-value contribution. Col invested $50,000 of assets measured at fair value for a 50 percent interest in the partnership. One can infer from Col's investment that the fair value of the partnership is $100,000 ($50,000 ÷ 50%). The implied fair value of the unidentifiable asset contributed by Cro is $8,000 because Cro also has a 50 percent interest in the partnership but only contributed identifiable assets with a fair value of $42,000.

The partnership agreement specifies equal capital interests, so we should adjust the capital account balances of Col and Cro to meet the agreement's conditions. Either of two approaches may be used to adjust the capital accounts—the bonus approach or the goodwill approach. Under the **bonus approach**, the unidentifiable asset is not recorded on the partnership books.

Because the total identifiable contributed capital is $92,000, each partner will start with $46,000 if the unidentifiable asset is not recorded. As a result, Col's capital will be reduced by $4,000, and Cro's capital will be increased by $4,000. This is recorded as follows:

| | | |
|---|---|---|
| Col capital (−OE) | 4,000 | |
| Cro capital (+OE) | | 4,000 |
| To establish equal capital interests of $46,000 by recording a $4,000 bonus from Col to Cro. | | |

When the **goodwill approach** is used, the unidentifiable asset contributed by Cro is measured on the basis of Col's $50,000 investment for a 50 percent interest. Col's investment implies total partnership capital of $100,000 ($50,000 ÷ 50%) and goodwill of $8,000 ($100,000 total capital −$92,000 identifiable assets). We record the unidentifiable asset as follows:

| | | |
|---|---:|---:|
| Goodwill (+A) | 8,000 | |
| Cro capital (+OE) | | 8,000 |
| To establish equal capital interests of $50,000 by recognizing Cro's investment of an $8,000 unidentifiable asset. | | |

Both approaches are equally effective in aligning the capital accounts with the agreement and are equitable in assigning capital interests to individual partners. A decision to use one approach over the other will depend on partner attitudes toward recording the $8,000 unidentifiable asset under the goodwill method and on Col's willingness to receive a $46,000 capital credit for a $50,000 investment under the bonus approach.

## ADDITIONAL INVESTMENTS AND WITHDRAWALS

The partnership agreement should establish guidelines for additional investments and withdrawals made after partnership operations have begun. Additional investments are credited to the investing partner's capital account at fair value at the time of the investment. Withdrawals of large and irregular amounts are ordinarily recorded directly in the withdrawing partner's capital account. The entry for such a withdrawal is:

| | | |
|---|---:|---:|
| Sam capital (−OE) | 20,000 | |
| Cash (−A) | | 20,000 |
| To record the withdrawal of cash. | | |

## Drawings

Partnership profits are the business rewards for partners, so partners do not have take-home pay as do the employees of the partnership business. Instead, active partners commonly withdraw regular amounts of money on a weekly or monthly basis in anticipation of their share of partnership profits. Such withdrawals are called **drawings**, **drawing allowances**, or sometimes **salary allowances,** and they are usually recorded in the partners' drawing accounts rather than directly in the capital accounts. For example, if Tow and Lee withdraw $1,000 from the partnership each month, they would record the monthly withdrawals as follows:

| | | |
|---|---:|---:|
| Tow drawing (−OE) | 1,000 | |
| Cash (−A) | | 1,000 |
| To record Tow's drawing allowance for January. | | |
| Lee drawing (−OE) | 1,000 | |
| Cash (−A) | | 1,000 |
| To record Lee's drawing allowance for January. | | |

Drawing accounts provide a record of each partner's drawings during an accounting period. This record may be compared with drawings allowed in the partnership agreement in order to establish an accounting control over excessive drawings. Drawings balances are also a factor in many profit- and loss-sharing agreements and are discussed later in the chapter.

If Tow draws $1,000 each month during the year, his drawing account balance at year-end is $12,000, and his drawing account is closed by the following entry:

| | | |
|---|---:|---:|
| Tow capital (−OE) | 12,000 | |
| Tow drawing (+OE) | | 12,000 |
| To close Tow's drawing account. | | |

Regardless of the name given to regular withdrawals by partners, such withdrawals are disinvestments of essentially the same nature as large and irregular withdrawals. Drawing accounts are closed to capital accounts before a partnership balance sheet is prepared.

## Loans and Advances

A partner may make a personal loan to the partnership. UPA section 401(d) specifies that "a partner, who in the aid of the partnership makes any payment or advance beyond the amount of capital which he agreed to contribute, shall be paid interest from the date of the payment or advance."[2] Such loans or advances and related accrued interest are regarded as liabilities of the partnership. Similarly, partnership loans and advances to an individual partner are considered partnership assets. Matters concerning loans and advances to or from partners should be covered in the partnership agreement.

## PARTNERSHIP OPERATIONS

LEARNING OBJECTIVE **16.3**

The operations of a partnership are similar in most respects to those of other forms of organizations operating in the same line of business. In measuring partnership income for a period, however, the expenses should be scrutinized to make sure that partners' personal expenses are excluded from the partnership's business expenses. If a partner's personal expenses are paid with partnership assets, the payment is charged to the drawing or capital account of that partner. Drawings and salary allowances are closed to the capital accounts of the partners rather than to an income summary account.

Partnership general-purpose financial statements include an income statement, a balance sheet, a statement of partnership capital, and a statement of cash flows. The statement of partnership capital is unique to the partnership form of organization and is illustrated here.

Assume that Rat and Yan are partners sharing profits in a 60:40 ratio, respectively. Data relevant to the partnership's equity accounts for 2016 are:

| | |
|---|---|
| Partnership net income 2016 | $34,500 |
| Rat capital January 1, 2016 | 40,000 |
| Rat additional investment 2016 | 5,000 |
| Rat drawing 2016 | 6,000 |
| Yan capital January 1, 2016 | 35,000 |
| Yan drawing 2016 | 9,000 |
| Yan withdrawal 2016 | 3,000 |

The statement of partners' capital that appears in Exhibit 16-1 reflects this information. Although other forms of presentation can be used, the format illustrated in Exhibit 16-1 provides a comparison of capital changes before and after the division of partnership net income. An ability to compare beginning capital balances and net contributed capital is helpful to the partners in setting investment and withdrawal policies and in controlling abuses of the established policies.

The additional investment by Rat and withdrawal by Yan have been directly recorded in their respective capital accounts. Partnership income and drawings are closed to each partner's capital accounts at year-end.

**EXHIBIT 16-1**

**Format for a Statement of Partners' Capital**

### RAT AND YAN
### STATEMENT OF PARTNERS' CAPITAL
### FOR THE YEAR ENDED DECEMBER 31, 2016

| | 60% Rat | 40% Yan | Total |
|---|---|---|---|
| Capital balances January 1, 2016 | $40,000 | $35,000 | $75,000 |
| Add: Additional investments | 5,000 | — | 5,000 |
| Deduct: Withdrawals | — | (3,000) | (3,000) |
| Deduct: Drawings | (6,000) | (9,000) | (15,000) |
| Net contributed capital | 39,000 | 23,000 | 62,000 |
| Add: Net income for 2016 | 20,700 | 13,800 | 34,500 |
| Capital balances December 31, 2016 | $59,700 | $36,800 | $96,500 |

Closing entries for the Rat and Yan partnership at December 31, 2016, are as follows:

*December 31, 2016*

| | | |
|---|---|---|
| Income summary (−OE) | 34,500 | |
|     Rat capital (+OE) | | 20,700 |
|     Yan capital (+OE) | | 13,800 |

   To divide net income 60% to Rat and 40% to Yan.

*December 31, 2016*

| | | |
|---|---|---|
| Rat capital (−OE) | 6,000 | |
| Yan capital (−OE) | 9,000 | |
|     Rat drawing (+OE) | | 6,000 |
|     Yan drawing (+OE) | | 9,000 |

To close partner drawing accounts to capital accounts.

## PROFIT- AND LOSS-SHARING AGREEMENTS

Equal division of partnership income is required in the absence of a profit- and loss-sharing agreement. However, partners generally agree to share profits in a specified ratio, such as the 60:40 division illustrated for the Rat and Yan partnership. Profit-sharing agreements also apply to the division of losses unless the agreement specifies otherwise.

Although agreements to share profits and losses equally or in specified ratios are common, more-complex profit-sharing agreements are also encountered in practice. The time that partners devote to the partnership business and the capital invested in the business by individual partners are frequently considered in determining the profit-sharing agreement. If one partner manages the partnership, the partnership agreement may allow that partner a salary allowance equal to the amount he or she could earn in an alternative employment opportunity before remaining profits are allocated. Similarly, if one partner invests significantly more than another in a partnership venture, the agreement may provide an interest allowance on capital investments before remaining profits are divided. As in the case of salary allowances, interest allowances are provisions of the partnership agreement and have no effect on the measurement of partnership income but do affect how much of that income is assignable to each partner.

### Service Considerations in Profit- and Loss-Sharing Agreements

As mentioned earlier, a partner who devotes time to the partnership business while other partners work elsewhere may receive a salary allowance. Salary allowances are also used to compensate for differences in the fair value of the talents of partners, all of whom devote their time to the partnership. Another variation in profit- and loss-sharing agreements provides salary allowances to active partners and a bonus to the managing partner to encourage profit maximization. These alternatives are illustrated for the partnership of Ann, Gar, and Kat. Ann is the managing partner, Gar is the sales manager, and Kat works outside the partnership.

### Salary Allowances in Profit-Sharing Agreements

Assume that Ann, Gar, and Kat's partnership agreement provides that Ann and Gar receive salary allowances of $12,000 each, with the remaining income allocated equally among the three partners. If partnership net income is $60,000 for 2016 and $12,000 for 2017, the income allocations are as shown in Exhibit 16-2. The total 2016 allocation is $24,000 each to Ann and Gar and $12,000 to Kat. The 2017 allocation is $8,000 income to Ann and Gar and a $4,000 loss to Kat. Note that the partnership agreement was followed in 2017 even though the salary allowances of $24,000 exceeded partnership net income of $12,000. The income allocation schedule follows the order of the profit-sharing agreement even when the partnership has a loss. Salary allowances increase the loss to be divided equally.

## INCOME ALLOCATION SCHEDULE—2016

|  |  | Ann | Gar | Kat | Total |
|---|---|---|---|---|---|
| Net income | $60,000 |  |  |  |  |
| Salary allowances to Ann and Gar | (24,000) | $12,000 | $12,000 |  | $24,000 |
| Remainder to divide | 36,000 |  |  |  |  |
| Divided equally | (36,000) | 12,000 | 12,000 | $12,000 | 36,000 |
| Remainder to divide | 0 |  |  |  |  |
| Net income allocation |  | $24,000 | $24,000 | $12,000 | $60,000 |

## INCOME ALLOCATION SCHEDULE—2017

|  |  | Ann | Gar | Kat | Total |
|---|---|---|---|---|---|
| Net income | $12,000 |  |  |  |  |
| Salary allowances to Ann and Gar | (24,000) | $12,000 | $12,000 |  | $24,000 |
| Remainder to divide | (12,000) |  |  |  |  |
| Divided equally | $12,000 | (4,000) | (4,000) | $(4,000) | (12,000) |
| Remainder to divide | 0 |  |  |  |  |
| Net income allocation |  | $8,000 | $8,000 | $(4,000) | $12,000 |

**EXHIBIT 16-2**

Salary Allowances
in Profit-Sharing
Agreements

Journal entries to distribute partnership income to individual capital accounts for 2016 and 2017 follow:

*December 31, 2016*

| | | |
|---|---|---|
| Income summary (−OE) | 60,000 | |
|     Ann capital (+OE) | | 24,000 |
|     Gar capital (+OE) | | 24,000 |
|     Kat capital (+OE) | | 12,000 |
|   Partnership income allocation for 2016. | | |

*December 31, 2017*

| | | |
|---|---|---|
| Income summary (−OE) | 12,000 | |
| Kat capital (−OE) | 4,000 | |
|     Ann capital (+OE) | | 8,000 |
|     Gar capital (+OE) | | 8,000 |
|   Partnership income allocation for 2017. | | |

In partnership accounting, partner salary allowances are not expenses in the determination of partnership net income. They are a means of achieving a fair division of income among the partners based on the time and talents devoted to partnership business.

Calculating partnership income after salary allowances is appropriate when comparing the performance of a partnership business with similar businesses operated under the corporate organizational form. Stockholders who devote their time to corporate affairs are employees, and their salaries are deducted in measuring corporate net income. Failure to adjust partnership income for salary allowances may result in inaccurate comparisons of a corporation's performance to a partnership's performance. Other adjustments, such as for corporate income taxes, also need to be made for accurate comparisons.

Calculation of partnership income after salary allowances is also appropriate in assessing the success of a business. The financial success of a partnership business lies in its earning a fair return for the services performed by partners, for capital invested in the business, and for the risks taken. If partnership income is not greater than the combined amounts that active partners could earn by working outside of the partnership, then the business is not a financial success. Income after salary allowances (or imputed salaries) should be sufficient to compensate for capital invested and risks undertaken.

**BONUS AND SALARY ALLOWANCES**   Assume that the partnership agreement of Ann, Gar, and Kat provides that Ann receive a bonus of 10 percent of partnership net income for managing the business; that Ann and Gar receive salary allowances of $10,000 and $8,000, respectively, for services rendered; and that the remaining partnership income be divided equally among the three partners. If partnership net income is $60,000 in 2016 and $12,000 in 2017, the partnership income is allocated as shown in Exhibit 16-3.

The allocation schedules follow the order of the profit-sharing agreement in allocating the bonus first, then the salary allowances, and finally the remainder to individual partners. The bonus is computed on the basis of partnership net income as the concept of "partnership net income" is generally understood in accounting practice (i.e., before salary allowances are deducted).

Partners may, however, require salary allowances to be deducted in determining the base for computing the bonus. If this had been the case here, the bonus illustrated for 2016 would have been $4,200 [($60,000 − $18,000) × 10%] rather than $6,000, and the final net income allocation would have been $26,800, $20,600, and $12,600 for Ann, Gar, and Kat, respectively.

Sometimes the partners may want the bonus, as well as salary allowances, to be deducted in determining the base for the bonus computation. Had this been the case in the Ann, Gar, and Kat partnership agreement, the bonus would have been $3,818, computed as follows:

$$\text{Let } B = \text{Bonus}$$
$$B = 0.1(\$60,000 - \$18,000 - B)$$
$$B = \$6,000 - \$1,800 - 0.1B$$
$$1.1B = \$4,200$$
$$\underline{B = \$3,818} \text{ (rounded)}$$

$$\textit{Check: } \$60,000 - \$18,000 - \$3,818 = \$38,182 \text{ bonus base}$$
$$\$38,182 \times 10\% = \$3,818 \text{ bonus}$$

In this scenario, the final net allocation would be $26,545, $20,727, and $12,728 for Ann, Gar, and Kat, respectively. The partnership agreement should be precise in specifying the measurement procedures to be used in determining the amount of a bonus.

**EXHIBIT 16-3**

Bonus and Salary
Allowances in Profit-
Sharing Agreements

**INCOME ALLOCATION SCHEDULE—2016**

| | | Ann | Gar | Kat | Total |
|---|---|---|---|---|---|
| Net income | $60,000 | | | | |
| Bonus to Ann | (6,000) | $ 6,000 | | | $ 6,000 |
| Remainder to divide | 54,000 | | | | |
| Salary allowances to Ann and Gar | (18,000) | 10,000 | $ 8,000 | | 18,000 |
| Remainder to divide | 36,000 | | | | |
| Divided equally | (36,000) | 12,000 | 12,000 | $12,000 | 36,000 |
| Remainder to divide | 0 | | | | |
| Net income allocation | | $28,000 | $20,000 | $12,000 | $60,000 |

**INCOME ALLOCATION SCHEDULE—2017**

| | | Ann | Gar | Kat | Total |
|---|---|---|---|---|---|
| Net income | $12,000 | | | | |
| Bonus to Ann | (1,200) | $ 1,200 | | | $ 1,200 |
| Remainder to divide | 10,800 | | | | |
| Salary allowances to Ann and Gar | (18,000) | 10,000 | $ 8,000 | | 18,000 |
| Remainder to divide | (7,200) | | | | |
| Divided equally | 7,200 | (2,400) | (2,400) | $(2,400) | (7,200) |
| Remainder to divide | 0 | | | | |
| Net income allocation | | $ 8,800 | $ 5,600 | $(2,400) | $12,000 |

## Capital as a Factor in Profit-Sharing Agreements

The capital contributions of partners are frequently considered in profit- and loss-sharing agreements. If capital is to be considered in the division of partnership income, the profit-sharing agreement should be specific with respect to which concept of capital is to be applied. For example, *capital* may refer to beginning capital balances, ending capital balances, or average capital balances. In addition, several interpretations of *average capital balances* are possible, and capital balances may be determined before or after drawing accounts are closed to the partners' capital accounts.

When beginning capital balances are used in allocating partnership income, additional investments during the accounting period may be discouraged because the partners making such investments are not compensated in the division of income until a later period. A similar problem exists when ending capital balances are used. Year-end investments are encouraged by their inclusion in determining each partner's share of income, but no incentive exists for a partner to make any investments before year end. Also, no penalty exists for withdrawals if the amounts withdrawn are reinvested before the period's end. Weighted average capital balances provide the fairest basis for allocating partnership income. A weighted average interpretation of capital should be assumed in the absence of evidence to the contrary.

Typically, the drawing allowances specified in a partnership agreement may be withdrawn without affecting the capital balances used in dividing partnership income. Drawing account balances up to the amounts specified in the agreement would not be deducted in determining the partners' average or year-end capital balances. For purposes of dividing partnership income, drawings in excess of allowable amounts are deducted from the partner's capital accounts in computing average or ending capital balances.

**INCOME ALLOCATED IN RELATION TO PARTNERSHIP CAPITAL**    The partnership of Ace and Soy was formed on January 1, 2016, with each partner investing $20,000 cash. Changes in the capital accounts during 2016 are summarized as follows:

|  | Ace | Soy |
|---|---|---|
| Capital balances January 1, 2016 | $20,000 | $20,000 |
| Investment April 1 | 2,000 | — |
| Withdrawal July 1 | — | (5,000) |
| Investment September 1 | 3,000 | — |
| Withdrawal October 1 | — | (4,000) |
| Investment December 31 | — | 8,000 |
| Capital balances December 31, 2016 | $25,000 | $19,000 |

The beginning, ending, and average capital amounts for Ace and Soy for 2016 are as follows (in thousands):

COMPARISON OF CAPITAL BASES

|  | Beginning Capital Investment | Ending Capital Investment | Weighted Average Capital Investment |
|---|---|---|---|
| Ace | $20 | $25 | $22.5 |
| Soy | 20 | 19 | 16.5 |
| Total | $40 | $44 | $39.0 |

Exhibit 16-4 shows computations of the weighted average capital investments of Ace and Soy. Actual investments are multiplied by the number of months outstanding to get dollar-month investment computations. Total dollar-month investments are divided by 12 to get weighted average annual capital balances.

**EXHIBIT 16-4**

Computations of
Weighted Average
Capital Investment

## WEIGHTED AVERAGE CAPITAL CALCULATIONS

| | Dollar-Month Investment | |
|---|---:|---:|
| *Weighted-Average Capital Investment of Ace* | | |
| $20,000 × 3 months (January 1 to April 1) | $60,000 | |
| $22,000 × 5 months (April 1 to September 1) | 110,000 | |
| $25,000 × 4 months (September 1 to December 31) | 100,000 | |
| 12 months | $270,000 | |
| Ace's weighted-average capital investment ($270,000 ÷ 12 months) | | $22,500 |
| | | |
| *Weighted-Average Capital Investment of Soy* | | |
| $20,000 × 6 months (January 1 to July 1) | $120,000 | |
| $15,000 × 3 months (July 1 to October 1) | 45,000 | |
| $11,000 × 3 months (October 1 to December 31) | 33,000 | |
| 12 months | $198,000 | |
| Soy's weighted-average capital investment ($198,000 ÷ 12 months) | | $16,500 |

Let's extend the Ace and Soy example by assuming that partnership net income is allocated on the basis of capital balances and that net income for 2016 is $100,000. Allocation of partnership income to Ace and Soy under each of the three capital bases is as follows:

| | |
|---|---:|
| *Beginning Capital Balances* | |
| Ace ($100,000 × 20/40) | $ 50,000.00 |
| Soy ($100,000 × 20/40) | 50,000.00 |
| Total income | $100,000.00 |
| | |
| *Ending Capital Balances* | |
| Ace ($100,000 × 25/44) | $ 56,818.18 |
| Soy ($100,000 × 19/44) | 43,181.82 |
| Total income | $100,000.00 |
| | |
| *Weighted-Average Capital Balances* | |
| Ace ($100,000 × 22.5/39) | $ 57,692.31 |
| Soy ($100,000 × 16.5/39) | 42,307.69 |
| Total income | $100,000.00 |

If the partnership agreement of Ace and Soy specifies that income is to be divided based on capital balances but fails to specify how capital balances are to be computed, the weighted average computation is used.

**INTEREST ALLOWANCES ON PARTNERSHIP CAPITAL** An agreement may provide for interest allowances on partnership capital in order to encourage capital investments, as well as salary allowances to recognize time devoted to the business. Remaining profits are then divided equally or in any other ratio specified in the profit-sharing agreement.

Consider the following information relating to the capital and drawing accounts of the Rus and Nag partnership for the calendar year 2016 (amounts in thousands):

| | Rus | Nag |
|---|---:|---:|
| *Capital Accounts* | | |
| Capital balances January 1, 2016 | $186 | $114 |
| Additional investments June 1, 2016 | 24 | 36 |
| Withdrawal July 1, 2016 | — | (10) |
| Capital balances December 31, 2016 (before drawings) | $210 | $140 |
| *Drawing Accounts* | | |
| Drawing account balances* December 31, 2016 | $ 10 | $ 12 |

---

* Account titles may be labeled partner salaries rather than partner drawings. In either case, the balances should be closed to partner capital accounts and not to the income summary.

The average capital balances for Rus and Nag are computed as follows (amounts in thousands):

|  | Dollar-Month Investment |  |
| --- | --- | --- |
| *Weighted-Average Capital Investment of Rus* |  |  |
| $186 × 5 months | $930 |  |
| $210 × 7 months | 1,470 |  |
| 12 months | $2,400 |  |
| Weighted-Average capital ($2,400 ÷ 12 months) |  | $200 |
| *Weighted-Average Capital Investment of Nag* |  |  |
| $114 × 5 months | $570 |  |
| $150 × 1 month | 150 |  |
| $140 × 6 months | 840 |  |
| 12 months | $1,560 |  |
| Weighted-Average capital ($1,560 ÷ 12 months) |  | $130 |

The partnership agreement provides that the partnership income is divided equally after salary allowances of $12,000 per year for each partner and after interest allowances at a 10 percent annual rate on average capital balances. Exhibit 16-5 shows the income allocations for 2016 under this agreement. Part A assumes that partnership net income for 2016 is $91,000, and Part B assumes a partnership loss for 2016 of $3,000.

Exhibit 16-5 shows that all provisions of the profit-sharing agreement are used in allocating partnership income, regardless of whether the partnership has net income or net loss. The full amount of salary allowances as provided in the agreement is included in the income division, even though Rus withdrew only $10,000 of the $12,000 allowable amount.

**PART A—PARTNERSHIP INCOME ASSUMED TO BE $91,000**
**INCOME ALLOCATION SCHEDULE**

|  |  | Rus | Nag | Total |
| --- | --- | --- | --- | --- |
| Net income | $91,000 |  |  |  |
| Salary allowances | (24,000) | $12,000 | $12,000 | $24,000 |
| Remainder to divide | 67,000 |  |  |  |
| Interest allowances |  |  |  |  |
| $200,000 × 10% | (20,000) | 20,000 |  | 20,000 |
| $130,000 × 10% | (13,000) |  | 13,000 | 13,000 |
| Remainder to divide | 34,000 |  |  |  |
| Divided equally | (34,000) | 17,000 | 17,000 | 34,000 |
| Remainder to divide | 0 |  |  |  |
| Net income allocation |  | $49,000 | $42,000 | $91,000 |

**PART B—PARTNERSHIP LOSS ASSUMED TO BE $3,000**
**INCOME ALLOCATION SCHEDULE**

|  |  | Rus | Nag | Total |
| --- | --- | --- | --- | --- |
| Net loss | $(3,000) |  |  |  |
| Salary allowances | (24,000) | $12,000 | $12,000 | $24,000 |
| Remainder to divide | (27,000) |  |  |  |
| Interest allowances |  |  |  |  |
| $200,000 × 10% | (20,000) | 20,000 |  | 20,000 |
| $130,000 × 10% | (13,000) |  | 13,000 | 13,000 |
| Remainder to divide | (60,000) |  |  |  |
| Divided equally | 60,000 | (30,000) | (30,000) | (60,000) |
| Remainder to divide | 0 |  |  |  |
| Net income (loss) allocation |  | $2,000 | $(5,000) | $(3,000) |

**EXHIBIT 16-5**

Interest and Salary Allowances in Profit-Sharing Agreements

In Part A of Exhibit 16-5, partnership income of $91,000 was divided $49,000 to Rus and $42,000 to Nag. The division of the $3,000 net loss in Part B was allocated as $2,000 income to Rus and a $5,000 loss to Nag. In both cases, the partnership agreement resulted in a $7,000 income difference between the two partners because of the difference in their weighted average capital balances. The amount of this difference was the same for the income and loss situations because the residual income amount was divided equally. A different division of income after salary and interest allowances would have resulted in a larger difference in Part A. For instance, if the income share was divided 60:40 then the difference between Rus and Nag would be $13,800. Rus's income would be $52,400 and Nag's $38,600. For Part B, Rus's allocation would be a loss of $4,000, and Nag's income would be $1,000. Thus, one must be careful in making generalizations about the effect of various profit-sharing provisions on final income allocations.

## CHANGES IN PARTNERSHIP INTERESTS

### Dissociation

Under UPA Section 601, a partner has the power to dissociate from the partnership at any time. Dissociation is the change in relationship caused by a partner ceasing to be associated with the carrying on of the business. Under UPA, the dissociation of the partner always results in either a buyout of the dissociated partner's interest or a dissolution and winding up of the business.

In addition to a partner providing notice to withdraw as a partner, other events that can give rise to dissociation include expulsion of the partner according to the terms of the partnership agreement by the vote of the other partners as well as expulsion by judicial decision because the partner engaged in wrongful conduct that adversely and materially affected the partnership business and breached the partnership agreement.

Here we discuss the dissociation of a partner that results in a buyout of the partner's interest. Chapter 17 discusses the dissolution and winding up of a business.

Dissociation does not necessarily result in the termination of the partnership operations or of the partnership as a separate business and accounting entity. **Partnership dissociation** under the UPA is "the change in the relation of the partners caused by any partner ceasing to be associated in the carrying on as distinguished from the winding up of the business."[3]

A question arises regarding whether the assets of the continuing partnership business should be revalued. Some argue that because legal dissolution terminates the old partnership, all assets transferred to the new partnership should be revalued in the same manner as if the assets had been sold to a corporate entity. Others argue that changes in partnership interests are not unlike changes in the stockholders of a corporation, and that private sales of ownership interests provide no basis for revaluation of the business entity. These alternative views reflect the concepts of the legal and business entities, respectively. Both views have merit, and this text does not emphasize either view. Instead, both views are discussed and illustrated in the following sections on changes in partnership interests. The revaluation approach is generally referred to as the *goodwill procedure*, and the absence of revaluation is referred to as the *bonus procedure*.

### Assignment of an Interest to a Third Party

A partnership is not dissolved when a partner assigns his or her interest in the partnership to a third party, because such an assignment does not in itself change the relationship of the partners. Such assignment only entitles the assignee to receive the assigning partner's interest in future partnership profits and in partnership assets in the event of liquidation. The assignee does not become a partner and does not obtain the right to share in management of the partnership (UPA Section 503). Because the assignee does not become a partner, the only change required on the partnership books is to transfer the capital interest of the assignor partner to his or her assignee.

We record the assignment by Mar to Sut of his 25 percent interest in the Hall–Mar partnership as follows:

| | | |
|---|---|---|
| Mar capital (−OE) | 50,000 | |
| Sut capital (+OE) | | 50,000 |

[3]© National Conference Of Commissioners On Uniform State Laws

The amount of the capital transfer is equal to the recorded amount of Mar's capital at the time of the assignment, and it is independent of the consideration received by Mar for his 25 percent interest. If the recorded amount of Mar's capital is $200,000, then the amount of the transfer entry is $50,000 ($200,000 × 0.25), regardless of whether Sut pays Mar $50,000 or some other amount.

## Admission of a New Partner

A new partner can be admitted with the consent of all continuing partners in the business. In the absence of a new profit-sharing agreement, all profits and losses in the new partnership are divided equally under UPA. A person may become a partner in an existing partnership with the consent of all continuing partners by purchasing an interest from one or more of the existing partners, or by investing money or other resources in the partnership.

Partnership admission can vary widely, from the simplest case of a single new partner entering into an existing and continuing partnership, to one multi-partner entity joining with another multi-partner entity. Because of this diversity of the levels of complexity, the partnership in question should be aware that traditional partnership accounting does not always follow current GAAP for business combinations (ASC 805). Most partnerships are privately held and managed, and therefore are only required to follow GAAP if the partnership is supplying financial statements to an external user that insists on GAAP as the basis of preparation.

If the partnership is one that follows GAAP and there is a partner admission, then the partnership should carefully evaluate if the admission meets the criteria for a business combination discussed earlier in this book. If the new partner admission does meet those criteria, then the partnership should account for the new admission by following GAAP (ASC 805). The following examples of the goodwill and bonus methods of revaluing partnership net assets are widely used by partnerships that do not follow GAAP. However, these methods do not conform to GAAP.

## PURCHASE OF AN INTEREST FROM EXISTING PARTNERS

LEARNING OBJECTIVE **16.4**

With the consent of all continuing partners, a new partner may be admitted into an existing partnership by purchasing an interest directly from the existing partners. The old partnership is dissolved, its books are closed, and a new partnership agreement governs the continuing business operations.

For example, Alf and Bal are partners with capital balances of $50,000 each, and they share profits and losses equally. Cob purchases one-half of Alf's interest from Alf for $25,000, and a new partnership of Alf, Bal, and Cob is formed such that Alf and Cob each have a 25 percent interest in the capital and profits of the new partnership. Bal's 50 percent interest is unchanged. The only entry required to record Alf's transfer to Cob is:

| | | |
|---|---|---|
| Alf capital (−OE) | 25,000 | |
|   Cob capital (+OE) | | 25,000 |
|   To record Cob's admission into the partnership with the purchase of one-half of Alf's interest. | | |

In this case, the capital and income interests are aligned before and after the admission of Cob, and the net assets of the old partnership were correctly valued on the books. Cob's payment of $25,000 for a 25 percent interest in the capital and future income of the partnership implies a total valuation for the partnership of $100,000 ($25,000 ÷ 0.25). The net assets of the old partnership were recorded at $100,000, so no basis for revaluation arises.

Now assume that Alf and Bal have capital balances of $50,000 and $40,000, respectively, that they share profits equally, and that they agree to take Cob into the partnership with a payment of $25,000 directly to Alf. The partners may agree that half of Alf's capital balance is to be transferred to Cob (as in the previous example), that the net assets are not to be revalued, and that future profits will be shared 25 percent, 50 percent, and 25 percent to Alf, Bal, and Cob, respectively. Although it seems equitable, there is no compelling reason for such an agreement, because the capital and income interests were not aligned either before or after the admission of Cob.

|  | Old Partnership | | | New Partnership | | |
|--|--|--|--|--|--|--|
|  | **Capital Investment** | | **Income Interest** | **Capital Investment** | | **Income Interest** |
| Alf | $50,000 | 5/9 | 50% | $25,000 | 5/18 | 25% |
| Bal | 40,000 | 4/9 | 50% | 40,000 | 8/18 | 50% |
| Cob | | | | 25,000 | 5/18 | 25% |
|  | $90,000 | | | $90,000 | | |

The $25,000 payment of Cob to Alf does not provide evidence regarding the correct valuation of partnership net assets, because the payment was for five-eighteenths of the partnership net assets but 25 percent of future partnership profits. If revaluation is desirable, the assets' fair values should be based on appraisals or evidence other than the amount of Cob's payment to Alf.

## Revaluation: Goodwill Approach

A third possibility is that Alf and Bal have capital balances of $50,000 and $40,000, respectively, that they share profits equally, and that Cob is admitted to the partnership with a total payment of $50,000 directly to the partners. Cob is to have a 50 percent interest in the capital and income of the new partnership. Alf and Bal will each have a 25 percent interest in future income of the partnership.

Several additional questions of fairness arise concerning the valuation of total partnership assets, the capital transfers to Cob, and the division of the $50,000 payment between Alf and Bal. Cob's $50,000 payment for a 50 percent interest in both capital and future income implies a $100,000 valuation for total partnership assets. If assets are to be revalued, the revaluation should be recorded prior to Cob's admission to the partnership. The partnership would record the revaluation as follows:

| | | |
|--|--|--|
| Goodwill (or identifiable net assets) (+A) | 10,000 | |
| Alf capital (+OE) | | 5,000 |
| Bal capital (+OE) | | 5,000 |

If the assets are revalued and identifiable asset accounts are adjusted, the amount of the adjustments are amortized or depreciated over the remaining asset lives. Although the revaluation procedure is commonly referred to as the goodwill approach, goodwill should not be recorded until all identifiable assets have been adjusted to their fair values. The approach is comparable to the approach used to record business combinations under the acquisition method or the acquisition of operating divisions or groups of assets.

The previous entry recording goodwill of $10,000 gives Alf and Bal capital balances of $55,000 and $45,000, respectively. If equal amounts of capital are to be transferred to Cob, the entry to record Cob's admission to the partnership is:

| | | |
|--|--|--|
| Alf capital (−OE) | 25,000 | |
| Bal capital (−OE) | 25,000 | |
| Cob capital (+OE) | | 50,000 |

The capital balances are summarized as follows:

### CAPITAL BALANCES

|  | **Before Revaluation** | **Revaluation** | **After Revaluation** | **Capital Transferred** | **Capital After Transfer** | |
|--|--|--|--|--|--|--|
| Alf | $50,000 | $ 5,000 | $ 55,000 | $(25,000) | $ 30,000 | (30%) |
| Bal | 40,000 | 5,000 | 45,000 | (25,000) | 20,000 | (20%) |
| Cob | | | | 50,000 | 50,000 | (50%) |
|  | $90,000 | $10,000 | $100,000 | $ 0 | $100,000 | |

Alternatively, it may be desirable to realign the capital balances of Alf and Bal in the new partnership such that each will have a 25 percent interest in the capital and income of the new partnership. In this case, the partnership would record the admission of Cob as follows:

| | | |
|--|--|--|
| Alf capital (−OE) | 30,000 | |
| Bal capital (−OE) | 20,000 | |
| Cob capital (+OE) | | 50,000 |

In this case, the capital changes are as follows:

**CAPITAL BALANCES**

|  | Before Revaluation | Revaluation | After Revaluation | Capital Transferred | Capital After Transfer | |
|---|---|---|---|---|---|---|
| Alf | $50,000 | $5,000 | $55,000 | $(30,000) | $25,000 | (25%) |
| Bal | 40,000 | 5,000 | 45,000 | (20,000) | 25,000 | (25%) |
| Cob |  |  |  | 50,000 | 50,000 | (50%) |
|  | $90,000 | $10,000 | $100,000 | $0 | $100,000 | |

## Nonrevaluation: Bonus Approach

If the assets of the new partnership are not to be revalued, but equal amounts of capital are to be transferred to Cob, the entry to record the transfer is:

| | | |
|---|---|---|
| Alf capital (−OE) | 22,500 | |
| Bal capital (−OE) | 22,500 | |
|     Cob capital (+OE) | | 45,000 |

Alf and Bal transfer equal amounts of capital and equal rights to future income to Cob, so each receiving $25,000 cash from Cob seems equitable. Each of the old partners receives $2,500 in excess of the amount of book capital transferred ($25,000 received less $22,500 capital transferred). The capital accounts before and after the admission of Cob are as follows:

**CAPITAL BALANCES**

|  | Per Books | Capital Transferred | Capital After Transfer | |
|---|---|---|---|---|
| Alf | $50,000 | $(22,500) | $27,500 | (30.6%) |
| Bal | 40,000 | (22,500) | 17,500 | (19.4%) |
| Cob |  | 45,000 | 45,000 | (50.0%) |
|  | $90,000 | $0 | $90,000 | |

Should Alf and Bal desire that their recorded capital and income interests in the new partnership are equal (that is, 25%), Alf would receive $30,000 of the amount paid by Cob, and Bal would receive $20,000. The entry to record the capital transfer in that case would be:

| | | |
|---|---|---|
| Alf capital (−OE) | 27,500 | |
| Bal capital (−OE) | 17,500 | |
|     Cob capital (+OE) | | 45,000 |

A summary of the capital balances follows:

**CAPITAL BALANCES**

|  | Per Books | Capital Transferred | Capital After Transfer | |
|---|---|---|---|---|
| Alf | $50,000 | $(27,500) | $22,500 | (25%) |
| Bal | 40,000 | (17,500) | 22,500 | (25%) |
| Cob |  | 45,000 | 45,000 | (50%) |
|  | $90,000 | $0 | $90,000 | |

Although the evidence supporting revaluation is not always convincing, a revaluation based on the price paid by an incoming partner does have the advantage of establishing a capital balance for that partner equal to the amount of his or her investment. For example, Cob's capital credit was equal to his $50,000 payment to Alf and Bal when the assets were revalued. It was only $45,000 when the assets were not revalued. Also, the amounts of capital transfer and cash allocations are easier to determine when assets are revalued because gains and losses relating to the old partnership are formally recorded in the accounts.

## INVESTING IN AN EXISTING PARTNERSHIP

A new partner may be admitted into an existing partnership by investing cash or other assets in the business or by bringing clients or abilities into the business that will contribute to future profitability. As in the case of a purchase of an interest from existing partners, the net assets contributed by the old partners' partnership may or may not be revalued. Because new assets are being invested in the business, the basis for a revaluation is not necessarily determined by the investment of the new partner. If the amount invested by the new partner implies that the old partnership has unrecorded asset values, a total revaluation of the new business based on the investment of the new partner seems appropriate. On the other hand, if the capital interest granted to the new partner is greater than the amount of his or her investment and the identifiable assets of the old partnership are recorded at their fair values, there is an implication that the new partner is bringing goodwill into the business. In this case, the valuation of the new business is determined by referring to the capital of the old partnership.

The evidence provided by the amount of an investment only relates to the total value of the business. Values for identifiable assets are determined on an individual asset basis by appraisal or other valuation techniques. The identifiable assets of the old partnership are recorded at their fair values, in the absence of evidence to the contrary. If identifiable assets of a partnership are to be revalued, the revaluation must be based on appraisals or other evidence relating to specific assets.

### Partnership Investment at Book Value

Dre and Boy have capital balances of $40,000 each and share profits equally. They agree to admit Cry to a one-third interest in capital and profits of a new Dre, Boy, and Cry partnership for a $40,000 cash investment. Cry's $40,000 investment is equal to the capital interest that she receives [($80,000 + $40,000)/3], so the issue of revaluation does not arise. Cry's investment is recorded on the partnership books as follows:

| | | |
|---|---|---|
| Cash (+A) | 40,000 | |
|     Cry capital (+OE) | | 40,000 |
|     To record Cry's $40,000 cash investment for a | | |
|     one-third interest in partnership capital and income. | | |

### Partnership Assets Revalued (Goodwill to Old Partners)

Now assume that Dre and Boy, who have capital balances of $40,000 each and share profits equally, agree to admit Cry to a one-third interest in the capital and profits of a new partnership for a cash investment of $50,000. Because Cry is willing to invest $50,000 for a one-third interest in the $80,000 recorded assets plus her $50,000 investment ($130,000 assets), the implication is that the old partnership had unrecorded asset values. The fair value of unrecorded assets is determined by referring to Cry's investment. By implication, the fair value of the new partnership's assets is $150,000 ($50,000 ÷ 1/3). The fair value of unrecorded assets is $20,000, the excess of the $150,000 total value less the $80,000 recorded assets plus the $50,000 new investment. If the assets contributed by the old partnership are revalued, the following entries are made:

| | | |
|---|---|---|
| Goodwill (+A) | 20,000 | |
|     Dre capital (+OE) | | 10,000 |
|     Boy capital (+OE) | | 10,000 |
|     To revalue the assets contributed by the old partnership | | |
|     based on the value of Cry's investment. | | |
| Cash (+A) | 50,000 | |
|     Cry capital (+OE) | | 50,000 |
|     To record Cry's investment in the partnership for a | | |
|     one-third interest in capital and income. | | |

The $20,000 recorded as goodwill in the first entry is credited to the old partners in their old profit- and loss-sharing ratios. Conceptually, the revaluation constitutes a final act of the old partnership, and all subsequent entries are those of the new partnership. The second entry records Cry's $50,000 cash investment and capital account in equal amounts. A summary of the capital balances before and after the $20,000 revaluation and the investment of Cry is as follows:

**CAPITAL BALANCES**

| | Before Revaluation | Revaluation | After Revaluation | New Investment | Capital After Investment | |
|---|---|---|---|---|---|---|
| Dre | $40,000 | $10,000 | $50,000 | | $50,000 | 1/3 |
| Boy | 40,000 | 10,000 | 50,000 | | 50,000 | 1/3 |
| Cry | | | | $50,000 | 50,000 | 1/3 |
| | $80,000 | $20,000 | $100,000 | $50,000 | $150,000 | |

## Partnership Assets Not Revalued (Bonus to Old Partners)

If the partners decide against revaluation, the entry required to record Cry's admittance into the partnership is as follows:

| | | |
|---|---|---|
| Cash (+A) | 50,000 | |
| Dre capital (+OE) | | 3,333 |
| Boy capital (+OE) | | 3,333 |
| Cry capital (+OE) | | 43,334 |

To record Cry's investment in the partnership and to allow Dre and Boy a bonus due to unrecorded asset values.

In this case, partnership net assets are increased only by the amount of the new investment. The new partner's capital account is credited for her one-third interest in the $130,000 ($80,000 book value of old partnership plus $50,000 contributed by Cry) capital of the new partnership. The difference between the investment ($50,000 contributed by Cry) and capital account ($43,334) of the new partner is allocated to the capital accounts of the old partners in relation to the old profit-sharing agreement.

This situation is referred to as a *bonus to old partners* because the old partners receive capital credits for a part of the new partner's investment. The capital balances before and after the admission of Cry are as follows:

**CAPITAL BALANCES**

| | Per Books | Investment | Capital After Investment | |
|---|---|---|---|---|
| Dre | $40,000 | $3,333 | $43,333 | 1/3 |
| Boy | 40,000 | 3,333 | 43,333 | 1/3 |
| Cry | | 43,334 | 43,334 | 1/3 |
| | $80,000 | $50,000 | $130,000 | |

## Partnership Assets Revalued (Goodwill to New Partner)

Suppose that Dre and Boy agreed to admit Cry into the partnership *for a 40 percent interest* in the capital and profit with an investment of $50,000. In this case, the implication is that Cry is bringing goodwill into the partnership. That is, Dre and Boy must be willing to admit Cry to a 40 percent interest in the $80,000 recorded assets plus her $50,000 investment (40% × $130,000 = $52,000) because they expect Cry's total contribution to exceed her cash investment. Accordingly, the total value of the partnership is determined by reference to the 60 percent interest retained in the new partnership capital and profits by Dre and Boy. Total capital of the new partnership is $133,333 ($80,000 old capital assumed to be fairly valued ÷ 60%), and the partnership records the admission of Cry as follows:

| | | |
|---|---|---|
| Cash (+A) | 50,000 | |
| Goodwill (+A) | 3,333 | |
| Cry capital (+OE) | | 53,333 |

To admit Cry to a 40 percent interest in capital and profits.

A summary of the capital balances before and after the admittance of Cry is as follows:

**CAPITAL BALANCES**

|  | Per Books | Investment Plus Goodwill | Capital After Investment | |
|---|---|---|---|---|
| Dre | $40,000 | | $40,000 | 30% |
| Boy | 40,000 | | 40,000 | 30% |
| Cry | | $53,333 | 53,333 | 40% |
| | $80,000 | $53,333 | $133,333 | |

## Partnership Assets Not Revalued (Bonus to New Partner)

Instead of recording goodwill attributable to the incoming partner, the bonus procedure can be used to ensure that the beginning partnership capital balances reflect the profit-sharing arrangement percentages. Under this procedure, the total assets of the new partnership are $130,000 ($80,000 contributed by Dre and Boy plus $50,000 contributed by Cry). Cry's share is $52,000 ($130,000 × 0.40), but she contributed only $50,000. The $2,000 difference between Cry's capital credit of $52,000 and her $50,000 investment is considered a bonus to Cry. Partnership assets are not revalued, so the excess $2,000 credited to Cry's account must be charged against the capital accounts of Dre and Boy in relation to their old profit- and loss-sharing ratios. The partnership records Cry's admittance under the bonus procedure as follows:

| | | |
|---|---|---|
| Cash (+A) | 50,000 | |
| Dre capital (−OE) | 1,000 | |
| Boy capital (−OE) | 1,000 | |
| Cry capital (+OE) | | 52,000 |

To record Cry's investment of $50,000 for a 40% interest in the partnership and allow her a $2,000 bonus.

The capital accounts of the partnership before and after admitting Cry are as follows:

**CAPITAL BALANCES**

|  | Per Books | Investment | Capital After Investment | |
|---|---|---|---|---|
| Dre | $40,000 | $(1,000) | $39,000 | 30% |
| Boy | 40,000 | (1,000) | 39,000 | 30% |
| Cry | | 52,000 | 52,000 | 40% |
| | $80,000 | $50,000 | $130,000 | |

LEARNING OBJECTIVE **16.5**

## DISSOCIATION OF A CONTINUING PARTNERSHIP THROUGH DEATH OR RETIREMENT

The retirement or death of a partner from a continuing partnership business results in dissociation and requires a settlement with the retiring partner or with the estate of the deceased partner. In the absence of a partnership agreement to the contrary, the settlement is in accordance with UPA Section 701.

According to UPA Section 701, "The buyout price of a dissociated partner's interest is the amount that would have been distributable to the dissociating partner under Section 807(b) if, on the date of dissociation, the assets of the partnership were sold at a price equal to the greater of the liquidation value or the value based on a sale of the entire business as a going concern without the dissociated partner and the partnership were wound up as of that date. Interest must be paid from the date of dissociation to the date of payment."[4] Notice that fair value is not included in the definition. However, valuation models could be used to determine the value of the entire business.

---

[4]© National Conference Of Commissioners On Uniform State Laws.

The valuation is at the date of dissolution, so partnership books are closed as of the date of death or retirement. When a time lag exists between death or retirement and final settlement, the capital balance of the deceased or retiring partner is reclassified as a liability. Any interest (or other return) accruing on the liability up to the date of final settlement is considered an expense of the continuing partnership entity.

If the retiring partner (or the estate of a deceased partner) is paid an amount equal to the final balance of his or her capital account, the only entry necessary is a debit to his or her capital account and a credit to cash for the amount paid. When the settlement with a retiring partner is more or less than the final capital account balance, the revaluation (goodwill) and non-revaluation (bonus) procedures provide alternate methods of accounting for the settlement.

To illustrate, assume that Ann, Mic, and Jus are partners with profit-sharing percentages of 40 percent, 20 percent, and 40 percent, respectively, and that Jus decides to retire. The capital and income interests of the three partners on the date of Jus's retirement are as follows:

|  | Capital Balances | Capital (%) | Profit and Loss (%) |
|---|---|---|---|
| Ann | $70,000 | 35% | 40% |
| Mic | 50,000 | 25 | 20 |
| Jus | 80,000 | 40 | 40 |
| Total capital | $200,000 | 100% | 100% |

## Excess Payment to Retiring Partner

The partners agree that the business is undervalued on the partnership books and that Jus will be paid $92,000 in final settlement of his partnership interest. The excess payment to Jus can be recorded by three methods: (1) Jus may be granted a bonus; (2) partnership capital may be revalued to the extent of the excess payment to Jus; or (3) partnership capital may be revalued based on the amount implied by the excess payment.

**BONUS TO RETIRING PARTNER**    The partnership would record Jus's withdrawal as follows under the bonus procedure:

| | | |
|---|---|---|
| Jus capital (−OE) | 80,000 | |
| Ann capital (−OE) | 8,000 | |
| Mic capital (−OE) | 4,000 | |
| Cash (−A) | | 92,000 |

Because Ann and Mic granted a $12,000 bonus to Jus, that amount reduces their capital accounts using their 40:20 relative profit-sharing ratios.

**GOODWILL EQUAL TO EXCESS PAYMENT IS RECORDED**    A second method of recording Jus's withdrawal is to record the $12,000 excess of cash paid to Jus over his capital account balance as goodwill:

| | | |
|---|---|---|
| Jus capital (−OE) | 80,000 | |
| Goodwill (+A) | 12,000 | |
| Cash (−A) | | 92,000 |

Under this approach, goodwill is recorded only to the extent paid by the continuing partnership to Jus. This approach only provides a revaluation of Jus's share of partnership assets; it does not provide a revaluation of Ann and Mic's capital interests.

**REVALUATION OF TOTAL PARTNERSHIP CAPITAL BASED ON EXCESS PAYMENT**    A third approach for recording Jus's retirement is to revalue total partnership capital on the basis of the $12,000 excess payment. Under this method, total partnership capital is revalued as follows:

| | | |
|---|---|---|
| Goodwill (other assets) (+A) | 30,000 | |
| Ann capital (+OE) | | 12,000 |
| Mic capital (+OE) | | 6,000 |
| Jus capital (+OE) | | 12,000 |

The total undervaluation of the partnership is measured by the amount implied by the excess payment. In this case, the $30,000 is computed by dividing the $12,000 excess payment by Jus's 40 percent profit-sharing percentage. The partnership then records Jus's retirement as follows:

| | | |
|---|---|---|
| Jus capital (−OE) | 92,000 | |
| Cash (−A) | | 92,000 |

## Payment to Retiring Partner Less than Capital Balance

Suppose that Jus is paid $72,000 in final settlement of his capital interest. In this case, the three partners may have agreed that the business is worth less than its book value.

**OVERVALUED ASSETS WRITTEN DOWN**    A retirement payment to Jus of $8,000 less than his final capital balance implies that existing partnership capital is overvalued by $20,000 [($80,000 − $72,000) ÷ 40%]. If the evidence available supports this implication, the overvalued assets should be identified and reduced to their fair values. The partnership records the revaluation and payment to Jus as follows:

| | | |
|---|---|---|
| Ann capital (−OE) | 8,000 | |
| Mic capital (−OE) | 4,000 | |
| Jus capital (−OE) | 8,000 | |
|     Net assets (−A) | | 20,000 |
| Jus capital (−OE) | 72,000 | |
|     Cash (−A) | | 72,000 |

This method of recording Jus's withdrawal is appropriate if the $72,000 paid to Jus is the result of a valuation provided for under UPA. However, it would not be appropriate if the $72,000 were determined by prior agreement of the partners without regard to total partnership capital at the time of withdrawal.

**BONUS TO CONTINUING PARTNERS**    If evidence indicates that partnership capital is fairly valued, the partnership would record the retirement of Jus under the bonus procedure as follows:

| | | |
|---|---|---|
| Jus capital (−OE) | 80,000 | |
|     Ann capital (+OE) | | 5,333 |
|     Mic capital (+OE) | | 2,667 |
|     Cash (−A) | | 72,000 |

This method of recording provides a bonus to Ann and Mic. The bonus is measured by the excess of Jus's capital balance over the cash paid by the partnership for his 40 percent interest.

## LIMITED PARTNERSHIPS

**LEARNING OBJECTIVE 16.6**

Under some circumstances, the unlimited liability characteristic of general partnerships may be circumvented by creating a special kind of partnership called a *limited partnership*. The Uniform Limited Partnership Act provides legal guidance for limited partnerships. The limited partnership consists of at least one general partner and one or more limited partners. The general partner is like any partner in a general partnership, and he or she has unlimited liability for partnership debts. The limited partner is basically an investor whose risk is limited to his or her equity investment in the partnership. The limited partner is *excluded* from the management of the business. If he or she takes part in management, he or she loses the limited partner status and becomes a general partner with unlimited liability.

A limited partnership is more difficult to form than a general partnership. The limited partnership agreement *must be written*, signed by the partners, and filed with the appropriate public official in the state where the partnership is created. If the statute is not carefully followed, the courts may find the partnership to be a general partnership rather than a limited partnership.

## Joint Ventures

Joint ventures have the characteristics of partnerships, except that the joint venture is usually set up for a specific limited purpose. When the activity is complete, the venture is terminated. For this reason, the agency power of joint ventures is limited. Joint ventures are covered in Chapter 11 of this book.

## SUMMARY

Partnership accounting procedures are similar to those for other forms of business organization, except for procedures relating to the measurement of partnership capital interests. Accounting measurements relating to the capital and income interests of partners are based on the partnership agreement or, in the absence of an agreement, on the UPA, except for partnerships in states that have not adopted the act. The partnership agreement should be in writing and should cover matters relating to the amount and valuation of capital contributions, additional investments with withdrawals, loans to partners, profit-sharing arrangements, changes in partnership interests, and various other matters.

## QUESTIONS

1. Explain why the noncash investments of partners should be recorded at their fair values.
2. Is there a conceptual difference between partner drawings and withdrawals? Is there a practical difference?
3. In the absence of an agreement for the division of profits, how are they divided under UPA? Does your answer also apply to losses? Does it apply if one partner invests three times as much as the other partners?
4. Why do some profit-sharing agreements provide for salary and interest allowances?
5. Are partner salary allowances expenses of the partnership?
6. When a profit-sharing agreement specifies that profits should be divided using the ratio of capital balances, how should capital balances be computed?
7. Explain how a partner could have a loss from partnership operations for a period even though the partnership had net income.
8. The concept of partnership dissociation has a technical meaning under the provisions of UPA. Explain the concept.
9. If a partner sells his or her partnership interest directly to a third party, the partnership may or may not be dissolved. Under what conditions is the partnership dissolved?
10. How does the purchase of an interest from existing partners differ from the acquisition of an interest by investment in a partnership?
11. What alternative approaches can be used in recording the admission of a new partner?
12. Why is the goodwill procedure best described as a revaluation procedure?
13. Explain the bonus procedure for recording an investment in a partnership. When is the bonus applicable to old partners, and when is it applicable to new partners?
14. The goodwill procedure was used to record the investment of a new partner in the XYZ Partnership, but immediately thereafter, the entire business was sold for an amount equal to the recorded capital of the partnership. Under what conditions would the amounts received in final liquidation of the partnership have been the same as if the bonus procedure had been used?
15. Bob invests $10,000 cash for a 25 percent interest in the capital and earnings of the BOP Partnership. Explain how this investment could give rise to (a) recording goodwill, (b) the write-down of the partnership assets, (c) a bonus to old partners, and (d) a bonus to Bob.

## EXERCISES

### E 16-1
### Computing initial partner investments

Car and Lam establish an equal partnership in both equity and profits to operate a used-furniture business under the name of C&L Furniture. Car contributes furniture inventory that cost $120,000 and has fair value of $160,000. Lam contributes $60,000 cash and delivery equipment that cost $80,000 and has a fair value of $60,000.

**REQUIRED:** Assume that the initial noncash contributions of the partners are recorded at fair market value. Compute the ending balance of each capital account under the bonus and goodwill approaches.

### E 16-2
### Partnership income allocation—Bonus

Arn, Bev, and Car are partners who share profits and losses 30:30:40, respectively, after Bev, who manages the partnership, receives a bonus of 10 percent of income, net of the bonus. Partnership income for the year is $198,000.

**REQUIRED:** Prepare a schedule to allocate partnership income to Arn, Bev, and Car.

### E 16-3
### Partnership income allocation—Salary allowance

Mel and Dav created a partnership to own and operate a health-food store. The partnership agreement provided that Mel receive a salary of $10,000 and Dav a salary of $5,000 to recognize their relative time spent in operating the store. Remaining profits and losses were divided 60:40 to Mel and Dav, respectively. Income of $13,000 for 2016, the first year of operations, was allocated $8,800 to Mel and $4,200 to Dav.

On January 1, 2017, the partnership agreement was changed to reflect the fact that Dav could no longer devote any time to the store's operations. The new agreement allows Mel a salary of $18,000, and the remaining profits and losses are divided equally. In 2017, an error was discovered such that the 2016 reported income was understated by $4,000. The partnership income of $25,000 for 2017 included this $4,000 related to 2016.

**REQUIRED:** Prepare a schedule to allocate the $25,000 reported 2017 partnership income to Mel and Dav.

### E 16-4
### Partnership income allocation—Salary allowance and interest

The partnership agreement of Dan, Hen, and Bai provides that profits are to be divided as follows:

- Bai receives a salary of $24,000, and Hen receives a salary of $18,000 for time spent in the business.
- All partners receive 10 percent interest on average capital balances.
- Remaining profits and losses are divided equally among the three partners.

On January 1, 2016, the capital balances were Dan, $300,000; Hen, $240,000; and Bai, $250,000. Dan invested an additional $40,000 on July 1 and withdrew $40,000 on October 1. Hen and Bai had drawings of $18,000 each during the year, which are allowed in the partnership agreement.

**REQUIRED:** Prepare a schedule to allocate partnership net income of $56,000 for 2016.

### E 16-5
### Partnership income allocation—Partnership capital statement

On December 31, 2016, the total partnership capital (assets less liabilities) for the Bir, Cag, and Den partnership is $186,000. Selected information related to the **pre-closing** capital balances follows:

|                     | Bir Capital | Cag Capital | Den Capital | Total Capital |
|---------------------|-------------|-------------|-------------|---------------|
| Balance January 1   | $60,000     | $45,000     | $70,000     | $175,000      |
| Investments 2016    |             | 10,000      | 10,000      | 20,000        |
| Withdrawals 2016    | (15,000)    |             | (15,000)    | (30,000)      |
| Drawings 2016       | (5,000)     | (5,000)     | (5,000)     | (15,000)      |
|                     | $40,000     | $50,000     | $60,000     | $150,000      |

**REQUIRED:** Prepare a statement of partnership capital for the Bir, Cag, and Den partnership at year-end 2016, assuming that no specific profit- or loss-sharing agreement exists.

## E 16-6
### Partnership income allocation—Assignment of interest to a third party

Capital balances and profit- and loss-sharing ratios of the partners in the BIG Entertainment Galley are as follows:

| | |
|---|---|
| Ben capital (50%) | $900,000 |
| Irv capital (30%) | 680,000 |
| Geo capital (20%) | 500,000 |
| Total | $2,080,000 |

Ben needs money and agrees to assign half of his interest in the partnership to Pet for $280,000 cash. Pet pays $280,000 directly to Ben.

### REQUIRED

1. Prepare a journal entry to record the assignment of half of Ben's interest in the partnership to Pet.

2. What is the total capital of the BIG partnership immediately after the assignment of the interest to Pet?

## E 16-7
### Recording new partner investment

The capital accounts of the Fax and Bel partnership on September 30, 2016, were:

| | |
|---|---|
| Fax capital (75% profit) | $140,000 |
| Bel capital (25% profit) | 60,000 |
| Total capital | $200,000 |

On October 1, Rob was admitted to a 40 percent interest in the partnership when he purchased 40 percent of each existing partner's capital for $120,000, paid directly to Fax and Bel.

### REQUIRED

1. Determine the capital balances of Fax, Bel, and Rob after Rob's admission to the partnership if goodwill is *not* recorded.

2. Determine the capital balances of Fax, Bel, and Rob after Rob's admission to the partnership if goodwill is recorded, assuming that the book value and fair value of recorded assets are equal.

## E 16-8
### Recording new partner investment—Revaluation case

Bow and Mon are partners in a retail business and divide profits 60 percent to Bow and 40 percent to Mon. Their capital balances at December 31, 2016, are as follows:

| | |
|---|---|
| Bow capital | $120,000 |
| Mon capital | 120,000 |
| Total capital | $240,000 |

Partnership assets and liabilities have book values equal to fair values. The partners agree to admit Joh into the partnership. Joh purchases a one-third interest in partnership capital and profits directly from Bow and Mon (one-third of each of their capital accounts) for $100,000.

**REQUIRED:** Prepare journal entries for the admission of Joh into the partnership, assuming that partnership assets are revalued.

## E 16-9
### Recording new partner investment—Revaluation cases

The capital balances and profits- and loss-sharing percentages for the Sip, Jog, and Run partnership at December 31, 2016, are as follows:

| | |
|---|---|
| Sip capital (30%) | $160,000 |
| Jog capital (50%) | $180,000 |
| Run capital (20%) | $140,000 |

The partners agree to admit Wal into the partnership on January 1, 2017, for a 20 percent interest in the capital and income of the business.

**REQUIRED**

1. Prepare the journal entry or entries to record Wal's admission to the partnership assuming that he invests $100,000 in the partnership for the 20 percent interest and that partnership capital is *revalued*. Assume that the book value of partnership assets equals the fair value.

2. Prepare the journal entry or entries to record Wal's admission to the partnership assuming that he invests $140,000 in the partnership for the 20 percent interest and that partnership capital is *revalued*.

## E 16-10
### Recording new partner investment—Nonrevaluation case

Capital balances and profit-sharing percentages for the partnership of Man, Eme, and Fot on January 1, 2016, are as follows:

| | |
|---|---|
| Man (36%) | $140,000 |
| Eme (24%) | 100,000 |
| Fot (40%) | 160,000 |
| | $400,000 |

On January 3, 2016, the partners agree to admit Box into the partnership for a 25 percent interest in capital and earnings for his investment in the partnership of $120,000. Partnership assets are not to be revalued.

**REQUIRED**

1. Determine the capital balances of the four partners immediately after the admission of Box.

2. What is the profit- and loss-sharing ratio for Man, Eme, Fot, and Box?

## E 16-11
### Partner retirement entries

Capital balances and profit- and loss-sharing ratios for the Nix, Man, and Per partnership on December 31, 2016, just before the retirement of Nix, are as follows:

| | |
|---|---|
| Nix capital (30%) | $128,000 |
| Man capital (30%) | $140,000 |
| Per capital (40%) | $160,000 |

On January 2, 2017, Nix is paid $170,000 cash on his retirement.

**REQUIRED:** Prepare the journal entry or entries to record Nix's retirement assuming that goodwill, as implied by the payment to Nix, is recorded on the partnership books.

## E 16-12
### Partner retirement entries—Fair value adjustment

A balance sheet at December 31, 2016, for the Bec, Dee, and Lyn partnership is summarized as follows:

| | | | |
|---|---|---|---|
| Assets | $800,000 | Liabilities | $200,000 |
| Loan to Dee | 100,000 | Bec capital (50%) | 300,000 |
| | $900,000 | Dee capital (40%) | 300,000 |
| | | Lyn capital (10%) | 100,000 |
| | | | $900,000 |

Dee is retiring from the partnership. The partners agree that partnership assets, excluding Dee's loan, should be adjusted to their fair value of $1,000,000 and that Dee should receive $310,000 for her capital balance net of the $100,000 loan. The bonus approach is used; therefore, no goodwill is recorded.

**REQUIRED:** Determine the capital balances of Bec and Lyn immediately after Dee's retirement.

## E 16-13
### Partnership income allocation—Salary allowance, bonus, and additional contributions during the year

Kat and Edd formed the K & E partnership several years ago. Capital account balances on January 1, 2016, were as follows:

|  |  |
|---|---|
| Kat | $496,750 |
| Edd | $268,250 |

The partnership agreement provides Kat with an annual salary of $10,000 plus a bonus of 5 percent of partnership net income for managing the business. Edd is provided an annual salary of $15,000 with no bonus. The remainder is shared evenly. Partnership net income for 2016 was $30,000. Edd and Kat each invested an additional $5,000 during the year to finance a special purchase. Year-end drawing account balances were $15,000 for Kat and $10,000 for Edd.

**REQUIRED**

1. Prepare an income allocation schedule.

2. Create the journal entries to update the equity accounts at the end of the year.

3. Determine the capital balances as of December 31, 2016.

## E 16-14
## Partnership retirement—Revaluation and bonus approaches

The capital account balances and profit- and loss-sharing ratios of the Byd, Box, Dar, and Fus partnership on December 31, 2016, after closing entries are as follows:

|  |  |
|---|---|
| Byd (30%) | $30,000 |
| Box (20%) | 25,000 |
| Dar (40%) | 25,000 |
| Fus (10%) | 20,000 |
| Total capital | $100,000 |

Box is retiring from the partnership, and the partners agree that he will receive a cash payment of $35,000 in final settlement of his interest. The book values of partnership assets and liabilities are equal to fair values, except for a building with a book value of $15,000 and a fair value of $25,000.

**REQUIRED**

1. Prepare the journal entry or entries to record Box's retirement assuming that assets are revalued to the basis implied by the excess payment to Box.

2. Prepare the journal entry or entries to record Box's retirement assuming the bonus approach is used.

## E 16-15
## Recording new partner investment and partner retirements—Various situations

1. Bil and Ken enter into a partnership agreement in which Bil is to have a 60 percent interest in capital and profits and Ken is to have a 40 percent interest in capital and profits. Bil contributes the following:

|  | Cost | Fair Value |
|---|---|---|
| Land | $10,000 | $20,000 |
| Building | 100,000 | 60,000 |
| Equipment | 20,000 | 15,000 |

There is a $30,000 mortgage on the building that the partnership agrees to assume. Ken contributes $50,000 cash to the partnership. Bil and Ken agree that Ken's capital account should equal Ken's $50,000 cash contribution and that goodwill should be recorded. Goodwill should be recorded in the amount of:

a  $10,000

b  $15,000

c  $16,667

d  $20,000

2. Tho and Mar are partners having capital balances of $50,000 and $60,000, respectively. They admit Jay to a one-third interest in partnership capital and profits for an investment of $65,000. If the goodwill procedure is used in recording Jay's admission to the partnership:

a  Jay's capital will be $58,333

b  Total capital will be $175,000

c  Mar's capital will be $70,000

d  Goodwill will be recorded at $15,000

**3.** On December 31, 2016, Tin and Web, who share profits and losses equally, have capital balances of $170,000 and $200,000, respectively. They agree to admit Zen for a one-third interest in capital and profits for his investment of $200,000. Partnership net assets are not to be revalued. Capital accounts of Tin, Web, and Zen, respectively, immediately after Zen's admission to the partnership are:

a **$170,000, $200,000, and $200,000**

b **$165,000, $195,000, and $200,000**

c **$175,000, $205,000, and $190,000**

d **$185,000, $215,000, and $200,000**

**4.** Fin and Rho have capital balances of $100,000 and $80,000, respectively, and they share profits equally. The partners agree to accept Che for a 25 percent interest in capital and profits for her investment of $90,000. If goodwill is recorded, the capital account balances of Fin and Rho immediately after Che's admittance to the partnership will be:

a **Fin, $100,000; Rho, $120,000**

b **Fin, $111,250; Rho, $91,250**

c **Fin, $145,000; Rho, $125,000**

d **Fin, $120,000; Rho, $120,000**

**5.** The balance sheet of the Fre, Gin, and Peg partnership on December 31, 2016, together with profit-sharing ratios, revealed the following:

| | | | |
|---|---|---|---|
| Cash | $240,000 | Fre capital (30%) | $200,000 |
| Other assets | 360,000 | Gin capital (30%) | 170,000 |
| | | Peg capital (40%) | 230,000 |
| | $600,000 | | $600,000 |

Gin is retiring from the partnership, and the partners agreed that she should receive $200,000 cash as payment in full for her share of partnership assets. If the goodwill implied by the settlement with Gin is recorded on the partnership books, total partnership assets after Gin's withdrawal should be:

a **$566,667**

b **$500,000**

c **$430,000**

d **$400,000**

## E 16-16
## Recording new partner investment and partner retirements—Various situations

**1.** Shi purchased an interest in the Ton and Olg partnership by paying Ton $40,000 for half of his capital and half of his 50 percent profit-sharing interest. At the time, Ton's capital balance was $30,000 and Olg's capital balance was $70,000. Shi should receive a credit to her capital account of:

a **$15,000**

b **$20,000**

c **$25,000**

d **$33,333**

**2.** Lin and Que are partners with capital balances of $50,000 and $70,000, respectively, and they share profits and losses equally. The partners agree to take Dun into the partnership for a 40 percent interest in capital and profits, while Lin and Que each retain a 30 percent interest. Dun pays $60,000 cash directly to Lin and Que for his 40 percent interest, and goodwill implied by Dun's payment is recognized on the partnership books. If Lin and Que transfer equal amounts of capital to Dun, the capital balances after Dun's admittance will be:

a **Lin, $35,000; Que, $55,000; Dun, $60,000**

b **Lin, $45,000; Que, $45,000; Dun, $60,000**

c **Lin, $36,000; Que, $36,000; Dun, $48,000**

d **Lin, $26,000; Que, $46,000; Dun, $48,000**

**Use the following information in answering questions 3 and 4:**

McC and New are partners with capital balances of $70,000 and $50,000, respectively, and they share profit and losses equally. Oak is admitted to the partnership with a contribution to the partnership of $50,000 cash for a one-third interest in the partnership capital and in future profits and losses.

**3.** If the goodwill is recognized in accounting for the admission of Oak, what amount of goodwill will be recorded?

a **$60,000**

b **$20,000**

c **$10,000**

d **$6,667**

**4.** If no goodwill is recognized, the capital balances of McC and New immediately after the admission of Oak will be:

a  *McC, $65,000; New, $45,000*
b  *McC, $66,667; New, $46,666*
c  *McC, $67,500; New, $47,500*
d  *McC, $70,000; New, $50,000*

**5.** The December 31, 2016, balance sheet of the Ben, Car, and Das partnership is summarized as follows:

| | | | |
|---|---|---|---|
| Cash | $100,000 | Car loan | $100,000 |
| Other assets, at cost | 500,000 | Ben capital | 100,000 |
| | | Car capital | 200,000 |
| | | Das capital | 200,000 |
| | $600,000 | | $600,000 |

The partners share profits and losses as follows: Ben, 20 percent; Car 30 percent; and Das, 50 percent. Car is retiring from the partnership, and the partners have agreed that "other assets" should be adjusted to their fair value of $600,000 at December 31, 2016. They further agree that Car will receive $244,000 cash for his partnership interest exclusive of his loan, which is to be paid in full, and that no goodwill implied by Car's payment will be recorded.

After Car's retirement, the capital balances of Ben and Das, respectively, will be:

a  *$116,000 and $240,000*
b  *$101,714 and $254,286*
c  *$100,000 and $200,000*
d  *$73,143 and $182,857*

## E 16-17
### Partnership income allocation and new partner investment—Various situations

**1.** Cob, Inc., a partner in TLC Partnership, assigns its partnership interest to Ben, who is not made a partner. After the assignment, Ben asserts the rights to:

I.  Participate in the management of TLC
II. Cob's share of TLC's partnership profits

Ben is correct as to which of these rights?

a  *I only*
b  *II only*
c  *I and II*
d  *Neither I nor II*

**2.** When property other than cash is invested in a partnership, at what amount should the noncash property be credited to the contributing partner's capital account?

a  *Fair value at the date of contribution*
b  *Contributing partner's original cost*
c  *Assessed valuation for property tax purposes*
d  *Contributing partner's tax basis*

**3.** Pla, a partner in the Bri Partnership, has a 30 percent participation in partnership profits and losses. Pla's capital account had a net decrease of $60,000 during the calendar year 2016. During 2016, Pla withdrew $130,000 (charged against his capital account) and contributed property with a fair value of $25,000 to the partnership. What was the net income of the Bri Partnership for 2016?

a  *$150,000*
b  *$233,333*
c  *$350,000*
d  *$550,000*

**4.** Fox, Gre, and How are partners with average capital balances during 2016 of $120,000, $60,000, and $40,000, respectively. Partners receive 10 percent interest on their average capital balances. After deducting salaries of $30,000 to Fox and $20,000 to How, the residual profit or loss is divided equally. In 2016, the partnership sustained a $33,000 loss before interest and salaries to partners. By what amount should Fox's capital account change?

a  *$7,000 increase*
b  *$11,000 decrease*
c  *$35,000 decrease*
d  *$42,000 increase*

5. Bec, an active partner in the Bec and Cri partnership, receives an annual bonus of 25 percent of partnership net income after deducting the bonus. For the year ended December 31, 2016, partnership net income before the bonus amounted to $300,000. Bec's 2016 bonus should be:

a **$56,250**

b **$60,000**

c **$62,500**

d **$75,000**

# E 16-18
## Partnership retirement—Various situations

1. Partners All, Bak, and Coe share profits and losses 50:30:20, respectively. The balance sheet at April 30, 2016, follows:

| Assets | | Equities | |
|---|---|---|---|
| Cash | $40,000 | Accounts payable | $100,000 |
| Other assets | 360,000 | All capital | 74,000 |
| | | Bak capital | 130,000 |
| | | Coe capital | 96,000 |
| | $400,000 | | $400,000 |

The assets and liabilities are recorded and presented at their respective fair values. Jon is to be admitted as a new partner with a 20 percent capital interest and a 20 percent share of profits and losses in exchange for a cash contribution. No goodwill or bonus is to be recorded. How much cash should Jon contribute?

a **$60,000**

b **$72,000**

c **$75,000**

d **$80,000**

2. Elt and Don are partners who share profits and losses in the ratio of 7:3, respectively. On November 5, 2016, their respective capital accounts were as follows:

| | |
|---|---|
| Elt | $70,000 |
| Don | 60,000 |
| | $130,000 |

On that date they agreed to admit Kra as a partner with a one-third interest in the capital and profits and losses upon his investment of $50,000. The new partnership will begin with a total capital of $180,000. Immediately after Kra's admission, what are the capital balances of Elt, Don, and Kra, respectively?

a **$60,000, $60,000, $60,000**

b **$63,000, $57,000, $60,000**

c **$63,333, $56,667, $60,000**

d **$70,000, $60,000, $50,000**

3. Wil desires to purchase a one-fourth capital and profit and loss interest in the partnership of Eli, Geo, and Dic. The three partners agree to sell Wil one-fourth of their respective capital and profit and loss interests in exchange for a total payment of $40,000. The capital accounts and the respective percentage interests in profits and losses immediately before the sale to Wil are as follows:

| | |
|---|---|
| Eli capital (60%) | $80,000 |
| Geo capital (30%) | 40,000 |
| Dic capital (10%) | 20,000 |
| | $140,000 |

All other assets and liabilities are fairly valued, and implied goodwill is to be recorded prior to the acquisition by Wil. Immediately after Wil's acquisition, what should be the capital balances of Eli, Geo, and Dic, respectively?

a **$60,000, $30,000, $15,000**

b **$69,000, $34,500, $16,500**

c **$77,000, $38,500, $19,500**

d **$92,000, $46,000, $22,000**

4. The capital accounts of the partnership of New, Sha, and Jac on June 1, 2016, are presented, along with their respective profit and loss ratios:

| | | |
|---|---|---|
| New | $139,200 | 1/2 |
| Sha | 208,800 | 1/3 |
| Jac | 96,000 | 1/6 |
| | $444,000 | |

On June 1, 2016, Sid was admitted to the partnership when he purchased, for $132,000, a proportionate interest from New and Sha in the net assets and profits of the partnership. As a result of this transaction, Sid acquired a one-fifth interest in the net assets and profits of the firm. Assuming that implied goodwill is *not* to be recorded, what is the combined gain realized by New and Sha upon the sale of a portion of their interests in the partnership to Sid?

   *a*  *$0*
   *b*  *$43,200*
   *c*  *$62,400*
   *d*  *$82,000*

5. Ker and Pat are partners with capital balances of $60,000 and $20,000, respectively. Profits and losses are divided in the ratio of 60:40. Ker and Pat decide to admit Gra, who invested land with a fair value of $15,000 for a 20 percent capital interest in the partnership. Gra's capital account should be credited for:

   *a*  *$12,000*
   *b*  *$15,000*
   *c*  *$16,000*
   *d*  *$19,000*

6. Dix, a partner in an accounting firm, decided to withdraw from the partnership. Dix's share of the partnership profits and losses was 20 percent. Upon withdrawing from the partnership, he was paid $74,000 in final settlement for his partnership interest. The total of the partners' capital accounts *before* recognition of partnership goodwill prior to Dix's withdrawal was $210,000. After his withdrawal, the remaining partners' capital accounts, excluding their share of goodwill, totaled $160,000. The total agreed-upon goodwill of the firm was:

   *a*  *$120,000*
   *b*  *$140,000*
   *c*  *$160,000*
   *d*  *$250,000*

7. On June 30, 2016, the balance sheet for the partnership of Wil, Bro, and Low, together with their respective profit and loss ratios, is summarized as follows:

| Assets, at cost | $300,000 | Wil loan | $15,000 |
|---|---|---|---|
| | | Wil capital (20%) | 70,000 |
| | | Bro capital (20%) | 65,000 |
| | | Low capital (60%) | 150,000 |
| | | | $300,000 |

Wil has decided to retire from the partnership, and by mutual agreement the assets are to be adjusted to their fair value of $360,000 at June 30, 2016. It is agreed that the partnership will pay Wil $102,000 cash for his partnership interest exclusive of his loan, which is to be repaid in full. Goodwill is to be recorded in this transaction, as implied by the excess payment to Wil. After Wil's retirement, what are the capital account balances of Bro and Low, respectively?

   *a*  *$65,000 and $150,000*
   *b*  *$97,000 and $246,000*
   *c*  *$73,000 and $174,000*
   *d*  *$77,000 and $186,000*

## E 16-19
## Partnership income allocation—Salary allowance and interest

The partnership agreement of Kra, Lam, and Man provides for the division of net income as follows:
1. Lam, who manages the partnership, is to receive a salary of $11,000 per year.
2. Each partner is to be allowed interest at 10 percent on beginning capital.
3. Remaining profits are to be divided equally.

   During 2016, Kra invested an additional $4,000 in the partnership. Lam withdrew $5,000, and Man withdrew $4,000. No other investments or withdrawals were made during 2016. On January 1, 2016, the capital balances were Kra, $65,000; Lam, $75,000; and Man, $70,000. Total capital at year-end was $252,000.

---

**REQUIRED:** Prepare a statement of partners' capital for the year ended December 31, 2016.

---

## E 16-20
## Recording new partner investment

After operating as partners for several years, Gro and Ham decided to sell one-half of each of their partnership interests to Lot for a total of $70,000, paid directly to Gro and Ham.

   At the time of Lot's admittance to the partnership, Gro and Ham had capital balances of $45,000 and $65,000, respectively, and shared profits 45 percent to Gro and 55 percent to Ham.

## REQUIRED

1. Calculate the capital balances of each of the partners immediately after Lot is admitted as a partner assuming that the assets are not revalued, and prepare a second calculation of the capital balances assuming that the assets are revalued at the time Lot is admitted.

2. In designing a new partnership agreement, how should profits and losses be divided?

3. If a new partnership agreement is not established, how will profits and losses be divided?

### E 16-21
### Partnership retirement—Various situations

The Cas, Don, and Ear partnership balance sheet and profit and loss percentages at June 30, 2016, are summarized as follows:

| Assets | $500,000 | Cas capital (30%) | $140,000 |
|---|---|---|---|
| | | Don capital (30%) | 175,000 |
| | | Ear capital (40%) | 185,000 |
| | $500,000 | | $500,000 |

On July 1, 2016, the partners agree that Cas is to retire immediately and receive $161,000 for her partnership interest.

**REQUIRED:** Prepare journal entries to illustrate *three* possible methods of accounting for the retirement of Cas.

## PROBLEMS

### P 16-1
### Partnership income allocation—Statement of partnership capital

Ell, Far, and Gar are partners who share profits and losses 30 percent, 30 percent, and 40 percent, respectively, after Ell and Far each receive a $32,000 salary allowance. Capital balances on January 1, 2016, are as follows:

| Ell (30%) | $69,000 |
|---|---|
| Far (30%) | 85,500 |
| Gar (40%) | 245,500 |

During 2016, Gar invested an additional $20,000 in the partnership, and Ell and Far each withdrew $32,000, equal to their salary allowances as provided by the profit- and loss-sharing agreement. The partnership net assets at December 31, 2016, were $481,000.

**REQUIRED:** Prepare a statement of partnership capital for the year ended December 31, 2016.

### P 16-2
### Recording new partner investment—Revaluation and nonrevaluation cases

The partnership of Mor and Osc is being dissolved, and the assets and equities at book value and fair value and the profit- and loss-sharing ratios at January 1, 2016, are as follows:

| | Book Value | Fair Value |
|---|---|---|
| Cash | $ 20,000 | $ 20,000 |
| Accounts receivable—net | 100,000 | 100,000 |
| Inventories | 50,000 | 200,000 |
| Plant assets—net | 100,000 | 120,000 |
| | $270,000 | $440,000 |
| Accounts payable | $ 50,000 | $ 50,000 |
| Mor capital (50%) | 120,000 | |
| Osc capital (50%) | 100,000 | |
| | $270,000 | |

Mor and Osc agree to admit Tre into the partnership for a one-third interest. Tre invests $95,000 cash and a building to be used in the business with a book value to Tre of $100,000 and a fair value of $120,000.

**REQUIRED**

1. Prepare a balance sheet for the Mor, Osc, and Tre partnership on January 2, 2016, just after the admission of Tre, assuming that the assets are revalued and goodwill is recognized.

2. Prepare a balance sheet for the Mor, Osc, and Tre partnership on January 2, 2016, after the admission of Tre, assuming that the assets are not revalued.

## P 16-3
## Partnership income allocation

Ash and Bar are partners with capital balances on January 1, 2016, of $70,000 and $80,000, respectively. The partnership agreement provides that each partner is allowed 10 percent interest on beginning capital balances; that Ash receives a salary allowance of $20,000 per year and a 20 percent bonus of partnership income after interest, salary allowance, and bonus; and that remaining income is divided equally.

**REQUIRED:** Prepare an income distribution schedule to show how the $160,000 partnership net income for 2016 should be divided.

## P 16-4
## Partnership income allocation—Complex, net loss

The partnership agreement of Ale, Car, and Eri provides that profits are to be divided as follows:

1. Ale is to receive a salary allowance of $10,000 for managing the partnership business.

2. Partners are to receive 10 percent interest on average capital balances. Drawings are excluded from computing these averages.

3. Remaining profits are to be divided 30 percent, 30 percent, and 40 percent to Ale, Car, and Eri, respectively.

Ale had a capital balance of $60,000 at January 1, 2016, and had drawings of $8,000 on July 1, 2016. Car's capital balance on January 1, 2016, was $90,000, and he invested an additional $30,000 on September 1, 2016. Eri's beginning capital balance was $110,000, and she withdrew $10,000 on July 1 but invested an additional $20,000 on October 1, 2016.

The partnership has a net loss of $12,000 during 2016, and the accountant in charge allocated the net loss as follows: $200 profit to Ale, $4,800 loss to Car, and $7,400 loss to Eri.

**REQUIRED**

1. A schedule to show the correct allocation of the partnership net loss for 2016

2. A statement of partnership capital for the year ended December 31, 2016

3. Journal entries to correct the books of the partnership at December 31, 2016, assuming that all closing entries for the year have been recorded.

## P 16-5
## Partnership income allocation—Profit-sharing based on beginning, ending, and average capital balances

A summary of changes in the capital accounts of the Kat, Lyn, and Mol partnership for 2016, before closing partnership net income to the capital accounts, is as follows:

|  | Kat Capital | Lyn Capital | Mol Capital | Total Capital |
|---|---|---|---|---|
| Balance January 1, 2016 | $80,000 | $80,000 | $90,000 | $250,000 |
| Investment April 1 | 20,000 |  |  | 20,000 |
| Withdrawal May 1 |  | (15,000) |  | (15,000) |
| Withdrawal July 1 | (10,000) |  |  | (10,000) |
| Withdrawal September 1 |  |  | (30,000) | (30,000) |
|  | $90,000 | $65,000 | $60,000 | $215,000 |

**REQUIRED:** Determine the allocation of the 2016 net income to the partners under each of the following sets of independent assumptions:

1. Partnership net income is $60,000, and profit is divided on the basis of average capital balances during the year.

2. Partnership net income is $50,000, Kat gets a bonus of 10 percent of income for managing the business, and the remaining profits are divided on the basis of beginning capital balances.

3. Partnership net loss is $35,000, Mol receives a $12,000 salary, each partner is allowed 10 percent interest on beginning capital balances, and the remaining profits are divided equally.

## P 16-6
## Partner income allocation—Correction of error

The partnership of Jon, Kel, and Gla was created on January 2, 2016, with each of the partners contributing cash of $30,000. Reported profits, withdrawals, and additional investments were as follows:

|  | Reported Net Income | Withdrawals | Additional Investments |
|---|---|---|---|
| 2016 | $19,000 | $4,000 Kel<br>5,000 Jon | $5,000 Gla |
| 2017 | 22,000 | 8,000 Gla<br>3,000 Kel | 5,000 Jon |
| 2018 | 29,000 | 2,000 Gla<br>4,000 Kel | 6,000 Gla |

The partnership agreement provides that partners are to be allowed 10 percent interest on the beginning-of-the-year capital balances, that Jon is to receive a $7,000 salary allowance, and that remaining profits are to be divided equally.

After the books were closed on December 31, 2018, it was discovered that depreciation had been understated by $2,000 each year and that the inventory taken at December 31, 2018, was understated by $8,000.

## REQUIRED

1. Calculate the balances in the three capital accounts on January 1, 2019.

2. Calculate the balances that should be in the three capital accounts on January 1, 2019, taking into account the corrections that must be made for errors made in the calculation of income in the prior years.

3. Give the journal entry (one entry) to correct the books on January 1, 2019.

## P 16-7
## Recording new partner investment and subsequent balance sheet

The partnership of Add and Bal is adding a new partner, Cat, and its assets and equities at book value and fair value just prior to her admission to the partnership on January 1, 2016, are as follows:

|  | Book Value | Fair Value |
|---|---|---|
| *Assets* |  |  |
| Cash | $15,000 | $15,000 |
| Accounts receivable—net | 45,000 | 40,000 |
| Inventories | 50,000 | 60,000 |
| Plant assets—net | 90,000 | 105,000 |
|  | $200,000 | $220,000 |
| *Equities* |  |  |
| Accounts payable | $30,000 | $30,000 |
| 15% note payable | 50,000 | 40,000 |
| Add capital (60%) | 64,000 |  |
| Bal capital (40%) | 56,000 |  |
|  | $200,000 |  |

On January 2, 2016, Add and Bal take Cat into the partnership of Add, Bal, and Cat for a 40 percent interest in capital and profits.

**REQUIRED**

1. Prepare journal entries for the admission of Cat into the partnership for an investment of $160,000 assuming that assets (including any goodwill) are revalued.

2. Prepare a balance sheet for the Add, Bal, and Cat partnership on January 2, 2016, just after the admission of Cat.

## P 16-8
## Recording new partner investment—Various situations

The capital accounts of the Ann, Bob, and Car partnership at December 31, 2016, together with profit-and loss-sharing ratios, are as follows:

| | |
|---|---|
| Ann (25%) | $75,000 |
| Bob (25%) | 100,000 |
| Car (50%) | 125,000 |

The partners agree to admit Dar into the partnership.

**REQUIRED:** Prepare the journal entry or entries to admit Dar into the partnership and calculate the partners' capital balances immediately after his admission under each of the following independent assumptions:

1. Car sells half of her interest to Dar for $90,000, and the partners agree to admit Dar into the partnership.

2. Dar invests $75,000 cash in the partnership for a 25 percent interest in the partnership capital and profits, and partnership assets are revalued.

3. Dar invests $80,000 cash in the partnership for a 20 percent interest in the capital and profits, and partnership assets are revalued.

4. Dar invests $90,000 cash in the partnership for a 30% interest in the capital and profits, and partnership assets are *not* revalued.

## P 16-9
## Recording new partner investment—Various situations

Three partners, Pat, Mic, and Hay, have capital balances and profit-sharing ratios at December 31, 2016, as follows:

| | | |
|---|---|---|
| Pat | $144,000 | profit ratio 2/5 |
| Mic | 216,000 | profit ratio 1/2 |
| Hay | 90,000 | profit ratio 1/10 |

On January 1, 2017, Con invests $85,080 in the business for a one-sixth interest in capital and income.

**REQUIRED**

1. Prepare journal entries giving *two* alternative solutions for recording Con's admission to the partnership.

2. Prepare journal entries giving *two* alternative solutions for recording Con's admission to the partnership if she purchased a one-sixth interest from each of the partners, rather than paying the $85,080 into the business.

## P 16-10
## Recording new partner investment—Various situations

The AT Partnership was organized several years ago, and on January 1, 2016, the partners agree to admit Car for a 40 percent interest in capital and earnings. Capital account balances and profit- and loss-sharing ratios at January 1, 2016, before the admission of Car, are as follows:

| | |
|---|---|
| Aid (50%) | $500,000 |
| Tha (50%) | 280,000 |

**REQUIRED:** Prepare journal entries to record the admission of Car for a 40 percent interest in the capital and rights to future profits under the following independent assumptions.

1. Car pays $450,000 directly to Aid and Tha for 40 percent of each of their interests, and the bonus procedure is used.

2. Car pays $600,000 directly to Aid and Tha for 40 percent of each of their interests, and goodwill is recorded.

3. Car invests $450,000 in the partnership for her 40 percent interest, and goodwill is recorded.

4. Car invests $600,000 in the partnership for her 40 percent interest, and goodwill is recorded.

## P 16-11
### Partnership income allocation—Multiple years

Har, Ion, and Jer formed a partnership on January 1, 2016, with each partner contributing $20,000 cash. Although the partnership agreement provided that Jer receive a salary of $1,000 per month for managing the partnership business, Jer has never withdrawn any money from the partnership. Har withdrew $4,000 in each of the years 2016 and 2017, and Ion invested an additional $8,000 in 2016 and withdrew $8,000 during 2017. Due to an oversight, the partnership has not maintained formal accounting records, but the following information as of December 31, 2017, is available:

| | |
|---|---|
| Cash on hand | $ 28,500 |
| Due from customers | 20,000 |
| Merchandise on hand (at cost) | 40,000 |
| Delivery equipment—net of depreciation | 37,000 |
| Prepaid expenses | 4,000 |
| Total Assets | $129,500 |
| Due to suppliers | $ 14,600 |
| Wages payable | 4,400 |
| Note payable | 10,000 |
| Interest payable | 500 |
| Total Liabilities | $ 29,500 |

### ADDITIONAL INFORMATION

1. The partners agree that income for 2017 was about half of the total income for the first two years of operations.

2. Although profits were not divided until 2017, the partnership agreement provides that profits, after allowance for Jer's salary, are to be divided each year on the basis of beginning-of-the-year capital balances.

**REQUIRED:** Prepare statements of partnership capital for the years ended December 31, 2016, and December 31, 2017.

## P 16-12
### Partnership income allocation

The partnership of Par and Boo was formed and commenced operations on March 1, 2016, with Par contributing $30,000 cash and Boo investing cash of $10,000 and equipment with an agreed-upon valuation of $20,000. On July 1, 2016, Boo invested an additional $10,000 in the partnership. Par made a capital withdrawal of $4,000 on May 2, 2016, but reinvested the $4,000 on October 1, 2016. During 2016, Par withdrew $800 per month, and Boo, the managing partner, withdrew $1,000 per month. These drawings were charged to Salaries to partners. A preclosing trial balance taken at December 31, 2016, is as follows:

|  | Debit | Credit |
|---|---|---|
| Cash | $9,000 | |
| Receivables—net | 15,000 | |
| Equipment—net | 50,000 | |
| Other assets | 19,000 | |
| Liabilities | | $17,000 |
| Par capital | | 30,000 |
| Boo capital | | 40,000 |
| Service revenue | | 50,000 |
| Supplies expense | 17,000 | |
| Utilities expense | 4,000 | |
| Salaries to partners | 18,000 | |
| Other miscellaneous expenses | 5,000 | |
| Total | $137,000 | $137,000 |

## REQUIRED

1. Journalize the entries necessary to close the partnership books assuming that there is no agreement regarding profit distribution.

2. Prepare a statement of partnership capital assuming that the partnership agreement provides for monthly salary allowances of $800 and $1,000 for Par and Boo, respectively, and for the division of remaining profits in relation to average capital balances.

3. Prepare a profit distribution schedule for the Par and Boo partnership assuming monthly salary allowances of $800 and $1,000 for Par and Boo, respectively; interest allowances at a 12 percent annual rate on average capital balances; and remaining profits divided equally.

## P 16-13
## Recording new partner investment—Complex non-revaluation and revaluation cases

A condensed balance sheet for the Pet, Qua, and She partnership at December 31, 2016, and their profit-and loss-sharing percentages on that date are as follows:

**Condensed Balance Sheet at December 31, 2016**

| Cash | $15,000 | Liabilities | $50,000 |
|---|---|---|---|
| Other assets | 185,000 | Pet capital (50%) | 75,000 |
| Total assets | $200,000 | Qua capital (30%) | 50,000 |
| | | She capital (20%) | 25,000 |
| | | Total liabilities and capital | $200,000 |

On January 1, 2017, the partners decided to bring Tom into the partnership for a one-fourth interest in the capital and profits of the partnership. The following proposals for Tom's admittance into the partnership were considered:

1. Tom would purchase one-half of Pet's capital and right to future profits directly from Pet for $60,000.

2. Tom would purchase one-fourth of each partner's capital and rights to future profits by paying a total of $45,000 directly to the partners.

3. Tom would invest $55,000 cash in the partnership for a 25 percent interest in capital. Future profits would be divided 37.5 percent, 22.5 percent, 15 percent, and 25 percent for Pet, Qua, She, and Tom, respectively.

**REQUIRED:** Prepare journal entries with supporting computations to show Tom's admittance into the partnership under each of the given proposals assuming that:

1. Partnership net assets are not to be revalued.

2. Partnership net assets are to be revalued.

### P 16-14
### Partnership income allocation

Tim and Las have been operating an accounting firm as partners for a number of years, and at the beginning of 2016, their capital balances were $60,000 and $75,000, respectively. During 2016, Tim invested an additional $10,000 on April 1 and withdrew $6,000 on August 30. Las withdrew $12,000 on May 1 and withdrew another $6,000 on November 1. In addition, Tim and Las withdrew their salary allowances of $18,000 and $24,000, respectively. At year-end 2016, total capital of the Tim-Las partnership was $182,000. Tim and Las share income after salary allowances in a 60:40 ratio.

#### REQUIRED

1. Determine average capital balances for Tim and Las for 2016.
2. Allocate 2016 partnership income to Tim and Las.

## PROFESSIONAL RESEARCH ASSIGNMENTS

Answer the following questions by reference to the Uniform Partnership Act of 1997. Include the appropriate reference in your response.

**PR 16-1** What defines a business as a partnership? What factors need to be examined to determine if an individual is a partner, and not some other type of participant in the business?

**PR 16-2** Under what circumstances can a partnership expel a partner?

# CHAPTER 17

# Partnership Liquidation

This chapter covers the situation in which a partnership is dissolved and the business ceases to operate. In this case, the business must be liquidated. The liquidation process, or winding up the business, includes paying liabilities, selling assets, and distributing monies to the partners.

**LEARNING OBJECTIVE 17.1**

## THE LIQUIDATION PROCESS

Usually, **partnership liquidation** involves the following:

■ Converting noncash assets into cash

■ Recognizing gains and losses and expenses incurred during the liquidation period

■ Settling all liabilities

■ Distributing cash to the partners according to the final balances in their capital accounts

This general description of the liquidation process assumes the following:

■ The partnership is solvent (i.e., partnership assets exceed partnership liabilities).

■ All partners have equity in partnership net assets.

■ No outstanding loan balances to any partner exist.

■ All assets are converted into cash before any cash is distributed to the partners.

As these assumptions are relaxed, the liquidation process becomes more complex. Accordingly, this chapter begins with simple liquidations for solvent partnerships and proceeds to installment liquidations and liquidations of insolvent partnerships.

The rules for distributing assets in the liquidation of a partnership are covered in Section 807 of the Uniform Partnership Act of 1997 (UPA). The rank order of payment is as follows:

1. Amounts owed to creditors other than partners and amounts owed to partners other than for capital and profits

2. Amounts due to partners liquidating their capital balance upon conclusion of the liquidation of partnership assets and liabilities

## Simple Partnership Liquidation

Simple partnership liquidation is a conversion of all partnership assets into cash with a single distribution of cash to partners in final settlement of the partnership's affairs. To illustrate a simple

**LEARNING OBJECTIVE 17.2**

liquidation, assume that the balance sheet of Hol and Kir at December 31, 2016, is as follows (amounts in thousands):

**HOL AND KIR**
**BALANCE SHEET**
**AT DECEMBER 31, 2016**

| Assets | | Liabilities and Equity | |
|---|---|---|---|
| Cash | $10 | Accounts payable | $40 |
| Accounts receivable—net | 30 | Loan from Hol | 10 |
| Inventory | 30 | Hol capital | 25 |
| Plant assets—net | 40 | Kir capital | 35 |
| | $110 | | $110 |

Hol and Kir share profits and losses 70 percent and 30 percent, respectively, and agree to liquidate their partnership as soon as possible after January 1, 2017. Assume that on January 5, 2017, the inventory items are sold for $25,000, plant assets are sold for $30,000, and $22,000 is collected in final settlement of the accounts receivable.

The balance sheet after these transactions are recorded (see Exhibit 17-1, Part A, for the journal entries) is as follows (amounts in thousands):

**HOL AND KIR**
**BALANCE SHEET**
**AT JANUARY 5, 2017**
*(IMMEDIATELY AFTER ASSET SALE AND RECEIVABLE COLLECTION)*

| Assets | | Liabilities and Equity | |
|---|---|---|---|
| Cash | $87 | Accounts payable | $40 |
| | | Loan from Hol | 10 |
| | | Hol capital | 8.9 |
| | | Kir capital | 28.1 |
| | $87 | | $87 |

As the final step in the partnership liquidation, the cash is distributed to the creditors and partners as follows (see Exhibit 17-1, Part B, for the journal entries):

| *Order of Payment* | |
|---|---|
| **I** To creditors for accounts payable | $40,000 |
| To Hol for his loan balance | 10,000 |
| **II** To Hol for his capital balance | 8,900 |
| To Kir for his capital balance | 28,100 |
| Total distribution | $87,000 |

We use the established profit- and loss-sharing ratios (in this example, 70% and 30%) during the liquidation period unless the partnership agreement specifies a different division of profits and losses during liquidation. In the case of partnership agreements that provide for salary and interest allowances, only the residual profit- and loss-sharing ratios would be applied during the liquidation period. This is because the gains and losses at liquidation are essentially adjustments of prior profits that would have been shared using the residual profit-sharing ratios if they had been recognized prior to dissolution.

A liquidating partnership should maintain a summary of transactions and balances during the liquidation stage. We present this summary of transactions and balances, called a partnership liquidation statement, for the Hol and Kir partnership in Exhibit 17-2.

## Debit Capital Balances in a Solvent Partnership

If liquidating partnerships are solvent, sufficient resources exist to pay creditors and distribute some cash to the partners. However, the process of liquidation may result in losses that force the capital accounts of some partners into debit balances. When this happens, those partners with debit balances have an obligation to partners with credit balances, and they can be required to use their personal

| | EXHIBIT 17-1 |
|---|---|
| | Simple Liquidation—Hol and Kir Partnership |

## JOURNAL ENTRIES TO RECORD THE LIQUIDATION

### PART A: JOURNAL ENTRIES TO RECORD ASSET SALE AND ACCOUNTS RECEIVABLE COLLECTION

| | | |
|---|---|---|
| Cash (+A) | 25,000 | |
| Hol capital (−OE) | 3,500 | |
| Kir capital (−OE) | 1,500 | |
| Inventory (−A) | | 30,000 |

To record sale of inventory items and allocation of the $5,000 loss to the partners' capital accounts in their residual profit- and loss-sharing ratios.

| | | |
|---|---|---|
| Cash (+A) | 30,000 | |
| Hol capital (−OE) | 7,000 | |
| Kir capital (−OE) | 3,000 | |
| Plant assets—net (−A) | | 40,000 |

To record sale of plant assets and allocation of the $10,000 loss to the partners' capital accounts in their residual profit- and loss-sharing ratios.

| | | |
|---|---|---|
| Cash (+A) | 22,000 | |
| Hol capital (−OE) | 5,600 | |
| Kir capital (−OE) | 2,400 | |
| Accounts receivable—net (−A) | | 30,000 |

To record collection of $22,000 of accounts receivable and to write off the remaining $8,000 receivables as a loss charged to the partners' capital accounts in their residual profit- and loss-sharing ratios.

### PART B: TO RECORD LIABILITY PAYMENT AND FINAL DISTRIBUTION TO PARTNERS

| | | |
|---|---|---|
| Accounts payable (−L) | 40,000 | |
| Cash (−A) | | 40,000 |

To record payment of nonpartner liabilities.

| | | |
|---|---|---|
| Loan from Hol (−L) | 10,000 | |
| Cash (−A) | | 10,000 |

To pay loan from Hol.

| | | |
|---|---|---|
| Hol capital (−OE) | 8,900 | |
| Kir capital (−OE) | 28,100 | |
| Cash (−A) | | 37,000 |

To distribute cash to partners in final liquidation of the partnership.

assets to settle their partnership obligations. If the partners with debit balances are without personal resources, the partners with positive equity absorb losses equal to the debit balances. Such losses are shared in the relative profit- and loss-sharing ratios of the partners with positive equity balances.

The partnership of Jay, Jim, and Joe is in the process of liquidation. The partnership accounts have the following balances after all assets have been converted into cash and all liabilities have been paid (amounts in thousands):

| | Debit | Credit |
|---|---|---|
| Cash | $25 | |
| Jay capital (40%) | 3 | |
| Jim capital (40%) | | $16 |
| Joe capital (20%) | | 12 |
| Total | $28 | $28 |

If Jay is personally solvent, he should pay $3,000 into the partnership to eliminate his debit capital account balance. His payment of $3,000 will bring the partnership cash up to $28,000, which can then be distributed to Jim and Joe in final liquidation of the partnership.

If Jay is unable to pay the debit balance, the debit balance represents a $3,000 loss to be absorbed by Jim and Joe according to their relative profit- and loss-sharing ratios. Jim's share of the loss is $2,000 ($3,000 × 0.4/0.6), and Joe's share is $1,000 ($3,000 × 0.2/0.6). In this case, the $25,000 is distributed $14,000 to Jim and $11,000 to Joe, and the partnership business is terminated.

EXHIBIT 17-2

Statement of
Partnership Liquidation

**HOL AND KIR PARTNERSHIP**
**STATEMENT OF PARTNERSHIP LIQUIDATION**
**FOR THE PERIOD JANUARY 1, 2017, TO JANUARY 31, 2017**
**(IN THOUSANDS)**

| | Cash | Noncash Assets | Priority Liabilities | Hol Loan | Hol Capital (70%) | Kir Capital (30%) |
|---|---|---|---|---|---|---|
| Balances January 1, 2017 | $10 | $100 | $40 | $10 | $25 | $35 |
| Sale of inventory | 25 | (30) | | | (3.5) | (1.5) |
| | 35 | 70 | 40 | 10 | 21.5 | 33.5 |
| Sale of plant assets | 30 | (40) | | | (7) | (3) |
| | 65 | 30 | 40 | 10 | 14.5 | 30.5 |
| Collection of receivables | 22 | (30) | | | (5.6) | (2.4) |
| | 87 | $ 0 | 40 | 10 | 8.9 | 28.1 |
| Payment of liabilities | (40) | | (40) | | | |
| | 47 | | $ 0 | 10 | 8.9 | 28.1 |
| Payment of Hol loan | (10) | | | (10) | | |
| | 37 | | | $ 0 | 8.9 | 28.1 |
| Final distribution to partners | (37) | | | | (8.9) | (28.1) |
| | $ 0 | | | | $ 0 | $ 0 |

UPA assigns higher payment priority in liquidation to amounts owed to partners other than their capital balances. This priority is usually abandoned and the legal doctrine of *right of offset* is applied when the partner has a debit capital balance. In this situation, the amount owed to the partner offsets up to the debit capital balance amount.

For example, assume that the partnership of Jay, Jim, and Joe had the following account balances (in thousands):

| | Debit | Credit |
|---|---|---|
| Cash | $25 | |
| Loan from Jay | | $5 |
| Jay capital (40%) | 8 | |
| Jim capital (40%) | | 16 |
| Joe capital (20%) | | 12 |
| Total | $33 | $33 |

Under the right of offset rule, the loan from Jay would not be paid even though it has a higher-priority ranking in liquidation than the capital interests of Jim and Joe. Instead, it would be offset against Jay's debit capital balance, leaving Jay with a $3,000 obligation to Jim and Joe. If Jay is personally solvent, he pays $3,000 to the partnership so that Jim and Joe can receive the balances in their capital accounts in final liquidation.

If Jay is personally insolvent, however, the situation is changed considerably. In this case, Jay's personal creditors would have a prior claim on any money paid to Jay because personal creditors have a prior claim on personal assets. If the right of offset is applied by the partnership, $25,000 cash would be paid: $14,000 to Jim and $11,000 to Joe.

If the right of offset was not applied, Jay's personal creditors would be paid the amount of their claims up to $5,000, leaving less than $25,000 for distribution to Jim and Joe. If the entire $5,000 is paid to Jay's creditors, only $20,000 would be distributed to Jim and Joe.

Because of insufficient evidence that the right of offset rule is generally accepted by the courts, it has been recommended that the rule not be applied without agreement from the partners when a partner-creditor is personally insolvent.[1] Upon dissolution and subject to the rights of creditors, partners can agree to different property distributions than provided for under UPA.[2]

## SAFE PAYMENTS TO PARTNERS

LEARNING OBJECTIVE **17.3**

Ordinarily, the process of liquidating a business takes considerable time. Some cash may become available for distribution to partners after all liabilities are paid but before all noncash assets are converted into cash. If the partners decide to distribute available cash before all noncash assets are sold (and before all gains or losses are recognized), the question arises as to how much cash can be safely distributed to the individual partners. **Safe payments** are distributions that can be made to partners with assurance that the amounts distributed will not need to be returned to the partnership at some later date to cover known liabilities or realign partner capital.

The calculation of safe payments is based on the following assumptions: (1) All partners are personally insolvent, and (2) all noncash assets represent possible losses. In addition, when calculating safe payments, the partnership may withhold specific amounts of cash on hand to cover liquidation expenses, unrecorded liabilities, and general contingencies. The amounts of cash withheld are contingent losses to the partners and are considered losses for purposes of determining safe payments.

### Application of a Safe Payments Schedule

Assume that the partnership of Buz, Max, and Nan is in the process of liquidation and that its account balances are as follows (in thousands):

| Debits | | Credits | |
|---|---|---|---|
| Cash | $80 | Loan payable to Nan | $20 |
| Loan due from Max | 10 | Buz capital (50%) | 50 |
| Land | 20 | Max capital (30%) | 70 |
| Buildings—Net | 140 | Nan capital (20%) | 110 |
| | $250 | | $250 |

All liabilities other than to partners have been paid, and the partners expect the sale of the land and buildings to take several months. Therefore, they agree that all cash on hand other than $10,000 to cover expenses and contingencies should be distributed immediately. Given this information, a schedule of safe payments (Exhibit 17-3) is prepared to determine the amount of cash that can be safely distributed to each partner.

The safe payments schedule begins with the equity of each partner shown on the top line. Partner equity is determined by combining the capital and loan balances for each of the partners. Possible losses are allocated to the partners in their profit- and loss-sharing ratios and are deducted from partner equity balances in the safe payments schedule in the same manner that actual losses would be deducted.

The possible losses shown in Exhibit 17-3 include the $160,000 book value of the land and buildings (the only noncash assets) and the $10,000 cash withheld from distribution. After possible losses are deducted from the equity of each partner for purposes of safe payment calculations, some partners may show negative equity. The negative amounts must be allocated to the partners with positive equity balances using their relative profit- and loss-sharing ratios. Allocations are continued until none of the partners shows negative equity. At that point, the sum of the amounts shown for partners with equity balances will be equal to the cash available for distribution. In Exhibit 17-3, the allocations are continued until Nan's equity shows a $70,000 balance and the equity of Buz and Max is zero. Thus, the $70,000 can be safely distributed to Nan, but nothing can be safely distributed to either Buz or Max.

---

[1]Stephen A. Zeff, "Right of Offset vs. Partnership Act in Winding-up Process," *Accounting Review* (January 1957), pp. 68–70.

[2]*Anderson v. Anderson*, 1958, 138 A.2d 880, 215 Md. 483.

EXHIBIT 17-3

Safe Payments Schedule

| BUZ, MAX, AND NAN PARTNERSHIP SCHEDULE OF SAFE PAYMENTS (AMOUNTS IN THOUSANDS) | Possible Losses | Buz Equity (50%) | Max Equity (30%) | Nan Equity (20%) |
|---|---|---|---|---|
| Partners' equities (capital ± loan balances) | | $50 | $60 | $130 |
| Possible loss on noncash assets | | | | |
| Book value of land and buildings | $160 | (80) | (48) | (32) |
| | | (30) | 12 | 98 |
| Possible loss on contingencies | | | | |
| Cash withheld for contingencies | 10 | (5) | (3) | (2) |
| | | (35) | 9 | 96 |
| Possible loss from Buz | | | | |
| Buz's debit balance allocated 60:40 to Max and Nan | | 35 | (21) | (14) |
| | | $ 0 | (12) | 82 |
| Possible loss from Max | | | | |
| Max's debit balance assigned to Nan | | | 12 | (12) |
| | | | $ 0 | $ 70 |

Note that the safe payments schedule is used *only* to determine the amount of advance distribution. The safe payments schedule does not affect account balances or the statement of partnership liquidation. Actual cash distributed to Nan is recorded in the usual fashion, with Nan's loan balance being reduced to zero before her capital account is reduced. The journal entry is as follows (in thousands):

| | | |
|---|---|---|
| Loan payable to Nan (−L) | 20 | |
| Nan capital (−OE) | 50 | |
| Cash (−A) | | 70 |

After this entry is recorded, the account balances of the Buz, Max, and Nan partnership are as follows (in thousands):

| **Debits** | | **Credits** | |
|---|---|---|---|
| Cash | $ 10 | Buz capital (50%) | $ 50 |
| Loan due from Max | 10 | Max capital (30%) | 70 |
| Land | 20 | Nan capital (20%) | 60 |
| Buildings—net | 140 | | |
| | $180 | | $180 |

The partnership loan to Max can be charged to the capital balance of Max at any time, subject to the approval of the partners. Ordinarily, partnership loans to partners should be charged against partner capital balances at the beginning of the liquidation process.

## Advance Distribution Requires Partner Approval

Any distribution to partners before all gains and losses have been realized and recognized requires approval of all partners. Assume that Vax, Yoo, and Zeb are partners sharing profits and losses equally and that the partnership is in the process of liquidation with the following account balances after all nonpartner liabilities have been paid (amounts in thousands):

| Debits | | Credits | |
|---|---|---|---|
| Cash | $30 | Vax loan | $15 |
| Equipment | 45 | Yoo capital | 30 |
| Vax capital | 10 | Zeb capital | 40 |
| | $85 | | $85 |

If available cash is to be distributed, $10,000 should be paid to Yoo and $20,000 to Zeb according to the following safe payments computations (in thousands):

| | Possible Losses | Vax Equity | Yoo Equity | Zeb Equity |
|---|---|---|---|---|
| Partners' equities | | $5 | $30 | $40 |
| Possible loss on noncash asset: | | | | |
| Equipment | $45 | (15) | (15) | (15) |
| | | (10) | 15 | 25 |
| Possible loss on Vax's debit | | | | |
| balance shared 50:50 | | 10 | (5) | (5) |
| Safe payments | | $0 | $10 | $20 |

Vax may object to the immediate distribution of the $30,000 cash to Yoo and Zeb because his $15,000 loan to the partnership has a higher priority in liquidation than the capital balances of Yoo and Zeb. The objection means that the partners do not agree to the advance distribution of cash, and accordingly, all distributions to partners are delayed until all assets are converted into cash and a final settlement can be made.

## INSTALLMENT LIQUIDATIONS

**Installment liquidation** involves the distribution of cash to partners as it becomes available during the liquidation period and before all liquidation gains and losses have been realized. The alternative is a simple liquidation, in which no cash is distributed to partners until all gains and losses on liquidation are realized and reflected in the partners' capital account balances.

### General Principles of Installment Liquidation

An orderly liquidation of a solvent partnership may be carried out with distributions of available cash on a regular basis until all noncash assets are converted into cash. Liabilities other than those to the partners must be paid before any distributions are made to the partners.

Once cash is available for distribution to partners, the amounts to be distributed to individual partners can be determined by preparing a schedule of safe payments for each installment distribution. A safe payments schedule will not be necessary, however, when the capital accounts at the start of the liquidation process are in the relative profit- and loss-sharing ratios of the partners and there are no partner loan or advance balances. In this case, all distributions to partners will be made in the relative profit- and loss-sharing ratios.

When installment payments to partners are determined using safe payments schedules, the order of distributions will be such that the remaining capital balances (equity balances if there are loans with partners) after each distribution will be ever closer to alignment with the profit- and loss-sharing ratios of the partners. Once all partners are included in an installment distribution, the remaining capital balances (equities) will be aligned, and further installment payments will be in the profit-sharing ratios. Thus, even though the capital accounts (equities) are not aligned at the start of the liquidation process, if all partners are included in the first installment, future installment payments to partners will be in the profit-sharing ratios, and additional safe payments schedules are not necessary.

### Installment Liquidation Illustration

The partnership of Deb, Ken, and Ren is to be liquidated as soon as possible after December 31, 2016. All cash on hand except for a $20,000 contingency balance is to be distributed at the end of each month until the liquidation is completed. Profits and losses are shared 50 percent, 30 percent, and 20 percent by Deb, Ken, and Ren, respectively. The partnership balance sheet at December 31, 2016, contains the following (in thousands):

**DEB, KEN, AND REN**
**BALANCE SHEET**
**AT DECEMBER 31, 2016**

| Assets | | Liabilities and Capital | |
|---|---|---|---|
| Cash | $ 240 | Accounts payable | $ 300 |
| Accounts receivable—net | 280 | Note payable | 200 |
| Loan to Ren | 40 | Loan from Ken | 20 |
| Inventories | 400 | Deb capital (50%) | 340 |
| Land | 100 | Ken capital (30%) | 340 |
| Equipment—net | 300 | Ren capital (20%) | 200 |
| Goodwill | 40 | | |
| | $1,400 | | $1,400 |

A summary of liquidation events is as follows:

*January 2017* — The loan to Ren is offset against his capital balance, the goodwill is written off, $200,000 is collected on account, inventory items that cost $160,000 are sold for $200,000, nonowner liabilities are settled at recorded values, and cash is distributed.

*February 2017* — Equipment with a book value of $80,000 is sold for $60,000, the remaining inventory items are sold for $180,000, liquidation expenses of $4,000 are paid, a liability of $8,000 is discovered and paid, and cash is distributed.

*March 2017* — The land is sold for $150,000, liquidation expenses of $5,000 are paid, and cash is distributed.

*April 2017* — Remaining equipment is sold for $150,000, the remaining receivables are written off, and all cash on hand is distributed in final liquidation of the partnership.

**JANUARY LIQUIDATION EVENTS**   The events of the Deb, Ken, and Ren partnership during the month of January 2017 are recorded as follows (in thousands):

| | | |
|---|---|---|
| Ren capital (−OE) | 40 | |
|     Loan to Ren (−A) | | 40 |
|   To offset loan against capital. | | |
| Deb capital (−OE) | 20 | |
| Ken capital (−OE) | 12 | |
| Ren capital (−OE) | 8 | |
|     Goodwill (−A) | | 40 |
|   To write off goodwill. | | |
| Cash (+A) | 200 | |
|     Accounts receivable (−A) | | 200 |
|   To record collection of receivables. | | |
| Cash (+A) | 200 | |
|     Inventories (−A) | | 160 |
|     Deb capital (+OE) | | 20 |
|     Ken capital (+OE) | | 12 |
|     Ren capital (+OE) | | 8 |
|   To record sale of inventory items at a gain. | | |
| Accounts payable (−L) | 300 | |
| Note payable (−L) | 200 | |
|     Cash (−A) | | 500 |
|   To record payment of nonpartner liabilities. | | |
| Loan from Ken (−L) | 20 | |
| Ken capital (−OE) | 100 | |
|     Cash (−A) | | 120 |
|   To record distribution of cash to Ken. | | |

In addition to being recorded in the accounts, each of the foregoing entries should be reflected in a statement of partnership liquidation, such as the one shown in Exhibit 17-4. A liquidation statement is a continuous record that summarizes all transactions and events during the liquidation period, and it will not be complete until the liquidation is finalized. The statement shown in Exhibit 17-4 for January events is really an interim statement. However, interim liquidation statements are probably more important than the final liquidation statement because interim statements show the progress that has been made toward liquidation to date and can provide a basis for current decisions as well as future planning. The completed liquidation statement can do little more than provide interested parties with an ability to check what has been done. The partnership liquidation statement may be an acceptable legal document for partnerships that are liquidated through a bankruptcy court.[3]

In the cash distribution that is made on January 31, 2017 (see Exhibit 17-4), the partnership has $140,000 in cash remaining after all nonpartner debts have been paid. Of this amount, $20,000 is retained by the partnership for contingencies, and $120,000 is available for distribution to the partners. The safe payments schedule that appears in Exhibit 17-5 shows that the full $120,000 should be distributed to Ken. The partnership has a $20,000 loan payable to Ken, so the first $20,000 distributed to Ken is applied to the loan, and the remaining $100,000 is charged to Ken's capital account.

**EXHIBIT 17-4**

Interim Statement of Partnership Liquidation

### DEB, KEN, AND REN
### STATEMENT OF PARTNERSHIP LIQUIDATION
### FOR THE PERIOD JANUARY 1, 2017, TO FEBRUARY 1, 2017 (AMOUNTS IN THOUSANDS)

| | Cash | Noncash Assets | Priority Liabilities | 50% Deb Capital | Ken Loan | 30% Ken Capital | 20% Ren Capital |
|---|---|---|---|---|---|---|---|
| Balances January 1 | $240 | $1,160 | $500 | $340 | $20 | $340 | $200 |
| Offset Ren loan | | (40) | | | | | (40) |
| Write-off of goodwill | | (40) | | (20) | | (12) | (8) |
| Collection of receivables | 200 | (200) | | | | | |
| Sale of inventory items | 200 | (160) | | 20 | | 12 | 8 |
| Predistribution balances January 31 | 640 | 720 | 500 | 340 | 20 | 340 | 160 |
| January distribution (see Exhibit 17-5) | | | | | | | |
| Creditors | (500) | | (500) | | | | |
| Ken | (120) | | | | (20) | (100) | |
| Balances February 1 | $ 20 | $ 720 | $ 0 | $340 | $ 0 | $240 | $160 |

### DEB, KEN, AND REN
### SCHEDULE OF SAFE PAYMENTS
### JANUARY 31, 2017 (AMOUNTS IN THOUSANDS)

**EXHIBIT 17-5**

First Installment—Safe Payments Schedule

| | Possible Losses | 50% Deb Capital | 30% Ken Capital and Loan | 20% Ren Capital |
|---|---|---|---|---|
| Partners' equities January 31, 2017 (see statement of liquidation) | | $340 | $360 | $160 |
| Possible loss on noncash assets (see statement of liquidation) | $720 | (360) | (216) | (144) |
| | | (20) | 144 | 16 |
| Possible loss on contingencies: Cash withheld | 20 | (10) | (6) | (4) |
| | | (30) | 138 | 12 |
| Possible loss from Deb: Debit balance allocated 60:40 | | 30 | (18) | (12) |
| | | $ 0 | $120 | $ 0 |

[3]When a partnership is liquidated under Chapter 7 of the Bankruptcy Act, court approval is required for all distributions.

**FEBRUARY LIQUIDATION EVENTS**    Journal entries to record the February 2017 events of the Deb, Ken, and Ren liquidation are as follows (in thousands):

| | | |
|---|---:|---:|
| Cash (+A) | 60 | |
| Deb capital (−OE) | 10 | |
| Ken capital (−OE) | 6 | |
| Ren capital (−OE) | 4 | |
|     Equipment—Net (−A) | | 80 |
| To record sale of equipment at a $20,000 loss. | | |
| Cash (+A) | 180 | |
| Deb capital (−OE) | 30 | |
| Ken capital (−OE) | 18 | |
| Ren capital (−OE) | 12 | |
|     Inventories (−A) | | 240 |
| To record sale of remaining inventory items at a $60,000 loss. | | |
| Deb capital (−OE) | 2 | |
| Ken capital (−OE) | 1.2 | |
| Ren capital (−OE) | .8 | |
|     Cash (−A) | | 4 |
| To record payment of liquidation expenses. | | |
| Deb capital (−OE) | 4 | |
| Ken capital (−OE) | 2.4 | |
| Ren capital (−OE) | 1.6 | |
|     Accounts payable (+L) | | 8 |
| To record identification of an unrecorded liability. | | |
| Accounts payable (−L) | 8 | |
|     Cash (−A) | | 8 |
| To record payment of accounts payable. | | |
| Deb capital (−OE) | 84 | |
| Ken capital (−OE) | 86.4 | |
| Ren capital (−OE) | 57.6 | |
|     Cash (−A) | | 228 |
| To record distribution of cash to partners. | | |

Exhibit 17-6 reflects these entries in a liquidation statement for the period January 1, 2017, to March 1, 2017. Exhibit 17-7 shows computations for the amount of cash distributed to partners on February 28, 2017. All the partners are included in the February 28 distribution, so all future distributions will be in the profit- and loss-sharing ratios, provided that the liquidation proceeds as planned.

The plan of distribution can be upset by events such as the distribution of noncash assets to specific partners. In the liquidation of a medical practice partnership, for example, doctors might withdraw equipment early in the liquidation process in order to continue their own practices. When noncash assets are distributed to partners, the fair value of such assets should be determined, and any difference between fair value and book value should be recognized as a partnership gain or loss. The distribution of noncash assets to specific partners and the valuation of the property distributed must be approved by all partners.

**MARCH AND APRIL LIQUIDATION EVENTS**    By March 2017, the liquidation of the Deb, Ken, and Ren partnership has progressed to a point at which partner capital balances are in their relative profit- and loss-sharing ratios. Journal entries for the events of March and April are as follows (in thousands):

| | | |
|---|---:|---:|
| *Entries for March* | | |
| Cash (+A) | 150 | |
|     Deb capital (+OE) | | 25 |
|     Ken capital (+OE) | | 15 |
|     Ren capital (+OE) | | 10 |
|     Land (−A) | | 100 |
| To record sale of land at a $50,000 gain. | | |
| Deb capital (−OE) | 2.5 | |
| Ken capital (−OE) | 1.5 | |
| Ren capital (−OE) | 1 | |
|     Cash (−A) | | 5 |
| To record payment of liquidation expenses. | | |

| | | | | |
|---|---|---|---|---|
| Deb capital (−OE) | 72.5 | | | |
| Ken capital (−OE) | 43.5 | | | |
| Ren capital (−OE) | 29 | | | |
|     Cash (−A) | | 145 | | |

To record the March distribution of cash to partners.

*Entries for April*

| | | |
|---|---|---|
| Cash (+A) | 150 | |
| Deb capital (−OE) | 35 | |
| Ken capital (−OE) | 21 | |
| Ren capital (−OE) | 14 | |
|     Equipment—net (−A) | | 220 |

To record sale of the remaining equipment at a $70,000 loss.

| | | |
|---|---|---|
| Deb capital (−OE) | 40 | |
| Ken capital (−OE) | 24 | |
| Ren capital (−OE) | 16 | |
|     Accounts receivable (−A) | | 80 |

To record write-off of remaining receivables.

| | | |
|---|---|---|
| Deb capital (−OE) | 85 | |
| Ken capital (−OE) | 51 | |
| Ren capital (−OE) | 34 | |
|     Cash (−A) | | 170 |

To record distribution of cash to partners in final liquidation.

## EXHIBIT 17-6

**Interim Statement of Partnership Liquidation**

**DEB, KEN, AND REN
STATEMENT OF PARTNERSHIP LIQUIDATION
FOR THE PERIOD JANUARY 1, 2017, TO MARCH 1, 2017 (AMOUNTS IN THOUSANDS)**

| | Cash | Noncash Assets | Priority Liabilities | Deb Capital (50%) | Ken Loan | Ken Capital (30%) | Ren Capital (20%) |
|---|---|---|---|---|---|---|---|
| Balances January 1 | $240 | $1,160 | $500 | $340 | $20 | $340 | $200 |
| Offset Ren loan | | (40) | | | | | (40) |
| Write-off of goodwill | | (40) | | (20) | | (12) | (8) |
| Collection of receivables | 200 | (200) | | | | | |
| Sale of inventory items | 200 | (160) | | 20 | | 12 | 8 |
| Predistribution balances January 31 | 640 | 720 | 500 | 340 | 20 | 340 | 160 |
| January distribution (see Exhibit 17-5) | | | | | | | |
|   Creditors | (500) | | (500) | | | | |
|   Ken | (120) | | | | (20) | (100) | |
| Balances February 1 | 20 | 720 | 0 | 340 | $0 | 240 | 160 |
| Equipment sale | 60 | (80) | | (10) | | (6) | (4) |
| Sale of inventory items | 180 | (240) | | (30) | | (18) | (12) |
| Liquidation expenses | (4) | | | (2) | | (1.2) | (.8) |
| Liability discovered | | | 8 | (4) | | (2.4) | (1.6) |
| Predistribution balances February 28 | 256 | 400 | 8 | 294 | | 212.4 | 141.6 |
| February distribution (see Exhibit 17-7) | | | | | | | |
|   Creditors | (8) | | (8) | | | | |
|   Partners | (228) | | | (84) | | (86.4) | (57.6) |
| Balances March 1 | $ 20 | $ 400 | $0 | $210 | | $126 | $84 |

## DEB, KEN, AND REN
## SCHEDULE OF SAFE PAYMENTS
## FEBRUARY 28, 2017 (AMOUNTS IN THOUSANDS)

| | Possible Losses | Deb Capital (50%) | Ken Capital (30%) | Ren Capital (20%) |
|---|---|---|---|---|
| Partners' equities February 28, 2017 (see statement of liquidation) | | $294 | $212.4 | $141.6 |
| Possible loss on noncash assets (see statement of liquidation) | $400 | (200) | (120) | (80) |
| | | 94 | 92.4 | 61.6 |
| Possible loss on contingencies: Cash withheld | 20 | (10) | (6) | (4) |
| | | $ 84 | $ 86.4 | $57.6 |

Exhibit 17-8 reflects these entries in a complete liquidation statement for the partnership. The complete liquidation statement covers the period January 1 to April 30, 2017. The March and April cash distributions to partners are in the relative profit- and loss-sharing ratios, so safe payments computations are not necessary. The $145,000 distributed to partners on March 31 is determined

## DEB, KEN, AND REN
## STATEMENT OF PARTNERSHIP LIQUIDATION
## FOR THE PERIOD JANUARY 1, 2017, TO APRIL 30, 2017 (AMOUNTS IN THOUSANDS)

| | Cash | Noncash Assets | Priority Liabilities | Deb Capital (50%) | Ken Loan | Ken Capital (30%) | Ren Capital (20%) |
|---|---|---|---|---|---|---|---|
| Balances January 1 | $240 | $1,160 | $500 | $340 | $20 | $340 | $200 |
| Offset Ren loan | | (40) | | | | | (40) |
| Write-off of goodwill | | (40) | | (20) | | (12) | (8) |
| Collection of receivables | 200 | (200) | | | | | |
| Sale of inventory items | 200 | (160) | | 20 | | 12 | 8 |
| Predistribution balances January 31 | 640 | 720 | 500 | 340 | 20 | 340 | 160 |
| January distribution (see Exhibit 17-5) | | | | | | | |
| Creditors | (500) | | (500) | | | | |
| Ken | (120) | | | | (20) | (100) | |
| Balances February 1 | 20 | 720 | 0 | 340 | $0 | 240 | 160 |
| Equipment sale | 60 | (80) | | (10) | | (6) | (4) |
| Sale of inventory items | 180 | (240) | | (30) | | (18) | (12) |
| Liquidation expenses | (4) | | | (2) | | (1.2) | (.8) |
| Liability discovered | | | 8 | (4) | | (2.4) | (1.6) |
| Predistribution balances February 28 | 256 | 400 | 8 | 294 | | 212.4 | 141.6 |
| February distribution (see Exhibit 17-7) | | | | | | | |
| Creditors | (8) | | (8) | | | | |
| Partners | (228) | | | (84) | | (86.4) | (57.6) |
| Balances March 1 | 20 | 400 | $ 0 | 210 | | 126 | 84 |

| Sale of land | 150 | (100) | | 25 | | 15 | 10 |
|---|---|---|---|---|---|---|---|
| Liquidation expenses | (5) | | | (2.5) | | (1.5) | (1) |
| Predistribution balances March 31 | 165 | 300 | | 232.5 | | 139.5 | 93 |
| March distribution (50:30:20) | (145) | | | (72.5) | | (43.5) | (29) |
| Balances April 1 | 20 | 300 | | 160 | | 96 | 64 |
| Sale of equipment | 150 | (220) | | (35) | | (21) | (14) |
| Write-off of receivables | | (80) | | (40) | | (24) | (16) |
| Predistribution balances April 30 | 170 | $  0 | | 85 | | 51 | 34 |
| April distribution (50:30:20) | (170) | | | (85) | | (51) | (34) |
| Liquidation completed April 30 | $  0 | | | $  0 | | $  0 | $  0 |

by subtracting the $20,000 cash reserve from the $165,000 cash balance immediately before the distribution. All remaining cash is remitted to the partners in the final installment distribution on April 30, 2017.

## CASH DISTRIBUTION PLANS

LEARNING OBJECTIVE **17.5**

Safe payments schedules are an effective method of computing the amount of safe payments to partners and of preventing excessive payments to any partner. However, the approach is inefficient if numerous installment distributions are made to partners, because a safe payments schedule must be prepared for each distribution until the capital balances are aligned with the profit- and loss-sharing ratios. The safe payments schedule approach is also deficient as a planning device because it does not provide information that will help the partners' project when they can expect to be included in cash distributions. These deficiencies of the safe payments approach can be overcome by preparing a cash distribution plan at the start of the liquidation process.

The development of a **cash distribution plan** (also referred to as a *cash predistribution plan*) for the liquidation of a partnership involves ranking the partners in terms of their vulnerability to possible losses, using the vulnerability ranking to prepare a schedule of assumed loss absorption, and developing a cash distribution plan from the assumed-loss-absorption schedule. In illustrating the preparation of a cash distribution plan, the Deb, Ken, and Ren example is used again.

### Vulnerability Ranking

At the inception of the liquidation process, Deb, Ken, and Ren had capital balances of $340,000, $340,000, and $200,000, respectively, but their equities (capital ± loan balances) were $340,000, $360,000, and $160,000, respectively. In determining their vulnerability to possible losses, the equity of each partner is divided by his or her profit-sharing ratio to identify the maximum loss that the partner could absorb without reducing his or her equity below zero. **Vulnerability rankings** for Deb, Ken, and Ren are determined as follows:

**DEB, KEN, AND REN VULNERABILITY RANKING**

| | Partner's Equity | | Profit-Sharing Ratio | | Loss Absorption Potential | Vulnerability Ranking (1 most vulnerable) |
|---|---|---|---|---|---|---|
| Deb | $340,000 | ÷ | 0.5 | = | $680,000 | 1 |
| Ken | 360,000 | ÷ | 0.3 | = | 1,200,000 | 3 |
| Ren | 160,000 | ÷ | 0.2 | = | 800,000 | 2 |

The vulnerability ranks indicate that Deb is most vulnerable to losses because her equity would be reduced to zero with a total partnership loss on liquidation of $680,000. Ken, on the other hand, is least vulnerable because his equity is sufficient to absorb his share of liquidation losses up to $1,200,000. This interpretation helps explain why Ken received all the cash distributed to partners in the first installment distribution in the previous illustration.

## Assumed Loss Absorption

A **schedule of assumed loss absorption** is prepared as a second step in developing the cash distribution plan. This schedule starts with the preliquidation equities and charges each partner's equity with its share of the loss that would exactly eliminate the equity of the most vulnerable partner. The next step is to charge each remaining partner's equity with its share of the loss that would exactly eliminate the equity of the next most vulnerable partner. This process is continued until the equities of all but the least vulnerable partner have been reduced to zero. A schedule of assumed loss absorption for the Deb, Ken, and Ren partnership is as follows (amounts in thousands):

### DEB, KEN, AND REN SCHEDULE OF ASSUMED LOSS ABSORPTION

|  | Deb (50%) | Ken (30%) | Ren (20%) | Total |
|---|---|---|---|---|
| Preliquidation equities | $340 | $360 | $160 | $860 |
| Assumed loss to absorb Deb's equity (allocated 50:30:20) | (340) | (204) | (136) | (680) |
| Balances | $0 | 156 | 24 | 180 |
| Assumed loss to absorb Ren's equity (allocated 60:40) |  | (36) | (24) | (60) |
| Balances |  | $120 | $ 0 | $120 |

The partnership loss that exactly eliminates Deb's equity is $680,000, an amount computed in preparing the vulnerability ranks. After Deb's equity is reduced to zero in the first step, losses are divided 60 percent to Ken and 40 percent to Ren until Ren's equity is reduced to zero. The additional partnership loss that reduces Ren's equity to zero is $60,000—Ren's $24,000 equity divided by his 40 percent profit-sharing ratio after Deb is eliminated from consideration (in other words, it is assumed that Deb is personally insolvent). After Ren's equity has been reduced to zero, the equity of Ken, the least vulnerable partner, stands at $120,000.

## Cash Distribution Plan

Ken should receive the first $120,000 distributed to the partners. A cash distribution plan for the Deb, Ken, and Ren partnership is prepared from the schedule of assumed loss absorption as follows:

### DEB, KEN, AND REN CASH DISTRIBUTION PLAN

|  | Priority Liabilities | Ken Loan | Deb | Ken | Ren |
|---|---|---|---|---|---|
| First $500,000 | 100% |  |  |  |  |
| Next $20,000 |  | 100% |  |  |  |
| Next $100,000 |  |  |  | 100% |  |
| Next $60,000 |  |  |  | 60 | 40% |
| Remainder |  |  | 50% | 30 | 20 |

In developing the cash distribution plan, the first cash available for distribution goes to nonpartner creditors. These consist of the $300,000 accounts payable and the $200,000 note payable of the Deb, Ken, and Ren partnership at December 31, 2016. The next $20,000 goes to Ken to settle his loan to the partnership, because partner loans have a higher priority than partner capital balances. The next $100,000 available is distributed to Ken in consideration of his capital balance. This distribution aligns the capital and profit-sharing ratios of Ken and Ren. The next $60,000 is shared 60 percent and 40 percent between Ken and Ren. This distribution completes the alignment of all capital balances and profit-sharing ratios, and the remaining distributions are in accordance with the profit-sharing ratios.

Ken can analyze the cash distribution plan on January 1, 2017, and determine that he will begin to receive cash after $500,000 has been paid to priority creditors. Similarly, Ren and Deb can use the plan to determine their chances of recovering some or all of their partnership equities. For example, if Deb expects $800,000 to be realized from all partnership assets, she can easily compute the amount she would receive [($800,000 − $680,000) × 50% = $60,000].

## Cash Distribution Schedule

Further application of the cash distribution plan can be illustrated by assuming that the Deb, Ken, and Ren partnership is liquidated in two installments, with $550,000 cash being distributed in the first installment and $250,000 in the second and final installment. Under these assumptions, the cash distribution plan would be used in preparing a **cash distribution schedule**, such as the following one (amounts in thousands):

**DEB, KEN, AND REN CASH DISTRIBUTION SCHEDULE**

| | Cash Distributed | Priority Liabilities | Ken Loan | Deb Capital | Ken Capital | Ren Capital |
|---|---|---|---|---|---|---|
| *First Installment* | | | | | | |
| Priority creditors | $500 | $500 | | | | |
| Ken loan | 20 | | $20 | | | |
| Ken capital (remainder) | 30 | | | | $ 30 | |
| | $550 | $500 | $20 | | $ 30 | |
| *Second Installment* | | | | | | |
| Ken capital | $ 70 | | | | $ 70 | |
| Ken and Ren (60:40) | 60 | | | | 36 | $24 |
| Remainder (50:30:20) | 120 | | | $60 | 36 | 24 |
| | $250 | | | $60 | $142 | $48 |

The $550,000 cash distributed in the first installment is allocated $500,000 to nonpartner liabilities and $20,000 to repay the loan from Ken. The remaining $30,000 is paid to Ken to reduce the balance of his capital account. In the second installment distribution, as shown in the cash distribution schedule, Ken receives the first $70,000 in order to align his capital balance with that of Ren. The next $60,000 is allocated to Ken and Ren in accordance with their 60:40 relative profit- and loss-sharing ratios, and the final $120,000 is allocated to Deb, Ken, and Ren in their 50:30:20 relative profit- and loss-sharing ratios.

The information from the cash distribution schedule is used in the same manner as information from safe payments schedules. The cash payments indicated by the cash distribution schedules are entered in the statement of partnership liquidation and in the partnership records as cash distributions are actually made.

The preparation of a cash distribution plan is more time-consuming than the preparation of a single safe payments schedule. However, as shown here, the cash distribution plan provides a flexible and efficient means of determining safe payments to partners. In addition, the cash distribution plan aids in planning.

## INSOLVENT PARTNERS AND PARTNERSHIPS

LEARNING OBJECTIVE **17.6**

The order for distributing assets in the liquidation of a partnership was listed earlier in this chapter as:

I. Amounts owed to creditors and amounts owed to partners other than for capital and profits

II. Amounts due to partners after liquidation

This order of distribution is specified in UPA section 807.

### Insolvent Partnership

When a partnership is insolvent, the cash available after all noncash assets have been converted into cash is not enough to pay partnership creditors.[4] Partnership creditors will obtain partial recovery from partnership assets and will call upon individual partners to use their personal resources to satisfy remaining claims.

Partnership creditors can seek recovery of their claims from the personal assets of any partner who is personally solvent. Partners are required to contribute the amounts necessary to satisfy partnership liabilities. UPA is specific in stating that a partner must contribute his or her share of the payment to satisfy the liabilities, as well as his or her relative share of the liabilities of any partners who are insolvent or who cannot or will not contribute their share of the liabilities (see UPA Sections

---

[4]In this chapter, *insolvent partnership* means that partnership liabilities exceed the fair value of partnership assets. Under the Bankruptcy Act of 1978, a partnership is insolvent if partnership liabilities exceed the fair value of partnership assets plus the excess of each general partner's personal assets over personal debts (11 *USC*, paragraph 101[26]B).

807[a] and [c]). A partner who pays more than his or her share of partnership liabilities does, of course, have a claim against partners with debit capital balances.

Rik, Fab, and Kat are partners sharing profits equally. Their partnership is in the process of liquidation. After all assets have been converted into cash and all available cash applied to payment of partnership liabilities, the following account balances remain on the partnership books (amounts in thousands):

| | |
|---|---|
| Liabilities | $90 CR |
| Rik capital (1/3) | 30 DR |
| Fab capital (1/3) | 30 DR |
| Kat capital (1/3) | 30 DR |

Provided that all partners have personal resources of at least $30,000, each partner should pay $30,000 into the partnership in full satisfaction of partnership liabilities. However, the creditors may collect the full $90,000 deficiency from any one of the partners. For example, creditors may collect the $90,000 from Rik, in which case the remaining partnership balances would be as follows (in thousands):

| | |
|---|---|
| Rik capital | $60 CR |
| Fab capital | 30 DR |
| Kat capital | 30 DR |

If Fab and Kat can each pay $30,000 into the partnership, the fact that the creditors proceeded against Rik is of no great concern. However, if the creditors proceeded against Rik because Kat is personally insolvent and Fab's net personal assets are only $35,000, the situation is changed considerably. In this case, Rik and Fab share equally the $30,000 loss on Kat's insolvency, after which Rik will have a $45,000 credit capital balance and Fab will have a $45,000 debit capital balance. Fab's personal assets are only $35,000, so Rik proceeds to collect the $35,000 from Fab, and the remaining $10,000 debit balance in Fab's capital account is written off as a loss to Rik.

The examples in this section illustrate some of the common problems that can arise in liquidations of partnerships that are insolvent or in which there are insolvent partners.

## SUMMARY

The liquidation of a partnership involves converting noncash assets into cash, recognizing gains and losses during the liquidation period, paying liabilities, and distributing cash to partners in final termination of the business entity. A *simple liquidation* refers to the conversion of all assets into cash before any distributions are made to partners.

A primary financial statement of a liquidating partnership is the statement of partnership liquidation, which summarizes all financial transactions and events during the liquidation period. This statement may also be used as a legal document for liquidations carried out under the jurisdiction of a court.

When partnerships are liquidated through installment distributions to partners, cash is distributed to partners after liabilities have been paid but before all gains and losses on liquidation are recognized in the accounts. To prevent excessive payments to any partner, the amount of cash to be distributed is computed on the basis of two assumptions—that all partners are personally insolvent and that all noncash assets are actual losses. Two approaches exist for computing the amounts that can be safely paid to partners in each installment distribution. A safe payments schedule may be prepared for each installment distribution, or a cash distribution plan may be prepared that can be used throughout the liquidation process.

The Uniform Partnership Act of 1997 (UPA) specifies priorities for the distribution of partnership assets in liquidations and for the distribution of the personal assets of insolvent partners. Partnership creditors rank first in recovering their claims from partnership property. Priorities for other claims depend on whether the partnership or the individual partners are insolvent, and each case requires separate analysis.

## QUESTIONS

1. How does partnership liquidation differ from partnership dissolution?
2. What is simple partnership liquidation, and how are distributions to partners computed?
3. UPA specifies a priority ranking for distribution of partnership assets in liquidation. What is the ranking?
4. What is the right of offset rule? How does it affect the amount to be distributed to partners in liquidation?
5. What assumptions are made in determining the amount of distributions (or safe payments) to individual partners prior to the recognition of all gains and losses on liquidation?
6. What are partner equities? Why are partner equities rather than partner capital balances used in the preparation of safe payments schedules?
7. How do safe payments computations affect partnership ledger account balances?
8. What is a statement of partnership liquidation, and how is the statement helpful to partners and other parties involved in partnership liquidation?
9. A partnership in liquidation has satisfied all of its nonpartner liabilities and has cash available for distribution to partners. Under what circumstances would it be permissible to divide available cash in the profit-and loss-sharing ratios of the partners?
10. What are vulnerability ranks? How are they used in the preparation of cash distribution plans for partnership liquidations?
11. If a partnership is insolvent, how is the amount of cash distributed to individual partners determined?
12. When all partnership assets have been distributed in the liquidation of a partnership, some partners may have debit capital balances and others may have credit capital balances. How are such balances eliminated if the partners with debit balances are personally solvent? What if they are personally insolvent?

## EXERCISES

### E 17-1
### Simple liquidation—Schedule of cash available

The partnership of Flo and Fay is in the process of liquidation. On January 1, 2016, the ledger shows account balances as follows:

| Cash | $10,000 | Accounts payable | $25,000 |
|------|---------|------------------|---------|
| Accounts receivable | 45,000 | Flo capital | 45,000 |
| Lumber inventory | 50,000 | Fay capital | 35,000 |

On January 10, 2016, the lumber inventory is sold for $40,000, and during January, accounts receivable of $41,000 is collected. No further collections on the receivables are expected. Profits are shared 60 percent to Flo and 40 percent to Fay.

**REQUIRED:** Prepare a schedule showing how the cash available on February 1, 2016, should be distributed.

### E 17-2
### Liquidation—Journal entries

After closing entries were made on December 31, 2016, the ledger of Mac, Nan, and Obe contained the following balances:

| Cash | $39,000 | Accounts payable | $5,000 |
|------|---------|------------------|--------|
| Inventory | 16,000 | Mac capital (40%) | 15,000 |
| | | Nan capital (30%) | 8,000 |
| | | Obe capital (30%) | 27,000 |

Due to unsuccessful operations, the partners decide to liquidate the business. During January some of the inventory is sold at cost for $10,000, and on January 31, 2017, all available cash is distributed. It is not known if the remaining inventory items can be sold.

**REQUIRED:** Prepare all journal entries necessary to account for the transactions of the partnership during January 2017.

## E 17-3
### Liquidation—Cash distribution computation, safe payments schedule

Fed, Ela, and Luc have decided to liquidate their partnership. Account balances on January 1, 2016, are as follows:

| | | | |
|---|---|---|---|
| Cash | $160,000 | Accounts payable | $60,000 |
| Other assets | 180,000 | Fed capital (30%) | 110,000 |
| | $340,000 | Ela capital (30%) | 50,000 |
| | | Luc capital (40%) | 120,000 |
| | | | $340,000 |

The partners agree to keep a $30,000 contingency fund and to distribute available cash immediately.

**REQUIRED:** Determine the amount of cash that should be paid to each partner.

## E 17-4
### Liquidation—Cash distribution computation, safe payments schedule

Jan, Kim, and Lee announce plans to liquidate their partnership immediately. The assets, equities, and profit- and loss-sharing ratios are summarized as follows.

| | | | |
|---|---|---|---|
| Loan to Kim | $ 20,000 | Accounts payable | $ 60,000 |
| Other assets | 180,000 | Jan capital (50%) | 59,000 |
| | $200,000 | Kim capital (30%) | 29,000 |
| | | Lee capital (20%) | 52,000 |
| | | | $200,000 |

The other assets are sold for $120,000, and an overlooked bill for landscaping services of $5,000 is discovered. Kim cannot pay her partnership debt at the present time, but she expects to have the money in a month or two.

**REQUIRED:** Determine how cash should be distributed to creditors and partners.

## E 17-5
### Liquidation—Capital balance computation correcting an error

The profit- and loss-sharing agreement of the partnership of Ali, Bob, and Kia provides a salary allowance for Ali and Kia of $10,000 each. Partners receive a 10 percent interest allowance on their average capital balances for the year. The remainder is divided 40 percent to Ali, 20 percent to Bob, and 40 percent to Kia. The December 31, 2016, after-closing balances are as follows:

| | | | |
|---|---|---|---|
| Net assets | $150,000 | Ali capital | $ 60,000 |
| | | Bob capital | 25,000 |
| | | Kia capital | 65,000 |
| | | | $150,000 |

In January 2017 the partners are preparing to liquidate the business and discover that the year-end inventory was erroneously undervalued by $25,000, resulting in an error in calculating the 2016 net income.

**REQUIRED:** Determine the correct capital balances of Ali, Bob, and Kia.

## E 17-6
### Safe payments schedule

A condensed balance sheet with profit-sharing percentages for the Eve, Fae, and Gia partnership on January 1, 2016, shows the following:

| | | | |
|---|---|---|---|
| Cash | $100,000 | Liabilities | $80,000 |
| Other assets | 500,000 | Eve capital (40%) | 100,000 |
| | | Fae capital (40%) | 250,000 |
| | | Gia capital (20%) | 170,000 |
| | $600,000 | | $600,000 |

On January 2, 2016, the partners decide to liquidate the business, and during January they sell assets with a book value of $300,000 for $170,000.

**REQUIRED:** Prepare a safe payments schedule to show the amount of cash to be distributed to each partner if all available cash, except for a $10,000 contingency fund, is distributed immediately after the sale.

## E 17-7
## Statement of partnership liquidation

The partnership of Ali, Bev, and Cal became insolvent during 2016, and the partnership ledger shows the following balances after all partnership assets have been converted into cash and all available cash distributed:

|  | Debit | Credit |
|---|---|---|
| Accounts payable |  | $ 30,000 |
| Ali capital |  | 20,000 |
| Bev capital | $120,000 |  |
| Cal capital |  | 70,000 |
|  | $120,000 | $120,000 |

Profit- and loss-sharing percentages for the three partners are Ali, 30 percent; Bev, 40 percent; and Cal, 30 percent. The personal assets and liabilities of the partners are as follows:

|  | Ali | Bev | Cal |
|---|---|---|---|
| Personal assets | $60,000 | $110,000 | $60,000 |
| Personal liabilities | 50,000 | 60,000 | 40,000 |

**REQUIRED:** Prepare a schedule to show the phaseout of the partnership and final closing of the books if the partnership creditors recover $30,000 from Bev.

## E 17-8
## Statement of partnership liquidation—Partner insolvency case

After all partnership assets were converted into cash and all available cash distributed to creditors, the ledger of the Dan, Edd, and Fed partnership showed the following balances:

|  | Debit | Credit |
|---|---|---|
| Accounts payable |  | $20,000 |
| Dan capital (40%) |  | 10,000 |
| Edd capital (30%) |  | 60,000 |
| Fed capital (30%) | $90,000 |  |
|  | $90,000 | $90,000 |

The percentages indicated are residual profit- and loss-sharing ratios. Personal assets and liabilities of the partners are as follows:

|  | Dan | Edd | Fed |
|---|---|---|---|
| Personal assets | $50,000 | $50,000 | $100,000 |
| Personal liabilities | 45,000 | 40,000 | 40,000 |

The partnership creditors proceed against Fed for recovery of their claims, and the partners settle their claims against each other in accordance with UPA.

**REQUIRED:** Prepare a schedule to show the phaseout of the partnership and final closing of the books.

## E 17-9
## Statement of partnership liquidation—Partner insolvency case

The partnership of Ace, Ben, Cid, and Don is dissolved on January 5, 2016, and the account balances at June 30, 2016, after all noncash assets are converted into cash, are as follows:

|  | Debits | Credits |
|---|---|---|
| Cash | $200,000 |  |
| Cid capital (20%) | 170,000 |  |
| Don capital (10%) | 80,000 |  |
| Accounts payable |  | $400,000 |
| Ace capital (50%) |  | 40,000 |
| Ben capital (20%) |  | 10,000 |
|  | $450,000 | $450,000 |

## ADDITIONAL INFORMATION

1. The percentages indicated represent the relevant profit- and loss-sharing ratios.

2. Personal assets and liabilities of the partners at June 30, 2016, are as follows:

|  | Personal Assets | Personal Liabilities |
|---|---|---|
| Ace | $600,000 | $300,000 |
| Ben | 100,000 | 150,000 |
| Cid | 400,000 | 300,000 |
| Don | 100,000 | 20,000 |

3. Ace pays $200,000 into the partnership, and partnership liabilities are paid on July 1, 2016.

4. On July 15, 2016, Cid pays $100,000 into the partnership and Don pays $80,000. No further contributions from either Cid or Don are possible.

5. Losses from the bankruptcy of Cid are divided among the solvent partners on July 15, 2016.

6. Available cash is distributed and the partnership books are closed on July 31, 2016.

**REQUIRED:** Prepare a liquidation statement for the Ace, Ben, Cid, and Don Partnership for the period June 30, 2016, to July 31, 2016.

## E 17-10
### Safe payments schedule

The partnership of Dee, Ema, Lyn, and Geo is being liquidated over the first few months of 2016. The trial balance at January 1, 2016, is as follows:

|  | Debits | Credits |
|---|---|---|
| Cash | $200,000 | |
| Accounts receivable | 56,000 | |
| Inventory | 142,000 | |
| Equipment (net) | 300,000 | |
| Land | 150,000 | |
| Loan to Dee | 20,000 | |
| Accounts payable | | $400,000 |
| Dee capital (20%) | | 170,000 |
| Ema capital (10%) | | 80,000 |
| Lyn capital (50%) | | 140,000 |
| Geo capital (20%) | | 78,000 |
| | $868,000 | $868,000 |

## ADDITIONAL INFORMATION

1. The partners agree to retain $20,000 cash on hand for contingencies and to distribute the rest of the available cash at the end of each month.

2. In January, half of the receivables were collected. Inventory that cost $75,000 was liquidated for $45,000. The land was sold for $250,000.

**REQUIRED:** Prepare a schedule of safe payments for the Dee, Ema, Lyn, and Geo partnership for January 31, 2016.

## E 17-11
### Installment liquidation—Various situations

The assets and equities of the Sam, Red, and Sal partnership at the end of its fiscal year on October 31, 2016, are as follows:

| Assets | | Equities | |
|---|---|---|---|
| Cash | $ 15,000 | Liabilities | $ 50,000 |
| Receivables—net | 20,000 | Loan from Sal | 10,000 |
| Inventory | 40,000 | Sam capital (30%) | 45,000 |
| Plant assets—net | 70,000 | Red capital (50%) | 30,000 |
| Loan to Red | 5,000 | Sal capital (20%) | 15,000 |
| | $150,000 | | $150,000 |

The partners decide to liquidate the partnership. They estimate that the noncash assets, other than the loan to Red, can be converted into $100,000 cash over the two-month period ending December 31, 2016. Cash is to be distributed to the appropriate parties as it becomes available during the liquidation process.

**1.** The partner most vulnerable to partnership losses on liquidation is:
  a  *Sam*
  b  *Red*
  c  *Red and Sam equally*
  d  *Sal*

**2.** If $90,000 is available for the first distribution, it should be paid to:

| | Creditors, Including Sal | Sam | Red | Sal (Capital) |
|---|---|---|---|---|
| a | $60,000 | $18,000 | $0 | $12,000 |
| b | 60,000 | 9,000 | 15,000 | 6,000 |
| c | 50,000 | 12,000 | 20,000 | 8,000 |
| d | 60,000 | 27,000 | 0 | 3,000 |

**3.** If a total amount of $7,500 is available for distribution to partners after all nonpartner liabilities are paid, it should be paid as follows:

| | Sam | Red | Sal |
|---|---|---|---|
| a | $7,500 | $0 | $0 |
| b | 0 | 3,750 | 3,750 |
| c | 2,250 | 3,750 | 1,500 |
| d | 2,500 | 2,500 | 2,500 |

# E 17-12
## Liquidation—Various situations

**1.** In partnership liquidation the final cash distribution to the partners should be made in accordance with the:
  a  *Partner profit- and loss-sharing ratios*
  b  *Balances of partner capital accounts*
  c  *Ratio of the capital contributions by partners*
  d  *Safe payments computations*

**2.** In accounting for the liquidation of a partnership, cash payments to partners after all nonpartner creditors' claims have been satisfied, but before final cash distribution, should be according to:
  a  *Relative profit- and loss-sharing ratios*
  b  *The final balances in partner capital accounts*
  c  *The relative share of gain or loss on liquidation*
  d  *Safe payments computations*

**3.** After all noncash assets have been converted into cash in the liquidation of the Mal and Max partnership, the ledger contains the following account balances:

| | Debit | Credit |
|---|---|---|
| Cash | $34,000 | — |
| Accounts payable | — | $25,000 |
| Loan payable to Mal | — | 9,000 |
| Mal capital | 8,000 | — |
| Max capital | — | 8,000 |

Available cash should be distributed as follows: $25,000 to accounts payable and:
  a  *$9,000 for loan payable to Mal*
  b  *$4,500 each to Mal and Max*
  c  *$1,000 to Mal and $8,000 to Max*
  d  *$8,000 to Mal and $1,000 to Max*

4. The partnership of Gee, Ben, and Sim is liquidating and the ledger shows the following:

| | |
|---|---|
| Cash | $80,000 |
| Inventories | 100,000 |
| Accounts payable | 60,000 |
| Gee capital (50%) | 40,000 |
| Ben capital (25%) | 45,000 |
| Sim capital (25%) | 35,000 |

If all available cash is distributed immediately:

a **Gee, Ben, and Sim should get $26,667 each**
b **Gee, Ben, and Sim should get $6,667 each**
c **Gee should get $10,000, and Ben and Sim should get $5,000 each**
d **Ben should get $15,000, and Sim $5,000**

5. The following balance sheet summary, together with residual profit-sharing ratios, was developed on April 1, 2016, when the Doc, Fae, and Hal partnership began its liquidation:

| | | | |
|---|---|---|---|
| Cash | $140,000 | Liabilities | $ 60,000 |
| Accounts receivable | 60,000 | Loan from Fae | 20,000 |
| Inventories | 85,000 | Doc capital (20%) | 75,000 |
| Plant assets—net | 200,000 | Fae capital (40%) | 200,000 |
| Loan to Doc | 25,000 | Hal capital (40%) | 155,000 |
| | $510,000 | | $510,000 |

If available cash except for a $5,000 contingency fund is distributed immediately, Doc, Fae, and Hal, respectively, should receive:

a **$0, $60,000, and $15,000**
b **$11,000, $22,000, and $22,000**
c **$0, $70,000, and $5,000**
d **$0, $27,500, and $27,500**

6. The partnership of Wes, Van, and Tom was dissolved on June 30, 2016, and account balances after noncash assets were converted into cash on September 1, 2016, are:

| | | | |
|---|---|---|---|
| Cash | $50,000 | Accounts payable | $120,000 |
| | | Wes capital (30%) | 90,000 |
| | | Van capital (30%) | (60,000) |
| | | Tom capital (40%) | (100,000) |

Personal assets and liabilities of the partners at September 1, 2016, are:

| | **Personal Assets** | **Personal Liabilities** |
|---|---|---|
| Wes | $80,000 | $90,000 |
| Van | 100,000 | 61,000 |
| Tom | 190,000 | 80,000 |

If Tom contributes $70,000 to the partnership to provide cash to pay the creditors, what amount of Wes's $90,000 partnership equity would appear to be recoverable?

a **$90,000**
b **$81,000**
c **$79,000**
d **None of the above**

## PROBLEMS

### P 17-1
### Cash distribution plan and entries—Installment

Ben, Bev, and Ron are partners in a business that is in the process of liquidation. On January 1, 2016, the ledger accounts show the balances indicated:

| | | | |
|---|---|---|---|
| Cash | $25,000 | Ben capital | $72,000 |
| Inventory | 72,000 | Bev capital | 28,000 |
| Supplies | 18,000 | Ron capital | 15,000 |

The cash is distributed to partners on January 1, 2016. Inventory and supplies are sold for a lump-sum price of $81,000 on February 9, 2016, and on February 10, 2016, cash on hand is distributed to the partners in final liquidation of the business.

### REQUIRED

1. Prepare the journal entry to distribute available cash on January 1, 2016. Include a safe payments schedule as proper explanation of who should receive cash.

2. Prepare journal entries necessary on February 9, 2016, to record the sale of assets and distribution of the gain or loss to the partners' capital accounts.

3. Prepare the journal entry to distribute cash on February 10, 2016, in final liquidation of the business.

### P 17-2
### Cash distribution plan

The December 31, 2016, balance sheet of the Cam, Doc, and Guy partnership, along with the partners' residual profit- and loss-sharing ratios, is summarized as follows:

| Assets | | Equities | |
|---|---|---|---|
| Cash | $ 120,000 | Accounts payable | $ 180,000 |
| Receivables | 240,000 | Loan from Doc | 100,000 |
| Inventories | 300,000 | Cam capital (20%) | 190,000 |
| Due from Cam | 30,000 | Doc capital (30%) | 320,000 |
| Other assets | 510,000 | Guy capital (50%) | 410,000 |
| | $1,200,000 | | $1,200,000 |

The partners agree to liquidate their partnership as soon as possible after January 1, 2017, and to distribute all cash as it becomes available.

REQUIRED: Prepare a cash distribution plan to show how cash will be distributed as it becomes available.

### P 17-3
### Cash distribution plan

Fed, Flo, and Wil announced the liquidation of their partnership beginning on January 1, 2016. Profits and losses are divided 30 percent to Fed, 20 percent to Flo, and 50 percent to Wil. Balance sheet items are summarized as follows:

| | | | |
|---|---|---|---|
| Cash | $ 45,000 | Accounts payable | $ 20,000 |
| Accounts receivable—net | 25,000 | Fed capital (30%) | 75,000 |
| Inventories | 25,000 | Flo capital (20%) | 30,000 |
| Plant assets—net | 80,000 | Wil capital (50%) | 60,000 |
| Flo loan | 10,000 | | |
| | $185,000 | | $185,000 |

REQUIRED: Prepare a cash distribution plan as of January 1, 2016, for the Fed, Flo, and Wil partnership.

## P 17-4
### Installment liquidation

The partnership of Gil, Hal, Ian, and Joe is preparing to liquidate. Profit- and loss-sharing ratios are shown in the summarized balance sheet at December 31, 2016, as follows:

| | | | |
|---|---|---|---|
| Cash | $100,000 | Other liabilities | $ 50,000 |
| Inventories | 100,000 | Gil capital (40%) | 150,000 |
| Loan to Hal | 10,000 | Hal capital (30%) | 160,000 |
| Other assets | 255,000 | Ian capital (20%) | 50,000 |
| | | Joe capital (10%) | 55,000 |
| | $465,000 | | $465,000 |

### REQUIRED

1. The partners anticipate an installment liquidation. Prepare a cash distribution plan as of January 1, 2017, that includes a $25,000 contingency fund to help the partners predict when they will be included in cash distributions.

2. During January 2017, the inventories are sold for $100,000, the other liabilities are paid, and $50,000 is set aside for contingencies. The partners agree that loan balances should be closed to capital accounts and that remaining cash (less the contingency fund) should be distributed to partners. How much cash should each partner receive?

## P 17-5
### Statement of partnership liquidation

Eli, Joe, and Ned agree to liquidate their consulting practice as soon as possible after the close of business on July 31, 2016. The trial balance on that date shows the following account balances:

| | Debits | Credits |
|---|---|---|
| Cash | $13,000 | |
| Accounts receivable | 12,000 | |
| Furniture and fixtures | 35,000 | |
| Accounts payable | | $ 6,000 |
| Eli capital | | 24,000 |
| Joe capital | | 15,000 |
| Ned capital | | 15,000 |
| | $60,000 | $60,000 |

The partners share profits and losses 20 percent, 30 percent, and 50 percent to Eli, Joe, and Ned, respectively, after Ned is allowed a monthly salary of $4,000.

August transactions and events are as follows:

1. The accounts payable are paid.

2. Accounts receivable of $8,000 are collected in full. Ned accepts accounts receivable with a face value and fair value of $3,000 in partial satisfaction of his capital balance. The remaining accounts receivable are written off as uncollectible.

3. Furniture with a book value of $25,000 is sold for $15,000.

4. Furniture with a book value of $4,000 and an agreed-upon fair value of $1,000 is taken by Joe in partial settlement of his capital balance. The remaining furniture and fixtures are donated to Goodwill Industries.

5. Liquidation expenses of $3,000 are paid.

6. Available cash is distributed to partners on August 31.

REQUIRED: Prepare a statement of partnership liquidation for the Eli, Joe, and Ned partnership for August.

## P 17-6
### Installment liquidation

Jon, Sam, and Tad are partners in a furniture store that began liquidation on January 1, 2016, when the ledger contained the following account balances:

| | Debit | Credit |
|---|---|---|
| Cash | $ 15,000 | |
| Accounts receivable | 20,000 | |
| Inventories | 65,000 | |
| Land | 50,000 | |
| Buildings | 100,000 | |
| Accumulated depreciation—buildings | | $ 40,000 |
| Furniture and fixtures | 50,000 | |
| Accumulated depreciation—furniture and fixtures | | 30,000 |
| Accounts payable | | 80,000 |
| Jon capital (20%) | | 40,000 |
| Sam capital (30%) | | 60,000 |
| Tad capital (50%) | | 50,000 |
| | $300,000 | $300,000 |

The following transactions and events occurred during the liquidation process:

*January*  Inventories were sold for $20,000 cash, collections on account totaled $14,000, and half of the amount due to creditors was paid.

*February*  Land costing $40,000 was sold for $60,000, the remaining land and buildings were sold for $40,000, half of the remaining receivables were collected, and the remainder was uncollectible.

*March*  Furniture and fixtures were written off. The remaining liabilities were paid, and available cash was distributed to the partners in final liquidation.

**REQUIRED:** Prepare a statement of liquidation for the Jon, Sam, and Tad partnership.

## P 17-7
### Installment liquidation

The after-closing trial balance of the Lin, Mae, and Nel partnership at December 31, 2016, was as follows:

| | Debit | Credit |
|---|---|---|
| Cash | $ 47,000 | |
| Receivables—net | 25,000 | |
| Inventories | 20,000 | |
| Plant assets—net | 50,000 | |
| Accounts payable | | $ 55,000 |
| Lin capital (50%) | | 55,000 |
| Mae capital (30%) | | 12,000 |
| Nel capital (20%) | | 20,000 |
| Total | $142,000 | $142,000 |

## ADDITIONAL INFORMATION

1. The partnership is to be liquidated as soon as the assets can be converted into cash. Cash realized on conversion of assets is to be distributed as it becomes available, except that $10,000 is to be held to provide for contingencies during the liquidation period.

2. Profits and losses on liquidation are to be divided in the percentages indicated in the trial balance.

**REQUIRED**

1. Prepare a cash distribution plan for the Lin, Mae, and Nel partnership.

2. If $25,000 cash is realized from the receivables and inventories during January 2017, how should the cash be distributed at the end of January? (Assume that this is the first distribution of cash during the liquidation period.)

## P 17-8
## Installment liquidation—Safe payments schedule

Jax, Kya, and Bud, who share partnership profits 50 percent, 30 percent, and 20 percent, respectively, decide to liquidate their partnership. They need the cash from the partnership as soon as possible but do not want to sell the assets at fire-sale prices, so they agree to an installment liquidation. A summary balance sheet on January 1, 2016, is as follows:

| | | | |
|---|---|---|---|
| Cash | $ 16,500 | Accounts payable | $ 21,000 |
| Accounts receivable | 28,000 | Jax capital | 69,000 |
| Inventory | 20,500 | Kya capital | 47,000 |
| Equipment—net | 101,000 | Bud capital | 43,000 |
| Loan to Jax | 14,000 | | |
| | $180,000 | | $180,000 |

Cash is distributed to the partners at the end of each month, with $5,000 retained for possible contingencies in the liquidation process.

During January 2016, Jax agreed to offset his capital balance with his loan from the partnership, $25,000 was collected on the accounts receivable, and the balance is determined to be uncollectible. Liquidation expenses of $2,000 were paid.

During February 2016, $18,000 was collected from the sale of inventories and $90,000 collected from the sale of equipment. Additional liabilities of $3,000 were discovered, and $2,000 of liquidation expenses were paid. All cash was then distributed in a final liquidation.

**REQUIRED:** Prepare a statement of partnership liquidation with supporting safe payments schedules for each cash distribution.

## P 17-9
## Installment liquidation—Safe payments schedules

The balance sheet of Ron, Sue, and Tom, who share partnership profits 30 percent, 30 percent, and 40 percent, respectively, included the following balances on January 1, 2016, the date of dissolution:

| | | | |
|---|---|---|---|
| Cash | $ 20,000 | Liabilities | $ 40,100 |
| Other assets | 130,000 | Loan from Ron | 5,000 |
| Loan to Sue | 10,000 | Ron capital | 9,900 |
| | | Sue capital | 45,000 |
| | | Tom capital | 60,000 |
| | $160,000 | | $160,000 |

During January 2016, parts of the firm's assets are sold for $40,000. In February the remaining assets are sold for $21,000. Assume that available cash is distributed to the proper parties at the end of January and at the end of February.

**REQUIRED:** Prepare a statement of partnership liquidation with supporting safe payments schedules for each cash distribution. (It will not be possible to determine the actual gains and losses in January.)

## E17-10
## Installment liquidation

Account balances for the Rob, Tom, and Val partnership on October 1, 2016, are as follows:

| | | | |
|---|---|---|---|
| Cash | $ 21,000 | Accounts payable | $ 80,000 |
| Accounts receivable | 63,000 | Note payable | 50,000 |
| Inventory | 120,000 | Rob capital (30%) | 43,600 |
| Equipment | 150,000 | Tom capital (50%) | 150,000 |
| Rob loan | 15,000 | Val capital (20%) | 45,400 |
| | $369,000 | | $369,000 |

The partners have decided to liquidate the business. Activities for October and November are as follows:

### October

**1.** Rob is short of funds, and the partners agree to charge her loan to her capital account.

**2.** $40,000 is collected on the accounts receivable; $4,000 is written off as uncollectible.

**3.** Half the inventory is sold for $50,000.

**4.** Equipment with a book value of $55,000 is sold for $60,000.

**5.** The $50,000 bank note plus $600 accrued interest is paid in full.

**6.** The accounts payable are paid.

**7.** Liquidation expenses of $2,000 are paid.

**8.** Except for a $5,000 contingency fund, all available cash is distributed to partners at the end of October.

### November

**9.** The remaining equipment is sold for $38,000.

**10.** Val accepts inventory with a book value of $20,000 and a fair value of $10,000 as payment for part of her capital balance. The rest of the inventory is written off.

**11.** Accounts receivable of $10,000 are collected. The remaining receivables are written off.

**12.** Liquidation expenses of $800 are paid.

**13.** Remaining cash, including the contingency fund, is distributed to the partners.

**REQUIRED:** Prepare a statement of partnership liquidation for the period October 1 through November 30.

## P 17-11
## Installment liquidation

The adjusted trial balance of the Jee, Moe, and Ole partnership at December 31, 2016, is as follows:

| | |
|---|---|
| Cash | $   50,000 |
| Accounts receivable—net | 100,000 |
| Nonmonetary assets | 800,000 |
| Expenses | 400,000 |
| Total debits | $1,350,000 |
| Accounts payable | $   80,000 |
| Jee capital | 250,000 |
| Moe capital | 450,000 |
| Ole capital | 370,000 |
| Revenue | 200,000 |
| Total credits | $1,350,000 |

## ADDITIONAL INFORMATION

**1.** Partnership profits are divided 20 percent, 40 percent, and 40 percent to Jee, Moe, and Ole, respectively, after salary allowances of $25,000 each to Jee and Moe for time devoted to the business.

**2.** Due to the disastrous results of 2016, the partners agreed to liquidate the business as soon as possible after January 1, 2017, and to distribute available cash on a weekly basis.

**3.** During the first week in January, $85,500 was collected on the accounts receivable, and cash was distributed on January 8, 2017.

## REQUIRED

**1.** Prepare the journal entries to close the partnership books at December 31, 2016.

**2.** Develop a cash distribution plan for the partnership as of January 1, 2017.

**3.** Prepare a cash distribution schedule for the January 8, 2017, distribution of available cash.

### P 17-12
### Installment liquidation

The after-closing trial balances of the Bea, Pat, and Tim partnership at December 31, 2016, included the following accounts and balances:

| | |
|---|---|
| Cash | $120,000 |
| Accounts receivable—net | 140,000 |
| Inventory | 200,000 |
| Plant assets—net | 200,000 |
| Trademarks | 20,000 |
| Total debits | $680,000 |
| Accounts payable | $150,000 |
| Notes payable | 100,000 |
| Bea capital (profit-sharing ratio, 50%) | 170,000 |
| Pat capital (profit-sharing ratio, 30%) | 180,000 |
| Tim capital (profit-sharing ratio, 20%) | 80,000 |
| Total credits | $680,000 |

The partnership is to be liquidated as soon as possible, and all available cash except for a $10,000 contingency balance is to be distributed at the end of each month prior to the time that all assets are converted into cash.

During January 2017, $100,000 was collected from accounts receivable, inventory items with a book value of $80,000 were sold for $100,000, and available cash was distributed.

During February 2017, Bea received plant assets with a book value of $60,000 and a fair value of $50,000 in partial settlement of her equity in the partnership. Also during February, the remaining inventory items were sold for $60,000, liquidation expenses of $2,000 were paid, and a liability of $8,000 was discovered. Cash was distributed on February 28.

During March 2017, the plant assets were sold for $110,000, the remaining noncash assets were written off, final liquidation expenses of $5,000 were paid, and cash was distributed. The dissolution of the partnership was completed on March 31, 2017.

**REQUIRED:** Prepare a statement of partnership liquidation for the Bea, Pat, and Tim partnership for the period January 1 to March 31, 2017.

## PROFESSIONAL RESEARCH ASSIGNMENTS

Answer the following questions by reference to the Uniform Partnership Act of 1997. Include the appropriate reference in your response.

**PR 17-1**  What events would require partnership liquidation?

# CHAPTER 18

# Corporate Liquidations and Reorganizations

This chapter examines accounting and legal matters related to financially distressed corporations.[1] Some corporations are able to recover from financial adversity through internal operating and policy changes, whereas others with more serious financial problems are forced to seek external remedies. These remedies are classified as direct agreements with creditors, reorganizations, and liquidations.

This chapter focuses on bankruptcies that result either in corporate liquidation or reorganization. We first provide an overview of U.S. bankruptcy law. We then discuss the requirements and procedures related to liquidations and reorganizations.

## BANKRUPTCY REFORM ACT OF 1978

LEARNING OBJECTIVE **18.1**

A debtor corporation is considered insolvent when it is unable to pay its debts as they come due, or when its total debts exceed the fair value of its assets. The inability to make payments on time is referred to as **equity insolvency**. Having total debts that exceed the fair value of total assets is referred to as **bankruptcy insolvency**. Debtor corporations that are insolvent in the equity sense may be able to avoid bankruptcy proceedings by negotiating an agreement directly with creditors. Debtor corporations that are insolvent in the bankruptcy sense ordinarily will be reorganized or liquidated under the supervision of a bankruptcy court.

Prior to 1898, state government legislation governed bankruptcy proceedings. The 1898 Bankruptcy Act, a federal law, preempted the state legislation. The 1898 Bankruptcy Act and its numerous amendments were repealed when Congress enacted Title 11 of the *United States Code*, the Bankruptcy Reform Act of 1978, which reflects the entire bankruptcy law and became effective October 1, 1979. The 1978 act established comprehensive bankruptcy law as well as new bankruptcy judges and new bankruptcy courts. The act has been amended several times since it was enacted, most recently in 2005.

Effective in October 2005, the Bankruptcy Abuse Prevention and Consumer Protection Act (BAPCPA) received a great deal of attention for its provisions, which made it more difficult for individual debtors to abuse the spirit behind bankruptcy provisions. BAPCPA also has ramifications for businesses, primarily through its limitations on the time frames allowed for plan exclusivity in Chapter 11 bankruptcies and real estate leases.

Under the current rules, a debtor company that files for bankruptcy has 120 days to submit a plan of reorganization to the court for approval. During this time, no other parties, such as creditors, can

---

[1]Municipalities, railroads, stockbrokers, and commodity brokers are excluded from the discussion in this chapter. Bankruptcies of these entities are covered by special provisions of Title 11 of the *United States Code*.

**EXHIBIT 18-1**

**Types of Bankruptcies**

| Type | Description |
|---|---|
| Chapter 7: Liquidation | A trustee is appointed to sell off the assets of the individual or company and pay claims to creditors. |
| Chapter 9: Adjustments of debts of a municipality | Municipalities (not covered here). |
| Chapter 11: Reorganization | The debtor corporation is expected to be rehabilitated, and the reorganization of the corporation is anticipated. <br>■ Either a trustee is appointed or the company performs the duties of a trustee (debtor in possession). <br>■ A plan of reorganization is negotiated with creditors, stockholders, employees, and others so that claims are settled and the company can continue to operate during bankruptcy proceedings and emerge from bankruptcy. <br>■ Although Chapter 11 also applies to individuals, Chapter 13 bankruptcy is usually easier. |
| Chapter 12: Farmers | Family farmers with regular income (not covered here). |
| Chapter 13: Adjustments of debts of an individual with regular income | Exclusively applies to individuals, including sole proprietorships. Unsecured debts less than $307,675 and secured debts less than $922,975 (not covered here). |

submit plans to the court. Before the enactment of BAPCPA, debtor companies could repeatedly ask for extensions of the exclusivity period, but BAPCPA limits the exclusivity period to a maximum of 18 months. This could speed up the process and allow creditors to recover more of their money since the debtor firm cannot delay the plan-writing process indefinitely.

Another change is that retail debtors now have only 120 days to assume or reject unexpired leases on nonresidential real property with a maximum 90-day extension. Only with the written consent of landlords are businesses able to extend this.

The bankruptcy law facilitates debt relief to individuals and corporations under various provisions, called chapters. Exhibit 18-1 summarizes the major bankruptcy-code chapters. The purposes of the bankruptcy law are to protect the interests of creditors, to ensure an equitable distribution of assets in settlement of liabilities, and to give debtors a "fresh start." Once the debtor has settled its debts through the bankruptcy process, the debtor can start anew without the constant threat of legal actions and collection agencies.

Chapter 11 reorganizations provide businesses and individuals with the time needed to put together a business plan. Hopefully, the plan will ensure the future survival of the corporation once it emerges from bankruptcy proceedings, as well as provide for the settlement of its existing debts. The bankruptcy court and creditors' committees must approve of the plan.

If a corporation cannot produce a plan the court approves, the court may force the corporation into Chapter 7 bankruptcy, or liquidation. Some companies (such as *Montgomery Ward, LTV Steel*, and *US Airways*) emerge from Chapter 11 bankruptcy and subsequently file for bankruptcy again because their business plan does not work.

Occasionally, corporations may file for bankruptcy protection even though they have sufficient fair value of assets to cover their debts, because they have liquidity problems and cannot meet debt payments as they come due. A few times in history, the bankruptcy court has allowed companies to file for bankruptcy even though they had sufficient liquidity to meet current debts, because they were parties to potentially large lawsuit findings. For example, *Dow Chemical* filed for bankruptcy as a result of silicon-breast-implant lawsuits; in 1985, *AH Robins* filed for bankruptcy as a result of Dalkon Shield IUD lawsuits; and *Johns Manville* filed for bankruptcy in 1982 as a result of threatened asbestos lawsuits. Unfortunately, in recent years, corporate accounting scandals have emerged as another reason firms file for bankruptcy. Some examples include *Enron, WorldCom*, and *Adelphia*. The most recent events in the world of corporate bankruptcy are also some of the most dramatic. The real estate and banking collapse of 2007 and 2008 led to half of the 20 largest U.S. public company bankruptcies taking place in 2007–2009.

It is clear to see how the great recession influenced the level of filings. In economic downturns, the accountants, lawyers, and courts that serve firms going thru bankruptcy are quite busy. However, even in periods of recovery and growth, there is a steady level of bankruptcy activity. The historically large spike in filings caused by the great recession is seen quite clearly in the following chart showing the level of yearly filings of Chapter 7 and Chapter 11.[2]

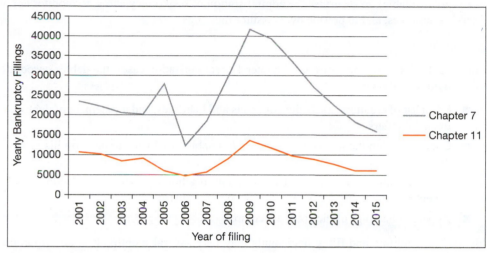

(Source: USCourts.gov).

When a firm files for bankruptcy protection, the court must decide if it has a role. If the court issues an **order of relief**, that order protects the debtor company from further litigation during the time the reorganization plan is being developed. Under court supervision, the creditors and the debtor work out a plan to settle the creditors' claims. The court is the final arbiter in such cases.

Sometimes companies are acquired by other companies as part of the reorganization plan. For example, *Montgomery Ward* filed for bankruptcy protection in 1997 and was acquired by *General Electric* (GE Capital) in 1999, bringing it out of bankruptcy. Despite an active plan to return the firm to profitability, Montgomery Ward again filed for bankruptcy in 2001, shuttered all of its stores, and set about liquidating its assets. *Lehman Brothers*, which filed for protection in 2008 with almost $700 billion in recorded assets, was sold to *Barclays and Nomura Holdings* for less than $2 billion.

The jurisdiction of the bankruptcy court covers all cases under Title 11 of the *U.S. Code*. A case begins with the filing of a petition under which a debtor is initially brought into bankruptcy court. Usually, the petition is filed in the U.S. bankruptcy court district where the debtor's principal place of business or principal assets have been located for at least 180 days. Either the debtor corporation or its creditors may file the petition. If the debtor corporation files the petition, the proceeding is termed a **voluntary bankruptcy proceeding**; if creditors file, it is an **involuntary bankruptcy proceeding**. Most bankruptcy filings are voluntary.

A petition commencing a case by or against a corporate debtor may be filed under either Chapter 7 or Chapter 11 of the bankruptcy act. **Chapter 7 of the Bankruptcy Reform Act** covers straight bankruptcy, under which liquidation of the debtor corporation is expected, and **Chapter 11 of the Bankruptcy Reform Act** covers rehabilitation of the debtor and anticipates reorganization of the debtor corporation.[3] The bankruptcy court has the power (subject to various requests and conditions) to dismiss a case, to enter the order for relief (in other words, accept the petition), or to convert a Chapter 11 reorganization case into a Chapter 7 liquidation case or vice versa.

## The Office of U.S. Trustee

The Bankruptcy Reform Act created the Office of U.S. Trustee, a branch of the Department of Justice, to be responsible for the administrative duties of bankruptcy cases. The U.S. Attorney

---

[2]USCourts.gov.

[3]Not all liquidations result from financial adversity. Voluntary liquidations are often based on the belief that the market value of the company's stock is less than the amount that could be realized by selling the company's assets. This type of liquidation does not involve restructurings or judicial remedies, and established accounting principles are applicable to winding up the company's affairs through liquidating dividends. For a discussion of voluntary liquidations, see Ronald J. Kudle, *Voluntary Corporate Liquidations* (Westport, CT: Quorum Books, Greenwood Press, 1988), or George E. Nogler and Kenneth B. Schwartz, "Financial Reporting and Auditors' Opinions on Voluntary Liquidations," *Accounting Horizons* (September 1989), pp. 12–20.

General appoints U.S. trustees for seven-year terms. The duties of the **U.S. trustee** are to maintain and supervise a panel of private trustees eligible to serve in Chapter 7 cases, to serve as trustee or interim trustee in some bankruptcy cases (such as in a Chapter 7 case in which a qualified private trustee is not available), to supervise the administration of bankruptcy cases, to monitor appointed creditors' committees, and to preside over creditor meetings.

### Duties of the Debtor Corporation

In both Chapter 7 liquidation cases and Chapter 11 reorganization cases, the debtor corporation is required to do the following:

- File a list of creditors, a schedule of assets and liabilities, and a statement of debtor's financial affairs
- Cooperate with the trustee as necessary to enable the trustee to perform his or her duties
- Surrender all property to the trustee, including books, documents, records, and papers relating to the estate in cases involving a trustee
- Appear at hearings of the court as required

Identifying creditors and filing documents may take several months. It is an important task because creditors who have been notified of the bankruptcy proceedings may receive only a percentage of their claims. Those creditors not notified are entitled to the full amount.

### Duties of the Bankruptcy Judge

The bankruptcy judge settles disputes that occur during the case and approves all payments of debts incurred before the bankruptcy filing, as well as other payments that are considered extraordinary.

### LIQUIDATION

The Administrative Office of the U.S. Courts reported that of the 25,227 business bankruptcy filings for the 12 months ended June 30, 2016, 15,551, or about 62 percent, were filed under Chapter 7 of the bankruptcy act. Chapter 7 liquidations are cheaper and faster than Chapter 11 reorganizations. A Chapter 7 liquidation case begins voluntarily when a debtor corporation files a petition with the bankruptcy court, or involuntarily through filing by three or more entities holding noncontingent, unsecured claims totaling at least $15,775.[4] A single creditor with an unsecured claim of $15,775[5] or more may also file a petition if there are fewer than 12 unsecured creditors.

The court will grant the order for relief (accept the petition) under Chapter 7 if the creditors prove their claims or if the debtor fails to contest the petition on a timely basis. The order for relief prevents creditors from seeking payment of their claims directly from the debtor. If the creditors fail to prove their alleged claims, the court will dismiss the case. The debtor may respond to the petition by filing for protection from creditors under Chapter 11, under which, instead of being liquidated, it can reorganize.

If an order for relief under Chapter 7 is granted, the U.S. trustee (or the court) appoints an interim trustee to take possession of the debtor corporation's estate until a trustee is elected. An interim trustee may be appointed at any time after commencement of a case if the court considers it necessary to preserve the property of the estate or prevent losses.

The election for trustee takes place at a meeting of creditors, and only unsecured creditors with undisputed claims are eligible to vote. A trustee is elected if creditors holding a minimum of 20 percent of the dollar amount of claims request an election, and one candidate obtains the votes of creditors holding a majority in the dollar amount of claims actually voting. If a trustee is not elected, the interim trustee serves as trustee. The unsecured creditors eligible to vote may also elect a creditors' committee of 3 to 11 members to consult with the trustee and to submit questions regarding the debtor's estate to the court.

---

[4]An *entity* under Title 11 means a person, an estate, a trustee, or a government unit. *Person* means an individual, a partnership, or a corporation, but not a government unit.

[5]Many of the threshold dollar amounts related to bankruptcy law are tied to inflation. U.S. Code, Title 11, section 104 spells out the process of inflation adjustments. This version of the text uses the figures that were current as of February 22, 2016.

## Duties of the Trustee in Liquidation Cases

The filing of a case creates an estate. The trustee takes possession of the estate, converts the estate assets into cash, and distributes the proceeds according to the priority of claims, as directed by the bankruptcy court. Other duties of the trustee in a liquidation case are as follows:

- To investigate the financial affairs of the debtor
- To provide information about the debtor's estate and its administration to interested parties
- To examine creditor claims and object to claims that appear to be improper
- To provide periodic reports and summaries of operations, a statement of receipts and disbursements, and other information as the court specifies, if they are authorized to operate the debtor's business
- To file final reports on trusteeship as required by the court

## Payment of Claims

Claims in a Chapter 7 liquidation case are paid in the order shown in Exhibit 18-2. Claims secured by valid liens are paid to the extent of the proceeds from property pledged as security. If the proceeds are insufficient to satisfy the claims of secured creditors, the amounts not satisfied are classified as unsecured nonpriority claims (or general unsecured claims). Unsecured claims are divided into priority and nonpriority classes for Chapter 7 liquidation cases (see Exhibit 18-2). Unsecured priority claims are paid in full before any distributions are made to unsecured nonpriority claims.

Claims within the unsecured priority claims class are ranked 1 through 6, such that claims in the first rank (administrative expenses) are paid in full before any distribution is made for claims in the second rank, and so forth. Within each of the six priority ranks, however, distributions are made on a pro rata basis when available cash is insufficient to pay all claims of that rank. Equivalent procedures apply to cash distributions in the four ranks included within the unsecured nonpriority class. Stockholders under a Chapter 7 liquidation case are included in distributions only when all valid creditor claims have been fully satisfied.

## ILLUSTRATION OF A LIQUIDATION CASE

Cam Corporation experienced a large operating loss in 2016 and the first half of 2017. By July 2017 its accounts payable were overdue, and its accounts receivable had been pledged to support a bank loan that was in default. Cam's creditors were unwilling to extend additional credit or to amend the

---

**I  Secured Claims**
  Claims secured by valid liens.
**II  Unsecured Priority Claims**
  1. Administrative expenses incurred in preserving and liquidating the estate, including trustee's fees and legal and accounting fees.
  2. Claims incurred between the date of filing an involuntary petition and the date an interim trustee is appointed.
  3. Claims for wages, salaries, and commissions earned within 180 days of filing the petition and not exceeding $12,475 per individual.
  4. Claims for contributions to employee benefit plans arising from services rendered within 180 days of filing the petition and limited to $12,475 per employee.
  5. Claims of individuals, not to exceed $2,775, arising from the purchase, lease, or rental of property that was not delivered or the purchase of services that were not provided by the debtor.
  6. Claims of governmental units for income or gross receipts taxes, property taxes, employment taxes, excise taxes, and customs duties that originated within one to four years before filing (periods vary for different claims). Taxes collected or withheld for which the debtor is liable and penalties related to the foregoing are also included.
**III  Unsecured Nonpriority Claims**
  1. Allowed claims that were timely filed.
  2. Allowed claims whose proof of claim was filed late.
  3. Allowed claims (secured and unsecured) for any fine, penalty, or forfeiture, or for multiple, exemplary, or punitive charges arising to the order for relief or appointment of trustee.
  4. Claims for interest on the unsecured priority claims or the unsecured nonpriority claims.
**IV  Stockholders' Claims**
  Remaining assets are returned to the debtor corporation or its stockholders.

**EXHIBIT 18-2**

Ranking of Claims in Chapter 7 Liquidation Cases

terms of any of their loans, and on August 1, 2017, Cam filed a voluntary petition for relief under Chapter 7 of the bankruptcy act.

Exhibit 18-3 presents a balance sheet prepared at the bankruptcy filing date. Although the balance sheet shows stockholders' equity of $13,000, historical cost valuations are not good indicators of financial condition for a liquidating company. An accounting statement that does provide relevant information for a liquidating company is the *statement of affairs*.

## Statement of Affairs

A trustee's duties may include filing a statement of financial affairs with the bankruptcy court. This statement is a legal document prepared for the bankruptcy court. The **statement of affairs** is a financial statement that emphasizes liquidation values and provides relevant information for the trustee in liquidating the debtor corporation. It also provides information that may be useful to creditors and to the bankruptcy court.

A statement of affairs is prepared at a specific date and shows balance sheet information. Assets are measured at expected net realizable values and are classified on the basis of availability for fully secured, partially secured, priority, and unsecured creditors. Liabilities are classified as priority, fully secured, partially secured, and unsecured. Historical cost valuations are included in the statement for reference purposes.

Exhibit 18-4 presents the statement of affairs for Cam Corporation. Information for the statement is derived from the balance sheet (see Exhibit 18-3) at the filing date and other sources, such as appraisals of the assets' expected liquidation values and contractual agreements with creditors. The

| EXHIBIT 18-3 |
| --- |
| Debtor Corporation's Balance Sheet at the Bankruptcy Filing Date |

**CAM CORPORATION**
**BALANCE SHEET**
**AUGUST 1, 2017**

| Assets | | |
| --- | --- | --- |
| *Current Assets* | | |
| Cash | $ 3,000 | |
| Marketable securities (at market) | 7,000 | |
| Accounts receivable (net of estimated uncollectible accounts) | 25,000 | |
| Inventories | 50,000 | |
| Prepaid expenses | 4,000 | $89,000 |
| | | |
| *Long-Term Assets* | | |
| Land | $ 15,000 | |
| Building—net | 40,000 | |
| Equipment—net | 30,000 | |
| Intangible assets | 6,000 | 91,000 |
| Total assets | | $180,000 |

| Liabilities and Stockholders' Equity | | |
| --- | --- | --- |
| *Current Liabilities* | | |
| Accounts payable | $ 65,000 | |
| Wages payable | 13,000 | |
| Property taxes payable | 2,000 | |
| Note payable—bank | 25,000 | |
| Notes payable—suppliers | 5,000 | |
| Interest payable | 7,000 | $117,000 |
| | | |
| *Long-Term Liabilities* | | |
| Mortgage payable | | 50,000 |
| Total liabilities | | 167,000 |
| | | |
| *Stockholders' Equity* | | |
| Capital stock | $200,000 | |
| Retained earnings | (187,000) | |
| Total stockholders' equity | | 13,000 |
| Total liabilities and stockholders' equity | | $180,000 |

**EXHIBIT 18-4**

**Statement of Affairs**

## CAM CORPORATION
## STATEMENT OF AFFAIRS
## ON AUGUST 1, 2017

### Assets

| Book Value | | Estimated Realizable Values Less Secured Creditor Liabilities | Estimated Realizable Value Available for Unsecured Creditors |
|---|---|---|---|
| | *Pledged for Fully Secured Creditors* | | |
| $55,000 | Land and buildings—net | $60,000 | |
| | Less: Mortgage payable | $50,000 | |
| | Interest payable | 5,000    55,000 | $5,000 |
| | *Pledged for Partially Secured Creditors* | | |
| 25,000 | Accounts receivable | $22,000 | |
| | Less: Note payable to bank | $25,000 | |
| | Interest payable | 2,000    27,000 | 0 |
| | *Available for Priority and Unsecured Creditors* | | |
| 3,000 | Cash | | 3,000 |
| 7,000 | Marketable securities | | 7,000 |
| 50,000 | Inventories | | 55,000 |
| 4,000 | Prepaid expenses | | 0 |
| 30,000 | Equipment—net | | 12,000 |
| 6,000 | Intangible assets | | 0 |
| | Total available for priority and unsecured creditors | | 82,000 |
| | Less: Priority liabilities | | 15,000 |
| | Total available for unsecured creditors | | 67,000 |
| | Estimated deficiency | | 8,000 |
| $180,000 | | | $75,000 |

### Liabilities and Stockholders' Equity

| Book Value | | Secured and Priority Claims | Unsecured Nonpriority Claims |
|---|---|---|---|
| | *Fully Secured Creditors* | | |
| $50,000 | Mortgage payable | $50,000 | |
| 5,000 | Interest payable | 5,000 | |
| | | $55,000 | |
| | *Partially Secured Creditors* | | |
| 25,000 | Note payable—bank | $25,000 | |
| 2,000 | Interest payable | 2,000 | |
| | | 27,000 | |
| | Less: Accounts receivable pledged | 22,000 | $5,000 |
| | *Priority Liabilities* | | |
| $13,000 | Wages payable | $13,000 | |
| 2,000 | Property taxes payable | 2,000 | |
| | | $15,000 | |
| | *Unsecured Creditors* | | |
| 65,000 | Accounts payable | | 65,000 |
| 5,000 | Notes payable to suppliers | | 5,000 |
| | *Stockholders' Equity* | | |
| 200,000 | Capital stock | | |
| (187,000) | Retained earnings | | |
| $180,000 | | | $75,000 |

mortgage payable, together with $5,000 interest payable, is secured by the land and building. All accounts receivable are pledged as security for the bank loan and $2,000 interest payable.

It is expected that Cam's assets can be converted into cash within three months. The estimated realizable values are as follows:

| | |
|---|---|
| Cash | $3,000 |
| Marketable securities | 7,000 |
| Accounts receivable | 22,000 |
| Inventories (net of selling expenses) | 55,000 |
| Prepaid expenses | — |
| Land and building | 60,000 |
| Equipment | 12,000 |
| Intangible assets | — |
| | $159,000 |

Assets pledged as security for creditor claims are offset against the estimated claims of secured creditors in the asset section of the statement of affairs. Any excess of the realizable value of assets pledged over related claims is carried to the righthand column of the statement to indicate the amount available for unsecured creditors. An excess of secured creditor claims over the estimated value of assets pledged as security indicates that these claims are only partially secured. The unsecured portion is shown in the liability section of the statement as an unsecured nonpriority claim. The value of total assets available to pay unsecured creditors is estimated to fall short by $8,000.

## Trustee Accounting

A trustee in a Chapter 7 bankruptcy case stewards the assets of the debtor corporation until being released by the bankruptcy court. The bankruptcy act does not cover procedural accounting details such as whether the trustee should create a new set of accounting records to establish accountability for the estate and show the eventual discharge of responsibility, or whether the corporation's existing accounting records should be continued under the direction of the trustee.

The trustee for Cam Corporation creates a new set of accounting records. The assets are recorded on the trustee's books at book values, rather than at expected realizable values, because of the subjectivity involved in estimating realizable amounts at the time of filing. Contra asset accounts are omitted from the trustee's books because they are not meaningful in a liquidation case and because it is desirable to keep the trustee accounts as simple as possible. The following entry could be prepared to open the trustee's books for Cam:

| | | |
|---|---|---|
| Cash (+A) | 3,000 | |
| Marketable securities (+A) | 7,000 | |
| Accounts receivable (+A) | 25,000 | |
| Inventories (+A) | 50,000 | |
| Prepaid expenses (+A) | 4,000 | |
| Land (+A) | 15,000 | |
| Building (+A) | 40,000 | |
| Equipment (+A) | 30,000 | |
| Intangible assets (+A) | 6,000 | |
| Accounts payable (+L) | | 65,000 |
| Wages payable (+L) | | 13,000 |
| Property taxes payable (+L) | | 2,000 |
| Note payable—bank (+L) | | 25,000 |
| Notes payable—suppliers (+L) | | 5,000 |
| Interest payable (+L) | | 7,000 |
| Mortgage payable (+L) | | 50,000 |
| Estate equity (+EE) | | 13,000 |
| To record custody of Cam Corporation in liquidation. | | |

After assuming custody of the estate, the trustee records gains, losses, and liquidation expenses directly in the estate equity account. This account represents the residual equity that shareholders can claim after the liquidation of assets and settlement of liabilities. Any unrecorded assets or liabilities that the trustee discovers are also entered in the estate equity account. To distinguish assets and liabilities included in the initial estate and those acquired or incurred by the trustee, the assets and liabilities recorded after the trustee takes charge of the estate are identified as "new."

Transactions and events during the first month of Cam's trusteeship are described and journal entries to record them in the trustee's books are illustrated as follows:

1. A previously unrecorded utility bill for $500 is received.

   | | | |
   |---|---|---|
   | Estate equity (−EE) | 500 | |
   | Utilities payable—new (+L) | | 500 |

2. Intangible assets are deemed worthless and are written off.

   | | | |
   |---|---|---|
   | Estate equity (−EE) | 6,000 | |
   | Intangible assets (−A) | | 6,000 |

3. All inventory items are sold for $48,000, of which $18,000 is on account and $30,000 is in cash.

   | | | |
   |---|---|---|
   | Cash (+A) | 30,000 | |
   | Accounts receivable—new (+A) | 18,000 | |
   | Estate equity (−EE) | 2,000 | |
   | Inventories (−A) | | 50,000 |

4. The equipment is sold for $14,200 cash.

   | | | |
   |---|---|---|
   | Cash (+A) | 14,200 | |
   | Estate equity (−EE) | 15,800 | |
   | Equipment (−A) | | 30,000 |

5. Wages and property taxes owed on August 1 (priority liabilities) are paid.

   | | | |
   |---|---|---|
   | Wages payable (−L) | 13,000 | |
   | Property taxes payable (−L) | 2,000 | |
   | Cash (−A) | | 15,000 |

6. Land and building are sold for $64,000 cash, and the mortgage payable and related interest are paid.

   | | | |
   |---|---|---|
   | Cash (+A) | 64,000 | |
   | Land (−A) | | 15,000 |
   | Building (−A) | | 40,000 |
   | Estate equity (+EE) | | 9,000 |
   | Mortgage payable (−L) | 50,000 | |
   | Interest payable (−L) | 5,000 | |
   | Cash (−A) | | 55,000 |

7. Insurance policies (included in prepaid expenses) are canceled, and a $1,000 cash refund is received.

   | | | |
   |---|---|---|
   | Cash (+A) | 1,000 | |
   | Prepaid expenses (−A) | | 1,000 |

8. Accounts receivable of $21,000 are collected from the amounts owed to Cam at August 1. The remaining $4,000 is uncollectible.

   | | | |
   |---|---|---|
   | Cash (+A) | 21,000 | |
   | Estate equity (−EE) | 4,000 | |
   | Accounts receivable (−A) | | 25,000 |

9. The $21,000 received on account is applied to the bank note payable and related interest.

   | | | |
   |---|---|---|
   | Interest payable (−L) | 2,000 | |
   | Note payable—bank (−L) | 19,000 | |
   | Cash (−A) | | 21,000 |

10. Estate administration expenses of $3,000 are paid.

    | | | |
    |---|---|---|
    | Estate equity (−EE) | 3,000 | |
    | Cash (−A) | | 3,000 |

**11.** Trustee fees of $2,000 are accrued.

| | | |
|---|---:|---:|
| Estate equity (−EE) | 2,000 | |
| Trustee's fee payable—new (+L) | | 2,000 |

After the transactions and events occurring through August 31 are entered on the trustee's books, financial statements can be prepared as needed to show progress toward liquidation and financial position at that date.

**STATEMENT OF CASH RECEIPTS AND DISBURSEMENTS**   The statement of cash receipts and disbursements is prepared directly from entries in the cash account. It appears in summary form here.

**CASH**

| | | | |
|---|---:|---|---:|
| Balance, August 1, 2017 | $3,000 | Wages and property taxes | $15,000 |
| Inventory items sold | 30,000 | Mortgage and interest payment | 55,000 |
| Equipment sold | 14,200 | Bank notes and interest | 21,000 |
| Land and building sold | 64,000 | Administrative expenses | 3,000 |
| Insurance refund | 1,000 | **Balance forward** | 39,200 |
| Accounts receivable | 21,000 | | $133,200 |
| | $133,200 | | |
| Balance, August 31, 2017 | $39,200 | | |

Exhibit 18-5 illustrates the trustee's interim statement of cash receipts and cash disbursements for the period August 1 to August 31, 2017. All disbursements require approval of the court, so the statement should be a useful financial summary.

**STATEMENT OF CHANGES IN ESTATE EQUITY**   The estate equity account in summary form is as follows:

**ESTATE EQUITY (DEFICIT)**

| | | | |
|---|---:|---|---:|
| Utility bill discovered | $500 | August 1, 2017, balance | $13,000 |
| Intangibles written off | 6,000 | Land and building gain | 9,000 |
| Inventory loss | 2,000 | | |
| Equipment loss | 15,800 | | |
| Accounts receivable written off | 4,000 | | |
| Administrative expenses | 3,000 | | |
| Trustee's fee | 2,000 | **Balance forward (deficit)** | 11,300 |
| | $33,300 | | $33,300 |
| Balance, August 31, 2017 | $11,300 | | |

**CAM CORPORATION IN TRUSTEESHIP**
**STATEMENT OF CASH RECEIPTS AND DISBURSEMENTS**
**FROM AUGUST 1 TO AUGUST 31, 2017**

| | | |
|---|---:|---:|
| Cash balance, August 1, 2017 | | $3,000 |
| Add: Cash receipts | | |
| Sale of inventory items | $30,000 | |
| Sale of equipment | 14,200 | |
| Sale of land and building | 64,000 | |
| Refund from insurance policy | 1,000 | |
| Collection of receivables | 21,000 | |
| Total cash receipts | | 130,200 |
| | | 133,200 |
| Deduct: Cash disbursements | | |
| Wages payable (priority claim) | $13,000 | |
| Property taxes payable (priority claim) | 2,000 | |
| Mortgage payable and interest (fully secured) | 55,000 | |
| Bank note payable and interest (for secured portion) | 21,000 | |
| Administrative expenses (priority item) | 3,000 | |
| Total cash disbursements | | 94,000 |
| Cash balance, August 31, 2017 | | $39,200 |

**CAM CORPORATION IN TRUSTEESHIP**
**STATEMENT OF CHANGES IN ESTATE EQUITY**
**FROM AUGUST 1 TO AUGUST 31, 2017**

| | | |
|---|---|---|
| Estate equity August 1, 2017 | | $13,000 |
| Less: Net loss on asset liquidation | $18,800 | |
| (see schedule below) | | |
| Liability for utilities discovered | 500 | |
| Administrative expenses | 3,000 | |
| Trustee's fee | 2,000 | |
| Net decrease for the period | | (24,300) |
| Estate deficit August 31, 2017 | | $(11,300) |

**SCHEDULE OF NET LOSSES ON ASSET LIQUIDATION**

| | Book Value August 1 | − | Proceeds on Realization | = | Gain (Loss) |
|---|---|---|---|---|---|
| Accounts receivable | $25,000 | | $21,000 | | $(4,000) |
| Inventories | 50,000 | | 48,000 | | (2,000) |
| Land and building | 55,000 | | 64,000 | | 9,000 |
| Equipment | 30,000 | | 14,200 | | (15,800) |
| Intangible assets | 6,000 | | 0 | | (6,000) |
| Net loss on liquidation of assets | | | | | $(18,800) |

Exhibit 18-6 illustrates the statement of changes in estate equity for Cam Corporation from August 1 to August 31, 2017. Observe that the statement separates gains and losses on asset realization from expenses involved in liquidating the corporation.

**BALANCE SHEET**   A balance sheet is prepared directly from the ledger account balances of the trustee and is presented in Exhibit 18-7. Two key amounts that appear in the balance sheet—cash and estate deficit—are supported by amounts from the statements of cash receipts and disbursements (Exhibit 18-5) and changes in estate equity (Exhibit 18-6). The statements presented in Exhibits 18-5, 18-6, and 18-7 are in a format familiar to accountants, but you will want to compare these financial statements with the traditional statement of realization and liquidation that is presented in Exhibit 18-8.

**STATEMENT OF REALIZATION AND LIQUIDATION**   A **statement of realization and liquidation** is an activity statement that shows progress toward the liquidation of a debtor's estate. It also informs the bankruptcy court and interested creditors of the accomplishments of the trustee. The bankruptcy act does not require such a statement; instead, the act allows the judge in a bankruptcy case to prescribe the form in which information is presented to the court.

**CAM CORPORATION IN TRUSTEESHIP**
**BALANCE SHEET**
**ON AUGUST 31, 2017**

| | |
|---|---|
| *Assets* | |
| Cash | $39,200 |
| Marketable securities | 7,000 |
| Accounts receivable—net | 18,000 |
| Prepaid expenses | 3,000 |
| Total assets | $67,200 |
| *Liabilities and Deficit* | |
| Accounts payable | $65,000 |
| Utilities payable—discovered | 500 |
| Trustee's fee payable—new | 2,000 |
| Note payable—bank (unsecured portion) | 6,000 |
| Notes payable—suppliers | 5,000 |
| Total liabilities | 78,500 |
| Less: Estate deficit | 11,300 |
| Total liabilities less deficit | $67,200 |

**EXHIBIT 18-8**

Statement of Realization and Liquidation

### CAM CORPORATION IN TRUSTEESHIP
### STATEMENT OF REALIZATION AND LIQUIDATION
### AUGUST 1, 2017, TO AUGUST 31, 2017

**Assets**

| | | | | | |
|---|---|---|---|---|---|
| *Assets to Be Realized* [Noncash assets at August 1] | | | *Assets Realized* [Proceeds from sale, disposal, or write-off] | | |
| Marketable securities | $7,000 | | Accounts receivable | $21,000 | |
| Accounts receivable | 25,000 | | Inventories | 48,000 | |
| Inventories | 50,000 | | Prepaid expenses | 1,000 | |
| Prepaid expenses | 4,000 | | Land and building | 64,000 | |
| Land | 15,000 | | Equipment | 14,200 | |
| Building | 40,000 | | Intangible assets | none | $148,200 |
| Equipment | 30,000 | | | | |
| Intangible assets | 6,000 | $177,000 | | | |
| *Assets Acquired* [New noncash assets received] | | | *Assets Not Realized* [Noncash assets at August 31] | | |
| Accounts receivable—new | | 18,000 | Marketable securities | $7,000 | |
| | | | Prepaid expenses | 3,000 | |
| | | | Accounts receivable—new | 18,000 | 28,000 |

**Liabilities**

| | | | | | |
|---|---|---|---|---|---|
| *Liabilities to Be Liquidated* [Liabilities at August 1] | | | *Liabilities Liquidated* [Amounts paid on liabilities] | | |
| Accounts payable | $65,000 | | Wages payable | $13,000 | |
| Wages payable | 13,000 | | Property taxes payable | 2,000 | |
| Property taxes payable | 2,000 | | Note payable—bank | 19,000 | |
| Note payable—bank | 25,000 | | Interest payable | 7,000 | |
| Notes payable—suppliers | 5,000 | | Mortgage payable | 50,000 | 91,000 |
| Interest payable | 7,000 | | | | |
| Mortgage payable | 50,000 | 167,000 | *Liabilities Not Liquidated* [Liabilities at August 31] | | |
| | | | Accounts payable | $65,000 | |
| *Liabilities Incurred or Discovered* [Amounts incurred or discovered but unpaid at August 31] | | | Note payable—bank | 6,000 | |
| | | | Notes payable—suppliers | 5,000 | |
| | | | Liability discovered for utilities | 500 | |
| Liability discovered for utilities | $500 | | Trustee's fee payable—new | 2,000 | 78,500 |
| Trustee's fee payable—new | 2,000 | 2,500 | | | |

**Income or Loss and Supplemental Items**

| | | | | | |
|---|---|---|---|---|---|
| *Supplementary Expenses* [Expenses excluding asset losses and write-offs] | | | *Supplementary Revenues* [Revenues excluding gains on assets or liability settlements] | | |
| Liability discovered for utilities | $500 | | None | | |
| Trustee's fee | 2,000 | | *Net Loss* | | 24,300 |
| Administrative expenses—new | 3,000 | 5,500 | | | |
| | | $370,000 | | | $370,000 |

Exhibit 18-8 presents a statement of realization and liquidation for Cam Corporation. The statement is presented in its traditional format except for bracketed explanations of the various categories. An examination of Cam's statement of realization and liquidation shows that the statement is complex and that its format is unusual. In addition, the logic of the statement's construction is not immediately apparent. Although a number of alternative formats for the statement have been proposed, many accountants feel that basic financial statements with supporting schedules provide more relevant information about liquidation activity than the statement of realization and liquidation.

## Winding up the Case

During September 2017, the trustee for Cam Corporation collected the $18,000 accounts receivable, sold the marketable securities for $7,300, sold supplies (included in prepaid expenses) for $995, wrote off the remaining prepaid expenses, and distributed cash in final liquidation of the estate. Journal entries to record these transactions and events are as follows:

| | | |
|---|---:|---:|
| Cash (+A) | 18,000 | |
|     Accounts receivable—new (−A) | | 18,000 |
|   Collection of receivable in full. | | |
| Cash (+A) | 7,300 | |
|     Marketable securities (−A) | | 7,000 |
|     Estate equity (+EE) | | 300 |
|   Sale of marketable securities for cash. | | |
| Cash (+A) | 995 | |
| Estate equity (−EE) | 2,005 | |
|     Prepaid expenses (−A) | | 3,000 |
|   Sale of supplies and write-off of prepaid expenses. | | |

Account balances after these entries are entered in the trustee's records are as follows:

| | Debit | Credit |
|---|---:|---:|
| Cash | $65,495 | |
| Accounts payable | | $65,000 |
| Utilities payable—new | | 500 |
| Trustee's fee payable—new | | 2,000 |
| Note payable—bank (unsecured portion) | | 6,000 |
| Notes payable—suppliers | | 5,000 |
| Estate equity | 13,005 | |
| | $78,500 | $78,500 |

The trustee's fee is a priority claim, so it is paid in full. The remaining claims of $76,500 (all first-rank unsecured creditors) receive 83¢ on the dollar ($63,495 ÷ $76,500) in final settlement of their claims. Entries to record the cash distributions are as follows:

| | | |
|---|---:|---:|
| Trustee's fee payable—new (−L) | 2,000 | |
|     Cash (−A) | | 2,000 |
|   To record payment of trustee's fee. | | |
| Accounts payable (−L) | 53,950 | |
| Utilities payable—new (−L) | 415 | |
| Note payable—bank (−L) | 4,980 | |
| Notes payable—suppliers (−L) | 4,150 | |
|     Cash (−A) | | 63,495 |
|   To record payment of 83¢ on the dollar to the general | | |
|   unsecured creditors. | | |

A case involving a corporation is closed when the estate is fully administered and the trustee is dismissed. The trustee makes the following entry in closing out the Cam Corporation case:

| | | |
|---|---:|---:|
| Accounts payable (−L) | 11,050 | |
| Utilities payable—new (−L) | 85 | |
| Note payable—bank (−L) | 1,020 | |
| Notes payable—suppliers (−L) | 850 | |
|     Estate equity (+EE) | | 13,005 |
|   To close the trustee's records. | | |

## REORGANIZATION

While the bulk of commercial bankruptcies are Chapter 7, there are still quite a few firms that believe they can successfully reorganize their way out of trouble. From 2001 through 2015, Chapter 7 filings averaged just fewer than 25,000 per year. During that period Chapter 11 filings were slightly greater than 8,500 per year. Chapter 11 reorganization cases usually involve very large organizations.

A firm initiates a Chapter 11 reorganization case voluntarily when a debtor corporation files a petition with the bankruptcy court or involuntarily when creditors file a petition. The same $15,775 claim threshold applicable to Chapter 7 filings apply here.

The act of filing commences the case and initiates a hearing before the bankruptcy court. As mentioned earlier, the court may enter an order for relief under Chapter 11, convert the case to a Chapter 7 liquidation, or dismiss the case (e.g., the case will be dismissed if the bankruptcy court believes that the filing was an act of bad faith). A U.S. trustee is appointed by the bankruptcy judge to be responsible for the administration of the Chapter 11 case.

## Trustee or Debtor in Possession

In a Chapter 11 case, a private trustee may be appointed for cause, but otherwise the debtor corporation is continued in possession of the estate and is referred to as a **debtor in possession**. A trustee may be appointed in cases involving fraud, dishonesty, or gross mismanagement, or if the court rules that appointment of a trustee is in the best interests of creditors, equity holders, and other parties with an interest in the estate. For the most part, bankruptcy judges have been reluctant to appoint private trustees to operate businesses in reorganization cases because company management is usually more qualified to operate and reorganize insolvent companies. However, trustees are occasionally appointed. In 2003, at the behest of a major creditor, a subsidiary of ***Boeing***, a trustee was appointed to operate ***Hawaiian Airlines***, which filed for bankruptcy on March 21, 2003.

If the court orders the appointment of a private trustee, one is appointed by the U.S. trustee or by the bankruptcy court in non-U.S. trustee districts. Within 30 days of the order to appoint a private trustee, any party of interest in the case may request the election of a disinterested person to serve as trustee, and the U.S. trustee will call a meeting of creditors for that purpose. The option to elect a trustee is an important change provided by the 1994 Bankruptcy Reform Act.

The duties of a trustee or debtor in possession include the following:

- Being accountable for the debtor's property, including operations of the debtor's business
- Filing a list of creditors, a schedule of assets and liabilities, and a statement of financial affairs (if not filed by the debtor)
- Furnishing information to the court about the debtor's estate and its administration
- Examining creditor claims and objecting to claims that appear to be improper (normally, only the trustee can object)
- Filing a reorganization plan or reporting why a plan will not be filed
- Filing final reports on the trusteeship as required by the court

Trustees and debtors in possession negotiate with the creditors, stockholders, and others in creating a plan of reorganization that will be approved by the bankruptcy court.

If a debtor in possession is appointed, an examiner will be appointed if loans to outsiders other than for goods and services exceed $5,000,000 or if the court concludes that such an appointment is in the interests of the creditors, equity holders, or other parties with an interest in the estate. A primary function of the examiner is to value the debtor's assets and report such valuations to the court.

## Committee Representation

**Creditors' committees** are responsible for protecting the interests of the creditors they represent and preserving the debtor's assets. The committees may review debtor transactions proposed to the court during bankruptcy, such as debtor-in-possession financing and disposal of assets. Committees can bring their objections to the court for consideration. All negotiations between prepetition creditors and the debtor in possession must take place through the creditors' committees.

Unlike in Chapter 7 cases, creditors' committees are not elected in Chapter 11 cases. A creditors' committee is appointed by the U.S. trustee as soon as practicable after the bankruptcy court grants an order for relief under Chapter 11. The creditors' committee (usually seven members) is selected from the largest unsecured creditors. Subsequently, the composition of that committee may be changed and other committees of creditors or equity holders may be appointed. The selection of creditors' committees can be extremely important to the final disposition of a reorganization case. If creditors' committees begin fighting each other, a simple and timely reorganization is nearly impossible.

Governmental units are generally not eligible to serve on creditors' committees. Prior to 1994, the Pension Benefit Guaranty Corporation (PBGC) sat on creditors' committees, but only as a nonvoting member. However, the 1994 Bankruptcy Reform Act gave the PBGC voting rights on creditors' committees.

## Operating Under Chapter 11

Reorganization may take from six months to several years. In the meantime, subject to restrictions of the Bankruptcy Code and the bankruptcy court, the debtor in possession continues operating the business while working out a reorganization plan that is acceptable to all parties concerned. On the day of the bankruptcy filing, the company's existing bank accounts and books are closed and new accounts and books opened.

Usually, the company will arrange a new line of credit with its banks to enable it to continue to operate. This is often referred to as *debtor-in-possession financing*. The bankruptcy court must approve new financing agreements.

**POSSIBLE BENEFITS OF CHAPTER 11 PROTECTION TO THE DEBTOR IN POSSESSION**     With the bankruptcy court's approval, the company may be able to reduce its labor costs through layoffs or wage reductions, or by terminating its pension plans. With the bankruptcy court's approval, the company can reject certain executory contracts and unexpired leases. (**Executory contracts** are those that have not been completely performed by both parties, such as purchase commitments.) Any claims for damages resulting from the cancellation of unfavorable contracts are treated as unsecured debt. Interest accrual on unsecured debt stops at the time of filing. This can be a big factor for some companies. Interest of nearly $3 million a day was accruing on ***Pennzoil's*** $10.3 billion award from ***Texaco*** until the date of Texaco's Chapter 11 filing.

Creditors subject to the jurisdiction of the bankruptcy court may not commence or continue a lawsuit to take possession of the debtor's property without permission of the bankruptcy court; however, secured creditors may receive payments to protect their interest in collateral that the debtor continues to use in its operations. This is particularly applicable when the debtor continues to use collateralized property subject to depreciation, depletion, or amortization. Payments to the secured creditor may reduce the loan balance as the value of the collateral declines.

Financially distressed companies that find it necessary to restructure or swap debt may have difficulty gaining the necessary support from bondholders without filing for bankruptcy. A debt-restructuring plan typically requires approval of 95 percent of each class of bondholders and a majority of stockholders. However, a debt restructuring under the bankruptcy court requires only two-thirds approval of each class of bondholders.

**DISADVANTAGES OF A CHAPTER 11 FILING**     A Chapter 11 filing creates the obvious disadvantage for the debtor corporation of losing the confidence of its lenders, suppliers, customers, and employees. Beyond this stigma of bankruptcy, there is the additional disadvantage of operating a business in competitive markets when capital expenditures, acquisitions, disposals of assets, borrowing money, and so on require prior approval of the court. Depending on the circumstances of a particular case, the bankruptcy court may impose so many restrictions on company management that even day-to-day operations of the business become difficult. The company may have to sell off its profitable units to meet creditor demands for emerging from Chapter 11.

The biggest disadvantage to the debtor is the cost of the bankruptcy proceedings.[6] Lawyers and other advisers are hired by the creditors' committees and the stockholders' committees, as well as by the debtor, but they are all paid from the debtor's assets. Expenses of the creditors' committees may also be reimbursed. Soaring fees in bankruptcy cases prompted some judges to cut fees that they considered unreasonable. The 1994 amendments to the bankruptcy act specifically granted the court the authority to award compensation less than the compensation requested when the fees seem unreasonable.

---

[6]*Finley Kumble* is a good example of how costly and drawn out bankruptcy cases can be. The company filed for bankruptcy in 1988. During the next six years while in Chapter 11, the trustee collected $60 million in cash for creditors. However, 80 percent of the money went for operating and administering the bankruptcy case, including $37 million for lawyers, trustees, and accountants (*The Wall Street Journal*, April 8, 1994, pp. B1, B5).

## The Plan of Reorganization

Confirmation of a **reorganization plan** that is "fair and equitable" to all interests concerned is the final objective of Chapter 11. Only the debtor corporation may file a plan during the first 120 days after the order for relief is granted. Subsequently, the debtor, the trustee, the creditors' committees, an equity security holders' committee, or other parties in interest may file plans.

To reduce bankruptcy expenses and reduce the time a debtor must operate under bankruptcy court restrictions, some firms file preapproved reorganization plans with the court at the same time as they file under Chapter 11 (often called a *prepackaged bankruptcy*). In other words, the terms of the debt restructuring have been worked out with creditors, and some or all creditors have agreed to the plan before the bankruptcy filing. In 2009, General Motors filed a prepackaged bankruptcy on June 1, and on July 9 emerged as a new continuing organization named General Motors, and a new organization that will liquidate named Motors Liquidation Company The prearrangement with creditors was critical in allowing General Motors to emerge in less than six weeks.

Chapter 11 provisions stipulate that the plan of reorganization must:

- Identify classes of claims (except for the administrative expenses, claims arising after an involuntary filing but before the order for relief or appointment of a trustee, and certain tax claims that are given priority)

- Specify any class of claims that is not impaired (a class of claims is *impaired* unless the plan leaves unaltered the legal rights of each claim in the class)

- Specify any class of claims that is impaired

- Treat all claims within a particular class alike

- Provide adequate means for the plan's execution (such as retention of property by the debtor, merger, modification of a lien, and extension of maturity dates)

- Prohibit the issuance of nonvoting equity securities

- Contain provisions for selection of officers and directors that are consistent with the interests of creditors, equity holders, and public policy

A reorganization plan may provide for the sale of the debtor's property and distribution of the proceeds. A debtor corporation may prefer to liquidate under Chapter 11 instead of Chapter 7 because it expects that an orderly sale by company management will raise more money than a liquidating sale by a trustee. **Circuit City** is an example of filing for Chapter 11 bankruptcy with the intent to liquidate.

The court may confirm a reorganization plan if it is accepted by each class of creditors and stockholders whose claims or interests will be impaired. Alternatively, the plan may be confirmed even if some impaired classes reject it, a "cramdown," if the bankruptcy judge determines the plan is fair and equitable.

Acceptance of a plan by a class of claim holders requires approval by at least two-thirds of those claim holders in dollar amount and more than half in number of claims. Classes of claim holders that are unimpaired are assumed to have accepted the plan, and classes that receive nothing are assumed to have rejected it without the necessity of a vote. In order for the bankruptcy court to confirm a plan, each class of claim holders must have accepted the plan or not be impaired under it. Within each class, each holder of a claim must either have accepted the plan or must receive (or retain an interest) not less than that holder would receive if the debtor corporation were liquidated.

After the necessary approval has been obtained, the court holds a confirmation hearing to entertain objections to confirmation and to confirm that the plan is "fair and equitable." Confirmation by the court constitutes discharge of the debtor except for claims provided for in the reorganization plan.

The ranking of unsecured creditors in a large reorganization case is seldom simple and is often the result of negotiation rather than rules. Professional investors who buy debt claims from the original holders at deep discounts and then push for settlements to turn a quick profit from their investment complicate many reorganizations.

Two years after R. H. Macy & Company filed for Chapter 11, Federated Department Stores purchased half of Macy's billion-dollar secured creditor claims held by Prudential Insurance Company of America for $449.3 million and took an option to buy the rest. This gave Federated the ability to block any takeover attempt by another retailer while it negotiated its own Macy takeover with the eight major creditors' committees.

Shareholders have also become more aggressive in bankruptcies. One reason for the increased shareholder activism is the increase in investors who speculate in the stock of companies in Chapter 11. Another reason is the rise of lawyers and financial advisers who specialize in leading equity committees against creditors and management. When solvent companies seek bankruptcy reorganization (e.g., AH Robins and Texaco), shareholders have equity to protect.

## FINANCIAL REPORTING DURING REORGANIZATION

LEARNING OBJECTIVE **18.3**

The reorganization process can take several years. The corporation must still prepare financial statements and filings for the SEC during this time period and after it emerges from reorganization.

Current GAAP (ASC 852) provides guidance for financial reporting by firms during Chapter 11 reorganization and when they emerge from Chapter 11. Accounting practices were diverse prior to this standard because no prescribed accounting for reorganization existed.

The objective of financial statements prepared for a company operating under Chapter 11 is to reflect the financial evolution during the bankruptcy proceedings. Therefore, the financial statements should distinguish the transactions and events directly related to the reorganization from the ongoing operations of the business.

### Effects of Chapter 11 Proceedings on the Balance Sheet

Unsecured liabilities (no collateral) and undersecured liabilities incurred before the company entered Chapter 11 proceedings are **prepetition liabilities subject to compromise**. The debtor corporation and creditors' committees negotiate payment of these liabilities, which may result in payment of less than the claimed amount. The company reports these liabilities as a separate line item on the balance sheet. The remainder of a company's liabilities is reported in the usual manner. These represent secured prepetition liabilities and postpetition liabilities. Recall that liabilities incurred after entering Chapter 11 must be preapproved by the bankruptcy court.

On its June 3, 2006, balance sheet, debtor in possession *Interstate Bakeries Corporation*, maker of Hostess Twinkies and Wonder Bread, reported liabilities subject to compromise of $287,080,000, which represented 19 percent of its total liabilities at that date.

Prepetition claims discovered after the Chapter 11 filing are included in the balance sheet at the court-allowed amount of the claims, rather than the amount at which they may be settled. Claims that cannot be reasonably estimated should be disclosed in notes to the financial statements according to GAAP. (ASC 450)

### Effects of Chapter 11 Proceedings on the Income Statement and the Statement of Cash Flows

Professional fees and similar expenses related directly to the Chapter 11 proceedings are expensed as incurred. "Income, expenses, realized gains and losses, and provisions for losses that result from the restructuring of the business should be reported separately in the income statement as *reorganization items*, except for those required to be reported as discontinued operations." (ASC 852)[7]

Hawaiian Airlines reported $115,063,000 of reorganization costs for the year ended December 31, 2003. Without these charges, Hawaiian's pretax operating income was $77,478,000. Over $14,000,000 of the reorganization costs were attributable to professional fees.

Recorded interest expense is the amount that will be paid during the proceedings, or the probable amount to be allowed as a priority, secured, or unsecured claim. Amounts by which reported interest expense differs from contractual interest should be disclosed. For example, Interstate Bakeries suspended accrual of interest on $100 million of prepetition liabilities. As a result, it parenthetically disclosed on its 2006 income statement that $6.0 million and $4.1 million of contractual interest expense was not accrued in 2006 and 2005, respectively.

Earnings per share for Chapter 11 companies should be reported as usual. Probable issuance of common stock or common stock equivalents under a reorganization plan should be disclosed.

Cash flow items relating to reorganization are disclosed separately from cash flow items relating to the ongoing operations of the business in the statement of cash flows. ASC 852-10-45-13 strongly recommends the direct method of presenting cash flows. The standard does allow for the use of the indirect method if accompanied by further disclosure.

---

[7]FASB ASC 852. Originally Statement of Financial Accounting "Business Combinations." Stamford, CT: Financial Accounting Standards Board, 2016.

## Supplementary Combined Financial Statements

The Financial Reporting Executive Committee of the AICPA concluded that consolidated financial statements that include one or more companies operating under Chapter 11 do not provide adequate information about the bankruptcy proceedings. Therefore, ASC 852 requires the presentation of *condensed combined financial statements* for all entities in reorganization proceedings, as supplementary information. Intercompany receivables and payables are disclosed, with receivables written down if necessary. Consolidation may be inappropriate for some subsidiaries in bankruptcy, particularly if a trustee is appointed to operate the company in bankruptcy.

## FINANCIAL REPORTING FOR THE EMERGING COMPANY

LEARNING OBJECTIVE **18.4**

Ordinarily, a corporate reorganization involves a restructuring of liabilities and capital accounts and a revaluation of assets. Participation of stockholders in the reorganized company depends on whether they are deemed to have an equitable interest by the bankruptcy court. Many companies cannot emerge from bankruptcy as independent companies, and their reorganization plans include the sale of the company. To aid in the plan's execution, the debtor corporation typically amends its charter to provide for the issuance of new securities for cash or in exchange for creditor claims.

The financial condition of companies filing for bankruptcy court protection varies drastically. Occasionally, profitable corporations file for protection under Chapter 11. Settlements under a reorganization plan are influenced by the ability of the interested parties to negotiate and manipulate their relative positions through creditors' and equity holders' committees. Bankruptcy judges also have broad discretionary powers in bankruptcy settlements. A provision of the Bankruptcy Code known as the *doctrine of equitable subordination* allows judges to move unsecured creditors ahead of secured creditors in certain situations in the interest of "fairness."

### Reorganization Value

Determining the reorganization value of the entity emerging from bankruptcy is an important part of the reorganization plan. The emerging entity's **reorganization value** approximates fair value of the entity without considering liabilities. Generally, the reorganization value is determined by discounting future cash flows for the reconstituted business, plus the expected proceeds from sale of assets not required in the new business. The discount rates should reflect the business and financial risks involved. (ASC 852)

The reorganization value determines how much creditors will recover and how much of the reorganized company's stock each class of creditors will receive when the company emerges from bankruptcy. For example, in the Macy bankruptcy case, senior creditors were owed $3.1 billion, and public bondholders were owed $1.2 billion. Macy's board of directors debated a $3.5 billion reorganization value under one plan and a $3.8 billion value under another. Senior creditors would receive a smaller stake in the reorganized company under the higher reorganization value, and bondholders would receive almost nothing under the lower value. The unsecured bondholders' committee pushed for a reorganization value of $4 billion, and another plan put forth by Federated Department Stores, a major creditor, was based on a $3.35 billion reorganization value. After months of negotiation, Federated and Macy filed a joint plan that called for the merger of the two companies and a reorganization value of $4.1 billion.

Financial reporting by a company whose reorganization plan has been confirmed by the court is determined by whether the reorganized entity is essentially a new company that qualifies for fresh-start reporting. GAAP (ASC 852) provides two conditions that must be met for **fresh-start reporting**:

1. The reorganization value of the emerging entity's assets immediately before the date of confirmation of the reorganization plan must be less than the total of all postpetition liabilities and allowed claims subject to compromise.

2. Holders of existing voting shares immediately before confirmation of the reorganization plan must receive less than 50 percent of the emerging entity. This loss of control must be substantive and not temporary.[8]

When firms meet both of these conditions, the emerging entity is in effect a new company and should adopt fresh-start reporting.

---

[8]FASB ASC 852. "Reorganizations." Stamford, CT: Financial Accounting Standards Board, 2014

## Fresh-Start Reporting

Fresh-start reporting results in a new reporting entity with no retained earnings or deficit balance.

**ALLOCATING THE REORGANIZATION VALUE TO IDENTIFIABLE ASSETS**    The reorganization value of the company should be allocated to tangible and identifiable intangible assets according to the acquisition method of accounting for transactions under GAAP. (ASC 805) Any amount of reorganization value not attributed to the tangible and identifiable intangible assets is reported as an unidentifiable intangible asset, "reorganization value in excess of amounts allocable to identifiable assets."[9]

**REPORTING LIABILITIES**    Liabilities, other than deferred income taxes, are reported at their current value at the confirmation date of the reorganization plan. GAAP (ASC 740) requires that deferred tax benefits realized from prior net operating loss carryforwards are applied first to reduction of the reorganization value in excess of amounts allocable to identifiable assets and to other intangibles until exhausted and, finally, as a reduction of income tax expense.

**FINAL STATEMENTS OF OLD ENTITY**    The final statements of the old entity as of and for the period ending on the date of confirmation of the plan disclose the effects of the adjustments on the individual asset and liability accounts resulting from adopting fresh-start reporting. The statements also show the effect of debt forgiveness. The ending balance sheet of the old entity is the same as the opening balance sheet of the new entity, including a zero retained earnings balance.

**DISCLOSURES IN INITIAL FINANCIAL STATEMENTS OF NEW ENTITY**    GAAP (ASC 852) requires the following disclosures to be included in notes to the initial financial statements of the new entity:

- Adjustments to the historical amounts of individual assets and liabilities
- The amount of debt forgiveness
- The amount of prior retained earnings or deficit eliminated
- Significant factors relating to the determination of reorganization value[10]

**COMPARATIVE FINANCIAL STATEMENTS**    The new entity's fresh-start financial statements are not comparable with those prepared by the predecessor company before confirmation of the reorganization plan. If the SEC or another regulatory agency requires predecessor statements, a clear distinction is made between the fresh-start statements of the new entity and the statements of the predecessor company.

## Reporting by Entities That Do Not Qualify for Fresh-Start Reporting

Companies emerging from reorganization that do not meet the criteria for fresh-start reporting report liabilities at present values using appropriate interest rates under GAAP. (ASC 835) Forgiveness of debt should be reported as an unusual item, or other gain. Quasi-reorganization accounting is *not* used for any entities emerging from bankruptcy court protection.

## ILLUSTRATION OF A REORGANIZATION CASE

Tig Corporation files for protection from creditors under Chapter 11 of the bankruptcy act on January 5, 2016. Tig is a debtor in possession and, at the time of filing, its balance sheet includes the following (amounts in thousands):

| | | |
|---|---:|---:|
| Current assets | | |
| Cash | $50 | |
| Accounts receivable—net | 500 | |
| Inventory | 300 | |
| Other current assets | 50 | $900 |
| Plant assets | | |
| Land | $200 | |
| Building—net | 500 | |
| Equipment—net | 300 | |
| Patent | 200 | 1,200 |
| | | $2,100 |

*(continued)*

[9]FASB ASC 805. Originally Statement of Financial Accounting "Business Combinations." Stamford, CT: Financial Accounting Standards Board, 2016.

[10]FASB ASC 852. "Reorganizations." Stamford, CT: Financial Accounting Standards Board, 2014.

| Current liabilities | | |
|---|---|---|
| Accounts payable | $600 | |
| Taxes payable | 150 | |
| Accrued interest on 15% bonds | 90 | |
| Note payable to bank | 260 | $1,100 |
| 15% bonds payable (partially secured with land and building) | | 1,200 |
| Stockholders' deficit | | |
| Capital stock | $500 | |
| Deficit | (700) | (200) |
| | | $2,100 |

On the filing date, Tig's bank accounts and books are closed, and a new set of books is opened. The company arranges short-term financing with a bank (with the bankruptcy court's approval) in order to continue operations while working out a reorganization plan.

During 2016, no prepetition liabilities are paid and no interest is accrued on the bank note or the bonds payable. The bankruptcy court allows Tig Corporation to invest $100,000 in new equipment in August 2016. This new equipment has a useful life of five years, and Tig uses straight-line depreciation calculated to the nearest half-year. The building's depreciation expense is $50,000 per year, and the old equipment's rate is $60,000 per year. Patent amortization is $50,000 per year.

Costs related to the bankruptcy, including all expenses of the creditors' committees and the equity holder committee, are expensed as incurred and paid in cash.

## Reclassification of Liabilities Subject to Compromise

At the beginning of 2016, Tig reclassifies the liabilities subject to compromise into a separate account. The entry to record the reclassification is as follows (in thousands):

| | | |
|---|---|---|
| Accounts payable (−L) | 600 | |
| Taxes payable (−L) | 150 | |
| Accrued interest payable on 15% bonds (−L) | 90 | |
| Note payable to bank (−L) | 260 | |
| 15% bonds payable (partially secured) (−L) | 1,200 | |
|     Liabilities subject to compromise (+L) | | 2,300 |
| To reclassify liabilities subject to compromise. | | |

The $2,300,000 prepetition claims are included in the December 31, 2016, balance sheet separately. A supplemental schedule shows details of these claims.

**DISCLOSING RECLASSIFIED LIABILITIES IN THE FINANCIAL STATEMENTS**    Exhibit 18-9 presents a combined income and retained earnings statement for 2016, as well as a balance sheet at December 31, 2016.

Although the reclassification of liabilities subject to compromise poses no difficulties in preparing balance sheets and income statements, it does complicate the preparation of the cash flows statement.

---

**EXHIBIT 18-9**

Balance Sheet and
Income Statement
During Chapter 11
Reorganization

**TIG CORPORATION**
**INCOME AND RETAINED EARNINGS STATEMENT**
**FOR THE YEAR ENDING DECEMBER 31, 2016**

| | |
|---|---|
| Sales | $1,000,000 |
| Cost of sales | (430,000) |
| Wages and salaries | (250,000) |
| Depreciation and amortization | (170,000) |
| Other expenses | (50,000) |
|     Earnings before reorganization items | 100,000 |
| Professional fees related to bankruptcy proceedings | (450,000) |
|     Net loss | (350,000) |
| Beginning deficit | (700,000) |
|     Deficit December 31, 2016 | $(1,050,000) |

*(continued)*

**EXHIBIT 18-9**

**Balance Sheet and
Income Statement
During Chapter 11
Reorganization
(*Continued* )**

## TIG CORPORATION
## BALANCE SHEET
## AT DECEMBER 31, 2016

| | | |
|---|---:|---:|
| Current assets | | |
| Cash | $150,000 | |
| Accounts receivable—net | 350,000 | |
| Inventory | 370,000 | |
| Other current assets | 50,000 | $920,000 |
| Plant assets | | |
| Land | $200,000 | |
| Building—net | 450,000 | |
| Equipment—net | 330,000 | |
| Patent | 150,000 | 1,130,000 |
| Total assets | | $2,050,000 |
| Current liabilities | | |
| Short-term borrowings | $150,000 | |
| Accounts payable | 100,000 | |
| Wages and salaries payable | 50,000 | $300,000 |
| Liabilities subject to compromise* | | 2,300,000 |
| Stockholders' deficit | | |
| Capital stock | $500,000 | |
| Deficit | (1,050,000) | (550,000) |
| Total liabilities and stockholders' deficit | | $2,050,000 |

**\*Liabilities subject to compromise:**

| | |
|---|---:|
| Partially secured 15% bonds payable plus $90,000 interest, | |
| secured by first mortgage on land and building | $1,290,000 |
| Priority tax claim | 150,000 |
| Accounts payable and unsecured note to bank | 860,000 |
| | $2,300,000 |

The year's changes in the account balances that are reclassified must be separated from changes that affect operations and cash flows for the period. Exhibit 18-10 presents the cash flows statement. Only the direct method of presenting the cash flows statement is illustrated because GAAP (ASC 852) recommends this format.

**EXHIBIT 18-10**

**Statement of Cash
Flows During Chapter 11
Reorganization**

## TIG CORPORATION
## STATEMENT OF CASH FLOWS
## FOR THE YEAR ENDED DECEMBER 31, 2016 (IN THOUSANDS)

| | | |
|---|---:|---:|
| *Cash Flows from Operating Activities* | | |
| Cash received from customers | | $1,150 |
| Cash paid to suppliers | | (400) |
| Cash paid to employees | | (200) |
| Cash paid for other expenses | | (50) |
| Net cash flows provided by operating activities | | |
| before reorganization items | | 500 |
| Operating cash flows from reorganization | | |
| Professional fees paid for services relating | | |
| to bankruptcy proceedings | | (450) |
| Net cash provided by operating activities | | 50 |
| *Cash Flows from Investing Activities* | | |
| Capital expenditures | $(100) | |
| Net cash used in investing activities | | (100) |
| *Cash Flows from Financing Activities* | | |
| Net short-term borrowings | 150 | |
| Net cash provided by financing activities | | $ 150 |
| Net increase in cash | | $ 100 |

(continued)

**EXHIBIT 18-10**

Statement of Cash Flows During Chapter 11 Reorganization (*continued*)

**TIG CORPORATION**
**STATEMENT OF CASH FLOWS**
**FOR THE YEAR ENDED DECEMBER 31, 2016 (IN THOUSANDS)**

| | |
|---|---:|
| Reconciliation of net loss to net cash provided by operating activities | |
| Net loss | $(350) |
| Adjustments to reconcile net loss to net cash provided by operating activities: | |
| Depreciation and amortization | 170 |
| Increase in postpetition payables (operating activities) | 150 |
| Decreases in accounts receivable | 150 |
| Increase in inventory | (70) |
| Net cash provided by operating activities | $50 |

One item unique to firms in reorganization is professional fees relating to bankruptcy proceedings. Cash paid for these items is classified as cash flows from operating activities, but separate disclosure of operating cash flows *before* and *after* the bankruptcy proceedings is recommended.

## Operations Under Chapter 11

During the next six months, Tig continues to operate under Chapter 11 of the Bankruptcy Code while it works out a reorganization plan, and by June 30, 2017, Tig has a plan. Balance sheet and income statement amounts reflecting operations for the first six months of 2017 are summarized as follows (in thousands):

### COMPARATIVE BALANCE SHEETS 2017

| | January 1 | June 30 | Change |
|---|---:|---:|---:|
| Cash | $150 | $300 | $ 150 |
| Accounts receivable | 350 | 335 | (15) |
| Inventory | 370 | 350 | (20) |
| Other current assets | 50 | 30 | (20) |
| Land | 200 | 200 | — |
| Building—net | 450 | 425 | (25) |
| Equipment—net | 330 | 290 | (40) |
| Patent | 150 | 125 | (25) |
| Assets | $2,050 | $2,055 | $5 |
| Liabilities subject to compromise | $2,300 | $2,300 | — |
| Short-term loan | 150 | 75 | $(75) |
| Accounts payable | 100 | 125 | 25 |
| Wages and salaries | 50 | 55 | 5 |
| Liabilities | 2,600 | 2,555 | (45) |
| Common stock | 500 | 500 | — |
| Deficit | (1,050) | (1,000) | 50 |
| Equities | $2,050 | $2,055 | $ 5 |

### INCOME AND RETAINED DEFICIT STATEMENT
### FOR SIX MONTHS ENDING JUNE 30, 2017

| | | |
|---|---:|---:|
| Sales | | $600 |
| Cost of sales | | (200) |
| Wages and salaries expense | | (100) |
| Depreciation and amortization | | |
| Building | $25 | |
| Old equipment | 30 | |
| New equipment | 10 | |
| Patent | 25 | (90) |
| Other expenses | | (30) |
| Earnings before reorganization items | | 180 |
| Professional fees related to bankruptcy proceedings | | (130) |
| Net income | | 50 |
| Beginning deficit | | (1,050) |
| Ending deficit | | $(1,000) |

## The Reorganization Plan

After extensive negotiations among the parties of interest, a reorganization value of $2,200,000 is agreed upon, and a plan of reorganization is filed with the court. The terms of Tig's proposed reorganization plan include the following:

1. Tig's 15 percent bonds payable were secured with the land and building. The bondholders agree to accept $500,000 new common stock, $500,000 senior debt of 12 percent bonds, and $100,000 current portion of senior debt payable on December 31, 2017.

2. The priority tax claims of $150,000 will be paid in cash as soon as the bankruptcy court confirms the reorganization plan.

3. The remaining unsecured, nonpriority, prepetition claims of $950,000 will be settled as follows:
   a. Creditors represented by the accounts payable will receive $275,000 subordinated debt and $140,000 common stock.
   b. The $90,000 accrued interest on the 15 percent bonds will be forgiven.
   c. The $260,000 note payable to the bank will be exchanged for $120,000 subordinated debt and $60,000 common stock.

4. Equity holders will exchange their stock for $100,000 common stock of the emerging company.

## Fresh-Start Reporting

The firm compares the reorganization value with the total postpetition liabilities and court-allowed claims at June 30 to determine if fresh-start reporting is appropriate (amounts in thousands):

| | |
|---|---:|
| Postpetition liabilities | $255 |
| Allowed claims subject to compromise | 2,300 |
| Total liabilities on June 30, 2017 | 2,555 |
| Less: Reorganization value | (2,200) |
| Excess liabilities over reorganization value | $355 |

The excess liabilities over reorganization value indicates that the first condition for fresh-start reporting is met. The reorganization plan calls for the old equity holders to retain less than a 50 percent interest in the emerging company, so the second condition also is met, and fresh-start reporting is appropriate. A summary of the proposed reorganized capital structure is as follows (in thousands):

| | |
|---|---:|
| Postpetition liabilities | $255 |
| Taxes payable | 150 |
| Current portion of senior debt, due December 31, 2017 | 100 |
| Senior debt, 12% bonds | 500 |
| Subordinated debt | 395 |
| Common stock | 800 |
| | $2,200 |

The plan is approved by each class of claims and confirmed by the bankruptcy court on June 30, 2017. Tig Corporation records the provisions of the reorganization plan and the adoption of fresh-start reporting in the books of the old entity as follows (in thousands):

| | | |
|---|---:|---:|
| Accounts payable (prepetition) (−L) | 600 | |
| Interest payable (prepetition) (−L) | 90 | |
| Note payable to bank (prepetition) (−L) | 260 | |
| 15% bonds payable (prepetition) (−L) | 1,200 | |
|     12% senior debt (+L) | | 500 |
|     12% senior debt—current (+L) | | 100 |
|     Subordinated debt (+L) | | 395 |
|     Common stock (new) (+SE) | | 700 |
|     Gain on debt discharge (+Ga, +SE) | | 455 |
| To record settlement of the prepetition claims. | | |

| | | |
|---|---|---|
| Common stock (old) (−SE) | 500 | |
| Common stock (new) (+SE) | | 100 |
| Additional paid-in capital (+SE) | | 400 |
| To record exchange of stock by equity holders. | | |

Tig's assets that have fair values different from their recorded book values on June 30, 2017, are summarized as follows (in thousands):

| | Fair Value | Book Value | Difference |
|---|---|---|---|
| Inventory | $375 | $350 | $25 |
| Land | 300 | 200 | 100 |
| Buildings—net | 350 | 425 | (75) |
| Equipment—net | 260 | 290 | (30) |
| Patent | 0 | 125 | (125) |
| | $1,285 | $1,390 | $(105) |

The entries to adjust Tig's assets for the fair value/book value differences and record the fresh start are as follows (in thousands):

| | | |
|---|---|---|
| Inventory (+A) | 25 | |
| Land (+A) | 100 | |
| Loss on asset revaluation (+Lo, −SE) | 105 | |
| Buildings—net (−A) | | 75 |
| Equipment—net (−A) | | 30 |
| Patent (−A) | | 125 |
| To adjust Tig's assets to their fair values. | | |
| Reorganization value in excess of identifiable assets (+A) | 250 | |
| Gain on debt discharge (−Ga, −SE) | 455 | |
| Additional paid-in capital (−SE) | 400 | |
| Loss on asset revaluation (−Lo, +SE) | | 105 |
| Deficit (+SE) | | 1,000 |
| To eliminate the deficit and additional paid-in capital and to record the excess reorganization value and the fresh start. | | |

Exhibit 18-11 presents working papers to show the effect of the reorganization plan on Tig's balance sheet.

The two leftmost columns of the working papers reflects the balance sheet at June 30, 2017, immediately before recognizing the terms of the reorganization plan and establishing fresh-start reporting. Entries a through e in the adjustment columns adjust the identifiable assets to their reorganization value, which approximates fair value. The excess reorganization value over the fair value of identifiable assets is entered. Working paper entries g through k impose the terms of the reorganization plan.

Note that the last column, Reorganized Balance Sheet, is both the final balance sheet of the old entity and the opening balance sheet of the emerging entity. Although the opening balance sheet of the new entity reflects the reorganization values of the assets, GAAP (ASC 852) provides that the adjustments to historical cost should be disclosed in notes to the initial financial statements. The new Tig Corporation should also disclose the amount of debt forgiveness, the deficit eliminated, and key factors used in the determination of the reorganization value.

**EXHIBIT 18-11**

**Working Papers to Show Confirmation of Reorganization Plan with Fresh-Start Reporting**

## TIG CORPORATION COMPARATIVE BALANCE SHEETS AT JUNE 30, 2017 (IN THOUSANDS)

| | Preconfirmation Balance Sheet | Adjustments to Record Confirmation of Plan | | Reorganized Balance Sheet |
|---|---|---|---|---|
| | | Debits | Credits | |
| **Assets** | | | | |
| Cash | $ 300 | | | $300 |
| Accounts receivable | 335 | | | 335 |
| Inventory | 350 | a    25 | | 375 |
| Other current assets | 30 | | | 30 |
| Land | 200 | b   100 | | 300 |
| Building | 425 | | c    75 | 350 |
| Equipment | 290 | | d    30 | 260 |
| Patent | 125 | | e   125 | — |
| Reorganization excess | — | f   250 | | 250 |
| | $2,055 | | | $2,200 |
| **Equities** | | | | |
| *Postpetition Claims* | | | | |
| Short-term bank loan | $75 | | | $75 |
| Accounts payable | 125 | | | 125 |
| Wages payable | 55 | | | 55 |
| *Prepetition Claims* | | | | |
| Accounts payable—old | 600 | h   600 | | — |
| Taxes payable | 150 | | | 150 |
| Interest payable | 90 | i    90 | | — |
| Bank note payable | 260 | j   260 | | — |
| 15% bonds payable | 1,200 | g 1,200 | | — |
| *Stockholders' Equity* | | | | |
| Capital stock—old | 500 | k   500 | | — |
| Deficit | (1,000) | c    75<br>d    30<br>e   125 | a    25<br>b   100<br>f   250<br>g   100<br>h   185<br>i     90<br>j     80<br>k   400 | — |
| *New Equities:* Current portion—bonds | — | | g   100 | 100 |
| 12% senior debt | — | | g   500 | 500 |
| Subordinated debt | — | | h   275<br>j   120 | 395 |
| Common stock—new | — | | g   500<br>h   140<br>j    60<br>k   100 | 800 |
| Retained earnings—new | — | | | 0 |
| | $2,055 | 3,255 | 3,255 | $2,200 |

## SUMMARY

A debtor corporation that cannot solve its financial problems internally may be able to obtain relief by direct negotiation with creditors. Failing this, the debtor may seek protection from creditors by filing a petition for bankruptcy under Title 11 of the *United States Code*. Either the debtor or the creditors can file a petition. A petition filed under Chapter 11 of the bankruptcy act covers reorganization of the debtor; a Chapter 7 filing covers liquidation of the debtor.

In a Chapter 7 liquidation case, a trustee and creditors' committee are elected by the unsecured creditors. The trustee takes possession of the debtor's estate, converts the assets into cash, and distributes the proceeds according to the priority of claims, as directed by the bankruptcy court.

In a Chapter 11 reorganization case, the U.S. trustee appoints a creditors' committee as soon as practicable after the filing. A trustee may be appointed for cause, but generally the debtor continues in possession. The debtor corporation continues operations while it works out a reorganization plan that is fair and equitable.

GAAP (ASC 852) prescribes financial reporting for companies operating under Chapter 11. Some companies emerging from Chapter 11 are essentially new companies and qualify for fresh-start reporting. Emerging companies that do not meet the criteria for fresh-start reporting account for their liabilities in accordance with GAAP. (ASC 835)

## QUESTIONS

1. What is the distinction between *equity insolvency* and *bankruptcy insolvency*?

2. Bankruptcy proceedings may be designated as *voluntary* or *involuntary*. Distinguish between the two types, including the requirements for filing of an involuntary petition.

3. What are the duties of the U.S. trustee under BAPCPA? Do U.S. trustees supervise the administration of all bankruptcy cases?

4. What obligations does a debtor corporation have in a bankruptcy case?

5. Is a trustee appointed in Title 11 cases? Is a trustee appointed in all Chapter 7 cases? In all Chapter 11 cases? Discuss.

6. Describe the duties of a trustee in a liquidation case under the BAPCPA 1978.

7. Which unsecured claims have priority in a Chapter 7 liquidation case? Discuss in terms of priority ranks.

8. Does the BAPCPA establish priorities for holders of unsecured nonpriority claims (i.e., general unsecured claims)?

9. What is the purpose of a statement of affairs, and how are assets valued in this statement?

10. Does filing a case under Chapter 11 of the bankruptcy act mean that the company will not be liquidated? Discuss.

11. What is a debtor-in-possession reorganization case?

12. When can a creditors' committee file a plan of reorganization under a Chapter 11 case?

13. Discuss the requirements for approval of a plan of reorganization.

14. Describe *prepetition liabilities subject to compromise* on the balance sheet of a company operating under Chapter 11 of the bankruptcy act.

15. The *reorganization value* of a firm emerging from Chapter 11 bankruptcy is used to determine the accounting of the reorganized company. Explain reorganization value as used in FASB ASC 852.

16. FASB ASC 852 provides two conditions that must be met for an emerging firm to use fresh-start reporting. What are these two conditions?

17. A firm emerging from Chapter 11 bankruptcy that does not qualify for fresh-start reporting must still report the effect of the reorganization plan on its financial position and results of operations. How is debt forgiveness reported in the reorganized company's financial statements?

## EXERCISES

### E18-1
### Differences among types of bankruptcy filings and other terminology related to bankruptcy law

1. Bankruptcy *Insolvency* means:
   a **Book value of assets is greater than liabilities**
   b **Fair value of assets is less than liabilities**
   c **Inability to meet financial obligations as they come due**
   d **Liabilities are greater than book value of assets**

2. Aside from liability discharge provided for in the reorganization plan, the discharge of a debtor corporation's liabilities occurs when:
   a **The plan is accepted by a majority of unsecured creditors**
   b **Each class of claims has accepted the plan or is not impaired under it**
   c **Each holder of a claim has accepted the plan or will receive at least as much as if the company were liquidated**
   d **The court confirms that the plan is fair and equitable**

3. A trustee's election in a Chapter 7 case requires:
   a **Approval by a majority of creditors**
   b **Approval by a majority of claims represented**
   c **Approval by a majority in dollar amount of voting creditors, and at least 20 percent of claims must vote**
   d **Approval of two-thirds in dollar amount and a majority of holders of all claims**

4. A corporation may *not* be a debtor in possession if:
   a **The case is initiated in a voluntary filing**
   b **The case is initiated in an involuntary filing**
   c **Loans other than for goods and services exceed $5,000,000**
   d **The court concludes that appointment of a trustee is in the best interests of creditors**

### E18-2
### Financial reporting during bankruptcy

Use the following information in answering questions 1 and 2:

Hal Company filed for protection from creditors under Chapter 11 of the bankruptcy act on July 1, 2016. Hal had the following liabilities at the time of filing:

| | |
|---|---:|
| 10% mortgage bonds payable, secured by a building with a book value and fair value of $100,000 | $200,000 |
| Accrued interest on mortgage (January 1–July 1) | 10,000 |
| Accounts payable | 80,000 |
| Priority tax claims | 50,000 |
| | $340,000 |

1. The December 31, 2016, balance sheet will show prepetition liabilities of:
   a **$340,000 (the claims at filing)**
   b **$240,000 (the original claims less the secured portion of the mortgage bonds)**
   c **$350,000 (the original claims plus six months' interest on the bonds)**
   d **$290,000 (the original claims less the priority tax claims)**

2. Two-and-a-half years after filing the petition for bankruptcy, Hal's management, its creditors, the equity holders, and other parties in interest agree on a reorganization value of $500,000. Which of the following statements is most likely?
   a **The reorganization value approximates the appraised value of the firm as a going concern less the prepetition liabilities.**
   b **The reorganization value approximates the fair value of the assets less the fair value of the prepetition and postpetition liabilities.**
   c **The reorganization value approximates the fair value of the assets less the book value of the postpetition liabilities and the estimated settlement value of the prepetition liabilities.**
   d **The reorganization value approximates the fair value of the entity without considering the liabilities.**

3. Uni, a parent company with five wholly owned operating subsidiaries, is in the process of preparing consolidated financial statements for the year. Two of Uni's subsidiaries are operating as debtors in possession under Chapter 11 of the bankruptcy act. Which of the following statements is correct?

a *ASC Topic 810, "Consolidation," prohibits Uni from consolidating the financial statements of the two subsidiaries in bankruptcy with those of the other affiliated companies.*

b *ASC Topic 810, "Consolidation," requires that the financial statements of all five of the subsidiaries be consolidated with those of the parent company.*

c *If Uni's consolidated financial statements include the operations of the two subsidiaries in bankruptcy, ASC Topic 852 requires that condensed combined financial statements for all entities in reorganization be presented as supplementary financial statements.*

d *If Uni's consolidated financial statements do not include the operations of the two subsidiaries in bankruptcy, those subsidiaries must be accounted for under the cost method.*

4. When fresh-start reporting is used, the initial financial statement disclosures should not include:

a *Adjustments made in the amounts of individual assets and liabilities*

b *The amount of debt forgiven*

c *The amount of prior retained earnings or deficit eliminated*

d *Current and prior-year EPS amounts*

## E18-3
## Financial reporting during bankruptcy—Distributions to creditors

Ram holds a $400,000 note receivable from Pat. It has been learned that Pat filed for Chapter 7 bankruptcy and that the expected recovery of nonsecured claims is 45¢ on the dollar. Inventory items with an estimated recoverable value of $80,000 secure Pat's note payable to Ram.

**REQUIRED:** Determine Ram's expected recovery on the note.

## E18-4
## Fresh-start reporting requirements

Bax has been operating under Chapter 11 of the Bankruptcy Code for the past 15 months. On March 31, 2016, just before confirmation of its reorganization plan, Bax's reorganization value is estimated at $3,000,000. A balance sheet for Bax prepared on the same date is summarized as follows:

| | |
|---|---|
| Current assets | $750,000 |
| Plant assets | 3,000,000 |
| | $3,750,000 |
| Postpetition liabilities | $1,200,000 |
| Prepetition liabilities subject to compromise* | 1,500,000 |
| Fully secured debt | 900,000 |
| Capital stock | 900,000 |
| Deficit | (750,000) |
| | $3,750,000 |

*Represents allowed claims. The reorganization plan calls for payment of $150,000 and issuance of $300,000 notes and $375,000 common stock in settlement of the prepetition liabilities.

**REQUIRED**

1. Does Bax qualify for fresh-start reporting on the basis of the reorganization value?
2. What other conditions must be met for fresh-start reporting? Show calculations.

## E18-5
## Financial reporting during bankruptcy—Distributions to creditors

Hol is in bankruptcy and is being liquidated by a court-appointed trustee. The financial report that follows was prepared by the trustee just before the final cash distribution:

| | |
|---|---|
| *Assets* | |
| Cash | $300,000 |
| *Approved Claims* | |
| Mortgage payable (secured by property that was sold for $100,000) | $180,000 |
| Accounts payable, unsecured | 160,000 |
| Administrative expenses payable, unsecured | 16,000 |
| Salaries payable, unsecured | 4,000 |
| Interest payable, unsecured | 20,000 |
| Total approved claims | $380,000 |

The administrative expenses are for trustee fees and other costs of administering the debtor corporation's estate.

**REQUIRED:** Show how the $300,000 cash will be distributed to holders of each of the claims.

## PROBLEMS

## P18-1
## Financial reporting during bankruptcy

The balance sheet of Sco appeared as follows on March 1, 2016, when an interim trustee was appointed by the U.S. trustee to assume control of Sco's estate in a Chapter 7 case.

| Assets | | Liabilities and Stockholders' Equity | |
|---|---|---|---|
| Cash | $4,000 | Accounts payable | $50,000 |
| Accounts receivable—net | 8,000 | Note payable—unsecured | 40,000 |
| Inventories | 36,000 | Revenue received in advance | 1,000 |
| Land | 20,000 | Wages payable | 3,000 |
| Buildings—net | 100,000 | Mortgage payable | 80,000 |
| Intangible assets | 26,000 | Capital stock | 40,000 |
| | | Retained earnings deficit | (20,000) |
| Assets | $194,000 | Liabilities and equity | $194,000 |

## ADDITIONAL INFORMATION

1. Creditors failed to elect a trustee; accordingly, the interim trustee became trustee for the case.

2. The land and buildings are pledged as security for the mortgage payable.

3. In January 2016, Sco received $1,000 from a customer as a payment in advance for merchandise that is no longer marketed.

4. Activities of the trustee during March are summarized as follows:

   **a.** $7,200 is collected on the receivables, and the balance is determined to be uncollectible.

   **b.** All inventories are sold for $19,400.

   **c.** Land and buildings bring a total of $90,000.

   **d.** Nothing is realized from the intangible assets.

   **e.** Administrative expenses of $8,200 are incurred by the trustee.

## REQUIRED

1. Prepare a separate set of books for the trustee to assume possession of the estate and convert its assets into cash.

2. Prepare financial statements on March 31 for Sco in trusteeship (balance sheet, cash receipts and disbursements, and changes in estate equity).

3. Prepare journal entries on the trustee's books to distribute available cash to creditors and close the case.

## P18-2
## Financial reporting during bankruptcy

Jut filed a petition under Chapter 7 of the bankruptcy act in January 2016. On March 15, 2016, the trustee provided the following information about Jut's financial affairs.

| | Book Values | Estimated Realizable Values |
|---|---|---|
| *Assets* | | |
| Cash | $20,000 | $10,000 |
| Accounts receivable—net | 100,000 | 70,000 |
| Inventories | 150,000 | 60,000 |
| Plant assets—net | 250,000 | 270,000 |
| Total assets | $520,000 | |
| *Liabilities* | | |
| Liability for priority claims | $80,000 | |
| Accounts payable—unsecured | 130,000 | |
| Note payable, secured by accounts receivable | 100,000 | |
| Mortgage payable, secured by all plant assets | 220,000 | |
| Total liabilities | $530,000 | |

### REQUIRED

1. Determine the amount expected to be available for unsecured claims.
2. Determine the expected recovery per dollar of unsecured claims.
3. Estimate the amount of recovery for each class of creditors.

## P18-3
## Claims rankings and cash distribution upon liquidation

Fab is being liquidated under Chapter 7 of the bankruptcy act. All assets have been converted into cash, and $374,500 cash is available to pay the following claims:

1. Administrative expenses of preserving and liquidating the debtor corporation's estate — $12,500
2. Merchandise creditors — 99,000
3. Local government for property taxes — 4,000
4. Local bank for unsecured loan (principal is $30,000 and interest is $4,500) — 34,500
5. State government for gross receipts taxes — 3,000
6. Employees for unpaid wages during the month before filing (includes $13,025 for the company president and less than $12,475 for each of the other employees) — 48,000
7. Customers for prepaid merchandise that was not delivered — 1,500
8. Holders of the first mortgage on the company's real estate that was sold for $240,000 (includes $220,000 principal and $8,500 interest) — 228,500

Assume that all the claims are allowed and that they were timely filed.

### REQUIRED

1. Rank the claims according to priority under the bankruptcy act.
2. Show how the available cash will be distributed in final liquidation of the corporation.

## P18-4
## Financial reporting during bankruptcy—Statement of affairs

Han filed a petition under Chapter 7 of the bankruptcy act on June 30, 2016. Data relevant to its financial position as of this date are:

| | Book Value | Estimated Net Realizable Values |
|---|---|---|
| Cash | $2,200 | $2,200 |
| Accounts receivable—net | 15,000 | 13,500 |
| Inventories | 20,000 | 22,500 |
| Equipment—net | 55,000 | 28,000 |
| Total assets | $92,200 | $66,200 |
| Accounts payable | $26,400 | |
| Rent payable | 7,600 | |
| Wages payable | 12,000 | |
| Note payable plus accrued interest | 31,000 | |
| Capital stock | 55,000 | |
| Retained earnings (deficit) | (39,800) | |
| Total liabilities and equity | $92,200 | |

### REQUIRED

1. Prepare a statement of affairs assuming that the note payable and interest are secured by a mortgage on the equipment and that wages are less than $4,000 per employee.

2. Estimate the amount that will be paid to each class of claims if priority liquidation expenses, including trustee fees, are $4,000 and estimated net realizable values are actually realized.

## P18-5
## Financial reporting during bankruptcy

The unsecured creditors of Dan filed a petition under Chapter 7 of the bankruptcy act on July 1, 2016, to force Dan into bankruptcy. The court order for relief was granted on July 10, at which time an interim trustee was appointed to supervise liquidation of the estate. A listing of assets and liabilities of Dan as of July 10, 2016, along with estimated realizable values, is as follows:

| | Book Values | Estimated Realizable Values |
|---|---|---|
| *Assets* | | |
| Cash | $80,000 | $80,000 |
| Accounts receivable—net | 210,000 | 160,000 |
| Inventories | 200,000 | 210,000 |
| Equipment—net | 150,000 | 60,000 |
| Land and buildings—net | 250,000 | 140,000 |
| Intangible assets | 10,000 | — |
| | $900,000 | $650,000 |
| Accounts payable | $400,000 | |
| Note payable | 100,000 | |
| Wages payable (from June and July) | 24,000 | |
| Taxes payable | 76,000 | |
| Mortgage payable $200,000, plus $5,000 unpaid interest to July 10 | 205,000 | |
| Capital stock | 300,000 | |
| Retained earnings deficit | (205,000) | |
| | $900,000 | |

### ADDITIONAL INFORMATION

1. Accounts receivable are pledged as security for the note payable.

2. No more than $1,000 is owed to any employee.

**3.** Taxes payable is a priority item.

**4.** Inventory items include $50,000 acquired on July 5, 2016; the unpaid invoice is included in accounts payable.

**5.** The mortgage payable and interest are secured by the land and buildings.

**6.** Trustee fees and other costs of liquidating the estate are expected to be $11,000.

### REQUIRED

**1.** Prepare a statement of affairs for Dan on July 10, 2016.

**2.** Develop a schedule showing how available cash will be distributed to each class of claims, assuming that (a) the estimated realizable values are actually received and (b) the trustee and other fees of liquidating the estate are $11,000.

### P18-6
### Financial reporting during bankruptcy

The balance sheet of Val at June 30, 2016, contains the following items:

| *Assets* | |
|---|---|
| Cash | $40,000 |
| Accounts receivable—net | 70,000 |
| Inventories | 50,000 |
| Land | 30,000 |
| Building—net | 200,000 |
| Machinery—net | 60,000 |
| Goodwill | 50,000 |
| | $500,000 |
| | |
| *Equities* | |
| Accounts payable | $110,000 |
| Wages payable | 60,000 |
| Property taxes payable | 10,000 |
| Mortgage payable | 150,000 |
| Interest on mortgage payable | 15,000 |
| Note payable—unsecured | 50,000 |
| Interest payable—unsecured | 5,000 |
| Capital stock | 200,000 |
| Retained earnings deficit | (100,000) |
| | $500,000 |

Val is in financial difficulty, and its stockholders and creditors have requested a statement of affairs for planning purposes. The following information is available:

**1.** The company estimates that $63,000 is the maximum amount collectible for the accounts receivable.

**2.** Except for 20 percent of the inventory items that are damaged and worth only $2,000, the cost of the other items is expected to be recovered in full.

**3.** The land and building have a combined appraisal value of $170,000 and are subject to the $150,000 mortgage and related accrued interest.

**4.** The appraised value of the machinery is $20,000.

**5.** Wages payable and property taxes payable are unsecured priority items that do not exceed any limitations of the bankruptcy act.

### REQUIRED

**1.** Prepare a statement of affairs for Val as of June 30, 2016.

**2.** Compute the estimated settlement per dollar of unsecured liabilities.

## P18-7
## Installment liquidation

Lop filed for relief under Chapter 11 of the bankruptcy act on January 2, 2016. A summary of Lop's assets and equities on this date, and at June 30, 2016, follows. Estimated fair values of Lop's assets at June 30 are also shown.

|  | January 2, 2016 | June 30, 2016 | |
|---|---|---|---|
|  | Per Books | Per Books | Estimated Fair Value |
| **Assets** |  |  |  |
| Cash | $200 | $6,700 | $6,700 |
| Trade receivables—net | 800 | 1,000 | 1,000 |
| Inventories | 2,000 | 1,600 | 2,000 |
| Prepaid items | 500 | — | — |
| Land | 1,000 | 1,000 | 2,000 |
| Buildings—net | 3,000 | 2,900 | 1,500 |
| Equipment—net | 2,000 | 1,800 | 1,800 |
| Patent | 4,500 | 4,000 | 0 |
|  | $14,000 | $19,000 | $15,000 |
| **Equities** |  |  |  |
| Accounts payable | $1,000 | $3,000 | |
| Wages payable | 500 | 1,000 | |
| Bank note payable (includes $500 interest) | 5,000 | | |
| Long-term note payable (secured with equipment) | 6,000 | | |
| Prepetition liabilities allowed | | 12,500 | |
| Common stock | 7,000 | 7,000 | |
| Deficit | (5,500) | (4,500) | |
|  | $14,000 | $19,000 | |

The parties in interest agree to a reorganization plan on July 1, 2016, and a hearing to confirm that the plan is fair and equitable is scheduled for July 8. Under the reorganization plan, the reorganization value is set at $16,000, and the debt and equity holders will receive value as follows:

|  | To Receive Cash Consideration | To Receive Noncash Consideration | |
|---|---|---|---|
| **Postpetition Claims** |  |  |  |
| Accounts payable (in full) | $3,000 | | |
| Wages payable (in full) | 1,000 | | |
| **Prepetition Claims** |  |  |  |
| Accounts payable (80%) | 800 | | |
| Wages payable (80%) | 400 | | |
| Bank note payable and | | $2,000 | note payable |
| interest (80%) | | 2,000 | common stock |
| Long-term note payable (80%) | | 1,800 | note payable |
| | | 3,000 | common stock |
| Common stockholders* | | 2,000 | common stock |
|  | $5,200 | $10,800 | |

*Reorganization value over consideration allocated to creditors.

The reorganization plan is confirmed on July 8, 2016, under the new name of Hip. There are no asset or liability changes between July 1 and July 8.

### REQUIRED

1. Is the reorganization of Lop eligible for fresh-start accounting? Show calculations.
2. Prepare journal entries to adjust Lop's accounts for the reorganization plan.
3. Prepare a fresh-start balance sheet for Hip as of July 8, 2016.

# PROFESSIONAL RESEARCH ASSIGNMENTS

Answer the following questions by reference to the FASB Codification of Accounting Standards. Include the appropriate reference in your response.

**PR 18-1** What are the special requirements for the presentation of financial statements for a firm that is operating under Chapter 11 Bankruptcy protection?

**PR 18-2** Under what circumstances does a firm emerging from bankruptcy qualify for fresh start reporting? Can you find an example of how a firm should report in a fresh start reporting situation?

# CHAPTER 19

## An Introduction to Accounting for State and Local Governmental Units

**H**ave you ever examined a set of financial statements for the city where you live, or have you wondered how your donation to the Red Cross is accounted for? The preceding 18 chapters of this book have highlighted issues affecting the accounting and financial reporting practices of commercial business organizations. Other organizations exist whose composition or operations differ to some extent from those of the commercial business organizations with which you have become most familiar as an accounting student. For example, governmental units, not-for-profit organizations, colleges and universities, and some healthcare entities are deemed different enough to warrant the establishment of accounting standards for their specific use. In fact, generally accepted accounting principles (GAAP) of state and local governments are established by the **Governmental Accounting Standards Board (GASB)** under the auspices of the Financial Accounting Foundation (FAF). As you will recall, GAAP for businesses and other nongovernment (essentially, private not-for-profit) organizations are established by the GASB's sister organization, the Financial Accounting Standards Board (FASB).

This chapter provides an overview of fund accounting and financial reporting for state and local governmental units. Chapters 20 and 21 illustrate fund accounting practices for specific funds of a local governmental entity. Chapter 22 provides an introduction to accounting principles and reporting practices for not-for-profit organizations.

### HISTORICAL DEVELOPMENT OF ACCOUNTING PRINCIPLES FOR STATE AND LOCAL GOVERNMENTAL UNITS

LEARNING OBJECTIVE **19.1**

According to the U.S. Census Bureau's 2012 *Census of Governments*, there are more than 91,000 general and special-purpose governmental entities in the United States. A governmental entity is generally created for the administration of public affairs and has one or more of the following characteristics:

- Popular election of officers or appointment (or approval) of a controlling majority of the members of the organization's governing body by officials of one or more state or local governments

- The potential for unilateral dissolution by a government with the net position reverting to a government

- The power to enact and enforce a tax levy[1]

---

[1]Guide for non profit entities, © AICPA

**LEARNING OBJECTIVES**

**19.1** Learn about the historical development of accounting principles for state and local governmental units.

**19.2** Understand the purposes of fund accounting and its basic premises.

**19.3** Perform transaction analysis using proprietary and governmental accounting models.

**19.4** Recognize various fund categories, as well as their measurement focus and basis of accounting.

**19.5** Review basic governmental accounting principles.

**19.6** Learn about the contents of a governmental entity's comprehensive annual financial report.

An organization may also be classified as a governmental entity if it possesses the ability to directly issue debt that is exempt from federal taxation.

With the exception of the federal government, state and local governmental units such as the State of Maine; Jefferson County, Milwaukee School District; and the City of Golden, Colorado, constitute the largest single category of nonprofit organizations in terms of the dollar volume of annual expenditures. Since 1984, the GASB has been the primary source of accounting principles for states, cities, counties, towns, villages, school districts, special districts and authorities, and other local governmental entities. Before 1984, the most important continuous source of accounting principles for state and local governmental units was the Municipal Finance Officers Association (MFOA) and its committees on governmental accounting.[2] The MFOA's National Committee on Governmental Accounting issued *Municipal Accounting and Auditing* in 1951 and *Governmental Accounting, Auditing, and Financial Reporting (GAAFR)* in 1968. These resources constituted the most complete frameworks of accounting principles specific to governmental units, and they provided standards for preparing and evaluating the financial reports of governmental units. In 1974 the AICPA issued its industry audit guide, *Audits of State and Local Governmental Units*, in which it noted that *GAAFR*'s accounting and reporting principles constituted generally accepted accounting principles (GAAP) except when they were modified by the audit guide. The American Institute of Certified Public Accountants' (AICPA) endorsement was important to the *GAAFR*'s authority and general acceptance by preparers, auditors, and users of governmental financial statements.

The AICPA's audit guide prompted the 1980 revision of *GAAFR* to update and clarify governmental accounting and financial reporting principles and to incorporate pertinent aspects of the audit guide. The MFOA established a new committee, the National Council on Governmental Accounting (NCGA), to develop the *GAAFR* restatement. As part of this project, the NCGA issued *Governmental Accounting and Financial Reporting Principles, Statement No. 1* (NCGA1) in 1979. The following year, a new *GAAFR* was issued as a comprehensive volume to explain and illustrate the principles of NCGA1. Shortly thereafter, the AICPA issued *Statement of Position 80-2*, which amended *Audits of State and Local Governmental Units* to recognize the principles of NCGA1 as GAAP. GAAFR and AICPA audit guides are updated periodically.

## The Governmental Accounting Standards Board

In 1984, the Financial Accounting Foundation (FAF, which also oversees the Financial Accounting Standards Board [FASB]) formed the Governmental Accounting Standards Board (GASB) to establish and improve standards for governmental accounting and financial reporting. FAF trustees appoint one full-time chair and six part-time members to serve on the board.

In July 1984, GASB issued GASB Statement No. 1, *Authoritative Status of NCGA Pronouncements and AICPA Industry Audit Guide*, designating all NCGA statements and interpretations issued and currently in effect as "generally accepted accounting principles" until changed or superseded.

The GASB in 1985 integrated all effective accounting and reporting standards into one publication called *Codification of Governmental Accounting and Financial Reporting Standards*. The *Codification* is revised annually to reflect all current GASB official pronouncements. In 1986, the AICPA declared that Rule 203 of its Rules of Conduct applies to the GASB's pronouncements. Therefore, GASB pronouncements constitute GAAP for governments. At this writing, the GASB has issued 81 statements of standards, 6 concept statements, and 6 interpretations that set forth governmental accounting and reporting requirements. The GASB issues technical bulletins, implementation guides, and user guides as well.

The GASB is widely respected for its "due process," but the scope of several of its projects have been controversial including GASB Statement No. 34 (discussed later in the chapter), nonfinancial performance reporting (which GASB calls SEA or Service Efforts and Accomplishments reporting), and reporting of Economic Condition. In 2013, the FAF reviewed concerns with GASB and instituted a few changes in the scope of GASB's authority.[3]

---

[2]The Municipal Finance Officers Association was renamed the Government Finance Officers Association in 1985.

[3]The FAF's project on the scope of GASB is summarized online at (http://www.accountingfoundation.org/jsp/Foundation/Page/FAFSectionPage&cid=1176162236146)

## GAAP Hierarchy for State and Local Governmental Entities

In June of 2015, GASB issued Statement No. 76, *The Hierarchy of Generally Accepted Accounting Principles for State and Local Governments* and in December of 2010, GASB issued Statement No. 62, *Codification of Accounting and Financial Reporting Guidance Contained in Pre-November 30, 1989 FASB and AICPA Pronouncements*. Statement 76 "reduces the GAAP hierarchy to two categories of authoritative GAAP and addresses the use of authoritative and nonauthoritative literature in the event that the accounting treatment for a transaction or other event is not specified within a source of authoritative GAAP."[4] The two categories are:

a. Officially established accounting principles—Governmental Accounting Standards Board (GASB) Statements and GASB Interpretations (Category A)

b. GASB Technical Bulletins; GASB Implementation Guides; and literature of the AICPA cleared by the GASB (Category B).[5]

If none of these provides adequate guidance, governmental entities should consider *other accounting literature* (including GASB Concepts Statements, Standards of the International Public Sector Accounting Standards Board, FASB standards not made applicable to governments by a GASB standard, and textbooks). Thus, when addressing an accounting issue, governmental financial statement preparers should first look to GASB statements and interpretations, followed by GASB technical bulletins, and so on. From a practical standpoint, *Statement on Auditing Standards (SAS) No. 69* requires independent auditors who audit governmental entities to express an opinion about whether the auditee has complied with GASB pronouncements. Bond rating agencies consider the audit opinion when assessing a governmental entity's rating for a municipal bond offering, which provides further incentive for compliance with GASB standards.

## OVERVIEW OF BASIC GOVERNMENTAL ACCOUNTING MODELS AND PRINCIPLES

LEARNING OBJECTIVE **19.2**

Governmental accounting and financial reporting differ from corporate accounting and financial reporting. Primary reasons for the differences are that governments lack a profit motive and must focus on demonstrating accountability to the public and governmental authorities.[6] Governments focus on their continuing ability to provide and fund goods and services, rather than on measures of income. Since GASB Statement 34 was issued in 1999, state and local governments must utilize two bases of accounting and two **measurement focuses**. This section introduces some of the unique aspects of governmental accounting. The discussion continues in Chapters 20 and 21.

State and local governmental units engage in both business-type activities and general governmental activities. **Business-type activities** provide services to users for fees that are intended to recover all, or at least the primary portion, of the costs of providing the services. Some of these activities provide services to entities outside the government, such as water and sewer services, electric service, golf courses, public docks and wharves, and transit systems. Others provide services to departments or agencies within the government, such as central motor pools, self-insurance activities, and central printing and data processing services.

**General governmental activities** provide goods and services to citizens without regard to their ability to pay. The level of goods and services provided is mandated by the citizens through their elected officials or is determined by persuasion from a higher level of government. General governmental activities (police and fire protection, road maintenance) are usually financed by taxes or intergovernmental grants and subsidies, and there may be no relationship between the people receiving the services and those paying for them (e.g., free immunizations provided to children of low-income families). Limited governmental resources are allocated by establishing fixed dollar budgets and legally restricting the use of resources to various general governmental projects and programs. For example, the City of Portland, Maine, may levy taxes to finance the construction of a new school, the State of Montana may provide monies to finance a drug prevention program at local levels, or Orange County, California, may borrow resources to finance a convention center addition. In each

---

[4]Summary of Statement No. 76 The Hierarchy of Generally Accepted Accounting Principles for State and Local Governments © 2015 GASB.

[5]Statement No. 55 of the Governmental Accounting Standards Board, © 2009 GASB.

[6]GASB White Paper, "Why Governmental Accounting and Financial Reporting Is—and Should Be—Different." Norwalk, CT, 2006.

of these cases, the resources collected are formally restricted for a specific purpose. The appropriate governmental bodies must approve expenditures beyond the allocated limits.

Because general governmental activities and business-type activities constitute two different models of financing and providing services, governments are said to have a dual nature. Furthermore, the existence of restrictions on most governmental resources is the primary reason for fund accounting, a major feature of governmental accounting that helps governments demonstrate compliance with resource restrictions.

**Fund accounting** supports the practice of restricting financial resource usage to specific purposes as a means of controlling governmental operations, and it also accommodates the differing accounting bases that general governmental activities and business-type activities use for resource allocation. It is a system that requires multiple accounting entities, called **funds**, for a single government. Governments use an individual fund to account for a certain business-type activity or a certain subset of general governmental financial resources that are set aside for a certain purpose or purposes. Indeed, not only are funds separate accounting entities, but they also use different accounting models for business-type activities and general governmental activities. Thus, just as governments have a dual nature, they also have dual accounting models.

## Fund Definition and Categories

GASB defines a fund as

> a fiscal and accounting entity with a self-balancing set of accounts recording cash and other financial resources, together with all related liabilities and residual equities or balances, and changes therein, which are segregated for the purpose of carrying on specific activities or attaining certain objectives in accordance with special regulations, restrictions, or limitations.[7]

Note that because a fund is an accounting entity, each fund has the following:

- Its own accounting equation
- Its own journals, ledgers, and other accounting records needed to account for the effects of external transactions or interfund activities on the net position/activities accounted for in the fund
- Financial statements that report on the fund itself

Business-type activities are accounted for in a category of funds called **proprietary funds**. General governmental activities are accounted for in **governmental funds**. There are two types of proprietary funds and five types of governmental funds. Fortunately, accounting for each of the two types of proprietary funds is quite similar, and accounting for each of the five types of governmental funds is also quite similar. Thus, once you learn to account for one type of proprietary fund, you will know most of what is needed to account for all other proprietary funds. Likewise, once you can account for one type of governmental fund, you know most of what is needed to account for all governmental funds.

A third category of funds is the **fiduciary** or **trust and agency funds**. Most transactions or interfund activities within funds in this category are accounted for like proprietary funds. Hence, learning how to account for proprietary funds enables one to account for most fiduciary funds as well. The following sections focus on accounting for proprietary funds and governmental funds, and they begin to discuss the various models of accounting.

## The Proprietary Fund Accounting Model

The most effective way to understand the nature and working of funds is to understand the basic accounting model or accounting equation. Proprietary funds are explained first because accounting for a proprietary fund is very similar to accounting for a commercial business. In fact, the GASB has incorporated a substantial portion of the FASB's standards for proprietary funds.

---

[7]*GASB Codification*, Section 1100.102. Printed with permission.

A simplified[8] accounting equation for a proprietary fund is:

$$\text{Current assets} + \text{Noncurrent assets} - \text{Current liabilities} - \text{Noncurrent liabilities} = \text{Net position}^9$$

With the exception of the term **net position**, which is used to represent **fund equity**, the same accounting equation is used for businesses and proprietary funds. Proprietary funds report revenues and expenses using the accrual basis of accounting, and they use the economic resources measurement focus. Because most proprietary fund transactions are accounted for and reported in the same manner as commercial businesses, your business accounting background is directly applicable to proprietary fund accounting. The transactions and events that are unique to governments or that are accounted for differently from a commercial business enterprise are the focus of much of the discussion of proprietary funds in Chapter 21.

## The Governmental Fund Accounting Model

Accounting for general governmental activities (e.g., public safety, general administration, and the judicial system) differs from the accounting for business-type activities. Governmental funds, in their purest and simplest form, are essentially working capital entities. A simplified accounting equation for a governmental fund is:

$$\text{Current assets} - \text{Current liabilities} = \text{Fund balance}$$

The measurement focus of governmental funds is current financial resources. Although this equation becomes complicated by practical considerations, it is important to continue to think of governmental funds as working capital entities, which focus on current assets and current liabilities, even as you address more advanced issues. In fact, governmental funds generally record **expenditures** to reflect the use of governmental fund working capital, instead of traditional "expenses." Expenditures normally represent the disbursement of working capital funds during a period, whether or not consumption of resources occurs.

Obviously, the governmental funds are not adequate to account for all the assets and liabilities of general governmental activities. When comparing the proprietary and governmental fund models, note that noncurrent assets (e.g., fixed assets) and long-term liabilities are excluded from the governmental fund equation. General governmental activities, however, require significant investments in fixed assets, and governments commonly incur large debt obligations associated with general governmental operations. General governmental fixed assets (i.e., all fixed assets except those of specific proprietary or similar fiduciary funds) are referred to as **general fixed assets**. Although governments do not account for and record these fixed assets and their depreciation within the governmental funds or governmental fund statements, they do maintain fixed asset records. The general fixed assets and related depreciation are reflected in government-wide financial statements, which are discussed later in the chapter.

General governmental long-term liabilities (i.e., all governmental long-term liabilities except those of specific proprietary or similar fiduciary funds) are referred to as **general long-term debt**. These long-term liabilities include bonds, notes, warrants, claims and judgments, unfunded pension obligations, and accumulated vacation and sick leave that will be paid with general governmental resources. As in the accounting for general fixed assets, governments do not account for and record long-term liabilities within the governmental funds or governmental fund statements. Again, debt records are maintained, and general long-term debt is reflected in government-wide financial statements, which are discussed later in the chapter.

Although the governmental fund model has never included noncurrent assets and liabilities, general fixed assets and general long-term debt have been historically reported in governmental-entity

---

[8]GASB Statement No. 63 creates reporting requirements for two additional financial statement elements, "deferred outflows of resources" and "deferred inflows of resources," which are described later in this chapter but not needed to explain the intuition about differences in the basic accounting models.

[9]As described later, GASB Statement No. 63 does not allow the term *net assets* for fiscal periods beginning after June 15, 2012. During the transition, students may see financial statements with the term *net assets*, which just means the reporting entity has not implemented Statement No. 63.

financial statements within account groups called the *general fixed asset account group* and the *general long-term debt account group*. GASB Statement No. 34, issued in 1999, eliminated these account groups, but it requires inclusion of these noncurrent items in government-wide financial statements. Many governmental entities may accomplish the recordkeeping requirements associated with the noncurrent items through maintenance of the account groups; however, in name, they no longer exist.

LEARNING
OBJECTIVE **19.3**

## Applying the Simplified Models—Transaction Analysis

To solidify your understanding of the proprietary (or business-type activity) fund accounting model and the governmental fund accounting model, consider the effects of several transactions on each of those models. The various types of governmental and proprietary funds are discussed later.

Some transactions have essentially the same impact on a proprietary fund as they would on a governmental fund. This is true for most events that affect only working capital accounts. Consider the analysis of the following four transactions from Exhibit 19-1:

**Transactions**

1. Incurred salary cost of $5,000.

2. Charges for services rendered, $2,500, were billed and collected immediately.

3. Borrowed $30,000 on a one-year, 6 percent note six months before year-end.

4. Year-end accrual of interest on the note.

Note that the analysis is identical except that net increases and decreases in proprietary fund asset and liability accounts affect net position, whereas net increases and decreases in governmental fund assets and liabilities affect fund balance. We would report transaction 1 as an *expense* of $5,000 in a proprietary fund and as an *expenditure* of $5,000 in a governmental fund. We would report transaction 2 as revenue of $2,500 in each case. Transaction 3 does not affect the operating statement of either a proprietary fund or a governmental fund. We would report transaction 4 as interest expense of $900 in a proprietary fund and as $900 of interest expenditures in a governmental fund.

In many other cases, identical transactions impact proprietary and governmental funds differently. This is particularly true for transactions that relate to long-term liabilities or fixed assets. The full effects of such transactions related to business-type activities are accounted for completely within a proprietary fund. The same transaction involving general governmental activity is handled quite differently, because governmental funds focus on current financial resources and are not equipped to record noncurrent assets and liabilities. Therefore, we make memorandum entries in fixed asset or long-term debt records to accommodate subsequent reporting of these items as appropriate within the financial statements. Consider the analysis of the following four transactions from Exhibit 19-2:

**Transactions**

5. Borrowed $15,000 by issuing a three-year note.

6. Purchased computer equipment costing $2,800 for cash.

7. Sold a truck for $1,000. It was originally purchased five years ago for $18,000, has an estimated residual value of $1,200, and is fully depreciated.

8. Computed depreciation on the computer equipment for the year, $875.

## EXHIBIT 19-1

**Transaction Analysis—Only Working Capital Accounts Affected**

| Proprietary Fund | Business-Type Activity | | | | Governmental Fund | General Governmental Activity | | | |
|---|---|---|---|---|---|---|---|---|---|
| | No. 1 | No. 2 | No. 3 | No. 4 | | No. 1 | No. 2 | No. 3 | No. 4 |
| Current assets | | +2,500 | +30,000 | | Current assets | | +2,500 | +30,000 | |
| Noncurrent assets | | | | | | | | | |
| Current liabilities | +5,000 | | +30,000 | +900 | Current liabilities | +5,000 | | +30,000 | +900 |
| Noncurrent liabilities | | | | | | | | | |
| Net position | −5,000 | +2,500 | | −900 | Fund balance | −5,000 | +2,500 | | −900 |

**EXHIBIT 19-2**

### Transaction Analysis—Nonworking Capital Accounts Affected

| Proprietary Fund | Business-Type Activity | | | | Governmental Fund | General Governmental Activity | | | |
|---|---|---|---|---|---|---|---|---|---|
| | No. 5 | No. 6 | No. 7 | No. 8 | | No. 5 | No. 6 | No. 7 | No. 8 |
| Current assets | +15,000 | −2,800 | +1,000 | | Current assets | +15,000 | −2,800 | +1,000 | |
| Noncurrent assets | | +2,800 | −1,200 | −875 | | | | | |
| Current liabilities | | | | | Current liabilities | | | | |
| Noncurrent liabilities | +15,000 | | | | | | | | |
| Net position | | | −200 | −875 | Fund balance | +15,000 | −2,800 | +1,000 | |

Notice the dramatic difference in the accounting and reporting of these transactions under the two models. Transactions 5 and 6 do not affect a proprietary fund's net position. However, both of these transactions do affect working capital. Therefore, the fund balance of a governmental fund is affected by both transactions. We report fund balance increases resulting from issuance of general long-term debt as other financing sources in governmental funds and refer to them as "long-term note proceeds, $15,000." Transaction 6 is reported as expenditures for capital outlay in the governmental fund and is capitalized as computer equipment in the proprietary fund.

Transaction 7 affects the proprietary fund net position and the fund balance in very different ways. A proprietary fund would report a $200 loss on disposal of fixed assets (book value less cash received) for transaction 7, whereas a governmental fund would report the $1,000 of "proceeds from the sale of fixed assets" as an other financing source, because it has experienced a cash inflow and carried no fixed assets in its fund balance sheet.

Transaction 8 requires that we report $875 of depreciation expense in the proprietary fund operating statement. However, if the computers are general fixed assets, we do not report depreciation in the governmental fund because depreciation is not a use of working capital, and we do not recognize the fixed asset within the fund.

After you have mastered the transaction analysis for a generic proprietary fund and that for a generic governmental fund, two primary elements remain to establish a good understanding of the basic governmental accounting model. The first is to know and distinguish the specific types of funds. The second is to understand the basis of accounting used for each type of fund. In addition, it is helpful to be able to identify and classify interfund transactions, which are simply transactions between two funds.

## Proprietary Fund Types

LEARNING OBJECTIVE **19.4**

Governments account for their business-type activities in one of two types of proprietary funds: enterprise funds and internal service funds. Some governments do not have any enterprise or internal service funds; other governments have several of each type. The primary distinction between the two types of proprietary funds is that governmental units use **internal service funds** to account for activities operated and financed on a business-type basis that provide goods or services either solely or almost solely to *internal customers*, that is, other departments or agencies of the government. Governments use **enterprise funds** to account for business-type activities that serve primarily *outside customers*, typically the public. Enterprise fund activities often provide services to internal customers as well, but those customers are not the predominant customers.

Exhibit 19-3 contains the formal definitions of the specific fund types. Common examples of activities accounted for in internal service funds include centralized data processing services, central motor pools and garages, centralized risk financing activities, and central inventory stores. Activities commonly accounted for in enterprise funds include public (government-owned) gas and electric utilities, water and sewer departments, government trash and garbage services, parking garages, civic centers, toll roads, mass transit services, and golf courses.

Governmental Fund* Types

- *General fund.* Accounts for all financial resources except those accounted for in another fund.
- *Special revenue funds.* Account for the proceeds of specific revenue sources that are restricted or committed to expenditure for specified purposes other than debt service or capital projects. Is not used for resources held in trust for individuals, private organizations, or other governments.
- *Capital projects funds.* Account for financial resources that are restricted, committed, or assigned to expenditure for capital outlays, including the acquisition or construction of capital facilities and other capital assets (excluding those financed by proprietary funds or in trust funds for individuals, private organizations, or other governments).
- *Debt service funds.* Account for financial resources that are restricted, committed, or assigned to expenditure for principal and interest (including financial resources accumulating for future principal and interest payments).
- *Permanent funds.* Report resources that are legally restricted to the extent that only earnings, and not principal, may be used for purposes that support the reporting government's programs—that is, for the benefit of the government or its citizenry.

Proprietary Fund Types

- *Enterprise funds.* Report any activity for which a fee is charged to external users for goods and services. Activities are required to be reported as enterprise funds if any of the following criteria are met: (a) The activity is financed with debt that is secured solely by a pledge of the net revenues from fees and charges of the activity; (b) laws and regulations require that the activity's costs of providing services, including capital costs (such as depreciation or debt service), be recovered with fees and charges, rather than with taxes or similar revenues; or (c) the pricing policies of the activity establish fees and charges designed to recover its costs, including capital costs (such as depreciation or debt service).
- *Internal service funds.* Report any activity that provides goods or services to other funds, departments, or agencies of the primary government and its component units, or to other governments, on a cost-reimbursement basis. Internal service funds should be used only if the reporting government is the predominant participant in the activity.

Fiduciary Fund Types

- *Trust and agency funds.* Report assets held in a trustee capacity for others that therefore cannot be used to support the government's own programs. The fiduciary fund category includes (a) pension (and other employee benefit) trust funds, (b) investment trust funds, (c) private-purpose trust funds, and (d) agency funds. (*GASB Codification, sec 1300*)

*The governmental fund definitions were updated in GASB Statement No. 54, *Fund Balance Reporting and Governmental Fund Definitions* issued in February of 2009 and effective for fiscal years ending after June 15, 2010.

Notice how the internal service fund definition in Exhibit 19-3 requires departments or agencies that provide goods or services to other departments or agencies on a cost-reimbursement basis to use these funds for accounting. A cost-reimbursement basis means that the fee charged is intended to cover the costs (expenses) of providing the good or service, rather than to produce net income. Proprietary funds, which provide goods and services to external parties, are more apt to produce net income. As noted earlier, the key distinction between the two types of proprietary funds is whether they primarily serve the public and external entities, or they predominantly serve internal departments and agencies.

## Governmental Fund Types

Five types of governmental funds are used to account for general governmental activities. Each is a working capital entity that accounts for only a portion of the general governmental working capital. The difference between these funds, then, is the purpose or purposes for which the working capital accounted for in each of them may or must be used. **Special revenue funds** account for general governmental financial resources restricted for specific purposes. **Permanent funds** report resources whose use is permanently restricted, but whose earnings are expendable for the benefit of the government or its citizens (this type is least common). A **capital projects fund** accounts for resources to be used to construct or acquire a major general governmental fixed asset and the related current liabilities. A **debt service fund** accounts for resources to be used to pay principal, interest, and related charges on general long-term debt. Finally, the **general fund** accounts for working capital available for general use. A government has only one general fund, but it may have any number of each of the other fund types. Recall that each of these governmental funds has the same accounting equation that was discussed and illustrated earlier for a generic governmental fund. The only added complexity is that we must understand which governmental fund is affected in order to account for general governmental activities properly.

## Fiduciary (Trust and Agency) Fund Types

As indicated in Exhibit 19-3, trust and agency funds include three types of trust funds as well as agency funds. Note that all fiduciary funds contain resources held for the benefit of parties other than the government itself. Pension trust funds account for government pension plans, if the government acts as a trustee. Investment trust funds account for the external portion of investment pools reported by the sponsoring government. **Private-purpose trust funds** report all other trust arrangements whose resources provide benefits to parties outside the government.

**Agency funds** are essentially "receive-hold-remit" or "bill-collect-hold-remit" accountability devices, which account for resources a government is holding as an agent on behalf of parties outside the government. For example, an agency fund may be used to record payroll taxes withheld and remitted to a higher government. The accounting equation for an agency fund is:

$$\text{Assets} = \text{Liabilities}$$

Every asset received by an agency fund results in a corresponding increase in liabilities or a decrease in another asset. Agency funds have no equity or fund balance and, therefore, have no operations to report. No revenues, expenditures or expenses, or transfers are reported in an agency fund.

## Applying the Model Using Specific Funds

A useful way to solidify your understanding of the funds and the model at this point is to expand your knowledge using transactions. Exhibit 19-4 analyzes the following general governmental transactions:

**Transactions**

1. Issued general obligation bonds, par value of $3,000,000, at 101 to finance construction of a government office building.

2. Transferred the premium on the bonds to the fund used to account for payment of principal and interest on the bonds.

3. Incurred and paid construction costs of $12,500 on the building.

4. Levied and collected sales taxes restricted to use for economic development, $6,000.

5. Paid general governmental employees' salaries, $4,500. Another $500 of salaries accrued but not paid.

6. Borrowed $7,500 on a six-month note to finance general operating costs of the government.

Note that the transaction analysis is the same as for general governmental activities in the previous section on applying the model, except that the exhibit identifies the specific governmental fund

| Governmental Fund | | Accounting Equation | | |
|---|---|---|---|---|
| No. | Fund | Current Assets | Current Liabilities | Fund Balance |
| 1 | Capital projects | +3,030,000 | | +3,030,000 |
| 2a | Capital projects | −30,000 | | −30,000 |
| 2b | Debt service | +30,000 | | +30,000 |
| 3 | Capital projects | −12,500 | | −12,500 |
| 4 | Special revenue | +6,000 | | +6,000 |
| 5 | General | −4,500 | +500 | −5,000 |
| 6 | General | +7,500 | +7,500 | |

**EXHIBIT 19-4**

General Governmental Transaction Analysis Using Specific Funds

affected by each transaction. Transaction 1 represents a long-term debt issuance. Because governmental funds do not record long-term liabilities, fund balance is increased by the amount of bond proceeds. Transaction 2 illustrates a transfer of resources between funds. The premium amount transferred from the capital projects fund to the debt service fund will be held for the purpose of debt repayment. The premium amount, which represents an increase to fund balance in the debt service fund is recognized as an "other financing source—nonreciprocal transfer from the capital projects fund." The premium is termed an "other financing source" to distinguish it from a revenue, and it is nonreciprocal because it will not be repaid to the capital projects fund. The transfer is reflected as "other financial use—nonreciprocal transfer to the debt service fund" in the capital projects fund. The remaining transactions affect current assets, current liabilities, and fund balance as you might anticipate.

## Basis of Accounting

Key aspects of the proprietary fund and governmental fund models are the *basis of accounting* and *measurement focus* used for each. Consistent with having fundamentally different accounting equations and models, governmental and proprietary funds use different bases of accounting in measuring financial position and operating results. The GASB specifies when the accrual and modified accrual bases of accounting are to be used.

In essence, the *accrual basis* refers to recognition of revenues and expenses as in business accounting. It follows an "economic resources" measurement focus, whereby all economic resources, whether current or noncurrent, are reported. We report proprietary funds using the accrual basis of accounting.

The *modified accrual basis* refers to recognition of revenues when resources become available to meet current obligations and recognition of expenditures when incurred. The modified accrual basis of accounting is consistent with a "flow of current financial resources" measurement focus, whereby funds report on current resources and current obligations. In general, we report governmental funds using the modified accrual basis of accounting, which is consistent with the governmental model introduced earlier in the chapter. In addition, governments prepare government-wide financial statements, which present governmental and proprietary funds together on the accrual basis of accounting.

It is important to understand the differences between the accrual basis of accounting and the modified accrual basis of accounting. We always report proprietary (or business-type) funds on the accrual basis of accounting, whereas we report governmental funds using the modified accrual basis of accounting in the fund statements and the accrual basis of accounting in the government-wide statements. Chapter 20 focuses on governmental funds and governmental fund financial statements. We record governmental fund transactions using the modified accrual basis of accounting. Later, when we prepare the government-wide statements, we make adjustments to reflect governmental fund activities under the accrual basis of accounting.[10] Chapter 21 discusses the accounting and financial reporting for proprietary and fiduciary funds in detail.

## Elements of Financial Statements

In 2007 the GASB issued Concepts Statement No. 4 and established seven basic elements (assets, liabilities, inflows of resources, outflows of resources, deferred inflows of resources, deferred outflows of resources, and net position). These elements become prominent for fiscal periods beginning after June 15, 2012, as they are required to be used per GASB Statement Nos. 63 and 65 when preparing financial statements. GAAP financial reports no longer use the term *net assets* as it has been replaced with *net position*. The balance sheets and statements of net position have two new categories; the debit side includes assets *plus deferred outflows of resources* while the credit side includes liabilities *plus deferred inflows of resources* and net position.

---

[10]Governments have three options for original entries in the governmental funds: (1) record using modified accrual during the year and make year-end adjustments to accrual for the government-wide statements, (2) record using accrual during the year and make year-end adjustments to modified accrual for the fund statements, or (3) record each event under both modified accrual and full accrual during the year. Due to its prevalence in practice, we present the first approach.

## Revenue Recognition

Governmental revenue sources are varied and include taxes, grant receipts, and collections of user fees and fines. Revenue recognition within governmental entities is determined by the nature of the underlying transaction. GASB Statement No. 33, *Accounting and Financial Reporting for Nonexchange Transactions*, characterizes revenue transactions as (1) exchange (and exchange-like) transactions or (2) nonexchange transactions. *Exchange transactions* are those "in which each party receives and gives up essentially equal values."[11] *Nonexchange transactions* are those "in which a government gives (or receives) value without directly receiving (or giving) equal value in exchange." Many of the transactions in governmental funds are nonexchange in nature, because general governmental activities often address the needs of the public and are funded by taxpayers who generally do not receive benefits in direct relation to their tax payments.

Exhibit 19-5 provides an overview of the four classifications of nonexchange transactions identified in GASB Statement No. 33 (derived tax revenues, imposed nonexchange revenues, government-mandated nonexchange transactions, and voluntary nonexchange transactions) and the criteria that must be met prior to revenue and asset recognition. Derived tax revenues include sales and income taxes, because they are assessed based on a value that a taxpayer spends or earns. Imposed nonexchange revenues include property taxes. Although the tax is assessed based on property value, the governmental resources available to the taxpayer (police and fire protection) are not necessarily relative to the amount paid. Government-mandated and voluntary nonexchange transactions, which include grant funds and donations, do not require an equal exchange by the governmental entity.

In general, a transaction should be substantially complete prior to revenue recognition. However, the modified accrual basis of accounting used for governmental funds also requires that revenues be objectively measurable and "available" in order to be recognized. To be available, the revenues must

**EXHIBIT 19-5**

**Recognition Criteria for Nonexchange Transactions**

| Class of Revenue | Recognition |
|---|---|
| *Derived Tax Revenues* Examples: Sales taxes, personal and corporate income taxes, motor fuel taxes, and similar taxes on earnings and consumption | *Assets* Period when underlying exchange has occurred or when resources are received, whichever is first. *Revenues* Period when underlying exchange has occurred. (Report advance receipts as liabilities.) When modified accrual accounting is used, resources should be "available." |
| *Imposed Nonexchange Revenues* Examples: Property taxes, most fines and forfeitures | *Assets* Period when an enforceable legal claim has arisen or when resources are received, whichever is first. *Revenues* Period when resources are required to be used or first period that use is permitted (e.g., for property taxes, the period for which levied). When modified accrual accounting is used, resources should be "available." |
| *Government-Mandated Nonexchange Transactions* Examples: Federal government mandates on state and local governments *Voluntary Nonexchange Transactions* Examples: Certain grants and entitlements, most donations | *Assets and Liabilities* Period when all eligibility requirements have been met or (for asset recognition) when resources are received, whichever is first. *Revenues and Expenses or Expenditures* Period when all eligibility requirements have been met. (Report advance receipts or payments for use in the following period as liabilities.) However, when a provider precludes the sale, disbursement, or consumption of resources for a specified number of years, until a specified event has occurred, or permanently (e.g., permanent and **term endowments**), report revenues and expenses or expenditures when the resources are received or paid, respectively, and report resulting net position as restricted. When modified accrual accounting is used, resources should be "available." |

*Source:* GASB Statement No. 33, p. 48. Printed with permission.

[11]GASB Statement No. 33. Printed with permission.

be "collectible within the current period or soon enough thereafter to pay liabilities of the current period."[12] Recognition of revenues that do not meet these "available" criteria must be *deferred* initially (recorded as a liability, but in an account title other than "deferred revenues," so as to avoid confusion with the new financial statement elements **Deferred Outflows of Resources** and **Deferred Inflows of Resources**). Then revenues are recognized when "available." (Thus, revenues may be recognized later in governmental funds than in proprietary funds.)

The criterion of being collected "soon enough" after the current period to pay liabilities for current expenditures is not defined in the GASB Codification. However, with respect to property tax revenue recognition, the *Codification* limits this period to not more than 60 days after the end of the fiscal year. Most government accountants extend this "not more than 60 days" limitation to all other **governmental fund revenues** as well. Governments are required to disclose their revenue recognition policies in the notes to the financial statements.

The GASB established an exception to the 60-day rule of thumb in GASB Statement No. 31, *Accounting and Financial Reporting for Certain Investments and for External Investment Pools*. This statement requires most investments to be reported at their fair value. In 2015, GASB issued Statement No. *79, Certain External Investment Pools and Pool Participants*, to provide conformity with SEC rules. As a result, many investment pools will not be able to report their pools at amortized cost.

Investment income of each fund of a government, therefore, is increased or decreased by the net change in the fair value of investments. Governments may report income as a single line item in the financial statements, with the effect of the change in fair value disclosed in the notes, or they may present details in the financial statements as follows:

| | |
|---|---|
| Interest income | XXX |
| Net increase (decrease) in fair value of investments | YYY |
| Total investment income | ZZZ |

A final point is that governmental funds recognize revenues on the net revenue approach. These funds recognize revenues net of allowances for uncollectible accounts, rather than at gross amounts earned or levied. Therefore, whereas a proprietary fund that levied charges on customers of $1,000 but expected $10 to prove uncollectible would report revenues of $1,000 and expenses of $10, a governmental fund in a similar scenario would report only the net realizable value, or $990, as revenues.

## Expense and Expenditure Recognition

The expenses of a governmental unit are similar to those of a commercial business enterprise. Expenses essentially reflect the cost of assets or services used by an entity, and they are recognized in the period incurred. Expenditures, unique to government accounting, typically reflect the use of governmental fund working capital. Thus, expenditures normally reflect the cost of goods or services acquired during a period, whether or not consumed, and the maturing of general long-term debt principal. With limited exceptions, governmental funds recognize expenditures in the period that the fund liability is incurred.

Recall that under fund accounting, proprietary funds recognize expenses using the accrual basis of accounting, whereas governmental funds recognize expenditures, based on the modified accrual basis. However, GASB Statement No. 34 requires both proprietary funds and governmental funds to report expenses within the government-wide statements. In fund statements, governmental funds report expenditures, whereas proprietary funds report expenses. Although this may sound confusing, examples in Chapters 20 and 21 should help clarify the difference between expenses and expenditures, as well as their treatment within the financial statements.

Many operating expenses and expenditures occur simultaneously. For instance, the use of electricity results in both an expense and an expenditure in the same amount at the same point in time. The same is true for salaries and wages of government employees. For other items, the timing of expense and expenditure recognition differs dramatically. The purchase of a fixed asset that is to be used by a governmental fund over a 10-year period results in a capital outlay *expenditure* in the year of acquisition and no additional expenditures over the next nine years. The same purchase within a proprietary fund results in a depreciation *expense* each year over the 10-year period of its

---

[12]*GASB Codification*, Section 1600.106. Printed with permission.

use, however. Note that a fixed asset acquired by a governmental fund is treated differently within a set of financial statements. In the fund statements, a governmental fund records an expenditure for the full cost of the asset in the year purchased. In the government-wide statements, an adjustment is made to capitalize and depreciate the same fixed asset. This occurs because of the unique bases of accounting used in the government-wide and fund financial statements.

Likewise, the government as a whole sometimes incurs liabilities that do not result in governmental fund liabilities being incurred at the same point in time. This may be true for general government claims and judgments, compensated absences, or pension contributions. For example, proceeds of general long-term debt issuances increase both the fund balance and the current assets of the governmental funds, but the liability is not recorded in the fund statements. In the fund statements, the recipient governmental fund will report the fund balance increase as bond issue proceeds, or a similar title, and show it as another financing source in the statement of revenues, expenditures, and changes in fund balance (a fund statement). Long-term debt appears as a long-term liability within the government-wide statement of net position.

The primary exception to recognizing expenditures when a governmental fund incurs a liability relates to interest and principal expenditures on general long-term debt. Governmental funds record these amounts "when due"; however, although they are never required to be reported before the legal due date, it is permissible to accrue such expenditures if (1) they are due early in the next year and (2) the financial resources for their payment have been provided in the current year.

## Interfund Activity

Governments use several funds to account for their activities, and numerous transactions between funds, or interfund transactions, occur annually. Examples include sales of services from an enterprise or internal service fund department to other departments, shifts of general fund resources to capital projects funds to cover part of the cost of a capital project, and interfund loans. *GASB Codification*, Section 1800.102, classifies interfund transactions into several types, each of which is reported differently in the financial statements.

**Interfund loans** are loans that are made by one fund to another and must be repaid. The receivable and payable resulting from an interfund loan appear in the lender and borrower funds. If prompt payment is not expected, the activity may require reclassification as a transfer. Interfund transfers occur when one fund provides resources to another for legally authorized purposes (an operating transfer) or when one fund helps to establish or enhance another (a **residual equity transfer**). Transfers are either reciprocal or nonreciprocal, depending on whether or not repayment is expected. Governmental funds record transfers as other financing sources/uses, whereas proprietary funds report transfers in a category following nonoperating revenues/expenses on the statement of revenues, expenses and changes in fund net position. Interfund services provided and used include sales and purchases between funds at approximate external market value. The seller fund records these activities as revenues, whereas the purchasing fund recognizes an expense or expenditure; however, unpaid amounts should be reported as interfund receivables and payables in the fund financial statements. An interfund **reimbursement** is necessary when an expenditure applicable to one fund is made by a different fund. Reimbursements are not reported in the financial statements.

## The Role of the Budget

Because resource use within governments typically must be authorized by laws or ordinances, the role and impact of the budget is dramatically more significant in governments than in business accounting.[13] In fact, every governmental unit is required to adopt a budget document, which is often considered more significant than the financial reports.[14] Governmental accounting systems are required to provide appropriate budgetary control either formally through the use of budgetary accounts (typical in the general fund, special revenue funds, and other governmental funds) or informally through the maintenance of separate budgetary records and comparisons. In addition, a comparison of actual and budgetary amounts is required to be included in the annual operating statements

---

[13]GASB White Paper 2006.
[14]*GASB Codification*, Section 1100.111.

(or in required supplementary information) of all governmental funds for which an annual budget has been adopted. (We will illustrate how budgets are used within fund accounting in Chapter 20.)

A **budget** is a plan of financial operation consisting of an estimate of proposed expenditures for a given period and the proposed means of financing them. Ordinarily, the preparation of a budget is the responsibility of the executive branch of government—the mayor, city manager, governor, and so on. Approval of a budget, however, is a legislative responsibility. A legislative body may approve a proposed budget as submitted by the chief executive, or it may amend the executive budget prior to approval. *When approved by the legislative body, the budget for expenditures becomes a spending ordinance that has the force of law. An approved revenue plan also has the force of law*, because it provides the governmental unit with the power to levy taxes, to sell licenses, to charge for services, and so on, in the amount or at the rate approved.

**Appropriations** are approved or authorized expenditures. They provide legislative control over the expenditure budget prepared by the executive branch. Such control may be in detail, such as when the legislative body makes appropriations for each item included in the budget. The legislative body, however, may approve expenditures (make appropriations) by category (e.g., by department) or in total. Line-item approval provides maximum control over the management by the legislative branch because the legislative body must approve any change in the budget. If a department makes appropriations, however, managers could allocate more resources to some items within a department (e.g., supplies) and less to others (e.g., salaries) without legislative approval of the change.

If an appropriation is allocated to a specific time period, it is termed an **allotment**. In other words, the yearly appropriations may be allotted to months or quarters to prevent expenditure of the appropriation too early in the year or during times of fiscal stress. Furthermore, allotments may be necessary for coordinating revenues collected with payments for expenditures (i.e., managing cash flows).

A current budget is normally for a one-year period, and it includes the operating budget as well as the capital budget for the current period. A **capital budget**, as used here, represents the current portion of a **capital program** (a plan of capital expenditures to be incurred each year over a fixed period of years).

## THE FINANCIAL REPORTING ENTITY

Many governments are closely associated with other entities or governmental units, which may or may not be economically dependent on the government. For example, Genesee County, New York, houses a local community college, and your hometown has probably established a public housing authority to provide low-cost housing to residents. When a government has such relationships, the complex question arises about how (or if) these entities should be reported in the financial statements of the government. GASB Statement No. 14, *The Financial Reporting Entity*, explains that the financial reporting entity is made up of the primary government and its component units. Each state government and each general-purpose local government (city, town, county, and so on) is a **primary government**, whereas a special-purpose government (e.g., a water district, hospital, or transit authority) is a primary government if it has a separately elected governing body, is legally separate, and is fiscally independent of other state or local governments. Component units are legally separate organizations for which the primary government is financially accountable. They can also be other organizations for which the nature and significance of their relationships with the primary government are such that their exclusion would result in the reporting entity's statements being misleading or incomplete.

Governments have two main options on how to report component units in their financial statements. The component units can be combined (a.k.a. *blended*) into the primary government, or they can be *discretely presented* in a separate column depending on how closely related the component is to the primary government. Determining the proper presentation has challenged preparers since Statement No. 14 was issued in 1991. GASB issued improvements via Statement No. 39 in 2002, Statement No. 61 in 2010, and Statement No. 80 in 2016. While the final determination requires professional judgment, the goal of the reporting entity is to include "only organizations for which the elected officials are financially accountable or that are determined by the government to be misleading to exclude."[15]

---

[15]GASB Statement No. 61 , p. ii. Printed with permission.

Component units are *blended* under three circumstances. First, blending is used when the governing body of the component is substantially the same as the primary government *and either* (a) there is a financial burden or benefit relationship between the primary government and the component unit *or* (b) management of the primary government has operational responsibility for the component unit. Second, blending is used for component units that exclusively or almost exclusively provide services for the benefit of the primary government, such as offering financing services or services to employees of the primary government. Third, blending is used for component units whose total debt, including leases, will be repaid entirely or almost entirely by the primary government.

If none of the criteria are met, the component unit is *discretely presented* in the reporting entity's financial statements. Discrete presentation requires the presentation of the component unit's financial data in a column or columns separate from the primary government's financial data in the government-wide statements. Supporting information for the individual component units should be provided in combining statements that follow the fund financial statements or in condensed financial statements included in the notes to the financial statements of the primary government.

## COMPREHENSIVE ANNUAL FINANCIAL REPORT

LEARNING OBJECTIVE **19.6**

All state and local governmental units must report their activities to residents and other interested parties. *GASB Codification*, Section 2200.101, states that "Every governmental entity should prepare and publish, as a matter of public record, a *comprehensive annual financial report* (CAFR) that encompasses all funds of the primary government (including its blended component units). The CAFR should also encompass all discretely presented component units of the reporting entity."[16]

In 1999, the GASB issued GASB Statement No. 34, *Basic Financial Statements—and Management's Discussion and Analysis—for State and Local Governments* (GASB 34), which instituted major changes to the manner in which governmental entities prepare and present their financial statements. GASB 34 retained traditional fund accounting and fund financial statements; however, it also introduced *government-wide financial statements*, which are prepared using accrual accounting for all of a government's activities—both governmental and business-type.

CAFRs contain three major sections (introductory, financial, and statistical) and are considered an entity's "official annual report." Exhibit 19-6 lists the contents of a GASB 34 CAFR, which are described in detail here.

### Introductory Section of a CAFR

The introductory section of a CAFR includes a table of contents, a letter of transmittal, a list of principal officers, and an organizational chart. It might also include copies of awards that were received for financial reporting. The transmittal letter provides an introduction to the financial report, describes management's responsibility for the statements, and outlines significant developments within the entity during the fiscal year. Prior to GASB 34 implementation, transmittal letters were quite extensive, but GASB 34 requires an in-depth analysis of the entity's economic condition in management's discussion and analysis, which is found in the financial section. Thus, transmittal letters are now relatively brief in comparison.

### Financial Section

The financial section includes the management's discussion and analysis, the auditor's report, the government-wide financial statements, and the fund financial statements.

**MANAGEMENT'S DISCUSSION AND ANALYSIS (MD&A)**   The MD&A is a new requirement under *GASB 34*. Considered *required supplementary information*, the MD&A precedes the financial statements and is comparable to the MD&A of a corporate annual report. Intended to "provide an objective and easily readable analysis of the government's financial activities based on the currently known facts, decisions, or conditions,"[17] the MD&A should include the following:

1. A brief discussion of the basic financial statements, including the relationships of the statements to each other, and the significant differences in the information they

---

[16]*GASB Codification, Section 2200.101*. Printed with permission.
[17]GASB Statement No. 34, paragraph 8.

## CAFR CONTENTS REQUIRED UNDER GASB 34

**Introductory Section.**

Table of contents
Letter of transmittal
List of principal officers
Organization chart

**Financial Section**

Management's discussion and analysis (MD&A)
Auditor's report
Basic financial statements
*Government-wide statements*
 Statement of net position (accrual basis)
 Statement of activities (accrual basis)
*Fund financial statements*
 Balance sheet—governmental funds (modified accrual basis)
 Statement of revenues, expenditures, and changes in fund balance—governmental funds (modified accrual basis)
 Statement of net position—proprietary funds (accrual basis)
 Statement of revenues, expenses, and changes in net position—all proprietary and similar trust fund types (accrual basis)
 Statement of cash flows—all proprietary and similar trust fund types (accrual basis)
 Statement of fiduciary net position—fiduciary funds (accrual basis)
 Statement of changes in fiduciary net position—fiduciary funds (accrual basis)
Notes to the financial statements
Required supplementary information other than MD&A
Combining statements and individual fund statements and schedules
**Statistical Section**

provide. This discussion should include analyses that assist readers in understanding why measurements and results reported in fund financial statements either reinforce information in government-wide statements or provide additional information.

2. Condensed financial information derived from government-wide financial statements comparing the current year to the prior year. At a minimum, governments should present the information needed to support their analysis of financial position and results of operations required in 3, later, including these elements:
   a. Total assets, distinguishing between capital and other assets
   b. Total liabilities, distinguishing between long-term liabilities and other liabilities
   c. Total net position, distinguishing among amounts invested in capital assets, net of related debt; restricted amounts; and unrestricted amounts
   d. Program revenues, by major source
   e. General revenues, by major source
   f. Total revenues
   g. Program expenses, at a minimum by function
   h. Total expenses
   i. Excess (deficiency) before contributions to term and permanent endowments or permanent fund principal, special items, and transfers
   j. Contributions
   k. Special items
   l. Transfers
   m. Change in net position
   n. Ending net position

3. An analysis of the government's overall financial position and results of operations to assist users in assessing whether financial position[18] has improved or deteriorated[19]

---

[18]The GASB had a controversial project on reporting "Economic Condition" in which it issued a Preliminary Views document in November of 2011. The project was placed on hold in November of 2012 pending resolution of the "Scope of GASB" effort noted in footnote 3. See https://algaonline.org/index.aspx?NID=376 for a summary of the controversy.

[19]Based on GASB SUMMARY OF STATEMENT NO. 34, © Anthony H Joseph

as a result of the year's operations. The analysis should address both governmental and business-type activities as reported in the government-wide financial statements and should include *reasons* for significant changes from the prior year, not simply the amounts or percentages of change. In addition, important economic factors, such as changes in the tax or employment bases that significantly affected operating results for the year, should be discussed.

4. An analysis of balances and transactions of individual funds. The analysis should address the reasons for significant changes in fund balances or fund net position and whether restrictions, commitments, or other limitations significantly affect the availability of fund resources for future use.

5. An analysis of significant variations between original and final budget amounts and between final budget amounts and actual results for the general fund (or its equivalent). The analysis should include any currently known reasons for those variations that are expected to have a significant effect on future services or liquidity.

6. A description of significant capital asset and long-term debt activity during the year, including a discussion of commitments made for capital expenditures, changes in credit ratings, and debt limitations that may affect the financing of planned facilities or services.

7. A discussion by governments that use the modified approach to report some or all of their infrastructure assets.

8. A description of currently known facts, decisions, or conditions that are expected to have a significant effect on financial position (net position) or results of operations (revenues, expenses, and other changes in net position).

A sample MD&A appears in the appendix to GASB Statement No. 34.

**AUDITOR'S REPORT** The auditor's report within the financial section of a CAFR indicates that the financial statements are the responsibility of the government's management. It identifies the financial statements that have been audited and expresses an opinion about whether the financial statements are presented in conformity with GAAP. It should also specify the information included within the CAFR that was unaudited.

**GOVERNMENT-WIDE FINANCIAL STATEMENTS** Government-wide statements that consist of the statement of net position and the statement of activities, provide consolidated information for the government as a whole and introduce the concept of operational accountability to governmental financial reporting. **Operational accountability** measures the extent of a government's success at meeting operating objectives efficiently and effectively and its ability to meet operating objectives in the future.[20]

The government-wide statements report governmental activities, business-type activities, and discretely presented component units; however, they do not include fiduciary funds. All data are reported on the accrual basis of accounting. Thus, it may be necessary to convert governmental fund balances to the accrual basis of accounting. Chapter 20 examines this conversion process.

The statement of net position was changed in several ways by GASB Statement No. 63 issued in June of 2011. Two notable changes: (1) The term *net assets* is no longer allowed, being replaced by *net position*, and (2) two new financial statement elements (a.k.a. categories) are now reported: (a) deferred inflows of resources and (b) deferred outflows of resources. Deferred outflows are reported below assets (sort-of like prepaid assets) while deferred inflows are reported below liabilities (sort-of like deferred revenue—but we cannot use this account title per GASB No. 65, which did not recommend an alternative account title). The only items that may be reported as deferred inflows or outflows are items expressly identified in a GASB pronouncement. Currently, only three GASB Statements make such identification: No. 53 on derivatives, No. 60 on service concession arrangements, and No. 65 on items previously reported as assets or liabilities. It is unclear at this point whether the dollar amounts of these deferred elements will be material.

[20]GASB Statement No. 34, p. 78. In the 2012 "Scope of GASB" independent academic report written by Professors Deis, Rubin, and Smith, the term *accountability* received substantial coverage and recommendations were made to improve clarity around the use of this term.

The statement of net position shall add assets and deferred outflows of resources and subtract liabilities and deferred inflows of resources to calculate *net position*. The balance sheet format may be used, for example, assets plus deferred outflows equals the total of liabilities, deferred inflows, and net position, though the preferred format is to end with net position.[21] The statement lists both assets and liabilities in terms of liquidity, though does not require deferred outflows or inflows to be in liquidity order. Net position is categorized as either: (1) invested in capital assets, net of related debt, (2) restricted, or (3) unrestricted.[22] The statement of net position contains columns for governmental activities, business-type activities, totals of the primary government, and component unit totals, if applicable. Columns for reporting entity totals and prior-year comparative data are optional. The governmental activities column aggregates all general governmental assets and liabilities, including fixed assets and general long-term debt, from the general, special revenue, permanent, debt service, and capital projects funds. This column also includes most internal service fund assets and liabilities, because general governmental departments are typically the largest customers of internal service funds. Exhibit 19-7 presents the statement of net position for the City of Golden, Colorado.

The statement of activities presents governmental and proprietary fund revenues and expenses on the same statement using full accrual accounting. The format, which appears quite complex at first glance, can be viewed as two distinct parts. The upper portion focuses on costs of services and reports to taxpayers both the total expenses and the net expenses of the government by functional area or program. The lower portion of the statement displays how the net program expenses incurred during the year compared with general revenues. The complete format of the statement of activities for the City of Golden, Colorado, appears in Exhibit 19-8.

For example, during 2014, $569,265 of expenses were incurred by the "business-activity" Splash Aquatic Park in Golden, while only $403,566 in revenues were recognized ($403,566 Charges for Services). Thus, this functional area (the Splash Park) was not totally self-financed and had a net expense of $(101,887) for the year. The $(101,887) net expense is subsidized by general governmental revenues, such as taxes or grant receipts. Note that this does not necessarily reflect negatively on the Splash Park or its operations, because a partial subsidy might be the city policy or goal. The financial statement simply informs taxpayers of the functions or activities that are partially supported by taxes.

*Program revenues* are defined as being "directly from the program itself or from parties outside the reporting government's constituency." They are categorized as charges for services, (program-specific) operating grants and contributions, or (program-specific) capital grants and contributions within the statement's columns. For example, revenues from the water and wastewater facilities or grants for the cemetery are program revenues. All revenues other than program revenues are considered *general revenues*. General revenues, which include all taxes (even those restricted to programs), grants and investment income not considered program revenue, contributions to endowments, special items, and transfers, are reported in the lower section. Note that governmental activities and business-type activities are distinguished both in the presentation of functional classifications (the rows) and in the presentation of net expenses or revenues and changes in net position (the columns).

**FUND FINANCIAL STATEMENTS**   Fund financial statements focus on fiscal accountability rather than operational accountability. Fiscal accountability is the responsibility of a government to demonstrate compliance with public decisions regarding the use of financial resources.[23] The individual fund statements include the following: balance sheet—governmental funds; statement of revenues, expenditures, and changes in fund balance—governmental funds; statement of net position—proprietary funds; statement of revenues, expenses, and changes in fund net position—all proprietary

---

[21]GASB Statement No. 63, p. 5.

[22]GASB Statement No. 46 provides additional guidance regarding the restricted net position classification. GASB Statement No. 54 provides new guidance for reporting fund balance in the governmental fund statements for fiscal years beginning after June 15, 2010. GASB Statement No. 54 does not change the reporting of net position and is illustrated in the next chapter.

[23]GASB Statement No. 34, p. 78.

**EXHIBIT 19-7**

**Statement of Net Position**

## CITY OF GOLDEN, COLORADO, STATEMENT OF NET POSITION DECEMBER 31, 2014

| | Primary Government | | | | Component Unit |
|---|---|---|---|---|---|
| | Governmental Activities | Business-Type Activities | Totals | | |
| | | | 2014 | 2013 | |
| *Assets* | | | | | |
| Cash and investments | $ 14,484,191 | $5,037,567 | $19,521,758 | $18,450,829 | $1,012,379 |
| Property taxes receivable | 5,414,737 | — | 5,414,737 | 5,294,909 | 1,553,395 |
| Accounts receivable | 3,735,364 | 1,980,767 | 5,716,131 | 4,815,467 | 233,929 |
| Internal balances | (1,519,197) | 1,519,197 | — | — | — |
| Prepaid expenses | 22,097 | — | 22,097 | 266,255 | 4,763 |
| Inventory | 45,784 | 117,863 | 163,647 | 147,246 | — |
| Restricted cash and investments | 331,005 | 465,371 | 796,376 | 1,346,064 | 525,111 |
| Capital assets not being depreciated | 18,883,557 | 22,449,147 | 41,332,704 | 41,508,061 | 1,009,149 |
| Capital assets (net of accumulated depreciation) | 72,454,606 | 77,142,295 | 149,596,901 | 144,741,394 | 3,981,011 |
| Total assets | $113,852,144 | $108,712,207 | $222,564,351 | $216,570,225 | $8,319,737 |
| *Deferred Outflows of Resources* | | | | | |
| Amount on Refunding of Bonds | 801,793 | 51,645 | 853,438 | 997,398 | — |
| Total Deferred Outflows of Resources | 801,793 | 51,645 | 853,438 | 997,398· | — |
| *Liabilities* | | | | | |
| Accounts payable and accrued liabilities | $1,814,868 | $763,283 | $2,578,151 | 1,992,737 | $213,005 |
| Accrued Interest Payable | 102,275 | 29,344 | 131,619 | 142,179 | — |
| Escrow Deposits and Other | 342,290 | 192,489 | 534,779 | 622,067 | — |
| Claims payable | 423,088 | — | 423,088 | 471,924 | — |
| Unearned revenue | 261,000 | 56,575 | 317,575 | 420,827 | — |
| Noncurrent liabilities | | | | | |
| Due within one year | 2,560,000 | 1,062,541 | 3,622,541 | 3,511,275 | 479,123 |
| Due in more than one year | 22,212,025 | 6,504,126 | 28,716,151 | 32,317,684 | — |
| Total liabilities | 27,715,546 | 8,608,358 | 36,323,904 | 39,478,693 | 692,128 |
| *Deferred Inflows of Resources* | | | | | |
| Property Tax Revenue | 5,414,737 | — | 5,414,737 | 5,294,909 | 1,553,395 |
| Total Deferred Inflows of Resources | 5,414,737 | — | 5,414,737 | 5,294,909 | 1,553,395 |
| *Net Position* | | | | | |
| Net investment in capital assets | 68,762,301 | 92,423,864 | 161,186,165 | 153,066,698 | 4,511,037 |
| Restricted for | | | | | |
| Parks & recreation | 791,208 | — | 791,208 | 1,294,991 | — |
| Capital projects | 238,814 | — | 238,814 | 190,421 | — |
| Cemetery perpetual care (nonexpendable) | 1,379,766 | — | 1,379,766 | 1,312,664 | — |
| Cemetery perpetual care (expendable) | 236,758 | — | 236,758 | 282,117 | — |
| Debt service | — | 465,371 | 465,371 | 663,144 | 500,000 |
| Emergency reserves | 980,000 | — | 980,000 | 940,000 | — |
| Unrestricted | 9,134,807 | 7,266,259 | 16,401,066 | 15,043,985 | 1,063,177 |
| Total net position | $81,523,654 | $100,155,494 | $181,679,148 | $172,794,020 | $6,074,214 |

*Source:* © City of Golden

EXHIBIT 19-8

Statement of Activities

## CITY OF GOLDEN, COLORADO, STATEMENT OF ACTIVITIES FOR THE YEAR ENDED DECEMBER 31, 2014

| Functions/Programs | Expenses | Program Revenues | | |
| --- | --- | --- | --- | --- |
| | | Charges for Services | Operating Grants and Contributions | Capital Grants and Contributions |
| *Primary Government* | | | | |
| Governmental activities | | | | |
| General government | $ 7,480,751 | $ 2,039,950 | $ 4,725 | $— |
| Planning & economic development | 1,915,287 | 284,859 | — | — |
| Police | 7,520,766 | 717,166 | 395,954 | — |
| Fire | 1,733,106 | 198,872 | — | — |
| Public works | 5,692,087 | 81,750 | 292,050 | 1,252,350 |
| Parks and recreation | 3,345,295 | 553,876 | — | 775,772 |
| Unallocated interest on long-term debt | 1,032,257 | — | — | — |
| Total governmental activities | 28,719,549 | 3,876,473 | 692,729 | 2,028,122 |
| Business-type activities | | | | |
| Water | 5,192,955 | 5,668,271 | — | 1,888,848 |
| Wastewater | 1,745,956 | 2,312,333 | — | 455,338 |
| Drainage | 709,625 | 959,494 | — | 428,641 |
| Fossil Trace Golf Course | 3,089,033 | 3,318,353 | — | — |
| Community Center | 2,663,568 | 1,798,031 | — | 68,700 |
| Splash Aquatic Park | 569,265 | 403,566 | — | 63,812 |
| Cemetery Operations | 481,036 | 450,091 | — | — |
| Rooney Road Sports Complex | 230,882 | 70,476 | — | — |
| Museums | 508,265 | 101,621 | 57,096 | 5,390 |
| Total business-type activities | 15,190,585 | 15,082,236 | 57,096 | 2,910,729 |
| Total Primary Government | $43,910,134 | $18,958,709 | $749,825 | $4,938,851 |
| *Component Unit* | | | | |
| Golden Urban Renewal Authority | $ 2,217,184 | $— | $— | $— |
| *General Revenues* | | | | |
| Taxes | | | | |
| Property | | | | |
| Sales and use | | | | |
| Franchise fees | | | | |
| Other | | | | |
| Grants and contributions not restricted to specific programs | | | | |
| Investment income | | | | |
| Miscellaneous | | | | |
| Gain on disposal of capital assets | | | | |
| *Transfers* | | | | |
| Total general revenues and transfers | | | | |
| Change in net position | | | | |
| Net position, beginning | | | | |
| Prior Period Adjustment (in fiscal year 2013) | | | | |
| Net position, beginning as restated | | | | |
| Net position, ending | | | | |

*Source:* © City of Golden

and similar trust fund types (if applicable); statement of cash flows—all proprietary and similar trust fund types (if applicable); statement of fiduciary net position—fiduciary funds; and statement of fund changes in fiduciary net position—fiduciary funds. Exhibits 19-9 through 19-13 present illustrative statements for the City of Golden, Colorado. (Fiduciary fund statements are shown in Chapter 21.)

**EXHIBIT 19-8**

Statement of Activities
*(continued)*

| Governmental Activities | Business-Type Activities | Totals 2014 | 2013 | Component Unit |
|---|---|---|---|---|
| \$(5,436,076) | \$— | \$(5,436,076) | \$(5,126,606) | \$— |
| (1,630,428) | — | (1,630,428) | (1,271,102) | — |
| (6,407,646) | — | (6,407,646) | (6,613,615) | — |
| (1,534,234) | — | (1,534,234) | (1,649,421) | — |
| (4,065,937) | — | (4,065,937) | (4,346,247) | — |
| (2,015,647) | — | (2,015,647) | (1,706,226) | — |
| (1,032,257) | — | (1,032,257) | (1,100,795) | — |
| (22,122,225) | — | (22,122,225) | (21,814,012) | — |
| — | 2,364,164 | \$2,364,164 | \$1,441,627 | — |
| — | 1,021,715 | 1,021,715 | 753,660 | — |
| — | 678,510 | 678,510 | 349,525 | — |
| — | 229,320 | 229,320 | (106,187) | — |
| — | (796,837) | (796,837) | 59,401 | — |
| — | (101,887) | (101,887) | (175,511) | — |
| — | (30,945) | (30,945) | (166,010) | — |
| — | (160,406) | (160,406) | (136,034) | — |
| — | (344,158) | (344,158) | (366,633) | — |
| — | 2,859,476 | 2,859,476 | 1,653,838 | — |
| (22,122,225) | 2,859,476 | (19,262,749) | (20,160,174) | — |
| — | — | — | — | (2,217,184) |
| 5,241,397 | — | 5,241,397 | 5,074,134 | 1,552,675 |
| 18,457,400 | — | 18,457,400 | 17,505,037 | 918,593 |
| 1,256,630 | — | 1,256,630 | 1,224,798 | — |
| 433,758 | — | 433,758 | 394,656 | — |
| 1,195,717 | — | 1,195,717 | 2,536,149 | — |
| 153,032 | 51,514 | 204,546 | 19,188 | 5,849 |
| 982,143 | 271,809 | 1,253,952 | 1,329,195 | 2,656 |
| 104,477 | — | 104,477 | 247,685 | — |
| 8,976 | (8,976) | — | — | — |
| 27,833,530 | 314,347 | 28,147,877 | 28,330,842 | 2,479,773 |
| 5,711,305 | 3,173,823 | 8,885,128 | 8,170,668 | 262,589 |
| 75,812,349 | 96,981,671 | 172,794,020 | 165,012,464 | 5,811,625 |
| — | — | — | (389,112) | — |
| 75,812,349 | 96,981,671 | 172,794,020 | 164,623,352 | 5,811,625 |
| \$81,523,654 | \$100,155,494 | \$181,679,148 | \$172,794,020 | \$6,074,214 |

Net (Expense) Revenue and Changes in Net Position

A significant change that GASB Statement No. 34 made to fund financial statements was the introduction of the concept of a *major fund*. The general fund is always a major fund. Other funds are considered major funds if they meet both of the following criteria:

1. Total assets, liabilities, revenues, or expenditures/expenses of that individual governmental or enterprise fund are at least 10 percent of the *corresponding* total (assets, liabilities, and so forth) for *all* funds of that *categoryy* or *type* (i.e., total governmental or total enterprise funds).

## EXHIBIT 19-9

**Balance Sheet—Governmental Funds**

### CITY OF GOLDEN, COLORADO, BALANCE SHEET—GOVERNMENTAL FUNDS DECEMBER 31, 2014

| | General | Sales and Use Tax Capital Improvement | Other Governmental Funds | Total Governmental Funds 2014 | 2013 |
|---|---|---|---|---|---|
| *Assets* | | | | | |
| Cash and investments | $ 4,246,359 | $4,499,227 | $962,346 | $9,707,932 | $11,308,701 |
| Property taxes receivable | 5,387,027 | — | 27,710 | 5,414,737 | 5,294,909 |
| Accounts and taxes receivable | 2,259,297 | 996,920 | 9,284 | 3,265,501 | 2,651,458 |
| Prepaid Items | 13,397 | — | — | 13,397 | 257,555 |
| Inventories | 45,784 | — | — | 45,784 | 34,449 |
| Advance to other funds | 1,717,611 | — | 1,431,343 | 3,148,954 | 3,300,000 |
| Due from other funds | — | — | — | — | 100,000 |
| Due from other governments | 91,572 | — | 309,617 | 401,189 | 693,535 |
| Restricted cash and investments | 331,005 | — | — | 331,005 | 682,920 |
| Total assets | $14,092,052 | $5,496,147 | $2,740,300 | $22,328,499 | $24,323,527 |
| *Liabilities and fund balance* | | | | | |
| Liabilities | | | | | |
| Accounts payable | $ 1,048,170 | $ 388,555 | $66,044 | $1,502,769 | $1,306,022 |
| Accrued liabilities | 118,432 | — | — | 118,432 | 102,947 |
| Escrow deposits and other | 342,290 | — | — | 342,290 | 443,796 |
| Advances from other funds | — | 4,668,150 | — | 4,668,150 | 4,819,197 |
| Unearned revenue | 261,000 | — | — | 261,000 | 193,647 |
| Total liabilities | 1,769,892 | 5,056,705 | 66,044 | 6,892,641 | 6,865,609 |
| *Deferred Inflows of Resources* | | | | | |
| Property tax revenue | 5,387,027 | — | 27,710 | 5,414,737 | 5,294,909 |
| Use Tax Revenue | 112,500 | — | — | 112,500 | 162,500 |
| Total Deferred Inflows of Resources | 5,499,527 | — | 27,710 | 5,527,237 | 5,457,409 |
| Fund balance | | | | | |
| Nonspendable: | | | | | |
| Prepaid items | 13,397 | — | — | 13,397 | 257,555 |
| Inventories | 45,784 | — | — | 45,784 | 34,449 |
| Permanent fund principal | — | — | 1,379,766 | 1,379,766 | 1,312,664 |
| Advance to other funds | 1,717,611 | — | — | 1,717,611 | 1,987,336 |
| Restricted for: | | | | | |
| TABOR reserve | 980,000 | — | — | 980,000 | 940,000 |
| Parks and recreation | — | — | 73,541 | 73,541 | 306,383 |
| Parking improvements | — | — | 33,678 | 33,678 | 65,946 |
| Cemetery Maintenance | — | — | 236,758 | 236,758 | 94,781 |
| Capital Projects | — | 439,442 | — | 439,442 | 2,149,387 |
| Debt Service | — | — | — | — | 250,430 |
| Assigned for: | | | | | |
| Street improvements | — | — | 205,136 | 205,136 | 124,475 |
| Parks and recreation | — | — | 717,667 | 717,667 | 988,608 |
| Future Year Expenditures | 1,300,000 | — | — | 1,300,000 | 1,610,812 |
| Unassigned | 2,765,841 | — | — | 2,765,841 | 1,877,683 |
| Total fund balance | 6,822,633 | 439,442 | 2,646,546 | 9,908,621 | 12,000,509 |
| Total liabilities and fund balance | $14,092,052 | $5,496,147 | $2,740,300 | | |

| | | |
|---|---|---|
| Amounts reported for governmental activities in the Statement of Net Position are different because: | | |
| Capital assets used in governmental activities are not financial resources and therefore are not reported in the funds. Capital assets for internal service funds of $3,646,150 have been deducted from total governmental net capital assets of $91,338,163. | 87,692,013 | 81,792,221 |
| Long-term assets are not available to pay current expenditures, and therefore, are deferred in the funds. | 112,500 | 162,500 |
| Internal service funds are used by management to charge the costs of certain activities to individual funds, such as insurance, fleet, and information technology management. The assets and liabilities of the internal service funds are included in governmental activities in the statement of net position. | 7,789,516 | 8,200,605 |
| Long-term liabilities, including bonds payable ($12,445,000), bond premium ($998,248), certificates of participation ($9,995,000), compensated absences ($1,300,859), accrued interest on long-term debt ($102,275), deferred refunding $801,793, and bond discount $60,593 are not due and payable in the current period and therefore are not reported in the funds. | (23,978,996) | (26,343,486) |
| Net Position of Governmental Activities | $81,523,654 | $75,812,349 |

*Source:* © City of Golden

EXHIBIT 19-10

Statement of Revenues, Expenditures, and Changes in Fund Balances—Governmental Funds

**CITY OF GOLDEN, COLORADO, STATEMENT OF REVENUES, EXPENDITURES, AND CHANGES IN FUND BALANCES—GOVERNMENTAL FUNDS FOR THE YEAR ENDED DECEMBER 31, 2014**

| | General | Sales and Use Tax Capital Improvement | Other Governmental Funds | Total Governmental Funds 2014 | 2013 |
|---|---|---|---|---|---|
| **Revenues** | | | | | |
| Taxes | $19,234,346 | $6,175,637 | $ 29,202 | $25,439,185 | $24,248,625 |
| Licenses and permits | 599,978 | — | — | 599,978 | 673,820 |
| Intergovernmental | 896,229 | 441,756 | 1,300,598 | 2,638,583 | 4,010,367 |
| Charges for services | 2,465,891 | — | 101,145 | 2,567,036 | 2,576,195 |
| Fines and forfeitures | 709,459 | — | — | 709,459 | 624,136 |
| Investment income | 55,240 | 34,250 | 21,957 | 111,447 | 2,539 |
| Miscellaneous | 722,432 | 254,099 | 5,612 | 982,143 | 837,458 |
| Total revenues | 24,683,575 | 6,905,742 | 1,458,514 | 33,047,831 | 32,973,140 |
| **Expenditures** | | | | | |
| Current | | | | | |
| General government | 6,366,726 | — | 37,765 | 6,404,491 | 5,761,247 |
| Planning & economic development | 1,918,795 | — | — | 1,918,795 | 1,630,787 |
| Police | 7,224,732 | — | — | 7,224,732 | 7,143,867 |
| Fire | 1,452,762 | — | — | 1,452,762 | 1,535,326 |
| Public works | 3,343,061 | — | — | 3,343,061 | 3,553,887 |
| Parks and recreation | 2,502,871 | — | — | 2,502,871 | 2,290,432 |
| Debt service | | | | | |
| Principal | — | 2,450,000 | — | 2,450,000 | 2,050,000 |
| Interest and other charges | — | 1,058,617 | — | 1,058,617 | 1,126,117 |
| Capital outlay | — | 6,605,005 | 2,264,381 | 8,869,386 | 6,776,520 |
| Total expenditures | 22,808,947 | 10,113,622 | 2,302,146 | 35,224,715 | 31,868,183 |
| Excess (deficiency) of revenues over expenditures | 1,874,628 | (3,207,880) | (843,632) | (2,176,884) | 1,104,957 |
| **Other Financing Sources (Uses)** | | | | | |
| Transfers in | 110,256 | 2,182,977 | 910,459 | 3,203,692 | 3,872,424 |
| Transfers (out) | (1,682,750) | (1,187,116) | (248,830) | (3,118,696) | (3,702,420) |
| Proceeds from Sale of Assets | — | — | — | — | 100,000 |
| Total other financing sources (uses) | (1,572,494) | 995,861 | 661,629 | 84,996 | 270,004 |
| Net change in fund balances | 302,134 | (2,212,019) | (182,003) | (2,091,888) | 1,374,961 |
| Fund balances, beginning | 6,520,499 | 2,651,461 | 2,828,549 | 12,000,509 | 10,625,548 |
| Fund balances, ending | $6,822,633 | $ 439,442 | $2,646,546 | $ 9,908,621 | $12,000,509 |

*Net Change in Fund Balances—Total Governmental Funds* $(2,091,888)

Amounts reported for governmental activities in the Statement of Activities are different because:

Governmental funds report capital outlays as expenditures. However, in the Statement of Activities, the cost of those assets is allocated over their estimated useful lives as depreciation expense. This is the amount by which capital additions $8,608,574 and developer contributions $1,252,672, less net dispositions ($124,770) and Internal Service Fund capital additions ($672,409), exceed depreciation ($4,325,242) less Internal Service Fund depreciation $963,112 in the current period. 5,701,937

Repayment of bond principal is an expenditure in the governmental funds, but the repayment reduces long-term debt liabilities in the Statement of Net Position. These include bond payments $1,825,000, certificate of participation $625,000, amortization of bond premium $162,532, amortization of loss on refunding ($133,632), accrued interest on outstanding debt $7,562, amortization of bond discount ($10,098), and an increase in accrued compensated absences of $85,981. 2,562,345

Receipt of payment of a long-term receivable is not reported as revenues in the Statement of Activities. (50,000)

Internal service funds are used by management to charge the costs of certain activities to individual funds, such as insurance, fleet, and information technology management. The net revenue (expense) of the internal service funds is reported with governmental activities. (411,089)

Change in Net Position of Governmental Activities $ 5,711,305

*Source:* © City of Golden

## CITY OF GOLDEN, COLORADO, STATEMENT OF NET POSITION—PROPRIETARY FUNDS DECEMBER 31, 2014

| | Business-Type Activities—Enterprise Funds | | |
|---|---|---|---|
| | Water Fund | Wastewater Fund | Drainage Fund |
| *Assets* | | | |
| Current assets | | | |
| Cash and cash equivalents | $2,190,876 | $1,256,477 | $44,224 |
| Accounts receivable | 1,245,680 | 431,442 | 193,434 |
| Prepaid expenses | — | — | — |
| Inventory | 18,526 | — | — |
| Due from other funds | 200,000 | — | — |
| Restricted cash and cash equivalents | 290,371 | — | 175,000 |
| Total current assets | 3,945,453 | 1,687,919 | 412,658 |
| Noncurrent assets | | | |
| Advances to other funds | — | 1,519,197 | — |
| Capital assets not being depreciated | 18,916,954 | — | 1,111,648 |
| Capital assets (net of accumulated depreciation) | 35,953,689 | 7,081,870 | 12,529,034 |
| Total noncurrent assets | 54,870,643 | 8,601,067 | 13,640,682 |
| Total assets | 58,816,096 | 10,288,986 | 14,053,340 |
| *Deferred Outflows of Resources* | | | |
| Amount on Refunding of Bonds | — | — | 51,645 |
| Total Deferred Outflows of Resources | — | — | 51,645 |
| *Liabilities* | | | |
| Current liabilities | | | |
| Accounts payable | 301,837 | 288,808 | 9,436 |
| Accrued liabilities | 45,191 | 763 | — |
| Accrued interest payable | 24,676 | — | 4,668 |
| Due to other funds | — | — | 200,000 |
| Claims payable | — | — | — |
| Unearned revenue | — | — | — |
| Compensated absences, current portion | 22,436 | 9,997 | 2,600 |
| Bonds payable, current portion | 700,000 | — | 300,000 |
| Due to other funds | | | |
| Total current liabilities | 1,094,140 | 299,568 | 516,704 |
| Noncurrent liabilities | | | |
| Accrued compensated absences | 102,207 | 45,541 | 11,845 |
| Bonds payable, long-term portion (net of unamortized premium) | 5,110,000 | — | 1,109,223 |
| Total noncurrent liabilities | 5,212,207 | 45,541 | 1,121,068 |
| Total liabilities | 6,306,347 | 345,109 | 1,637,772 |
| *Net Position* | | | |
| Net invested in capital assets | 49,060,643 | 7,081,870 | 12,283,104 |
| Restricted for debt service | 290,371 | — | 175,000 |
| Unrestricted | 3,158,735 | 2,862,007 | 9,109 |
| Total net position | $52,509,749 | $9,943,877 | $12,467,213 |

*Source:* © City of Golden

2. Total assets, liabilities, revenues, or expenditures/expenses of that individual governmental or enterprise fund are at least 5 percent of the *corresponding* total for all governmental and enterprise funds *combined*.

Using the concept of major fund reporting, the required governmental fund statements will include a separate column for each major governmental fund and a column with aggregated information for all other governmental funds, as well as a total column for all governmental funds. Proprietary fund statements will include a separate column for each major enterprise fund, a column with

**EXHIBIT 19-11**

Statement of Net Position—Proprietary Funds *(continued)*

| Fossil Trace Golf Course Fund | Community Center Fund | Total Nonmajor Proprietary Funds | Totals | | Governmental Activities—Internal Service Funds |
| --- | --- | --- | --- | --- | --- |
| | | | 2014 | 2013 | |
| $ 119,265 | $ 350,127 | $1,076,598 | $ 5,037,567 | $ 2,247,688 | $4,776,259 |
| 17,365 | 66,863 | 25,983 | 1,980,767 | 1,406,354 | 68,673 |
| — | — | — | — | — | 8,700 |
| 90,851 | — | 8,486 | 117,863 | 112,797 | — |
| — | — | — | 200,000 | 350,000 | — |
| — | — | — | 465,371 | 663,144 | — |
| 227,481 | 416,990 | 1,111,067 | 7,801,568 | 4,779,983 | 4,853,632 |
| — | — | — | 1,519,197 | 1,519,197 | — |
| 2,024,661 | 182,890 | 212,994 | 22,449,147 | 23,829,913 | — |
| 7,262,163 | 7,041,397 | 7,274,142 | 77,142,295 | 76,678,381 | 3,646,150 |
| 9,286,824 | 7,224,287 | 7,487,136 | 101,110,639 | 102,027,491 | 3,646,150 |
| 9,514,305 | 7,641,277 | 8,598,203 | 108,912,207 | 106,807,474 | 8,499,782 |
| — | — | — | 51,645 | 61,973 | — |
| — | — | — | 51,645 | 61,973 | — |
| 54,567 | 80,021 | 28,614 | 763,283 | 562,446 | 193,667 |
| 109,869 | 34,760 | 1,906 | 192,489 | 75,324 | — |
| — | — | — | 29,344 | 32,342 | — |
| — | — | — | 200,000 | 450,000 | — |
| — | — | — | — | — | 423,088 |
| 31,468 | 25,107 | — | 56,575 | 227,180 | — |
| 11,931 | 9,270 | 6,307 | 62,541 | 61,275 | — |
| — | — | — | 1,000,000 | 975,000 | — |
| 207,835 | 149,158 | 36,827 | 2,304,232 | 2,383,567 | 616,755 |
| 54,351 | 42,230 | 28,729 | 284,903 | 279,140 | 93,511 |
| — | — | — | 6,219,223 | 7,225,068 | — |
| 54,351 | 42,230 | 28,729 | 6,504,126 | 7,504,208 | 93,511 |
| 262,186 | 191,388 | 65,556 | 8,808,358 | 9,887,775 | 710,266 |
| 9,286,824 | 7,224,287 | 7,487,136 | 92,423,864 | 92,370,199 | 3,646,150 |
| — | — | — | 465,371 | 663,144 | — |
| (34,705) | 225,602 | 1,045,511 | 7,266,259 | 3,948,328 | 4,143,366 |
| $9,252,119 | $7,449,889 | $8,532,647 | $100,155,494 | $96,981,671 | $7,789,516 |

aggregated information for all other enterprise funds, a total column for all enterprise funds, and a column with aggregated information for *all* internal service funds. (In addition to the general fund, the city has one other major governmental fund—sales and use tax capital improvement—and five major proprietary funds: Water, Wastewater, Drainage, Fossil Trace Golf Course, and Community Center Fund.) Governmental officials may also present a separate column for any nonmajor fund that they feel is particularly important and therefore should be presented to financial statement users. For both governmental and proprietary fund statements, whenever a nonmajor total column is used, a combining statement must be presented.

**EXHIBIT 19-12**

Statement of Revenues, Expenses, and Changes in Fund Net Position— Proprietary Funds

## CITY OF GOLDEN, COLORADO, STATEMENT OF REVENUES, EXPENSES AND CHANGES IN FUND NET POSITION—PROPRIETARY FUNDS FOR THE YEAR ENDED DECEMBER 31, 2014

| | Business-Type Activities—Enterprise Funds | | |
| --- | --- | --- | --- |
| | Water Fund | Wastewater Fund | Drainage Fund |
| *Operating revenues* | | | |
| Charges for services | $5,668,271 | $2,312,333 | $959,494 |
| Intergovernmental | — | — | 58,352 |
| Miscellaneous | 34,172 | — | — |
| Total operating revenues | 5,702,443 | 2,312,333 | 1,017,846 |
| *Operating Expenses* | | | |
| Personnel services | 1,421,656 | 455,415 | 133,983 |
| Operating | 2,266,525 | 1,040,309 | 135,879 |
| Depreciation and amortization | 1,279,693 | 250,232 | 384,266 |
| Claims | — | — | — |
| Premiums | — | — | — |
| Total operating expenses | 4,967,874 | 1,745,956 | 654,128 |
| Operating income (loss) | 734,569 | 566,377 | 363,718 |
| *Nonoperating revenues (expenses)* | | | |
| Investment income | 18,261 | 16,055 | 958 |
| Investment expense | (225,081) | — | (55,497) |
| Gain (loss) on sale of capital assets | — | — | — |
| Total nonoperating revenues (expenses) | (206,820) | 16,055 | (54,539) |
| Income (loss) before transfers and capital contributions | 527,749 | 582,432 | 309,179 |
| Transfers in | — | — | — |
| Transfers (out) | — | — | — |
| Capital contributions | 1,888,848 | 455,338 | 370,289 |
| Change in net position | 2,416,597 | 1,037,770 | 679,468 |
| Net position, beginning | 50,093,152 | 8,906,107 | 11,787,745 |
| Prior Period Adjustment (2013) | — | — | — |
| Net position, beginning, as restated | 50,093,152 | 8,906,107 | 11,787,745 |
| Net position, ending | $52,509,749 | $9,943,877 | $12,467,213 |

*Source:* © City of Golden

Because governmental funds are accounted for using the accrual basis of accounting in the government-wide statements and using the modified accrual basis of accounting in the fund statements, a reconciliation between the government-wide statements of net position and activities and the fund balance sheet and statement of revenues, expenditures, and changes in fund balances is required either on the face of the fund financial statements or in an accompanying schedule. (See Golden's reconciliations at the bottom of Exhibits 19-9 and 19-10.)

The information in the business-type activities column of the government-wide financial statements is basically the same as that provided by the enterprise fund columns within the fund financial statements.

**BUDGETARY COMPARISONS**   Governments must present budgetary comparison information for the general fund and each special revenue fund that has a legally adopted annual budget. The comparison may be presented as a comparison statement within the basic financial statements or as a schedule within CAFR-required supplementary information. The statement or schedule must disclose the budgetary basis of accounting and include columns presenting the original budget, the final appropriated budget, and actual balances (on the budgetary basis) for the fiscal year. Variance columns are optional. Exhibit 19-14 presents the budgetary comparison statement for Golden, Colorado.

| Fossil Trace Golf Course Fund | Community Center Fund | Total Nonmajor Proprietary Funds | Totals | | Governmental Activities—Internal Service Funds |
|---|---|---|---|---|---|
| | | | 2014 | 2013 | |
| $3,318,353 | $1,798,031 | $1,025,754 | $15,082,236 | $13,551,450 | $5,455,282 |
| — | — | 57,096 | 115,448 | 57,934 | 59,225 |
| 161,668 | 38,433 | 37,536 | 271,809 | 491,737 | 59,038 |
| 3,480,021 | 1,836,464 | 1,120,386 | 15,469,493 | 14,101,121 | 5,573,545 |
| | | | | | |
| 1,187,637 | 1,357,230 | 786,756 | 5,342,677 | 5,235,529 | 882,441 |
| 1,233,162 | 860,112 | 587,105 | 6,123,092 | 6,024,643 | 1,416,559 |
| 668,234 | 346,905 | 415,587 | 3,344,917 | 3,205,432 | 963,112 |
| — | — | — | — | — | 1,807,344 |
| — | — | — | — | — | 1,010,855 |
| 3,089,033 | 2,564,247 | 1,789,448 | 14,810,686 | 14,465,604 | 6,080,311 |
| 390,988 | (727,783) | (669,062) | 658,807 | (364,483) | (506,766) |
| | | | | | |
| 2,636 | 3,397 | 10,207 | 51,514 | 12,639 | 41,585 |
| — | — | — | (280,578) | (369,521) | — |
| — | (99,321) | — | (99,321) | (58,127) | 104,477 |
| 2,636 | (95,924) | 10,207 | (328,385) | (415,009) | 146,062 |
| 393,624 | (823,707) | (658,855) | 330,422 | (779,492) | (360,704) |
| — | 401,020 | 290,004 | 691,024 | 950,343 | — |
| (700,000) | — | — | (700,000) | (1,050,000) | (76,020) |
| — | 68,700 | 69,202 | 2,852,377 | 2,937,706 | 25,635 |
| (306,376) | (353,987) | (299,649) | 3,173,823 | 2,058,557 | (411,089) |
| 9,558,495 | 7,803,876 | 8,832,296 | 96,981,671 | 95,149,196 | 8,200,605 |
| — | — | — | — | (226,082) | — |
| 9,558,495 | 7,803,876 | 8,832,296 | 96,981,671 | 94,923,114 | 8,200,605 |
| $9,252,119 | $7,449,889 | $8,532,647 | $95,149,196 | $96,981,671 | $7,789,516 |

**REQUIRED SUPPLEMENTARY INFORMATION**    Governments are required to supply supplementary information, including schedule(s) of funding progress of pension plans, schedule(s) of employer contributions to pension plans, budgetary comparison schedules for the general and special revenue funds, and information about infrastructure assets reported using the modified approach (if applicable).

**NOTES TO THE FINANCIAL STATEMENTS**    The basic financial statements also include notes to the financial statements. The GASB Codification provides details regarding required CAFR note disclosure.[24] The purpose of the notes is to communicate information essential for fair presentation of the financial statements that is not displayed on the face of the financial statements. Given this, the notes are an integral part of the basic financial statements. The notes should focus on the primary government—specifically, its governmental activities, business-type activities, major funds, and nonmajor funds in the aggregate.

---

[24]*GASB Codification*, Section 2300.103.

EXHIBIT 19-13

Statement of Cash
Flows—Proprietary
Funds

## CITY OF GOLDEN, COLORADO, STATEMENT OF CASH FLOWS—PROPRIETARY FUNDS FOR THE YEAR ENDED DECEMBER 31, 2014

|  | Business-Type Activities—Enterprise Funds | | |
|---|---|---|---|
|  | Water Fund | Wastewater Fund | Drainage Fund |
| *Cash Flows from Operating Activities* | | | |
| Cash received from customers/users | $5,291,126 | $2,222,292 | $1,016,893 |
| Cash paid to suppliers | (2,248,215) | (846,079) | (143,359) |
| Cash paid to employees | (1,437,254) | (459,673) | (124,239) |
| Cash paid to providers | — | — | — |
| Cash paid to claimants | — | — | — |
| Net cash provided (used) by operating activities | 1,605,657 | 916,540 | 749,295 |
| *Cash Flows from Noncapital Financing Activities* | | | |
| Transfers to other funds | — | — | — |
| Transfers from other funds | — | — | — |
| Interfund loan made | (200,000) | — | 200,000 |
| Repayment of interfund loan | 350,000 | — | (350,000) |
| Net cash provided (used) by noncapital financing activities | 150,000 | — | (150,000) |
| *Cash Flows from Capital Financing Activities* | | | |
| Purchase of Capital Assets | (1,071,290) | (435,676) | (256,738) |
| Proceeds from Sale of Capital Assets | — | — | — |
| Proceeds from Issuance of Debt | — | — | — |
| Interest paid | (227,565) | — | (56,013) |
| Principal payments | (700,000) | — | (275,000) |
| Contributed capital | 1,851,490 | 455,338 | — |
| Net cash provided (used) by capital financing activities | (147,365) | 19,662 | (587,751) |
| *Cash flows from investing activities* | | | |
| Interest received | 18,261 | 16,055 | 958 |
| Net cash provided (used) by investing activities | 18,261 | 16,055 | 958 |
| Net increase (decrease) in cash and cash equivalents | 1,626,553 | 952,257 | 12,502 |
| Cash and cash equivalents, beginning | 854,694 | 304,220 | 206,722 |
| Cash and cash equivalents, ending | $2,481,247 | $1,256,477 | $ 219,224 |
| *Reconciliation of Operating Income (Loss) to Net Cash Provided (Used) by Operating Activities* | | | |
| Operating income (loss) | $ 734,569 | $ 566,377 | $ 363,718 |
| Adjustments to reconcile operating income (loss) to net cash provided (used) by operating activities | | | |
| Depreciation expense | 1,279,693 | 250,232 | 379,782 |
| Amortization expense | — | — | 4,484 |
| Changes in assets and liabilities | | | |
| Accounts receivable | (411,317) | (90,041) | (953) |
| Inventory | (5,494) | — | — |
| Accounts payable | 18,729 | 194,230 | (7,480) |
| Accrued liabilities | 5,075 | — | — |
| Claims payable | — | — | — |
| Unearned revenue | — | — | — |
| Accrued compensated absences | (15,598) | (4,258) | 9,744 |
| Total adjustments | 871,088 | 350,163 | 385,577 |
| Net cash provided (used) by operating activities | $1,605,657 | $ 916,540 | $ 749,295 |
| *Noncash Transactions* | | | |
| Capital assets contributed by (to) other funds | $ 37,358 | $— | $ 370,289 |

*Source:* © City of Golden

**EXHIBIT 19-13**

Statement of Cash
Flows—Proprietary
Funds *(continued)*

| Fossil Trace Golf Course Fund | Community Center Fund | Total Nonmajor Proprietary Funds | Totals 2014 | Totals 2013 | Governmental Activities—Internal Service Funds |
|---|---|---|---|---|---|
| $3,347,297 | $1,745,358 | $1,101,511 | $14,724,477 | $14,192,691 | $5,568,996 |
| (1,128,492) | (854,568) | (589,572) | (5,810,285) | (6,024,585) | (1,347,163) |
| (1,186,456) | (1,352,579) | (775,318) | (5,335,519) | (5,205,159) | (908,332) |
| — | — | — | — | — | (1,010,855) |
| — | — | — | — | — | (1,856,180) |
| 1,032,349 | (461,789) | (263,379) | 3,578,673 | 2,962,947 | 446,466 |
| (700,000) | — | — | (700,000) | (1,050,000) | (76,020) |
| — | 401,020 | 290,004 | 691,024 | 950,343 | — |
| — | — | — | — | 100,000 | — |
| (75,000) | — | (25,000) | (100,000) | (100,000) | — |
| (775,000) | 401,020 | 265,004 | (108,976) | (99,657) | (76,020) |
| (170,290) | (767) | (42,593) | (1,977,354) | (3,726,895) | (672,409) |
| — | — | — | — | 1,600 | 142,199 |
| — | — | — | — | 2,900,000 | — |
| — | — | — | (283,578) | (384,735) | — |
| — | — | — | (975,000) | (3,710,000) | — |
| — | — | — | 2,306,828 | 1,516,184 | — |
| (170,290) | (767) | (42,593) | (929,104) | (3,403,846) | (530,210) |
| 2,636 | 3,397 | 10,206 | 51,513 | 12,640 | 41,583 |
| 2,636 | 3,397 | 10,206 | 51,513 | 12,640 | 41,583 |
| 89,695 | (58,139) | (30,762) | 2,592,106 | (527,916) | (118,181) |
| 29,570 | 408,266 | 1,107,360 | 2,910,832 | 3,438,748 | 4,894,440 |
| $ 119,265 | $ 350,127 | $1,076,598 | $ 5,502,938 | $2,910,832 | $4,776,259 |
| $ 390,988 | $(727,783) | $(669,062) | $ 658,807 | $ (364,483) | $(506,766) |
| 668,234 | 346,905 | 415,587 | 3,340,433 | 3,231,671 | 963,113 |
| — | — | — | 4,484 | (26,240) | — |
| (893) | (52,332) | (18,875) | (574,411) | 74,660 | (4,550) |
| 2,236 | — | (1,808) | (5,066) | (4,886) | 69,396 |
| (7,435) | 3,452 | (659) | 200,837 | (6,233) | — |
| 109,869 | 2,092 | 129 | 117,165 | 10,474 | — |
| — | — | — | — | — | (48,836) |
| (131,831) | (38,774) | — | (170,605) | 16,911 | — |
| 1,181 | 4,651 | 11,309 | 7,029 | 31,073 | (25,891) |
| 641,361 | 265,994 | 405,683 | 2,919,866 | 3,327,430 | 953,232 |
| $1,032,349 | $ (461,789) | $ (263,379) | $ 3,578,673 | $2,962,947 | $ 446,466 |
| $ — | $ 68,700 | $ 69,202 | $ 545,549 | $1,421,522 | $ 25,635 |

## CITY OF GOLDEN, COLORADO, BUDGETARY COMPARISON STATEMENT, GENERAL FUND, FOR THE YEAR ENDED DECEMBER 31, 2014

| | Budgeted Amounts | | | Variance with Final Budget Positive (Negative) | Actual 2013 |
|---|---|---|---|---|---|
| | Original | Final | Actual | | |
| Budgetary fund balance, beginning | $3,808,091 | $6,520,499 | $6,520,499 | $— | $6,960,463 |
| Resources (inflows) | | | | | |
| Taxes | 18,275,075 | 18,275,075 | 19,234,346 | 959,271 | 18,386,308 |
| Licenses and permits | 493,800 | 493,800 | 599,978 | 106,178 | 673,820 |
| Intergovernmental | 650,060 | 650,060 | 896,229 | 246,169 | 756,434 |
| Charges for services | 2,402,699 | 2,402,699 | 2,465,891 | 63,192 | 2,521,468 |
| Fines and forfeitures | 580,482 | 580,482 | 709,459 | 128,977 | 624,136 |
| Investment income | 50,068 | 50,068 | 55,240 | 5,172 | 55 |
| Miscellaneous | 610,287 | 610,287 | 722,432 | 112,145 | 647,329 |
| Transfers in | 107,625 | 107,625 | 110,256 | 2,631 | 105,000 |
| Total Resources | $23,170,096 | $23,170,096 | $24,793,831 | $1,623,735 | $23,714,550 |
| Amounts available for appropriation | $26,978,187 | $29,690,595 | $31,314,330 | $1,623,735 | $30,675,013 |
| Charges to Appropriations (outflows) | | | | | |
| Current | | | | | |
| General government | $6,139,298 | $6,139,300 | $6,366,726 | ($227,426) | $5,745,219 |
| Planning & economic development | 1,678,483 | 1,678,483 | 1,918,795 | (240,312) | 1,630,787 |
| Police | 7,369,428 | 7,369,428 | 7,224,732 | 144,696 | 7,143,867 |
| Fire | 1,592,113 | 1,592,113 | 1,452,762 | 139,351 | 1,535,326 |
| Public works | 3,296,029 | 3,296,027 | 3,343,061 | (47,034) | 3,553,887 |
| Parks and recreation | 2,532,807 | 2,532,807 | 2,502,871 | 29,936 | 2,290,432 |
| Transfers out | 2,172,750 | 2,172,750 | 1,682,750 | 490,000 | 2,254,996 |
| Total charges to appropriations | 24,780,908 | 24,780,908 | 24,491,697 | 289,211 | 24,154,514 |
| Budgetary fund balance, ending | 2,197,279 | 4,909,687 | 6,822,633 | 1,912,946 | 6,520,499 |
| Total Appropriations | $26,978,187 | $29,690,595 | $31,314,330 | $1,623,735 | $30,675,013 |

**Budget-to-GAAP Reconciliation**

| | | | | | |
|---|---|---|---|---|---|
| Resources (Inflows) | | | | | |
| Actual amounts (budgetary basis) available for appropriation | | | $31,314,330 | | $30,675,013 |
| Differences—budget to GAAP | | | | | |
| The fund balance at the beginning of the year is a budgetary resource but is not a current-year revenue for financial reporting purposes | | | (6,520,499) | | (6,960,463) |
| Transfers from other funds are inflows of budgetary resources but are not revenue for financial reporting purchase | | | (110,256) | | (105,000) |
| Total revenues as reported on the statement of revenues, expenditures, and changes in fund balances—governmental funds | | | $24,683,575 | | $23,609,550 |
| Charges to Appropriations (Outflows) | | | | | |
| Actual amount (budgetary basis) of total charges to appropriations | | | 24,491,697 | | 24,154,514 |
| Differences—budget to GAAP | | | | | |
| Transfers to other funds are outflows of budgetary resources but are not expenditures for financial reporting purposes | | | (1,682,750) | | (2,254,996) |
| Total expenditures as reported on the statement of revenues, expenditures and changes in fund balances—governmental funds | | | $22,808,947 | | $21,899,518 |

*Source:* © City of Golden

**INFRASTRUCTURE** The most controversial portion of GASB Statement No. 34 regards capital assets, particularly infrastructure assets. Prior to the issuance of GASB 34, capital assets acquired by governmental funds (general governmental assets) were not capitalized and recorded as assets in governmental funds. They were treated as expenditures in the period of acquisition and also were recorded in a general fixed asset account group. (GASB Statement No. 34 eliminated account groups.)

Infrastructure assets, which are long-lived capital assets that are normally stationary in nature and include roads, bridges, drainage systems, and other public-domain capital assets, were not required to be reported in governmental financial statements. Depreciation was also optional. Under GASB 34, general governmental assets, including infrastructure assets, are capitalized and depreciated within the government-wide statements.

For many governments, the historical costs of infrastructure assets, such as roads and sidewalks, may be somewhat difficult to ascertain. Expenditures may not have been closely traced to infrastructure projects, because financial statement reporting of these assets was not required. Many infrastructure assets, such as sidewalks and streets, were constructed long ago, and costs are not readily available or may have little current economic meaning. Understandably, finance directors and preparers of governmental financial statements strongly opposed GASB 34's infrastructure reporting requirements. To alleviate the difficulty of complying with the new infrastructure requirements, the GASB allowed prospective reporting of general infrastructure assets during a transition period ending in 2005. For fiscal years beginning after June 15, 2005, governments with total annual revenues in excess of $100 million are required to retroactively report the estimated historical cost of infrastructure assets acquired or significantly improved or reconstructed in fiscal years ending after June 30, 1980.

GASB 34 also allows adoption of a modified approach for handling infrastructure assets that are part of a network. Under the modified approach, a government must maintain an up-to-date inventory of eligible infrastructure assets, perform condition assessments of the assets a minimum of every three years using a measurement scale, and estimate the annual amount necessary to maintain and preserve the eligible assets at a condition established by the government. If the infrastructure assets are shown to be preserved at the condition level determined by the government, all expenditures for these assets (except for additions and improvements, which should be capitalized) should be expensed in the period incurred, and depreciation will not be necessary.

**COMBINING AND INDIVIDUAL FUND STATEMENTS**    In each of the government-wide and fund financial statements, column data often include the activity of several individual funds. Combining financial statements aggregate individual fund account balances and produce relevant totals by classification or activity (e.g., governmental, business-type, type of program revenue). The combining statement total data correspond to an aggregated column on an associated financial statement. Individual fund balances are combined to arrive at totals that agree with the appropriate columns on the proprietary fund statement of net position shown in Exhibit 19-11. The *GASB Codification* requires that CAFRs include combining financial statements; however, inclusion of combining statements that detail the aggregation of nonmajor funds is optional.

## Statistical Section

The final required section of a CAFR contains statistical tables with comparative data from several periods of time. The tables, which focus on social and economic data, financial trends, and the fiscal capacity of the government, include both accounting and nonaccounting information.

As you can well imagine, the CAFR of a large metropolitan government amounts to hundreds of pages of information. Although the preceding discussion has provided a brief description of CAFR contents, each CAFR is unique, especially in terms of its transmittal letter and MD&A presentation. Although it is not required, many governments also publish other information, such as Single Audit reports, with their annual CAFR.

## Additional Reporting

In recent years, the GASB has suggested that governments supplement CAFR reporting with non-financial information that is deemed important to their citizens.[25] Service efforts and accomplishment (SEA) reporting is a form of performance measurement that provides more-complete information about an entity's performance than is found in the CAFR. SEA indicators are concerned with the *results* of services delivered by the government and the assessment of whether an entity is

---

[25]GASB, *Suggested Guidelines for Voluntary Reporting SEA Performance Information.* Norwalk, CT, 2010. See also the GASB SEA Web site at http://www.seagov.org.

progressing toward stated goals. Governments gather information about the *outputs* and *outcomes* of the services they provide and the relationship between the use of resources of those outputs and outcomes. SEA indicators enable management and citizens to evaluate the manner and effectiveness with which a branch or agency of a political system functions, operates, or behaves in carrying out a given task.

## SUMMARY

Accounting principles for state and local governmental units were initially developed through the efforts of the MFOA and, more recently, the GASB. The *GASB Codification of Governmental Accounting and Financial Reporting Standards* provides GAAP for the financial statements of more than 90,000 state and local governmental units. The development of accounting standards is a fluid and at times controversial process, with recent controversy around the "scope" of GASB and how to define and understand accountability.

Governmental entities utilize fund accounting as a means of ensuring and demonstrating compliance with formal budgetary constraints. There are five governmental fund types, which generally follow the modified accrual basis of accounting and maintain a focus on current financial resources, and two proprietary fund types, which follow the accrual basis of accounting and maintain an economic resources measurement focus. Fiduciary fund types are also reported in governmental financial statements.

The formal financial report of a governmental unit is called a CAFR. A CAFR under GASB Statement No. 34, a statement that initiated major changes to governmental financial reporting, contains three major sections: introductory, financial, and statistical.

## QUESTIONS

1. What organization provides accounting standards for state and local governmental units? What hierarchy of authority do they use?

2. What is the *GAAFR*? Who creates the *GAAFR*?

3. What are the characteristics of a government?

4. Why do governmental entities use fund accounting? How many funds might be used by a single governmental unit? How many fund types?

5. Distinguish between governmental funds, proprietary funds, and fiduciary funds. Which funds are classified as governmental funds?

6. List the five types of governmental funds. What are the primary distinctions among them?

7. What are the simplified and complete accounting equations for a governmental fund?

8. List the two types of proprietary funds. What distinguishes them from each other?

9. What are the simplified and complete accounting equations for a proprietary fund?

10. Why aren't fixed assets recorded in the accounts of a general fund? Where are they recorded?

11. What is the modified accrual basis of accounting? Which funds utilize the modified accrual basis of accounting?

12. What does *measurement focus* mean? What two focuses are used in governmental accounting? Which fund types use each?

13. What types of revenue do governments have? How do nonexchange transactions differ from exchange transactions?

14. How does the accounting treatment of a nine-month note payable differ from the accounting treatment of a five-year note payable within a governmental fund? Why?

15. Are interfund transfers expenditures or expenses? Explain.

16. What is an appropriation? How can budgetary approval be arranged to give the legislative body maximum control over the budget? How can it be arranged to give the executive maximum flexibility?

17. List the required governmental fund and proprietary fund financial statements. On what basis of accounting are these statements prepared?

18. How do nonreciprocal transfers differ from reciprocal transfers?

19. List the authoritative documents available to financial statement preparers and auditors related to governmental accounting and financial reporting. Which is the most authoritative?

20. Distinguish between the various types of interfund activity.

21. How does an expenditure differ from an expense? Identify the funds that report expenditures and those that report expenses.
22. What are the three sections of a CAFR? Briefly identify the contents of each section.
23. How do operational accountability and fiscal accountability differ? In what context are they used?

## EXERCISES

### E 19-1
### Multiple choice

1. Which of the following items has the greatest GAAP authority under *SAS 69*?
   a  *GASB implementation guides*
   b  *Consensus positions of GASB's Emerging Issues Task Force*
   c  *GASB statements and interpretations*
   d  *FASB statements and interpretations*

2. The primary emphasis in accounting and reporting for governmental funds is on:
   a  *Flow of current financial resources*
   b  *Income determination*
   c  *Capital transfers*
   d  *Transfers relating to proprietary activities*

3. The term *appropriation*, as used in governmental accounting, is:
   a  *A budget request*
   b  *A commitment*
   c  *An authorization to spend*
   d  *An allotment*

4. Which of the following will not appear in financial statements prepared under *GASB 34?*
   a  *Government-wide statements*
   b  *Fund financial statements*
   c  *Management's discussion and analysis*
   d  *General long-term debt account group*

5. Ketchum County issues general obligation serial bonds to finance construction of a new high school. Which of the following funds are affected by the transaction?
   a  *Special revenue fund*
   b  *Capital projects fund and general fund*
   c  *Capital projects fund, general fund, and debt service fund*
   d  *Capital projects fund and debt service fund*

### E 19-2
### Multiple choice [AICPA adapted]

1. Depreciation expense accounts would likely be found in the
   a  *General fund*
   b  *Capital projects fund*
   c  *Debt service fund*
   d  *Enterprise fund*

2. The government-wide statements of a state government
   a  *May not be issued separately from the comprehensive annual financial report*
   b  *Are prepared on both the accrual and modified accrual bases of accounting*
   c  *Include both governmental and proprietary funds*
   d  *Contain more-detailed information regarding the state government's finances than is contained in the comprehensive annual financial report*

3. Under the modified accrual basis of accounting for a governmental unit, revenues should be recognized in the accounting period in which they
   a  *Are earned and become measurable*
   b  *Are collected*
   c  *Become available and measurable*
   d  *Become available and earned*

4. Authority granted by a legislative body to make expenditures and to incur obligations is the definition of an
   a *Appropriation*
   b *Allowance*
   c *Encumbrance*
   d *Expenditure*

5. An expense would be reported in which of the following funds?
   a *Special revenue funds*
   b *Capital projects funds*
   c *Enterprise funds*
   d *Permanent funds*

## E 19-3
## Multiple choice

1. Which of the following is considered an exchange transaction under GASB 33?
   a *A city receives a federal grant*
   b *A bus driver collects bus fare from a rider*
   c *Property taxes are collected from a homeowner*
   d *An employer withholds state income tax from employee paychecks*

2. One would not expect to find fixed asset accounts in the
   a *Governmental fund financial statements*
   b *Proprietary fund financial statements*
   c *Government-wide financial statements*
   d *Financial statements of a governmental entity*

3. The cash received from the sale of vehicles used by the sheriff's office should be recorded in
   a *The general fund*
   b *The general fixed assets account group*
   c *A capital projects fund*
   d *A debt service fund*

4. Which fund follows the modified accrual basis of accounting?
   a *General fund*
   b *Special revenue fund*
   c *Debt service fund*
   d *All of the above*

5. The simplified governmental fund accounting model is as follows:
   a *Assets = Liabilities + Fund Balance*
   b *Current Assets − Current Liabilities = Fund Balance*
   c *Current Assets + Noncurrent Assets − Current Liabilities − Noncurrent Liabilities = Fund Balance*
   d *Current Assets + Noncurrent Assets − Current Liabilities − Noncurrent Liabilities = Net Position*

## E 19-4
## Multiple choice

1. Which of the following is not a governmental fund?
   a *Special revenue fund*
   b *Debt service fund*
   c *Trust fund*
   d *General fund*

2. Which of these funds generally follows the accrual basis of accounting?
   a *General fund*
   b *Internal service fund*
   c *Debt service fund*
   d *Special revenue fund*

3. Which of the following funds will report fixed assets in the fund financial statements?
   a *General fund*
   b *Special revenue fund*
   c *Debt service fund*
   d *None of the above*

**4.** Which of the following funds would not be included in governmental fund financial statements?
   a *Debt service fund*
   b *General fund*
   c *Pension trust fund*
   d *Permanent fund*

**5.** Which of the following funds would be used to account for an activity that provides goods or services to other funds?
   a *General fund*
   b *Enterprise fund*
   c *Debt service fund*
   d *Internal service fund*

# E 19-5
## Multiple choice

**1.** Which of the following are eliminated from the financial statements under GASB 34?
   a *General long-term debt account group*
   b *General fixed asset account group*
   c *Both a and b*
   d *None of the above*

**2.** An expense would be reported in which of the following funds?
   a *General fund*
   b *Internal service fund*
   c *Debt service fund*
   d *Special revenue fund*

**3.** A component unit
   a *Is financially accountable to the primary government*
   b *Must be discretely presented in a primary government's CAFR*
   c *Is excluded from a primary government's CAFR*
   d *Is a legally separate organization for which the primary government is financially accountable*

**4.** Budgetary comparison information must be presented for the
   a *Debt service fund*
   b *General fund*
   c *Pension fund*
   d *Permanent trust fund*

**5.** Required supplementary information includes
   a *Schedule(s) of funding progress of pension plans*
   b *Schedule(s) of employer contributions to pension plans*
   c *Budgetary comparison schedules for the general and special revenue funds*
   d *All of the above*

# E 19-6
## Identification of fund type

Identify each of the fund types described.
1. A fund that is used to report assets held in a trustee capacity for others and that cannot be used to support the government's own programs.
2. A fund used to report any activity for which a fee is charged to external users for goods and services.
3. A fund used to account for all financial resources except those required to be accounted for in another fund.
4. A fund used to account for the accumulation of resources for, and the payment of, general long-term debt principal and interest.
5. A fund used to report resources that are legally restricted to the extent that only earnings, and not principal, may be used for purposes that support the reporting government's programs—that is, for the benefit of the government or its citizenry.
6. A fund used to account for the proceeds of specific revenue sources (other than trusts for individuals, private organizations, or other governments or for major capital projects) that are legally restricted to expenditures for specified purposes.
7. A fund used to report any activity that provides goods or services to other funds, departments, or agencies of the primary government and its component units, or to other governments, on a cost-reimbursement basis.
8. A fund used to account for financial resources to be used for the acquisition or construction of major capital facilities (other than those financed by proprietary funds or in trust funds for individuals, private organizations, or other governments).

### E 19-7
### Transaction analysis—governmental funds

Use transaction analysis to determine the effects of each of the following transactions in the general fund.
1. Salaries paid totaled $30,000. Additional salaries incurred, but not paid, totaled $2,500.
2. Levied property taxes of $100,000; $98,000 was collected during the year. The balance is expected to be uncollectible.
3. Borrowed $60,000 by issuing a nine-month note bearing interest at 7 percent.
4. Repaid the note plus interest when due.
5. Borrowed $600,000 by issuing bonds at par. The bonds mature in 10 years.
6. Purchased equipment costing $25,000 with cash.
7. Sold equipment at the end of its expected useful life. The equipment had no expected residual value when acquired (at a cost of $13,000), but it sold for $1,200.
8. Determined that it is probable that a lawsuit involving a claim against a department will result in a settlement of at least $50,000. However, it is not expected that any payments will be required for two years or more.

### E 19-8
### Transaction analysis—proprietary funds

Repeat Exercise 19-7, this time assuming that the transactions involve a proprietary activity instead of a general governmental activity.

### E 19-9
### Identification of fund type

For each of the following events or transactions, identify the fund or funds that will be affected.
1. The principal, interest, and related charges from a city's general long-term debt bond issue will be handled in a fund established for that purpose.
2. A wealthy citizen donates $10,000,000 for city park maintenance. The principal cannot be spent.
3. A wealthy citizen donates $10,000,000 for city park maintenance. The principal may be spent as needed.
4. A village collects cigarette taxes from vendors. The tax funds must be remitted to the state.
5. The city issued general obligation bonds at par to finance construction of a government office building.

### E 19-10
### Identification of fund type

For each of the following events or transactions, identify the fund or funds that will be affected.
1. The Board of County Commissioners approved the construction of a new town band shell.
2. A central computing center was established to handle the data processing needs of a municipality.
3. A local municipality provides water and sewer services to residents of nearby communities for a fee.
4. A village receives a grant from the state government. The funds are to be used solely for preserving wetlands.
5. Property taxes are levied by a city government.

### E 19-11
### Identification of fund type

For each of the following events or transactions, identify the fund or funds that will be affected.
1. A new city government establishes an employee pension program.
2. A utility department constructs a new building.
3. A truck is purchased for use at the centralized storage center.
4. A new fleet of police cars is purchased.
5. Property taxes are collected by a city government.

### E 19-12
### Identification of fund type and transaction analysis

The City of Sioux Falls entered into a number of transactions for the current fiscal year. Identify the fund or funds affected by each transaction and determine how each transaction will affect the accounting equation of the particular fund.
1. Sioux Falls paid salaries to general government employees, $95,000.
2. Sioux Falls purchased an automobile by issuing a $25,000, 8 percent note to the vendor. The purchase occurred at midyear, and the note is a one-year note.
3. The city sold general fixed assets with an original cost of $300,000 for $30,000 at the end of their useful life. The use of the resources received is not restricted.
4. In the second fiscal year, the city repaid the principal and interest on the note issued in transaction 2 at the due date of the note.
5. "Profits" of $500,000 from the airport enterprise fund were transferred to the general fund of the city to subsidize general fund operations.
6. Interest income collected on Sioux Falls's general fund investments totaled $70,000 for the year.

## E 19-13
## Identification of fund type and transaction analysis

Perez County entered into a number of transactions for the current fiscal year. Identify the fund or funds affected by each transaction and determine how each transaction will affect the accounting equation of the particular fund.

1. Perez County issued $10 million of general obligation bonds at par to finance construction of a new county office building.
2. The county purchased a truck for a general governmental department. The cost of the truck, $22,000, was paid in cash.
3. The county-owned and operated electric utility billed residents and businesses $500,000 for electricity sales.
4. The county paid $2 million to High Rise Construction Company during 2008 for work completed during the year.
5. The county paid general governmental employee salaries of $4,500. Another $500 of salaries accrued but has not been paid.
6. The county borrowed $7,500 on a six-month note to finance general operating costs of the government.

---

# INTERNET ASSIGNMENT

1. Visit the GASB's Web site. Click on Standards & Guidance menu and select Pronouncements. What is the title of the most recently issued GASB standard? When was it issued? What is its effective date?

2. Locate the Web site for a municipality (city, county, town, parish, etc.) in which your college or university is located. Is the municipality's financial report available on the Web site? If so, review the CAFR and answer the following questions:

   a. How many governmental funds does the government have? List the name of one special revenue fund.

   b. Does the government have a capital projects fund? For what purpose was it created?

   c. How many enterprise funds does the government have? List the name of one enterprise fund.

   d. How many trust and agency funds does the government have? List the name of one such fund.

---

## SELECTED READINGS

[1] AICPA. State and Local Governmental, Audit and Accounting Guide. New York: American Institute of Certified Public Accountants, 2015.

[2] Deis, Donald R., Marc A. Rubin, and Kenneth A. Smith. Independent Academic Study of the Scope of GASB: Accounting and Accountability—Topics and Processes. July 24, 2012. Available online at the FAF Web site.

[3] Freeman, Robert J., Craig D. Shoulders, Gregory S. Allison, and G. Robert Smith, Jr. Governmental and Non-Profit Accounting (10th ed.). New York: Prentice Hall, 2013.

[4] Governmental Accounting Standards Board. Codification of Governmental Accounting and Financial Reporting Standards. Norwalk, CT: Governmental Accounting Standards Board, 2013.

[5] Governmental Accounting Standards Board. SEA Performance Information. Norwalk, CT: Governmental Accounting Standards Board, 2010.

[6] Governmental Accounting Standards Board. Statement No. 34, "Basic Financial Statements—and Management's Discussion and Analysis—for State and Local Governments." Norwalk, CT: Governmental Accounting Standards Board, 1999.

[7] Government Finance Officers Association of the United States and Canada. Governmental Accounting, Auditing, and Financial Reporting. Chicago: Municipal Finance Officers Association of the United States and Canada, 2012.

[8] National Council on Government Accounting. Governmental Accounting and Financial Reporting Principles, Statement 1. Chicago: Municipal Finance Officers Association of the United States and Canada, 1979.

[9] U.S. General Accounting Office. Government Auditing Standards. Washington, D.C.: Government Printing Office, 2011.

# 20

# Accounting for State and Local Governmental Units—Governmental Funds

Chapter 19 introduced accounting and financial reporting practices applicable to state and local governments. This chapter begins with a summary of recent changes to how we report fund balances and define governmental funds. It then continues the discussion of fund accounting by illustrating the proper accounting for governmental funds. It also provides examples of fund statements for governmental funds and outlines the process of converting the modified-accrual-basis financial information in the governmental fund statements into the accrual-basis information presented in the government-wide statements.

Recall that governmental funds include the general fund as well as special revenue, permanent, capital projects, and debt service funds. Every governmental entity has one general fund and may have zero, one, or many of each of the other four governmental funds. The general governmental activities included within governmental funds are accounted for in the same manner, regardless of specific fund type. This chapter reviews transactions in the general fund and each of the other four governmental funds so that you may recognize the different purpose of each governmental fund.

## RECENT CHANGES TO GOVERNMENTAL FUND ACCOUNTING

LEARNING OBJECTIVE **20.1,2**

As noted in the previous chapter, GASB Statement No. 34 (GASB 34) was a major change in governmental accounting and reporting. Perhaps the most significant change was that governmental funds essentially report financial statements on two bases of accounting with different goals for each reporting basis. The modified accrual basis focusing on current resources helps users assess budgetary compliance and fiscal accountability. The accrual basis focusing on all economic resources helps users assess long-term financial and operational accountability.

One area of inconsistent application of the GASB 34 reporting model was the reporting of Fund Balance. There was also confusion about reserved versus restricted fund balances in the governmental funds and government-wide statements, respectively. Issued in March 2009, GASB Statement No. 54, *Fund Balance Reporting and Government Fund Type Definitions*, establishes five classifications of governmental fund balance listed in decreasing order of spending constraints:

- **Nonspendable fund balance**—amounts not in spendable form, such as inventories, or amounts that must be maintained, such as the principal of an endowment.
- **Restricted fund balance**—amounts can only be spent for the specific purposes stipulated by constitution, external resource providers, or through enabling legislation.

### LEARNING OBJECTIVES

**20.1** Prepare journal entries to record transactions in governmental funds, including the new fund balance classifications.

**20.2** Learn about accounting methods unique to government accounting: budgetary issues, encumbrance accounting, and interfund transactions.

**20.3** Determine the appropriate governmental fund to be used.

**20.4** Prepare governmental fund financial statements.

**20.5** Convert governmental fund financial statements to government-wide financial statements.

CHAPTER 20

■ Committed fund balance—amounts can only be spent for the specific purposes determined by a formal action of the government's highest level of decision-making authority.

■ Assigned fund balance—amounts intended to be used by the government for specific purposes but do not meet the criteria to be classified as restricted or committed. In governmental funds other than the general fund, assigned fund balance represents the remaining amount that is not restricted or committed.

■ Unassigned fund balance—the residual classification for the government's general fund and includes all spendable amounts not contained in the other classifications. In other funds, the unassigned classification should be used only to report a deficit balance resulting from overspending for specific purposes for which amounts had been restricted, committed, or assigned.[1]

Governments are required to disclose information about the processes through which constraints are imposed on amounts in the committed and assigned classifications. They also must disclose their policies regarding how they determine the amounts in each classification that have been spent. The use of "reserved" and "unreserved" fund balance is no longer permitted for governmental funds. The new classifications are required for fiscal periods starting after June 15, 2010. GASB Statement No. 54 (GASB 54) also refined the definitions of the governmental funds as listed in Exhibit 19-3.

## THE GENERAL FUND

Governments use the *general fund (GF)* to account for all unrestricted resources except those accounted for in a specific fund. In more descriptive terms, the GF is the governmental fund used to account for the general operations of government, including the revenue received and the expenditures made in providing public goods and services to citizens. If a general-purpose government has only one fund accounting entity, that fund is a GF. Recall that the GF follows the modified accrual basis of accounting.[2]

## ACCOUNTING FOR THE GENERAL FUND

This chapter uses the small town of Grantville to demonstrate accounting for the GF. The postclosing trial balance of the Town of Grantville GF at September 30, 2015, shows the following ledger account balances:

| | |
|---|---|
| *Debits* | |
| Cash | $310,000 |
| Taxes receivable—delinquent | 150,000 |
| Accounts receivable | 30,000 |
| Supplies inventory | 60,000 |
| Total debits | $550,000 |
| *Credits* | |
| Allowances for uncollectible taxes—delinquent | $10,000 |
| Vouchers payable | 140,000 |
| Note payable (short-term) | 150,000 |
| Fund balance—reserved | 90,000 |
| Fund balance—unreserved | 160,000 |
| Total credits | $550,000 |

[1]Based on GASB SUMMARY OF STATEMENT NO. 54, © Anthony H Joseph.

[2]Governments may choose to record governmental fund transactions under the accrual basis of accounting and later adjust balances to the modified accrual basis for presentation in fund financial statements. This book presents the traditional fund accounting approach to accounting for governmental funds, whereby transactions in governmental funds are initially recorded on the modified accrual basis of accounting. Governments also may record transactions under both methods, thus having two sets of books throughout the year—one on the accrual basis and the other on the modified accrual basis. GAAP does not require a method for internal record-keeping, but it does require both methods in a complete financial report.

Events for the town during the year October 1, 2015, to September 30, 2016, that involve the GF include reclassifying the fund balance to comply with GASB 54, recording an approved budget, accounting for revenues from various sources, accounting for expenditures with encumbrance controls, preparing year-end adjusting and closing entries, and preparing the fund financial statements.

## Fund Balance Reclassification

We assume this is the first year that the Town of Grantville implements the new fund balance classifications of GASB 54 in order to illustrate how to do reclassification entries. Grantville determines that $60,000 is *nonspendable* because it is tied up in inventory; $90,000 is *committed* because the town council voted at the September 15, 2015, council meeting to make the appropriation binding for next period[3]; and $100,000 is *unassigned*.

*General Fund—Beginning Fund Balance Reclassification Entry*

| | | |
|---|---|---|
| Fund balance—unreserved | 160,000 | |
| Fund balance—reserved | 90,000 | |
| Fund balance—nonspendable | | 60,000 |
| Fund balance—committed | | 90,000 |
| Fund balance—unassigned | | 100,000 |

To reclassify opening fund balances to comply with GASB 54.

## The Budget

The Town of Grantville approved the following GF budget for the fiscal year October 1, 2015, to September 30, 2016:

**TOWN OF GRANTVILLE**
**GENERAL FUND BUDGET SUMMARY**
**FOR THE YEAR OCTOBER 1, 2015, TO SEPTEMBER 30, 2016**

| | |
|---|---|
| *Revenue Sources* | |
| Taxes | $2,075,000 |
| Licenses and permits | 205,000 |
| Intergovernmental revenue | 400,000 |
| Charges for services | 557,000 |
| Fines and forfeitures | 118,000 |
| Investment income | 100,000 |
| Miscellaneous revenues | 45,000 |
| Total budgeted revenues | $3,500,000 |
| | |
| *Expenditures* | |
| Current services | |
| General government | $477,500 |
| Public safety | 897,750 |
| Highways and streets | 825,000 |
| Sanitation | 525,000 |
| Health and welfare | 175,000 |
| Recreation | 270,000 |
| Capital outlays | 150,000 |
| Total appropriations | $3,320,250 |
| | |
| *Other Financing Sources (Uses)* | |
| Transfers out | (115,000) |
| Budgeted increase in fund balance | $ 64,750 |

*Source:* © Anthony H Joseph

The budgeted GF activity includes revenue from various sources, expenditures, and a category of "other sources and uses" of working capital funds. Section 1100.112 of the *GASB Codification* addresses classification requirements for revenue and expenditure accounts. As required, the town classifies budgeted GF revenue items by source (taxes, licenses and permits, and so on). Budgeted

[3]The government's policies will determine the classification of fund balance for prior period encumbrances, though it is possible they could be any three of the four expendable classes: restricted, committed, or assigned. Encumbrance accounting is illustrated later in this chapter.

expenditures are organized by character class (current services, capital outlays) and by function within each character category (general government, public safety). If desired, the town could further classify expenditures for each of the functions by specific departments or units within the organization (such as police department and fire department). It could also present expenditures in each of the organizational units in terms of the object of expenditure (such as personal services, supplies, and other services and charges). The classification scheme is an important part of operational control over expenditures, because most governmental entities limit expenditures within a functional or object category to the amount of the formal budget approval. Any excess requires administrative approval.

**RECORDING THE BUDGET**   At the beginning of the fiscal year, the approved budget of Grantville is recorded. Although many business entities adopt and approve budgets, only governmental entities formally prepare journal entries to record the budget within the accounting records. The town makes the following general journal entry to record the budget in the accounts of the GF.

| *General Fund—Budgetary Entry* | | |
|---|---|---|
| Estimated revenues | 3,500,000 | |
|     Appropriations | | 3,320,250 |
|     Estimated other financing uses—transfers out | | 115,000 |
|     Fund balance—unassigned | | 64,750 |
|   To record the budget for the year October 1, 2015, to September 30, 2016. | | |

The entry records total estimated revenues, total appropriations, and estimated other financing uses in the general ledger and credits the budgeted excess to the fund balance—unassigned account. Some governments require budgeted revenues to exceed appropriations, resulting in a balanced budget. Other governments are allowed to legally include beginning fund balance in order to balance the budget, such that budgeted appropriations may exceed budgeted revenues as long as beginning fund balance exceeds the shortfall.

T-accounts for all GF transactions appear in Exhibit 20-1. Journal entry numbers correspond to entries in the T-accounts. The beginning balances in the T-accounts are obtained from the postclosing trial balance at September 30, 2015, on page 644.

**SUBSIDIARY LEDGERS**   Although budgets may be approved in terms of broad categories, governments record details of the planned revenues (such as property taxes, sales taxes, and license revenue) and appropriations (such as police supplies, mayor's office expenses, and maintenance of the town hall) in subsidiary revenue and expenditure ledgers. Recording estimated revenues for individual items as debits in the subsidiary revenue ledger and recording actual revenue items as credits allows the outstanding subsidiary account balances during the year to reveal differences between actual and budgeted revenue for each item to date, as well as the final excess or deficiency at year-end. Similarly, recording appropriations as credits and recording actual expenditures or commitments for expenditures (encumbrances) as debits helps the government monitor expenditures. The account balances shown in the individual accounts of the subsidiary expenditure ledger represent unencumbered, unexpended appropriations (or amounts that remain to be spent) for each expenditure item. These subsidiary ledger techniques provide the means of achieving formal budgetary control over the items included in the approved budget. The financial statements or their notes will report budget compliance for the general and budgeted special revenue funds (SRF), as illustrated in Chapter 19.

## Transactions and Interfund Activities for the Year

**ACCOUNTING FOR PROPERTY TAXES**   Recall that under the modified accrual basis of accounting, revenues are generally recognized in the period in which they become measurable and available to finance expenditures of the period. Governments recognize property tax revenues, which are considered imposed nonexchange revenues under GASB Statement No. 33,[4] when taxpayers are billed for the amount of taxes levied, if the resources collected can be used in that period.

---

[4]The classifications from GASB Statement No. 33 are summarized in Exhibit 19-5.

## EXHIBIT 20-1

### General Fund Transactions

**Cash**

| Debit | | Credit | |
|---|---|---|---|
| beg. | 310,000 | 5,000 | 14) |
| 2) | 1,900,000 | 164,250 | 15) |
| 5) | 200,000 | 150,000 | 16) |
| 6) | 1,240,000 | 3,143,500 | 18) |
| | 3,650,000 | 3,462,750 | |
| Adj. bal. | 187,250 | | |
| bal. | | | |

**Accounts receivable**

| Debit | | Credit | |
|---|---|---|---|
| beg. | 30,000 | 150,000 | 4) |
| | 180,000 | 180,000 | |
| Adj. bal. | | | |
| bal. | | | |

**Taxes receivable—delinquent**

| Debit | | Credit | |
|---|---|---|---|
| beg. | 150,000 | 140,000 | 2) |
| Adj. 2 | 240,000 | 10,000 | 3) |
| | 390,000 | 150,000 | Adj. bal. |
| | 240,000 | | bal. |

**Taxes receivable—current**

| Debit | | Credit | |
|---|---|---|---|
| beg. | 0 | 1,760,000 | 2) |
| 1) | 2,000,000 | 240,000 | Adj. 2 |
| | 2,000,000 | 2,000,000 | Adj. bal. |
| | 0 | | bal. |

**Allowance for u/c taxes—delinquent**

| Debit | | Credit | |
|---|---|---|---|
| | | 10,000 | beg. |
| | | 20,000 | Adj. 2 |
| 3) | 10,000 | 30,000 | Adj. bal. |
| | | 20,000 | bal. |

**Allowance for u/c taxes—current**

| Debit | | Credit | |
|---|---|---|---|
| | | 0 | beg. |
| | | 20,000 | 1) |
| Adj. 2 | 20,000 | 20,000 | Adj. bal. |
| | | 0 | bal. |

**Supplies inventory**

| Debit | | Credit | |
|---|---|---|---|
| beg. | 60,000 | 30,000 | Adj. 1 |
| 13c) | 60,000 | 30,000 | |
| Adj. bal. | 120,000 | | |
| bal. | 90,000 | | |

**Vouchers payable**

| Debit | | Credit | |
|---|---|---|---|
| | | 140,000 | beg. |
| | | 200,000 | 7) |
| | | 140,000 | 10) |
| | | 85,000 | 12b) |
| | | 60,000 | 13c) |
| | | 2,843,500 | 17) |
| 18) | 3,143,500 | 3,468,500 | Adj. bal. |
| | 3,143,500 | 325,000 | bal. |

**Notes payable**

| Debit | | Credit | |
|---|---|---|---|
| | | 150,000 | beg. |
| 16) | 150,000 | 150,000 | Adj. bal. |
| | | 0 | bal. |

**Revenue collected in advance**

| Debit | | Credit | |
|---|---|---|---|
| | | 0 | beg. |
| | | 50,000 | 4) |
| | | 50,000 | Adj. bal. |
| | | 50,000 | bal. |

**Encumbrances**

| Debit | | Credit | |
|---|---|---|---|
| beg. | 0 | 150,000 | 9) |
| 8) | 150,000 | 90,000 | 12a) |
| 11) | 90,000 | 60,000 | 13b) |
| 13a) | 60,000 | 50,000 | reclass-end |
| 13d) | 50,000 | 350,000 | |
| Adj. bal. | 350,000 | | |
| bal. | 0 | | |

**Reserve for encumbrances**

| Debit | | Credit | |
|---|---|---|---|
| 9) | 150,000 | 150,000 | beg. |
| 12a) | 90,000 | 90,000 | 8) |
| 13b) | 60,000 | 60,000 | 11) |
| 13d) | 50,000 | 50,000 | 13a) |
| reclass-end | 350,000 | 350,000 | Adj. bal. |
| | | 0 | bal. |

**Fund balance—committed**

| Debit | | Credit | |
|---|---|---|---|
| | | 0 | beg. |
| reclass-end | 40,000 | 90,000 | reclass-beg |
| | 40,000 | 90,000 | Adj. bal. |
| | | 50,000 | bal. |

**Fund balance—nonspendable**

| Debit | | Credit | |
|---|---|---|---|
| | | 0 | beg. |
| | | 60,000 | reclass-beg |
| | | 30,000 | reclass-end |
| | | 90,000 | Adj. bal. |
| | | 90,000 | bal. |

**Other financing uses**

| Debit | | Credit | |
|---|---|---|---|
| beg. | 0 | 164,250 | close 2 |
| 15) | 164,250 | | |
| Adj. bal. | 164,250 | | |
| bal. | 0 | | |

**Other financing sources**

| Debit | | Credit | |
|---|---|---|---|
| | | 0 | beg. |
| | | 45,000 | 14) |
| | | 45,000 | Adj. bal. |
| close 2 | 45,000 | 0 | bal. |

**Expenditures—PY**

| Debit | | Credit | |
|---|---|---|---|
| beg. | 0 | 85,000 | close 2 |
| 12b) | 85,000 | | |
| Adj. bal. | 85,000 | | |
| bal. | 0 | | |

**Expenditures**

| Debit | | Credit | |
|---|---|---|---|
| beg. | 0 | 3,263,500 | close 2 |
| 7) | 200,000 | | |
| 10) | 140,000 | | |
| 14) | 50,000 | | |
| 17) | 2,843,500 | | |
| Adj. 1 | 30,000 | | |
| Adj. bal. | 3,263,500 | | |
| bal. | 0 | | |

**Revenue**

| Debit | | Credit | |
|---|---|---|---|
| | | 0 | beg. |
| | | 1,980,000 | 1) |
| | | 100,000 | 4) |
| | | 200,000 | 5) |
| | | 1,240,000 | 6) |
| | | 3,520,000 | Adj. bal. |
| close 2 | 3,520,000 | 0 | bal. |

**Fund balance—unreserved**

| Debit | | Credit | |
|---|---|---|---|
| reclass-beg | 160,000 | 160,000 | beg. |
| | | 160,000 | Adj. bal. |
| | 160,000 | 0 | bal. |

**Fund balance—reserved**

| Debit | | Credit | |
|---|---|---|---|
| reclass-beg | 90,000 | 90,000 | beg. |
| | | 90,000 | Adj. bal. |
| | | 0 | bal. |

**Fund balance—unassigned**

| Debit | | Credit | |
|---|---|---|---|
| | | 0 | beg. |
| | | 100,000 | reclass-beg |
| | | 64,750 | bud. |
| | | 10,000 | reclass-end |
| | | 174,750 | Adj. bal. |
| close 1 | 64,750 | 52,250 | close 2 |
| Adj. bal. | 64,750 | 227,000 | |
| | | 162,250 | bal. |

**Estimated other financing uses**

| Debit | | Credit | |
|---|---|---|---|
| | | 0 | beg. |
| | | 115,000 | bud. |
| | | 115,000 | Adj. bal. |
| close 1 | 115,000 | 0 | bal. |

**Appropriations**

| Debit | | Credit | |
|---|---|---|---|
| | | 0 | beg. |
| | | 3,320,250 | bud. |
| | | 3,320,250 | Adj. bal. |
| close 1 | 3,320,250 | 0 | bal. |

**Estimated revenues**

| Debit | | Credit | |
|---|---|---|---|
| beg. | 0 | 3,500,000 | close 1 |
| bud. | 3,500,000 | | |
| Adj. bal. | 3,500,000 | | |
| bal. | 0 | | |

The treasurer of Grantville records the following entry when property tax bills of $2,000,000 are mailed:

*General Fund—Entry 1*

| | | |
|---|---|---|
| Taxes receivable—current | 2,000,000 | |
|     Allowance for uncollectible taxes—current | | 20,000 |
|     Revenue | | 1,980,000 |
| To record the property tax levy. | | |

This entry assumes that 1 percent of property tax levies are not collectible and that the rest of the taxes will be collected either during the current year or within not more than 60 days thereafter. Therefore, it recognizes revenue for 99 percent of the amount billed. However, governments must record a liability, instead of revenue, for taxes not collected by year-end or within 60 days thereafter, because they are not "available." Likewise, governments record taxes collected in a period before they become legally available to finance expenditures in an account with a title that does not include the word *deferred*, such as "taxes collected in advance," in order to comply with GASB Statement No. 63 as described in Chapter 19. Governments cannot recognize revenue until the period when it becomes legally available to cover expenditures.

Uncollectible taxes are not expenditures in governmental accounting; instead, they are revenue adjustments. Like accounts receivable, taxes receivable is a control account for individual amounts owed. The current designation for taxes receivable distinguishes current taxes receivable from taxes that are past due. Governments also reclassify any balances remaining in the "taxes receivable—current" and "allowance for uncollectible taxes—current" accounts after the due date for payment as "taxes receivable—delinquent" and "allowance for uncollectible taxes—delinquent." Note that the postclosing trial balance for the Town of Grantville's GF at September 30, 2015, includes a debit account, "taxes receivable—delinquent," of $150,000 and a credit account, "allowance for uncollectible taxes—delinquent," of $10,000.

The town records collection of current property taxes of $1,760,000 and past-due taxes of $140,000 in the usual manner for receivables as follows:

*General Fund—Entry 2*

| | | |
|---|---|---|
| Cash | 1,900,000 | |
|     Taxes receivable—current | | 1,760,000 |
|     Taxes receivable—delinquent | | 140,000 |
| To record collection of property taxes. | | |

When specific delinquent property tax bills totaling $10,000 are determined to be uncollectible, the town writes them off with the following entry:

*General Fund—Entry 3*

| | | |
|---|---|---|
| Allowance for uncollectible taxes—delinquent | 10,000 | |
|     Taxes receivable—delinquent | | 10,000 |
| To record write-off of uncollectible accounts. | | |

**DERIVED TAX REVENUES** Derived tax revenues, such as sales and income taxes, require the merchant or taxpayer to determine the tax base. Under GASB Statement No. 33, governments recognize derived tax revenues when the underlying exchange (e.g., the sale) has occurred; however, within governmental funds, the resources must also be measurable and available. Thus, the taxing authority should accrue sales taxes collected and held by merchants at the end of the fiscal year if they will be remitted in time to pay liabilities of the current period.[5]

Governments recognize sales tax revenue when tax returns are received from merchants, and the taxes are expected to be remitted to the government by year-end (or within 60 days thereafter).

---

[5]Although the 60-day rule applies to property tax revenue collections only, many governments choose to use the same criterion for other revenues. Thus, revenues collected within 60 days of year-end are considered available to meet the liabilities of the current period. GASB 38 requires governments to disclose the length of time used to define "available" in the financial statement note that summarizes significant accounting principles.

The entry to record $150,000 in sales taxes reported on tax returns, of which three equal payments are required to be remitted by the fifteenth day of October 2016, November 2016, and December 2016, is as follows:

*General Fund—Entry 4*

| | | |
|---|---|---|
| Accounts receivable | 150,000 | |
|     Revenue | | 100,000 |
|         Revenue collected in advance | | 50,000 |
|     To record sales tax activity. | | |

Because October 15, 2016, and November 15, 2016, fall within 60 days of the September 30, 2016, fiscal year-end, two of the payment amounts will be available to meet current obligations and thus should be recognized as income under the modified accrual basis of accounting. The amount scheduled to be received in December is recorded in a liability account, revenue collected in advance.

### REVENUE FROM OTHER SOURCES

Unlike levied or derived taxes, other imposed nonexchange revenues, such as revenues from licenses, permits, fines, and the like, cannot be measured objectively until cash is actually received. Therefore, revenues from these sources are usually recognized when cash is collected. Thus, the town records the collection of fees ($200,000) from business licenses as follows:

*General Fund—Entry 5*

| | | |
|---|---|---|
| Cash | 200,000 | |
|     Revenue | | 200,000 |
|     To record collection of business license fees. | | |

Other revenues for the 2015–2016 fiscal year are recognized as cash is received. The amount in the following entry includes all revenue items not listed individually:

*General Fund—Entry 6*

| | | |
|---|---|---|
| Cash | 1,240,000 | |
|     Revenue | | 1,240,000 |
|     To summarize other revenue items for the year. | | |

Although the general ledger ordinarily includes only one revenue account, remember that a government has to record the detailed revenue sources individually in a subsidiary revenue ledger.

### RECORDING EXPENDITURES

Expenditures are decreases in the net financial resources of a governmental fund, as noted earlier. Under modified accrual accounting, we normally record expenditures when the related fund liability is incurred. Do not confuse this concept with the expense recognition concept, in which proprietary funds recognize expenses when the funds use the related goods or services. Under modified accrual accounting, governmental funds recognize salaries, supplies, utilities, as well as fixed asset purchases as expenditures when they incur the related liabilities.

When salaries ($200,000) are vouchered for payment (i.e., a payroll document is prepared and approved), the town records the following GF entry:

*General Fund—Entry 7*

| | | |
|---|---|---|
| Expenditures | 200,000 | |
|     Vouchers payable | | 200,000 |
|     To record accrual of salaries. | | |

### ACCOUNTING FOR ENCUMBRANCES

The law limits expenditures for each period, as measured on a government's budgetary basis, to those for which appropriations have been made. Thus, it is extremely important to keep expenditures within authorized levels. Approving expenditures without considering outstanding purchase orders or unperformed contracts could result in overspending appropriations. For example, assume that total appropriations for the year exceed actual expenditures to date by $4,000 and that an unknowing employee approves an additional equipment purchase for $3,000. If $2,000 worth of supplies are already on order and expenditures are made for both the equipment and the supplies, actual expenditures for the period will exceed appropriations by $1,000. Encumbrance accounting helps prevent this type of situation by maintaining a running total of outstanding purchase commitments. *Encumbrance* means "commitment," and **encumbrance accounting** records commitments made for goods on order and for unperformed contracts in order to provide additional control over expenditures.

During the year, the town orders snow-removal equipment expected to cost $150,000. Grantville makes the following encumbrance entry *at the time the purchase order is placed* to recognize a commitment to pay for the equipment when it is received:

*General Fund—Entry 8*

| | | |
|---|---|---|
| Encumbrances | 150,000 | |
| Reserve for encumbrances | | 150,000 |

To record a purchase order for $150,000 of snow-removal equipment.

This information helps prevent overspending because encumbrances can be deducted from unexpended appropriations to determine unencumbered appropriations (i.e., maximum additional authorizations):

| | |
|---|---|
| Appropriations (authorized expenditures) | $X |
| Less: Expenditures to date | Y |
| Unexpended appropriations | X–Y |
| Less: Encumbrances (commitments for expenditures) | Z |
| Unencumbered appropriations | $X–Y–Z |

The remaining expenditure authority for the budgetary period appears in the amount of unencumbered appropriations.

When the snow-removal equipment is received, Grantville reverses the entry recording the encumbrance:

*General Fund—Entry 9*

| | | |
|---|---|---|
| Reserve for encumbrances | 150,000 | |
| Encumbrances | | 150,000 |

To reverse the encumbrance entry for snow-removal equipment.

The entry to record the receipt of the equipment is unaffected by the encumbrance entries and reflects the actual amount of the invoice. Assuming that the actual cost of the equipment purchased is $140,000, the town records the expenditure as follows:

*General Fund—Entry 10*

| | | |
|---|---|---|
| Expenditures | 140,000 | |
| Vouchers payable | | 140,000 |

To record the purchase of snow-removal equipment.

As noted in the transaction analysis in the previous chapter, the acquisition of fixed assets (such as the snow-removal equipment) by a governmental fund decreases working capital and the fund balance. Therefore, under the modified accrual basis of accounting, we do not record fixed assets as assets in the GF, and they will not appear in the fund statements; however, we maintain fixed asset records and include governmental **fund fixed assets** in the government-wide statements, which we prepare on the accrual basis of accounting. Thus, fixed assets are one of the reconciling items between the fund financial statements and the government-wide financial statements.

Note that the amount of the encumbrance was an estimate of the actual cost, which was $10,000 less than the estimate. Like formal budgetary accounting, encumbrance accounting does not affect the recording of actual transactions and events.

If a governmental unit does not spend the full amount of an appropriation during the period covered by an appropriation, a question arises about whether the unexpended portion can be carried over as authorization for expenditures in the succeeding year. Although laws of the governmental unit will cover this matter, a common position is that all appropriations lapse at the end of the year for which they are made, with the exception of committed appropriations (i.e., encumbrances outstanding), which can continue to serve as authorizations for items on order or under contract.

Prior to GASB 54, total expenditures for the period and outstanding encumbrance amounts at fiscal year end were closed to fund balance at year-end while reserve for encumbrance credits remained in the accounting records as reservations of fund balance within the governmental fund statements. Note that the 2015 postclosing trial balance for the Town of Grantville at the beginning of the chapter includes a credit account, "Fund balance—reserved," of $90,000. This account represents a commitment of fund balance to appropriations from a prior fiscal period. The new classifications from GASB 54 require the government to be more specific about the level of constraints and the end of period reports must move the amounts from reserved and unreserved fund balance to fund balance classified as either nonspendable, restricted, committed, assigned, or unassigned.

Grantville has a long tradition of using encumbrance accounting and decides to keep its record-keeping entries as similar to pre–GASB 54 methods as possible. Thus, it decides to continue recording all initial encumbrances as in entry 8 with a debit to Encumbrances and a credit to Reserve for encumbrances. At year-end, any encumbrances still open will be closed with a reversing entry debiting Reserve for encumbrances and crediting Encumbrances. A final reclassification entry will be done for all fund balance categories based on an analysis of the spending constraints at year-end. This bookkeeping method retains the useful internal control aspects of encumbrance accounting while also improving external reporting to outsiders.

For those encumbrances that were closed at the end of the year and for which the legal and accounting policies allow them to be paid in the subsequent year, such as the $90,000 in the opening trial balance, Grantville reinstates the encumbrance:

*General Fund—Entry 11*

| | | |
|---|---|---|
| Encumbrances | 90,000 | |
|     Reserve for encumbrances | | 90,000 |
|     To reinstate the prior period encumbrance. | | |

This entry would be done at the beginning of every fiscal period.

In October 2015, Grantville receives the equipment that was ordered in the previous fiscal year and for which an encumbrance of $90,000 had been reinstated. If the actual invoice is $85,000, the entries to record receipt of the equipment are as follows:

*General Fund—Entry 12a*

| | | |
|---|---|---|
| Reserve for Encumbrances | 90,000 | |
|     Encumbrances | | 90,000 |
|     To reverse the encumbrance upon receipt of equipment. | | |

*General Fund—Entry 12b*

| | | |
|---|---|---|
| Expenditures—prior year | 85,000 | |
|     Vouchers payable | | 85,000 |
|     To record receipt of equipment ordered during the prior year and chargeable against the prior year's budget. | | |

**SUPPLIES**    Within governmental funds, a government may treat supply acquisitions as expenditures either when purchased (purchases method) or when used (consumption method), as long as it reports *significant* amounts of inventory in the balance sheet.[6] Although the consumption method is similar

---

[6]GASB Codification, Section 1600.123.

to the manner in which commercial businesses record supplies, the purchases method better allows for comparison of expenditures and appropriations. Thus, if a government's annual appropriations include all inventory acquisitions for the period, the government will likely select the purchases method. Under the purchases method, a government with significant inventory balances at year-end will recognize the balances as assets in the fund balance sheet and establish an accompanying increase in fund balance—nonspendable to reflect the fact that the supply amount is not an available financial asset.

Under the consumption method, which is preferred by the GASB, we record the process of acquiring supplies as follows:

*General Fund—Entry 13a*

| | | |
|---|---|---|
| Encumbrances | 60,000 | |
| Reserve for encumbrances | | 60,000 |

To record the purchase order for operating supplies.

*General Fund—Entry 13b*

| | | |
|---|---|---|
| Reserve for encumbrances | 60,000 | |
| Encumbrances | | 60,000 |

To reverse the encumbrance entry upon receipt of the supplies.

*General Fund—Entry 13c*

| | | |
|---|---|---|
| Supplies inventory | 60,000 | |
| Vouchers payable | | 60,000 |

To record receipt of operating supplies.

Depending on their policies, governments may follow a "perpetual" approach, increasing fund balance—nonspendable when supplies are acquired and reducing fund balance—nonspendable when supplies are consumed. Grantville chooses instead to use a "periodic" approach with year-end reclassification entries to fund balance when it adjusts inventory and expenditures for the amount consumed and on hand.

When an additional $50,000 of supplies is ordered, the entry is:

*General Fund—Entry 13d*

| | | |
|---|---|---|
| Encumbrances | 50,000 | |
| Reserve for encumbrances | | 50,000 |

To record encumbrances for a purchase order for supplies.

These supplies have not been received at year-end, September 30, 2016.

**CAPITAL LEASE** Lease agreements of state and local governments fall under the provisions of FASB Statement No. 13, *Accounting for Leases*, as amended and interpreted by NCGA Statement No. 5, *Accounting and Financial Reporting Principles for Lease Agreements of State and Local Governments*, and by GASB Statement No. 13, *Accounting for Operating Leases with Scheduled Rent Increases*. A lease agreement that is financed from general government resources must be accounted for under governmental fund accounting principles. (See *GASB Codification*, Section L20.)

When governments use capital leases to acquire general fixed assets, the governmental fund acquiring the general fixed asset records an expenditure and another financing source, as if long-term debt had been issued (*GASB Codification*, Section L20.115).

The Town of Grantville enters into a general government capital lease for a fixed asset with an initial down payment of $5,000 and a present value of lease payments of $50,000 and records the following entry:

*General Fund—Entry 14*

| | | |
|---|---|---|
| Expenditures | 50,000 | |
| Cash | | 5,000 |
| Other financing sources—capital lease | | 45,000 |

At the same time, the town notes a liability (capital lease payable) in the general long-term debt account records for the amount remaining due ($45,000) and adds an asset to the general fixed asset account records at the present value of the lease payments determined by FASB 13 criteria ($50,000). The asset and liability, as well as associated depreciation, will appear in the government-wide financial statements; however, only an expenditure and other financing source appear in the governmental fund statements. The town may record future capital lease payments as expenditures of principal and interest in the GF or transfer resources to the debt service fund, which will recognize the expenditures. The notes to the financial statements disclose lease payments for each of the following five years and in five-year increments thereafter.

**INTERFUND TRANSACTIONS**    During the year, the GF transfers funds to three other governmental funds. (The transactions are covered from the perspectives of the other funds later in this chapter.) The town transfers a total of $50,000 to establish an SRF balance, $100,000 to help finance a capital project, and $14,250 to the debt service fund to finance general long-term debt payments. (Note that the $50,000 transfer was not appropriated in the GF budget and therefore will require administrative or legislative approval.) A summary entry for these transfers is as follows:

*General Fund—Entry 15*

| | | |
|---|---|---|
| Other financing uses—nonreciprocal transfer to town hall capital project fund (CPF) | 100,000 | |
| Other financing uses—reciprocal transfer to special revenue fund (SRF) | 50,000 | |
| Other financing uses—nonreciprocal transfer to debt service fund (DSF) | 14,250 | |
|     Cash | | 164,250 |

    To record transfers to town hall CPF, the SRF, and the DSF.

This entry recognizes slight differences between the interfund transfers. GASB 34 distinguishes between reciprocal and nonreciprocal transfers. **Reciprocal transfers** are loans for which a fund expects repayment, whereas nonreciprocal transfers represent flows of assets that do not require repayment. Furthermore, GASB Statement No. 38, *Certain Financial Statement Note Disclosures*, requires note disclosure of significant transfers that are considered nonroutine or are inconsistent with the activities of the fund making the transfer.[7] The transfers in the previous entry include nonreciprocal transfers to the capital projects and debt service funds (DSF) and a reciprocal transfer (loan) to an SRF. Each of these transfers is considered routine and consistent with the activities of the general fund.

**OTHER TRANSACTIONS FOR THE YEAR**    The short-term note payable that was outstanding at September 30, 2015, becomes due and is paid:

*General Fund—Entry 16*

| | | |
|---|---|---|
| Note payable | 150,000 | |
|     Cash | | 150,000 |

Here is a summary entry for the remainder of the various expenditures throughout the year:

*General Fund—Entry 17*

| | | |
|---|---|---|
| Expenditures | 2,843,500 | |
|     Vouchers payable | | 2,843,500 |
|   Summary entry for accrual of salaries, purchase of supplies, and other expenditures. | | |

*General Fund—Entry 18*

| | | |
|---|---|---|
| Vouchers payable | 3,143,500 | |
|     Cash | | 3,143,500 |
|   To record payment of vouchers during the year in summary form. | | |

---

[7]GASB Codification, Section 2300.120–121.

## Year-End Procedures

**ADJUSTING ENTRIES**    If supplies with a historical cost of $90,000 are on hand at the balance sheet date, the town needs to make a $30,000 adjusting entry under the consumption method of accounting for inventory balances as follows: $60,000 beginning balance + $60,000 purchased − $90,000 remaining. (Under the purchases method, the town would adjust supplies inventory and fund balance—nonspendable.)

*General Fund—Adjusting Entry 1*

| | | |
|---|---|---|
| Expenditures | 30,000 | |
|     Supplies inventory | | 30,000 |

    To adjust the supplies inventory and supplies expen-
ditures accounts using consumption method.

Assume that uncollected taxes on September 30, 2016, are past due but will be collected within 60 days of year-end.[8] Accordingly, the $240,000 taxes receivable—current and the $20,000 allowance for uncollectible taxes—current are reclassified as delinquent. The entry for this reclassification is as follows:

*General Fund—Adjusting Entry 2*

| | | |
|---|---|---|
| Taxes receivable—delinquent | 240,000 | |
| Allowance for uncollectible taxes—current | 20,000 | |
|     Taxes receivable—current | | 240,000 |
|     Allowance for uncollectible taxes— delinquent | | 20,000 |

To reclassify past-due taxes receivable as delinquent.

By year-end, Grantville created accounting policies related to fund balance classifications that were approved by the Council. First, all open encumbrances and the related reserves are closed via reversal. Second, all of the open encumbrances are analyzed for the level of spending constraints. The Council approved a default policy where end of period encumbrances constitute "commitments" unless otherwise acted upon by the Council. Finally, all of the fund balance accounts are reviewed for possible adjustments, and a reclassification entry is made to adjust the fund balance accounts to the proper classification—the unassigned category is the plug account.

Grantville needs to make two fund balance adjustments. The first is to update the nonspendable category for the $30,000 increase in inventory. The second is to update the committed category for the $40,000 decrease in open encumbrances at the end of the period (remember the outstanding encumbrances at the beginning of the fiscal year are $90,000 and the outstanding encumbrances at the end of the fiscal year are $50,000). Note the open encumbrance for $50,000 at the end of the year is represented by the postclosing balance of $50,000 in fund balance—committed from the commitment to purchase supplies in entry 13d. This amount will be classified as committed rather than nonspendable because the supplies have not yet been delivered.

*General Fund—Ending Fund Balance Reclassification Entry*

| | | |
|---|---|---|
| Reserve for encumbrances | 50,000 | |
| Fund balance—committed | 40,000 | |
|     Encumbrances | | 50,000 |
|     Fund balance—nonspendable | | 30,000 |
|     Fund balance—unassigned | | 10,000 |

    To reverse end of year encumbrances and adjust
related fund balance classifications.

---

[8]If the taxes are not expected to be collected within 60 days of year-end, the revenue would be reclassified as a liability account such as "Revenue collected in advance" because it would not be available to meet current obligations.

Grantville's adjusted GF trial balance at September 30, 2016, includes the following accounts and balances:

| Debits | |
| --- | --- |
| Cash | $187,250 |
| Taxes receivable—delinquent | 240,000 |
| Accounts receivable | 180,000 |
| Supplies inventory | 90,000 |
| Estimated revenues | 3,500,000 |
| Expenditures | 3,263,500 |
| Expenditures—prior year | 85,000 |
| Other financing uses | 164,250 |
| **Total debits** | **$7,710,000** |
| Credits | |
| Allowance for uncollectible taxes—delinquent | $20,000 |
| Vouchers payable | 325,000 |
| Revenue collected in advance | 50,000 |
| Fund balance—nonspendable | 90,000 |
| Fund balance—committed | 50,000 |
| Fund balance—unassigned | 174,750 |
| Appropriations | 3,320,250 |
| Revenues | 3,520,000 |
| Estimated other financing uses—transfers out | 115,000 |
| Other financing sources | 45,000 |
| **Total credits** | **$7,710,000** |

**CLOSING ENTRIES**    By year-end, the budgetary accounts will have served their purpose and must be closed. The most direct method of closing budgetary accounts is to reverse the original entry used to record the budget. At September 30, 2016, Grantville could close its accounts as follows:

*General Fund—Closing Entry 1*

| | | |
| --- | --- | --- |
| Appropriations | 3,320,250 | |
| Estimated other financing uses—transfers out | 115,000 | |
| Fund balance—unassigned | 64,750 | |
| Estimated revenues | | 3,500,000 |
| To close the budgetary accounts. | | |

The town closes actual revenues and expenditures directly to the fund balance—unassigned account. The adjusted trial balance shows that Grantville had revenue of $3,520,000, expenditures of $3,263,500 for the current year and $85,000 for the prior year, other financing sources of $45,000, and other financing uses of $164,250 at September 30, 2016. The entry to close these accounts is as follows:

*General Fund—Closing Entry 2*

| | | |
| --- | --- | --- |
| Revenues | 3,520,000 | |
| Other financing sources—capital lease (OFS) | 45,000 | |
| Expenditures | | 3,263,500 |
| Expenditures—prior year | | 85,000 |
| Other financing uses (OFU)—nonreciprocal transfer to town hall CPF | | 100,000 |
| Other financing uses—reciprocal transfer to SRF | | 50,000 |
| Other financing uses—nonreciprocal transfer to DSF | | 14,250 |
| Fund balance—unassigned | | 52,250 |
| To close revenues, expenditures, and OFS/OFU accounts. | | |

This entry reveals that actual revenues and other financing sources exceeded expenditures and other financing uses by $52,250, which is the change in fund balance shown later in Exhibit 20-3.

## Special Revenue Funds

An *SRF* is the entity that a government uses to account for the proceeds of specific revenue sources (other than resources for permanent funds (PF), major capital projects, or debt service on general long-term debt) that are restricted by law or administrative action to expenditures for specified purposes. Although a government has only one GF, it can have many SRFs, or none at all. If specific revenue sources are earmarked for education, the government may use a special revenue education fund to account for the earmarked resources.[9] Similarly, if a city receives state or federal funds specifically designated for highway maintenance, the government may create an SRF to account for such fund resources.

Governments account for earmarked revenues in separate SRFs to show compliance with legal or administrative requirements. GASB 54 requires that an SRF fund balance is classified as nonspendable, restricted, committed, or assigned. The fund balance cannot be classified as unassigned in an SRF, unless there is a deficit. Outside of the need to separate earmarked revenue sources and the limited use of unassigned fund balance, there is no essential difference between an SRF and a GF. Indeed, if an SRF is not legally or contractually required, governments have the option of accounting for a special revenue source in the GF. Both types of funds are governmental funds, use the modified accrual basis for fund statements, and typically integrate their budgets into their accounting systems. Because the accounting requirements for SRFs are essentially the same as for a GF, this chapter illustrates only SRF entries used to record grant proceeds.

GRANTS   Governments often receive **grants** from other governments or private sources. For example, the federal government provides grant funds for public safety at the local level, and private organizations donate grant funds for senior citizen activities. If the grant funds are restricted to a specific purpose other than a capital acquisition, they will usually be accounted for in an SRF. Grant revenues can be recognized when all eligibility requirements set forth in the grant contract have been met, if the funds are available to meet current liabilities. If the grant funds are disbursed to the government prior to the eligibility requirements having been met, they must be accounted for as Revenue collected in advance.

In July 2016, the state awards a highway beautification grant of up to $50,000 to the Town of Grantville for the purchase and placement of trees on the major highway within town jurisdiction. Because the grant funds are not paid to the town until after approved expenditures have been incurred, the GF "loans" cash of $50,000 to the SRF. (Recall the interfund transfer entry in the GF.) During July and August, the town incurs $38,000 in approved expenditures and records the following entries in an SRF:

| | | |
|---|---|---|
| *Special Revenue Fund—Highway Beautification* | | |
| Cash | 50,000 | |
|    Other financing sources—reciprocal transfer from GF | | 50,000 |
|   To record a transfer of cash from the general fund. | | |
| *Special Revenue Fund—Highway Beautification* | | |
| Expenditures | 38,000 | |
|    Vouchers payable | | 38,000 |
|   To record expenditures related to highway beautification. | | |
| *Special Revenue Fund—Highway Beautification* | | |
| Accounts receivable—grant | 38,000 | |
|    Grant revenue | | 38,000 |
|   To recognize grant revenue related to approved grant expenditures. | | |

Note that the town recognizes revenue and a receivable equal to the amount of acceptable expenditures, because the state will reimburse Grantville the $38,000 of approved expenditures. This amount is now measurable and should be available soon enough to meet current obligations.

---

[9]GASB 54 clarifies that GAAP does not require the use of specific funds for specific activities or specific revenues (paragraph 110). Thus, some governments may record specific revenues in the General Fund and some governments may record multiple revenue sources in a single SRF. GAAP provides flexibility for preparers to best communicate their financial activities and position.

In July 2016, the Town of Grantville receives $20,000 from the state to be used for police and fire officer training sessions on the proper installation of child car seats. The town records the following entry:

*Special Revenue Fund—Officer Training*

| | | |
|---|---|---|
| Cash | 20,000 | |
|     Revenue collected in advance | | 20,000 |
|     To record the receipt of grant funds from the state. | | |

When expenditures have been incurred for the training sessions in the amount of $18,500, the entry is as follows:

*Special Revenue Fund—Officer Training*

| | | |
|---|---|---|
| Expenditures | 18,500 | |
|     Vouchers payable | | 18,500 |
|     To record expenditures for an officer training program. | | |

*Special Revenue Fund—Officer Training*

| | | |
|---|---|---|
| Revenue collected in advance | 18,500 | |
|     Grant revenue | | 18,500 |
|     To recognize grant revenue. | | |

If additional training will take place in the time span identified in the grant agreement (if any), then the SRF can remain open. If the town has completed all training related to the grant's purpose and will not spend the remaining $1,500, the town will return the money to the state and close the SRF.

At the end of the year, the town will prepare closing entries for SRF revenues and expenditures (including encumbrances, if any), as well as budgetary accounts, in the same manner as was illustrated for the GF earlier in the chapter.

## PERMANENT FUNDS

GASB 34 created a new governmental fund category, permanent funds, for nonexpendable resources set aside for support of a government's programs or citizenry. *PF* typically account for contributions for which the grantor specifies that a principal amount must be maintained but for which interest accumulation or asset appreciation, or both, are to be used for a specified purpose. (Such resources were previously referred to as **nonexpendable trust funds**.) In contrast, if funds are **expendable** (i.e., they can be spent), a government accounts for them in an SRF; or, if the contribution benefits parties external to the government, it should be accounted for in a private-purpose trust fund.

In April 2016, the Town of Grantville receives a gift of $500,000 in bonds. The 5 percent bonds pay interest semiannually in September and March. The contributor wants to ensure that the seal exhibit at the town zoo is maintained for years to come. He instructs that the principal shall be maintained, but all interest income and asset appreciation may be used for the benefit of the seal exhibit. During the year, the town receives an interest installment and incurs $3,000 in approved expenditures. The town makes the following entries in a permanent fund:

*Permanent Fund—Seal Exhibit*

| | | |
|---|---|---|
| Investments—bonds | 500,000 | |
|     Revenues—additions to permanent endowments | | 500,000 |
|     To record the receipt of a permanent endowment. | | |

*Permanent Fund—Seal Exhibit*

| | | |
|---|---|---|
| Cash | 12,500 | |
|     Revenues—investment income—interest | | 12,500 |
|     To record the receipt of interest ($500,000 $\times$ 5% $\times$ $\frac{1}{2}$ year) | | |

*Permanent Fund—Seal Exhibit*

| | | |
|---|---|---|
| Expenditures | 3,000 | |
|     Cash | | 3,000 |
|     To record allowable expenditures. | | |

The town may constrain the spending of the expendable interest in the permanent fund until the funds are used for the seal exhibit, or it may transfer the expendable funds to an SRF (or the GF); however, the interest must be earmarked for the seal exhibit with an appropriate classification of fund balance as restricted due to the external resource provider.

According to GASB Statement No. 31, *Accounting and Financial Reporting for Certain Investments and for External Investment Pools*, governments should record investments with determinable fair values at fair value. In 2015, however, GASB issued Statement No. 79, *Certain Investment Pools and Pool Participants*, which allows the use of amortized cost to measure investments if certain criteria are met. Thus, if the fair value of the bonds, excluding accrued interest, had changed, the town could have needed to make an entry to reflect the fair market value of the bonds. The value of the bonds in this example remained unchanged.

At the end of the year, the town will close the permanent fund's revenues and expenditures (including encumbrances, if any), as well as budgetary accounts, in the same manner as was illustrated for the GF earlier in the chapter.

## CAPITAL PROJECTS FUNDS

Governments account for the acquisition of most general fixed assets from expenditures of annual appropriations in the GF or SRFs; however, *major*[10] general fixed assets are seldom financed through appropriations of these funds. The purpose of *capital projects funds (CPF)* is to account for resources segregated for the acquisition or construction of capital facilities or other capital assets other than those financed by trust and proprietary funds. Typical sources of financing include the proceeds of bond issues, grants and **shared revenues**, transfers from other funds, and contributions from property owners.

CPF are governmental funds that account for working capital to be used for general governmental capital projects. CPF use modified accrual accounting and revenue and expenditure accounts. Governments use encumbrance accounting procedures to account for commitments made to contractors and for material and supply orders. Ordinarily, a governmental unit will create a separate CPF to account for each significant capital project that has been legally authorized. Once created, a CPF exists for the life of the project. CPF typically do not use formal budgetary accounting unless numerous capital projects are financed through the same fund or facilities are being constructed with the governmental unit as the primary contractor.

The next section illustrates the accounting and reporting for a CPF during a two-year construction period.

### Accounting for a Capital Projects Fund

The Town of Grantville authorizes an addition to the town hall on December 15, 2015, in the amount of $1,000,000. Financing for the project consists of $500,000 from a 6.5 percent serial bond issue, $400,000 from a federal grant, and $100,000 from the GF. Transactions and events during the life of the project are as follows:

**2015–2016 Fiscal Year**

1. The town transfers $100,000 from the GF to the town hall addition capital projects fund (a CPF created to account for the town hall construction).

2. Planning and architect's fees are paid in the amount of $40,000.

3. The contract is awarded to the lowest bidder for $950,000.

4. The bonds are sold for $502,000 (at a premium of $2,000).

5. The amount of the premium is transferred to the debt service fund.

6. The construction is certified to be 50 percent complete, and a bill for $475,000 is received from the contractor.

7. Contract payable, less a 10 percent retained percentage, is paid.

8. The books are closed and financial statements are prepared.

---

[10]GASB 54 changed the definition of capital projects funds and removed the requirement that the capital expenditures be for "major" projects. Capital projects funds may now be used for any capital facilities or other capital assets.

**2016–2017 Fiscal Year**

9. The amount due from the federal grant is received.

10. Construction is completed and the contractor is paid.

11. Closing entry is recorded.

12. Remaining cash is transferred to the GF.

**CREATION OF THE CPF**    When the town hall addition CPF is created, the town makes a memorandum entry in the CPF noting the $1,000,000 authorization.

> *Capital Projects Fund*
> Memorandum—town hall project authorization                $1,000,000

**INTERFUND TRANSFER (1)**    Transaction 1 increases CPF current assets and fund balance. As discussed earlier, the town classifies this interfund transaction as a nonreciprocal transfer, because it does not expect it to be repaid. The town reports fund balance increases from transfers as other financing sources, not as revenues, in the fund receiving the transfer. Likewise, it records this transaction, which decreases GF current assets and fund balance, as an other financing use, not an expenditure, in the fund transferring the cash. The $100,000 transfer requires an entry in both funds. Recall the interfund transfer entry in the GF. The corresponding entry in the capital projects fund to receive the $100,000 is as follows:

> *Capital Projects Fund*
> Cash                                                       100,000
>     Other financing sources—nonreciprocal transfer                        100,000
>         from general fund
>     To record receipt of funds from the GF.

**RECORDING EXPENDITURES (2)**    The town records payments for planning and architect's fees as follows:

> *Capital Projects Fund*
> Expenditures                                               40,000
>     Cash                                                           40,000
>     To record payments for planning and architect's fees.

**RECORDING ENCUMBRANCES (3)**    When the contract is awarded to a contractor, the town makes an encumbrance entry for the full amount of the contract:

> *Capital Projects Fund*
> Encumbrances                                               950,000
>     Reserve for encumbrances                                       950,000
>     To record encumbrances for the amount of the contract.

**ACCOUNTING FOR THE BOND PROCEEDS (4 AND 5)**    Governments recognize the proceeds of bond issues in the CPF at the time the bonds are sold. The sale of the bonds increases CPF current assets (cash). The bond liability is long-term, so the town does not account for it in the CPF; rather, it includes it in long-term debt records. As in the GF treatment of the capital lease, this debt will appear on the government-wide statements; however, within the CPF, the fund balance increases by the amount of the bond proceeds ($502,000). The increase is classified as an other financing source (bond issue proceeds), not as revenue.

The town sold the bonds at a premium. Although the following entry places the full amount of the proceeds in the CPF, the premium is not available to finance the project; however, premiums often are set aside to service the debt. Thus, a second entry transfers the premium to the debt service fund through which the bond liability will be serviced. (The corresponding entry for the debt service fund is illustrated later in this chapter.) Journal entries for the sale of bonds and transfer of the premium are as follows:

*Capital Projects Fund*

| | | |
|---|---|---|
| Cash | 502,000 | |
|     Other financing sources—proceeds from bond issue | | 502,000 |
|   To record sale of bonds. | | |
| Other financing uses—nonreciprocal transfer to debt<br>    service fund | 2,000 | |
|     Cash | | 2,000 |
|   To transfer the premium to the town hall addition debt service fund. | | |

When bonds sell at a discount, bond proceeds equal the amount received. Governments selling bonds at a discount must reduce the project authorization or transfer additional resources to the CPF.

**PROGRESS PAYMENTS AND RETAINED PERCENTAGES (6 AND 7)**   A construction contract often stipulates that a portion of the contractor's remuneration be withheld until completion of the construction project and final inspection. Note that the fixed asset (construction in progress) is not recorded in the CPF, because it is a governmental fund. The fixed asset does not represent CPF working capital. Instead, the incurrence of the contract payable liability increases CPF liabilities and decreases CPF fund balance. Governments report this fund balance decrease as an expenditure. Accounting entries for the amount owed on partial completion of the contract and the first progress payment on the contract appear as follows:

*Capital Projects Fund*

| | | |
|---|---|---|
| Reserve for encumbrances | 475,000 | |
|     Encumbrances | | 475,000 |
|   To reverse half of the amount encumbered. | | |
| Expenditures | 475,000 | |
|     Contracts payable | | 427,500 |
|     Contracts payable—retained percentage | | 47,500 |
|   To record expenditures and a 10% retained percentage<br>    on the town hall construction. | | |
| Contracts payable | 427,500 | |
|     Cash | | 427,500 |
|   To record partial payment to the contractor. | | |

## Adjusting and Closing Entries (8)

At the end of the fiscal year, the town closes the CPF books and prepares financial statements. The town hall construction project has not been completed, and the statements for the CPF are interim statements from the standpoint of the project.

**INTERGOVERNMENTAL REVENUE**   The grant from the federal government is intergovernmental revenue. Under modified accrual accounting, a governmental fund recognizes revenue on restricted grants when qualifying costs have been incurred (and other significant conditions, if any, have been met), assuming that the funds are measurable and available.

Because the CPF did not receive the federal grant proceeds for the town hall project at the time the books were closed, the town will prepare an accrual entry, provided that the commitment is firm. Just as previously discussed in the section on SRFs, governments recognize revenue if the receivable will be collected and available to meet current obligations. Otherwise, they must credit Revenue collected in advance. Failure to recognize revenue from the grant could make the CPF appear to be in financial difficulty for interim reporting purposes when, in fact, it has progressed as planned.

*Capital Projects Fund (Adjusting Entry)*

| | | |
|---|---|---|
| Due from federal government | 400,000 | |
|     Grant revenue | | 400,000 |
|   To recognize revenue from the federal grant. | | |

This entry assumes that the federal government has agreed to contribute $400,000 to the project regardless of the total cost. Therefore, because more than $400,000 of costs were incurred in 2016, the town records the full $400,000 as revenue. If the grant had specified that the federal government would pay a percentage of the cost of the project up to $400,000, the town would prorate the amounts in the entry.

**CLOSING ENTRY—SEPTEMBER 30, 2016**    To determine the classification of the fund balance, the accounting staff reviewed the documentation accompanying all of the funding sources and determined that all of them made a legally binding restriction on the use of the funds only for the capital project. The town records a closing entry for the CPF as follows:

*Capital Projects Fund (Closing Entry)*

| | | |
|---|---|---|
| Grant revenue | 400,000 | |
| Other financing sources—nonreciprocal transfer from general fund | 100,000 | |
| Other financing sources—proceeds from bond issue | 502,000 | |
| Reserve for encumbrances | 475,000 | |
|     Expenditures | | 515,000 |
|     Other financing uses—nonreciprocal transfer to debt service fund | | 2,000 |
|     Encumbrances | | 475,000 |
|     Fund balance—restricted | | 485,000 |

To close the books at the end of fiscal year 2016.

**UNISSUED BONDS AT AN INTERIM STATEMENT DATE**    The bonds to finance the town hall capital project have been issued by September 30, 2016, but in some cases there will be authorized but unissued bonds at an interim reporting date. The existence of the unissued bonds would be disclosed only in a statement note. The authorization of the bonds does not represent a CPF asset. Assets are received only upon bond issuance.

## Entries for 2016 to 2017

The following entries illustrate the proper accounting treatment for the completion of a capital project; however, they will not be reflected in the October 1, 2015, to September 30, 2016, financial statements at the end of the chapter.

**REINSTATEMENT OF ENCUMBRANCES**    At the start of the 2016–2017 fiscal year, the $475,000 encumbrance that was closed at the end of the prior fiscal year is reinstated in the accounts as follows:

*Capital Projects Fund*

| | | |
|---|---|---|
| Encumbrances | 475,000 | |
|     Reserve for encumbrances | | 475,000 |

To reinstate the encumbrances.

It is not necessary to denote the encumbrance in the CPF as related to the prior year, because capital projects are budgeted by project rather than on an annual basis.

**RECEIPT OF GRANT (9)**    When the federal grant is received, it is recorded:

*Capital Projects Fund*

| | | |
|---|---|---|
| Cash | 400,000 | |
|     Due from federal government | | 400,000 |

To record receipt of the federal grant.

**COMPLETION OF THE PROJECT (10)** The journal entries to record completion of construction and payment to the contractor are as follows:

*Capital Projects Fund*

| | | |
|---|---|---|
| Reserve for encumbrances | 475,000 | |
|     Encumbrances | | 475,000 |
|   To remove encumbrances when construction is complete. | | |
| Expenditures | 475,000 | |
|     Contracts payable | | 475,000 |
|   To record expenditures on town hall construction. | | |
| Contracts payable | 475,000 | |
| Contracts payable—retained percentage | 47,500 | |
|     Cash | | 522,500 |
|   To record final payment to contractor. | | |

**CLOSING ENTRY—SEPTEMBER 30, 2017 (11)** The town makes an entry to close expenditures:

*Capital Projects Fund*

| | | |
|---|---|---|
| Fund balance—restricted | 475,000 | |
|     Expenditures | | 475,000 |
|   To close the expenditures to fund balance. | | |

**NONRECIPROCAL TRANSFER (12)** The town records the transfer of the remaining fund balance to the GF in final termination of the town hall addition CPF as follows:

*Capital Projects Fund*

| | | |
|---|---|---|
| Other financing uses—nonreciprocal transfer to GF | 10,000 | |
|     Cash | | 10,000 |
|   To record transfer of cash to the general fund. | | |
| Fund balance—restricted | 10,000 | |
|     Other financing uses—nonreciprocal transfer to GF | | 10,000 |
|   To close town hall addition CPF ledger. | | |

A corresponding entry is required in the GF to receive the cash transferred. That entry is as follows:

*General Fund*

| | | |
|---|---|---|
| Cash | 10,000 | |
|     Other financing sources—nonreciprocal transfer from CPF | | 10,000 |
|   To record receipt of cash from town hall addition CPF. | | |

The $10,000 transfer to the GF is a nonreciprocal transfer because the fund is being terminated. It should be presented separately as an increase or decrease in fund balance in the financial statements. Also, the appropriate fund balance classification will need to be used when the GF closes the other financing sources—whether it is unassigned or in some way constrained per the terms of the financing providers.

## SPECIAL ASSESSMENT ACTIVITIES

Governments sometimes finance public improvements that benefit a limited group of property owners through special taxes levied against these residents. These special tax levies are known as *special assessment levies*, or just **special assessments**. The more common types of special assessment projects include street paving, the construction of sidewalks, and the installation of sewer lines. Ordinarily, a special assessment project originates when property owners in an area petition the government to construct the improvements desired. If the project is authorized, the government obtains the financing, makes the improvement, and levies special assessments on the property owners for some or all of the cost incurred. If the project will benefit the general citizenry, the government may pay a portion of the cost.

The property owners may pay the special assessments immediately, in which case the governmental unit is repaid for the resources it uses in constructing the improvement, and the special assessment project is terminated. In many cases, however, the government issues special assessment bonds to pay the construction costs and collects the assessment in installments over the term of the special assessment bond issue. Interest charged on the unpaid balances of special assessment receivables covers the interest on the special assessment bonds. If special assessments are not paid as they come due, the governmental unit has the power to enforce collection through seizure of the real property against which special assessments are levied.

The GASB requires that governments account for capital improvements related to special assessment projects in CPF. If the special assessment involves general obligation debt that will be repaid, in part, from special assessments, or if *the government is obligated in some manner* for debt repayment, the government should report the debt in the governmental activities column of the government-wide statement of net position. If, however, *the governmental unit is not obligated in any manner*, it should not report the special assessment obligation in its financial statements.[11] In this case, special assessment receipts can be accounted for in an agency fund, and the related special assessment obligation is only disclosed in notes to the financial statements.

## DEBT SERVICE FUNDS

*DSF* are governmental funds that account for the receipt of resources from designated sources (such as taxes or transfers from the GF) and for the use of these resources to make principal and interest payments on general long-term debt obligations. Ordinarily, governments create a separate DSF to account for servicing each general long-term debt issue, but some use one DSF for all governmental fund debt. Although DSF make interest and principal payments on general long-term debt, they do not record the liability for general long-term debt. You will recall that governments maintain internal records of general long-term debt, which coordinate with the records of debt service. When long-term debt matures, governments record the appropriate expenditures in DSF and reduce the liability for the debt in the internal debt records and the appropriate financial statements.

DSF generally follow the modified accrual basis of accounting. *GASB Codification*, Section 1600.122, identifies a major exception for DSF expenditures. Because resources for debt service are often appropriated in other funds and transferred to a DSF, the DSF may recognize principal and interest expenditures on general long-term debt when due (i.e., in the year of payment). This exception is made to avoid showing an expenditure and a liability for debt service in one period and the transfer of resources from the GF or other sources to pay the liability in the following period.[12]

The operations of DSF for serial bond issues differ from those for term bond issues. In the case of a serial bond issue, in which bonds are retired at regular intervals, resources typically are received as needed to service the debt, and no significant balances are carried over from one period to the next. However, DSF for term bond issues accumulate resources over time to retire all of the debt at maturity as well as make periodic interest payments. DSF for term bond issues accommodate both sinking fund operations and operations for current debt service. Thus, they are more complex than those for serial bond issues. Formal budgetary accounting is ordinarily needed for term bond issues but not for serial bond issues. This chapter illustrates only debt service fund operations for serial bond issues.

## ACCOUNTING FOR THE DEBT SERVICE FUND

Assume that the $500,000, 6.5 percent serial bond issue of the Town of Grantville that was issued for $502,000 on April 3, 2016, has interest payment dates of April 1 and October 1 of each year.

---

[11]GASB Codification, Section S40.

[12]Accrual is permitted, but not required, if two conditions are met. First, the resources to be used for payment must be available in the DSF by year-end. Second, the payment must be due early (the first few weeks) in the next year.

Principal amounts of $50,000 are due each year starting on April 1, 2017, and cash for all debt service is to be provided by transfers from the GF. The town transfers amounts needed for debt service payments from the GF during the month before the due date. Under these assumptions, the required journal entries for the town hall addition debt service fund for the 2015–2016 and 2016–2017 fiscal years are as follows:

*Debt Service Fund—April 3, 2016*

| | | |
|---|---|---|
| Cash | 2,000 | |
|     Other financing sources—nonreciprocal transfer from town hall CPF | | 2,000 |
|   To record receipt of issue premium from town hall addition CPF. | | |

*Debt Service Fund—September 2016*

| | | |
|---|---|---|
| Cash | 14,250 | |
|     Other financing sources—nonreciprocal transfer from general fund | | 14,250 |
|   To record receipt of resources for the October 1, 2016, interest payment from the general fund, less the $2,000 already accumulated. | | |

($500,000 × 6.5% × $\frac{1}{2}$ year) − $2,000 = $14,250.

*Debt Service Fund—Adjusting Entry—September 30, 2016*

| | | |
|---|---|---|
| Expenditures—interest payment | 16,250 | |
|     Matured interest payable | | 16,250 |
|   To accrue payment of interest due on 6.5% serial bond issue, due October 1. | | |

*Debt Service Fund Closing Entries—September 30, 2016*

| | | |
|---|---|---|
| Other financing sources—nonreciprocal transfer from town hall CPF | 2,000 | |
| Other financing sources—nonreciprocal transfer from general fund | 14,250 | |
|     Expenditures—interest payment | | 16,250 |
|   To close the accounts. | | |

The following entries illustrate the proper accounting treatment for debt service transactions; however, they will not be reflected in the October 1, 2015, to September 30, 2016, financial statements at the end of the chapter.

*Debt Service Fund—October 1, 2016*

| | | |
|---|---|---|
| Matured interest payable | 16,250 | |
|     Cash | | 16,250 |
|   To record payment of interest on the serial bond issue. | | |

*Debt Service Fund—March 2017*

| | | |
|---|---|---|
| Cash | 66,250 | |
|     Other financing sources—nonreciprocal transfer from general fund | | 66,250 |
|   To record receipt of $16,250 for interest payment plus $50,000 for the first serial payment due April 1, 2017. | | |

*Debt Service Fund—April 1, 2017*

| | | |
|---|---|---|
| Expenditures—principal payment | 50,000 | |
| Expenditures—interest payment | 16,250 | |
|     Cash | | 66,250 |
|   To record payment of principal and interest on the serial bond issue. | | |

*Debt Service Fund—September 2017*

| | | |
|---|---|---|
| Cash | 14,625 | |
|     Other financing sources—nonreciprocal transfer from general fund | | 14,625 |
|   To record receipt of cash from GF for the October 1, 2017, interest payment ($450,000 × 6.5% × ¹⁄₂ year). | | |

*Debt Service Fund—Adjusting Entry—September 30, 2017*

| | | |
|---|---|---|
| Expenditures—interest payment | 14,625 | |
|     Matured interest payable | | 14,625 |
|   To accrue payment of interest due. | | |

*Debt Service Fund Closing Entries—September 30, 2017*

| | | |
|---|---|---|
| Other financing sources—nonreciprocal transfer from general fund | 80,875 | |
|     Expenditures—principal payment | | 50,000 |
|     Expenditures—interest payment | | 30,875 |
|   To close the accounts. | | |

**NONRECIPROCAL, ROUTINE TRANSFERS**   The receipts of cash from the GF in September 2016, March 2017, and September 2017 are nonreciprocal, routine transfers made in connection with the normal operations of government. Such recurring transfers are not revenues or expenditures of either fund in the transaction. Instead, governments report recurring transfers as "other financing sources (uses)." In this case, the town reports the $2,000 transfer of the bond premium on April 3, 2016, the $14,250 nonreciprocal, routine transfer in September 2016 for the payment of interest; the $66,250 recurring transfer in March 2017 for interest and the first principal payment; and the $14,625 nonreciprocal, routine transfer in September 2017 for interest as other financing sources in the DSF and as other financing uses in the GF or in the CPF.

Note that interest payable was accrued on September 30, 2016 and 2017, for interest payments due on October 1, 2016 and 2017. The interest could be accrued because the amounts payable are due on October 1, and resources are available in the DSF at year-end to cover the interest payments due early in the next fiscal year. Interest could not be accrued at September 30 if the GF nonreciprocal, routine transfers were made on October 1 to pay interest on October 1.

## GOVERNMENTAL FUND FINANCIAL STATEMENTS

LEARNING OBJECTIVE **20.4**

As noted in discussing the GASB 34 financial reporting model, the required governmental fund financial statements include a statement of net position or balance sheet and a statement of revenues, expenditures, and changes in fund balance. Exhibits 20-2 and 20-3 present examples of these statements for Grantville's 2015–2016 fiscal year governmental activities. In addition, governments must present budgetary comparison information for the GF and each SRF that has a legally adopted annual budget. Exhibit 20-4 illustrates one accepted method of presenting this information for the Town of Grantville GF.

The balance sheet in Exhibit 20-2 contains separate columns for the GF, the seal exhibit permanent fund, and the town hall capital projects fund. Each of these funds meets the criteria of a *major fund* outlined in Chapter 19. The balance sheet also has a column for the debt service fund, which was not considered a major fund in this example; however, the town's management opted to disclose the fund because they felt it was important to financial statement users. Also, just prior to a totals column, there is a column for other governmental funds, where all nonmajor governmental fund balances are presented in aggregate. The SRFs within the chapter example that the town used to account for the highway beautification grant and the state grant for police and fire officer training are included in this column, because they are relatively small in dollar amount, and their separate presentation on the face of the balance sheet is not essential. Note that the balance sheet does not include fixed assets or long-term debt.

The total fund balance reported on the balance sheet is the same as the ending fund balance reported in the statement of revenues, expenditures, and changes in fund balance in Exhibit 20-3. This governmental fund operating statement has the same columns as the balance sheet and lists

EXHIBIT 20-2

Balance Sheet—Governmental Funds

## TOWN OF GRANTVILLE BALANCE SHEET—GOVERNMENTAL FUNDS SEPTEMBER 30, 2016

| | General Fund | Seal Exhibit Permanent Fund | Debt Service Fund | Town Hall Capital Projects Fund | Other Governmental Funds | Total Governmental Funds |
|---|---|---|---|---|---|---|
| *Assets* | | | | | | |
| Cash and cash equivalents | $187,250 | $9,500 | $16,250 | $132,500 | $95,605 | $441,105 |
| Investments | — | 500,000 | — | — | 11,435 | 511,435 |
| Receivables | | | | | | |
| Taxes receivable—delinquent (net of $20,000 estimated uncollectible taxes) | 220,000 | — | — | — | — | 220,000 |
| Accounts receivable | 180,000 | — | — | — | 14,950 | 194,950 |
| Due from other governments | — | — | — | 400,000 | 53,225 | 453,225 |
| Supplies inventory | 90,000 | — | — | — | — | 90,000 |
| Total assets | $677,250 | $509,500 | $16,250 | $532,500 | $175,215 | $1,910,715 |
| *Liabilities and Fund Balances* | | | | | | |
| Liabilities | | | | | | |
| Vouchers payable | $325,000 | — | — | — | $58,000 | $383,000 |
| Matured interest payable | — | — | $16,250 | — | — | 16,250 |
| Contracts payable | — | — | — | $47,500 | — | 47,500 |
| Revenue collected in advance | 50,000 | — | — | — | 5,000 | 55,000 |
| Total liabilities | 375,000 | — | 16,250 | 47,500 | 63,000 | 501,750 |
| *Fund balances* | | | | | | |
| Nonspendable | 90,000 | $500,000 | — | — | — | 590,000 |
| Restricted | — | 9,500 | — | 485,000 | — | 494,500 |
| Committed | 50,000 | — | — | — | 112,215 | 162,215 |
| Assigned | — | — | — | — | — | 0 |
| Unassigned | 162,250 | — | — | — | — | 162,250 |
| Total fund balance | 302,250 | 509,500 | 0 | 485,000 | 112,215 | 1,408,965 |
| Total liabilities and fund balance | $677,250 | $509,500 | $16,250 | $532,500 | $175,215 | $1,910,715 |

*Source:* © Anthony H Joseph

revenues, expenditures, and other financing sources (uses) to illustrate changes in the fund balance (working capital) for the governmental funds.

Finally, Exhibit 20-4 presents a budgetary comparison schedule for the GF. This statement, which is required supplementary information for the GF and for all SRFs with legally adopted budgets, includes columns for the original budget, the final budget, actual amounts, and variances (optional). It typically includes the same classifications as the GAAP operating statement. Often, however, the amounts reported for revenues, expenditures, and fund balance differ between the two statements. Differences exist when a government uses a non-GAAP basis of accounting for budgeting purposes, as Grantville does because of its use of encumbrance accounting. The budget and actual comparison statement must be presented on the budgetary basis of accounting even if it differs from GAAP. The differences between the two statements must be reconciled on the face of the statements, as done here, or in the notes to the financial statements. The reconciliation can explain differences between GAAP-basis and budgetary-basis fund balance amounts or differences between the excess of revenues and other financing sources over expenditures and other financing uses reported in the two statements.

The exhibits do not present budgetary data for the SRFs, because it appears that they did not have legally adopted budgets. You can see that the $50,000 transfer of cash from the GF to the SRF was not originally budgeted. Transfers of $115,000 were originally budgeted for debt service and

Statement of Revenues, Expenditures, and Changes in Fund Balance

## TOWN OF GRANTVILLE GOVERNMENTAL FUNDS STATEMENT OF REVENUES, EXPENDITURES, AND CHANGES IN FUND BALANCE FOR THE FISCAL YEAR ENDED SEPTEMBER 30, 2016

| | General Fund | Seal Exhibit Permanent Fund | Debt Service Fund | Town Hall Capital Projects Fund | Other Governmental Funds | Total Governmental Funds |
|---|---|---|---|---|---|---|
| *Revenues* | | | | | | |
| Taxes | $2,080,000 | — | — | — | $5,250 | $2,085,250 |
| Licenses and permits | 203,000 | — | — | — | — | 203,000 |
| Intergovernmental revenues | 400,000 | — | — | $400,000 | 61,500 | 861,500 |
| Charges for services | 563,000 | — | — | — | — | 563,000 |
| Fines and forfeitures | 122,000 | — | — | — | — | 122,000 |
| Addition to permanent endowments | 0 | $500,000 | — | — | — | 500,000 |
| Investment income | 110,000 | 12,500 | — | — | — | 122,500 |
| Miscellaneous revenue | 42,000 | — | — | — | 8,200 | 50,200 |
| Total revenues | $3,520,000 | $512,500 | — | $400,000 | $74,950 | $4,507,450 |
| *Expenditures* | | | | | | |
| Current services | | | | | | |
| General government | $896,000 | — | — | — | $6,150 | $902,150 |
| Public safety | 927,750 | — | — | — | 23,500 | 951,250 |
| Highways and streets | 528,750 | — | — | — | 38,000 | 566,750 |
| Sanitation | 427,000 | — | — | — | — | 427,000 |
| Health and welfare | 175,000 | — | — | — | 4,200 | 179,200 |
| Recreation | 204,000 | $3,000 | — | — | — | 207,000 |
| Capital outlays | 190,000 | — | — | $515,000 | — | 705,000 |
| Debt service | — | — | $16,250 | — | — | 16,250 |
| Total expenditures | 3,348,500 | 3,000 | 16,250 | 515,000 | 71,850 | 3,954,600 |
| Excess of revenues over expenditures | 171,500 | 509,500 | (16,250) | (115,000) | 3,100 | 552,850 |
| *Other Financing Sources (Uses)* | | | | | | |
| Bond proceeds | — | — | — | 502,000 | — | 502,000 |
| Capital lease | 45,000 | — | — | — | — | 45,000 |
| Transfers in | — | — | 16,250 | 100,000 | 50,000 | 166,250 |
| Transfers out | (164,250) | — | — | (2,000) | — | (166,250) |
| Excess of revenues and other financing sources over expenditures and other financing uses | 52,250 | 509,500 | 0 | 485,000 | 53,100 | 1,099,850 |
| Fund balance at October 1, 2015 | 250,000 | 0 | 0 | 0 | 59,115 | 309,115 |
| Fund balance at September 30, 2016 | $302,250 | $509,500 | $0 | $485,000 | $112,215 | $1,408,965 |

capital projects only. Note, however, that the town's elected officials must have approved the transfers and amendments to the budget during the year. In fact, each time the actual expenditures or outflows of the GF exceeded budget, approvals had to be sought and the budget had to be amended. This demonstrates the legal level of control that a governmental entity's budget has over spending. GASB 34 requires disclosure of the original and final budget information, along with actual figures, in budgetary comparison disclosures. Thus a user of the financial statements can examine the extent of budgetary amendments that were necessary during the financial statement period.

## TOWN OF GRANTVILLE BUDGETARY COMPARISON SCHEDULE—GENERAL FUND FOR THE YEAR ENDED SEPTEMBER 30, 2016

| | Original Budget | Final Budget | Actual Amounts (Budgetary Basis) | Variance with Final Budget, Positive (Negative) |
|---|---|---|---|---|
| **Revenues** | | | | |
| Taxes | $2,075,000 | $2,075,000 | $2,080,000 | $5,000 |
| Licenses and permits | 205,000 | 205,000 | 203,000 | (2,000) |
| Intergovernmental revenues | 400,000 | 400,000 | 400,000 | — |
| Charges for services | 557,000 | 557,000 | 563,000 | 6,000 |
| Fines and forfeitures | 118,000 | 118,000 | 122,000 | 4,000 |
| Investment income | 100,000 | 105,000 | 110,000 | 5,000 |
| Miscellaneous revenue | 45,000 | 45,000 | 42,000 | (3,000) |
| Total revenues | $3,500,000 | $3,505,000 | $3,520,000 | $15,000 |
| **Expenditures and Encumbrances** | | | | |
| Current services | | | | |
| General government | $477,500 | $477,500 | $475,000 | $2,500 |
| Public safety | 897,750 | 897,750 | 892,750 | 5,000 |
| Highways and streets | 825,000 | 830,000 | 828,750 | 1,250 |
| Sanitation | 525,000 | 527,000 | 527,000 | — |
| Health and welfare | 175,000 | 175,000 | 175,000 | — |
| Recreation | 270,000 | 275,000 | 275,000 | — |
| Capital outlays | 150,000 | 150,000 | 140,000 | 10,000 |
| Total expenditures and encumbrances | 3,320,250 | 3,332,250 | 3,313,500* | 18,750 |
| Excess of revenues over expenditures and encumbrances | 179,750 | 172,750 | 206,500 | 33,750 |
| **Other Financing Sources (Uses)** | | | | |
| Capital lease | — | 45,000 | 45,000 | — |
| Transfers out | (115,000) | (164,250) | (164,250) | — |
| Net change in fund balance | 64,750 | 53,500 | 87,250 | 33,750 |
| Budgetary fund balance—beginning | 160,000 | 160,000 | 160,000 | — |
| Add: Excess prior year encumbrance over actual expenditure | — | — | 5,000 | 5,000 |
| Budgetary fund balance—ending | $224,750 | $213,500 | $252,250 | $38,750 |
| Encumbrances outstanding at September 30, 2016 | | | 50,000 | |
| Fund balance—ending | | | $302,250 | |

* Actual expenditures on a budgetary basis include the $50,000 supplies purchase commitment chargeable against the 2016 appropriations, but exclude the $85,000 expenditure chargeable against the prior year's carryover appropriation.

Source: © Anthony H Joseph

## PREPARING THE GOVERNMENT-WIDE FINANCIAL STATEMENTS

In addition to the fund financial statements illustrated previously, a government must include governmental fund activities in the government-wide statements. You may recall, however, that the government-wide statements are prepared on the accrual basis of accounting, whereas the fund financial statements for the governmental funds are prepared on the modified accrual basis of accounting.

Thus, governments must convert governmental fund financial information to the accrual basis of accounting for inclusion in the government-wide statements of activities and net position. This conversion, illustrated for the Town of Grantville in Exhibit 20-5, includes the following actions. (The letters in the list correspond with those in the exhibit.)

**a.** Governments must capitalize governmental fund fixed assets, which were recorded as expenditures in the fund statements, at cost in the government-wide statements. During the year, Grantville purchased $190,000 in equipment. For simplicity, we treat the equipment purchases as the only fixed assets in this example; however, most governmental entities possess extensive general fixed asset balances, which must be reinstated in total each year as part of the conversion process.

**b.** Grantville must also record depreciation associated with the governmental fixed assets in the government-wide statements. If the equipment has a 10-year estimated useful life and the town uses straight-line depreciation, depreciation expense and accumulated depreciation amount to $19,000. Until the equipment is retired or sold, this $19,000, as well as annual depreciation expense, will be reinstated as accumulated depreciation in the conversion process.

**c.** Grantville should recognize capital projects fund construction expenditures as "construction in progress" in the government-wide statements. These expenditures will later be reclassified as "buildings" once construction of the town hall addition is completed.

**d.** Governments must report governmental **fund long-term liabilities**, where applicable, in the government-wide statements. Thus, Grantville's capital lease, which was recorded as an "other financing source," should be recognized as a long-term liability, "capital lease payable."

**e.** Similar to the capital lease in (d), Grantville recorded bond proceeds as an "other financing source" and must reclassify them as a long-term liability, "bonds payable," on the government-wide statements.

**f.** Governments must also adjust for instances when revenue recognition differs between the modified accrual and accrual bases of accounting. The sales tax revenue in Grantville's GF that was deferred because it would not be collected within 60 days of year-end was earned within the fiscal year, so it should be recognized under the accrual basis of accounting. Thus, for Grantville, the $50,000 GF "Revenue collected in advance" will be treated as government-wide revenue.

**g.** Because the government-wide statement is, in essence, a combined financial statement, it is necessary to eliminate interfund balances within the governmental funds. For Grantville, the $166,250 transfers between funds are eliminated.

**h.** Internal service funds primarily provide goods and services within a governmental entity. Therefore, internal service funds are reported with the governmental activities in the government-wide statements. In the statement of net position, internal service fund balance sheet accounts are included in the governmental activities column; however, the statement of activities will include only those internal service fund transactions involving entities other than the primary reporting entity. Thus, internal service fund revenues (and expenditures) resulting from transactions with parties external to the government are added to the statement of activities, and internal governmental transactions are excluded from government-wide statements.

This chapter does not review the accounting for internal service funds for Grantville, so internal service balances are noted as zero, but the column is included to show how internal service funds would be treated in the conversion worksheet.

Note that the conversion worksheet is an internal, optional document that will never be presented in the financial statements. It is simply helpful for use in preparing the government-wide statement of net position and statement of activities, as well as required reconciliations.

**STATEMENT OF NET POSITION**   We can prepare the governmental activities column of the government-wide statement of net position by transferring the converted balance sheet numbers from the conversion worksheet to the statement of net position. Exhibit 20-6 presents a sample statement of net position.

**EXHIBIT 20-5**

**Conversion Worksheet**

| | Fund Financial Statement Balances—Governmental Funds | | Adjustments/Eliminations | | Internal Service Funds | Total Governmental Activities | | | |
| --- | --- | --- | --- | --- | --- | --- | --- | --- | --- |
| | DR | CR | DR | CR | | Statement of Activities DR | Statement of Activities CR | Statement of Net Position DR | Statement of Net Position CR |
| Cash and cash equivalents | 441,105 | | | | x | | | 441,105 | |
| Investments | 511,435 | | | | x | | | 511,435 | |
| Taxes receivable | 220,000 | | | | x | | | 220,000 | |
| Accounts receivable | 194,950 | | | | x | | | 194,950 | |
| Due from other governments | 453,225 | | | | x | | | 453,225 | |
| Supplies inventory | 90,000 | | | | x | | | 90,000 | |
| Vouchers payable | | 383,000 | | | x | | | | 383,000 |
| Matured interest payable | | 16,250 | | | x | | | | 16,250 |
| Contracts payable | | 47,500 | | | x | | | | 47,500 |
| Revenue collected in advance | | 55,000 | (f) 50,000 | | x | | | | 5,000 |
| Fund balances/Net position, beg. | | 309,115 | | | x | | | | 309,115 |
| Revenues | | 4,507,450 | | (f) 50,000 | x | | 4,557,450 | | |
| Expenditures | 3,954,600 | | (b) 19,000 | (a) 190,000 | x | 3,268,600 | | | |
| | | | | (c) 515,000 | | | | | |

*Source:* © Anthony H Joseph

EXHIBIT 20-5

**Conversion Worksheet (*continued*)**

| Account | Debit | Credit | Adjustments Dr | Adjustments Cr | | Statement of Activities Dr | Statement of Activities Cr | Statement of Net Position Dr | Statement of Net Position Cr |
|---|---|---|---|---|---|---|---|---|---|
| OFS—Bond proceeds | | 502,000 | (e) 502,000 | | x | | | | |
| OFS—Capital lease | | 45,000 | (d) 45,000 | | x | | | | |
| OFS—Transfers in | | 166,250 | (g) 166,250 | | x | | | | |
| OFU—Transfers out | 166,250 | | | (g) 166,250 | x | | | | |
| Construction in progress | | | (c) 515,000 | | x | | | 515,000 | |
| Equipment | | | (a) 190,000 | | x | | | 190,000 | |
| Accumulated depreciation | | | | (b) 19,000 | x | | | | 19,000 |
| Capital leases payable | | | | (d) 45,000 | x | | | | 45,000 |
| Bonds payable | | | | (e) 500,000 | x | | | | 500,000 |
| Premium on bonds payable | | | | (e) 2,000 | x | | | | 2,000 |
| Total | 6,031,565 | 6,031,565 | 1,487,250 | 1,487,250 | | 3,268,600 | | | 1,326,865 |
| Change in net position | | | | | | 1,288,850 | | | 1,288,850 |
| Total | | | | | | 4,557,450 | 4,557,450 | 2,615,715 | 2,615,715 |

CR, credit; DR, debit; OFS, other financing source; OFU, other financing use.

GASB 34 requires a reconciliation between the fund and government-wide financial statements to be presented either at the bottom of the fund financial statements or in an accompanying schedule. We can easily prepare the reconciliation by referencing adjustments on the conversion schedule. An acceptable format for the reconciliation follows:

| | |
|---|---|
| Total fund balance—governmental funds | $1,408,965 |
| Amounts reported for *governmental activities* in the statement of net position differ from those in the governmental fund balance sheet because: | |
| Capital assets (net) used in governmental activities are not financial resources and therefore are not reported in the fund balance sheet | 686,000 |
| Revenues reported as collected in advance on the fund balance sheet using the 60-day criteria are recognized as revenue in the government-wide statement | 50,000 |
| Long-term liabilities (bonds and capital lease payable) are not due and payable in the current period and therefore are not reported in the governmental fund balance sheet | (547,000) |
| Net position—governmental funds | $1,597,965 |

**STATEMENT OF ACTIVITIES** Governmental activities reported on the government-wide statement of activities correspond to figures on the conversion worksheet. Exhibit 20-7 presents the statement of

**EXHIBIT 20-6**

Government-Wide Statement of Net Position

**TOWN OF GRANTVILLE STATEMENT OF NET POSITION SEPTEMBER 30, 2016**

| | Governmental Activities | Business-Type Activities | Total |
|---|---|---|---|
| *Assets* | | | |
| Cash and cash equivalents | $441,105 | $ xxx,xxx | $ x,xxx,xxx |
| Investments | 511,435 | xxx,xxx | x,xxx,xxx |
| Receivables | | | |
| Taxes receivable—delinquent (net of $20,000 estimated uncollectible taxes) | 220,000 | xx,xxx | xxx,xxx |
| Accounts receivable | 194,950 | xxx,xxx | xxx,xxx |
| Due from other governments | 453,225 | xx,xxx | xxx,xxx |
| Supplies inventory | 90,000 | xx,xxx | xxx,xxx |
| Capital assets, net | 686,000 | xxx,xxx | x,xxx,xxx |
| Total assets | $2,596,715 | $x,xxx,xxx | $ x,xxx,xxx |
| *Liabilities and Fund Balances* | | | |
| Liabilities | | | |
| Vouchers payable | $383,000 | $ xxx,xxx | $ xxx,xxx |
| Matured interest payable | 16,250 | xx,xxx | xx,xxx |
| Contracts payable | 47,500 | xx,xxx | xx,xxx |
| Revenue collected in advance | 5,000 | xx,xxx | xx,xxx |
| Capital leases payable | 45,000 | xx,xxx | xxx,xxx |
| Bonds payable | 500,000 | xxx,xxx | x,xxx,xxx |
| Premium on bonds payable | 2,000 | x,xxx | x,xxx |
| Total liabilities | 998,750 | xxx,xxx | x,xxx,xxx |
| Net position | | | |
| Invested in capital assets, net of related debt | 139,000 | x,xxx,xxx | x,xxx,xxx |
| Restricted for debt service | — | xxx,xxx | xxx,xxx |
| Restricted for capital projects | 485,000 | xxx,xxx | xxx,xxx |
| Restricted for other purposes | 9,500 | xx,xxx | xxx,xxx |
| Unrestricted | 964,465 | x,xxx,xxx | x,xxx,xxx |
| Total net position | $1,597,965 | $x,xxx,xxx | $xx,xxx,xxx |

*Source:* © Anthony H Joseph

EXHIBIT 20-7

Government-Wide Statement of Activities

# TOWN OF GRANTVILLE STATEMENT OF ACTIVITIES FOR THE FISCAL YEAR ENDED SEPTEMBER 30, 2016

| Functions/Programs | Expenses | Charges for Services | Operating Grants and Contributions | Capital Gains and Contributions | Governmental Activities | Business-Type Activities | Total |
|---|---|---|---|---|---|---|---|
| **Governmental activities** | | | | | | | |
| General government | $921,150 | $138,250 | — | $405,000 | $(377,900) | — | $(377,900) |
| Public safety | 951,250 | 129,650 | — | 18,500 | (803,100) | — | (803,100) |
| Highways and streets | 566,750 | 25,350 | $400,000 | 38,000 | (103,400) | — | (103,400) |
| Sanitation | 427,000 | 390,750 | — | — | (36,250) | — | (36,250) |
| Health and welfare | 179,200 | 102,200 | — | — | (77,000) | — | (77,000) |
| Recreation | 207,000 | 152,000 | 12,500 | — | (42,500) | — | (42,500) |
| Debt service | 16,250 | — | — | — | (16,250) | — | (16,250) |
| Total governmental activities | 3,268,600 | 938,200 | 412,500 | 461,500 | (1,456,400) | — | (1,456,400) |
| **Business-type activities** | | | | | | | |
| Utilities | x,xxx,xxx | x,xxx,xxx | — | xxx,xxx | — | xx,xxx | xx,xxx |
| Parking facilities | xx,xxx | xx,xxx | x,xxx | — | — | x,xxx | x,xxx |
| Total business-type activities | x,xxx,xxx | x,xxx,xxx | x,xxx | xxx,xxx | — | xx,xxx | xx,xxx |
| Total government | $x,xxx,xxx | $x,xxx,xxx | $ xxx,xxx | $x,xxx,xxx | ($1,456,400) | $xx,xxx | $x,xxx,xxx |

| General Revenues | Governmental Activities |
|---|---|
| Property taxes | $1,980,000 |
| Sales taxes | 155,250 |
| Investment earnings | 110,000 |
| Special item—permanent fund contribution | 500,000 |
| Total general revenues and special items | 2,745,250 |
| Change in net position | 1,288,850 |
| Net position—beginning | 309,115 |
| Net position—ending | $1,597,965 |

*Source:* © Anthony H Joseph

activities for the Town of Grantville. You can trace the total expenses of $3,268,600 to the conversion worksheet. Also, the various revenues ($938,200 + $412,500 + $461,500 + $2,745,250) agree with the $4,557,450 on the conversion worksheet.[13]

GASB 34 also requires a reconciliation between the change in fund balance reported on the fund statement of revenues, expenditures, and changes in fund balance and the change in net position reported on the statement of activities. This reconciliation may be presented either on the face of the fund financial statements or in an accompanying schedule. Again, the conversion worksheet is helpful. An acceptable format for the reconciliation follows:

| | |
|---|---:|
| Net change in fund balance—total governmental funds | $1,099,850 |
| Amounts reported for *governmental activities* in the statement of activities differ from those in the governmental fund statement of revenues, expenditures, and changes in fund balance because: | |
| Governmental funds report capital outlays as expenditures; the assets are capitalized and depreciated in the government-wide statements | 686,000 |
| Revenues in the statement of activities that do not provide current financial resources are not reported as revenues in the governmental funds | 50,000 |
| Bond proceeds provide current financial resources in the fund statement, but issuing debt increases long-term liabilities in the statement of net position | (502,000) |
| A capital lease is treated as an expenditure in the governmental funds in the year that the lease agreement is entered into; however, it increases long-term liabilities in the statement of net position | (45,000) |
| Change in net position of governmental activities | $1,288,850 |

Although the two reconciliations between governmental fund financial statements and government-wide statements will include many of the same items, they will not be identical, and reconciling items will often differ between the two schedules.

## SUMMARY

Governmental funds are used to account for general governmental activities affecting a governmental entity. They generally follow the modified accrual basis for accounting and reporting within the fund financial statements. This chapter has included a review of appropriate accounting for the GF, as well as the special revenue fund, permanent fund, capital projects fund, and DSF using the governmental fund model introduced in Chapter 19.

Accounting for each of the governmental funds is the same, but the purpose of each fund type differs. The essential difference between a GF and an SRF lies in the fact that a GF includes revenues available to finance the general needs of government, whereas the revenues of SRFs are restricted to specific uses. PF are used to account for nonexpendable resources set aside for support of a government's programs or citizenry. CPF are used to account for the acquisition of capital assets, and DSF are used to account for the receipt and use of resources to service general long-term debt obligations.

General and special revenue activities normally are controlled with formal budgetary procedures and accounting practices. Compliance with the budget is demonstrated by presenting budgetary comparison statements comparing actual and budgeted revenues and expenditures. Required fund financial statements for governmental funds include a statement of net position or balance sheet and a statement of revenues, expenditures, and changes in fund balance. Those governments that record governmental fund transactions in the accounting records on the modified accrual basis of accounting must convert governmental fund statement data into their government-wide statement counterparts.

## QUESTIONS

**1.** What is the accounting equation for a governmental fund?
**2.** What classifications of fund balance are currently allowed and which ones are no longer allowed?

[13]Criteria for classification of the "converted" revenues and expenses into the program and function categories are provided in GASB Statement No. 34, paragraphs 38–56.

3. If property tax bills totaling $200,000 are mailed to taxpayers and 97 percent are deemed collectible, what amount should be recorded as revenue?

4. What are encumbrances, and how does encumbrance accounting help control expenditures?

5. List the required governmental fund financial statements under GASB 34. On what basis of accounting are these statements prepared?

6. What is the purpose of a capital projects fund? Are all general fixed assets of a governmental unit acquired through capital projects funds? Explain.

7. How are capital projects funds financed, and when would a capital projects fund be terminated?

8. How do the purchases and consumption methods of accounting for inventory differ?

9. Are debt service funds used to account for debt service on all long-term obligations of a governmental unit? If not, which long-term debt obligations are excluded?

10. Describe a transaction that would affect the general fund and the debt service fund at the same time.

11. How do special assessment levies differ from general tax levies?

12. Which funds may be used to account for the activities of a general governmental special assessment construction project with long-term financing? Explain.

13. How are capital leases recorded in governmental funds?

14. Assume that supplies on hand at the beginning of the year amount to $60,000 and that supply purchases during the year are $400,000. Supplies on hand at year-end are $40,000, and the consumption basis of accounting for supplies is used. What adjusting entry for supplies should be made at year-end?

15. What is the role of a subsidiary ledger in a governmental entity?

16. The Village of Lester had appropriations of $250,000 for the current fiscal year. If $175,000 worth of items has been ordered but only $150,000 of the $175,000 has been received, what amount can city officials order prior to year-end? What happens if they have not spent the full $250,000 prior to year-end?

17. How does a permanent fund differ from a special revenue fund? A private-purpose trust fund?

18. How can you determine whether or not a governmental fund should be considered major?

19. What is included on a budgetary comparison schedule? Is such a schedule required to be included in a CAFR?

20. How is a conversion worksheet used? Why is it necessary?

21. List three items that might appear on the reconciliation between the governmental fund balance sheet and the government-wide statement of net position. List three items that might appear on the reconciliation between the governmental fund operating statement and the government-wide statement of activities.

## EXERCISES

### E 20-1
### Multiple choice

1. Which of the following statements regarding budgetary accounting is true?
   a *When the budget is recorded, estimated revenues are debited.*
   b *Budgetary accounts are never closed.*
   c *Encumbrance is another term for appropriation.*
   d *Budgeted revenues can be classified by source or character class.*

2. The encumbrance account of a governmental unit is debited when:
   a *The budget is recorded*
   b *A purchase order is approved*
   c *Goods are received*
   d *A voucher payable is recorded*

3. Encumbrance outstanding at year end in a state's general fund could be reported as a:
   a *Liability in the general fund*
   b *Fund balance—committed in the general fund*
   c *Liability in the general long-term debt account group*
   d *Expenditure in the general fund*

4. For the budgetary year ending December 31, 2016. Emerald City's general fund expects the following inflows of resources:

| | |
|---|---|
| Property taxes, licenses, and fees | $9,000,000 |
| Proceeds of debt issue | 5,000,000 |
| Interfund transfers for debt service | 1,000,000 |

In the budgetary entry, what amount should Emerald record for estimated revenues?

a $9,000,000
b $10,000,000
c $14,000,000
d $15,000,000

5. During its fiscal year ended June 30, 2016, the City of Ingalls issued purchase orders totaling $5,000,000, which were properly charged to encumbrances at that time. Ingalls received goods and related invoices at the encumbered amounts totaling $4,500,000 before year-end. The remaining goods of $500,000 were not received until after year-end. Ingalls paid $4,200,000 of the invoices received during the year. What amount of Ingalls's encumbrances was outstanding at June 30, 2016?

a $0
b $300,000
c $500,000
d $800,000

## E 20-2
## Multiple choice

1. The accounts "estimated revenues" and "appropriations" appear in the trial balance of the general fund. These accounts indicate:
   a *The use of cash-basis accounting*
   b *The use of accrual-basis accounting*
   c *The formal use of budgetary accounts*
   d *The informal use of budgetary accounts*

2. When a complete system of encumbrance accounting is used, the authorizations remaining available for expenditures at any interim date will be equal to:
   a *Appropriations less encumbrances*
   b *Appropriations less expenditures*
   c *Appropriations plus encumbrances less expenditures*
   d *Appropriations less expenditures and encumbrances*

3. Encumbrance accounting is designed to:
   a *Prevent overspending of amounts appropriated*
   b *Replace expenditure accounting for governmental organizations*
   c *Prevent excessive appropriations*
   d *Prevent or reduce waste in governmental spending*

4. Reserve for encumbrance accounts in general fund balance sheets at year-end indicate:
   a *The amount of net position required to complete the transaction(s) in the succeeding period*
   b *Noncompliance with GAAP*
   c *Cash on hand*
   d *Valuation reserves*

5. The reserve for encumbrances—past-year account typically represents amounts recorded by a governmental unit for:
   a *Anticipated expenditures in the next year*
   b *Expenditures for which purchase orders were made in the prior year but for which expenditure and disbursement will be in the current year*
   c *Excess expenditures in the prior year that will be offset against the current-year budgeted amounts*
   d *Unanticipated expenditures of the prior year that become evident in the current year*

## E 20-3
## Multiple choice

1. When equipment was purchased with general fund resources, which of the following accounts would have been increased in the general fund?
   a *Due from general fixed assets account group*
   b *Expenditures*
   c *Appropriations*
   d *No entry should be made in the general fund*

**2.** Which of the following funds would not be included in governmental fund financial statements?

*a  Debt service fund*

*b  General fund*

*c  Permanent fund*

*d  Pension trust fund*

**3.** When the purchases method of accounting for supplies is used, the financial statements of the related fund entity:

*a  Need not show material amounts of supplies on hand as an asset*

*b  Must disclose the cost of supplies used during the period*

*c  Are substantially the same as they would be under the consumption method*

*d  Must disclose fund balance unexpendable for material amounts of supplies on hand*

**4.** When the consumption basis of accounting for supplies is used, the financial statements of the related fund entity must:

*a  Show supply purchases as expenditures of the period*

*b  Show a fund balance restriction for material amounts of supplies on hand*

*c  Reflect the fact that perpetual inventory procedures have been used in accounting for supplies*

*d  Show supplies on hand as an asset*

**5.** The receipts from a special tax levy to retire and pay interest on general obligation bonds should be recorded in a:

*a  Debt service fund*

*b  Capital projects fund*

*c  Revolving interests fund*

*d  Special revenue fund*

## E 20-4
## Multiple choice

**1.** Howard City should use a capital projects fund to account for:

*a  Proceeds of a capital grant to finance a new civic center that will not provide services primarily on a user-charge basis*

*b  Construction of sewer lines by the water and sewer utility to be financed by user costs*

*c  The accumulation of resources to retire bonds issued to construct the town hall*

*d  Construction of an addition to the airport terminal owned by the Howard City Municipal Airport, an enterprise fund*

**2.** When a capital projects fund is dissolved by paying any remaining assets to another fund, the decrease in fund balance is a (an):

*a  Expenditure*

*b  Operating transfer*

*c  Residual equity transfer*

*d  Reimbursement*

**3.** Which of the following items would be least likely to appear in the account titles of a capital projects fund?

*a  Due from federal government (for grant)*

*b  Due from general fund*

*c  Proceeds from bond issue*

*d  Construction in progress*

**4.** Three financial statements may be required to present the results of operations and financial position of a special revenue fund. Which of the following is not one of these required statements?

*a  Statement of cash flows*

*b  Statement of revenues, expenditures, and changes in fund balance*

*c  Statement of revenues, expenditures, and changes in fund balance—budget and actual*

*d  Balance sheet*

**5.** Assets financed through a capital projects fund should be capitalized in the government-wide financial statements:

*a  Only when construction is completed*

*b  On the basis of expenditures to date in Construction in Progress*

*c  On the basis of expenditures and encumbrances to date in Construction in Progress*

*d  On the basis of amounts paid to date in Construction in Progress*

## E 20-5
## Multiple choice [Based on AICPA]

1. If numerous funds are maintained, which of the following transactions would typically not be reported in a municipality's general fund?

   a   The collection of property taxes

   b   The purchase of office equipment

   c   The receipt of grant funds for local youth programs

   d   The payment of salaries to municipal employees

2. Other financing sources—proceeds of general obligation bonds is an account of a governmental unit that typically would be included in the:

   a   Enterprise fund

   b   Special revenue fund

   c   Capital projects fund

   d   Government-wide financial statements

3. Equipment in general governmental service that had been constructed 10 years before by a capital projects fund was sold. The receipts were accounted for as an other financing source. Entries are necessary in the:

   a   General fund and capital projects fund

   b   General fund only

   c   General fund, capital projects fund, and enterprise fund

   d   General fund, capital projects fund, and general fixed assets account group

4. Martha County issues general obligation serial bonds at a premium to finance construction of a sheriff's office. Which of the following are affected by the transaction?

   a   Special revenue

   b   Capital projects fund and general fund

   c   Capital projects fund, general fund, and debt service fund

   d   Capital projects fund and debt service fund

5. Property taxes are considered:

   a   Derived tax revenues

   b   Imposed nonexchange revenues

   c   Government-mandated nonexchange transactions

   d   Voluntary nonexchange transactions

## E 20-6
## Multiple choice [AICPA adapted]

1. The following information pertains to Walnut Corners:

   | | |
   |---|---|
   | 2016 governmental fund revenues that became measurable and available in time to be used for payment of 2016 liabilities | $16,000,000 |
   | Revenues earned in 2014 and 2015 and included in the $16,000,000 indicated | 2,000,000 |
   | Sales taxes collected by merchants in 2016 but not required to be remitted to Walnut Corners until January 2017 | 3,000,000 |

   For the year ended December 31, 2016, Walnut Corners should recognize revenues of:

   a   $14,000,000

   b   $16,000,000

   c   $17,000,000

   d   $19,000,000

2. Capital City was awarded a $3,000,000 grant from the state. Of this grant, $1,500,000 was sent to the city and recorded in a special revenue fund. Qualified expenditures of that fund totaled $900,000 in the year that the grant was received. What amount of revenues should the city recognize with respect to the grant?

   a   $0

   b   $900,000

   c   $1,500,000

   d   $3,000,000

**3.** The following information pertains to property taxes levied by Coral City for the calendar year 2016:

| | |
|---|---:|
| Collections during 2016 | $500,000 |
| Expected collections during the first 60 days of 2017 | 100,000 |
| Expected collections during the balance of 2017 | 60,000 |
| Expected collections during January 2018 | 30,000 |
| Estimated to be uncollectible | 10,000 |
| Total levy | $700,000 |

What amount should Coral City report for 2016 net property tax revenues?

a  *$700,000*
b  *$690,000*
c  *$600,000*
d  *$500,000*

**4.** The following information pertains to Tedfred's general fund for 2017:

| | |
|---|---:|
| Appropriations | $6,500,000 |
| Expenditures | 5,000,000 |
| Other financing sources | 1,500,000 |
| Other financing uses | 2,000,000 |
| Revenues | 8,000,000 |

In 2017, Tedfred's total fund balance increased by:

a  *$3,000,000*
b  *$2,500,000*
c  *$1,500,000*
d  *$1,000,000*

**5.** The following information pertains to Amber Township's general fund at December 31, 2016:

| | |
|---|---:|
| Total assets, including $200,000 of cash | $1,000,000 |
| Total liabilities | 600,000 |
| Fund balance—restricted | 100,000 |

Appropriations do not lapse at year-end. At December 31, 2016, what amount should Amber report as fund balance—unassigned in its general fund balance sheet?

a  *$800,000*
b  *$400,000*
c  *$300,000*
d  *$100,000*

## E 20-7
### General fund journal entries (property taxes)

The following events and transactions relate to the levy and collection of property taxes for Jedville Township:
   March 21, 2016—Property tax bills for $2,500,000 are sent to property owners. An estimated 2 percent of the property tax levies are uncollectible. The taxes are due on May 1.
   May 4, 2016—$1,900,000 in taxes have been collected. The remaining receivables are reclassified as delinquent.
   May 5 to December 31, 2016—An additional $150,000 of taxes are collected.
   November 1, 2016—A $5,000 tax receivable account is determined to be uncollectible and is written off.
   January 1, 2017, to February 28, 2017—An additional $87,750 of 2016 taxes are collected.

### REQUIRED

**1.** Prepare summary journal entries for the events and transactions described for the Jedville general fund.

**2.** How will property taxes be presented in the December 31, 2016, balance sheet?

**3.** What amount of property tax revenues should be reported for 2016?

## E 20-8
### Governmental fund closing entries

A general ledger trial balance for Any City contained the following balances at June 30, 2013, just before closing entries were made:

| | |
|---|---:|
| Due from other funds | $600 |
| Fund balance—unassigned | 3,000 |
| Estimated revenues | 18,000 |

| | |
|---|---|
| Revenues | 17,380 |
| Appropriations | 17,500 |
| Expenditures—current year | 16,450 |
| Expenditures—prior year | 1,900 |
| Encumbrances | 1,000 |
| Nonreciprocal transfer in | 3,200 |
| Reserve for encumbrances | 1,000 |
| Reserve for encumbrances—prior year | 2,000 |

**REQUIRED:** Prepare the necessary closing entries.

## E 20-9
## Preparation of fund balance sheet

A general ledger trial balance at June 30, 2013, for Millar City is as follows:

| | Debits | Credits |
|---|---|---|
| Cash | $12,000 | — |
| Taxes receivable | 30,000 | — |
| Allowance for uncollectible taxes | — | $2,000 |
| Due from other funds | 3,000 | — |
| Supplies inventory, June 30, 2013 | 4,000 | — |
| Estimated revenues | 300,000 | — |
| Expenditures | 290,000 | — |
| Expenditures—prior year | 5,000 | — |
| Encumbrances | 6,000 | — |
| Vouchers payable | — | 13,000 |
| Due to other funds | — | 5,000 |
| Reserve for encumbrances | — | 6,000 |
| Reserve for encumbrances—prior year | — | 5,000 |
| Fund balance—nonspendable | — | 4,000 |
| Fund balance—unassigned | — | 10,000 |
| Appropriations | — | 300,000 |
| Revenues | — | 305,000 |
| | $650,000 | $650,000 |

Millar City uses a purchases basis in accounting for supplies. Open encumbrances are considered constrained by the highest decision-making level of the city.

**REQUIRED:** Prepare a fund balance sheet as of June 30, 2013.

## E 20-10
## Preparation of a fund statement of revenues, expenditures, and changes in fund balance

The trial balance of the general fund of Madelyn City before closing at December 31, 2013, contained the following accounts and balances:

| | |
|---|---|
| Fund balance—unassigned | $25,000 |
| Estimated revenues | 100,000 |
| Appropriations | 95,000 |
| Encumbrances | 4,000 |
| Reserve for encumbrances | 4,000 |
| Reserve for encumbrances—prior year | 5,000 |
| Revenues | 101,000 |
| Expenditures | 94,000 |
| Expenditures—prior year | 4,800 |
| Nonreciprocal transfers out | 18,000 |
| Reciprocal transfers in | 27,000 |

**REQUIRED:** Prepare a statement of revenues, expenditures, and changes in (total) fund balance for Madelyn City's general fund in 2013. (Details of revenue and expenditure accounts are omitted to simplify the requirement.)

## E 20-11
## General fund journal entries

Prepare entries in the general fund to record the following transactions and events:
1. Estimated revenues for the fiscal year were $250,000 and appropriations were $248,000.
2. The tax levy for the fiscal year, of which 99 percent is believed to be collectible, was $200,000.
3. Taxes collected were $150,000.
4. A short-term loan of $15,000 was made to the special revenue fund.
5. Orders for supplies were placed in the amount of $18,000. Use the purchases method.
6. The items ordered in transaction 5 were received. Actual cost was $18,150, and vouchers for that amount were prepared.
7. Materials were acquired from the stores fund (an internal service fund) in the amount of $800 (without encumbrance).
8. A $5,000 payment (transfer) was made to the debt service fund.
9. A cash payment of $15,000 was made for the purchase of equipment.
10. Licenses were collected in the amount of $3,000.
11. The balance of taxes receivable became delinquent.
12. Delinquent taxes of $30,000 were collected before year-end. The remaining net realizable value of delinquent taxes is expected to be collected uniformly over the first four months of the next fiscal year.

## E 20-12
## General fund journal entries

Prepare the journal entries required to record the following transactions in the general fund of Rochester Township.
1. Borrowed $75,000 by issuing six-month tax anticipation notes.
2. Ordered equipment with an estimated cost of $33,000.
3. Received the equipment along with an invoice for its actual cost, $33,250.
4. Transferred $200,000 of general fund resources to a debt service fund.
5. On January 1, the township levied property taxes of $1,000,000. The township expects to collect all except $100,000 by the end of the fiscal year or within not more than 60 days thereafter. Of the remaining $100,000, half is expected to prove uncollectible.
6. The township received a $100,000 restricted grant for certain library programs from another unit of government. The grant will be accounted for in the general fund.
7. The township incurred $75,000 of expenditures for the programs covered by the library grant.

## E 20-13
## Governmental fund journal entries

For each of the following transactions, note the fund(s) affected, and prepare appropriate journal entries.
1. General obligation bonds with a par value of $750,000 are issued at $769,000 to finance construction of a government office building.
2. A Community Block Development Grant in the amount of $450,000 is awarded for residential services within a city.
3. Upon approval of a new town band shell, the general fund transfers $500,000 to create a new fund.
4. A wealthy citizen donates $10,000,000 for city park maintenance. The principal cannot be spent.
5. Automobiles and vans for general governmental use are purchased for $375,000.
6. General fixed assets with an original cost of $300,000 sold for $30,000 at the end of their useful life.
7. Sold equipment at the end of its expected useful life. The equipment had no expected residual value when acquired (at a cost of $13,000), but it sold for $1,200. Equipment is used in general fund.
8. The general fund transfers $50,000 for an interest payment on debt. The interest payment is made.

## E 20-14
## Governmental fund reconciliation to total net position

The postclosing trial balance for the Village of Alantown general fund at June 30, 2016, shows the following ledger account balances:

| Debits | |
|---|---|
| Cash | $410,000 |
| Investments | 300,000 |
| Tax receivable—delinquent | 150,000 |
| Accounts receivable | 30,000 |
| Supplies inventory | 60,000 |
| Total debits | $950,000 |
| Credits | |
| Allowances for uncollectible taxes—delinquent | $10,000 |
| Vouchers payable | 140,000 |
| Revenue collected in advance | 40,000 |
| Note payable (short-term) | 150,000 |
| Fund balance—committed | 90,000 |
| Fund balance—unassigned | 520,000 |
| Total credits | $950,000 |

## ADDITIONAL INFORMATION

1. The village owns general fixed assets with a historical cost of $100,000 and accumulated depreciation totaling $65,000.

2. General long-term debt recorded in the internal debt records is $100,000. This was recorded as an other financing source in the general fund.

3. A capital lease payable in the amount of $75,000 is noted in the internal debt records. This was recorded as an other financing source in the general fund.

4. Revenues reported as collected in advance on the fund balance sheet using the 60-day criteria are recognized as revenue in the government-wide statement.

**REQUIRED:** Determine the village's general fund net position that will appear on the government-wide statement of net position.

### E 20-15
### Governmental fund reconciliation to total net position

The following data are available from the City of Boulder's financial records on September 30, 2016:

a. The net change in fund balance—total governmental funds for the city is $1,408,950.

b. The city purchased general fixed assets at a historical cost of $225,000 during the year. No depreciation is recorded in the year of purchase.

c. Grants receivable in the amount of $165,000 are recorded as revenue collected in advance in the fund statements but would be recognized as revenue under accrual accounting.

d. A capital lease payable in the amount of $75,000 has been recorded as an expenditure in the general fund. The related long-term debt at year-end is $55,000.

e. General long-term debt in the amount of $350,000 has been issued and recorded in the general fund.

**REQUIRED:** Determine the city's change in net position of governmental activities that will appear in the government-wide statements.

## PROBLEMS

### P 20-1
### Preparation of a general fund balance sheet

The unadjusted trial balance for the general fund of the City of Orchard Park at December 31, 2016, is as follows:

|  | Debit | Credit |
|---|---|---|
| Accounts receivable | $25,000 | — |
| Allowance for bad debts | — | $2,000 |
| Allowance for uncollectible taxes | — | 30,000 |
| Appropriations | — | 900,000 |
| Cash | 40,000 | — |
| Due from agency fund | 10,000 | — |
| Due to utility fund | — | 20,000 |
| Encumbrances | 50,000 | — |
| Estimated revenues | 910,000 | — |
| Expenditures | 858,000 | — |
| Fund balance—unassigned | — | 26,000 |
| Reserve for encumbrances | — | 50,000 |
| Revenues | — | 910,000 |
| Taxes receivable—delinquent | 210,000 | — |
| Taxes received in advance | — | 10,000 |
| Vouchers payable | — | 155,000 |
|  | $2,103,000 | $2,103,000 |

Supplies on hand at December 31, 2016, are $3,000. The $50,000 encumbrance relates to equipment ordered November 28 for the Department of Public Works but not received by year-end. The equipment purchase was approved by the City Council.

**REQUIRED:** Prepare a balance sheet for the general fund of the City of Orchard Park at December 31, 2016.

## P 20-2
## Preparation of general fund statements

The preclosing account balances of the general fund of the City of Batavia on June 30, 2017, were as follows:

| | |
|---|---:|
| *Debits* | |
| Cash | $80,000 |
| Taxes receivable—delinquent | 160,000 |
| Due from County | 18,000 |
| Estimated revenues | 1,000,000 |
| Expenditures | 940,000 |
| Nonreciprocal transfers out | 10,000 |
| Encumbrances | 20,000 |
| | $2,228,000 |
| *Credits* | |
| Allowance for uncollectible taxes—delinquent | $30,000 |
| Vouchers payable | 58,000 |
| Notes payable | 60,000 |
| Reserve for encumbrances | 20,000 |
| Fund balance—unassigned | 120,000 |
| Revenues | 980,000 |
| Appropriations | 960,000 |
| | $2,228,000 |

The fund balance—unassigned at the beginning of the year was $80,000, and there were no carryover encumbrances at the beginning of the fiscal year. The end-of-year encumbrances are a result of enabling legislation.

**REQUIRED**

1. Prepare a statement of revenues, expenditures, and changes in total fund balance for the year ended June 30, 2017.

2. Prepare a general fund balance sheet at June 30, 2017.

## P 20-3
## Governmental fund journal entries, budgetary comparison, and reconciling items

The Town of Tyler approved the following general fund budget for the fiscal year July 1, 2016, to June 30, 2017:

**TOWN OF TYLER GENERAL FUND BUDGET SUMMARY**
**FOR THE YEAR JULY 1, 2016 TO JUNE 30, 2017**

| | |
|---|---:|
| *Revenue Sources* | |
| Taxes | $250,000 |
| Licenses and permits | 20,000 |
| Intergovernmental revenue | 40,000 |
| Charges for services | 60,000 |
| Fines and forfeits | 15,000 |
| Rents and royalties | 10,000 |
| Miscellaneous revenues | 5,000 |
| Total budgeted revenues | $400,000 |

*(Continued)*

**TOWN OF TYLER GENERAL FUND BUDGET SUMMARY
FOR THE YEAR JULY 1, 2016 TO JUNE 30, 2017**

| | |
|---|---:|
| *Expenditures* | |
| Current services | |
| General government | $45,000 |
| Public safety | 140,000 |
| Highways and streets | 90,000 |
| Sanitation | 55,000 |
| Health and welfare | 20,000 |
| Recreation | 30,000 |
| Capital outlays | 15,000 |
| Total appropriations | $395,000 |
| Budgeted increase in fund balance | $5,000 |

The after-closing trial balance of the Town of Tyler general fund at June 30, 2016, shows the following ledger account balances:

| | |
|---|---:|
| *Debits* | |
| Cash | $31,000 |
| Tax receivable—delinquent | 15,000 |
| Accounts receivable | 3,000 |
| Supplies inventory | 6,000 |
| Total debits | $55,000 |
| *Credits* | |
| Allowances for uncollectible taxes—delinquent | $1,000 |
| Vouchers payable | 14,000 |
| Note payable (short-term) | 15,000 |
| Fund balance—committed | 9,000 |
| Fund balance—nonspendable | 6,000 |
| Fund balance—unassigned | 10,000 |
| Total credits | $55,000 |

**1.** Prepare journal entries to record the budget and each of the following transactions:
  **a.** *The treasurer of Tyler sends out property tax bills of $200,000; 1 percent is considered uncollectible.*
  **b.** *Current property taxes of $176,000 and past-due taxes of $14,000 were collected.*
  **c.** *A specific property tax bill ($1,000) is determined to be uncollectible.*
  **d.** *Fees in the amount of $20,000 are collected for hunting licenses.*
  **e.** *Other revenues in the amount of $200,000 are collected.*
  **f.** *The payroll for salaries of $20,000 is vouchered for payment.*
  **g.** *Playground equipment expected to cost $15,000 is ordered.*
  **h.** *The playground equipment is received and has an actual cost of $14,000.*
  **i.** *Tyler received equipment that had been ordered in the previous fiscal year. The actual cost was $9,500.*
  **j.** *Supplies in the amount of $11,000 were ordered. By year-end, only $5,000 worth of these supplies has been received. The consumption method is used.*
  **k.** *The note payable that was outstanding at June 30, 2016, becomes due and is paid.*
  **l.** *Various expenditures are paid throughout the year totaling $348,040.*
  **m.** *Supplies in the amount of $3,000 are on hand at year-end.*
  **n.** *Assume that uncollected taxes on June 30, 2016, are past due.*
  **o.** *Closing entries are made.*

**2.** Prepare a budgetary comparison statement for the Tyler general fund.

**3.** Identify the transactions above that will be reconciling items between the fund financial statements and the government-wide financial statements.

## P 20-4
### Governmental fund conversion worksheet

The postclosing trial balance for the City of Fort Collins governmental funds at June 30, 2016, shows the following ledger account balances:

| | DR | CR |
|---|---|---|
| Cash and cash equivalents | $541,100 | |
| Investments | 520,000 | |
| Taxes receivable | 520,000 | |
| Accounts receivable | 187,500 | |
| Due from other governments | 364,970 | |
| Supplies inventory | 290,000 | |
| Vouchers payable | | $379,500 |
| Contracts payable | | 47,500 |
| Revenue collected in advance | | 55,000 |
| Fund balance/net position, beginning | | 912,720 |
| Revenues | | 3,507,450 |
| Expenditures | 3,043,600 | |
| OFS—Bond proceeds | | 500,000 |
| OFS—Capital lease | | 65,000 |
| OFS—Transfers in | | 75,250 |
| OFU—Transfers out | 75,250 | |
| | $5,542,420 | $5,542,420 |

### ADDITIONAL INFORMATION

1. During the year, Fort Collins purchased $9,000 in equipment, which was not depreciated.

2. Fort Collins also has other fixed assets with a historical cost of $95,000 and accumulated depreciation of $65,000.

3. Fort Collins has capital project fund construction expenditures totaling $20,000.

4. During the year, the city issued a bond at $500,000 par value.

5. During the year, the city entered into a lease agreement. The entire amount should be recognized as general long-term debt.

6. The city's revenue collected in advance would be treated as revenue under accrual accounting.

7. The transfers in and out were made between governmental funds.

8. The city does not report internal service funds.

**REQUIRED:** Prepare a conversion worksheet to determine the change in net position and the net position balance for the city's governmental funds.

## P 20-5
### Reconstruct general fund journal entries [AICPA adapted]

The following summary of transactions was taken from the accounts of the Oslo School District general fund before the books had been closed for the fiscal year ended June 30, 2016:

| | Postclosing Balances June 30, 2015 | Preclosing Balances June 30, 2016 |
|---|---|---|
| Cash | $400,000 | $700,000 |
| Taxes receivable | 150,000 | 170,000 |
| Estimated uncollectible taxes | (40,000) | (70,000) |
| Estimated revenues | — | 3,000,000 |
| Expenditures | — | 2,842,000 |
| Expenditures—prior years | — | — |
| Encumbrances | — | 91,000 |
| | $510,000 | $6,733,000 |

*(Continued)*

|  | Postclosing Balances June 30, 2015 | Preclosing Balances June 30, 2016 |
|---|---|---|
| Vouchers payable | $80,000 | $408,000 |
| Due to other funds | 210,000 | 142,000 |
| Fund balance—committed | 60,000 | 91,000 |
| Fund balance—unassigned | 160,000 | 182,000 |
| Revenues from taxes | — | 2,800,000 |
| Miscellaneous revenues | — | 130,000 |
| Appropriations | — | 2,980,000 |
|  | $510,000 | $6,733,000 |

## ADDITIONAL INFORMATION

1. The estimated taxes receivable for the year ended June 30, 2016, were $2,870,000, and current-year taxes collected during the year totaled $2,810,000.

2. Estimated uncollectible taxes from the prior year were written off.

3. An analysis of the transactions in the vouchers payable for the year ended June 30, 2016, follows:

|  | Debit (Credit) |
|---|---|
| Current expenditures | $(2,700,000) |
| Expenditures for prior years | (58,000) |
| Vouchers for payment to other funds | (210,000) |
| Cash payments during the year | 2,640,000 |
| Net change | $(328,000) |

4. During the year the general fund was billed $142,000 for services performed on its behalf by other city funds.

5. On May 2, 2016, commitment documents were issued for the purchase of new textbooks at a cost of $91,000.

## REQUIRED:

Based on the data presented, reconstruct the original detailed journal entries that were required to record all transactions for the fiscal year ended June 30, 2016, including the recording of the current year's budget. Do not prepare closing entries at June 30, 2016.

## P 20-6
## Journal entries from trial balance [AICPA adapted]

The following information was abstracted from the accounts of the general fund of the City of Lahti after the books had been closed for the fiscal year ended June 30, 2016:

|  | Trial Balance June 30, 2015 | Transactions July 1, 2015, to June 30, 2016 | | Postclosing Trial Balance June 30, 2016 |
|---|---|---|---|---|
|  |  | Debit | Credit |  |
| Cash | $700,000 | $1,820,000 | $1,852,000 | $668,000 |
| Taxes receivable | 40,000 | 1,870,000 | 1,828,000 | 82,000 |
|  | $740,000 |  |  | $750,000 |
| Allowances for uncollectible taxes | $8,000 | 8,000 | 10,000 | $10,000 |
| Vouchers payable | 132,000 | 1,852,000 | 1,840,000 | 120,000 |
| Fund balance: |  |  |  |  |
| Committed | — | 1,000,000 | 1,070,000 | 70,000 |
| Unassigned | 600,000 | 140,000 | 60,000 |  |
|  |  |  | 30,000 | 550,000 |
|  | $740,000 |  |  | $750,000 |

**ADDITIONAL INFORMATION:** The budget for the fiscal year ended June 30, 2016, provided for estimated revenues of $2,000,000 and appropriations of $1,940,000.

**REQUIRED:** Prepare journal entries to record the budgeted and actual transactions for the fiscal year ended June 30, 2016.

## P 20-7
### Preparation of a fund statement of revenues, expenditures, and changes in fund balance

The following information regarding the fiscal year ended December 31, 2016, was drawn from the accounts and records of the Volendam County general fund:

| | |
|---|---|
| *Revenues and Other Asset Inflows* | |
| Taxes | $10,000,000 |
| Licenses and permits | 2,000,000 |
| Intergovernmental grants | 300,000 |
| Proceeds of short-term note issuances | 1,000,000 |
| Collection of interfund advance to other fund | 450,000 |
| Receipt of net position of terminated fund | 2,000,000 |
| *Expenditures and Other Asset Outflows* | |
| General government expenditures | 8,000,000 |
| Public safety expenditures | 1,500,000 |
| Judicial system expenditures | 1,000,000 |
| Health and welfare expenditures | 1,200,000 |
| Equipment purchases | 600,000 |
| Payment to debt service fund to cover future debt service on general government bonds | 320,000 |
| Fund balance—unassigned, January 1, 2016 | $3,130,000 |

**REQUIRED:** Prepare a statement of revenues, expenditures, and changes in fund balance for the Volendam County general fund for the year ended December 31, 2016.

## P 20-8
### Debt service fund journal entries

The Town of Lilehammar has $3,000,000 of 6 percent bonds outstanding. Interest on the general obligation, general government indebtedness is payable semiannually each March 31 and September 30. December 31 is the fiscal year-end. Record the following transactions in the town's debt service fund.

**1.** Received a transfer from the general fund to provide financing for the March 31, interest payment.

**2.** Paid the interest due on March 31.

**3.** Received a transfer from the general fund to provide financing for the September 30, interest payment and retirement of $1,000,000 of the bonds.

**4.** Paid the interest on September 31, and repaid $1,000,000 of the bonds.

**5.** December 31 is the fiscal year-end. Record any appropriate adjustments.

**6.** Received a transfer from the general fund to provide financing for the March 31 interest payment for year 2 of the bond.

**7.** Paid the interest due on March 31 for year 2 of the bond.

**REQUIRED:** Prepare a statement of revenues, expenditures, and changes in fund balance for the Town of Lilehammar debt service fund for the year ended December 31, 2016.

## P 20-9
### Capital projects fund journal entries

The City of Stockholm authorized construction of a $600,000 addition to the municipal building in September 2016. The addition will be financed by $200,000 from the general fund and a $400,000 serial bond issue to be sold in April 2017.

**REQUIRED:** Prepare journal entries for the capital projects fund and any other fund involved to the extent of requiring journal entries to record the transactions described.

1. On October 1, 2016, the general fund transferred $200,000 to the capital projects fund.

2. On November 1, 2016, a contract for the addition was awarded to Crooked Construction for $580,000.

3. On April 15, 2017, the $400,000, 7 percent bonds were sold for $401,000, and the premium was transferred to the debt service fund.

4. On May 2, 2017, construction was completed, and Crooked Construction submitted a bill for $580,000.

5. On May 12, 2017, the bill to Crooked Construction was paid in full. The CPF was closed, and the remaining cash was transferred to the general fund.

## P 20-10
### Journal entries associated with a capital project

On June 15, 2016, Malmo City authorizes the issuance of $500,000 par of 6 percent serial bonds to be issued on July 1, 2016, and to mature in annual serials of $100,000 beginning on July 1, 2017. The proceeds of the bond issue are to be used to finance a new tourist rest area.

During the fiscal year ended June 30, 2017, the following events and transactions occurred:

> July 1—A contract for construction of the rest area is awarded to Gunnarsson Construction Company for $480,000.
>
> July 1—$250,000 par value of 6 percent serial bonds are sold at a premium of 2 percent.
>
> December 20—A bill is received from Gunnarsson Construction Company for one-third of the contract price.
>
> January 1—Gunnarsson Construction Company is paid for work completed to date, less a 10 percent retained percentage to ensure performance.
>
> January 1—Bond interest due is paid with funds transferred from the general fund and from the premium that was made available for interest payments.
>
> June 30—A bill is received from Gunnarsson Construction Company for one-third of the contract price.

### REQUIRED

1. Prepare journal entries in each of the affected funds to account for the transactions and events described. Identify the fund for each journal entry.

2. Prepare a closing journal entry for the capital projects fund at June 30, 2017.

## P 20-11
### Capital projects fund journal entries and balance sheet [AICPA adapted]

In a special election held on May 1, 2016, the voters of the City of Cerone approved a $10,000,000 issue of 6 percent general obligation bonds maturing in 20 years. The proceeds of this sale will be used to help finance the construction of a new civic center. The total cost of the project was estimated at $15,000,000. The remaining $5,000,000 will be financed by a state grant, which has been awarded. A capital projects fund was established to account for this project and was designated the civic center construction fund. The formal project authorization was appropriately recorded in a memorandum entry.

The following transactions occurred during the fiscal year beginning July 1, 2016, and ending June 30, 2017.

1. On July 1 the general fund loaned $500,000 to the civic center construction fund for defraying engineering and other expenses.

2. Preliminary engineering and planning costs of $320,000 were paid to Eminem Engineering Company. There had been no encumbrance for this cost.

3. On December 1 the bonds were sold at 101. The premium on the bonds was transferred to the debt service fund.

**4.** On March 15 a contract for $12,000,000 was entered into with Candu Construction Company for the major part of the project.

**5.** Orders were placed for materials estimated to cost $55,000.

**6.** On April 1 a partial payment of $2,500,000 was received from the state.

**7.** The materials that were previously ordered were received at a cost of $51,000 and paid.

**8.** On June 15 a progress billing of $2,000,000 was received from Candu Construction for work done on the project. As per the terms of the contract, the city will withhold 6 percent of any billing until the project is completed.

**9.** The general fund was repaid the $500,000 previously loaned.

### REQUIRED

**1.** Prepare journal entries to record the transactions in the civic center construction fund for the period July 1, 2016, through June 30, 2017, and the appropriate closing entries at June 30, 2017.

**2.** Prepare a balance sheet for the civic center construction fund on June 30, 2017.

## P 20-12
## Capital projects fund journal entries and financial statements

The City of Catalina authorized the construction of a new recreation center at a total cost of $1,000,000 on June 15, 2016. On the same date, the city approved a $1,000,000, 8 percent, 10-year general obligation serial bond issue to finance the project. During the year July 1, 2016, to June 30, 2017, the following transactions and events occurred relative to the recreation center project:

**1.** On July 1, 2016, the city sold $500,000 par of the authorized bonds, with interest payment dates on December 31 and June 30 and the first serial retirement to be made on June 30, 2017. The bonds were sold at 102.

**2.** On July 5, 2016, a construction contract for the recreation center was created in the amount of $960,000.

**3.** On December 15, 2016, the contractor's bill for $320,000 was received based on certification that the work was one-third completed.

**4.** The contractor was paid for one-third of the contract less a 10 percent retained percentage to ensure performance.

**5.** On December 30, 2016, the GF transferred $30,000 to the fund responsible for servicing the serial bonds.

**6.** Interest on the serial bonds was paid on December 31, 2016, with the money transferred from the GF and the CPF.

**7.** On June 15, 2017, the contractor's bill for $320,000 was received based on certification that the work was two-thirds completed.

**8.** On June 28, 2017, the GF transferred $90,000 to the fund responsible for servicing the serial bonds: $20,000 for interest and $50,000 for principal.

**9.** Interest and principal on the serial bonds were paid on June 30, 2017.

**10.** On June 30, 2017, the city sold the remaining $500,000 par of authorized bonds at par.

### REQUIRED

**1.** Prepare all journal entries in the funds necessary to account for the transactions and events given. (If amounts are not known, use xxx.)

**2.** Prepare financial statements for the CPF for the year ended June 30, 2017.

## INTERNET ASSIGNMENT

1. Choose a CAFR from a city, county, or other local government. Review the CAFR and answer the following questions:
   a. How many governmental funds does the government have? List the name of one special revenue fund.
   b. Does the government have a capital projects fund? For what purpose was it created? Is it a major fund?
   c. Does the government use a debt service fund?
   d. Does the government use encumbrance accounting? How can you tell?
   e. Has the government implemented *GASB Statement No. 54*? How can you tell?
   f. Locate the reconciliations between the fund and government-wide statements. List two reconciling items.
   g. Locate the budgetary comparison statement or schedule for the general fund. Comment on the extent of the differences between the original and final budgets.
2. Locate the Web site for the municipality in which your college or university is located. List one major event that has occurred recently and will be recorded in the accounting records. What fund or funds will be affected by this event?
3. Locate the Web site for the county in which your college or university is located. Has the county recorded any new debt this year in its governmental funds? How much? How can you tell?

# 21

# Accounting for State and Local Governmental Units—Proprietary and Fiduciary Funds

T his chapter concludes coverage of state and local governmental accounting practices with a review of accounting and reporting procedures applicable to proprietary funds (internal service funds and enterprise funds), fiduciary funds (trust funds and agency funds), and accounting for pensions and other post-employment benefits (OPEB), the latter of which was substantially updated in 2012 through 2016. Recall that governments use proprietary funds to account for business-type activities, while they use fiduciary funds to account for resources that are held for the benefit of others.

## PROPRIETARY FUNDS

LEARNING OBJECTIVE **21.1**

Governmental units use *proprietary funds* to account for business-type activities that provide goods and services to users and that finance those services largely from user charges. The objective of proprietary funds is to maintain capital or to produce income, or both, and full accrual accounting procedures apply. Thus, proprietary funds have revenue and expense, not expenditure, accounts. Within proprietary funds, governments recognize revenues in the accounting period in which they are earned (or in which similar recognition criteria have been met) and become measurable, and they recognize expenses in the period incurred, if measurable. The availability criterion for governmental fund revenue recognition does not apply to proprietary fund and similar trust fund revenue recognition.

Recall that the simplified[1] accounting equation for proprietary funds is:

$$\text{Current assets} + \text{Noncurrent assets} - \text{Current liabilities} - \text{Noncurrent liabilities} = \text{Net position}$$

Unlike governmental funds, the fixed assets of proprietary funds and long-term liabilities expected to be serviced by proprietary fund revenues are both reported in proprietary fund financial statements. Long-term liabilities incurred by a proprietary fund and expected to be serviced from its revenues are fund liabilities, rather than general long-term debt. Lease agreements of proprietary funds are accounted for entirely within the fund under the same provisions as *FASB Statement No. 13,* Accounting for Leases, except for operating leases with scheduled rent increases.[2] When governments report operating leases with scheduled rent increases in proprietary funds and similar trust funds, they recognize rental revenue as it accrues over the lease term.

---

[1]Chapter 19 discusses the changes from *GASB Statement No. 63,* which no longer allows *net assets,* and instead uses *net position.* It also adds two financial statement elements "deferred outflows of resources," which is reported with assets and "deferred inflows of resources," which is reported with liabilities.

[2]Leasing standards are being updated with FASB issuing ASU 2016-02 early in 2016 and GASB anticipating issuing a new standard in December 2016. Please see their websites for the most recent information.

As noted in Chapter 19, GASB Statement No. 34 requires the preparation of three fund financial statements for proprietary funds. The required statements are a statement of net position; a statement of revenues, expenses, and changes in fund net position; and a statement of cash flows.

Because proprietary funds account for transactions in much the same manner as commercial business organizations, the Governmental Accounting Standards Board (GASB) incorporated several aspects of Financial Accounting Standards Board (FASB) statements into the GASB codification via *GASB Statement No. 62,* Codification of Accounting and Financial Reporting Guidance Contained in Pre-November 30, 1989 FASB and AICPA Pronouncements, which was issued in 2010. This statement reduces confusion since preparers no longer have to consult both FASB and GASB guidance; the guidance for governmental proprietary activities is now solely within the GASB Codification.

The two types of funds within the proprietary fund classification are internal service funds (ISF) and enterprise funds (EF). The key difference between an ISF and an EF lies in the user group for which the goods and services are intended. EFs provide goods and services primarily to the general public, whereas ISFs provide their goods and services primarily to other departments or agencies within the same governmental unit (or, on a limited basis, to other governmental units). Even though the user groups for enterprise funds and ISFs differ, the accounting treatment is similar. Under GASB Statement No. 34, however, presentation within both the government-wide and fund financial statements differs for internal service funds and EFs. This chapter discusses and illustrates these differences.

## INTERNAL SERVICE FUNDS

ISF are proprietary funds that a government uses to account for governmental activities that provide goods and services to other departments or agencies of the governmental unit, or to other governmental units, on a cost-reimbursement basis. The account classifications used by an ISF are those that would be used in accounting for similar operations of a private business enterprise.

Centralized purchasing, motor pools, printing shops, and self-insurance are examples of ISF operations. Each activity offers potential efficiencies through economies of scale, improved services, and better control.

In many cases, governmental units provide the initial financing of an ISF through a contribution of cash or operating facilities, while expecting the ISF to be self-sustaining in future periods. Alternatively, the governmental unit may provide a loan to an ISF to be repaid from future operating flows of the fund. A contribution is classified as a nonreciprocal transfer, which flows through the statement of revenues, expenses, and changes in fund net position, whereas a loan is recorded as a liability of the ISF in the statement of net position.

### Accounting for an Internal Service Fund

The Village of Tara creates a central motor pool fund with a cash contribution of $200,000 from the general fund and a contribution of existing motor vehicles with a book value of $120,000. Because the cash is not expected to be repaid, the village will record the cash contribution as a $200,000 nonreciprocal transfer. The village will also remove the transferred equipment from the records of general fixed assets at its original cost, or at book value if accumulated depreciation has been recorded. In the records of the central motor pool fund, the appropriate journal entry is as follows:

| | | |
|---|---|---|
| *Internal Service Fund* | | |
| Cash | 200,000 | |
| Motor vehicles | 120,000 | |
|     Nonreciprocal transfer from GF | | 200,000 |
|     Contributed capital from municipality | | 120,000 |
|   To record establishment of the fund. | | |

The village also records the transfer in the general fund:

| | | |
|---|---|---|
| *General Fund* | | |
| Other financing use—nonreciprocal transfer to ISF | 200,000 | |
|     Cash | | 200,000 |
|   To record the transfer of resources to establish an ISF. | | |

Note that there is no need to reflect the fixed asset contribution in the general fund accounting system; however, we will remove the assets from the general fixed asset *records* and record them as ISF fixed assets. Because ISFs are reported as governmental activities on the government-wide statement of net position, this interfund activity will not affect the amount of fixed assets reported in the governmental activity column of the government-wide statement of net position.

The village obtains a maintenance facility at a cost of $100,000, purchases equipment for $50,000, and acquires operating supplies for $20,000. The village records these cash expenditures, in summary form, as follows:

| | | |
|---|---|---|
| *Internal Service Fund* | | |
| Building | 100,000 | |
| Equipment | 50,000 | |
| Supplies on hand | 20,000 | |
|     Cash | | 170,000 |
|       To record purchase of building, equipment, and supplies. | | |

Notice how the building and equipment are recorded in the ISF, as it is a proprietary fund. Depreciation expense will also be recognized.

During the first year of operation, the central motor pool fund provides motor pool vehicles to municipal departments and bills these departments at a predetermined rate based on miles driven. The rate is set to cover all costs of operating the motor pool and servicing the vehicles, including the cost of replacing worn-out vehicles. Note the similarity to business accounting entries.

When the ISF bills user funds, individual funds will record entries at the amount charged. Governments record short-term interfund receivables/payables as "Due to" in the fund that gets billed and "Due from" in the fund that sends the bill.

| | | |
|---|---|---|
| *Internal Service Fund* | | |
| Due from general fund | 100,000 | |
| Due from special revenue fund | 30,000 | |
|     Service revenue | | 130,000 |
|       To charge user funds for vehicle services. | | |
| *General Fund* | | |
| Expenditures | 100,000 | |
|     Due to internal service fund | | 100,000 |
|       To record user charges for vehicle services. | | |
| *Special Revenue Fund* | | |
| Expenditures | 30,000 | |
|     Due to internal service fund | | 30,000 |
|       To record user charges for vehicle services. | | |

Similarly, collection of the user charges triggers entries in the funds involved:

| | | |
|---|---|---|
| *Internal Service Fund* | | |
| Cash | 100,000 | |
|     Due from general fund | | 100,000 |
|       To record collections from user funds. | | |
| *General Fund* | | |
| Due to internal service fund | 100,000 | |
|     Cash | | 100,000 |
|       To record payment of user charges for vehicle services. | | |

If revenue is received from external parties, the village will record ISF revenue in the following manner:

| | | |
|---|---|---|
| *Internal Service Fund* | | |
| Cash | 1,000 | |
|     Interest revenue | | 1,000 |
|       To record interest revenue. | | |

ISFs record expenses as they are incurred. The predetermined billing rate was designed to cover such expenses:

| Internal Service Fund | | |
|---|---|---|
| Salaries expense | 40,000 | |
| Utilities expense | 18,000 | |
| Insurance expense | 16,000 | |
| Cash | | 74,000 |
| To record payments for expense items. | | |

Adjusting and closing entries are similar to those noted in a commercial enterprise:

| Internal Service Fund—Adjusting Entries | | |
|---|---|---|
| Supplies expense | 15,000 | |
| Supplies on hand | | 15,000 |
| To adjust supplies expense and supplies on hand accounts at year-end. | | |
| Salaries expense | 4,000 | |
| Accrued salaries payable | | 4,000 |
| To accrue salaries. | | |
| Depreciation expense—building | 5,000 | |
| Accumulated depreciation—building | | 5,000 |
| To record depreciation on building ($100,000 ÷ 20 years). | | |
| Depreciation expense—motor vehicles | 20,000 | |
| Accumulated depreciation—motor vehicles | | 20,000 |
| To record depreciation on vehicles (200,000 miles driven × 10 cents per mile). | | |
| Depreciation expense—equipment | 10,000 | |
| Accumulated depreciation—equipment | | 10,000 |
| To record depreciation on equipment ($50,000 ÷ 5 years). | | |

| Internal Service Fund—Closing Entries | | |
|---|---|---|
| Nonreciprocal transfer from GF | 200,000 | |
| Net position, unrestricted | | 200,000 |
| To close transfer to net position. | | |
| Contributed capital from municipality | 120,000 | |
| Net position, invested in capital assets, net of related debt | | 120,000 |
| To close contributed capital to net position. | | |
| Service revenue | 130,000 | |
| Interest revenue | 1,000 | |
| Supplies expense | | 15,000 |
| Insurance expense | | 16,000 |
| Salaries expense | | 44,000 |
| Utilities expense | | 18,000 |
| Depreciation expense—building | | 5,000 |
| Depreciation expense—motor vehicles | | 20,000 |
| Depreciation expense—equipment | | 10,000 |
| Net position, unrestricted | | 3,000 |
| To close revenue and expense accounts to net position. | | |
| Net position, unrestricted | 150,000 | |
| Net position, invested in capital assets, net of related debt | | 150,000 |
| To transfer unrestricted net position to net position invested in capital assets. | | |
| Net position, invested in capital assets, net of related debt | 35,000 | |
| Net position, unrestricted | | 35,000 |
| To transfer depreciation expense to unrestricted net position. | | |

Notice that the ISF had revenues in excess of expenses in the amount of $3,000. This slight income figure indicates that the predetermined rate charged to users was reasonable.

### Reporting Internal Service Funds in the Financial Statements

LEARNING OBJECTIVE **21.2**

ISFs are officially designated as proprietary funds; however, their intended purpose is to provide goods and services to governmental and EFs of the governmental entity. Thus, they possess a unique nature, and, under GASB Statement No. 34, governments report them in a unique manner. In the fund financial statements, governments include ISFs with the proprietary funds. Due to their nature, though, they are never considered major funds, and all ISFs are aggregated into a single column within the proprietary fund statement of net position, the statement of revenues, expenses, and changes in fund net position, and the statement of cash flows. The column containing ISF activities is captioned Governmental Activities. Exhibits 21-1, 21-2, and 21-3 use this format for the sample proprietary fund financial statements for the Village of Tara.

Within the government-wide statements, governments report ISFs with the governmental activities. The ISF balance sheet accounts are included in the governmental activities column of the statement of net position. However, the statement of activities will include only those ISF transactions involving entities other than the primary reporting entity. Thus, governments add external ISF

**EXHIBIT 21-1**

Proprietary Fund Statement of Net Position

## VILLAGE OF TARA STATEMENT OF NET POSITION—PROPRIETARY FUNDS
### JUNE 30, 2016

| | Business-Type Activities—Enterprise Funds | | | | Governmental Activities |
| | Utilities | Parking Facilities | Other Enterprise Funds | Totals | Internal Service Funds |
|---|---|---|---|---|---|
| **Assets** | | | | | |
| Current assets | | | | | |
| Cash and cash equivalents | $ 614,635 | $75,000 | $30,000 | $719,635 | $57,000 |
| Receivables, net | 235,915 | 20,000 | 5,000 | 260,915 | — |
| Due from other funds | — | — | — | — | 30,000 |
| Due from other governments | 32,112 | — | — | 32,112 | — |
| Supplies | 61,443 | 1,000 | — | 62,443 | 5,000 |
| Total current assets | 944,105 | 96,000 | 35,000 | 1,075,105 | 92,000 |
| Noncurrent assets | | | | | |
| Restricted cash and cash equivalents | 185,000 | — | — | 185,000 | — |
| Land | 45,000 | 50,000 | — | 95,000 | — |
| Buildings and equipment | 1,000,000 | 850,000 | 140,000 | 1,990,000 | 150,000 |
| Vehicles | 220,000 | — | — | 220,000 | 120,000 |
| Less accumulated depreciation | (520,000) | (450,000) | (35,000) | (1,005,000) | (35,000) |
| Total noncurrent assets | 930,000 | 450,000 | 105,000 | 1,485,000 | 235,000 |
| Total assets | $1,874,105 | $546,000 | $140,000 | $2,560,105 | $327,000 |
| **Liabilities** | | | | | |
| Current liabilities | | | | | |
| Accounts payable | $45,000 | $20,000 | $3,000 | $68,000 | — |
| Accrued liabilities | 19,000 | 20,000 | 5,000 | 44,000 | $4,000 |
| Due to other funds | — | — | 4,000 | 4,000 | — |
| Compensated absences | 3,000 | 2,000 | — | 5,000 | — |
| Bonds and notes payable | 20,000 | 50,000 | 10,000 | 80,000 | — |
| Total current liabilities | 87,000 | 92,000 | 22,000 | 201,000 | 4,000 |
| Noncurrent liabilities | | | | | |
| Customer deposits | 185,000 | — | — | 185,000 | — |
| Compensated absences | 230,000 | 65,000 | — | 295,000 | — |
| Bonds and notes payable | 275,000 | 100,000 | 90,000 | 465,000 | — |
| Total noncurrent liabilities | 690,000 | 165,000 | 90,000 | 945,000 | — |
| Total liabilities | $ 777,000 | $257,000 | $112,000 | $1,146,000 | $4,000 |
| **Net Position** | | | | | |
| Invested in capital assets, net of related debt | $450,000 | $278,000 | $5,000 | $755,000 | $235,000 |
| Restricted | 185,000 | — | — | 185,000 | — |
| Unrestricted | 462,105 | 11,000 | 23,000 | 474,105 | 88,000 |
| Total net position | $1,097,105 | $289,000 | $28,000 | $1,414,105 | $323,000 |

*Source: © Anthony H Joseph*

**VILLAGE OF TARA STATEMENT OF REVENUES, EXPENSES, AND CHANGES IN FUND NET POSITION—PROPRIETARY FUNDS FOR THE YEAR ENDED JUNE 30, 2016**

| | Business-Type Activities—Enterprise Funds | | | | Governmental Activities |
|---|---|---|---|---|---|
| | Utilities | Parking Facilities | Other Enterprise Funds | Totals | Internal Service Funds |
| *Operating Revenues* | | | | | |
| Charges for services | $680,000 | $500,000 | $40,000 | $1,220,000 | $130,000 |
| Miscellaneous | — | — | — | — | — |
|   Total operating revenues | 680,000 | 500,000 | 40,000 | 1,220,000 | 130,000 |
| *Operating Expenses* | | | | | |
| Salaries | 167,000 | 25,000 | 12,000 | 204,000 | 44,000 |
| Contractual services | — | 275,000 | — | 275,000 | — |
| Utilities | 60,000 | 24,000 | — | 84,000 | 18,000 |
| Repairs and maintenance | 78,000 | 11,000 | — | 89,000 | — |
| Insurance expense | 15,000 | 8,000 | — | 23,000 | 16,000 |
| Supplies and other expenses | 132,000 | 1,200 | 3,000 | 136,200 | 15,000 |
| Depreciation | 42,000 | 65,000 | 18,000 | 125,000 | 35,000 |
|   Total operating expenses | 494,000 | 409,200 | 33,000 | 936,200 | 128,000 |
|     Operating income (loss) | 186,000 | 90,800 | 7,000 | 283,800 | 2,000 |
| *Nonoperating Revenues (Expenses)* | | | | | |
| Interest revenue | — | — | — | — | 1,000 |
| Miscellaneous revenue (expense) | — | — | — | — | — |
| Interest expense | 2,000 | 12,000 | 5,000 | 19,000 | — |
|   Total nonoperating revenue (expense) | (2,000) | (12,000) | (5,000) | (19,000) | 1,000 |
|     Income (loss) before contributions and transfers | 184,000 | 78,800 | 2,000 | 264,800 | 3,000 |
| Capital contributions | 50,000 | — | — | 50,000 | 120,000 |
| Transfers in | — | — | — | — | 200,000 |
| Transfers out | — | — | — | — | — |
|   Change in net position | 234,000 | 78,800 | 2,000 | 314,800 | 323,000 |
| Total net position—beginning | 863,105 | 210,200 | 26,000 | 1,099,305 | — |
| Total net position—ending | $1,097,105 | $289,000 | $28,000 | $1,414,105 | $323,000 |

*Source:* © Anthony H Joseph

revenues (and expenses) to the statement of activities, while they exclude internal governmental transactions. For example, Tara includes only the $1,000 of ISF interest revenue in the governmental activities totals in the government-wide statement of activities. This, in essence, eliminates double counting of interfund transactions, much like consolidated entities eliminate intercompany transactions. This process is reviewed later in the chapter.

## ENTERPRISE FUNDS

EFs are proprietary funds that a government uses to account for activities that are financed and operated similarly to those of private business enterprises. Typically, EFs provide goods and services to the general public on a continuing basis, with the costs being financed primarily through user charges. Governments may use EFs to record any business activities for which a user fee is charged. However, they are required to use an EF for activities that (1) are financed with debt secured solely by net revenue from fees and charges to external users; (2) operate under laws or regulations requiring that the activity's costs of providing services, including capital costs, be recovered with fees and charges; or (3) have prices established by management to cover the costs (including capital costs)

**VILLAGE OF TARA STATEMENT OF CASH FLOWS—PROPRIETARY FUNDS FOR THE YEAR ENDED JUNE 30, 2016**

**EXHIBIT 21-3**

**Proprietary Fund Cash Flow Statement**

| | Business-Type Activities—Enterprise Funds | | | | Governmental Activities |
| --- | --- | --- | --- | --- | --- |
| | Utilities | Parking Facilities | Other Enterprise Funds | Totals | Internal Service Funds |
| *Cash Flows from Operating Activities* | | | | | |
| Cash received from customers | $640,000 | $489,000 | $32,000 | $1,161,000 | $100,000 |
| Cash paid to suppliers | (132,000) | (2,000) | (6,000) | (140,000) | (20,000) |
| Cash paid for salaries | (150,000) | (25,000) | (11,000) | (186,000) | (40,000) |
| Cash paid for utilities | (60,000) | (24,000) | — | (84,000) | (18,000) |
| Cash paid for contractual services | — | (275,000) | — | (275,000) | — |
| Cash paid for insurance | (15,000) | (8,000) | — | (23,000) | (16,000) |
| Cash paid for repairs and maintenance | (78,000) | (11,000) | — | (89,000) | — |
| Net cash provided (used) by operating activities | 205,000 | 144,000 | 15,000 | 364,000 | 6,000 |
| *Cash Flows from Noncapital Financing Activities* | | | | | |
| Cash received from general fund | — | — | 3,000 | 3,000 | 200,000 |
| Net cash provided (used) by noncapital financing activities | — | — | 3,000 | 3,000 | 200,000 |
| *Cash Flows from Capital and Related Financing Activities* | | | | | |
| Purchase of building | — | — | — | — | (100,000) |
| Purchase of equipment | — | (12,000) | (6,000) | (18,000) | (50,000) |
| Principal paid on capital debt | — | (75,000) | — | (75,000) | — |
| Interest paid on capital debt | — | (12,000) | — | (12,000) | — |
| Net cash provided (used) by capital and related financing activities | — | (99,000) | (6,000) | (105,000) | (150,000) |
| *Cash Flows from Investing Activities* | | | | | |
| Interest and dividends | — | — | — | — | 1,000 |
| Net cash provided by investing activities | — | — | — | — | 1,000 |
| Net (decrease) increase in unrestricted cash and cash equivalents | 205,000 | 45,000 | 12,000 | 262,000 | 57,000 |
| Balances—beginning | 409,635 | 30,000 | 18,000 | 457,635 | — |
| Balances—ending | $614,635 | $75,000 | $30,000 | $719,635 | $57,000 |

*Source:* © Anthony H Joseph

of providing services.[3] As you can imagine, EF operations are about as diverse as those found in private enterprise. They range from the operation of electric and water utilities, which are intended to produce income, to swimming pool and golf course operations, in which costs are intended to be

---

[3]GASB Statement No. 34, paragraph 387.

recovered primarily from user charges, to activities such as mass transit authorities and civic centers, which are often heavily subsidized from general governmental revenues.

The objective of an EF is to maintain capital or to generate net income, or both; thus, full accrual accounting procedures are applicable. Like ISFs, EFs are proprietary funds that use revenue and expense accounts and accrual accounting practices similar to those of private business enterprises. EF fixed assets and long-term liabilities are fund fixed assets and fund long-term liabilities. Therefore, governments record them in the EF. Often, the long-term debt obligations are in the form of *revenue bonds* secured only by EF operations. If such bonds are also secured by the "full faith and credit" of the governmental unit, they are called *general obligation bonds*, or G.O. bonds. For G.O. bonds, the EF still records the liability in the fund, but the notes to the financial statements will also disclose a contingent liability, indicating the extent of general government responsibility for repayment.

Initial financing of many EFs is typically the same as for an ISF. The governmental unit makes a capital contribution (a transfer from the general fund) or provides a long-term interfund loan to the EF. Future operations are expected to cover all costs, including depreciation on fund fixed assets, so operations can continue indefinitely without further capital contributions.

The following section presents sample entries related to a utility department's operations. Because the accounting for EFs is quite similar to accounting for commercial business enterprises, the discussion and examples are abbreviated.

## Accounting for an Enterprise Fund

Utility-type EFs often require customer deposits to assure timely payment for services. The utility normally collects the deposit before service starts and refunds the money after a minimum holding period has elapsed or when service is terminated. Land developers may also be required to make good-faith deposits to finance the cost of extending utility service lines. Governments segregate such assets and report them as restricted assets in the EF balance sheet. Customer deposits remain in current liabilities until they are applied against unpaid billings or refunded to customers. Entries related to customer deposits are as follows:

| | | |
|---|---|---|
| *Enterprise Fund* | | |
| Restricted cash | 10,000 | |
|     Customer deposits | | 10,000 |
|    To record customer deposits collected. | | |
| *Enterprise Fund* | | |
| Customer deposits | 3,000 | |
|     Restricted cash | | 3,000 |
|    To record customer deposit refunds. | | |

An EF records customer billings and receipts as follows:

| | | |
|---|---|---|
| *Enterprise Fund* | | |
| Accounts receivable | 680,000 | |
|     Charges for services | | 680,000 |
|    To record customer charges for utility services. | | |
| *Enterprise Fund* | | |
| Cash | 640,000 | |
|     Accounts receivable | | 640,000 |
|    To record collection from customers for utility services. | | |

EFs often receive intergovernmental grants that are designated for operations (operating grants) or capital asset acquisition (capital grants). For example, the Gator County Waste Management Facility may receive grant funds from the Environmental Protection Agency designated for pollution control. Governments report operating grants as nonoperating revenues in proprietary funds, whereas they recognize capital grants as contributed capital, not as revenues. Under GASB Statement No. 33, EFs recognize grant revenues and capital contributions in the period in which qualifying expenses are incurred, assuming any other significant conditions have been met. If funds are received before qualifying expenses are incurred, Revenue collected in advance[4] is recorded. The entry to record an intergovernmental capital grant once qualified expenses have been made is as follows:

*Enterprise Fund*

| | | |
|---|---|---|
| Due from other governments | 50,000 | |
| Contributed capital—grant | | 50,000 |
| To recognize capital grant for qualified expenses. | | |

If a new generator is purchased by issuing a note payable, the EF entry will be as follows:

*Enterprise Fund*

| | | |
|---|---|---|
| Equipment | 35,000 | |
| Notes payable | | 35,000 |
| To record the purchase of equipment. | | |

Using accrual accounting, EFs record other operating expenses as they are incurred:

*Enterprise Fund*

| | | |
|---|---|---|
| Salaries expense | 150,000 | |
| Repairs and maintenance expense | 78,000 | |
| Supplies expense | 132,000 | |
| Utilities expense | 60,000 | |
| Insurance expense | 15,000 | |
| Cash | | 435,000 |
| To record payments for expense items. | | |

Adjusting and closing entries are similar to those recorded in ISFs:

*Enterprise Fund—Adjusting Entries*

| | | |
|---|---|---|
| Salaries expense | 17,000 | |
| Accrued salaries payable | | 17,000 |
| To accrue salaries. | | |
| Interest expense | 2,000 | |
| Interest payable | | 2,000 |
| To accrue interest on note payable. | | |
| Depreciation expense | 42,000 | |
| Accumulated depreciation | | 42,000 |
| To record depreciation for the year. | | |

*Enterprise Fund—Closing Entries*

| | | |
|---|---|---|
| Charges for services | 680,000 | |
| Salaries expense | | 167,000 |
| Repairs and maintenance expense | | 78,000 |
| Supplies expense | | 132,000 |
| Depreciation expense | | 42,000 |
| Interest expense | | 2,000 |
| Utilities expense | | 60,000 |
| Insurance expense | | 15,000 |
| Net position, unrestricted | | 184,000 |
| To close revenue and expense accounts to net position. | | |
| Contributed capital—grant | 50,000 | |
| Net position, restricted | | 50,000 |
| To close contributed capital to net position. | | |

---

[4]As discussed in Chapter 19, GASB 65 no longer allows the use of the word *deferred* in account titles, such as *deferred revenue*. GASB did not offer a required alternate title. This text uses *Revenue collected in advance* to replace *Deferred revenue*.

## PROPRIETARY FUND FINANCIAL STATEMENTS

Required fund financial statements for proprietary funds consist of a statement of net position; a statement of revenues, expenses, and changes in fund net position; and a statement of cash flows. Each of these statements includes a column for each EF that is considered a major fund, as well as a column totaling all nonmajor EF activity.[5] As noted earlier, proprietary fund statements report ISFs with the EFs. The fund financial statements aggregate all ISFs in a single column. Exhibits 21-1, 21-2, and 21-3 illustrate this format for the sample proprietary fund financial statements for the Village of Tara.

The financial statements of proprietary funds are similar to those of a business enterprise, with a few exceptions. Internal service funds and EFs do not pay property taxes or income taxes, and thus these items are noticeably absent from the operating statement. The funds may exhibit interfund activity; therefore, governmental entity financial statements may include interfund account titles such as due from general fund (for utility charges or supply acquisitions), advance from general fund (for long-term financing), and transfers.

In addition, proprietary funds do not have capital stock or paid-in capital. In place of stockholders' equity, their statement of net position (balance sheet) shows a net position section, such as the following:

| | |
|---|---:|
| *Net position* | |
| Invested in capital assets, net of related debt | $500,000 |
| Restricted | 150,000 |
| Unrestricted | 300,000 |
| Total net position | $950,000 |

*Net position invested in capital (fixed) assets, net of related debt* is equal to the fixed assets of the fund less all fixed-asset-related debt, whether current or long-term. *Restricted net position* is composed of restricted assets reduced by liabilities and deferred inflows of resources related to those assets. Restrictions are imposed externally by creditors, grantors, donors, or laws and regulations of other governments, or internally by constitutional provisions or enabling legislation. The restrictions must be narrower than the purposes of the fund being reported. *Unrestricted net position* is the net amount of the assets, deferred outflows of resources, liabilities, and deferred inflows of resources that are not included in the two other components.[6] Restricted net position must be reclassified as unrestricted when the government satisfies the restriction.

<table>
<tr><td>LEARNING<br>OBJECTIVE</td><td>**21.3**</td></tr>
</table>

## Statement of Cash Flows for Proprietary Funds

The statement of cash flows for proprietary funds also differs slightly from its commercial business counterpart. First of all, GASB Statement No. 34 makes the direct method mandatory for statement presentation. Also, cash flow classifications have been modified. You may recall that FASB Statement No. 95 specifies a three-section format for cash flow statements of business enterprises: operating activities, investing activities, and financing activities. *GASB Statement No. 9*, Reporting Cash Flows of Proprietary and Nonexpendable Trust Funds and Governmental Entities That Use Proprietary Fund Accounting, which establishes standards for cash flow reporting for proprietary funds, separates financing activities into noncapital- and capital-related. Therefore, a proprietary fund cash flow statement has four separate sections: cash flows from operating activities, cash flows from noncapital financing activities, cash flows from capital and related financing activities, and cash flows from investing activities. The following sections review the content of the four separate sections of the statement of cash flows for proprietary funds and government entities that use proprietary fund accounting. A proprietary fund cash flow statement for the Village of Tara is presented in Exhibit 21-3.

---

[5]Recall from Chapter 19 that a fund is considered a major fund if it meets both of the following criteria: (a) Total assets, liabilities, revenues, or expenditures/expenses of that individual governmental or enterprise fund are at least 10 percent of the *corresponding* total (assets, liabilities, and so forth) for *all* funds of that *category* or *type* (i.e., total governmental or total enterprise funds), and (b) total assets, liabilities, revenues, or expenditures/expenses of that individual governmental or enterprise fund are at least 5 percent of the *corresponding total* for all governmental *and* enterprise funds *combined*.

[6]GASB Statement No. 63, p. 33.

**CASH FLOWS FROM OPERATING ACTIVITIES**    Cash inflows of the operating activities section include the following:

> Receipts from sales of goods or services
>
> Receipts from interfund services provided
>
> Receipts from interfund reimbursements[7]
>
> All other receipts not included in one of the other three sections

Cash outflows of the operating activities section include the following:

> Payments for materials used in providing services or manufacturing goods for resale
>
> Principal payments to suppliers of those materials or goods on account or under short-term or long-term notes payable
>
> Payments to suppliers for other goods and services
>
> Payments to employees for salaries
>
> Payments to other governments as grants for operating activities
>
> Payments for taxes and in lieu of taxes
>
> All other cash payments not included in one of the other three sections[8]

**CASH FLOWS FROM NONCAPITAL FINANCING ACTIVITIES**    Items to be considered cash inflows for the noncapital financing activities section include the following:

> Proceeds from bonds and notes not clearly issued specifically for the acquisition, construction, or improvement of capital assets
>
> Receipts from grants and subsidies and receipts from other funds (except those restricted for capital purposes or operating activities)
>
> Receipts from property taxes and other taxes collected for the governmental enterprise and not restricted for capital purposes

Cash outflows for this section include the following:

> Repayments of amounts borrowed (including interest payments) other than those related to acquiring or constructing capital assets
>
> Amounts paid for grants and subsidies (except those for specific operating activities of the grantor government)
>
> Cash paid to other funds, except for interfund services used

**CASH FLOWS FROM CAPITAL (FIXED ASSET) AND RELATED FINANCING ACTIVITIES**    Capital and related activities include acquiring and disposing of capital assets used in providing goods and services, including borrowing money to finance fixed asset construction or acquisition and repaying it with interest. Cash inflows include amounts from capital grants (i.e., grants for the sole purpose of acquiring, constructing, or improving a fixed asset), contributions, special assessments, insurance proceeds, and so on, as long as they are received specifically to defray the cost of acquiring, constructing, or improving capital assets. Cash received from sale or disposal of fixed assets is included in this section also.

Cash outflows include amounts to acquire, construct, or improve capital assets, and to repay amounts borrowed (including interest), as long as the purpose of the borrowing was directly related to acquiring, constructing, or improving capital assets.

**CASH FLOWS FROM INVESTING ACTIVITIES**    Investing activities include making and collecting loans and acquiring and disposing of investments in debt or equity instruments. Cash inflows include collections of loans and sales of investment securities (other than from cash equivalents) and the receipt of interest and dividends. Cash outflows include making loans and payments to acquire investment securities (other than for cash equivalents).

---

[7]FASB ASC 230. Originally 'Statement of Cash flows' Norwalk, CT: Financial Accounting Standards Board.

[8]FASB ASC 230. Originally 'Statement of Cash flows' Norwalk, CT: Financial Accounting Standards Board.

## FIDUCIARY FUNDS

Governmental units use **fiduciary funds** to account for assets held in a trustee or agency capacity on behalf of others external to the governmental entity. Such resources cannot be used for the benefit of the government's own programs. The fiduciary grouping includes trust funds (private-purpose, investment, and pension) and agency funds, which are similar in the sense that the governmental unit acts in a fiduciary capacity for both types of funds. The accounting emphasis for trust and agency funds lies in demonstrating how the government's fiduciary responsibilities have been met. The basic difference between the two fund types is that a trust agreement, which mandates the degree of management involvement and the duration of the trust, typically exists for trust fund resources. Furthermore, agency funds are more temporary in nature.

Accounting for fiduciary funds follows the accrual basis of accounting; however, agency funds do not have revenues or expenses because their operations are of a custodial nature. Governments report fiduciary funds in the fund financial statements on a statement of fiduciary net position and a statement of changes in fiduciary net position. Fiduciary funds are not included in the government-wide statements.

### Agency Funds

*Agency funds* are fiduciary funds used to account for resources that governments hold in a custodial or agency capacity. For example, a local government acts as an agent for the federal government when it withholds income and Social Security taxes, which will later be remitted to other government agencies, from employee payrolls. Also, an agency fund reports the debt service transactions of a special assessment bond issue for which the government is not obligated in any manner in order to reflect the fact that the government's duties are limited to acting as an agent for the assessed property owners and bondholders. Thus, the government acts as an agent for the property owners in collecting special assessments and remitting the amounts collected to bondholders.

Governments utilize agency funds when their agency responsibilities involve numerous transactions, include several different governmental units, or do not arise from normal and recurring operations of any other fund. For example, if a county unit of government serves as a tax collection agency for all towns and cities located within the county, the county will create an agency fund to demonstrate acceptance of responsibility for collecting and remitting taxes for other governmental units. To use an agency fund, however, the governmental entity should only act as a cash conduit, collecting and dispersing cash. If the governmental entity undertakes any administrative duties, such as determining who will receive the cash or monitoring recipient eligibility, it cannot use an agency fund.

The accounting treatment for agency funds is quite simple, as reflected in the following accounting equation:

$$Assets = Liabilities$$

There is no fund balance or equity. Assets and liabilities are recognized at the time that the government becomes responsible for the assets.

### Accounting for an Agency Fund

Assume that Morris County collects property taxes for its own purposes as well as for the cities of Howard Lake, Brownsville, and Clute, and that total property tax levies for the 2015–2016 fiscal year are as follows:

| | | |
|---|---|---|
| Morris County | $100,000 | 50% |
| Howard Lake | 50,000 | 25% |
| Brownsville | 20,000 | 10% |
| Clute | 30,000 | 15% |
| Total | $200,000 | 100% |

When the tax levies are certified to the county for collection, a tax agency fund records the county's custodial responsibility for collecting the taxes:

*Agency Fund*

| | | |
|---|---|---|
| Taxes receivable for local governmental units | 200,000 | |
|     Liability to Morris County | | 100,000 |
|     Liability to Howard Lake | | 50,000 |
|     Liability to Brownsville | | 20,000 |
|     Liability to Clute | | 30,000 |
|     To record tax levy. | | |

The county collects $180,000 of the levy for remittance to the respective units of government during the year. Ninety percent of the taxes are collected for Morris County and each of the three cities. The following entry is made to record the collection:

*Agency Fund*

| | | |
|---|---|---|
| Cash | 180,000 | |
|     Taxes receivable for local governmental units | | 180,000 |
|     To record collection of taxes receivable. | | |

If Morris County charges Howard Lake, Brownsville, and Clute a fee of 1 percent of taxes collected, the total charges would be $900 ($90,000 collected for these three cities multiplied by 1%), recorded as follows:

*Agency Fund*

| | | |
|---|---|---|
| Liability to Howard Lake | 450 | |
| Liability to Brownsville | 180 | |
| Liability to Clute | 270 | |
|     Due to general fund (of Morris County) | | 900 |
|     To charge cities a 1% fee for taxes collected for them. | | |

*General Fund*

| | | |
|---|---|---|
| Due from other governments | 900 | |
|     Miscellaneous revenues | | 900 |
|     To record fees charged to cities. | | |

The following entries reflect the remittance:

*Agency Fund*

| | | |
|---|---|---|
| Due to general fund | 900 | |
| Liability to Morris County | 90,000 | |
| Liability to Howard Lake | 44,550 | |
| Liability to Brownsville | 17,820 | |
| Liability to Clute | 26,730 | |
|     Cash | | 180,000 |
|     To record remittance of taxes collected net of 1% fee. | | |

*General Fund*

| | | |
|---|---|---|
| Cash | 900 | |
|     Due from other governments | | 900 |
|     To record collection of fees. | | |

## Financial Statements for the Agency Fund

Morris County includes the tax collection agency fund in the statement of fiduciary net position shown in Exhibit 21-4. Because agency funds do not have revenues and expenses, they need not be included in the statement of changes in fiduciary net position. Agency funds are not included in the government-wide statements.

## Trust Funds

*Investment trust funds* are fiduciary funds used to account for multigovernment external investment pools sponsored by the governmental entity. For example, a county government may offer to pool

**EXHIBIT 21-4**

Statement of Fiduciary
Net Position

## MORRIS COUNTY STATEMENT OF FIDUCIARY NET POSITION—FIDUCIARY FUNDS JUNE 30, 2016

|  | Tax Collection Agency Fund | School Library Trust Fund |
|---|---|---|
| *Assets* |  |  |
| Cash and cash equivalents | 0 | 0 |
| Investments | 0 | $100,000 |
| Taxes receivable | $20,000 | 0 |
| Interest receivable | 0 | 1,667 |
| Total assets | $20,000 | $101,667 |
| *Liabilities* |  |  |
| Liability to Morris County | 10,000 | 0 |
| Liability to Howard Lake | 5,000 | 0 |
| Liability to Brownsville | 2,000 | 0 |
| Liability to Clute | 3,000 | 0 |
| Total liabilities | $20,000 | $0 |
| *Net Position* |  |  |
| Available for distribution to school libraries | 0 | 1,667 |
| Held in trust for endowment | 0 | 100,000 |
| Total net position | $0 | $101,667 |

*Source:* © Anthony H Joseph

the cash available for investment from cities located within its boundaries. Because the cash is not an asset of the county government and cannot be used for its benefit, the resources should be accounted for in a fiduciary fund. Furthermore, if a formal agreement exists and income will be recognized in the fund, it would be appropriate to establish a trust. GASB Statement No. 31 describes the accounting for investment trust funds. Accounting for investment trust funds is beyond the scope of this chapter, so the following discussion focuses on private-purpose and pension trust funds.

*Private-purpose trust funds* are fiduciary funds used to account for resources (other than investment pools and employee benefits) that are held for the benefit of parties outside the governmental entity.[9] *Pension trust funds* are fiduciary funds used when a government acts as trustee for defined benefit and defined contribution pension plans of a government or for other employee benefit programs.

### Accounting for a Private-Purpose Trust Fund

Assume that on July 2, 2016, Morris County receives a $100,000 contribution from the Hurricane Valley Historical Society. A trust agreement specifying that the income from the contribution must be distributed each May 15 to the three school libraries in Morris County accompanies the contribution. The principal amount is intended to remain intact indefinitely. The county establishes a private-purpose trust fund to account for the contribution and associated activities, because the county itself will not benefit from these resources. The entry is as follows:

*Trust Fund*

| Cash | 100,000 | |
| Contributions—foundations | | 100,000 |
| To record a contribution received. | | |

This principal amount is not expendable and will remain in the trust fund. Expendable income amounts may be either accounted for within the same trust fund or transferred to a separate **expendable trust fund**.

---

[9]Recall that permanent funds are used to account for restricted resources that will benefit the government or its citizens.

On September 1, the county invests the contribution in bonds, which yield 5 percent annually (payable on March 1 and September 1):

| | | |
|---|---|---|
| *Trust Fund* | | |
| Investments | 100,000 | |
|     Cash | | 100,000 |
|       To record an investment in bonds. | | |

On March 1, the county receives the first interest payment:

| | | |
|---|---|---|
| *Trust Fund* | | |
| Cash | 2,500 | |
|       Interest income | | 2,500 |
|       To record the collection of interest. | | |

On May 15, Morris County distributes the interest to local school libraries:

| | | |
|---|---|---|
| *Trust Fund* | | |
| Distribution to school libraries | 2,500 | |
|       Cash | | 2,500 |
|       To record the distribution of interest. | | |

On June 30, the county adjusts and closes its accounts:

| | | |
|---|---|---|
| *Trust Fund—Adjusting Entry* | | |
| Interest receivable | 1,667 | |
|     Interest income | | 1,667 |
|       To accrue interest income ($100,000 × .05 × 4/12) | | |
| *Trust Fund—Closing Entry* | | |
| Interest income | 4,167 | |
| Contributions—foundations | 100,000 | |
|     Distribution to school libraries | | 2,500 |
|     Net position held in trust for school libraries—nonexpendable | | 100,000 |
|     Net position held in trust for school libraries—expendable | | 1,667 |
|       To close accounts. | | |

## Financial Statements for the Trust Fund

Morris County includes the school library trust fund in the statement of fiduciary net position (Exhibit 21-4) and the statement of changes in fiduciary net position (Exhibit 21-5). Note how a statement of changes in fiduciary net position reports fund additions and deductions to reflect funds held on behalf of others and distributed to parties outside the government. Trust funds are not included in the government-wide statements.

**EXHIBIT 21-5**

Statement of Changes in Fiduciary Net Position

**MORRIS COUNTY STATEMENT OF CHANGES IN FIDUCIARY NET POSITION—TRUST FUND FOR THE YEAR ENDED JUNE 30, 2016**

| | | |
|---|---|---|
| *Additions* | | |
| Contributions | | |
|   Foundations | $100,000 | |
|     Total contributions | | $100,000 |
| Investment earnings | | |
|   Interest | 4,167 | |
|     Total investment earnings | | 4,167 |
|     Total additions | | 104,167 |
| *Deductions* | | |
| Distributions to school libraries | 2,500 | |
|   Total deductions | | 2,500 |
| Change in net position | | 101,667 |
| Net position—beginning of the year | | 0 |
| Net position—end of the year | | $101,667 |

*Source: © Anthony H Joseph*

## Accounting for a Pension Trust Fund

Governments account and report for public employee retirement systems (PERS) through pension trust funds. There are two primary types of pension plans: defined benefit and defined contribution. A defined benefit plan specifies the amount of benefits that will be provided to the employee after retirement, and a defined contribution plan specifies the amount of resources that the government will invest on behalf of employee retirement during the employee's employment. Pension plans are further classified as single-employer plans if they involve only one government or multiple-employer if they include more than one government. Finally, for multiple-employer plans, a cost-sharing plan pools the cost of financing pensions, while an agent plan maintains separate actuarial calculations for each participating government.

PERS are not subject to the regulations of ERISA (the federal government's Employee Retirement Income Security Act). Consequently, some governmental pension plans are fully funded, others are partially funded, and still others make all pension payments from current revenue. Pension accounting and financial reporting requirements were changed substantially in 2012 as set forth in *GASB Statement No. 67,* Financial Reporting for Pension Plans: An amendment of GASB Statement No. 25 and *GASB Statement No. 68,* Accounting and Financial Reporting for Pensions: An amendment of GASB Statement No. 27.[10] FASB pension accounting guidance had never been previously applied by governments.

Nearly 1,000 individuals or groups responded during GASB's due process from 2009 to 2012, making this one of the most deliberated standards in its history. Among the many comments, respondents focused on the discount rate, the display in footnotes versus the financial statements, and whether pension expense should approximate pension funding. The GASB decided to reduce variability in practice and prescribed the discount rate to compute the net present value of the net pension liability. The discount rate is the long-term expected rate of the actual assets in the plan, but only if there are enough assets to cover the obligations. At the point where there are not enough expected assets, the discount rate becomes a municipal borrowing rate (tax-exempt AA/Aa or higher for 20-year bonds).

The GASB also decided to display the net pension liability on the face of the financial statements. Finally, the GASB decided to move away from a *funding-based* approach to measuring and reporting pension expense to an *accounting-based* approach. Upon issuance of GASB Statement No. 67 in June 2012, GASB stated in its plain language summary (p. 2), "The Board crafted its new Statements with the fundamental belief that funding is squarely a policy decision for elected officials to make as part of the government budget approval process."[11] Accounting and reporting for pension trust funds is quite complex, thus, pension trust fund accounting is not examined in detail here.

In addition to pensions, many state and local governmental employers provide other postemployment benefits (OPEB) to qualified employees. OPEB includes postemployment healthcare as well as other forms of postemployment benefits (e.g., life insurance) provided separately from a pension plan. Issued in 2015, *GASB Statement No. 74*, Financial Reporting for Postemployment Benefit Plans Other Than Pension Plans, and *GASB Statement No. 75,* Accounting and Financial Reporting for Postemployment Benefits Other Than Pensions, establish standards for the reporting, measurement, recognition, and display of OPEB expenses/expenditures and related liabilities (assets), note disclosures, and, if applicable, required supplementary information (RSI) in the financial reports of state and local governmental employers.

## PREPARING THE GOVERNMENT-WIDE FINANCIAL STATEMENTS

The government-wide statements include a column for business-type activities. This column includes EF amounts only. Because the government-wide statement of activities and statement of net position report all items using the accrual basis of accounting, conversion between the EF and government-wide statements is not necessary. Governments can simply transfer EF figures from the proprietary fund statements to the government-wide statements, *with one exception*: Governments must either eliminate internal balances or report them as interfund balances in the asset section of the statement of net position. For example, in the Village of Tara illustration, $4,000 is due to other funds from

---

[10]GASB issued several updates to Statements 67 and 68 to deal with implementation issues, including GASB Statements No. 71, 73, and 78.

[11]© 2013 GASB, Financial Accounting Foundation.

an EF. Because the EF owes this interfund payable to a governmental fund, the village will report the amount as an "internal balance." It appears in the asset section of the statement of net position as a debit in the governmental activities column (for the governmental fund receivable) and as a credit in the business-type activity column (for the EF payable). Internal balances account for the only difference between enterprise fund balances on the fund statements and the government-wide statements, so no reconciliations are necessary.

Recall that government-wide statements report ISFs with governmental activities. When preparing the government-wide statements, governments add ISF assets and liabilities to governmental fund assets and liabilities,[12] as was indicated in the conversion worksheet in Exhibit 20-5; however, note that internal balances among governmental activities are eliminated. For example, in the Village of Tara illustration, Tara will eliminate the $30,000 due to the ISF from the special revenue fund in the governmental activities column. Also, Tara will eliminate the $200,000 transfer in from the general fund. Any revenues from external parties, such as the $1,000 interest revenue recognized earlier in the chapter, will be included in governmental totals reported on the statement of activities. However, because the ISF benefited the governmental funds only, debiting ISF net position and crediting **governmental fund expenditures** eliminate the intragovernmental operating revenue and expenses for the ISF. This adjustment ensures that figures in the governmental activity column are not "grossed up."

## REQUIRED PROPRIETARY FUND NOTE DISCLOSURES

EFs follow the accrual basis of accounting and are therefore able to report long-term debt within their funds. If an EF issues debt that is backed by its revenue-generating activity (i.e., revenue-backed debt instruments), the government must present certain detailed segment information in the notes to the financial statements.[13] The information helps creditors and financial statement users to determine if the segment that has issued the debt is generating the proceeds to fund the debt. The segment disclosure includes a description of the type of goods and services provided by the segment, as well as condensed statements of net position; revenues, expenses, and changes in fund net position; and cash flows.

## SUMMARY

Governmental units use proprietary funds to account for business-type activities and use fiduciary funds to account for assets held in a trustee or agency capacity on behalf of others external to the governmental entity. This chapter has reviewed the appropriate accounting and financial reporting for proprietary and fiduciary funds, which generally follow the accrual basis for accounting and reporting.

Accounting for each of the proprietary funds is the same; however, financial statement presentation differs. Within the proprietary fund financial statements, each major EF appears in a separate column, whereas nonmajor EF activities are totaled and reported in a single column. A separate column reports the total of all ISF balances. Within the government-wide statements, however, EFs appear in a column labeled Business-Type Activities, whereas ISFs are included with governmental activities. Governmental funds financial statements report fiduciary funds in separate fund statements, but government-wide statements do not include these funds. Pension accounting standards were revised in 2012 while accounting for other postemployment benefits (OPEB) were revised in 2015. Governments must now report the net pension or OPEB liability on the face of the financial statements.

## QUESTIONS

**1.** How are enterprise and internal service funds similar? How are they different?

**2.** Cite some governmental operations that might be accounted for through an internal service fund.

---

[12]Preparers would also need to combine any balances that may exist in the new categories of Deferred Outflows of Resources and Deferred Inflows of Resources, per GASB Statement No. 63.

[13]GASB Statement No. 34, paragraph 122.

3. What fund financial statements are needed for an enterprise fund to meet the requirements for fair presentation in accordance with GAAP? Which government-wide statements include enterprise fund data?

4. Which fund financial statements include internal service fund data? Which government-wide statements include internal service fund data?

5. How does the presentation of an enterprise *major* fund differ from the presentation of an internal service *major* fund?

6. Because proprietary funds are accounted for in much the same manner as commercial business organizations, is it appropriate for FASB pronouncements to be used for their accounting?

7. Why is it important for internal service funds to differentiate between revenues generated by interfund transactions and transactions with external parties?

8. How does a proprietary fund statement of cash flows differ from a commercial enterprise's statement of cash flows?

9. What fund types are included in the fiduciary fund category? Where are they reported in the financial statements?

10. How might an internal service fund be financed initially? How will the financing appear in the fund financial statements?

11. How does a private-purpose trust fund differ from a permanent fund?

12. How many columns (not including total columns) are needed for a government-wide statement of net position of a governmental unit with a general fund, two special revenue funds, three internal service funds, four enterprise funds, and a component unit? Explain.

13. Do governmental financial statements indicate whether a pension plan is fully funded? Explain.

14. What is the accounting equation for an agency fund?

15. Under what circumstances will a proprietary fund be required to report segment information?

16. How might the enterprise fund amounts on the proprietary fund statement of net position differ from the amounts reported as "business-type activities" on the government-wide statement of net position?

## EXERCISES

### E 21-1
### Multiple choice

1. Internal service funds are reported:
   a *With governmental funds on the fund financial statements*
   b *With governmental activities on the government-wide statement of net position*
   c *With proprietary funds on the government-wide statement of net position*
   d *All of the above*

2. Which of the following is not a fiduciary fund?
   a *Agency fund*
   b *Trust fund*
   c *Permanent fund*
   d *All of the above are fiduciary funds*

3. The proprietary fund statement of cash flows includes all of the following sections except:
   a *Cash flows from operating activities*
   b *Cash flows from investing activities*
   c *Cash flows from capital and related financing activities*
   d *Cash flows from noncapital investing activities*

4. The simplified accounting equation for proprietary funds is:
   a *Current assets − Noncurrent assets − All liabilities = Fund balance*
   b *Current assets − Noncurrent assets − All liabilities = Net position*
   c *Current assets + Noncurrent assets − All liabilities = Net position*
   d *Assets = Liabilities*

5. The accounting equation for agency funds is:
   a *Current assets − Noncurrent assets − All liabilities = Fund balance*
   b *Current assets − Noncurrent assets − All liabilities = Net position*
   c *Current assets + Noncurrent assets − All liabilities = Net position*
   d *Assets = Liabilities*

## E 21-2
## Multiple choice [Based on AICPA]

1. The billings for transportation services provided to other governmental units are recorded by the internal service fund as:
   a  *Interfund exchanges*
   b  *Intergovernmental transfers*
   c  *Transportation appropriations*
   d  *Operating revenues*

2. Which of the following transactions would not be allowed in an internal service fund?
   a  *The purchase of capital items*
   b  *Borrowing from another fund*
   c  *Transfers from other funds*
   d  *None of the above*

3. Initial financing for internal service fund activities may be obtained from
   a  *Advances from another fund*
   b  *Transfers from another fund*
   c  *Transfer of related materials held by governmental departments*
   d  *All of the above*

4. Carlton City serves as a collecting agency for the local independent school district and for a local water district. For this purpose, Carlton has created a single agency fund and charges the other entities a fee of 1 percent of the gross amounts collected. (The service fee is treated as a general fund revenue.) During the latest fiscal year, a gross amount of $268,000 was collected for the independent school district and $80,000 for the water district. As a consequence of the forgoing, Carlton's general fund should:
   a  *Recognize receipts of $348,000*
   b  *Recognize receipts of $344,520*
   c  *Record revenue of $3,480*
   d  *Record encumbrances of $344,520*

5. Through an internal service fund, Floyd County operates a centralized data processing center to provide services to Floyd's other departments. In 2014, this internal service fund billed Floyd's parks and recreation fund $75,000 for data processing services. What account should Floyd's internal service fund credit to record this $75,000 billing to the parks and recreation fund?
   a  *Operating revenues*
   b  *Interfund exchanges*
   c  *Intergovernmental transfers*
   d  *Data processing department expenses*

## E 21-3
## Multiple choice

1. Charges for services are a major source of revenue for:
   a  *A debt service fund*
   b  *A trust fund*
   c  *An enterprise fund*
   d  *A capital projects fund*

2. A city provides initial financing for its enterprise fund with the stipulation that the amount advanced be returned to the general fund within five years. The general fund expects prompt repayment. In recording the payment to the enterprise fund, the general fund should:
   a  *Debit the contribution to enterprise fund account*
   b  *Debit the expenditures account*
   c  *Debit a reserve for advance to enterprise fund account*
   d  *Debit a due from enterprise fund account*

3. If enterprise fund assets are financed through general obligation bonds, rather than revenue bonds, the debt:
   a  *Is not an enterprise fund liability*
   b  *Must be serviced through a debt service fund*
   c  *Is an enterprise fund liability if enterprise fund revenues are intended to service the debt*
   d  *Is reported both as a long-term fund liability and a general obligation liability*

**4.** An internal service fund would most likely be created to provide:

   *a*  *Debt service*

   *b*  *Centralized purchasing*

   *c*  *Perpetual care of cemeteries*

   *d*  *Tax collection and recording services*

**5.** Enterprise funds should be used in accounting for governmental activities that involve:

   *a*  *Providing goods and services to the public*

   *b*  *Providing goods and services to other departments of the government*

   *c*  *Providing goods and services to the public if a substantial amount of revenue is derived from user charges*

   *d*  *Collection of money from the public*

## E 21-4
## Multiple choice

**1.** Fiduciary funds include four different types of funds. Which of the following is *not* one of these types?

   *a*  *Agency funds*

   *b*  *Tax collection funds*

   *c*  *Private-purpose trust funds*

   *d*  *Pension trust funds*

**2.** Agency funds maintain accounts for:

   *a*  *Liabilities*

   *b*  *Revenues*

   *c*  *Net position*

   *d*  *Expenditures*

**3.** Funds for which a government entity has fiduciary responsibilities:

   *a*  *Must be accounted for in trust and agency funds according to GAAP*

   *b*  *May be accounted for as liabilities of the general fund*

   *c*  *Are infrequently encountered in accounting for governments*

   *d*  *Arise whenever assets are placed in trust for particular purposes*

**4.** If Hudack County established a separate fund entity to account for state income taxes collected and remitted to the state, the fund would likely be:

   *a*  *An agency fund*

   *b*  *An internal service fund*

   *c*  *An endowment fund*

   *d*  *A trust fund*

**5.** The accounting and financial reporting concepts are virtually the same for which of the following fund types?

   *a*  *Private-purpose trust funds and permanent funds*

   *b*  *Permanent funds and pension trust funds*

   *c*  *Pension trust funds and investment trust funds*

   *d*  *Permanent funds and agency funds*

## E 21-5
## Multiple choice [AICPA adapted]

**1.** The following revenues were among those reported by Arvida Township in 2016:

| | |
|---|---|
| Net rental revenue (after depreciation) from a parking garage owned by Arvida | $40,000 |
| Interest earned on investments held for employees' retirement benefits | 100,000 |
| Property taxes | 6,000,000 |

What amount of the foregoing revenues should be accounted for in Arvida's governmental funds?

   *a*  *$6,140,000*

   *b*  *$6,100,000*

   *c*  *$6,040,000*

   *d*  *$6,000,000*

**2.** Taylor City issued the following long-term obligations:

| | |
|---|---|
| Revenue bonds to be repaid from admission fees collected from users of the city swimming pool | $1,000,000 |
| General obligation bonds issued for the city water and sewer fund that will service the debt | $1,800,000 |

Although these bonds are expected to be paid from enterprise funds, the full faith and credit of the city has been pledged as further assurance that the obligations will be paid. What amount of these bonds should be accounted for in the proprietary funds?

*a* $0
*b* $1,000,000
*c* $1,800,000
*d* $2,800,000

**3.** The following proceeds received by Glad City in 2017 are legally restricted to expenditure for specified purposes:

| | |
|---|---|
| Donation by a benefactor mandated to provide meals for the needy | $200,000 |
| Sales taxes to finance the maintenance of tourist facilities owned by the city | 800,000 |

What amount should be accounted for in Glad's fiduciary funds?

*a* $0
*b* $200,000
*c* $800,000
*d* $1,000,000

**4.** In connection with Thurman Township's long-term debt, the following cash accumulations are available to cover payment of principal and interest on:

| | |
|---|---|
| Bonds for financing of water treatment plant construction | $1,000,000 |
| General long-term obligations | 400,000 |

The amount of these cash accumulations that should be accounted for in Thurman's debt service funds is:

*a* $0
*b* $400,000
*c* $1,000,000
*d* $1,400,000

Use the following information in answering questions 5 and 6:
On December 31, 2016, Cane City paid a contractor $3,000,000 for the total cost of a new municipal annex built in 2016 on city-owned land. Financing was provided by a $2,000,000 general obligation bond issue sold at face amount on December 31, 2016, with the remaining $1,000,000 transferred from the general fund.

**5.** What account and amount should be reported in Cane's 2016 financial statements for the general fund?
*a* Other financing uses, $1,000,000
*b* Other financing sources, $2,000,000
*c* Expenditures, $3,000,000
*d* Other financing sources, $3,000,000

**6.** What accounts and amounts should be reported in Cane's 2016 financial statements for the capital projects fund?
*a* Other financing sources, $2,000,000; general long-term debt, $2,000,000
*b* Revenues, $2,000,000; expenditures, $2,000,000
*c* Other financing sources, $3,000,000; expenditures, $3,000,000
*d* Revenue, $3,000,000; expenditures, $3,000,000

## E 21-6
## Agency fund statement of net position

The City of Laramee established a tax agency fund to collect property taxes for the City of Laramee, Bloomer County, and Bloomer School District. Total tax levies of the three governmental units were $200,000 for 2016, of which $60,000 was for the City of Laramee, $40,000 for Bloomer County, and $100,000 for Bloomer School District.

The tax agency fund charges Bloomer County and Bloomer School District a 2 percent collection fee that it transfers to the general fund of the City of Laramee in order to cover costs incurred for agency fund operations.

During 2016 the tax agency fund collected and remitted $150,000 of the 2016 levies to the various governmental units. The collection fees associated with the $150,000 were remitted to Laramee's general fund before year-end.

**REQUIRED:** Prepare a statement of fiduciary net position for the City of Laramee Tax Agency Fund at December 31, 2016.

## E 21-7
### Enterprise fund journal entries and reporting

Prepare journal entries to record the following grant-related transactions of an enterprise fund activity. Explain how these transactions should be reported in the enterprise fund's financial statements, including the statement of cash flows.
1. Received an operating grant in cash from the state, $3,000,000.
2. Incurred qualifying expenses on the grant program, $1,200,000.
3. Received a federal grant to finance construction of a processing plant, $7,000,000. (The cash was received in advance.)
4. Incurred and paid construction costs on the processing plant, $4,000,000.

## E 21-8
### Identification of fund type

For each of the following events or transactions, identify the fund or funds that will be affected.
1. A governmental unit operates a municipal pool. Costs are intended to be recovered primarily from user charges.
2. A bond offering was issued at par to subsidize the construction of a new convention center.
3. A bond offering was issued at a premium to subsidize the construction of a new convention center.
4. A town receives a donation of cash that must be used for the benefit of the town's bird sanctuary, which is not operated by the town.
5. A central computing center was established to handle the data processing needs of a municipality.
6. A local municipality provides water and sewer services to residents of nearby communities for a fee.
7. A village receives a grant from the state government. The funds are to be used solely for preserving wetlands.
8. Property taxes are levied by a city government.
9. A county government serves as a tax collection agency for all towns and cities located within the county.
10. A county government offers to pool the cash available for investment from cities located within its boundaries. A formal agreement exists, and income will be recognized in the fund.

## E 21-9
### Journal entries—various funds

For each of the following events or transactions, prepare the necessary journal entry or entries, and identify the fund or funds that will be affected.
1. A governmental unit collects fees totaling $4,500 at the municipal pool. The fees are charged to recover costs of pool operation and maintenance.
2. A county government that serves as a tax collection agency for all towns and cities located within the county collects county sales taxes totaling $125,000 for the month.
3. A $1,000,000 bond offering was issued, with a premium of $50,000, to subsidize the construction of a city visitor center.
4. A town receives a donation of $50,000 in bonds. The bonds should be held indefinitely, but bond income is to be donated to the local zoo. The zoo is not associated with the town.
5. A central printing shop is established with a $150,000 nonreciprocal transfer from the general fund.
6. A $1,000,000 revenue bond offering was issued at par by a fund that provides water and sewer services to residents of nearby communities for a fee. The funds are to be used for facility expansion.
7. A village is awarded a grant of $250,000 from the state government for highway beautification. The general fund provides a $50,000 loan, because grant funds will be disbursed after valid expenditures are documented.
8. Property taxes of $5,000,000 are levied by a city government. One percent is considered uncollectible, and the taxes will be used to fund current obligations.

## E 21-10
### Net position classification

For an enterprise fund, note how each of the following transactions affects (a) net investment in capital assets (net of related debt), (b) restricted net position, and (c) unrestricted net position. (Record N/A if there is no effect on the net position section.)
1. The sale of a building for a gain
2. Depreciation of an asset

3. The issuance of capital asset-related debt
4. The payment of capital asset-related debt
5. Property taxes are levied and collected
6. Supplies are purchased and used

## P 21-1
### Internal service fund journal entries

The City of Thomasville established an internal service fund to provide printing services to all city offices and departments. The following transactions related to the fund took place in 2016:

1. On January 15, the general fund transferred equipment with a book value of $550,000 and provided a $500,000 loan to the internal service fund.

2. On February 1, the internal service fund acquired $200,000 worth of printing equipment and computers. The assets have a five-year life with no salvage, and the city uses straight-line depreciation. Assume half-year depreciation in the year of acquisition. They paid cash.

3. Throughout the year, the internal service fund billed various departments $345,000 for service rendered and collected $300,000 of the amount billed.

4. Various expenses for the year were as follows: wages and salaries, $180,000; payroll taxes, $37,800; repayment to the general fund, $50,000; and other operating expenses, $120,000. They paid cash.

**REQUIRED:** Prepare all necessary journal entries for the printing services internal service fund for the year ended December 31, 2016.

## P 21-2
### Enterprise fund journal entries and trial balance

The following transactions relate to the Fiedler County Utility Plant, a newly established municipal facility financed with debt secured solely by net revenue from fees and charges to external users.

1. The general fund made a $30,000,000 contribution to establish the working capital of the new utility enterprise fund.

2. The utility fund purchased a utility plant for $25,250,000 with cash.

3. The utility fund issued a $5,000,000 revenue bond for renovations to the facility.

4. Utility bills of $4,500,000 were mailed to customers.

5. Utility collections totaled $4,400,000.

6. Renovations of $3,500,000 were completed during the year and recorded as building improvements. They paid cash.

7. Salaries of $700,000 were paid to employees.

8. Interest expense of $300,000 related to the revenue bonds was paid during the year, and $100,000 was accrued at year-end.

9. Operating expenses totaling $1,000,000 were paid during the year, and an additional $100,000 of operating expenses was accrued at year-end.

10. Depreciation of $1,050,000 was recorded.

**REQUIRED:** Prepare all necessary journal entries and an adjusted trial balance for the utility enterprise fund for the year.

## P 21-3
## Preparation of internal service fund statements

Comparative adjusted trial balances for the motor pool of Douwe County at June 30, 2016, and June 30, 2017, are as follows:

|  | June 30, 2017 | June 30, 2016 |
|---|---|---|
| Cash | $37,000 | $44,000 |
| Due from general fund | — | 8,000 |
| Due from electric fund | 4,000 | 3,000 |
| Supplies on hand | 14,000 | 12,000 |
| Autos | 99,000 | 80,000 |
| Supplies used | 68,000 | 60,000 |
| Salaries expense | 25,000 | 20,000 |
| Utilities expense | 9,000 | 8,000 |
| Depreciation expense | 16,000 | 15,000 |
| Operating transfer to general fund | 12,000 | — |
|  | $284,000 | $250,000 |
| Accumulated depreciation—autos | $56,000 | $40,000 |
| Accounts payable | 11,000 | 10,000 |
| Advance from general fund (current) | 5,000 | 5,000 |
| Contribution from general fund | 50,000 | 50,000 |
| Net position (beginning) | 42,000 | 35,000 |
| Revenue from billings | 120,000 | 110,000 |
|  | $284,000 | $250,000 |

**REQUIRED:** Prepare fund financial statements for the motor pool for the year ended June 30, 2017. (The statement of cash flows is to be included. Assume all expenses are paid in cash.)

## P 21-4
## Preparation of trust fund statements

On January 1, 2016, J. G. Monee created a student aid trust fund to which he donated a building with a fair value of $400,000 (his cost was $250,000), bonds having a market value of $500,000, and $100,000 cash. The trust agreement stipulated that principal was to be maintained intact and earnings were to be used to support needy students. Consider gains on investments and depreciation as adjustments of earnings rather than of trust fund principal.

### Activities for 2016

1. During the year, net rentals of $40,000 were collected for building rental.

2. The bonds were sold for $550,000 on June 30, 2016. Of the proceeds, $30,000 represented interest accrued from January 1 to June 30.

3. Stocks were purchased for $600,000 cash.

4. Depreciation on the building was calculated at $20,000 for the year.

5. Dividends receivable of $60,000 were recorded at December 31, 2016.

**REQUIRED:** Prepare a statement of fiduciary net position and a statement of changes in fiduciary net position for this private-purpose trust fund at December 31, 2016.

## P 21-5
## Preparation of trust fund statements

On July 1, 2016, Duchy County receives a $500,000 contribution from the local chapter of Homeless No More. A trust agreement specifying that the income from the contribution be distributed each May 15 to the downtown homeless shelter accompanies the contribution. The principal amount is intended to remain intact indefinitely. The following transactions related to the contribution occur during the fiscal year:

1. On September 1, the county invests the contribution in bonds, which yield 4.5 percent annually (payable on March 1 and September 1).

**2.** On March 1, the county receives the first interest payment.

**3.** On May 15, the county distributes the interest to the homeless shelter.

**4.** On June 30, the county closes its accounts.

**REQUIRED:** Prepare a statement of fiduciary net position and a statement of changes in fiduciary net position for this private-purpose trust fund at June 30, 2017.

## P 21-6
### Internal service fund journal entries [AICPA adapted]

The City of Meringen operates a central garage through an internal service fund to provide garage space and repairs for all city-owned and operated vehicles. The central garage fund was established by a contribution of $200,000 from the general fund, when the building was acquired several years ago. The postclosing trial balance at June 30, 2016, was as follows:

|  | Debit | Credit |
|---|---|---|
| Cash | $150,000 |  |
| Due from general fund | 20,000 |  |
| Inventory of materials and supplies | 80,000 |  |
| Land | 60,000 |  |
| Building | 200,000 |  |
| Accumulated depreciation—building |  | $10,000 |
| Machinery and equipment | 56,000 |  |
| Accumulated depreciation—machinery and equipment |  | 12,000 |
| Vouchers payable |  | 38,000 |
| Contribution from general fund |  | 200,000 |
| Net position |  | 306,000 |
|  | $566,000 | $566,000 |

The following information applies to the fiscal year ended June 30, 2017:

**1.** Materials and supplies were purchased on account for $74,000.

**2.** The inventory of materials and supplies at June 30, 2017, was $58,000, which agreed with the physical count taken.

**3.** Salaries and wages paid to employees totaled $230,000, including related costs.

**4.** A billing was received from the enterprise fund for utility charges totaling $30,000, and it was paid.

**5.** Depreciation of the building was recorded in the amount of $5,000. Depreciation of the machinery and equipment totaled $8,000.

**6.** Billings to other departments for services rendered to them were as follows:

| | |
|---|---|
| General fund | $262,000 |
| Water and sewer fund | 84,000 |
| Special revenue fund | 32,000 |

**7.** Unpaid interfund receivable balances at June 30, 2017, were as follows:

| | |
|---|---|
| General fund | $6,000 |
| Special Revenue Fund | 16,000 |

**8.** Vouchers payable at June 30, 2017, were $14,000.

**REQUIRED**

**1.** For the period July 1, 2016, through June 30, 2017, prepare journal entries to record all the transactions in the central garage fund accounts.

**2.** Prepare closing entries for the central garage fund at June 30, 2017.

### P 21-7
### Enterprise fund statement of cash flows

Caleb County had a beginning cash balance in its enterprise fund of $714,525. During the year, the following transactions affecting cash flows occurred:

1. Acquired equity investments totaling $165,000 for cash

2. Receipts from sales of goods or services totaled $3,276,500

3. Payments for materials used in providing services were made in the amount of $2,694,500

4. A capital grant, whose proceeds of $750,000 are restricted for the acquisition of constructing or improving a fixed asset, was awarded (cash was received during the year).

5. Payments to employees for salaries amounted to $479,300

6. The fund's allocated portion of property taxes was $217,000

7. Other cash expenses for operations were $819,200

8. Capital assets used in providing goods and services were sold for $522,000. They had a book value of $550,000

9. Long-term debt payments totaled $515,000; not associated with capital assets

**REQUIRED:** Prepare a statement of cash flows for the Caleb County enterprise fund.

## INTERNET ASSIGNMENT

1. Choose a CAFR from a city, county, or other local government. Review the CAFR and answer the following questions:
   a. How many proprietary funds does the government have? List the name of one enterprise fund.
   b. Does the government have an internal service fund? What product or service does it provide?
   c. Does the government have an agency fund? What is its title?
   d. What type of pension fund is reported in the financial statements? Are the required disclosures contained in the CAFR?
   e. What type of other postemployment benefits are reported in the footnotes? Is the net OPEB liability reported on the face of the financial statements?
2. Locate the Web site for the municipality in which your college or university is located. Does this municipality provide utilities, sewer, or water to its residents? Are these activities accounted for in the appropriate fund?
3. Locate the Web site for your hometown. Does this municipality provide local transit service (i.e., bus, subway, etc.)? If so, how is it funded? Did the government receive any capital or operating grants during the year?

# CHAPTER 22

# Accounting for Not-for-Profit Organizations

T his chapter provides an introduction to accounting principles and reporting practices of not-for-profit (NFP) entities, which include voluntary health and welfare organizations (VHWOs), other NFP organizations (such as churches and museums), healthcare entities, and colleges and universities. Each of these organizational types is important for the resources it controls and for its impact on society.

Although these four NFP organizational types often share a focus on service objectives, their sources of financing and degree of autonomy vary significantly. Also, some NFP organizations are governments required to follow the pronouncements of the Governmental Accounting Standards Board (GASB), whereas others are nongovernmental NFP organizations, whose standards are established by the Financial Accounting Standards Board (FASB). This chapter describes NFP organizations, introduces the *FASB Accounting Standards Codification* (FASB ASC) sections applicable to nongovernmental NFPs, and provides detailed examples of journal entries and financial statements for nongovernmental NFP organizations.

| LEARNING OBJECTIVE | **22.1** |

## THE NATURE OF NOT-FOR-PROFIT ORGANIZATIONS

You can distinguish a not-for-profit (NFP) entity from a commercial business enterprise by examining its underlying characteristics. An NFP entity (1) receives contributions of significant amounts of resources from resource providers who do not expect commensurate or proportionate pecuniary return, (2) operates for purposes other than to provide goods or services at a profit, and (3) does not possess ownership interests like those of business enterprises. (ASC 958)

Once designated as such, an NFP organization finds itself in a quite diverse sector of entities whose members are public and private, charitable and self-promoting, and tax-exempt and taxable. Although the term *not-for-profit* conjures up thoughts of the Salvation Army or your local church, NFP entities can fall into one of four categories: voluntary health and welfare organizations (VHWOs, such as the Salvation Army), other NFP organizations (such as churches and museums), healthcare entities, and colleges and universities. The accounting and financial reporting methods of each type of NFP vary. NFP entities are first designated as governmental or nongovernmental to determine whether they should follow Governmental Accounting Standards Board (GASB) or Financial Accounting Standards Board (FASB) standards.

A governmental NFP organization meets the aforementioned NFP criteria and also possesses one of the following characteristics: Officers are elected by popular vote or appointment by a state or local government; a government can unilaterally dissolve the entity, with the assets reverting back to the government; or the entity has the power to enact and enforce a tax levy.[1] Unlike *general-purpose governments*, such as the state and local municipalities discussed in Chapters 20 to 21, the GASB defines other legally separate governmental entities as *special-purpose governments*. Governmental NFP organizations are therefore special-purpose governments and are generally required to follow GASB standards; however, their reporting requirements are often less than those of general-purpose governments. GASB Statements No. 34 and 35 require special-purpose governments with more than one governmental program or both governmental and business-type activities to present both government-wide and fund financial statements, as well as the management's discussion and analysis (MD&A), notes, and required supplementary information. Special-purpose governments with only one governmental program may combine fund and government-wide statements, whereas those with only business-type activities should report only the financial statements required for enterprise funds, as well as the MD&A, notes, and required supplementary information. Because accounting and financial reporting under GASB 34 was covered extensively in previous chapters, the remainder of this chapter is devoted to the accounting and financial reporting required for nongovernmental NFP entities, and mention of governmental NFPs is limited.

**LEARNING OBJECTIVE 22.2**

**Nongovernmental not-for-profit organizations** are NFP entities that lack the governmental element. All nongovernmental, NFP organizations—whether VHWOs, healthcare organizations, colleges and universities, or other—use essentially the same basic guidance, although the nature of their transactions differs. The *FASB Accounting Standards Codification* (FASB ASC) became the sole source of authoritative generally accepted accounting principles (GAAP) for interim and annual periods ending after September 15, 2009. FASB ASC 958 incorporates the prior FASB standards that provided guidance for NFPs, primarily FASB Statement No. 116, *Accounting for Contributions Received and Contributions Made*, which established accounting standards for contributions, and Statement No. 117, *Financial Statements of Not-for-Profit Organizations*, which identified the required statements to be presented by nongovernmental, NFP organizations.

**LEARNING OBJECTIVE 22.3**

## NOT-FOR-PROFIT ACCOUNTING PRINCIPLES

The model for developing and disseminating accounting guidance changed in 2009 with FASB's publication of the Codification. FASB will now issue ASU (Accounting Standard Updates) that will be pending until formally incorporated into the Codification.[2] The FASB also created a Not-for-Profit Advisory Committee (NAC) in October of 2009 to provide advice on existing guidance, current projects, and future issues. Concurrently, the AICPA continues its Not-for-Profit Organization Committee, which updated the *AICPA Audit and Accounting Guide: Not-for-Profit Entities* in 2016. The AICPA guide incorporates three of the prior audit guides (VHWOs, colleges and universities, and "other" NFP organizations), includes FASB NFP standards, and contains additional guidance for such organizations. The AICPA also updated its Audit and Accounting guide for healthcare entities in 2015.

### Financial Statements

GAAP (ASC 958-205) requires NFP organizations to provide a set of financial statements that includes a statement of financial position, statement of activities, statement of cash flows, and accompanying notes. VHWOs must also provide a statement of functional expenses.

Within the financial statements, NFP organizations classify net assets, revenues, expenses, gains, and losses according to three classes of **net assets**—unrestricted, temporarily restricted, and permanently restricted—based on the existence or absence of donor-imposed restrictions. The three classes of net assets are defined as follows:

■ **Permanently restricted net assets** are the portion of net assets whose use is limited by donor-imposed stipulations that do not expire by time and cannot be removed by action of the NFP entity.

---

[1]An organization may also be considered a government if it has the ability to issue tax-exempt debt directly; however, if this is the only governmental characteristic that it possesses, the organization can dispute the presumption that it is governmental in nature.

[2]FASB published a notice to constituents that explains the scope, structure, and usage of FASB ASC. Constituents can read the notice and the full ASC at https://asc.fasb.org/ at no charge in a basic view.

- **Temporarily restricted net assets** are the portion of net assets whose use is limited by donor-imposed stipulations that either expire (time restrictions) or can be removed by the organization fulfilling the stipulations (purpose restrictions).
- **Unrestricted net assets** are the portion of net assets that carry no donor-imposed stipulations.[3]

Organizations can report revenues, gains, and losses in each net asset class, but expenses are reported only in the unrestricted net assets class.

**STATEMENT OF FINANCIAL POSITION**   The statement of financial position or balance sheet reports assets, liabilities, and net assets. It reports net assets in total and by the three classes of net assets—unrestricted, temporarily restricted, and permanently restricted. Permanently and temporarily restricted amounts appear on the face of the balance sheet or in notes. Assets received with donor-imposed restrictions that limit their use to long-term purposes should be separated from assets available for current use. Comparative statements from the prior period are not required.

**STATEMENT OF ACTIVITIES**   The statement of activities provides information about the change in amount and nature of net assets and reports how resources are used to provide various programs or services. NFP organizations account for revenues and expenses using the accrual basis of accounting. NFP organizations that issue GAAP-basis financial statements must recognize depreciation expense on long-lived assets. NFP organizations should record depreciation even if the assets are gifts; however, certain works of art and certain historical treasures that meet the definition of "collections" need not be capitalized or depreciated.

The statement of activities focuses on the organization as a whole. It reports the amount of change in net assets, ending with a net asset figure that is the same as net assets on the balance sheet. The statement presents revenues, expenses, gains, and losses by net asset class; thus, there are columns or sections reporting the amount of change in permanently restricted net assets, temporarily restricted net assets, and unrestricted net assets.

NFP revenues, described in detail later, increase unrestricted net assets unless use of the assets received is limited by donor-imposed restrictions. Gains and losses on investments are increases or decreases in unrestricted net assets unless their use is restricted by explicit donor stipulations or by law. Expenses always decrease unrestricted net assets; thus, they cannot appear in the temporarily restricted or permanently restricted net asset classes. Temporarily restricted or permanently restricted net assets consist of donor-restricted contributions whose restrictions have not yet been met. If restrictions placed on donor-restricted contributions are met in the same reporting period in which the contribution is made, the organization may report the contribution as unrestricted as long as the organization follows a consistent policy. Reclassifications between net asset classes are reported separately.

Generally, NFP organizations report revenues and expenses at gross amounts. Gains and losses from peripheral or incidental transactions or events beyond the control of the organization may be reported at net amounts, and investment income is reported net of related expenses. Further classifications of revenues, expenses, gains, and losses (such as operating or nonoperating, recurring or nonrecurring, and so on) are optional, except for VHWOs which must report functional expenses.

NFP organizations report expenses by functional classification—major classes of program services and supporting services—in the statement or notes. *Program services* are the activities that distribute goods and services that fulfill the purpose or mission of the organization to beneficiaries, customers, or members. *Supporting services* are all activities other than program services. Supporting services include the following:

- **Management and general.**  Oversight, business management, general record-keeping, budgeting, financing, and related administrative activities
- **Fund-raising.**  Publicizing and conducting fund-raising campaigns; maintaining donor mailing lists; conducting special fund-raising events; preparing and distributing fund-raising manuals, instructions, and other materials; and other activities to solicit contributions
- **Membership-development activities.**  Soliciting for prospective members and membership dues, membership relations, and so on

---

[3]Based on FSB ASC 958, © Anthony H Joseph

**STATEMENT OF FUNCTIONAL EXPENSES** VHWOs must report expenses classified by function and by natural classification (salaries, rent, etc.) in a matrix format as a separate statement. Other NFP organizations are encouraged, but not required, to provide this additional expense information.

**STATEMENT OF CASH FLOWS** NFP organizations use the same cash flow classifications and definitions as business enterprises, except that the description of financing activities is expanded to include resources that are donor restricted for long-term purposes. The NFP statement of cash flows reports investing activities of permanent endowments as cash flows of investing activities.

When preparing the balance sheet, organizations cannot aggregate cash restricted for long-term purposes with cash available for current uses in the balance sheet. Similarly, they should exclude cash and cash equivalents that are restricted for long-term purposes from cash in the cash flows statement.

NFP organizations are encouraged to use the direct method for presenting cash flows, but are allowed to use the indirect method. Organizations that select the direct method must provide a schedule to reconcile the change in net assets in the statement of activities to net cash flows from operating activities.

## Contributions

For some NFP entities, contributions are a major source of revenue. GAAP defines a **contribution** as "an unconditional transfer of cash or other assets to an entity or a settlement or cancellation of its liabilities in a voluntary, nonreciprocal transfer by another entity acting other than as an owner."[4] Examples of other assets include buildings, securities, the use of facilities or services, and unconditional promises to give. GAAP describes a *promise to give* as a written or oral agreement to contribute cash or other assets to another entity. The promise should be verifiable by evidence such as pledge cards or tape recordings of oral promises. A promise to give may be conditional or unconditional.

A **conditional promise to give** depends on the occurrence of a specified future and uncertain event to bind the promisor.[5] For example, a church parishioner may pledge to contribute a sum of money if a local government approves a proposed church renovation. Organizations recognize conditional promises to give as contribution revenue and receivables when the conditions are substantially met (in other words, when the conditional promise to give becomes unconditional); however, they account for a conditional gift of cash or other asset that may have to be returned to the donor if the condition is not met as a refundable advance (liability). Disclosures in notes to the financial statements for conditional promises to give include the total amounts promised and a description and amount for any group of promises having similar characteristics (i.e., a specific project or goal).

An **unconditional promise to give** depends only on the passage of time or demand by the promisee for performance.[6] Promises to give are unconditional if the possibility that a condition will not be met is remote. Organizations recognize unconditional promises to give as contribution revenue and receivables in the period in which the promise is received. They report such promises as restricted support (in other words, as contribution revenues in temporarily restricted net assets, based on the time restriction), even if the resources are not restricted for specific purposes, until cash is received and available for expenditure.[7] NFP entities should disclose both anticipated time frame for receipt (amounts of unconditional promises receivable in less than one year, in one to five years, and in more than five years) and the allowance for uncollectible promises receivable.

Generally, NFP organizations measure restricted and unrestricted contributions at fair value and recognize them as revenues or gains in the period in which they are received. As previously noted, contributions are separated into the three classes of net assets on the statement of activities: those that increase unrestricted net assets, those that increase temporarily restricted net assets, and those that increase permanently restricted net assets.

**DONOR-IMPOSED RESTRICTIONS OR CONDITIONS** A **donor-imposed condition** provides that the donor's money is returned or the donor is released from the promise to give if the condition is not met.

---

[4]FASB ASC 720-25. Originally 'Other Expenses.' Norwalk, CT: Financial Accounting Standards Board, 2014.

[5]From Paragraph 22, Statement of Financial Accounting Standards No. 116, Accounting for Contributions Received and Contributions Made © 1993 FASB

[6]From Appendix D: GLOSSARY, Statement of Financial Accounting Standards No. 116, Accounting for Contributions Received and Contributions Made © 1993 FASB.

[7]An exception is provided when the donor explicitly stipulates that the contribution is intended to support current-period activities, in which case it is reported as unrestricted support.

**Donor-imposed restrictions** simply limit the use of contributed assets. If it is unclear whether donor stipulations are conditions or restrictions, the organization should presume that the promise is conditional. A donor-imposed restriction expires in the period in which the restriction is satisfied (i.e., when a time restriction is met or a purpose restriction satisfied). If a given contribution is subject to more than one restriction, the restrictions expire in the period in which the last restriction is satisfied.

When a temporary restriction is met (either by the passage of time or by the incurrence of expenses for the restricted purpose), organizations reclassify resources from the temporarily restricted net assets category to the unrestricted net assets category. On the statement of activities, they report the reclassified amount as net assets released from restrictions. These assets increase unrestricted net assets and decrease temporarily restricted net assets. If donor-imposed restrictions are met in the same period in which the contributions are received, organizations may report the contributions as unrestricted if the following conditions are met: (1) The policy must be disclosed in the notes and followed consistently, and (2) the organization must have the same policy for temporarily restricted investment income whose restrictions are met in the same period as income is recognized.

GIFTS OF LONG-LIVED ASSETS    Gifts of long-lived assets may be restricted or unrestricted, depending on the organization's accounting policy or the donor's restriction. If the donor restricts contributed long-lived assets for use over a certain period of time, recipients report the assets as restricted support in temporarily restricted net assets. Later, the recipient organization recognizes depreciation by reclassifying the amount of the depreciation from temporarily restricted to unrestricted net assets and recording an expense in unrestricted net assets.

If the donor contributes the long-lived assets with no restrictions or if the assets are purchased with contributions restricted to the acquisition of long-lived assets, the organization can choose either of two accounting methods, which should be used consistently. The accounting policy must be disclosed in notes to the financial statements. The two acceptable methods are as follows:

1. The organization may adopt an accounting policy that implies a time restriction that *expires over the useful life* of the donated asset. As in the case of contributed long-lived assets with an explicit donor-imposed time restriction, the gift is reported as restricted support in temporarily restricted net assets. Depreciation is recorded as an expense in unrestricted net assets, and a reclassification for the amount of the depreciation from temporarily restricted to unrestricted net assets. (This also applies to assets purchased with cash that was restricted to the purchase of long-lived assets.)

2. If no policy implying a time restriction exists and there are no donor-imposed restrictions, the gifts are *unrestricted support.*

INVESTMENTS AND INVESTMENT INCOME    NFP organizations initially record purchased investments at their cost and contributed investments at fair value in the appropriate net asset classification. They recognize investment income as earned and report the income as an increase in unrestricted, temporarily restricted, or permanently restricted net assets, depending on donor-imposed restrictions on the use of the investment income. GAAP (ASC 958-320) requires organizations to report investments in debt securities at their fair values. Investments in equity securities that have readily determinable fair values also must be reported at fair values. Changes in fair values are reported in the statement of activities. The fair-value accounting requirement does not apply to equity investments that are accounted for by the equity method or investments in consolidated subsidiaries.

## Transfers That Are Not Contributions

Contributions do not include several items: transfers that are exchange transactions; transfers in which the NFP enterprise is acting as an agent, trustee, or intermediary for the donor; or possibly gifts in kind.

EXCHANGE TRANSACTIONS    Exchange transactions are reciprocal transfers in which both parties give and receive approximately equal value. Sales of products and services are exchange transactions. Exchange transactions are sometimes difficult to distinguish from contributions. Assume that an NFP organization sends calendars (premiums) to potential donors in a fund-raising appeal. The recipients keep the premium whether or not they make a donation. In this case, the donations that result from the calendar mailing are contributions, and the cost of premiums is a fund-raising expense. The same is true if the NFP organization gives the premiums only to donors, but the premiums are nominal in relation to the donations. If donors receive gifts that approximate the value of their donations, however, the transaction is an exchange.

Dues charged to members of NFP entities may have characteristics of both contributions and exchange transactions. The portion of the dues representing contributions will be recognized as revenue when received, but the portion representing an exchange transaction will be recognized as revenue as it is earned.

Resources received in exchange transactions are classified as unrestricted revenues and unrestricted net assets even if the resource provider limits use of the resources.

**AGENCY TRANSACTIONS**    An agency transaction is one in which assets are transferred to the NFP organization, but the NFP organization has little or no discretion over the use of those assets, and the assets are passed on to a third party. The resource provider is using the NFP entity as an agent or intermediary to transfer assets to a third-party donee. For example, the United Way often acts as an agent by collecting contributions for distribution to a number of local organizations. Under GAAP (ASC 958-605), the receipt of assets in an agency transaction increases the assets and liabilities of the NFP agent, and disbursement of those assets decreases assets and liabilities. No contribution revenue or program expense is recorded by the agent.[8] The NFP agent reports the cash received and paid as cash flows from operating activities in the statement of cash flows.

**GIFTS IN KIND**    Gifts in kind are noncash contributions, such as clothing, furniture, and services. They are contributions if the NFP entity has discretion over the disposition of the resources. Otherwise, the entity will account for the gifts as agency transactions. Organizations measure gifts in kind that are contributions at fair value, if practicable. When fair value cannot be reasonably determined, NFP entities should not record the gifts as contributions. Instead, they record the items as sales revenue when they are sold. Cost of sales is the cost of getting the inventory ready for sale. GAAP (ASC 958-605-25-16) limits the recognition of contributed services to those that (1) create or enhance nonfinancial assets of the organization or (2) require specialized skills, are provided by individuals possessing those skills, and would typically need to be purchased if not provided by donation.[9] If contributed services do not meet these criteria, they should not be recognized; however, information about services contributed to the organization's programs and activities should be described in the financial statement notes.

## Measurement Principles

NFP organizations measure contributions at fair value. Quoted market prices are the best estimate of fair values for both monetary and nonmonetary assets. Other valuation methods that might be used include quoted market prices for similar assets or independent appraisals. If a reasonable estimate for fair value cannot be made, the contribution should not be recognized.

Recall that NFP organizations record unconditional promises to give when pledges are made. If the fair value of the contributed asset changes significantly between the pledge date and the date the asset is received, the NFP entity accounts for the contribution as follows:

- No additional revenue is recognized if the fair value increases.
- If the fair value decreases, the difference is recognized in the period the decrease occurred and is reported as a change in the net asset class in which the revenue was originally reported or in the class where the net assets are represented.

---

[8]There is pressure on not-for-profits to report a high percentage of their expenses going to programs rather than management or fund-raising expenses. If an entity booked both contribution revenues and program expenses, it would improve (a.k.a overstate) the "program ratio," usually defined as program expenses divided by total expenses. Thus, it matters for accountability purposes to not record "pass-through" funds on the statement of activities.

[9]Accounting Standards Update No. 2013–06 provides clarification if the person donating services works for an affiliate of the not-for-profit, since there was divergence in practice. These donated services should be recorded at the cost of the personnel if this does not significantly over- or understate the value of the service received; otherwise, the organization can elect to record the services at either the cost or fair value.

An NFP entity may record unconditional promises to give that it expects to collect within one year of the financial statement date at their net realizable value (gross amount less an allowance for uncollectible accounts). However, the entity should measure unconditional promises to give that are not expected to be collected within the year at the present value of the amounts expected to be collected (estimated future cash flows).[10]

## Collections

Collections of works of art, historical treasures, and similar items may be capitalized but are not required to be so long as the following conditions are satisfied:

- They are held for public exhibition, education, or research in furtherance of public service rather than financial gain.
- They are protected, kept encumbered, cared for, and preserved.
- They are subject to an organizational policy that requires proceeds from sales of collection items to be used to acquire other items for collections.[11]

Organizations that choose not to capitalize collections should describe the collections in the notes to the financial statements. Contributed collection items are recognized as revenues or gains if the collection is capitalized.

When collection items are not recognized, the costs of collection items, proceeds from sales, and proceeds from insurance recoveries appear as increases or decreases of the appropriate net asset class on the activities statement, separately from revenues, expenses, gains, and losses.

## Fund Accounting

NFP entities receive resources from contributions, charges for services, grants, appropriations, and so on, and the use of some of these resources is restricted for specific activities or purposes. Fund accounting principles provide a convenient method for segregating the accounting records of resources restricted for specific purposes. Many NFP organizations choose to use fund accounting for internal accounting, although FASB issuances and the AICPA guide do not require fund accounting. Although GAAP allows fund reporting as additional information, fund information is rarely presented in financial statements of nongovernmental NFP organizations.

## VOLUNTARY HEALTH AND WELFARE ORGANIZATIONS

LEARNING OBJECTIVE **22.4**

VHWOs encompass a diverse group of NFP entities that are supported by and provide voluntary services to the public. They may expend their resources to solve basic social problems in the areas of health or welfare either globally, nationally, at the community level, or on an individual basis. Examples include charities such as the March of Dimes or the American Cancer Society, Girl Scouts of the USA, Boy Scouts of America, and Meals on Wheels. VHWOs follow FASB standards, and the 2016 *AICPA Audit and Accounting Guide: Not-for-Profit Entities* provides additional, but no longer authoritative, guidance.

## Accounting for a VHWO

A group of concerned citizens organized a VHWO called Neighbors Helping Neighbors (NHN). The following journal entries provide examples of some typical accounting procedures for this organization.

CONTRIBUTIONS    As part of its fund-raising effort in 2016, NHN distributed decals to all residents in the community. The decals cost NHN $145. As a result of the campaign, the organization received unrestricted cash contributions of $4,000 and unconditional promises to give totaling $6,000. Of this $6,000 contribution receivable, $2,000 is not collectible until 2017. A presumption exists that

---

[10]See FASB ASC 820 for general coverage of fair value and FASB ASC 985-605-30 for specific guidance related to not-for-profits.

[11]© Anthony H Joseph

the $2,000 due in 2017 is restricted for use in 2017. NHN estimates that 10 percent of the pledges will be uncollectible and makes the following entries in 2016:

| | | |
|---|---:|---:|
| Expenses—supporting services—fund-raising | 145 | |
|     Cash | | 145 |
| To record payment for decals used in fund-raising. | | |
| Cash | 4,000 | |
|     Unrestricted support—contributions | | 4,000 |
| To record cash contributions. | | |
| Contributions receivable | 6,000 | |
|     Allowance for uncollectible contributions | | 600 |
|     Unrestricted support—contributions | | 3,600 |
|     Temporarily restricted support—contributions | | 1,800 |
| To record unrestricted promises to give, promises restricted for use in 2017, and estimated uncollectibles. | | |

NHN collected $3,600 of the contributions receivable due in 2016 and wrote off the remaining $400 as uncollectible:

| | | |
|---|---:|---:|
| Cash | 3,600 | |
| Allowance for uncollectible contributions | 400 | |
|     Contributions receivable | | 4,000 |
| To record collection of contributions receivable. | | |

The following two journal entries do *not* pertain to 2016, and thus are not utilized in the closing entries on pages 727–728. Assume NHN collects the full $2,000 due in 2017 during that year. When the receivables are collected, NHN reports any difference between the estimated amount of uncollectibles and the actual amount as a gain or loss in the appropriate net asset class. The implied time restriction is met, so NHN reclassifies $1,800 of temporarily restricted net assets as unrestricted net assets:

| | | |
|---|---:|---:|
| Cash | 2,000 | |
| Allowance for uncollectible contributions | 200 | |
|     Contributions receivable | | 2,000 |
|     Unrestricted support—contributions | | 200 |
| To record collection of receivables and recognize support for the difference between the estimated and actual allowance for uncollectible amounts. | | |
| Temporarily restricted net assets—reclassifications out | 1,800 | |
|     Unrestricted net assets—reclassifications in | | 1,800 |
| To reclassify net assets for which the restriction has been met. | | |

A donor gives NHN $1,000 that is restricted for a playground project. NHN purchases supplies for the playground project for $900 and reports the expenses as changes in unrestricted net assets. The organization makes an entry to reclassify $900 of temporarily restricted net assets. The reclassification is entered even though unrestricted resources were used to pay for the playground supplies:

| | | |
|---|---:|---:|
| Cash | 1,000 | |
|     Temporarily restricted support—contributions | | 1,000 |
| To record a gift restricted for a special project. | | |
| Expenses—program services—community service | 900 | |
|     Cash | | 900 |
| To record purchase of supplies used in the playground project. | | |
| Temporarily restricted net assets—reclassifications out | 900 | |
|     Unrestricted net assets—reclassifications in | | 900 |
| To reclassify net assets restricted for the playground project for which the restriction has been met. | | |

As shown earlier, a VHWO classifies its expenses as program services or supporting services and reports them on a functional basis under these classifications (e.g., community service, recreation programs, and fund-raising). Program services relate to the expenses incurred in providing the organization's social service activities. Supporting services consist of administrative expenses and fund-raising costs.

**DONATED LONG-LIVED ASSETS**    NHN has a policy of implying a time restriction on donated fixed assets over the life of each asset. On January 1, 2016, Martin Construction donated a used van to the organization. The fair value of the van is $1,500, and it has a three-year remaining useful life. The van will be used in the organization's community service program.

NHN initially records the donated van as temporarily restricted support. Later, NHN records depreciation expense on the van as a program expense. The amount of depreciation expense is reclassified from temporarily restricted net assets to unrestricted net assets, because all expenses decrease unrestricted net assets.

| | | |
|---|---|---|
| Equipment | 1,500 | |
|     Temporarily restricted support—contributions | | 1,500 |
|   To record receipt of donated van. | | |
| Expenses—program services—community service | 500 | |
|     Accumulated depreciation—equipment | | 500 |
|   To record depreciation. | | |
| Temporarily restricted net assets—reclassifications out | 500 | |
|     Unrestricted net assets—reclassifications in | | 500 |
|   To record reclassification of net assets for which the temporary restriction is satisfied. | | |

**SPECIAL EVENT FUND-RAISERS**    A fund-raising event for NHN featured a dinner and dance. Ticket sales for the dinner totaled $950, and expenses of the fund-raiser amounted to $650. VHWOs generally report gross revenues and expenses for special events related to the major ongoing activities of the organization in which attendees receive a benefit. If the special event is incidental to the activities of the organization, the organization may report the proceeds of the special event as gains net of direct costs:

| | | |
|---|---|---|
| Cash | 950 | |
|     Unrestricted gains—special event | | 950 |
|   To record proceeds from a fund-raising event. | | |
| Unrestricted gains—special event | 650 | |
|     Cash | | 650 |
|   To charge costs of fund-raising event against support from the event. | | |

**GIFTS IN KIND**    Throughout the summer, NHN receives donations of used housewares and furniture that are then sold at a rummage sale held in August. Fair values for the donated items cannot be reasonably determined, but the cost of storing and moving the items to the rummage sale location is $550. Proceeds from the sale are $6,595. Because the fair value cannot be determined, NHN cannot record the items as contributions:

| | | |
|---|---|---|
| Cost of goods sold | 550 | |
|   Cash | | 550 |
|   To pay costs of storing and moving rummage sale items. | | |
| Cash | 6,595 | |
|     Unrestricted revenues—sales | | 6,595 |
|   To record proceeds from rummage sale. | | |

Alternatively, if the fair value of donated items can be reasonably determined, the gifts in kind are recorded as contributions. Office-Mate Company donates office supplies with a fair value of

$390 to NHN. Office-Mate puts no restrictions on the use of the donated items. The organization records the gift as follows:

| | | |
|---|---|---|
| Materials and supplies inventory | 390 | |
| Unrestricted support—contributions | | 390 |
| To record receipt of office supplies. | | |

**MEMBERSHIP FEES**   Memberships give members certain benefits, such as the right to receive the organization's newsletters. Dues from members may represent exchange transactions, contributions, or both, depending on the benefits provided to members. Revenues from exchange transactions are classified as unrestricted and are recognized as revenue as benefits are provided. Dues received when member benefits are negligible are recognized as contributions when received with a credit to "unrestricted support—contributions."

In cases in which the fair value of member benefits is less than the amount of dues, VHWOs divide the transfers between contributions and revenues. An organization may have different levels of memberships, but the more-expensive memberships do not necessarily entitle the members to additional benefits. The excess payments are classified as contributions. NHN offers regular memberships for $10 and sustaining memberships for $50 and over. All members are entitled to the same newsletter and local discount coupons that are distributed when the dues are received. NHN received 500 regular memberships ($5,000) and 130 sustaining memberships ($6,500), which it records as follows:

| | | |
|---|---|---|
| Cash | 11,500 | |
| Unrestricted revenues—dues | | 6,300 |
| Unrestricted support—contributions | | 5,200 |
| To record revenue and support from the sale of memberships. | | |

**DONATED SECURITIES AND INVESTMENT INCOME**   NHN receives securities (fair value of $5,000) with a stipulation that they permanently endow a park enhancement project. Income earned on the securities is restricted to use for the park enhancement project. Dividend income is $475:

| | | |
|---|---|---|
| Securities | 5,000 | |
| Permanently restricted support—contribution | | 5,000 |
| To record receipt of securities permanently restricted for a park enhancement project. | | |
| Cash | 475 | |
| Temporarily restricted revenue—investment income | | 475 |
| To record investment income restricted for a park enhancement project. | | |

**SUPPLIES**   NHN had supplies on hand of $1,600 at January 1, 2016. The organization purchased supplies for $1,500 during the year and received donations of supplies that had a fair value of $2,050 in addition to the $390 already received. At the end of 2016, the inventory on hand was $750. The supplies used were allocated to recreation programs, $2,000; community service programs, $1,400; fund-raising expenses, $600; and management and general $790:

| | | |
|---|---|---|
| Materials and supplies inventory | 3,550 | |
| Unrestricted support—contributions | | 2,050 |
| Cash | | 1,500 |
| To record donated materials and supplies and to record purchase of supplies. | | |
| Expenses—supporting services—management and general | 790 | |
| Expenses—program services—recreation programs | 2,000 | |
| Expenses—program services—community service | 1,400 | |
| Expenses—supporting services—fund-raising | 600 | |
| Materials and supplies inventory | | 4,790 |
| To record allocation of supplies expense. | | |

**DONATED SERVICES AND PAYMENT OF SALARIES**  An accounting firm donated its services to audit the books of NHN. The audit would have cost the association $1,200 if the services had not been donated. NHN also paid salaries allocated to program services and supporting services as follows: recreation programs, $6,000; community services, $4,000; management and general, $1,500; and fund-raising $500:

| | | |
|---|---:|---:|
| Expenses—supporting services—management and general | 1,200 | |
|     Unrestricted support—donated services | | 1,200 |
|   To record donated services allocated to management and general expenses. | | |
| Expenses—program services—recreation programs | 6,000 | |
| Expenses—program services—community service | 4,000 | |
| Expenses—supporting services—management and general | 1,500 | |
| Expenses—supporting services—fund-raising | 500 | |
|     Cash | | 12,000 |
|   To record salaries allocated to program services and supporting services. | | |

**DEPRECIATION**  Equipment owned by NHN is used to travel through the neighborhood and provide park programs. There are no explicit or implicit donor-imposed restrictions on the fixed assets, so the equipment has been recorded as an unrestricted asset. The organization allocates the $8,000 depreciation expense on the equipment to its program services and supporting services as follows:

| | | |
|---|---:|---:|
| Expenses—program services—recreation programs | 3,000 | |
| Expenses—program services—community service | 4,000 | |
| Expenses—supporting services—management and general | 1,000 | |
|     Accumulated depreciation | | 8,000 |
|   To record depreciation allocated to program services and supporting services. | | |

**FIXED ASSET PURCHASE WITH RESTRICTED RESOURCES**  NHN purchased equipment costing $4,000. The equipment was financed by $3,000 from contributions with donor-imposed restrictions that were accumulated for the purchase of the equipment and $1,000 from general resources:

| | | |
|---|---:|---:|
| Equipment | 4,000 | |
|     Cash | | 4,000 |
|   To record payment for the purchase of equipment. | | |
| Temporarily restricted net assets—reclassifications out | 3,000 | |
|     Unrestricted net assets—reclassifications in | | 3,000 |
|   To record reclassification of temporarily restricted net assets. | | |

**CLOSING ENTRIES**  NHN's closing entries for 2016 are as follows:

| | | |
|---|---:|---:|
| Unrestricted support—contributions | 15,240 | |
| Unrestricted revenues—dues | 6,300 | |
| Unrestricted support—donated services | 1,200 | |
| Unrestricted revenues—sales | 6,595 | |
| Unrestricted gains—special event | 300 | |
| Unrestricted net assets—reclassifications in | 4,400 | |
|     Expenses—program services—community service | | 10,800 |
|     Expenses—program services—recreation programs | | 11,000 |
|     Expenses—supporting services—fund-raising | | 1,245 |
|     Expenses—supporting services—management and general | | 4,490 |
|     Cost of goods sold | | 550 |
|     Unrestricted net assets | | 5,950 |

| | | |
|---|---:|---:|
| Temporarily restricted support—contributions | 4,300 | |
| Temporarily restricted revenue—investment income | 475 | |
| Temporarily restricted net assets—reclassifications out | | 4,400 |
| Temporarily restricted net assets | | 375 |
| Permanently restricted support—contribution | 5,000 | |
| Permanently restricted net assets | | 5,000 |

## Financial Reporting

Exhibits 22-1 to 22-4 present sample financial statements for NHN. The basic financial statements of nongovernmental VHWOs include the same statements required for other NFP organizations (a statement of financial position, a statement of activities, and a statement of cash flows). The statement of activities reports revenues in the net asset class to which they relate, using the accrual basis of accounting. Revenues with no donor-imposed restrictions increase unrestricted net assets; revenues with donor-imposed restrictions increase temporarily restricted or permanently restricted net assets. Expenses decrease unrestricted net assets only. Note that expenses are classified as either program services or supporting services and are reported on a functional basis under these classifications (e.g., community service, recreation programs). The functional basis of reporting expenses results in an informative but highly aggregated form of statement presentation. To overcome the limitations of aggregation, VHWOs prepare an additional, separate statement of functional expenses, as shown in Exhibit 22-4. This statement reconciles the functional classifications with basic object-of-expense classifications such as salaries, supplies, professional fees, and depreciation.

A national VHWO may have financially interrelated local affiliates. Unless the local organizations are independent of the national organization, with separate purposes and separate governing boards, the financial statements of the national and local organizations are combined for reporting in accordance with GAAP.

---

**EXHIBIT 22-1**

Balance Sheet for
Nongovernmental
Voluntary Health and
Welfare Organization

**NEIGHBORS HELPING NEIGHBORS (A VHWO)**
**STATEMENTS OF FINANCIAL POSITION**
**DECEMBER 31, 2016, AND 2015**

| | 2016 | 2015 |
|---|---:|---:|
| *Assets* | | |
| Cash and cash equivalents | $22,375 | $14,000 |
| Inventories | 750 | 1,600 |
| Contributions receivable (less allowance of $300 in 2016 and $100 in 2015) | 2,200 | 400 |
| Short-term investments | 1,000 | 1,000 |
| Land, buildings, and equipment (less accumulated depreciation of $16,500 in 2016 and $8,000 in 2015) | 34,000 | 37,000 |
| Assets restricted for endowment | 10,000 | 5,000 |
| Total assets | $70,325 | $59,000 |
| | | |
| *Liabilities and Net Assets* | | |
| Liabilities | | |
| Accounts payable | $ 2,300 | $ 2,300 |
| Grants payable | 1,550 | 1,550 |
| Mortgage payable | 3,000 | 3,000 |
| Interest payable | 50 | 50 |
| Total liabilities | $ 6,900 | $ 6,900 |
| | | |
| Net assets | | |
| Unrestricted | $24,350 | $18,400 |
| Temporarily restricted | 29,075 | 28,700 |
| Permanently restricted | 10,000 | 5,000 |
| Total net assets | 63,425 | 52,100 |
| Total liabilities and net assets | $70,325 | $59,000 |

**EXHIBIT 22-2**

**Statement of Activities**

**NEIGHBORS HELPING NEIGHBORS (A VHWO)**
**STATEMENT OF ACTIVITIES**
**FOR THE YEAR ENDED DECEMBER 31, 2016**

| | | | |
|---|---:|---:|---:|
| *Changes in Unrestricted Net Assets* | | | |
| Revenues and gains | | | |
| Contributions | | $15,240 | |
| Membership dues | | 6,300 | |
| Donated services | | 1,200 | |
| Sales, net | | 6,045 | |
| Special event | $950 | | |
| Less: Direct costs | 650 | 300 | |
| Total unrestricted revenues and gains | | | $29,085 |
| Net assets released from restrictions | | | |
| Satisfaction of program restriction | | 900 | |
| Expiration of time restriction | | 3,500 | |
| Total net assets released from restrictions | | | 4,400 |
| Total unrestricted revenues, gains, and | | | 33,485 |
|    other support | | | |
| Expenses and losses | | | |
| Program services | | | |
| Community service | | 10,800 | |
| Recreation programs | | 11,000 | 21,800 |
| Supporting services | | | |
| Fund-raising | | 1,245 | |
| Management and general | | 4,490 | 5,735 |
| Total expenses and losses | | | 27,535 |
| Increase in unrestricted net assets | | | 5,950 |
| | | | |
| *Changes in Temporarily Restricted Net Assets* | | | |
| Contributions | | 4,300 | |
| Income on investments | | 475 | |
| Net assets released from restrictions | | (4,400) | |
| Increase in temporarily restricted net assets | | | 375 |
| *Changes in Permanently Restricted Net Assets* | | | |
| Contributions | | | 5,000 |
| Increase in net assets | | | 11,325 |
| Net assets at the beginning of the year | | | 52,100 |
| Net assets at the end of the year | | | $63,425 |

**EXHIBIT 22-3**

**Statement of Cash
Flows (Indirect Method)**

**NEIGHBORS HELPING NEIGHBORS (A VHWO)**
**STATEMENT OF CASH FLOWS—INDIRECT METHOD**
**FOR YEAR ENDED DECEMBER 31, 2016**

| | | |
|---|---:|---:|
| *Cash Flows from Operating Activities* | | |
| Change in net assets | | $11,325 |
| Adjustments to reconcile change in net assets to net | | |
|   cash provided by operating activities | | |
| Depreciation | $8,500 | |
| Increase in net contributions receivable | (1,800) | |
| Decrease in inventories | 850 | |
| Noncash contribution of equipment | (1,500) | |
| Noncash contribution of securities | (5,000) | 1,050 |
| Net cash provided by operating activities | | 12,375 |
| | | |
| *Cash Flows from Investing Activities* | | |
| Cash paid for equipment | (4,000) | |
| Net cash used for investing activities | | (4,000) |
| | | |
| *Cash Flows from Financing Activities* | | |
| Net cash used in financing activities | | — |
| Increase in cash and cash equivalents | | 8,375 |
| Cash and cash equivalents at beginning of year | | 14,000 |
| Cash and cash equivalents at end of year | | $22,375 |

**EXHIBIT 22-4**

Statement of Functional Expenses

## NEIGHBORS HELPING NEIGHBORS (A VHWO)
## STATEMENT OF FUNCTIONAL EXPENSES
## FOR THE YEAR ENDED DECEMBER 31, 2016

|  | Total | Community Service | Recreation Programs | Fund-Raising | Management and General |
|---|---|---|---|---|---|
| Salaries | $12,000 | $ 4,000 | $ 6,000 | $  500 | $1,500 |
| Supplies | 5,835 | 2,300 | 2,000 | 745 | 790 |
| Professional fees | 1,200 | — | — | — | 1,200 |
| Depreciation | 8,500 | 4,500 | 3,000 | — | 1,000 |
|  | $27,535 | $10,800 | $11,000 | $1,245 | $4,490 |

## "OTHER" NOT-FOR-PROFIT ORGANIZATIONS

As noted earlier, NFP classifications include four categories corresponding to four previously published AICPA audit and accounting guides: VHWOs, health care entities, colleges and universities, and other NFP organizations. The "other" category encompasses a variety of organizations, such as cemetery associations, civic organizations, libraries, museums, social organizations, political organizations, and religious organizations. The accounting and financial reporting for each of these entities is quite similar to that for the VHWO illustrated previously, although the statement of functional expenses would be optional. In fact, "other" NFPs follow the same FASB ASC and are discussed in the 2016 umbrella *AICPA Audit and Accounting Guide: Not-for-Profit Entities*, which supersedes and consolidates the AICPA guides for VHWOs, colleges and universities, and other NFP organizations. Because the accounting for other NFP organizations is similar to the previous example provided, this book chapter does not provide further illustrations.

## NONGOVERNMENTAL NOT-FOR-PROFIT HOSPITALS AND OTHER HEALTH CARE ORGANIZATIONS

Hospitals and other health care providers constitute a significant area of accounting, both in terms of the entities represented and the cost of services provided. Health care providers include clinics, ambulatory care organizations, continuing-care retirement communities, health maintenance organizations, home health agencies, hospitals, government-owned health care entities, and nursing homes that provide health care. Health care entities may be organized as NFP entities, governmental entities, or private business enterprises owned by investors (stockholders, partners, or sole proprietors).

Since 2009, the authoritative source of GAAP for nongovernmental NFP health care organizations has been FASB ASC 958 on NFP organizations (discussed earlier) and FASB ASC 954[12] on health care organizations (discussed in the following section). Topic Code 954 relates to both for-profit and NFP health care organizations, while GASB is the source of GAAP for governmental health care organizations. As with NFP organizations, the AICPA maintains an industry "audit and accounting guide," revised in 2016 to reflect the FASB ASC. The AICPA guide provides guidance (not authoritative since 2009) on accounting and reporting for both governmental and nongovernmental health care organizations, even though there are significant differences between the two. Although the FASB and GASB have responsibility for setting accounting standards, the AICPA guide is likely to continue as a useful resource for both accounting and auditing professionals.

The discussion in this chapter generally refers to hospitals as a matter of convenience, but the principles apply to other health care organizations as well. Accounting and reporting for a nongovernmental NFP hospital are based on the same standards and principles as for any other nongovernmental NFP organization. However, there are unique characteristics of a health care entity that warrant specific discussion. First, health care entities have unique revenue sources,

---

[12]As noted earlier, the FASB created the NAC (Not-for-profit Advisory Committee) in 2009. Some of the members of the advisory group are health care experts. To reduce divergence in practice, the FASB issued four Accounting Standards Updates: 2010-23 on charity care; 2010-24 on insurance claims and recoveries; 2011-07 on patient revenue and bad debts; and 2012-01 on refundable advances in retirement communities. Current activities of the NAC are online at www.fasb.org/jsp/FASB/Page/SectionPage&cid=1176156543050.

such as patient service revenues and premium fees, and their expense classifications are relatively specialized. Also, health care organizations present a statement of financial position, a statement of operations, a statement of changes in net assets, and a statement of cash flows. The health care audit guide requires that the statement of operations, which replaces the statement of activities reported by other NFP organizations, report a performance measurement (such as excess of revenues over expenses or earned income) and the change in unrestricted net assets. These differences are covered in detail here.

## Accounting for a Nongovernmental Not-for-Profit Hospital

The following situations review typical activities often unique to a health care entity. The sample journal entries demonstrate how the activities are reflected in the accounting system of a nongovernmental, NFP hospital.

**PATIENT SERVICE REVENUE**    **Patient service revenues** include room and board, nursing services, and other professional services. Patient revenues are recorded at full established rates when service has been provided. However, because a hospital's objective is to report the amount of revenues that it will ultimately collect, adjustments are made for deductions from revenues, such as the following:

- **Courtesy allowances**. Discounts for doctors and employees
- **Contractual adjustments.** Discounts arranged with third-party payors (Medicare and Blue Cross, e.g.) that frequently have agreements to reimburse at less-than-established rates

Courtesy allowances and contractual adjustments are not expenses. They are revenue deductions that are subtracted from gross patient service revenues to arrive at the net patient service revenue reported in the statement of operations. In addition, bad debt expense is recorded and allowance accounts are used to reduce net receivables for estimated bad debts. **Charity care** services—those provided free of charge to patients who qualify under a hospital's charity care policy—are excluded from both gross and net patient service revenues, because they are not expected to generate cash flow.

Community General Hospital is a nongovernmental NFP hospital. Gross charges at established rates for services rendered to patients amounted to $1,300,000 during 2015. The hospital had contractual adjustments with insurers and Medicare of $300,000. Hospital staff and their dependents received courtesy discounts of $9,000. Bad debts are estimated at 2 percent of gross patient revenues. Community General records these transactions as follows:

| | | |
|---|---|---|
| Patient accounts receivable | 1,300,000 | |
|     Patient service revenues—unrestricted | | 1,300,000 |
|   To record patient service charges at established rates. | | |
| Courtesy discounts | 9,000 | |
| Contractual adjustments | 300,000 | |
|     Patient accounts receivable | | 309,000 |
|   To record courtesy discounts and contractual adjustments. | | |
| Bad debt expense | 26,000 | |
|     Allowance for uncollectible patient accounts receivable | | 26,000 |
|   To establish an allowance for uncollectible receivables. | | |

**PREMIUM FEES**    Premium fees, also known as subscriber fees or capitation fees, are revenues from agreements under which a hospital provides any necessary patient services (perhaps from a contractually established list of services) for a specific fee. The fee is usually a specific fee per member per month. Hospitals earn the agreed-upon fee whether the standard charges for services actually rendered are more or less than the amount of the fee—that is, without regard to services actually provided in the period. Therefore, hospitals report premium fees, which constitute a growing portion of revenues in many hospitals, separately from patient service revenues.

Community General Hospital receives premium revenue from capitation agreements totaling $454,000. The revenues are recognized as follows:

| | | |
|---|---|---|
| Cash | 454,000 | |
|     Premium revenue—unrestricted | | 454,000 |
| To record premium revenue from capitation agreements. | | |

**OTHER OPERATING REVENUES**   The "other operating revenue" classification includes revenue from services to patients other than for health care and revenues from sales and services provided to non-patients. This classification might include tuition from schools operated by the hospital, rentals of hospital space, charges for preparing and reproducing medical records, and proceeds from cafeterias, gift shops, and snack bars.

Throughout the year, Community General Hospital offers several health care courses, for which it charges tuition. Revenue for hospital space rental was $72,000 for the year, and the tuition charges for courses were $24,000. The hospital also receives revenue from the gift shop ($85,000) and cafeteria ($135,000). Community General records these other revenues as follows:

| | | |
|---|---|---|
| Cash (or accounts receivable) | 316,000 | |
|     Other operating revenue—unrestricted | | 316,000 |
| To record revenue from rentals, fees charged for courses, and gift shop and cafeteria proceeds. | | |

**GIFTS AND BEQUESTS**[13]   Community General Hospital received unrestricted cash donations of $25,000 and a $250,000 donation for a pediatric care room:

| | | |
|---|---|---|
| Cash | 275,000 | |
|     Unrestricted support—nonoperating gains | | 25,000 |
|     Temporarily restricted support | | 250,000 |
| To record receipt of contributions. | | |

**DONATED ASSETS**   Community General Hospital received marketable equity securities with a fair value of $500,000 that were donor restricted for the purchase of diagnostic equipment. (Income from the securities is also restricted.) Community General records the donation in a restricted fund until the funds are used to purchase the equipment:

| | | |
|---|---|---|
| Investments | 500,000 | |
|     Temporarily restricted support | | 500,000 |
| To record donation of securities. | | |

At year-end, Community General determined that the market value of the investment increased by $40,000:

| | | |
|---|---|---|
| Investments | 40,000 | |
|     Net realized and unrealized gains on investments—temporarily restricted | | 40,000 |
| To record receipt of investment appreciation restricted to the acquisition of diagnostic equipment. | | |

Assume that these securities, which now have a book value of $540,000, are sold for $600,000. The hospital uses the proceeds to purchase the diagnostic equipment, which costs $560,000, and records the following entries:

---

[13]Many hospitals have a separate fund-raising entity typically called a foundation, regardless of whether the hospital is governmental, not-for-profit, or investor-owned. Foundations collect unrestricted, temporarily restricted, and permanently restricted endowments. The results and condition of foundations can be reported separately, discretely presented with the hospital, or blended (i.e., combined) into the parent hospital depending on the circumstances.

| Cash | 600,000 | |
| Investments | | 540,000 |
| Temporarily restricted support—gain on the sale of investments | | 60,000 |

To record sale of securities.

| Equipment | 560,000 | |
| Cash | | 560,000 |

To record purchase of diagnostic equipment.

| Temporarily restricted net assets—reclassifications out | 560,000 | |
| Unrestricted net assets—reclassifications in | | 560,000 |

To record reclassification of net assets for which the temporary restriction is satisfied.

**OPERATING EXPENSES** Hospitals record operating expenses on an accrual basis and normally specify functional categories for nursing services (medical and surgical, intensive care, nurseries, operating rooms), other professional services (laboratories, radiology, anesthesiology, pharmacy), general services (housekeeping, maintenance, laundry), fiscal services (accounting, admissions, credits and collections, data processing), administrative services (personnel, purchasing, insurance, governing board), interest, and depreciation provisions.

The hospital accrues salaries and wages allocated to functional categories as follows: nursing services, $355,000; other professional services, $115,000; fiscal services, $112,000; and administrative services, $120,000:

| Nursing services expense | 355,000 | |
| Other professional services expense | 115,000 | |
| Fiscal services expense | 112,000 | |
| Administrative services expense | 120,000 | |
| Wages and salaries payable | | 702,000 |

To record accrual of payroll.

The hospital purchases materials and supplies for $110,000. The supplies usage by the major functional categories during the year is as follows: nursing services, $50,000; other professional services, $40,000; fiscal services, $5,000; and administrative services, $8,000:

| Inventory of materials and supplies | 110,000 | |
| Cash (or accounts payable) | | 110,000 |

To record purchase of supplies.

| Nursing services expense | 50,000 | |
| Other professional services expense | 40,000 | |
| Fiscal services expense | 5,000 | |
| Administrative services expense | 8,000 | |
| Inventory of materials and supplies | | 103,000 |

To record usage of materials and supplies.

Community General Hospital recognizes depreciation on its equipment ($50,000) and building ($20,000):

| Depreciation expense | 70,000 | |
| Accumulated depreciation—equipment | | 50,000 |
| Accumulated depreciation—building | | 20,000 |

To record depreciation on major equipment and building.

## Statement of Operations and Other Hospital Financial Statements

Basic statements for nongovernmental NFP health care entities consist of a balance sheet, or statement of financial position, a statement of operations, a statement of changes in net assets, and a statement of cash flows. Exhibits 22-5 to 22-8 illustrate these basic statements for a fictitious nongovernmental NFP hospital unrelated to the preceding journal entries. Note that the statement of operations and the statement of changes in net assets taken together present essentially the same information as a statement of activities. Also, in Exhibit 22-6, Care Hospital reports the excess of revenues, gains, and other support over expenses and losses, as well as the increase in unrestricted net assets. The statement of cash flows illustrated in Exhibit 22-8 is prepared using the indirect method.

**EXHIBIT 22-5**

Nongovernmental
Not-for-Profit Hospital
Statement of Financial
Position

### CARE HOSPITAL
### STATEMENT OF FINANCIAL POSITION
### DECEMBER 31, 2015

| | | | |
|---|---|---|---|
| *Current Assets* | | | |
| Cash and cash equivalents | | | $     60,000 |
| Investments | | | 540,000 |
| Accounts receivable—patients, less $120,000 | | | |
| estimated uncollectible receivables | | | 1,080,000 |
| Accounts receivable—Medicare | | | 400,000 |
| Receivable from limited-use assets | | | 100,000 |
| Inventories and prepaid items | | | 170,000 |
| Total current assets | | | 2,350,000 |
| | | | |
| *Noncurrent Assets* | | | |
| Assets whose use is limited | | | |
| by board for capital improvements | | | 230,000 |
| Property, plant, and equipment: | | | |
| Land | | $650,000 | |
| Buildings | $5,000,000 | | |
| Fixed equipment | 2,000,000 | | |
| Movable equipment | 1,500,000 | | |
| | 8,500,000 | | |
| Less: Accumulated depreciation | 2,800,000 | 5,700,000 | |
| Total property, plant, and equipment | | | 6,350,000 |
| Assets restricted for plant purposes | | | 300,000 |
| Assets restricted for endowment | | | 1,420,000 |
| Total assets | | | $10,650,000 |
| | | | |
| *Current Liabilities* | | | |
| Accounts payable | | | $    300,000 |
| Accrued interest | | | 150,000 |
| Accrued salaries | | | 210,000 |
| Payroll taxes payable | | | 140,000 |
| Accrued pension expense | | | 50,000 |
| Current portion of long-term debt | | | 100,000 |
| Total current liabilities | | | 950,000 |
| | | | |
| *Long-Term Debt* | | | |
| Notes payable | | | 500,000 |
| Bonds payable (net of current portion) | | | 900,000 |
| Mortgage payable | | | 3,000,000 |
| Total long-term liabilities | | | 4,400,000 |
| Total liabilities | | | 5,350,000 |
| | | | |
| *Net Assets* | | | |
| Unrestricted | | | $ 3,220,000 |
| Temporarily restricted | | | 660,000 |
| Permanently restricted | | | 1,420,000 |
| Total net assets | | | 5,300,000 |
| Total liabilities and net assets | | | $10,650,000 |

**CARE HOSPITAL**
**STATEMENT OF OPERATIONS**
**FOR THE YEAR ENDED DECEMBER 31, 2015**

| | | |
|---|---:|---:|
| *Unrestricted Revenues, Gains, and Other Support* | | |
| Net patient service revenues | $7,740,000 | |
| Other operating revenues | 950,000 | |
| Unrestricted donations | 150,000 | |
| Unrestricted income from endowments | 120,000 | |
| Income from board-designated funds | 20,000 | |
| Net assets released from restrictions upon satisfaction of program restrictions | 50,000 | |
|     Total unrestricted revenues, gains, and other support | | $9,030,000 |
| *Expenses and Losses* | | |
| Nursing services | $2,700,000 | |
| Other professional services | 1,800,000 | |
| General services | 1,500,000 | |
| Fiscal services | 500,000 | |
| Administrative services | 300,000 | |
| Medical malpractice costs | 180,000 | |
| Provision for uncollectible accounts | 600,000 | |
| Provision for depreciation | 400,000 | |
|   Total expenses and losses | | 7,980,000 |
| Excess (deficiency) of revenues, gains, and other support over expenses and losses | | 1,050,000 |
| Net assets released from restrictions for plant-asset purposes | | 20,000 |
| Increase in unrestricted net assets | | $1,070,000 |

**CARE HOSPITAL**
**STATEMENT OF CHANGES IN NET ASSETS**
**FOR THE YEAR ENDED DECEMBER 31, 2015**

| | Unrestricted | Temporarily Restricted | Permanently Restricted | Total |
|---|---:|---:|---:|---:|
| Balance, January 1, 2015 | $2,150,000 | $450,000 | $1,010,000 | $3,610,000 |
| Excess of revenues, gains, and other support over expenses and losses | 1,050,000 | — | — | 1,050,000 |
| Contributions | — | 270,000 | 300,000 | 570,000 |
| Restricted investment income | —. | 10,000 | 110,000 | 120,000 |
| Net assets released from restrictions | 20,000 | (70,000) | — | (50,000) |
| Changes in net assets | 1,070,000 | 210,000 | 410,000 | 1,690,000 |
| Balance, December 31, 2015 | $3,220,000 | $660,000 | $1,420,000 | $5,300,000 |

## PRIVATE NOT-FOR-PROFIT COLLEGES AND UNIVERSITIES

The primary objective of a college or university is to provide educational services to its constituents. Like governmental entities, colleges and universities often provide their services on the basis of social desirability and finance them, at least in part, without reference to those receiving the benefits. For example, very bright students may receive a full academic scholarship, or needy students might receive federal subsidies and financial aid to cover the costs of their education. The objectives of college and university accounting are to show the sources from which resources have been received and to demonstrate how those resources have been utilized in meeting educational objectives.

The primary authority over accounting principles for private (nongovernmental) colleges and universities is the FASB ASC. FASB standards have been incorporated into the *AICPA Audit and Accounting Guide: Not-for-Profit Entities*, which provides accounting and reporting guidance (nonauthoritative since 2009) for private colleges and universities as well as VHWOs and other NFP organizations. In addition to the audit guide, much college and university implementation guidance comes from the *Financial Accounting and Reporting Manual*, an accounting manual prepared by

EXHIBIT 22-8

Nongovernmental
Not-for-Profit Hospital
Statement of Cash
Flows

**CARE HOSPITAL**
**STATEMENT OF CASH FLOWS (INDIRECT METHOD)**
**FOR THE YEAR ENDED DECEMBER 31, 2015**

| | | |
|---|---:|---:|
| *Cash Flows from Operating Activities and Gains and Losses* | | |
| Change in net assets | | $1,690,000 |
| Adjustments to reconcile change in net assets to net cash provided by operating activities | | |
| Provision for depreciation | $400,000 | |
| Provision for uncollectible accounts | 600,000 | |
| Decrease in Medicare accounts receivable | 40,000 | |
| Decrease in unearned interest (limited-use assets) | 15,000 | |
| Increase in accounts payable and accrued expenses | 60,000 | |
| Increase in patient accounts receivable | (195,000) | |
| Increase in inventories and supplies | (40,000) | 880,000 |
| Net cash provided by operating activities and gains and losses | | 2,570,000 |
| *Cash Flows from Investing Activities* | | |
| Purchase of property, plant, and equipment | (2,280,000) | |
| Purchase of investments | (300,000) | |
| Cash invested in limited-use assets | (350,000) | |
| Net cash used by investing activities | | (2,930,000) |
| *Cash Flows from Financing Activities* | | |
| Proceeds from contributions restricted for investment in endowment | 300,000 | |
| Other financing activities | | |
| Proceeds from long-term note payable | 500,000 | |
| Repayment of bonds payable | (100,000) | |
| Repayment of mortgage note payable | (800,000) | |
| Net cash used by financing activities | | (100,000) |
| Net decrease in cash for 2015 | | (460,000) |
| Cash and cash equivalents at beginning of year | | 520,000 |
| Cash and cash equivalents at end of year | | $60,000 |

the National Association of College and University Business Officers (NACUBO). The required financial statements of private NFP colleges and universities are the same as those for VHWOs, except for the statement of functional expenses.

Colleges and universities maintain accounts and reports on an accrual basis; thus, revenues are recognized when earned, and expenses are recognized when the related materials or services are received. They report expenses by function, either on the face of the financial statements or in the notes. As with other NFP organizations, private institutions classify net assets, revenues, expenses, gains, and losses based on the existence or absence of donor-imposed restrictions (unrestricted, temporarily restricted, or permanently restricted), in accordance with the FASB ASC.

## Accounting for a Private Not-for-Profit College or University

This section presents several journal entries to illustrate the recording of typical events and transactions that would occur in a private NFP college or university.

**TUITION AND FEES** Private colleges and universities recognize the full amount of tuition and fees (net of refunds) assessed against students for educational purposes as revenue. Tuition waivers for scholarships appear in a contra revenue account, while estimated bad debts are recorded as institutional support expenses.

Student tuition and fees for Cane College total $1,000,000. Student tuition and fees also include $50,000 of tuition reductions provided under a fellowship program that requires no services on the part of the student. The college estimates bad debts at 3 percent of gross revenue from student tuition and fees, or $30,000. The following entries, recorded in the unrestricted category, reflect these events:

| | | |
|---|---|---|
| Accounts receivable | 1,000,000 | |
|     Unrestricted revenues—tuition and fees | | 1,000,000 |
|   To record tuition and fees. | | |
| Tuition reduction: Unrestricted—student aid | 50,000 | |
|     Accounts receivable | | 50,000 |
|   To record tuition reductions. | | |
| Expenses—educational and general—institutional support | 30,000 | |
|     Allowance for uncollectible accounts | | 30,000 |
|   To record allowance for uncollectible accounts. | | |

**APPROPRIATIONS FROM FEDERAL, STATE, AND LOCAL GOVERNMENTS**    Appropriations include unrestricted amounts for current operations that are received, or made available, from legislative acts or from a local taxing authority. Institutions may classify restricted appropriations as unrestricted if the governing board can change a restriction without going through a legislative process. Cane College receives appropriations on a per-student basis from the state totaling $700,000. The funds are unrestricted:

| | | |
|---|---|---|
| Cash | 700,000 | |
|     Unrestricted revenues—state appropriation | | 700,000 |
|   To record appropriations from the state government. | | |

**STUDENT FINANCIAL AID**    Universities often receive financial aid funds from third parties that are intended to be used by students to cover educational costs. For example, Cane College receives federal grants through the Pell Grant program in the amount of $150,000 for its students. Cane College plays an agency role by holding the funds until they are disbursed to the students. The funds are not considered revenue for the college:

| | | |
|---|---|---|
| Cash | 150,000 | |
|     Grant funds held for students | | 150,000 |
|   To record the receipt of Pell Grant funds. | | |
| Grant funds held for students | 150,000 | |
|     Cash | | 150,000 |
|   To record the distribution of Pell Grant funds. | | |

**CONTRIBUTIONS**    Universities record contributions that carry no specifications regarding the time period or purpose of use as unrestricted revenue, whereas they must record contributions that may only be expended after a point in time or for a specific purpose as temporarily restricted. Cane College received contributions totaling $300,000; $225,000 were unrestricted, and $75,000 were for alumni center renovations. An additional $12,000 was pledged for the center:

| | | |
|---|---|---|
| Cash | 300,000 | |
| Contributions receivable | 12,000 | |
|     Unrestricted revenues—contributions | | 225,000 |
|     Temporarily restricted revenues—contributions | | 87,000 |
|   To record contributions received and pledged. | | |

**ENDOWMENTS**    Universities record contributions of principal that must be held indefinitely but whose income is available for restricted or unrestricted purposes as special contributions termed *endowments*. At Cane College, an elderly alumnus established a $50,000 endowment to provide book scholarships for athletes. During the year, investment income on the endowment was $4,000, and book scholarships for Cane athletes totaled $2,500:

| | | |
|---|---:|---:|
| Cash | 50,000 | |
|     Permanently restricted revenues—endowment contribution | | 50,000 |
| To record receipt of an endowment. | | |
| Cash | 4,000 | |
|     Temporarily restricted revenues—endowment income | | 4,000 |
| To record endowment income. | | |
| Expenses: Unrestricted—student aid | 2,500 | |
|     Cash | | 2,500 |
| To record payment of scholarships. | | |
| Temporarily restricted net assets—reclassifications out | 2,500 | |
|     Unrestricted net assets—reclassifications in | | 2,500 |
| To record reclassification of net assets for which the temporary restriction is satisfied. | | |

**SALES AND SERVICES OF AUXILIARY ENTERPRISES**   The revenue of **auxiliary enterprises** includes amounts earned in providing facilities and services to faculty, staff, and students. It includes amounts charged for residence halls, food services, intercollegiate athletics, and college student unions, as well as sales and receipts from college stores, barber shops, movie houses, and so on. Colleges and universities classify all revenue and expenses directly related to the operations of auxiliary enterprises as "auxiliary" and report them as unrestricted.

The dining hall at Cane College had sales of $60,800 and purchased $30,000 worth of supplies during May. The supplies used by the auxiliary enterprise during the period amounted to $28,000. Salaries paid to auxiliary employees were $31,000. Summary entries are as follows:

| | | |
|---|---:|---:|
| Cash | 60,800 | |
|     Revenues—auxiliary enterprises | | 60,800 |
| To record sales and services related to auxiliary enterprises. | | |
| Supplies inventory | 30,000 | |
|     Cash (or accounts payable) | | 30,000 |
| To record purchase of supplies. | | |
| Expenses—auxiliary enterprises—supplies | 28,000 | |
|     Supplies inventory | | 28,000 |
| To record utilization of supplies related to auxiliary enterprises. | | |
| Expenses—auxiliary enterprises | 31,000 | |
|     Cash | | 31,000 |
| To record expenses for salaries of auxiliary enterprises. | | |

**SALES AND SERVICES OF EDUCATIONAL ACTIVITIES**   The sale of goods and services that are related incidentally to educational activities of the university can generate unrestricted revenue. Often, the goods and services sold are a by-product of training or instruction. An example of this revenue category is the dairy creamery of Cane College, which has $550 revenue from sales of its products.

| | | |
|---|---:|---:|
| Cash | 550 | |
|     Revenue—educational and general | | 550 |
| To record sales related to educational activities. | | |

**EXPENSES**   For reporting purposes, colleges and universities classify unrestricted expenses broadly, as either educational and general or as auxiliary enterprises. Expenses are further classified on a functional basis in the statement of activities. Functional classifications include the following:

- **Instruction.** Expenses for educational programs
- **Research.** Expenses to produce research outcome
- **Public service.** Expenses for activities to provide noninstructional services to external groups
- **Academic support.** Expenses to provide support for instruction, research, and publications (i.e., computing, libraries)
- **Student services.** Amounts expended for admissions and registrar, and amounts expended for students' emotional, social, and physical well-being
- **Institutional support.** Amounts expended for administration and the long-range planning of the university
- **Operation and maintenance of plant.** Expenses of operating and maintaining the physical plant (net of amounts to auxiliary enterprises and university hospitals)
- **Student aid.** Expenses from restricted or unrestricted funds in the form of grants, scholarships, or fellowships to students

Cane College incurred the following expenses in June: instruction, $45,000; research, $22,000; student services, $12,000; and institutional support, $3,500:

| | | |
|---|---|---|
| Expenses—educational and general—instruction | 45,000 | |
| Expenses—educational and general—research | 22,000 | |
| Expenses—educational and general—student services | 12,000 | |
| Expenses—educational and general—institutional support | 3,500 | |
| Cash (or payables) | | 82,500 |

To record expenses for June.

**PURCHASE OF PLANT ASSETS** Recall that property, plant, and equipment acquired by a NFP organization with unrestricted or restricted resources may be recorded at acquisition as unrestricted or temporarily restricted. If temporarily restricted, the assets are reclassified when depreciation is recognized.

Cane College purchases equipment with unrestricted assets in the amount of $35,000. Depreciation expense for the year is $3,500, and the equipment is allocated to each of the functional categories as shown here. The entries for the year are as follows:

| | | |
|---|---|---|
| Equipment | 35,000 | |
| Cash | | 35,000 |

To record purchase of equipment with unrestricted funds.

| | | |
|---|---|---|
| Expenses—educational and general—instruction | 1,300 | |
| Expenses—educational and general—research | 800 | |
| Expenses—educational and general—student services | 1,000 | |
| Expenses—educational and general—institutional support | 400 | |
| Accumulated depreciation | | 3,500 |

To record depreciation of equipment.

Cane College purchases land adjacent to the campus. The land costs $200,000, and financial resources were previously restricted for the purchase. The entries to record this transaction are as follows:

| | | |
|---|---|---|
| Land | 200,000 | |
| Cash | | 200,000 |

To record payment for the purchase of land.

| | | |
|---|---|---|
| Temporarily restricted net assets—reclassifications out | 200,000 | |
| Unrestricted net assets—reclassifications in | | 200,000 |

To record reclassification of temporarily restricted net assets.

## Financial Statements of Private Not-for-Profit Colleges and Universities

The required financial statements of private NFP colleges and universities include a statement of financial position, a statement of activities, and a statement of cash flows. There are several acceptable alternatives for the statement of activities, so long as revenues, expenses, and reclassifications are clearly shown and changes in net assets are presented by classification (unrestricted, temporarily restricted, and permanently restricted). One popular, acceptable alternative to the statement of activities is to present two other statements: a statement of unrestricted revenues, expenses, and other changes in unrestricted net assets; and a statement of changes in net assets. The statement of financial position need not be classified, but assets are generally shown in order of liquidity. The statement of cash flows may be prepared using either the direct or the indirect method.

Exhibits 22-9 to 22-11 illustrate sample statements for a fictitious university. (The statements are for illustrative purposes only. They have no relationship to the preceding sample journal entries for Cane College.)

**EXHIBIT 22-9**

Private Not-for-Profit College or University Statement of Activities

**ALMA MATER UNIVERSITY**
**STATEMENT OF ACTIVITIES**
**FOR THE YEAR ENDED JUNE 30, 2016**

| | |
|---|---:|
| *Revenues* | |
| Tuition and fees (net of allowances of $150,000) | $1,000,000 |
| State appropriations | 1,200,000 |
| Federal grants and contracts | 50,000 |
| Private grants and gifts | 400,000 |
| Endowment income | 75,000 |
| Sales and services of educational departments | 60,000 |
| Sales and services of auxiliary enterprises | 800,000 |
| Total current revenues | 3,585,000 |
| *Total net assets released from* | |
| *restrictions for operations* | 370,000 |
| Total revenues and reclassifications | 3,955,000 |
| *Expenses* | |
| Educational and general | |
| Instruction | 1,640,000 |
| Research | 850,000 |
| Public service and extension | 100,000 |
| Academic support | 50,000 |
| Student services | 40,000 |
| Institutional support | 90,000 |
| Operation and maintenance of plant | 80,000 |
| Student aid | 150,000 |
| Educational and general expenditures | 3,000,000 |
| Auxiliary enterprises | |
| Expenses | 865,000 |
| Total operating expenses | 3,865,000 |
| Net increase in unrestricted net asset | 90,000 |
| *Changes in temporarily restricted net assets:* | |
| Federal grants and contracts | 100,000 |
| Private grants and gifts | 250,000 |
| Endowment income | 20,000 |
| Net assets released from restrictions | (370,000) |
| Increase in temporarily restricted net assets | 0 |
| *Changes in permanently restricted net assets:* | |
| Private grants and gifts | 100,000 |
| Increase in permanently restricted net assets | 100,000 |
| Change in net assets | 190,000 |
| Net assets, July 1, 2015 | 535,000 |
| Net assets, June 30, 2016 | $ 725,000 |

**ALMA MATER UNIVERSITY**
**STATEMENT OF FINANCIAL POSITION**
**FOR THE YEAR ENDED JUNE 30, 2016**

| | 2016 | 2015 |
|---|---|---|
| *Assets* | | |
| Cash and cash equivalents | $ 95,000 | $25,000 |
| Investments | 500,000 | 400,000 |
| Accounts receivable (net of allowances) | 70,000 | 44,500 |
| Accrued interest receivable | 5,000 | — |
| Contributions receivable (net of allowances) | 20,000 | 15,000 |
| Loans to students | 7,500 | 5,000 |
| Inventories | 12,000 | 5,000 |
| Property, plant, and equipment (net of accumulated depreciation) | 175,500 | 190,500 |
| Total assets | $885,000 | $685,000 |
| *Liabilities* | | |
| Accounts payable | $ 90,000 | $75,000 |
| Students' deposits | 25,000 | 25,000 |
| Bonds payable | 45,000 | 50,000 |
| Total liabilities | 160,000 | 150,000 |
| *Net Assets* | | |
| Unrestricted | 190,000 | 100,000 |
| Temporarily restricted | 35,000 | 35,000 |
| Permanently restricted | 500,000 | 400,000 |
| Total net assets | 725,000 | 535,000 |
| Total liabilities and net assets | $885,000 | $685,000 |

**ALMA MATER UNIVERSITY**
**STATEMENT OF CASH FLOWS—INDIRECT METHOD**
**FOR THE YEAR ENDED JUNE 30, 2016**

| | | |
|---|---|---|
| *Cash Flows from Operating Activities* | | |
| Change in net assets | | $190,000 |
| Adjustments to reconcile change in net assets to net cash provided by operating activities | | |
| Depreciation | $15,000 | |
| Increase in investments | (100,000) | |
| Increase in net accounts receivable | (25,500) | |
| Increase in accrued interest receivable | (5,000) | |
| Increase in net contributions receivable | (5,000) | |
| Increase in inventories | (7,000) | |
| Increase in accounts payable | 15,000 | (112,500) |
| Net cash provided by operating activities | | 77,500 |
| *Cash Flows from Investing Activities* | | |
| Increase in loans to students | (2,500) | |
| Net cash used by investing activities | | (2,500) |
| *Cash Flows from Financing Activities* | | |
| Payment of bonds payable | (5,000) | |
| Net cash used by financing activities | | (5,000) |
| Increase in cash and cash equivalents | | 70,000 |
| Cash and cash equivalents at beginning of year | | 25,000 |
| Cash and cash equivalents at end of year | | $ 95,000 |

## Internal Accounting and Control—The AICPA Model

Traditionally, colleges and universities used fund accounting practices within their accounting systems. Many adopted a fund structure referred to as the *AICPA model*. Although NFP colleges and universities are now only required to report their resources based on restrictions rather than funds, the fund structure is often used for internal accounting and control. For this reason, the current

*AICPA Audit and Accounting Guide: Not-for-Profit Entities* includes the AICPA fund structure. The structure includes the following fund classifications: current operating, loan, endowment, annuity and life income, plant, and agency.

The **current operating funds** grouping includes resources that are expendable for operating purposes. The current operating funds grouping contains two subgroups—one for **unrestricted current funds** and the other for **restricted current funds**.

The **loan funds** group accounts for resources held by colleges and universities under agreements to provide loans to students (and possibly faculty and staff). The **endowment fund** group consists of gifts with specifications about the manner in which the cash or donated item should be maintained and distributed. A separate fund is used for each endowment. **Annuity and life income funds** account for special types of endowment funds whereby the donor or a specified beneficiary receives a return from the gift for a specified period of time. After that time, the remainder of the gift belongs to the educational institution.

The *plant funds* group comprises four subgroups: unexpended plant funds, renewal and replacement funds, retirement of indebtedness funds, and investment in plant accounts. Colleges and universities use the first three funds to account for their financial resources, and the last subgroup (the investment in plant accounts) to account for the physical plant and related long-term debt. Institutions use **unexpended plant funds** to account for resources held for additions and improvements to the physical plant, whereas they use **renewal and replacement funds** for resources held for renewal and replacements of the existing plant. Fund assets of a **retirement of indebtedness fund** consist of liquid resources for current debt service and investments held for future debt retirement, including sinking fund investments. The assets of the **investment in plant accounts** consist of the physical plant (land, buildings, improvements other than buildings, and equipment, which includes library books).

*Agency funds* are used to account for assets held by the college or university for individual students and faculty members and for their organizations. As with the agency funds of governmental entities, transactions of college and university agency funds only affect asset and liability accounts and do not result in revenues and expenses.

## SUMMARY

NFP organizations include a diverse group of governmental and private entities. Governmental NFP organizations must follow the GASB standards covered in prior chapters, whereas private NFP organizations look to the FASB for primary accounting guidance and the AICPA for supplemental accounting guidance. In recent years, the FASB has issued several statements aimed at improving comparability in the financial statements of all nongovernmental NFP entities that issue statements in accordance with GAAP. Thus, nongovernmental VHWOs, health care entities, and colleges and universities prepare a set of financial statements that present unrestricted net assets, temporarily restricted net assets, permanently restricted net assets, and total net assets, as well as changes in each class of net assets and in total.

Financial statements of nongovernmental NFP entities include the statement of financial position, statement of activities, and statement of cash flows. VHWOs also prepare a statement of functional expenses. Healthcare entities prepare a statement of operations and a statement of changes in net assets instead of the statement of activities. The financial statements and notes include all information required by GAAP and from which NFP entities are not specifically exempt, as well as information required by applicable specialized accounting and reporting principles and practices. The focus of the financial statements is on the entity as a whole.

## QUESTIONS

1. What statements are included in a set of financial statements for nongovernmental not-for-profit entities?
2. How does one determine whether a hospital, college, or voluntary health and welfare organization should be reported in accordance with FASB standards or GASB standards?
3. What is the authoritative status of *AICPA Audit and Accounting Guides* for not-for-profit and health care organizations as of 2016?
4. For nongovernmental NFP, explain the difference between a conditional promise to give and an unconditional promise to give.

5. For nongovernmental NFP, explain the difference between donor-imposed conditions and donor-imposed restrictions.

6. For nongovernmental NFP, how are unconditional promises to give with collections due in the next period accounted for?

7. For nongovernmental NFP, how is the expiration of a time restriction recognized?

8. For nongovernmental NFP, are gifts in kind always reported as unrestricted support that increases unrestricted net assets?

9. Expenses of voluntary health and welfare organizations include classifications for program services and supporting services. Explain these classifications.

10. What is the purpose of the statement of functional expenses of voluntary health and welfare organizations?

11. Are contributed services reported in the statement of activities of a nongovernmental voluntary health and welfare organization?

12. Health care entities frequently provide charity care to qualified individuals. How is charity care reported in the financial statements of a hospital?

13. How are net patient service revenues of hospitals measured, and in which hospital financial statement are they reported?

14. What are the major revenue groupings of hospitals? Give an example of a revenue item that would be included in each grouping.

15. Are provisions for bad debts and depreciation of hospitals reported as expenses? Explain.

16. Describe the difference in a set of financial statements for a governmental university and a private not-for-profit university.

17. When is the AICPA college guide model used?

18. Other than FASB standards and the AICPA guide, where can you find guidance on accounting and reporting issues for colleges and universities?

19. Describe the reporting requirements for a governmental not-for-profit entity with both governmental and business-type activities.

20. Identify the functional expense classifications for a university. Provide an example of each.

21. Discuss the two options that not-for-profit organizations have for recording donated fixed assets.

## EXERCISES

### E 22-1
### Multiple choice

1. Contributions that are restricted by a donor to a nongovernmental not-for-profit organization are reported as a part of:
   a  *Permanently restricted net assets*
   b  *Temporarily restricted net assets*
   c  *Unrestricted net assets*
   d  *Either permanently restricted or temporarily restricted net assets, depending on the terms of the restriction*

2. Unconditional promises to give are recognized as contribution revenue under GAAP when:
   a  *The promise is received*
   b  *The related receivable is collected*
   c  *The time or purpose restriction is satisfied*
   d  *The future event that binds the promisor occurs*

3. Which of the following is not a characteristic of a conditional promise to give?
   a  *It depends on the occurrence of a specified future and uncertain event to bind the promisor.*
   b  *The gift may have to be returned to the donor if the condition is not met.*
   c  *It is recognized as contribution revenue when the conditions are substantially met.*
   d  *It depends on demand by the promisee for performance.*

4. Contributed long-lived assets that are donor restricted for a certain time period are reported by a nongovernmental not-for-profit entity as:
   a  *Unrestricted support in unrestricted net assets*
   b  *Restricted support in permanently restricted net assets*
   c  *Restricted support in temporarily restricted net assets*
   d  *Unrestricted support in temporarily restricted net assets*

5. Long-lived assets are purchased by a nongovernmental not-for-profit entity with cash that was restricted for that purpose. The assets are reported in temporarily restricted net assets. Depreciation expense is reported in unrestricted net assets.

   a   *The depreciation expense is incorrectly reported.*

   b   *An amount equal to the depreciation is reclassified from temporarily restricted to unrestricted net assets.*

   c   *An amount equal to the depreciation is reclassified from unrestricted to temporarily restricted net assets.*

   d   *An amount equal to the depreciation is reported as revenues.*

## E 22-2
## Multiple choice

1. When a temporary restriction on resources of a nongovernmental not-for-profit entity is met by the incurrence of an expense for the restricted purpose:

   a   *The expense is reported in the statement of activities as an increase in unrestricted net assets.*

   b   *Amounts reported in the temporarily restricted net assets are reclassified as unrestricted net assets.*

   c   *The entry is a debit to expense and a credit to the program services.*

   d   *The expense is reported in restricted net assets.*

2. A nongovernmental not-for-profit entity gives donors a sweatshirt imprinted with its logo when they pay $25 dues. The value of the sweatshirt is approximately $25. This transaction is most likely reported as:

   a   *An exchange transaction*

   b   *An agency transaction*

   c   *A contribution*

   d   *A gift in kind*

3. How will a nongovernmental not-for-profit entity record an agency transaction in which it receives resources?

   a   *No entry is made in the accounts.*

   b   *Debit the asset account and credit contribution revenue.*

   c   *Debit the asset account and credit temporarily restricted net assets.*

   d   *Debit the asset account and credit a liability account.*

4. Unconditional promises to give that are collectible within one year of the financial statement date:

   a   *Should be reported at their gross amount*

   b   *Should be reported at the gross amount less an allowance for uncollectible accounts*

   c   *Should be reported at the present value of the amounts expected to be collected, using the donor's incremental borrowing rate*

   d   *Should not be reported until collected*

5. In preparing the statement of cash flows for a nongovernmental not-for-profit entity, cash contributions that are restricted for long-term purposes are classified as:

   a   *Operating activities*

   b   *Investing activities*

   c   *Financing activities*

   d   *None of the above*

## E 22-3
## Multiple choice

1. Which of the following statements is not required for nongovernmental voluntary health and welfare organizations that issue financial statements in accordance with GAAP?

   a   *Balance sheet*

   b   *Statement of support, revenues, and expenses, and changes in retained earnings*

   c   *Statement of functional expenses*

   d   *Statement of cash flows*

2. Voluntary health and welfare organizations:

   a   *Are required to use fund accounting principles to segregate unrestricted and restricted net assets*

   b   *May report fund accounting information as additional information*

   c   *Must report by funds if fund accounting principles are used for internal accounting purposes*

   d   *Are prohibited from reporting by funds, even if fund accounting is used for internal accounting purposes*

3. Fund-raising costs of voluntary health and welfare organizations are classified as:

   a   *Functional expenses*

   b   *Program services*

   c   *Supporting services*

   d   *Management and general expenses*

4. Volunteers collect money and nonperishable food for the Food Pantry, a nongovernmental VHWO, by going house to house once each year for donations. The services of the volunteers should be accounted for as follows:

   a  *The fair value of the service is estimated and recorded as contributions that increase unrestricted net assets.*

   b  *The fair value of the service is estimated and recorded as contributions that increase either unrestricted net assets or temporarily restricted net assets, depending on donor-imposed restrictions on the resources collected.*

   c  *The per diem wage rates of the donors are recorded in unrestricted net assets.*

   d  *None of the above*

5. Unconditional promises to give (pledges) of nongovernmental voluntary health and welfare organizations are recognized as revenue and support in the period in which:

   a  *The pledges are received*

   b  *Cash is received from the pledges*

   c  *All restrictions on pledged resources have been removed*

   d  *Pledged resources are expended*

## E 22-4
## Multiple choice

1. A university that is considered a special-purpose government:

   a  *Is generally required to follow GASB standards*

   b  *Is generally required to follow FASB standards*

   c  *Should refer to the AICPA Audit and Accounting Guide for governmental colleges and universities*

   d  *May choose whether to follow FASB, GASB, or AICPA guidelines*

2. The operations of dormitories and dining halls for colleges and universities are reported as:

   a  *Operating income*

   b  *Auxiliary operations*

   c  *Restricted income*

   d  *Specific-purpose income*

3. A university that follows the AICPA college model for internal control may have all of the following funds, *except*:

   a  *Property, plant, and equipment*

   b  *Loan*

   c  *Life income*

   d  *Endowment*

4. Required financial statements for a private, nongovernmental not-for-profit college include which of the following?

   a  *A statement of cash flows*

   b  *A statement of functional expenses*

   c  *A statement of changes in fund balances*

   d  *A statement of revenues, expenses, and other changes*

5. Grant funds received from the federal government and remitted directly to students provide an example of:

   a  *An exchange transaction*

   b  *An endowment*

   c  *An agency transaction*

   d  *A restricted contribution*

## E 22-5
## Multiple choice

1. Tuition waivers for scholarships are:

   a  *Not reflected in the accounting records*

   b  *Recorded in a contra revenue account*

   c  *Recorded as institutional support expenses*

   d  *None of the above*

2. Auxiliary enterprises in a college and university include all of the following, *except*:

   a  *Bookstore*

   b  *Research*

   c  *Cafeteria*

   d  *Dormitories*

3. Under GASB Statement No. 35, a state university (governmental) with only business-type activities may present:
   a *Fund financial statements*
   b *Government-wide financial statements*
   c *Only the financial statements required of enterprise funds*
   d *Condensed financial information*

4. Contributions of principal that must be held indefinitely but whose income is available for restricted or unrestricted purposes are termed:
   a *Bequests*
   b *Annuities*
   c *Endowments*
   d *Support*

5. Scholarships are classified as:
   a *Academic support*
   b *Student services*
   c *Institutional support*
   d *Student aid*

### E 22-6
### Multiple choice

1. A principal source of revenue for hospitals is from patient services. Patient services revenue for hospitals is recorded at:
   a *Amounts actually billed to patients*
   b *The hospital's full established rates for services provided*
   c *Amounts actually received from patients*
   d *Amounts actually billed to patients less discounts granted*

2. Premium fees:
   a *Are earned whether the standard charges for services actually rendered are more or less than the amount of the fee*
   b *Are earned only to the extent of services actually provided in the period*
   c *Must be returned to the subscriber if services are not provided*
   d *Are initially recorded as revenues collected in advance*

3. Oliver Hardwick, a roofing contractor, repaired the roof on the Mosely Clinic, a nongovernmental health care entity, at no charge to the clinic. The estimate for the job was $3,000.
   a *The donated services meet the criteria in FASB ASC and should be reported in the statement of operations as unrestricted support–donated services.*
   b *The donated services should be described in notes to the financial statements, but not included in the statement of operations.*
   c *Only donated services that directly provide health care to patients can be recognized in the financial statements.*
   d *The donated services are a direct addition to the current fund.*

4. Charity care provided by a not-for-profit hospital:
   a *Is reported as an operating expense in the statement of operations of unrestricted funds*
   b *Is reported as a deduction from gross patient service revenues in the statement of operations of unrestricted funds*
   c *Is excluded from both gross patient service revenue and expense*
   d *Is reported in the statement of functional expenses*

5. Discounts allowed to third-party payors in hospital accounting are recorded as:
   a *Charity care*
   b *Contractual adjustments*
   c *Courtesy allowances*
   d *Mandatory discounts*

### E 22-7
### Multiple choice

1. Hospital room charges for telephone and television rentals should be classified as:
   a *Patient service revenues*
   b *Other operating revenues*
   c *Nonoperating gains*
   d *Premium fees*

**2.** A hospital bills patients at gross rates and provides for courtesy allowances for employees when they settle their accounts at less than gross rates. In accordance with this system, the journal entry to record courtesy allowances would appear as:

*a Debit—cash; debit—courtesy allowance; credit—accounts receivable*
*b Debit—courtesy discount; credit—allowance for courtesy discounts*
*c Debit—cash; debit—patient service revenue; credit—accounts receivable*
*d Debit—accounts receivable; credit—courtesy allowances; credit—patient service revenue*

**3.** Unrestricted income from a nongovernmental health care entity's permanent endowment investments should be reported:

*a In the permanently restricted net assets as unrestricted support—nonoperating gains*
*b In the statement of operations as unrestricted support—operating gains*
*c In the statement of operations as unrestricted revenues—investment income*
*d In the permanently restricted net assets as restricted revenues—investment income*

**4.** Depreciation and amortization of hospital property and equipment:

*a Are required for both governmental and nongovernmental hospitals*
*b Are not recorded in the statement of operations, but accumulated depreciation is disclosed in the statement of financial position*
*c Are reported in the plant replacement and expansion fund of hospitals that use fund accounting*
*d Are optional on donated property*

**5.** A nongovernmental health care entity receives a gift of cash that is specified by the donor to be used for cancer research. The contribution will most likely be reported in:

*a Unrestricted net assets*
*b Temporarily restricted net assets*
*c Permanently restricted net assets*
*d Either a or b, depending on the mission and activities of the health care entity*

## E 22-8
## Not-for-profit expense classifications

A voluntary health and welfare organization summarizes its expenses by function, as follows:

| | |
|---|---|
| Education | $20,400 |
| Fund-raising | 11,400 |
| Management and general | 5,500 |
| Public health | 15,700 |
| Research | 12,000 |

**REQUIRED:** Determine the expenses for program services and for supporting services.

## E 22-9
## Journal entries—Various not-for-profit organizations

**1.** A nongovernmental VHWO receives $20,000 of unconditional promises to give with no donor-imposed restrictions. Of this amount, $14,000 is due during the current period and $6,000 is due in the next period. The organization estimates that 3 percent of the pledges will be uncollectible.

**2.** A nongovernmental VHWO receives a $200 cash gift that is restricted for use in a project to provide immediate assistance to qualified people with temporary hardships. Money is given to a qualified individual during the same period.

**3.** The Uptown Restaurant donated restaurant equipment to the Food Kitchen, a nongovernmental VHWO. The equipment had a fair value of $6,000 and a remaining useful life of four years, with no scrap value. No restrictions were imposed on the use of the equipment, either by the Uptown Restaurant or the Food Kitchen.

**4.** A donor contributed $8,000 to a homeless shelter that was restricted to the purchase of a new truck. The money was invested in a CD that pays 5 percent interest. Accrued interest on the investment totaled $215 at year-end. The income from the investment was also restricted for the purchase of a truck.

**5.** Orleans Community College assessed its students $750,000 tuition for the 2016 fall term. The college estimates bad debts will be 1 percent of the gross assessed tuition. Orleans's scholarship program provides for tuition waivers totaling $65,000. Because of class cancellations, $15,000 is refunded to the students.

**6.** Your State University received donations of $3 million in 2016 that were restricted to certain research projects on the feasibility of growing tobacco for pharmaceutical uses. The university incurred $1.2 million of expenses on this research in 2016.

**REQUIRED:** Prepare journal entries to account for these transactions. Include net asset classifications, where applicable.

## PROBLEMS

### P 22-1
### Journal entries—Various not-for-profit organizations

Three wealthy friends, Tom, Grant, and Karen, each decided to donate $5,000,000 to the not-for-profit organization of their choice. Each donation was made on May 21, 2016. Prepare the entries required for each of the recipient organizations under the following scenarios.

1. Tom chose to contribute to a local voluntary health and welfare organization, and no restrictions were placed on the use of the donated resources.
   a. Prepare the May 21, 2016, entry.
   b. Prepare any entries necessary in 2017 if $2,300,000 of the gift is used to finance operating expenses.

2. Grant contributed to a local private university, and the donation was restricted to research.
   a. Prepare the May 21, 2016, entry.
   b. Prepare any entries necessary in 2017 if $2,300,000 of the gift is used to finance research expenses.

3. Karen gave to the local hospital, and the donation was restricted for construction of a fixed asset.

   a. Prepare the May 21, 2016, entry.
   b. Prepare any entries necessary in 2017 if $2,300,000 of the gift is used to finance construction costs.

### P 22-2
### Journal entries—Voluntary health and welfare organization

At the beginning of 2016, the citizens of North Ptarmigan created Share Shop, a voluntary health and welfare organization. Share receives donations of money, nonperishable groceries, and household items from contributors. The food and household items are distributed free of charge to families on the basis of need. Share allocates expenses 80 percent to community services and 20 percent to management and general services, unless otherwise noted.

Share has one paid administrator with a yearly salary of $14,600. An accountant donates accounting services to Share that have a fair value of $900 and are allocated to management and general. Work is also performed by regular volunteers whose services cannot be measured.

A local transit company has provided free warehouse space for the operations of Share Shop. Fair value of rent for the warehouse is $3,000 a year. Utilities of $1,800 are paid by Share for 2016.

During the year, Share purchased supplies for $300. At December 31, 2016, the supplies inventory was insignificant. Expenses incurred in determining which families were eligible for Share's services, and other accounting and reporting expenses totaled $6,000.

Donated assets for 2016 included nonperishable groceries with a fair value of $60,000 and household items with a fair value of $40,000. During the year, Share Shop distributed three-fourths of the groceries and half of the household items. No portion of these distributions was allocated to management and general services.

In addition to the donated assets, Share received cash donations of $10,000 and pledges of $20,000. Share estimated that 10 percent of the pledges would be uncollectible. At year-end 2016, $15,000 of the pledges had been collected. Share estimates that only $1,000 of the remaining pledges will be uncollectible.

The town council of North Ptarmigan made a $25,000 grant to Share Shop that will be paid in January 2017.

**REQUIRED:** Prepare summary entries for Share Shop for 2016.

## P 22-3
## Statement of operations—Nongovernmental not-for-profit health care organization

The following selected items were taken from the accounts of Hometown Memorial Hospital, a not-for-profit hospital, at December 31, 2016:

*Debits*

| | |
|---|---|
| Administrative services | $310,000 |
| Contractual allowances | 400,000 |
| Depreciation | 200,000 |
| Employee discounts | 100,000 |
| General services | 290,000 |
| Loss on sale of assets | 50,000 |
| Nursing services | 1,000,000 |
| Other professional services | 500,000 |
| Provision for bad debts | 150,000 |

*Credits*

| | |
|---|---|
| Donated medicine | 300,000 |
| Income from investment in affiliate | 80,000 |
| Patient service revenues | 2,500,000 |
| Television rentals to patients | 50,000 |
| Unrestricted donations | 200,000 |
| Unrestricted income from investments of endowment funds | 270,000 |
| Restricted donations for fixed asset purchases | 300,000 |
| Restricted donations for specific operating purposes | 100,000 |

**REQUIRED:** Use the information given to prepare a statement of operations for Hometown Memorial Hospital for the year ending December 31, 2016. Assume that $80,000 of expenses were for purposes for which restricted donations were available and that fixed assets costing $97,000 were purchased from donations restricted for their purchase.

## P 22-4
## Journal entries and statement of activities—Nongovernmental not-for-profit college

The following information relates to revenues and expenses for a private not-for-profit college:

| | |
|---|---|
| *Tuition and Fees* | |
| Total assessed | $2,000,000 |
| Tuition waivers | 120,000 |
| *Appropriations* | |
| State | 800,000 |
| Local | 300,000 |
| *Auxiliary Enterprises* | |
| Sales | 500,000 |
| Expenses | 480,000 |
| *Endowment Income* | |
| Temporarily restricted to research | 70,000 |
| Unrestricted | 20,000 |
| *Private Gifts and Grants* | |
| Temporarily restricted to student scholarships | 300,000 |
| Unrestricted | 80,000 |
| *Expenses* | |
| Instruction | 2,100,000 |
| Research | 100,000 |
| Student services | 120,000 |
| Operation of plant | 180,000 |
| Scholarships (does not include tuition waivers) | 200,000 |

**REQUIRED:** Prepare journal entries and a statement of activities for the college. Assume all scholarships and research expenses were obtained from temporarily restricted funds.

### P 22-5
### Statement of activities—Nongovernmental not-for-profit organization

The following information was taken from the accounts and records of the Community Society, a nongovernmental not-for-profit organization. The balances are as of December 31, 2016, unless otherwise stated:

| | |
|---|---:|
| Unrestricted support—contributions | $3,000,000 |
| Unrestricted support—membership dues | 400,000 |
| Unrestricted revenues—investment income | 83,000 |
| Temporarily restricted gain on sale of investments | 5,000 |
| Expenses—education | 300,000 |
| Expenses—research | 2,300,000 |
| Expenses—fund-raising | 223,000 |
| Expenses—management and general | 117,000 |
| Temporarily restricted support—contributions | 438,000 |
| Temporarily restricted revenues—investment income | 22,500 |
| Permanently restricted support—contributions | 37,000 |
| Unrestricted net assets, January 1, 2016 | 435,000 |
| Temporarily restricted net assets, January 1, 2016 | 5,000,000 |
| Permanently restricted net assets, January 1, 2016 | 40,000 |

The unrestricted support from contributions was all received in cash during the year. Additionally, the society received pledges totaling $425,000. The pledges should be collected during 2017, except for the estimated uncollectible portion of $16,000. The society spent $3,789,000 of restricted resources on construction of a major capital facility during 2016, and $500,000 of research expenses were for research financed from restricted donations. Assume pledges of $425,000 are not recorded.

**REQUIRED:** Prepare the statement of activities for the Community Society for 2016.

### P 22-6
### Journal entries—Nongovernmental not-for-profit university

Prepare journal entries to record the following transactions in the appropriate funds of a nongovernmental not-for-profit university:

1. Tuition and fees assessed total $6,000,000. Eighty percent is collected by year-end, scholarships are granted for $200,000, and $100,000 is expected to be uncollectible.

2. Revenues collected from sales and services of the university bookstore, an auxiliary enterprise, were $800,000.

3. Salaries and wages were paid, $2,600,000. Of this amount, $170,000 was for employees of the university bookstore.

4. Unrestricted resources were used to service the long-term mortgage on the university's buildings, $1,000,000.

5. Mortgage payments totaled $960,000, of which $600,000 was for interest.

6. Restricted contributions for a specific academic program were received, $440,000.

7. Expenses for the restricted program were incurred and paid, $237,000.

8. Equipment was purchased from resources previously set aside for that purpose, $44,000.

### P 22-7
### Journal entries—Voluntary health and welfare organization

The Good Grubb Food for the Hungry Institute is a nongovernmental not-for-profit organization that provides free meals for the destitute in a large metropolitan area. Record the following transactions in the accounts of Good Grubb.

1. Cash gifts that were received last year, but designated for use in the current year, totaled $20,000. The cash was used in the current year for expenses.

2. Unrestricted pledges of $65,000 were received. Five percent of pledges typically prove uncollectible. Additional cash contributions during the year totaled $35,000.

**3.** Donations of food totaled $150,000. The inventory of food on hand decreased by $1,200 during the year.

**4.** Expenses were incurred as follows: salary of director, $10,000; facility rental, $8,000; purchases of food, $70,000; and supplies, $27,000. Supplies inventory increased by $5,000 during the year.

**5.** Restricted pledges of $300,000 were received during the year. The pledges are restricted for use in constructing a new kitchen and dining hall. Of the pledges received, 5 percent is expected to be uncollectible.

## P 22-8
### Journal entries—Nongovernmental not-for-profit health care organization

The Fort Collins Health Center is a nongovernmental not-for-profit health care organization. During the current year, the following occurred:

**1.** Gross charges at established rates for services rendered to patients amounted to $102,300. The clinic had contractual adjustments with insurers and Medicare of $30,000. Bad debts are estimated at 2 percent of gross charges.

**2.** The health center receives premium revenue from capitation agreements totaling $54,000.

**3.** The center also receives revenue of $16,000 from the pharmacy housed in its building.

**4.** The center paid salaries and wages allocated to functional categories as follows: nursing services, $35,000; other professional services, $11,000; general services, $10,000; fiscal services, $2,000; and administrative services, $20,000.

**5.** The health center receives a federal grant for $12,000. The money must be used for medical equipment.

**6.** Supplies costing $13,000 were purchased during the month, and $6,700 in nursing supplies were used.

**REQUIRED:** Prepare journal entries to account for these transactions. Include net asset classifications, where applicable.

## INTERNET ASSIGNMENT

1. Search the Internet for the financial statements of the United Way or a charity of your choice.
   a. Print a copy of the financial statements and bring them to class for discussion.
   b. Is the charity a VHWO? How can you tell?
   c. Are net assets properly classified into three categories?
   d. Are expenses classified into function categories on the face of the financial statements or in the notes?
   e. Were any temporarily restricted net assets reclassified as unrestricted? Can you determine the nature of the restrictions that were met?
2. Visit the AICPA's Web site. Select Publications and then select *Journal of Accountancy*. Find an article related to not-for-profits. Read the article and prepare a one-page summary.
3. Visit NACUBO's Web site. Locate the Accounting Advisory Reports. Select Business and Policy Areas and then choose Accounting. Under Accounting select Advisory Reports. View the most recent advisory report related to institutions of higher learning, and prepare a one-paragraph summary of its purpose.
4. Visit the GuideStar Web site and obtain the Form 990 for a local not-for-profit organization.
   a. Examine Part VIII of the 990 to determine gross receipts of the organization.
   b. Examine Part IX of the 990. What category contained the majority of the organization's expenses?
   c. From Part VII, note the salaries of officers.
   d. After examining Parts VII–IX, look at the mission in Part III. Do you think spending is in line with the organization's mission?

## SELECTED READINGS

American Institute of Certified Public Accountants. AICPA Audit and Accounting Guide: Health Care Organizations. New York: AICPA, 2016.

American Institute of Certified Public Accountants. AICPA Audit and Accounting Guide: Not-for-Profit Entities. New York: AICPA, 2016.

Benson, Martha L., Alan S. Glazer, and Henry R. Jaenicke. "Coping with NPO Standards—It's Not Difficult." Journal of Accountancy (September 1998), pp. 67–74.

Booker, Quinton. "Accounting for Transfers to Non-Profits That Raise or Hold Contributions for Others: An Overview of SFAS No. 136." National Public Accountant (February/March 2001), p. 14.

Financial Accounting and Reporting Manual for Higher Education. Washington, DC: National Association of College and University Business Officers, 2003. (Now available only as an online subscription service.)

Governmental Accounting Standards Board. Statement No. 29. "The Use of Not-for-Profit Accounting Principles by Governmental Entities." Norwalk, CT: Governmental Accounting Standards Board, 1995.

Governmental Accounting Standards Board. Statement No. 34. "Basic Financial Statements—and Management's Discussion and Analysis—for State and Local Governments." Norwalk, CT: Governmental Accounting Standards Board, 1999.

Governmental Accounting Standards Board. Statement No. 35. "Basic Financial Statements— and Management's Discussion and Analysis—for Public Colleges and Universities." Norwalk, CT: Governmental Accounting Standards Board, 1999.

Henry, Elaine, Oscar J. Holzmann, and Ya-wen Yang. "Fair Value Measurements, The Next Step." The Journal of Corporate Finance & Accounting (September/October 2007), pp. 89–94.

Statement of Financial Accounting Standards No. 93. "Recognition of Depreciation by Not-for-Profit Organizations." Stamford, CT: Financial Accounting Standards Board, 1987.

Statement of Financial Accounting Standards No. 116. "Accounting for Contributions Received and Contributions Made." Norwalk, CT: Financial Accounting Standards Board, 1993.

Statement of Financial Accounting Standards No. 117. "Financial Statements of Not-for-Profit Organizations." Norwalk, CT: Financial Accounting Standards Board, 1993.

Statement of Financial Accounting Standards No. 124. "Accounting for Certain Investments Held by Not-for-Profit Organizations." Norwalk, CT: Financial Accounting Standards Board, 1995.

Statement of Financial Accounting Standards No. 136. "Transfers of Assets to a Not-for-Profit Organization or Charitable Trust That Raises or Holds Contributions for Others." Norwalk, CT: Financial Accounting Standards Board, 1999.

Statement of Financial Accounting Standards No. 157. "Fair Value Measurements." Norwalk, CT: Financial Accounting Standards Board, 2006.

Statement of Financial Accounting Standards No. 159. "The Fair Value Option for Financial Assets and Financial Liabilities—Including an amendment of FASB Statement No. 115." Norwalk, CT: Financial Accounting Standards Board, 2007.

Statement of Financial Accounting Standards No. 164. "Not-for-Profit Entities: Mergers and Acquisitions— Including an amendment of FASB Statement No. 142." Norwalk, CT: Financial Accounting Standards Board, 2009.

# 23

# Estates and Trusts

Accountants often refer to estate and trust accounting as **fiduciary accounting**. This is because estate and trust managers operate in a good-faith custodial or stewardship relationship with beneficiaries of the estate or trust property. A *fiduciary* is a person who is held in particular confidence by other people. Fiduciaries may be executors, trustees, administrators, and guardians, depending on the nature of their duties and the demands of custom.

In legal terms, a **fiduciary** is an individual or an entity authorized to take possession of the property of others. Upon taking possession of estate or trust property, the fiduciary (e.g., trustee of a trust) has an obligation to administer it in the best interest of all beneficiaries. Although similar practices are used in accounting for estates and trusts, there are a number of differences between the two types of entities. These include the manner in which the entities are created, the objectives of their activities, and the life of their existence. This chapter discusses these differences and reviews and illustrates accounting practices for estates and trusts.

This chapter provides an overview of accounting for estates and trusts. You should recognize that these are very complex areas, from both accounting and legal viewpoints. Estates are subject to probate laws, which vary widely across the 50 states. Estates and trusts may also be subject to taxation. There are potential taxes on the value of estate assets (often referred to as *inheritance taxes*) at both the federal and state levels. Estates and trusts may also be subject to income taxes, once again at both the state and federal levels. Calculations of inheritance and income taxes may differ at the state and federal levels, and across the 50 states. More detailed coverage of these topics is left to advanced courses in law and tax accounting.

## CREATION OF AN ESTATE

An estate comes into existence at the death of an individual. If the deceased (**decedent**) had a valid will in force at the time of death, he or she is said to have died **testate**.[1] In the absence of a valid will, the decedent is said to have died **intestate**. The estate consists of the property of the decedent at the time of death. Ordinarily, a probate court appoints a **personal representative** of the decedent to take control of the property, but flexibility is provided if a valid will is in force. In this case, the personal representative may leave real or tangible personal property under the control of the person entitled to it under the terms of the will.

---

[1]People with sizable estates usually have an attorney draw up their wills. The attorney can provide for the eventual validation of the will and also help with estate planning so that property is distributed according to the client's wishes and taxes are minimized.

## PROBATE PROCEEDINGS

The personal representative of the deceased files a petition with the appropriate probate court requesting that an existing will be **probated**, that is, for the will to be validated. The hearing of the probate court to establish validity is called a **testacy proceeding** because it determines whether the deceased died testate or intestate. Under the **Uniform Probate Code (UPC)**, the term *personal representative* includes both executor and administrator, as well as other designations for persons who perform the same functions.

### Confirmation

A confirmation by a probate court that a will is valid means that the decedent died testate. Ordinarily, this leads to appointment of the personal representative named in the will as **executor** of the will. It also leads to the presumption that estate property will be distributed in accordance with the provisions of the will, in the absence of extenuating circumstances.

A person dies intestate when he or she dies without leaving a will. Failure of the probate court to validate a will submitted for probate also means that the decedent died intestate. In either case, the court appoints an **administrator** to take control of the estate and supervise the distribution of estate assets in accordance with applicable state laws.

### Uniform Probate Code

The state laws governing probate and distribution of estate property vary considerably and do not provide a uniform basis for classifying the legal and accounting characteristics of estates. Therefore, this chapter bases its discussion and illustrations on the UPC, which was approved by the National Conference of Commissioners on Uniform State Laws. The UPC has been approved by the American Bar Association, even though most states have not adopted it.

## ADMINISTRATION OF THE ESTATE

The executor or administrator of the estate is a fiduciary who is expected to observe the standards of care applicable to trustees. Appointment by a probate court gives the executor authority to carry out the written instructions of the decedent, including settlement and distribution of the estate. The executor is expected to perform this duty as expeditiously and efficiently as possible.

Within 30 days after appointment, the executor or administrator must inform the heirs and devisees of his or her appointment and provide selected information about certain other matters. **Heirs** are the persons entitled to the property of the decedent under the statutes of intestate succession. **Intestate succession** is the order in which estate property is distributed to the surviving spouse, parents, children, and so on, if any estate property is not effectively distributed by will. **Devisees** are those persons designated in a will to receive a *devise* (a testamentary disposition of real or personal property). Under the UPC, "to devise" means to dispose of real or personal property by will. A *specific devise* is the gift of an object, and a *general devise* is a gift of money.

### Intestate Succession

Under the UPC, as amended, the entire estate of a person who dies intestate passes to the spouse if (1) the decedent has no living descendants or (2) all surviving descendants are also descendants of the surviving spouse. If there are descendants from a prior marriage or relationship, the surviving spouse receives the first $100,000 (the amount varies by state) and one-half of the remaining intestate estate. The remaining part of the estate not passing to the spouse (or the entire estate if there is no surviving spouse) passes to the descendants as directed in the state code.

### Inventory of Estate Property

The executor or administrator is required to prepare and file an inventory of property owned by the deceased within three months of appointment. This inventory must list the property in reasonable detail and show the fair market value on the date of death for each item of property. Any encumbrance on the property (such as a lien or other claim) must also be disclosed for each item. This inventory is filed with the probate court, and additional copies must be provided to interested persons on request. If appraisers are employed to assist in valuing the property, their names and addresses must accompany the inventory. Subsequent discovery of property omitted from the inventory, or errors in valuing certain items, are corrected by preparing and filing a new or supplementary inventory. Personal items of limited value are usually excluded from the inventory.

## Exempt Property and Allowances

The UPC entitles the surviving spouse to a **homestead allowance** that is exempt from, and has priority over, all claims against the estate. The amount of the allowance varies, but in some states it is $15,000. In the absence of a surviving spouse, the minor children would share the allowance equally. The surviving spouse also has an entitlement of up to $10,000 (varies by state) in household furniture, automobiles, and personal effects from the estate, depending on whether or not the property has been used to secure a loan. In the absence of a surviving spouse, the minor children share this property jointly.

The surviving spouse and minor children who were dependent on the deceased are also entitled to a reasonable **family allowance** to be paid out of the estate property during the period in which the estate is being administered. This family allowance is exempt from and has priority over all claims except the homestead allowance.

## Claims Against the Estate

Under the UPC, the personal representative publishes a notice in a newspaper of general circulation in the county for three consecutive weeks. The purpose is to announce his or her appointment and to notify creditors to present their claims within four months of the date of first publication of the notice.

Claims against the estate *that arose before death* and were not presented within four months (or three years, if the required notice to creditors was not published) are barred forever against the estate, the personal representative, the heirs, and the devisees.

All claims against the decedent's estate *that arose after death* are barred as claims against the estate, the personal representative, the heirs, and the devisees unless presented as:

1. A claim based on a contract with the personal representative within four months after performance is due and discharged
2. Any other claim within four months after it arises

**CLASSIFICATION OF CLAIMS**   When estate assets are insufficient to pay all claims in full, the UPC provides that payments are made as follows:

1. Costs and expenses of administration of the estate
2. Reasonable funeral expenses and reasonable and necessary medical and hospital expenses of the last illness of the decedent
3. Debts and taxes with preference under federal or state law
4. All other claims

No preference is given for payment within a given class of claims.

**SECURED CLAIMS**   Payment of secured claims against the estate depends on the amount allowed if the creditor surrenders his or her security. However, if the assets of the estate are encumbered by mortgage, pledge, lien, or other security interest, the personal representative may pay the encumbrance if it appears to be in the best interests of the estate.

## ACCOUNTING FOR THE ESTATE

LEARNING OBJECTIVE **23.1**

The executor records the inventory of estate property in a self-balancing set of accounts that show:

1. The property for which responsibility has been assumed
2. The manner in which that responsibility is subsequently discharged

The executor does not accept responsibility for obligations of the decedent (testator), so the liabilities of the estate are not recorded until paid.

## Estate Principal and Income

The focus of fiduciary accounting lies in distinguishing between principal and income. That focus applies to accounting for both estates and trusts. Estates frequently realize income from investments between the time that the property inventory is filed by the executor and the time the estate is fully administered. A primary reason for dividing estate principal and income is that the beneficiaries are likely to be different. For example, some devises specified in the will are distributed from estate principal, but the income may accrue to the residual beneficiaries. **Residual beneficiaries** are those entitled to the remainder of the estate after all other rightful claims on the estate have been satisfied.

The National Conference of Commissioners on Uniform State Laws approved a Revised Uniform Principal and Income Act to provide guidance in distinguishing between estate principal and income. The act provides that expenses incurred in settling a decedent's estate be charged against the principal of the estate. These expenses include debts, funeral expenses, estate taxes, interest and penalties, family allowances, attorney's fees, personal representative's fees, and court costs.

Alternatively, income (less expenses) earned after death on assets included in the decedent's estate is distributed to the specific devisee to whom the property was devised. Any remaining income that accrues during the period of estate administration is distributed to the devisees in proportion to their interests in the undivided (residual) assets of the estate.

**ESTATE INCOME, GAINS, AND LOSSES**   In accounting for a decedent's estate, receipts due but unpaid at the date of death are a part of the estate principal. These include items such as interest, dividends, rents, royalties, and annuities due at the time of death. After death, earnings from income-producing property are estate income, unless the will specifically provides otherwise. That is, amounts earned for the items listed would be classified as income, rather than principal, if they came due during the period of estate administration. In accounting for interest income on bond investments included in the estate, no provision is made for amortization of bond premiums and discounts. This is because bonds (and other securities) are included in the inventory at fair market value, and any gains or losses on disposal are adjustments of estate principal.

Depreciation is a related matter that requires interpretation under the Uniform Principal and Income Act. The act provides that a reasonable allowance for depreciation be made on depreciable property of the estate, except that no depreciation is to be made on real property used by a beneficiary as a residence or on personal property held by a trustee who is not then making a depreciation allowance.

## ILLUSTRATION OF ESTATE ACCOUNTING

On April 1, 2015, Harry Olds entered the hospital with a terminal illness. He died on May 1, 2015, at the age of 70. Laura Hunt, Harry's daughter, was appointed executor of the estate by the probate court, which also confirmed that Harry had died testate. The will provided specific devises at estimated values to be awarded as follows:

| | |
|---|---:|
| Summer home to his daughter, Laura Hunt | $145,000 |
| 2012 Ford Taurus to his grandson, Gary Hunt | 12,000 |
| 200 shares of FFF stock to his friend, Michael Wallace | 10,000 |
| All other personal effects to Harry's widow, Gloria Olds | |

The following general devises of cash were also provided:

| | |
|---|---:|
| Laura Hunt, in lieu of fees as executor | $20,000 |
| Sara Tyson, Harry's housekeeper | 10,000 |
| First Methodist Church | 10,000 |
| Humane Society | 10,000 |
| Gloria Olds is to receive the income earned during the administration of the estate. | |
| The residue of the estate is to be placed in trust, with the income used to support Harry's widow during her lifetime. Upon her mother's death, Laura gets the remainder of the estate. | |

**EXHIBIT 23-1**

Inventory of Estate Assets

**HARRY OLDS, TESTATOR
INVENTORY OF ESTATE ASSETS
AS OF THE DATE OF DEATH ON MAY 1, 2015**

| Description of Property | Fair Value |
|---|---|
| Cash in Commercial National Bank | $30,000 |
| Cash in savings account at First National Bank, 6% annual interest | 93,000 |
| Certificate of deposit, 8 percent, 18 months, due August 1, 2015 (includes $10,000 accrued interest) | 110,000 |
| Certificate of deposit, 9 percent, one year, due July 1, 2015 (includes $7,500 interest) | 107,500 |
| Note receivable plus $1,500 accrued interest from George Stein, 10 percent, due June 1, 2015 | 21,500 |
| Rocky Mountain Power common stock, 1,000 shares | 40,000 |
| Southern Natural Gas common stock, 2,000 shares | 30,000 |
| Danville City 9 percent, $50,000 par municipal bonds | 58,000 |
| Interest on Danville City bonds, due June 1, 2015 | 1,875 |
| Dividends receivable—utility stocks | 1,500 |
| Summer home | 145,000 |
| FFF common stock, 200 shares | 10,000 |
| 2014 Ford Mustang | 12,000 |
| Personal effects* | — |
| | $660,375 |

*The probate court permitted Laura to exclude Harry's personal effects other than specific devises from the inventory. Submitted by Laura Hunt, executor, on June 15, 2015.

Laura informed the heirs and devisees of her appointment as executor of Harry's estate on May 19, 2015, and at the same time, placed the required notice to creditors in the newspaper. On June 15, 2015, she filed the estate inventory that appears in Exhibit 23-1 with the probate court.

Laura subsequently prepared the following entries to record transactions and events during the period of estate administration (all during 2015)[2]:

**MAY 19** Memorandum: Placed a notice in the *Montgomery News Messenger* that creditors of the estate of Harry Olds should present claims against the estate within four months.

**JUNE 15** Recorded the inventory of estate assets as of May 1:

| | | |
|---|---|---|
| Cash—principal (+A) | 30,000 | |
| Savings account (+A) | 93,000 | |
| Certificate of deposit, due August 1, 2015 (+A) | 100,000 | |
| Certificate of deposit, due July 1, 2015 (+A) | 100,000 | |
| Note receivable—George Stein (+A) | 20,000 | |
| Rocky Mountain Power common stock (+A) | 40,000 | |
| Southern Natural Gas common stock (+A) | 30,000 | |
| FFF Company common stock (+A) | 10,000 | |
| Danville municipal bonds (+A) | 58,000 | |
| Summer home (+A) | 145,000 | |
| 2014 Ford Mustang (+A) | 12,000 | |
| Interest receivable on CDs (+A) | 17,500 | |
| Interest receivable—George Stein (+A) | 1,500 | |
| Interest receivable—municipal bonds (+A) | 1,875 | |
| Dividends receivable—common stock (+A) | 1,500 | |
| Estate principal (+SE) | | 660,375 |

[2]This chapter treats the estate principal as a stockholders' equity–type account, to be consistent with other topics in the text.

**JUNE 16**   Cashed dividend checks received May 5 on utility stock:

| | | |
|---|---|---|
| Cash—principal (+A) | 1,500 | |
|     Dividends receivable—common stock (−A) | | 1,500 |

**JUNE 18**   Collected interest of $2,250 on Danville City bonds. Interest of $375 was earned after the date of death:

| | | |
|---|---|---|
| Cash—principal (+A) | 1,875 | |
| Cash—income (+A) | 375 | |
|     Interest receivable—municipal bonds (−A) | | 1,875 |
|     Estate income (R, +SE) | | 375 |

**JUNE 23**   Funeral expenses of $4,500 were paid:

| | | |
|---|---|---|
| Funeral expenses (E, −SE) | 4,500 | |
|     Cash—principal (−A) | | 4,500 |

**JUNE 24**   Collected the $20,000 George Stein note and $1,650 interest. Interest of $150 was earned after the date of death:

| | | |
|---|---|---|
| Cash—principal (+A) | 21,500 | |
| Cash—income (+A) | 150 | |
|     Note receivable—George Stein (−A) | | 20,000 |
|     Interest receivable—George Stein (−A) | | 1,500 |
|     Estate income (R, +SE) | | 150 |

**JUNE 25**   Discovered and cashed a certificate of deposit that matured on April 15 and was excluded from the estate inventory. The proceeds were $10,800:

| | | |
|---|---|---|
| Cash—principal (+A) | 10,800 | |
|     Assets subsequently discovered (−A) | | 10,800 |

**JUNE 28**   Paid hospital and medical bills in excess of amounts paid by Medicare and private health insurance policies:

| | | |
|---|---|---|
| Hospital and medical expenses (E, −SE) | 19,000 | |
|     Cash—principal (−A) | | 19,000 |

**JULY 1**   Cashed the certificate of deposit that was due on July 1:

| | | |
|---|---|---|
| Cash—principal (+A) | 107,500 | |
| Cash—income (+A) | 1,500 | |
|     Certificate of deposit (−A) | | 100,000 |
|     Interest receivable on CDs (−A) | | 7,500 |
|     Estate income (R, +SE) | | 1,500 |

**JULY 12**   Paid cash to general devisees as provided in the will:

| | | |
|---|---|---|
| Devise—Laura Hunt (E, −SE) | 20,000 | |
| Devise—Sara Tyson (E, −SE) | 10,000 | |
| Devise—First Methodist Church (E, −SE) | 10,000 | |
| Devise—Humane Society (E, −SE) | 10,000 | |
|     Cash—principal (−A) | | 50,000 |

**AUGUST 1**   Received interest from savings account for the quarter ending July 31:

| | | |
|---|---|---|
| Cash—income (+A) | 1,395 | |
|     Estate income (R, +SE) | | 1,395 |

**AUGUST 1**    Cashed in the certificate of deposit due August 1:

| | | |
|---|---|---|
| Cash—principal (+A) | 110,000 | |
| Cash—income (+A) | 2,000 | |
|     Certificate of deposit (−A) | | 100,000 |
|     Interest receivable on CDs (−A) | | 10,000 |
|     Estate Income (R, +SE) | | 2,000 |

**AUGUST 5**    Received dividend checks on utilities stock:

| | | |
|---|---|---|
| Cash—income (+A) | 1,500 | |
|     Estate income (R, +SE) | | 1,500 |

**AUGUST 15**    Paid a $500 mechanics bill on the Ford that was incurred on April 10, and submitted for payment on August 10:

| | | |
|---|---|---|
| Debts of decedent paid (E, −SE) | 500 | |
|     Cash—principal (−A) | | 500 |

**AUGUST 15**    Delivered specific devises as provided in the will. Personal effects not included in the estate inventory were left with the widow, Gloria Olds:

| | | |
|---|---|---|
| Devise—Laura Hunt (E, −SE) | 145,000 | |
| Devise to Gary Hunt (E, −SE) | 12,000 | |
| Devise to Michael Wallace (E, −SE) | 10,000 | |
|     Summer home (−A) | | 145,000 |
|     2014 Ford Mustang (−A) | | 12,000 |
|     FFF Company common stock (−A) | | 10,000 |

**AUGUST 28**    Payment of attorney fees and court costs:

| | | |
|---|---|---|
| Attorney fees paid (E, −SE) | 4,500 | |
| Court costs paid (E, −SE) | 500 | |
|     Cash—principal (−A) | | 5,000 |

**AUGUST 31**    Distribution of estate income to Gloria Olds:

| | | |
|---|---|---|
| Distribution to Gloria Olds (E, −SE) | 6,920 | |
|     Cash—income (−A) | | 6,920 |

## Closing Entries

Entries to close the nominal accounts to estate income and estate principal on August 31 are as follows:

| | | |
|---|---|---|
| Estate principal (−SE) | 246,000 | |
|     Funeral expenses (−E, +SE) | | 4,500 |
|     Hospital and medical expenses (−E, +SE) | | 19,000 |
|     Devise—Laura Hunt (−E, +SE) | | 165,000 |
|     Devise—Sara Tyson (−E, +SE) | | 10,000 |
|     Devise—First Methodist Church (−E, +SE) | | 10,000 |
|     Devise—Humane Society (−E, +SE) | | 10,000 |
|     Debts of decedent paid (−E, +SE) | | 500 |
|     Devise to Gary Hunt (−E, +SE) | | 12,000 |
|     Devise to Michael Wallace (−E, +SE) | | 10,000 |
|     Attorney fees paid (−E, +SE) | | 4,500 |
|     Court costs paid (−E, +SE) | | 500 |
| Estate income (−R, −SE) | 6,920 | |
|     Distribution to Gloria Olds (−E, +SE) | | 6,920 |
| Assets subsequently discovered (+A) | 10,800 | |
|     Estate principal (+SE) | | 10,800 |

After these closing entries are made, the remaining account balances are as follows:

| | |
|---|---:|
| Cash—principal | $204,175 |
| Savings account | 93,000 |
| Rocky Mountain Power common stock | 40,000 |
| Southern Natural Gas common stock | 30,000 |
| Danville municipal bonds | 58,000 |
| Estate principal | $425,175 |

**AUGUST 31**  Laura Hunt transfers estate property to Ed Jones, trustee for Gloria Olds, in accordance with the income trust established by Harry Olds's will:

| | | |
|---|---:|---:|
| Estate principal (−SE) | 425,175 | |
| Cash—principal (−A) | | 204,175 |
| Savings account (−A) | | 93,000 |
| Rocky Mountain Power common stock (−A) | | 40,000 |
| Southern Natural Gas common stock (−A) | | 30,000 |
| Danville municipal bonds (−A) | | 58,000 |

## Charge–Discharge Statement

The **charge–discharge statement** is a document prepared by the personal representative (executor or administrator) to show accountability for estate property received and maintained or disbursed in accordance with the will (or the probate court in intestate cases). A charge–discharge statement shows progress in the administration of the estate and termination of responsibility when the will has been fully administered. Exhibit 23-2 shows a final charge–discharge statement by Laura Hunt for her father's estate. The statement consists of two major parts: one for estate principal and one for estate income. The extent of detail is determined by the complexity of the estate, number of devises, and instructions from the probate court.

## ACCOUNTING FOR TRUSTS

LEARNING OBJECTIVE **23.3**

The will of Harry Olds resulted in the creation of an income trust for Gloria Olds. A trust created pursuant to a will is referred to as a **testamentary trust**. The fiduciary that administers a trust is the **trustee**. A trustee may be a business entity or a natural person. As in the case of estates, guidance in accounting for trusts comes from state laws, the Uniform Trusts Act, the UPC, and the Revised Uniform Principal and Income Act.

The entry made by Ed Jones, the trustee, to open the books for the creation of the Gloria Olds Trust is as follows:

| | | |
|---|---:|---:|
| Cash (+A) | 204,175 | |
| Savings account (+A) | 93,000 | |
| Rocky Mountain Power common stock (+A) | 40,000 | |
| Southern Natural Gas common stock (+A) | 30,000 | |
| Danville municipal bonds (+A) | 58,000 | |
| Trust fund principal (+SE) | | 425,175 |
| To record receipt of property transferred from Laura Hunt, executor. | | |

A primary concern in accounting for trust entities is distinguishing between principal and income. This is especially true of income trusts such as the one created for Gloria Olds because the principal amount of the trust is to be maintained intact to provide income for Mrs. Olds's care until her death. Separate trust fund principal and trust fund income accounts are used to separate principal and income balances for accounting purposes. The use of separate principal and income cash accounts, however, is of limited value, and is usually unnecessary.

**EXHIBIT 23-2**

Charge–Discharge
Statement

## ESTATE OF HARRY OLDS
## CHARGE–DISCHARGE STATEMENT
## FOR THE PERIOD OF ESTATE ADMINISTRATION
## MAY 1 TO AUGUST 31, 2015

**Estate Principal**

| | | |
|---|---:|---:|
| *I charge myself for:* | | |
| Assets included in estate inventory | $660,375 | |
| Assets discovered after inventory | 10,800 | $671,175 |
|    Total estate principal charge | | $671,175 |
| | | |
| *I credit myself for:* | | |
| Funeral expenses paid | $4,500 | |
| Hospital and medical expenses paid | 19,000 | |
| Mechanic's bill paid | 500 | |
| Attorney fees and court costs | 5,000 | $29,000 |
| Devises paid in cash to: | | |
|   Laura Hunt | $20,000 | |
|   Sara Tyson | 10,000 | |
|   First Methodist Church | 10,000 | |
|   Humane Society | 10,000 | 50,000 |
| Devises distributed in kind to: | | |
|   Laura Hunt (summer home) | $145,000 | |
|   Gary Hunt (2014 Ford Mustang) | 12,000 | |
|   Michael Wallace (FFF stock) | 10,000 | 167,000 |
| Transferred to Ed Jones, trustee for Gloria Olds: | | |
|   Cash—principal | $204,175 | |
|   Savings account | 93,000 | |
|   Rocky Mountain Power Company stock | 40,000 | |
|   Southern Natural Gas Company stock | 30,000 | |
|   Danville municipal bonds | 58,000 | 425,175 |
|    Total estate principal discharge | | $671,175 |

**Estate Income**

| | | |
|---|---|---:|
| *I charge myself for:* | | |
| Estate income received during estate administration | | $ 6,920 |
| | | |
| *I credit myself for:* | | |
| Payment of estate income to Gloria Olds as directed by the will | | $ 6,920 |

Respectfully submitted: Laura Hunt, Estate Executor, August 31, 2015.

---

After the original entry to record the creation of the trust, trust accounting essentially parallels accounting for an estate. Income and distributions are recorded following the terms of the trust agreement. A trustee may also be responsible for supervising the investment trust assets, once again in accordance with the original trust agreement. If the trust has a termination date, the trustee must prepare a charge and discharge statement indicating the final disposition of all trust assets.

## ESTATE TAXATION

An estate may be subject to taxation (referred to as estate, or inheritance, taxes) at both the state and federal levels. Accountants and attorneys play a vital role in estate planning to minimize these tax burdens for their clients and heirs. State taxes vary considerably across the 50 states and will not be discussed further here. Estate planning services are also critical for larger estates subject to state-level taxation.

### Estate Taxes

The Economic Growth and Tax Relief Reconciliation Act of 2001 proposed a reduction of the estate tax, and a total repeal in 2010. However, the tax returned in 2011 because Congress did not vote to make the repeal permanent. As of this writing, the IRS offers an exemption of $5,430,000 for 2015. Amounts in excess are taxed at a 40 percent rate.

The taxable amount of an estate is based on fair values of all estate assets at the date of death. Assets include real and personal property, as well as life insurance policies. The estate fair value is reduced by funeral expenses, settlement of estate liabilities, bequests to qualified charities, an unlimited marital deduction/exemption for properties given to a spouse, state-level taxes, expenses of estate administration (e.g., executor's fees), and the tax-exempt amount of $5,430,000.

Michael Dennyson dies on August 1, 2015, leaving taxable estate assets with a fair value of $8,400,000. Michael is survived by his widow, Danielle. Details of the estate are as follows:

| | |
|---|---:|
| Fair value of gross estate | $8,400,000 |
| Funeral expenses | (20,000) |
| Executor's fees | (50,000) |
| Estate liabilities | (500,000) |
| Bequest to local symphony | (400,000) |
| Bequest to church | (200,000) |
| Bequest to State University | (400,000) |
| Marital deduction | (6,830,000) |
| Taxable value of estate | $0 |
| Estate tax due | $0 |

Under this scenario, no federal estate tax is due. However, the $6,830,000 marital deduction becomes a part of Danielle's estate, subject to taxation upon her demise.

Suppose instead that Michael's sole heir is his niece, Jennifer. The marital deduction is no longer available, leaving a taxable estate value of $6,830,000. The estate tax is calculated as follows:

| | |
|---|---:|
| Taxable value of estate | $6,830,000 |
| Estate tax exemption | (5,430,000) |
| Estate subject to tax | $1,400,000 |
| Estate tax due (assuming 40% maximum rate) | $ 560,000 |
| Jennifer's net inheritance | $6,270,000 |

Notice that with proper planning, Michael could have provided a $560,000 combined greater benefit to his favorite charities and his niece. If Michael had bequeathed an additional $1,400,000 to the three charities, the remaining $5,430,000 would have been exempt from federal estate tax. Jennifer's net inheritance would have been reduced to $5,430,000.

The taxable estate can also be reduced through gifts to an unlimited number of donees before a person's death. However, these may be subject to federal gift taxes beyond a certain level. Annual gift amounts are indexed to inflation, currently standing at $14,000 per donee ($28,000 for a married couple). The exclusion from gift taxation is further subject to a lifetime maximum. Bequests to qualified charities are not considered gifts. The 2001 Economic Growth and Tax Relief Reconciliation Act did not eliminate gift taxes.

## Income Taxes on Estate Income

In addition to federal and state estate and inheritance taxes, trusts and estates are also subject to federal (and possibly state) income taxes. An estate is a taxable entity and is subject to tax on income earned from the date of death until final settlement of the estate. The tax may be paid by the estate or by the beneficiary if estate property has already been distributed to the beneficiary.

Estates and trusts file federal income tax returns on Form 1041, U.S. Income Tax Return for Estates and Trusts. The beneficiary's share of income is reported on Schedule K-1 of Form 1041. Income for estates and trusts and applicable tax rates are defined in essentially the same manner as for individuals. Income includes interest and dividends, rent, and so on. Deductions and/or exemptions for estate administration fees, charitable donations, and distributions to beneficiaries reduce taxable income. Distributions to beneficiaries may be taxable income amounts in their personal tax returns. There is also a tax exemption for estates and trusts with taxable income less than $600. The fiduciary of the estate must provide applicable information to the beneficiary on Schedule K-1.

## SUMMARY

When a person dies without a valid will, he or she is said to have died intestate. The deceased person's estate is distributed under the statutes of intestate succession. When the decedent has a valid will in force, he or she dies testate. The probate court normally names the personal representative named in the will as executor of the estate. The executor is a fiduciary charged with carrying out the provisions of the will, including the settlement and distribution of the estate.

The executor records an inventory of the estate in a self-balancing set of accounts; however, obligations of the decedent are not recorded until paid. The executor must distinguish estate principal and income in accounting for the estate. Guidance for distinguishing estate principal and estate income is found in the Uniform Principal and Income Act. The executor prepares a charge–discharge statement to show accountability for estate property and progress in the administration of the estate. A final charge–discharge statement is prepared when the estate has been fully administered.

## QUESTIONS

1. Does accounting for a trust follow GAAP?
2. Briefly summarize differences between principal and income transactions for estates and trusts. Why is the classification important in estate and trust accounting?
3. What is the meaning of a devise in estate accounting?
4. What does it mean to die intestate?
5. What is meant by a homestead, or family, allowance?
6. Does the calculation of the federal estate tax permit any deductions?
7. How should assets and liabilities be measured in the accounting records of an estate?
8. Is it possible to avoid estate taxation by giving assets as gifts prior to death?
9. Briefly summarize how income earned on estate property should be treated by a beneficiary for purposes of filing a federal tax return. Where should the beneficiary look to provide this information?
10. Summarize reasons why it may be important to have a will.
11. Are estate income taxes the responsibility of the estate or its beneficiaries?

## EXERCISES

### E 23-1
### Prepare journal entries for an estate

You serve as the executor for the estate of John Seagull. The following transactions occur during June 2015:

a   John's estate included a municipal bond with a fair value of $1,000,000. On the date of death, there was $8,800 of accrued but unpaid interest. On June 5, you received a check in the amount of $18,000, representing the normal semiannual interest payment.

b   Included in the specific devises of John's will was a bequest to the Atlanta Animal Shelter in the amount of $200,000. You decide that estate assets will be more than adequate to meet all obligations of the estate and to pay all specific devises, and you issue a check for $200,000 to the animal shelter on June 10.

c   On June 20, you pay funeral expenses for John, in the amount of $16,400.

d   You receive an interest check in the amount of $6,000 from First Atlanta National Bank on June 24 and realize that an unknown investment in a certificate of deposit in the amount of $100,000 was omitted in the original inventory of estate assets, along with $2,400 of accrued interest.

**REQUIRED:** Prepare journal entries for the listed transactions. You can ignore estate and income taxes.

## E 23-2
## Prepare journal entries for an estate

You serve as the executor for the estate of Maribeth Rainy. The following transactions occur during July 2015:

a  *The Rainy estate included a certificate of deposit in the amount of $600,000. On the date of death, there was $11,600 of accrued but unpaid interest. On July 15, you received a check in the amount of $15,000, representing the normal semiannual interest payment.*

b  *Included in the specific devises of Maribeth's will was a bequest to the local symphony orchestra in the amount of $150,000. You decide that estate assets will be more than adequate to meet all obligations of the estate and to pay all specific devises, and you issue a check for $150,000 to the orchestra on July 18.*

c  *You pay a probate court fee of $2,800 on July 24.*

d  *On July 20, you pay funeral expenses in the amount of $12,800.*

e  *On July 28, you receive a bill from the local hospital for costs not covered by Maribeth's insurance in the amount of $44,000. The liability was unknown and not included in your initial estate inventory.*

**REQUIRED:** Prepare journal entries for the listed transactions. You can ignore estate and income taxes.

## E 23-3
## Prepare journal entries for an estate

You serve as the executor for the estate of Matthew Troy. Matthew's will provides that all remaining assets other than specific items in the will pass to his longtime friend Melanie Matthews. The following transactions occur during October and November 2015:

a  *The Troy estate included 100,000 shares of common stock of the Board of Water & Light, with a fair value of $62 per share. On the date of death, there were no outstanding dividends receivable. On October 15, you note that a dividend of $3 per share has been declared, payable on October 25.*

b  *Included in the specific devises of Matthew's will was a bequest to the Philadelphia Art Museum in the amount of $150,000.*

c  *You pay a probate court fee of $3,800 on October 24.*

d  *On October 29, you pay funeral expenses in the amount of $11,600.*

e  *On October 28, you receive and pay a bill from the local hospital for costs not covered by Matthew's insurance in the amount of $37,000. The liability was unknown and not included in your initial estate inventory.*

f  *On October 29, you receive a dividend check from the Board of Water & Light in the amount of $300,000.*

**REQUIRED:** Prepare journal entries for the listed transactions. You may ignore estate and income taxes.

## E 23-4
## Accounting for an estate

K.T. Tim has been appointed to serve as executor for the estate of Ms. Lisa Triciao, who passed away on August 15, 2015. Ms. Triciao's assets consisted of the following:

| Asset | Book Value | Fair Value |
|---|---|---|
| Cash | $118,225 | $118,225 |
| Savings accounts | 250,000 | 250,000 |
| ViaReggio common stock | 67,500 | 225,000 |
| City of Roma municipal bonds | 381,500 | 412,000 |
| Mercedes sports car | 57,500 | 41,000 |
| Condominium on Italian Riviera | 399,700 | 1,265,500 |
| Atlanta personal residence | 225,700 | 430,000 |
| Collection of rare hand puppets | 11,145 | 85,000 |
| Fully restored Model T Ford | 1,750 | 125,000 |

The probate court has ruled that other personal effects may be excluded from the estate inventory.

**REQUIRED:** Prepare the estate inventory as of August 15, 2015.

## E 23-5
## Journal entries and accounting for an estate

You serve as the executor for the estate of Jeff Carpenter, who passed away on August 25, 2015, at the age of 102. Jeff's estate consisted of two certificates of deposit totalling $800,000 and a $15,000 balance in his checking account. Total accrued interest on the CDs at the date of death amounted to $7,000. Jeff left a valid will, which provided that most of the estate be inherited by his sole surviving nephew, J.J. Kara. The will further provided that $100,000 be transferred to a trust account for his faithful dog, Sooner XXV. Income from the trust would be used to care for Sooner. Upon Sooner's demise, the trust would end, and remaining trust principal would transfer to J.J. Kara. Jeff's personal effects were minimal and excluded from the estate. Ms. Colleen Ryan, a trust officer at the Oxford National Bank, serves as estate executrix and as fiduciary for the trust. Ms. Ryan determines that no federal or state inheritance taxes are due. The limited estate income is also free from any federal or state income tax. The following transactions occur during September 2015:

*a* On September 12, received a check in the amount of $11,500, representing the normal semiannual interest payment on the certificates of deposit.

*b* On September 13, cashed out the certificates of deposit for $800,000.

*c* On September 15, transferred $100,000 to a trust account at Oxford National Bank to provide care for Sooner XXV. Also, on the way to the bank, Sooner was dropped off at Puppy Paradise, his new home.

*d* On September 18, paid funeral expenses for Jeff in the amount of $7,200.

*e* On September 20, paid herself the $2,500 executor's fee specified in Jeff's will.

*f* On September 28, finalized the estate and transferred the balance of the estate assets to Jeff's nephew, J. J. Kara.

### REQUIRED

1. Prepare an estate inventory at the date of death.

2. Prepare journal entries to record the estate transactions during September.

3. Prepare the estate closing entries on September 28.

4. Prepare the charge–discharge statement for the estate of Jeff Carpenter for the period August 25 through September 28, 2015.

## E 23-6
## Prepare journal entries for a trust

You serve as the trustee for the Sooner XXV trust. The following transactions occur during 2015:

| | |
|---|---|
| **September 15** | Open the Sooner XXV trust account, depositing the $100,000 transferred from the estate of Jeff Carpenter. |
| **September 16** | Deposit the $100,000 into an insured money market fund earning 5 percent annually, in accordance with the trust agreement. |
| **October 16** | Deposit $417 interest received from the money market fund into the trust checking account. |
| **October 19** | Write a $300 check to Puppy Paradise to cover Sooner's November room and board costs. Costs to November 1 had been prepaid by the estate. |
| **October 27** | Write a check for $22 to cover chew toys for Sooner. |
| **November 16** | Deposit $417 interest received from the money market fund into the trust checking account. |
| **November 22** | Write a $300 check to Puppy Paradise to cover Sooner's December room and board costs. |
| **December 16** | Deposit $417 interest received from the money market fund into the trust-checking account. |
| **December 28** | Puppy Paradise informs you of Sooner's passing. Pay $700 for Sooner's funeral and burial costs. |
| **December 31** | Pay yourself the agreed $100 trust administration fee. |
| **December 31** | Distribute all remaining trust principal by transferring the title to the money market fund and cash to J. J. Kara. |

**REQUIRED:** Prepare journal entries for the listed transactions. You may ignore taxes.

### E 23-7
### Prepare charge and discharge statement for the Sooner XXV trust

Use information from E 23-6 to prepare a charge and discharge statement for the trust for the period September 15, 2015 through December 31, 2015.

### E 23-8
### Prepare journal entries for a trust

You serve as the trustee for the Lisa Wyatt Trust. The following transactions occur during June and July 2015:

| | |
|---|---|
| **June 1** | Open the trust account, depositing the $1,000,000 transferred from the estate of Cheri James into a non-interest-bearing checking account to be used for trust investment and administration and for accumulation of interest and dividends received from trust investments. |
| **June 2** | Deposit $500,000 into a two-year certificate of deposit earning 6 percent annually, with interest paid monthly. |
| **June 3** | Invest the remaining $500,000 in a stock mutual fund. |
| **July 2** | Record deposit of one month's interest from the certificate of deposit to the trust-checking account. |
| **July 3** | Pay bank's trust administration monthly fee of $41. |

**REQUIRED:** Prepare journal entries for the listed transactions. You may ignore taxes.

### E 23-9
### Prepare journal entries for a trust

You serve as the trustee for the Josephine Frederick testamentary income trust. The trust was created by the will of her late husband, John. Under the terms of John's will, all assets are transferred to the trust to cover living expenses for his spouse. Upon her demise, trust assets will be sold, with the proceeds distributed to their six children. Each is to receive an equal share.

The probate court ruled that household furnishings and John's personal effects could be excluded from the estate. The executor has paid all inheritance and income taxes on estate income for the period of estate administration. The estate inventory prepared by John's estate executor showed the following assets:

| Asset | Cost | Fair Value |
|---|---|---|
| Cash | $218,220 | $218,220 |
| Savings accounts | 300,000 | 300,000 |
| Microsystems common stock | 163,400 | 400,000 |
| Big Casino common stock | 181,500 | 120,000 |
| Vintage sports car | 17,500 | 31,000 |
| Mountain cottage | 39,700 | 114,500 |
| Personal residence | 209,900 | 457,500 |

**REQUIRED:** Prepare the journal entries for the creation of the trust.

### E 23-10
### Estate tax calculation

Mr. Dogbert dies on March 1, 2015, and leaves his entire estate, with a fair value of $10,600,000 (after settlement of all estate expenses and liabilities) to his sole surviving family member, his daughter Emily.

### REQUIRED

1. Calculate the federal tax on Mr. Dogbert's estate. (You may ignore any state-level inheritance taxes and assume that federal taxes are paid at the 40 percent rate.)

2. Offer suggestions as to how the estate tax might be avoided, leaving Dogbert's daughter Emily better off financially.

### E 23-11
### Estate tax calculation

Mr. Chuck Rainy dies on May 21, 2015, and leaves his entire estate, with a fair value of $7,200,000 (after settlement of all estate expenses and liabilities) to be equally divided among his sole surviving family members, his daughters Emily and Laura, and his son Tom.

**REQUIRED:** Calculate the federal tax on Mr. Rainy's estate. (You may ignore any state-level inheritance taxes and assume that federal taxes are paid at the 40 percent rate.)

## E 23-12
## Estate tax calculation

Ms. Jacki Jerome, a famous rock superstar, dies on November 28, 2015, and leaves her entire estate, with a fair value of $23,400,000 (after settling all estate expenses and liabilities) to her cousin Maggie.

**REQUIRED:** Calculate the federal tax on Ms. Jerome's estate. (You may ignore any state-level inheritance taxes and assume that federal taxes are paid at the 40 percent rate.)

## PROBLEMS

## P23-1
## Estate accounting

Jimmy Olson died on June 15, 2015, at the age of 75, after a brief illness. Jimmy is survived by his wife, Lois, and two adult sons, Clark and Kent. Jimmy left a valid will, requesting that Clark serve as executor of his estate. Jimmy's widow will maintain the family residence, which was owned jointly.

Jimmy's will provided the following specific devises:

| | |
|---|---|
| 2014 Corvette to his son, Clark | $35,000 |
| Summer cottage on Lake Michigan to his son Kent | 40,000 |
| Stock investments to be shared equally between his two sons | 400,000 |
| Miscellaneous personal effects to his widow, Lois | — |

Jimmy's will also provided the following general devises of cash:

| | |
|---|---|
| Clark—to cover executor's services | $5,000 |
| Ms. Lana Lang, Jimmy's personal trainer | 200,000 |
| Jimmy's church | 50,000 |
| The local symphony orchestra | 50,000 |

Jimmy's will further provides that Lois should receive any excess of income over expenses during the administration of his estate. All remaining assets are to be placed in a trust to support Lois for the remainder of her lifetime. Upon Lois's death, the remainder of the estate is to be divided equally between Clark and Kent.

Clark filed notice of his appointment as executor on June 25 and placed the required notice to potential creditors in *The Daily Planet*, the local newspaper. Clark prepared and filed the following estate inventory with the probate court on July 15:

**Jimmy Olson, Testator**
**Inventory of Estate Assets**
**As of the Date of Death on June 15, 2015**
*Submitted by Clark Olson, executor, on July 15*

| Property Description | Fair Value |
|---|---|
| Cash checking and savings accounts in Metropolis National Bank | $750,000 |
| Certificate of deposit (6 percent, 36 months, matures December 31) (includes $5,000 accrued interest) | 505,000 |
| Stocks held by Perry White brokerage | 460,000 |
| Dividends receivable on stocks | 12,000 |
| Lake Michigan cottage | 40,000 |
| 2014 Corvette | 35,000 |
| Personal effects* | — |
| | $1,802,000 |

*The probate court permitted Clark to exclude Jimmy's personal effects from the inventory.

The following events occurred during June and July 2015:

| | |
|---|---|
| **June 22** | Received a check in the amount of $15,000, representing interest on the certificates of deposit, including the amount accrued at the date of death. |
| **June 24** | Received a dividend check in the amount of $12,000. |
| **June 30** | Paid $250 to repair a roof leak on the Lake Michigan cottage. |
| **July 4** | Paid $4,900 in funeral expenses for Jimmy. |
| **July 12** | Cashed out the certificate of deposit for $501,300. The additional $1,300 represented interest income from June 23 through July 12. The bank waived the fees for early withdrawal because Jimmy had been a loyal, long-term customer. |
| **July 15** | Filed the estate inventory with the probate court. |
| **July 20** | Distributed the general property devises as provided in Jimmy's will. |
| **July 21** | Distributed the general cash devises as provided in Jimmy's will. |
| **July 22** | Closed the accounts, finalizing the estate administration, paid remaining estate income to Lois, and transferred remaining estate assets to Lois Olson testamentary income trust. |

### REQUIRED

1. Prepare journal entries for the transactions related to the estate during 2015.

2. Prepare entries to terminate the estate and transfer remaining assets to the trust.

3. Prepare the final charge–discharge statement for the estate of Jimmy Olson for the period June 15, 2015 through July 22, 2015.

## P23-2
## Creation of a trust

You have been hired as trustee for the testamentary trust created by the will of Jimmy Olson. The trust is created on July 22, 2015. (Use the information provided in P 23-1.)

The trust initially invests the proceeds from the estate in a checking account that pays 3 percent per year. Interest is paid monthly. On July 23, the trust invests $300,000 in a certificate of deposit at Metropolis National Bank. The certificate earns 6 percent interest per year, paid monthly. On July 25, the trust invests $500,000 in the Super Stock Mutual Fund. On July 31, the trust invests $100,000 in 10-year, 10 percent Smallville Municipal Bonds, which will mature on July 31, 2023. The bonds pay interest semiannually on January 31 and July 31. On August 22, you receive a check for $1,500, representing one month's interest on the certificate of deposit. On August 23, you receive the statement on the checking account indicating a deposit of $405 for one month's interest on the checking account. The statement also indicates the bank's monthly fee of $100 for maintaining the trust. On August 31, you send a check to Lois Olson for $3,700 to cover her monthly living expenses.

**REQUIRED:** Prepare the entry to record the creation of the Olson trust on July 22. Prepare all additional required entries to account for trust activities through August 31.

## P23-3
## Estate accounting

George Wilson dies on March 1, 2015, leaving a valid will. The will reads as follows:

> *I leave my home, furnishings, remaining bank account balances and personal posses-sions to my wife Helen. I leave my automobile to my nephew, Dennis. I leave my stock investment accounts to my niece, Denise. I leave income on my estate to be divided equally between Dennis and Denise. Estate expenses are to be paid from principal, not from estate income. All remaining property is to be placed in a trust for my four children. I name my nephew, Dennis, as executor of my estate.*

Dennis prepares an estate inventory for all assets discovered and files the appropriate notice to potential creditors on March 15:

**George Wilson, Testator**
**Inventory of Estate Assets**
**As of March 1, 2015**

| Assets | Fair Value |
| --- | --- |
| Cash—checking | $16,500 |
| Cash—savings | 50,000 |
| Dividends receivable on stocks | 400 |
| Interest receivable on bonds | 2,400 |
| Life insurance—payable to the estate | 500,000 |
| Personal residence | 325,000 |
| Household furnishings and personal effects | 76,000 |
| 2000 Thunderbird Convertible | 21,000 |
| Investments in stocks | 25,000 |
| Investments in bonds | 200,000 |
| | $1,216,300 |

The following transactions occurred during March and April:

| | |
| --- | --- |
| **March 25** | Dennis pays funeral expenses of $2,800. |
| **March 30** | Dennis receives a check from the life insurance company for $500,000. |
| **April 9** | Dennis discovers title to a small parcel of lakefront property in George's safe deposit box. The title indicates that George purchased the land for $10,000. |
| **April 15** | A check for $3,000 in bond interest is received. |
| **April 19** | Dennis receives an appraiser's report on the lakefront property, valuing it for $28,000. |
| **April 28** | Dennis pays $13,250 to settle all liabilities of the estate, including property taxes and George's medical bills. |
| **April 29** | A check for $500 in stock dividends is received. |
| **April 30** | Dennis makes all remaining payments and property transfers and closes the estate. |

**REQUIRED:** Prepare all journal entries required to account for the estate of George Wilson. You may ignore taxes.

## P23-4
### Charge and discharge statement for an estate

Use the information in P 23-3 to prepare a charge–discharge statement for the estate of George Wilson for the period March 1, 2015 through April 30, 2015.

## P23-5
### Creation of a trust

You have been hired as trustee for the testamentary trust created by the will of George Wilson. The trust is created on April 30, 2015. (Use the information provided in P 23-3 and P 23-4.) The trust initially invests the proceeds from the estate in a checking account, which pays 3 percent per year. Interest is paid quarterly. On May 3, the trust invests $450,000 in a certificate of deposit at the local bank. The certificate earns 6 percent interest per year, paid monthly. On May 25, the trust sells the land for $31,300 in cash. On May 31 and June 30, you pay the $165 monthly service fees to the bank. On June 3, you receive a check for $2,250, representing the first month's interest on the certificate of deposit. On June 15, you send a check to Jimmy Wilson (George's oldest son) for $8,700 to cover his fall semester tuition, room, and board at Big State University.

**REQUIRED:** Prepare the entry to record the creation of the Wilson Family Trust on April 30. Prepare all required entries to account for trust activities through June 30.

## P23-6
## Estate accounting

Tom Josephson dies on May 16, 2015, leaving a valid will. The will reads as follows:

> *I leave my automobile to my niece, Pat. I leave my stock investment accounts to my niece, Sue. I leave income on my estate to the local humane society. Estate expenses are to be paid from principal, not from estate income. All remaining property is to be placed in a trust for my two children, Megan and Ryan. I name my niece, Prima, as executrix of my estate, for which she should be paid a fee of $2,500.*

Prima prepares an estate inventory for all assets discovered and files the appropriate notice to potential creditors on May 31. Prima excludes the personal residence, furnishings, and bank accounts from the inventory, as these were jointly owned by Tom and his wife, Corinne.

**Tom Josephson, Testator**
**Inventory of Estate Assets**
**As of May 16, 2015**

| Assets * | Fair Value |
|---|---:|
| Dividends receivable on stocks | $1,200 |
| Interest receivable on bonds | 6,750 |
| Life insurance—payable to the estate | 750,000 |
| 2014 Volkswagen | 2,600 |
| Investments in stocks | 52,000 |
| Investments in bonds | 400,000 |
| | $1,212,550 |

*The probate court allowed exclusion of Tom's personal effects.

The following transactions occurred during May and June:

| | |
|---|---|
| **June 5** | Prima discovers government bonds with a face value of $200,000 in Tom's safe deposit box. The box also contains an additional life insurance policy in the amount of $50,000. |
| **June 15** | Prima receives a check from the life insurance company for $750,000. |
| **June 16** | A check for $8,000 in bond interest is received. |
| **June 18** | Prima pays funeral expenses of $4,300. |
| **June 22** | Prima cashes in the government bonds for $215,000, which includes accrued interest at the date of death. The bonds matured several years earlier and were no longer accruing interest. |
| **June 23** | Prima receives a check from the insurance company on the subsequently discovered policy for $50,000. |
| **June 24** | Prima pays $18,250 to settle all liabilities of the estate, including property taxes and Tom's medical bills. |
| **June 28** | A check for $1,600 in stock dividends is received. |
| **June 30** | Prima makes all remaining payments (including her fee as executrix) and property transfers and closes the estate. |

**REQUIRED:** Prepare all journal entries required to account for the estate of Tom Josephson. You may ignore taxes.

## P23-7
## Charge and discharge statement for an estate

Use the information in P 23-6 to prepare a charge–discharge statement for the estate of Tom Josephson for the period May 16, 2015 through June 30, 2015.

## P23-8
## Creation of a trust

You have been hired as trustee for the testamentary trust created by the will of Tom Josephson. The trust is created on June 30, 2015. (Use the information provided in P 23-6 and P 23-7.) The trust initially invests the proceeds from the estate in a checking account, which pays 3 percent per year. Interest is paid quarterly. On July 5, the trust invests $750,000 in a certificate of deposit at the local bank. The certificate earns 6 percent interest per year, paid monthly. On July 31, you pay the $275 quarterly trust service fees to the bank. On August 5, you receive a check for $3,750, representing the first month's interest on the certificate of deposit. On August 19, you send a $15,000 check to Superprivate Academy to cover fall semester tuition, room, and board for Megan and Ryan.

**REQUIRED:** Prepare the entry to record the creation of the Josephson Family Trust on June 30, 2015. Prepare all required entries to account for trust activities through August 31.

# GLOSSARY

**Acquisition:** a business combination in which one corporation acquires control over the operations of another entity. Acquisitions are recorded based on the fair value of net assets.

**Acquisition Method:** accounting method to record business combinations based on fair value of net assets acquired. Replaces the prior purchase method.

**Actual Retirement:** the repurchase and retirement of bonds by the issuing affiliate.

**Additions (Governmental Colleges and Universities):** increases to the fund balance of fund groupings other than current unrestricted funds and current restricted funds to the extent that expenditures have not been made.

**Administrator:** the court-appointed representative who takes control of the estate of a person who died intestate and supervises the estate's distribution.

**Affiliate:** a subsidiary in a technical sense, although the term is sometimes used to refer to 20%- to 50%-owned equity investees.

**Agency Funds (Governmental Accounting):** used to account for resources held by the governmental unit as agent for other funds, other governmental units, or individuals.

**Agency Theory:** theory of intercompany bond holdings that allocates constructive gains and losses to the issuing affiliate.

**Allotments:** divisions of the appropriation authority by time period.

**Annuity Funds:** a college and university fund type to account for resources acquired under the condition that stipulated periodic payments be made to individuals as directed by the donor of the resources.

**Appropriations:** budget authorizations of expenditures.

**Assigned Fund Balance (governmental):** amounts intended to be used by the government for specific purposes but do not meet the criteria to be classified as restricted or committed.

**Auxiliary Enterprises:** a college and university activity encompassing student unions, dormitories, resident halls, and intercollegiate athletics that are intended to be self-sustaining.

**Bankruptcy Insolvency:** a condition in which an entity has total debts in excess of the fair market value of its assets.

**Bargain Purchase:** the excess of the fair market value of assets acquired in a purchase business combination over the investment cost. Under current FASB guidance, this is termed a bargain purchase, and recognized as a gain to the acquirer. Previously referred to as negative goodwill.

**Bonus Approach (Partnerships):** the adjustment of partner capital balances as an alternative to revaluing partnership assets or recording goodwill.

**Budget:** a plan of financial operations including proposed expenditures for a period and the means of financing them.

**Business Combination:** a uniting of previously separate business entities through acquisition by one entity of another entity's net assets or a majority of its outstanding voting common stock, or through an exchange of common stock.

**Capital Budget (Governmental Accounting):** the current portion of a capital program.

**Capital Program (Governmental Accounting):** a plan of capital expenditures by year over a fixed period of years.

**Capital Projects Funds (Governmental Accounting):** used to account for resources to be used for acquisition or construction of major general government capital facilities.

**Cash Distribution Plan (Partnerships):** a plan developed at the beginning of the liquidation period that shows how cash will be distributed throughout the phase-out period.

**Cash Distribution Schedule (Partnerships):** a schedule of cash distributions made to creditors and partners in a partnership liquidation.

**Cash Flow Hedge:** a hedge of the exposure to variability in the cash flows of a recognized asset or liability, or of a forecasted transaction, that is attributable to a particular risk.

**Chapter 11 of the Bankruptcy Reform Act:** Chapter 11 covers rehabilitation of the debtor and anticipates a reorganization of the debtor corporation.

**Chapter 7 of the Bankruptcy Reform Act:** Chapter 7 covers straight bankruptcy under which the debtor entity is expected to be liquidated.

**Charge-Discharge Statement (Estates and Trusts):** a document prepared by the executor or administrator of an estate to show accountability for property received and disbursed.

**Charity Care:** hospital terminology for services provided free of charge to qualifying patients.

**Committed Fund Balance (Governmental):** amounts can only be spent for the specific purposes determined by a formal action of the government's highest level of decision-making authority.

**Conditional Promise to Give (Not-for-Profit Accounting):** a pledge that is dependent upon the occurrence of a specified future and uncertain event to bind the promisor.

**Conglomeration:** the combination of firms in unrelated and diverse product lines and/or service functions.

**Connecting Affiliates Relationship:** a type of affiliation structure involving indirect or mutual holdings between a parent company and its subsidiaries.

**Consolidation:** (1) a business combination in which a new corporation is formed to take over two or more business entities that then go out of existence; (2) in a generic sense, it means the same as acquisition or merger; (3) the process of combining parent-company and subsidiary financial statements.

**Constructive Retirement of Bonds:** the repurchase of bonds of one affiliate by another so that the bonds are held within the parent–subsidiary affiliation and, in effect, retired.

**Constructive Retirement of Preferred Stock:** the purchase of a subsidiary's preferred stock by the parent company that results in a retirement of the preferred stock from the viewpoint of the consolidated entity.

**Contemporary Theory:** the current theory underlying consolidated financial statements; it reflects certain aspects of both entity and parent-company theories.

**Contribution (Not-for-Profit Accounting):** a transfer of cash or other assets to an entity or a settlement or cancellation of its liabilities from a voluntary nonreciprocal transfer.

**Controlling Share of Net Income:** share of consolidated net income available to the controlling interest shareholders.

**Conventional Approach of Accounting for Mutually Held Common Stock:** parent-company stock held by a subsidiary is accounted for as being constructively retired for consolidation purposes.

**Corporate Joint Venture:** a joint venture organized under the corporate form of business organization.

**Creditors' Committees:** a group of people who represent a company's creditors in a bankruptcy proceeding.

**Current Operating Funds:** a college and university fund grouping to account for resources expendable for operating purposes; includes unrestricted current funds and restricted current funds.

**Current Rate:** the exchange rate in effect at the balance sheet date or the transaction date.

**Current Rate Method:** translation of all assets, liabilities, revenues, and expenses at current exchange rates.

**Debt Service Funds (Governmental Accounting):** used to account for the accumulation of resources for payment of principal and interest on general long-term debt.

**Debtor in Possession:** a Chapter 11 case in which the debtor corporation keeps control of the business and performs the duties of a trustee.

**Decedent:** a person who is deceased.

**Deferred Inflows of Resources (Governmental Accounting):** an acquisition of net assets by the government that is applicable to a future reporting period. Under new GASB guidance, deferred inflows of resources are reported separately and have a negative effect on net position, similar to liabilities.

**Deferred Outflows of Resources (Governmental Accounting):** a consumption of net assets by the government that is applicable to a future reporting period. Under new GASB guidance, deferred outflows of resources are reported separately and have a positive effect on net position, similar to assets.

**Denominated:** to denominate in a currency is to fix the amount in units of that currency.

**Derivative:** a security whose price is dependent upon or derived from one or more underlying assets.

**Devisees:** those persons designated in a will to receive real or personal property.

**Direct Holdings:** direct investments in voting stock of one or more investee companies.

**Direct Quotation:** the expression of an exchange rate in U.S. dollars (U.S. dollar equivalent).

**Dissolution of a Partnership:** the change in the relation of partners when any partner is no longer involved in carrying on the business. The business may continue as an operating business despite the dissolution of the partnership.

**Donor-Imposed Conditions (Not-for-Profit Accounting):** the occurrence or failure to occur of an uncertain future event that releases the donor from its obligation.

**Donor-Imposed Restrictions (Not-for-Profit Accounting):** specifications of how or when the assets promised or received must be used.

**Downstream Sale:** sales or other intercompany transactions from parent company to subsidiary.

**Drawings (Partnerships):** regular partner withdrawals as provided in the partnership agreement and closed to partner capital at year-end. (Also *Salary Allowances (Partnerships)*.)

**EDGAR System:** the SEC's Electronic Data Gathering, Analysis, and Retrieval system. Forms filed with the SEC can be downloaded from the EDGAR system at www.sec.gov/edaux/searches.htm by providing the form desired and company name.

**Encumbrance Accounting:** recording commitments made for goods on order and for unperformed contracts to prevent overspending of amounts appropriated.

**Endowment Funds (Not-for-Profit Accounting):** used to account for gifts and bequests received from donors under endowment agreements (hospitals); a fund type for colleges and universities to account for resources received from donors or outside agencies with the stipulation that the principal be maintained in perpetuity and income be used as directed.

**Enterprise Funds (Governmental Accounting):** used to account for operations that are financed and operated in a manner similar to private enterprise.

**Entity Theory:** a theory under which consolidated financial statements are prepared from the view of the total business entity.

**Equity Adjustment on Translation:** an exchange gain or loss that is reported as a stockholders' equity adjustment (and in other comprehensive income). (Also *Translation Adjustment*.)

**Equity Insolvency:** the inability of an entity to pay its debts as they come due.

**Equity in Subsidiary Realized Income:** the parent company's or controlling interest's share of subsidiary income adjusted for intercompany gains and losses and amortization of fair value/book value differentials.

**Equity Method:** accounting for a common stock investment on an accrual basis; earnings increase the investment and dividends decrease it.

**Exchange Rate:** the ratio between a unit of one currency and the amount of another currency for which it can be exchanged at a particular time.

**Executor:** the court-appointed representative who takes control of the estate of a decedent who died testate and supervises its distribution.

**Executory Contracts:** contracts that have not been completely performed by the parties to the contract (e.g., purchase commitments and leases).

**Expendable Funds:** those in which resources can be expended to meet the objective of the fund.

**Expendable Trust Funds:** a trust fund in which the assets can be expended as needed to meet the fund's objectives.

**Expenditures:** decreases in the net financial resources of a governmental type fund other than those caused by transfers or other similar financing uses.

**Fair Value/Cost Method (for Equity Investments):** if the stock is not marketable, a common stock investment is accounted for at its original cost. If the stock is marketable, the investment is carried at fair market value with an associated adjunct/contra equity account for the change in value from original cost (assuming an available-for-sale security). In both cases, dividends received are recorded as income from the investment.

**Fair Value Hedge:** a hedge of the exposure to changes in the fair value of a recognized asset or liability, or of an unrecognized firm commitment, both attributable to a particular risk.

**Family Allowance:** an allowance to a surviving spouse and minor children to be paid out of estate property during the period of estate administration.

**Father-Son-Grandson Relationship:** a type of affiliation structure involving indirect or mutual holdings between a parent company and its subsidiaries.

**Fiduciary:** an individual or entity authorized to take possession of the property of others.

**Fiduciary Accounting:** a term used to describe accounting for estates and trusts whose managers have a custodial or stewardship relationship with the trust or estate beneficiaries.

**Fiduciary Funds:** a category of funds to account for assets held by the government as trustee or agent; includes expendable, nonexpendable, and pension trust funds and agency funds.

**Fixed Exchange Rates:** exchange rates set by a government and subject to change only by that government. (Also *official exchange rates*.)

**Floating Exchange Rates:** exchange rates that are market driven and reflect supply and demand factors, inflation, and so on. (Also *free exchange rates*.)

**Foreign Currency:** a currency other than the entity's functional currency.

**Foreign Currency Cash Flow Hedge:** a derivative instrument that hedges against the effect of the change in the relative value of two currencies because of the inherent exposure in forecasted transactions denominated in the foreign currency.

**Foreign Currency Commitment:** a contract or agreement that will result in a foreign currency transaction at a later date.

**Foreign Currency Fair Value Hedge:** a derivative instrument that hedges against the effect of the change in the relative value of two currencies because of the inherent exposure of holding an asset, liability, or firm commitment denominated in a foreign currency.

**Foreign Currency Statements:** the financial statements of a foreign subsidiary or other foreign entity and expressed in its local currency.

**Foreign Currency Transactions:** transactions whose terms are denominated in a currency other than the entity's functional currency.

**Foreign Transactions:** transactions between entities in different countries.

**Form 8-K:** form to disclose significant changes in firm policies, financial condition, and so on, to the SEC.

**Form 10-K:** basic form for the annual report that firms file with the SEC.

**Form 10-Q:** form for quarterly reports that firms file with the SEC.

**Forward Contracts:** a customized contract between two parties to buy or sell an asset at a specified price on a future date.

**Free Exchange Rates:** exchange rates that are market driven and reflect supply and demand factors, inflation, and so on. (Also *floating exchange rates*.)

**Fresh-Start Reporting:** accounting under a reorganization plan that meets prescribed conditions and enables the new entity to eliminate its prior deficit and report zero retained earnings.

**Functional Currency:** the currency of the primary economic environment in which an entity operates.

**Fund:** a fiscal and accounting entity with a self-balancing set of accounts that records cash and other assets together with related liabilities and residual balances.

**Fund Accounting:** financial systems that are segmented into separate accounting and reporting entities (funds) on the basis of their objectives and restrictions on their operations and resources.

**Fund Equity:** an amount equal to assets less liabilities of a fund.

**Fund Fixed Assets (Governmental Accounting):** fixed assets related to specific proprietary or trust funds and accounted for in those funds.

**Fund Long-Term Liabilities (Governmental Accounting):** long-term liabilities of proprietary and trust funds are designated fund long-term liabilities and are accounted for in those funds.

**Futures Contracts:** a contractual agreement, generally made on the trading floor of a futures exchange, to buy or sell a particular commodity or financial instrument at a pre-determined price in the future.

**General Fixed Assets (Governmental Accounting):** all fixed assets not classified as fund fixed assets; general fixed assets are reported for in the government-wide financial statements.

**General Fund (Governmental Accounting):** used to account for all financial resources not accounted for in another fund.

**General Governmental Activities:** in a simple situation, they are essentially taxpayer-financed activities made available to all members of a government's constituency without charges for use. These activities commonly include general administration, public safety, education, the judicial system, and so on.

**General Long-Term Debt (Governmental Accounting):** all unmatured long-term liabilities other than fund long-term liabilities; reported in the government-wide financial statements.

**General Partnership:** an association in which each partner has unlimited liability.

**Goodwill Approach (Partnerships):** the adjustment of assets and liabilities to fair values and recording goodwill as an alternative to adjusting partner equity balances (also, a partnership revaluation approach).

**Governmental Accounting Standards Board (GASB):** the standards-setting body for state and local governmental accounting and financial reporting in the United States.

**Governmental Fund Expenditures:** decreases in fund financial resources other than from interfund transfers and other financing uses.

**Governmental Fund Revenues:** increases in fund financial resources other than from transfers, debt issue proceeds, and interfund reimbursement transactions.

**Governmental Funds:** a category of funds used to account for most governmental functions that are basically different from private enterprise; they include the general fund, special revenue funds, capital projects funds, debt service funds and permanent funds.

**Grants:** contributions from other governmental units to be used for specific purposes.

**Hedge:** combined transaction of an existing position and a derivative contract that is designed to manage the risks the firm faces by holding the existing position alone.

**Hedge of Net Investment in a Foreign Subsidiary:** combined transaction of an existing investment in a foreign subsidiary and a derivative contract that is designed to manage the risks the firm faces from the foreign currency translation of that investment.

**Hedging Operations:** purchase or sale of a foreign currency contract to offset the risks of holding receivables or payables denominated in a foreign currency.

**Heirs:** the persons entitled to the property of the decedent under the statutes of intestate succession.

**Historical Rate:** the exchange rate in effect at the time a specific transaction or event occurred.

**Homestead Allowance:** an allowance to a surviving spouse that has priority over all other claims against the estate.

**Horizontal Integration:** the combination of firms in the same business lines or markets.

**IASC:** International Accounting Standards Committee.

**Indirect Holdings:** investments that enable an investor company to control an investee that is not directly owned through an investee that is directly owned.

**Indirect Quotation:** the expression of an exchange rate in foreign currency units (foreign currency per U.S. dollar).

**Installment Liquidation (Partnerships):** distribution of cash as it becomes available during the liquidation period.

**Interfund Loans:** loans made by one fund to another and that must be repaid.

**Intergovernmental Revenue:** revenues received from other governmental units.

**Interim Financial Reports:** unaudited financial reports that are issued for periods of less than a full year and are frequently called quarterly reports.

**Internal Service Funds (Governmental Accounting):** used to account for financing goods and services provided by one department to other departments on a cost-reimbursement basis.

**Intestate:** having died without a valid will.

**Intestate Succession:** the order in which intestate estate property is distributed to the surviving spouse, descendants, parents, and so on.

**Investment in Plant Accounts:** used by colleges and universities to account for the physical plant, which includes land, buildings, improvements other than buildings, and equipment including library books, and for related debt.

**Involuntary Bankruptcy Proceedings:** the filing is involuntary if the creditors file the bankruptcy petition.

**Joint Venture:** a business entity that is owned, operated, and jointly controlled by a small group of investors (venturers) for a specific undertaking; it may be temporary or relatively permanent, and it may be corporate or partnership.

**Leveraged Buyout:** acquisition of a public-held company directly from its shareholders in a transaction financed primarily by debt.

**Life Income Funds:** a college and university fund type to account for resources acquired under the condition that the income be paid to a designated individual until death.

**Limited Partnership:** an association in which one or more partners have limited liability and at least one partner has unlimited liability.

**Loan Funds:** a college and university fund grouping to account for resources available for student and faculty loans.

**Local Currency:** the currency of the country being referred to.

**Local Transactions:** transactions within a country that are measured in the currency of that country.

**Measurement Focuses (Governmental Accounting):** governmental funds focus on "current financial resources" while proprietary funds focus on "economic resources."

**Merger:** a business combination in which one corporation takes over the operations of another entity and that entity goes out of existence; also, a business combination or an acquisition in a generic sense.

**Mixed-Attribute Model:** (Hedge Accounting) is a model where more than one measurement attribute is used to record account values

**Monetary Assets and Liabilities:** are assets and liabilities in which the amounts are fixed in currency units. If the value of the currency unit changes, it is still settled with the same number of units.

**Multiple Exchange Rates:** fixed exchange rates with preferential rates set for different kinds of transactions.

**Mutual Agency (Partnerships):** each partner has the power to bind all other partners, in the absence of notification to the contrary.

**Mutual Holdings:** two or more affiliated companies that hold stock in each other.

**Net Assets (Not-for-profit- Accounting):** the title for the equity section of the balance sheet in not-for-profit financial reporting. Three categories include unrestricted, temporarily restricted, and restricted. No longer used for governmental organization (see Net Position).

**Net Position (Governmental Accounting):** under new guidance from the GASB, the title for the equity section of the entity-wide statement of financial position. Includes three categories: net investment in capital assets, restricted, and unrestricted. The term Net Assets is no longer used in governmental reporting.

**Net Settlement:** a feature of many derivative contracts that allows the parties to settle the contract without delivering the underlying commodity.

**Noncontrolling Interest:** the stockholder interest in a subsidiary not owned by the parent company.

**Nonexpendable Trust Funds:** principal is maintained intact but income may or may not be expendable.

**Nonmonetary Items:** are items that would change with changes in market price or changes in the value of the currency.

**Nonprofit or Not-for-Profit Entities:** nonbusiness organizations that have neither individual ownership nor private-profit objectives.

**Nonspendable Fund Balance (Governmental Accounting):** represents amounts not in spendable form, such as inventories, or amounts that must be maintained, such as the principal of an endowment.

**Offering Circular:** similar to a prospectus, but with fewer disclosure requirements.

**Official Exchange Rates:** exchange rates set by a government and subject to change only by that government. (Also *fixed exchange rates*.)

**One-Line Consolidation:** another name for the equity method of accounting; under the equity method the investor's income and the controlling interest share of consolidated net income are equal.

**Operating Profit Test:** a test to determine if an operating segment is a reportable segment of the enterprise.

**Operating Segment:** a component of an enterprise engaged in providing goods and services to unaffiliated or affiliated customers for a profit.

**Options:** a financial derivative that represents a contract sold by one party to another party. The contract offers the buyer the right, but not the obligation, to buy or sell a security or other financial asset at an agreed-upon price during a certain period of time or on a specific date.

**Parent-Company Theory:** a theory under which consolidated financial statements are prepared from the view of parent-company stockholders.

**Parent–Subsidiary Relationship:** a relationship that gives one corporation the power to control another corporation through its majority common stock ownership.

**Partnership:** an association of two or more persons to carry on as co-owners in a business for profit.

**Partnership Agreement:** a contract between partners covering duties of partners, investments, withdrawals, profit sharing, and so on. Without this agreement, these issues are settled by the Uniform Partnership Act.

**Partnership Dissociation:** a change in the relationship of the partners caused by any partner ceasing to be associated in the carrying on of the business.

**Partnership Liquidation:** the process of converting assets into cash, settling all liabilities, and distributing any remaining cash to partners.

**Par Value Theory:** a theory of intercompany bond holdings that allocates constructive gains or losses between the purchasing and issuing affiliates on the basis of the par value of the bonds.

**Patient Service Revenue (Hospitals):** revenue from board and room, nursing services, and other professional services, and recorded on an accrual basis.

**Pay-Fixed, Receive-Variable Interest Rate Swap:** a derivative contract where the purchaser pays a fixed amount and receives a variable amount based on an agreed upon interest rate.

**Pay-Variable, Receive-Fixed Interest Rate Swap:** a derivative contract where the purchaser pays a variable amount based on an agreed upon interest rate and receives a fixed amount.

**Payments in Lieu of Taxes:** payments by one governmental unit to another for revenues lost because governments cannot tax each other. Also, similar payments from a government's enterprise fund to its other tax-supported funds.

**Permanently Restricted Net Assets (Not-for-Profit-Accounting):** the portion of a not-for-profit entity's net assets whose use is limited by donor-imposed stipulations that do not expire and cannot be removed by action of the entity.

**Personal Representative:** a person named by the probate court to take control of a decedent's estate.

**Piecemeal Acquisition:** a corporation gains control of a subsidiary through a series of separate stock purchases.

**Plant Funds:** a college and university fund grouping to account for unexpended plant funds, renewal and replacement funds, retirement of indebtedness funds, and investment in plant accounts.

**Pooling of Interests Method:** accounting method that records business combinations based on book values of net assets acquired rather than fair values. Not an acceptable method for business combinations initiated after 2001.

**Preacquisition Dividends:** dividends paid on an equity investment prior to the date the investment was acquired during the year.

**Preacquisition Earnings:** year-to-date earnings for an interim business combination, prior to the date of the acquisition.

**Preliminary Prospectus:** a preliminary communication about securities to be issued that also explains how to get a copy of the prospectus filed with the SEC.

**Prepetition Liabilities Subject to Compromise:** unsecured and undersecured liabilities incurred before a Chapter 11 bankruptcy filing.

**Primary Beneficiary:** the entity that is required to consolidate a variable interest entity.

**Probate:** to probate a will is to validate a will.

**Proprietary Funds (Governmental Accounting):** a category of funds to account for operations that are similar to those of private business enterprises; including enterprise funds and internal service funds.

**Pro Rata or Proportionate Consolidation:** a practice in accounting for joint ventures in which each investor-venturer accounts for its share of assets, equities, revenues, and expenses.

**Prospectus:** information about an SEC registrant firm that includes its type of business, company background, and financial statements; it is a part of the SEC registration statement.

**Push-Down Accounting:** establishment of a new basis of subsidiary accounting based on the price paid by the parent company.

**Registration Statements:** statements required to be filed with the SEC for firms that issue securities to the public, and for firms whose shares are traded on national stock exchanges.

**Regulation S:** a 1990 regulation to clarify the applicability of security laws across national boundaries.

**Reimbursements:** transactions between two funds of a government that constitute reimbursements of a fund for expenditures or expenses initially made from it that are properly applicable to another fund. Reimbursements are recorded as expenditures or expenses in the reimbursing fund and as reductions of expenditures or expenses in the reimbursed fund.

**Remeasurement:** the conversion of a foreign entity's financial statements from another currency into its own functional currency.

**Renewal and Replacement Funds (Colleges and Universities):** used to account for the resources held by colleges and universities for renewal and replacement of the physical plant.

**Reorganization Items:** income, expenses, realized gains and losses, and provisions for losses that result from restructuring a business under Chapter 11 of the Bankruptcy Act.

**Reorganization Plan:** a plan for rehabilitation of the debtor corporation in a Chapter 11 case; to be confirmed, the plan must be fair and equitable to all interests concerned.

**Reorganization Value:** an approximation of the amount a willing buyer would pay for the assets of the corporation at the time of restructuring.

**Reportable Operating Segment:** an operating segment for which information is required to be reported.

**Reporting Currency:** the currency in which consolidated financial statements are prepared.

**Residual Beneficiaries:** those entitled to the remainder of an estate after all other rightful claims have been satisfied.

**Residual Equity Transfer (Governmental Accounting):** nonrecurring or nonroutine transfers of equity between funds.

**Restricted Current Funds (Colleges and Universities):** encompasses resources expendable currently but restricted to expenditures for specified operating purposes.

**Restricted Fund Balance (Governmental):** amounts can only be spent for the specific purposes stipulated by constitution, external resource providers, or through enabling legislation.

**Retained Earnings (Ending):** total retained earnings at the end of the year.

**Retirement of Indebtedness Fund:** used in college and university accounting for liquid resources held for current debt service, and investments held for future debt retirement.

**Safe Payments (Partnerships):** distributions that can be made to partners with assurance that the amounts distributed will not need to be returned to the partnership at some later date.

**Salary Allowances (Partnerships):** partner salary allowances are drawings authorized in lieu of salaries because partner rewards come from sharing in partnership earnings. (Also *Drawings (Partnerships)*.)

**Schedule of Assumed Loss Absorption:** used in developing the cash distribution plan in a partnership liquidation. Each partner's equity is charged with a loss amount to eliminate the equity of the most vulnerable partner, and so on.

**Shared Revenues (Governmental Accounting):** specific revenue sources shared with other governmental units; sales taxes and gasoline taxes are examples.

**Special Assessments:** special tax levies against benefited property owners for improvements that benefit the owner's property.

**Special Revenue Funds (Governmental Accounting):** used to account for proceeds from specific revenue sources that are legally restricted to specified purposes.

**Spot Rate:** the exchange rate in effect for immediate delivery of the currencies exchanged.

**Statement of Affairs:** a financial statement that shows liquidation values of a bankrupt entity and provides estimates of possible recovery for unsecured creditors.

**Statement of Functional Expenses (Voluntary Health and Welfare Organizations):** a financial statement that shows the costs associated with the program services or other activities of the organization.

**Statement of Realization and Liquidation:** statement showing progress toward liquidation in a bankruptcy case.

**Step-by-Step Acquisitions:** acquiring an equity interest in a series of separate stock purchases.

**Subsidiary:** a corporation in which the controlling stockholders' interest lies with a parent company that controls its decisions and operations.

**Swaps:** a type of derivative where two counterparties agree to exchange payments with each other. These payments will vary in amount based on the price of some underlying instrument.

**Temporal Method:** translation of items carried at past, current, and future prices in a manner that retains their measurement bases.

**Temporarily Restricted Net Assets (Not-for-Profit- Accounting):** the portion of a not-for-profit entity's net assets whose use is limited by donor-imposed stipulations that either expire or can be removed by fulfilling the stipulations.

**Temporary Differences:** differences in taxable income and accounting income that originate in one accounting period and reverse in a later period.

**Term Endowments:** a college and university fund type to account for resources received from donors or outside agencies with the stipulation that the principal may be expended after a period of time or the occurrence of some event.

**Testacy Proceeding:** a hearing of a probate court to determine if the deceased died testate or intestate (that is, with or without a valid will).

**Testamentary Trust:** a trust that is created pursuant to a will.

**Testate:** having died with a valid will in force.

**Total Assets of Consolidated Entity:** the total of all assets for the consolidated reporting entity.

**Total Equities of Consolidated Entity:** the total of all liabilities and shareholders' equity accounts for the consolidated reporting entity.

**Traditional Theory:** GAAP for consolidated financial statement preparation prior to 2001. Traditional theory combines elements of parent-company and entity theories.

**Translation:** expressing functional currency measurements in the reporting currency.

**Translation Adjustment:** an exchange gain or loss that is reported as an equity adjustment in other comprehensive income. (Also *Equity Adjustment on Translation*.)

**Treasury Stock Approach:** accounting for parent-company stock held by a subsidiary as treasury stock in consolidated statements.

**Trust and Agency Funds:** used to account for assets held in a trustee capacity or as agent for individuals, private organizations, and other governmental units.

**Trustee:** a lawyer appointed by the U.S. trustee or by the bankruptcy court to assume control of the debtor's estate and coordinate its administration with the court.

**Unassigned Fund Balance (Governmental):** the residual classification for the government's general fund and includes all spendable amounts not contained in the other classifications. In other funds, the unassigned classification should be used only to report a deficit balance resulting from overspending for specific purposes for which amounts had been restricted, committed, or assigned.

**Unconditional Promises to Give (Nonprofit Accounting):** a pledge without conditions.

**Undivided Interest (Joint Ventures):** an ownership arrangement in which two or more parties own property and title is held individually to the extent of each party's interest.

**Unexpended Plant Funds:** used by colleges and universities to account for resources held for additions and improvements to the physical plant.

**Uniform Probate Code:** a document prepared by the National Conference of Commissioners on Uniform State Laws that provides guidelines for estate and trust administration.

**Unlimited Liability:** each partner is liable for all partnership debts. Limited partners in a limited partnership, which is allowed in some states, do not have unlimited liability.

**Unrestricted Current Funds (Colleges and Universities):** encompasses resources received and expended for instruction, research, extension, and public services, as well as auxiliary enterprises.

**Unrestricted Net Assets (Not-for-Profit Accounting):** the portion of net assets of a not-for-profit entity that carries no donor-imposed restrictions.

**Upstream Sale:** sales or other intercompany transactions from subsidiary to parent company.

**U.S. Trustee:** an administrative officer of the bankruptcy court; appointed by the attorney general for five-year terms.

**Variable Interest Entities (VIEs):** special purpose entities that require consolidation under GAAP.

**Venturers:** the owner participants in a joint venture.

**Vertical Integration:** the combination of firms with operations in different but successive stages of production and/or distribution.

**Voluntary Bankruptcy Proceedings:** the filing is voluntary if the debtor files the bankruptcy petition.

**Voluntary Health and Welfare Organizations:** a diverse group of nonprofit entities that is supported by donations and seeks to solve basic social problems of health and welfare.

**Vulnerability Ranking (Partnerships):** a ranking of partners on the basis of the amount of partnership losses they could absorb without reducing their capital accounts below zero.

# INDEX